Tort Law

PEARSON

At Pearson, we take learning personally. Our courses and resources are available as books, online and via multi-lingual packages, helping people learn whatever, wherever and however they choose.

We work with leading authors to develop the strongest learning experiences, bringing cutting-edge thinking and best learning practice to a global market. We craft our print and digital resources to do more to help learners not only understand their content, but to see it in action and apply what they learn, whether studying or at work.

Pearson is the world's leading learning company. Our portfolio includes Penguin, Dorling Kindersley, the Financial Times and our educational business, Pearson International. We are also a leading provider of electronic learning programmes and of test development, processing and scoring services to educational institutions, corporations and professional bodies around the world.

Every day our work helps learning flourish, and wherever learning flourishes, so do people.

To learn more please visit us at: www.pearson.com/uk

Tort Law

Fourth Edition

Nicholas J. McBride
Fellow of Pembroke College, Cambridge

Roderick Bagshaw
Fellow of Magdalen College, Oxford

PEARSON

Harlow, England • London • New York • Boston • San Francisco • Toronto • Sydney
Auckland • Singapore • Hong Kong • Tokyo • Seoul • Taipei • New Delhi
Cape Town • São Paulo • Mexico City • Madrid • Amsterdam • Munich • Paris • Milan

Pearson Education Limited
Edinburgh Gate
Harlow
Essex CM20 2JE
England

and Associated Companies throughout the world

Visit us on the World Wide Web at:
www.pearson.com/uk

First published 2001
Second edition published 2005
Third edition published 2008
Fourth edition published 2012

© Pearson Education Limited 2001, 2012

ISBN 978-1-4082-5270-3

British Library Cataloguing-in-Publication Data
A catalogue record for this book is available from the British Library

Library of Congress Cataloging-in-Publication Data
McBride, Nicholas J.
  Tort law / Nicholas J. McBride, Roderick Bagshaw. — 4th ed.
    p. cm.
  Includes bibliographical references and index.
  ISBN 978-1-4082-5270-3
  1. Torts—England. I. Bagshaw, Roderick. II. Title.
  KD1949.M38 2012
  346.4203—dc23   2012001768

10 9 8 7 6 5 4 3 2 1
16 15 14 13 12

Typeset in 10/12pt Minion by 35
Printed and bound by Ashford Colour Press Ltd., Gosport

111711

To
Liz, Corin and Arthur
and
Barbara, Chris, Ben and Damian

Brief contents

Acknowledgements *xv*

Preface *xvii*

Table of cases *xxi*

Table of statutes, statutory
instruments and conventions *xlviii*

1 The basics *1*

2 Trespass to the person *35*

3 The Human Rights Act 1998 *69*

4 Claims in negligence *92*

5 Duty of care – Introduction *99*

6 Duty of care – Acts *124*

7 Duty of care – Omissions *207*

8 Breach of duty *244*

9 Causation *277*

10 Actionability *328*

11 Occupiers' liability *358*

12 Product liability *381*

13 Liability for animals *398*

14 Trespass to land *405*

15 Private nuisance *415*

16 The rule in *Rylands* v *Fletcher 466*

17 Torts to things *485*

18 Torts to intangible property *508*

19 Defamation *522*

20 Harassment *579*

21 Invasion of privacy *589*

22 Breach of statutory duty *626*

23 Public nuisance *639*

24 The economic torts *655*

25 Abuse of power torts *705*

26 Defences *716*

27 Nominal damages *749*

28 Compensatory damages *754*

29 Aggravated damages *789*

30 Exemplary damages *796*

31 Gain-based damages *805*

32 Vindicatory damages *820*

33 Injunctions *832*

34 Wrongful death claims *844*

35 Other third party claims *854*

36 Accessory liability *860*

37 Vicarious liability *865*

38 Loss compensation schemes *893*

Bibliography *904*

Index of problems *919*

Index *920*

Contents

Acknowledgements xv

Preface xvii

Table of cases xxi

Table of statutes, statutory instruments and conventions xlviii

1
The basics 1

1 The function of tort law 1
2 Rights and duties 2
3 The range of torts 5
4 Torts and wrongs 8
5 The importance of being a victim 10
6 The loss compensation model of tort law 13
7 The residual wrongs model of tort law 16
8 Tort law and contract law 17
9 Tort law and equity 19
10 Tort law and statute law 21
11 Tort law and criminal law 23
12 Tort law and property law 24
13 Tort law and strict liability 25
14 Insurance 27
15 Paying for tort law 29
16 Tort law as a foreign country 32

2
Trespass to the person 35

1 The basics 35
2 Conduct requirements 38
3 Fault requirements 42
4 Consent 45
5 Necessity 50
6 Statutory authority 58
7 Mistakes 61
8 Remedies 65

3
The Human Rights Act 1998 69

1 The basics 69
2 Direct effect 74
3 Indirect effect 85

4
Claims in negligence 92

1 The basics 92
2 Negligence and intention 93
3 Negligence and other wrongs 94
4 Remedies for negligence 97

5
Duty of care – Introduction 99

1 The basics 99
2 Duty of care tests 104
3 Duty of care factors 108
4 Duty-skepticism 119
5 Risk and harm 121

6
Duty of care – Acts 124

1 The basics 124
2 Physical injury (1): the basic rule 129
3 Physical injury (2): harm caused by a third party 137
4 Psychiatric illness (1): general principles in accident cases 140
5 Psychiatric illness (2): the caselaw on accident cases 142
6 Psychiatric illness (3): non-accident cases 151
7 Pure distress 158
8 *Wilkinson* v *Downton* 161
9 Harm to property 162

10 Pure economic loss (1): *Hedley Byrne* – the basic principle *172*

11 Pure economic loss (2): *Hedley Byrne* – the extended principle *180*

12 Pure economic loss (3): *Hedley Byrne* – two misconceptions *187*

13 Pure economic loss (4): some difficult cases *188*

14 Pure economic loss (5): explanation of the difficult cases *196*

7
Duty of care – Omissions *207*

1 The basics *207*

2 Assumption of responsibility *217*

3 Creation of danger *222*

4 Interference *228*

5 Control *231*

6 Occupiers *234*

7 Landlords *234*

8 Employers *235*

9 Bailees *237*

10 Carriers *237*

11 Child carers *238*

8
Breach of duty *244*

1 The basics *244*

2 Objectivity *248*

3 Balancing *252*

4 Common practice *256*

5 Public powers *258*

6 Breach through others *260*

7 Proof *267*

9
Causation *271*

1 The basics *271*

2 The 'but for' test *275*

3 Divisible and indivisible harm *279*

4 Evidential difficulties (1): the standard approach *281*

5 Evidential difficulties (2): the *Fairchild* exception *285*

6 Evidential difficulties (3): loss of a chance cases *291*

7 *Gregg* v *Scott* *296*

8 Overdetermination *300*

9 Another solution to overdetermination? *303*

10 Coincidences *305*

11 Coincidental overdetermination *309*

12 Break in the chain of causation *311*

13 Alternative approaches to causation *317*

14 Fact and policy *325*

10
Actionability *328*

1 The basics *328*

2 Remoteness of damage *331*

3 Scope of duty *339*

4 The *SAAMCO* principle *342*

5 Wrongful pregnancy/birth *346*

6 Mitigation *350*

7 No double recovery *353*

8 Public policy *353*

11
Occupiers' liability *358*

1 The basics *358*

2 Occupiers' Liability Act 1957 *360*

3 Occupiers' Liability Act 1984 *366*

4 Warnings, disclaimers, exclusions *370*

5 Liability under the general law of negligence *376*

12
Product liability *381*

1 The basics *381*

2 Product *383*

3 Defect *384*

4 Defendants *387*

5 Damage *388*

6 Defences *390*

7 Remedies *393*

8 Discussion *394*

13
Liability for animals 398
1 The basics 398
2 Section 2(2) 399
3 Defences 404

14
Trespass to land 405
1 The basics 405
2 Conduct requirements 406
3 Intention and fault 408
4 Defences 409
5 Title to sue 411
6 Remedies 413

15
Private nuisance 415
1 The basics 415
2 Ways of committing the tort 416
3 Emanation cases (1): establishing an interference 419
4 Emanation cases (2): reasonable interferences 422
5 Emanation cases (3): establishing an unreasonable interference 429
6 Encroachment cases 434
7 Obstruction cases 435
8 Affront cases 438
9 Responsibility 440
10 Defences 446
11 Title to sue 448
12 Remedies 454
13 Peculiar forms of the tort 464

16
The rule in *Rylands* v *Fletcher* 466
1 The basics 466
2 Rationale 468
3 Scope of liability 471
4 Strict liability? 477

5 Remedies 479
6 Analogous liability rules 480

17
Torts to things 485
1 The basics 485
2 Some key concepts 487
3 Conversion 494
4 Trespass to goods 500
5 Bailment 503
6 Remedies 504

18
Torts to intangible property 508
1 The basics 508
2 Intellectual property 511
3 Goodwill 513
4 Contractual rights 516
5 Virtual property 519

19
Defamation 522
1 The basics 522
2 What is defamatory? 530
3 Reference to the claimant 535
4 Publication to a third party 538
5 Title to sue 543
6 Consent 546
7 Justification 547
8 Honest (or fair) comment 549
9 Absolute privilege 555
10 Qualified privilege 557
11 *Reynolds* privilege 562
12 Other defences 568
13 Remedies 570
14 Options for reform 572

20
Harassment 579
1 The basics 579
2 Protection from Harassment Act 1997 580
3 Equality Act 2010 585

21
Invasion of privacy 589

1 The basics 589

2 Wrongful disclosure of private information 591

3 Private information 594

4 Freedom of expression 605

5 Striking the balance 611

6 Fault elements 613

7 Wrongfully obtaining access to private information 614

8 Remedies 617

9 Cases not involving wrongful disclosure or access 621

22
Breach of statutory duty 626

1 The basics 626

2 Resolving hard cases 630

3 Health and safety at work 634

4 Highways 635

5 Defective premises 636

6 Equality Act 2010 637

23
Public nuisance 639

1 The basics 639

2 Unreasonable Interference 641

3 Responsibility 647

4 Special damage 650

24
The economic torts 655

1 The basics 655

2 Inducing a breach of contract 660

3 Analogous torts 672

4 Intentionally causing loss by unlawful means 672

5 Two-party cases 681

6 Lawful means conspiracy 683

7 Unlawful means conspiracy 688

8 Deceit 692

9 Malicious falsehood 696

10 Recoverable harm 698

25
Abuse of power torts 705

1 The basics 705

2 Malicious prosecution 706

3 Analogous torts 707

4 Misfeasance in public office 709

26
Defences 716

1 The basics 716

2 Lack of capacity 718

3 Act of state 720

4 Sovereign and diplomatic immunity 720

5 Trade union immunity 721

6 Witness immunity 721

7 Abuse of process 723

8 Death 725

9 *Volenti non fit injuria* 725

10 Exclusion of liability 728

11 Illegality (1): the common law 730

12 Illegality (2): statute 737

13 More good than harm 738

14 Limitation 739

15 Contributory negligence 743

16 The impact of Article 6 of the ECHR 743

27
Nominal damages 749

1 The basics 749

2 Reasons 750

3 Theories 751

28
Compensatory damages 754

1 The basics 754

2 Techniques 755

3 Assessment 758

4 Reduction (1): receipt of benefit 765

5 Reduction (2): contributory negligence 773

6 Third party losses 779

7 Theories 781

29
Aggravated damages 789

1 The basics 789

2 Requirements 789

3 Theories 792

30
Exemplary damages 796

1 The basics 796

2 Requirements 797

3 Further points 801

4 Reform 802

31
Gain-based damages 805

1 The basics 805

2 Disgorgement damages 810

3 Licence fee damages 814

4 Theories 816

32
Vindicatory damages 820

1 The basics 820

2 Examples? 822

3 The *Lumba* decision 827

4 The future 829

33
Injunctions 832

1 The basics 832

2 Classification of injunctions 834

3 When will an interim injunction be granted? 834

4 When will a final injunction be granted? 837

5 Reform 841

34
Wrongful death claims 844

1 The basics 844

2 Dependant 845

3 The parasitical nature of wrongful death claims 845

4 Loss of support 846

5 Bereavement 851

6 Funeral expenses 852

7 Limitation 852

8 Non-wrongful death 852

35
Other third party claims 854

1 The basics 854

2 Congenital disabilities 854

3 Recovery of state losses 857

4 The principle of transferred loss 858

36
Accessory liability 860

1 The basics 860

2 Requirements 860

3 Limits 862

37
Vicarious liability 865

1 The basics 865

2 Situations of vicarious liability 867

3 Who is an employee? 869

4 'Borrowed' employees 873

5 The Salmond test 874

6 The *Lister* test 878

7 Theories of vicarious liability 886

8 Two final points 890

38
Loss compensation schemes 893

1 The basics 893

2 Features of loss compensation schemes 893

3 Four loss compensation schemes 895

4 Evaluating loss compensation schemes 899

Bibliography 904

Index of problems 919

Index 920

Acknowledgements

We would like to thank our outstanding editor, Cheryl Cheasley, for all the support and encouragement she has provided during the writing of the fourth edition of this textbook. She has played a hugely significant role in the production of this book: encouraging us to revisit its basic structure, working with us on getting the layout of the book exactly right, and providing extremely helpful comments on draft chapters. We could not have wished for a better editor to work with us on the book. We would also like to thank all the other people at Pearson Education who have helped with the production of this book, in particular, Joe Vella, Colin Reed, Carol Abbott, Robert Chaundy and Jill Birch. We would both also like to acknowledge the huge role played by our students in helping us understand how best to help them understand what can – at first sight – seem like one of the most difficult subjects in English law.

Nick McBride writes: My work on this book, and my general understanding of tort law, has profited hugely from conversations with John Goldberg and Ben Zipursky, Rob Stevens, Sandy Steel, Jason Varuhas, John Murphy, and – of course – Rod.

Completing this fourth edition was a huge task, made much easier as a result of the support of my mother, my brothers, and my friends – in particular, Isabel Haskey, Ines Anoustis, Bridget Callaghan, Shamima Dawood, Siobhan Sparkes McNamara and Charlie Brearley.

My work on the book was largely completed while teaching in Hong Kong in the summer of 2011. I hugely appreciate all the support and encouragement of my colleagues at HKU, in particular Lusina Ho, Lee Mason and Po Jen Yap. Most of the book was written at Pembroke College, Cambridge. I continue to be extremely grateful to Pembroke for employing me to work alongside some wonderful colleagues, and to teach such fantastic students.

Roderick Bagshaw writes: I would particularly like to thank my wife – Liz – and sons – Corin and Arthur, for being so generous and supportive. Producing a book like this imposes burdens on many people beyond those whose names appear on the cover, but the willingness of close family not merely to tolerate this, but to facilitate and encourage, is a wonderful blessing for any author. Thank you.

Most of my work on this book was done using libraries and databases at Magdalen College and the University of Oxford. I am very grateful to my colleagues at Magdalen and in the Law Faculty at Oxford for all the assistance they provide, directly and indirectly, consciously and unknowingly. For the final two months of preparing this edition Roderick was an academic visitor at the National University Singapore and he would also like to express his warm gratitude to the Law Faculty there for welcoming him so hospitably into a rich academic environment.

As in previous editions I would like to place on record my great thanks to Nick. While the names of both of us appear on the cover it is only appropriate to disclose that Nick takes on a far greater share of the writing and all the other tasks involved in ensuring that this book meets its goals. In particular, it is Nick who has made sure that the revisions to the structure, layout and style of the book in this edition will all contribute to making tort law less daunting for students.

Preface

It is a striking feature of most textbooks that they tend not to change that much from edition to edition, in terms of their basic structure. We have bucked this trend by completely rewriting and restructuring our textbook for its fourth edition. In the previous three editions, we adopted what seemed to us the most rational way of setting out the law of tort – that is, by in one part of the book setting out the torts recognised by English law and in a subsequent part setting out what remedies would be available when someone committed a tort. The final part of the book dealt with a number of liability rules that are customarily dealt with in tort law textbooks because they make a defendant liable to pay *compensation* to a claimant, but which are difficult to rationalise as actually being part of the law of tort because the defendant does not have to have done anything *wrong* to incur a liability to pay compensation under these rules.

We continue to think that this is the most rational way of setting out tort law as a body of legal rules and principles: it has the twin virtues of enabling those rules and principles to be presented in a way that is very clear and involves no repetitions. However, we acknowledge that the most *rational* way of setting out the law of tort may not be the most *convenient* for tort law teachers or students. Separating out the issue of when someone will commit a tort from the issue of what remedies will be available when someone commits a tort meant that readers had to look in two different parts of the book to find out everything they needed to know about (say) the law of negligence – one part to find out when someone will commit the tort of negligence, and one part to find out what remedies will be available when that tort is committed. Moreover, readers wanting to compare the remedies available to a claimant in (a) negligence, and (b) under the Consumer Protection Act 1987 when the claimant's car was wrecked by a dangerously defective tyre might have found it disconcerting to have our discussion of those issues separated by 700-odd pages.

So, for this edition, we have opted for a much more conventional way of presenting tort law. So, for example, after we conclude our discussion of the law of negligence, we do not move on to another tort (as we did in previous editions), but instead talk about the law on causation and actionability. Convenience demands that we do so, as these areas of law are crucial to the outcome of any negligence case. But what is convenient also carries with it some dangers, as these areas of law are relevant to all tort cases where a claimant is suing for compensatory damages (as he or she almost always is) and discussing these areas of law before other torts may tend to obscure that fact. Again, for reasons of practical convenience, we talk about the Consumer Protection Act 1987 in chapter 12 of this book, as opposed to chapter 43 in the previous edition. And again, some dangers are involved in doing this. When we come to the 'remedial' chapters in this edition (chapters 26–37), and make statements starting 'When a defendant commits a tort in relation to a claimant . . .', the reader may well wonder, 'Does that include a situation where the defendant is liable to the claimant under the Consumer Protection Act 1987?' The short and obvious answer is, 'No – it does not' – but the potential for confusion is created by dealing with the 1987 Act *before* talking about the remedies available when a tort has been committed, rather than *after* (as in previous editions). However, we are alert – in a way that writers who go along as a matter of course with conventional presentations of the law of tort might not be – to the dangers of confusion created by setting out tort law in a convenient way, and have sought to warn the reader of those dangers all along the way.

Radically rewriting and restructuring this textbook has also freed us up to make some further innovations in this edition. Two in particular should be noted:

(1) *Theory*. In this edition, we discuss various academic views about the basis of tort law or various features of the law of tort in far more depth than we have in previous editions. We have three reasons for doing this.

First, we do so for the sake of students who read this book for the purpose of learning about tort law. We firmly believe that tort law is easier for students to come to grips with and remember if they have some understanding of the principles underlying the cases and provisions making up the body of tort law. To draw an analogy, chess masters and grandmasters have the ability to remember thousands and thousands of different positions on a chessboard. But if you lay out some pieces on a chessboard randomly, not even the most distinguished chess player will be able to remember how the pieces were arranged. The reason is that we are only capable of remembering things that form some sort of order or pattern; our memories cannot cope with randomness. Students who can discern some sort of order underpinning the rules and doctrines that make up tort law will find those rules and doctrines far easier to remember than students for whom those rules and doctrines are only noise.

Secondly, we do so for the sake of the future of tort law, which can only function effectively and fairly if those who administer it know what they are doing and why. There is a saying from the Bible that 'Where there is no vision, the people perish.'[1] The same is true of the law. Where there is no lively understanding – albeit, perhaps, unspoken – among the judges as to *why* the law says what it does, they will not know how to develop the law in a consistent and principled way in deciding novel cases; moreover, they will have no reason to stick to the letter of the law in cases where their sympathies are on the side of the party whose case has no legal merits. The courts will become a casino where the outcome of your case will be largely a matter of chance. There are some signs that the absence of any understanding among the judges as to what tort law is for is already resulting in tort cases no longer being decided in any kind of principled way. It is quite remarkable how many recent Court of Appeal decisions in the field of tort law have been badly reasoned or decided. A particular nadir was reached in the case of *Shell UK Ltd v Total UK Ltd* (2010) where counsel's argument for the defendants in that case was dismissed on the ground that it would be 'legalistic' to deny the claimants' claim.[2] What are the courts for, if not to be 'legalistic'?

Thirdly, we do so for the sake of academics whose painstaking researches into, and arguments about, tort law are in danger of being lost unless they are assimilated into a work such as this one. Worldwide pressure on academics to produce more and more 'research outputs' in order to ensure continued state funding to their institutions has resulted in a huge profusion of articles and books on all areas of law, including tort law. But it is difficult for anyone to be heard properly when everyone is speaking at once – and there is a real danger at the moment that the profusion of research into tort law is actually making it more difficult, rather than making it easier, for real progress to be made in understanding

---

[1] Proverbs 29:18 (KJV).
[2] [2011] QB 86, at [132].

tort law. We do not really need any more law journals, carrying more and more articles about aspects of the law. What we are desperately in need of are meta-journals: journals that report and reflect on what is in the law journals, so as to bring the flood of research pouring out of the universities under control, disperse it into the tributaries of various legal specialisms, and thereby enrich their development. In the absence of such meta-journals, it falls on textbook writers – paradoxically, the most despised breed of writer under the current systems for evaluating a university's or faculty's worth – to do the necessary work of assimilating and communicating to others the current state of legal research.

(2) *Problems*. The reader will find at various points throughout this edition that we have included a number of difficult tort law-related problem scenarios. A full glossary of these problems may be found at the back of this book.

We have done so, in part, for educational reasons. The problem questions are fun, and interesting, and help the reader see how tort law can be fun, and interesting. This is particularly important when a lot of the tort law problem questions a typical student reader might be confronted with in the course of his or her studies reduce down to 'Can you remember the case or cases that are relevant to this situation?' We hope the problem scenarios scattered throughout this book show that tort law can be a *lot* more interesting than *that*.

But we have also done so in order to make a general point about tort law. The mathematical and scientific revolutions of the seventeenth century led many thinkers to believe that human institutions such as law could be given a mathematical/scientific basis.[3] As Roger Berkowitz explains in his book *The Gift of Science: Leibniz and the Modern Legal Tradition* (Fordham, 2010):

> The grand insight of seventeenth-century natural scientists was not simply to rediscover Euclid and ancient mathematical reasoning; rather it was to extend the mathematical method from logical beings to actual beings in the world.[4]

So the mathematician Gottfried Wilhelm Leibniz (who – simultaneously with Isaac Newton – invented calculus)

> expresse[d] his ambition to discover a method for the determination of fundamental principles that would decide all legal cases, even the most difficult and perplexing ones, with certainty.[5]

Leibniz thought he had found this method in 'this single principle: the fact that justice is the charity of the wise.'[6] This single principle, he thought, lay at the base of the law and would yield up rules and sub-principles that could determine – with mathematical certainty – any legal case.

It may be that history is now repeating itself. While this edition was being written, the BBC screened a three part Adam Curtis documentary series called *All Watched Over By Machines Of Loving Grace*. The essential thesis of Curtis' documentary was that the computer revolution has had a fundamental effect on the way we think of ourselves and the world. We tend to think of ourselves, and the world we live in, as programmed to achieve certain outcomes, in a stable and determinate way. Just like a computer. It might be that this mental conditioning explains why so many academics are happy to endorse

---

[3] Our thanks to Sandy Steel for first suggesting to us this historical parallel.
[4] Berkowitz 2010, 18–19.
[5] Berkowitz 2010, 29.
[6] Berkowitz 2010, 64, quoting from a letter written by Leibniz in May 1677.

accounts of tort law that see it as giving effect to one 'single principle' – such as 'Maximise wealth!' or 'Preserve the equal freedom of every agent to determine what purposes he will pursue!' or 'Do what is most beneficial for society!' – that will (it is thought) determine *for certain* what the outcome of *any* tort case should be.

The problem scenarios scattered throughout this book are intended as a corrective to this – in our view – overly simplistic view of tort law. Even if tort law gives effect to one 'single principle' – something which is very doubtful – such a principle will never be able to determine for certain what decision a court should make in the sort of difficult scenarios that are set out in this book.[7] How those sorts of cases are to be resolved requires judgment and wisdom; and we hope some of that will come through in reading this book.

---

[7] A topic pursued further in Bagshaw 2011b.

Table of cases

Case navigator cases are in **bold**.

A v B [2002] EWCA Civ 337, [2003] QB 195 *606, 607, 608, 836*

A v Bottrill [2002] UKPC 44, [2003] 1 AC 449 *97, 797, 822*

A (children) (conjoined twins: medical treatment), Re [2001] Fam 147 *54–5*

A v Essex County Council [2003] EWCA Civ 1848, [2004] 1 WLR 1881 *13, 118, 132, 717*

A v Hoare [2008] UKHL 6, [2008] 1 AC 884; reversing [2006] EWCA Civ 395, [2006] 1 WLR 2320; applied [2008] EWHC 1573 (QB) *161, 741–2*

A v Leeds Teaching Hospital NHS Trust [2004] EWHC 644, [2005] QB 506 *181*

A v National Blood Authority [2001] 3 All ER 289 *384, 391, 397*

A & J Fabrication (Batley) Ltd v Grant Thornton (a firm) [1999] PNLR 811 *189*

AB v Ministry of Defence [2010] EWCA Civ 1317 *742*

AB v South West Water Services Ltd [1993] QB 507 *791, 798*

AB v Tameside & Glossop Health Authority (1997) 35 BMLR 79 *152*

Abbahall v Smee [2002] EWCA Civ 1831, [2003] 1 WLR 1472 *444*

Abbott v Refuge Assurance Co Ltd [1962] 1 QB 432 *707*

Abouzaid v Mothercare (UK) Ltd, The Times, February 20 2001 *130, 135–6, 387, 394*

Acrow (Automation) Ltd v Rex Chainbelt Inc [1971] 1 WLR 1676 *672*

Adams v Ursell [1913] 1 Ch 269 *424, 425, 454*

Adams-Araphoe School District No 28-J v Celotex Corp, 637 F Supp 1207 (1986) *341*

Addis v Crocker [1961] 1 QB 11 *556*

Adorian v Commissioner of Police of the Metropolis [2009] EWCA Civ 18, [2009] 1 WLR 1859; applied [2010] EWHC 3861 (QB) *737–8*

Ajinomoto Sweeteners SAS v Asda Stores Ltd
    [2010] EWCA Civ 609, [2011] QB 497 *535,*
    698, 703
Akenzua v Secretary of State for the Home
    Department [2002] EWCA Civ 1470, [2003] 1
    WLR 741 *713*
Akerhielm v De Mare [1959] AC 789 *694*
Aksoy v Turkey (1997) 23 EHRR 533 *83*
Al-Adsani v United Kingdom (2002) 34 EHRR
    273 *745*
Alain Bernardin et Compagnie v Pavilion
    Properties Ltd [1967] RPC 581 *514*
Al-Amoudi v Brisard [2006] EWHC 1062 (QB),
    [2007] 1 WLR 113 *524*
Alcoa Minerals of Jamaica Inc v Broderick
    [2002] 1 AC 371 *763*
Alcock v Chief Constable of the South Yorkshire
    Police [1992] 1 AC 310 *142–5, 147–9, 152,*
    158, 159
Alexander v Home Office [1988] 1 WLR
    968 *790*
Alexander v The North Eastern Railway Company
    (1865) 6 B & S 340, 122 ER 1221 *548*
Alfred McAlpine Construction Ltd v Panatown
    Ltd [2001] 1 AC 518 *859*
Ali v City of Bradford MDC [2010] EWCA Civ
    1282 *649*
Aliakmon, The, see Leigh & Sillavan Ltd v
    Aliakmon Shipping Co Ltd
Al-Kandari v J R Brown & Co [1988] QB
    665 *95, 159*
Allen v Flood [1898] AC 1 *4–5, 11, 657, 658,*
    659, 660, 661, 687, 705
Allen v Gulf Oil [1981] AC 1001 *447*
Alliance & Leicester Building Society v Edgestop
    Ltd [1993] 1 WLR 1462 *773*
Allied Maples Group Ltd v Simmons &
    Simmons [1995] 1 WLR 1602 *295*
Allin v City & Hackney HA [1996] 7 Med LR
    167 *153*
Al-Skeini v United Kingdom, July 7 2011,
    unreported *720*
Ambergate, Nottingham and Boston and
    Eastern Junction Railway Company, The v
    The Midland Railway Company (1853) 2 E &
    B 793, 118 ER 964 *498*
American Cyanamid v Ethicon Ltd [1975] AC
    396 *835, 837*
Anchor Brewhouse Developments Ltd v Berkley
    House Ltd [1987] 2 EGLR 173 *412*
Andreae v Selfridge & Co Ltd [1938] Ch 1 *420,*
    434, 437

Andrews v Secretary of State for Health, June 19
    1998, unreported *157*
Andrews v Television New Zealand Ltd [2009] 1
    NZLR 220 *596*
Aneco Reinsurance Underwriting Ltd v Johnson
    & Higgins Ltd [2001] UKHL 51 *342*
Anglo-Cyprian Agencies v Paphos Industries
    [1951] 1 All ER 873 *751*
Anns v Merton London Borough Council
    [1978] AC 728 *104, 106, 131, 139, 211, 323,*
    324
Anthony v Haney (1832) 8 Bing 186, 131 ER
    372 *499*
Anufrijeva v Southwark LBC [2003] EWCA Civ
    1406, [2004] QB 1124 *80, 82, 84, 85*
Archer v Brown [1985] QB 401 *791, 792, 799*
Argent v Minister of Social Security [1968] 1
    WLR 1749 *871*
Armagas Ltd v Mundogas Ltd [1986] AC
    717 *868*
Armonienė v Lithuania (2009) 48 EHRR 53
    598
Armory v Delamirie (1721) 1 Stra 505, 93 ER
    664 *491, 498*
Arnup v White [2008] EWCA Civ 447 *850–1*
Arpad, The [1934] P 189 *335, 336*
Arscott v The Coal Authority [2004] EWCA Civ
    892 *434*
Arthur v Anker [1997] QB 564 *501*
Arthur J S Hall v Simons [2002] 1 AC 615 *116,*
    182, 724
ASG v GSA [2009] EWCA Civ 1574 *605*
Ashby v Tolhurst [1937] 2 KB 242 *487, 496*
Ashby v White (1794) 6 Mod 45, 87 ER
    810 *823, 827*
Ashdown v Samuel Williams Ltd [1957] 1 QB
    409 *371*
Ashdown v Telegraph Group Ltd [2001] EWCA
    Civ 1142, [2002] Ch 149 *839*
Ashley v Chief Constable of Sussex Police [2008]
    UKHL 25, [2008] 1 AC 962 *63, 66, 67, 791,*
    793, 794, 825
Associated British Ports v Transport and
    General Workers' Union [1989] 1 WLR
    939 *672*
Associated Newspapers plc v Insert Media Ltd
    [1991] 1 WLR 571 *515*
Associated Picture Houses Ltd v Wednesbury
    Corp [1948] 1 KB 223 *712*
Aston Cantlow and Wilmcote with Billesley
    Parochial Church Council v Wallbank [2003]
    UKHL 37, [2004] 1 AC 546 *75, 76, 77*

Aswan Engineering Ltd v Lupdine [1987] 1
  WLR 1 168, 169
AT v Dulghieru [2009] EWHC 225 (QB) 24,
  799, 800, 801, 816, 818, 819
Atkinson v The Newcastle and Gateshead
  Waterworks Company (1877) 2 Ex D 441 632
Attia v British Gas [1988] QB 304 341
Attorney-General v Blake [2001] 1 AC 268 807,
  808, 809, 819
Attorney-General v De Keyser's Royal Hotel
  [1920] AC 508 720
Attorney-General v Doughty (1752) Ves Sen
  453, 28 ER 290 436
Attorney-General v Guardian Newspapers Ltd
  (No 2) [1990] 1 AC 109 811
Attorney-General v Manchester Corporation
  [1893] 2 Ch 87 841
Attorney-General v Newspaper Publishing Plc
  [1988] Ch 333 619
Attorney-General v Prince [1998] 1 NZLR
  262 240
Attorney-General v PYA Quarries [1957] 2 QB
  169 643, 645
Attorney-General v Times Newspapers Ltd
  [1992] 1 AC 191 619
Attorney-General v Tod Heatley [1897] 1 Ch
  560 650
Attorney-General v Wilcox [1938] Ch 394 643
Attorney-General for the British Virgin Islands
  v Hartwell [2004] UKPC 12, [2004] 1 WLR
  1273 130, 884
Attorney-General of Trinidad and Tobago v
  Ramanoop [2005] UKPC 15, [2006] 1 AC
  328 821
Attorney-General's Reference (No 2 of 1999)
  [2000] QB 796 267
Aubry v Editions Vice-Versa Inc [1998] 1 SCR
  591 623
Austin v Commissioner of Police of the
  Metropolis [2009] UKHL 5, [2009] 1 AC 545;
  affirming [2007] EWCA Civ 989, [2008] QB
  660; affirming [2005] EWHC 480 (QB) 36–7,
  54, 59, 88
Australian Broadcasting Corporation v Lenah
  Game Meats Pty Ltd (2001) HCA 63, (2001)
  208 CLR 199 598, 604
Auty v National Coal Board [1985] 1 WLR
  784 848
Ayers v Jackson, 525 A 2d 287 (1987) 228

B (a child) v McDonald's Restaurants Ltd [2002]
  EWHC 490 386

B v An NHS Hospital Trust [2002] EWHC
  429 53
B v Attorney-General [2003] UKPC 61, [2003] 4
  All ER 833 240
B v Nugent Care Society [2009] EWCA Civ 827,
  [2010] 1 WLR 516 741, 742
Bailey v HSS Alarms Ltd, The Times, 20 June
  2000 187
Bailey v Ministry of Defence [2008] EWCA Civ
  883, [2009] 1 WLR 1052 280
Bailiffs of Dunwich v Sterry (1831) 1 B & Ad
  831, 109 ER 995 503
Baker v T E Hopkins [1959] 1 WLR 966 131
Baker v Willoughby [1970] AC 467 302–3
Baldacchino v West Wittering Council [2008]
  EWHC 3386 (QB) 363
Balfour v Barty-King [1957] 1 QB 496 481
Bamford v Turnley (1862) 3 B & S 66, 122 ER
  27 422
Banbury v Bank of Montreal [1918] AC 626
  220
Bank of New Zealand v Greenwood [1984] 1
  NZLR 525 459
Bank voor Handel en Scheepvart NV v Slatford
  [1953] 1 QB 248 872
Banque Bruxelles Lambert SA v Eagle Star
  Insurance Co Ltd, see South Australia Asset
  Management Corporation v York Montague
  Ltd
Barber v Somerset County Council [2004]
  UKHL 13, [2004] 1 WLR 1089 155, 156, 236
Barclays Mercantile Finance Ltd v Sibec
  Developments Ltd [1992] 1 WLR 1253 496
Barker v Corus UK Ltd [2006] UKHL 20, [2006]
  2 AC 572 287, 290, 301
Barker v Furlong [1891] 2 Ch 172 502
Barker v Herbert [1911] 2 KB 633 648, 650
Barlow Clowes International v Eurotrust
  International [2005] UKPC 37, [2006] 1 WLR
  1476 863
Barnard v Restormel BC [1998] 3 PLR 27 710
Barnett v Chelsea & Kensington Hospital
  Management Committee [1969] 1 QB
  428 181, 220, 275–6
Barnett v Cohen [1921] 2 KB 461 846–7
Barr v Biffa Waste Services Ltd [2011] EWHC
  1003 (TCC) 425, 428, 431
Barrett v Enfield London Borough Council
  [2001] 2 AC 550, reversing [1998] QB 367 89,
  238, 239, 240
Barrett v Ministry of Defence [1995] 1 WLR
  1217 112, 137, 229

Barretts & Baird (Wholesale) Ltd v Institution of Professional Civil Servants [1987] IRLR 3 *680*

Basébé v Matthews (1867) LR 2 CP 684 *706*

Baxter v Woolcombers Ltd (1963) 107 SJ 553 *774*

Bazley v Curry [1999] 2 SCR 534 *878, 881, 882–3, 887, 888*

BBMB Finance (Hong Kong) Ltd v Eda Holdings Ltd [1990] 1 WLR 409 *506*

Beatty v Gillbanks (1882) 9 QBD 308 *37*

Beaudesert Shire Council v Smith (1966) 120 CLR 145 *627*

Beaulieu v Finglam (1401) YB 2 Hen IV fo 18, pl 16 *483*

Bee v Jenson [2007] EWCA Civ 923, [2007] 4 All ER 791 *764*

Beechwood Birmingham Ltd v Hoyer Group UK Ltd [2010] EWCA Civ 647, [2011] QB 357 *765*

Behrens v Bertram Mills Circus Ltd [1957] 2 QB 1 *398*

Bellefield Computer Services Ltd v E Turner & Sons Ltd [2000] BLR 97 *170*

Bellinger (FC) v Bellinger [2003] UKHL 21, [2003] 2 AC 467 *86*

Bennett v Chemical Construction (GB) Ltd [1971] 1 WLR 1571 *268*

Berezovsky v Michaels [2000] 1 WLR 1024 *526, 529*

Berkoff v Burchill [1996] 4 All ER 1008 *530, 531*

Bernard v Attorney-General of Jamaica [2004] UKPC 47 *875*

Bernstein v Skyviews [1978] QB 479 *412, 440*

Berry v Humm [1915] 1 KB 627 *847*

Bhamra v Dubb [2010] EWCA Civ 13 *128–9, 136*

Bici v Ministry of Defence [2004] EWHC 786 (QB) *43, 44, 251, 720*

Biffa Waste Services Ltd v Maschinenfabrik Ernst Hese GmbH [2008] EWCA Civ 1257, [2009] QB 725 *263, 264*

Billings v Riden [1945] KB 11 *741*

Bin Mahfouz v Ehrenfeld [2005] EWHC 1156 (QB) *525*

Bird v Jones (1845) 7 QB 742, 115 ER 668 *40*

Birmingham Development Co Ltd v Tyler [2008] EWCA Civ 859 *439*

Bisset v Wilkinson [1927] AC 177 *693*

Blake v Galloway [2004] EWCA Civ 814, [2004] 1 WLR 2844 *48, 94, 251*

Blake v Lanyon (1795) 6 TR 221, 101 ER 521 *662*

Bloodworth v Gray (1844) 7 Man & Gr 334, 135 ER 140 *545*

Blue Circle Industries plc v Ministry of Defence [1999] Ch 289 *165, 294, 421*

Blundy, Clark & Co Ltd v London North Eastern Railway [1931] 2 KB 334 *652*

Bocardo SA v Star Energy UK Onshore Ltd [2010] UKSC 35, [2011] 1 AC 380 *405, 412–3, 414, 814*

Bolam v Friern Hospital Management Committee [1957] 1 WLR 582 *247, 257, 258, 564*

Bolitho v City and Hackney Health Authority [1998] AC 232 *247, 257, 258*

Bollinger, J v Costa Brava Wine Co [1960] 1 Ch 262 *515*

Bolton v Stone [1951] AC 850 *132, 253*

Bolton (Engineering) Ltd, H L v T J Graham & Sons Ltd [1957] 1 QB 159 *266*

Bone v Seale [1975] 1 WLR 797 *451, 460*

Bonnard v Perryman [1891] 2 Ch 269 *836*

Bonnick v Morris [2002] UKPC 31, [2003] 1 AC 300 *836*

Bonnington Castings Ltd v Wardlaw [1956] AC 613 *279*

Borders v Commissioner of Police of the Metropolis [2005] EWCA Civ 197 *799, 800*

Bottomley v Bannister [1932] KB 458 *131*

Bourhill v Young [1943] AC 92 *11–12, 92*

Bourne Leisure Ltd v Marsden [2009] EWCA Civ 671 *364*

Bower v Hill (1835) 1 Bing NC 549, 131 ER 1229 *751*

Box v Jubb (1879) 4 Ex D 76 *478*

Bradburn v Great Western Railway Co (1874) LR 10 Ex 1 *768, 769*

Bradburn v Lindsay [1983] 2 All ER 408 *445*

Bradford Corporation v Pickles [1895] AC 587 *433, 435, 437, 438, 705*

Bradford-Smart v West Sussex County Council [2002] EWCA Civ 7 *239*

Brady v Norman [2008] EWHC 2481 (QB) *568*

Braithwaite v South Durham Steel Co Ltd [1958] 1 WLR 986 *406*

Brandeis Goldschmidt & Co v Western Transport [1981] QB 864 *749*

Breeden v Lampard, 21 March 1985, unreported *401*

Bretton v Hancock [2005] EWCA Civ 404 *628*

Brice v Brown [1984] 1 All ER 997 *335*

Bridlington Relay Ltd v Yorkshire Electricity
  Board [1965] Ch 436 *435*
Briess v Woolley [1954] AC 333 *694*
Brimelow v Casson [1924] 1 Ch 302 *668*
Brink's Global Services Inc v Igrox Ltd [2010]
  EWCA Civ 1207 *885–6*
Briscoe v Lubrizol [2000] ICR 694 *201*
Bristol & West Building Society v May, May &
  Merrimans (No 2) [1988] 1 WLR 336 *769*
British Celanese Ltd v A H Hunt (Capacitors)
  Ltd [1969] 1 WLR 959 *421*
British Chiropractic Association v Singh [2010]
  EWCA Civ 350, [2011] 1 WLR 133 *524,
  551–2*
British Diabetic Association v Diabetic Society
  Ltd [1995] 4 All ER 812 *515*
British Economical Lamp Co v Empire Mile End
  (Limited) (1913) 29 TLR 386 *495*
British Industrial Plastics v Ferguson [1940] 1
  All ER 479 *665*
British Motor Trade Association v Salvadori
  [1949] Ch 556 *662, 663*
British Railways Board v Herrington [1972] AC
  877 *366, 377*
British Road Services v Slater [1964] 1 WLR
  498 *650*
Brooke v Bool [1928] 2 KB 578 *869*
Brooks v Commissioner of Police of the
  Metropolis [2005] UKHL 24, [2005] 1 WLR
  1495 *114*
Broome v Cassell & Co Ltd [1972] AC 1027,
  affirming [1971] 2 QB 354 *571, 572, 792, 798,
  799*
Brown v Ministry of Defence [2006] EWCA Civ
  546 *292*
Brown v Raphael [1958] 1 Ch 636 *693*
Brown v Robinson [2004] UKPC 56 *875*
Brownlie v Campbell (1880) 5 App Cas 925 *694*
Bryan v Moloney (1995) 182 CLR 609 *341*
Bryanston Finance v de Vries [1975] 1 QB
  703 *561*
Buckle v Holmes [1926] 2 KB 125 *407, 408*
Buckley v Gross (1863) 3 B & S 566, 122 ER
  213 *492*
Bunt v Tilley [2006] EWHC 407 (QB), [2007] 1
  WLR 1243 *540*
Burgess v Florence Nightingale Hospital for
  Gentlewomen [1955] 1 QB 349 *847*
Burmah Oil v Lord Advocate [1965] AC 75 *410,
  720*
Burnard v Haggis (1863) 14 CB (NS) 45, 143 ER
  360 *718*

Burnett v British Waterways Board [1973] 1
  WLR 700 *365*
Burnie Port Authority v General Jones Pty Ltd
  (1994) 179 CLR 520 *469*
Burns v Edman [1970] 2 QB 541 *848*
Buron v Denman (1848) 2 Exch 167, 154 ER
  450 *720*
Burton v Islington Health Authority [1992] 3 All
  ER 833 *854–5*
Butchart v Home Office [2006] EWCA Civ 239,
  [2006] 1 WLR 1155 *226*
Butterworth v Butterworth and Englefield
  [1920] P 126 *7*
Byrne v Deane [1937] 1 KB 818 *540*

C v D [2006] EWHC 166 *154, 161*
Cable v Bryant [1908] 1 Ch 259 *437*
Cadbury Schweppes Pty Ltd v Pub Squash Co
  Pty Ltd [1981] RPC 429 *509*
CAL No 14 v Motor Accidents Board (2009) 239
  CLR 390 *225*
Caldwell v Fitzgerald [2001] EWCA Civ
  1054 *251*
Calgarth, The [1927] P 93 *362, 363*
Caltex Oil Pty Ltd v The Dredge 'Willemstaad'
  (1976) 136 CLR 529 *205*
Calveley v Chief Constable of the Merseyside
  Police [1989] AC 1228 *114, 711*
Calvert v William Hill [2008] EWCA Civ 1427,
  [2009] Ch 330, affirming [2008] EWHC 454
  (Ch) *276, 302, 303*
**Cambridge Water Co v Eastern Counties
  Leather Plc** [1994] 2 AC 264 *426, 463, 465,
  469, 472, 473, 474, 476–7*
Camden Nominees Ltd v Slack (or Forcey)
  [1940] Ch 352 *662*
Cameron v Network Rail Infrastructure Ltd
  [2006] EWHC 1133, [2007] 1 WLR 163 *75,
  81*
Caminer v Northern and London Investment
  Trust [1951] AC 88 *379, 650*
Campbell v Frisbee [2002] EWCA Civ 1374,
  [2003] ICR 141 *600*
Campbell v MGN Ltd [2004] UKHL 22, [2004]
  2 AC 457; reversing [2002] EWCA Civ 1373,
  [2003] QB 633 *589, 591, 592, 593, 594, 595,
  596, 597, 598, 600, 601, 602, 603, 605, 606,
  608, 611, 612, 614*
Candler v Crane, Christmas & Co [1951] 2 KB
  164 *109, 173, 178*
Candlewood Navigation Corporation Ltd v
  Mitsui OSK Lines Ltd [1986] AC 1 *110*

Caparo Industries plc v Dickman [1990] 2 AC
  605 *100, 104, 106, 107, 108, 131, 174, 198,*
  344–5
Capital and Counties plc v Hampshire County
  Council [1997] QB 1004 *12, 208, 209, 219,*
  221
Carmathenshire County Council v Lewis [1955]
  AC 549 *232*
Carmichael v National Power plc [1999] 1 WLR
  2042 *869*
Carrie v Tolkien [2009] EWHC 29 (QB) *546*
Carr-Saunders v Dick McNeil Associates Ltd
  [1986] 1 WLR 922 *456, 806*
Carslogie Steamship Co Ltd v Royal Norwegian
  Government [1952] AC 292 *306–7*
Carson v Here's Johnny Portable Toilets Inc, 698
  F 2d 831 (1983) *623*
Cassidy v Daily Mirror Newspapers Ltd [1929] 2
  KB 331 *534–5*
Cassidy v Ministry of Health [1951] 2 KB
  343 *263, 268*
Castle v St Augustine's Links (1922) 38 TLR
  615 *653*
Cattanach v Melchior (2003) 215 CLR 1 *347*
Cattle v Stockton Waterworks Co (1875) LR 10
  QB 453 *110, 205, 472, 477*
CBS Inc v Ames Records & Tapes Ltd [1982] Ch
  91 *861*
CBS Songs v Amstrad Consumer Electronics
  plc [1988] AC 1013 *94, 97, 110, 139, 861,*
  862
CC v AB [2006] EWHC 3083 *603, 609*
CDE v MGN Ltd [2010] EWHC 3308 (QB) *606*
Chadwick v British Transport Commission
  [1967] 1 WLR 912 *145, 146, 149*
Chaplin & Co Ltd, W H v Mayor of Westminster
  [1901] 2 Ch 329 *642*
Chapman v Lord Ellesmere [1932] 2 KB
  431 *546*
Charing Cross Electricity Supply Co v Hydraulic
  Power Co [1914] 3 KB 772 *471*
Charleston v News Group Newspapers Ltd
  [1995] 2 AC 65 *532*
Chastey v Ackland [1895] 2 Ch 389 *436*
Chatterton v Gerson [1981] 1 QB 432 *45, 46*
Chatterton v Secretary of State for India in
  Council [1895] 2 QB 189 *557*
Chaudhry v Prabhakar [1989] 1 WLR 29 *178*
Chester v Afshar [2004] UKHL 41, [2005] 1 AC
  134 *98, 281–2, 307, 308, 323–4, 826–7*
Chic Fashions Ltd v Jones [1968] 2 QB 299 *409*
Child v Stenning (1879) 11 Ch D 82 *749*

Childs v Desormeaux [2006] 1 SCR 643 *223,*
  224, 225
China Pacific SA v Food Corporation of India,
  The Winson [1982] AC 939 *498*
Christie v Davey [1893] 1 Ch 316 *432, 438*
Christie v Leachinsky [1947] AC 573 *58*
Chute Farms v Curtis, The Times, 10 October
  1961 *181*
Cinnamond v BAA [1980] 1 WLR 582 *409*
City of London Corporation v Appleyard [1963]
  1 WLR 982 *492*
City of New York v Keene Corp, 513 NYS 2d
  1004 (1987); affirming, 505 NYS 2d 782
  (1986) *341*
City of New York v Lead Industries Ass'n, Inc,
  644 NYS 2d 919 (1996) *341*
Clark v Associated Newspapers Ltd [1998] 1
  WLR 1559 *516*
Clark v Bowlt [2006] EWCA Civ 978 *402*
Clayton v Le Roy [1911] 2 KB 1031 *498*
Clift v Slough Borough Council [2010] EWCA
  Civ 1484, [2011] 1 WLR 1774 *558–60, 573*
Club Cruise Entertainment v Department of
  Transport [2008] EWHC 2794 (Comm)
  495
Clunis v Camden and Islington Health
  Authority [1998] QB 978 *355, 731*
Coleman v British Gas, 27 February 2002,
  unreported *126*
Colledge v Bass Mitchells & Butlers Ltd [1988] 1
  All ER 536 *767*
Collingwood v Home & Colonial Stores Ltd
  [1936] 3 All ER 200 *482*
Collins v Wilcock [1984] 1 WLR 1172 *49, 88,*
  502
Colls v Home & Colonial Stores Ltd [1904] AC
  179 *436*
Colour Quest Ltd v Total Downstream UK Plc
  [2009] EWHC 540 (Comm) *479, 644, 646,*
  647, 652
Columbia Picture Industries Inc v Robinson
  [1987] 1 Ch 38 *793*
Commissioner of Police of the Metropolis v
  Lennon [2004] EWCA Civ 130, [2004] 2 All
  ER 266 *178*
Conarken Group Ltd v Network Rail
  Infrastructure Ltd [2011] EWCA Civ 644,
  affirming [2010] EWHC 1852 (TCC) *407,*
  409
Condon v Basi [1985] 1 WLR 866 *130, 251*
Congregational Union v Harriss and Harriss
  [1988] 1 All ER 15 *182*

Connor v Surrey CC [2010] EWCA Civ 286, [2011] QB 429 *259–60*

Consolidated Company v Curtis & Son [1892] 1 QB 495 *496*

Conway v George Wimpey & Co Ltd [1951] 2 KB 266 *877*

Cook v Cook (1986) 162 CLR 376 *249*

Cook v Lewis [1951] SCR 830 *284, 285, 303, 304*

Co-operative Group v Pritchard [2011] EWCA Civ 329 *773*

Cope v Sharpe (No 2) [1912] 1 KB 496 *410*

Corbett v Hill (1870) LR 9 Eq 671 *412*

Corby Group Litigation, Re [2008] EWCA Civ 463, [2009] QB 335; applied [2009] EWHC 1944 (TCC) *644, 653*

Cornwell v Myskow [1987] 1 WLR 630 *530*

Corporacion Nacional de Cobre v Sogemin [1997] 1 WLR 1396 *773*

Corr v IBC Vehicles Ltd [2008] UKHL 13, [2008] 1 AC 884 *316, 326, 774, 775–6, 845*

Costello v Chief Constable of Derbyshire Constabulary [2001] EWCA Civ 381, [2001] 1 WLR 1437 *492*

Costello v Chief Constable of Northumbria Police [1999] 1 All ER 550 *228–9*

Coulson v Coulson [1887] 3 TLR 846 *836*

Countryside Residential (North Thames) Ltd v Tugwell [2000] 34 EG 87 *412*

Cox v Hockenhull [2000] 1 WLR 750 *847*

Coxall v Goodyear GB Ltd [2003] 1 WLR 536 *236*

Cream Holdings Ltd v Banerjee [2004] UKHL 44, [2005] 1 AC 253 *619, 836*

Credit Lyonnais Bank Nederland NV v Export Credit Guarantee Department [2000] AC 486 *672, 860, 862, 867, 891–2*

Crocker v Sundance Northwest Resorts Ltd [1988] 1 SCR 1186 *138*

Crofter Hand Woven Harris Tweed Co v Veitch [1942] AC 435 *685, 686, 687*

Croke (a minor) v Wiseman [1982] 1 WLR 171 *762*

Cross v Kirkby, The Times, 5 April 2000 *50, 734*

Crowhurst v Amersham Burial Board (1878) 4 CPD 5 *473*

Cullen v Chief Constable of the Royal Ulster Constabulary [2003] UKHL 39, [2003] 1 WLR 1763 *633, 750*

Cummings v Grainger [1977] 1 QB 397 *400, 401, 404*

Curtis v Betts [1990] 1 WLR 459 *400, 401*

Customs & Excise Commissioners v Barclays Bank [2006] UKHL 28, [2007] 1 AC 181 *110, 114, 118, 175, 177, 188*

Cutler v Wandsworth Stadium Ltd [1949] AC 398 *628*

D v East Berkshire Community Health NHS Trust [2005] UKHL 23, [2005] 2 AC 373 *8, 13, 88, 115, 118–9, 120, 240–1, 717*

D & F Estates v Church Commissioners [1989] AC 177 *110, 131, 183, 340, 341*

Daiichi Pharmaceuticals UK Ltd v Stop Huntingdon Animal Cruelty [2003] EWHC 2337, [2004] 1 WLR 1503 *585*

Dakhyl v Labouchere [1908] 2 KB 325n *551*

Dalton v Angus (1881) 6 App Cas 740 *436, 437*

Daly v General Steam Navigation Co Ltd [1981] 1 WLR 120 *781*

Daly v Liverpool Corporation [1939] 2 All ER 142 *774*

Darbishire v Warran [1963] 1 WLR 1067 *764*

Darby v National Trust [2001] EWCA Civ 189 *366*

Darker v Chief Constable of the West Midlands Police [2001] 1 AC 435 *723*

David v Abdul Cader [1963] 1 WLR 834 *710*

Davidson v Chief Constable of North Wales [1994] 2 All ER 597 *40*

Davie v New Merton Board Mills Ltd [1959] AC 604 *262*

Davies v Taylor [1972] 1 QB 286 *847*

Davis v Radcliffe [1990] 1 WLR 821 *208*

Daw v Intel Corporation (UK) Ltd [2007] EWCA Civ 70 *156*

Dawkins v Lord Paulet (1869) LR 5 QB 94 *557*

Dawkins v Lord Rokeby (1875) LR 7 HL 744 *556*

Dawson v Vansandau (1863) 11 WR 516 *707*

De Beers Abrasive Products Ltd v International General Electric Co of New York [1975] 1 WLR 972 *698*

De Francesco v Barnum (1890) 63 LT 514 *662*

Deane v Ealing London Borough Council [1993] ICR 329 *792*

Deatons Pty Ltd v Flew (1949) 79 CLR 370 *876*

Dee v Telegraph Media Group Ltd [2010] EWHC 924 (QB) *530, 531*

Dennis v Ministry of Defence [2003] EWHC 793 *427, 429, 454*

Densmore v Whitehorse [1986] 5 WWR 708 *187, 219*

Derbyshire County Council v Times Newspapers Ltd [1993] AC 534 *543–4, 575*

Derry v Peek (1889) 14 App Cas 337 *694*

Devenish Nutrition Ltd v Sanofi-Aventis SA [2008] EWCA Civ 1086, [2009] Ch 390 *800, 808–9, 813, 815, 817*

Deyong v Shenburn [1946] KB 227 *237*

DFT v TFD [2010] EWHC 2335 (QB) *605*

Dickins v O2 Plc [2008] EWCA Civ 1144 *280*

Dimond v Lovell [2002] 1 AC 384 *312, 781*

Dixon v Bell (1816) 5 M & S 198, 105 ER 1023 *129, 130, 137*

Dobson v North Tyneside Health Authority [1997] 1 WLR 596 *488*

Dobson v Thames Water Utilities Ltd [2009] EWCA Civ 28 *420, 451, 454, 462, 749*

Dodd Properties (Kent) Ltd v Canterbury City Council [1980] 1 WLR 433 *763*

Dodwell v Burford (1670) 1 Mod 24, 86 ER 703 *38*

Doltis Ltd, J v Issac Braithwaite & Sons (Engineers) Ltd [1957] 1 Lloyds Rep 522 *481*

Dominion Natural Gas Co v Collins [1909] AC 640 *129, 130*

Donachie v Chief Constable of Greater Manchester [2004] EWCA Civ 405 *140, 337*

Donald v Ntuli [2010] EWCA Civ 1276, [2011] 1 WLR 294 *599, 609*

Donnelly v Joyce [1974] QB 454 *780*

Donoghue v Folkestone Properties Ltd [2003] EWCA Civ 231, [2003] QB 1008 *363, 368*

Donoghue v Stevenson [1932] AC 562 *1–2, 3, 4, 5–6, 7, 9, 13, 92, 104, 105, 106, 122, 129, 130, 136, 171, 172, 184, 187, 341, 376, 377*

Dooley v Cammell Laird & Co Ltd [1951] 1 Lloyds Rep 271 *146, 147, 149*

Dorset Yacht Co Ltd v Home Office [1970] AC 1004 *232–3*

D'Orta-Ekenaike v Victoria Legal Aid [2005] HCA 12 *182*

Doughty v Turner Manufacturing Co Ltd [1964] 1 QB 518 *122, 333*

Douglas v Hello! Ltd (No 3) [2007] UKHL 21, [2008] 1 AC 1; reversing [2005] EWCA Civ 595, [2006] QB 125 *592, 593, 596, 618, 624, 680–1, 811–2*

Downs v Chappell [1997] 1 WLR 426 *695*

Doyle v Olby (Ironmongers) Ltd [1969] 2 QB 158 *338*

DPP v Jones [1999] 2 AC 240 *409*

Drane v Evangelou [1978] 1 WLR 455 *791, 799*

Drayton Public School District No 19 v WR Grace & Co, 728 F Supp 1410 (1989) *341*

Drummond-Jackson v British Medical Association [1970] 1 WLR 688 *532*

Dubai Aluminium Co Ltd v Salaam [2002] UKHL 48, [2003] 2 AC 366 *262, 866, 878, 879, 880, 881, 888, 889*

Dudgeon v UK (1981) 4 EHRR 149 *599*

Duffy v Eastern Health & Social Services Board [1992] IRLR 251 *792, 801*

Duke of Brunswick, The v Harmer (1849) 14 QB 185, 117 ER 75 *542–3*

Dulieu v White & Sons [1901] 2 KB 669 *161*

Dunlop v Maison Talbot (1904) 20 TLR 579 *696*

Dunlop v Woollahara MC [1982] AC 158 *710*

Dutton v Bognor Regis United Building Co [1972] 1 QB 373 *131*

Dwyer v Mansfield [1946] 1 KB 437 *642*

E (a child) v Souls Garages Ltd, The Times, 23 January 2001 *137*

Easson v London and North Eastern Railway Company [1944] 1 KB 421 *268*

East v Maurer [1991] 1 WLR 461 *693, 694*

East Suffolk Rivers Catchment Board v Kent [1941] AC 74 *208*

Eastern & South African Telegraph Co v Cape Town Tramways Co [1902] AC 381 *471, 473*

Eastwood v Holmes (1858) 1 F & F 347, 175 ER 758 *537*

Ecclestone v Telegraph Media Group Ltd [2009] EWHC 2779 (QB) *531*

Edelsten v Edelsten (1863) 1 De G J & S 185, 46 ER 72 *811*

EDG v Hammer [2003] 2 SCR 459 *882*

Edgington v Fitzmaurice (1885) 29 Ch D 459 *551, 693*

Edward Wong Finance Co Ltd v Johnson Stokes & Master [1984] 1 AC 296 *258*

Edwards v Lee's Administrators, 96 SW 2d 1028 (1936) *812–3*

Edwards v Mallan [1908] 1 KB 1002 *181*

Edwards v Railway Executive [1952] AC 737 *361*

Edwin Hill v First National [1989] 1 WLR 225 *668*

EETPU v Times Newspapers Ltd [1980] QB 585 *543*

Eglantine Inn Ltd v Smith [1948] NI 29 *539*

Elguzouli-Daf v Commissioner of the Police of the Metropolis [1995] QB 335 *218*

Elliott *v* London Borough of Islington [1991] 1
  EGLR 167 *458, 459*
Ellis *v* Home Office [1953] 2 All ER 149 *224*
Elvin & Powell Ltd *v* Plummer Roddis Ltd
  (1934) 50 TLR 158 *499*
Emeh *v* Kensington Area Health Authority
  [1985] 1 QB 1012 *351, 352*
Emerald Construction *v* Lowthian [1966] 1
  WLR 691 *665, 666*
Emmanuel Ltd, H & N *v* GLC [1971] 2 All ER
  835 *481, 482*
Emmens *v* Pottle (1885) 16 QBD 354 *540*
Empire Jamaica, The [1957] AC 386 *277*
Environment Agency *v* Empress Car Co
  (Abertilly) Ltd [1999] 2 AC 22 *316–7*
Erven Warnink Besloten Vennootschap *v* J
  Townend & Sons (Hull) Ltd [1979] AC
  731 *515*
Essa *v* Laing [2004] EWCA Civ 2 *337, 338, 339*
Esser *v* Brown (2004) 242 DLR (4th) 112 *163*
Esso Petroleum Co Ltd *v* Mardon [1976] QB
  801 *178*
Esso Petroleum Co Ltd *v* Southport Corporation
  [1956] AC 218, reversing [1954] 2 QB 182,
  affirming [1953] 3 WLR 773 *410, 440, 446,*
  647
ETK *v* News Group Newspapers Ltd [2011]
  EWCA Civ 439 *603, 605*
European Commission *v* United Kingdom
  [1997] All ER (EC) 481 *391*
Eurymedon, The, see New Zealand Shipping
  Co Ltd *v* A M Satterthwaite & Co Ltd
Evans *v* London Hospital Medical College
  (University of London) [1981] 1 WLR
  184 *556*
Everett *v* Comojo (UK) Ltd [2011] EWCA Civ
  13 *363, 376–7*
Experience Hendrix *v* PPX Enterprises [2003]
  EWCA Civ 323 *815*

F (mental patient: sterilisation), Re [1990] 2 AC
  1 *43, 45, 49, 50, 52, 53, 54*
F *v* Wirral MBC [1991] Fam 69 *8*
Fairchild *v* Glenhaven Funeral Services Ltd
  [2002] UKHL 22, [2003] 1 AC 32; reversing,
  [2001] EWCA Civ 1891, [2002] 1 WLR
  1052 *13, 98, 285–7, 288, 289, 290, 291, 301,*
  302, 363
Farley *v* Skinner [2001] UKHL 49, [2002] 2 AC
  732 *160*
Farrugia *v* Great Western Railway Co [1947] 2
  All ER 565 *136*

Fashion Brokers Ltd *v* Clarke Hayes [2000]
  PNLR 473 *177*
Fayed *v* Al-Tajir [1988] 1 QB 712 *557*
Fayed *v* United Kingdom (1994) 18 EHRR
  393 *745*
Femis-Bank *v* Lazar [1991] Ch 391 *836*
Fennelly *v* Connex South Eastern Ltd [2001]
  IRLR 390 *884*
Ferguson *v* British Gas [2009] EWCA Civ 46,
  [2010] 1 WLR 785 *584*
Ferguson *v* Welsh [1987] 1 WLR 1553 *361*
Fields *v* Davis [1955] CLY 1543 *531*
Fish *v* Kapur [1948] 2 All ER 176 *181*
Fisher *v* Prowse (1862) 2 B & S 770, 121 ER
  1258 *643*
Fitzgerald *v* Lane [1989] AC 328 *775*
Flood *v* Times Newspapers Ltd [2010] EWCA
  Civ 804, [2011] 1 WLR 153; reversing [2009]
  EWHC 2375 (QB) *565, 567, 577*
FM (a child) *v* Singer [2004] EWHC 793
  (QB) *114*
Fogarty *v* United Kingdom (2001) 34 EHRR
  302 *745*
Forrester *v* Tyrell (1893) 9 TLR 257 *544*
Forsyth-Grant *v* Allen [2008] EWCA Civ
  505 *800, 806, 812, 815*
Foskett *v* McKeown [2001] 1 AC 102 *26, 818*
Foster *v* Stewart (1814) 3 M & S 191, 105 ER
  582 *815*
Foster *v* Warblington UDC [1906] 1 KB 648 *450*
Fouldes *v* Willoughby (1841) 8 M & W 540, 151
  ER 1153 *495*
Fowler *v* Lanning [1959] 1 QB 426 *42, 43, 44,*
  408, 500
Franklin *v* The South Eastern Railway Company
  (1858) 3 H & N 211, 157 ER 448 *846*
Fraser *v* Evans [1969] 1 QB 349 *836*
Freeman *v* Higher Park Farm [2008] EWCA Civ
  1185 *402–3, 404*
French *v* Chief Constable of Sussex Police
  [2006] EWCA Civ 312 *148, 236*
Friends for All Children *v* Lockheed
  Corporation Inc, 746 F 2d 816 (1984) *228*
Froom *v* Butcher [1976] QB 286 *775*
Frost *v* Chief Constable of the South Yorkshire
  Police [1999] 2 AC 455 *145–6, 148, 161,*
  236, 727

G & K Landenbau (UK) Ltd *v* Crawley & De
  Reya [1978] 1 WLR 266 *258*
Gaca *v* Pirelli General plc [2004] EWCA Civ
  373, [2004] 1 WLR 2683 *769*

Gäfgen v Germany (2011) 52 EHRR 1 51

Galoo v Bright Grahame Murray [1994] 1 WLR 1360 177

Gammell v Wilson [1982] AC 27 762, 779

Gardiner v Moore [1969] 1 QB 55 766

Garret v Taylor (1620) Cro Jac 567, 79 ER 485 673

Gartside v Outram (1857) 26 LJ Ch 113 603

Gaunt v Fynney (1872–3) LR 8 Ch App 8 424

Geest plc v Lansiquot [2002] UKPC 48, [2002] 1 WLR 3111 351

George v Skivington (1869–70) LR 5 Ex 1 129

Ghaidan v Godin-Mendoza [2004] UKHL 30, [2004] 2 AC 557 86

Gibbons v Caraway, 565 NW 2d 663 (1997) 727

Giblan v National Amalgamated Labourers' Union of Great Britain and Ireland [1903] 2 KB 600 686

Gilding v Eyre (1861) 10 CB NS 592, 142 ER 584 709

Giles v Thompson [1994] 1 AC 142 781

Giles v Walker (1890) 24 QBD 656 473

Gillette UK Ltd v Edenwest Ltd [1994] RPC 279 515

Gillick v West Norfolk Area Health Authority [1986] AC 112 48

Gillingham BC v Medway (Chatham) Dock Co Ltd [1993] QB 343 430, 431

Gladwell v Steggal (1839) 5 Bing NC 733, 132 ER 1283 181

Glaister v Appleby-in-Westmorland Town Council [2009] EWCA Civ 1325 366

Glinski v McIver [1962] AC 726 707

Godfrey v Demon Internet Ltd [2001] QB 201 540, 569–70

Godwin v Uzoigwe [1993] Fam Law 65 682, 701, 702

Gold v Essex County Council [1942] 2 KB 293 263

Golder v United Kingdom (1975) 1 EHRR 524 744

Goldman v Hargrave [1967] 1 AC 645 93, 96, 252, 378, 379, 445, 448, 482

Goldsmith v Bhoyrul [1998] QB 459 544

Goldsmith v Sperrings [1977] 1 WLR 478 574

Goldsoll v Goldman [1914] 2 Ch 603 669

Goodes v East Sussex County Council [2000] 1 WLR 1356 635

Goodwill v British Pregnancy Advisory Service [1996] 1 WLR 1397 196, 202

Goodwin v United Kingdom (2002) 35 EHRR 18 593

Gordon v Harper (1796) 7 TR 9, 101 ER 828 491–2

Gorham v British Telecommunications plc [2001] 1 WLR 2129 202, 352, 778

Gorringe v Calderdale MBC [2004] UKHL 15, [2004] 1 WLR 1057 13, 96, 114, 118, 209, 210, 211, 221–2, 240, 242, 717

Gorris v Scott (1874) LR 9 Ex 125 329, 342, 629

Gough v Thorne [1966] 1 WLR 1387 774

Grainger v Hill (1838) 4 Bing NC 212, 132 ER 769 709

Gran Gelato Ltd v Richcliff (Group) Ltd [1992] Ch 560 177, 777

Gravil v Carroll [2008] EWCA Civ 689 884, 886, 888, 889

Gray v Thames Trains Ltd [2009] UKHL 33, [2009] 1 AC 1339 310, 330, 730, 731, 733, 748

Greatorex v Greatorex [2000] 1 WLR 1970 150

Green Corns Ltd v Claverley Group Ltd [2005] EWHC 958 (QB) 604

Greene v Associated Newspapers Ltd [2004] EWCA Civ 1462, [2005] QB 972 836

Greenfield v Irwin [2001] EWCA Civ 113, [2001] 1 WLR 113 347

Greenock Corporation v Caledonian Railway Co [1917] AC 556 478

Gregg v Scott [2005] UKHL 2, [2005] 2 AC 176 293, 295, 296–9, 762

Gregory v Portsmouth City Council [2000] AC 419 708–9

Greig v Insole [1978] 1 WLR 302 661, 668

Greystoke Castle, The, see Morrison Steamship Co Ltd v Greystoke Castle (Cargo Owners)

Griffin v UHY Hacker Young & Partners [2010] EWHC 146 (Ch) 733

Grimshaw v Ford Motor Co, 119 Cal App 3d 757 (1981) 246

Grobbelaar v News Group Newspapers Ltd [2002] UKHL 40, [2002] 1 WLR 3024 549, 571

Grote v Chester and Holyhead Railway (1848) 2 Ex 251, 154 ER 485 129

Group B Plaintiffs v Medical Research Council [2000] Lloyds Rep Med 161 157

Groves v Wimborne [1898] 2 QB 402 631

Guardian News and Media Ltd, In Re [2010] UKSC 1, [2010] 2 AC 697 573, 613

Guerra v Italy (1998) 26 EHRR 357 453

Gulf Oil (Great Britain) Ltd v Page [1987] Ch 327 836

Gwilliam v West Hertfordshire Hospitals NHS Trust [2002] EWCA Civ 1041, [2003] QB 443 260–1, 365–6

H v AB [2009] EWCA Civ 1092 *706*

H v News Group Newspapers Ltd [2011] EWCA Civ 42, [2011] 1 WLR 1645 *620*

Hale v Jennings Bros [1938] 1 All ER 579 *472*

Haley v London Electricity Board [1965] AC 778 *136*

Halford v United Kingdom (1997) 24 EHRR 523 *83*

Halifax Building Society v Thomas [1996] Ch 217 *813*

Hall v Beckenham Corp [1949] 1 KB 716 *440*

Hall v Simons, see Arthur J S Hall v Simons

Halsey v Esso Petroleum [1961] 1 WLR 683 *425, 440, 463*

Hamilton Jones v David & Snape (a firm) [2003] EWHC 3147 (Ch), [2004] 1 WLR 924 *160*

Hansen v Mountain Fuel Supply Co, 858 P 2d 970 (1993) *228*

Harakas v Baltic Mercantile and Shipping Exchange Ltd [1982] 1 WLR 958 *836*

Hardaker v Idle DC [1896] 1 QB 335 *649*

Hardwick v Hudson [1999] 1 WLR 1770 *781*

Hardy v Brooks, 118 SE 2d 492 (1961) *222*

Harooni v Rustins [2011] EWHC 1362 (TCC) *475*

Harper v G N Haden & Sons Ltd [1933] Ch 298 *641, 642*

Harris v Birkenhead Corporation [1976] 1 WLR 279 *360*

Harris v Evans [1998] 1 WLR 1285 *114, 192*

Harris v Perry [2008] EWCA Civ 907, [2009] 1 WLR 19 *253, 254–5*

Harriton v Stephens (2006) 80 AJLR 791 *856*

Hartley v Moxham (1842) 3 QB 701, 114 ER 675 *501*

Harvey v Plymouth City Council [2010] EWCA Civ 860 *362–3*

Haseldine v Daw [1941] 2 KB 343 *187, 210*

Haskett v Trans Union of Canada (2003) 224 DLR (4th) 419 *199*

Hasselblad (GB) Ltd v Orbinson [1985] QB 475 *556*

Hatton v Sutherland [2002] EWCA Civ 76 *149, 155*

Hatton v United Kingdom (2003) 37 EHRR 28 *453*

Hawkins v Smith (1896) 12 Times LR 532 *129*

Hawley v Luminar Leisure Ltd [2006] EWCA Civ 18 *873, 874*

Hay v Hughes [1975] 1 QB 790 *849*

Hayden v Hayden [1992] 1 WLR 986 *850, 851*

Haynes v Harwood [1935] 1 KB 146 *311, 726*

Heasmans v Clarity Cleaning Co [1987] ICR 949 *875, 885, 886*

Heaven v Pender (1883) 11 QBD 503 *104, 105, 106*

Hedley Byrne & Co Ltd v Heller & Partners Ltd [1964] AC 465 *106, 173–4, 175, 176, 177, 179, 180, 181, 183, 184, 186, 187, 188, 189, 190, 191, 192, 195, 204, 205, 206, 217, 218, 220, 263, 340, 342, 343, 345, 740, 776, 777*

Heil v Rankin [2001] QB 272 *759*

Hemmens v Wilson Browne [1995] 2 Ch 223 *201*

Henderson v Merrett Syndicates Ltd [1995] 2 AC 145 *96, 177, 184–7, 217*

Henly v Mayor of Lyme (1828) 5 Bing 91, 130 ER 995 *711*

Hepburn v Lordan (1865) 2 H & M 345, 71 ER 497 *439*

Herbage v Pressdram [1984] 1 WLR 1160 *836*

Herd v Weardale Steel, Coal and Coke Company Ltd [1915] AC 67 *47*

Hern v Nichols (1700) 1 Salk 289, 91 ER 256 *887*

Herring v Metropolitan Board of Works (1865) 19 CB NS 510, 144 ER 886 *642*

Hewison v Meridian Shipping Services Pte Ltd [2002] EWCA Civ 1821 *735*

Hibbert v McKiernan [1948] 2 KB 142 *492*

Hicks v Chief Constable of South Yorkshire Police [1992] 2 All ER 65 *158, 340*

Hicks v Faulkner (1881–2) LR 8 QBD 167 *707*

Hilbery v Hatton (1864) 2 H & C 822, 159 ER 341 *861*

Hill v Chief Constable of West Yorkshire [1989] AC 53 *12, 102, 106, 109, 208, 216, 241*

Hill v Tupper (1863) 2 H & C 121, 159 ER 51 *412*

Hinz v Berry [1970] 2 QB 40 *158*

Hiort v Bott (1874) LR 9 Ex 86 *499*

Hiort v The London and North Western Railway Company (1879) 4 Ex D 188 *494*

Hirst v UK (No 2) (2006) 42 EHRR 41 *71*

HL v United Kingdom (2005) 40 EHRR 32 *41*

Hobbs (Farms) Ltd, E v Baxenden Chemicals [1992] 1 Lloyds Rep 54 *227*

Hodgson v Trapp [1989] 1 AC 807 *769*

Holbeck Hall Hotel Ltd v Scarborough Council [2000] QB 836 *96, 252, 378, 444*

Holden v Chief Constable of Lancashire [1987] 1 QB 380 *801*

Hole v Barlow (1858) 4 CB NS 334, 140 ER 1113 *424*

Holley v Smyth [1998] QB 726 *836*

Holliday v National Telephone Co [1899] 2 QB 392 *649*

Hollins v Fowler (1875) LR 7 HL 757 *500*

Hollis v Vabu Pty Ltd (2001) 207 CLR 21 *886*

Hollywood Silver Fox Farm Ltd v Emmett [1936] 2 KB 468 *433, 434, 438*

Holtby v Brigham & Cowan (Hull) Ltd [2000] 3 All ER 421 *279*

Honeywill & Stein v Larkin Brothers [1934] 1 KB 191 *263, 264, 870*

Hooper v Rogers [1975] Ch 43 *439*

Horrocks v Lowe [1975] AC 135 *557*

Horsley v McClaren [1971] 2 Lloyds Rep 410, affirming [1970] 1 Lloyds Rep 257 *131*

Hosking v Runting [2005] 1 NZLR 1 *601*

Hotson v East Berkshire Health Authority [1987] AC 750 *282, 283, 292–3*

Houghland v R R Low (Luxury Coaches) Ltd [1962] 1 QB 694 *269*

Housecroft v Burnett [1986] 1 All ER 332 *780*

Howard E Perry v British Railways Board [1980] 1 WLR 1375 *495, 506*

Howard Marine & Dredging Co v A Ogden (Excavations) Ltd [1978] QB 574 *177, 178*

HRH Prince of Wales v Associated Newspapers Ltd [2006] EWCA Civ 1776, [2008] Ch 57 *592, 598*

HSBC Rail (UK) Ltd v Network Rail Infrastructure Ltd [2005] EWCA Civ 1437, [2006] 1 WLR 643 *492*

Hubbard v Pitt [1976] QB 142 *440*

Huckle v Money (1763) 2 Wils KB 405, 95 ER 768 *822*

Hudson v Ridge Manufacturing Co Ltd [1957] 2 QB 348 *253*

Hughes v Lord Advocate [1963] AC 837 *332*

Hulton & Co, E v Jones [1910] AC 20 *536*

Hunt v Great Northern Railway Company [1891] 2 QB 189 *560*

Hunt v Severs [1994] 2 AC 350 *780–1*

Hunt v Star Newspaper Ltd [1908] 2 KB 309 *551*

Hunter v British Coal Corp [1999] QB 140 *146–7*

Hunter v Canary Wharf Ltd [1997] AC 655 *96, 165, 418, 420, 421, 422, 424, 430, 431, 438, 440, 449, 450, 451, 460, 463, 464, 469, 471, 579, 643, 653*

Hunter v Chief Constable of the West Midlands Police [1982] AC 529 *723*

Huntley v Thornton [1957] 1 WLR 321 *686, 687*

Hussain v Lancaster City Council [2000] QB 1 *208, 440, 441, 442*

Hussain v New Taplow Paper Mills [1988] 1 AC 514 *769, 771*

Hussey v Eels [1990] 1 All ER 449 *772*

Huth v Huth [1915] 3 KB 32 *539–40*

Hyett v Great Western Railway Company [1948] 1 KB 345 *311*

IBL Ltd v Coussens [1991] 2 All ER 133 *506*

Ilott v Wilkes (1820) 3 B & Ald 304, 106 ER 674 *69*

Imbree v McNeilly (2008) 82 AJLR 1374 *249*

Imerman v Tchenguiz [2010] EWCA Civ 908 *502, 592, 614–5, 616*

Inland Revenue Commissioners v Muller & Co's Margarine Ltd [1901] AC 217 *509, 513*

Inniss v Attorney-General of Saint Christopher & Nevis [2008] UKPC 42 *821*

International Factors v Rodriguez [1979] 1 QB 751 *493*

Inverugie Investments Ltd v Hackett [1995] 1 WLR 713 *815*

Iqbal v Dean Manson Solicitors [2011] EWCA Civ 123 *583*

Iqbal v Prison Officers Association [2009] EWCA Civ 1312, [2010] QB 732 *12, 41, 44, 714*

Iqbal v Whipps Cross University Hospital NHS Trust [2007] EWCA Civ 1190 *762*

Irvine v Talksport Ltd [2002] EWHC 367 (QB), [2002] 1 WLR 2355 *515, 623*

Irving v Penguin Books Ltd, 11 April 2000, unreported *552*

Isaack v Clark (1615) 2 Bulstr 306, 80 ER 1143 *494*

Island Records, Ex parte [1978] 1 Ch 122 *630*

Islington LBC v University College London Hospital NHS Trust [2005] EWCA Civ 956 *110, 780*

Iveson v Moore (1699) 1 Ld Raym 486, 91 ER 1224 *651*

Jacobi v Griffiths [1999] 2 SCR 570 *878, 882, 883, 890*

Jaggard v Sawyer [1995] 1 WLR 269 *455, 456, 806, 838, 840*

Jain v Trent Strategic HA [2009] UKHL 4, [2009] 1 AC 853 *115, 192–3, 194*

Jameel (Mohammed) v Wall Street Journal Europe SPRL [2006] UKHL 44, [2007] 1 AC 359 545, 546, 562, 564, 565, 566, 568, 577, 610

Jameel (Yousef) v Dow Jones & Co Inc [2005] EWCA Civ 75, [2005] QB 946 524, 538, 541, 545

James v Attorney General of Trinidad and Tobago [2010] UKSC 23 821

James v United Kingdom (1986) 8 EHRR 123 744

James McNaughton Paper Group Ltd v Hicks Anderson & Co [1991] 2 QB 113 177

Jameson v Central Electricity Generating Board [2000] 1 AC 455 767

Jan de Nul (UK) Ltd v NV Royale Belge [2002] EWCA Civ 209, affirming [2000] 1 Lloyd's Rep 700 644, 651, 652

Janvier v Sweeney [1919] 2 KB 316 154

JEB Fasteners Ltd v Marks Bloom & Co [1983] 1 All ER 583 695

Jebson v Ministry of Defence [2000] 1 WLR 2055 237–8

Jennings v Rundall (1799) 8 TR 335, 101 ER 1419 718

Jeyaretnam v Goh Chok Tong [1989] 1 WLR 1109 551

Jobling v Associated Dairies Ltd [1982] AC 794 276, 302, 303, 309, 310, 759

Jockey Club v Buffham [2002] EWHC 1866 (QB), [2003] QB 462 619

Joe Lee Ltd v Lord Dalmeny [1927] 1 Ch 300 661

John v Associated Newspapers Ltd [2006] EWHC 1611 (QB) 601

John v MGN Ltd [1997] QB 586 572

John Hudson & Co Ltd v Oaten, 19 June 1980, unreported 860

John Young & Co v Bankier Distillery Co [1893] AC 691 437

Johnson v BJW Property Developments Ltd [2002] EWHC 1131 (QB), [2002] 3 All ER 574 481, 482

Johnstone v Pedlar [1921] 2 AC 262 720

Jolley v Sutton London Borough Council [2000] 1 WLR 1082, reversing [1998] 1 WLR 1546 331–2, 334, 340

Jones v Kaney [2011] UKSC 13 116, 722, 724

Jones v Livox Quarries Ltd [1952] 2 QB 608 778

Jones v Llanrwst UDC [1911] 1 Ch 393 411

Jones v Pritchard [1908] 1 Ch 630 445

Jones v Ruth [2011] EWCA Civ 804 339, 583–4

Jones v Swansea CC [1990] 1 WLR 54 709, 711

Jones Brothers (Hunstanton) Ltd v Stevens [1955] 1 QB 275 662

Jones (Insurance Brokers) Ltd, LE v Portsmouth City Council [2002] EWCA Civ 1723, [2003] 1 WLR 427 445

Jordan House Ltd v Menow [1974] SCR 239 225

Joseph v Spiller [2010] UKSC 53, [2011] 1 AC 852 549, 550, 551, 553, 554, 555, 576

Joyce v Sengupta [1993] 1 WLR 337, [1993] 1 All ER 897 697, 703

Junior Books Ltd v Veitchi Co Ltd [1983] 1 AC 520 183, 184, 187, 729, 730

K v Secretary of State for the Home Dept [2002] EWCA Civ 1983 233

Kambadzi v Secretary of State for the Home Dept [2011] UKSC 23 61

Kane v New Forest DC [2001] EWCA Civ 878, [2002] 1 WLR 312 223, 224

Kapfunde v Abbey National plc [1999] ICR 1 199

Karagozlu v Metropolitan Police Comr [2006] EWCA Civ 1691, [2007] 1 WLR 1881 714

KD v Chief Constable of Hampshire [2005] EWHC 2550 (QB) 45–6

Kearns v General Council of the Bar [2003] EWCA Civ 331, [2003] 1 WLR 1357 568

Kelly v DPP [2003] Crim LR 43 582

Kelsen v Imperial Tobacco Co [1957] 2 QB 334 412

Kemsley v Foot [1952] AC 345 550, 553

Kennaway v Thompson [1981] QB 88 457–8

Kent v Griffiths [2001] QB 36 12, 220–1, 222, 228

Keown v Coventry Healthcare NHS Trust [2006] EWCA Civ 39, [2006] 1 WLR 953 364

Keppel Bus Co v Sa'ad bin Ahmed [1974] 1 WLR 1082 876

Ketley v Gooden (1996) 73 P & CR 305 456

Ketteman v Hansel Properties [1987] AC 189 182

KGM v News Group Newspapers Ltd [2011] EWCA Civ 808, affirming [2010] EWHC 3145 (QB) 595

Khodaparast v Shad [2000] 1 WLR 618 696–7, 703, 791

Khorasandjian v Bush [1993] QB 727 450–1, 579

King v Lewis [2004] EWCA Civ 1329 526

Kirkham v Chief Constable of the Greater Manchester Police [1990] 2 QB 283 316

KJO v XIM [2011] EWHC 1768 (QB) 603

KLB v British Columbia [2003] 2 SCR 403
  867

Klein v Caluori [1971] 1 WLR 619 868

Knight v Fellick [1977] RTR 316 267–8

Knight v Home Office [1990] 3 All ER 237 252

Knightley v Johns [1982] 1 WLR 349 312

Knupffer v London Express Newspaper Ltd
  [1944] AC 116 537

Koehler v Cerebos (2005) 222 CLR 44 156

Koursk, The [1924] P 140 766, 862

Kralj v McGrath [1986] 1 All ER 54 97, 791

Kreski v Modern Wholesale Electric Supply Co,
  415 NW 2d 178 (1987) 727

Kruber v Grzesiak [1963] VR 621 741

Kuddus v Chief Constable of Leicestershire
  [2001] UKHL 29, [2002] 2 AC 122 798, 802

Kuwait Airways Corpn v Iraqi Airways Co
  (Nos 4 & 5) [2002] UKHL 19, [2002] 2 AC
  883 338, 413, 493–4, 496, 505, 810, 814

Lagden v O'Connor [2003] UKHL 64, [2004] 1
  AC 1067 311–2, 764

Lamb v Camden LBC [1981] QB 625 139

Lancashire County Council v Municipal Mutual
  Insurance Ltd [1997] QB 897 802

Lancashire Waggon Co v Fitzhugh (1861) 6 H
  & N 502, 158 ER 206 496

Land Securities plc v Fladgate Fielder [2009]
  EWCA Civ 1402, [2010] Ch 467 709

Langbrook Properties Ltd v Surrey CC [1970] 1
  WLR 161 437

Langley v Liverpool City Council [2005] EWCA
  Civ 1173, [2006] 1 WLR 375 58

Langridge v Levy (1837) 2 M&W 519, 150 ER
  863 130

La Société Anonyme de Remourquage a Hélice v
  Bennetts [1911] 1 KB 243 28, 110

Latimer v AEC [1953] AC 643 253

Lavis v Kent County Council (1992) 90 LGR
  416 635

Law Debenture Corp v Ural Caspian Ltd [1995]
  Ch 152, reversing [1993] 1 WLR 138 672

Law Society v KPMG Peat Marwick [2000] 1
  WLR 1921 177

Law Society v Sephton & Co [2006] UKHL 22,
  [2006] 2 AC 543 740

Lawrence v Pembrokeshire CC [2007] EWCA
  Civ 446, [2007] 1 WLR 2991 8, 115

Laws v Florinplace [1981] 1 All ER 659 438–9

Lawton v BOC Transhield [1987] 2 All ER
  608 109

League Against Cruel Sports v Scott [1986] QB
  240 408

Leakey v National Trust for Places of Historic
  Interest or Natural Beauty [1980] QB 485 96,
  378, 443, 444, 445

Lee Ting Sang v Chung Chi-Keung [1990] 2 AC
  374 870

Leichhardt Municipal Council v Montgomery
  [2007] HCA 6 866

Leigh & Sillavan Ltd v Aliakmon Shipping Co
  Ltd [1986] AC 785, affirming [1985] QB
  350 110, 163, 164, 165, 858, 859

Le Lievre v Gould [1893] 1 QB 491 106

Lemmon v Webb [1895] AC 1 407, 435

Lennard's Carrying Co Ltd v Asiatic Petroleum
  Co Ltd [1915] AC 705 266

Letang v Cooper [1965] 1 QB 232 43

Levine v Morris [1970] 1 WLR 71 130, 210

Lewis v Daily Telegraph Ltd [1964] AC 234
  547

Ley v Hamilton (1935) 153 LT 384 790, 791

Liesbosch, The [1933] AC 449 312

Lightly v Clouston (1808) 1 Taunt 112, 127 ER
  774 815

Lim v Camden Area Health Authority [1980]
  AC 174 756

Limpus v London General Omnibus Company
  (1862) 1 H & C 526, 158 ER 995 875, 886

Lingens v Austria (1986) 8 EHRR 407 575

Lipkin Gorman v Karpnale Ltd [1991] 2 AC
  548 500, 810

Lippiatt v South Gloucestershire CC [2000] QB
  51 441, 442

Lister v Hesley Hall Ltd [2001] UKHL 22,
  [2002] 1 AC 215 262, 264, 866, 874, 878–81,
  882, 883, 886, 888, 890

Lister v Romford Ice and Cold Storage Co Ltd
  [1957] AC 555 891

Litchfield-Speer v Queen Anne's Gate Syndicate
  (No 2) Ltd [1919] 1 Ch 407 834

Livingstone v Rawyards Coal Company (1880) 5
  App Cas 25 813

Lloyd v Grace, Smith & Co [1912] AC 716 264,
  868, 878, 879

Lloyds Bank Ltd v E B Savory and Co [1933] AC
  201 258

LMS International Ltd v Styrene Packaging &
  Insulation Ltd [2005] EWHC 2065 (QB) 482

London Artists Ltd v Littler [1969] 2 QB
  375 552

London County Council v Cattermoles
  (Garages) Ltd [1953] 1 WLR 997 876

Lonrho v Fayed [1992] 1 AC 448, affirming [1990] 2 QB 479 *674*

Lonrho v Shell Petroleum (No 2) [1982] AC 173 *627, 673*

Lopez Ostra v Spain (1995) 20 EHRR 277 *453*

Lord Browne of Madingley v Associated Newspapers Ltd [2007] EWCA Civ 295, [2008] QB 103; reversing [2007] EWHC 202 (QB) *592, 595, 600*

Lord Napier and Ettrick v Hunter [1993] AC 713 *27, 768*

Lord Strathcona SS Co v Dominion Coal Co [1926] AC 108 *663*

Loutchansky v Times Newspapers Ltd [2001] EWCA Civ 536, [2002] QB 321 *563*

Loutchanksy v Times Newspapers Ltd (Nos 2–5) [2001] EWCA Civ 1805, [2002] QB 783 *567, 568*

Louth District Council v West (1896) 65 LJ (QB) 535 *653*

Lowe v Guise [2002] EWCA Civ 197, [2002] QB 1369 *781*

Lowery v Walker [1911] AC 10 *362*

Lowns v Woods (1996) 36 NSWLR 344 *243*

Lucasfilm Ltd v Ainsworth [2011] UKSC 39 *512*

Lumba v Secretary of State for the Home Dept [2011] UKSC 12 *59–61, 67, 278, 749, 821–2, 827–9*

Lumley v Gye (1853) 2 E & B 216, 118 ER 749 *660, 662, 667, 669, 703*

Lunn Poly Ltd v Liverpool and Lancashire Properties Ltd [2006] EWCA Civ 430 *807*

Lynch v Knight (1861) 9 HLC 577, 11 ER 854 *313–4*

Lyons & Sons, J v Wilkins [1899] 1 Ch 255 *440*

Lyons, Sons & Co v Gulliver [1914] 1 Ch 631 *652*

Maga v Trustees of the Birmingham Archdiocese of the Roman Catholic Church [2010] EWCA Civ 256, [2010] 1 WLR 1441 *885, 886, 890*

Magill v Magill (2006) 226 CLR 551 *692*

Mahon v Rahn (No 2) [2000] 1 WLR 2150 *556, 706*

Mainstream Properties v Young [2007] UKHL 21, [2008] 1 AC 1 *665*

Maitland v Raisbeck [1944] KB 689 *130*

Majrowski v Guy's and St Thomas's NHS Trust [2006] UKHL 34, [2007] 1 AC 224 *581, 585, 888, 889*

MAK v United Kingdom (2010) 51 EHRR 14 *8, 115*

Malyon v Plummer [1964] 1 QB 330 *847*

Manchester Airport plc v Dutton [2000] QB 133 *412*

Manchester Corporation v Farnworth [1930] AC 171 *457*

Mansfield v Weetabix Ltd [1998] 1 WLR 1263 *251, 719*

Marcic v Thames Water Utilities Ltd [2003] UKHL 66, [2004] 2 AC 42; reversing [2002] EWCA Civ 64, [2002] QB 929 *444*

Marc Rich & Co AG v Bishop Rock Marine Co Ltd [1996] AC 211, affirming [1994] 1 WLR 1071 *111, 166, 170–1, 211*

Marcq v Christie's [2003] EWCA Civ 731, [2004] QB 286 *495, 496, 500, 504*

Mardas v New York Times Co [2008] EWHC 3135 (QB) *541–2*

Marengo v Daily Sketch and Sunday Graphic (1948) 65 RPC 242 *515*

Mariola Marine Corp v Lloyd's Register of Shipping [1990] 1 Lloyd's Rep 547 *189*

Market Investigations Ltd v Minister for Social Security [1969] 2 QB 173 *870, 871, 872*

Marrinan v Vibart [1963] 1 QB 528 *722*

Martin v Watson [1996] 1 AC 74 *706*

Mason v Levy Auto Parts [1967] 2 QB 530 *482*

Matthews v Ministry of Defence [2003] UKHL 4, [2003] 1 AC 1163 *744, 745–6, 747*

Mattis v Pollock [2003] EWCA Civ 887, [2003] 1 WLR 2158; reversing [2002] EWHC 2177 (QB) *884, 886*

Mayfair Ltd v Pears [1987] 1 NZLR 459 *338, 413*

Mayfair Property Co v Johnston [1894] 1 Ch 508 *441*

Maynard v West Midlands Regional Health Authority [1984] 1 WLR 634 *257*

Mayne v Silvermere Cleaners [1939] 1 All ER 693 *268*

Maynegrain Pty Ltd v Compafina Bank (1984) 58 ALJR 389 *500*

Mbasogo v Logo Ltd [2006] EWCA Civ 1370, [2007] QB 846; affirming [2005] EWHC 2034 (QB) *40, 701–2*

McAuley v Bristol City Council [1992] 1 QB 134 *235*

McAuley v London Transport Executive [1958] 2 Lloyd's Rep 500 *314*

MCC Proceeds Inc v Lehman Bros International (Europe) [1998] 4 All ER 675 *164, 493*

McCafferty v Metropolitan District Receiver [1977] 1 WLR 1073 *236*

McCall v Abelesz [1976] 1 QB 585 *632*

McCann v United Kingdom (1996) 21 EHRR 97 *84*

McCarey v Associated Newspapers Ltd (No 2) [1965] 2 QB 86 *792*

McCartan Turkington Breen v Times Newspapers Ltd [2001] 2 AC 277 *562*

McDermid v Nash Dredging & Reclamation Ltd [1987] 1 AC 906 *261*

McElhinney v Ireland (2001) 34 EHRR 322 *745*

McFarlane v E E Caledonia Ltd [1994] 2 All ER 1 *148*

McFarlane v Tayside Health Board [2000] 2 AC 59 *137, 330, 347, 348, 349, 351, 352, 356*

McGeown v Northern Ireland Housing Executive [1995] 1 AC 233 *368*

McGhee v National Coal Board [1973] 1 WLR 1 *279, 280–1, 283, 291*

McHale v Watson (1966) 115 CLR 199 *718*

McIntyre v Harland & Wolff plc [2006] EWCA Civ 287, [2006] 1 WLR 2577 *850*

McKay v Essex Area Health Authority [1982] 1 QB 1166 *856*

McKenna v British Aluminum, The Times, 25 April 2002 *453*

McKennitt v Ash [2006] EWCA Civ 1714, [2008] QB 73 *592, 593, 597, 609*

McKenny v Foster [2008] EWCA Civ 173 *401, 402, 403*

McKew v Holland & Hannen & Cubitts (Scotland) Ltd [1969] 3 All ER 1621 *313*

McKie v Swindon College [2011] EWHC 469 (QB) *199*

McKinnon Industries v Walker [1951] 3 DLR 577 *423*

McLoughlin v Grovers [2001] EWCA Civ 1743, [2002] QB 1312 *187*

McLoughlin v O'Brian [1983] 1 AC 410 *102, 126, 144–5, 147, 152, 159, 160*

McManus v Beckham [2002] EWCA Civ 939, [2002] 1 WLR 2982 *571*

McMillan v Singh (1984) 17 HLR 120 *789–90, 791*

McWilliams v Sir William Arrol & Co Ltd [1962] 1 WLR 295 *276*

Meade v Haringey LBC [1979] 1 WLR 637, [1979] 2 All ER 1016 *672*

Meah v McCreamer [1985] 1 All ER 367 *355, 356, 731*

Meah v McCreamer (No 2) [1986] 1 All ER 943 *355, 356*

Mediana (Owners of Steamship) v Comet (Owners of Lightship) [1900] AC 113 *814, 823, 824, 825*

Meering v Grahame-White Aviation Company Ltd (1920) 122 LT 44 *41*

Melvin v Reid, 121 Cal App 285 (1931) *603*

Mercer v South Eastern & Chatham Railway Companies' Managing Committee [1922] KB 549 *230*

Meretz Investments NV v ACP Ltd [2007] EWCA Civ 1303, [2008] Ch 244 *664, 665*

Meridian Global Funds Management Asia Ltd v Securities Commission [1995] 2 AC 500 *266, 267*

Merkur Island Shipping Corp v Laughton [1983] 2 AC 570 *673*

Merlin v BNFL [1990] 2 QB 557 *484*

Merrett v Babb [2001] EWCA Civ 214, [2001] QB 1174 *188, 189*

Mersey Docks & Harbour Board v Coggins & Griffith (Liverpool) Ltd [1947] AC 1 *874*

Messenger Newspapers Group Ltd v National Graphical Association [1984] IRLR 397 *791, 793*

Metall und Rohstoff AG v Donald Lufkin & Jenrette Inc [1990] 1 QB 391 *672, 708*

Metropolitan Asylum District Managers v Hill (1881) 6 App Cas 193 *447*

Metropolitan International Schools Ltd v Designtechnica Corporation [2009] EWHC 1765 (QB) *540, 574*

Metropolitan Properties Ltd v Jones [1939] 2 All ER 202 *432*

MGN Ltd v United Kingdom (2011) 53 EHRR 5 *527*

Michaels v Taylor Woodrow Developments Ltd [2001] Ch 493 *688*

Midland Bank v Hett, Stubbs and Kemp [1979] Ch 383 *181*

Midler v Ford Motor Co, 849 F 2d 460 (1988) *623*

Miller v Inglis, 567 NW 2d 253 (1997) *727*

Miller v Jackson [1977] QB 966 *97, 133, 253, 255, 256, 457, 458, 486, 837*

Mills v Winchester Diocesan Board of Finance [1989] Ch 428 *189*

Milne v Express Newspapers Ltd [2004] EWCA Civ 664, [2005] 1 WLR 772 *570*

Miner v Gilmour (1858) 12 Moore PC 131, 14 ER 861 *437*

Mineral Transporter, The, see Candlewood Navigation Corporation Ltd v Mitsui OSK Lines Ltd

Ministry of Defence v Ashman [1993] 2 EGLR 102 *814*

Ministry of Defence v Meredith [1995] IRLR 539 *791, 794*

Ministry of Defence v Thompson [1993] 2 EGLR 107 *814*

Ministry of Housing v Sharp [1970] 2 QB 223 *163, 191, 204*

Mint v Good [1951] 1 KB 517 *647, 649, 650*

Minter v Priest [1930] AC 558 *556*

Mirage Studios v Counter-Feat Clothing Company Ltd [1991] FSR 145 *516*

Mirvahedy v Henley [2003] UKHL 16, [2003] 2 AC 491; affirming [2001] EWCA Civ 1749, [2002] QB 749 *400–1, 402, 403, 404*

Mistry v Thakor [2005] EWCA Civ 953 *653*

Mitchell v Glasgow City Council [2009] UKHL 11, [2009] 1 AC 874 *112, 223, 225, 226, 448*

Moeliker v Reyrolle [1977] 1 All ER 9 *755*

Mogul Steamship Co Ltd v McGregor, Gow & Co [1892] AC 25 *683–4, 685, 687*

Monsanto v Tilly [2000] Env LR 313 *410, 411*

Montgomery v Johnson Underwood Ltd [2001] EWCA Civ 318 *872*

Moore v Regents of University of California, 271 Cal Rptr 146 (1990) *489*

Moorgate Mercantile Co Ltd v Finch and Read [1962] 1 QB 701 *496*

Morgan v Odhams Press Ltd [1971] 1 WLR 1239 *536–7*

Morgan Crucible Co plc v Hill Samuel & Co Ltd [1991] Ch 295 *198, 345*

Morgans v Launchbury [1973] AC 127 *868*

Morris v C W Martin [1966] 1 QB 716 *262, 729, 879*

Morris v Murray [1991] 2 QB 6 *725*

Morris v Redland Bricks Ltd [1970] AC 652 *455*

Morrison Sports Ltd v Scottish Power Plc [2010] UKSC 37, [2010] 1 WLR 1934 *630*

Morrison Steamship Co Ltd v Greystoke Castle (Cargo Owners) [1947] AC 265 *172, 195*

Morriss v Marsden [1952] 1 All ER 925 *719*

Mosley v News Group Newspapers [2008] EWHC 687 (QB), [2008] EWHC 1777 (QB) *596, 603, 607, 609, 610, 617, 618, 825*

Mosley v United Kingdom [2011] ECHR 774 *611*

Mount Isa Mines Ltd v Pusey (1970) 125 CLR 383 *152*

Mulcahy v Ministry of Defence [1996] QB 732 *114, 133–4*

Mulgrave v Ogden (1591) Cro Eliz 219, 78 ER 475 *497*

Mullin v Richards [1998] 1 WLR 1304 *134, 718*

Murphy v Brentwood District Council [1991] 1 AC 398 *110, 131, 169, 183, 188, 195, 203, 211, 340*

Murphy v Culhane [1977] 1 QB 96 *773, 845*

Murray v Express Newspapers plc [2008] EWCA Civ 446, [2009] Ch 481 *590, 599, 600*

Murray v Ministry of Defence [1988] 1 WLR 692 *42*

Musgrove v Pandelis [1919] 2 KB 43 *482*

Mutual Life and Citizens' Assurance Co Ltd v Evatt [1971] AC 793 *178, 184*

Muuse v Secretary of State for the Home Department [2010] EWCA Civ 453 *797, 798, 802, 803*

My Kinda Town v Soll [1983] RPC 407, reversing [1982] FSR 147 *811*

National Coal Board v England [1954] AC 403 *10, 734*

National Coal Board v J E Evans & Co (Cardiff) Ltd [1951] 2 KB 861 *500*

National Union of General and Municipal Workers v Gillian [1946] KB 81 *543*

Naylor v Payling [2004] EWCA Civ 560 *366*

Nayyar v Denton Wilde Sapte [2009] EWHC 3218 (QB) *733*

Needler Financial Services v Taber [2002] 3 All ER 501 *771*

Neil Martin Ltd v The Commissioners for Her Majesty's Customs & Excise [2007] EWCA Civ 1041 *194*

Nelson v Raphael [1979] RTR 437 *868*

Nettleship v Weston [1971] 2 QB 691 *93, 249*

Network Rail Infrastructure Ltd v CJ Morris [2004] EWCA Civ 172 *423*

New South Wales v Budjoso [2005] HCA 76 *224*

New South Wales v Ibbett [2006] HCA 57 *802*

New South Wales v Lepore (2003) 212 CLR 511 *94, 239, 262, 263, 264, 866, 878, 879, 880, 881, 883, 886, 888*

New York Times Co v Sullivan (1964) 376 US 254 *524, 526, 576, 577*

New Zealand Shipping Co Ltd v A M Satterthwaite & Co Ltd [1975] AC 154 *729*

Newstead v London Express Newspaper Ltd [1940] 1 KB 377 *536, 750*

Ng Chun Pui v Lee Chuen Tat [1988] RTR 298 *268*

Nicholas H, The, see Marc Rich & Co AG v
Bishop Rock Marine Co Ltd
Nicholls v Ely Beet Sugar Factory [1931] 2 Ch
84 *412*
Nicholls v Ely Beet Sugar Factory (No 2) [1936]
1 Ch 343 *420, 462, 749*
Nicholls v F Austin (Leyton) Ltd [1946] AC
493 *342*
Nichols v Marsland (1876) 2 Ex D 1 *478*
Nissan v Attorney-General [1970] AC 179 *720*
Noble v Harrison [1926] 2 KB 332 *650*
Nocton v Lord Ashburton [1914] AC 465 *181*
Nolan v Dental Manufacturing Co Ltd [1958] 1
WLR 936 *276*
Norman Kark Publications Ltd v Hutton-Wild
Communications Ltd [1990] RPC 576 *514*
Northern Territory v Mengel (1995) 185 CLR
307 *627, 711*
Norwich CC v Harvey [1989] 1 WLR 828 *729*
NWL Ltd v Woods [1979] 1 WLR 1294 *836*
Nykredit Plc v Edward Erdman Ltd [1997] 1
WLR 1627 *342*

OBG Ltd v Allan [2007] UKHL 21, [2008] 1 AC
1 *516–8, 519, 660, 661, 662, 664, 665, 666,
667, 669, 670, 672, 673, 674, 675, 676, 677,
678, 679, 680, 681, 682, 689, 690, 691, 700*
O'Byrne v Aventis Pasteur MSD Ltd [2010]
UKSC 23, [2010] 1 WLR 1412 *392*
Ocean Accident & Guarantee Corp v Ilford Gas
Co [1905] 2 KB 493 *411, 473*
Ocean Frost, The, see Armagas Ltd v Mundogas
Ltd
Odhavji Estate v Woodhouse [2003] 3 SCR
263 *710*
Ogopogo, The, see Horsley v McClaren
O'Grady v Westminster Scaffolding Ltd [1962] 2
Lloyds Rep 238 *763*
Ogwo v Taylor [1988] AC 431 *131, 727*
Oliver v Ashman [1962] 2 QB 210 *762*
Oliver v Saddler & Co [1929] AC 584 *129*
OLL Ltd v Secretary of State for Transport
[1997] 3 All ER 897 *230–1*
Olwell v Nye & Nissen, 173 P 2d 652 (1946)
811
OPQ v BJM [2011] EWHC 1059 (QB) *619*
Orchard v Lee [2009] EWCA Civ 295 *251*
O'Reilly v National Rail & Tramway Appliances
Ltd [1966] 1 All ER 499 *262*
Organ Retention Litigation, In re [2004] EWHC
644 (QB), [2005] QB 506 *149, 488*
Orjula, The [1995] 2 Lloyds Rep 395 *203*

Ormrod v Crosville Motor Services Ltd [1953] 1
WLR 1120 *868*
Oropesa, The [1943] P 32 *313*
O'Rourke v Camden London Borough Council
[1998] AC 188 *634*
Osborn v Thomas Boulter & Son [1930] 2 KB
226 *544, 561*
Osman v Ferguson [1993] 4 All ER 344 *89*
Osman v United Kingdom [1999] FLR 193 *23,
79, 80, 89, 242*
Otto v Bolton & Norris [1936] 2 KB 46 *131*
Oughton v Seppings (1830) 1 B & Ad 241, 109
ER 776 *810, 811, 818*
Overseas Tankship (UK) Ltd v Miller Steamship
Co Pty [1967] 1 AC 617 *127, 132, 332, 334,
337, 463*
Overseas Tankship (UK) Ltd v Morts Dock &
Engineering Co Ltd [1961] AC 388 *334, 337,
339*

P v B [2001] 1 FLR 1041 *692*
Pacific Associates v Baxter [1990] 1 QB 993 *110*
Page v Smith [1996] AC 155 *126, 127, 137,
140–1, 149, 156, 157, 202, 335, 336–7*
Page v Smith (No 2) [1996] 1 WLR 855 *336*
Palmer v Cornwall County Council [2009]
EWCA Civ 456 *232*
Palmer v Tees Health Authority [1999] Lloyds
Rep Med 351 *233*
Palsgraf v Long Island Railroad, 248 NY 339
(1928) *11*
Paris v Stepney London Borough Council
[1951] AC 367 *253*
Parish v Judd [1960] 1 WLR 867 *130*
Parker v British Airways Board [1982] QB
1004 *492*
Parker-Knoll Ltd v Knoll International Ltd
[1962] RPC 265 *514*
Parkinson v St James and Seacroft NHS Hospital
[2001] EWCA Civ 530, [2002] QB 266 *137,
349, 350*
Parmiter v Coupland (1840) 6 M & W 105, 151
ER 340 *531*
Parry v Cleaver [1970] AC 1 *770, 771*
Patrick v Colerick (1838) 3 M & W 483, 150 ER
1235 *499*
Peabody Donation Fund v Sir Lindsay Parkinson
& Co Ltd [1985] AC 210 *106, 208*
Peck v United Kingdom (2003) 36 EHRR
719 *600, 613*
Pemberton v Southwark London Borough
Council [2000] 1 WLR 672 *450*

Penarth Dock Engineering Co v Pounds [1963]
1 Lloyd's Rep 359 814
Penfold v Westcote (1806) 2 B & P (NR) 335,
127 ER 656 531
Penny v Wimbledon Urban District Council
[1899] 2 QB 72 649
Percy v Hall [1997] QB 924 64, 65
Performance Cars Ltd v Abraham [1962] 1 QB
33 764
Performing Right Society Ltd v Mitchell &
Booker (Palais de Danse) Ltd [1924] 1 KB
762 870
Perl P (Exporters) Ltd v Camden LBC [1984]
QB 342 130
Perre v Apand Pty Ltd (1999) 198 CLR
180 193–4, 200, 204
Perrett v Collins [1998] 2 Lloyd's Rep 255 132
Perrin v Northampton Borough Council [2007]
EWCA Civ 1353, [2008] 1 WLR 1307 435
Perry v Kendricks Transport Ltd [1956] 1 WLR
85 478, 482
Peters v Prince of Wales Theatre [1943] KB
73 473, 479
Pfeifer v Austria (2007) 48 EHRR 175 573
PG v United Kingdom [2001] ECHR 546 597
Phelps v Hillingdon London Borough Council
[2001] 2 AC 619, reversing [1999] 1 WLR
500 89, 117, 174, 188, 190–1, 197, 198, 200,
201, 239
Philcox v Civil Aviation Authority, The Times, 8
June 1995 171
Philips v William Whiteley Ltd [1938] 1 All ER
566 182, 264
Phillips v Britannia Hygienic Laundry Co [1923]
2 KB 832 631
Phipps v Rochester Corporation [1955] 1 QB
450 364
Photo Production Ltd v Securicor Transport Ltd
[1980] AC 827 264, 879
Pickering v Liverpool Daily Post [1991] 2 AC
370 750
Pickett v British Rail Engineering Ltd [1980] AC
126 762
Pidduck v Eastern Scottish Omnibuses Ltd
[1990] 1 WLR 993 850
Pigney v Pointer's Transport Services Ltd [1957]
1 WLR 1121 316
Pilcher v Rawlins (1872) LR 7 Ch App 259 493
Pioneer Container, The [1994] 2 AC 324 504,
729
Pippin v Sherrard (1822) 11 Price 400, 147 ER
512 181

Pitts v Hunt [1991] 2 QB 24 727, 735
Platform Home Loans v Oyston Shipways Ltd
[2000] 2 AC 190, reversing [1998] Ch
466 342, 777
Plato Films Ltd v Speidel [1961] AC 1090 571
Plon v France (58148/00), 18 May 2004,
unreported 604
Poland v John Parr & Sons [1927] 1 KB 236 875
Polemis and Furness Withy & Co, Re [1921] 3
KB 560 334
Polhill v Walter (1832) 3 B & Ad 114, 110 ER
43 657
Polly Peck (Holdings) plc v Trelford [1986] 1
QB 1000 549
Poplar Housing and Regeneration Community
Association Ltd v Donoghue [2001] EWCA
Civ 595, [2002] QB 48 76
Poppleton v Trustees of the Portsmouth Youth
Activities Committee [2008] EWCA Civ
646 231
Popplewell v Hodkinson (1869) LR 4 Ex
248 437
Port Line Ltd v Ben Line Steamers Ltd [1958]
QB 146 663
Port Swettenham Authority v T W Wu & Co
[1979] AC 580 269
Potter v Firestone Tire and Rubber Co, 863 P 2d
795 (1993) 157, 228
Powell v Boladz [1998] Lloyd's Rep Med
116 688, 691
Powell v Fall (1880) 5 QBD 597 471
Powell v McFarlane (1977) 38 P & CR 452 411
Powell and Rayner v United Kingdom (1990) 12
EHRR 355 453, 745
Pratt v DPP [2001] EWHC 483 (Admin) 583
Price v Hilditch [1930] 1 Ch 500 420
Pride & Partners v Institute of Animal Health
[2009] EWHC 685 (QB) 165–6, 194
Prison Service v Johnson [1997] ICR 275 791
Pritchard v J H Cobden Ltd [1988] Fam
22 353–4
Proform Sports Management Ltd v Proactive
Sports Management Ltd [2006] EWHC 2903
(QB) 661
Pullman v Hill & Co [1891] 1 QB 524 539
Purnell v Business F1 Magazine Ltd [2007]
EWCA Civ 774, [2008] 1 WLR 1 571
Pye (Oxford) Ltd, JA v Graham [2002] UKHL
30, [2003] 1 AC 419 411

Quartz Hill Consolidated Gold Mining Co v
Eyre (1863) 11 QBD 674 708

Quartz Hill Consolidated Mining Co v Beal
    (1882) 20 Ch D 501 *836*
Quinland v Governor of Swaleside Prison
    [2002] EWCA Civ 174, [2003] QB 306 *64*
Quinn v Leathem [1901] AC 495 *338, 685–6,
    687*
Quinton v Pearce [2009] EWHC 912 (QB) *702*

R v Adomako [1995] 1 AC 171 *217*
R v Bishop [1975] QB 274 *533*
R v Bournewood Community and Mental
    Health NHS Trust, ex parte L [1999] 1 AC
    458 *41*
R v Broadcasting Standards Commission ex p
    BBC [2001] QB 885 *604*
R v Brown [1994] 1 AC 212 *45*
R v Buxton [2010] EWCA Crim 2923, [2011] 1
    WLR 857 *585*
R v Chan-Fook [1994] 1 WLR 689 *55*
R v Chilworth Gunpowder Co (1888) 4 TLR
    557 *439, 641*
R v Collins [1973] QB 100 *361*
R v Cross (1812) 3 Camp 224, 170 ER 1362 *642,
    643*
R v Curtis [2010] EWCA Crim 123, [2010] 1
    WLR 2770 *582, 583*
R v Deputy Governor of Parkhurst Prison, ex
    parte Hague; Weldon v Home Office [1992] 1
    AC 58 *57*
R v Dica [2004] EWCA Civ 1103, [2004] QB
    1257 *46, 132*
R v Evans [2009] EWCA Crim 650, [2009] 1
    WLR 1999 *224, 225*
R v Gibbins and Proctor (1919) 13 Cr App Rep
    134 *238*
R v Governor of Blundeston Prison, ex parte
    Gaffney [1982] 1 WLR 696 *64, 65*
R v Governor of Brockhill Prison, ex parte Evans
    [1997] QB 443 *64*
R v Governor of Brockhill Prison, ex parte Evans
    (No 2) [2001] 2 AC 19, reversing [1999] QB
    1043 *64–5*
R v H (assault of child: reasonable chastisement)
    [2001] EWCA Crim 1024 *55*
R v Henson (1852) Dears 24, 169 ER 621 *644*
R v Hills [2001] Crim LR 318 *583*
R v Ireland [1998] AC 147 *39*
R v Jones (1812) 3 Camp 230, 170 ER 1364 *642*
R v Kelly [1999] QB 621 *488*
R v Kennedy [2007] UKHL 38, [2008] 1 AC
    269 *315, 322, 323, 326*
R v Lambert [2001] UKHL 7, [2002] 2 AC 545 *86*

R v Lister (1856–7) 7 Dears & B 209, 169 ER
    979 *439, 641*
R v Lloyd (1802) 4 Esp 200, 170 ER 691 *645*
R v Madden [1975] 1 WLR 1379 *644*
R v Miller [1983] 2 AC 161 *227*
R v Moore (1832) 3 B & Ad 184, 110 ER 68 *441*
R v R [1992] 1 AC 599 *7*
R v Rimmington, R v Goldstein [2005] UKHL
    63, [2006] 1 AC 459 *641, 645*
R v Saskatchewan Wheat Pool [1983] 1 SCR
    205 *638*
R v Shorrock [1994] QB 279 *648*
R v Tabassum [2000] 2 Cr App Rep 328 *46*
R v Train (1862) 2 B & S 640, 121 ER 1129 *643*
R v Vantandillo (1815) 4 M & S 73, 105 ER
    762 *644*
R v Watts (1703) 1 Salk 357, 91 ER 311 *649*
R v Williams [1923] 1 KB 340 *45*
R v Williams (Gladstone) [1987] 3 All ER
    411 *63*
R (a minor) (wardship: medical treatment), Re
    [1992] Fam 11 *48*
R (Al-Skeini) v Secretary of State for Defence
    [2007] UKHL 26, [2008] 1 AC 153 *720*
R (Greenfield) v Secretary of State for the Home
    Department [2005] UKHL 14, [2005] 1 WLR
    673 *82, 83, 84, 85*
R (Heather) v Leonard Cheshire Foundation
    [2002] EWCA Civ 366 *76*
R (KB) v London and South and West Region
    Mental Health Review Tribunal [2003]
    EWHC 193 (Admin), [2004] QB 936 *83*
R (Moos and McClure) v Commissioner of
    Police of the Metropolis [2011] EWHC 957
    (Admin) *38*
R (Smeaton) v Secretary of State for Health
    [2002] EWHC 610 (Admin) *352*
R (Smith) v Oxfordshire Assistant Deputy
    Coroner [2010] UKSC 29, [2011] 1 AC 1 *720*
R (Weaver) v London & Quadrant Housing
    Trust [2009] EWCA Civ 587, [2010] 1 WLR
    363 *78*
R (Williamson) v Secretary of State for
    Education and Employment [2002] EWCA
    Civ 1926, [2003] QB 1300 *55*
Rabone v Pennine Care NHS Trust [2010]
    EWCA Civ 698 *81, 83*
Racz v Home Office [1994] 2 AC 45 *711*
Rahman v Arearose Ltd [2001] QB 351 *280*
Rainham Chemical Works Ltd v Belvedere Fish
    Guano Co Ltd [1921] 2 AC 465 *471, 473,
    474, 482*

Ramzan v Brookwide Ltd [2011] EWCA Civ 985 *412*

Rantzen v MGN (1986) Ltd [1994] QB 670 *571, 572*

Ratcliff v McConnell [1999] 1 WLR 670 *368*

Ratcliffe v Evans [1892] 2 QB 524 *696, 697*

Rawlinson v Rice [1998] 1 NZLR 454 *711*

Ray v Fairway Motors (Barnstaple) Ltd (1969) 20 P & CR 261 *437*

RCA Corp v Pollard [1983] Ch 135 *678*

Read v J Lyons & Co [1947] AC 156 *468, 469, 471, 473, 476*

Read v The Great Eastern Railway Company (1868) LR 3 QB 555 *846*

Ready Mixed Concrete (South East) Ltd v Minister of Pensions and National Insurance [1968] 2 QB 497 *872*

Reay v BNFL, Hope v BNFL [1994] PIQR P171 *484*

Reckitt & Colman Products Ltd v Borden Inc [1990] 1 WLR 491 *514*

Reddaway v Banham [1896] AC 199 *514*

Redland Bricks Ltd v Morris [1970] AC 632 *455, 838*

Reeman v Department of Transport [1997] 2 Lloyds Rep 648 *345*

Rees v Darlington Memorial Hospital NHS Trust [2003] UKHL 52, [2004] 1 AC 309 *347, 348–9, 350, 826, 828, 829*

Reeves v Commissioner of the Police of the Metropolis [2000] AC 360 *98, 229, 274, 316, 727, 773, 775, 776*

Regan v Paul Properties Ltd [2006] EWCA Civ 1391, [2007] Ch 135 *456*

Reid v Rush & Tompkins Group plc [1990] 1 WLR 212 *237*

Renault UK Ltd v Fleetpro Technical Services Ltd [2007] EWHC 2541 (QB) *813*

Revenue and Customs Commissioners v Total Network SL [2008] UKHL 19, [2008] 1 AC 1174 *677, 684, 685, 686, 687, 688–92, 699, 862*

Revill v Newbery [1996] QB 567 *377, 734*

Reynolds v Commissioner of Police of the Metropolis [1984] 3 All ER 649 *707*

Reynolds v Times Newspapers Ltd [2001] 2 AC 127 *562–4, 571, 610, 750*

Ribee v Norrie (2001) 33 HLR 777 *361, 481*

Rich v Basterfield (1847) 4 CB 783, 136 ER 715 *441*

Richardson v Atkinson (1723) 1 Stra 576, 93 ER 710 *497*

Richardson v LRC Products [2000] Lloyds Rep Med 280 *137, 352*

Riches v News Group Newspapers Ltd [1986] 1 QB 256 *537, 801*

Rickards v Lothian [1913] AC 263 *473, 478*

Ricket v Metropolitan Railway Co (1867) LR 2 HL 175 *652*

Rigby v Chief Constable of Northamptonshire [1985] 1 WLR 1242 *410*

Robb v Salamis [2006] UKHL 56 *635*

Roberts v Chief Constable of the Cheshire Constabulary [1999] 1 WLR 662 *58*

Roberts v Gable [2007] EWCA Civ 721, [2008] QB 502 *566–7*

Roberts v Ramsbottom [1980] 1 All ER 7 *251*

Robinson v Balmain New Ferry Company Ltd [1910] AC 295 *41*

Robinson v Jones (Contractors) Ltd [2011] EWCA Civ 9 *18, 183–4*

Robinson v Kilvert (1889) 41 Ch D 88 *423, 429*

Roche v United Kingdom (2006) 42 EHRR 30 *746–7, 748*

Roe v Minister of Health [1954] 2 QB 66 *135*

Rogers v Night Riders [1983] RTR 324 *264*

Roncarelli v Duplessis [1959] SCR 121 *710*

Rondel v Worsley [1969] 1 AC 191 *114, 116*

Rookes v Barnard [1964] AC 1129 *24, 97, 657, 674, 679–80, 682, 792, 796, 798, 799, 800, 801, 802, 803, 804, 805*

Rose v Miles (1815) 4 M & S 101, 105 ER 773 *651*

Rose v Plenty [1976] 1 WLR 141 *875*

Rothwell v Chemical & Insulating Co Ltd [2007] UKHL 39, [2008] 1 AC 281; affirming [2006] EWCA Civ 27 *111, 126, 157, 202, 295, 341*

Rowe v Herman [1997] 1 WLR 1390 *649*

Rowley v Secretary of State for Work and Pensions [2007] EWCA Civ 598, [2007] 1 WLR 2861 *201*

Rowling v Takaro Properties Ltd [1988] AC 473 *106*

Roy v Prior [1971] AC 470 *707*

Royal Brunei Airlines v Tan [1995] 2 AC 378 *672*

Rushmer v Polsue & Alferi [1906] 1 Ch 234 *432*

Rylands v Fletcher (1868) LR 3 HL 330; affirming (1866) LR 1 Ex 265; reversing (1865) 3 H & C 774, 159 ER 737 *14, 15, 26, 231, 421, 464, 466–7, 468, 469, 472, 473, 475, 484, 650, 888*

S (a child) (identification: restrictions on publication), Re [2004] UKHL 47, [2005] 1 AC 593 *593, 611, 839*

S (adult: refusal of medical treatment), Re [1993] Fam 123 *54*

S and Marper *v* United Kingdom (2008) 48 EHRR 50 *593*

Safeway Stores Ltd v Twigger [2010] EWCA Civ 1472, [2011] 2 All ER 841 *733*

Salmon *v* Seafarer Restaurants Ltd [1983] 1 WLR 1264 *727*

Sanders *v* Snell (1998) 196 CLR 329 *661*

Sanix Ace, The [1987] 1 Lloyd's Rep 465 *824*

Saunders *v* Vautier (1841) Cr & Ph 240, 41 ER 482 *493*

Savage *v* South Essex Partnership NHS Foundation Trust [2008] UKHL 74, [2009] 1 AC 681; applied [2010] EWHC 865 (QB) *79, 81, 83, 84*

Savill *v* Roberts (1698) 12 Mod Rep 208, 88 ER 1267 *708*

Scala Ballroom (Wolverhampton) Ltd *v* Ratcliffe [1958] 1 WLR 1057 *686*

Scally *v* Southern Health and Social Services Board [1992] 1 AC 294 *631*

Schellenberg *v* British Broadcasting Corp [2000] EMLR 296 *541*

Schofield *v* Chief Constable of West Yorkshire [1999] ICR 193 *140*

Scott *v* London and St Katherine Docks Company (1865) 3 H & C 595, 159 ER 665 *268*

Scott *v* Shepherd (1773) 2 Black W 892, 96 ER 525 *38*

Scout Association *v* Barnes [2010] EWCA Civ 1476 *253, 254, 256*

Scruttons Ltd *v* Midland Silicones Ltd [1962] AC 446 *729*

Scullion *v* Bank of Scotland [2011] EWCA Civ 693 *198*

Seaga *v* Harper [2009] UKPC 26, [2009] 1 AC 1 *567*

Seaman *v* Netherclift (1876) 2 CPD 53 *556*

Sedleigh-Denfield *v* O'Callaghan [1940] AC 880 *442–3, 444, 445, 447, 448, 647, 648, 650*

Sefton (Earl) *v* Tophams [1967] 1 AC 50, reversing [1965] Ch 1140, affirming [1964] 1 WLR 1408 *663*

Selvanayagam *v* University of West Indies [1983] 1 WLR 585 *351*

Sevenoaks DC *v* Vinson Ltd [1984] Ch 211 *464*

Severn Trent Water Ltd *v* Barnes [2004] EWCA Civ 570 *813*

Shah *v* Standard Chartered Bank [1999] QB 241 *533*

Shearman *v* Folland [1950] 2 KB 43 *765, 768*

Shelfer *v* City of London Electric Lighting Co [1895] 1 Ch 287 *456, 457, 458, 840*

Shell UK Ltd v Total UK Ltd [2010] EWCA Civ 180, [2011] QB 86; reversing [2009] EWHC 540 (Comm) *163–5, 479, 644, 646, 647*

Shelley *v* Paddock [1980] QB 348 *702*

Shevill *v* Presse Alliance [1995] 2 AC 18, [1996] AC 959 *526*

Shiffman *v* Order of St John [1936] 1 All ER 557 *471*

Shimp *v* New Jersey Bell Telephone Co, 368 A 2d 408 (1976) *98, 837*

Ship *v* Crosskill (1870) LR 10 Eq 73 *694, 696*

Shore *v* Sedgwick Financial Services Ltd [2008] EWCA Civ 863 *740*

Shoreham-by-Sea UDC *v* Dolphin Canadian Proteins Ltd (1973) 71 Local Government Reports 261 *646*

Short *v* J W Henderson Ltd (1946) 62 TLR 427 *870*

Shrosbery *v* Osmaston (1877) 37 LT 792 *707*

Sienkiewicz *v* Greif (UK) Ltd [2011] UKSC 10 *279, 283, 284, 288–90, 291, 301, 327*

Silver *v* United Kingdom (1991) 13 EHRR 582 *83*

Sim *v* Stretch [1936] 2 All ER 1237 *531*

Simaan General Contracting Co *v* Pilkington Glass (No 2) [1988] QB 758 *110, 183*

Simmons *v* British Steel plc [2004] UKHL 20 *140*

Simmons *v* Lillystone (1853) 8 Ex 431, 155 ER 1417 *497*

Simms *v* Leigh Rugby Football Club [1969] 2 All ER 923 *365*

Simpson & Co *v* Thomson (1877) 3 App Cas 279 *110*

Sirros *v* Moore [1975] QB 118 *114*

Six Carpenters' Case, The (1610) 8 Co Rep 146a, 77 ER 695 *409*

Slater *v* Clay Cross Co Ltd [1956] 2 QB 264 *376, 726*

Slater *v* Swann (1730) 2 Stra 872, 93 ER 906 *501, 749*

Slater *v* Worthington's Cash Stores (1930) Ltd [1941] 1 KB 488 *647*

Slim *v* Daily Telegraph [1968] 2 QB 157 *535*

Slipper *v* BBC [1991] 1 QB 283 *337, 571*

Smeaton v Ilford Corp [1954] Ch 450 *473*

Smith v Baker [1891] AC 325 *236*

Smith v Chadwick (1884) 9 App Cas 187 *693–4, 695*

Smith v Chief Constable of Sussex Police [2008] EWCA Civ 39 *73, 241*

Smith v Eric S Bush, Harris v Wyre Forest District Council [1990] 1 AC 831 *174, 175, 188, 197–8, 200, 201*

Smith v Leech Brain & Co Ltd [1962] 2 QB 405 *335*

Smith v Linskills (a firm) [1996] 1 WLR 763 *724*

Smith v Littlewoods Organisation Ltd [1987] AC 241 *139, 378–9, 447*

Smith v London and South Western Railway Co (1870) LR 6 CP 14 *335*

Smith v Manchester (1974) 17 KIR 1 *755*

Smith v Ministry of Defence [2011] EWHC 1676 (QB) *114, 134*

Smith v Northamptonshire County Council [2009] UKHL 27 *635*

Smith v Scott [1973] Ch 314 *442*

Smith v Stages [1989] 1 AC 928 *876*

Smith v Stone (1647) Style 65, 82 ER 533 *406*

Smith v Western Electric Co, 643 SW 2d 10 (1982) *98, 837*

Smith and Grady v United Kingdom (2000) 29 EHRR 493 *83*

Smith New Court Securities v Scrimgeour Vickers (Asset Management) Ltd [1997] AC 254 *338*

SmithKline Beecham v Avery [2009] EWHC 1488 (QB) *585*

Smoker v London Fire Authority [1991] 2 AC 502 *770*

Sochacki v Sas [1947] 1 All ER 344 *481, 483*

Société Anonyme de Remourquage à Hélice, La v Bennetts [1911] 1 KB 243 *28, 110*

Soltau v De Held (1851) 2 Sim NS 133, 61 ER 291 *432*

Somerset v Stewart (1772) Lofft 1, 98 ER 499 *69*

Sorrell v Paget [1950] 1 KB 252 *498*

Sorrell v Smith [1925] AC 700 *685, 686*

South Australia Asset Management Corporation v York Montague Ltd [1997] AC 191 *342, 343*

South Hetton Coal Company Ltd v North-Eastern News Association Ltd [1894] 1 QB 133 *532, 543*

South Wales Miners' Federation v Glamorgan Coal Co [1905] AC 239 *667, 668, 670*

Southwark LBC v Tanner [2001] 1 AC 1 *425, 441–2*

Southwark LBC v Williams [1971] 1 Ch 734 *410*

Spartan Steel & Alloys Ltd v Martin & Co (Contractors) Ltd [1973] 1 QB 27 *101, 172, 340*

Spencer v S Franses Ltd [2011] EWHC 1269 (QB) *498*

Spencer-Franks v Kellogg, Brown and Root Ltd [2008] UKHL 46 *635*

Spring v Guardian Assurance Ltd [1995] 2 AC 296 *95, 116, 178, 189–90, 199*

St George v Home Office [2008] EWCA Civ 1068, [2009] 1 WLR 1670 *779*

St George's Healthcare NHS Trust v S [1999] Fam 26 *54*

St Helen's Smelting v Tipping (1865) 11 HLC 642 *419, 424, 430, 465*

Stadium Capital Holdings (No 2) Ltd v St Marylebone Property Co Ltd [2010] EWCA Civ 952 *813*

Standard Chartered Bank v Pakistan National Shipping Corporation (No 2) [2002] UKHL 43, [2003] 1 AC 959 *773*

Stansbie v Troman [1948] 2 KB 48 *187, 218, 316*

Steel and Morris v United Kingdom [2005] EMLR 15 *528, 572, 575*

Stephenson Jordan & Harrison Ltd v MacDonald & Evans (1951) 69 RPC 10 *872*

Stern v Piper [1997] QB 123 *533*

Stevens v Bermondsey & Southwark Group Hospital Management Committee (1963) 107 Sol J 478 *345*

Stevens v Midland Counties Railway (1854) 10 Ex 352, 156 ER 480 *707*

Stewart v Pettie [1995] 1 SCR 131 *225*

Stockwell v Society of Lloyd's [2007] EWCA Civ 930, [2008] 1 WLR 2255 *711*

Stoke-on-Trent City Council v W & J Wass Ltd [1988] 1 WLR 1406 *464, 806, 812, 818*

Stone v Bolton [1949] 1 All ER 237 *646*

Stone & Rolls Ltd v Moore Stephens [2009] UKHL 39, [2009] 1 AC 1391 *267, 736*

Storey v Ashton (1869) LR 4 QB 476 *876*

Stovin v Wise [1996] AC 923 *114, 208, 209, 211, 213, 215, 378*

Strand Electric Engineering Co Ltd v Brisford Entertainments [1952] 2 QB 246 *814*

Stubbings v United Kingdom [1997] 1 FLR 105 *744*

Stubbings v Webb [1993] AC 498 *741, 744*

Stupple v Royal Insurance Co Ltd [1971] 1 QB
  50 269
Sullivan v Moody (2001) 207 CLR 562 115
Summers v Tice, 199 P 2d 1 (1948) 285
Sunbolf v Alford (1838) 3 M & W 248, 150 ER
  1135 49
Supply of Ready Mixed Concrete (No 2), Re
  [1995] 1 AC 456 266, 267
Surtees v Kingston-upon-Thames Borough
  Council [1991] 2 FLR 559 238, 250
Sutcliffe v Pressdram Ltd [1991] 1 QB 153 572,
  790, 791
Sutherland Shire Council v Heyman (1985) 127
  CLR 424 104, 118
**Sutradhar v Natural Environment Research
  Council** [2006] UKHL 33 208
Swinney v Chief Constable of the Northumbria
  Police [1997] QB 464 187, 219
Swinney v Chief Constable of Northumbria
  Police (No 2), The Times, 25 May 1999 219
Swiss Bank Corp v Lloyds Bank Ltd [1982] AC
  584 663
Swordheath Properties v Tabet [1979] 1 WLR
  285 814
Sykes v Harry [2001] EWCA Civ 167, [2001] QB
  1014 234, 235
Sykes v Midland Bank Executor & Trustee Co
  [1971] 1 QB 113 749
Szalatnay-Stacho v Fink [1947] KB 1, [1946] 1
  All ER 303 557

T (adult: refusal of medical treatment), Re
  [1993] Fam 95 53
T v BBC [2007] EWHC 1683 (QB) 599, 613
T v Surrey County Council [1994] 4 All ER
  577 131
Tadd v Eastwood [1985] ICR 132 556
Tai Hing Cotton Mill v Liu Chong Hing Bank
  [1986] AC 80 156
Tamares Ltd v Fairpoint Properties Ltd (No 2)
  [2007] EWHC 212 (QB), [2007] 1 WLR
  2167 456, 806
Tamworth BC v Fazeley Town Council (1978) 77
  LGR 238 464
Tang Man Sit v Capacious Investments Ltd
  [1996] AC 514 808
Tanks and Vessels Industries Ltd v Devon Cider
  Company Ltd [2009] EWHC 1360 (Ch) 506
Tarasoff v Regents of the University of
  California, 551 P 2d 334 (1976) 233
Tarleton v M'Gawley (1793) Peake 270, 170 ER
  153 673

Tarry v Ashton (1876) 1 QBD 314 379, 650
Tate & Lyle Industries Ltd v GLC [1983] 2 AC
  507 652
Taunoa v Attorney General [2007] NZSC 70 821
Taylor v Director of the Serious Fraud Office
  [1999] 2 AC 177 556, 723
Tear v Freebody (1858) 4 CB (NS) 228, 140 ER
  1071 494
Telnikoff v Matusevitch [1992] 2 AC 343 553
Tempest v Snowden [1952] 1 KB 130 707
Tesco Stores Ltd v Pollard [2006] EWCA Civ
  393 385
Tesco Supermarkets Ltd v Natrass [1972] AC
  153 265
Tetley v Chitty [1986] 1 All ER 663 442
Tharpe v Stallwood (1843) 5 M & G 760, 134 ER
  766 502
Theaker v Richardson [1962] 1 WLR 151 539
Theakston v MGN Ltd [2002] EWHC 137
  (QB) 591
Thomas v Bridgend County Borough Council
  [2011] EWCA Civ 862 86
Thomas v Lewis [1937] 1 All ER 137 479
Thomas v National Union of Mineworkers
  (South Wales Area) [1986] 1 Ch 20 40, 440
Thomas v News Group Newspapers Ltd [2001]
  EWCA Civ 1233 582, 584
Thompson v Commissioner of Police of the
  Metropolis [1998] QB 498 790, 791, 792, 802
Thompson v Hill (1870) LR 5 CP 564 789, 791
Thompson-Schwab v Costaki [1956] 1 WLR
  335 439
Thomson, DC v Deakin [1952] Ch 646 661
Thornton v Telegraph Media Group Ltd [2010]
  EWHC 1414 (QB) 530, 532
Three Rivers DC v Governor and Company of
  the Bank of England (No 3) [2003] 2 AC
  1 709, 710, 711, 712, 713, 714
Thunder Air Ltd v Hilmarsson [2008] EWHC
  355 488
Tidman v Reading Borough Council [1994]
  Times LR 592 177
Tillett v Ward (1882) 10 QBD 17 483
Tinnelly & Sons Ltd v United Kingdom (1998)
  27 EHRR 249 745
TJ Hooper, The, 60 F 2d 737 (1932) 245
Tojo Maru, The [1972] AC 242 738
Tolstoy Miloslavsky v United Kingdom (1995)
  20 EHRR 442 572
Tomlinson v Congleton BC [2003] UKHL 47,
  [2004] 1 AC 46; reversing [2002] EWCA Civ
  309 30–1, 109, 112, 253, 254, 256, 363, 369

Topp *v* London Country Bus (South West) Ltd [1993] 1 WLR 976 *139*

Torquay Hotel *v* Cousins [1969] 2 Ch 106 *661, 662*

Transco plc *v* Stockport Metropolitan Borough Council [2003] UKHL 61, [2004] 2 AC 1 *421, 464, 467, 468, 469, 470, 471, 472, 473, 474, 475, 476, 478, 482, 484, 653*

Tremain *v* Pike [1969] 1 WLR 1556 *334*

Trevett *v* Lee [1955] 1 WLR 113 *641*

TRM Copy Centres (UK) Ltd *v* Lanwall Services Ltd [2009] UKHL 35, [2009] 1 WLR 1375 *503*

Trotman *v* North Yorkshire County Council [1999] LGR 584 *878, 879*

Trumm *v* Norman [2008] EWHC 116 (QB) *568*

TSE *v* News Group Newspapers Ltd [2011] EWHC 1308 (QB) *599*

Tse Wai Chun *v* Cheng [2001] EMLR 777 *550, 555*

Tubantia, The [1924] P 78 *490*

Tuberville *v* Savage (1669) 1 Mod 3, 86 ER 684 *39*

Tuttle *v* Buck, 119 NW 946 (1909) *658, 659*

Tutton *v* A D Walter Ltd [1986] QB 61 *408*

Twinsectra Ltd *v* Yardley [2002] UKHL 12, [2002] 2 AC 164 *863*

Ultramares Corporation *v* Touche, 174 NE 441 (1931) *111, 195*

United Australia Ltd *v* Barclays Bank Ltd [1941] AC 1 *808*

United States *v* Carroll Towing, 159 F 2d 169 (1947) *245*

University of Oxford *v* Broughton [2008] EWHC 75 (QB) *581*

Uren *v* Corporate Leisure [2011] EWCA Civ 66 *256*

Uren *v* John Fairfax & Sons Pty Ltd (1965–66) 117 CLR 118 *793*

Uxbridge Permanent Benefit Building Society *v* Pickard [1939] 2 KB 248 *868*

Van Colle *v* Chief Constable of the Hertfordshire Police [2008] UKHL 50, [2009] 1 AC 225; reversing [2007] EWCA Civ 325 [2007] 1 WLR 1821 *73, 81, 83, 87, 208, 241, 822*

Vancouver *v* Ward [2010] 2 SCR 28 *821*

Van Oppen *v* Clerk to the Bedford Charity Trustees [1990] 1 WLR 235 *110, 239*

Vanderpant *v* Mayfair Hotel [1930] 1 Ch 138 *432, 479*

Various Claimants *v* The Catholic Child Welfare Society [2010] EWCA Civ 1106 *887, 889*

Vaughan *v* Menlove (1837) 3 Bing NC 468, 132 ER 490 *135, 248*

Veakins *v* Kier Islington [2009] EWCA Civ 1288 *581*

Vellino *v* Chief Constable of Greater Manchester Police [2001] EWCA Civ 1249, [2002] 1 WLR 218 *112, 732, 734*

Vernon v Bosley (No 1) [1997] 1 All ER 577 *159, 160*

Viasystems (Tyneside) Ltd *v* Thermal Transfer (Northern) Limited [2005] EWCA Civ 1151, [2006] QB 510 *873, 874*

Vincent *v* Lake Erie Transportation Co, 124 NW 221 (1910) *410*

Vine *v* Waltham Forest LBC [2000] 1 WLR 2383, [2000] 4 All ER 169 *501*

Von Hannover *v* Germany (2005) 40 EHRR 1 *593, 601, 604, 606, 609, 624*

Vowles *v* Evans [2003] EWCA Civ 318, [2003] 1 WLR 1607 *182*

W (a minor) (medical treatment), Re [1993] Fam 64 *48*

W *v* Essex County Council [2001] 2 AC 592 *147, 149*

W *v* Meah, D *v* Meah [1986] 1 All ER 935 *355, 791*

Wagon Mound, The, see Overseas Tankship (UK) Ltd *v* Morts Dock & Engineering Co Ltd

Wagon Mound (No 2), The, see Overseas Tankship (UK) Ltd *v* Miller Steamship Co Pty

Wainwright *v* Home Office [2003] UKHL 53, [2004] 2 AC 406 *93, 131, 153–4, 158–9, 161, 162, 589, 615, 622, 659, 660, 702*

Wakley *v* Cooke and Healey (1849) 4 Ex 511, 154 ER 1316 *548*

Walker *v* Brewster (1867) LR 5 Eq 25 *441*

Walker *v* Medlicott & Son [1999] 1 WLR 727 *352*

Walker *v* Northumberland County Council [1995] 1 All ER 737 *155*

Walkin *v* South Manchester HA [1995] 1 WLR 1543 *137*

Wallis *v* Meredith [2011] EWHC 75 (QB) *542*

Walpole *v* Partridge & Wilson (a firm) [1994] 1 All ER 385 *724*

Walsh *v* Ervin [1952] VLR 361 *651, 652*

Walter *v* Selfe (1851) 4 De G & Sm 315, 64 ER 849 *423, 429*

Walters v Sloan, 571 P 2d 609 (1977) *727*

Wandsworth Board of Works v United Telephone Co Ltd (1884) 13 QBD 904 *412*

Wandsworth LBC v Railtrack PLC [2001] EWCA Civ 1236, [2002] QB 756; affirming [2001] 1 WLR 368 *643, 650*

Ward v Hobbs (1878) 4 App Cas 13 *692*

Warner v Basildon Development Corp (1991) 7 Const LJ 146 *740*

Warren v Henleys Ltd [1948] 2 All ER 935 *876*

Waters v Commissioner of Police of the Metropolis [2000] 1 WLR 1607 *236*

Watkins v Secretary of State for the Home Department [2006] UKHL 17, [2006] 2 AC 395; reversing [2004] EWCA Civ 966 *714, 749, 750, 752*

Watson v British Board of Boxing Control Ltd [2001] 1 QB 1134 *223*

Watson v Croft Promosport Ltd [2009] EWCA Civ 15 *455, 458, 840*

Watson v M'Ewan [1905] AC 480 *556, 722*

Watson v Wilmott [1991] 1 QB 140 *851*

Watt v Longsdon [1930] 1 KB 130 *557–8, 560*

Watts v Aldington, The Times, December 16 1993 *572*

Watts v Times Newspapers Ltd [1997] QB 650 *561*

Waverley Borough Council v Fletcher [1996] QB 334 *492*

WBA v El-Safty [2005] EWHC 2866 *110*

Webb v Chief Constable of Merseyside Police [2000] QB 427 *736*

Weir v Chief Constable of Merseyside Police [2003] EWCA Civ 111 *883*

Weller & Co v Foot and Mouth Disease Research Institute [1966] 1 QB 569 *110*

Wells v First National Commercial Bank [1998] PNLR 552 *201*

Wells v Wells [1999] 1 AC 345 *756, 761*

Welsh v Chief Constable of Merseyside Police [1993] 1 All ER 692 *218*

Welsh v Stokes [2007] EWCA Civ 796, [2008] 1 WLR 1224 *401, 403*

Welsh Ambulance Services NHS Trust v Williams [2008] EWCA Civ 81 *848*

Welton v North Cornwall District Council [1997] 1 WLR 570 *176*

Wennhak v Morgan (1888) 20 QBD 635 *538*

Wentworth v Wiltshire CC [1993] QB 654 *635*

West v Bristol Tramways Co [1908] 2 KB 14 *471, 473*

West v East Tennessee Pioneer Oil Co, 172 SW 3d 545 (2005) *139*

Westcott v Westcott [2008] EWCA Civ 818, [2009] QB 407 *40, 556, 706, 723*

Western Engraving Co v Film Laboratories Ltd [1936] 1 All ER 106 *473*

Westminster City Council v Ocean Leisure Ltd [2004] EWCA Civ 970 *641, 642*

Westwood v The Post Office [1974] AC 1 *778*

Whalley v Lancashire and Yorkshire Railway Co (1884) 13 QBD 131 *434*

Whatford v Carty, The Times, October 29 1960 *499*

Wheat v E Lacon & Co Ltd [1966] AC 552 *360, 361*

Wheeler v J J Saunders Ltd [1996] Ch 19 *430*

White v Blackmore [1972] 2 QB 651 *373*

White v Chief Constable of the South Yorkshire Police, see Frost v Chief Constable of the South Yorkshire Police

White v Jones [1995] 2 AC 207 *98, 165, 175, 191, 196, 197, 200–2, 352, 729, 730, 778, 859*

White v Mellin [1895] AC 154 *697*

White v Morris (1852) 11 CB 1015, 138 ER 778 *502*

White v Samsung Electronics America Inc, 971 F 2d 1395 (1992) *623*

White v Withers [2009] EWCA Civ 1122 *501–2, 503, 750, 751*

Whiteley Limited v Hilt [1918] 2 KB 808 *506*

Whitwham v Westminster Brymbo Coal & Coke Company [1896] 2 Ch 538 *814*

WHPT Housing Association Ltd v Secretary of State for Social Services [1981] ICR 737 *870*

Wieland v Cyril Lord Carpets Ltd [1969] 3 All ER 1006 *313*

Wilkes v Hungerford Market Co (1835) 2 Bing NC 281, 132 ER 110 *651*

Wilkinson v Downton [1897] 2 QB 57 *131, 153, 154, 161, 162, 579*

Williams v Natural Life Health Foods Ltd [1998] 1 WLR 830 *174, 175, 179–80, 189, 204*

Willis (R H) & Son v British Car Auctions Ltd [1978] 1 WLR 438 *496*

Wilsher v Essex Area Health Authority [1988] 1 AC 1074, affirming [1987] 1 QB 730 *182, 250, 251, 282–3, 290, 291*

Wilson v Pringle [1987] 1 QB 237 *43*

Wilson v Waddell (1876) 2 App Cas 95 *473*

Wilsons & Clyde Coal Co Ltd v English [1938] AC 57 *261*

Wingrove v Prestige & Co Ltd [1954] 1 WLR 524 *628*

Winkfield, The [1902] P 42 *504*

Winnipeg Condominium Corporation No 36 v
Bird Construction Co Ltd [1995] 1 SCR
85 *341*

Winsmore v Greenbank (1745) Willes 577, 125
ER 1330 *7*

Winterbottom v Lord Derby (1867) LR 2 Ex
316 *652*

Winterbottom v Wright (1842) 2 M & W 109,
152 ER 402 *2, 7*

Wise v Kaye [1962] 1 QB 638 *772*

Withers v Perry Chain Co Ltd [1961] 1 WLR
1314 *236*

Wong v Parkside Health NHS Trust [2001]
EWCA Civ 1721, [2003] 3 All ER 932 *65,
161, 162*

Woodward v Hutchins [1977] 2 All ER 751 *597*

Wooldridge v Sumner [1963] 2 QB 43 *251*

Worsley v Tambrands Ltd [2000] PIQR P95 *386*

Wright v Cambridge Medical Group [2011]
EWCA Civ 669 *299, 304, 308–9*

Wringe v Cohen [1940] 1 KB 229 *647, 650*

Wrotham Park Estate Company Ltd v Parkside
Homes Ltd [1974] 1 WLR 798 *807, 819*

WWF v WWF [2006] EWHC 184 (QB) *817*

X v Bedfordshire County Council [1995] 2 AC
633 *12, 13, 87, 118, 192, 239, 241, 556, 627,
629, 632, 634, 717, 722–3*

X v Y [2004] EWCA Civ 662 *603*

X and Y v London Borough of Hounslow
[2009] EWCA Civ 286 *221*

X and Y v Persons Unknown [2006] EWHC
2783 (QB) *594*

XA v YA [2010] EWHC 1983 (QB) *238*

Yachuk v Oliver Blais Co Ltd [1949] AC 386 *774*

Yearworth v North Bristol NHS Trust [2009]
EWCA Civ 37, [2010] QB 1 *237, 488, 489,
507*

Yetkin v Mahmood [2010] EWCA Civ 776,
[2011] QB 827 *210*

Yewens v Noakes (1880) 6 QBD 530 *870*

YL v Birmingham City Council [2007] UKHL
27, [2008] 1 AC 95 *76, 77, 78*

Young v Hichens (1844) 6 QB 606, 115 ER
228 *490*

Youssoupoff v Metro-Goldwyn-Mayer Pictures
Ltd (1934) 50 TLR 581 *531, 544*

Yuen Kun Yeu v Attorney-General for Hong
Kong [1988] AC 175 *106, 179, 208*

Z v Finland (1997) 25 EHRR 371 *598*

Z v United Kingdom [2001] 2 FLR 612 *80, 87,
89, 241, 744*

Zelenko v Gimbel Bros, 287 NYS 134
(1935) *229–30*

Table of statutes, statutory instruments and conventions

Statutes

Administration of Justice Act 1982: s.1 *762*; s.2 *7*; s.6 *756*; s.8 *780*

Animals Act 1971 *231, 408*; s.1 *398, 407*; s.2 *399–404, 483, 852*; s.3 *399*; s.4 *399, 407, 483*; s.5 *404, 483*; s.6 *399*; s.7 *483, 498*; s.8 *408*; s.9 *498*; s.10 *404, 483, 852*; s.11 *483*

Bill of Rights 1688: Article 9 *555, 738*

Broadcasting Act 1990: s.166 *545*

Cheques Act 1957: s.4 *500*

Children Act 2004: s.58 *55*

Civil Aviation Act 1982: s.76 *412, 745*

Civil Evidence Act 1968: s.11 *269*; s.13 *549*

Civil Liability (Contribution) Act 1978 *890*; s.1 *113*; s.2 *113, 353*; s.3 *766*

Compensation Act 2006: s.1 *256*; s.3 *288, 289, 290*

Congenital Disabilities (Civil Liability) Act 1976 *854–7*; s.1 *855, 856*; s.1A *855, 856*; s.2 *28, 856*

Consumer Protection Act 1987 *14, 15, 136, 272, 352, 382, 852, 857, 888*; s.1 *383, 387*; s.2 *382*; s.3 *384*; s.4 *390–2*; s.5 *169, 388–90*; s.6 *393, 394, 853, 857*; s.7 *394*; s.45 *383, 388*; s.46 *383*

Contracts (Rights of Third Parties) Act 1999 *674, 729*; s.1 *729*; s.3 *729*

Copyright, Designs and Patents Act 1988 *512*; s.1 *512*; s.96 *512, 513*; s.97 *512, 513*; s.213 *512*; s.229 *512*; s.233 *512*

Corporate Manslaughter and Corporate Homicide Act 2007 *217*

Countryside and Rights of Way Act 2000 *363, 367*

Courts and Legal Services Act 1990: s.8 *572*

Courts Act 2003: s.100 *757*

Criminal Damage Act 1971 *227*

Criminal Justice Act 1988: s.133 *57*

Criminal Justice Act 2003: s.329 *730, 737*

Criminal Law Act 1967: s.3 *55*

Crown Proceedings Act 1947: s.2 *64, 719, 868*; s. 10 *746*; s.11 *720*

Damages Act 1996: s.2 *757*; s.3 *762, 846*

Damages (Asbestos-related Conditions) (Scotland) Act 2009: s.1 *295*

Defamation Act 1952: s.2 *545*; s.3 *697*; s.5 *548* ; s.6 *554*

Defamation Act 1996: s.1 *568–9*; s.2 *570*; s.3 *570*; s.4 *570*; s.9 *525, 573*; s.13 *555*; s.14 *557*; s.15 *561, 562*; Sch 1, Part I *562*; Sch 1, Part II *562*

Defective Premises Act 1972 *131, 740*; s.1 *636–7*; s.2 *636*; s.4 *234–5*

Education Act 1996: s.548 *55*; s.550A *55*

Employers' Liability (Defective Equipment) Act 1969: s.1 *262*

Equality Act 2010 *579, 582, 585*; s.4 *637*; s.13 *637*; s.14 *637*; s.19 *637*; s.26 *579, 585–6*; s.28 *586*; s.29 *586*; s.32 *587*; s.33 *586*; s.35 *587*; s.40 *587*; s.44 *587*; s.47 *587*; s.53 *587*; s.57 *587*; s.58 *587*; s.84 *587*; s.85 *587*; s.91 *587*; s.101 *580*; s.102 *580*; s.108 *587*; s.109 *587*; s.114 *637* ; s.119 *580*; s.120 *637*; s.124 *580, 588*

Family Law Reform Act 1969: s.8 *47*

Fatal Accidents Act 1976 *13, 81, 272, 289, 393, 397, 762, 767, 825, 844, 846, 854*; s.1 *845*; s.1A *851*; s.3 *846, 849, 852*; s.4 *850, 851*; s.5 *394, 846*

Fire Prevention (Metropolis) Act 1774: s.86 *480*

Health and Safety at Work Act 1974: s.2 *634*; s.15 *634*; s.47 *634*

Health and Social Care Act 2008: s.145 *78*

Health and Social Care (Community Health and Standards) Act 2003: s.150 *857–8*; s.153 *858*

Highways Act 1980: s.41 *368, 635*; s.58 *635*

Human Rights Act 1998 *3, 8, 21, 23, 68, 95, 115, 208, 241, 242, 558–9, 589, 720, 738, 821, 822*; s.3 *81, 86*; s.6 *72, 73, 74, 79, 80–1, 85, 453, 592*; s.7 *81*; s.8 *21, 72, 81, 82, 84, 85*; s.9 *85*; s.12 *619, 836*

Latent Damage Act 1986:
s.3 *858*

Law Reform (Contributory
Negligence) Act 1945 *22,
394*; s.1 *773*; s.4 *773*

Law Reform (Married Women
and Joint Tortfeasors) Act
1935: s.3 *868*

Law Reform (Miscellaneous
Provisions) Act 1934:
s.1 *543, 723, 747, 802, 803,
825*

Law Reform (Miscellaneous
Provisions) Act 1970: s.4 *7*;
s.5 *7*

Law Reform (Personal Injuries)
Act 1948: s.2 *315*

Limitation Act 1980: s.2 *740*;
s.4A *542, 743*; s.11 *740, 741*;
s.11A *392, 393*; s.12 *852*;
s.14 *740, 741*; s.32 *740, 743*;
s.32A *743*; s.33 *741, 742,
852*

Matrimonial Causes Act 1857:
s.33 *7*

Mental Capacity Act 2005:
s.1 *53*; s.3 *52*; s.4 *54*;
s.4A *53*; s.5 *52*; s.6 *52–3*

Mental Health Act 2007:
s.50 *53*

Misrepresentation Act 1967:
s.3 *728*

National Parks and Access to
the Countryside Act
1949 *363, 367*

Nuclear Installations Act 1965:
s.7 *484*; s.12 *484* ; s.13 *484*

Occupiers' Liability Act
1957 *234, 237, 358, 362, 369,
370, 373, 376*; s.1 *99, 237,
360, 363, 364, 370*; s.2 *261,
360, 363, 364, 365, 368, 371*

Occupiers' Liability Act
1984 *22, 234, 358, 362,
363, 366, 369, 373, 404*;
s.1 *367–8, 373, 374, 377*

Offences Against the Person
Act 1847: s.45 *65*; s.47 *45,
55*

Parliamentary Papers Act 1840:
s.1 *555*

Partnership Act 1890: s.10 *868*

Patents Act 1977: s.60 *512*;
s.61 *512*; s.62 *512, 513, 811*

Police Act 1996: s.88 *868*

Police and Criminal Evidence
Act 1984: s.17 *409*; s.18 *409*;
s.19 *492, 499*; s.24 *56*;
s.24A *56*; s.34 *58*; s.37 *58*;
s.40 *58*

Policing and Crime Act 2009:
s.34 *832*

Prison Act 1952: s.12 *57*

Private International Law
(Miscellaneous Provisions)
Act 1995 *720*

Protection from Harassment
Act 1997 *339, 451*; s.1 *21,
579, 580, 584, 585*; s.2 *580*;
s.3 *21, 579, 580, 585*;
s.3A *585*; s.5 *585*; s.7 *581,
585*

Railways and Transport Safety
Act 2003: s.111 *635*

Rehabilitation of Offenders Act
1974 *549*

Registered Designs Act
1949 *512*; s.7 *513*; s.9 *513*

Road Traffic Act 1988:
s.149 *727, 728*

Road Traffic (NHS Charges)
Act 1999 *28*

Senior Court Act 1981:
s.32A *756*; s.37 *832*;
s.50 *455, 839*; s.69 *572*

Slander of Women Act 1891:
s.1 *545*

Social Security (Recovery of
Benefits) Act 1997 *767, 857*

Theatres Act 1968: s.4 *545*;
s.7 *545*

Torts (Interference with
Goods) Act 1977: s.1 *493*;
s.2 *237, 497*; s.3 *506*;
s.5 *505, 506*; s.6 *506*;
s.11 *496, 773*

Trade Marks Act 1994:
s.10 *513*; s.14 *513*

Trade Union and Labour
Relations (Consolidation)
Act 1992: s.219 *659, 721,
748, 837*; s.220 *721*;
s.221 *837*; s.222 *721*;
s.223 *721*; s.224 *721*;
s.225 *721*; s.244 *721*

Trustee Act 2000 *97*

Unfair Contract Terms Act
1977 *371, 374*; s.1 *372, 374*;
s.2 *22, 176, 359, 360, 372,
373, 375, 728*; s.13 *372*;
s.14 *373*

Vaccine Damage Payments Act
1979 *897–8*; s.1 *898*

Water Industry Act 1991:
s.209 *483*

Statutory instruments

Conservation of Habitats and
Species Regulations 2010 *9*

Construction (Health, Safety
and Welfare) Regulations
1996 *634*

Control of Substances
Hazardous to Health
Regulations 2002 *635*

Damages (Variation of
Periodical Payments)
Order 2005 *757*

Fire Precautions (Workplace)
Regulations 1997 *634–5*

Management of Health and
Safety at Work and Fire
Precautions (Workplace)
(Amendment) Regulations
2003 *635*

Management of Health and
Safety at Work Regulations
1999 *635*

Personal Protective Equipment
at Work Regulations
1992 *634*

Provision and Use of Work
Equipment Regulations
1998 *635*

Regulatory Reform (Vaccine
Damage Payments Act 1979)
Order 2002 *898*

Unfair Terms in Consumer
Contracts Regulations
1999 *728*

Workplace (Health, Safety and
Welfare) Regulations
1992 *634*

Conventions

European Convention on
Human Rights: Art 2 *23, 70,
71, 79, 80, 84, 87*; Art 3 *70,
71, 80, 87, 241*; Art 4 *70*;
Art 5 *37, 70, 83, 85, 88*;
Art 6 *23, 70, 72, 79, 89–90*;
Art 7 *70*; Art 8 *23, 70, 90,
453–4, 559, 560, 592–3, 611*;

Art 9 *70*; Art 10 *3, 23, 70,
72, 90–1, 528, 572, 575,
593, 605, 611*; Art 11 *70*;
Art 12 *70, 79*; Art 14 *70*;
Art 34 *81*; Art 41 *82*

First Protocol to the European
Convention on Human
Rights: Art 1 *70*; Art 2 *70*;
Art 3 *70, 71*

1 The basics

1.1   The function of tort law *1*

1.2   Rights and duties *2*

1.3   The range of torts *5*

1.4   Torts and wrongs *8*

1.5   The importance of being a victim *10*

1.6   The loss compensation model of tort law *13*

1.7   The residual wrongs model of tort law *16*

1.8   Tort law and contract law *17*

1.9   Tort law and equity *19*

1.10 Tort law and statute law *21*

1.11 Tort law and criminal law *23*

1.12 Tort law and property law *24*

1.13 Tort law and strict liability *25*

1.14 Insurance *27*

1.15 Paying for tort law *29*

1.16 Tort law as a foreign country *32*

Overview

This is the only chapter in the book that does not begin with a section on 'The basics'. That is because the whole of this chapter is concerned with 'the basics' of tort law. Section 1.1 explains the importance of tort law. Sections 1.2 to 1.4 are concerned to get the reader going in understanding some of the basic concepts (such as rights, and duties owed to another) and terminology (such as the names for different torts) that are essential for any tort lawyer to understand. Section 1.5 deals with an important limit on who may sue for a remedy when a tort has been committed. Sections 1.6 to 1.7 present two alternative views of tort law to the one presented in this book, and explain why those views are inadequate. Having got some understanding of tort law's territory, we start to explore tort law's relationship with some neighbouring areas of law in sections 1.8 to 1.13. Sections 1.14 to 1.15 discuss the impact of tort law on the real world – how tort law is paid for, and who pays for the fact that we have a system of tort law. Section 1.16 aims to provide some reassurance for students starting off in this subject: there is a lot about tort law that is unfamiliar and takes getting used to, but with the right preparation it won't take long before reasoning like a tort lawyer becomes second nature to you.

1.1 THE FUNCTION OF TORT LAW

Tort law is one of the most fundamental legal subjects that you can study. This is because the function of tort law is to determine what legal rights[1] we have against other people, free of charge and without our having to make special arrangements for them, and what remedies will be available when those rights are violated.

In *Donoghue* v *Stevenson* (1932), Mrs Donoghue and a friend of hers went to a café in Paisley, Scotland. Donoghue's friend ordered an ice cream 'float' for Donoghue. Francis Minchella, the café owner, served Donoghue with a tumbler of ice cream and an opaque bottle of ginger beer. Minchella poured some of the beer over the ice cream to create the

---

[1] From now on, whenever we use the word 'right', we mean by that a legal right, not a moral right.

'float' and left the bottle – now half full – on Donoghue's table. After Donoghue had eaten some of the 'float', she topped it up by pouring onto it some more ginger beer. As she did so, the decomposing remains of a snail slid out of the ginger beer bottle. Donoghue was taken ill. She brought a claim in tort against David Stevenson, the manufacturer of the ginger beer bottle. She argued that Stevenson had been careless in allowing a snail to get into the bottle, and as a result he should be held liable in tort to compensate her for the illness she had suffered after drinking the bottle's contents (dead snail remains and all).

In bringing her claim against Stevenson, Donoghue faced an uphill battle. The available authorities that applied to her case indicated that:

(1) If Donoghue wanted to sue Stevenson in tort, she had first of all to show that she had a right against Stevenson that he take care that the ginger beer in her bottle was safe to drink. If she could not show this, then even if Stevenson had been careless in allowing a snail to get into the ginger beer bottle, he would have done no wrong – committed no tort – to Donoghue in being careless.

(2) Donoghue could only have had a right against Stevenson that he take care that the ginger beer in the bottle was safe to drink if she and he had entered into a contract – a legally binding agreement – under which Stevenson undertook to take such care in manufacturing the ginger beer bottle.[2] Obviously, this requirement was not satisfied in this case. Donoghue and Stevenson were complete strangers. Donoghue did not even have a contract with Minchella, the café owner who had served her the ginger beer, as the ginger beer had been bought from Minchella by her friend, and not her.

When the case came to the House of Lords, the Law Lords decided – by a 3:2 majority – that (2) was incorrect. It decided that even though Donoghue and Stevenson were complete strangers, Donoghue still had a right that Stevenson take care that the ginger beer in her bottle was safe to drink. *Donoghue* v *Stevenson* established that a consumer would *not* have to enter into a contract with a manufacturer if she wanted to have a right that the manufacturer take care that his goods were safe for the consumer to use. Instead a consumer would have such a right automatically.

What the House of Lords did in *Donoghue* v *Stevenson* was exactly what tort law does generally. Tort law tells us what rights we have against other people automatically – free of charge and without us having to make any special arrangements for them – and what remedies will be available when those rights are violated. To save words, let's call these rights that tort law gives us, *basic rights*. So the function of tort law is to determine what basic rights we have against other people, and what remedies will be available when those rights are violated.[3] The major task of a tort textbook is to set out what these basic rights are, and what remedies will be available when they are violated.

1.2 RIGHTS AND DUTIES

Because lawyers use the word 'right' in different ways, saying – as we do – that tort law determines what basic rights we enjoy against other people can create confusion. Lawyers use the word 'right' in at least three different ways:

(1) To describe what A has when A has a power to perform some kind of legal act, such as suing someone for damages, or terminating a contract. So if A has the power to sue B for

---

[2] *Winterbottom* v *Wright* (1842) 2 M & W 109, 152 ER 402.
[3] For an excellent presentation of this view of tort law, see Tettenborn 2000a.

damages, lawyers say that A has a 'right' to sue B for damages. Similarly, if A has the power to terminate a contract that A has with B because B has failed to perform her side of the contract in some serious way, then we say that A has a 'right' to terminate his contract with B.

(2) To describe what A has when the law imposes a legal duty on B to do *x*, and the law imposes that duty on B for A's benefit. In such a situation, lawyers will say that A has a 'right' against B that B do *x*. This right is correlative to the duty that (lawyers say) B *owes* A to do *x*. The right and the duty are two sides of the same coin. The right does not arise out of the duty. The duty does not arise out of the right. The duty and the right are two sides of the same coin.

So, for example, we said above that the issue in *Donoghue* v *Stevenson* was whether Donoghue had a right against Stevenson that he take care that the ginger beer in her bottle was safe to drink. But an exactly identical way of expressing this point is to say that the issue in *Donoghue* v *Stevenson* was whether Stevenson owed Donoghue a duty to take care that the ginger beer in her bottle was safe to drink. And that was the way the case was argued in the House of Lords – in terms of duties, not rights. But it makes no difference whether you discuss that case in terms of Stevenson owing a duty of care to Donoghue, or in terms of Donoghue having a right against Stevenson that he take care. It comes to the same thing.

(3) To describe what A has when the law takes steps to protect some freedom or interest of A's from being interfered with by other people. So, for example, it is correct to say that you have a 'right' to freedom of speech. This is because the law takes special steps to protect your freedom of speech – in two ways.

First, the Human Rights Act 1998 makes it unlawful for a public body to interfere with your freedom of speech if doing so serves no legitimate purpose,[4] or if doing so does serve a legitimate purpose but would have a disproportionate effect on your freedom of speech.

Secondly, the law grants you immunities, or exemptions, from certain legal rules that would otherwise have the effect of allowing other people to unacceptably interfere with your freedom of speech. For example, it is normally the case that if you defame someone else – say something bad about them – then the person you have defamed will be entitled to sue you for damages. But applying that rule across the board would have the effect of unacceptably interfering with your freedom of speech – for example, when what you have to say about someone else is damaging but true, or when you occupy some position that makes it important that you be able to say what you think about someone else without fear of being sued. In order to prevent people's freedom of expression being unacceptably interfered with in this way, the law grants us certain immunities, or exemptions, from the law on defamation.

So if you say something bad about A, but what you say about A is substantially true, then you will almost always have a defence to being sued by A for defamation. Again, if a journalist in good faith publishes an article that makes damaging allegations about B, then the journalist will have a defence to being sued by B for defamation if the article was on a matter of public interest, and the journalist acted responsibly in publishing the article. And again, a Member of Parliament who makes damaging allegations against C on the floor in

---

[4] Article 10(2) of the European Convention on Human Rights provides that it may be legitimate to limit freedom of speech 'in the interests of national security, territorial integrity or public safety, for the prevention of disorder or crime, for the protection of health or morals, for the protection of the reputation or rights of others, for preventing the disclosure of information received in confidence, or for maintaining the authority and impartiality of the judiciary.'

Parliament cannot be sued at all by C – and this is so even if the MP in question knew that what he was saying about C was untrue when he said it.

When we say that the function of tort law is to determine what basic rights we have against other people, and what remedies are available when those rights are violated, we are using the word 'right' in the *second* sense above. This is a very important point, because people often mix up the second and third types of rights and say things like – 'In *Donoghue* v *Stevenson*, Donoghue was entitled to sue Stevenson because he violated her right *to* bodily integrity'. No – Donoghue was entitled to sue Stevenson because she had a right *that* he take care that the ginger beer in her bottle was safe to drink, and he (we can suppose) violated that right.[5]

Remedies in tort law are based on the violation of a 'right *that* . . .', not a 'right *to* . . .'. Tort law does not do what it does because we have various 'rights to . . .' (bodily integrity, freedom of speech, reputation, property, trade, vote, freedom from discrimination, and so on).[6] On the contrary: our 'rights to . . .' (bodily integrity, freedom of speech, reputation, property, trade, vote, freedom from discrimination, and so on) exist because tort law does what it does in giving us particular rights against other people that they not act in particular ways. It is because we have *those* rights that we can say we have rights to bodily integrity, freedom of speech, reputation, and so on.[7]

In *Allen* v *Flood* (1898) Allen represented ironworkers who were employed by the Glengall Iron Company to repair a ship. The ironworkers were employed on a 'day to day' basis. In other words, if they were working on the ship one day, the Glengall Iron Company had no contractual duty to employ them to work on the ship the next day. But equally, they had no contractual duty to turn up to work on the ship the next day. So each day, the ironworkers would present themselves at the yard for work, and see if they would be taken on for that day. Flood and Taylor were also employed on a 'day to day' basis by the Glengall Iron Company to work on the ship, repairing its woodwork. The ironworkers objected to working alongside Flood and Taylor because Flood and Taylor had previously done some ironwork on another ship, and the ironworkers regarded such work as exclusively theirs to do. So Allen told the Glengall Iron Company that if the company carried on employing Flood and Taylor, the ironworkers would no longer work on their ship. The result was that the next day, Flood and Taylor were told they were no longer needed to work on the ship.

Flood and Taylor sued Allen. They won at first instance, and in the Court of Appeal. When the case reached the House of Lords, nine Law Lords heard the case. Such was the importance of the case, the nine Law Lords asked eight judges to sit in on the hearings and advise them as to what decision they should give in the case. Of those eight judges, six (Hawkins, Cave, North, Wills, Grantham and Lawrance JJ) said that Flood and Taylor were entitled to sue Allen, and only two (Mathew and Wright JJ) said they were not. However, the nine Law Lords decided by six (Lords Watson, Herschell, Macnaghten, James, Shand and Davey) to three (Lord Halsbury LC, and Lords Ashbourne and Morris) that Flood and Taylor had no claim in this case. All in all, 21 judges heard arguments in *Allen* v *Flood* (including one judge at first instance, and three in the Court of Appeal) – 13 found for Flood and Taylor, and only eight for Allen.

---

[5] In fact, the issue of whether Stevenson failed to take care that Donoghue's ginger beer was safe to drink was never tried. The only issue the House of Lords had to decide was whether Stevenson owed Donoghue a duty of care. The case was then sent back down to a lower court to resolve the issue of whether Stevenson breached that duty of care. But the case was settled – Stevenson paid Donoghue damages out of court – before that issue came to court.

[6] Again, it should be remembered (see fn 1, above) that we are talking of legal rights here, not moral rights.

[7] See McBride 2011 for a much more detailed exposition of this basic point.

Allen v *Flood* illustrates just how important it is to bear in mind that you can only sue someone in tort for doing *x* if you can show that you had a right against them *that* they not do *x*. This point was overlooked by the 13 judges who ruled for the claimants in *Allen* v *Flood*. Those judges all took the view that Flood and Taylor should be allowed to sue Allen because they had a 'right to trade' that had been unjustifiably interfered with by Allen. But whether or not Flood and Taylor had a 'right to trade' was irrelevant. The real issue was whether Flood and Taylor had a right against Allen *that* he not persuade the Glengall Iron Company not to re-employ them the next day by threatening that if the company did so, the ironworkers represented by Allen would no longer work on the company's ship. The House of Lords decided that Flood and Taylor had no such right against Allen.

The only (relevant) rights that Flood and Taylor did have against Allen were: (1) a right that Allen not persuade the Glengall Iron Company to breach any contract it had with Flood and Taylor, and (2) a right that Allen not intentionally cause Flood and Taylor loss using means that were independently unlawful. Flood and Taylor could not sue Allen because neither of those rights had been violated in this case. Right (1) was not violated because the Glengall Iron Company was under no contractual obligation to employ Flood and Taylor the next day. Right (2) was not violated because the means by which Allen caused Flood and Taylor loss in this case was to threaten that the ironworkers that he represented would not turn up to work the next day. As the ironworkers were under no contractual duty to turn up for work the next day, it was not independently unlawful for Allen to make this threat.

1.3 THE RANGE OF TORTS

In principle, there are as many different torts as there are different basic rights that tort law gives us against other people.[8] In practice, this is not true as there is one tort, *negligence*, that encompasses the violation of a large number of different rights that we have against other people that they take care not to harm us in some way, or take care to help us in some way. The range of torts recognised under English law can be divided up into a number of different groups:

(1) *Torts of trespass to the person*. These include battery (unlawfully touching another), assault (unlawfully making someone think that they are about to be touched), and false imprisonment (unlawfully confining someone's movements to a particular area).

(2) *Negligence*. This tort covers any situation where a defendant has breached a duty of care owed to a claimant. There are a large number of different duties of care recognised under the law, and a large number of different situations in which one person will owe another a duty of care. Periodic attempts have been made to come up with a master formula that will tell us in any given situation whether or not one person will owe another a duty of care, and if so, what sort of duty. The most famous was Lord Atkin's in *Donoghue* v *Stevenson*, where he argued that 'in English law there must be, and is, some general conception of relations giving rise to a duty of care, of which the particular cases found in the books are but instances' and went on to suggest that the particular cases to be found in the books (that is, the law reports) were based on the general proposition that 'You must take

---

[8] Rudden 1991–1992 provides us with a list of over 70 torts which have been recognised at one time or another in the common law jurisdictions. But it is doubtful whether some of the listed 'torts' are actually torts – for example, 'homicide' or 'products liability'.

reasonable care to avoid acts or omissions which would be likely to injure your neighbour', where 'your neighbour' is someone who is 'so closely and directly affected by my act that I ought reasonably to have them in contemplation as being so affected when I am directing my mind to the acts or omissions which are called in question.'[9]

In truth, all such attempts to come up with such a master formula have failed. Either the formula has been wrong (as Lord Atkin's was, in eliding the fundamental distinction in English tort law between acts and omissions) or the formula has amounted to nothing more than saying 'A will owe B a duty of care if it would be "fair, just and reasonable" for him to do so' – which may be true, but is hardly informative.

(3) *Torts to land.* This group of torts includes the tort of trespass to land (unlawfully going on to someone else's land) and the tort of private nuisance (unlawfully interfering with the amenity value of land in someone else's possession), as well as any forms of the tort of negligence that involve breaching a duty to take care not to do something that is liable to damage someone else's land or a duty to take care to do something to protect someone else's land from being damaged.

(4) *Torts to goods.* Again, the tort of negligence is relevant here, or at least any forms of the tort that involve breaching a duty to take care not to do something that is liable to damage someone else's goods, or a duty to take care to do something to protect someone else's goods from being damaged. The latter kind of duty will be owed in a bailment situation – where A is entrusted with the job of looking after B's goods. Other torts that belong to this group are trespass to goods (unlawfully touching another's goods) and conversion (treating another's goods as though they are your own to dispose of). A further tort, detinue (which involved refusing to hand over goods to the person entitled to them), was abolished in 1977, and this type of wrong is now treated as a form of conversion.

(5) *Personality torts.* These torts involve acting in ways that impinge on someone's ability to function as a person, or to interact with other people. They include defamation, harassment and the new tort of invasion of privacy (or, more accurately, unlawful disclosure of private information to a third party).

(6) *The economic torts.* The torts that belong to this group are so-called because they all involve inflicting some kind of economic harm on someone else. These torts including the tort of inducing a breach of contract, the intentional infliction of economic loss using unlawful means to do so, conspiracy (in both its 'lawful means' form – combining together with one or more people to cause someone loss for no good reason – and its 'unlawful means' form – combining together with one or more people to cause someone loss, using unlawful means to do so), deceit (intentionally or recklessly lying to someone so as to get them to act in a particular way), passing off (trading on the goodwill attached to someone's name or business, or trading in a way that might endanger the goodwill attached to someone's name or business), and malicious falsehood (deliberately telling a third party lies about someone with the object of causing that someone loss). In theory, this group also involves any form of the tort of negligence that involves a breach of a duty to take care not to harm, or to safeguard, someone else's economic welfare.

(7) *Abuse of power torts.* This group includes misfeasance in public office (which either involves a public official unlawfully and intentionally causing someone loss, or involves a public official knowingly doing something unlawful that he knew would cause someone

[9] [1932] AC 562, at 580.

loss) and malicious prosecution (which involves A instituting criminal proceedings against an innocent person for no legitimate reason).

(8) *Statutory torts*. We will discuss these in more detail shortly,[10] but for the time being: A will commit a statutory tort if: (1) he breaches a duty that Parliament has imposed on him for the benefit of B; and (2) Parliament intended that a breach of that duty should be actionable in tort – that is, Parliament intended that the same remedies that are available against someone who commits one of the torts set out above should also be available against A.

The range of torts recognised under English law expands and contracts over time, to reflect changing social notions as to what basic rights we should have against other people. We have already seen how in *Donoghue v Stevenson*, the House of Lords was confronted with the question: Should a consumer automatically have a right against the manufacturer of a product she is using that the manufacturer take care that that product is safe to use? Previous decisions had indicated that a consumer should not: that if a consumer wanted such a right, she would have to go to the manufacturer and bargain for it. Such decisions reflected a desire not to impose too many burdens on businesses and expose them to the risk of a multiplicity of lawsuits:

> The only safe rule is to confine the right to recover [for harm caused by a defective product] to those who enter into [a] contract [with the manufacturer]; if we go one step beyond that, there is no reason why we should not go fifty.[11]

But by the time *Donoghue v Stevenson* was decided, the pendulum had swung, and the majority in the House of Lords was more concerned to enhance the degree of protection enjoyed by consumers than it was to protect businesses from too many lawsuits.

Donoghue v Stevenson was an example of changes in society triggering an expansion in the basic rights we enjoy against each other; but social change can also result in a contraction in our basic rights. For example, it used to be the case that if a man was married, he would normally have a right against other men that they not sleep with his wife,[12] that they not encourage his wife to leave him, and that if his wife did leave him, that they not give her a place to stay.[13] As McCardie J frankly admitted in *Butterworth v Butterworth and Englefield* (1920), the reason for this was that a 'wife was in substance regarded by the common law as the property of her husband'[14] – so interfering with a man's wife was regarded as being akin to interfering with his property. Now that society has rejected the idea that a man's wife is his property, the idea that a married man will have a right against other men that they not interfere with his marriage has also been rejected. So it is not a tort anymore to interfere with someone else's marriage.[15]

[10] See § 1.10, below.
[11] *Winterbottom v Wright* (1842) 2 M & W 109, at 115 (per Alderson B).
[12] Matrimonial Causes Act 1857, s 33.
[13] *Winsmore v Greenbank* (1745) Willes 577, 125 ER 1330.
[14] [1920] P 126, 130.
[15] Section 4 of the Law Reform (Miscellaneous Provisions) Act 1970 provides that 'no person shall be entitled to . . . claim . . . damages from any other person on the ground of adultery with the wife of the first-mentioned person'. Section 5 of the 1970 Act provides that '[no] person shall be liable in tort . . . (a) to any other person on the ground only of his having induced the wife . . . of that other person to leave or remain apart from [that person]; . . . (c) to any other person for harbouring the wife . . . of [that person] . . .' Section 2 of the Administration of Justice Act 1982 provides that '[no] person shall be liable in tort . . . to a husband on the ground only if having deprived him of the services or society of his wife'. The last remaining traces of the idea that a man's wife is his property were removed from the law by the House of Lords in *R v R* [1992] 1 AC 599, ruling that a man is not allowed to have sexual intercourse with his wife without her consent.

However, the pendulum might swing again, particularly under the influence of Article 8 of the European Convention on Human Rights, which provides that 'Everyone has the right to respect for his private and family life, his home and his correspondence.' It could be argued that it is unrealistic to look at a family as an atomistic collection of individuals that have nothing to do with each other. Every member of a family's welfare is bound up with the fate of the family as a whole – so anything that happens to disrupt or harm the family as a whole has a serious effect on the welfare of each member of that family. Given this, it could be argued that the law should recognise that parents have a right that other people not harm their children; and children have a right that other people not harm, or break up, their parents.

So far, attempts to argue for the existence of parental rights that social workers take care not to take the parents' children out of the family home for no good reason,[16] or that social workers not unjustifiably interfere with parents' relationships with their children by placing them with foster parents or having them adopted[17] – have fallen on stony ground because of a desire on the part of the courts to let social workers get on with their jobs, and do what they think is right, free from the fear that their decisions may result in their being sued. However, it is easy to imagine that such parental rights will be recognised in future, as society comes to take a different view of where the balance should be struck between the need to protect good families from being broken up, and the need to allow social workers to do their jobs properly.[18]

1.4 TORTS AND WRONGS

A tort is often said to be a form of *civil wrong*.[19] What do we think?

A wrong involves the breach of a legal duty.[20] Whenever someone does something he is not allowed to do under the law, we can say that he had a duty not to do what he did, and we can also say that he has committed a (legal) wrong. All wrongs can be divided up into *private* wrongs and *public* wrongs.

A private wrong involves the breach of a legal duty that has been imposed on someone for the benefit of a specific individual. So, for example, if you take any two given individuals, A and B, A will have a legal duty not to beat B up. That duty is imposed on A for B's benefit. It is not imposed on A for anyone else's benefit – such as B's wife or children. No doubt they have an interest in B's not being beaten up. But their interest in B's not being beaten up is not the reason why A has a duty not to beat B up. A's duty not to beat B up is

---

[16] See *D v East Berkshire Community Health NHS Trust* [2005] 2 AC 373; *Lawrence v Pembrokeshire County Council* [2007] 1 WLR 2991.

[17] See *F v Wirral MBC* [1991] Fam 69.

[18] The European Court of Human Rights has already ruled in *MAK v United Kingdom* (2010) 51 EHRR 14 that a public authority will violate a parent's Article 8 rights if it unreasonably reaches the incorrect conclusion that the parent's child is at risk of abuse (physical or sexual) in the family home and as a result takes the child into care. This may prod the UK courts into recognising that parents have rights under the common law not to have their children taken away from them unreasonably. But there is no need for the courts to do this to bring UK law into compliance with the European Convention on Human Rights as the existence of the Human Rights Act 1998 now means there is an adequate remedy when a parent's Article 8 rights are violated in the way they were in *MAK*. For criticism of the *MAK* decision – and, in particular, its failure to pay attention to the concern that in cases of suspected abuse, doctors and the social services need to be shielded from the risk of litigation by parents who have had their children taken away from them, if there is to be a proper investigation of the allegations of abuse – see Greasley 2010.

[19] See Birks 1995.

[20] From now on, whenever we use the word 'duty' we mean by that a legal duty, not a moral duty.

imposed on him because B has an interest in not being beaten up. Because A's duty not to beat B up is imposed on A for the benefit of B, we can say that A will commit a private wrong *in relation to B* if A beats B up. We saw in the previous section, if the law imposes a duty on A to do *x* for the benefit of B, we can say that A *owes* B a duty to do *x*, and – what comes to exactly the same thing – we can also say that B has a right against A that A do *x*. So we can say that a private wrong involves the breach of a legal duty owed to someone else, or – what comes to exactly the same thing – that someone who commits a private wrong violates a right that someone else had against him.

It is quite different with public wrongs. A public wrong involves the breach of a legal duty that has been imposed on someone not for the benefit of a specific individual, but for the benefit of society as a whole. So, for example, you are under a duty not to damage or destroy the breeding site or resting place of a wild animal that belongs to a 'European protected species'. This is because regulation 41(d) of the Conservation of Habitats and Species Regulations 2010 makes it a criminal offence to do such a thing. That duty is not imposed on you for the benefit of a particular individual. So you cannot be said to owe that duty to a particular individual; nor can it be said that any particular individual has a right that you not damage or destroy a protected animal's breeding site or resting place. Rather, your duty not to do such a thing is imposed on you for the benefit of society as a whole. So if you do damage or destroy a protected animal's breeding site or resting place, you will commit a public wrong, not a private wrong.

With that all said, let us now turn to civil wrongs. There are two popular ways of defining what a civil wrong is:

(1) A private wrong. That is, a breach of a duty owed to another, or – to put it another, exactly equivalent way – the violation of a right that one person had against another.[21]

On this definition, we would agree that a tort is a form of civil wrong. Clearly, everything we have said so far indicates that we take the view that someone who commits a tort commits a private wrong.

(2) Any kind of wrong – private or public – that is capable of giving rise to a right to bring an action (known as a 'civil action') against the person who committed that wrong for damages.[22]

On this definition, we would again agree that a tort is a form of civil wrong. Someone who commits a tort commits a wrong, and one of the remedies that *may* be made available against them is an order to pay damages to someone else. But strong emphasis needs to be placed on the word 'may'. If someone commits a tort, it is not necessarily the case that they will *always* have to pay damages to someone else. Consider the **Two Burglars Problem**:

> *Greedy* and *Nasty* break into *Owner's* house and attempt to open *Owner's* safe with some explosives that they have brought with them. *Greedy* carelessly drops the explosives, with the result that they go off, and *Nasty* is injured.

In this sort of case, it seems to us obvious that *Greedy* has committed a tort to *Nasty*: the tort of negligence. *Greedy* owed *Nasty* a duty to take care not to drop the explosives for the same reason that the defendant in *Donoghue* v *Stevenson* owed the claimant a duty to take care to see that her ginger beer was safe to drink – because it was reasonably foreseeable

---

[21] See Birks 1995, at 33.
[22] See Birks 1995, at 40.

that if care was not taken, someone would get injured. But the available authorities indicate that in Two Burglars, *Nasty* will not be entitled to sue *Greedy* for damages for his injuries.[23] *Greedy* will be able to raise a defence of 'illegality' to *Nasty*'s claim. So here we have a situation where *Greedy* has committed a tort in relation to *Nasty*, but *Nasty* is not entitled to sue *Greedy* for damages. But we can still say – in line with definition (2), above – that *Greedy* has committed a civil wrong here. The sort of tort that *Greedy* committed when he dropped the explosives – negligence – is one which is capable of giving rise to an action for damages, even if no action for damages is available on the particular facts of this case.

1.5 THE IMPORTANCE OF BEING A VICTIM

When a tort has been committed, usually only the victim of the tort will be entitled to seek a remedy. (If he does so, he is known in English law as a 'claimant', and as a 'plaintiff' in all other countries whose legal systems derive from English law. English courts stopped using the term 'plaintiff' after 1999 in an attempt to make the process of suing someone else more 'user-friendly'.)

Now – suppose that A has committed a tort by doing *x*. Who is the victim of A's tort? It's the person who had a right that A not do *x*. Or to put it another, exactly equivalent way, it's the person to whom A owed a duty not to do *x*. By doing *x*, A has committed a tort *in relation to* that person. And that person will normally be the only person entitled to bring a claim against A for what he has done. Consider, for example, the **Gullible Lovers Problem**:

Envy hates *Handsome* because *Handsome* is going out with *Beauty*, *Envy*'s ex-girlfriend. *Envy* keeps his feelings to himself, and pretends to be *Handsome*'s friend. One day, he hits on a plan to hurt *Handsome*. He tells *Handsome* that he has found out from a friend that X Corp is just about to announce that it has discovered a cure for AIDS. This is not true. In fact, *Envy* has found out that X Corp is about to announce that it is insolvent. *Envy* urges *Handsome* to buy as many shares in X Corp as he can afford. *Handsome* spends £20,000 of his own money on X Corp shares. *Handsome* also tells *Beauty* about the news about X Corp, and she spends £75,000 of her own money on X Corp shares. A week later, X Corp announces that it is insolvent, and both *Handsome* and *Beauty*'s shares become worthless.

In this situation, *Envy* has committed a tort – it was a tort for *Envy* to lie to *Handsome* with the object of getting *Handsome* to act in a particular way and with the result that *Handsome* did act in that way. The tort *Envy* committed was the tort of deceit (or fraud). Now – who was the victim of *Envy*'s tort? Who had a right against *Envy* that he not lie to *Handsome* with the object of getting *Handsome* to act in a particular way and with the result that *Handsome* did act in that way? To put it another way, the duty *Envy* had not to lie to *Handsome* etc – for whose benefit was that duty imposed on *Envy*? The answer is obvious: *Handsome* had a right that *Envy* not lie to him etc; the duty *Envy* had not to lie to *Handsome* etc was imposed on him for the benefit of *Handsome*. So *Handsome* was the victim of *Envy*'s tort. It follows that *Handsome* will be entitled to sue *Envy* for compensation for the losses he suffered as a result of *Envy*'s lies.

If *Beauty* wants to sue *Envy* for compensation for the losses *she* has suffered, it is not enough for her to show that she suffered those losses as a result of *Envy*'s committing a tort in relation to *Handsome*. She will have to show that *Envy*, in acting as he did, *also* committed a tort in relation to *her*, and not just a tort in relation to *Handsome*. *Beauty* will find it very

---

[23] *National Coal Board* v *England* [1954] AC 403.

hard to do this. She will find it very hard to establish that *she* had a right against *Envy* that *Envy* not lie to *Handsome*. To put it another way, she will find it very hard to show that *Envy* owed *her* a duty not to lie to *Handsome*.

However, there is one right *Beauty* may be able to rely on to bring a claim against *Envy* in this situation. *Beauty* will have had a right against *Envy* that he not intentionally cause her loss using unlawful means to do so. That right was recognised in the case of *Allen* v *Flood*, which we came across earlier. All of us are given this right against everyone else by the law of tort. So – *Beauty might* be able to establish that *Envy* committed a tort in relation to *her* in Gullible Lovers. To do this, she will have to show that *Envy* intended to cause *her* (as well as *Handsome*) to suffer loss when he lied to *Handsome*. If she can show this, she has everything she needs to establish that *Envy* committed the tort of intentional infliction of harm by unlawful means in relation to *her* when he lied to *Handsome*: (1) she suffered loss as a result of *Envy*'s lying to *Handsome*; (2) *Envy* intended that she should suffer that loss; and (3) *Envy* used unlawful means – lies – to cause her to suffer that loss. Unfortunately for *Beauty*, it is unlikely that *Envy did* intend to cause *her* to suffer loss when he lied to *Handsome*. The more plausible scenario is that he intended *Handsome* to lose a lot of money as a result of relying on his lies, and that he did not contemplate that *Beauty* would also invest in X Corp – or if he did, he regarded that as an unfortunate side-effect of his main plan, which was to ruin *Handsome*, his rival.

There are plenty of cases that make it clear that only the victim of a tort will normally be entitled to a remedy for the fact that that tort has been committed. The most famous of them is an American case, *Palsgraf* v *Long Island Railroad* (1928). In that case, a traveller, T, attempted to get onto a train as it was moving away. A porter standing nearby, D, tried to help T onto the train. In doing so, D carelessly knocked a package that T was carrying to the ground. Unfortunately, the package contained fireworks, and when the package hit the ground, the fireworks exploded. The plaintiff (this was an American case, and in America people who bring legal actions are known as plaintiffs, not claimants) in the *Palsgraf* case was a woman called Helen Palsgraf, who was standing some way away. The shock of the explosion caused a weight scale, that Helen Palsgraf was standing next to, to fall over and hit her. She sued for compensation. The New York Court of Appeals dismissed her claim. As Cardozo CJ explained, D had not committed a tort *in relation to Palsgraf* in knocking T's package to the ground. He had owed T a duty to take care not to knock the package to the ground, as it was reasonably foreseeable that doing so would damage the package. But he had not owed *Palsgraf* a duty to take care not to knock the package to the ground as it was not – the contents of the package not being apparent to a person in D's position – reasonably foreseeable that Palsgraf would suffer any harm as a result of the package being knocked to the ground. So as Palsgraf was not the victim of any tort committed by D, she could not sue for damages.

The English version of the *Palsgraf* case is *Bourhill* v *Young* (1943). In that case, John Young was riding too fast on his motorbike and crashed into a car driven by a third party. Young died of the injuries that he suffered in the crash. At the time of the crash, Mrs Bourhill was about 50 feet away: she was on a tram and was about to get off. By the time she reached the scene of the accident, Young's body had been taken to hospital and all she could see was some of his blood on the road. Bourhill fell ill – either because of the shock of hearing the crash, or the shock of seeing the blood, or a combination of the two – and later miscarried a baby she was eight months pregnant with at the time of the accident. She sued Young's estate for damages. Her claim was dismissed by the House of Lords. It held that Young had not owed Bourhill a duty to take care not to crash his bike. It had simply not been foreseeable that doing so would result in someone like Bourhill – someone standing 50 feet away – being injured as a result of Young's crashing his bike. Of course, in carelessly crashing his bike, Young committed a tort in relation to the third party into whose car he crashed. But it was not enough for Bourhill to show that she had suffered harm as a result of Young's committing a tort in relation to that third party. She had to show that Young, in acting as he did, also committed a tort in relation to *her* – and this she could not do, for the reasons just explained.

The same point arose in a recent case, *Iqbal v Prison Officers Association* (2009).[24] In that case, members of the defendant association of prison officers went on strike, unlawfully. As a result, the claimant – a prisoner at HMP Wealstun – was not let out of his cell at the time he would normally be let out. He sued, claiming that the prison officers had committed a tort in failing to let him out of his cell. His claim failed. No doubt the prison officers had done something wrong in failing to let the claimant, and the other prisoners at Wealstun, out of their cells at the appointed time. But they did not do anything wrong *to the claimant*. They did something wrong to the Governor of the prison, who had a contractual right that the officers working at her prison turn up to work that day and follow her orders – which they did not. The claimant suffered loss as a result of the officers' wrong, but that was not enough for him to be allowed to sue. In order to sue, he had to show that the prison officers had committed a tort *in relation to him* by failing to let him out of his cell. This he could not do: the fundamental distinction drawn by English tort law between acts and omissions stood in his way. The claimant had no right that the prison officers make him better off by letting him out of his cell. The only right that he had against them was that they not make him worse off, by locking him up when he was entitled to be free (a violation of which right would amount to the tort of false imprisonment). But as the prison officers had not done this, but merely failed to let the claimant out of his cell, they had not done anything wrong to him.

This is a point that students always need to bear in mind whenever they consider cases where a defendant is employed to protect the interests of a person, or class of people, and then fails to do that job properly. Cases like *Hill v Chief Constable of West Yorkshire* (1989) (where the police failed to catch the serial killer known as the 'Yorkshire Ripper' in time before he could kill his last victim, Jacqueline Hill), or *X v Bedfordshire County Council* (1995) (where social workers failed to investigate adequately allegations that the five children in that case were being abused or neglected) or *Capital and Counties plc v Hampshire County Council* (1997) (where, in two of the situations considered in that case, a fire brigade failed to put out a fire on business premises effectively, with the result that the fire later flared up again and burned the premises down), or *Kent v Griffiths* (2000) (where the claimant, who was having an asthma attack, stopped breathing and suffered brain damage – something that could have easily been prevented had the ambulance workers who had been summoned to take the claimant to hospital not taken so long to get to her house). There is no doubt that the defendants in all these cases failed to do their jobs properly. In so doing they did something wrong *to their employers*. But for a tort lawyer, that is irrelevant to the question of whether the claimants in these cases should have been allowed to sue the defendants. That question depends on whether the defendants, in failing to do their jobs properly, did anything wrong *to the claimants*. In other words, did the *claimants* (as opposed to the defendants' employers) have a basic right that the defendants

---

[24] Noted, Varuhas 2010.

take reasonable steps to protect their interests? And the answer is normally 'no' – tort law does not normally give us a basic right that other people save us from harm.

So students must always be on guard against the temptation to think, 'The defendants did something wrong here, and the claimants suffered loss as a result, so the claimants must be entitled to sue.' This is an easy mistake to fall into: and one from which our judges are not immune. For example, some judges are fond of beginning their judgments in cases analogous to the ones we have just mentioned by invoking, 'the rule of public policy that has first claim on the loyalty of the law: that wrongs should be remedied.'[25] But the fact that A has committed a wrong does not tell us anything about whether B – who has suffered a loss as a result of A's actions – should be entitled to a remedy. What is crucial is to determine whether B is a victim of A's wrong – and no amount of braying that 'wrongs should be remedied' will get us any closer to understanding whether B can claim to have been a victim of A's wrong.

There is hardly any rule in English law that does not have an exception to it, and the rule that it is only the victim of a tort who will be entitled to a remedy is no exception. The most important exception to this rule applies in *wrongful death* cases – where A has committed a tort in relation to B and B has died as a result. In such a case, B's estate will be entitled to sue for damages for the actionable losses that B suffered before he died. But B's family will also usually be entitled to sue A for damages under the Fatal Accidents Act 1976. This is so even though it was B who was a victim of A's tort, and not B's family. B's family will, first of all, be able to sue A for 'loss of support' – that is for any loss of economic support that they would have received in the future from B had he not been killed as a result of A's tort. If B was married, then B's wife will also be able to sue A for the fixed sum of £11,800 as damages for 'bereavement'. If B was a child then B's parents will be able to sue for the bereavement damages. B's funeral costs will also be recoverable from A at the suit of his estate.

1.6 THE LOSS COMPENSATION MODEL OF TORT LAW

Let us now turn to consider, in this section and the next, two alternative views of tort law that can be found in other books and articles about tort law.

By far the most dominant alternative view of tort law is the *loss compensation model* of tort law, according to which tort law determines, in a case where A has caused B some kind of loss, when A will be entitled to sue B for compensation for that loss. So, for example, Lord Bingham remarked in the case of *Fairchild v Glenhaven Funeral Services Ltd* that, 'The overall object of tort law is to define cases in which the law may justly hold one party liable to compensate another.'[26]

On this view, tort law does not just cover the case where A commits a private wrong in relation to B, and B suffers some loss as a result, and B is entitled to sue A for compensation for that loss. Tort law *also* covers the case where A causes B to suffer some loss *without having done anything wrong* but A is still held liable to compensate B for that loss. For example, we saw earlier that the House of Lords' decision in *Donoghue v Stevenson* established that the manufacturer of consumer goods will owe a consumer using one of his products a duty to take care that that product is safe to use. What happens if a modern day David Stevenson

---

[25] See *X v Bedfordshire CC* [1995] 2 AC 633, at 663 (per Sir Thomas Bingham MR); *Gorringe v Calderdale MBC* [2004] 1 WLR 1057, at [2] (per Lord Steyn); *A v Essex CC* [2004] 1 WLR 1881, at [43] (per Hale LJ); *D v East Berkshire Community NHS Trust* [2005] 2 AC 373, at [24]–[25] (per Lord Bingham).

[26] [2003] 1 AC 32, at [9].

manufactures glass bottles using the safest bottle production line in the world, but nevertheless one in every million of the bottles that he produces is liable to fracture because of microscopic and undetectable impurities in the glass? If A is injured as a result of one of these bottles fracturing, A will not be able to sue the manufacturer in negligence – as he took all reasonable steps to see that the bottle would be safe to use – but A will *still* be entitled to sue the manufacturer for compensation for his injuries under the Consumer Protection Act 1987, which makes manufacturers *strictly liable* for harm done to persons as a result of their products being dangerously defective. This is an example of 'compensation without wrongdoing' – even though it is impossible to say that the manufacturer did anything wrong in making glass bottles on the safest production line in the world, he is still liable to pay compensation in those one in a million cases where a bottle leaves his production line with an infinitesimally small flaw in it, and as a result fractures and injures someone.

We reject the loss compensation model of tort law, for a number of different reasons:

(1) The loss compensation model of tort law completely ignores the many non-compensatory remedies that are standardly available in tort cases. The most important of these non-compensatory remedies is the *injunction*, which is a court order requiring someone who is continually committing a tort to stop doing it. Another non-compensatory remedy that is available in some tort cases is *gain-based damages*, which require someone who has committed a tort to give up, or pay a reasonable sum for, some gain which he has obtained as a result of committing that tort. And the loss compensation model of tort law simply cannot account for the development of new non-compensatory remedies in tort, such as *vindicatory damages*.

(2) The loss compensation model of tort law cannot account for the existence of torts that are actionable *per se*: that is, torts that can be committed without causing anyone else any loss. For example, suppose that while A is on holiday, B – A's neighbour, and to whom A has given a spare key – watches the TV in A's house because hers is broken. A is not aware of this. In this situation, B has committed the tort of trespass to land – she went onto A's land without his permission. The fact that A has suffered no loss as a result of B's trespass is irrelevant: trespass to land is a tort that is actionable *per se*. The fact that B can be held liable for committing a tort in this situation is something that the loss compensation model of tort law simply cannot comprehend.

(3) The loss compensation model of tort law simply does not fit the way we think and speak about tort law.

For example, we have just seen that under the loss compensation model of tort law, liability arising under the Consumer Protection Act 1987 is counted as a form of tort liability. But no one would ever seriously say that a manufacturer who is held liable under the 1987 Act has committed a *tort* – and that is because, at the very deepest level, we must subscribe to the idea that committing a tort involves doing something wrong to someone else.

Similarly, what is called 'the rule in *Rylands* v *Fletcher*' says that if A brings onto his land something that is liable to do damage to his neighbour B's land if it escapes from A's land, then if that thing does escape and damage B's land, A will be held liable to compensate B for the damage – and this is so even if A took all due care to prevent the thing escaping. On the loss compensation model of tort law, liability arising under the rule in *Rylands* v *Fletcher* counts as a form of tort liability. But there is some significance in the fact that we talk about the *rule* in *Rylands* v *Fletcher* – hardly anyone ever talks about the *tort* in *Rylands* v *Fletcher*. Again, that must be because we subscribe at a very deep level to the idea that committing a tort involves doing something wrong to someone else – and someone who is held liable under the *Rylands* v *Fletcher* has not necessarily done anything wrong to anyone else.

Again, if the government lawfully expropriates someone else's land (say) to build a new motorway, it is required to pay the landowner the fair value of the land. Interestingly, this is not an example of 'compensation without wrongdoing' that has ever gotten into the tort textbooks. When one of us once asked an extremely distinguished writer on tort law why this was, the response was, 'Well, it's a liability that only the State is subject to'. Surely the more convincing answer is that no one thinks that the government has committed a tort in this situation. This is again because we subscribe at a very deep level to the idea that committing a tort involves doing something wrong to someone else – and the government does no wrong when it lawfully expropriates other people's property.

Despite its fundamental flaws, the loss compensation model of tort law has proved highly influential in determining the current shape of tort law textbooks. Liability under the Consumer Protection Act 1987, and liability under the rule in *Rylands* v *Fletcher* are both in. The availability of injunctions in tort cases is not mentioned, or downplayed. Gain-based damages are not mentioned or reconceptualised as really compensatory in nature. Torts that are actionable *per se* are relegated to one chapter at the end of the book. Tort law in these textbooks becomes a ragbag of causes of action, which are treated as having nothing in common except the remedy – compensation – that you get at the end. It is no wonder that such textbooks confess that tort law is very difficult to understand, that it is impossible to ascribe any one aim or function to tort law, and that it is impossible to define with any precision what a tort actually is. But if tort law as presented in the textbooks is in a mess, it is a mess that the academics have created by subscribing to the loss compensation model of tort law. The reality is that: (i) tort law – if looked at right – is quite simple to understand, and (ii) it is possible to say clearly what the aim or function of tort law in one sentence, and (iii) it is perfectly easy to define what a tort is.

In previous editions of this textbook, we attempted to clear up the mess that the academics have made of tort law by carefully separating out cases where A would be held liable to pay B compensation for some loss that he had caused B to suffer even though he has not committed a wrong in relation to B, and dealing with those cases at the very end of the book under the generic heading 'Alternative Sources of Compensation'. However, some tort law teachers found it disconcerting that about 600 pages separated our discussion of liability in negligence and liability under the Consumer Protection Act 1987, and that there was a similar gap between our discussion of liability in private nuisance and liability under the rule in *Rylands* v *Fletcher*. And we have to admit that there is some pedagogical advantage in discussing those topics alongside each other. So in this edition, we have adopted a more conventional structure and the reader will find mixed in with all the normal instances of tort liability, instances of compensation without wrongdoing. One disadvantage of this mixing is the potential it creates for confusing you, the reader, about what sort of conduct amounts to a tort and what does not, which then in turn creates the potential for confusion on your part about what exactly is being said when we say – in chapters dealing with the remedies available when someone commits a tort – such things as, 'If a defendant has committed a tort in relation to a claimant, then the claimant may be entitled to sue the defendant for . . .' or 'If *Employee* has committed a tort in relation to *Victim* in the course of his employment by *Employer*, then *Victim* may be entitled to sue *Employer* . . .' The best way of avoiding falling into such confusion is always to remember that whenever we use the word 'tort', we are using the word in its *correct* sense – as denoting a private wrong that A has committed in relation to B – and whatever we say does *not* apply to any situation where it is *not* possible to say that A has committed a private wrong in relation to B.

1.7 THE RESIDUAL WRONGS MODEL OF TORT LAW

The second alternative view of tort law that we need to discuss is the *residual wrongs model of tort law*, according to which tort law is made up of all civil wrongs that are not dealt with under some other area of law – such as the law of contract, or the law of equity. (We will discuss both of these areas of law very shortly.)[27] On this view, it makes no sense to talk of tort law as having a 'function' or to think that the various torts recognised in English law have anything in common. The only function 'tort law' performs is to provide us with a title under which we can group the civil wrongs that are left over once we deduct the civil wrongs that we can make sense of as belonging to some determinate area of law such as the law of contract, or the law of equity. And the only thing that the various torts recognised in English law have in common is their orphan status as wrongs that cannot be classified as belonging to some such determinate area of the law. As Tony Weir has joked, 'Tort is what is in the tort books and the only thing holding it together is the binding.'[28]

We disagree. The various torts gathered together in the tort law textbooks are not orphans, and nor are they unrelated to each other. The very fact that their daddy is not the law of contract or the law of equity tells us something about who their daddy actually is. The torts gathered together in the tort law textbooks owe their status as wrongs to a consensus, evolving over time, among our law makers as to what the law should do by way of requiring each of us to look out for the interests of other people.[29] This consensus underlies *all* of the torts that are gathered together in the tort textbooks: it is imprinted on their DNA. It could hardly be otherwise. The courts could hardly draw on one moral–political vision as to what the law should do by way of requiring us to look out for each other's interests in deciding a negligence case, and then draw on a completely different vision in deciding a false imprisonment case.[30]

Some might argue, against what we have said in the preceding paragraph: 'But what about public nuisance? That is a completely different kind of tort to all the other torts gathered together in the tort law textbooks. Surely that shows that the residual wrongs view of tort law is correct, and that the various torts gathered together in the textbooks really have nothing in common?' Indeed, public nuisance is a very strange 'tort'. To explain: there are many different ways of committing a public nuisance, but for our purposes, you should just consider the case where A blocks the highway for a long time, or dumps oil into the

---

[27] See §§ 1.8, 1.9, below.

[28] Weir 2006, ix.

[29] There are, at the moment, at least three rival accounts as to what private law – the bit of the law that requires us to look out for other people's interests – should do. There is the increasingly influential view (advanced by Weinrib 1995, and Ripstein 2006a, 2006b, 2007b, 2009) that private law should give effect to the demands of *Kantian right*, according to which each of us is entitled to determine for ourselves – independently of anyone else – what purposes we will pursue, and private law should prevent people from acting in ways that subvert our independence as persons. There is the *Rawlsian/contractualist* view (originating in Rawls 1971) that private law should give effect to whatever legally enforceable rights we would all agree that we should have against each other if we made such an agreement under fair conditions. And there is the *natural law view* (originating in Finnis 1980, now Finnis 2011) according to which private law should, by giving us legally enforceable rights against each other, aim to enable each of us to live a flourishing life; that is, a life which participates in a full range of objective human goods.

[30] Though this is not to deny that their understanding of these matters can evolve over time.

sea. In such a case, A will be guilty of committing a wrong – the wrong of public nuisance. Now, suppose various people have suffered loss as a result of A's actions. In such a case, only those who have suffered 'special damage' as a result of A's actions – that is, damage that is significantly worse than that suffered by everyone else – will be entitled to sue A for damages. This is a very different rule from the normal rule that applies when A has committed a tort – where, as we have seen, only the victim of A's tort will normally be entitled to sue A for damages, and this is so even if the victim of A's tort has suffered a comparatively trivial loss as a result and someone else has suffered a devastating loss.

But does this show that the residual wrongs view of tort law is correct? Not really. It could be argued – and we would argue – that public nuisance is not a tort at all. It is not a private wrong. Rather, it is a public wrong – involving the breach of a duty imposed for the benefit of society as a whole – akin to the wrong of disturbing a protected animal's habitat. The only reason it has gotten into the tort textbooks is because they are wedded either to the loss compensation model of tort law (under which claims for compensation for loss under the law on public nuisance count as part of the law of tort) or to the residual wrongs model of tort law (under which public nuisance counts as a tort because it is a wrong that is capable of giving rise to a civil action for damages and cannot be classified as arising under the law of contract or the law of equity).

So the strangeness of the law on public nuisance does not, of and in itself, establish that the residual wrongs view of tort law is correct. Proponents of such a view would be on firmer ground if they could show that the various well-established torts – such as negligence, or the various forms of trespass to the person, or the various torts to property – have *nothing* to do with each other. But no one has ever convincingly managed to do this.

1.8 TORT LAW AND CONTRACT LAW

As we have seen, it is tort law that determines what basic rights we enjoy against other people, and what remedies will be available when those rights are violated. It is contract law that provides us with the facility to alter the rights that tort law provides us with – either by entering into contracts that give us extra rights against other people that tort law does not give us (contracting *on top of* tort law) or by entering into contracts that reduce the rights that tort law gives us against other people (contracting *out of* tort law).

Tort law draws a fundamental distinction between acts and omissions – that is, between doing something that makes someone worse off than they would have been if you had done nothing, and failing to do something that would have made them better off than they would have been if you had done nothing. Tort law is far more willing to give us rights that people not make us worse off, than it is to give us rights that other people make us better off. Generally speaking, if you want to have a right that someone do something for you that will make you better off, then you need to enter into a contract with them that provides that they will act in that way. But to obtain such a right, you will normally need to pay. Promises are not normally contractually binding unless something – called *consideration* by the lawyers – has been given in return for them. So tort rights come free of charge, but are limited in what they will do for you; contract rights can do far more for you, but you normally need to pay for them.

The need to contract on top of tort law, and the iron distinction between tort rights and contract rights, has been lessened in the past thirty years or so by the increasing willingness of the courts to recognise that if A 'assumes a responsibility' to B, then B will have a right in tort that A take care to do whatever it is that he 'assumed a responsibility' for doing. It is not entirely clear what 'assuming a responsibility' to someone else involves – but the available authorities indicate that A will 'assume a responsibility' to B if he indicates to B (or reasonably appears to be indicating to B) that she can rely on him to act in a particular way, and she does so rely on him. So tort rights arising out of 'assumptions of responsibility' do not have to be paid for, but they only arise in special circumstances – to establish such a right against someone else, you have to show that they encouraged you to rely on them and you did so rely.

Turning to the topic of contracting out of tort law, it is an interesting question whether any of the basic rights that tort law gives us are *inalienable* – that is, they simply cannot be given up, no matter how much you might want to give them up. In considering this question, we need to draw a distinction between giving up a right here and now, and giving up rights in the future. So far as giving up a right here and now is concerned, the law recognises that '*volenti non fit injuria*' – no wrong (*injuria*) is done to the willing (*volenti*). If you are happy for someone to lock you up or beat you up you cannot later turn round and complain that your rights have been violated. (Though the courts will require clear evidence before they will accept that you were genuinely *volenti* as to what was done to you.)

But how far can you contract to give up your basic rights in the future? – So that someone would be allowed in the future to lock you up or beat you up, even if you were *not* happy to be treated that way at the time they were locking you up or beating you up? It is now recognised that a cinema that sells you a ticket to watch a film on its premises does thereby, and for the duration of the film, surrender the right that it would normally have as a landowner that you not stay on its premises if you have been asked to leave. (Though the cinema will still have a right that you leave the premises if you start being a nuisance to other customers.) At the opposite extreme, a contract of slavery will be void – so if you agreed with a TV production company to be locked up in a house for six months and have your doings in the house continuously televised, it seems highly unlikely that they would be allowed to keep you locked in if you demanded to be let out after three weeks.

So far, we have been looking at how people can contract on top of tort law to give themselves contractual rights that tort law will not provide them for free, and how far people can contract out of tort law to modify the rights and remedies for violation of those rights that tort law would otherwise give them. But the very act of entering into a contract can give rise to rights in tort:

(1) If *Worker* undertakes in a contract with *Homeowner* to install a new kitchen in *Homeowner*'s house, *Worker* will almost invariably be found by the courts to have 'assumed a responsibility' to install the kitchen with a reasonable degree of care and skill – with the result that he will owe *Homeowner* a duty in tort to install that kitchen with a reasonable degree of care and skill.[31] So if he carelessly fails to do a good job, *Homeowner* can not only sue him for committing a breach of contract; she can also sue him (concurrently) in tort (under the tort of negligence) for failing to do a good job in installing the kitchen.

(2) If *Magician* undertakes in a contract with *Mother* to perform at a birthday party *Mother* is throwing for her son, then *Mother* will have a right against everyone else that they not persuade *Magician* to breach his contract with *Mother* unless they have a really good reason for doing so. Anyone who violates this right will commit the tort of *inducing a breach of contract* in relation to *Mother*.

---

[31] Though see the strange decision of the Court of Appeal in *Robinson* v *Jones* (Contractors) Ltd [2011] EWCA Civ 9 (criticised below, § 6.11(A)), which seems hostile to finding an 'assumption of responsibility' here.

1.9 TORT LAW AND EQUITY

Before the end of the nineteenth century, the English legal system could be roughly divided into three parts. There was, first of all, Parliament (once known, more grandly, as the 'High Court of Parliament') which changed the law by enacting *statutes*, which all English courts were and are required to give effect to under the doctrine of *Parliamentary supremacy*, or *sovereignty*. Secondly, there were the Courts of Common Law, from which the *common law* emerged, made up of the rules and principles given effect to by the common law judges deciding cases argued before them. Thirdly, there was the Court of Chancery, which would in its judgments supplement or modify the common law as given effect to by the Courts of Common Law. The rules and principles given effect to by the Court of Chancery were known as *equity*. Equity modified and supplemented the common law in three significant ways:

(1) *Enforcing common law rights*. Where a claimant's rights at common law were being violated, or in danger of being violated, by a defendant but damages (the only remedy he would be able to get from the Courts of Common Law for the violation of his rights) would be an inadequate remedy, the Court of Chancery would grant the claimant an *injunction*, requiring the defendant not to violate the claimant's rights and threatening him with imprisonment if he did.[32]

(2) *Recognising equitable rights*. Where a claimant had no rights that were enforceable in the Courts of Common Law, but the Court of Chancery thought that justice demanded that they should recognise that the claimant had a right against someone else, the Court of Chancery would recognise that the claimant had such a right – called an *equitable right* – and grant the claimant remedies – *equitable remedies* – when that right was violated (which violation would be known as an *equitable wrong*).

So, for example, if *Settlor* transferred property to *Owner* on the understanding that *Owner* would apply that property for the benefit of *Beneficiary* (or, in lawyer's language, on the understanding that *Owner* would hold the property '*on trust*' for *Beneficiary*), if *Owner* took that property and used it for his own benefit, the Courts of Common Law would not allow *Beneficiary* to sue *Owner*. So far as the Courts of Common Law were concerned, *Owner* was the absolute legal owner of the property and could do with it what he liked. The Court of Chancery took the view that this was very unjust, and recognised that *Beneficiary* had a right against *Owner* that *Owner* use the property for *Beneficiary*'s benefit, and would hold *Owner* accountable if he committed a 'breach of trust' by, for example, using the property to enrich himself, or failing to invest it properly so as to produce an income for *Beneficiary*. In this way, *trusts* became part of English law – arrangements whereby the absolute owner of property under the common law (or, more simply, 'at law') would be under an obligation to apply that property for the benefit of someone else (who would be known as 'the *beneficiary*' of the trust, or the '*equitable owner*' of the trust property or – in traditional legal language – the '*cestui que trust*'[33]).

(3) *Modifying common law rights*. If a claimant did have rights that were enforceable in the Courts of Common Law, but the Court of Chancery took the view that it would be unjust – or *unconscionable* – for the claimant to be allowed to exercise those rights, then the Court of Chancery would prevent the claimant enforcing those rights by issuing an injunction

---

[32] This is where we get the saying 'Equity acts *in personam*' from: '*in personam*' here means 'against the body'. If you didn't do what the Court of Chancery told you to do, you would be thrown into prison, rather than having your goods seized (which was the way the Courts of Common Law would enforce their judgments).

[33] Pronounced 'settee kee trust'.

against the claimant. This created tensions between the Courts of Common Law and the Court of Chancery that were only resolved by a declaration of King James I in 1615 that in any conflict between the common law and equity, equity was to prevail.

Tort law was a creation of the Courts of Common Law. Claims in tort were brought in the Courts of Common Law, and could only succeed if the claimant had a right that was recognised under the common law. As we have just seen, the Court of Chancery was willing to grant injunctions to tort claimants for whom damages were an inadequate remedy, but that was the Court of Chancery's only involvement in the law of tort. The equitable rights that were recognised in the Court of Chancery and enforced by the Court of Chancery had nothing to do with the law of tort. To say that an equitable wrong was a tort would have been regarded as complete nonsense by a nineteenth century lawyer.

At the end of nineteenth century, the formal distinction between the Courts of Common Law and the Court of Chancery was abolished by the Judicature Acts, which created one unified court system, known as the 'Supreme Court of Judicature'.[34] No longer would claimants have to choose which court to plead their case in. All courts would from now on practise the same law. But that law was made up of three parts, corresponding to the three parts of the legal system before the Judicature Acts: statute law, common law, and equity. Fusion of the courts did not abolish the distinction between common law and equity; and those branches of the law continued evolving along their own paths. While claimants now all go to the same court to have their cases heard, those cases are still presented as being 'a claim at common law' or 'a claim in equity' or even 'a claim at common law and in equity', and the remedies that are available to a claimant do still vary – at least in language, if not in substance – depending on whether he or she is making 'a claim at common law' or a 'claim in equity'.

The fact that fusion did not eliminate the difference between common law and equity means that among lawyers the concept of a 'tort' has retained its roots in the common law. You would still get some very funny looks from practising lawyers if you attempted to assert that a breach of trust is a tort. A breach of trust is a wrong, but because it is a wrong that has its roots in the law of equity, practising lawyers do not think of it as being a tort. And they are right to do so. It is dangerous to use old words in new ways: associations that have built up around the old word may infect the new usage in undesirable ways. Perhaps one day this textbook will evolve into a book on 'The Law of Wrongs' (or 'Wrongs Law'), and will treat of all the rights we have against each other and what remedies will be available when those rights are violated, without making any distinction between which rights, historically, are 'legal' in nature and which 'equitable'. That would be a more rational development than trying to assert, as a matter of linguistic *fiat*, that 'all wrongs are torts' and that a tort textbook will deal with all wrongs.

One wrong which, because of its history, escapes clear classification as a tort or an equitable wrong is the wrong of *invasion of privacy* – or, more accurately, the wrong of *unauthorised disclosure of private information to another*. It has its formal roots in the equitable wrong of breach of confidence, which involves disclosing to a third party secrets that you have been told by someone else. As a result, most judges regard the wrong of invasion of privacy (to use the simpler expression for the moment) as being an equitable wrong and not a tort. However, the wrong of invasion of privacy seems to have very little in common with the equitable wrong of breach of confidence: you can sue someone for committing the wrong

---

[34] Renamed the 'Supreme Court of England and Wales' by s 1(1) of the Supreme Court Act 1981, and then re-renamed the 'Senior Courts of England and Wales' by s 59 of the Constitutional Reform Act 2005, to avoid confusion with the 'Supreme Court of the United Kingdom', which replaced the House of Lords as the highest court in the UK on October 1 2009.

of invasion of privacy even if what they are disclosing was not told to them by you or anyone else, and even if what they are disclosing is not secret anymore. Moreover, the remedies available for the wrong of invasion of privacy seem to have more in common with the remedies available for a tort than an equitable wrong. For example, you can claim compensatory damages if someone invades your privacy – when the idea of compensatory damages being available for equitable wrongdoing is one that is still alien to most equity lawyers. Given this, there does not seem to be any danger involved in calling the wrong of 'invasion of privacy' a tort – and indeed, we do deal with that wrong in this book. In any case, given the close links between the law on privacy and other well-established areas of tort law, such as the law of defamation, the law of malicious falsehood, the law on trespass to land, and the law on passing off, it would be strange not to deal with actionable invasions of privacy in a tort book.

1.10 TORT LAW AND STATUTE LAW

While tort law has its origins in the decisions of the Courts of Common Law, statute law does have an effect on tort law in a number of different ways:

A. Creating new torts

Parliament can create *statutory torts*, by endowing people with statutory rights and making it clear that the violation of those rights is to be *actionable in tort* – that is, remedied in the same way as a normal common law tort.

Parliament creates a statutory right whenever it imposes a duty on someone for the benefit of a particular individual. For example, s 1 of the Protection from Harassment Act 1997 provides (with certain exceptions) that if you know or ought to know that your doing *x* would amount to harassment of a particular individual, you must not do *x*. That duty is imposed on you for the benefit of the particular individual who would be harassed by your doing *x*, and so that individual has a statutory right that you not do *x*. Violation of that right will amount to a statutory tort as s 3 of the 1997 Act provides that 'an actual or apprehended breach of s 1 may be the subject of a claim in civil proceedings by the person who is or may be the victim of the course of conduct in question.'

What if Parliament creates a statutory right and makes it clear that a violation of that right is to be remedied in a particular way, but not in the same way as a normal common law tort? This is the case with the Human Rights Act 1998, which gives each of us a right that public bodies not act in ways that are inconsistent with our rights as set out in the European Convention on Human Rights (ECHR). Section 8 of the 1998 Act sets down specific rules as to how a breach of the Act is to be remedied: a 'just and appropriate' remedy is to be awarded, and such a remedy is not to include an order to pay damages unless such an award 'is necessary to afford just satisfaction to the person in whose favour it is made'. This is a very different set of remedial rules from those that obtain when a normal common law tort is committed, under which the victim of a tort can normally expect to obtain damages for any losses caused by the tort that are not too remote a consequence of that tort's being committed. Given the remedial regime set out in s 8 of the 1998 Act, it would be wrong (because liable to create confusion) to say that a public body will commit a 'tort' if it acts inconsistently with someone's rights as set out in the ECHR. It will commit a private wrong (a breach of statutory duty), but not a tort.

What if Parliament creates a statutory right but does not make it clear one way or the other whether or not violation of such a right is to be actionable in tort? Unfortunately, this is often the case – either because of Parliamentary *optimism* (Parliament may assume no one would ever fail to do what Parliament tells them to do) or because of Parliamentary *cowardice* (imposing statutory duties is an easy way of gaining popularity with the people who benefit from those duties, while specifying what unpleasant consequences should follow if the duty is breached is an easy way of losing popularity with those who are subject to those duties). The most straightforward solution would be to say that when such a right is violated the only remedy is to seek a declaration that it has been violated, or when it is clear that such a right might be violated, the only remedy is to seek an injunction to prevent the violation. Unfortunately, the courts have bravely decided that even in such cases, it should be possible – if one looks hard enough – to determine whether or not Parliament intended that a violation of such a right should be actionable in tort, thus generating a huge amount of very uninteresting caselaw on whether the violation of a particular statutory provision does or does not amount to a statutory tort.

B. Modifying tort law

The second way statute law can have an effect on tort law is by modifying or extending: (1) the rights that we enjoy under tort law; and (2) the remedies that may be obtained when someone commits a tort.

For example, under the common law, an occupier of premises would only owe a trespasser on his land a duty to take steps to protect him from some danger on his land if 'common humanity' demanded that he offer him such protection. This rule was replaced by the Occupiers' Liability Act 1984, which provided that an occupier would owe a trespasser a duty to take steps to protect him from some danger on his land if: (i) the occupier knew or ought to know of the danger; (ii) the occupier knew or ought to know that a trespasser might come into the vicinity of that danger; and (iii) the danger was one which the occupier reasonably could be expected to offer some protection against.

A common law rule that affected the remedies available to the victim of a tort went like this: if *Fool* committed the tort of negligence in relation to *Victim* by breaching a duty of care owed to *Victim*, and *Victim* was partly to blame for the losses he suffered as a result of *Fool*'s breach, then *Victim* could not sue *at all* for compensation for those losses. This very strict rule was replaced by the Law Reform (Contributory Negligence) Act 1945, which provided that *Victim* should be allowed to sue for compensation for her losses, but the damages recoverable should be reduced so far as is 'just and equitable having regard to' how far *Victim* was to blame for the fact that she suffered those losses.

C. Preventing contracting out of tort law

The third way that statute law can have an effect on tort law is by preventing people 'contracting out' of tort law. The most obvious example of this is s 2(1) of the Unfair Contract Terms Act 1977, which provides that any contractual provision which purports to prevent an individual or his estate suing a business in negligence for killing or injuring him is automatically of no effect.

D. Requiring the courts to develop tort law in certain ways

The fourth way that statute law can have an effect on tort law is by imposing duties on the courts to develop tort law in certain ways. There is only one example of this, and it is arguable how far this example goes.

Under the Human Rights Act 1998, the courts count as public bodies, and therefore have a duty under the 1998 Act – like other public bodies – not to act in ways that are inconsistent with individuals' rights as set out in the ECHR. So the courts have a duty under the 1998 Act to make sure that tort law – as it is applied in the UK courts – does not work in ways that violate individuals' rights under the ECHR to freedom of speech (Article 10), or to a fair trial of their civil rights and obligations (Article 6), and so on. That is not controversial.

What is more controversial is the argument that the courts have a duty under the Human Rights Act 1998 to develop tort law as it applies *between private individuals* so as to give greater protection to people's rights under the ECHR to life (Article 2), not to be subjected to inhuman or degrading treatment (Article 3), and to respect for their private and family life (Article 8) greater protection than they have at the moment. The argument is that just as a police officer would be acting inconsistently with an individual's right to life under Article 2 of the ECHR if he watched that individual being stabbed to death and did nothing to intervene,[35] the courts also act inconsistently with people's rights to life under Article 2 when they sit on their hands and fail to develop tort law so that it does more to protect people from being killed, by – for example – failing to get rid of the rule that there is normally no liability in tort for failing to save a stranger from drowning. The argument is very strained, for two reasons.

First of all, it is clear in the case of the police officer that if he intervened, then the stab victim's life would probably be saved. It is not at all clear that making people liable in tort for failing to save strangers from drowning would have the net effect of saving more people's lives. Secondly, even if UK law could do more than it does at the moment to protect people's rights to life, it is not clear why the burden of doing more to save people's lives should fall on *tort* law, rather than some other area of the law, such as the criminal law.

1.11 TORT LAW AND CRIMINAL LAW

We have already seen one link between tort law and criminal law. If Parliament makes it a criminal offence for A to harm B, we can normally say (assuming that Parliament made it unlawful for A to harm B in order to protect B's interests) that B has a statutory right that A not harm B (or, in other words, that A owes B a statutory duty not to harm B). It may be that a violation of that right will be actionable in tort: it will depend on whether Parliament intended that a violation of that right should be actionable in tort.

However, there is a deeper link between tort law and criminal law in that the core of the criminal law – made up of offences such as murder, manslaughter, rape, assault, theft, and criminal damage to property – exists to punish people who deliberately or recklessly violate the basic rights that we are supplied with by tort law. In this way, the criminal law helps protect our rights from being violated. So there are many cases where someone who commits a tort – known in legal parlance as a *tortfeasor* – will commit a crime as well. If A hits B for no good reason, that is a tort and a crime – battery, in both cases. If a man has sexual intercourse with a woman without her consent, that is a tort – battery. If he had no reasonable grounds for believing that she was consenting to have sex with him, then he will also have committed a crime – rape. If a doctor fails to treat a patient properly with the result that the patient dies, the doctor will have committed a tort – negligence. If the doctor's failure to treat the patient properly was so culpable as to be worthy of punishment, then the doctor will also have committed a crime – gross negligence manslaughter. If A drives off B's car

---

[35] *Osman v United Kingdom* [1998] EHRR 101.

without B's consent, he will have committed two torts – trespass to goods (touching someone else's property without their permission) and conversion (treating someone else's property as your own to dispose of). If A, in driving away B's car, acts dishonestly and with the intent permanently to deprive B of the car, he will also commit a crime – theft.

The overlap between tort law and criminal law often leads students into blunders in the way they talk about claims in tort. If A has committed a tort in relation to B, it would be wrong to say that B can *prosecute* A for committing that tort. No – B can *sue* A for committing that tort. If A is going to be prosecuted for what he has done, it will be by the State, and only if his actions amounted to a crime. If A has committed a crime in acting as he did, it would be wrong to say that A can be held *liable* for committing that crime. People are held liable for committing torts, not crimes. Getting back to the tort that A has committed in relation to B, it would be inappropriate to say that A is *guilty* of committing a tort in relation to B. The language of 'guilt' and 'innocence' should be confined to the criminal sphere.

While the core of the criminal law exists to protect the rights that tort law supplies us with from being violated by other people, by threatening to punish people who intentionally or recklessly violate those rights, tort law performs much the same role in making awards of exemplary (or punitive) damages against tortfeasors who deliberately violate other people's rights. Under English law, such awards can only be made against public officials who have acted in an 'oppressive, arbitrary or unconstitutional way' in committing a tort, or against someone who has deliberately committed a tort figuring that the gain he will make from committing that tort will exceed what he will have to pay by way of compensatory damages for committing that tort.[36] In order to avoid the risk of a tortfeasor whose tort also amounts to a crime being punished twice over for his actions, exemplary damages may not be awarded against a tortfeasor whose actions have already been the subject of a criminal prosecution.[37]

1.12 TORT LAW AND PROPERTY LAW

In order to teach students law, law schools are forced to divide the law up into digestible subjects – contract law, tort law, criminal law, land law, constitutional law, administrative law, and so on. One unfortunate side effect of this need to divide up the law is that it creates the impression that there is a clear cut division between these different areas of law. So it is with tort law and property law. Many academics seem to be under the impression that a given legal rule or principle can be allocated either to the realm of tort law, or the realm of property law, but cannot belong to both.[38] The reality is that there is a substantial overlap between tort law and property law.

---

[36] *Rookes* v *Barnard* [1964] AC 1129.

[37] Though see the strange case of *AT* v *Dulghieru* [2009] EWHC 225 (QB), criticised below, § 30.2.

[38] Calabresi and Melamed 1972 may have helped to create this impression, by suggesting that tort law was a matter of 'liability rules' (making people pay money for the losses caused by their acting in a particular way) and property law was a matter of 'property rules' (requiring people to act in a particular way), and that all private nuisance cases (where B complains that her use and enjoyment of land is being interfered with by the way A is using his land) could be solved either by the application of a liability rule (allowing A to use his land as he likes so long as he compensates B for the interference that this will cause to her use and enjoyment of land) or a property rule (requiring A not to use his land in a way that will interfere with B's use and enjoyment of her land) or no rule at all (allowing A to use his land as he likes without requiring him to compensate B for the interference that this will cause to her use and enjoyment of land). The problem with this 'view of the cathedral' of the common law, as Calabresi and Melamed put it, is that tort law does not deal in liability rules. In Calabresi and Melamed's terms, it deals in property rules – it tells people to act in certain ways, and provides a variety of remedies when people fail to do what tort law tells them to do.

In terms of a Venn diagram, tort law and property law are two intersecting circles within a rectangle that represents the entirety of English law. The area covered by both the tort law circle and the property law circle is made up of rules and principles which belong to both areas of law. These rules and principles define what basic rights someone with a given interest in property will have against other people, and what remedies will be available when those rights are violated. These rules and principles belong to tort law, because it is tort law that defines what basic rights we have against other people, and what remedies will be available when those rights are violated. But these rules and principles also belong to property law, because they concern what rights are enjoyed by people who have a particular interest in property, and what remedies will be available when those rights are violated.

So what rules and principles belong exclusively to tort law and do not have anything to do with property law? And what rules and principles belong exclusively to property law and have nothing to do with tort law? On the tort law side, if we have a basic right against someone else but we are given that right not because we have some kind of interest in property, but for some other reason – then that right has nothing to do with property law. So, for example, the right A will have that B not lie to him and induce him to act in a particular way (the violation of which amounts to the tort of deceit, or fraud) has nothing to do with property law – he does not have that right because he has a particular interest in property, but because he is a human being whose autonomy (or freedom to choose what to do, free from other people's manipulations) is deserving of respect.

On the property law side, all the rules and principles that define what can amount to property, what interests someone can have in property, and how those interests may be acquired and lost, belong exclusively to property law and have nothing to do with tort law. Tort law only comes in after someone has acquired an interest in property, to define what rights that interest-holder has against other people by virtue of his holding that interest. Tort law has nothing to say about what sort of interests people can have in property, and how those interests may be acquired and lost. It is a rule of property law, and not tort law, that no more than four people can own land as joint tenants, and that if Blackacre is conveyed to A, B, C, D, E and F in undivided shares, then Blackacre will be legally owned by A, B, C and D as joint tenants, and held on trust by them for A, B, C, D, E and F.[39] Where tort law comes in, and where tort law and property law overlap, is in determining what rights these various people have against other people by virtue of the interests they have in Blackacre. (Though because Blackacre is in this situation held on trust for A, B, C, D, E and F, equity will also have something to say about what rights – in equity's case, equitable rights – these various individuals will have against other people by virtue of the fact that they each have a *beneficial interest* in Blackacre.)

1.13 TORT LAW AND STRICT LIABILITY

Strict liability exists when the fact that a particular event has occurred means that a claimant can obtain a remedy against a defendant, but the defendant was not necessarily at fault, or to blame, for that event occurring. There is strict liability both within, and outside, tort law.

Strict liability within tort law is not usually objectionable where the remedy being sought against a defendant is an *injunction* or some sort of specific order that the defendant act in a particular way. For example, suppose that *Dealer* acquires an antique watch that

[39] Law of Property Act 1925, s 34.

was stolen from *Owner*. If *Owner* finds out that *Dealer* has his watch, *Owner* will be able to obtain an order that *Dealer* hand the watch over to him.[40] The fact that *Dealer* was not at fault for the fact that *Owner*'s watch has come into her hands makes no difference. It is *Owner*'s watch and *Dealer* must now give it back. In this case, strict liability is unobjectionable.[41]

Where strict liability within tort law becomes more questionable is where the remedy being sought against the defendant is *damages*. For example, suppose that *Hiker* is going for a walk along a public pathway marked out on a map that he is carrying. But suppose the map is wrong and leads *Hiker* onto *Rich*'s land. In this case, *Hiker* will have committed a tort (the tort of trespass to land) in relation to *Rich*. The fact that *Hiker* was not at fault for walking on to *Rich*'s land does not affect the matter. The map maker's mistake cannot abridge the right *Rich* had against *Hiker* that *Hiker* stay off her land. Now: the English courts are strongly committed to the idea that if A has committed a tort in relation to B, and B has suffered loss as a result, then B should in principle be entitled to recover damages from A – and they will not give A a defence to being sued for damages by B in cases where A was not at fault, or not to blame, for the fact that he committed that tort. The upshot is that *Hiker* may be held liable to pay *Rich* damages for trespassing on her land, even though he was not at fault for going onto her land.

Instances of strict liabilities to pay damages *outside* tort law (properly understood) are, strangely enough, easier to justify. We have already come across a couple of examples:

(1) A producer of a dangerously defective product will be held liable for the harm done by that product under the Consumer Protection Act 1987 even if he was not necessarily to blame for the fact that the product was dangerously defective.

(2) If A, in the course of using his land in a non-natural way, brings onto his land, or collects on his land, something that is liable to do damage if it escapes, then if that thing does escape and damages B's land, B will be entitled to sue A under the rule in *Rylands* v *Fletcher* for compensation for that damage even if A was not necessarily at fault for the fact that that thing escaped off his land.[42]

Both examples of strict liability can be explained as being based on an *enterprise risk* rationale. That is: if you engage in some enterprise for your own benefit which involves some inherent risk of harm to others, then if that risk materialises, you should compensate those others for the harm you have suffered. It's only fair: if you want to keep the benefits from your enterprise, then you should shoulder the burdens associated with that enterprise.

Such an enterprise risk rationale may underlie a very well-established rule of strict liability associated with tort law. This is the rule of *vicarious liability* that says: If *Employee*

---

[40] Such an order – for what is called *specific restitution of goods* (what Roman lawyers would have known as *vindicatio*) – will only be available if being paid the value of the watch would be an inadequate remedy for *Owner*. We have made the watch an antique watch in order to satisfy this condition. If this condition were not satisfied, *Dealer* would be given the option of either returning the watch, or paying *Owner* its value.

[41] Things become tougher on A if A bought the watch or if A has spent money in the belief that the watch was his to keep (perhaps on a display case for the watch) or if A has given away something of value in the belief that the watch was his to keep (perhaps another, inferior, example of the antique watch that A owned before he came into possession of B's watch). In such situations, A will be left out of pocket if he is required to hand over B's watch. But A will still be required to hand over the watch. There is no defence of what is called *change of position* to a proprietary claim: *Foskett* v *McKeown* [2001] AC 102.

[42] These *are* examples of liability rules in Calabresi and Melamed's terminology (see above, § 1.12), in that they attach a cost to something that someone is allowed to do (manufacturing products, bringing dangerous things onto his land in the course of using that land in a non-natural way).

commits a tort in relation to *Victim* in the course of *Employee*'s employment by *Employer*, then *Victim* will be entitled to sue *Employer* for whatever sum in damages she is entitled to recover from *Employee*; and this is so even if *Employer* was not necessarily at fault for the tort committed by *Employee*. This is one of the most important rules associated with tort law as tortfeasors rarely have enough money to be worth suing. It is only companies and public bodies that usually have pockets deep enough to satisfy tort claimants seeking damages – and it is the law on vicarious liability that allow those pockets to be picked. If there were no law on vicarious liability, the law reports would contain very few instances of tort claims. However, it is possible to argue that the law on vicarious liability exists to do more than keep tort lawyers in employment, and give tort claimants someone to sue. It can be argued that if *Employer* seeks to profit from having *Employee* work for him, and there is a risk associated with the work that *Employee* is employed to do that he will commit a particular tort, then it is only fair that if that risk materialises, *Employer* should be held liable for the losses suffered by the victim of *Employer*'s tort.

1.14 INSURANCE[43]

Insurance has a role to play at both ends of a tort claim – the claimant's end and the defendant's end.

A. Claimants

At the claimant's end, the claimant may have suffered loss that is covered by an insurance policy (under what is called 'first party insurance'). If the loss takes the form of a physical injury, then the law allows the claimant to sue the defendant in tort for compensation for her injury *and* claim from her insurance company the sum payable under her insurance policy for that injury. The law does not regard this as a form of 'double recovery'. It takes the view that people may put a special value on their bodies and if the special value that they put on their bodies has led them to take out insurance to cover harm to their bodies (such as a pianist insuring his hands, or a model insuring her legs and her face), then they should be allowed to claim on that insurance policy in full if their bodies are harmed, whatever rights they might simultaneously have under tort law to claim damages for the harm that they have suffered.

If the loss suffered by the claimant takes some other form – such as damage to property or an economic loss – then the law says that the claimant's right to sue the defendant in tort for compensation for that loss will *not* be affected if she has already recovered compensation for that loss under her insurance policy. The defendant cannot take advantage of arrangements that the claimant put in place to protect herself, and for which the claimant paid good money, in order to reduce his liability to the claimant. *However*, if the claimant has already recovered compensation for the loss she has suffered under her insurance policy then:

(1) If she subsequently sues the defendant in tort for compensation for that loss, she must hand over the damages she wins to her insurance company.[44]

(2) If she – having claimed on her insurance policy – is not interested in suing the defendant in tort for compensation for the loss she has suffered, her insurer can bring a

---

[43] See, generally, Merkin 2010.
[44] *Lord Napier and Ettrick* v *Hunter* [1993] AC 713.

claim in tort against the defendant *in the claimant's name* for such compensation and can keep any damages that it recovers.

It is a little puzzling why insurance companies have this right, which arises under the law of subrogation (under which the insurance company, having paid out on the claimant's insurance policy, is said to be *subrogated to* the claimant's rights to sue the defendant). The law is clear that an insurance company that has had to pay out to the victim of a tort cannot bring a claim *in its own name* against the person who committed that tort for the loss it has suffered as a result of that tort being committed.[45] So why do the courts allow an insurance company to bring effectively the same claim *in the name of the victim of the tort*? Three possible explanations may be given:

(a) The terms of the contract between the insurer and insured may provide that the insurer can do this, and the courts are simply giving effect to this contract.
(b) Public policy demands that the loss suffered as a result of a tortfeasor's conduct should ultimately fall on the tortfeasor, so as to penalise him for what he has done – and allowing the insurer to sue in the insured's name where the insured has been compensated by the insurer is a good way of ensuring this happens.
(c) This whole area of law represents an unprincipled concession to the insurance industry, designed to help keep their costs (and the costs of premiums) down.

B. Defendants

At the defendant's end, the defendant may be carrying liability insurance (called 'third party insurance'), which will cover him if he is held liable to the claimant. Officially, the fact that a liability insurer, and not the defendant, will end up paying the bill for any damages awarded to the claimant is not supposed to have any effect on whether the defendant is held liable to pay damages to the claimant. However, it is hard to imagine that the existence of liability insurance has not played a role in shaping the following features of tort law:

(1) The courts will readily find that a motorist has breached the duty he will owe nearby drivers and pedestrians to take care not to drive dangerously if he is guilty of a momentary lapse of attention – even though experiments have shown that no driver can be humanly expected to keep his eyes on the road all the time. The fact that it is not the driver, but his liability insurer, that will foot the bill for any claim made against the driver for harm done as a result of his momentary lapse of attention may explain why the courts are happy to adopt such a strict attitude in negligence cases involving motorists.

(2) Staying with motorists, the Road Traffic (NHS Charges) Act 1999 provides that if A is liable to compensate B for injuries that B has suffered as a result of a motor vehicle accident, and B's injuries have been treated by the National Health Service, then A will be liable to compensate the government for the money spent on B's care. Again, the fact that A will almost always be carrying liability insurance must account for why Parliament is happy to impose such a liability on A.

(3) The same fact makes it easy to understand the otherwise strange provision in s 2 of the Congenital Disabilities (Civil Liability) Act 1976, that a pregnant woman who is driving will owe her unborn child a duty to take care to drive carefully – so that if she breaches that

---

[45] *La Société Anonyme de Remourquage a Hélice* v *Bennetts* [1911] 1 KB 243. This case provides another example of the principle discussed in the previous section, that where a tort has been committed, it is normally only the victim of the tort who is allowed to sue.

duty and her child is, as a result born disabled, the child can sue its mother for compensation for its disability. A right to sue for such compensation could not help the child if its mother were paying the compensation out of her own pocket – the compensation payment would merely represent money that the mother would have to spend on her child's care anyway. However, as the child's injuries were sustained as a result of a motor accident, the compensation payment will not come from the mother, but her motor liability insurer – so giving the child a right to sue its mother will provide a way of tapping into the mother's liability insurance policy so as to cover the future costs of catering for the child's disabilities.

(4) The fact that private defendants (whether the defendant is a company or an individual) almost invariably carry liability insurance – it is, after all, the 'deep pockets' that their liability insurance gives them that make them a target for litigation – means that the courts have never had to give any thought to whether successful claimants in tort cases should recover anything other than full compensation for the actionable losses that they have suffered.[46] As a result, damages awarded in tort claims can easily run up to hundreds of thousands of pounds – amounts way beyond the ability of a normal individual to pay. If liability insurance were not allowed to exist – as was once the case in England (on the basis that it was against public policy to allow people who had acted unlawfully to escape the consequences of their illegal behaviour) – our courts would have long ago switched to a system where the damages payable in tort cases would be much smaller on average, and would reflect what individuals could afford to pay.

The fact that there may be an insurance company at both ends of a tort claim – so that an award of damages in a tort case may represent nothing more than a payment from one insurance company (a liability insurer) to another insurance company (a property insurer) – should make anyone wonder whether tort law is worth retaining in its current form. Do we pay too high a price for the benefits we obtain from having a system of tort law?

1.15 PAYING FOR TORT LAW

At first sight, it seems to be employers (through the law on vicarious liability) and insurance companies (through liability insurance policies) who pay the price for tort law's existence. It is they, predominantly, who have to meet the cost of the (justified) damages claims that are made by tort victims. However, a second look at the situation tells us that it is in fact the general public that pays the cost of meeting those claims through higher prices for the goods and services that employers exist to provide, and through higher insurance premiums. In that sense the cost of meeting the claims made by tort claimants is 'spread' throughout the population. At the same time, the general public does not just cover the cost of meeting those claims, but also the costs involved in paying for the courts and the lawyers that are needed to keep the tort system functioning. So tort law can be seen as a system for taking money out of the pockets of the general public and funnelling it into the hands of: (1) tort victims; (2) tort lawyers; and (3) the civil court bureaucracy.

But none of that matters to the task of assessing whether we pay too high a price for having a system of tort law. From the point of view of society as a whole, it is impossible to tell whether the redistribution of income effected by tort law has – of and in itself – a negative or a positive effect. So in order to assess whether it is worth having a system of tort,

---

[46] Goldberg 2006 argues that *fair* compensation, rather than *full* compensation, should be (and once was) the standard remedy for committing a tort.

we need to look at the social benefits and social costs of having a system of tort law that exist independently of tort law's redistributive effects.

The social benefits are, it seems to us, *potentially* threefold:

(B1) Vesting people with basic rights gives people *more control* over their lives than they would have otherwise. Under a system of law where there was no tort law, people would become wholly dependent on the criminal law, and what security they could purchase out of their own pockets, to protect them from being harmed by other people.

(B2) People *feel better* if they are vested with basic rights. They feel that the state is, first of all, respecting them enough to give them a certain minimum level of protection that they are entitled to simply by virtue of who they are, and is, secondly, respecting them enough to give them the ability to control whether or not they take advantage of that minimum level of protection.

(B3) People are *better protected* in a legal system that includes a system of tort law than one that does not. Tort law gives people another layer of protection, above and beyond what protection they might enjoy under the criminal law. Moreover, because tort law is a self-administered system of protection, tort law is likely to provide a more reliable level of protection than will the criminal law, which depends for its effectiveness on the competence, concern, and integrity of public officials.

These social benefits are only potential in nature. The less use people make of tort law, and the less relevant it is to their daily life and the way they are treated by other people, the more attenuated these benefits will be. In a country where tort law is perceived to be something that only rich people can take advantage of, these social benefits will be virtually zero.

The social costs from having a system of tort law that exist independently of its redistributive effects are, it seems to us, also threefold:

(C1) The fact that you might be sued if you fail to conform to tort law's demands means that people will often do much more than tort law requires them to do in order to ensure that they will not incur the risk of being sued. This 'overkill' response to tort law's demands represents a social cost because it is wasteful – but it is something that is an unavoidable by-product of the existence of a system of tort law. People do not like to be sued, and will always go out of their way to avoid the risk that they might be sued.

(C2) The 'overkill' response to the existence of tort law becomes even more costly when it takes the form of avoiding doing things that are socially beneficial, or getting in the way of other people doing things that are socially beneficial. The classic example of this is provided by the case of *Tomlinson v Congleton Borough Council* (2004).

That case centred around a lake in a park run by the defendant council. There were a number of beaches around the lake which hundreds of people would relax on during the summer. When it got very hot, some people would go for a swim in the lake, ignoring the 'No Swimming' signs that the council had posted all around the lake. The council became concerned that if someone got injured while swimming, they would sue the council for compensation. The council decided that to avoid this risk, it would turn the beaches around the lake into swampland, so that no one would ever want to go near the lake. But before the council got the chance to put its plans into action, John Tomlinson dived into the lake, hit his head on the bottom, and was paralysed. The council's worst fear was realised: Tomlinson sued the council, arguing that they had owed him a duty to do more than they had done to stop him endangering himself.

The House of Lords dismissed his claim. They ruled that tort law did not demand that the council destroy the valuable social amenity represented by the beaches around the lake so as to save people like Tomlinson from harming themselves:

> . . . it is not, and should never be, the policy of the law to require the protection of the foolhardy or reckless few to deprive, or interfere with, the enjoyment by the remainder of society of the liberties and amenities to which they are rightly entitled. Does the law require that all trees be cut down because some youths may climb them and fall? Does the law require the coastline and other beauty spots to be lined with warning notices? Does the law require that attractive waterside picnic spots be destroyed because of a few foolhardy individuals who choose to ignore warning notices and indulge in activities dangerous only to themselves? The answer to all these questions is, of course, no. But this is the road down which your Lordships, like other courts before, have been invited to travel . . . In truth, the arguments for the claimant have involved an attack upon the liberties of the citizen which should not be countenanced. They attack the liberty of the individual to engage in dangerous, but otherwise harmless, pastimes at his own risk and the liberty of citizens as a whole fully to enjoy the variety and quality of the landscape of this country. The pursuit of an unrestrained culture of blame and compensation has many evil consequences and one is certainly the interference with the liberty of the citizen.[47]

The House of Lords' decision in *Tomlinson* was intended to reassure local councils that all the law of negligence required them to do by way of protecting people from harm on their land was to act reasonably. However, the House of Lords missed the point as to why the council in *Tomlinson* was happily proposing to destroy the beaches around the lake before Tomlinson's accident. To *win* a negligence case, all you may have to show is that you acted reasonably. (Though it is worth pointing out that the council in *Tomlinson* lost in the Court of Appeal.) To *avoid being sued at all*, you *may* have to go beyond what is reasonable and take *unreasonable steps* to minimise the risk of people being injured on your watch. And it is the desire to avoid being sued at all that motivates actors like the council in *Tomlinson* – not the desire to give yourself a good chance of winning if you are sued – and attempting to avoid being sued at all can involve acting in ways that are contrary to the public interest.

(C3) The third potential social cost associated with tort law lies in the fact that anyone who is continually exposed to a risk of being sued in tort needs to carry liability insurance. This gives insurance companies a huge amount of power over the insured, to dictate to the insured what they must and must not do – threatening that if the insured does not do as they are told, they will lose their liability insurance. This transfer of power to insurance companies represents a considerable social cost because of the loss of autonomy, responsibility and accountability involved in transferring to insurance companies the power to make decisions as to what precautions the insured should take to avoid harm to others. If we lived in a rational world, there is simply no way an insurance company would be given the power to decide, for example, whether a teacher needed to be on duty at a school on a Saturday when the school hall was being used for a wedding reception, or whether a play area in a park should have a merry-go-round on it. But that is the world we live in it at the moment.

It does not seem to us that these are merely potential costs of having a system of tort law. They are costs that are *always* present whenever a system of tort law exists, and so far as the size of these costs are concerned, they seem to loom very large at present.

---

[47] [2004] 1 AC 46, at [81] (per Lord Hobhouse).

The conclusion we are moving towards is a pessimistic one: that the social costs of having a system of tort law seem at the moment to outweigh the social benefits. However, this conclusion does not necessarily suggest that we should *abolish* tort law. *Reforming* tort law so as to reduce the social costs associated with its existence and maximise its social benefits would seem a more sensible, and promising option. Such a programme of reform would involve both cutting tort law down to size and strengthening its application. Rolling back the scope of tort law would reduce the power of liability insurance companies to dictate to individuals, companies and public bodies what they should do. The need to carry liability insurance might also be lessened by reducing the size of damages awards and relating them to individual defendants' ability to pay. Simplifying tort law in this way would also help to strengthen tort law's application – a simpler tort law would help individuals re-connect with tort law, and understand what it is here for, and what it does for them. Simplifying and speeding up the procedures for bringing tort claims would also help individuals feel that tort law is not just a rich man's luxury, but an area of law that exists to protect everyone.

1.16 TORT LAW AS A FOREIGN COUNTRY

Our survey of the basics of English tort law is now over. To a novice student reading this chapter, tort law must seem like a foreign country. People who live in this country speak an unfamiliar language, full of strange terms and phrases like 'conversion', '*volenti non fit injuria*', 'duty of care', and 'misfeasance in public office'. The boundaries of the country are hard to make out – it is hard to know when you are still in tort law, and when you have strayed beyond tort law into some other area of law. It is also hard to know what the relations between tort law and its neighbours are like. The country has its strange customs, which take some getting used to – such as only allowing people to sue if they are 'victims' of a tort; or allowing the victim of a tort not only to sue the person who committed that tort, but also her employer. The layout of the country seems so complicated, it is easy to get confused, and go wrong, and lose your way.

The reaction is understandable, but it is important that newcomers to tort law do not get put off. The longer you spend in this country, the more familiar it becomes, and the easier it gets. So, for example, we would suggest that if you have gotten this far in reading this book, that you turn back to page one and start reading again. You can't expect to have learned in one go everything we have been trying to tell you in this first chapter. As well as spending time getting used to tort law and its ways, it is also important that you start trying as soon as possible to talk like a tort lawyer, by writing essays and problem answers and conducting moots. Of course, like any beginner in a foreign language, you are likely to get some things wrong. But getting things wrong is the first step towards getting things right.

Before we go further in exploring the difficult terrain of tort law, we would like to suggest one analogy that it might be worth keeping a hold of, so as to make tort law seem a bit less unfamiliar and a bit easier to understand. Tort law, stripped down to its essentials, is something you have been familiar with since you were a child playing at school. At school, there were lots of rules designed to make the school run smoothly: get into school and be in class by 8 am, no pushing in line in the lunch queue, no playing dangerous games in the playground. If you broke those rules and were caught, you would be liable to be punished by the school in some way. There were other rules that were aimed to help you do your best as a student – no submitting homework late, no copying other children's work, no talking during tests. Again, if you broke those rules you were liable to be punished. Finally, there was a third set of rules that were more concerned with placing limits on what you could do to other children – no fighting, no bullying, no stealing. If you broke those rules, then you were again liable to be punished – but you would also be required to make things up with the child who you had maltreated, usually by saying sorry and shaking their hand. Doing that would get your relationship with the child you had maltreated back to normal, and allow both of you to put the past behind you and get on with your life. Tort law is like the third set of school rules. It tells you how you should treat other people and specifies what you must do to make things up to them if you fail to treat them right. Tort law is simply playground morality, writ very large indeed.

Further reading

John Goldberg's 'Ten half-truths about tort law' (2008) 41 *Valpairiso University Law Review* 1221 provides the reader with a wonderful overview of the history of tort law, and contending views about the nature and function of tort law. The same author's **'Unloved: tort law in the modern legal academy'** (2002) 55 *Vanderbilt Law Review* 1501 is also highly recommended.

For particular views of tort law, see **Lord Bingham, 'The uses of tort'** (2010) 1 *Journal of European Tort Law* 3 (tort law exists to discourage undesirable behaviour); **Jolowicz, 'Civil litigation: what's it for?'** (2008) 67 *Cambridge Law Journal* 508 (tort law exists to provide people with a peaceful means of obtaining redress for the wrongs done to them and to resolve disputes in a just manner); and **Tettenborn, 'Professional negligence: free riders and others' in Economides** *et al* (eds), *Fundamental Values* (Hart Publishing, 2000), **chapter 17** (tort law exists to determine what basic rights we have against each other and what remedies will be available when those rights are violated). The Tettenborn piece may be hard to get hold of: an alternative and extended summary of this last view of tort law can be found in **McBride, 'Rights and the basis of tort law' in Nolan and Robertson (eds),** *Rights and Private Law* (Hart Publishing, 2011), chapter 12.

John Goldberg and Benjamin Zipursky are the academics who are nowadays most strongly associated with the view that tort law exists to provide the victims of wrongs with a peaceful means of obtaining redress for the wrongs they have suffered, but an early statement of this view can be found in **J.M. Kelly, 'The inner nature of the tort action'** (1967) 2 *Irish Jurist* *(New Series)* 279.

The view that tort law exists to provide people who have unjustly suffered loss a means of obtaining compensation for that loss (condemned as long ago as 1971 by Tony Weir as encouraging tort law to go 'a-whoring after false gods' (see Veitch and Miers, 'Assault on the law of tort' (1975) 38 *Modern Law Review* 139, fn 35)) is gradually falling out of favour but **Patrick Atiyah's** *The Damages Lottery* (Hart Publishing, 1997) provides a good example of (1) someone who takes such a view of tort law; and (2) the despair, and the desire to abolish tort law and come up with something better in its stead, that adopting such a view of tort law promotes. Atiyah's book is well summarised and criticised in **Ripstein, 'Some recent obituaries of tort law'** (1998) 48 *University of Toronto Law Journal* 561.

The extent to which our system of tort law inflicts a social cost in the form of creating a 'compensation culture' is addressed in **Williams, 'State of fear: Britain's compensation culture reviewed'** (2005) 25 *Legal Studies* 499; Lewis, Morris and Oliphant, 'Tort personal injury claims statistics: is there a compensation culture in the United Kingdom?' (2006) 14 *Torts Law Journal* 158; and **Morris, 'Spiralling or stabilising? The compensation culture and our propensity to claim damages for personal injury'**

(2007) 70 *Modern Law Review* 349. Political attempts to come to grips with our 'compensation culture' (if we have one) are summarised and assessed in **Mullender, 'Blame culture and political debate: finding our way through the fog' (2011) 27 *Professional Negligence* 64** and **Morris, ' "Common sense common safety": the compensation culture perspective' (2011) 27 *Professional Negligence* 82**.

If we have a compensation culture in the UK, its existence is often blamed on the ability claimants now have to bring claims financed on a 'no win, no fee' basis, a system of funding tort litigation that has long existed in the United States as a means of enabling impecunious claimants to obtain some justice from those who have wronged them. **Jonathan Harr's book *A Civil Action* (Century, 1996)** provides a fascinating account of a real-life American case fought on a 'no win, no fee' basis.

The relationship between tort law and insurance is excellently explored in **Rob Merkin, 'Tort and insurance: some insurance law perspectives' (2010) 26 *Professional Negligence* 194** and **Tom Baker, 'Liability insurance as tort regulation: six ways that liability insurance shapes tort law in action' (2005) 12 *Connecticut Insurance Law Journal* 1**.

Visit **www.mylawchamber.co.uk/mcbride** to access tools to help you develop and test your knowledge of Tort law, including interactive multiple choice questions, practice exam

premium
mylawchamber
unrivalled support for legal education

questions with guidance, weblinks, legal newsfeed, additional case summaries, legal updates and tips on answering problem and essay questions.

Use **Case Navigator** to read in full some of the key cases referenced in this chapter with commentary and questions:

POWERED BY LexisNexis

- Fairchild *v* Glenhaven Funeral Services Ltd
- Tomlinson *v* Congleton Borough Council

2 Trespass to the person

2.1 The basics *35*

2.2 Conduct requirements *38*

2.3 Fault requirements *42*

2.4 Consent *45*

2.5 Necessity *50*

2.6 Statutory authority *58*

2.7 Mistakes *61*

2.8 Remedies *65*

Overview

In this chapter, we will be looking at three torts that involve a direct interference with someone else's person: *assault*, *battery* and *false imprisonment*. For historical reasons, these three torts are normally grouped together under the name '*trespass to the person*'. After introducing these torts in section 1, we explain how they are committed in sections 2.2 to 2.3. In sections 2.4 and 2.5, we look at two defences that a defendant might be able to rely on if he is sued for committing a trespass to the person: *consent* ('the claimant agreed that I could do what I did') and *necessity* ('I had to do what I did, either in the claimant's interests or in my interests or the interests of a third party'). Section 2.6 is a very difficult section that explains some of the complications that arise when a defendant purports to rely on the defence that he was authorised by statute to interfere with the claimant's person. Section 2.7 deals with the issue of what happens if a defendant mistakenly believed he was entitled to interfere with the claimant's person when he was not. Finally, section 2.8 briefly sets out the sort of remedies that will be available when a defendant commits a trespass to the person against a claimant.

2.1 THE BASICS

We begin our exploration of the torts recognised by English law with some of the oldest forms of wrongdoing for which claimants would be able to obtain a remedy from the English courts. These are the torts that are known, collectively, as torts involving a 'trespass to the person'.

The name of these torts goes back to the birth of the common law – a general system of law administered by the King's courts. A claimant seeking a remedy for some wrong that he or she alleged they had suffered could only gain access to the King's courts with the aid of a *writ*, which was an order issued by the King's representative that the claimant's case be heard in the King's court. Originally, the only writ that the sort of claimant that we would nowadays classify as a 'tort' claimant could obtain was a *writ of trespass*. Writs of trespass came in a variety of different forms: the writ of *trespass de vi et armis* (available where the claimant claimed that he or she had suffered personal injury as a result of the defendant's direct and forceful misconduct), the writ of *trespass quare clausum fregit* (available where the claimant claimed that the defendant had gone onto the claimant's land), and the writ of *trespass de bonis asportatis* (available where the claimant claimed that the defendant had damaged his or her goods by carrying them away).

For some time, claimants who wanted to sue for some other kind of wrong in the King's court would not be able to have their case heard because their case simply was not covered by the writ of trespass. However, in the fourteenth century, the King's representatives were granted the power to issue new writs of *trespass on the case* if they thought a particular case, while not covered by the writs of trespass, was sufficiently similar to a trespass case as to be deserving of a remedy. The law of negligence – which we will start to look at in a couple of chapters' time – has its origins in the power to issues writs of trespass on the case. But the law of trespass came first. And rightly so: no legal system worthy of the name could allow the sort of wrongs originally dealt with by the writs of trespass to go unremedied. The minimum aim of any decent legal system – which is to preserve a certain degree of stability in the lives of the people governed by that system – could not be achieved if people were free to beat each other up, or imprison each other without cause, or steal their property, or go onto their land.[1]

We will look later on at the trespass torts that protect people's property.[2] For the moment, we are concerned with the trespass torts that protect people's persons. There are three of them: *battery, assault,* and *false imprisonment.* A will commit the tort of battery in relation to B if he touches her when he has no lawful justification for doing so. A will commit the tort of assault in relation to B if he makes her think he is about to touch her when he has no lawful justification for doing so. A will commit the tort of false imprisonment in relation to B if he does something to limit her freedom of movement to a confined space when he has no lawful justification for doing so.

The existence of these torts confers on each of us a certain zone of liberty, within which we enjoy some freedom from interference with our bodily integrity and our ability to move about. However, this zone of liberty becomes weakened and attenuated the more occasions the law allows other people to intrude into it, arguing that they have a lawful justification for doing so. Those who would seek to violate this zone of liberty do not just include the wicked and selfish and ill-disposed, but also those who claim that they are acting in the *public interest* by depriving us of freedoms that the common law would otherwise give us. So the courts, in dealing with trespass cases, are often called upon to decide when it would be lawful for a representative of the State to interfere with someone else's liberty. These cases – dealing as they do with fundamental political questions about the relative importance of the individual and the collective – are some of the most interesting a law student can study.

For example, on 1 May 2000, the police suffered a major humiliation when anti-capitalist demonstrators ran riot through London, destroying a branch of McDonalds and defacing the Cenotaph and the statue of Winston Churchill in Whitehall. The following year, the police were better prepared. Acting on intelligence that the demonstrators were planning to assemble in Oxford Circus before dispersing around the capital, at 2 pm on 1 May 2001, the police set up a cordon at the junction at Oxford Circus, trapping within the cordon a large number of would-be demonstrators as well as a lot of people who were simply out shopping. About 3,000 people were trapped within the cordon, and they were held there until 9.30 pm, at which point the police judged that the steam had gone out of the would-be demonstrators and that it was safe to let them go. Lois Austin – a would-be demonstrator – was one of the people trapped within the cordon. When she requested the police to let her out, so that she could pick her baby up from a creche, her request was

---

[1] For a discussion of the minimum aims of a legal system, see Hart 1994, 193–200.
[2] See below, chapter 14 and § 17.4.

denied. She was told that she and everyone else were being held in order to 'bore you into submission' and was told that she only had herself to blame if she was unable to pick up her baby. Lois Austin sued the police, arguing that they had acted unlawfully in holding her in the cordon; a tactic that has become known as 'kettling'.

At first instance and in the Court of Appeal it was held that the police tactic of kettling demonstrators at Oxford Circus had been lawful.[3] Even though innocent shoppers had been caught up in the police cordon, it was still lawful to hold people within the cordon for almost eight hours because doing so was necessary to prevent a breach of the peace. By the time the case reached the House of Lords, Lois Austin's lawyers were reduced to arguing that holding within the cordon was unlawful, not under the common law, but under the Human Rights Act 1998, which – among other things – requires public bodies not to violate people's rights to liberty under Art 5 of the European Convention on Human Rights. Under Art 5, everyone has a 'right to liberty and security of person' and someone can only be deprived of their liberty in certain exceptional circumstances, which did not apply on the facts of the case in *Austin*. The House of Lords held that Art 5 had not been violated as holding someone in a cordon for almost eight hours did not amount to depriving someone of their liberty.[4] As a result, they upheld the lawfulness of kettling as a police tactic for handling demonstrations that are liable to become violently out of control.[5]

It is surprising that of the nine judges who ended up considering the case of *Austin* v *Commissioner of Police of the Metropolis*, not one could be found to speak for the idea that it is unlawful to imprison an innocent person, whether or not doing so is necessary in order to prevent a breach of the peace. This is surprising for two reasons.

First, the courts have traditionally struck a more individualistic note in determining where the line is to be drawn between protecting individual liberty and promoting collective security.[6] The traditional position is well represented by Tony Weir, who has observed that:

> no one in Britain, *no one*, can justify deliberately touching even a hair on [a claimant's] head, or entering her garden – much less depriving her of her liberty – merely on the ground that it was reasonable to do so . . .[7]

Secondly, in cases like *Austin* it is not easy to decide which set of values should prevail – those of individual liberty, or those of collective security. It is simply not possible to say that whenever the public interest conflicts with individual liberties, individual liberties must give way. Human fallibility on the issue of what is actually in the public interest guarantees that every society that has been founded on the principle of the supremacy of

---

[3] [2005] EWHC 480 (QB) (Tugendhat J); [2008] 1 QB 660.

[4] [2009] 1 AC 564.

[5] The House of Lords' judgments were handed down on 28 January 2009. They bore immediate, and bitter, fruit on 2 April 2009, when the police used kettling as a tactic for handling demonstrators at the G20 economic summit in London. The police tactics were widely blamed for turning an initially peaceful anti-bankers demonstration outside the Bank of England into a violent confrontation between demonstrators and police that resulted in windows being smashed in at branches of HSBC and the Royal Bank of Scotland, and the death of a newspaper vendor, Ian Tomlinson, who was pushed over by a policeman in the aftermath of the demonstration. Widespread criticism of the police tactics at the G20 summit led to their initiating a review of the practice of kettling demonstrators. Supporters of kettling may have taken some grim comfort from the events in late 2010, when – in the absence of kettling – demonstrators against plans to raise student university fees were allowed to run riot in London, smashing in windows at the Conservative Party headquarters, and threatening the Prince of Wales and Duchess of Cornwall.

[6] See, for example, *Beatty* v *Gillbanks* (1882) 9 QBD 308 (it is not unlawful to organise a march just because the march will be met with violence by the organisers' opponents).

[7] Weir 2004, 322 (emphasis in original).

the collective over the individual has eventually descended into a charnel house. A due concern for individual liberty must sometimes be allowed to trump our desire to protect and advance the public interest. But it is very hard to say when that should be the case. *Austin* certainly does not seem to be an easy case where it was obvious that the public interest should have been allowed to prevail over the interests of individual liberty. Given this, it is surprising that none of the judges who decided *Austin* seemed to feel much discomfort about finding that the 'kettling' in *Austin* was lawful.[8]

2.2 CONDUCT REQUIREMENTS

Each of the torts under discussion in this chapter has two different aspects: a conduct requirement, and a fault requirement. A defendant who is sued for committing a particular trespass tort has to satisfy both before he can be found to have committed the tort. In this section, we look at the conduct requirements for each of the trespass to the person torts.

A. Battery

For the tort of battery to be committed, a defendant must have *directly* and *voluntarily* applied *force* to the claimant's body. Let us take each of these italicised terms in turn, in reverse order.

(1) *Force*. This requirement will obviously be satisfied if the defendant touches the claimant. It will also be satisfied if the claimant is hit by something thrown by the defendant, whether or not the defendant intended to throw the thing *at* the claimant.[9] It has also been held that this requirement will be satisfied if the defendant removes (or does something that has the effect of removing) something that the claimant is sitting on, with the result that the claimant falls to the ground.[10]

(2) *Voluntariness*. This requirement will not be satisfied in cases where the defendant was not in control of his body at the time he touched the claimant (or otherwise directly applied force to the claimant's body). So, for example, if A and B are both standing in a train and the train suddenly brakes, with the result that A is thrown against B, A will not have committed the tort of battery in relation to B. A was not in control of his body at the time he touched B.

(3) *Directly*. The requirement that the defendant directly apply force to the claimant's body is a major limit on the scope of the tort of battery. The requirement of directness is better explained by example, rather than by definition. If A pushes B into a hole, that is a battery.

---

[8] Since the decision in *Austin*, the courts have sought to restrict its impact, ruling – for example – in *R (Moos and McClure) v Commissioner of Police of the Metropolis* [2011] EWHC 957 (Admin), at [56] that kettling may only be employed lawfully as a 'last resort [tactic] catering for situations about to descend into violence.' The court emphasised that 'It is only when the police reasonably believe that there is no other means whatsoever to prevent an imminent breach of the peace that they can as a matter of necessity curtail the lawful exercise of their rights by third parties. The test of necessity is met only in truly extreme and exceptional circumstances. The action taken has to be both reasonably necessary and proportionate and taken in good faith.' The court added, for good measure, that '*Austin* . . . was a very exceptional case.'

[9] *Scott v Shepherd* (1773) 2 Black W 892, 96 ER 525 (defendant threw a lighted firework into a marketplace and the firework was thrown from trader to trader in an attempt to get rid of it, and ended up exploding in the claimant's face; held that the defendant was liable for battery).

[10] *Dodwell v Burford* (1670) 1 Mod 24, 86 ER 703 (defendant struck claimant's horse with the result that it bolted and the claimant was thrown from the horse; held that the defendant was liable for battery).

If A digs a hole in the road and B later on falls into it, that is not a battery. If A injects a poison into B's body, that is a battery. If A puts poison in B's drink and B later drinks it, that is not a battery.

B. Assault

For the tort of assault to be committed, a defendant must have performed a positive act that made the claimant *think* that someone is *about* to apply force directly and voluntarily to their body. Again, let us take these italicised terms in turn, in reverse order.

(1) *About.* There is no assault on a claimant unless the claimant is made to think that they are in *imminent danger* of being attacked.

In *Tuberville* v *Savage* (1669), it was held that Tuberville did not commit an assault when he drew his sword on Savage and said, 'If it were not assize-time I should not take such language from you.' As it *was* assize time (that is, the time when the courts had set up in town to hear any criminal or civil cases), Tuberville's words did *not* lead Savage to believe that Tuberville was about to strike him with his sword.

In *Thomas* v *National Union of Mineworkers (South Wales Area)* (1986), the claimants were coal miners who wished to go to work during the miners' strike. As they entered the colliery where they worked they suffered abuse and threats from massed pickets at the colliery gates. They sought to obtain an injunction against the massed picketing, claiming among other things that the pickets were committing the tort of assault in abusing and threatening them as they entered the colliery. This claim was rejected by Scott J on the ground that the claimants were always driven into the colliery and were separated from the pickets by ranks of policemen – given this, it could hardly be said that the abuse and threats the claimants received when they entered the colliery put them in fear that they were *about* to be beaten up by the pickets.

It is not clear *how* imminent the threat of an attack has to be for an assault to have been committed. In *R* v *Ireland* (1998) (a criminal case), the defendant made a series of malicious telephone calls to three women – when they answered he would remain silent. The women all developed psychiatric illnesses as a result of their treatment at the hands of the defendant. The defendant was charged with committing the offence of assault occasioning actual bodily harm and was convicted. The House of Lords upheld the conviction, holding that his silent telephone calls could have led the women in question to believe they were about to be attacked by whoever was on the other end of the line. This was so even though there would have been some interval of time before the defendant could get from wherever he was phoning the women from to their houses. It seems that it was enough, for the assault to be established, that the women were put in *uncertainty* as to whether they were *about* to be attacked. That is, they were made to think that they *might* be *about* to be attacked.

(2) *Think.* For an assault to be committed, the claimant must be made to think that she is about to be attacked. So if A creeps up on B from behind and hits her on the head with a plank of wood, that is a battery, but not an assault. At no point was B made to think that she was about to be attacked. It is enough, for an assault to be committed, that the claimant was made to *think* that she was about to be attacked. It does *not* (repeat *not*) have also to be shown either: (i) that the claimant *was* about to be attacked; or (ii) that the claimant was *afraid* of being attacked. So, for example, if A points a fake gun at B and says 'I'm going to shoot you' and B is unaware that the gun is fake, that is an assault. It does not matter that

A was incapable of shooting B with the gun, and nor will it matter if B would actually welcome being shot because he is suicidally depressed.[11]

C. False imprisonment

For the tort of false imprisonment to be committed, a defendant must have performed a *positive act* that *directly resulted* in the claimant's freedom of movement being *completely restricted or restricted to a defined area*. Let us take each of the italicised terms in turn, in reverse order.

(1) *Restriction.* If *Policeman* wrongfully arrests *Innocent* and drags *Innocent* to a nearby police station, *Innocent* is falsely imprisoned while she is being taken to the station: her freedom of movement has been completely restricted by *Policeman*. Once *Innocent* is placed in a police cell, she is still falsely imprisoned, but this time because her freedom of movement has been restricted to a defined area. The requirement that a claimant's freedom of movement be completely restricted, or restricted to a defined area, was not satisfied in *Bird* v *Jones* (1845). In that case, a public right of way ran through an enclosure created by the defendants for the purpose of viewing a boat race. The claimant, in an attempt to use the right of way, entered the enclosure. The defendants prevented the claimant from walking through the enclosure and instead instructed him to turn back and use another route to reach his destination. The claimant refused to move and stayed in the enclosure for half an hour. When the matter came to court, it was held that the claimant had not been falsely imprisoned. The claimant's freedom of movement had only been restricted in one direction (the direction he wanted to go). He had been free to go back where he came from and leave the enclosure that way, and so his freedom of movement had not been completely restricted to a defined area.

(2) *Directly resulted.* It does not have to be shown that the defendant *himself* restricted the claimant's freedom of movement – it just has to be shown that the defendant did something positive that *directly resulted* in the claimant's freedom of movement being restricted. But the defendant's actions must have the *direct* effect of restricting the claimant's freedom of movement. For example, in a case where A tips off the authorities that B may be guilty of wrongdoing, with the result that B is arrested, the Court of Appeal has held that A can only be found guilty of false imprisonment if A *persuaded, encouraged,* or *requested* the authorities to arrest B.[12] Given this, it is unlikely that *Mule* could sue *Smuggler* for

---

[11] In *Mbasogo* v *Logo Ltd* [2006] EWCA Civ 1370, the Court of Appeal said of the *Thomas* v *NUM* case (at [75]) that: 'The threats made by pickets to those miners who sought to go to work were not an assault because the pickets had no capacity to put into effect their threats of violence while they were held back from the vehicles which the working miners were within.' This suggests that if A threatens to shoot B if B does not do as he says, then A's threat will *not* amount to an assault if A did not have the capacity to shoot B at the time he made his threat. This cannot be right. In *Mbasogo* v *Logo* itself, the claimant – the head of state of Equatorial Guinea – attempted to sue a group of people who, he alleged, had attempted to overthrow him by paying for mercenaries to invade Equatorial Guinea and kill him. The main body of the mercenaries were arrested in Zimbabwe before they could fly to Equatorial Guinea. The claimant alleged that he was the victim of an assault when he received the news that the mercenaries had been arrested because that made him think that he might be about to be attacked, perhaps by a second group of mercenaries already in the country. The claim was dismissed on the ground that the claimant was not *in fact* in danger. Again, this cannot be right.

[12] *Davidson* v *Chief Constable of North Wales* [1994] 2 All ER 597 (a store detective reported to the police his suspicions that the claimant had been stealing from the store; the police arrested the claimant, who turned out to be completely innocent; held, the store detective was not guilty of false imprisonment because he was not trying to persuade the police to arrest the claimant when he contacted them – he was content to leave it up to the police to decide what to do). Though see now *Westcott* v *Westcott* [2009] QB 407, holding that someone reporting a crime to the police enjoys absolute immunity from being sued for doing so.

false imprisonment just because he planted drugs in her luggage that resulted in her being arrested by the police.

(3) *Positive act*. The requirement that for the tort of false imprisonment to be committed, a positive act has to be performed was recently reaffirmed by the Court of Appeal in *Iqbal v Prison Officers Association* (2010).[13] In that case, a number of prison warders failed (in breach of their contracts of employment) to turn up to work, with the result that the claimant prisoner could not be let out of his cell at the time he would normally be let out. It was held that the prison warders' *failure* to turn up to work did not make them liable to the claimant for false imprisonment.

In *R v Bournewood Community and Mental Health NHS Trust, ex parte L* (1999), a patient, L, was staying at a mental health ward at Bournewood Hospital. The ward was unlocked and no attempts were made physically to restrain L from leaving. However, the staff there decided that if L attempted to leave, they would section him under the Mental Health Act 1983 and prevent him from leaving. L did in fact eventually attempt to leave and was sectioned under the Act. When L was eventually discharged, he sued the hospital, claiming that its employees had falsely imprisoned him in the period between his entering the hospital and his being sectioned.

The House of Lords dismissed L's claim, by a majority of three to two. The fact that the staff had decided to stop L leaving if he attempted to leave could not, of and in itself, sustain a finding of false imprisonment: the staff could not imprison L just through having a certain mental state. However, there was evidence that the staff had taken positive steps to make it harder for L to leave the ward, in that they kept him constantly sedated and dissuaded family members and friends from visiting him. The European Court of Human Rights found that the staff's conduct had violated L's right to liberty under Art 5 of the European Convention of Human Rights.[14] Had greater emphasis been placed on the staff's conduct, rather than their mental state, in the House of Lords, it is hard to imagine they would not also have been found liable for false imprisonment.

(4) *No requirement of awareness*. It should be noted that there is *no* (repeat *no*) requirement that the claimant be *aware* that he has been imprisoned for him to be able to sue for false imprisonment.[15] As Atkin LJ remarked in *Meering v Grahame-White Aviation Company Ltd*:

> It appears to me that a person could be imprisoned without his knowing it. I think a person can be imprisoned while he is asleep, while he is in a state of drunkenness, while he is unconscious and while he is a lunatic. Those are cases where it seems to me that the person might properly complain if he were imprisoned, though the imprisonment began and ceased while he was in that state. Of course, the damages might be diminished and would be affected by the question of whether he was conscious of it or not.[16]

---

[13] This requirement also provides a possible explanation of the Privy Council decision in *Robinson v Balmain New Ferry Company Ltd* [1910] AC 295. The claimant in that case wanted to take a ferry from a wharf operated by the defendants. Entrance or exit from the wharf was through a turnstile and anyone wanting to use the turnstile had to pay a penny to the defendants. The claimant paid his penny, went through the turnstile and waited for the ferry. He then changed his mind about catching the ferry and demanded to be let back through the turnstile without paying another penny for the privilege. The defendants refused to let him through. A claim for false imprisonment against the defendants failed. One possible explanation is that the defendants did not do anything *positive* in this situation to imprison the claimant: they merely failed to release him from the situation in which he had put himself.

[14] *HL v United Kingdom* (2005) 40 EHRR 32 (noted, Pedain 2005).

[15] The same point would apply to battery: if A has sex with B while she is passed out, and she has no awareness of what he is doing, and feels no ill effects from what he has done, he has still committed the tort of battery.

[16] (1920) 122 LT 44, 53–4.

These *dicta* were endorsed by the House of Lords in *Murray* v *Ministry of Defence*.[17] So if A locks a room in which B is sleeping and then unlocks the room before B awakes, A may be liable for falsely imprisoning B – the fact that B was unaware that she was sleeping in a locked room will be completely immaterial.[18]

2.3 FAULT REQUIREMENTS

As we have already seen Tony Weir observe, if you are being sued for committing one of the trespass torts, it is no defence simply to say that 'I acted reasonably under the circumstances.' To that extent, the trespass torts are torts of strict liability: the fact that you were not at fault for what happened will not necessarily absolve you of liability. Having said that, before we can find a defendant liable for committing one of the trespass torts, we do need to inquire into his or her mental state at the time he or she acted. But what sort of mental state a defendant needs to have been in to have committed one of the trespass torts varies from tort to tort.

A. Battery

Diplock J's decision in *Fowler* v *Lanning* (1959) established that merely showing that the conduct requirements for a battery have been satisfied is not enough to show that a defendant has committed the tort of battery. In that case, the claimant sued the defendant for damages. His statement of claim said, 'on November 19, 1957 at Vinyard Farm, Corfe Castle, in the county of Dorset the defendant shot the [claimant]. By reason of the premises[19] the [claimant] sustained personal injuries . . .' The defendant applied to have the claimant's claim struck out on the ground that the statement of claim did not disclose a good cause of action against the defendant. Diplock J agreed, holding that in this kind of case it would have to be shown at the very least that the defendant *carelessly* shot the claimant before he could be sued.

At first sight, this seems to make the tort of battery redundant. Were it be established that the defendant either carelessly or, worse, intentionally shot the claimant, the claimant would of course have been able to sue the defendant in negligence for his injuries. So what role is there for the tort of battery? We would submit that battery still has a useful role to play in dealing with cases where a defendant *intentionally* touched the claimant, and (i) the defendant's touching the claimant caused the claimant to suffer no loss, or no loss that the law of negligence could compensate the claimant for (such as pure distress); or (ii) the defendant's touching the claimant was reasonable under all the circumstances. If either (i) or (ii) is true, a claim in negligence will not help the claimant, and the only way the claimant will be able to sue the defendant is by bringing a claim for battery. Where a defendant *carelessly* touched the claimant and either (i) or (ii) is true, there is nothing in *Fowler* v *Lanning* that would prevent the claimant suing the defendant in battery, but we are doubtful whether the courts would allow the claimant to evade the limits on when someone can sue another in negligence by that route.

---

[17] [1988] 1 WLR 692, 701–3.
[18] Most jurisdictions in the United States take the view that a claim for false imprisonment could *not* be made here.
[19] 'By reason of the premises' means here 'As a result of this'.

So the decision in *Fowler* v *Lanning* has effectively limited the tort of battery to cases of *intentional* touchings (or other direct applications of force to the claimant's body).[20] Since *Fowler* v *Lanning*, various attempts to tighten up still further the ambit of the tort of battery have been made, but with no success. In *Letang* v *Cooper* (1965), Lord Denning MR suggested that a defendant could only commit the tort of battery if he *intended to injure* the claimant.[21] This suggestion was disapproved in *Wilson* v *Pringle* (1987): '[an] intention to injure is not essential to an action for [battery]'.[22] But in the very same case – in which a schoolboy playfully pulled on a schoolbag that a friend was carrying over his shoulder, with the result that the friend fell to the ground and injured his hip – the Court of Appeal held that a defendant could not be held to have committed the tort of battery unless he had acted in a *hostile* way.[23] They accordingly declined to find that a battery had been committed on the facts of *Wilson* v *Pringle* and sent the case back down for a hearing to determine whether the defendant, in acting as he did, had acted with the requisite degree of hostility. Tony Weir has remarked of this decision that 'it is perfectly clear that this is nonsense'[24] and indeed in *Re F* (1990), Lord Goff disapproved the Court of Appeal's suggestion in *Wilson* v *Pringle* that a touching has to be 'hostile' before it can amount to a battery:

> I respectfully doubt whether that is correct. A prank that gets out of hand; an over-friendly slap on the back; surgical treatment by a surgeon who mistakenly thinks that the patient has consented to it – all these things may transcend the bounds of lawfulness, without being characterised as hostile. Indeed the suggested qualification is difficult to reconcile with the principle that any touching of another's body is, in the absence of lawful excuse, capable of amounting to a battery . . .[25]

B. Assault

Suppose that *Paranoid* thinks that anyone who rubs their nose in front of her is indicating that they are about to attack her. *Fidget* rubs his nose while he is talking to *Paranoid*, and as a result *Paranoid* thinks that *Fidget* is about to attack her. The conduct elements for an

---

[20] It need not be shown that the defendant intended to apply the force to the *claimant's* body, so long as he intended to apply force to *someone's* body and ended up applying force to the claimant's body. So A will also commit the tort of battery in relation to B if he directly applies force to B's body with the intention of applying that force to C's body: *Bici* v *Ministry of Defence* [2004] EWHC 786 (QB), at [68]–[71] (soldiers operating in Kosovo committed tort of battery in shooting MB even though they were aiming to hit FB when they opened fire). Beever 2009 criticises the reasoning of the judge in *Bici* (which involves transplanting the criminal doctrine of 'transferred malice' (under which A will be guilty of murder if he intends to kill C and accidentally ends up killing B instead) to tort law. But he supports the result in *Bici* on the basis that 'the soldiers intended to shoot the occupants of the car and that class of persons included [MB]' (at 416). But he can only make this argument by endorsing a *very* wide view of intention whereby what you intend is not restricted to that your 'aim, want or purpose' is, but also covers whatever you are aware will happen as a result of your actions 'in the ordinary course of events' (415). This very wide concept of intention has no support in the modern day law, either in the criminal law (which only goes so far as to say that you *can* be held to intend what you foresee is *virtually certain* to result from your actions) or tort law (which generally sticks with the idea that you intend a certain consequence only if it is your aim or purpose to bring that consequence about). Goldberg 2006 argues (at fn 81) that if A aims to shoot at B and accidentally ends up shooting C instead, C's cause of action against A should be in negligence, not in a battery.

[21] [1965] 1 QB 232, 239.

[22] [1987] 1 QB 237, 249.

[23] [1987] 1 QB 237, 250: 'for there to be . . . a battery there must be something in the nature of hostility.'

[24] Weir 1998a, 109.

[25] [1990] 2 AC 1, 73.

assault are satisfied here, but has *Fidget* assaulted *Paranoid*? To discuss this issue, we need to distinguish the following cases:

(i) *Fidget* knew about *Paranoid*'s belief about the significance of nose rubbing and he rubbed his nose in front of her with the intention of making her think that she was about to be attacked.

(ii) *Fidget* knew about *Paranoid*'s belief and he intentionally rubbed his nose in front of her, but not in order to make her think that she was about to be attacked but in order to stop his nose itching. At the time he rubbed his nose, he realised the effect his rubbing his nose would have on *Paranoid*, but thought it was a price worth paying for relieving the itch on his nose.

(iii) *Fidget* knew about *Paranoid*'s belief but was so distracted by an itch on his nose that he rubbed his nose in front of her without even thinking about what effect this might have on *Paranoid*.

(iv) *Fidget* was not aware of *Paranoid*'s belief but ought to have been aware of it (he had been warned about it before by *Fidget*'s friends and family, but had either forgotten or not paid attention).

(v) *Fidget* was not aware of *Paranoid*'s belief and had no reason to know about it.

There is clearly an assault in situation (i), and we think it follows from *Fowler* v *Lanning* (1959) that there is clearly not an assault in situation (v). We think that (ii) would also amount to an assault, unless *Fidget* could argue that he had a lawful justification for rubbing his nose under the circumstances. (iii) and (iv) are examples of 'careless assaults' and – as we have seen – there is nothing in *Fowler* v *Lanning* to rule out the possibility that a claim in trespass could be made against a defendant who is merely careless. But it must be doubtful whether the courts would allow a claim for assault to be made against a defendant who was merely careless as to what effect his conduct would have on the claimant.[26]

C. False imprisonment

Suppose that *Owner* locks a room in which *Child* is inside. To determine whether *Owner* is liable for falsely imprisoning *Child*, we again need to distinguish a variety of different situations:

(i) *Owner* knew *Child* was inside the room, and *Owner* intended to lock *Child* in the room.

(ii) *Owner* did not know *Child* was inside the room, but ought to have known. (*Owner* could reasonably have been expected to check inside the room before locking the door, and had *Owner* done so, he would have seen *Child*.)

(iii) *Owner* did not know *Child* was inside the room, and had no reason to know *Child* was inside the room. (Before locking the room, *Owner* had checked there was no one inside, and saw no one as *Child* was inside a wardrobe at the time, looking for a secret entrance to Narnia.)

Situation (i) will clearly give rise to a claim for false imprisonment (subject to the possibility of *Owner*'s having a justification for locking *Child* up). *Fowler* v *Lanning* (1959) seems to rule out a claim for false imprisonment in situation (iii), as *Owner* was not at all careless in locking *Child* in the room. In *Iqbal* v *Prison Officers Association* (2010), Smith LJ took the view that 'with false imprisonment . . . the claimant must show . . . an intention to deprive the claimant of his liberty.'[27] If this is right, *Child* will not be able to sue for false imprisonment in situation (ii) as *Owner* had no intention of locking *Child* in when he

---

[26] In *Bici* v *Ministry of Defence* [2004] EWHC 786 (QB), Elias J held that for a defendant to be held liable to a claimant in assault, it has to be shown that the defendant intended to put the claimant 'personally in fear of imminent violence . . . The fact that [putting someone in fear of imminent violence may have been the consequence of [the defendant's] actions, even a foreseeable consequence, is not enough to fix [him] with liability in trespass' (at [77]).

[27] [2010] QB 732, at [72].

locked the door. If this is right, then an *intention to imprison* is an essential element to any claim for false imprisonment.

2.4 CONSENT

In *Re F* (1990), Lord Goff remarked that:

> as a general rule physical interference with another person's body is lawful if he consents to it; though in certain limited circumstances the public interest may require that his consent is not capable of rendering the act lawful.[28]

Lord Goff's qualification to his 'general rule' was designed to cover cases where consent is no defence to someone being charged under criminal law with an offence against the person. For example, in *R v Brown* (1994), a group of sado-masochists who inflicted various wounds on each other for sexual pleasure were convicted of assault occasioning actual bodily harm, contrary to s 47 of the Offences Against the Person Act 1861. However, if A invites B to wound him for their mutual sexual pleasure, it is very doubtful – if B takes up A's invitation – whether A could sue B, claiming that B had violated his rights in wounding him.

Given this, we can amend Lord Goff's *dictum* to say that 'physical interference with another person's body is *always* lawful *for the purposes of tort law* if he consents to it; though in certain limited circumstances the public interest may require that his consent is not capable of rendering the act lawful *for the purposes of the criminal law.*' But this simple statement conceals a host of difficulties, which we will now explore.

A. Validity of consent

If A has touched B in some way, B will obviously not have validly consented to A's touching her in the way he did if B did not agree that A could touch her in the way he did. So suppose *Patient* went to hospital for a tonsillectomy but *Surgeon* – due to an administrative mix-up – performed an appendectomy instead. In such a case, it could not be said that *Patient* validly consented to *Surgeon's* touching her in the way he did.[29]

Even if B formally agreed that A could touch her in the way he did, it still cannot be said that she validly consented to A's touching her in that way, if, when she agreed, she did not really understand what A was proposing to do. So suppose *Doctor* proposed to *Patient* that he treat her condition by giving her an 'intrathecal injection of phenol solution nerve block'. If *Patient* agreed that *Doctor* could do this but did not actually understand what *Doctor* was proposing to do – because *Doctor* did not bother to explain to *Patient* what such an injection involved – then it cannot be said that *Patient* validly consented to *Doctor's* giving her such an injection.[30]

A difficult issue is whether B has validly consented to A's touching her if she understood what A was doing in touching her, but had been misled as to A's *motives* in touching her. For example, in *KD v Chief Constable of Hampshire* (2005), the claimant became distressed while she was being interviewed by a police constable about her sexual history with a former boyfriend (who, it was alleged, had sexually abused the claimant's daughter). The constable hugged the claimant – but not, as the claimant thought, with the intention of

---

[28] [1990] 2 AC 1, 72.

[29] *Chatterton v Gerson* [1981] 1 QB 432, 443.

[30] ibid. Cf. *R v Williams* [1923] 1 KB 340 where the defendant – who had been engaged to give singing lessons to one Vera Howley – persuaded Howley to allow him to have sexual intercourse with her by pretending that he was performing a surgical operation on her to improve her voice. He was convicted of rape; she had not validly consented to the defendant's having sex with her as she did not really understand what he was proposing to do when she agreed that he could have sex with her.

cheering her up, but because he was attracted to her. It was held that the constable committed a battery in hugging the claimant – so while the claimant consented to being hugged by the constable, her consent must have been rendered invalid by her being misled as to the reasons why the constable was hugging her.[31]

B. Vitiation of consent

An apparently valid consent will be vitiated, and rendered invalid, if it was procured through illegitimate pressure or through the illegitimate exercise of some influence over the person giving their consent. Suppose, for example, that *Surgeon* performed an abortion on *Girl* but *Girl* only agreed to the abortion because her father threatened to kill her if she did not have it. In this case, it cannot be said that *Girl* validly consented to *Surgeon*'s performing the abortion on her. This is not to say that *Girl* could sue *Surgeon* for battery in this case. But if *Surgeon* is to establish a lawful justification for what he did, he cannot do so by claiming that *Girl* consented to the abortion. The topic is further explored below.[32]

It is well-established that an apparently valid consent will *not* be vitiated merely because it is not *informed*. So, for example, if *Beauty* consents to have sex with *Handsome*, a man she has met through an Internet dating site, her consent to have sex with *Handsome* will not be rendered invalid merely because he turns out to be HIV+ and she would never have agreed to have sex with him had she known of that fact.[33] In *Chatterton v Gerson* (1981), the claimant had an operation which left her with an extremely painful scar. The claimant consulted the defendant – who was a specialist in treating pain – and he suggested that she have an operation to block the sensory nerve behind the scar which was transmitting pain signals to her brain. The claimant agreed and the defendant carried out the operation. After the operation, the claimant discovered that the area around her scar was numb and she had suffered a loss of muscle power in that area. The claimant sued the defendant, claiming that the defendant had committed the tort of battery in operating on her. She argued that she had not validly consented to the operation performed by the defendant because she had not been informed that there was a risk she would experience numbness and loss of muscle power if she had that operation. This argument was rejected: as the claimant had known perfectly well the nature of the operation the defendant was proposing to carry out on her when she agreed that the defendant could carry out that operation, she validly consented to that operation's being carried out. The fact that she was unaware that the operation involved some risk for her did not vitiate her consent in any way.

C. Withdrawal of consent

A continuing interference with someone's person may be initially consented to, but what happens if consent is subsequently withdrawn? The general rule is that withdrawal of consent will render any further interference unlawful. So if A is having sex with his girlfriend, B, with her consent and she tells him to stop having sex with her, he will commit a battery if he ignores her and carries on having sex with her.

---

[31] Cf. *R v Tabassum* [2000] 2 Cr App Rep 328 (defendant persuaded a number of women to let him touch their breasts by telling them (falsely) that he was a doctor and he could guide them as to the best way to check themselves for lumps in their breasts; held that he was rightly convicted of indecent assault – the women had not validly consented to being touched by the defendant given that they were consenting to a touching that was wholly different in nature from the way he was touching them).

[32] See below, § 2.7(A).

[33] *R v Dica* [2004] QB 1257, at [39].

There is an important exception to this general rule, which applies where it would not be reasonable to expect the initially consented-to interference to stop immediately once consent has been withdrawn. In such a case, once consent is withdrawn, the defendant will be given a reasonable period of time to bring the interference to an end, and will only be held liable for continuing the interference if it carries on beyond that period of time. So, for example, suppose *Beauty* is giving *Handsome* a lift on the back of her motorbike, with *Handsome* holding onto her leather jacket, when she suddenly remembers that *Handsome's* hands will be really filthy from doing some work on the bike before they set off. If *Beauty* tells *Handsome* to stop touching her jacket, it will be lawful for *Handsome* to continue holding on until *Beauty* has stopped the bike and it is safe for him to let go.

In *Herd v Weardale Steel, Coal and Coke Company Ltd* (1915), the claimant was a miner who descended to the bottom of a pit at the start of his shift. He then refused to do certain work and asked to be lifted up to the surface. The claimant was only allowed to go back up to the surface at the end of the morning shift and even then he was only permitted to go back up once all the miners on the morning shift had been taken to the surface. The claimant sued, claiming that he had been falsely imprisoned. The House of Lords dismissed his claim. One explanation of the decision is that this was a withdrawal of consent case where the claimant initially consented to be left at the bottom of the pit, and then withdrew his consent.[34] Given this, under the law, the defendants were allowed a reasonable period of time to release the claimant from the bottom of the pit, and on the facts of the case, it was reasonable for the defendants to wait until the end of the shift to release the claimant: there was no reason why they should go to the trouble and inconvenience of arranging for the claimant to be taken back to the surface on his own.

D. Possibility of consent

Some people are incapable of giving a valid consent to having their person interfered with in a given way. If B's level of maturity, intelligence and understanding was not such that B could be safely left to decide for herself whether or not A could touch her in the way he did, any consent that B gave to A's touching her will not be valid.

If, at the time B agreed that A could touch her in the way he did, B was an adult (over 18) and not mentally unstable or acting under the influence of drugs or alcohol, it will be automatically presumed that B's level of maturity, intelligence and understanding was such that she could be safely left to decide for herself whether or not A could touch her in the way he did.

Section 8 of the Family Law Reform Act 1969 provides that 'the consent of a minor who has attained the age of 16 years to any surgical, medical or dental treatment which, in the absence of consent, would constitute [a battery], shall be as effective as it would be if he were of full age . . .' The effect of this is that if *Doctor* treated *Child* with *Child's* agreement and *Child* was between 16 and 18 at the time, it will be automatically presumed that *Child* was of a level of maturity, intelligence and understanding that she could be safely left to decide for herself whether or not *Doctor* could treat her in the way he did – just as would have been the case if *Child* had been over 18 when she agreed to being treated by *Doctor*.

If, when B agreed A could touch her in the way he did, B was less than 16 years old then no fixed rules will apply – all the circumstances will have to be looked at to determine whether, when B agreed A could touch her in the way he did, B's level of

---

[34] See Tan 1981 for this explanation of the decision in *Herd*, though he doubts whether the case was correctly decided on the facts.

maturity, intelligence and understanding was such that she could be safely left to decide for herself whether or not A could touch her in the way he did. If B was of such a level of maturity, intelligence and understanding, she is known as being 'Gillick competent', after the case in which the rule for determining B's competence to give consent was laid down.[35]

E. Consent on behalf of others

In a case where an under 16 year old is not *Gillick* competent to consent to medical treatment, medical treatment will still be lawful if it is carried out with the consent of one of the child's parents.

A much more difficult situation is where *Child*, who is over 16 or *Gillick* competent, is *refusing* treatment that one of *Child*'s parents is consenting to – is it lawful in that situation to treat *Child*? The available *dicta* are confused.[36] The issue is most likely to arise in two situations: (i) where *Child* has moral beliefs not shared by his or her parents (for example, where a 15 year old refuses to have an abortion when her parents want her to have one); and (ii) where *Child* is engaging in short-term thinking about what is in their best interests while his or her parents are engaging in long-term thinking about what is in the child's best interests (for example, where a 10 year old is refusing to have braces fixed on his teeth to adjust them because it will ruin his last year in primary school). One way of resolving the conflict between *Child* and parent in these kind of situations might be to let the parent's wishes prevail where the treatment is medically important but not radically invasive, but only allow radically invasive treatment (for example, an abortion) against *Child*'s wishes when it is necessary to save *Child*'s life.

F. Consent to risks

In principle, a valid consent to the *risk* of having one's person interfered with in some way should afford just as much a defence to being sued in trespass as a valid consent to the *fact* of one's person being interfered with does. And so it proves, for the most part.

For example, in *Blake* v *Galloway* (2004), the claimant was a 15 year old who joined a group of similarly aged children who were playfully throwing twigs and bits of bark at each other. The claimant threw a bit of bark at the defendant, that hit the defendant in the chest. The defendant threw the bark back in the direction of the claimant. Unfortunately, the bark hit the claimant in the face, injuring one of his eyes. The claimant sued for damages for the injury in negligence and battery. His claim was dismissed. While he had not consented to being hit in the eye by the bark thrown by the defendant, he *had* consented to the *risk* of being hit in the eye by the sort of playful throwing of the bark that the defendant had engaged in. Of course, if the defendant had intentionally aimed the bark at the claimant's eye or had thrown it at him at very high velocity, not caring where it hit the claimant, it

---

[35] *Gillick* v *West Norfolk and Wisbech Area Health Authority* [1986] AC 112.

[36] *Dicta* in favour of the view that it would be lawful to treat *Child* despite their positive refusal to be treated can be found in *Re R (a minor) (wardship: consent to treatment)* [1992] Fam 11, 23–5 (per Lord Donaldson MR); *Re W (a minor) (medical treatment)* [1993] Fam 64, 76 (per Lord Donaldson MR), 87 (per Balcombe LJ). *Dicta* in favour of the view that it would be unlawful to treat *Child* if they are positively refusing to be treated can be found in *Re R (a minor) (wardship: medical treatment)* [1992] Fam 11, 27 (per Staughton LJ). The latter view rests heavily on some *obiter dicta* of Lord Scarman's in *Gillick* v *West Norfolk and Wisbech Area Health Authority* [1986] AC 112, 188–189: '. . . I would hold that as a matter of law the parental right to determine *whether* or not their minor child below the age of 16 will have medical treatment *terminates* if and when the child achieves a sufficient understanding and intelligence to enable him or her to understand fully what is proposed' (emphasis added).

could not be said that the claimant consented to the risk of being hit by a piece of bark that was thrown like that – such a throw would have been well outside the expectations of the participants in the game. But as the defendant's throw was purely playful and not reckless, the claimant had consented to the risk of being hit in the eye by that kind of throw.

The idea that consent to the risk of one's person being interfered with affords a lawful justification for that interference may also be seen to underlie Goff LJ's suggestion in *Collins* v *Wilcock* (1984) that an application of force to another's person that is 'generally acceptable in the conduct of daily life'[37] will not amount to a battery. So if A and B are at a noisy party, and A grabs B's arm to get her attention, then that will not amount to a battery. If you go to a noisy party, you consent to the risk of that sort of thing happening to you.[38] In *Collins* v *Wilcock* itself, a policewoman grabbed a prostitute by the arm to stop her from walking away when she was trying to question her. The Court of Appeal held that the policewoman committed the tort of battery in restraining the prostitute – the policewoman's conduct went well beyond what is 'generally acceptable in the conduct of daily life'.

The idea that consenting to the risk of one's person being interfered with in some way provides a lawful justification for one's person being interfered with in that way runs into difficulty in cases where people try to exploit that idea to subvert the monopoly of violence that the State is supposed to possess in enforcing people's rights. Consider the **Restaurant–Dungeon Problem:**

> *Rich* goes to a very exclusive and expensive restaurant for a meal. He is warned when he makes the reservation at the restaurant that people who do not pay for their meals will be kept in a dungeon underneath the restaurant until someone comes to pay their bill. There are also numerous notices to this effect at the entrance to the restaurant and on the menu. *Rich* enjoys an excellent meal, but when he comes to pay the bill, he discovers he has left his wallet at home. He is forcibly dragged into the underground dungeon by the kitchen staff and has to wait there for 36 hours, until his ex-wife comes to pay the bill.

If *Rich* tries to sue the restaurant for false imprisonment, can they argue that they had a lawful justification for imprisoning him based on the fact that he consented to the risk that he might be imprisoned if he did not have enough money on him to pay the bill? In principle, the restaurant should be able to argue this. However, such an argument runs into, and against, the argument that debts should be enforced through the courts, and not through private force. It is likely that this latter argument would prevail, and the courts would find that the restaurant was liable for false imprisonment in this case.[39]

Having said that, as we will see later on,[40] if A unlawfully parked his car in the restaurant car park, the restaurant *would* – as the law stands at the moment – be allowed to detain A's car until he had paid the fine or fee for parking where he did, so long as they had given A enough notice that unlawfully parked cars would be detained. So detaining someone's property to enforce a debt that they owe you can be made lawful so long as the owner has consented to the risk that his property might be detained – but detaining someone's body

---

[37] [1984] 1 WLR 1172, 1177.

[38] It should be noted that in *Re F* [1990] 2 AC 1, Lord Goff thought that this rationalisation of his suggestion in *Collins* v *Wilcock* was 'artificial' (at 72).

[39] See Tan 1981, 167: 'a creditor cannot imprison his debtor in the absence of statutory authority' (quoting Glanville Williams). The only authority on point does not really tell us very much. In *Sunbolf* v *Alford* (1838) 3 M & W 248, 150 ER 1135, the claimant was forcibly restrained from leaving the defendant's restaurant when he failed to pay the bill. It was held that the defendant was liable for false imprisonment. But in that case, there were no notices telling people that they might be detained if they tried to leave without paying.

[40] See below, § 17.4.

to enforce a debt that they owe you cannot be made lawful even if the owner has consented to the risk that his body might be detained.

2.5 NECESSITY

Returning to Lord Goff's judgment in *Re F* (1990), immediately after the couple of sentences quoted at the start of the last section, Lord Goff observed, 'There are also specific cases where physical interference without consent may not be unlawful – chastisement of children, lawful arrest, the prevention of crime, and so on.'[41] We will be grouping these specific cases under the heading of 'necessity'.

The term 'necessity' needs some explanation here. Normally, the word 'necessity' is used to describe the plea of someone who claims 'I *had* to act as I did'. Normally, such a plea is unconvincing: very few people *had* to act as they did. Even if someone has been made an offer 'he can't refuse', he can actually refuse the offer and face the consequences. However, in this section we intend to give the word 'necessity' a much wider meaning, under which someone relies on a necessity defence whenever they say that it was, on balance, *good* for them to do as they did. Necessity – in this sense – is not, of and in itself, a defence to being sued for trespass to the person. Merely saying 'I did a good thing in acting as I did' is no more of a defence than merely saying 'It was reasonable for me to act as I did.' However, there are plenty of situations where the law does allow one person to interfere with another's person on the basis that it is good for them to act in that way.

Such situations can be grouped into four categories. First, *self-interested interference*: A interfered with B in order to protect himself from being harmed in some way. Secondly, *paternalistic interference*: A interfered with B in order to protect B from being harmed in some way. Thirdly, *interference to protect third parties*: A interfered with B in order to protect a third party from being harmed in some way. Fourthly, *interference based on the public interest*: A interfered with B because it was generally in the public interest to do so. We will now look at each of these categories in turn.

A. Self-interested interference

Under the law on *self-defence*, if B poses an unjustified threat to A's life or person, A is allowed to use reasonable force against B in order to protect himself. In such a case, B will have a lawful justification for his actions.

The case of *Cross v Kirkby* (2000) provides an example of a case where such a defence was successfully made out. In that case, Kirkby was a farmer who allowed the local hunt to ride over his land while hunting foxes. Cross was a hunt saboteur. While the local hunt was riding over Kirkby's land, Cross walked onto Kirkby's land in an attempt to disrupt the hunt. Kirkby attempted to remove Cross from his land with the result that Cross attacked Kirkby with a baseball bat, jabbing him in the chest and throat with the bat and eventually hitting Kirkby twice on the arm with the bat. Kirkby managed to grab the bat from Cross and hit Cross with it. Cross sustained a fracture of the skull as a result of the blow and sued Kirkby. Kirkby claimed that he had acted reasonably in self-defence in hitting Cross and had therefore done no wrong in hitting Cross.

The trial judge considered scientific evidence as to how heavy Kirkby's blow had been, found that the blow had been a 'heavy' one and held that Kirkby had used excessive force

---

[41] [1990] 2 AC 1, 72.

in striking Cross. He therefore found for Cross, awarding him £52,000 in damages. However, the Court of Appeal allowed Kirkby's appeal, finding that Kirkby had acted reasonably in self-defence. Beldam LJ – with the agreement of Otton LJ – thought that the correct test to apply, for the purpose of determining whether Kirkby acted reasonably in self-defence, was to ask: '[Did Kirkby] in a moment of unexpected anguish only [do] what he honestly and instinctively thought was necessary?' As Kirkby had only hit Cross in order to bring the attack on him to an end, the answer was 'yes'. All the Court of Appeal judges emphasised that the trial judge was wrong to find that Kirkby had used excessive force in hitting Cross because his blow was estimated to be 10% harder than a blow delivered with average force. Beldam LJ remarked that 'the judge [in reaching such a finding] . . . fell into the error . . . [of] "using jeweller's scales to measure reasonable force" '. Judge LJ remarked that the victim of violence cannot be expected, when acting in self-defence, 'to measure [the force used by him in self-defence] with mathematical precision'.[42]

Are there are any limits on what can amount to 'reasonable force'? Consider the **Dead Man Walking Problem**:

Evil invites *Patsy* round to his house, and serves her with a glass of wine when she arrives. When *Patsy* drinks the wine, he remarks that it has a funny taste. *Evil* tells *Patsy* that he poisoned it with a toxin that invariably proves fatal within two hours of being drunk. *Evil* further tells *Patsy* that he has left the antidote to the poison at a location within a 15 minute drive of the hotel where *Patsy*'s best friend is currently staying. *Evil* hands *Patsy* a gun and says that he will tell *Patsy* where the antidote is once *Patsy* visits her best friend in his hotel room and shoots her best friend dead. *Patsy* refuses to do any such thing.

Is *Patsy* allowed to torture *Evil* in this situation to extract the information as to where the antidote is?[43] Would torture count as 'reasonable force' in this situation? It seems doubtful that the courts could ever countenance regarding torture as 'reasonable force'. Doing so would open the door to the State torturing suspected terrorists to extract information about terrorist plots. The point is reinforced by Article 3 of the European Convention on Human Rights, which provides that 'No one shall be subjected to torture or to inhuman or degrading treatment or punishment.' This is one of the few rights laid down by the European Convention that is completely unqualified – there are no exceptions to it.[44] Even the right to life (Article 2) may be abridged 'if it results from the use of force which is no more than absolutely necessary . . . in defence of any person from unlawful violence'. However, refusing to allow *Patsy* to torture *Evil* in this situation does create a paradox. If

---

[42] See, to the same effect, s 76 of the Criminal Justice and Immigration Act 2008 (which only applies in criminal contexts), subsection 3 of which provides that 'In deciding [whether the defendant has used reasonable force] the following considerations are to be taken into account . . . – (a) that a person acting for a legitimate purpose may not be able to weigh to a nicety the exact measure of any necessary action; and (b) that evidence of a person's having only done what the person honestly and instinctively thought was necessary for a legitimate purpose constitutes strong evidence that only reasonable action was taken by that person for that purpose.'

[43] Slapping or punching A would probably not be regarded as torture, at least if not prolonged. Putting needles under A's fingernails or ripping out A's fingernails certainly would be.

[44] A Grand Chamber of the European Court of Human Rights held in *Gäfgen* v *Germany* (2011) 52 EHRR 1 (noted, Bjorge 2011) that Article 3 forbade the torturing of a kidnapper to find out the location of a child he had kidnapped: 'the prohibition on ill-treatment of a person applies irrespective of the conduct of the victim or the motivation of the authorities. Torture, inhuman or degrading treatment cannot be inflicted even in circumstances where the life of an individual is at risk. No derogation is allowed even in the event of a public emergency threatening the life of the nation. Article 3, which has been framed in unambiguous terms, recognises that every human being has an absolute, inalienable right not to be subjected to torture or to inhuman or degrading treatment under any circumstances, even the most difficult' (at [107]).

Evil came at *Patsy* with a syringe full of deadly poison, *Patsy* would be allowed under the law to shoot *Evil* dead in order to protect herself. But not killing *Evil* and merely putting *Evil* through excruciating pain instead is not regarded as an acceptable way of saving *Patsy*'s life.

B. Paternalistic interference

The law does not allow you to interfere with someone else on paternalistic grounds if they are an adult, capable of making up their own mind what they want, and want to be left alone. But it is different in the case of adults who cannot be asked what they want, or are not mentally fit to decide for themselves what they want. For example, it is well established that if B is in danger of being hit by some moving object, A will commit no battery if he drags B out of the way.[45] Similarly, it is well established that if B is brought unconscious into hospital, A, the attending doctor, will commit no battery if he gives B the medical treatment she needs to bring her back to good health.[46]

In *Re F* (1990), the House of Lords gave formal expression to the principle underlying this last example and ruled that: if A has medically treated B, an adult, without her consent, A will not have committed a battery in so treating B if: (i) it was in B's best interests for A to treat her in the way he did; (ii) B did not validly decline to be treated by A in the way he treated her; and (iii) B was incapable of validly consenting to be treated by A in the way he treated her (either because she was drunk or because she was mentally unstable or because she was unconscious at the time she was treated by A).[47]

Parliament has now intervened to put the area of law governed by *Re F* on a statutory footing. Under s 5 of the Mental Capacity Act 2005, D will act lawfully in doing

> an act in connection with the care or treatment of another person ('P') . . . if –
>
> (a) before doing the act, D takes reasonable steps to establish whether P lacks capacity in relation to the matter in question, and
> (b) when doing the act, D reasonably believes –
>   (i) that P lacks capacity in relation to the matter, and
>   (ii) that it will be in P's best interests for the act to be done.

provided that P is not under 16.[48]

Under s 2 of the 2005 Act, 'a person lacks capacity in relation to a matter if at the material time he is unable to make a decision for himself in relation to the matter because of an impairment of, or a disturbance in the functioning of, the mind or brain'. And s 3(1) provides that, 'For the purposes of [s] 2, a person is unable to make a decision for himself if he is unable – (a) to understand the information relevant to the decision, (b) to retain that information, (c) to use or weigh that information as part of the process of making the decision, or (d) to communicate his decision.'

Section 6 of the 2005 Act places an important limit on the scope of s 5. It deals with the situation where D 'restrains' P – that is, the situation where D 'uses, or threatens to use, force

---

[45] *Re F* [1990] 2 AC 1, 74.

[46] ibid.

[47] In *Re F*, F was a voluntary in-patient in a mental hospital. She was 36 years old but had the mental age of a small child. When she showed signs that she was about to become sexually active, F's mother sought to have her sterilised on the grounds that it would be harmful to F's mental health if she became pregnant. The House of Lords held that the hospital staff at F's mental hospital would commit no battery if they sterilised F without her consent: it would be in F's best interests to be sterilised; F had not validly declined to be sterilised; and F's mental age meant that F was incapable of validly consenting to be sterilised.

[48] Point (3) is a consequence of s 2(5) of the 2005 Act, which provides that 'No power which a person ("D") may exercise under this Act – (a) in relation to a person who lacks capacity, or (b) where D reasonably thinks a person lacks capacity, is exercisable in relation to a person under 16.'

to secure the doing of an act which P resists, or' the situation where D 'restricts P's liberty of movement, whether or not P resists'. Section 6 provides that if we want to establish that D is acting lawfully in 'restraining' P, it will not be enough to show that conditions set out in s 5, above, are satisfied. It will *also* have to be shown that: 'D reasonably believes that it is necessary to do the act in order to prevent harm to P' *and* 'the act is a proportionate response to – (a) the likelihood of P's suffering harm, and (b) the seriousness of that harm'.[49]

We can illustrate how the 2005 Act works by considering two cases that were decided under the old law, as set out in *Re F.*

In *B v An NHS Hospital Trust* (2002), the claimant suffered from spinal problems which resulted in her being paralysed from the neck down. This meant that she could not breathe without the assistance of a ventilator. The claimant had an operation to make her better, but it was unsuccessful. The claimant was bitterly disappointed with this and decided that she did not wish to live any more. She asked for her ventilator to be switched off. The claimant's doctors declined to do this, and so the claimant took them to court. It was held that *Re F* did not apply; and so the doctors were acting unlawfully in continuing to treat the claimant. Even if it were in the claimant's best interests to be kept alive, the claimant was old enough and intelligent enough to decide for herself whether she wanted to continue being treated, and so her refusal to be treated any more was perfectly valid.

It is likely that the same result would be reached under the 2005 Act. The claimant here did not lack capacity to decide for herself how she was to be treated: she was able to understand the information relevant to that decision; she was able to retain that information, use it and weigh it; and to communicate her decision about how she was to be treated. The fact that her decision may have been coloured by her bitter disappointment that her operation had not been more successful did not prevent her from having the 'capacity' to make that decision: under s 1(4) of the 2005 Act, 'A person is not to be treated as [being] unable to make a decision merely because he makes an unwise decision.'

In *Re T* (1993), T was injured in a car accident when she was 34 weeks pregnant. She was admitted into hospital where she went into labour. She was told that the baby would have to be delivered by Caesarian section and that it might be necessary to give her a blood transfusion to replenish her blood after the operation. After conversations with her mother, T told the hospital staff that she was a Jehovah's Witness and did not want to have a blood transfusion after her Caesarian. After the Caesarian was carried out – and before T had regained consciousness – T's condition suddenly deteriorated and she was transferred to an intensive care unit where she was put on a ventilator and paralysing drugs were administered. She was then given a blood transfusion at the behest of T's father and boyfriend. The Court of Appeal had to decide whether the hospital had committed a battery in giving T a blood transfusion.

The court thought that the House of Lords' decision in *Re F* established that the hospital did not commit a battery in treating T in the way it did: the court thought that it had been in T's best interests to give her a blood transfusion (she might have died without it); T had not validly declined to be given a blood transfusion in the circumstances in which she was given it; and at the time the blood transfusion was administered T was incapable of validly consenting to its being given to her. The court gave two reasons for thinking that T had not validly declined to be given a blood transfusion in the circumstances in which she was given

---

[49] Even if all these conditions are satisfied, this will not authorise D to do anything to P which would deprive P of his liberty: s 4A of the 2005 Act (as amended by the Mental Health Act 2007, s 50) provides that subject to certain narrow exceptions, 'This Act does not authorise any person . . . to deprive any other person . . . of his liberty'; and s 6(5) of the 2005 Act provides that 'D does more than merely restrain P if he deprives P of his liberty within the meaning of Article 5(1)' of the European Convention on Human Rights.

it. First, when T declined to be given a blood transfusion after her Caesarian she was simply declining to be given a blood transfusion in order to replenish her blood – she did not mean to indicate that if it was necessary for her to receive a blood transfusion to save her life, she still did not want to be given a blood transfusion. Secondly, when T declined to be given a blood transfusion after her Caesarian, she did so under pressure from her mother.

It is, again, likely that the same result would be reached under the 2005 Act. One important difference between the law under the 2005 Act, and the old law as stated in *Re F*, is that to establish that their treatment of T was lawful under the 2005 Act, her doctors would merely have to show that they reasonably believed that T lacked capacity at the time they gave her a blood transfusion, and that giving her a blood transfusion was in her best interests. There is no doubt that T lacked the capacity whether or not to decide to have a blood transfusion at the time it was administered, and it is highly likely that T's doctors would have been able to establish that they reasonably thought giving her a blood transfusion was in her best interests at the time it was administered. Section 4(6) of the 2005 Act does provide that in determining what is in a person's ('P's') best interests, the person making that determination ('D') must consider 'so far as is reasonably ascertainable – (a) [P]'s past and present wishes and feelings . . . , [and] (b) the beliefs and values that would be likely to influence his decision if [P] had [the] capacity [to make that decision] . . .' However, even taking these factors into account, T's doctors would be able to argue convincingly that they reasonably thought that it was in T's best interests to have a blood transfusion: the fact that she did not want a blood transfusion to replenish her blood did not mean that she did not want a blood transfusion to save her life.

C. Interference to protect third parties

The law on when someone can interfere with another's person in order to protect a third party from harm is still developing. The law on self-defence will apply to allow you to use force against someone who poses an unjustified threat to someone else's life or person in order to protect the threatened person. And we have already seen in the *Austin* v *Commissioner of Police of the Metropolis* (2009) case that the courts are prepared to accept that the police can imprison even completely innocent people who pose no danger to anyone else if there is no other way of preventing a breach of the peace.

In *Re S* (1993), the President of the Family Division, Sir Stephen Brown, ruled that a doctor who performs a Caesarian section on a pregnant patient in order to save the life of her foetus will commit no battery even if the patient has validly declined to undergo a Caesarian section.[50] However, in *St George's Healthcare NHS Trust* v *S* (1999), the Court of Appeal held that Sir Stephen Brown was wrong: if a pregnant patient validly declines to undergo a Caesarian section, a doctor who performs such an operation on the patient will commit a battery even if it is necessary to perform the operation in order to save the life of the patient's foetus.

Re A (2001) concerned a pair of conjoined twins, Jodie and Mary. Mary was much the weaker of the twins and relied on Jodie's heart and lungs to keep her alive. If an operation was not carried out to separate Mary from Jodie, Jodie's heart would fail within six months and they both would die. However, if such an operation were carried out, Mary would certainly die as a result. The Court of Appeal held that Mary and Jodie's doctors would act lawfully if they carried out the operation. The doctors were entitled to rely on a defence of

---

[50] In so holding he was following a suggestion of Lord Donaldson MR's in *Re T (adult: refusal of medical treatment)* [1993] Fam 95, 102: 'An adult patient who . . . suffers from no mental incapacity has an absolute right to choose whether to consent to medical treatment, to refuse it or to choose one rather than another of the treatments being offered. The only possible qualification is a case in which the choice may lead to the death of a viable foetus.'

necessity in this case as Mary posed a (passive) threat to Jodie's life and removing Mary from Jodie was the only way of saving Jodie's life. It is submitted that the decision is to be confined to its own facts – it does not, for example, authorise A to kill B if both are stranded in some wilderness and one needs to eat the other in order to survive; nor does it authorise a doctor to kill a terminally ill patient by removing his heart and lungs in order to give them to another patient who is in need of them.

D. Interference based on the public interest

There are a number of different occasions where the law gives people the power to interfere with other people's persons on the basis that it is in the public interest for people to have that power.

(1) *Public defence.* Section 3 of the Criminal Law Act 1967 provides that '[a] person may use such force as is reasonable in the circumstances in the prevention of crime, or in effecting or assisting in the lawful arrest of offenders or suspected offenders or of persons unlawfully at large'.[51] So if A runs out of a store with some goods which he has stolen, B – one of the store's security guards – will commit no battery if she chases A and wrestles him to the ground in an attempt to apprehend him.

(2) *Lawful chastisement.* If A hits B to punish her for misbehaving, A will not usually be able to argue that he acted lawfully in hitting B. It used to be that there were two exceptions to this general rule. *First*, parents were allowed to use reasonable force to discipline their children. *Secondly*, a schoolteacher, acting *in loco parentis*, was allowed to use reasonable force to punish the children in his care if they misbehaved.

The second exception no longer survives: s 548 of the Education Act 1996 provides that 'Corporal punishment given by, or on the authority of, a member of staff to a child . . . cannot be justified in any proceedings on the ground that it was given in pursuance of a right exercisable by the member of the staff by virtue of his position . . .'.[52]

The first exception has now been qualified by s 58(3) of the Children Act 2004, which provides that 'Battery of a child causing actual bodily harm to the child cannot be justified in any civil proceedings on the ground that it constituted reasonable punishment.' So a parent, A, will have committed a tort in using force to discipline his or her child, B, if – either: (1) in doing so, A caused B to suffer actual bodily harm;[53] or (2) A failed to use reasonable force in disciplining B.[54] It is unlikely that this state of affairs will satisfy those who think it unacceptable for force ever to be used on children,[55] and further reform of this area of the law must be expected.

---

[51] See also the Education Act 1996, s 550A, which provides that 'A member of the staff of a school may use, in relation to any pupil at the school, such force as is reasonable in the circumstances for the purpose of preventing the pupil from doing (or continuing to do) any of the following, namely – (a) committing any offence, (b) causing personal injury to, or damage to the property of, any person (including the pupil himself), or (c) engaging in any behaviour prejudicial to the maintenance of good order and discipline at the school or among any of its pupils, whether that behaviour occurs during a teaching session or otherwise.'

[52] In *R (Williamson)* v *Secretary of State for Education and Employment* [2005] 2 AC 246, the House of Lords rejected a claim that this provision violated the applicants' rights to manifest their religion or beliefs under Art 9 of the European Convention on Human Rights and Art 2 of the First Protocol to the Convention.

[53] Under s 58(4) of the 2004 Act, 'For the purposes of subsection (3) "actual bodily harm" has the same meaning as it has for the purposes of section 47 of the Offences against the Person Act 1847.' The courts have interpreted 'actual bodily harm' under the latter Act as meaning any hurt or injury that was 'not so trivial as to be wholly insignificant': *R* v *Chan-Fook* [1994] 1 WLR 689, at 696 (per Hobhouse LJ).

[54] In judging what amounts to reasonable force, the courts must 'consider the nature and context of the defendant's behaviour, its duration, its physical and mental consequences in relation to the child, the age and personal characteristics of the child and the reasons given by the defendant for administering punishment': *R* v *H (assault of child: reasonable chastisement)* [2001] 2 FLR 431, at [31].

[55] See, for example, Bitensky 1998.

(3) *Powers of arrest.* In granting people powers to arrest others, the law draws a distinction between ordinary citizens (effecting a 'citizen's arrest') and the police. The table below sums up the powers of arrest conferred by ss 24 and 24A of the Police and Criminal Evidence Act 1984 (where s 24 deals with 'Arrest without warrant: constables' and s 24A deals with 'Arrest without warrant: other persons'):

	. . . is about to commit an offence	. . . is committing an offence	. . . has committed an offence
B . . .	B can be arrested by a constable so long as the constable has reasonable grounds for believing the arrest is necessary: (a) to enable the name or address of the arrestee to be ascertained; *or* (b) to prevent physical injury, loss or damage to property, public indecency, or an unlawful obstruction of the highway; *or* (c) to protect a child or other vulnerable person from the arrestee; *or* (d) to aid the investigation or prosecution of the offence. B cannot be arrested by an ordinary citizen.	B can be arrested by a constable so long as the constable has reasonable grounds for believing the arrest is necessary on one of the grounds (a) – (d) set out on the left. B can also be arrested by an ordinary citizen so long as: (i) the offence is an indictable one; *and* (ii) the person making the arrest has reasonable grounds for believing the arrest is necessary to prevent physical injury or loss or damage to property or to stop the arrestee making off before a constable can assume responsibility for him; *and* (iii) it appears to the person making the arrest that it is not reasonably practicable for a constable to make it instead.	B can be arrested by a constable so long as the constable has reasonable grounds for believing the arrest is necessary on one of the grounds (a) – (d) set out on the far left. B can also be arrested by an ordinary citizen so long as conditions (i), (ii) and (iii) set out on the left are satisfied.
A has reasonable grounds for suspecting B . . .	A can arrest B if A is a constable and A has reasonable grounds for believing that the arrest is necessary on one of the grounds (a) – (d) set out above. A cannot arrest B if A is an ordinary citizen.	A can arrest B if A is a constable and A has reasonable grounds for believing that the arrest is necessary on one of the grounds (a) – (d) set out above left. A can also arrest B if A is an ordinary citizen so long as conditions (i), (ii) and (iii) set out above are satisfied.	A can arrest B if A is a constable and A has reasonable grounds for believing that the arrest is necessary on one of the grounds (a) – (d) set out above far left. A can also arrest B if A is an ordinary citizen so long as the offence for which he is arresting B has *actually been committed* (by someone, not necessarily B) and conditions (i), (ii) and (iii) set out above left are satisfied.

For further details on when the police can lawfully arrest an individual, and what procedures have to be followed when they do so, we refer the reader to any textbook on constitutional law, or police powers.

(4) *Prisons*. Section 12(1) of the Prison Act 1952, provides that '[a] prisoner, whether sentenced to imprisonment or committed to prison on remand or pending trial or otherwise, may be lawfully confined in any prison'. This is so even if it is subsequently established that the prisoner was wrongly convicted of the offence for which he was imprisoned. In such a case, the prisoner will not be able to sue anyone *in tort* for imprisoning him – for no one did him any legal wrong in locking him up – but he may be entitled to some statutory compensation under s 133 of the Criminal Justice Act 1988 for the fact that he was detained in prison for an offence he did not commit.[56] We will deal in the next section with what the position is where a prisoner is held in jail longer than he should have been, but we should note at this stage the decision of the House of Lords in The House of Lords' decision in *R v Deputy Governor of Parkhurst Prison, ex parte Hague*.[57]

That decision actually dealt with two cases – the *Hague* case and *Weldon v Home Office*. In the *Hague* case, the claimant – a prisoner at Parkhurst Prison – claimed he had been falsely imprisoned because he had been kept in isolation for 28 days, contrary to the Prison Rules 1964. In the *Weldon* case, the claimant – a prisoner at Leeds Prison – claimed he had been falsely imprisoned because he had been detained in a strip cell. Lord Bridge remarked that the 'primary and fundamental issue' raised by the *Hague* and *Weldon* cases was:

> [Does] any restraint within defined bounds imposed upon a convicted prisoner whilst serving his sentence by the prison governor . . . but in circumstances where the particular form of restraint is not sanctioned by the prison rules, amounts for that reason to the tort of false imprisonment.[58]

The House of Lords answered this question in the negative and dismissed the claims of both the claimant in the *Hague* case and the claimant in the *Weldon* case.

The reason the House of Lords gave for answering Lord Bridge's question in the negative was that a governor's authority to detain a prisoner under s 12(1) of the 1952 Act did not come with any limits attached to it. So a governor could not act unlawfully in detaining a prisoner under s 12(1) of the 1952 Act merely because the way in which he chose to imprison the prisoner breached the Prison Rules 1964.

However, s 12(1) only makes it lawful for the *prison governor* (and those acting with the governor's authority) to detain a prisoner, however he happens to be detained. The House of Lords was very clear that if A, a fellow prisoner of B's, locks B in a prison shed, then A will have committed the tort of false imprisonment.[59] Similarly, the House of Lords held that if A, a prison officer, locks B in a cell and does so in bad faith – knowing that he has no authority from the governor of the prison to do so – then A will have committed the tort of false imprisonment.[60]

The decision in the *Hague* case seems quite legalistic, resting as it does on a wide interpretation of the powers granted to a prison governor under s 12(1) of the 1952 Act. However, it may be that the real basis of the decision in *Hague* was that the House of Lords was simply trying to avoid the government being swamped with claims for compensation from prisoners, each alleging that their detention was unlawful because it technically breached the Prison Rules 1964.

(5) *Mental health*. People suffering from various mental disorders may in certain circumstances be arrested or detained in hospital. For example, s 136 of the Mental Health Act 1983 provides that if

---

[56] For an excellent summary of who will, and who will not, be entitled to compensation under s 133, see Spencer 2010.
[57] [1992] 1 AC 58.
[58] ibid, 162.
[59] [1992] 1 AC 58, 164, 166, 178.
[60] [1992] 1 AC 58, 164.

... a constable finds in a place to which the public have access a person who appears to him to be suffering from mental disorder and to be in immediate need of care or control, the constable may, if he thinks it necessary to do so in the interests of that person or for the protection of other persons, remove that person to a place of safety ...

2.6 STATUTORY AUTHORITY

The above section gave us a number of different examples where people are given *statutory powers* to interfere with other people's persons. The position of a defendant who wishes to rely on the fact that he was given a statutory power to interfere with another's person in order to establish he had a lawful justification for acting as he did is complicated by the fact that the *valid* exercise of a statutory power will normally be subject to a number of conditions. These conditions are of two types:

A. Statutory conditions

These conditions are expressly or impliedly laid out in the statute. They take the form: 'If x is true, then D will have the power to [interfere with C's person]'. If x is not satisfied, then the statute will not give D a power to interfere with C's person and D will not be able to rely on the statute to justify his interfering with C's person.

For example, s 34(1) of the Police and Criminal Evidence Act 1984 provides that 'A person arrested for an offence shall not be kept in police detention except in accordance with the provisions of ... Part [IV] of this Act.' One of those provisions[61] provides that the custody officer of a police station where an arrestee is being detained should periodically review the arrestee's detention to see whether:

> ... his detention without being charged is necessary to secure or preserve evidence relating to an offence for which he is under arrest or to obtain such evidence by questioning him.[62]

This condition was not observed in the case of *Roberts* v *Chief Constable of the Cheshire Constabulary* (1999), where the claimant was arrested on suspicion of conspiracy to burgle and held in police custody for six hours before his detention was reviewed by the custody officer. It was held that his detention should have been reviewed at least four and a half hours after his arrest, and that he was therefore falsely imprisoned for the one and a half hours that he was detained in custody without having his detention reviewed when it should have been.[63]

B. Public law conditions

Where a statutory power to interfere with other people's persons has been created, the courts will readily infer that Parliament intended that the exercise of that power should be subject to a number of different conditions:

> (1) that the power not be exercised for an *improper purpose*; (2) that the power only be exercised after the power-holder has considered all *relevant considerations* (and has put out of his mind any

---

[61] Police and Criminal Evidence Act 1984, s 40(1).

[62] Police and Criminal Evidence Act 1984, s 37(1).

[63] See also *Christie* v *Leachinsky* [1947] AC 573 (arrest of claimant without warrant declared unlawful as statute under which he was arrested gave no power to arrest without warrant); and *Langley* v *Liverpool City Council* [2006] 1 WLR 375 (police constable had no power to take child into custody in order to protect child from harm under Children Act 1999 unless there were compelling reasons to do so, which did not exist in this case).

irrelevant considerations); (3) that the power not be exercised in a way that is *wholly unreasonable*; (4) that (in certain cases) that the grantee of the power not exercise it before having given the person against whom the power is exercised a *fair hearing*; (5) that the grantee of the power not exercise it in a way that would disappoint for no good reason other people's *legitimate expectations* as to how that power would be exercised; (6) that the grantee of the power be *open about the reasons* why he has exercised the power in the way he was; (7) that the grantee of the power exercise that power in a way that is not inconsistent with the *European Convention on Human Rights*.[64]

The courts will infer that Parliament intended that the exercise of a statutory power to interfere with other people's persons should be subject to such conditions because they assume that Parliament is committed to the idea that statutory powers should only be exercised in a responsible manner; and all of the above conditions are designed to ensure that is the case.

If D is granted a statutory power[65] to interfere with C's person and he exercises that power in a way that violates one or more of the above conditions, he is said to have exercised the power in breach of a *public law duty*.[66] The question of whether, and if so when, the breach of a public law duty will prevent a defendant claiming that he had a lawful justification for interfering with the claimant's person was addressed by the Supreme Court in the recent case of *Lumba* v *Secretary of State for the Home Department* (2011).[67]

That case had its roots in the revelation in April 2006 that 1,023 foreign nationals who had been imprisoned in the UK for committing various criminal offences – including five who had committed sex offences against children – had not been considered for deportation after they were released from prison. This caused a media outcry and the Home Secretary, Charles Clarke, was subsequently replaced by John Reid, who declared the Home Office 'unfit for purpose'. Eager to avoid further bad publicity, the Home Office revised its policy on when it would exercise its powers under the Immigration Act 1971 to detain a foreign national prisoner (FNP) who had been released from prison. (The 1971 Act allows the Home Office to deport from the UK anyone who is not a British citizen if his 'deportation [is deemed] to be conducive to the public good' and allows a foreign national who has been designated for deportation to be detained pending his deportation.) At the time, the Home Office's *official* policy was that they would only detain an FNP who had been released from prison if it was necessary to do so. But in order to avoid the media outrage that would inevitably result if an FNP was not detained after having been released from prison and took advantage of his freedom to commit a serious criminal offence, the Home Office instituted a *secret* policy that *any* FNP who was released from prison should be detained pending deportation.

---

[64] See any textbook on constitutional or administrative law for a more in-depth discussion of these conditions and the key authorities that establish that the valid exercise of a statutory power is subject to these conditions. It should be noted that these conditions can only really apply to powers that the power-holder has some *choice* about exercising. In the case of a power such as the power to imprison under s 12(1) of the Prisons Act 1952 (discussed above, § 2.5(D)(4)), where a prison governor really has *no choice but* to detain a prisoner, it makes no sense to say that the valid exercise of that power is conditional on requirements (1)–(7) being observed. That is why in the *Hague* case (ibid), the House of Lords ruled that there were no limits on the power to detain under s 12(1).

[65] It should be noted that the valid exercise of a power under the *common law* to interfere with someone else's person is also subject to the above conditions. For example, it was assumed in *Austin* v *Commissioner of Police of the Metropolis* [2009] 1 AC 564 that the police would not have validly exercised their powers to prevent a breach of peace if in doing so they had violated Art 5 of the European Convention on Human Rights.

[66] The word 'duty' may be a bit of a misnomer here. It is not so much that a power holder has a *duty* to exercise the power in accordance with conditions (1)–(7), but that the power holder will *not be entitled* to exercise that power unless he abides by conditions (1)–(7).

[67] The case is reported at [2011] 2 WLR 671 and will be referred to below simply as '*Lumba*'.

The claimants in *Lumba* were detained after being released from prison pursuant to this secret policy; though it was not disputed that the seriousness of the offences for which the claimants had been imprisoned meant that they would have been detained even under the Home Office's official policy. The Supreme Court agreed in *Lumba* that the Home Office had breached a public law duty – the requirement that they be open about the reasons why they were detaining the claimants – in exercising their powers under the Immigration Act 1971 to detain the claimants. However, the Supreme Court divided over the issue of whether that breach meant that the claimants had been falsely imprisoned. Of the nine Supreme Court Justices who decided *Lumba*, six took the view that the claimants had been falsely imprisoned (but for different reasons), and three took the view that they had not been falsely imprisoned.

In the majority, Lords *Dyson* and *Collins* and Lady *Hale* took the straightforward position that there was no lawful justification for imprisoning the claimants in *Lumba* because the Home Office's decision to detain the claimants was invalid as a matter of public law.[68] The decision to detain the claimants was made in pursuance of a policy that the Home Office was not entitled to pursue. It did not matter – so far as the claim that the claimants had been falsely imprisoned was concerned – that the Home Office *could* have lawfully detained the claimants under its official policy.[69] The fact that the claimants *might* have been lawfully detained did not mean that they *had* been lawfully detained.[70]

The other members of the majority in *Lumba* (and, indeed, the minority) were more cautious about adopting the line that *any* breach of a public law duty that had a bearing on, and was relevant to,[71] the decision to exercise a statutory power to interfere with a claimant's person would mean that there was no lawful justification for that interference. Lord *Kerr* took the view that there was no lawful justification for detaining the claimants in *Lumba* because the reasons for detaining them frustrated the purpose for which the Home Office had been given the power to detain foreign nationals like the claimants.[72] The fact that the claimants had been detained pursuant to a secret policy made it much harder (if not impossible) for the claimants to determine whether their detention was justified. Lords *Hope* and *Walker* argued that there was no lawful justification for detaining the claimants because their detention amounted to a serious 'abuse of power'.[73]

In the minority, Lord *Brown* (with whom Lord *Rodger* agreed) objected to the majority's finding that the claimants in *Lumba* had been falsely imprisoned on the basis that 'not every decision to detain affected by a public law breach necessarily carries in its wake an unanswerable claim for false imprisonment.'[74] Where the public law breach 'consists of applying, in place of [the government's] published policy, an unpublished policy less

---

[68] *Lumba*, at [68]–[69] (per Lord Dyson), [207] (per Lady Hale). Lord Collins expressed agreement with Lord Dyson's judgment at [219], but perhaps departed from the spirit of Lord Dyson's judgment by emphasising at [219] that 'the *serious* breach of public law in this case has the result that the detention of the [claimants] was unlawful. Any other result would negate the rule of law.'

[69] Though this feature of the case had the effect of reducing the damages payable to the claimants to a nominal level: see below, § 9.2.

[70] *Lumba*, at [71] (per Lord Dyson), [208] (per Lady Hale), [221] (per Lord Collins); also [175] (per Lord Hope), and [239]–[241] (per Lord Kerr).

[71] *Lumba*, at [68] (per Lord Dyson): 'the breach of public law must bear on and be relevant to the decision to detain.' Lady Hale held (at [207]) that 'the breach of public law duty must be material to the decision to detain and not to some other aspect of the detention and it must be capable of affecting the result'.

[72] *Lumba*, at [250]–[251].

[73] *Lumba*, at [170] (per Lord Hope), and [193] (per Lord Walker).

[74] *Lumba*, at [358].

favourable to those subject to the detaining power'[75] Lord Brown took the view that only a claimant who would have been entitled to be released under the published policy could sue for false imprisonment.[76] He pointed out the paradox involved in saying that the claimants had been falsely imprisoned when had they 'sought to challenge [their] continued detention by judicial review (or habeas corpus), the court would have been likely to [decline] in its discretion to order the [claimants'] release.'[77] How then, he asked, could one justify awarding 'damages to those conceded to have been rightly detained?'[78]

None of these positions are particularly satisfactory. The position taken by Lord *Dyson et al* gives rise to the problem that the House of Lords may have been trying to avoid in the *Hague* case: the problem of technical breaches of public law requirements resulting in the government being held liable for false imprisonment.[79] But at least their position has the virtue of making the law reasonably certain, which is more than can be said of Lords *Kerr*, *Hope* or *Walker*'s judgments. On the other hand, Lord *Brown*'s judgment would create an unsustainable distinction between cases where a defendant exercises a statutory power to interfere with a claimant's person in breach of an expressed or implied condition on its exercise in the statute (in which case Lord Brown would be in favour of finding liability, even if the defendant could have exercised his power to interfere with the claimant's person without breaching any condition)[80] and cases where a defendant's exercise of a statutory power to interfere with a claimant's person breached a public law condition on the exercise of a statutory power.

2.7 MISTAKES

We have already quoted Tony Weir as saying that:

> no one in Britain, *no one*, can justify deliberately touching even a hair on [a claimant's] head, or entering her garden – much less depriving her of her liberty – merely on the ground that it was reasonable to do so . . .

In the same passage, Tony Weir immediately went on to say:

> . . . or on the more insidious ground that he reasonably thought he was entitled to do so. Trespass trips up the zealous bureaucrat, the eager policeman and the officious citizen; indeed, punitive damages can be awarded against the first two. It is not enough to *think* you are entitled; you must actually *be* entitled.[81]

The quote suggests there is no room for a defendant to escape liability in trespass by claiming they mistakenly believed they were entitled to interfere with the claimant's person. The reality is more complex, and requires very careful discussion.

---

[75] *Lumba*, at [353].
[76] *Lumba*, at [355]. Lord Phillips, also in the minority, took the view (at [321]–[323]) that where there was a disparity between the government's official policy as to how it would exercise its detention powers and its actual policy, only those who had a 'legitimate expectation' that they would not be detained under the official policy could claim they had been falsely imprisoned, and the claimants in *Lumba* did not fall into that category.
[77] *Lumba*, at [359].
[78] *Lumba*, at [361].
[79] See the subsequent case of *Kambadzi* v *Secretary of State for the Home Department* [2011] UKSC 23, where the detention of a foreign national who was being held pending deportation – having served time in prison for sexual assault – was rendered unlawful merely because his continued detention had not been reviewed as regularly as the Home Office had said it would review it in a policy document.
[80] *Lumba*, at [347](2).
[81] Weir 2004, 322 (emphasis in original).

A. Mistaken belief in consent

Let us first take the case where a defendant mistakenly believes that the claimant has consented to his touching her in some way. Consider the **Gullible Student Problem**:

> *Hopeful* attends a party at *Beauty*'s house. As the party finishes very late, *Beauty* agrees that *Hopeful* and some other friends can sleep over in the front room, while she goes to bed. *Hopeful*'s friends tell him that *Beauty* has told them that she would like *Beauty* to wake her with a kiss. *Hopeful* has always liked *Beauty* and is very happy to hear this. He wakes himself up at 6.30 am, goes upstairs to *Beauty*'s room and kisses her on the lips. *Hopeful*'s kissing her wakes *Beauty* up, and *Beauty* – who never said that she wanted *Hopeful* to kiss her awake – is disgusted to find *Hopeful* kissing her.

It is very likely in this case that *Beauty* could sue *Hopeful* for what he has done. Even though *Hopeful* is completely innocent, it cannot be the case that what *Hopeful*'s friends told him deprived *Beauty* of the right she had not to be subjected to unwelcome physical attentions from people like *Hopeful*. Only *Beauty* could waive that right. But what should we say about the **Changing Mind Problem**?

> *Beauty* and *Hopeful* are both at a party. *Beauty* tells *Hopeful* that she would like him to kiss her. *Hopeful* has always liked *Beauty* and is very happy to hear this. *Hopeful* leans in to kiss *Beauty*, but before he does, *Beauty* has a sudden change of heart. She thinks of her boyfriend (who is not at the party) and who would be very hurt by her kissing someone else. *Beauty* decides that she does not want *Hopeful* to kiss her, but before she has a chance to say anything, *Hopeful* has kissed her on the lips.

In this situation, *Beauty* did not consent to *Hopeful*'s kissing her at the time he actually did kiss her, any more than she did in Gullible Student. The only difference between the two situations is that in Gullible Student, *Hopeful*'s friends made *Hopeful* think *Beauty* wanted him to kiss her; in Changing Mind, *Beauty* made *Hopeful* think she wanted him to kiss her. Should it make a difference who told *Hopeful* that *Beauty* wanted him to kiss her? We think it should and that *Beauty* should not be entitled to sue *Hopeful* in Changing Mind.

One elegant way of reaching this result is by invoking the law on *estoppel*. The law on estoppel now has many different branches, but it originated as a part of the law of evidence. Under the law on estoppel, *Beauty* would be prevented (or estopped) from claiming that she did not consent to *Hopeful*'s kissing her in Changing Mind. This is because she represented to *Hopeful* that she wanted him to kiss her, and he relied on that representation by kissing her. Given this, she cannot now go back on her representation and say in court that, actually, when *Hopeful* kissed her, she was not consenting. It would be different if, when *Hopeful* leaned in to kiss *Beauty*, he saw the confusion in her eyes and realised she was hesitating about kissing him, and decided to quickly steal a kiss before it was too late. In such a case, *Hopeful* could not argue that he relied on *Beauty*'s representation that she wanted him to kiss her. When he kissed her, he was no longer acting in good faith on the basis of her representation, and was simply trying to take advantage of the situation. In such a case, *Beauty* would not be estopped from claiming that she did not consent to the kiss, and would be able to sue *Hopeful* for battery.

B. Mistaken belief in self-defence

The issue of whether a defendant to a trespass claim could rely on a mistaken belief that he was being attacked by the claimant to defeat that claim was considered by the House of Lords in the case of *Ashley* v *Chief Constable of Sussex Police* (2008).

In that case, PC Christopher Sherwood was one of a group of armed police officers who conducted a drugs raid on James Ashley's house at 4.20 am on 15 January 1998. Ashley was asleep at the time the police broke into his house. Sherwood was the first into Ashley's bedroom. By then, Ashley was standing in the middle of the room, naked. There was no light on. Sherwood shot Ashley dead. When Sherwood was tried for murder, he was acquitted. He argued that he had shot Ashley because he honestly thought that Ashley might be about to fire a gun at him. Under the criminal law, a defendant who honestly (though mistakenly) acts on facts which, if they had been true, would have given him a defence of self-defence is entitled to be acquitted.[82]

When Ashley's family brought a claim in tort against the police, the police argued that a similar rule should apply under the civil law, and that the courts should find that Sherwood did no wrong in shooting Ashley if he honestly (though mistakenly) thought his life was in danger. The House of Lords unanimously rejected this argument, and quite rightly too. Ashley could not suddenly have lost the rights he would otherwise have had not to be shot just because Sherwood decided that his life was in danger. It would have been different if Ashley had *done something* to give Sherwood reasonable grounds for believing that his life was in danger. In such a case, Ashley's actions would have deprived him of his rights not to be shot: people who play with fire can expect to be burned.[83]

But what would have been the situation had Ashley not done anything to make it reasonable for Sherwood to believe that his life was in danger, but Sherwood still reasonably thought his life was in danger, and he shot Ashley for that reason? Suppose, for example, that Sherwood had been briefed before the raid by his commanders that Ashley was an extremely dangerous individual and that if he were allowed to make any movement at all before he was brought under police control, the lives of the police officers conducting the drugs raid would be in danger? Three of the Law Lords who decided *Ashley* left the question open as to whether, in such a case, Sherwood would have done anything wrong in shooting Ashley.[84] Lord Carswell thought that any kind of reasonable belief that Sherwood's life was in danger would have entitled Sherwood to shoot Ashley.[85] Lord Bingham said nothing on the issue.

The concern about allowing a defence in this type of case – where Sherwood reasonably believed his life was in danger, but not because of anything Ashley did – is that allowing such a defence suggests that what was said in a briefing room some miles away from Ashley's house could deprive Ashley of his rights not to be shot. This would seem counter-intuitive. If what *Hopeful*'s friends said to him in the Gullible Student could not strip *Beauty* of her rights that she would otherwise have had not to be kissed by someone she was repulsed by, then a police briefing could not have stripped Ashley of the rights that he would otherwise have had not to be shot. Given this, we favour the view that it would only have been lawful (under the law of tort) for Sherwood to shoot Ashley if *Ashley* had done

---

[82] *R v Williams (Gladstone)* [1987] 3 All ER 411.

[83] Though see Lord Scott in the *Ashley* case ([2008] 1 AC 962, at [20]), who seems to have taken the view that in this sort of case, Ashley's family would still have been entitled to sue Sherwood, subject to a discount in the damages for contributory negligence.

[84] [2008] 1 AC 962, at [20] (per Lord Scott), [55] (per Lord Rodger), and [90] (per Lord Neuberger).

[85] [2008] 1 AC 962, at [76] (per Lord Carswell).

something to make it reasonable for Sherwood to believe his life was in danger. If *someone else* had done something to make it reasonable for Sherwood to believe this, that would not give him a defence.

C. Mistaken belief in validity of byelaw

In *Percy v Hall* (1997), the claimants were arrested over 150 times for trespassing on land in the vicinity of a military communications installation in North Yorkshire in breach of the HMS Forest Moor and Menwith Hill Station Byelaws 1986. These byelaws were actually invalid at the time the claimants were arrested because they were insufficiently precise. When this was discovered, the claimants sued the constables for false imprisonment. The claimants' claims were dismissed by the Court of Appeal: the fact that the constables had mistakenly believed the byelaws were valid, and would have been failing in their duties had they not enforced those apparently valid byelaws, was enough to give them a defence to being sued for false imprisonment. Tony Weir calls the decision 'disgraceful'.[86] It certainly seems inconsistent with the next set of cases.

D. Unduly prolonged detention in prison

Suppose that someone makes a mistake in determining how long *Prisoner* should spend in prison and as a result he is imprisoned for three months longer than he ought to have been. Can *Prisoner* sue his prison *Governor* on the ground that he was falsely imprisoned for those three months? If it was the *courts* that made the mistake in calculating *Prisoner's* sentence, then *Prisoner* will *not* be able to sue *Governor* for falsely imprisoning him.[87] *Governor* will be able to argue that he was duty-bound to imprison *Prisoner* for as long as he did, and that he therefore had a lawful justification for imprisoning *Prisoner* for the extra three months that *Prisoner* should not have served.

If, however, it was *Governor* who made the mistake in calculating *Prisoner's* sentence, then *Prisoner will* be able to sue *Governor* for falsely imprisoning him – and this is so even if the prison governor's mistake was an entirely reasonable one to make. This was established by the House of Lords' decision in *R v Governor of Brockhill Prison, ex parte Evans (No 2)* (2001).[88] In that case, the claimant was a woman named Evans who was sent to prison to serve several terms of imprisonment, running concurrently. At the time Evans was sent to prison, the Divisional Court had ruled – in a case called *R v Governor of Blundeston Prison, ex parte Gaffney* (1982) – that the release date of a prisoner serving several concurrent sentences should be calculated in a certain way (call this 'Method X'). The governor, abiding by the decision in *Gaffney*, applied Method X to determine when Evans should be released. However, while Evans was still in prison, she went to court and persuaded the Court of Appeal to rule that the governor should have used a different method for calculating her release date – let's call this method 'Method Y'.[89] The Court of

---

[86] Weir 2004, 354.

[87] *Quinland v Governor of Swaleside Prison* [2003] QB 306. A will not be able to sue the *courts* for falsely imprisoning him by virtue of s 2(5) of the Crown Proceedings Act 1947, which provides that 'No proceedings shall lie against the Crown by virtue of this section in respect of anything done or omitted to be done by a person while discharging or purporting to discharge any responsibilities of a judicial nature vested in him, or any responsibilities which he has in connection with the execution of judicial process.'

[88] Noted, Cane 2001a.

[89] *R v Governor of Brockhill Prison, ex parte Evans* [1997] QB 443.

Appeal thereby overruled the decision of the Divisional Court in *Gaffney*. According to Method Y, Evans should have *already* been released and, accordingly, she was released on the same day as the Court of Appeal overruled *Gaffney*. In fact, according to Method Y, Evans should have been released 59 days before she was actually released. Evans sued the prison governor, claiming that she had been falsely imprisoned in being detained for those 59 days. The House of Lords allowed her claim.

It is hard to reconcile this decision with the decision in *Percy* v *Hall*. If the constables in *Percy* v *Hall* had a lawful justification for arresting the claimants in that case based on the fact that they were duty-bound to arrest the claimants when they did, it is hard to see why the governor of Evans's prison did not have a similar lawful justification for detaining Evans for as long as he did.[90] After all, until *Gaffney* was overruled, the governor of Evans's prison was – for all practical purposes[91] – *required* to calculate Evans's release date using Method X and to detain Evans in prison until that date.[92]

2.8 REMEDIES

The victim of a trespass to the person will normally be able sue for compensation for any actionable losses that the tort caused her to suffer.[93] (An exception exists under s 45 of the Offences Against the Person Act 1861, which prevents someone who has brought a private prosecution against someone for assault or battery in the magistrates' court subsequently suing the same person in tort for assault or battery.)[94] Aggravated damages and exemplary (or punitive) damages may also be available if the tortfeasor acted in a sufficiently outrageous way in committing the tort.[95] Even if the victim has suffered no loss as a result of the trespass tort being committed, he or she will still be able to sue for nominal damages (about £5) to mark the fact that his or her rights have been violated.[96]

It has been suggested that the mere violation of a right should attract a more substantial award than merely nominal damages, and that consequently someone whose rights have been violated should be able to sue – in the absence of any other remedy being available to them – for something known as *vindicatory damages*: damages designed to mark the fact that someone's rights have been violated.[97]

---

[90] Which is *not* to say that Evans should not have been entitled to recover something for the extra days she was kept in prison. She should probably have been allowed to bring a *non-tortious* claim for compensation, just as people who are wrongly convicted of committing an offence and sent to prison are allowed to bring a non-tortious claim for compensation for the time they have spent in prison (see above, fn 56). See, to the same effect, Cane 2001a, 10.

[91] It might be argued that, technically, it would have been open to the governor to say, 'I think *Gaffney* was wrongly decided – I will make up my own mind how long to detain Evans'; but it was also open to the officers in *Percy* v *Hall* to say, 'These bye-laws do not look valid to us; we are not going to enforce them', and that did not stop the Court of Appeal finding that – for all practical purposes – the officers in *Percy* v *Hall* were duty-bound to enforce the bye-laws.

[92] See Judge LJ's remarks in the Court of Appeal in *R* v *Governor of Brockhill Prison, ex parte Evans (No 2)* [1999] QB 1043, 1071: 'The governor was blameless. Indeed if he had not continued to detain [Evans] he would have been acting in defiance of the earlier decisions of the Divisional Court . . . So in detaining [Evans] for as long as he did the governor was responsibly performing his duties.'

[93] See below, chapter 9, for the law on causation, and chapter 10, for the law on actionability.

[94] A case where this provision was applied to stop the claimant suing for battery was *Wong* v *Parkside NHS Trust* [2003] 3 All ER 932.

[95] Aggravated damages are discussed in more detail below, chapter 29; exemplary damages in chapter 30.

[96] Nominal damages are discussed in more detail below, chapter 27.

[97] Vindicatory damages are discussed in more detail below, chapter 32.

The possibility that the victim of a trespass tort might be able to sue for such damages was first raised by Lord Scott in the case of *Ashley* v *Chief Constable of Sussex Police* (2008), the facts of which have already been set out above.[98] In that case, Ashley's family were not only claiming that Sherwood had acted unlawfully (under the law of tort) in shooting Ashley. They also claimed that the police officers who had organised the raid had acted negligently in failing to brief properly the officers conducting the raid (including Sherwood) and that their negligence had contributed to Ashley's death, in the sense that had Sherwood been briefed properly, he might not have been so quick to fire at Ashley when he went into Ashley's bedroom. The defendant – the Chief Constable of Sussex Police – was prepared to admit negligence, and had offered to settle the family's claim and pay them all the damages they were seeking on the basis that the officers who had organised the raid were negligent. But the defendant was not prepared to admit that Sherwood had acted unlawfully (under the law of tort) in shooting Ashley. Ashley's family therefore declined the Chief Constable's settlement offer and wanted the case to go to trial, in order to have it publicly established that Sherwood had done something wrong (under the law of tort) in shooting Ashley.

The issue the House of Lords was asked to resolve was whether Ashley's family could do this, or whether their continuing attempts to sue the Chief Constable should be struck out on the basis that they amounted to an abuse of process, given that the Chief Constable had already admitted negligence and was prepared on that basis to pay the family all the damages they could possibly recover by taking their claim to trial. The House of Lords decided, by three to two, that Ashley's family should be allowed to proceed with their claim against the Chief Constable. Lord Rodger and Lord Bingham thought that, as Ashley's family had an arguable claim that a battery had been committed against Ashley, there was no basis for striking out an attempt to have that claim tried in court, whatever the motives of Ashley's family in wanting to take their case to court. Lord Scott (with whom Lord Rodger agreed) went further, arguing that it was entirely legitimate for Ashley's family to want to have it publicly established that Ashley had been (under the law of tort) wrongfully killed:

> the Ashleys are determined, if they can, to take the assault and battery case to trial not for the purpose of obtaining a larger sum by way of damages than they have so far become entitled to pursuant to the chief constable's concessions, but in order to obtain a public admission or finding that the deceased Mr Ashley was unlawfully killed by PC Sherwood. They want a finding of liability on their assault and battery claim in order to obtain a public vindication of the deceased's right not to have been subjected to a deadly assault, a right that was infringed by PC Sherwood. They have pleaded a case that, if reasonably arguable on the facts, cannot be struck out as being unarguable in law. Why therefore should they be denied the chance to establish liability at trial? It is open to the chief constable to avoid a trial by admitting liability on the assault and battery claim . . . But the chief constable declines . . . That being so, I can see no ground upon which it can be said that it would be inappropriate for the claim to proceed for vindicatory purposes.[99]

Furthermore, Lord Scott thought that if it were established that Ashley had been unlawfully killed (under the law of tort), Ashley's estate might be entitled to 'vindicatory damages', which were 'essentially rights-centred, awarded in order to demonstrate that the right in

---

[98] See above, § 2.7.
[99] [2008] 1 AC 962, at [23].

question should not have been infringed at all.'[100] The fact that vindicatory damages might be available to Ashley's estate was, for Lord Scott, an additional reason why the claim for battery in *Ashley*'s case had to be allowed to continue: 'The chief constable has conceded compensatory damages. He has not conceded vindicatory damages and he cannot do so unless he concedes liability on the assault and battery claim.'[101]

In the subsequent case of *Lumba* v *Secretary of State for the Home Department* (2011), the Supreme Court was radically divided over the issue of whether vindicatory damages would be available in a trespass case, with three Supreme Court Justices ruling that vindicatory damages had no place in the law of tort, and four Supreme Court Justices indicating their willingness to allow such damages to be claimed, at least in some circumstances. This aspect of the *Lumba* decision is discussed in much more detail below.[102]

The emphasis placed in some of the judgments in *Ashley* and *Lumba* on the vindicatory element of the remedies that are available for the trespass torts finds strong echo in the work of Tony Weir, who argues that in thinking about what remedies should be available when A commits a trespass to the person in relation to B, we should separate out *compensatory* remedies from *vindicatory* remedies. B, he argues, should only be able to sue A for compensation if she has a claim in negligence against A for such remedies. On the other hand, vindicatory remedies – such as an injunction, or a declaration that A acted wrongfully in relation to B – should be available to B whether or not A was at fault for what happened:

> where the [claimant] is seeking compensation for harm, the rules of negligence seem so appropriate nowadays as to be almost mandatory, whereas they have, or ought to have, no place where the [claimant] is seeking, not compensation for harm, but rather vindication of the rights by whose infringement he is aggrieved. It is not a great step to move from the proposition that no harm need be established in a trespass claim to the position that if harm is alleged, the rules of negligence apply.[103]

One problem with this suggestion is that the law on trespass to the person protects some interests that are not well protected under the law of negligence – such as an interest in being free to move about, or being free from threats of harm. Weir's proposal would make it harder for a claimant who was falsely imprisoned or assaulted to recover compensation for the frustration of having one's liberty taken away, or any distress caused by being threatened with imminent attack. Another, more philosophical, problem with this proposal is that it is not clear that it is possible to separate out compensation from vindication. As we will see,[104] some academics argue that the reason why the victim of a tort (B) can sue the person who committed that tort (A) for compensation is to vindicate B's rights against A. The award of compensation is meant to give B the monetary equivalent of whatever right of B's it is that A violated in acting as he did. If these academics are right, then compensation should be payable whenever a right has been violated, whether or not the violator was at fault for the violation.

---

[100] [2008] 1 AC 962, at [22].
[101] [2008] 1 AC 962, at [29].
[102] See below, § 32.3.
[103] Weir 1998a, 109–110. See also Weir 2006, 134–5.
[104] See below, § 28.7.

Further reading

The modern-day dominance of the law of negligence within tort law – and in particular, tort law as it is taught in the universities – means there is not much decent writing on the torts dealt with in this chapter. What writing there is is usually flawed by characterising these torts as *intentional* torts – which confuses these torts with a separate set of torts (dealt with in the chapter on 'Economic Torts', below) which require for their commission that the defendant acted with an *intention to harm* the claimant. See, for example, **David Howarth's essay 'Is there a future for the intentional torts?' in Birks (ed),** *The Classification of Obligations* **(OUP, 1997), 233–281**, which groups *together* assault, battery, false imprisonment *and* the economic torts under the heading 'intentional torts'.

Tony Weir's views on the torts discussed here have been summed up above, but are well worth reading in the original: **Weir,** *An Introduction to Tort Law*, **2nd edn (Clarendon Press, 2006), ch 9**. He takes the view that the torts discussed here are very different in function from the tort of negligence that we are just about to look at in detail. The trespass torts are concerned with vindicating rights; negligence is concerned with compensating for harm. For similar views, see **Peter Cane, 'Justice and justifications for tort liability' (1982) 2** *Oxford Journal of Legal Studies* **30**; and **Jason Varuhas, 'A tort-based approach to damages under the Human Rights Act 1998' (2009) 72** *Modern Law Review* **750**.

Visit **www.mylawchamber.co.uk/mcbride** to access tools to help you develop and test your knowledge of Tort law, including interactive multiple choice questions, practice exam questions with guidance, weblinks, legal newsfeed, additional case summaries, legal updates and tips on answering problem and essay questions.

3 The Human Rights Act 1998

3.1   The basics 69

3.2   Direct effect 74

3.3   Indirect effect 85

Overview

In this chapter, we will be looking at the effects of the Human Rights Act 1998; both its direct effect – making it unlawful for public authorities to act in ways that are incompatible with the rights found in the European Convention on Human Rights and creating the possibility for claimants to obtain damages under s 8 of the Act where they are victims of incompatible acts – and its indirect effects – obliging judges to interpret statutes as far as possible to make them compatible with the rights found in the European Convention on Human Rights and pressuring the UK courts to develop the common law.

3.1 THE BASICS

English law has had a law on human rights as long as it has had a law of tort. That is because most of the rights that tort law recognises us as having are enjoyed by us by virtue of our humanity. The reason why we have rights under the law of trespass not to be touched without our consent, and not to be threatened with imminent violence, and not to be falsely imprisoned is because our basic dignity as human beings means that it would be wrong to treat us in those ways. And the reason why the English law of tort developed *beyond* the law of trespass was because the law of trespass – with its emphasis on the direct interference with another's person – was inadequate to give effect to the full range of rights that our humanity deserves. Of course, there are some rights that tort law gives us that cannot be said to rest on our basic dignity as human beings; for example, rights emerging out of 'assumptions of responsibility' by one person to another.[1] But if we ask, in relation to most of the rights we have under the law, 'Why do we have *these* rights, and not some inferior set of rights?' the answer will invariably be, 'Because all human beings should have at least *these* rights.'

Perhaps it sounds odd to claim that the law of tort, for the most part, rests on a vision of what human rights we have.[2] If it does sound surprising then this is probably due to the

---

[1] See below, §§ 6.10–6.11.

[2] The idea occasionally peeps through in the caselaw, such as *Ilott v Wilkes* (1820) 3 B & Ald 304, 106 ER 674, holding that an occupier of premises who sets a spring gun on his premises to deter trespassers must give trespassers as much notice as possible of the existence of the spring gun on the ground that 'Humanity requires that the fullest notice possible should be given, and the law of England will not sanction what is inconsistent with humanity' (per Best J, at 319 (B & Ald), 680 (ER)). Also the great judgment of Lord Mansfield in *Somerset v Stewart* (1772) Lofft 1, 98 ER 499, holding that a slave who has arrived in England cannot be held against his will by his purported master: 'The state of slavery is . . . so odious, that nothing can be suffered to support it, but positive law. Whatever inconveniences, therefore, may follow from a decision, I cannot say this case is allowed or approved by the law of England . . .' (at 19 (Lofft), 510 (ER)).

fact that when the language of 'human rights' entered popular culture[3] the human rights concerned were primarily thought of as rights that individuals had, or ought to have had, against their governments. Thus in the 1970s dissidents in Eastern Europe argued that their governments were violating their 'human rights', and anti-Communist politicians and journalists in the West beat out a similar message. Similarly, when in the 1980s, politicians and journalists on the left also started talking the language of human rights, it was usually to argue that governments in the West were also guilty of human rights violations, particularly in relation to the way intelligence agencies and police forces operated. Of course since then the language of human rights has been used in a much wider range of contexts. Indeed, today it is plausible to argue that 'if the discourse of peacetime global society can be said to have a common moral language, it is that of human rights.'[4] But it is still the case that most of the plethora of pleas, demands and complaints, which are made using the language of human rights are directed at governments. Nonetheless, while this means that we most often *hear* human rights invoked in contexts where the key issue is the relationship between individuals and their governments, there is no reason why we cannot acknowledge that most of the rights that individuals have against other individuals are similarly founded on the equal dignity and freedom of all human beings. Moreover, as we will see, there are important connections between the rights that individuals can invoke against their governments and the rights that they can rely on in a tort claim.

For your purposes, the most important document on human rights that you have to know about is the European Convention on Human Rights (or 'ECHR', for short). This Convention was drawn up in 1950, in the aftermath of the Second World War, and set out a number of different 'human rights' that states signing the Convention pledged to observe. They include the right to life (Article 2), the right not to be subjected to torture or to inhuman and degrading treatment (Article 3), the right not to be enslaved or compelled to perform forced labour (Article 4), the right to liberty and security of person (Article 5), the right to a fair trial (Article 6), the right not to be retrospectively convicted of committing an offence (Article 7), the right to respect for private and family life (Article 8), the right to freedom of thought, conscience and religion (Article 9), the right to freedom of expression (Article 10), the right to freedom of peaceful assembly and freedom of association (Article 11), the right to marry (Article 12), the right not to be discriminated against in the enjoyment of the other rights and freedoms (Article 14), the right to peaceful enjoyment of possessions (First Protocol, Article 1), the right to education (First Protocol, Article 2), and the right to free elections (First Protocol, Article 3).

All the member states of what is called the 'Council of Europe' are signatories to the ECHR. This now comprises 47 states – virtually all of the European states, including Russia and other states from the former Soviet Union. Importantly, the ECHR is not a product of the European Union (comprising 27 states) – a point sometimes lost on journalists who regularly ascribe responsibility for decisions of the European Court of Human Rights

---

[3] It is not easy to date when the notion of 'human rights' entered general discourse. Thus while the United Nations proclaimed the Universal Declaration of Human Rights in 1948, George Orwell's classic anti-totalitarian work *1984* – written in the same year – contains plenty of references to humanity, the importance of 'staying human' and the significance of the 'human mind' as vehicle for grasping and hanging onto the truth; but not one reference to 'human rights'. Many commentators would argue that the relevant date was during the 1970s: for example, Moyn 2010 reports (at p 4) that in 1977 the *New York Times* used the phrase 'human rights' approximately five times more frequently than in any previous year.

[4] Beitz 2009, 2.

(ECtHR) to the European Union.[5] Students should be careful not to fall into the same error. The ECtHR – which sits in Strasbourg, France – is a wholly different institution from the Court of Justice, often called the European Court of Justice by English lawyers,[6] which sits in Luxembourg and interprets and applies the law of the European Union.

Although English lawyers played a large part in drafting the original text of the ECHR, there are two major inconsistencies between that text and the centuries-old understanding of what human rights we enjoy against each other that was developed under the English law of tort.

(1) *Exigibility*. The ECHR only imposes obligations on the states that have signed it. It does not impose obligations, directly, on private individuals. This is understandable. The lawyers who drafted the ECHR had in mind the state-sponsored atrocities that took place in Nazi Germany after 1933, and wanted to put the ECHR in place to prevent such atrocities ever taking place again. But the idea of human rights only being exigible against the state is a paradoxical one, and one that did not form part of the traditional understanding of human rights as developed under the English law of tort. On that understanding, the rights we were given by the English law of tort were exigible against everyone.

(2) *Acts and omissions*. The ECHR – as it has been subsequently interpreted by the ECtHR – not only imposes *negative* obligations on the states who are bound by it not to do something positive that would violate someone's rights under the ECHR, such as the right to life (Article 2), or the right not to be subjected to torture or to inhuman or degrading treatment or punishment (Article 3). It also imposes *positive* obligations on signatory states to take reasonable steps to protect people's rights under the ECHR, such as the right to life, and the right not to be subjected to inhuman or degrading treatment. So a state – or representative of the state – that fails to respond adequately to reports that it has received that *Bethan* is in imminent danger of being killed by an ex-boyfriend, or that *Benedict* is being sexually abused by his parents, may be found to have violated their rights under the ECHR as a result of its failure to act. The idea that we might have a human right to be saved from harm by the state, or by its representatives, is inconsistent with the English law of tort's traditional understanding of what rights we have against each other. That understanding is summed up by the old saying: 'Not doing is no trespass'. Under the law of trespass, if you did not do anything, you could not be found to have done anything wrong to anyone else. While the law of tort expanded beyond the law of trespass, it never abandoned the idea that, absent special circumstances, there is nothing wrong with failing to save someone else from harm. Even today, strangers are allowed to walk past people lying unconscious in the street without any legal sanction at all.

---

[5] For example, the *Yorkshire Post* of 3 November 2010 carried the headline: 'EU court ruling means prisoners will have right to vote'. The article under the headline referred to a 2005 decision of the European Court of Human Rights – *Hirst v UK (No 2)* (2006) 42 EHRR 41 – that a blanket ban on prisoners being allowed to vote was inconsistent with Article 3 of the First Protocol to the ECHR. (Article 3 provides that 'The High Contracting Parties undertake to hold free elections at reasonable intervals by secret ballot, under conditions which will ensure the free expression of the opinion of the people in the choice of the legislature.') The same mistake was made in a comment piece by Jenny McCartney, a columnist for the *Daily Telegraph*, which appeared on the Telegraph website on 27 November 2010: she criticised the same decision under the headline 'Europe has got too big for its boots', and said that the decision 'chimes . . . with the popular feeling that the European Union is increasingly overstepping the mark . . .'.

[6] Officially, the Court of Justice is one of three parts of an institution called the Court of Justice of the European Union.

These inconsistencies between the ECHR and the indigenous understanding of what rights we have proved relatively unproblematic for the first 45 years of the ECHR's existence. This is because the ECHR was unenforceable in UK courts. So the UK courts only had to apply one understanding – the indigenous understanding – of what rights we have against each other when deciding whether or not a particular defendant had wronged a particular claimant. If an individual wanted to complain that the United Kingdom had not granted her the rights that it undertook to provide when it signed the ECHR then she had to head to Strasbourg, and bring a claim against the United Kingdom there, before the ECtHR. That all changed with the enactment of the Human Rights Act 1998 ('HRA' for short), which made the ECHR enforceable in UK courts, and came into effect on 2 October 2000.

The *direct* effect of the HRA is to make it unlawful (under s 6) for 'a public authority to act in a way which is incompatible with a Convention right' and to confer on the courts the power (under s 8) to 'grant such relief or remedy, or make such order, within its powers as it considers just and appropriate' when a public authority has acted in a way which was incompatible with a Convention right. As a result, a claimant who wants to sue a public body in an English court for damages for something it has done after 2 October 2000 need no longer rely exclusively on the law of tort to bring her claim; she could try instead to argue that the public body has violated her rights under the ECHR and obtain a remedy that way. In cases where a public body is merely guilty of an omission – a failure to save the claimant from harm – this is a boon for claimants. As we will see,[7] claimants cannot normally sue a public body for an omission under the law of tort, but as we have just seen, it *is* possible in certain circumstances for claimants to argue that a public body has violated their Convention rights through a mere omission.

The *indirect* effects of the HRA have been twofold. First, in situations where the scope of tort law depends on statutes the UK courts are now obliged to interpret those statutes, so far as it is possible to do so, to make them compatible with Convention rights.[8] Secondly, in situations where the rules of tort law are part of the common law the courts have been put under pressure to develop and reshape those rules to make them more 'Convention-friendly'. This pressure takes a variety of different forms.

(1) *Negative obligations.* Under s 6(3) of the HRA, 'a court or tribunal' counts as a 'public authority' for the purposes of s 6 of the HRA. This has the effect of subjecting UK courts to the ECHR, including the *negative* obligations it imposes on states not to do something *positive* that would violate someone's rights under the ECHR. So, since the HRA was enacted, the UK courts have had to be careful not to decide tort cases in a way that could allow the losing party to say that the court directly violated his rights under the ECHR in the way it decided the case. The courts have been particularly mindful, in the way they decide tort cases, of the possibilities: (i) that, by dismissing a claimant's claim too peremptorily, they might violate the claimant's rights under Article 6 of the ECHR to 'a fair and public hearing' in 'the determination of his civil rights and obligations'; and (ii) that, by sanctioning something a defendant has said, or by preventing through an injunction a defendant from saying something he wants to say, they might violate the defendant's rights under Article 10 to 'freedom of expression'. How the courts have reacted to these possibilities will be discussed further below.

---

[7] See below, chapter 7.
[8] HRA, s 3.

(2) *Positive obligations*. Because 'a court or tribunal' counts as a 'public authority' for the purposes of s 6 of the HRA, it has been argued that the HRA has the effect of imposing on the courts the *positive* obligations that the ECHR imposes on states to take reasonable steps to protect people's enjoyment of the rights they have under the ECHR. Some have argued that the courts are, as a result, legally required under the HRA to develop and expand the law of tort to give greater protection (in tort) to the rights that people are granted by the ECHR.[9] If this view is correct – and one of us is very firmly of the view that it is not[10] (and the other fully agrees) – then it might be argued that the courts are duty-bound under the HRA to revise the well-established tort rule that absent special circumstances there is no liability for omissions, at least in cases where life or freedom from cruel treatment is at stake. The argument is based on the premise that the existence of such a rule means that the law of tort is not doing as much it could and should to protect people's rights to life and to be free from cruel treatment under the ECHR, and that therefore the courts are in breach of their obligations under the HRA by maintaining such a rule.

While the judges might deny this, it is hard to avoid the impression that it was arguments such as these that led them, soon after the enactment of the HRA, to sweep away the traditional tort law rule that there is no free-standing right not to have one's privacy invaded, with the result that the legal protection for people's Article 8 rights 'to respect for [their] private and family life, [their] home and [their] correspondence' was considerably enhanced.[11]

(3) *Pressure for harmony*. Even in situations where the courts are not obliged to develop the law in some way it would be surprising if the courts did not feel some awkwardness or embarrassment when faced by a claimant who can sue a defendant under the HRA but not under the law of tort. If tort law cannot help those who have been badly treated or let down by public officials or state institutions then this tends to make the homegrown law of tort seem fusty and undeveloped compared with the newer and more vigorous HRA. If the claimant's rights were actually violated (as a claim under the HRA demonstrates), why does the law of tort not recognise this?

For example, in *Van Colle v Chief Constable of Hertfordshire Police* (2009), it was argued that in a case where the police had failed to save someone from being killed or seriously injured by an attacker, the House of Lords should eliminate any distinction between the law of negligence and the HRA and allow the police to be sued in negligence if the police's failure to act violated the deceased's right to life under Article 2 of the ECHR. With the notable exception of Lord Bingham, the House of Lords rejected this argument. Lord Bingham argued that:

> one would ordinarily be surprised if conduct which violated a fundamental right or freedom of the individual did not find a reflection in a body of law ordinarily as sensitive to human needs as the common law . . . I agree . . . that 'where a common law duty covers the same ground as a Convention right, it should, so far as practicable, develop in harmony with it.'[12]

Lord Bingham argued that harmony would be achieved in this case if the common law adopted a 'liability principle' which said that

---

[9] See, in particular, Hunt 1998.
[10] See Bagshaw 2011b.
[11] See below, chapter 21.
[12] [2009] 1 AC 225, at [58], quoting Rimer LJ in *Smith v Chief Constable of Sussex Police* [2008] EWCA Civ 39, at [45].

if a member of the public (A) furnishes a police officer (B) with apparently credible evidence that a third party whose identity and whereabouts are known presents a specific and imminent threat to his life or physical safety, B owes A a duty [under the law of negligence] to take reasonable steps to assess such threat and, if appropriate, take reasonable steps to prevent it being executed.[13]

There was no precedent in English law for the existence of such a principle: it was proposed that it be adopted purely and simply to bring the common law into harmony with the right under Article 2 of the ECHR.

The other Law Lords rejected Lord Bingham's arguments, with Lord Hope holding that 'the common law, with its own system of limitation periods and remedies, should be allowed to stand on its own feet side by side with the alternative remedy [under the HRA].'[14] But the fact that the majority thought that there was no *necessity* to bring the law of tort into harmony with the right under Article 2 does not mean that other judges will not be subject to *pressure* to make other parts of the law of tort harmonious with other Convention rights.

3.2 DIRECT EFFECT

Section 6(1) of the HRA makes it unlawful for a 'public authority to act in a way which is incompatible with a Convention right', except where s 6(2) applies. So: if A, a public authority, acts in a way which is incompatible with a 'Convention right' in circumstances where s 6(2) does not apply and B suffers loss as a result, B may be able to claim damages from A under s 8 of the 1998 Act in respect of that loss. This raises a number of issues which we will deal with in this section.

A. Public authority

The HRA does not define what a 'public authority' is. It states that courts and tribunals *are* 'public authorities',[15] and that neither of the Houses of Parliament, nor any person exercising functions in connection with proceedings in Parliament, is a 'public authority'.[16] Beyond these classes, however, the Act merely provides that the term 'public authority' *includes* 'any person certain of whose functions are functions of a public nature'[17] *but* that such a person will not be a 'public authority' by virtue only of this provision 'if the nature of the act is private'.[18]

After reading this provision it might be thought that the question whether A is a 'person certain of whose functions are functions of a public nature' is the principal test for whether A is a 'public authority'. This, however, is not what Parliament intended.[19] Parliament intended that there should be two classes of 'public authorities'. First, there are *core* or *pure* public authorities, such as government departments, local authorities, the police and the

---

[13] [2009] 1 AC 225, at [44].

[14] [2009] 1 AC 225, at [82].

[15] HRA, s 6(3)(a). The special problems arising from liability for judicial acts are discussed below, at § 3.2(G).

[16] Section 6(3)(b).

[17] ibid.

[18] Section 6(5).

[19] When interpreting a statute it is Parliament's intention which is crucial. Here, however, the best evidence of Parliament's intentions is the statements of government ministers who were involved in steering the HRA onto the statute book.

armed forces,[20] which are treated as 'public authorities' for *all* activities. Secondly, there are *hybrid* or *functional* authorities, which are only treated as 'public authorities' with regard to acts which are part of their public functions, as opposed to acts of a private nature.[21] In the parliamentary debates leading to the passing of the 1998 Act, Railtrack plc[22] was regularly used as an example of a *hybrid* or *functional* authority. Thus the Lord Chancellor suggested that Railtrack would have to act compatibly with 'Convention rights' when carrying out its *public* functions in relation to safety, but not when performing *private* acts as a property developer.[23] The Home Secretary identified the churches and the governing bodies of certain sports as further authorities which might be treated as *hybrid*.[24] Another example might be a private security company which provides services to corporate clients (private acts) and also runs a 'private' prison (public function).

How do the courts determine whether a body is a *core* or *pure* 'public authority'? In *Aston Cantlow* v *Wallbank* (2004), Lord Nicholls said that the 'nature' of such bodies was 'governmental', and that factors leading to such a classification were likely to include 'the possession of special powers, democratic accountability, public funding in whole or in part, an obligation to act only in the public interest, and a statutory constitution'.[25] As we noted above, examples of *core* public authorities include government departments, local authorities, the police and the armed forces.

The test for whether a body is a *hybrid* public authority, because some of its functions are 'of a public nature', has proved more difficult for judges to agree on. In *Aston Cantlow* v *Wallbank* (2004), Lord Nicholls concluded that 'there is no single test of universal application' which can determine whether a particular function is 'of a public nature' because of 'the diverse nature of governmental functions and the variety of means by which these functions are discharged today'.[26] He went on, however, to identify several *relevant* factors, and subsequent cases have also adopted a 'factor-based' approach. Within such an approach

---

[20] These are the examples given by Lord Nicholls in *Aston Cantlow and Wilmcote with Billesley Parochial Church Council* v *Wallbank* (henceforth '*Aston*') [2004] 1 AC 546, at [7].

[21] In *Aston* the two classes are referred to (at [11]) as 'core public authorities' and 'hybrid public authorities'. But in its reports the Joint Committee on Human Rights, *The Meaning of Public Authority under the Human Rights Act, Seventh Report of the Session 2003–4* (HL Paper 39, HC 382) and *The Meaning of Public Authority under the Human Rights Act, Ninth Report of the Session 2006–7* (HL Paper 77, HC 410), prefers the terms 'pure' and 'functional'. For evidence that two classes were intended see, for example, Lord Irvine of Lairg LC, Hansard (HL Debates), 24 November 1997, col. 784, 'There are obvious public authorities . . . which are covered in relation to the whole of their functions by [s 6(1)]. Then there are some bodies some of whose functions are public and some private. If there are some public functions the body qualifies as a public authority but not in respect of acts which are of a private nature.' See also Jack Straw MP, Home Secretary, Hansard (HC Debates), 16 February 1998, col 775.

[22] The private company in which the infrastructure of the railway system was vested after privatisation. In 2001, Railtrack was put into administration, changed its name, and was purchased by Network Rail Ltd.

[23] Hansard (HL Debates), 24 November 1997, col 784. Many of Railtrack's duties relating to the *regulation* of safety were removed by the Railways (Safety Case) Regulations 2000 (SI 2000/2688) and in *Cameron* v *Network Rail Infrastructure Ltd* [2007] 1 WLR 163 Sir Michael Turner held that the company was not *thereafter* a 'public authority' under the Human Rights Act.

[24] Hansard (HC Debates), 20 May 1998, col 1020. At col 1017 he stated that 'the two most obvious examples' of churches carrying out *public* functions 'relate to marriages and to the provision of education in Church schools'. Despite pressure Parliament did not exclude churches from the scope of s 6 but instead sought to allay concerns by accepting the amendment which became s 13 of the HRA. In *Aston* the House of Lords confirmed that parochial church councils, an emanation of the Church of England, were a hybrid body.

[25] *Aston*, at [7]. He drew attention to Oliver 2000, where it is suggested (at 492) that the test for a *core* public authority should 'place emphasis on whether it enjoys special powers and authority, and whether it is under constitutional duties to act only in the public interest which are "enforceable", *inter alia*, via mechanisms of democratic accountability'.

[26] *Aston*, at [12].

'[a] number of factors may be relevant, but none is likely to be determinative on its own and the weight of different factors will vary from case to case'.[27] Note, the question whether a particular function is 'of a public nature' can be important in two ways: (1) a body cannot be a *hybrid* or functional public authority *at all* unless *at least one* of its functions is 'of a public nature'; and (2) even if at least one of its functions is of a public nature such a body will cease to be a public authority when it is performing a private act, and an act is unlikely to be classified as 'private' if it is central to the performance of one of its public functions.[28]

So what factors are relevant to determine if a function is 'of a public nature'? To answer this question it is necessary to look in detail at the case of *YL v Birmingham City Council* (2008), where the House of Lords had to decide whether Southern Cross Healthcare Ltd (SCH), a private company operating a care home for profit, was performing a function 'of a public nature' by providing YL, an elderly sufferer from Alzheimer's disease, with residential care in its care home. Most of the fees for this care were being paid by Birmingham City Council, which had a statutory duty to 'make arrangements for providing' residential care for YL. Thus the case raised the more general question of whether companies and charities delivering services under contracts with pure public authorities, particularly local government bodies, are *hybrid* or *functional* 'public authorities'.[29] A majority of the House of Lords held that SCH, when caring for YL, was not carrying out 'functions of a public nature'.[30]

One factor which Lord Nicholls identified as relevant in *Aston Cantlow v Wallbank* was 'the extent to which in carrying out the relevant function the body is publicly funded'.[31] But while the majority in the *YL* case accepted that 'public funding' was relevant, they thought that it was important to distinguish between a company which was seeking to make a profit by receiving a commercial fee under a contract with a public authority and a company receiving a 'subsidy' from public funds.[32] A 'subsidy' would point towards the body carrying out 'functions of a public nature' while obtaining a commercial fee from a public source, equal to what a private client would be charged for the same service, would not.

The majority in the *YL* case also agreed with Lord Nicholls that a second relevant factor was 'the extent to which in carrying out the relevant function the body ... is exercising statutory powers'.[33] Indeed the majority treated the fact that SCH enjoyed no special powers as particularly significant in the *YL* case, because SCH provided similar residential care for both publicly-funded and privately-funded clients, and it would be anomalous if the nature of its function changed from client to client.[34]

---

[27] *YL v Birmingham City Council* (henceforth, '*YL*') [2008] 1 AC 95, at [5] (per Lord Bingham). Although Lord Bingham was in the minority with regard to the outcome of this appeal his general description of a 'factor-based' approach is *not* what divided the House of Lords. The matters which did divide the court are discussed in the next paragraphs of the text.

[28] There is no simple answer to the question how closely connected with a 'public function' an act must be in order to prevent it from being a 'private act'.

[29] Important cases *before* the *YL* case included *Poplar Housing and Regeneration Community Association Ltd v Donoghue* [2002] QB 48 and *R (Heather) v Leonard Cheshire Foundation* [2002] 2 All ER 936. These were criticised in Craig 2002 and by the Joint Committee on Human Rights, *The Meaning of Public Authority under the Human Rights Act, Seventh Report of the Session 2003–4* (HL Paper 39, HC 382), paras 16–17: 'A serious gap has opened in the protection which the Human Rights Act was intended to offer.'

[30] The majority comprised Lord Scott, Lord Mance and Lord Neuberger. Lord Bingham and Baroness Hale dissented.

[31] *Aston*, at [12].

[32] *YL*, at [27] (per Lord Scott), [105] (per Lord Mance), [165] (per Lord Neuberger).

[33] *Aston*, at [12] (per Lord Nicholls); *YL*, at [28] (per Lord Scott), [102] (per Lord Mance), [160] (per Lord Neuberger).

[34] *YL*, at [117]–[119] (per Lord Mance), [151] (per Lord Neuberger).

Two further factors identified by Lord Nicholls in *Aston Cantlow* v *Wallbank* were 'the extent to which in carrying out the relevant function the body . . . is taking the place of central government or local authorities, or is providing a public service'.[35] The majority in the *YL* case, however, were cautious about how these factors might be understood. In particular they thought that very little weight could be attached to the fact that a function had previously been performed by a *core* public authority, or could have been performed by a *core* public authority instead of being 'contracted out'. Lord Mance argued that the fact that a function was sometimes performed by *core* public authorities did not establish that it was a '*public* function' because the HRA applies to *all* functions, public or private, when they are performed by *core* public authorities,[36] and Lord Neuberger drew attention to the wide range of functions undertaken by *core* public authorities.[37] In contrast, the minority in the *YL* case attached considerable importance to whether the state had 'assumed responsibility' for seeing that a particular task was performed[38] and to whether it was in the public interest for it to be performed, something that might be demonstrated by the task being regulated by the state. But the majority doubted the significance of both regulation[39] and 'the public interest' in a service being performed.[40] The minority also attached more significance than the majority to whether the improper performance of a function was likely to lead to the violation of an individual's 'Convention rights'.[41]

In summary, we can see that for the majority the most important two factors were: (a) whether the body received public funding, particularly by way of a grant or subsidy rather than through charging a market-rate for its services; and (b) whether the body was exercising any special statutory powers. The majority also accepted that three further factors were relevant, though it attached less importance to them than the minority would have done: (c) whether the task had previously been done by a core public authority, or might otherwise have had to be done by such an authority; (d) the public interest in the task being performed, often demonstrated by its performance being regulated; and (e) whether the task being done improperly was likely to lead to a person's human rights being violated.

Standing back, we think that it is possible to describe the majority in the *YL* case as having concentrated on how a function might appear from the perspective of the body performing it, while the minority focused on the perspective of the person whose 'Convention rights' were at stake. Thus SCH probably would have described its function as to provide a service under a contract for a commercial fee, while YL's relatives probably would have described her as a vulnerable person receiving the essential care which it is the state's responsibility to provide. It seems to us that the wording of the Act does not indicate which of these perspectives should be decisive, and as a result many arguments about the

---

[35] *Aston*, at [12].

[36] *YL*, at [110] (per Lord Mance), 'it is a fallacy to regard all functions and activities of a core public authority as inherently public in nature', citing Oliver 2004.

[37] *YL*, at [144] (per Lord Neuberger), 'Apart from anything else, there must be scarcely an activity which cannot be carried out by some core public authority.' See also [30] (per Lord Scott).

[38] *YL*, at [7] and [15] (per Lord Bingham), [66] (per Baroness Hale).

[39] *YL*, at [116] (per Lord Mance), 'Regulation by the state is no real pointer towards the person regulated being a state or governmental body or a person with a function of a public nature, if anything perhaps the contrary.' See also [134] (per Lord Neuberger). To the contrary, [9] (per Lord Bingham).

[40] *YL*, at [134] (per Lord Neuberger): 'The fact that a service can fairly be said to be to the public benefit cannot mean, as a matter of language, that it follows that providing the service itself is a function of a public nature. Nor does it follow as a matter of logic or policy. Otherwise, the services of all charities, indeed, it seems to me, of all private organizations which provide services which could be offered by charities, would be caught by section 6(1).' To the contrary, [67] (per Baroness Hale).

[41] *YL*, at [11] (per Lord Bingham), [71] (per Baroness Hale).

issue are primarily about whether it would be better for the HRA to apply more broadly or more narrowly.[42] Indeed the actual result in the *YL* case was subsequently reversed by Parliament,[43] but without overturning the majority's *approach* to the general issue.[44]

Even if a body will sometimes be a *hybrid* public authority, because *some* of its functions are 'of a public nature', it may still be necessary to consider whether the particular 'act' that is alleged to be incompatible with a Convention right is 'private', because s 6(5) HRA 1998 provides that a body will not count as a *hybrid* public authority 'if the nature of the act is private'.[45]

This issue caused considerable disagreement in the Court of Appeal in *R (Weaver)* v *London & Quadrant Housing Trust* (2010), where the defendant was a registered social landlord and the claim arose out of it seeking possession from a tenant who had not paid her rent.[46] All the parties accepted that registered social landlords have *some* functions 'of a public nature', since they have special statutory powers with regard to anti-social behaviour and the like. But since the defendant had not exercised any of these special powers against the claimant their existence clearly did not determine whether seeking possession for non-payment of rent was a 'private' act, and consequently outside the scope of the HRA 1998.

A majority in the Court of Appeal suggested that a decision as to whether an act is 'private' can be divided into two stages. First, it must be determined if the act was 'in pursuance of, or at least connected with, performance of functions of a public nature'.[47] This means that the 'factor based' approach from *Aston* and *YL* must be applied to the particular function that the act was connected with in order to decide if *that* function was 'of a public nature'. Secondly, the degree of connection between the act and the function must be determined. Thus an act which was 'inextricably linked' to a function 'of a public nature' will be a public act, while an act which was 'purely incidental or supplementary' to that function may still be 'private'.[48] In the particular case the majority concluded that 'management of social housing' by a registered social landlord was a function 'of a public nature' – emphasising that registered social landlords receive a significant subsidy from public sources and enter 'allocation agreements' which give local authorities substantial control over who obtains tenancies – and the act of terminating the claimant's tenancy was

---

[42] Palmer 2008 argues, at 602, that there was a 'fundamental policy and ideological difference between the majority and the minority judges' in the *YL* case as to whether 'social welfare' was 'considered a responsibility of the government in the United Kingdom'. Her article concludes, however, with a series of general reasons why it would be beneficial for the HRA to apply more broadly (at 604): 'Considering the intention of the HRA "to bring rights home," the decision in *YL* is disappointing. It will not encourage a culture of human rights to flourish but, rather, will excuse private institutions and actors that exercise public functions from fully implementing basic human rights standards. Human rights values must traverse the public–private divide if there is to be a change of culture in institutions delivering public services.'

[43] Health and Social Care Act 2008, s 145(1).

[44] The UK Parliament's Joint Committee on Human Rights has been critical of the approach adopted by the majority in the *YL* case (see its reports *The Meaning of Public Authority under the Human Rights Act, Seventh Report of the Session 2003–4* (HL Paper 39, HC 382) and *The Meaning of Public Authority under the Human Rights Act, Ninth Report of the Session 2006–7* (HL Paper 77, HC 410)). For an impressive academic analysis of the issues from a comparative perspective see Donnelly 2007.

[45] This makes it very important to distinguish between *core* and *hybrid* public authorities: *all* of the acts of *core* public authorities must be compatible with Convention rights (unless s 6(2) applies), but the *private* acts of *hybrid* public authorities fall outside the HRA 1998.

[46] The claimant alleged that the defendant had violated her right to respect for private and family life under Article 8.

[47] [2010] 1 WLR 363, at [95] (per Lord Collins). The two judges in the majority differed in the importance they attached to this issue: Elias LJ thought that it was highly relevant to the classification of the relevant act while Lord Collins thought that it was an 'essential pre-requisite' to a conclusion that the act was 'public'.

[48] See [76] (per Elias LJ) and [102] (per Lord Collins).

sufficiently linked to that function to make it a public act. They suggested, however, that other acts, such as terminating a contract with a window-cleaner or builder, would be very likely to be classified as 'private', because they would be far less closely connected to the public functions of the landlord.[49]

B. When will a public authority act inconsistently with a Convention right?

The scope of this book does not allow us to deal with this issue comprehensively or in detail; the interested reader should consult a standard work on the HRA. However, a few preliminary points may be made here.

(1) *Convention rights*. The term 'Convention rights' refers to the rights and fundamental freedoms set out in Articles 2 to 12 and 14 of the ECHR and in Articles 1 to 3 of the First Protocol and Articles 1 to 2 of the Sixth Protocol.[50]

Many of these 'Convention rights' stretch beyond the interests currently protected by the law of tort. To pick two examples, there is no tort designed to protect directly a person's right to a fair trial (Article 6) or a person's right to marry (Article 12). Further, some of the 'Convention rights' offer greater protection for particular interests than is provided by the law of tort.[51] Consequently, it seems likely that there will be attempts to claim damages under s 8 of the HRA for violations of many, if not all, of these 'Convention rights'.[52]

(2) *Qualified rights*. It is important to bear in mind that not all of these rights are *absolute*. Many of the rights *expressly* permit restrictions, provided that such restrictions can be demonstrated to be 'prescribed by law' and 'necessary in a democratic society' in order to fulfil certain listed purposes. Where a public authority's act goes no further than a permitted restriction or interference it will not be incompatible with a 'Convention right'. Moreover, even some of the rights that are not *expressly* qualified, such as the right to a fair trial (Article 6), turn out not to make *absolute* demands when they are interpreted by the ECtHR.

(3) *Acts and omissions*. 'Failures to act' by a public authority are treated as 'acts' for the purpose of determining whether it has acted in a way which is incompatible with a 'Convention right'.[53] This provision is particularly important in those contexts where it has been held that the ECHR imposes a *positive* obligation on states to protect 'Convention rights'.

---

[49] See [76] (per Elias LJ) and [96] (per Lord Collins). The third judge, Rix LJ, doubted whether 'management' of social housing by registered social landlords was a function 'of a public nature' at all, and also thought that 'management' could be sub-divided so that even if 'allocation' of social housing was a 'public function' the termination of an individual tenancy was a 'private' act (see [160]).

[50] These articles are all set out in Sch 1 to the HRA.

[51] A good example is provided by Article 2, the right to life. In *Osman v United Kingdom* [1999] 1 FLR 193, the ECtHR held that Article 2 puts a broader duty on police to take steps to deal with threats to life by criminals than is imposed on the police by the common law. See also *Savage v South Essex Partnership NHS Foundation Trust* [2009] 1 AC 681 (staff in an NHS hospital where a patient has been detained pursuant to s 3 of the Mental Health Act 1983 to do all that can reasonably be expected to prevent the patient from committing suicide if they know or ought to know that there is a 'real and immediate' risk of the patient committing suicide, though the House of Lords thought that in such a case there would already be a common law duty of care: at [76] (per Lord Rodger) and [99] (per Baroness Hale)).

[52] Of course, in practice, some of the 'Convention rights' are violated by public authorities far more often than others.

[53] HRA, s 6(6).

For instance, in *Osman* v *United Kingdom* (1999), the European Court of Human Rights ('ECtHR' for short) ruled that Article 2 imposed a positive obligation on a state to protect an individual whose life was at risk from criminal acts, and that this included an obligation on the police to 'do all that could be reasonably expected of them to avoid a real and immediate risk to life of which they have or ought to have knowledge'.[54] Similarly, in *Z* v *United Kingdom* (2001), the ECtHR held that there was a parallel positive obligation under Article 3 on local authorities to take all steps that could reasonably be expected of them to avoid a real and immediate risk of ill-treatment of children of which they knew or ought to have had knowledge.[55] In *Anufrijeva* v *Southwark LBC* (2004), the Court of Appeal accepted that Article 8 also imposed a positive obligation which extended beyond the obligation under Article 3 where a family unit was involved.[56] The Court offered the following guidance on when inaction would constitute a lack of respect for private and family life:

> [T]here must be some ground for criticising the failure to act. There must be an element of culpability. At the very least there must be knowledge that the claimant's private and family life were at risk . . . Where the domestic law of a state imposes positive obligations in relation to the provision of welfare support, breach of those positive obligations of domestic law may suffice to provide the element of culpability necessary to establish a breach of article 8, provided that the impact on private or family life is sufficiently serious and was foreseeable.[57]

There is, however, an important exception to the rule that the HRA generally covers omissions as well as acts: s 6(6) makes it clear that a failure to introduce a proposal for legislation or to make a remedial order cannot be treated as an unlawful 'act'. So a Minister will not act unlawfully under the HRA if all he or she fails to do is to propose a Bill to better protect a Convention Right.

C. Section 6(2)

Section 6(2) of the 1998 Act provides that a public authority will not be liable for an act which violates a 'Convention right' if:

(a) as the result of one or more provisions of primary legislation, the authority could not have acted differently; or

(b) in the case of one or more provisions of, or made under, primary legislation which cannot be read or given effect in a way which is compatible with the Convention rights, the authority was acting so as to give effect to or enforce those provisions.

This provision means that a public authority cannot be liable for performing a statutory duty, even if this leads to a violation of a 'Convention right'. In such circumstances the most that a UK court will be able to do is to declare that the statutory provision is incompatible with a 'Convention right'. Similarly, a public authority will not be liable for enforcing or giving effect to an incompatible statute or delegated legislation, where that legislation

---

[54] [1999] 1 FLR 193, 223. On the facts, though, the European Court of Human Rights found that there had not been a violation of Article 2.

[55] [2001] 2 FLR 612, at [73].

[56] [2004] QB 1124, at [43]. The Court suggested that where only an individual's welfare was involved it was unlikely that Article 8 would require the State to provide positive support unless the individual's predicament was sufficiently severe to engage Article 3.

[57] [2004] QB 1124, at [45]. This passage clearly involves a jumble of conditions. It seems that the Court of Appeal intended that three elements should be relevant (the degree to which the public authority was at fault, whether the inaction breached a statutory duty, and the effect on the claimant) and that a decision whether there had been a breach of Article 8 should turn on the combined effect of these three elements.

cannot be given effect to in any way which is compatible. Of course, if it is possible to interpret the statute so that it does not impose a duty which will lead to the violation of a 'Convention right', or in such a way that it can be enforced or given effect without any such right being violated, then s 3 of the 1998 Act will oblige a UK court to adopt this interpretation,[58] and as a result the protection that s 6(2) might have provided for a public authority will evaporate.

D. The availability of remedies: victims

If a public authority has acted incompatibly with a 'Convention right' a claimant will only be able to obtain damages, or any other remedy, if he or she was a 'victim' of the public authority's unlawful act.[59] The HRA expressly relies on the definition of 'victim' developed in individual claims to the ECtHR under Article 34 of the ECHR.[60] A person will have no difficulty in establishing that she is a 'victim' if she has been 'directly affected' by the public authority's unlawful act. In certain circumstances, however, the ECtHR has also allowed claims by 'indirect victims', for instance, close relatives of a person whose right to life was violated.[61] Thus in *Savage v South Essex Partnership NHS Foundation Trust* (2010) Mackay J held that the adult daughter of a woman who committed suicide was a 'victim' of an NHS Hospital's violation of its positive obligation to protect her mother's life.[62]

Companies and other associations with legal personality can be 'victims',[63] but *core* public authorities cannot be.[64]

E. The quantification of damages: principles

Where a court finds that a public authority has acted incompatibly with a 'Convention right' it may only award damages if it is a type of court which can award damages in civil proceedings.[65]

Section 8(3) of the HRA states that a court should not award damages unless, taking account of all the circumstances of the case, it 'is satisfied that the award is necessary to afford just satisfaction to the person in whose favour it is made'.[66] In considering whether

---

[58] Discussed below, § 3.3(A).

[59] HRA, s 7(1). See, generally, Miles 2000.

[60] Section 7(7).

[61] In *Savage v South Essex Partnership NHS Foundation Trust* [2010] EWHC 865 (QB), at [91], Mackay J reported that decisions of the ECtHR have treated the range of relatives having 'the necessary standing to bring a claim based on an Article 2 violation' as including: 'siblings . . . ; parents . . . ; the . . . son of the deceased . . . ; and a nephew . . .' In *Van Colle v Chief Constable of the Hertfordshire Police* [2007] 1 WLR 1821, at [114], the Court of Appeal left open for 'future consideration' the question whether an 'indirect victim' can recover damages for his or her *own* losses, as opposed to obtaining an award as a representative of the 'direct victim'. The point is of some importance because in some cases – for instance, *Cameron v Network Rail Infrastructure Ltd* [2007] 1 WLR 163 – relatives of a person who has been killed have brought claims under the HRA in circumstances where they could not have successfully obtained damages under the Fatal Accidents Act 1976. For discussion of the relevant provisions of the Fatal Accidents Act 1976 see below, § 34.2.

[62] In *Rabone v Pennine Care NHS Trust* [2010] EWCA Civ 698, at [92], Jackson LJ stated that he agreed with Mackay J's conclusion on this point.

[63] Provided that the right that they are asserting is one which can be enjoyed by such a body.

[64] *Aston*, at [8]: 'A core public authority seems inherently incapable of satisfying the Convention description of a victim' (per Lord Nicholls).

[65] HRA, s 8(1). This is thought to prevent awards by magistrates and the Crown Court. The position of the Court of Appeal (Criminal Division) is unclear.

[66] See, generally, Fairgrieve 2001.

it is necessary to make such an award, and, if so, the amount, courts are instructed to 'take into account the principles applied by the European Court of Human Rights in relation to the award of compensation under Article 41 of the Convention'.[67] This instruction might seem relatively loose, since it is an instruction 'to take into account', not 'to follow'; and it refers to 'principles', not 'detailed practice'. But in *R (Greenfield)* v *Secretary of State for the Home Department* (2005) the House of Lords unanimously held that domestic courts should follow the Strasbourg court's guidance with regard to both *when* an award should be made and the *amount* because 'the purpose of incorporating the Convention in domestic law through the 1998 Act was not to give victims better remedies at home than they could recover in Strasbourg but to give them the same remedies without the delay and expense of resort to Strasbourg.'[68]

Before the HRA came into force the Law Commission carried out a survey of the 'principles' applied by the ECtHR,[69] and concluded that 'the only principle which is clearly stated in the Strasbourg caselaw is that of *restitutio in integrum*.'[70] That is: the victim should be returned, as far as possible, to the position that he or she would have been in had there not been a breach of a 'Convention right'. The Court of Appeal has described this as 'the fundamental principle' and has derived from it the proposition that 'where the breach of a Convention right has clearly caused significant pecuniary loss, this will usually be assessed and awarded'. But despite describing the *restitutio in integrum* principle as 'fundamental' the Court of Appeal went on to emphasise the further principle that, 'in considering whether to award compensation and, if so, how much, there is a balance to be drawn between the interests of the victim and those of the public as a whole'.[71] This means that the claimant's interest in receiving compensation must be weighed against the interest of the wider public in the continued funding of public services.

The Law Commission also identified five specific factors which appear to have been regularly taken into account by the ECtHR in determining whether or not to make an award of damages.[72]

(1) *A finding of a violation may constitute 'just satisfaction'.* Where an applicant has not suffered pecuniary loss as a result of a breach, the ECtHR has often concluded that the mere decision that there was a violation is sufficient to constitute 'just satisfaction'. This factor has been most influential in cases where convicted criminals have claimed that while they were being investigated or tried there were violations of a procedural type.[73]

(2) *The degree of loss suffered must be sufficient to justify an award of damages.* Although the ECtHR has generally been more willing to award damages for forms of mental distress

---

[67] Section 8(4).

[68] [2005] 1 WLR 673, [19]. This approach is strongly criticised by Varuhas 2009, who argues that damages under the HRA should instead be based on the principles used in the rest of English tort law.

[69] Law Com. No. 266, *Damages Under the Human Rights Act 1998* (2000).

[70] ibid, para 3.78.

[71] *Anufrijeva* v *Southwark LBC* [2004] QB 1124 at [56].

[72] Law Com. No. 266, para 4.44.

[73] In *R (Greenfield)* v *Secretary of State for the Home Department* [2005] 1 WLR 673, the House of Lords decided that no damages should be awarded to a prisoner whose Article 6 'Convention right' was violated when a deputy controller, who was not an independent and impartial tribunal, decided that he had committed a prison disciplinary offence. The court concluded, however, a procedural violation could lead to an award of damages if the violation led to the claimant being 'deprived of a real chance of a better outcome' (at [14]–[15]) or caused 'anxiety and frustration' (at [16]).

falling short of psychiatric injury than English courts dealing with tort claims, it has also usually insisted that something beyond mere annoyance or frustration must be shown before an award of damages will be appropriate.[74] Consistently with this, in *R (KB)* v *London and South and West Region Mental Health Review Tribunal* (2004), Stanley Burnton J concluded that mental health patients who had suffered frustration and distress because of inordinate delay in processing their claims to mental health review tribunals in violation of Article 5(4) were only entitled to compensation for significant distress, which he took to be distress at the level that might be recorded in clinical notes.

But while the ECtHR has been more willing to award damages for mental distress than English courts dealing with tort claims this difference is largely offset by the fact that the ECtHR does not tend to make awards for an invasion of a right *per se*. Thus English courts in tort claims often give damages for harms such as 'loss of liberty' without looking for any form of further *consequential* loss, while the ECtHR will in parallel situations only award damages for mental distress or other forms of *consequential* loss.[75]

In some circumstances, however, a loss may justify a 'symbolic' award. For example, in *Savage* v *South Essex Partnership NHS Foundation Trust* (2010) Mackay J made an award of £10,000 to the adult daughter of a mother who had committed suicide as a 'symbolic acknowledgment that the defendant ought properly to give her some compensation to reflect her loss'.[76]

(3) *The seriousness of the violation will be taken into account.* Generous awards have been made for both pecuniary and non-pecuniary losses where there has been a serious violation, for instance, deliberate torture.[77] At the same time, however, the ECtHR has expressly refused to award 'aggravated damages'[78] and 'exemplary damages'.[79] But it seems that despite this refusal the ECtHR does take account of 'aggravating features' in assessing damages, particularly for distress, anxiety and injury to feelings.

(4) *The conduct of the public authority may be taken into account.* This may include both the conduct giving rise to the claim and any record of previous violations by the state. Although the ECtHR has expressly refused to award 'exemplary damages' it tends to be more generous in compensating for non-pecuniary loss when the behaviour of the public authority in question has been particularly reprehensible[80] or forms part of a pattern of

---

[74] *Silver* v *United Kingdom* (1991) 13 EHRR 582. In *R (Greenfield)* v *Secretary of State for the Home Department* [2005] 1 WLR 673, the House of Lords did not suggest that feelings of 'anxiety and frustration' had to reach any particular pitch before an award of damages could be made *but* nonetheless refused to make an award to the claimant in the case confronting them. The court apparently attached weight to the facts that although the claimant had demonstrated 'structural bias' the conduct of the adjudication was exemplary and he was not treated in an unexpected way or differently from anyone else (see [29]).

[75] For further analysis of this distinction see Steele 2008, 630–634.

[76] [2010] EWHC 865 (QB), at [97]. In *Rabone* v *Pennine Care NHS Trust* [2010] EWCA Civ 698, at [107], Jackson LJ stated that he would have awarded £10,000 in total, £5000 to each parent, if he had found that a violation of Article 2 had led to their teenage daughter's suicide. In *Van Colle* v *Chief Constable of the Hertfordshire Police* [2007] 1 WLR 1821, at [97], the Court of Appeal awarded £7500 to each of the parents of a man who was killed as a result of what was held to be a violation of Article 2. The House of Lords overturned the conclusion that there had been a violation of Article 2: [2009] 1 AC 225.

[77] *Aksoy* v *Turkey* (1997) 23 EHRR 553.

[78] Discussed in Chapter 29, below.

[79] Discussed in Chapter 30, below.

[80] Two cases involving the United Kingdom provide good examples of this factor in action: *Halford* v *United Kingdom* (1997) 24 EHRR 523 (£10,000 awarded for stress caused by phone-tapping); *Smith and Grady* v *United Kingdom* (2000) 29 EHRR 493 (£19,000 awarded for non-pecuniary loss suffered as a result of investigation and dismissal from the armed forces because of sexual orientation).

violations.[81] In *Anufrijeva v Southwark LBC* (2004), the Court of Appeal treated the wording of s 8 as precluding an award of exemplary damages.[82]

The question has been asked whether a claimant will have to show that a breach of Convention rights was the result of a public authority's carelessness in order to claim damages.[83] The simple answer to this question must be 'no'. But the more detailed answer will add the qualifications that *in some circumstances* the claimant will have to show fault on the part of the public authority in order to establish that the authority acted incompatibly with a particular Convention right,[84] and *in some circumstances* the fault of the public authority may be decisive in demonstrating that an award of compensation is necessary as 'just satisfaction' and reflects the appropriate balance between the interests of the victim and those of the public as a whole.

(5) *The conduct of the applicant will be taken into account.* An award will be reduced where the applicant's conduct made a violation more likely or contributed to the damage suffered as a result of a violation.[85] There is also some evidence of a general reluctance to compensate criminals for violations of their 'Convention rights'.[86]

F. Quantification of damages: deciding the amount

The Law Commission's review concluded that

> in many cases – probably the majority of cases – the terms of section 8, read in the light of our review of the Strasbourg case-law, will not require [a court] awarding damages under the [HRA] to apply measures which are significantly different to those it would reach were the claim one in tort.[87]

But in *R (Greenfield) v Secretary of State for the Home Department* (2005), as we noted above, the House of Lords insisted that courts should look instead primarily to awards made by the ECtHR and 'should not aim to be significantly more or less generous than [that] court might be expected to be'.[88] Thus claimants usually present their claims by drawing comparisons with precedents from Strasbourg. Before the HRA came into force Lord Woolf also expressed the view, extra-judicially, that awards made by English courts

---

[81] Cases involving excessive length of legal proceedings in Italy provide the best example of this factor in action: Law Com. No. 266, paras 3.52–3.53.

[82] [2004] QB 1124, at [55]. The House of Lords has suggested, however, that one reason why an award of damages may be appropriate, rather than a finding of a violation being held to be just satisfaction, is if 'there is felt to be a need to encourage compliance [with their duties under the Convention] by individual officials or classes of official: *R (Greenfield) v Secretary of State for the Home Department* [2005] 1 WLR 673, at [19].

[83] Fairgrieve 2001, 698.

[84] For instance, where the Convention right imposes a positive obligation to take *reasonable* steps to protect someone's life under Article 2, a claimant will only be able to show that an omission to take steps was incompatible with Article 2 if it would have been *reasonable* to take such steps. In *Savage v South Essex Partnership NHS Foundation Trust* [2009] 1 AC 681, Baroness Hale suggested (at [100]) that in judging what steps it would have been reasonable to take to prevent someone from committing suicide it would be necessary to take into account the importance of that person's liberty and autonomy and the available resources.

[85] In *McCann v United Kingdom* (1996) 21 EHRR 97, the ECtHR found a violation of Article 2 (right to life) with respect to three IRA terrorists suspected of planning a bomb attack on Gibraltar, but refused to award compensation because of the applicants' behaviour.

[86] Law Com. No. 266, para. 3.57 discusses the different views on this matter.

[87] Law Com. No. 266, para 4.97. Similarly, in *Anufrijeva v Southwark LBC* [2004] QB 1124, Lord Woolf MR instructed courts making awards for kinds of harm not commonly compensated by common law damages to consider the level of awards for such harm commonly made by the Parliamentary Ombudsman and Local Government Ombudsman.

[88] [2005] 1 WLR 673, at [19].

under s 8 for non-pecuniary losses should be 'moderate',[89] and this comment has been judicially endorsed.[90]

G. Liability for judicial acts

Section 9(3) of the HRA states that 'In proceedings under this Act in respect of a judicial act done in good faith, damages may not be awarded otherwise than to compensate a person to the extent required by Article 5(5) of the Convention'. Article 5(5) provides that 'Everyone who has been the victim of arrest or detention in contravention of the provisions of this Article [5] shall have an enforceable right to compensation.' In practice, the ECtHR has not interpreted Article 5(5) as requiring that every victim of a violation of Article 5 must be awarded compensation. Indeed, the Strasbourg Court has often ruled that the finding that Article 5 was violated is itself sufficient 'just satisfaction'.

Section 9(3) may be important, however, in that it precludes an award of damages for a good faith violation by a judge of, for instance, Article 6 (right to a fair trial) or Article 8 (right to respect for private or family life). To an extent, it may be possible to circumvent this by attributing the violation to the act of some other public authority, for instance, a public prosecutor. This will not always be possible, however, because s 9(5) defines 'judicial act' as including 'an act done on the instructions, or on behalf, of a judge'.

H. Liability for legislative acts

For the avoidance of doubt it is worth stating that because the term 'public authority' does not include 'either House of Parliament or a person exercising functions in connection with proceedings in Parliament'[91] there will be no liability under s 8 of the HRA for the passing of legislation which violates a 'Convention right'. Further, because, as we noted above, 'act' does not include 'a failure to (a) introduce in, or lay before, Parliament a proposal for legislation, or (b) make any primary legislation or remedial order',[92] there will be no liability under s 8 of the HRA for a ministerial failure to correct legislation which violates a 'Convention right'.

3.3 INDIRECT EFFECT

We noted above that the indirect effect of the HRA is twofold. First, it obliges UK courts to interpret statutes in a particular way, and this can lead to those statutes giving rise to tort claims (or *not* giving rise to tort claims) in different circumstances from what would have been the case if the statutes had been interpreted literally. Secondly, the HRA has had an indirect effect on the common law of tort, by pressurising, or encouraging, UK courts to develop the common law. These indirect effects can best be understood by describing a situation where the obligation to interpret statutes might make a difference, and then by

---

[89] Woolf 2000, 434.

[90] *Anufrijeva* v *Southwark LBC* [2004] QB 1124, at [73]. Lord Woolf also stated extra-judicially that awards should be 'normally on the low side by comparison to tortious awards', but in the same paragraph that endorsed his view that awards should be 'moderate' the Court of Appeal said that the 'on the low side' comment 'should in future be ignored'. In *R (Greenfield)* v *Secretary of State for the Home Department* [2005] 1 WLR 673, [19], the House of Lords suggested that damages under the HRA might seem modest alongside tort awards because in HRA cases the finding of a violation would always be 'an important part' of a claimant's remedy.

[91] HRA, s 6(3)(b).

[92] Section 6(6).

looking at a few of the Articles of the ECHR in turn, and seeing what indirect effect those Articles have had on English common law since the HRA was enacted.

A. HRA, s 3(1)

This provision states that 'So far as it is possible to do so, primary legislation and subordinate legislation must be read and given effect in a way which is compatible with the Convention rights.' Consequently if, for example, a statute created a tort which appeared to restrict free expression to an unjustifiable extent, then a court which was asked by a claimant to apply that statute would have to consider whether it was possible to interpret the statute in some way that prevented it restricting free expression to this extent. Similarly, if a statutory tort offered some protection to a Convention right, but on a literal reading fell somewhat short of providing all the protection that the state was obliged to provide, then when asked to apply the statute a court would have to consider if it could be interpreted so as to provide the required protection.

An illustrative example, from a context outside tort law, is provided by *Thomas* v *Bridgend County Borough Council* (2011). In that case the claimants were seeking compensation under Part I of the Land Compensation Act 1973 for depreciation in the value of their houses attributable to noise and other nuisance from a newly built road, but a provision in the Act said that they could not obtain such compensation if the road concerned became 'maintainable at the public expense' more than three years after it opened. Unfortunately for the claimants the three year period had been exceeded in this case, but this was apparently because of delays by a developer, which had actually undertaken to indemnify the Council for any compensation which was payable under the Act. The Court of Appeal held that if the claimants were left without compensation for the loss they had suffered then this would violate their rights under Article 1 of the First Protocol (peaceful enjoyment of possessions) and to prevent this they interpreted the statute so that the three year limit did not apply in the circumstances. Carnwath LJ said that it was not necessary for the Court to determine exactly how the statute should be interpreted, but seemed inclined to read into it some provision preventing the three year limit from precluding a claim where the road 'should reasonably have become so maintainable within that period'.[93]

This example is particularly useful because it demonstrates that the UK courts regard an obligation to do what is 'possible' as permitting them to read new words into a statute.[94] There are, however, limits beyond which a judge should not go, though it is not easy to define them with any precision. One of the most commonly quoted explanations of the limits was provided by Lord Hope in *Bellinger* v *Bellinger* (2003): 'the obligation [imposed by s 3(1)], powerful though it is, is not to be performed without regard to its limitations. The obligation applies to the interpretation of legislation, which is the judges' function. It does not give them power to legislate.'[95]

---

[93] [2011] EWCA Civ 862, at [67]–[68].

[94] See also *Ghaidan* v *Godin-Mendoza* [2004] 2 AC 557, at [32] (per Lord Nicholls): 'Section 3 enables language to be interpreted restrictively or expansively. But section 3 goes further than this. It is also apt to require a court to read in words which change the meaning of the enacted legislation, so as to make it Convention-compliant. In other words, the intention of Parliament in enacting section 3 was that, to an extent bounded only by what is "possible", a court can modify the meaning, and hence the effect, of primary and secondary legislation.'

[95] [2003] 2 AC 467, at [67]. He was drawing on his own previous speech in *R* v *Lambert* [2002] 2 AC 545, at [79].

B. Pressure to develop the common law

We will now seek to illustrate the indirect effect that the HRA has had on the law of torts through pressurising, or encouraging, UK courts to develop the common law. We will do this by looking at a few of the Articles of the ECHR in turn, and seeing what indirect effect those Articles have had on English common law since the HRA was enacted.

(1) We start with *Article 2(1)*, which provides that:

> Everyone's right to life shall be protected by law. No one shall be deprived of his life intentionally ... [96]

This Article has not, so far, had much of an indirect effect on English tort law. As we have seen, in *Van Colle* v *Chief Constable of Hertfordshire Police* (2009), the House of Lords – with one exception – rejected an attempt to argue that the police's liabilities in negligence should be expanded so as to make them liable in negligence for failing to protect someone whom they know is in danger of being killed or injured by someone else. Given this, it seems doubtful that – for the time being at least – the courts will accept that their obligations under the Human Rights Act require them to modify the general rule in English tort law against liability for omissions (absent special circumstances) so as to protect more effectively people's rights to life under Article 2.

(2) Turning to *Article 3*, this provides that:

> No one shall be subjected to torture or to inhuman or degrading treatment or punishment.

Unlike Article 2, Article 3 has had a very significant indirect effect on English tort law. The story is told in more detail below,[97] but briefly: until the HRA came into effect, the English courts had maintained that local authorities could not be sued in negligence for failing properly to investigate allegations that children were in danger of being abused or neglected. The courts could have justified this rule by reference to the general rule in English tort law against liability for omissions.[98] Instead, the courts held that it was necessary for local authorities not to be held liable in negligence for their failures to protect children from abuse or neglect because the prospect of their being held liable might cause them to adopt a very defensive mindset and take a lot of children into care who were not in fact in any danger of being abused or neglected.[99] However, after the HRA came into force it became clear that local authorities that had failed to take steps to protect children whom they knew were in danger of being abused or neglected could be sued *under the 1998 Act* for violating those children's rights under Article 3.[100] Given this, the courts no longer thought there was any point in ruling that local authorities could not be sued *in negligence* for failing to protect children from being abused or neglected and in 2004, the Court of Appeal held that a local authority that received a report that a child was in danger or being

---

[96] The remainder of Article 2(1), which creates an exception where someone is killed intentionally 'in the execution of a sentence of a court following his conviction of a crime for which this penalty is provided by law' has been made redundant by the UK's ratification (in October 2003) of the Thirteenth Protocol to the ECHR, Article 1 of which provides that 'The death penalty shall be abolished. No one shall be condemned to such penalty or executed.'

[97] See below, § 7.11.

[98] Though this would not have been sufficient in those cases where a local authority caused damage (usually psychiatric harm) by intervening and removing a child from its parents unnecessarily.

[99] See *X* v *Bedfordshire CC* [1995] 2 AC 633, 650.

[100] See *Z* v *United Kingdom* [2001] 2 FLR 612.

abused or neglected *would* owe that child a duty to take care to investigate that report properly.[101] Had the HRA never been enacted, it is very doubtful that this development in the law of negligence would have happened.

(3) *Article 5(1)* provides that:

> Everyone has the right to liberty and security of person. No one shall be deprived of his liberty save in the following cases and in accordance with a procedure prescribed by law:
>
> (a) [imprisonment after conviction];
> (b) [arrest or detention for disobeying a court order];
> (c) [arrest or detention of a person to bring him to court on reasonable suspicion of having committed an offence, or to prevent him committing an offence, or fleeing the scene of an offence];
> (d) [detention of a minor for educational supervision];
> (e) [detention of persons to prevent spreading of infectious diseases, or persons of unsound mind, alcoholics, drug addicts or vagrants];
> (f) [detention of persons to stop them entering into the country illegally, or to deport or extradite them].

It was conceded in *Austin* v *Commissioner of Police of the Metropolis* (2009)[102] that the police's 'kettling' of Lois Austin and about 3,000 other people would not be lawful under the law on false imprisonment if 'kettling' violated those people's rights under Article 5(1). As it turns out, the House of Lords found that, in this case, Article 5(1) was not engaged. They held that 'measures of crowd control that are undertaken in the interests of the community will not infringe the Article 5 rights of individual members of the crowd whose freedom of movement is restricted by them' provided that the measures are 'resorted to in good faith' and 'proportionate to the situation which has made the measures necessary'.[103]

The case is now being taken to the European Court of Human Rights and many commentators think that they will take a different view to the House of Lords. If so, then Article 5(1) will have an indirect effect on the law on false imprisonment, in that its existence will severely limit the circumstances in which the police can justify temporarily imprisoning someone on the ground that it is necessary to do so to prevent a breach of the peace.

More widely, in a case where a *private* person imprisons someone else, it is not yet clear whether the courts will be tempted severely to restrict the circumstances under which that imprisonment can be justified so as to ensure the better protection of people's Article 5(1) rights not to be deprived of their liberty save in the very limited circumstances set out in Article 5(1). For example, suppose that *Husband* and *Wife* are having an argument and *Wife* is made so angry by what *Husband* is saying that she tries to leave, but *Husband* physically prevents her from walking out on the basis that what they are arguing about is too important for her to walk away without their having resolved the issue. *Husband* could, arguably, justify his conduct at the moment on the basis that it was 'generally acceptable in the conduct of daily life'.[104] However, *if Husband*'s conduct does deprive *Wife* of her liberty here, the courts might be tempted to refuse to allow *Husband* to take advantage of this defence so as to give more protection to *Wife*'s Article 5(1) rights not to be deprived of her liberty except in certain exceptional circumstances, none of which apply here.

---

[101] *D* v *East Berkshire Community Health NHS Trust* [2004] QB 558.
[102] Discussed above, § 2.1.
[103] At [34] (per Lord Hope). See, similarly, at [59]–[60] (per Lord Neuberger).
[104] *Collins* v *Wilcock* [1984] 1 WLR 1172.

(4) *Article 6(1)* provides that

> In the determination of his civil rights and obligations or of any criminal charge against him, everyone is entitled to a fair and public hearing within a reasonable time by an independent and impartial tribunal established by law . . .

Like Article 3 and Article 5 – and unlike the next two Articles we will be looking at – this Article gives people an *unqualified* right: that is, a right that cannot be abridged under any circumstances. However, the ECtHR has interpreted this right in a qualified way, holding that state actions which prevent A's civil rights and obligations being determined at a fair and public hearing in court will not violate A's Article 6(1) rights provided those actions serve a legitimate purpose and do not have a disproportionate effect on A's interests.

It was thought at one time that Article 6(1) would have a major impact on the English law of tort. In the case of *Osman* v *Ferguson* (1993), it was claimed that the police were liable for the tort of negligence because they had failed to take sufficient steps to protect a schoolboy and his family from a deputy headmaster at the boy's school who had developed an obsession with the boy. The deputy headmaster ended up injuring the boy and killing the boy's father. The Court of Appeal dismissed the family's claims against the police on the basis that even if the police were as incompetent as the family alleged, the police could still not be sued as they had not owed the boy or the rest of his family a duty of care to protect them from the deputy headmaster. Disturbed by the perception that the Court of Appeal was here giving effect to a blanket ban on the police being sued in negligence, regardless of the merits of the case, the ECtHR found, in the case of *Osman* v *UK* (1999), that the Court of Appeal's finding that the police had not owed a duty of care in this case violated the family's rights under Article 6(1).

The immediate effect of the *Osman* decision was to make the courts very cautious about striking out negligence claims on the basis that no duty of care was owed to the claimant.[105] However, in the later case of *Z* v *United Kingdom* (2001), the ECtHR confessed that in *Osman* it had misunderstood the English law of negligence, and that it now realised that no one under English law enjoyed the benefit of a blanket ban from being sued under the law of negligence.[106] Given this, the English courts would not violate people's rights under Article 6(1) if, after having seriously considered the allegations made by a claimant, they dismissed the claimant's claim on the basis that even if those allegations were true, the claimant would still have no case because no duty of care was owed to him. Since then, the English courts have not been troubled by any suggestions that dismissing claims in negligence on the basis that no duty of care was owed to the claimant would result in their violating the claimant's Article 6(1) rights.

Having said that, there are defendants who do, under English law, enjoy the benefit of blanket bans from being sued in tort for their actions. For example, you cannot sue a Member of Parliament for what he or she has said on the floor of the House of Commons. No matter how outrageous his or her conduct, no matter how malicious or corrupt his or her actions, you cannot sue them – ever. So if you do try to sue an MP for defaming you on the floor of the House of Commons, no court in the land will hear your claim. By refusing to

---

[105] See *Barrett* v *Enfield LBC* [2001] 2 AC 550 (refusal to strike out a claim that a local authority had owed a boy in care a duty of care to raise him properly and not shuffle him from school to school); *Phelps* v *Hillingdon LBC* [2001] 2 AC 619 (refusal to strike out a claim that a local authority had owed special needs children a duty of care to provide them with an education appropriate to their needs).

[106] Five of the seventeen judges in the ECtHR dissented, and continued to insist that the ECtHR had been correct to find a violation of Article 6(1) in *Osman* v *UK* (1999).

listen to your claim, will the courts violate your Article 6(1) rights? If so, then the enactment of the HRA, and the existence of Article 6(1) might have an indirect effect on tort law in that it might force the courts to modify some or all of the blanket bans on being sued that *do* exist in English law. The issue of when a claimant can argue that their Article 6(1) rights have been violated because their claim in tort against someone else has been thrown out is so complex that we will not deal with it here. Instead, the interested reader is referred to our extended discussion of this issue in a later section, in the chapter on 'Defences'.[107]

(5) *Article 8* provides that:

1. Everyone has the right to respect for his private and family life, his home and his correspondence.

2. There shall be no interference by a public authority with the exercise of this right except such as in accordance with the law and necessary in a democratic society in the interests of national security, public safety or the economic well-being of the country, for the prevention of disorder or crime, for the protection of health or morals, or for the protection of the rights and freedoms of others.

There is no doubt that this Article has had a major indirect effect on English tort law, in encouraging the courts to abandon the long-standing rule that there was no free-standing right to sue a defendant in tort for invading your privacy.[108] Over the last 15 years, the courts have developed the law on when someone can be sued for breaching another's confidence so as to give better protection to people's Article 8(1) rights to respect for their private and family life. Indeed this area of the law has developed so far from its roots that we think that the new cause of action should be treated as an independent tort: 'wrongful disclosure of private information'. Our detailed discussion of this tort, and the even more recently-recognised wrong of 'wrongfully obtaining access to private information', is below, in our chapter on 'Invasion of Privacy'.[109]

It has also been argued[110] that the courts are required by the combined effect of the HRA and Article 8 to develop the law on private nuisance so that non-owners of land are allowed to sue in nuisance when their quiet enjoyment of the land they are living on is interfered with by someone else. There are severe problems with this argument, which we will address in our chapter on 'Private Nuisance'.[111]

(6) *Article 10* provides that:

1. Everyone has the right to freedom of expression. This right shall include freedom to form opinions and to receive and to impart information and ideas without interference by public authority and regardless of frontiers . . .

2. The exercise of these freedoms, since it carries with it duties and responsibilities, may be subject to such formalities, conditions, restrictions or penalties as are prescribed by law and are necessary in a democratic society, in the interests of national security, territorial integrity or public safety, for the prevention of disorder or crime, for the protection of health or morals, for

---

[107] See below, § 26.16.
[108] See Arden 2010, at 147: 'Convention rights have had a powerful influence and they have led to the development of a right of action for breach of confidence, but not for invasions of privacy generally. The right of action for breach of confidence has been developed along the lines of Convention rights, not because English judges were compelled to do this, but because it was generally felt that the law did not provide adequate remedies against the intrusions by the paparazzi. The English courts chose to accept the Convention value of privacy as interpreted by the Strasbourg court.'
[109] See below, chapter 21.
[110] See, for example, Hunt 1998.
[111] See below, § 15.11.

the protection of the reputation or rights of others, for preventing the disclosure of information received in confidence, or for maintaining the authority and impartiality of the judiciary.

In developing the law on invasion of privacy, the courts have had to be careful not to develop the law in such a way that defendants' rights under Article 10 are violated. So the courts have ended up saying that in order to decide whether or not to find liability in a 'wrongful disclosure of private information' case, they have to weigh the claimant's interests in having their privacy protected against the defendant's interests in being allowed freely to talk about the claimant's private life. The complexities of this weighing process are explained more fully below.[112]

More generally, the courts' obligations under the HRA – together with the existence of Article 10 – mean that they have a continual obligation to monitor the law of defamation to ensure that that area of law does not have a disproportionately adverse effect on freedom of expression. The question of whether the law of defamation, as it stands at the moment, does have such an impact on freedom of expression is, again, a question we will address later on.[113]

Further reading

So many interesting books and articles have been written about the Human Rights Act 1998, claims for damages under it, and its relation to tort law, that it seems invidious to highlight only a handful. Nonetheless, we think that **Jenny Steele, 'Damages in tort and under the Human Rights Act: remedial or functional separation?' (2008) 67** *Cambridge Law Journal* **606** discusses some particularly important questions about the relationship between tort remedies and remedies under the 1998 Act. Jason Varuhas also deals with similar questions in his article, **'A Tort-Based Approach to Damages under the Human Rights Act 1998' (2009) 72** *Modern Law Review* **750**, though he is far more confident as to what the answer ought to be. With regard to the effect that the 1998 Act has had on the law of tort, and other parts of private law, useful recent accounts can be found in **David Hoffman (ed),** *The Impact of the UK Human Rights Act on Private Law* **(Cambridge, 2011)**. We also expect that **Jane Wright,** *Tort Law and Human Rights*, **2nd edn (Hart Publishing, 2012)** will be an important resource for anyone inclined to research in depth the issues covered in this chapter.

Visit **www.mylawchamber.co.uk/mcbride** to access tools to help you develop and test your knowledge of Tort law, including interactive multiple choice questions, practice exam questions with guidance, weblinks, legal newsfeed, additional case summaries, legal updates and tips on answering problem and essay questions.

premium
my**law**chamber
unrivalled support for legal education

---

[112] See below, § 21.5.
[113] See below, § 19.14.

4 Claims in negligence

4.1   The basics *92*

4.2   Negligence and intention *93*

4.3   Negligence and other wrongs *94*

4.4   Remedies for negligence *97*

Overview

This chapter begins our journey into the law on negligence. Section 4.1 sets out the basic elements that have to be established if a claimant wants to sue in negligence. Section 4.2 sorts out some confusions that students are often prone to when thinking about the concept of negligence. Section 4.3 charts the relationship between negligence and other types of wrong recognised under the law. Section 4.4 sets out the basic principles governing what remedies will be available to a claimant who successfully sues someone else in negligence.

4.1 THE BASICS

If a claimant wants to sue a defendant in negligence, he will have to show four things:

(1) that the defendant owed the claimant *a duty of care*;
(2) that the defendant *breached* that duty of care;
(3) that the defendant's breach *caused* the claimant to suffer some kind of loss; and
(4) at least one of the losses that the defendant's breach caused the claimant to suffer is *actionable*.

For those who find it hard to remember the above, it might be useful to note that these four requirements correspond with the first four letters of the alphabet: D (for duty of care), B (for breach), C (for causation) and A (for actionability).

Duty comes *first*:

> The law takes no cognizance of carelessness in the abstract. It concerns itself with carelessness only where there is a duty to take care and where failure in that duty has caused damage. In such circumstances carelessness assumes the legal quality of negligence and entails the consequences of negligence.[1]

Some university lecturers on the law of negligence prefer to leave the topic of duty to the end, after they have dealt with the law on breach of duty (usually lectured on under the heading 'fault'), and causation, and actionability (usually lectured on under the heading 'remoteness of damage'). We have two reasons for not following their example.

First, in a negligence case, the courts do not simply ask – Was the defendant careless? They ask – Did the defendant breach a duty of care owed to the claimant? And what factors the courts take into account in answering that question will depend crucially on what *sort* of duty it was that the defendant owed the claimant. For example, the duty of care a

---

[1] *Donoghue* v *Stevenson* [1932] AC 562, 618–619 (per Lord Macmillan). See also *Bourhill* v *Young* [1943] 1 AC 92, 116 (per Lord Porter).

landowner owes his neighbours to protect them from dangers arising on his land requires him simply to do his best, given the resources he has, to deal with any such dangers.[2] In contrast, the duty of care a driver owes nearby users of the road to take care not to drive dangerously does not just require him to do his best to drive safely, but to drive to the standards of a normal, qualified driver – even if he is incapable of reaching that standard.[3] So you simply cannot understand the authorities on when the courts will find that a defendant breached a duty of care owed to the claimant without a good prior understanding of what sort of duties of care we owe each other.

Secondly, just as there is no such thing as carelessness in the abstract, neither is there such a thing as causation in the abstract. Whether or not a defendant's breach of a duty of care will be held to have caused the claimant to have suffered a particular kind of loss will depend on what sort of duty of care the defendant is supposed to have owed the claimant. Consider the **Unfortunate Rock Star Problem**:

> *Star* goes everywhere with his *Bodyguard*. *Driver* carelessly runs over *Star* while *Star* is crossing the road. *Envy* – who suspects that *Star* is having an affair with his wife and who has been following *Star* to confirm his suspicions – takes advantage of the fact that *Star* is lying in the middle of the road to go up to *Star* and kick him in the head (something which causes *Star* to suffer severe brain damage). *Bodyguard* does nothing to stop *Envy* doing this, because he is unhappy with *Star* for sleeping with *Bodyguard*'s latest girlfriend.

In this case, we have two people – *Bodyguard* and *Driver* – who owed *Star* duties of care (in *Driver*'s case, a duty to take care not to drive dangerously, and in *Bodyguard*'s case, a duty to take reasonable steps to save *Star* from being attacked). *Driver* and *Bodyguard* each breached the duties of care they owed *Star*. *Star* would not have suffered the brain damage that he did had *Driver* and *Bodyguard* not *each* breached the duties of care that they respectively owed him. But only *Bodyguard*'s breach of his duty of care will be held to have *caused Star*'s brain damage. That is because of the nature of the particular duty of care that *Bodyguard* owed *Star* – a duty to prevent the very kind of attack that brought about *Star*'s brain damage.[4] But it is impossible to appreciate this point if you have no idea what sort of duties of care *Driver* and *Bodyguard* owed *Star* in this case.

4.2 NEGLIGENCE AND INTENTION

Sir Percy Winfield once suggested that someone would commit the tort of negligence if, and only if, he 'breach[ed] a legal duty to take care by an *inadvertent* act or omission'.[5] This seems wrong.[6] Suppose *Driver* drives down a street at 80 miles an hour and as a result runs over *Pedestrian*. *Pedestrian* attempts to sue *Driver* in negligence for compensation for her injuries. Could *Driver* really rebut *Pedestrian*'s claim by arguing that while he admittedly owed *Pedestrian* a duty to take care not to drive dangerously, he did not commit the tort of negligence in relation to B in driving as he did because he *deliberately* drove down the road

---

[2] *Goldman* v *Hargrave* [1967] AC 645. See below, § 11.5.
[3] *Nettleship* v *Weston* [1971] 2 QB 691. See below, § 8.2.
[4] See below, § 9.12.
[5] Winfield 1926, 184 (emphasis added).
[6] It is also inconsistent with the House of Lords' ruling in *Wainwright* v *Home Office* [2004] 2 AC 406 that if A *deliberately* lies to B, telling her that her husband has been injured when he has not, and B is made physically sick as a result of hearing this, then B will be able to sue A for damages in negligence. See below, § 6.8.

at 80 miles an hour? The answer must be 'no'. A breach of a duty of care is still a breach, even if the breach was committed intentionally.

Perhaps acknowledging this point, Winfield later suggested that someone would commit the tort of negligence if: (1) he breached a duty of care owed to another *and* (2) when he breached that duty he did not intend to harm that other.[7] Again, there does not seem any reason for this limitation on the scope of the tort of negligence. Suppose, for example, that *Mother-in-Law* visited *Husband* in his house. While she was in the house, she put her foot through a rotten floorboard on the staircase which *Husband* had neglected to replace and as a result twisted her ankle. Now suppose that *Mother-in-Law* sues *Husband* in negligence, claiming that her injury happened as a result of *Husband*'s breach of the duty of care that he owed her as an occupier to take reasonable steps to see that she would be reasonably safe while she was on his premises. Could *Husband* really defeat *Mother-in-Law*'s claim by arguing that 'When I found out that the floorboard was rotten and liable to give way, I deliberately left it untouched in the hope that when my *Mother-in-Law* came visiting she would put her foot through it'? Surely not[8] – the fact that *Husband* breached the duty of care he owed *Mother-in-Law* as his visitor with the intention of harming her would not stop any court from concluding that *Husband* had committed the tort of negligence in this case.

4.3 NEGLIGENCE AND OTHER WRONGS[9]

Negligence is one of very few torts that is not, on its face, geared towards protecting people from suffering a particular *kind* of harm. Unlike torts such as defamation (which protects reputation) or battery (which protects someone's physical integrity) or false imprisonment (which protects someone's freedom of movement), negligence seems simply to focus on what the defendant *did*, rather than on what harm he caused. This gives negligence, as a tort, the potential to range very wide indeed. In any case where a defendant acted unreasonably and a claimant suffered harm as a result, the claimant *might* be able to argue that the defendant is liable in negligence to compensate him for the harm he has suffered, on the basis that the defendant owed him, and breached, a duty to take care not to act as he did, and the harm suffered by the claimant resulted from that breach.

Lawyers have not been slow to seize on negligence's potential to provide a remedy in any case where unreasonable conduct has resulted in harm being suffered. As Lord Templeman remarked in *CBS Songs* v *Amstrad plc* (1988), when making a negligence claim 'it is always easy to draft a proposition which is tailor-made to produce the desired result.'[10] And the courts have sometimes allowed lawyers to make claims in negligence for compensation in respect of harms which other areas of the law of tort are concerned to protect people against. All of which means there is now some overlap between the law of negligence and a range of other wrongs. In this section we want to chart the areas of overlap and see how far they go:

(1) *Battery*. Unlike negligence, battery is a tort that is actionable *per se*. So a claimant suing in battery has no need to show that he has suffered any loss. Nor does he have to show

---

[7] Winfield 1934, 41.
[8] Cf. *New South Wales* v *Lepore* (2003) 212 CLR 511, at [162] (per McHugh J): '[a claimant] may, if he or she chooses, sue in negligence for the intentional infliction of harm'; also *Blake* v *Galloway* [2004] 1 WLR 2844, at [17] (per Dyson LJ): 'If the defendant . . . [had] deliberately aimed the piece of bark at the claimant's head, then [the claimant might have been able to sue the defendant in negligence].'
[9] See Weir 1998a.
[10] [1988] 1 AC 1013, 1059.

that the defendant acted unreasonably in touching him – all he has to do is show that the defendant intentionally or carelessly touched him. This means that battery, rather than negligence, will be the tort a claimant will sue under if he has suffered no tangible harm as a result of being touched by the defendant or if the defendant acted reasonably in touching him. But in cases where a defendant *carelessly* touched a claimant, and physical injury or a psychiatric illness resulted, a claim in negligence may well be available, as well as a claim in battery. In practice, such cases tend to be pleaded as negligence cases, rather than battery cases. Certainly, in a case where *Driver* has carelessly run down *Pedestrian* in the street, it would be regarded as peculiar for *Pedestrian* to sue *Driver* in battery, rather than in negligence.

(2) *False imprisonment.* In theory, false imprisonment can only be alleged where a defendant intentionally locked up a claimant.[11] So if a defendant carelessly did something that resulted in a claimant being imprisoned, negligence is the only tort that might provide the claimant with a remedy – provided, of course, that the imprisonment resulted in the claimant suffering some tangible harm. (If the defendant is a public authority, a claim under the Human Rights Act 1998 might also be available.) This was the case in *Al-Kandari* v *Brown* (1988), where the defendant firm of solicitors was acting for the claimant's husband in a child custody dispute between the claimant and her husband. Because the husband had a record of violence and kidnapping his and the claimant's children, the courts had ordered that the husband's passport be held by the defendants. Due to the defendants' carelessness, the husband was allowed to get his passport back, and he promptly kidnapped the claimant and their children. The claimant was left tied up in the back of a van, and the claimant's children were spirited out of the country and she never saw them again. The claimant successfully sued the defendants in negligence for damages for the physical and psychiatric injuries she had suffered as a result of being kidnapped.

(3) *Defamation.* A substantial overlap between the law of negligence and the law of defamation was created by the House of Lords' decision in *Spring* v *Guardian Assurance* (1995). In that case, the claimant was seeking a job selling life insurance policies. His prospective employer contacted the firm for which he used to work for a reference. The firm responded that the claimant was 'a man of little or no integrity and could not be regarded as honest'. This was doubly unfortunate: first, the reference resulted in the claimant not getting the job; second, the reference was extremely unfair. Had the claimant sued his old firm in defamation, his claim would have been dismissed as the firm would have had a defence of 'qualified privilege' to his claim.[12] So the claimant sued the firm in negligence instead, and won. It is surprising that claimants have – post-*Spring* – not attempted to make more attempts to circumvent the rules on when someone can sue in defamation by invoking the law of negligence. But the result is that it is still very unclear how far the law of negligence goes to help protect people from suffering loss as a result of having their reputation besmirched.

(4) *Breach of statutory duty.* We have already seen,[13] that if A breaches a statutory duty imposed on him for the benefit of B, and B suffers loss as a result, B may be able to bring a claim (a claim for 'breach of statutory duty') for compensation for that loss. But he will only be able to do so if Parliament intended that a breach of that statutory duty be

---

[11] See above, § 2.3.
[12] See below, § 19.10(1).
[13] See above, § 1.10.

actionable in tort. But what if it is clear that Parliament did not so intend? In such a case, B might be tempted to bring a claim in negligence against A instead, arguing that A owed him a duty to take care not to act as he did. Due to the almost single-handed efforts of Lord Hoffmann, it seems that this option is now closed off to B unless there are special circumstances in B's case that would justify the courts in finding that A owed B a duty of care. The mere fact that A was subject to a statutory duty not to act as he did will not be enough on its own to justify the courts in finding that A owed B a duty to take care not to act as he did:

> If a statute actually imposes a duty, it is well settled that the question of whether it was intended to give rise to a private right of action depends upon the construction of the statute . . . If the statute does not create a private right of action, it would be, to say the least, unusual if the mere existence of the statutory duty could generate a common law duty of care.[14]

(5) *Private nuisance.* As we will see, the tort of private nuisance – very roughly speaking – exists to protect the value of a claimant's land as something to be used and enjoyed.

The tort extends far enough to allow *Owner* to sue *Neighbour* when he knows or ought to know that a problem has arisen on his land that creates a foreseeable risk that *Owner's* land will be damaged, and fails to take reasonable steps to deal with that problem, with the result that *Owner's* land is in fact damaged. (*Neighbour's* liability in this case is known as liability for 'adopting or continuing' a nuisance.) In such a case, *Owner* can sue *Neighbour* in private nuisance for the harm done to his land, but there is authority that he can choose to sue in negligence as well.[15] However, nowadays the claim would usually be made in nuisance,[16] and there seems no advantage in bringing the claim in negligence instead: *Owner* would still have to prove fault on the part of *Neighbour* for what happened, and would probably only be able to recover damages for the harm done to his land, just as would be the case in nuisance.[17]

One potential overlap between the law of private nuisance and the law of negligence has been eliminated by the House of Lords' insistence that claims cannot be brought in private nuisance for personal injury.[18] As a result, a landowner who suffers physical injury as a result of inhaling smoke coming from his neighbour's land can only sue in negligence, rather than private nuisance. It is unclear what the position is if it is the landowner's cattle that are poisoned as a result of inhaling the smoke from the defendant's land. In such a case, it may be that a claim in private nuisance will be available,[19] thus giving the landowner the option of suing his neighbour either in negligence or in private nuisance.

(6) *Breach of contract.* Moving away from tortious wrongs and into other wrongs now, some overlap between the tort of negligence and the wrong of breach of contract was created by the House of Lords' decision in *Henderson v Merrett Syndicates Ltd* (1995), which ruled that if A has, in a contract with B, 'assumed a responsibility' to B to perform a certain task carefully, and then fails to perform that task carefully, B will not only be able to sue A for breach of contract; he will also be able to sue A in negligence (provided, of course, that A's carelessness has caused B to suffer an actionable loss).

---

[14] *Gorringe* v *Calderdale MBC* [2004] 1 WLR 1057, at [23] (per Lord Hoffmann).
[15] *Goldman* v *Hargrave* [1967] AC 645.
[16] See *Leakey* v *National Trust* [1980] QB 485 and *Holbeck Hall Hotel Ltd* v *Scarborough BC* [2000] QB 836.
[17] See below, § 11.5(C).
[18] *Hunter* v *Canary Wharf* [1997] AC 655, 696 (per Lord Lloyd) and 707 (per Lord Hoffmann).
[19] The question is discussed further below, § 15.12.

(7) *Equitable wrongs*. While a trustee who holds money on trust for a beneficiary will owe that beneficiary a duty to invest that money carefully,[20] that duty is equitable in nature. As such, breach of that duty will amount to an equitable wrong, rather than a tort. The courts have generally set their face against allowing those with a merely equitable interest in property to take advantage of the law of tort to obtain remedies when that property is misapplied.[21] As a result, there is no real overlap between the law of negligence and the law of equitable wrongs. However, where a third party carelessly damages property that is held on trust for the claimant, the Court of Appeal has now allowed that the claimant might be able to sue the third party for damages.[22]

4.4 REMEDIES FOR NEGLIGENCE

Negligence seems to be a peculiar tort in that most people think that compensatory damages are the *only* remedy available to a claimant in a negligence case.

In *Kralj* v *McGrath* (1986), Woolf J held that in a negligence case, aggravated damages (damages designed to assuage a claimant's feelings of outrage at the way the defendant has treated him) will *never* be available. It is hard to see why: there is no other tort for which aggravated damages will never be available. Woolf J held that allowing such damages to be awarded in negligence cases would 'be wholly inconsistent with the general approach to damages in this area, which is to compensate the [claimant] for the loss that she has actually suffered'.[23] But that begs the question of whether compensatory damages *should* be the only type of damages available in negligence cases.

In principle, exemplary damages (damages designed to punish a defendant who has flouted the law by deliberately committing a tort) should be available in negligence cases so long as the defendant's breach of a duty of care was sufficiently culpable, has not been punished under the criminal law, and falls within the rules laid down in *Rookes* v *Barnard* (1964) for when exemplary damages may be awarded. There is one New Zealand case – *A* v *Bottrill* (2003) – where exemplary damages were awarded against a doctor who was negligent in adopting a completely out of date method for examining the claimant's cervical smear tests for cancer. The New Zealand Court of Appeal declined to award exemplary damages against the doctor, on the ground that he was not conscious of doing anything wrong when he acted as he did. The Privy Council held that in principle exemplary damages could be awarded so long as it was established that the defendant's conduct was so outrageous as to be worthy of punishment. The case shows a willingness on the part of at least some English judges to allow exemplary damages to be awarded in appropriate negligence cases – but there is, at the moment, no authority where such damages *were* awarded by an English court.

There is, similarly, no English precedent where an injunction has ever been awarded against a defendant to stop him breaching a duty of care.[24] Indeed, there seems to be no precedent anywhere in the common law world, apart from two obscure American cases

---

[20] Trustee Act 2000, ss 1, 2 and Sched 1.
[21] See below, § 17.2(D)(5).
[22] For further discussion, see below, § 6.9.
[23] *Kralj* v *McGrath* [1986] 1 All ER 54, 61.
[24] See *Miller* v *Jackson* [1977] QB 966, at 980: 'there is no case, so far as I know, where [an injunction] has been granted to stop a man being negligent' (per Lord Denning MR). In *CBS Songs plc* v *Amstrad* [1988] AC 1013, 'damages and an injunction for negligence [were] sought' (ibid, at 1060) against the defendants, but no duty of care was found to be owed in that case: see below, § 5.3, fn 30.

where an injunction was awarded against an employer, forcing him to comply with the duty of care he owed his employees to take care to protect them against risks of injury arising in the workplace.[25] (In both cases, the risk was of developing cancer from being exposed to second hand smoke in the workplace.) The lack of authority does not, we think, indicate that we are not actually required by the courts to observe the duties of care we owe other people. (There are, for example, plenty of cases where the courts are willing to distort the rules on when a person can sue another in negligence in order to ensure that a defendant suffers some kind of sanction for breaching a duty of care that he owed someone else and isn't allowed to 'get away with' breaching that duty.)[26] The difficulty lies in the fact that duties of care are rarely breached on a continuing basis. When a duty of care is breached, it tends to be a one-off event that happens without warning to the person who is owed the duty of care. As a result, there is never any chance for a claimant to seek an injunction, to force a defendant to comply with a duty of care that he owes the claimant. By the time the claimant finds out about the breach, it is too late – it has already happened.

---

[25] *Shimp* v *New Jersey Bell Telephone Co*, 368 A 2d 408 (1976) and *Smith* v *Western Electric Co*, 643 SW 2d 10 (1982).
[26] Notable examples are: *White* v *Jones* [1995] 2 AC 207 (discussed below, § 6.13); *Reeves* v *Commissioner of Police of the Metropolis* [2000] AC 360 (§ 7.4); *Fairchild* v *Glenhaven Funeral Services Ltd* [2003] 1 AC 32 (§ 9.5); and *Chester* v *Afshar* [2005] 1 AC 134 (§ 9.10).

5 Duty of care – Introduction

5.1   The basics 99

5.2   Duty of care tests 104

5.3   Duty of care factors 108

5.4   Duty-skepticism 119

5.5   Risk and harm 121

Overview

We continue our look at the law of negligence by introducing the most fundamental concept in the law of negligence: the idea of a duty of care. We will be exploring in the next few chapters when exactly one person will owe another a duty to be careful of one kind or another. This chapter lays the groundwork for the chapters coming up. After making a few basic points about the notion of a duty of care in section 5.1, we criticise in section 5.2 the idea that there can exist a 'test' for determining whether or not one person owes another a duty of care in a given situation. In section 5.3 we set out a range of factors that the courts will take into account in determining whether or not to find that a duty of care was owed in a given situation. Sections 5.4 and 5.5 are quite theoretical. Section 5.4 considers the views of those who are skeptical as to whether the law actually requires someone who is subject to a duty of care to do anything, and who think that saying that A owes B a duty of care merely amounts to saying that 'If A carelessly harms B, A will be liable for that carelessness.' Section 5.5 considers the views of those who think that our duties of care are duties not to *harm* someone by acting carelessly, as opposed to being duties to act *carefully*.

5.1 THE BASICS

As we have seen, the first thing a claimant needs to establish – if he or she wants to bring a claim in negligence against a defendant – is that the defendant owed him or her a duty of care of some kind. Three points need to be made at this stage about duties of care:

A. Different types of duty

There are many different kinds of duty of care that people can owe each other. We can categorise the duties of care that we might owe each other in three different ways: (1) according to what they require someone to do; (2) according to what sort of interest they are designed to protect; and (3) according to how they arise.

Looking at (1) first, we can begin by splitting the various duties of care recognised in English law into *negative duties* and *positive duties*. A negative duty of care requires a defendant to take care *not to act* in a certain way. A positive duty of care requires a defendant *to act* in a certain way. We can then split up our positive duties of care into two groups. Some positive duties of care require a defendant to take reasonable steps to ensure a particular outcome. An example is an occupier's duty to take reasonable steps to see that a visitor on her premises is reasonably safe for the purposes for which she is on those premises.[1] Other

---

[1] Occupiers' Liability Act 1957, s 1.

positive duties of care require a defendant to perform a particular task with a reasonable degree of care and skill. An example is the duty a doctor will owe his patient to treat her with a reasonable degree of care and skill.

Turning to (2), the various duties of care that we might owe each other are designed to protect a variety of interests: physical, mental, and economic. For example, suppose that a driver carelessly crashes into a bus shelter, killing most of the people waiting at the bus shelter. The driver will have owed the people waiting at the bus shelter a duty to take care not to crash into the bus shelter. That duty will have been designed to protect those people's physical integrity. But he will also have owed anyone who puts themselves in danger rescuing people in the aftermath of the accident a duty to take care not to crash into the bus shelter. That duty of care will have been imposed on him to protect potential rescuers from the mental scars they might suffer as a result of what they see during the course of their rescue efforts. And the driver will also have owed the company that owns the bus shelter a duty to take care not to crash into the bus shelter. That duty is designed to protect the company's economic interest in not having its property damaged.

With regard to (3), some duties arise merely because it is foreseeable that acting in a particular way will result in someone else suffering harm of some kind. A driver's duty to take care not to act dangerously is one such duty – a driver has that duty merely because it is reasonably foreseeable that if he drives dangerously, other people nearby will get hurt. For other duties, foreseeability of harm is not enough. There are some duties that a defendant will only be subject to if he has 'assumed a responsibility' to someone else. For example, in giving advice to someone else as to what is the best way of investing their money, I will only owe them a duty to take care not to give them bad advice if I 'assume a responsibility' to them not to give them bad advice – which requirement will only be satisfied if I do something to make them think that they can safely rely on my advice and don't need to get anyone else's opinion.

B. The duty–harm relationship

As we will see later,[2] if a claimant wants to sue a defendant in negligence for compensation for a particular harm that she has suffered, then she has to show that the defendant owed her a duty of care that was geared towards protecting her from suffering *that kind of harm*. As Lord Bridge of Harwich observed in *Caparo Industries plc v Dickman* (1990): 'It is never sufficient simply to ask whether A owes B a duty of care. It is always necessary to determine the scope of the duty by reference to the kind of damage from which A must take care to hold B harmless.'[3]

As a result of this, a claimant has to be quite selective about what sort of duty of care she will use to base her claim against the defendant on. Consider, for example, the **Forgetful Investor Problem**:

> One morning, *Commuter* reads something in the newspapers that makes her think that she needs to sell all her shares in *Dodgy plc*. She then takes a train to work, resolving that once she gets into work, she will call her broker and have him sell her shares. Unfortunately, due to the carelessness of the *Train Driver*, *Commuter's* train de-rails. *Commuter* is unharmed, but is so shaken by the accident that she completely forgets to sell her shares in *Dodgy*. By the time she remembers, the value of shares in *Dodgy* has plummeted.

---

[2] See below, § 10.3.
[3] [1990] 2 AC 605, 627.

Commuter may want to sue *Train Driver* in negligence for the money she has lost as a result of forgetting to sell up her interest in *Dodgy*. But in order to get her claim off the ground, she cannot rely on the fact that *Train Driver*'s negligence in breaching the duty he owed her – and each of the other people on the train – to take care not to drive the train dangerously caused her to lose a lot of money (in that had he not been negligent, she would have remembered to sell her shares and would have done so at a much higher price than she can now get for her shares). This is because the duty *Train Driver* owed *Commuter* to take care not to drive dangerously was designed to protect *Commuter* from suffering some kind of physical harm, not economic harm. If *Commuter* wants to sue *Train Driver* in negligence for the economic loss that she has suffered, she will have to show that he owed her a duty of care that was geared towards protecting her from suffering *that kind of loss*. This she will not be able to do. Duties of care that exist to protect people from suffering some kind of pure economic loss – that is a loss not consequent on physical injury or property damage – generally only exist between people with some kind of special relationship between them; which is obviously not the case between *Commuter* and *Train Driver*.

In cases where a claimant suffers two *independent* (that is, not causally related to each other) harms as a result of a defendant's actions, if she wants to sue the defendant in negligence for compensation for each of those harms, she will have to show that the defendant owed her *two* duties of care: the first geared towards protecting her from the first kind of harm she wants to sue for, the second geared towards the second kind of harm. The duties of care in question could be identical in content – they could each require the defendant to do exactly the same thing – but they will be distinct in respect of the reason why they exist.

For example, in *Spartan Steel & Alloys Ltd* v *Martin* (1973), the defendants carelessly cut through a power line that supplied electricity to the claimants' factory. The power cut had two independent effects on the claimants. First of all, it stopped the claimants from working on some 'melts' that they were processing – with the result that the 'melts' were damaged. Secondly, it stopped the claimants doing any work at all for a number of hours. The claimants wanted to sue the defendants in negligence for compensation for these harms they had suffered – the harm to the melts, and the harm to their business. The Court of Appeal held that the claimants could recover for the first harm, but not the second. Why?

Well, the defendants *had* owed the claimants a duty to take care not to cut through the power line. But this duty was imposed on the defendants because it was reasonably foreseeable that cutting through the power line might cause people like the claimants to suffer some kind of property damage. So the defendants had owed the claimants a property-protecting duty of care, and the claimants could rely on that to sue the defendants in negligence for the harm done to their 'melts'. But in order to sue for the harm to their business, the claimants had to establish that the defendants owed them a business-protecting duty to take care not to cut through the power line. And this they could not do. Such a duty – which would have the effect of protecting the claimants against suffering a form of pure economic loss – generally only exists between people in some kind of special relationship, and no such relationship existed between the claimants and the defendants in *Spartan Steel*.

C. Duties of care and public policy

There are three views on the relevance of public policy – in other words, the public interest – in determining whether one person owes another a duty of care.

(1) *Policy minimalists* take the view that question of whether A owed B a duty of care should be decided without any reference at all to public policy.[4] An early statement of the policy minimalist position can be found in the judgment of Lord Scarman in *McLoughlin* v *O'Brian* (1983), in which he argued,

> The distinguishing feature of the common law is [the] judicial development and formation of principle. Policy considerations will have to be weighed: but the objective of the judges is the formulation of principle. And, if principle inexorably requires a decision which entails a degree of policy risk, the court's function is to adjudicate according to principle, leaving policy curtailment to the judgment of Parliament.[5]

Lord Scarman thought that principle demanded that the courts should find that A owed B a duty to take care not to injure C if it was reasonably foreseeable that A's injuring C would result in B suffering a psychiatric illness. He wondered at the same time whether such a position would be 'socially desirable':

> I foresee social and financial problems if damages for [psychiatric illnesses] should be made available to persons other than parents and children who without seeing or hearing the accident, or being present in the immediate aftermath, suffer [a psychiatric illness] in consequence of it. There is, I think, a powerful case for legislation [to restrict claims in this area] . . .[6]

Why, then, Lord Scarman asked, should the courts not try to draw the line and come up with some rule on when a duty of care would be owed that would work in a socially acceptable way? His answer was:

> Simply, because the policy issue as to where to draw the line is not justiciable. The problem is one of social, economic, and financial policy. The considerations relevant to a decision [as to where to draw the line] are not such as to be capable of being handled within the limits of the forensic process.[7]

(2) *Policy maximalists* take the view that the public interest is *always* relevant to the question of whether A owed B a duty of care. Policy considerations can be invoked as a reason for *denying* that A owed B a duty of care; and they can be invoked as a reason for *claiming* that A owed B a duty of care. For example, in *Hill* v *Chief Constable of West Yorkshire* (1989) the House of Lords had to decide whether the police had owed a murder victim a duty to take reasonable steps to apprehend her killer before he got a chance to kill her. The House of Lords found that the police had not owed the murder victim a duty of care. *Part*[8] of their reason for denying that a duty of care was owed in *Hill* was that finding that the police owed the potential victims of crime a duty of care would be contrary to the public interest:

> The general sense of public duty which motivates police forces is unlikely to be appreciably reinforced by the imposition of . . . liability so far as concerns their function in the investigation and suppression of crime. From time to time they make mistakes in the exercise of that function, but it is not be doubted that they apply their best endeavours to the performance of it. In some

---

[4] See Stevens 2007 and Beever 2007 for two policy minimalist presentations of the law of negligence.
[5] [1983] AC 410, at 430.
[6] [1983] AC 410, at 431.
[7] ibid.
[8] It is almost always forgotten that in Lord Keith of Kinkel's leading speech in the *Hill* case, the policy reasons that he gave for refusing to find a duty of care was owed occupy *one* paragraph at the end of a 14 paragraph judgment, and that last paragraph begins 'That is sufficient for the disposal of the appeal' – thus clearly indicating that there were sufficient reasons to dismiss the claim that a duty of care was owed in *Hill* without needing to rely on the public interest at all.

instances the imposition of liability may lead to the exercise of a function being carried on in a detrimentally defensive frame of mind ... Further it would be reasonable to expect that if potential liability were to be imposed it would be not uncommon for actions to be raised against police forces on the ground that they had failed to catch some criminal as soon as they might have done, with the result that he went on to commit further crimes. While some such actions might involve allegations of a simple and straightforward type of failure – for example that a police officer negligently tripped and fell while pursuing a burglar – others would be likely to enter deeply into the general nature of a police investigation, as indeed the present action would seek to do ... A great deal of police time, trouble and expense might be expected to have to be put into the preparation of the defence to the action and the attendance of witnesses at the trial. The result would be a significant diversion of police manpower and attention from their most important function, that of the suppression of crime. Closed investigations would require to be reopened and retraversed, not with the object of bringing any criminal to justice but to ascertain whether or not they had been competently conducted.[9]

A policy maximalist would think it entirely legitimate to take such concerns into account in deciding a case like *Hill*. But a policy maximalist would also think it legitimate to take into account policy considerations as a reason, not for *denying* that a duty of care was owed in a case like *Hill*, but as a reason *for* finding that a duty of care was owed in a case like *Hill*.

For example, suppose that Lord Keith was wrong in the first two sentences of the above quote. Suppose that it could be established that the police are generally lazy and uninterested in catching criminals and preventing crime, and a useful way of galvanising them into action would be to hold over them the prospect that if they failed to do their jobs properly, they could be sued in negligence by victims of crimes that would never have occurred if the police had not been incompetent. A policy maximalist would think it legitimate to take that into account as a positive reason for finding that a duty of care was owed in a case like *Hill*.

(3) Finally, there is *our position*,[10] which is that if *everything else* indicates that it would be *wrong* for the law to impose a particular duty of care on a class of people, the public interest cannot make it *okay* for the law to impose that duty of care on that class of people. But if *everything else* indicates that the law *should* impose a particular duty of care on a class of people, it would still be *wrong* for the law to impose that duty of care on that class of people if doing so would be contrary to the public interest.

For example, let's suppose there are lots of reasons that indicate that it would be wrong for the law to impose on the police a duty of care to catch criminals, which duty would be owed to potential victims of those criminals' crimes. (To save words, we'll call such a duty a *criminal-catching* duty of care.) For example, it might be objected that imposing a criminal-catching duty of care on the police would result in the law subjecting the police to a special disadvantage that they had done nothing to deserve. If it would be wrong to impose a criminal-catching duty of care on the police for reasons like this, then it it would still be wrong to impose such a duty of care on the police even if doing so would result in their doing a better job.

By way of contrast, we saw earlier that a case could be made for saying that the law should impose on the social services a duty to take care not to take a child out of the family home when there is no good reason to, where that duty would be owed to the parents of the child.[11] But even if that were true, it might still be wrong for the law to impose such a

---

[9] [1989] 1 AC 53, 63 (per Lord Keith of Kinkel).
[10] See McBride 2011, 364–5; also Robertson 2011, text at n 26.
[11] See above, § 1.3.

duty of care on the social services, if doing so would impair their efficiency in protecting children at risk of harm.

5.2 DUTY OF CARE TESTS

Over the years, a number of different judges have attempted to come up with 'tests' that can be applied to determine whether or not a given defendant owed a claimant a duty of care of some description:

The *Heaven* v *Pender* test (1883):

> whenever one person is by circumstances placed in such a position with regard to another that every one of ordinary sense who did think would at once recognise that if he did not use ordinary care and skill in his own conduct with regard to those circumstances he would cause danger of injury to the person or property of the other, a duty arises to use ordinary care and skill to avoid such danger.[12]

Lord Atkin's 'neighbour principle' (1932):

> You must take reasonable care to avoid acts or omissions which you can reasonably foresee would be likely to injure your neighbour. Who, then, in law is my neighbour? The answer seems to be – persons who are so closely and directly affected by my act that I ought reasonably to have them in contemplation as being so affected when I am directing my mind to the acts or omissions which are called in question.[13]

The *Anns* test (1978):

> in order to establish that a duty of care arises in a particular situation, it is not necessary to bring the facts of that situation within those of previous situations in which a duty of care has been held to exist. Rather the question has to be approached in two stages. First one has to ask whether, as between the alleged wrongdoer and the person who has suffered damage there is a sufficient relationship of proximity or neighbourhood such that, in the reasonable contemplation of the former, carelessness on his part may be likely to cause damage to the latter – in which case a prima facie duty of care arises. Secondly, if the first question is answered affirmatively, it is necessary to consider whether there are any considerations which ought to negative, or to reduce or limit the scope of the duty or the class of person to whom it was owed or the damages to which a breach of it may give rise . . .[14]

The 'incremental test' (1985):

> It is preferable, in my view, that the law should develop novel categories of negligence incrementally and by analogy with established categories, rather than by a massive extension of a prima facie duty of care restrained only by indefinable 'considerations which ought to negative, or to reduce or limit the scope of the duty or the class of the person to whom it is owed.'[15]

The *Caparo* test (1990):

> in addition to . . . foreseeability of damage, necessary ingredients in any situation giving rise to a duty of care are that there should exist between the party owing the duty and the party to whom it is owed a relationship characterised by the law as one of 'proximity' or 'neighbourhood' and that the situation should be one in which the court considers it fair, just and reasonable that the law should impose a duty of a given scope upon the one party for the benefit of the other.[16]

---

[12] *Heaven* v *Pender* (1883) 11 QBD 503, 509 (per Brett MR).
[13] *Donoghue* v *Stevenson* [1932] AC 562, 580 (per Lord Atkin).
[14] *Anns* v *Merton LBC* [1978] AC 728, 751–752 (per Lord Wilberforce).
[15] *Sutherland Shire Council* v *Heyman* (1985) 127 CLR 424, 481 (per Brennan J).
[16] *Caparo Industries plc* v *Dickman* [1990] 2 AC 605, 617–618 (per Lord Bridge of Harwich).

A number of different points need to be made about these tests for finding whether or not a duty of care was owed in a given case.

A. The need for tests

Lower courts only need to use a test to determine whether or not a defendant owed a claimant a duty of care in a novel case – where the issue of whether or not the defendant owed the claimant a duty of care has not yet been settled. If it has been settled, then they simply apply the law as it stands at the moment. As a result, there are fewer and fewer occasions when the lower courts – courts of first instance and the Court of Appeal – have to use these tests to determine whether or not a duty of care was owed. This is because, as more and more cases are decided on whether a duty of care was owed in a given situation, fewer and fewer cases can be genuinely said to raise a genuinely novel issue as to whether or not the defendant owed the claimant a duty of care.

It is different for the UK Supreme Court, which is not bound by the decisions of the lower courts, or by its own decisions, or by the decisions of the House of Lords, which was the UK Supreme Court's predecessor as the highest court in the UK. So even in a case where the law on whether the defendant owed the claimant a duty of care seems to be settled, the UK Supreme Court is free to 'unsettle' the law, and find (or refuse to find) that a duty of care was owed when all the precedents indicated that a duty of care was not owed (or was owed). In reaching its decision, the UK Supreme Court may want to employ a test for whether or not the defendant owed the claimant a duty of care, both to focus its mind on what it should take into account in determining whether the settled law on this issue is satisfactory or needs changing, and to give everyone the impression that the UK Supreme Court is not free to decide the case however it likes, but is instead bound by rules that it has to observe in reaching that decision.

It is an interesting question whether a student answering a problem question that raises the issue of whether the defendant owed the claimant a duty of care should do so from the perspective of a lower court judge or a Justice of the UK Supreme Court. We think most students would be expected to answer the question as though they were a lower court judge and should therefore have very little need to draw on any tests for whether or not the defendant owed the claimant a duty of care. Unless the problem question raises a genuinely novel issue, there should be ample authorities available to the student to be able to say – without need for recourse to any tests – whether or not a duty of care was owed in the situation under consideration.

B. The fate of the tests

Both Brett MR's test in *Heaven* v *Pender* and Lord Atkin's 'neighbour principle' were inspired by the idea that the existing authorities on when a defendant would owe a claimant a duty of care must have something in common – and if that 'common element' could be identified, then that would provide the courts with a guide as to what they should be looking for in future cases that raised the question of whether or not a defendant owed a claimant a duty of care. So Lord Atkin argued in *Donoghue* v *Stevenson*: 'in English law there *must* be, and is, some general conception of relations giving rise to a duty of care, of which the particular cases found in the books are but instances.'[17] But it soon became clear

---

[17] [1932] AC 562, 580 (emphasis added). To similar effect, see Brett MR in *Heaven* v *Pender* (1883) 11 QBD 503, 509.

that the 'common element' that they both seized on – foreseeability of harm – was not a satisfactory criterion for determining whether or not a duty of care was owed in any given case; in particular, cases where the defendant had *failed to save* the claimant from suffering some kind of harm, and cases where the defendant had done some positive act that resulted in the claimant suffering some kind of *pure economic loss*.[18] As a result, Lord Atkin's 'neighbour principle' had very little impact in terms of being used by the courts after *Donoghue* v *Stevenson* to determine whether or not a defendant owed a claimant a duty of care.[19]

And there the matter rested until the 1970s, when litigants became more determined to test the scope of the tort of negligence – in particular, by bringing claims in negligence against public bodies – and the courts felt the need to come up with a test for whether or not a duty of care was owed in a given case that would help them deal with all the novel duty claims that were being made to them. The test that the House of Lords provided the courts with was the *Anns* test – a duty of care will be owed if it is reasonably foreseeable that the defendant's conduct would result in the claimant suffering harm, and there are no policy considerations that would weigh against finding that such a duty was owed. The *Anns* test quickly came under fire[20] for making it too easy for the courts to find that a duty of care was owed in a particular case, and for making the law on when one person would owe another a duty of care intolerably uncertain.

The 'incremental test' suggested by Brennan J in the High Court of Australia and the *Caparo* test (sometimes referred to by the courts as the 'threefold test') were both reactions against the *Anns* test. Requiring that a claimant show that his case was analogous to cases where it had already been established that a duty of care would be owed, and requiring that the claimant show that there existed a relationship of 'proximity' between him and the defendant and that it was 'fair, just and reasonable' that the courts find a duty of care between the claimant and the defendant were simply ways of making it harder for claimants to convince the courts to recognise that a duty of care was owed in a novel case, and thereby reintroduce some kind of stability into this area of the law.

It is not clear that either of these tests were intended to do anything more than that. Certainly their authors could not have thought that either of these tests provided the courts with any concrete *guidance* as to what they should look for in determining whether a duty of care was owed in a novel case. A court seeking to apply the 'incremental test' to determine

[18] As Brett MR himself acknowledged, when – having become Lord Esher MR – in *Le Lievre* v *Gould* [1893] 1 QB 491, he declined to apply his *Heaven* v *Pender* test to a case where a surveyor's carelessness had resulted in the owner of land losing money that he had paid in advance to a builder for the construction of buildings on that land (the advance payments being made on the strength of the surveyor's certificates that the work was going as planned).

[19] For example, in the most important negligence case that was decided between 1940 and 1970 – *Hedley Byrne* v *Hellers & Partners Co Ltd* [1964] AC 465 – counsel for the claimants placed great reliance on *Donoghue* v *Stevenson* (arguing (at 472) that 'it should apply to words as well as deeds') but when the case was decided, Lord Reid only cited *Donoghue* v *Stevenson* to say that it was of no assistance (ibid, at 482: 'I do not think it has any direct bearing on this case') and Lord Devlin cited *Donoghue* v *Stevenson* as authority in favour of his not deciding the case in a way that would leave the law in a defective state (at 516: 'The common law is tolerant of much illogicality, especially on the surface, but no system of law can be workable if it has not got logic at the root of it') while going on to hold that counsel for the claimants had gone too far in trying to apply *Donoghue* v *Stevenson* 'literally to a certificate or a bankers' reference' (at 525). He held that 'The real value of *Donoghue* v *Stevenson* . . . is that it shows how the law can be developed to solve particular problems . . . As always in English law, the first step in such an inquiry is to see how far the authorities have gone, for new categories in the law do not spring into existence overnight' (at 525).

[20] Particularly from Lord Keith of Kinkel: *Peabody Donation Fund* v *Sir Lindsay Parkinson & Co Ltd* [1985] AC 210, 240–1; *Yuen Kun Yeu* v *Att-Gen for Hong Kong* [1988] AC 175, 190–4; *Rowling* v *Takaro Properties Ltd* [1988] AC 473, 501; and *Hill* v *Chief Constable of West Yorkshire* [1989] AC 53, 60.

whether or not a duty of care was owed in a novel case would inevitably end up asking: *How close* does this case have to be to a situation where it is established that a duty of care was owed before we can find that a duty of care was owed in this case? But the incremental test does not tell them. And even at the moment the *Caparo* test was set out by Lord Bridge of Harwich in *Caparo Industries plc v Dickman*, he admitted that:

> the concepts of proximity and fairness embodied [in this test] are not susceptible of any such precise definition as would be necessary to give them utility as practical tests, but amount in effect to little more than convenient labels to attach to the features of different specific situations which, on a detailed examination of all the circumstances, the law recognises pragmatically as giving rise to a duty of care of a given scope.[21]

C. The *Caparo* test

Despite its vagueness, the *Caparo* test still to this day provides the courts with a formula that they will invariably invoke if they need to resolve a debate over whether or not a defendant owed the claimant a duty of care in a given case. It is worth, then, looking at the *Caparo* test in more detail. The *Caparo* test essentially says that a defendant will have owed the claimant a duty of care in a given case if: (1) it was reasonably foreseeable that the claimant would suffer harm as a result of the defendant's actions or inaction; (2) there was a relationship of proximity between the defendant and the claimant; and (3) it would be 'fair, just and reasonable' to find that the defendant owed the claimant a duty of care.

The key leg of this formula is the last one. Essentially, the *Caparo* test tells the courts: find that A owed B a duty of care if, and only if, it would be 'fair, just and reasonable' to do so.

In some cases (usually involving A doing something positive that foreseeably resulted in B's person or property being harmed), this requirement will be satisfied merely by showing that it was reasonably foreseeable that A's actions would result in B suffering some kind of harm. In such cases, the courts will say that because (1) is true, (2) and (3) are also true – the fact that it was foreseeable that B would suffer harm as a result of A's actions also establishes that there was a sufficient relationship of 'proximity' between them, and that it would be 'fair, just and reasonable' to find that A owed B a duty of care.

But in other cases (such as cases where A has failed to save B from harm, or has done something positive that foreseeably resulted in B suffering some kind of pure economic loss or psychiatric illness), the mere fact that it was foreseeable that B would suffer some kind of harm if A acted as he did will *not* make it 'fair, just and reasonable' to find that A owed B a duty of care. Something more will be required – some kind of special relationship, or special circumstances, that would justify the courts in finding that A owed B a duty of care. In such cases, the courts will not find that (2) and (3) are made out unless such a special relationship, or special circumstances, are made out.

In each type of case, the courts' decision as to what needs to be established in order to show that there was sufficiently 'proximate' relationship between A and B (mere foreseeability of harm, or a special relationship or special circumstances) will be driven by its view as to when it would be 'fair, just and reasonable' to find that A owed B a duty of care. The same point was made by Lord Oliver of Aylmerton in *Caparo Industries plc v Dickman*:

---

[21] [1990] 2 AC 605, 618.

it is difficult to resist a conclusion that what have been treated as three separate requirements are, at least in most cases, in fact merely facets of the same thing, for in some cases the degree of foreseeability is such that it is from that alone that the requisite proximity can be deduced, whilst in others the absence of that special relationship can most rationally be attributed simply to the court's view that it would not be fair and reasonable to hold the defendant responsible. 'Proximity' is, no doubt, a convenient expression so long as it is realised that it is no more than a label which embraces not a definable concept but merely a description of circumstances from which, pragmatically, the courts conclude that a duty of care exists.[22]

The fact that the *Caparo* test amounts to nothing more than an instruction to the courts to act reasonably in determining whether or not a defendant owed a claimant a duty of care not only establishes that the *Caparo* test does not really function as a 'test' for determining when a duty of care will be owed. It also means that the *Caparo* test does not really provide us with any kind of concrete guidance that will help us predict when the courts will and will not find that a defendant owed a claimant a duty of care. For that, we need to abandon all talk of 'tests' and focus instead on what kind of *factors* the courts will take into account in determining whether or not a duty of care was owed in a particular case.

5.3 DUTY OF CARE FACTORS[23]

So what sort of factors will the courts take into account in deciding whether or not it would be 'fair, just and reasonable' to find that a duty of care was owed in a particular case? This is a list of the more important factors:

A. Reasonable foreseeability of harm

As we have already seen, the courts will not find that A owed B a duty of care if it was not reasonably foreseeable that B would be affected by A's actions. This is because the law of negligence would become unduly uncertain if it simply said, 'You must not do x if someone somewhere will be harmed by your doing x.' If the law did say this then A would never know whether he was allowed to do x or not because he could never be certain whether or not his doing x would harm someone somewhere in the world. So the law of negligence allows A to do x if it is not reasonably foreseeable that someone else will be harmed by A's doing x. If A wants to know whether he is allowed to do x, all he has to do is take reasonable steps to check and see if anyone will be harmed by his doing x, and if it does not look as though anyone will be, he will know he is free to go ahead and do x.

B. Reasonableness

One of the differences between the law of trespass and the law of negligence is that you can't be held liable in negligence for acting reasonably.[24] So the courts will not find that A owed B a duty of care not to do x if it was reasonable for A to act in that way; nor can A be said to have owed B a duty of care to do x if it would have been unreasonable for A to do x.

---

[22] [1990] 2 AC 605, 633.
[23] See Stapleton 1998, Stanton 2007b, Hartstone 2008.
[24] See above, §§ 2.3, 2.5, 2.7, for examples of situations where someone can be held liable in trespass despite acting reasonably.

We have already seen an example of this principle at work in the case of *Tomlinson v Congleton BC* (2004),[25] where it was contended that the defendant local council owed people who might endanger themselves by swimming in a lake in the council's park a duty to turn the beaches around the lake into marshland so that no one in their right mind would ever want to go anywhere near the lake. As we have seen, the House of Lords rejected in the strongest terms the idea that the council was subject to a duty to do something so ridiculous.[26]

For the same reason, an employer will not owe an ex-employee a duty to hide the truth about that ex-employee's performance at work when writing a reference for the ex-employee, even if it is reasonably foreseeable that telling the truth about the ex-employee will stop him getting the job.[27]

C. Acts and omissions

English law draws a fundamental distinction between acts and omissions – between cases where A does something that makes B worse off than she would have been had A done nothing, and cases where A fails to do something that would have had the effect of making B better off than she currently is. So if A pushes B into a lake, then that is an 'act'. If someone else pushes B into the lake, and A fails to rescue B, that is an omission.[28]

The courts are far more willing to find that a duty of care was owed in an 'act' case than in an 'omission' case. We will fully explore the reasons for this in Chapter 8, but for the time being it suffices to point out that a duty not to do *x* is far less intrusive on individual liberty (because it leaves the person subject to it free to do anything but *x*) than a duty to do *x* is (because the person subject to a duty to do *x* is not free to do anything except *x*). The courts will usually only find that A owed B a duty of care to make B better off in some way if there existed some kind of 'special relationship' between A and B. If there was not, they will usually deny that A owed B a duty of care on the ground that there was no 'proximity' between the parties. For example, in *Hill* v *Chief Constable of West Yorkshire* (1989), the police failed to save Jacqueline Hill from being killed by the 'Yorkshire Ripper', Peter Sutcliffe. But as there existed no special relationship between Jacqueline Hill and the police, the House of Lords found that the police did not owe Jacqueline Hill a duty to take reasonable steps to catch Peter Sutcliffe before he could kill again. There was not a sufficient relationship of 'proximity' between them to warrant finding that a duty of care was owed.

---

[25] Discussed above, § 1.15.

[26] ibid.

[27] *Lawton* v *BOC Transhield* [1987] 2 All ER 608.

[28] There are some cases where the distinction between an act and an omission can be difficult to apply. Take the case – considered *obiter* in *Candler* v *Crane, Christmas & Co* [1951] 2 KB 164, at 183 and 194 – of the marine hydrographer who omits a reef from a map of the seabed. A ship's captain, using the map, steers his ship in such a way that it collides with the reef. This looks like an omission case – the hydrographer failed to save the ship from colliding with the reef because he failed to alert the captain to the existence of the reef. If it is, then the members of the Court of Appeal who considered this case in *Candler* were right to think that the hydrographer did not owe the ship's owner a duty of care in preparing his map of the seabed: there was no 'special relationship' between the two that would justify finding that a duty of care was owed. But we might be able to say that this case is an act case if, had the map not been drawn up, the ship's captain would have relied on his own eyes or other charts, spotted the reef and steered the ship clear of it. If this is the case, then we can say that the marine hydrographer made things worse by drawing up his map – had he not drawn up his map, the ship would not have been damaged. If this is the case, then it could be said that the hydrographer owed the ship's owner a duty of care in drawing up his map, even in the absence of a 'special relationship' between the two: see below, § 6.2.

D. Seriousness of harm

In an 'act' case, whether the courts are willing to find that A owed B a duty of care not to act as he did will turn on a number of factors. One of the most important is the seriousness of the harm that B stood to suffer if A acted as he did. If it was reasonably foreseeable that B would suffer *physical injury* or *damage to his property* as a result of A's actions, then the courts will readily find that A owed B a duty of care not to act as he did.

If, on the other hand, it was *merely* foreseeable that B would suffer *pure economic loss* as a result of A's actions, the courts will not find that A owed B a duty of care not to act as he did. The loss that B stood to suffer if A acted as he did was not serious enough[29] to warrant the law's intervening to require A to look out for B's interests.[30] This is not to say that the courts will always refuse to find that A owed B a duty of care in a case where he did something that merely made B economically worse off. It is merely to say that the *mere* fact that it was reasonably foreseeable that B would lose money as a result of A's actions will not

---

[29] For an interesting argument that cases of someone's suffering pure economic losses are always more trivial than cases of someone's suffering property damage (because property is more important to our personalities than stocks of wealth), see Witting 2001.

[30] Cases where a duty of care was denied because the only ground for imposing it would have been that it was foreseeable that the defendant would suffer economic loss as a result of the claimant's actions include: *Cattle* v *Stockton Waterworks Co* (1875) LR 10 QB 453 (no duty of care owed to contractors not to delay them in their work, thereby making their contract to do that work less profitable); *Simpson & Co* v *Thomson* (1877) 3 App Cas 279 (no duty of care owed to insurer not to damage insured property); *Société Anonyme de Remourquage à Hélice* v *Bennetts* [1911] 1 KB 243 (no duty of care owed by defendants not to sink ship being towed by tug, thereby preventing the tug earning a fee for towing the ship); *Weller & Co* v *Foot and Mouth Disease Research Institute* [1966] 1 QB 569 (virus causing foot and mouth disease escaped from defendants' premises and caused outbreak of foot and mouth disease in area with the result that claimants' business as cattle auctioneers was temporarily suspended; no duty of care not to release virus owed by defendants to claimants); *Candlewood Navigation Corporation Ltd* v *Mitsui OSK Lines Ltd, The Mineral Transporter* [1986] AC 1 (no duty of care owed to claimants not to damage ship which claimants did not have proprietary interest in but which the claimants had to pay hire for even if the ship was damaged); *Leigh & Sillavan Ltd* v *Aliakmon Shipping Co Ltd, The Aliakmon* [1986] AC 785 (no duty of care owed to claimant not to damage goods which the claimant had contracted to pay for but which he had not yet acquired ownership or possession of); *Simaan General Contracting Co* v *Pilkington Glass Ltd (No 2)* [1988] QB 758 (job of constructing building in Saudi Arabia given to claimant; building was to include a green glass curtain wall and the job of constructing the wall was subcontracted to F; job of constructing the glass that would make up the wall was sub-contracted to defendant; defendant's glass panels were not the right shade of green with the result that the fee payable to the main contractor for constructing the building was reduced; held, that defendant had not owed the claimant a duty of care in constructing the panels); *CBS Songs* v *Amstrad Consumer Electronics plc* [1988] AC 1013 (no duty of care owed to claimant recording company whose royalties might be reduced as a result of defendants' marketing tape-to-tape recording machine which would allow illegal copies of cassette tapes to be made); *Van Oppen* v *Clerk to the Bedford Charity Trustees* [1990] 1 WLR 235 (no duty of care owed by school to pupil to arrange insurance on his behalf against his being injured playing rugby at the school); *Pacific Associates* v *Baxter* [1990] 1 QB 993 (no duty of care owed by engineers employed to judge whether contractors should be paid for the work they have done to use reasonable skill and care in making those judgments); *Islington LBC* v *University College London Hospital NHS Trust* [2005] EWCA Civ 596 (no duty of care owed to local authority that foreseeably would have to spend money providing residential care to person who suffered stroke as a result of defendant hospital's negligence); *WBA* v *El-Safty* [2005] EWHC 2866 (doctor does not owe football club a duty of care to treat one of their footballer's injuries properly); *Customs and Excise Commissioners* v *Barclays Bank* [2007] 1 AC 181 (where A is suing B and has obtained a 'freezing order' over B's bank account to stop B transferring money from the account out of the country and beyond A's reach, B's bank will not owe A a duty of care to stop B withdrawing money from his account). It is customary to mention, alongside these cases, cases such as *D & F Estates* v *Church Commissioners* [1989] AC 177 and *Murphy* v *Brentwood DC* [1991] 1 AC 398 (held in both cases, no action maintainable in negligence against builders of a dangerously defective house for the cost of repairing the defects in the building). However, in those cases a duty of care *was* owed (see below, § 6.2): the real significance of those cases was that they set a limit on the losses that someone would be liable for if he or she breached that duty of care. An explanation of the House of Lords' rulings in *D & F Estates* and *Murphy* is set out below, at § 10.3.

be enough to justify a finding that A owed B a duty of care. Something more will be required, such as the existence of a 'special relationship' between A and B.

Similarly, if the only loss that it could be foreseen that B would suffer as a result of A's actions was that B would suffer *distress*, the courts will not find that A owed B a duty of care not to act as he did unless there existed some kind of 'special relationship' between A and B.[31] The mere fact that it was reasonably foreseeable that B would suffer distress as a result of A's actions will not be enough to warrant finding that A owed B a duty of care not to act as he did.[32]

So – *Driver* will owe nearby pedestrians a duty of care not to drive dangerously because it is reasonably foreseeable that they will be physically injured if she drives dangerously. She will not owe a nearby pedestrian's *Employer* a duty of care not to drive dangerously. This is because the only loss that it is foreseeable *Employer* will suffer if *Driver* drives dangerously and runs down the pedestrian is economic loss – the disruption his business will suffer as a result of his employee being run down – and there exists no 'special relationship' between *Driver* and *Employer* that would tip the scales in favour of a finding that *Driver* owes *Employer* a duty of care not to drive dangerously. Similarly, *Driver* will not owe the nearby pedestrian's uncles and aunts a duty of care not to drive dangerously – the only loss that it is foreseeable they will suffer if she drives dangerously and runs down the pedestrian is distress.

E. Fairness

One factor that the courts will always take into account in determining whether a duty of care was owed in a given situation is the need to be 'fair'. 'Fairness' is a slippery term, but best encapsulates the reason why the courts will sometimes refuse to find that a duty of care was owed in a particular case if doing so might expose a defendant to a 'liability in an indeterminate amount for an indeterminate time to an indeterminate class'.[33] If there is a danger that finding that A owed B a duty of care will result in A's liability for the harm he caused B getting out of all proportion to his fault in causing that harm, the courts may well refuse to find that a duty of care was owed.

For example, in *The Nicholas H* (1996), a certification society certified that a ship was fit to sail when it was not. When the ship sank with all its cargo on board, the cargo owners sued the certification society in negligence for compensation for the loss of the cargo, claiming that the defendant had owed them a duty of care not to certify the ship as being fit to sail when it was not. The House of Lords held that the certification society had not owed a duty of care to the cargo owners. This was so even though *The Nicholas H* was an 'act' case (without the certificate from the certification society the ship could not have sailed, so issuing the certificate made the cargo owners worse off than they were before the certificate was issued) and it was plainly foreseeable that the cargo owners would suffer property damage if the ship was certified as being fit to sail when it was not. Part of the reason for denying that a duty of care was owed in this case may have been that if a duty of care was found in this case, the certification society's liability could have run into millions of pounds – depending on the value of the cargo on board the ship – and got out of all proportion to the society's initial fault in approving the ship as being fit to sail.

---

[31] See below, § 6.7, for an account of when someone may sue in negligence for compensation for mere distress.
[32] See *Rothwell* v *Chemical & Insulating Co Ltd* [2006] EWCA Civ 27, at [63]: 'The law does not recognise a duty to take reasonable care not to cause anxiety.'
[33] *Ultramares Corporation* v *Touche*, 174 NE 441 (1931), at 444, per Cardozo CJ.

F. Individual responsibility

If finding that a duty of care was owed in a particular case might tend to undermine people's sense of individual responsibility, then that is a factor which will weigh heavily (though not conclusively) against a finding that a duty of care was owed. There are two ways in which a finding of a duty of care might undermine people's sense of individual responsibility.

(1) Finding a duty of care might allow a responsible adult to escape some or all of the consequences of his own foolhardiness by giving him the right to sue someone else in negligence for compensation for self-inflicted injuries. For example, in *Vellino* v *Chief Constable of Greater Manchester Police* (2002), the police arrested the claimant, a habitual thief, in his flat. He attempted to escape arrest by jumping out of his kitchen window. He fell very badly and was severely injured. The Court of Appeal held that the police had not owed the claimant a duty to take reasonable steps to stop him escaping from police custody. Similarly, in *Barrett* v *Ministry of Defence* (1995) a soldier died after he had too much to drink at a party held in his barracks. It was argued that the soldier's commanding officer owed the soldier a duty to take reasonable steps to ensure that he did not drink too much at the party. The Court of Appeal rejected this claim, holding that it would not be 'fair, just and reasonable' to find that the commanding officer had owed the soldier such a duty.[34] *Tomlinson* (2004) is another case in the same vein, with Lord Hoffmann holding in that case that:

> A duty to protect against obvious risks of self-inflicted harm exists only in cases in which there is no genuine or informed choice, as in the case of employees whose work requires them to take the risk, or some lack of capacity, such as the inability of children to recognise danger . . . or the despair of prisoners which may lead them to inflict injury on themselves . . .[35]

(2) The second way in which finding that a duty of care was owed in a particular case might undermine people's sense of individual responsibility is if finding that a duty was owed might allow an admitted wrongdoer to escape being held liable to compensate the victim of his wrong for the harm that he did her. For example, in *Mitchell* v *Glasgow City Council* (2009), Mitchell was killed by a 'neighbour from hell' about whom he had complained to the council. The council had held a meeting with the neighbour – who had a history of violence – and disclosed to him at the meeting that Mitchell had made a video of the neighbour threatening Mitchell. The neighbour became very angry and left the meeting. The council made no attempt to warn Mitchell that he might be in danger from his neighbour; and sadly, shortly after the meeting ended, the neighbour attacked and killed Mitchell with an iron bar. The House of Lords held that the council had *not* owed Mitchell a duty to warn him that he might be in danger – despite the fact that one of the situations where A will owe B to save him from harm is in a situation where A has put B in danger of suffering that harm.[36]

It is hard to avoid the impression that at least part of the reason for the House of Lords' decision was that they thought that if they held that the council had owed Mitchell a duty of care in this case, that would have the effect of diluting the neighbour's liability for what he did to Mitchell. Instead of suing the neighbour, who was primarily responsible for what

---

[34] However, once the soldier fell into a drunken stupor and the officers in charge undertook to look after him, they owed him a duty to look after him with a reasonable degree of care and skill: [1995] 1 WLR 1217, 1223. See below, § 7.4.

[35] [2004] 1 AC 46, at [46].

[36] See below, § 7.3, where the *Mitchell* case is discussed in further detail.

happened to Mitchell, Mitchell's estate would be encouraged to target the council instead, which was – at best – secondarily responsible for the tragic turn of events. Moreover, even if Mitchell's estate did sue the neighbour, the neighbour would have been allowed – if the council had owed Mitchell a duty of care – to seek to make the council share some of the cost of compensating Mitchell's estate under the law on contribution. The law of contribution applies in cases where *Defendant One* and *Defendant Two* are *both* liable in tort to compensate *Victim* for some loss that she has suffered, and *Victim* successfully sues *One* for compensation for that loss. *One* can then make a claim in contribution against *Two*, arguing that as *Two* was also liable to *Victim*, he should be made to contribute towards the cost of compensating *Victim* by paying *One* a 'just and equitable' sum that reflects *Two*'s responsibility for what happened to *Victim*.[37] So here: if Mitchell's estate had sued his neighbour for damages for the injuries he suffered before he died, and the House of Lords had held that the council had owed Mitchell a duty of care and was therefore potentially liable in negligence for what happened to Mitchell, Mitchell's neighbour might have been able to escape some of the burden of compensating Mitchell's estate for what he did to Mitchell by making a claim in contribution against the council.

G. Parliament's intentions

The courts are subordinate to Parliament. It follows that the courts cannot find that A owes B a duty of care if to do so would undermine Parliament's intentions in passing a particular piece of legislation.

For example, imagine that Parliament placed the Identity and Passport Service (IPS, for short) under a statutory duty to process people's passport applications within eight weeks of their being submitted. Imagine also that Parliament provided that breach of this statutory duty should *not* be actionable in tort. So if *Traveller* received a new passport 12 weeks after submitting her application for a new passport, she would *not* be able to bring an action for breach of statutory duty against the IPS. Could she instead argue that the IPS owed her a duty of care in negligence to process her application within eight weeks of its being submitted? The answer is, 'Without more – no. If the *only* basis for saying that the IPS owed *Traveller* a duty of care in this case is the fact that it was under a statutory duty to process her application within eight weeks of its being submitted, then the courts cannot find that the IPS owed *Traveller* a duty of care in processing her application.'

The reason why the courts cannot do this is that to do so would undermine Parliament's intention that the IPS's breach of statutory duty in *Traveller*'s case should not be actionable in tort. If the courts were to find that the IPS owed *Traveller* a duty of care in processing her application based *only* on the fact that the IPS owed *Traveller* a statutory duty to process her application speedily, then the courts would effectively be making the IPS's breach of statutory duty actionable in tort. The statutory duty that the IPS was under to process *Traveller*'s passport application speedily would give rise to a parallel duty of care, and *Traveller* would be able to bring a claim in negligence against the IPS if the IPS breached its statutory duty to process her passport application speedily. It is for this reason that Lord Hoffmann, in particular, has repeatedly insisted that:

> If [a public authority's failure to perform a statutory] duty does not give rise to a private right to sue for breach, it would be unusual if it nevertheless gave rise to a duty of care at common law

---

[37] Civil Liability (Contribution) Act 1978, ss 1, 2.

which made the public authority liable to pay compensation for foreseeable loss caused by the duty not being performed. It will often be foreseeable that loss will result if, for example, a benefit or a service is not provided. If the policy of the Act [imposing the statutory duty in question was] not to create a statutory liability to pay compensation, the same policy should ordinarily exclude the existence of a common law duty of care.[38]

H. Divided loyalties

The courts will often refuse to find that a duty of care was owed in a specific case because doing so would harm the public interest. The most obvious way in which this might happen is where the prospect of being sued might cause a public official to 'take his eye off the ball' and not do his job properly because he is more concerned about avoiding litigation that he is with performing his responsibilities in the way they should be performed.

There are many situations where the courts will refuse to find that a duty of care is owed because they fear that the existence of such a duty will tempt a public official not to do his job properly and opt instead to do whatever will expose him to the least risk of being sued:

(1) *Judges.* A judge deciding a civil case will not owe the parties to the case a duty to decide the case with a reasonable degree of care and skill.[39] If a judge feared he might be sued by the losing party in a civil case, he might be less concerned about giving the right decision and more concerned about 'splitting the difference' between the parties so as to avoid annoying either of them with his decision.

(2) *Military commanders.* A military officer will not owe a duty of care to the soldiers under his command in the heat of battle.[40] If he did, he might be tempted not to put them in harm's way – so as to avoid being sued later by soldiers injured in the battle and the families of soldiers who were killed – when doing so is required to achieve his military objectives.

(3) *Police.* If the police suspect A of committing a crime, they will not owe A a duty of care in carrying out their investigations into whether or not he committed that crime.[41] Moreover, if A presents himself to the police as being a witness to a crime, the police will *not* owe A a duty of care to treat him properly as a witness, and a potential victim of crime.[42] The courts fear that finding that the police are subject to either of these duties of care will divert them from their central task of investigating crime.

(4) *Health and safety inspectors.* The Court of Appeal ruled in *Harris v Evans* (1998) that a health and safety inspector did *not* owe a duty of care to a claimant whose business was severely disrupted by the health and safety inspector making what turned out to be unjustified demands on the claimant. The Court of Appeal was fearful that if it found

---

[38] *Stovin v Wise* [1996] AC 923, 952–3. See also Lord Hoffmann's judgments in *Gorringe v Calderdale MBC* [2004] 1 WLR 1057, at [23] ('If the statute does not create a private right of action, it would be, to say the least, unusual if the mere existence of the statutory duty could generate a common law duty of care'); and in *Customs and Excise Commissioners v Barclays Bank plc* [2007] 1 AC 181, at [39] ('you cannot derive a common law duty of care directly from a statutory duty'). To the same effect, see Lord Scott in *Gorringe v Calderdale MBC* [2004] 1 WLR 1057, at [71]: 'if a statutory duty does not give rise to a private right to sue for breach, the duty cannot create a duty of care that would not have been owed at common law if the statute were not there.'

[39] *Rondel v Worsley* [1969] 1 AC 191, 270 (per Lord Pearce); *Sirros v Moore* [1975] QB 118; *FM (a child) v Singer* [2004] EWHC 793.

[40] *Mulcahy v Ministry of Defence* [1996] QB 732; *Smith v Ministry of Defence* [2011] EWHC 1676 (QB).

[41] *Calveley v Chief Constable of Merseyside Police* [1989] AC 1228.

[42] *Brooks v Commissioner of Police of the Metropolis* [2005] 1 WLR 1495.

that health and safety inspectors owed duties of care to businesses affected by their findings and decisions, inspectors would – out of a desire to avoid being sued – become very cautious about making any decisions or findings that might adversely affect someone's business.[43]

(5) *Social services.* In D v *East Berkshire Community NHS Trust* (2005), the House of Lords held that if the social services investigate allegations that *Parent* is abusing his *Daughter*, the *only* person the social services will owe a duty of care to in carrying out their investigations is *Daughter*. They will *not* owe *Parent* a duty to carry out their investigations with a reasonable degree of care and skill.[44] Their Lordships feared that if the social services owed *Parent* such a duty of care, they would become excessively cautious about taking *Daughter* into care, for fear that they might be sued by *Parent* if they made a mistake and took *Daughter* into care when she was not actually at risk. So if a duty of care were owed to *Parent*, it might cause the social services to neglect their fundamental responsibility to safeguard *Daughter*'s interests.[45]

(6) *Councils.* A concern not to do anything that might cause public officials to neglect their core responsibilities may also explain why the House of Lords refused to find that a duty of care was owed in the *Mitchell* case, discussed above. Some of the Law Lords expressed themselves concerned that if they found that a duty of care was owed by the council to Mitchell in this case, that might have the effect of discouraging councils generally from tackling the problem of 'neighbours from hell' on the basis that if the councils didn't get involved in the first place, they couldn't get sued when their getting involved had tragic consequences for individuals complaining to councils about their neighbours.[46]

One of the reasons why *policy minimalists* think that considerations of public policy should *not* be taken into account in determining whether or not a defendant owed a claimant a duty of care is that – they argue – judges are simply *not competent* to determine correctly whether or not deciding a case one way or the other would be contrary to the public interest. If this is right, then one implication is that whether or not a particular judge is convinced by a public policy argument that he should decide a case in a particular way will become a matter of *chance* – as there is no guarantee that the objective strength of that argument will determine whether or not the judge accepts it or not. While we have criticised *policy minimalism* above, it must be admitted that it does seem that it is just a matter of chance whether or not the courts will deny a duty of care on the basis of what we might call a *divided loyalty* argument. There are plenty of cases where the courts have not been convinced by such arguments to deny that a duty of care was owed in a particular case, and it is very difficult to say why *divided loyalty* arguments won the day in the situations above, but were dismissed in the situations discussed below.

---

[43] [1998] 1 WLR 1285, 1298 (per Sir Richard Scott V-C). See also *Jain* v *Trent Strategic HA* [2009] 1 AC 853. Both *Harris* and *Jain* are discussed below, § 6.13.

[44] See also *Lawrence* v *Pembrokeshire County Council* [2007] 1 WLR 2991. The position is the same in Australia (*Sullivan* v *Moody* (2001) 207 CLR 562, at [62]) and New Zealand (*B* v *Attorney General* [2003] 4 All ER 833).

[45] Though see now *MAK* v *United Kingdom* (2010) 51 EHRR 14 holding that *Parent*'s rights under Article 8 of the European Convention on Human Rights will be violated if the social services unreasonably reach the wrong conclusion that *Daughter* is being abused and as a result take her into care. If the UK courts follow *MAK*, *Parent* will be entitled to sue the social services under the Human Rights Act 1998 for unreasonably taking *Daughter* into care. If this happens, the divided loyalty argument against finding that the social services owed *Parent* a duty of care under the common law will fall away as the potential for being sued under the Human Rights Act 1998 will mean that the social services' loyalties will *already* be divided.

[46] [2009] 1 AC 874, at [27]–[28] (per Lord Hope), and at [77] (per Baroness Hale).

(1) *Doctors*. The courts have never hesitated to find that doctors owe duties of care to their patients in treating them, despite widely expressed fears that doing so only encourages doctors to practise 'defensive medicine', giving patients excessive tests and treatments in an attempt to demonstrate publicly that everything has been done for the patient and avoid litigation.[47]

(2) *Referees*. In *Spring* v *Guardian Assurance* (1995), the House of Lords dismissed fears that if they found that an *Employer* will owe an *Ex*-employee a duty of care in writing a reference for him, *Employer* would become excessively cautious about saying anything negative about *Ex* in his reference. This was so even though *Employer* will normally owe the *Prospective Employer* to whom the reference is sent a duty to take care to provide an accurate reference and admitting that he *also* might owe a duty to *Ex* in writing a reference might create a real conflict between *Employer*'s desire to perform his primary duty to provide *Prospective Employer* with an accurate reference and *Employer*'s desire not to say anything that might result in his being sued by *Ex*. Moreover, in the law of defamation, references are protected by qualified privilege precisely because it is feared that if they were not, referees would become unduly cautious about expressing themselves frankly in their references.[48]

(3) *Barristers*. It used to be the law that a barrister would not owe a duty to his or her client to conduct that client's case in court with a reasonable degree of care and skill. One of the reasons for this was that

> A barrister has an overriding duty to the court to act with independence in the interests of justice: he must assist the court in the administration of justice and must not knowingly or recklessly mislead the court[49]

and it was feared that if barristers owed their clients a duty of care, a desire to avoid

> the possibility of being sued in negligence would at least subconsciously lead some counsel to undue prolixity which would not only be harmful to [his or her] client but against the public interest in prolonging trials.[50]

However, in *Arthur J S Hall* v *Simons* (2002)[51] the House of Lords was less concerned about this and as a result swept away the no-duty rule in relation to barristers.

(4) *Expert witnesses*. Almost ten years later, in *Jones* v *Kaney* (2011) the Supreme Court also swept away the rule that an expert witness who was hired (or volunteered) to give evidence in court on behalf of a claimant or a defendant would not owe their client an actionable duty of care in giving that evidence. Under the Civil Procedure Rules, such witnesses have an overriding duty to the court 'to help the court on matters within their expertise'. The Supreme Court dismissed fears that finding that an expert witness owed a duty of care to his client might tempt the witness to breach this overriding duty by not saying anything that might prove damaging to the client's case for fear that if he did so, he might end up being sued by his client.

---

[47] American studies estimate the cost of defensive medicine in the United States as being in the tens of *billions* of dollars: see, for example, US Congress Office of Technology Assessment, *Defensive Medicine and Medical Malpractice*, OTA-H-602 (1994); Kessler and McClellan 1996.

[48] For an account of the law on qualified privilege, see below, § 19.10.

[49] Code of Conduct of the Bar of England and Wales, para 302.

[50] *Rondel* v *Worsley* [1969] 1 AC 191, 229 (per Lord Reid).

[51] Noted, Seneviratne 2001.

I. Waste of resources

Another way in which finding that a duty of care was owed in a concrete case may harm the public interest is where doing so would encourage a lot of groundless litigation against a public body, which would in turn take up *valuable time and resources* to deal with. As we have seen, this was one of the reasons why, in the *Hill* case, the House of Lords thought that it would *not* be 'fair, just and reasonable' to find that the police owed potential victims of a criminal on the loose a duty to take reasonable steps to arrest him.[52]

In other cases, this argument for finding that it would not be 'fair, just and reasonable' to find that one person will owe another a duty of care has been less successful. In *Phelps* v *London Borough of Hillingdon* (2001), Lord Nicholls – with the agreement of Lord Jauncey of Tullichettle – suggested that the time had come to recognise that teachers owe their students a duty to teach them with reasonable skill and care. He acknowledged some would be concerned that taking such a step would adversely affect the public interest:

> The principal objection [to recognising that the teacher of a normal student will owe that student a duty to teach him or her with a reasonable degree of care and skill] is the spectre of a rash of 'gold digging' actions brought on behalf of under-achieving children by discontented parents, perhaps years after the events complained of. If teachers are liable, education authorities will be vicariously liable, since the negligent acts and omissions were committed in the course of the teachers' employment. So, it is said, the limited resources of education authorities and the time of teaching staff will be diverted away from teaching and into defending unmeritorious legal claims. Further, schools will have to prepare and keep full records, lest they be unable to rebut negligence allegations, brought out of the blue years later. For one or more of these reasons [it is argued], the overall standard of education given to children is likely to suffer if a legal duty of care were held to exist.[53]

However, Lord Nicholls felt able to dismiss these concerns: 'I am not persuaded by these fears.'[54]

J. Novelty

The more novel a claim that a duty of care was owed in a particular case, the less likely it is that the courts will accept it. There are two reasons for this.

First of all, while the courts do sometimes act as legislators and create new law with their decisions, they do not like to advertise this fact for fear of attracting accusations that they are acting undemocratically and usurping the role of Parliament. So when the courts are invited in a particular case to create new law, they are unlikely to accept the invitation unless they can dress up the innovation that they will be introducing into the law as a marginal, or incremental, development of the existing law.

Secondly, just as Parliament can make mistakes in reforming the law, so can the courts. Indeed, the courts are more prone than Parliament in one respect to making mistakes in reforming the law. This is because when the courts are invited to reform the law in some way, they will often be unable to tell what the full effects will be of reforming the law in the way proposed. As a result, the courts will often find it difficult to tell whether a given reform of the law will be beneficial in the long run. Given this, the courts are rightly wary of using their powers to reform the law in radical ways, and are happier to make

[52] See above, § 5.1.
[53] [2001] 2 AC 619, 667.
[54] ibid.

small changes in the law, where the effects of those changes can be more easily estimated and assessed.

These concerns about the wisdom of the courts' developing the law on when one person will owe another a duty of care underlay Brennan J's adoption of the 'incremental test' for when a defendant will owe a claimant a duty of care in *Sutherland Shire Council* v *Heyman* (1985), which was set out above.[55] However, there are problems with applying the incremental test in practice.

First of all, it can be argued that it places too tight a constraint on the courts' ability to find a duty of care in a novel case. Secondly, it is often arguable whether one case is genuinely analogous to another. Thirdly, it is unclear – as we have already observed – how close a given case needs to be to an already established duty situation for the incremental test to be satisfied in that case. For these reasons, in *Customs and Excise Commissioners* v *Barclays Bank plc* (2007), Lord Bingham dismissed the 'incremental test' for determining whether a duty of care was owed in a novel case as 'of little value as a test in itself'.[56]

The same case does, however, provide a great deal of support for Brennan J's view that the courts should be wary of making radical changes in the law on when one person will owe another a duty of care. So Lord Bingham conceded that

> The closer the facts of the case in issue to those of a case in which a duty of care has been held to exist, the readier a court will be [to find a duty of care in the case in issue] . . . The converse is also true.[57]

And Lord Mance made it clear that he viewed 'incrementalism' as an 'important cross-check'[58] on finding a duty of care in a novel case, on the basis that 'caution and analogical reasoning are generally valuable accompaniments to judicial activity, and this is particularly true in the present area'.[59]

K. The importance of remedying wrongs

In our list of factors that the courts will take into account in deciding whether A owed B a duty of care in a novel case, we have left until last a factor that some judges like to mention first in deciding whether a duty of care was owed in a novel case. This factor is: 'the rule of public policy that has first claim on the loyalty of the law: that wrongs should be remedied.'[60]

As a factor to be taken into account in judging whether A owed B a duty of care in a novel case, this is very puzzling. The very reason we want to know whether A owed B a duty of care is to find out whether or not A *wronged* B in acting as he did. So to say that one of the things we should take into account in judging whether A owed B a duty of care is the fact that A *did* wrong B, and that that wrong needs to be remedied by allowing B to sue A for damages, seems to be a fairly spectacular case of putting the cart before the horse. As Lord Rodger observed in the case of *D* v *East Berkshire Community NHS Trust* (2005):

---

[55] See above, § 5.2.
[56] [2007] 1 AC 181, at [7].
[57] ibid.
[58] [2007] 1 AC 181, at [93].
[59] [2007] 1 AC 181, at [84].
[60] See *X* v *Bedfordshire CC* [1995] 2 AC 633, at 663 (per Sir Thomas Bingham MR); *Gorringe* v *Calderdale MBC* [2004] 1 WLR 1057, at [2] (per Lord Steyn); *A* v *Essex CC* [2004] 1 WLR 1881, at [43]; *D* v *East Berkshire Community NHS Trust* [2005] 2 AC 373, at [24]–[25] (per Lord Bingham).

In [inquiring into whether a defendant owed a claimant a duty of care] I do not actually find it helpful to bear in mind – what is in any event obvious – that the public policy consideration which has first claim on the loyalty of the law is that wrongs should be remedied. Harm which constitutes a 'wrong' in the contemplation of the law must, of course, be remedied. But the world is full of harm for which the law furnishes no remedy. For instance, a trader owes no duty of care to avoid injuring his rivals by destroying their long-established businesses. If he does so and, as a result, one of his competitors descends into a clinical depression and his family are reduced to penury, in the eyes of the law they suffer no wrong and the law will provide no redress – because competition is regarded as operating to the overall good of the economy and society. A young man whose fiancée deserts him for his best friend may become clinically depressed as a result, but in the circumstances the fiancée owes him no duty of care to avoid causing this suffering. So he too will have no right to damages for his illness. The same goes for a middle-aged woman whose husband runs off with a younger woman. Experience suggests that such intimate matters are best left to the individuals themselves. However badly one of them may have treated the other, the law does not get involved . . .[61]

We agree, and do not think that this factor should play any part in a court's decision as to whether or not a duty of care was owed in a novel case.

5.4 DUTY-SKEPTICISM[62]

A skeptic is someone who harbours doubts about the truth of some proposition. There are people who are skeptical about the truth of the following two propositions about duties of care:

(1) *That it is an essential element of the law of negligence that a claimant in negligence show that the defendant owed her a duty of care.* We can say that people who are skeptical about this proposition are skeptics about the *essentiality* of the notion of a duty of care to the law of negligence.

(2) *That when the courts find that a defendant owed the claimant a duty of care, the defendant was actually legally required to act carefully in some respect.* We can say that people who are skeptical about this proposition are skeptics about the *reality* of duties of care in negligence.

Let's now look at each of these forms of duty-skepticism in detail, to see if there is anything to them.

A. Skepticism about the essentiality of the duty concept to the law of negligence

Skeptics of this kind fall into two camps.

There are, first, those who think that a claimant who is suing a defendant in negligence should not need to show that a defendant owed her a duty of care because the defendant will *always* have owed the claimant a duty not to cause her to suffer foreseeable harm by

---

[61] [2005] 2 AC 373, at [100].

[62] This section and the following section are quite theoretical. A student seeking simply to understand how negligence cases are decided in the courts does not need to read either of these sections. However, a student who wants to gain a deeper undestanding of *why* negligence cases are decided the way they are should read on – but slowly.

acting carelessly. So if the claimant can establish that the defendant acted carelessly in some way, and that the claimant suffered some kind of foreseeable harm as a result of the defendant's carelessness, then we can *take it as read* that the defendant did something wrong to the claimant in acting as he did. To ask then, 'Did the defendant owe the claimant a duty of care not to act as he did?' seems to be wholly redundant. Of course he did. On this view, then, the duty of care requirement acts as a 'fifth wheel on the coach', in William Buckland's memorable phrase.[63] So let's call people who think like this, *fifth wheelers*.[64]

There are, second, those who think that a claimant who is suing a defendant in negligence should not need to show that a defendant owed her a duty of care because the outcome of the claimant's case should not depend on whether or not the defendant did anything *wrong* to the claimant in acting as he did. For the claimant to win her case, it should be enough for her to show that the defendant was careless and she suffered loss as a result. If she can show this, then it is only just that the claimant should be able to sue the defendant for compensation. As between the defendant and the claimant, the defendant was to blame for the loss suffered by the claimant, and the claimant was not. So the loss suffered by the claimant should fall on the defendant, not the claimant. Let's call people who think like this, *fault fans* – in that, they think that the courts should focus on fault rather than wrongdoing in determining whether a defendant is liable to a claimant in negligence.

There are plenty of tort academics who are either fifth wheelers or fault fans. But we are neither. We are not fifth wheelers because it seems to us impossible to say that, as a matter of positive law, A will *always* owe B a duty to be careful if it is reasonably foreseeable that B will suffer some kind of harm if A is careless. As Lord Rodger pointed out in *D v East Berkshire Community NHS Trust* (2005), there are plenty of times when the law allows people to be careless, even though doing so may foreseeably cause harm to others.[65] We are not fault fans because a system of law which was genuinely based on a 'fault principle' that losses should fall on those who were at fault for causing them would destabilise society – both because people would be paralysed from doing anything by the fear that if their conduct was judged to have fallen below the standard of a 'reasonable man' they might be fixed with a huge bill for damages, and because the normal business of the courts would collapse under the weight of the claims for compensation with which they would be flooded by claimants arguing that someone else was to blame for their misfortunes.

B. Skepticism about the reality of duties of care in negligence[66]

Skeptics of this kind think that when the courts *say* that A owed B a duty of care, they don't really *mean* that A was under a duty to B to act carefully in some respect. Rather, when the courts say that A owed B a duty of care, they are simply saying that A will be held liable to pay B compensation if A's lack of care results in B suffering some kind of harm. And – more importantly – when the courts say that A did *not* owe B a duty of care, they are simply saying that, for one reason or another, B will *not* be allowed to sue A for compensation if A's lack of care results in B suffering some kind of harm. On this view, then, the duty

---

[63] See Buckland 1935, at 641.

[64] The great tort lawyer Sir Percy Winfield was a fifth wheeler, arguing in Winfield 1934 (at 66) that the duty requirement in negligence was 'superfluous' and 'might well be eliminated from the tort of negligence.'

[65] [2005] 2 AC 373, at [100].

[66] For in-depth explorations of this topic, see McBride 2004, and Goldberg and Zipursky 2006.

concept in negligence acts as a convenient 'control device' which helps to stop the scope of claims for compensation in negligence getting out of control.[67]

There are, again, plenty of tort academics who are skeptics about the reality of duties of care in negligence. But we are not. It seems to us that there is plenty of evidence that the courts mean what they say when they say that a defendant owed a claimant a duty to act carefully in some respect. For example, we have already seen that the courts are willing to distort the rules on causation to make sure that a defendant who is in admitted breach of a duty of care is not allowed to 'get away' with breaching that duty, but instead will incur some kind of sanction for his breach.[68] If the courts did not mean people to abide by the duties of care that the courts say that people owe others, why would they do this? Similarly, the fact that, in theory, exemplary damages may be available in a case where someone has deliberately breached a duty of care owed to another (provided, of course, that various other conditions are satisfied)[69] indicates that when the courts say we owe someone else a duty of care, we are meant to abide by that duty, and not meant to think that the courts are simply putting us on notice that if we are careless, we will be held liable to pay compensation.

5.5 RISK AND HARM

There is a saying that 'damage is the gist of negligence'.

Some people interpret this as meaning that the duty of care that *Driver* owes nearby *Pedestrian* is a duty not to injure *Pedestrian* by driving carelessly. So if *Driver* is drunk at the wheel and his car is veering madly across the road, he will not do anything wrong to *Pedestrian* if he just misses hitting *Pedestrian*. He may have been driving carelessly, but his duty was not to *injure* Pedestrian by driving carelessly and *Driver* did not injure her. So in the case where *Driver* just avoids hitting *Pedestrian* despite driving really badly, *Pedestrian* cannot complain that he has been negligent towards her.

On this view, the only duty *Driver* owes *Pedestrian* is *conduct plus result-focused* (or 'CPR-focused' for short). We reject this view. We think that *Driver* owes *Pedestrian* a duty to take care not to drive dangerously. This duty of care is purely conduct-focused (or 'C-focused' for short). Whether he *also* owes *Pedestrian* a CPR-focused duty not to injure *Pedestrian* by driving badly is a matter of debate.[70] But we think the view that the *only* duty of care *Driver* owes is a CPR-focused duty is untenable, for the following reasons:

(1) In the case where *Driver* is drunk at the wheel, and veering madly across the road, but just misses hitting *Pedestrian*, most people would think that *Driver* has done something morally wrong to *Pedestrian* in driving as he did. He took a huge chance with *Pedestrian*'s life. The risk that he created may not have materialised; but he still took a risk, and that was a bad thing to do. It would be strange if the law of negligence – which (as we have said

---

[67] See Fleming 1998, 135–6: 'The basic problem in the "tort" of negligence is that of limitation of liability. One or more control devices were required to prevent the incidence of liability from getting out of hand. Among these, "duty of care" occupies today a paramount position.'

[68] See above, § 4.1; also below, §§ 9.5, 9.12.

[69] See above, § 4.4.

[70] Ripstein and Zipursky 2001 argue (at 220) that *Driver* owes *Pedestrian* a C-focused duty to take care not to drive dangerously *and* a CPR-focused duty not to injure *Pedestrian* by breaching the C-focused duty that he owes *Pedestrian*.

before) is based, in part, on a moral vision of what we can legitimately demand that other people do for us – took a completely different view of *Driver*'s conduct and said that, in law, *Driver* did nothing wrong to *Pedestrian* in driving as he did.

(2) The point of legal duties is to guide people's behaviour. Only legal duties that are C-focused can do this effectively. Legal duties that are CPR-focused leave people uncertain as to what they can do. They tell people – you can drive as carelessly as you like down the road, just so long as you don't hit anyone. But if you do not know whether you are going to hit anyone or not before you start driving, such 'guidance' amounts to no guidance at all. There is a reason why parents tell their children to go to bed at 7 pm on the dot, and don't tell them, 'You can stay up as long as you like, so long as are not tired in the morning.'

(3) The courts frequently find that a given defendant has breached a duty of care owed to the claimant, but that breach has not caused the claimant any harm. It would not be possible for them to come to this conclusion if causation of harm had to be shown as a precondition of establishing that a defendant breached a duty of care owed to a claimant.

(4) The most famous statement in English law as to what duties of care we owe each other is Lord Atkin's 'You must take reasonable care to avoid acts or omissions which you can reasonably foresee would be likely to injure your neighbour.'[71] That statement is unambiguously C-focused. Lord Atkin did *not* say 'You must avoid injuring your neighbour by failing to take reasonable care to avoid acts or omissions that reasonably foreseeably would have that effect.'

(5) As we will see,[72] in cases where it is uncertain whether A's breach of a duty of care owed to B has caused B harm, the courts will sometimes hold A liable for that harm because they think that A should not 'get away' with breaching his duty of care, but should instead incur some kind of sanction. And there are other cases[73] where the normal rules on causation indicate that A's breach did *not* cause B harm, but the courts will distort the normal rules on causation to ensure that A's breach incurs some kind of sanction. The only way of explaining these cases is to adopt a C-focused view of the duties of care we owe each other. A CPR-focused interpretation of our duties of care is unable to explain these cases. If we are uncertain whether A's actions have caused B harm, or we know that A's actions have *not* caused B harm, then – if the CPR-focused view of the duties of care we owe each other is correct – it is not possible to say that A has done anything wrong to B; in which case, why are we twisting the law to ensure that he is held liable to B?

---

[71] *Donoghue* v *Stevenson* [1932] AC 562, 580. See also Diplock LJ in *Doughty* v *Turner Manufacturing Co Ltd* [1964] 1 QB 518, 531: 'the law of negligence . . . is the application of common morality and common sense to the activities of the common man. He must take reasonable care to avoid acts or omissions which he can reasonably foresee would be *likely* to injure his neighbour . . .' (emphasis added).

[72] See below, § 9.5.

[73] See below, § 9.12.

Further reading

On the utility of 'tests' to determine whether we owe another a duty of care, see **Smith and Burns, '***Donoghue* v *Stevenson* **– the not so golden anniversary' (1983) 46 *Modern Law Review* 147**, and **Morgan, 'The rise and fall of the general duty of care?' (2006) 22 *Professional Negligence* 206**.

It might be an interesting idea to compare our list of factors that judges take into account in determining whether one person owed another a duty of care with Jane Stapleton's (**Stapleton, 'Duty of care factors: a selection from the judicial menus' in Cane and Stapleton (eds), *The Law of Obligations: Essays in Honour of John Fleming* (OUP, 1998)**) and consider what accounts for the differences.

The idea that our duties of care really exist is defended in **McBride, 'Duties of care – do they really exist?' (2004) 24 *Oxford Journal of Legal Studies* 417**, and **Goldberg and Zipursky, 'The Restatement (Third) and the place of duty in negligence law' (2001) 54 *Vanderbilt Law Review* 657** and, by the same authors, **'Seeing tort law from the internal point of view: Holmes and Hart on legal duties' (2006) 75 *Fordham Law Review* 1563**. In response to these arguments, David Howarth concedes that duties of care really exist, but argues that we are all subject to just one duty of care, a duty to take care not to harm others: see **Howarth, 'Many duties of care – or a duty of care? Notes from the underground' (2006) 26 *Oxford Journal of Legal Studies* 449**.

6 Duty of care – Acts

6.1 The basics *124*

6.2 Physical injury (1): the basic rule *129*

6.3 Physical injury (2): harm caused by a third party *137*

6.4 Psychiatric illness (1): general principles in accident cases *140*

6.5 Psychiatric illness (2): the caselaw on accident cases *142*

6.6 Psychiatric illness (3): non-accident cases *151*

6.7 Pure distress *158*

6.8 *Wilkinson* v *Downton* *161*

6.9 Harm to property *162*

6.10 Pure economic loss (1): *Hedley Byrne* – the basic principle *172*

6.11 Pure economic loss (2): *Hedley Byrne* – the extended principle *180*

6.12 Pure economic loss (3): *Hedley Byrne* – two misconceptions *187*

6.13 Pure economic loss (4): some difficult cases *188*

6.14 Pure economic loss (5): explanation of the difficult cases *196*

Overview

In this chapter, we will be looking at when a defendant will be found to have owed a claimant a duty of care in a case where the defendant has performed a positive act that has resulted in the claimant suffering some kind of harm. The different sections of this chapter are divided up according to the type of harm that the claimant might have suffered: sections 6.2 and 6.3 deal with physical injury cases; sections 6.4, 6.5 and 6.6 with cases where the defendant's positive act has resulted in the claimant suffering a psychiatric illness; section 6.7 with the case where the defendant's act caused the claimant to suffer pure distress; section 6.9 with cases where the claimant's property was harmed as a result of the defendant's actions; and sections 6.10 to 6.14 with cases where the defendant's actions result in the claimant suffering a form of pure economic loss – that is, economic loss not consequent on the claimant suffering an injury to her body, mind or property. The odd one out is section 6.8. This deals with what is known as the tort in *Wilkinson* v *Downton*, which allows a claimant to recover from a defendant whose outrageous treatment of her has resulted in her suffering physical injury or a psychiatric illness. Properly understood, this tort has now been subsumed within the law of negligence, and that is why we deal with it here.

6.1 THE BASICS

We are mainly concerned in this chapter with cases where a defendant has performed a *positive* act that has resulted in the claimant suffering some kind of harm. It must be emphasised that – unless the contrary is made clear – everything we say in this chapter (and especially in this introductory section) as to when a defendant will owe a claimant a duty of care will *only* apply to cases where a defendant has performed a positive act that has resulted in a claimant suffering harm. The law on when a defendant will owe a claimant a duty to save her from suffering some kind of harm, with the result that a defendant can be held liable for a *failure to act*, will be dealt with in the next chapter.

So – a defendant has performed a positive act that has resulted in the claimant suffering some kind of harm, and the claimant wants to sue the defendant in negligence for what he has done. As we have seen, in order to get her claim off the ground, the claimant will have to show that the defendant breached a duty of care that he owed to her in acting as he did. But – as we have also seen, when discussing the Forgetful Investor Problem[1] – it will not be enough for the claimant to show that the defendant breached any old duty of care in acting as he did. The claimant has to show that the defendant breached a duty of care that was geared towards protecting her from the harm for which she wants to sue the defendant. So in a case where the defendant's act has resulted in the claimant suffering some kind of physical injury, she needs to show that the defendant – in acting as he did – breached a duty of care that was geared towards protecting her from suffering physical injury. In the same way, in a case where the defendant's act has resulted in the claimant suffering some kind of pure economic loss, she needs to show that the defendant – in acting as he did – breached a duty of care that was geared towards protecting her from suffering pure economic loss.

It is a lot harder to establish that a defendant owed a claimant a duty of care that was geared towards protecting her from suffering pure economic loss than it is to establish that a defendant owed the claimant a duty of care that was geared towards protecting her from suffering physical injury. The table below gives a rough summary of what a claimant will have to show if she wants to show that the defendant owed her a duty of care geared towards protecting her from suffering a particular kind of harm. The different kinds of harm in the first column are arranged according to how easy it is to establish that a defendant owed a claimant a duty of care geared towards protecting the claimant from suffering that kind of harm:

Duty of care geared towards protecting claimant from –	What has to be established
Physical harm	It was reasonably foreseeable that the defendant's actions would result in the claimant suffering some kind of physical injury.
Property damage	It was reasonably foreseeable that the defendant's actions would result in property being damaged, and the claimant had a sufficient interest in the property at the time it was damaged as a result of the defendant's actions.
Psychiatric illness	It was reasonably foreseeable that the defendant's actions would result in the claimant suffering some form of psychiatric illness, and there was a sufficient degree of proximity between the defendant's actions and the claimant's suffering of psychiatric illness (where what counts as a sufficient degree of proximity depends on how the claimant's psychiatric illness was triggered).
Pure economic loss	There was a special relationship between the defendant and the claimant, or special circumstances that would make it 'fair, just and reasonable' to find that the defendant owed the claimant a duty of care geared towards protecting the claimant from suffering some kind of pure economic loss.
Pure distress	There was a contractual relationship between the defendant and the claimant, under which the defendant undertook to perform some task for the claimant with reasonable skill and care, and an important object of the defendant's undertaking was to secure some mental satisfaction for the claimant, or save the claimant from some sort of mental distress.

[1] See above, § 5.1.

If we look down the list of harms in the first column, we will see that – as a general rule – the law makes it harder for a claimant to establish that a defendant owed her a duty of care that was geared towards protecting her from suffering a particular kind of harm, the less serious the harm in question is. But there is an important exception to this rule. It is easier for the claimant to establish that the defendant owed her a duty of care geared towards protecting her property from being damaged, than it is for a claimant to establish that a defendant owed her a duty of care that was geared towards protecting her mind from being damaged. It is a difficult question whether the restrictive stance of the law towards finding duties of care designed to protect people from being made mentally ill is justified. (As we have already seen,[2] Lord Scarman in *McLoughlin* v *O'Brian* (1983) was in favour of the courts simply finding such a duty of care whenever it was reasonably foreseeable that a defendant's actions would result in a claimant suffering a psychiatric illness – though he also acknowledged that such a position might create social problems that it would be up to Parliament to deal with.) We will attempt to address that question later on, after you have gained a better appreciation of what the law currently says as to when a defendant will owe the claimant a duty of care that is geared towards protecting her from suffering some kind of psychiatric illness.

Psychiatric illness cases are also special in another respect. Consider the facts of *Page* v *Smith* (1996). The defendant carelessly ran into the claimant's car while the claimant was sitting in it. The claimant was uninjured, but the experience caused him to suffer a renewed onset of chronic fatigue syndrome (CFS) – a condition that the claimant had suffered from in the past, but which he had managed to overcome. The claimant sued the defendant in negligence for compensation for his CFS. This was a claim for damages for psychiatric illness. Given this, we would expect the claimant to have to show that the defendant breached a duty of care that was geared towards protecting the claimant from suffering a psychiatric illness. But the House of Lords held that this was unnecessary. It was enough if the claimant could establish that his psychiatric illness resulted from the defendant's breaching a duty of care that was geared towards protecting the claimant from suffering a *physical injury*. The claimant was easily able to satisfy this condition. The defendant had owed him a duty to take care not to crash into the claimant's car based on the fact that it was reasonably foreseeable that doing so would result in the claimant suffering some kind of physical injury. The defendant breached this duty when he carelessly crashed into the claimant's car, and the claimant's psychiatric illness resulted from that breach of duty.

Page v *Smith* (1996) is unorthodox in that it allows a claimant to sue for one kind of harm based on the breach of a duty of care geared towards protecting the claimant from suffering another kind of harm. Given this, in *Rothwell* v *Chemical & Insulating Co Ltd* (2007), the House of Lords sought to limit *Page* v *Smith* to cases where a claimant has suffered a psychiatric illness as an *immediate* result of the defendant breaching a duty of care owed to the claimant that was geared towards protecting the claimant from suffering a physical injury.[3] So *Page* v *Smith* did not apply to a case like *Coleman* v *British Gas* (2002) where the defendant installed a gas heater in the claimants' house. The gas heater was defective: it leaked carbon monoxide. The problem with the heater was only discovered seven years

---

[2] See above, § 5.1.
[3] [2008] 1 AC 281, at [55] (per Lord Hope), [77] (per Lord Scott), [95] (per Lord Rodger), and [104] (per Lord Mance).

later. Amazingly, the claimants suffered no physical ill effects from breathing in carbon monoxide for so many years. But after the problem with the heater was discovered, they each developed a psychiatric illness as a result of worrying that they *had* been poisoned by the carbon monoxide leaking from their heater. It was held that the claimants could not sue the defendant for their psychiatric illness. The defendant had owed the claimants a duty to take care not to install a defective gas heater in their house. This duty of care arose because it was reasonably foreseeable that installing a defective heater in the claimants' house would result in their being physically injured. So this duty of care was geared towards protecting the claimants from suffering a physical injury. But the claimants had not suffered any physical injury as a result of the defendant's breaching this duty of care. They had, instead, suffered a psychiatric illness: the wrong kind of loss. *Page v Smith* did not apply to save the claimants' claim because the claimants' psychiatric illness was not an *immediate* consequence of the defendant's negligence, in the same way as the psychiatric illness of the claimant in *Page v Smith* had been immediately triggered by the defendant in that case crashing into the claimant's car. The claimants' psychiatric illness in the *Coleman* case resulted from their worrying, seven years after their heater had been installed, that they had been poisoned. If the claimants wanted to recover for their psychiatric illnesses, they would have to establish, in the normal way, that the defendant had breached a duty of care owed to the claimants that was geared towards protecting them from psychiatric illness. This the claimants could not do. As the above table indicates, in order to do this they would have had to show (at the very least) that it was reasonably foreseeable that installing a defective heater in the claimants' house would result in the claimants suffering some kind of psychiatric illness. And they could not do this.

Clearly, the concept of reasonable foreseeability plays a major role (though not a deciding role, in cases where a claimant has suffered a psychiatric illness or pure economic loss or mere distress as a result of a defendant's positive act) in determining whether or not a defendant owed the claimant a duty of care in the sort of cases we are concerned with in this chapter – cases where a claimant has suffered harm as a result of a defendant's positive act. So how do we determine whether it was reasonably foreseeable that a defendant's actions would result in a claimant suffering some kind of harm? Some guidance is provided by the decision of the Privy Council in *The Wagon Mound (No 2)* (1967) (the facts of which we need not worry about for the time being).[4] In that case, Lord Reid – delivering the judgment of the Privy Council – indicated that questions of reasonable foreseeability can be resolved by asking whether the possibility of the claimant being harmed in some way by the defendant's action would, before the event, have been regarded as being so 'fantastic or far-fetched that no reasonable man would have paid any attention to it'.[5] If, before the event, a reasonable person would have thought that there was a 'real . . . risk'[6] that the claimant would be harmed in some way as a result of the defendant's actions, then it will have been reasonably foreseeable that the defendant's actions would result in the claimant

---

[4] For a summary of the facts, see below, § 10.2 fn 14.
[5] [1967] 1 AC 617, at 641.
[6] [1967] 1 AC 617, at 642. Lord Reid actually spoke of a 'real *and substantial* risk' (emphasis added), but the following paragraph of his judgment indicated that he thought that in a case where it was established that the defendant's regularly acting in a particular way (here, playing cricket) would result in harm to someone like the claimant (someone passing outside the defendant's cricket ground – who might be hit on the head by a ball hit out of the ground) once every thousand years counted as a risk that was 'plainly foreseeable' and was not 'fantastic or far-fetched', even though it was 'infinitesimal' (ibid). Given this, we think the qualifier 'substantial' can be dropped.

suffering that kind of harm. Applying that standard to the *Coleman* case, we have to ask whether, when the defendant installed the heater in the claimants' house, a reasonable person would have thought that there was a real risk that if the heater turned out to be defective, the claimants would suffer a psychiatric illness as a result, or would have dismissed such a possibility as being 'far-fetched or fantastic'. On this approach, we have little doubt that the judge reached the right decision that it was *not* reasonably foreseeable that the claimants would develop a psychiatric illness if the defendant installed a defective gas heater in their house.

Other cases are more difficult. In *Bhamra v Dubb* (2010), the issue was whether the defendant caterer in that case had owed a guest at a Sikh wedding reception a duty to take care not to serve food that contained egg. The guest suffered from an egg allergy and died as a result of eating a dish ('ras malai') that was served by the defendant at the reception and which contained egg. The guest never asked anyone whether the dish contained egg, because Sikhs are prohibited from consuming meat, fish or eggs – so he must have thought that there was no chance he would be served a dish made out of eggs at the reception. The question of whether the defendant caterer owed the guest a duty of care came down to whether it was reasonably foreseeable that serving a dish made out of eggs at the reception would result in one of the guests falling ill. Statistical evidence was introduced to show that one in every thousand people suffers from an egg allergy. That meant that if 100 people attended the wedding reception, there was a 10% chance (approximately) that at least one of them would suffer from an egg allergy.[7] If 500 people attended the reception, that probability rises to 40% (approximately).[8] So, clearly, there was a real risk, and not a 'far-fetched or fantastic possibility' that someone with an egg allergy would attend the wedding reception. But that is not enough to establish that it was reasonably foreseeable that serving an egg dish at the reception would result in one of the wedding guests being harmed. The crucial issue – once it is accepted that someone with an egg allergy could be expected to attend the wedding reception – is: How could someone with an egg allergy be expected to behave at the reception? Could he be expected to keep his guard up, to refuse to rely on the wedding caterer to observe the religious prohibitions on serving meat, fish or eggs at a Sikh wedding, and to turn away any dishes that looked suspicious (or at least not to eat from them without having first obtained assurances that they were egg-free)? Or could he be expected to let his guard down, and partake freely of all the dishes on offer at the reception, confident that the caterer would do everything required to observe the religious prohibition on serving egg at a Sikh wedding reception? If the first, then we might conclude that there was not a real risk that serving an egg dish at the reception would result in harm to one of the guests – any guests that suffered from an egg allergy could have been expected to guard against the possibility that they would be served an egg dish at the wedding. If the second, then there would obviously be a real risk that serving an egg dish at the reception would result in harm to one of the guests – anyone who suffered from an egg allergy attending the reception would be a sitting duck, so to speak, if an egg dish were served at the reception.

---

[7] We calculate this probability by saying that the chance that any one guest would not suffer from an egg allergy is 0.999. So the probability that every single guest did not suffer from an egg allergy at a wedding reception attended by 100 guests is $0.999 \times 0.999 \times 0.999 \ldots$ etc until we have done 100 multiplications. In other words 0.999^{100}. This comes to 0.905 (rounding up to three decimal places). So the probability that at least one guest would suffer from an egg allergy is 0.095 – that is, just under 10%.

[8] $1 - 0.999^{500} = 0.394$ (rounded up to three decimal places).

The courts (at first instance, and in the Court of Appeal) held that a guest suffering from an egg allergy could be expected to let his guard down at the reception, and eat from all the dishes served at the reception without worrying about whether they contained egg. This conclusion is questionable given: (1) the potential extreme downside for a guest who had an egg allergy of eating a dish containing egg; and (2) the lack of any prior, or special, relationship between the guests and the caterer, that might have encouraged a guest who suffered from an egg allergy to think that the caterer would not cut any corners in what dishes he served at the reception. However, the decision of the courts in the *Bhamra* case is *only* questionable – it is not clear what the right answer is in this case.

The use of statistical evidence in the *Bhamra* case shows just how extraordinary the 'reasonable person' (from whose perspective we determine what is reasonably foreseeable) can be. The 'reasonable person' is someone who can not only afford to take the time to contemplate questions such as 'Is there a real risk that someone with an egg allergy might be at the wedding reception?', but is also armed with the statistical information required to answer that question. The fact that the 'reasonable person' is endowed with superpowers of forethought, insight and knowledge that could not reasonably be expected to be shared by any ordinary member of the public creates a danger for the law of negligence. By making the existence of our duties of care dependent on what such an abstract 'reasonable person' could have been expected to foresee, there is a danger that people may end up being fixed with duties of care that they could not reasonably be expected to have known that they were subject to at the time they acted. This seems unfair, though the unfairness is mitigated by the consideration that the bill for paying damages to a claimant in a negligence is usually not ultimately borne by the person who was negligent, but by his or her employer or insurance company.

6.2 PHYSICAL INJURY (1): THE BASIC RULE

Before *Donoghue* v *Stevenson* (1932) was decided, there were plenty of cases where a defendant had been held liable in negligence for carelessly performing a positive act that resulted in a claimant suffering physical injury.

Examples of such cases that were mentioned in Lord Atkin's judgment in *Donoghue* v *Stevenson* are: *Dixon* v *Bell* (1816) (where the defendant asked a very young maidservant to fetch a gun for him, and while she was carrying the gun, she fired it, with the result that the claimant was injured); *Grote* v *Chester and Holyhead Railway* (1848) (where the claimant was a train passenger who was injured when a bridge over which the claimant's train was passing collapsed; the bridge had been built by the defendant); *George* v *Skivington* (1869) (where the claimant was injured using a shampoo that was manufactured by the defendant and that contained harmful ingredients); *Hawkins* v *Smith* (1896) (where the claimant dock worker was injured as a result of using a defective sack which had been supplied by the defendants); *Dominion Natural Gas Co Ltd* v *Collins* (1909) (where the defendants supplied gas to some business premises, installing a pressure safety valve that allowed gas that was building up in the system to escape into the premises, rather than the open air; as a result, a quantity of gas built up inside the premises and an explosion occurred in which the claimant was injured); and *Oliver* v *Saddler & Co* (1929) (where a dock worker was killed when a sling that was supplied by the defendants, and that was being used to lift a load from a ship to the dockside, broke).

What Lord Atkin did in his judgment in *Donoghue* v *Stevenson* was to suggest that the decisions in all these cases rested on a common principle, that applied to determine when one person will owe another a duty of care. As we have already seen, the 'neighbour principle' that Lord Atkin formulated to explain the outcome of the decisions in all these cases were seriously inadequate in that it failed to distinguish between cases where a defendant had caused a claimant harm by performing a positive act and those involving an omission, and failed to note that in cases where a defendant's actions resulted in suffering less serious harm – such as pure economic loss – foreseeability of harm alone cannot ground a duty of care.[9] However, a narrower formulation of Lord Atkin's neighbour principle does, we think, adequately explain both the outcome of the above cases and many other cases decided since *Donoghue v Stevenson*. According to this narrower formulation: A will *normally* owe B a duty to take care not to do a positive act *x*, if it is reasonably foreseeable that A's doing *x* will result in someone like B suffering some kind of physical injury. Such a formulation explains, we think, why there is a duty of care in the following cases:

(1) If A sells goods to B, A will normally owe B a duty to take care not to sell him goods that are unsafe to use or consume in the way they are intended to be used or consumed.[10]

(2) If A manufactures a product that is being used by B, A will normally owe B a duty to take care to see that that product is reasonably safe to use.[11]

(3) If A is out driving, A will owe other users of the road in the vicinity a duty to take care not to drive dangerously; similarly, if A is parking his car, A will owe other users of the road a duty to take care not to park the car in a dangerous fashion.[12]

(4) If A and B are playing football and A attempts to tackle B, A will owe B a duty to take care not to execute the tackle in an unnecessarily dangerous manner.[13]

(5) If A is in possession of a dangerous thing – such as a loaded firearm, a poison, or an explosive[14] – and B is incapable of handling that thing properly, A will normally owe B and anyone else who might be harmed by the thing's improper use a duty not to entrust it to B's care.[15]

(6) If A owns a car and B – who is obviously drunk – asks A for the keys to his car, intending to go for a drive in it, A will owe users of the highway a duty not to give B the keys to his car.[16]

(7) If A, a highway authority, places signs alongside a highway, A will owe each driver on that highway a duty to take care not to position those signs in such a way that that driver will be unreasonably endangered.[17]

---

[9] See above, § 5.3(D).

[10] *Langridge v Levy* (1837) 2 M&W 519, 150 ER 863; *Abouzaid v Mothercare (UK) Ltd*, The Times, 20 February 2001.

[11] *Donoghue v Stevenson* [1932] AC 562.

[12] *Maitland v Raisbeck* [1944] KB 689; *Parish v Judd* [1960] 1 WLR 867.

[13] *Condon v Basi* [1985] 1 WLR 866.

[14] *Dominion Natural Gas Co v Collins* [1909] AC 640, 646.

[15] *Dixon v Bell* (1816) 5 M & S 198, 199, 105 ER 1023, 1024; *Attorney-General for the British Virgin Islands v Hartwell* [2004] 1 WLR 1273.

[16] *P Perl (Exporters) Ltd v Camden LBC* [1984] QB 342, 359; *Yetkin v London Borough of Newham* [2010] EWCA Civ 776.

[17] *Levine v Morris* [1970] 1 WLR 71; also *Yetkin v London Borough of Newham* [2010] EWCA Civ 776 (bush planted by defendant authority allowed to grow to such an extent that it obstructed drivers' line of sight, with the result that there was accident in which claimant was injured).

(8) If A is building a house, A will normally owe any future occupants of that house a duty to take care not to build the house in such a way that it will become unreasonably dangerous to live in.[18]

(9) If it is reasonably foreseeable that C will be put in danger if A sets a building on fire, and that someone like B will attempt to rescue C if this happens, thereby putting himself in danger, A will owe B a duty to take care not to set that building on fire.[19]

(10) If B is married to C, A will owe B a duty to take care that he does not misinform her that C has been killed or injured if it is reasonably foreseeable that she will be made physically sick by this news.[20]

(11) If A is labelling bottles of medicine, he will owe B a duty to take care that he does not mislabel those bottles of medicine if it is reasonably foreseeable that someone like B will suffer some kind of physical injury if those bottles are mislabelled.[21]

(12) If B's mother asks A, a local authority, whether T would make a suitable child-minder for B, A will owe B a duty not to tell B's mother that T would make a suitable child-minder for B if A knows, or ought to know, that such advice will be acted on and that T has violent tendencies that mean that B will in fact be in danger of being killed or injured if she is looked after by T.[22]

(13) If B wants to adopt a child through A, an adoption agency, A will normally owe B a duty not to place with her a child which A knows or ought to know suffers from a

---

[18] *Dutton v Bognor Regis United Building Co Ltd* [1972] 1 QB 373, overruling *Bottomley v Bannister* [1932] KB 458 and *Otto v Bolton & Norris* [1936] 2 KB 46. The decision in *Dutton* was subsequently affirmed by the House of Lords in *Anns v Merton LBC* [1978] AC 728. The House of Lords has now disapproved both *Dutton* and *Anns: D & F Estates v Church Commissioners* [1989] AC 177; *Murphy v Brentwood DC* [1991] 1 AC 398. The better view of those decisions, we submit, is that they did *not* disapprove of the view taken in *Dutton* and *Anns* that if A builds a house he will owe B, a subsequent occupier of that house, a duty to take care to ensure that he does not build that house in such a way that it will become dangerous to live in. In *D & F Estates* and *Murphy* the House of Lords disapproved the view taken in *Dutton* and *Anns* that if (1) A builds a house and in doing so breaches the duty he owes B, a subsequent occupier of that house, to take care not to build the house in such a way that it will become dangerous to live in and (2) as a result, B is put to expense making the house safe to live in then, other things being equal, (3) B will be entitled to sue A in negligence so as to be reimbursed for the expense she was put to. The reason why B will not be able to sue A in negligence is that there is no relation between the harm that B has suffered here (pure economic loss) and the harm that A's duty was imposed on him in order to avoid (physical injury, and damage to B's possessions): see above, § 5.1, and below, § 10.3. The fact that B will not be entitled to sue A *in negligence* to recover the money she spent on repairing her house does not, of course, mean that B will not be entitled to sue A *at all* to recover that money. She may have an action under the Defective Premises Act 1972 (on which, see below, § 22.5). For an interesting argument that she would be entitled to bring a claim in restitution against A to recover the expense incurred by her in making her house safe to live in, see Moran 1997.

[19] *Ogwo v Taylor* [1988] AC 431. More difficult is the situation where A owes C a duty to save him from harm, A breaches that duty, and B attempts to save C instead, thereby endangering himself. One cannot use the formula discussed here to establish that A owed *B* a duty to rescue C because A is merely guilty of an omission and it is not clear why the fact that A owed *C* a duty to rescue her should mean that he also owed *B* a duty to rescue C. That A *will* have owed B a duty to rescue C in this situation is established by the decision of the Court of Appeal in *Baker v T E Hopkins* [1959] 1 WLR 966, though the Supreme Court of Canada took a different view in *Horsley v MacLaren, The Ogopogo* [1971] 2 Lloyd's Rep 410.

[20] *Wilkinson v Downton* [1897] 2 QB 57, as reinterpreted by *Wainwright v Home Office* [2004] 2 AC 406, at [40] (per Lord Hoffmann): 'the law [is] able comfortably to accommodate the facts of *Wilkinson v Downton* . . . [within] the law of . . . negligence.' See below, § 6.8, for an account of the case of *Wilkinson v Downton* and its significance.

[21] *Caparo Industries plc v Dickman* [1990] 2 AC 605, 636C.

[22] *T v Surrey County Council* [1994] 4 All ER 577.

personality disorder which means that the child is very likely to injure B if he is placed with B.[23]

(14) If A is asked to certify that an aircraft is ready to fly, he will owe those who are due to fly on the aircraft a duty not to say that the aircraft is ready to fly if he knows or ought to know that the aircraft is not fit to fly.[24]

A number of different aspects of the formula we advanced above – that A will *normally* owe B a duty to take care not to do a positive act *x*, if it is reasonably foreseeable that A's doing *x* will result in someone like B suffering some kind of physical injury – need further explanation.

A. Normally

A will not *always* owe B a duty of care not to do something that foreseeably will result in B's being injured. The exceptions to the normal rule that a duty of care will be owed in this kind of situation can be grouped under three headings: (1) *volenti non fit injuria*; (2) reasonable conduct; (3) public policy.

(1) *Volenti.* We have already come across the concept of *volenti non fit injuria* – the idea that 'no wrong is done to the willing'.[25] For example, if A is HIV+, it is reasonably foreseeable that B will become HIV+ if A has unprotected sex with her. But if B – in full knowledge of A's condition – wants to have unprotected sex with him, then A will do no wrong to B by having unprotected sex with her.[26] The maxim that *volenti non fit injuria* will be discussed more fully below, in our chapter on 'Defences'[27] – though it should be noted that, technically, the maxim does not operate in this context as a defence (that protects an admitted wrongdoer from being sued) but as a way of establishing that the defendant did not commit a tort at all in the way he behaved.

(2) *Reasonable conduct.* We have also already seen that a defendant cannot be sued in negligence for acting reasonably.[28] So if it was reasonable for A to act in a particular way, B cannot argue that A owed her a duty to take care not to act in that way even if A's acting in that way exposed her to a reasonably foreseeable risk of being physically injured. For example, in *Bolton* v *Stone* (1951), the claimant was standing outside the defendants' cricket ground when she was hit by a cricket ball that had been hit for six out of the ground. The House of Lords dismissed the claimant's claim for damages. The defendants had acted quite reasonably in carrying on playing cricket on their ground without taking any special precautions to avoid the risk of people outside the ground being hit by flying cricket balls. This was because the risk of someone being hit by a cricket ball while standing outside the defendants' ground was infinitesimally small.[29] Given this, it was reasonable for the defendants not to do anything about the risk.

---

[23] *A* v *Essex CC* [2004] 1 WLR 1881.
[24] *Perrett* v *Collins* [1998] 2 Lloyd's Rep 255 (discussed, Witting 2000a).
[25] See above, § 2.4.
[26] *R* v *Dica* [2004] QB 1257.
[27] See below, chapter 26.
[28] See above, § 5.3(B).
[29] In *Overseas Tankship (UK) Ltd* v *The Miller Steamship Co Pty Ltd, The Wagon Mound (No. 2)* [1967] 1 AC 617, 642 Lord Reid estimated that the risk of someone being hit by a ball hit out of the defendants' ground was such that it would only happen once every thousand years or so.

It was different in *Miller* v *Jackson* (1977), which was also a case involving claimants being harmed by flying cricket balls. In that case, the claimants' property adjoined the defendants' cricket ground and the risk that the claimants would be harmed by a cricket ball that was knocked out of the ground was quite substantial. The only way to avoid this risk was for the defendants to stop playing cricket on their ground. Two of the three judges who decided the case in the Court of Appeal – Geoffrey Lane and Cumming-Bruce LJJ – took the view that it was not reasonable for the defendants to carry on playing cricket on their ground. The risk of injury created by the defendants' activity was too high. Accordingly, these two judges were happy to find that the defendants owed the claimants a duty not to carry on playing cricket on their ground – though they disagreed over whether it would be right to grant an injunction to *force* the defendants to stop playing cricket. The third judge was Lord Denning MR, who took the view that the social value involved in the defendants' playing cricket was such that it was reasonable for them to carry on, despite the risks involved for the defendants' neighbours.

Miller illustrates how judging whether it was reasonable for a defendant to act in a particular way can often require us to weigh the costs and benefits of the defendant's actions. Sometimes that weighing exercise has already been done by Parliament, in deciding whether or not to make a particular activity illegal. If Parliament has made a particular activity illegal (for example, driving at 50 miles per hour in a built up area), the courts will accept Parliament's judgment that the costs associated with that activity outweigh its benefits, and that acting in that way is unreasonable. As a result, if it is reasonably foreseeable that B will be physically injured if A acts in a way that Parliament has made illegal, the courts will readily find that A owes B a duty to take care not to act in that way. This piece of common sense is often distorted by academics and judges, who sometimes say things like 'a breach of statutory duty is evidence of negligence' or 'a breach of statutory duty amounts to negligence *per se*'. This is not true. Suppose that A is driving down the road and B is walking beside the road some way up ahead. The speed limit applying to the road is 30 mph. In such a situation, we can argue that A owes B a duty to take care not to drive at more than 30 mph. It is, of course, reasonably foreseeable that A's driving faster than 30 mph will result in B's being injured, in the sense that it would not be 'fantastic or far-fetched' to suggest that A's breaking the speed limit will create a risk of B's being injured. The fact that it is independently unlawful for A to drive faster than 30 mph will mean that A cannot argue that it would be reasonable for him to drive faster than 30 mph, and that it would therefore be wrong for the courts to find that he owed B a duty to take care not to drive faster than 30 mph. However, A's duty in this situation will be *to take care* not to break the speed limit. So if A does end up breaking the speed limit, that does not show that he has breached the duty of care that he owes B. It still has to be shown that A's breaking the speed limit was a result of lack of care on his part, and was not – for example – because a faulty speedometer led A to believe he was under the speed limit.

(3) *Public policy*. Considerations of public policy will rarely result in A being exempted from the duty he would normally have to take care not to do something that foreseeably would result in B being physically injured. One example of a case where a policy-based exception was created to the normal rule that foreseeability of injury gives rise to a duty of care is *Mulcahy* v *Ministry of Defence* (1996). In that case, the claimant was a soldier serving with a British Army artillery unit during the Gulf War. While his unit was deployed in Saudi Arabia firing a howitzer into Iraq, his gun commander ordered him to fetch some water from in front of the howitzer. While the claimant was in front of the gun, the gun

commander fired the gun. As a result the claimant's hearing was severely affected. The claimant sued the Ministry of Defence for damages, claiming that the gun commander had been negligent in firing the gun and that the Ministry of Defence was vicariously liable in respect of the gun commander's negligence. The claimant's claim was turned down. The Court of Appeal held that the gun commander had not owed the claimant a duty of care in operating the howitzer. Crucial to the Court of Appeal's reasoning was the fact that the howitzer had been fired in the course of battle, and a fear that if military commanders were held to owe a duty of care to their soldiers to take care not to expose them to an unreasonable risk of harm, then commanders would become over-cautious about risking their soldiers' lives in battle, for fear that in the event of casualties, they would be sued.[30]

B. Positive act

It cannot be emphasised enough that the formula for when one person will owe another a duty of care under discussion here applies only in cases where it is foreseeable that A's performing a *positive act* will result in B being made worse off than she is at the moment. The fact that it is foreseeable that B will suffer harm if A does not intervene to save B from that harm is not, on its own, enough to justify A's owing B a duty of care to rescue B. This is a point we will discuss further below.[31]

C. Reasonable foreseeability

We have already discussed in outline when we can say that it was reasonably foreseeable that A's acting in a particular way would result in B's suffering some kind of harm. Here we want to flesh out that idea a bit more.

If A knew that his actions could have the effect of harming B, then the requirement of reasonable foreseeability is automatically satisfied. If A did not know, the issue of whether it was or was not reasonably foreseeable that A's actions would result in B's being harmed depends on what a *reasonable person in A's position* could have been expected to foresee at the time A acted. This raises the further issue of – what attributes do we give this reasonable person in determining what he or she could have been expected to foresee?

The authorities are clear that the reasonable person should be given the same *age* as A. So we judge what was reasonably foreseeable from the perspective of someone who was the same age as the defendant. In *Mullin v Richards* (1998), two 15-year-old school children – Teresa Mullin and Heidi Richards – were playfully fencing with plastic rulers when one of the rulers snapped and a fragment of plastic from the snapped ruler entered Mullin's right eye, blinding her in that eye. Mullin sued Richards in negligence. The Court of Appeal dismissed the claim, holding that Richards had not owed Mullin a duty of care in fencing with her. This was because, judged from the perspective of a *reasonable 15 year old*, it was not reasonably foreseeable that the fencing match would result in Mullin suffering some kind of harm. (Though presumably the result would have been different if the fencing match had been a particularly violent one.)

---

[30] For further discussion of the scope of what has been called 'combat immunity' see *Smith v Ministry of Defence* [2011] EWHC 1676 (QB), refusing to strike out claims alleging that the defendant Ministry of Defence was negligent in failing to provide British soldiers patrolling in Iraq with better equipment, to protect them against the risk of being killed by roadside bombs.

[31] See below, § 7.1.

It does not seem that the law makes any further concessions to A's frailties and imperfections in determining what characteristics the reasonable person has. It is established that if A is particularly stupid, that will not be taken into account in judging what he or she could reasonably be expected to have foreseen.[32] The consensus of academic opinion is that the same position holds even in the case where A suffers from some disability which means that A has a much lower mental age than his or her physical age. That, too, will not be taken into account in judging what a reasonable person in A's position could have been expected to foresee.[33] To take any other line, it seems, would open up the door to stupid and thoughtless defendants claiming that, like one's mental age, their stupidity or thoughtlessness is a genetic condition which should be taken into account in judging what a reasonable person in their position would have realised.[34]

Whether or not A owed B a duty of care under the formula discussed here depends crucially on what was reasonably foreseeable *at the time A acted*. For example, in *Roe* v *Minister of Health* (1954), each of the claimants went into hospital for an operation. In both cases, their spines were injected with nupercaine at the start of the operation to anaesthetise them. Unfortunately, the nupercaine in question had been stored in ampoules which had, in turn, been stored in phenol, a disinfectant. Some of this phenol passed through tiny invisible cracks in the ampoules and contaminated the nupercaine which was injected into the claimants' spines. As a result, the claimants were permanently paralysed. Before the nupercaine was injected into the claimants' spines the ampoules had been inspected for cracks but none was visible and as a result the claimants' doctors thought that it was safe to inject the claimants' spines with the nupercaine; at the time, nobody realised that it was possible that ampoules of nupercaine might suffer from invisible cracks as a result of which the nupercaine contained in those ampoules might become contaminated.

It follows that, once the claimants' doctors had inspected the ampoules of nupercaine for visible cracks and found that there were none, the doctors did *not* owe the claimants a duty not to inject their spines with nupercaine under the physical danger principle. *At that time* (when the injections were administered), a reasonable person in the position of the claimants' doctors would not have thought that there was a real risk that the claimants would suffer some form of physical injury if their spines were injected with nupercaine. Of course, thanks to the experience of people like the claimants in *Roe* we now know better – we now know that if you inject someone's spine with nupercaine which comes from an ampoule which has no visible cracks, there is still a real risk that that nupercaine is contaminated and that someone will suffer some form of physical injury as a result of being injected with that nupercaine. However, the crucial thing in *Roe* was that at the time the claimants were operated on, nobody realised this – as a result, it was not possible to argue that the claimants' doctors in *Roe* had owed the claimants a duty not to inject their spines with nupercaine on the basis that it was reasonably foreseeable *at that time* that doing so would result in harm to the claimants.

Similarly, in *Abouzaid v Mothercare (UK) Ltd* (2001), the claimant was a 12-year-old boy who attempted to attach a sleeping bag to a pushchair. The sleeping bag was attached to the pushchair by passing two elasticated straps attached to either side of the sleeping bag around the back of the pushchair and buckling them together using a metal buckle attached to the end of one of the straps. Unfortunately, when the claimant attempted to buckle the

---

[32] *Vaughan* v *Menlove* (1837) 3 Bing NC 468, 132 ER 490.
[33] See Moran 2003, 18–26.
[34] For criticism of this argument, see Moran 2003, 28–31; also Mullender 2000.

straps together, they slipped from his grasp and the strap with the metal buckle at the end recoiled, hitting the claimant in his left eye. (Presumably the claimant was standing in front of or beside the pushchair when he let go of the straps; had he been standing behind the pushchair, the straps would have recoiled away from him when he let go of them.) The claimant's left eye was blinded as a result and he sued the defendants, who sold the sleeping bag through their stores, for compensation.

His claim in negligence was dismissed: he could not establish that the defendants had owed him a duty not to market the sleeping bag.[35] The reason was that *at the time the defendants marketed the sleeping bag*, a reasonable person in the position of the defendants would not have realised that there was a real risk that people like the claimant might suffer some form of physical injury as a result of the sleeping bag being designed the way it was. Before the claimant was injured, there was no reason for anyone to think that someone using the sleeping bag could suffer this kind of accident – presumably because everyone assumed that anyone attaching the sleeping bag to a pushchair would do so by standing behind the pushchair and pulling the straps attached to the sleeping bag towards them; not by standing beside or in front of the pushchair and pulling the straps away from them. Of course we now know better and, as a result, it may well be that stores nowadays owe their customers (and their customers' children) a duty not to market sleeping bags designed in the same way as the sleeping bag in the *Abouzaid* case.

D. Someone like

It would be difficult for any claimant to show that it was reasonably foreseeable at the time the defendant acted that the defendant's actions would result in that *particular* claimant being injured. Instead, all the claimant has to show is that it was reasonably foreseeable that *someone like* the claimant would be injured as a result of the defendant's actions. To see whether this condition is satisfied, we focus in on a particular feature of the claimant that played a part in the claimant's being injured as a result of the defendant's actions and ask whether it was reasonably foreseeable that the defendant's actions would result in someone with that feature being injured. Depending on the particular circumstances of the case, we might end up asking whether it was reasonably foreseeable that the defendant's actions would injure someone who was using the defendant's products;[36] or someone who was in the vicinity of the defendant's vehicle;[37] or someone who was blind;[38] or someone who suffered from an egg allergy.[39]

E. Physical injury

The duty formula under discussion here only applies in cases where it is foreseeable that B will suffer some kind of *physical injury* as a result of A's doing x – where the term 'physical injury' covers death or lesser harms that any normal person would regard as forms of

---

[35] The claimant was, however, allowed to sue for compensation under the Consumer Protection Act 1987: see below, § 12.3.

[36] As in *Donoghue v Stevenson* [1932] AC 562.

[37] As in *Farrugia v Great Western Railway Co* [1947] 2 All ER 565, where the claimant was injured by a load falling off the defendant's lorry.

[38] As in *Haley v London Electricity Board* [1965] AC 778, where the claimant fell into a hole dug in the street by the defendants.

[39] As in *Bhamra v Dubb* [2010] EWCA Civ 13, discussed above, § 6.1.

'physical injury', such as wounds or bruises.[40] It should be noted that the term 'physical injury' does *not* cover any form of *psychiatric illness*.[41] As we are about to see, mere foreseeability that one's actions will result in someone else suffering a psychiatric illness is not usually enough to give rise to a duty of care. Something extra usually has to be established before the courts will accept that A owed B a duty to take care not to act in a way that foreseeably resulted in B suffering a psychiatric illness.

6.3 PHYSICAL INJURY (2): HARM CAUSED BY A THIRD PARTY

A difficult issue is whether the duty formula under discussion in the previous section applies in a case where A has done something unreasonable that has resulted in B's either physically harming *herself* or physically harming a *third party*, C.

In cases where B is – to borrow a term from the criminal law – an 'innocent agent' who was not really responsible for the harm she did to herself or C, there is no real problem: if it was reasonably foreseeable that A's actions would have the result they did, then the courts will readily find that A had a duty to take care not to act as he did, with that duty being owed either to B (in the case where B harmed herself) or to C (in the case where B harmed C). We have already seen an example of this in the case of *Dixon* v *Bell* (1816), where the defendant asked a very young maidservant to fetch a gun for him, and while she was carrying the gun, she fired it, with the result that the claimant was injured. The defendant was held to have owed a duty of care to the claimant in this case because it was reasonably foreseeable that giving the gun to such a young girl who had no experience of safely handling such things might result in someone like the claimant being shot.

Much more difficult are cases where B is *not* an innocent agent, and was responsible for the harm that she did either to herself or to C. Two examples of 'harm to self' cases where the issue of whether a duty of care was owed to the claimant by a defendant who had put the claimant in a position to harm himself are *E (a child)* v *Souls Garages* (2001) and *Barrett* v *Ministry of Defence* (1995).

In the *E* case, a petrol station manager broke the law by selling petrol in a can to the claimant, a 13-year-old boy. Unknown to the manager (though he could have guessed, had he thought about it), the claimant wanted to get high by sniffing the petrol. The claimant and a friend of his spent some time sniffing the petrol, in the course of which they managed to spill a fair amount of petrol on their clothes. After a while, they decided to smoke a cigarette, with the predictable consequence that the claimant's clothes were set alight. The claimant ended up with burns on 56% of his body. It was held that the petrol station manager could be sued for the claimant's injuries: as it had been reasonably foreseeable that selling the claimant the petrol would have the result it did, the manager had owed the claimant a duty not to sell him the petrol.

---

[40] It also seems to cover getting pregnant, which not many people would regard as a form of physical injury: see *Walkin* v *South Manchester HA* [1995] 1 WLR 1543; *Richardson* v *LRC Products* [2000] Lloyd's Rep Med 280; *Parkinson* v *St James and Seacroft NHS Hospital* [2002] QB 266; though the House of Lords was more equivocal in *McFarlane* v *Tayside Health Board* [2000] 2 AC 59, with Lords Steyn (at 81) and Millett (at 107) saying that pregnancy is a form of physical injury, Lord Slynn saying that it is not (at 74), and Lords Hope (at 86–87) and Clyde (at 102) saying that pregnancy is *analogous* to a physical injury. If pregnancy is a form of physical injury, then if A has sexual intercourse with B using contraception that he knows or ought to know is unreliable and B gets pregnant as a result and carries the child to term, will she be entitled to sue A for damages on the basis that he owed her, and breached, a duty to take care that he did not use unreliable contraception in having sex with her?

[41] Though the courts in other contexts do sometimes treat a psychiatric illness as though it were a form of physical injury: see *Page* v *Smith* [1996] AC 155, discussed above, § 6.1.

It was different in *Barrett*. In that case, a soldier got drunk at a Hawaiian party that had been organised by the defendants at the soldier's barracks. It was the soldier's birthday and he had recently been promoted, so he had a double reason to celebrate. He ended up drinking so much that he collapsed and eventually died from choking on his own vomit. A claim that the defendants had owed the soldier a duty to stop serving him alcohol when it became clear he had had too much was rejected by the Court of Appeal:

> I can see no reason why it should not be fair, just and reasonable for the law to leave a responsible adult to assume responsibility for his own actions in consuming alcoholic drink. No one is better placed to judge the amount that he can safely consume or to exercise control in his own interest as well as in the interest of others. To dilute self-responsibility and to blame one adult for another's lack of self-control is neither just nor reasonable and in the development of the law of negligence an increment too far.[42]

The fact that the soldier in *Barrett* was an adult, and the claimant in *E* a child may account for the difference in the two cases: the child's responsibility for his harming himself in *E* may not have been as great, because of his immaturity, as the soldier's responsibility for harming himself in *Barrett*. Similarly, if B were *already* drunk, and then A did something unreasonable that resulted in B's harming himself, the courts may be more ready to find that A owed B a duty of care not to give B a chance to harm himself. B's drunkeness will dilute (though not negate) his responsibility for the harm he did to himself. This may explain the result in the Canadian case of *Crocker v Sundance Northwest Resorts* (1988), where the defendant was held liable for supplying the claimant – who was obviously drunk – with ski equipment, with the result that the claimant, in his drunken state, injured himself in a subsequent ski race.

What about the case – which Robert Rabin calls an 'enabling tort' case[43] – where A's unreasonable act contributes in some way to B's harming C, and B is responsible for what has happened to C? John Goldberg and Benjamin Zipursky provide us with some examples of this sort of case:

> A person cosigns a friend's application for a car loan, knowing that the friend has the propensity to be overcome by 'road rage.' . . . [T]he friend carelessly runs into [someone] during a bout of rage. A fertilizer manufacturer is aware that its product can be converted into a powerful bomb by determined terrorists . . . [It fails] to take steps to reduce the risk of such misuse [with the result that its fertilizer is used in a bombing]. A woman is aware of her ex-boyfriend's violent jealousy, as well as his occasional appearances at a bar located in their small town. She nonetheless agrees to meet a date for a drink at the bar . . . [H]er ex-boyfriend shows up and proceeds to pummel her date . . . A website permits users to create individual accounts and to post messages offering and seeking goods and services, but it declines to monitor the type of transactions being consummated. One account holder maintains a posting offering 'full body massage therapy'. Another takes up the offer, agreeing to pay for a hotel room in which they will meet. The buyer, in fact, uses the occasion to assault and rob the masseuse . . .[44]

In such cases, C will face two formidable obstacles in the way of his establishing that A owed him a duty to take care not to 'enable' B to harm C:

---

[42] [1995] 1 WLR 1217, 1224 (per Beldam LJ). A claim that the defendants had owed the dead soldier a duty of care *after* he collapsed, to see that he did not choke on his own vomit, did succeed (at 1225), and is explained below, § 7.4.

[43] Rabin 1999.

[44] Goldberg and Zipursky 2009, 1217.

(1) C would obviously have to show that it was reasonably foreseeable that A's actions would result in B harming C. But the authorities indicate that in this kind of case, the requirement of reasonable foreseeability will *not* be satisfied merely by showing that a reasonable person would have thought there was a 'real risk' that if A did what he did, B would end up harming C. Instead, it will have to be shown – these authorities indicate – that it was *very likely*[45] or *probable*[46] that B would harm C if A did what he did. In *Topp v London Country Bus (South West) Ltd* (1993), the defendants left a bus outside a pub with the keys in the ignition, with the result that someone took the bus for a joyride and ended up running over and killing the claimant's wife. It was held that the defendants had not owed the claimant's wife a duty to take care not to act as they did because it was not reasonably foreseeable – in the sense of *very likely* or *probable* – that their actions would result in this kind of harm occurring.

(2) In a case in which B has committed a tort in relation to C, the courts will hold that A *also* committed that tort if he was an *accessory* to B's tort. Under the law on accessory liability in tort,[47] *assisting* someone to commit a tort will *not* make you an accessory to that tort. Given this, it seems unlikely that the courts would undermine this aspect of the law on accessory liability by finding that someone who has 'enabled' someone else to commit a tort will be liable in negligence instead. In *CBS Songs plc v Amstrad* (1988), the claimants sued the defendants for breach of copyright, arguing that they were liable as an accessory for the millions of acts of breach of copyright that had been committed by people using the defendants' stereos to make copies of cassette tapes that had been bought in shops. The claim was dismissed: the defendants could not be held liable as accessories to those acts of breach of copyright merely because they had enabled those acts to be performed. As an alternative, the claimants sued the defendants in negligence. Lord Templeman dismissed the claim in scathing terms:

> Since *Anns v Merton London Borough Council* [1978] AC 728 put the floodgates on the jar, a fashionable [claimant] alleges negligence. The pleading assumes that we are all neighbours now, Pharisees and Samaritans alike, that foreseeability is a reflection of hindsight and that for every mischance in an accident-prone world someone solvent must be liable in damages . . . In the present proceedings damages and an injunction for negligence are sought against Amstrad for a breach of statutory duty which Amstrad did not commit and in which Amstrad did not participate . . . Under and by virtue of that [statute] Amstrad owed a duty not to infringe copyright and not to authorise an infringement of copyright. They did not owe a duty to prevent or discourage or warn against infringement.[48]

Even if C can overcome these hurdles (and it is not clear whether hurdle (ii) can ever be overcome), it submitted that – in line with the decision of the Court of Appeal in *Barrett*, above – that A will only have owed C a duty to take care in an 'enabling tort' case where B's responsibility for the harm he did C is attenuated by some lack of capacity, such as B's being a child, or B's being drunk.

If this is right, then it is unlikely that a UK court would find that a duty of care would be owed in any of the cases described by Goldberg and Zipursky, as the principal wrongdoers in those cases (the road rage driver, the terrorists, the jealous boyfriend, and the robber) are all substantially responsible for the harm they did their victims. Closer to the line is a situation such as the one in *West v East Tennessee Pioneer Oil Co* (2005), where two of the

---

[45] *Lamb v Camden LBC* [1981] QB 625, 642 (per Oliver LJ).
[46] *Smith v Littlewoods LBC* [1987] AC 241, 258 (per Lord Mackay).
[47] This area of the law is set out below, in chapter 36.
[48] [1988] AC 1013, 1059, 1060.

defendants' employees helped an obviously drunk driver fill his car up with petrol.[49] The driver then drove onto the wrong side of the road, and after driving south on a northbound carriageway for two miles, hit the claimants' car head-on, causing the claimants to suffer serious injuries. The Supreme Court of Tennessee held that the defendants' employees had owed the claimants a duty of care not to 'enable' the drunk driver to drive any further. The fact that the driver was *already* drunk, with the result that his responsibility for what happened after he went back onto the road was diluted (though, obviously, not negated), may mean that a UK court would reach the same conclusion.

6.4 PSYCHIATRIC ILLNESS (1): GENERAL PRINCIPLES IN ACCIDENT CASES

There are many different ways in which a defendant's positive act might result in a claimant suffering a psychiatric illness. In this section we will focus on cases where a defendant carelessly performs a positive act that results in an accident occurring, in which someone is injured or almost injured, and the claimant suffers a psychiatric illness as a result. Three such cases can be distinguished:

A. Injury to the claimant

B was injured in an accident brought about by A's carelessly doing *x*. B's injuries result in B later on developing a psychiatric illness.

This is the most straightforward case, and the one which troubles the courts the least. In this sort of case, B should find it relatively easy to establish that A owed her a duty to take care not to do *x*, arguing that it was reasonably foreseeable that someone like her would suffer injury as a result of A's doing *x*. If A did owe B a duty of care on that basis, then A's breach has initially resulted in B suffering the right kind of loss – physical injury. In suing for damages for that physical injury, she can also recover compensation for any psychiatric illness that she suffered as a result of being injured, no matter how unforeseeable.[50] So, as long as it was reasonably foreseeable that A's doing *x* would result in B suffering some kind of physical injury, B should be able to sue A in negligence for compensation for her psychiatric illness.

B. Almost injury to the claimant

A caused an accident as a result of carelessly doing *x*, and B was almost injured as a result. The experience resulted in B developing a psychiatric illness.

We have already seen an example of this sort of situation in the caselaw: *Page* v *Smith* (1996).[51] In this case, the claimant – whose chronic fatigue syndrome had revived as a result

---

[49] Our thanks to Kyle Lawson for bringing this case to our attention.

[50] *Simmons* v *British Steel plc* [2004] UKHL 20 (accident at work resulting in physical injury and consequent severe depressive illness caused by employee's anger at employers' failure to heed his warnings that his working conditions were dangerous).

[51] See above, § 6.1. See also *Schofield* v *Chief Constable of West Yorkshire* [1999] ICR 193 (claimant police officer suffered post-traumatic stress disorder when colleague unexpectedly discharged gun three times in her presence, thus exposing her to foreseeable risk of physical injury); *Donachie* v *Chief Constable of Greater Manchester Police* [2004] EWCA Civ 405 (claimant police officer was given the job of installing a tracking device on the bottom of a car owned by a criminal gang; unfortunately the batteries in the tracking device did not work properly, and the claimant had to go back to the car nine times to replace the tracking device, an experience that both exposed him to a foreseeable risk of physical injury and caused him to develop post-traumatic stress disorder).

of the defendant's carelessly crashing into the claimant's car while the claimant was in it – was able to establish that the defendant had owed him a duty of care not to crash into the claimant's car by relying on the fact that it was reasonably foreseeable that crashing into the claimant's car would result in the claimant being injured. Although the claimant did not suffer any physical injury as a result of the defendant's breaching this duty of care, it was held that the claimant could still sue for the psychiatric illness resulting from the defendant's breach. The claimant did not even have to prove that the psychiatric illness was a foreseeable consequence of the defendant's breach – it was enough that some physical injury could be foreseen as resulting from the breach.

Page v *Smith* indicates that in the general situation set out above, B will be able to sue A in negligence for his psychiatric illness provided he can show that A owed him a duty to take care not to do *x* based on the fact that it was reasonably foreseeable that A's doing *x* would result in B's being physically injured.

C. Injury or almost injury to a third party

A's carelessly doing *x* resulted in an accident in which C was killed or injured, or almost killed or injured, and B suffered a psychiatric illness as a result.

This sort of psychiatric illness-resulting-from-an-accident situation is the one that the courts have found most troublesome to resolve, and the one that dominates the caselaw on when a claimant can sue a defendant in negligence for a psychiatric illness. Two reasons can be given for why these kinds of cases have proved so difficult to resolve.

First, unlike the first two accident situations considered above, the courts will not usually be able to find that A owed B a duty to take care not to do *x* based on the fact that it was reasonably foreseeable that *B* would suffer some kind of *physical injury* if A did *x*. While it may have been reasonably foreseeable that C (who is known in the caselaw as the 'primary victim' of A's conduct) would suffer some kind of physical injury as a result of A's doing *x*, the same will not usually be true of B (who is known in the caselaw as the 'secondary victim' of A's conduct). So if the courts want to find that A owed B a duty of care in this situation, they will have to base that duty of care on something other than foreseeability of physical harm to B.

Secondly, in searching for some rule or formula that they can apply to decide whether or not A owed B a duty of care, the courts have had to be wary of employing a rule or formula that could have the effect of exposing A to lawsuits from a substantial number of people, with the result that the scope of the liabilities incurred by A as a result of his killing or injuring (or almost injuring) C could get out of all proportion to his fault.

The rule or formula that the courts have ended up employing in these kinds of situations is a very complex one. First of all, it has to be shown that it was reasonably foreseeable that A's actions would result in B's developing a psychiatric illness. This requires B to show that:

(1) B was in a 'close and loving relationship' with C, and what happened to C was sufficiently serious as to make it reasonably foreseeable that someone like B would suffer a psychiatric illness as a result; OR

(2) In the aftermath of the accident carelessly caused by A's doing *x*, B helped to assist C, and what B saw or experienced in trying to assist C made it reasonably foreseeable that B would suffer a psychiatric illness as a result; OR

(3) B reasonably, but wrongly, felt responsible for what happened to C, and what happened to C was sufficiently serious as to make it reasonably foreseeable that B would suffer a psychiatric illness as a result; OR

(4) B saw what happened to C, and what B saw was so horrific that it was reasonably foreseeable that B would suffer a psychiatric illness as a result.

But foreseeability of a psychiatric illness is not enough to establish a duty of care. In order to keep the scope of A's liabilities within manageable bounds, the courts will require B to establish something more before they will find that A owed B a duty of care. What this 'something more' ('SM') is depends on the basis on which B is arguing that it was reasonably foreseeable that she would suffer a psychiatric illness as a result of A's actions.

(1–SM) If B is basing her claim on the fact that she was in a 'close and loving relationship' with C, she has to show that her psychiatric illness was triggered by the shock of *witnessing the accident* in which C was killed or injured or almost injured, or seeing C in the *immediate aftermath* of that accident.[52]

(2–SM) If B is basing her claim on the fact that she helped to assist C in the aftermath of the accident caused by A, B will have to show that she was, or thought she was, in danger at the time she was trying to help C.

(3–SM) If B is basing her claim on the fact that she felt responsible for what happened to C, B will have to show that she was present at the scene of the accident in which C was killed or injured or almost injured.

(4–SM) If B is basing her claim on the fact that she witnessed what happened to C, and what B saw was so horrific that someone like her – a mere bystander – could have been expected to develop a psychiatric illness as a result, the courts seem to have taken the position that A will not have owed B a duty of care – no matter how foreseeable B's psychiatric illness might have been.

6.5 PSYCHIATRIC ILLNESS (2): THE CASELAW ON ACCIDENT CASES

In this section, we will look in more detail at the caselaw dealing with when a claimant can recover for psychiatric illness in an 'injury or almost injury to a third party' case. We will divide up the caselaw according to the four different types of 'injury or almost injury to a third party' situations in which a claimant might be able to establish that it was reasonably foreseeable that the defendant's actions would result in her developing a psychiatric illness. Having looked at these situations, we will consider a fifth situation (the case where a defendant foreseeably caused the claimant to develop a psychiatric illness by injuring, or almost injuring, *himself*) which deserves separate consideration.

A. Close and loving relationship

The leading case in this area is *Alcock* v *Chief Constable of South Yorkshire* (1992). That case arose out of the Hillsborough disaster where 95 football fans were crushed to death and hundreds more were injured at the Leppings Lane end of Hillsborough Football Stadium

---

[52] So if B's psychiatric illness is triggered by her grief at C's dying, or as a result of the strain of tending to C after he is injured in the accident, she will not be able to establish that A owed her a duty of care: see *Alcock* v *Chief Constable of South Yorkshire* [1992] 1 AC 310, 396 (per Lord Keith), 400 (per Lord Ackner).

in Sheffield before an FA Cup semi-final between Liverpool and Nottingham Forest. The immediate cause of the disaster was the decision of the police to open an outer gate to the Leppings Lane end of the Hillsborough Stadium without cutting off access to spectator pens 3 and 4 at that end, which were already full. Football fans rushed through the opened gate into pens 3 and 4 with the result that those at the front of those pens were crushed. The claimants in *Alcock* were relatives of the dead who had developed various forms of post-traumatic stress disorder in the aftermath of the disaster. None of the claimants whose cases were decided by the House of Lords in *Alcock* succeeded in their claims for compensation; none of them could establish that the police owed them a duty to take care not to cause the disaster at Hillsborough.[53]

Most of the claimants in *Alcock* failed to establish that the police owed them a duty of care because they could not show that it was reasonably foreseeable that they would develop a psychiatric illness as a result of the accident at Hillsborough occurring. The only way they could show that it was reasonably foreseeable that they would develop a psychiatric illness as a result of the Hillsborough tragedy occurring was by showing that they were in a close and loving relationship with someone killed or injured at Hillsborough. But the House of Lords held that most of the *Alcock* claimants had not established that they were in a close and loving relationship with anyone killed or injured at Hillsborough. For example, Brian Harrison suffered post-traumatic stress disorder when he lost his two brothers at Hillsborough. His claim that the police owed him a duty to take care not to cause the accident at Hillsborough failed because there was nothing in the evidence before the House of Lords to suggest that he enjoyed a sufficiently close and loving relationship with his brothers as to make it reasonably foreseeable that he would develop a psychiatric illness as a result of their being killed and the House of Lords was not prepared to presume that Brian Harrison enjoyed such a relationship with his brothers.

It was different in the case of Mr and Mrs Copoc, who lost their son at Hillsborough and subsequently suffered post-traumatic stress disorder. In their case, the House of Lords *was* prepared to presume – in the absence of any evidence going the other way – that they enjoyed such a close and loving relationship with their son that it was reasonably foreseeable that they would develop a psychiatric illness in the aftermath of the Hillsborough disaster. Their claims that the police owed them a duty to take care not to cause the accident at Hillsborough failed because they could not establish that their psychiatric illnesses were triggered by their witnessing the Hillsborough disaster unfold or its immediate aftermath. They *did* see live pictures of the Hillsborough disaster unfolding on television but the fact that broadcasting guidelines forbade the transmission of live pictures showing scenes of recognisable human suffering led the House of Lords to think that what the Copocs saw on television could not have accounted for their subsequently developing post-traumatic stress disorder. The pictures they saw were insufficiently shocking – they gave rise to anxiety, but nothing more. Nor could the Copocs establish that they developed their psychiatric illnesses as a result of seeing their son in the *immediate* aftermath of the Hillsborough tragedy. Only one of the Copocs – Mr Copoc – travelled to Sheffield after the disaster and he only saw his son's body the next day, long after the disaster had occurred. The real reason

---

[53] One claimant succeeded in his claim for compensation at first instance: William Pemberton, who went by coach with his son to the match. His son had a ticket to watch the match; Pemberton stayed on in the coach, intending to watch the match on the coach's television. Pemberton watched the disaster unfold on the television and then searched for his son. His son had in fact died in the disaster and Pemberton identified his body at around midnight. No appeal was made against the first instance judge's decision that the police had owed Pemberton a duty to take care not to cause the accident at Hillsborough: [1992] 1 AC 310, 339, 348, 351, 365.

why the Copocs suffered post-traumatic stress disorder in the aftermath of the Hillsborough disaster was because of what they *imagined* their son had gone through – not because of what they *saw*.

The House of Lords was only prepared to presume that one other *Alcock* claimant enjoyed a close and loving relationship with someone killed or injured in the Hillsborough tragedy. This was Alexandra Penk. She lost her fiancé, Carl Rimmer, at Hillsborough and subsequently suffered post-traumatic stress disorder.[54] But again, Alexandra Penk's claim that the police owed her a duty to take care not to cause the accident at Hillsborough to occur failed because she could not establish that her psychiatric illness was caused by her witnessing the Hillsborough tragedy unfold or its immediate aftermath. All Alexandra Penk saw were live pictures of the tragedy unfolding – and they were insufficiently shocking for her post-traumatic stress disorder to be attributed to her witnessing them.

The fact that the claims of the Copocs and Alexandra Penk failed in *Alcock* leads some unwary students to conclude that in a 'close and loving relationship' case, it is not enough – for the purposes of establishing that the defendant owed the claimant a duty of care – to show that the claimant's psychiatric illness was triggered by watching live television pictures of the claimant's loved one being killed or injured. Not so:[55] the crucial element in the *Alcock* case was that the television pictures the Copocs and Alexandra Penk saw were not clear enough for them to be able to say that they saw their son and fiancé, respectively, being killed or injured. But what if the television companies had breached broadcasting guidelines and zoomed in on scenes of identifiable human beings being crushed to death? If such television scenes would have shown the Copocs and Alexandra Penk what was happening to their loved ones, it is submitted that the police would have been found to have owed the Copocs and Alexandra Penk a duty of care – but their claims would still have failed. This is because the police would have been able to argue that their breach of duty to the Copocs and Alexandra Penk did not *cause* their psychiatric illnesses. Those illnesses were caused by the deliberate, voluntary, informed and unreasonable decision of the television companies to breach broadcasting guidelines and show scenes of identifiable people suffering. That decision would have broken the chain of causation between the police's negligence and the psychiatric illnesses suffered by the Copocs and Alexandra Penk, and absolved them of responsibility for those illnesses. It may be that, in such a case, the Copocs and Alexandra Penk would have been able to sue the television companies, arguing that they owed them a duty to take care not to broadcast such distressing pictures. The issue will be discussed in the next section, when we look at cases where a defendant causes a claimant to suffer a psychiatric illness by doing something other than causing an accident.

Let's now take a closer look at Mr Copoc. How soon after the Hillsborough tragedy unfolded would he have had to have seen his son's dead body for him to be able to argue that his psychiatric illness was triggered as a result of seeing his son in the immediate aftermath of the Hillsborough tragedy? In *McLoughlin* v *O'Brian* (1983), the claimant's daughter was

---

[54] Would the House of Lords have been prepared to presume that she was in a close and loving relationship with Carl Rimmer had they actually been married at the time of the Hillsborough tragedy? One would have thought so, but see Lord Keith's remarks in *Alcock*: '[the] kinds of relationship which may involve close ties of love and affection . . . may be present in family relationships or those of close friendship and may be stronger in the case of engaged couples than in that of persons who have been married to each other for many years': [1992] 1 AC 310, 397.

[55] [1992] 1 AC 310, 405 (per Lord Ackner: 'simultaneous broadcasts of a disaster cannot in all cases be ruled out as providing the equivalent of the actual sight or hearing of event or of its immediate aftermath'), 417 (per Lord Oliver: 'there may well be circumstances where the element of visual perception is provided by witnessing the actual injury to the primary victim on simultaneous television'). Lord Jauncey of Tullichettle declined to express a view: [1992] 1 AC 310, 423.

killed and her husband and other two children were injured in a car accident. The claimant was at home when the accident happened, and was only told of it two hours later.[56] She was driven to the hospital (which would have taken about thirty minutes, according to Google maps) where her husband and surviving children were being looked after. The House of Lords was happy to accept in this case that the claimant's subsequent psychiatric illness had been triggered by her witnessing the 'immediate aftermath' of the accident involving her husband and children. So two and a half hours is not too long. Lords Ackner and Jauncey of Tullichettle expressed doubt in *Alcock* as to whether someone who identified a loved one's body eight or nine hours after the accident in which they were killed could be said to have been witnessed the *immediate* aftermath of the accident.[57]

B. Rescue

The decision in *Alcock* to reject all of the claims made by relatives of those who had died in the Hillsborough tragedy created some difficulty for the House of Lords seven years later when, in *Frost* v *Chief Constable of South Yorkshire Police* (1999),[58] five police officers who had been on duty on the day of the Hillsborough tragedy sought to sue their police force for the psychiatric illnesses they claimed to have suffered as a result of witnessing what happened that day.

The police officers' claim for damages was based on an earlier authority – *Chadwick* v *British Transport Commission* (1967) – where a claimant suffered a psychiatric illness as a result of what he saw and heard in attending to the survivors of a train crash that happened 200 yards from his house, and that was caused by the defendant train company's carelessness. It was held that the defendants had owed the claimant a duty to take care not to cause the train crash on the basis that it was foreseeable that if such a crash did occur, a rescuer like the claimant would suffer a psychiatric illness as a result. The police officers claimed that they were rescuers, like the claimant in *Chadwick*, and given that it had been reasonably foreseeable that their rescue activities on the day of the Hillsborough tragedy would result in their suffering a psychiatric illness, their senior officers had owed them a duty to take care not to cause the disaster at Hillsborough.

It would have been very embarrassing for the House of Lords to allow the police officers' claims in *Frost*.[59] The blameless relatives in *Alcock* would have been outraged to have their claims for compensation turned down while members of the police – who bore sole responsibility for what happened at Hillsborough – had their claims allowed. As a result, the Law Lords must have been on the look-out for any feature of the facts in *Frost* that would allow them to distinguish that case from *Chadwick*. They found it in the element of physical danger. In *Chadwick*, the claimant had spent nine hours crawling through wreckage from the train crash, trying to get people out from under the wreckage. In contrast, in *Frost*, two of the claimants helped carry the dead, two of the claimants tried unsuccessfully to resuscitate injured spectators in the stadium, one of the claimants assisted at a mortuary to which the dead were taken: and none of them were ever in any physical danger at all.

---

[56] The House of Lords had it that she was told an 'hour or so' after the accident ([1983] AC 410, 417 (per Lord Wilberforce), but the Court of Appeal judgment is clearer that the accident happened at 4 pm, and the claimant was told about it at about 6 pm: [1981] 1 QB 599, 603 (per Stephenson LJ).

[57] [1992] 1 AC 310, 405 (per Lord Ackner) and 424 (per Lord Jauncey of Tullichettle). Lord Oliver seems to have been of the same view: 410.

[58] The case is also known as '*White* v *Chief Constable of South Yorkshire Police*'. Some of the complications in the decision are very well discussed in Case 2010.

[59] As Lords Steyn and Hoffmann frankly acknowledged in *Frost*: [1999] 2 AC 455, at 499, and 510 respectively.

The House of Lords seized on this aspect of the case in *Frost* as a reason for dismissing the claimants' claims, ruling that in a case where A carelessly causes an accident and B suffers psychiatric illness trying to rescue the victims of that accident, A will only have owed B a duty to take care not to cause that accident if B was, or thought he was, in physical danger at some point in his rescue effort. Lord Goff dissented, thinking that this was a profoundly unsatisfactory basis on which to determine whether a defendant who had caused an accident owed a duty of care to a rescuer who had suffered a psychiatric illness in that accident:

> Suppose that there was a terrible train crash and that there were two Chadwick brothers living nearby, both of them small and agile window cleaners distinguished by their courage and humanity. Mr A. Chadwick worked on the front half of the train, and Mr B. Chadwick on the rear half. It so happened that, although there was some physical danger present in the front half of the train, there was none in the rear. Both worked for 12 hours or so bringing aid and comfort to the victims. Both suffered [post traumatic stress disorder] in consequence of the general horror of the situation. [According to the decision of the majority], Mr A. would recover but Mr B. would not. To make things worse, the same conclusion must follow even if Mr A. was unaware of the existence of the physical danger present in his half of the train. This is surely unacceptable.[60]

C. Responsibility

This category of case where a duty of care might be owed to a claimant who suffered a psychiatric illness as a result of a defendant's carelessness was first recognised in *Dooley* v *Cammell Laird & Co Ltd* (1951).

In that case, the claimant was a crane driver. The claimant was in his crane and was lowering a sling-load of materials into a hold when the rope which attached the sling-load to his crane snapped. The sling-load of materials fell into the hold where several of the claimant's colleagues were working. Fortunately, no one was injured. However, the claimant, sitting high up in his crane, did not know that and, thinking he was responsible for the accident that had occurred, developed a psychiatric illness at the thought of what he had done. In fact the accident was the fault of the claimant's employers – who had failed to check that the rope was strong enough for lifting purposes – and the firm that had manufactured the rope. The claimant sued both of them for damages. His claim was allowed. It was held that the defendants had owed the claimant a duty to take care not to cause the accident that had occurred on the ground that because the claimant thought he was responsible for the accident that occurred, it was reasonably foreseeable that the claimant would develop a psychiatric illness as a result of that accident's occurring.

However, just as the decision in *Chadwick* was substantially qualified by the decision of the House of Lords in *Frost*, so the decision in *Dooley* has been substantially qualified by the decision of the Court of Appeal in *Hunter* v *British Coal Corp* (1999). In that case, the claimant was employed by the defendants to work at their coal mine. He was driving a vehicle along a track when he became aware of a water hydrant protruding into the track. The claimant tried to manoeuvre the vehicle round the hydrant but the track was too narrow and the claimant managed to strike the hydrant, causing water to flow from it. The claimant stopped his vehicle and got out and tried to stop the flow of water from the hydrant with the assistance of a fellow employee, one Tommy Carter. The claimant ran off, looking for a water hose that he could use to channel the flow of water from the hydrant, while Carter continued to attempt to shut the hydrant off. When the claimant was 30 metres away from the hydrant, it burst and Carter was killed in the explosion. The claimant

---

[60] [1999] 2 AC 455, 487.

only learned that Carter had died on his way back to the scene of the accident. Feeling responsible for Carter's death, the claimant developed a deep depression. In fact, the defendants were responsible for the accident that occurred: it was their fault the track down which the claimant had been driving had been too narrow with the result that the claimant's vehicle struck the hydrant, with tragic consequences.

The claimant sued the defendants. The Court of Appeal turned down his claim, holding that the defendants had not owed the claimant a duty of care not to cause the accident that had triggered his depression because the claimant had not *witnessed* the accident. The Court of Appeal may have wanted to limit the scope of *Dooley* by imposing a requirement that a *Dooley*-style claimant witness the accident for which he felt responsible out of a fear that in the absence of such a requirement, someone who caused an accident might end up being found to have owed duties of care to a wide range of people who felt responsible for it. For example, if a motorist ran down a little girl in the street, it is conceivable that quite a few people might feel responsible for the girl's death and develop psychiatric illnesses as a result: the parents who let their girl go out on her own, the people who the little girl was on her way to visit, the policeman who did not ask the little girl where she was going and take her there himself. If the motorist were to be held to have owed all of these people a duty to take care not to run down the little girl, then his eventual liability would grow out of all proportion to his fault in running her down. (Though it should be noted that that liability would be borne by his insurance company.)

Hunter may not contain the last word on the issue of what has to be established before a duty of care will be found in a *Dooley*-type case. In *W* v *Essex CC* (2001), the claimant foster parents each developed a psychiatric illness when a boy who had been placed with them sexually abused their children. They sued the local authority who had placed the boy with them. The House of Lords refused to strike out the claimants' claims, holding that it was arguable that the local authority had owed them a duty not to place the boy with them. The House of Lords thought that a duty of care might have been owed to the claimants in this case because they *felt responsible* for what had happened to their children.[61] If so, then the decision in *W* casts doubt on whether *Hunter* was correctly decided as, of course, the claimants were not present when their children were sexually abused.

D. Bystanders

In *McLoughlin* v *O'Brian* (1983), Lord Wilberforce observed that in 'injury or almost injury to third party' cases, where the

> possible range [of people who might want to make claims in such cases goes from] the closest of family ties – of parent and child, or husband and wife – [to] the ordinary bystander . . . [e]xisting law recognises the claims of the first: it denies that of the second, either on the basis that such persons must be assumed to be possessed of fortitude sufficient to enable them to endure the calamities of modern life, or that defendants cannot be expected to compensate the world at large.[62]

However, some of the Law Lords in *Alcock* v *Chief Constable of South Yorkshire* (1992) took the view that in the right kind of case – where A has caused an accident that was so horrific that it was reasonably foreseeable that B, a mere bystander witnessing the accident, would develop a psychiatric illness as a result – B might be able to argue that A owed him a duty to take care not to cause the accident that triggered B's psychiatric illness:

---

[61] [2001] 2 AC 592, 601.
[62] [1983] AC 410, 422.

Psychiatric injury to [a mere bystander] would not ordinarily, in my view, be within the range of reasonable foreseeability, but could not perhaps be entirely excluded from it if the circumstances of a catastrophe occurring very close to him were particularly horrific.[63]

As regards [bystanders], while it may be very difficult to envisage the case of a stranger, who is not actively and foreseeably involved in a disaster or its aftermath, other than in the role of rescuer, suffering shock-induced psychiatric injury by the mere observation of apprehended or actual injury of a third person in circumstances that could be considered reasonably foreseeable, I see no reason why he should not, if in the circumstances, a reasonably strong-nerved person would have been so shocked. In the course of argument your Lordships were given, by way of example, that of a petrol tanker careering out of control into a school in session and bursting into flames. I would not be prepared to rule out a potential claim by a passer-by so shocked by the scene as to suffer psychiatric illness.[64]

I would not exclude the possibility . . . of a successful claim, given circumstances of such horror as would be likely to traumatise the most phlegmatic spectator, by a mere bystander.[65]

Despite these *dicta*, both the Court of Appeal – in *McFarlane* v *E E Caledonia Ltd* (1994)[66] – and the House of Lords – in *Frost* v *Chief Constable of South Yorkshire* (1999)[67] – have held that the House of Lords decided in *Alcock* that someone who suffers a psychiatric illness simply as a result of witnessing an accident occur will *only* be able to sue in negligence for compensation for that illness if he or she was in a sufficiently 'close and loving relationship' with someone involved in the accident. On this reading of *Alcock*, the decision of the House of Lords in that case establishes that in a case where a bystander has developed a psychiatric illness as a result of witnessing an accident carelessly caused by A, the bystander will *never* be able to argue that A owed her a duty of care not to cause the accident that traumatised her: she will not have been in a sufficiently 'close and loving relationship' with anyone involved in the accident.

This reading of *Alcock* is simply wrong and completely inconsistent with the *dicta* from *Alcock* cited above. In fact, this reading of *Alcock* gets *Alcock* backwards. *Alcock* did *not* say that a bystander who develops a psychiatric illness as a result of witnessing an accident occur will only be able to sue in negligence for compensation for her illness if she was in a 'close and loving relationship' with someone involved in the accident. What *Alcock* said was that someone who develops a psychiatric illness because she was in a 'close and loving relationship' with someone who was involved in the accident will only be able to sue in negligence for compensation for her illness if her illness was triggered by her witnessing the accident or the immediate aftermath.

So what went wrong? How could the courts get *Alcock* so wrong? The fault lies, we suggest, in the fact that some judges seem to take the view that whether or not a duty of care was owed to a claimant who suffers a psychiatric illness as a result of an accident occurring will depend on whether the claimant was a 'primary' or 'secondary' victim of that accident. The idea being that one rule will apply to determine whether or not a duty of care was owed to you if you are a 'primary victim' and another rule will apply to determine whether or not a duty of care was owed to you if you are a 'secondary victim'.

---

[63] [1992] 1 AC 310, 397 (per Lord Keith of Kinkel).

[64] [1992] 1 AC 310, 403 (per Lord Ackner).

[65] [1992] 1 AC 310, 416 (per Lord Oliver).

[66] [1994] 2 All ER 1, at 14. See also *French* v *Chief Constable of Sussex* [2006] EWCA Civ 312 (ruling that police officers could not sue in negligence for psychiatric illness that resulted from shooting of a third party).

[67] [1999] 2 AC 455, 462 (per Lord Griffiths), 472 (per Lord Goff), 496–497 (per Lord Steyn), 502 (per Lord Hoffmann). Lord Browne-Wilkinson, the other judge in *White*, agreed with the judgments of Lords Steyn and Hoffmann: [1999] 2 AC 455, 462.

Now – the claimants in *Alcock* were 'secondary victims' of the Hillsborough tragedy. The House of Lords ruled in *Alcock* that the defendants in that case could only have owed the claimants a duty of care if: (1) the claimants were in a 'close and loving relationship' with the primary victims of the defendants' carelessness; and (2) the claimants' psychiatric illnesses were triggered as a result of their witnessing the primary victims being killed or injured or almost injured, or the immediate aftermath thereof. If you think that there is *one* rule that determines when a duty of care will be owed to the 'secondary victim' of an accident who has developed a psychiatric illness as a result of that accident occurring, then you will naturally think that the House of Lords was laying down in *Alcock* – a 'secondary victim' case – what that rule was: you have to show a 'close and loving relationship' and proximity in 'space and time' to the accident in which the primary victims of the accident were killed or injured or almost injured. And such a rule would rule out a duty of care ever being owed to a bystander who suffers a psychiatric illness as a result of witnessing an accident occur, as the bystander is also – like the claimants in *Alcock* – a 'secondary victim' but not in a 'close and loving relationship' with anyone involved in the accident.

But the truth is there is no *one* rule that determines when a 'secondary victim' can sue. As we observed above, the law in this area is much more complex. The simplistic view that there is *one* rule introduces all sorts of complications into our understanding of the law. How, for example, are we to account for the fact that a duty of care *was* owed to the claimant in *Dooley* v *Cammell Laird & Co Ltd* (1951) and to the claimant in *Chadwick* v *British Transport Commission* (1967), even though those claimants were obviously not in a 'close and loving relationship' with the primary victims of the defendants' carelessness in those cases? The only way is to reclassify those claimants as 'primary victims'.[68] But if we do this, the distinction between 'primary victims' and 'secondary victims' becomes meaningless and consequently useless as a means of organising, and discussing, this area of the law.[69]

---

[68] Lord Oliver suggested in *Alcock* that the claimant in *Dooley* was a 'primary victim' ([1992] 1 AC 310) and Lord Slynn seemed to endorse this suggestion in *W* v *Essex CC* ([2001] 2 AC 592, 601). Other Law Lords have tried to stick with the sensible (and intelligible) view that you only count as a 'primary victim' of A's causing an accident if A owed you a duty to take care not to cause that accident because it was reasonably foreseeable that doing so would cause you to suffer some kind of physical injury: see Lord Lloyd's judgment in *Page* v *Smith* [1996] AC 155, and Lord Steyn in *Frost* v *Chief Constable of South Yorkshire* [1999] 2 AC 455, 496.

[69] Cf. Teff 1998, 113–14: 'preoccupation with a victim's "primary" or "secondary" status only adds a further layer of obfuscation, distracting attention from the central issue . . . The primary/secondary divide . . . is . . . a recipe for more litigation and further confusion.' Regrettably, some judges seem to regard the distinction between 'primary' and 'secondary' victims as of crucial importance for the purpose of determining whether a duty of care was owed in *any* case where someone has suffered a psychiatric illness as a result of someone else's actions. See, for example, *Hatton* v *Sutherland* [2002] 2 All ER 1, at [19]–[22]. That case concerned the question of whether an employer owed an employee a duty not to make her do stressful work without giving her any assistance or counselling. It beggars belief that the courts think that the (vague) distinction between 'primary' and 'secondary' victims can be applied outside the context of a situation where a defendant's actions have resulted in someone's being killed or injured or almost injured and someone else has suffered a psychiatric illness as a result. In a case where A has made B do particularly stressful work which has resulted in B's suffering a psychiatric illness, it makes absolutely no sense whatsoever to ask whether B is a 'primary' or 'secondary' victim of A's actions. See Case 2010, at 50: 'a better approach would be to return the primary/secondary distinction to its original function: that is, "primary" and "secondary" victim status should only be relevant for dealing with claimants suffering lasting psychiatric trauma as a result of sudden traumatic events or accidents, and where they are otherwise "legal strangers" to the defendants.' Also *In Re Organ Retention Group Litigation* [2005] QB 506 (also known as *AB* v *Leeds Teaching Hospital NHS Trust*), where – in a case where the parents of dead children were suing a hospital for retaining organs from their chidren's bodies without their consent – it was (correctly) submitted (ibid, at [196]) that 'the primary/secondary victim dichotomy has no relevance to these claims' but Gage J rejected (at [197]) that 'tempting' proposition on the basis that 'the House of Lords has made it clear that those claiming for psychiatric injury must be placed in one or other category . . .'.

E. Self-harm

Let us now look at the situation where B foreseeably suffers a psychiatric illness because A's actions result in A being killed or injured or almost injured. In such a case, could B argue that A owed B a duty to take care not to kill or injure or almost injure *himself* (A)?

The issue came up in *Greatorex v Greatorex* (2000). In that case, the claimant's son was out driving in a friend's car when he crashed it and was injured as a result. The claimant – acting in his capacity as a fire officer – attended the scene of the car crash and saw his son unconscious, injured and trapped in the car. As a result of seeing this, the claimant developed a psychiatric illness. The claimant then sued his son for damages. (This was not as heartless as it seems. While the son was not insured to drive his friend's car, the Motor Insurers' Bureau would have covered any judgment entered against the son.) The claimant argued that his son owed him a duty to take care not to crash the car he was driving, on the basis that it was reasonably foreseeable that if he did so, the claimant would suffer a psychiatric illness as a result. Now, on the basis of what has already been said, one would expect the court to have ruled that the son *did* owe the claimant a duty to take care not to crash the car. The claimant was in a close and loving relationship with his son and developed his psychiatric illness as a result of attending the immediate aftermath of the accident in which his son was injured. However, Cazalet J ruled that no duty of care had been owed to the claimant in this case, for two reasons.

First of all, Cazalet J thought that the son's 'right of self-determination' would have been unacceptably limited if he had owed the claimant a duty to take care not to crash the car he was driving.[70] It is not clear that this is correct. If someone *wants* to kill himself, there is a case for saying that he will *not* owe those members of his family who might be affected by his death a duty not to kill himself – the existence of such a duty would, it is true, completely take away his 'right of self-determination'.[71] But the claimant's son was not *trying* to kill himself when he crashed his friend's car. Given this, it is not clear why his 'right to self-determination' would have been infringed if he had owed C a duty to take care that he did not crash his friend's car.

Cazalet J's second reason for denying that a duty of care was owed in this case was that to find a duty of care in this kind of case would 'open up the possibility of a particularly undesirable type of litigation between the family, involving questions of relative fault as between its members'. He continued:

> To take an example, A, while drunk, seriously injures himself. B, his wife, [develops a psychiatric illness as a result of seeing A injure himself]. What if A raises, by way of a defence, the fact that he had drunk too much because B had unjustifiably threatened to leave him for another man or had fabricated an allegation of child sexual abuse against him? Should the law of tort concern itself with this issue? In a case where A's self-harm is deliberate, the possibility that B's claim may be met by a defence of contributory negligence, alleging that B's behaviour caused A to harm himself, is an alarming one.[72]

---

[70] [2000] 1 WLR 1970, 1984.

[71] It is submitted that the would-be suicide will still owe other people a duty not to commit suicide in such a way that, it can reasonably be foreseen, will result in their suffering some kind of physical injury. So someone who wants to commit suicide will have a duty not to do it by taking a plane flight and blowing it up in mid-flight. Similarly, he will have a duty not to commit suicide by throwing himself off the top of a skyscraper if it is reasonably foreseeable that people walking around the base of the skyscraper will suffer some kind of physical injury if he does so.

[72] [2000] 1 WLR 1970, 1985.

Once again, this is not wholly convincing. Suppose, to take Cazalet J's example, A – in his drunken state – carelessly set fire to the family home and B only escaped the fire after she had been severely burned. In this case, the law will not prevent B from suing A in negligence in respect of her burns – even though allowing her to bring such an action will give rise to the same sort of difficulties as Cazalet J thought would arise if, in his example, B were allowed to sue A in negligence in respect of her psychiatric illness.

6.6 PSYCHIATRIC ILLNESS (3): NON-ACCIDENT CASES

So far, we have been looking at cases where a defendant performs a positive act that causes an accident that in turn results in a claimant suffering a psychiatric illness, either because the claimant is injured or almost injured in the accident, or because a third party (or even the defendant) is killed or injured or almost injured in the accident. There are, however, other ways that a defendant can cause a claimant to suffer a psychiatric illness:

(1) *Bad news*. A tells B some bad news and as a result B develops a psychiatric illness.

(2) *Humiliating or degrading treatment*. A treats B in a way that is particularly humiliating or degrading and B develops a psychiatric illness as a result.

(3) *Stress at work*. A makes his employee, B, do work that is so stressful or difficult for B that B ends up suffering a psychiatric illness.

(4) *Fear of future harm*. A has done something to put B in danger of suffering some kind of physical harm. B has not yet actually suffered any physical harm as a result of A's actions, but develops a psychiatric illness as a result of worrying that he will suffer physical harm in the future.

In each of these cases, there would be little fear of A's liability getting out of all proportion to his fault if A were found to owe B a duty of care. B is, after all, the only one in a position to sue A in these kinds of situations. However, the courts have still had to be cautious about developing the law on when a duty of care will be owed in some of these situations, for fear that being too ready to find that a duty of care was owed will deter people from acting in ways that are desirable or, at least, reasonable.

For example, people do sometimes need to be told bad news – and the bearers of that bad news should not be put off saying what they need to say for fear that what they say will result in their being sued. Again, while no one is in favour of people being treated in a humiliating or degrading way, saying that A will owe B a duty to take care not to humiliate or degrade B may have the effect of discouraging people from engaging in behaviour that is on the borderline of being humiliating or degrading – for example, a chef bawling out a trainee who has messed up a dish, or a football manager giving the 'hairdryer treatment' to a footballer who has played particularly badly. Finally, if the courts are too willing to find that an employer owes his employee a duty to take care not to make the employee do work that is too stressful or difficult for him, on the basis that it is reasonably foreseeable that doing so will result in the employee suffering a nervous breakdown, they could add considerably to the costs of an employer's enterprise (in that the employer will need to take on more workers to handle the work, or reduce the workload, of employees who cannot cope with the work they are expected to do) and could discourage employees from employing people with poor mental health records.

With that in mind, let us now look at how the courts approach the task of finding whether or not a duty of care was owed in each of the above four situations.

A. Bad news

In *Alcock* v *Chief Constable of South Yorkshire Police* (1992), Lord Ackner observed that, 'Even where the nervous shock and the subsequent psychiatric illness could have been reasonably foreseen, it has generally been accepted that damages for merely being informed of, or reading, or hearing about the accident are not recoverable.'[73] However, there he was thinking of a claimant who was trying to sue the defendant who *caused* the accident.[74] But could a claimant ever sue a defendant who had caused her to develop a psychiatric illness by telling her bad news?

For the claimant's claim to succeed, it would first of all have to be shown that her psychiatric illness was in response to what the defendant *said*, rather than the *event* that the defendant was telling the claimant about. So it would have to be shown that:

(1) the claimant's psychiatric illness was triggered by the *insensitive* way in which the defendant broke some bad news to her (for example, telling someone whose daughter has been run over and killed, 'You're never going to see your brat again'); *or*

(2) the claimant's psychiatric illness was triggered by her being *misinformed* that something bad happened, when in fact it had not (for example, telling someone 'I'm sorry to tell you that your daughter died this morning at school', when in fact the daughter is absolutely fine and it was her schoolmate who died).

With regard to situation (1), in *Mount Isa Mines Ltd* v *Pusey* (1970), a decision of the High Court of Australia, Windeyer J was hostile to the suggestion a duty of care might be owed in that kind of situation:

> If the sole cause of shock be what is told or read of some happening then I think, unless there be an intention to cause a nervous shock, no action lies against . . . the bearer of the bad tidings. There is no duty in law to break bad news gently . . .[75]

However, times have changed and in *AB* v *Tameside & Glossop Health Authority* (1997), a case where a health authority informed 114 patients by letter that they may be HIV+ because they had been treated by a HIV+ health worker, it was conceded by counsel for the defendant health authority – which was being sued by patients who complained that they had developed a psychiatric illness as a result of the way they were told this news – that the defendant health authority had owed the patients a duty to take care not to break this news to them in an insensitive way. The claim against the health authority was still dismissed by the Court of Appeal, but on the ground that the health authority had not really acted in such an insensitive manner by writing to the patients to let them know they were at risk before they had sorted out any counselling facilities that could be made available to patients who were worried about their health. So breach, rather than duty, was the focus of the decision in *AB*.

---

[73] [1992] 1 AC 310, 400.
[74] The same point could be made of similar *dicta* by Lord Wilberforce in *McLoughlin* v *O'Brian* [1983] AC 410, 423 and Lord Keith in *Alcock* [1992] 1 AC 310, 398.
[75] (1970) 125 CLR 383, 407.

Allin v *City and Hackney HA* (1996) was an example of situation (2). The claimant gave birth at the defendants' hospital. The baby was delivered, after a protracted labour, through an emergency Caesarian. The baby was in a very poor condition after it was born, having lost 80% of its blood. After the mother was taken back to the pregnancy ward of the hospital from the operating theatre, two doctors told her that her baby had died. This was not true, as the claimant discovered six hours later. The good news that her baby was alive came too late to prevent the claimant subsequently developing post-traumatic stress disorder. It was held at first instance that the claimant could sue the defendants in negligence for damages for her psychiatric illness. The issue of whether the claimant had been owed a duty of care not to misinform her of the fate of her baby was not explicitly addressed: the judge seems to have assumed that such a duty existed.[76]

Nicholas Mullany, in discussing the above cases, says that, 'Foreseeability of psychiatric injury is what matters . . .'[77] It may be doubted how often it will be the case that it will be reasonably foreseeable that someone will develop a full-blown psychiatric illness simply as a result of being treated insensitively or thinking temporarily that a tragedy has occurred. Given this, we could expect duties of care to arise rarely in 'liability for giving bad news' cases.

B. Humiliating or degrading treatment

In *Wainwright* v *Home Office* (2004), a man named Patrick O'Neill was arrested and taken into custody on a charge of murder. His mother and his brother went to visit him in prison. When they arrived at the prison they were strip-searched to check that they were not carrying any drugs that they could hand over to O'Neill. The strip-search was conducted by ordering the mother and the brother to undress; though the prison guards did touch the brother in the course of the strip-search. The mother was very distressed by the whole experience. The consequences of the strip-search for the brother were more serious: it was found that the strip-search had caused him to suffer a psychiatric illness.

The mother and the brother sued the prison authorities for damages. The mother could not sue the prison authorities in negligence because it is well established that you cannot normally sue in negligence for damages for pure distress.[78] And the brother did not need to rely on the law of negligence to sue the prison authorities: he could argue that the prison guards committed the tort of battery in touching him, and sue them for damages on the basis that his psychiatric illness was triggered by their committing that tort. The interesting question for our purposes is whether the brother *could* have sued the prison authorities in *negligence* for compensation for his psychiatric illness, by arguing that they owed him a duty of care not to subject him to the distressing and humiliating experience of being strip-searched.

---

[76] If Lord Hoffmann was right to think in *Wainwright* v *Home Office* (2004) that by 1919, 'the law was able comfortably to accommodate the facts of *Wilkinson* v *Downton* . . . in the law of nervous shock caused by negligence' ([2004] 2 AC 406, at [40]) then *Wilkinson* v *Downton* (1897) – where the defendant told the claimant (falsely) that her husband was a few miles away with both of his legs broken – is silent authority for the existence of a duty of care in an *Allin* type situation. For discussion of the 'tort in *Wilkinson* v *Downton*', see below, § 6.8.

[77] Mullany 2008, 384. This is in line with the general view taken in Mullany and Handford 1993, that psychiatric illness should be treated as a form of physical injury, with the result that foreseeability of psychiatric harm should normally give rise to a duty of care.

[78] See below, § 6.7. Instead, the mother sought to sue the prison authorities on the basis: (1) that the common law recognises a tort of invasion of privacy and the prison authorities committed that tort when they ordered her to undress; and (2) that the prison authorities committed the tort in *Wilkinson* v *Downton* by ordering her to undress. The House of Lords dismissed the mother's claim, holding that: (1) the common law does not recognise a general tort of invasion of privacy (see below, § 21.1); and (2) that the tort in *Wilkinson* v *Downton* should be subsumed within the tort of negligence and that therefore a claim cannot be brought under *Wilkinson* v *Downton* where a claim in negligence would not be available (see below, § 6.8).

Let's assume for the purposes of discussing this question that: (1) it was reasonably foreseeable that strip-searching the brother would result in his suffering a psychiatric illness; and (2) the prison authorities acted unreasonably in strip-searching the brother.

Given these two assumptions, could the brother have argued that the prison authorities owed him a duty of care not to order him to undress? The House of Lords' decision in *Wainwright* is frustratingly unclear on the issue.[79] In favour of the answer 'yes' is Lord Hoffmann's treatment in *Wainwright* of the case of *Janvier* v *Sweeney* (1919). In that case, the claimant was made physically sick as a result of the defendants' threatening her. She sued the defendants for damages and was allowed to recover on the ground that the defendants had committed a tort in relation to her in threatening her – the tort in *Wilkinson* v *Downton*.[80] Lord Hoffmann made it clear that he thought: (1) that the claimant in *Janvier* v *Sweeney* could have sued the defendants in negligence; and (2) that the claimant would have been entitled to succeed against the defendants even if she had merely suffered a psychiatric illness as a result of their threats.[81]

But if this is right, and the claimant in *Janvier* could have argued that the defendants in that case owed her a duty of care not to threaten her, then the claimant in *Wainwright* could equally well have argued that the defendants in that case owed him a duty of care not to order him to undress, and he could have sued the defendants in negligence for the psychiatric illness that he developed as a result of the defendants' breach of that duty. However, there is a *dictum* in *Wainwright* that goes against this. In his judgment, Lord Scott observed, 'I agree with the Court of Appeal [in *Wainwright*], and with your Lordships, that if there had been no touching, as there was not in [the mother's] case, no tort would have been committed.'[82] If this is right then if no one had touched the brother, the brother would not have been able to sue the prison authorities in negligence or anything else – and this is so even if the whole experience of being strip-searched caused the brother to suffer a psychiatric illness.

Our own view, for what it is worth, is that Lord Scott was wrong and that the brother in *Wainwright* could have sued the prison authorities in negligence had he chosen to do so.[83]

C. Stress at work

We are concerned here with the situation where B develops a psychiatric illness as a result of the stress created by the type of work that her employer, A, makes her do. In order to

---

[79] This is perhaps understandable given the way *Wainwright* was argued.

[80] For an account of the tort in *Wilkinson* v *Downton*, see below, § 6.8.

[81] [2004] 2 AC 406, at [40]: 'By the time of *Janvier* v *Sweeney* . . . the law was able comfortably to [deal with this kind of case] in the law of *nervous shock caused by negligence*' (emphasis added).

[82] [2004] 2 AC 406, at [60].

[83] In support of this it may be observed that Lord Scott seemed completely to forget that the brother in *Wainwright* suffered a psychiatric illness: see [2004] 2 AC 406, at [57]: 'The essence of the complaint of each claimant is that he or she was subjected to conduct by the prison officers . . . that was calculated to, and did, cause humiliation and distress' (this was of course *not* the essence of the brother's complaint); and at [58]: 'there is an important difference between the case of [the brother] and that of [the mother]. In the course of, and as part of, the strip-search . . . one of the prison officers [touched the brother] . . .' (the other important difference, unnoted by Lord Scott, is of course that the brother suffered a psychiatric illness and the mother did not). The decision of Field J in *C* v *D* [2006] EWHC 166 (QB) also supports our analysis. In that case, when the claimant was a schoolboy, on one occasion the claimant's headmaster pulled the claimant's trousers down while he was in the school infirmary and stared at the claimant's genitals; the claimant developed a psychiatric illness as a result. Field J held that the headmaster was liable in tort to compensate the claimant for his psychiatric illness. Admittedly, the tort in question was the tort in *Wilkinson* v *Downton* (see below, § 6.8), but if it is right that a claim in negligence can be made whenever a claim under *Wilkinson* v *Downton* can be made, then Field J's decision implies that the headmaster owed the claimant a duty of care not to act in the way he did.

establish that A owed her a duty of care not to make her do that work – or at least not to make her do that work without some kind of help that would make the work less stressful – the very first thing that B has to establish is that it was *reasonably foreseeable* that she would develop a psychiatric illness if she were made to do that kind of work. But even if B can do this, that may not be enough to show that A owed B a duty of care not to make her do the work that triggered her psychiatric illness.

In *Walker* v *Northumberland County Council* (1995), the claimant was employed by the defendant local authority as an area social services officer from 1970 to 1987. He was responsible for managing teams of social services fieldworkers in an area which had a high proportion of child care problems. In 1986 the claimant had a nervous breakdown as a result of the stress his job was putting on him. When he came back to work he discovered that there was a considerable backlog of work waiting for him to clear up and within six months he had another nervous breakdown which led to his stopping work permanently. When he was dismissed by the defendant local authority on grounds of permanent ill health, the claimant sued the defendant local authority in negligence so as to be compensated for the loss of income resulting from his second, irremediable, nervous breakdown. Coleman J allowed the claimant's claim, holding that when the claimant came back to work, the defendant local authority had owed the claimant a duty of care which required them to provide the claimant with some kind of assistance to perform his work. The basis for finding that the local authority had owed the claimant such a duty of care was that it had been reasonably foreseeable when the claimant came back to work that he would suffer a second breakdown if the local authority insisted that he perform his duties without giving him any kind of assistance.

It was crucial to the outcome of the case that the claimant in *Walker* had *already* suffered a nervous breakdown. It was that first breakdown that made his second breakdown reasonably foreseeable. The decision of the Court of Appeal in *Hatton* v *Sutherland* (2002) makes it clear that an employee who suffers a nervous breakdown as a result of being made to do particularly stressful work without any assistance or counselling will find it *very* difficult to show that her breakdown was reasonably foreseeable if nothing was done or nothing happened before her breakdown to alert her employers to the fact that she was having difficulty coping with the amount or type of work that she had to do. In that case, the Court of Appeal was hostile to the idea that the mere nature of an employee's work may be enough to make it reasonably foreseeable that she will develop a psychiatric illness if she is made to do that work without any kind of assistance or counselling.[84] The court went on to observe that, '*Unless he knows of some particular problem or vulnerability, an employer is entitled to assume that his employee is up to the normal pressures of the job.*'[85]

The decision of Coleman J in the *Walker* case seems to suggest that if it is reasonably foreseeable that an employee will develop a psychiatric illness if her employer makes her do some kind of work, then the employer will owe her a duty of care not to make her do that kind of work without giving her some kind of assistance. However, since *Walker* was decided, the courts have shown themselves uneasy at the idea that an employee can demand to be excused from, or given assistance to perform, some or all of her contractual

---

[84] [2002] 2 All ER 1, at [12] and at [24].

[85] [2002] 2 All ER 1, at [29] (emphasis in original). In *Barber* v *Somerset County Council* [2004] 1 WLR 1089, the House of Lords expressed broad agreement with this statement: ibid, at [5] (per Lord Scott: '[The Court of Appeal's decision in *Hatton* succeeds] in succinctly and accurately expressing the principles that ought to be applied') and, more tepidly, at [64] (per Lord Walker: '[The Court of Appeal's decision in *Hatton* provides] useful practical guidance, but it must be read as that, and not as having anything like statutory force').

duties merely because it is reasonably foreseeable that if she performs those duties without assistance, she will develop a psychiatric illness. As Lord Rodger observed in *Barber* v *Somerset County Council* (2004):

> The contract of employment will usually regulate what is to happen if an employee becomes unable, due to illness or injury, to carry out his duties. There may be provision for a defined period on full pay, followed by a further defined period on reduced pay, followed by termination of the contract. At the end of the process the employer is free to make new arrangements. While the timetable is likely to be definite, the exact legal analysis of the employee's position when off work under such provisions is by no means free from difficulty. Whatever the position, however, the introduction of a tortious duty of reasonable care on the employer to provide assistance so that the employee can return to work and draw his normal pay, but do less than his full duties for an indefinite period, does not sit easily with such contractual arrangements. Nor does it seem likely to promote efficiency within the enterprise or department.[86]

In *Koehler* v *Cerebos* (2005), the High Court of Australia went further, holding that

> An employer may not be liable for psychiatric injury to an employee brought about by the employee's performance of the duties originally stipulated in the contract of employment . . . Insistence upon performance of a contract cannot be in breach of a duty of care.[87]

If this is right, it severely narrows the scope of situations where an employee who has suffered a perfectly foreseeable psychiatric illness as a result of being made to do stressful work can sue in negligence for compensation for that illness. In effect, she would only be able to sue if she did not originally agree to do that kind (or level) of work when she started working for her employer, but her employer subsequently required her to do that kind (or level) of work.[88]

It is still unclear whether the English courts will follow these *dicta*. However, it may be suggested that, given the scope of the powers enjoyed by the courts to imply terms into contracts of employment to protect the interests of employees when it would be fair, just and reasonable to do so, this is one of those occasions when there is no point 'in searching for a liability in tort where the parties are in a contractual relationship'.[89] In other words, if the law of contract does not protect an employee who has developed a psychiatric illness as a result of the work she was made to do, it is hard to understand why the law of negligence should do any more for her. The reasons why the employee cannot bring a claim in contract for her psychiatric illness will apply with equal force to stop the employee bringing a claim in negligence for that illness.

D. Fear of future harm

Here we are concerned with cases that are like *Page* v *Smith* (1996),[90] in that the defendant in these cases has carelessly done something that foreseeably might have resulted in the claimant being physically injured, but unlike *Page* v *Smith* in that the claimant did not develop a psychiatric illness as a result of being almost injured by the defendant's carelessness but as a result of worrying that the defendant's carelessness will result in her being injured *in the future*.

---

[86] [2004] 1 WLR 1089, at [34].

[87] (2005) 222 CLR 44, at [29].

[88] (2005) 222 CLR 44, at [37]. This was the case in *Daw* v *Intel Corporation (UK) Ltd* [2007] EWCA Civ 70, where the claimant worked for the defendants as a mergers and acquisitions payroll integration analyst and suffered a nervous breakdown when poor management resulted in her being loaded with more and more responsibilities with which she could not cope.

[89] *Tai Hing Cotton Mill* v *Liu Chong Hing Bank* [1986] AC 80, at 107 (per Lord Scarman).

[90] See above, § 6.1.

In such cases, the House of Lords has made it clear that the claimant will *not* be able to rely on *Page* v *Smith* to recover damages for her psychiatric illness.[91] So, in suing the defendant, the claimant will not be able to rely on the fact that her psychiatric illness resulted from the breach of a duty of care that the defendant owed her and that was geared towards protecting her from being *physically injured*. She will have to show that the claimant owed her an independent duty of care not to act as he did that was geared towards protecting her from suffering a *psychiatric illness*. For that – it is submitted – she will have to show that it was reasonably foreseeable that the defendant's actions would cause her developing a psychiatric illness centred on her fear that she would suffer physical harm in future as a result of what the defendant did.

One 'fear of future harm' case where such a duty of care seems to have been established went as follows.[92] Between 1959 until 1985, the government ran a National Human Growth Hormone Programme (NHGHP), designed to treat children whose growth was naturally stunted with human growth hormone (hGH). About 1,800 children received hGH under this programme. From 1977 onwards, questions began to be asked about the health risks associated with receiving hGH that had been harvested from dead bodies. In 1985, the NHGHP was terminated when someone who had been treated with hGH on the programme died of Creutzfeldt–Jakob Disease (CJD). CJD is incurable. It attacks a carrier's nerve cells in the brain, resulting in dementia, body spasms, speech impairment, and eventual death. It was suspected that the hGH given to the deceased had been contaminated with a virus that causes CJD. Those suspicions were correct. To date, over 40 people who were given hGH as a part of the government programme have died of CJD.

The claimants in the 'fear of future harm' case under discussion here had all received hGH, and knew that that hGH might have been contaminated. At the time the case was decided, none of the claimants showed any symptoms that they had CJD, but – understandably – they had all developed psychiatric illnesses as a result of worrying that they might develop CJD in the future. Obviously, once it became reasonably foreseeable (in 1977) that injecting the claimants with hGH would make them ill, the government had owed the claimants a duty to take care to stop injecting them with hGH. That duty was geared towards protecting the claimants from being physically injured. And the claimants had not – so far – suffered physical injury, but a psychiatric illness instead. *Page* v *Smith* did not apply because the claimants' psychiatric illnesses were not a consequence of the shock of *almost* being injured, but a consequence of their worrying about being injured in the future as a result of the government's actions.

Despite this, the claimants who had received hGH injections after 1977 were allowed to sue for damages for their psychiatric illness. The courts accepted that after 1977, it was reasonably foreseeable that the claimants would develop a 'fear of future harm'-related psychiatric illness if the government continued to inject them with hGH, and that gave rise to a duty of care that could support the claimants' actions for their psychiatric illnesses.[93]

---

[91] See *Rothwell* v *Chemical & Insulating Co Ltd* [2008] 1 AC 281; above, § 6.1.

[92] The 'case' is actually two cases, centred on the same facts but dealing with different issues: *Group B Plaintiffs* v *Medical Research Council* [2000] Lloyd's Rep Med 161 (discussed, O'Sullivan 1999), and *Andrews* v *Secretary of State for Health*, 19 June 1998, unreported.

[93] Nolan 2004 notes (at 15) that in California, such a claim for a 'fear of future harm' psychiatric illness could only be brought if it was more likely than not that the claimant would suffer physical harm as a result of the defendant's negligence in the future: *Potter* v *Firestone Tire and Rubber Co*, 863 P 2d 795 (Cal. 1993) (claim for psychiatric illness as a result of fear of developing cancer in the future from exposure to dump filled with carcinogenic waste by the defendants). It is unlikely that the claimants in the litigation discussed here could have satisfied this requirement, given a rate of 40 deaths from 1,800 people who were treated with hGH.

6.7 PURE DISTRESS

In this section we are looking at situations where A's positive act has resulted in B's suffering, not a psychiatric illness, but pure distress. By 'pure distress', we mean distress (which can take the form of grief, fear, upset, anger, embarrassment, humiliation or sorrow – and that is not meant to be an exhaustive list) that is not consequent on B's being injured, or B's property being damaged. In such a case, can B ever establish that A owed her a duty to take care not to act as he did?

In *Hinz* v *Berry* (1970), Lord Denning MR held that:

> in English law, no damages are awarded for grief or sorrow caused by a person's death. No damages are to be given for the worry about the children, or for the financial strain or stress, or the difficulties of adjusting to a new life.[94]

In *Alcock* v *Chief Constable of South Yorkshire* (1992), Lord Ackner was similarly negative about the possibility of suing in negligence for pure distress: 'Mere mental suffering, though reasonably foreseeable, if unaccompanied by physical injury, is not a basis for a claim for damages.'[95]

These *dicta* were borne out by the decision of the House of Lords in *Hicks* v *Chief Constable of South Yorkshire* (1992), which was another case that arose out of the Hillsborough tragedy. That case concerned two sisters – Sarah and Victoria Hicks – who were crushed to death at the Leppings Lane end of the ground. The defendant police force had, of course, owed the Hickses a duty to take care not to cause the spectator pens where they were standing to become overcrowded as it was reasonably foreseeable that spectators like the Hickses would be physically injured if those pens did become overcrowded. However, the *Hicks* case was decided on the basis that the defendants' breach of this duty of care did not ever cause the Hickses to suffer physical injury – that what physical injuries they did suffer as a result of being crushed to death were suffered at the same moment as their death. The only loss that the Hickses suffered before they died – it was supposed – was the terror they went through as they were slowly crushed to death. The House of Lords held that damages for this form of pure distress were not recoverable in negligence:

> It is perfectly clear law that fear by itself, of whatever degree, is a normal human emotion for which no damages can be awarded. Those trapped in the crush at Hillsborough who were fortunate enough to escape without injury have no claim in respect of the distress they suffered in what must have been a truly terrifying experience. It follows that fear of impending death felt by the victim of a fatal injury before that injury is inflicted cannot by itself give rise to a cause of action which survives for the benefit of the victim's estate.[96]

Although the distress felt by the Hickses as they were crushed to death resulted from the defendants' breach of a duty of care that they owed the Hickses, that duty of care was geared towards protecting the Hickses from suffering physical injury, not pure distress. And there was – evidently – nothing in the facts of the *Hicks* case that led the House of Lords to think that the defendant police force owed the Hickses a duty to take care not to put them through such a 'truly terrifying experience'.

In *Wainwright* v *Home Office* (2004) – which was a case, as we have seen, where the defendants caused one of the claimants to suffer pure distress by making her strip before allowing her

---

[94] [1970] 2 QB 40, 42.
[95] [1992] 1 AC 310, 401.
[96] [1992] 2 All ER 65, 69.

to see her son in prison – Lord Hoffmann expressed himself open to the possibility of 'abandoning the rule that damages for mere distress are not recoverable' but made it clear that if such a step in the law were to be taken, it could not be taken via the law of negligence, where the mere careless infliction of harm can give rise to liability: 'The defendant must have acted in a way which he knew to be unjustifiable and either intended to cause harm or at least acted without caring whether he caused harm or not.'[97] And Lord Hoffmann went on to express doubts whether even that might justify a claim in tort for pure distress:

> In institutions and workplaces all over the country, people constantly do and say things with the intention of causing distress and humiliation to others. This shows lack of consideration and appalling manners but I am not sure that the right way to deal with it is always by litigation.[98]

Hicks and *Wainwright* were cases where there was no 'special relationship' between the claimants and the defendants.[99] Could such a 'special relationship' give rise to a duty of care geared towards protecting a claimant from suffering mere distress?

Vernon v Bosley (No 1) (1997) seems to indicate a negative answer. In that case, the defendant was a nanny who was charged with the job of looking after the claimant's two children. One day, the defendant was driving a car with the children in it. She carelessly lost control of the car, and it crashed down a 30 foot bank into a river that flowed alongside the road. The defendant managed to escape from the car, but the children were trapped. The claimant – who was working at a nearby factory – was called to the scene of the accident by the police. There, he and his wife watched the attempts to rescue their children. The attempts were unsuccessful, and the children died. The claimant suffered a recognised psychiatric illness – pathological grief disorder – in the aftermath of his children's deaths. The majority of the Court of Appeal accepted that the claimant's illness was a consequence of his being on the scene of the accident (as opposed to the loss of his children) and as a result found, in line with the authorities we have already discussed, that the defendant owed the claimant a duty of care on which he could base a claim for his psychiatric illness.

There was, in fact, no need to invoke authorities like *McLoughlin v O'Brian* (1983) and *Alcock v Chief Constable of South Yorkshire* (1992) to establish that the defendant owed the claimant a duty of care here. As we will see,[100] the fact that the defendant 'assumed a responsibility' to the claimant to look after his children meant that she owed the claimant a duty to look after those children with a reasonable degree of care and skill. What, then, would have happened had the claimant not suffered a recognised pathological grief disorder as a result of the defendant's breach of this duty of care, but merely grief? Would he have been entitled to sue for damages for that grief, given that there was in this case a 'special relationship' between the parties? The Court of Appeal was clear that mere grief would not have been actionable in *Vernon v Bosley*: 'Damages for mental injury do not include compensation for feelings of grief and bereavement which are not themselves symptomatic of illness.'[101]

---

[97] [2004] 2 AC 406, at [45].

[98] [2004] 2 AC 406, at [46].

[99] See also *Al-Kandari v Brown* [1988] 1 QB 665, where it was held (at 675) that the trial judge had been right to hold that 'he was not entitled to award damages for grief or sorrow' in a case where the defendant firm of solicitors – who were not in any kind of 'special relationship' with the claimant – carelessly allowed the claimant's husband to get hold of his passport from the defendants, with the result that he immediately kidnapped the claimant's children and left the country. But the claimant could sue for the physical injury and psychiatric illness she had suffered as a result of the defendants' breach of the duty of care that they owed the claimant.

[100] See below, § 7.2.

[101] [1997] 1 All ER 507, 604.

As against this must be set *Hamilton Jones v David & Snape (a firm)* (2004), where the defendant firm of solicitors were employed by the claimant to represent her in custody proceedings against the husband. The claimant told the defendants she was worried her husband – a Tunisian national – would attempt to take her children to Tunisia with him. To stop this happening, in February 1994 the defendants informed the UK Passport Agency that the claimant's husband was prohibited from removing the children from the claimant's care, and the Passport Agency undertook that for the next 12 months they would do their best to ensure that the claimant's husband was not issued with a British passport, and told the defendants to tell them at the end of the 12 months if they wanted the Passport Agency to renew this undertaking for the next 12 months. This the defendants failed to do. As a result, the claimant's husband – who had by now become a British citizen – had no trouble obtaining a British passport in June 1996. Shortly after that, he added the claimant's children's names to the passport. And shortly after *that*, he took the children to Tunisia. The claimant sued the defendants for damages for the distress she felt at losing her children. Neuberger J held that the claimant could sue the defendants for such damages either by bringing a claim against the defendants for breach of contract or by suing them in negligence. (The relevant duty of care that was breached in this case was a duty to represent the claimant with reasonable skill and care, which duty was based on the contractual 'assumption of responsibility' that the defendants made to the claimant when they took on her case.)

Andrew Burrows has sought to sum up the effect of the *Hamilton Jones* decision by saying that:

> . . . mental distress damages are recoverable in [negligence] provided they would be recoverable in that situation for breach of contract. In other words, mental distress damages will be recoverable provided one can show that an important object of the services was to provide mental satisfaction or freedom from distress . . .[102]

(In contract law, the 'object of the contract' is an important limit on the availability of damages for pure distress resulting from a breach of contract.)[103] But where does that leave *Vernon v Bosley*? There must have been a contract in that case, and an important object of that contract would have been to relieve the claimant from having to worry about his children and to give him the mental satisfaction of knowing they were safe. Perhaps grief is special and is simply non-actionable under any circumstances.

Two reasons may be given why the courts might regard grief as being something that is always non-actionable. First, grief for the loss of a loved one is something that the claimant may have had to go through anyway at some stage in his life, and so should not be actionable even if a defendant has accelerated the moment at which the claimant has to go through that experience.

Secondly, a couple of judges have expressed concern at the effect that litigation may have on the depth and duration of a claimant's psychiatric illness:

> Both at the bar and on the bench I have listened to doctors and particularly psychiatrists saying in cases of psychiatric illness that no further recovery is to be expected until the litigation is finished. I have often heard medical opinion suggest that litigation prolongs symptoms of psychiatric illness, making it more deep-seated and difficult to treat. May we not by giving the remedy aggravate the illness? Surely health is better than money.[104]

---

[102] Burrows 2004, 337–8.
[103] *Farley* v *Skinner* [2002] 2 AC 732.
[104] *McLoughlin* v *O'Brian* [1981] 1 QB 599, 624 (per Griffiths LJ), quoted in Nolan 2004, 20.

Where there is generally no prospect of recovery, such as in the case of injuries sustained in sport, psychiatric harm appears not to obtrude often. On the other hand, in the case of industrial accidents, where there is often a prospect of recovery of compensation, psychiatric harm is repeatedly encountered and often endures until the process of claiming compensation comes to an end . . . The litigation is sometimes an unconscious disincentive to rehabilitation.[105]

It may be that the courts are wary of the effect that the prospect of litigation might have on the grieving process, turning something that can be healing into something pathological.

6.8 *WILKINSON V DOWNTON*

Before we go on to see when a defendant will owe a claimant a duty of care geared towards protecting the claimant's property from being damaged, we should first of all mention the 'tort in *Wilkinson* v *Downton*', which has been alluded to a number of times above.

In *Wilkinson* v *Downton* (1897), the defendant played a joke on the claimant by telling her that her husband had met with a serious accident and that both his legs had been broken. In fact, as the defendant well knew, this was not true. The claimant was so upset to receive this news that she was physically sick. The claimant subsequently sued the defendant for compensation. At the time the case was decided, there existed a rule that you could not sue a defendant in negligence for compensation for some physical injury that you had suffered if the defendant had caused you to suffer that physical injury by making you distressed or upset.[106] Wright J, who decided *Wilkinson* v *Downton*, got round this rule by holding that the claimant was not confined to suing the defendant in negligence but could sue the defendant on the ground that he had committed a quite different tort in relation to her. This tort was subsequently dubbed 'the tort in *Wilkinson* v *Downton*'.

Subsequent case law[107] has made it clear that A will have committed the tort in *Wilkinson* v *Downton* in relation to B if: (1) B has suffered a physical injury or a psychiatric illness as a result of A's treating her in an unjustifiable way, and (2) A's conduct was intended to cause B to suffer such harm, or A knew that his conduct might cause B to suffer such harm, or it was highly likely that A's conduct would cause B to suffer such harm.

However, if (1) and (2) are made out, then there is no reason why B should not be able to sue A in *negligence*, claiming that A owed her a duty of care not to act in the way he did, and that A's breach of that duty of care caused her to suffer a physical injury or a psychiatric illness. So the tort in *Wilkinson* v *Downton* is completely redundant – no claimant will have to rely on it to sue a defendant in tort successfully.[108] If the claimant can bring a claim under the tort in *Wilkinson* v *Downton*, then he or she can also bring a claim in negligence. As a result, the Court of Appeal has urged that claims that could formerly have been brought under *Wilkinson* v *Downton* should now be brought in negligence: 'It seems preferable for the law to develop along conventional modern lines rather than through recourse to this obscure tort, whose jurisprudential basis remains unclear.'[109] However, as Lord Hoffmann observed

---

[105] *Frost* v *Chief Constable of South Yorkshire* [1999] 2 AC 455, 494 (per Lord Steyn).

[106] This rule was subsequently abolished in *Dulieu* v *White & Sons* [1901] 2 KB 669.

[107] *Wong* v *Parkside Health NHS Trust* [2003] 3 All ER 932, at [12]; *Wainwright* v *Home Office* [2004] 2 AC 406, at [41] and [44]; *C* v *D* [2006] EWHC 166, at [94] and [99].

[108] A former Professor of Law at Oxford University used to say that if A poisoned B's drink and B was made sick as a result of drinking the poison, the only tort B could sue A under was the tort in *Wilkinson* v *Downton*. But there seems no reason why B could not sue A in negligence here: A owed B a duty to take care not to poison her drink and he clearly breached that duty by putting poison in her drink. Negligence liability covers intentional acts, as well as careless acts: see above, § 4.2.

[109] *A* v *Hoare* [2006] 1 WLR 2320, at [136].

in *Wainwright* v *Home Office*, 'Commentators and counsel have . . . been unwilling to allow *Wilkinson* v *Downton* to disappear beneath the surface of the law of negligence'[110] and so it is as well for students to know about the existence of this tort, and to mention that it has been committed in answering any problem question where (1) and (2), above, are established.

The tort in *Wilkinson* v *Downton* would still have some role to play if a claim for damages for pure distress could be made under it: as we have seen, such claims cannot easily be made in negligence.[111] However, the Court of Appeal[112] and the House of Lords[113] have firmly rejected the idea that the claimant in *Wilkinson* v *Downton* could still have sued the defendant had she merely been distressed, and not been made physically sick, by the defendant's practical joke.

In *Wainwright* v *Home Office*, Lord Hoffmann observed that because claims under the tort in *Wilkinson* v *Downton* can be made merely on the basis that it was *highly likely* that B would suffer harm as a result of A's actions, it would not be desirable to allow claimants to make claims for pure distress under the tort in *Wilkinson* v *Downton*. It cannot be a tort merely to do something that is *highly likely* to make someone else suffer distress.[114] Lord Hoffmann suggested that *at a minimum* it would have to be shown that: 'The defendant must actually have acted in a way that he knew [was] unjustifiable and [he] either intended to cause [distress] or at least acted without caring whether he caused [distress] or not.'[115] But even if this could be shown, he wished to reserve his position on whether in such a case a defendant would be liable for causing a claimant to suffer pure distress.[116]

6.9 HARM TO PROPERTY

We are concerned here with the situation where a defendant has performed a positive act that has resulted in an item of property P being harmed. If a claimant wants to show that the defendant owed her a duty of care not to act as he did, the claimant will have to show that: (1) she had a sufficient interest in P at the time it was harmed as a result of the defendant's act; and (2) it was reasonably foreseeable that the defendant's act would result in property like P being harmed. If (1) and (2) are made out, the courts will normally find that the defendant owed the claimant a duty of care, geared towards protecting P from being harmed. All this raises a number of issues.

A. Property

The above formula for establishing that a defendant owed a claimant a duty of care will only apply in the case where the defendant's positive act has resulted in a *tangible* item of property – an item of property you can touch, such as a computer or a book or a house or a piece of land – being harmed.

Intangible items of property – items of property that you cannot touch, such as a patent (giving the holder a monopoly over a particular idea) or an easement (a right over someone

---

[110] [2004] 2 AC 406, at [41].

[111] See above, § 6.7.

[112] *Wong* v *Parkside Health NHS Trust* [2003] 3 All ER 932.

[113] *Wainwright* v *Home Office* [2004] 2 AC 406.

[114] [2004] 2 AC 406, at [44]–[45].

[115] [2004] 2 AC 406, at [45].

[116] [2004] 2 AC 406, at [46]. The tort of intentional infliction of harm by unlawful means (dealt with below, chapter 24) might have proved useful to claimants seeking some redress against a defendant who intentionally caused them to suffer distress. However, the courts seem to have ruled out the possibility that damages for pure distress might be recoverable under this tort: see below, § 24.10.

else's land) or a charge (a right to the proceeds of the sale of an item of property) – are not protected by the above formula. Mere foreseeability that A's acting in a particular way will destroy, or get in the way of B's exploiting, an intangible item of property that B has an interest in will not give rise to a duty of care on A's part not to act in that way.[117]

B. Sufficient interest

In a case where A has done something positive that has resulted in an item of property P being harmed, and it was reasonably foreseeable that A's actions would have that kind of effect, then A will normally have had a duty to take care not to act as he did. But that duty is only owed to – in other words, imposed for the benefit of[118] – people who had a *sufficient interest* in P *at the time it was harmed*. But what counts as a sufficient interest?

Until the recent decision of the Court of Appeal in *Shell UK Ltd* v *Total UK Ltd* (2010), it had been thought – on very high authority[119] – that A's duty would only have been owed to those who had a *legal* interest in P, or were in *possession* of P, at the time it was harmed. However, the Court of Appeal ruled in *Shell* that:

(1) A's duty will *also* have been owed to anyone for whom P was held on trust at the time it was harmed;

(2) *but* anyone for whom P was held on trust at the time it was harmed will *not* be able to sue in their own right for the losses they have suffered as a result of P being harmed *unless* they make the legal owner of P at the time it was harmed a party to their claim against A.

Shell was concerned with the aftermath of the explosion at the Buncefield oil depot on 11 December 2005. The oil depot – which was owned by Total UK – was capable of carrying 60m gallons of fuel. A gauge on a storage tank that was being filled with unleaded fuel stopped working, which meant that no one could tell the tank was full. As a result fuel kept on being pumped into the tank, and soon overflowed the tank. The overflowing fuel gave rise to a vapour cloud which ignited, for reasons never identified. The resulting explosion was the largest in peacetime Europe. It damaged numerous pipelines leading away from Buncefield. These pipelines were owned by a shell company, WLPS Ltd, and were held on trust for four oil companies, including Shell, that used the pipelines to supply oil to their customers.[120] Shell sued Total in negligence, claiming that Total had owed Shell a duty to

---

[117] *Esser* v *Brown* (2004) 242 DLR (4th) 112 (a notary who destroyed the claimant's interest in a ranch she owned with her husband when he executed a sale of the ranch to a third party which the claimant had not agreed to (her husband had forged her signature on the contract of sale) had not owed the claimant a duty of care not to destroy her interest in the ranch). Though see the decision in *Ministry of Housing* v *Sharp* (1970) 2 QB 223 (discussed below, § 6.13), where it was held that the defendant – whose carelessness in informing the purchaser of land that there were no charges over the land meant that the claimant lost his charge over the land when it was purchased – had owed the claimant a duty of care.

[118] See above, § 1.2.

[119] See *Leigh & Sillavan Ltd* v *Aliakmon Shipping Ltd, The Aliakmon* [1986] AC 785 (K-M shipped steel coils to be delivered to L&S, price to be paid in full on delivery (whatever condition the coils were in) and L&S only to acquire title to the goods once they had paid for them; the coils were damaged in transit as a result of D's carelessness; L&S still had to pay in full for the coils and sought to recover their loss from D; held, D had not owed a duty of care to L&S not to damage the coils as L&S was not the legal owner of the coils at the time they were damaged; nor was it in possession of the coils at that time).

[120] The pipelines were owned by a shell company because of the rule of law mentioned above, in § 1.12, that no more than four people can own land legally as joint tenants (Law of Property Act 1925, s 34). As there were originally more than four oil companies that wanted to have an interest in the pipelines leading away from Buncefield, it was thought best to vest legal ownership in a shell company and have that company hold the pipelines on trust for the oil companies that would be using those pipelines.

take care not to damage the pipelines owned by WLPS Ltd, and seeking to recover the loss of profits that Shell had suffered when the pipelines were damaged, as a result of being unable to supply their customers with oil, and having to supply what oil they could through more expensive means of transport.

Shell's claim was dismissed at first instance, but was allowed in the Court of Appeal. The Court of Appeal could see no problem in allowing Shell's claim, holding that 'it is legalistic to deny Shell a right to recovery . . . It is, after all, Shell who is (along with BP, Total and Chevron) the "real" owner, the "legal" owner being little more than a bare trustee of the pipeline.'[121] The 'high authority' adverted to above (the House of Lords' decision in *The Aliakmon* (1986)) was distinguished as merely requiring a claimant who wanted to sue a defendant in negligence for damaging property that was held on trust for the claimant to join the legal owner of the property in the claim. Once this is done, the claimant's action will be able to proceed and she will be able to recover damages for the losses that *she* has suffered as a result of the property being damaged.[122]

The decision of the Court of Appeal has come in for some fierce academic criticism.[123] Four criticisms can be made of the decision.

(1) Claims in negligence are claims under the common law, and it is not clear why the common law *should* get involved with protecting the beneficiary under a trust from losses that he or she has suffered as a result of the trust property being damaged. It is also not clear whether the common law *can* get involved with protecting the beneficiary without unacceptably disrupting and confusing the existing equitable rules on when a beneficiary can sue for losses suffered as a result of a third party interfering with trust property.[124]

(2) There is an argument to be made that where A holds property on trust for B, B does not actually have an interest in the trust property. All B has are rights *in* or *against* the rights A holds over the trust property.[125] If this is correct, then the Court of Appeal was wrong to think in *Shell* that Shell was (along with the other oil companies who used the pipelines at Buncefield) the 'real' owner of the pipelines that were damaged in this case. The *only* owner was WLPS Ltd; and all Shell had were rights against WLPS. If this is right, then Shell's claim was, in effect, one for pure economic loss, and one that could not have been allowed without overturning the restrictive rules on when a duty of care will be owed in a pure economic loss case.[126]

(3) If Total *had* owed Shell a duty of care in this case, it is not clear why Shell had to join WLPS to its claim against Total in order for *Shell* to sue Total in negligence for the losses suffered by *Shell* as a result of Total's breach of a duty of care owed to *Shell*. The requirement that Shell join WLPS to its claim was intended to get round the inconvenient authority of *The Aliakmon* (1986). But the Court of Appeal might have done better if, instead of

---

[121] [2011] QB 86, at [132].

[122] [2011] QB 86, at [129]–[130]. Strangely, a point of law (as to whether a beneficiary for whom property is held on trust can sue for his own loss if he joins the legal owner in *his* claim) that was 'not resolve[d]' (by the decision in *The Aliakmon*) in para [131] becomes 'clear' by para [137] ('it is clear that the beneficial owner can sue if he joins the legal owner').

[123] See Low 2010; Turner 2010.

[124] A consideration which led the Court of Appeal in *MCC Proceeds Inc v Lehman Bros International (Europe)* [1998] 4 All ER 675 (discussed below, § 17.2(D)(5)) to refuse to allow B to sue in conversion where trust property which is held on trust for B by A is interfered with by C. (*MCC Proceeds* was cited to the Court of Appeal in argument in *Shell* but not referred to in its judgment.)

[125] See Low 2010, 507, and references cited therein.

[126] See below, § 6.10.

distinguishing *The Aliakmon* on utterly specious grounds, they had complied with the rules of precedent and dismissed Shell's claim as inconsistent with *The Aliakmon*.

(4) The Court of Appeal confessed itself in *Shell* as having been influenced by 'the impulse to do practical justice'.[127] One can see why 'justice' might have seemed to dictate that Shell be afforded a remedy here. It was only s 34 of the Law of Property Act 1925[128] that led Shell and the other oil companies that used the pipelines at Buncefield to vest legal title to the pipelines in WLPS. Had s 34 not existed, Shell and the other companies might have made themselves joint legal owners of the pipelines, and there would then have been no obstacle in the way of Shell suing for the economic losses it suffered as a result of those pipelines being damaged and destroyed. However, one virtue of s 34 is that it limits the number of legal owners to a piece of land to *four*. By holding in *Shell* that a defendant who has damaged trust property will have owed a duty of care not only to the legal owner of that property, but also anyone for whom the property was held on trust, the Court of Appeal opens the defendant to the possibility of claims being made against him by a potentially unlimited number of claimants, as there is no limit on how many people for whom property can be held on trust. Suppose, for example, that a *hundred* different oil companies had used the pipelines at Buncefield, and those pipelines were held on trust for all of them. It is not clear whether it would be just to hold a defendant liable to a hundred different claimants, each suing for losses running into hundreds of thousands or millions of pounds, when the defendant was guilty of a trivial fault that resulted in the pipelines blowing up.

The Supreme Court allowed Total's application for leave to appeal the Court of Appeal's decision in *Shell*.[129] However, Total subsequently settled with Shell, and the Supreme Court was deprived of the chance to reverse the Court of Appeal's decision in *Shell* and restore order to this area of law. Until another such case reaches the Supreme Court, the position is that in the case we are considering – where it was reasonably foreseeable that property P would be harmed as a result of A's doing x – A will have owed a duty to take care not to do x *not just* to whoever legally owned P or possessed P at the time it was harmed, *but also* to whomever P was held on trust for at the time it was harmed. (Though a claimant for whom P was held on trust at the time it was harmed will only be able to sue A in negligence if the claimant joins the legal owner of P to the claim.)

C. Harm

What counts as 'harming' property for the purposes of the duty formula discussed here?

Obviously, destroying or damaging an item of property P will amount to harming it.[130] Property will count as having been damaged if it undergoes 'a physical change which renders [it] less useful or less valuable.'[131] So, in *Hunter v Canary Wharf* (1997), the Court of Appeal held that the deposit of excessive dust on a carpet could amount, of and in itself, to damage to the carpet. And in *Blue Circle Industries v Ministry of Defence* (1999), the Court of Appeal was willing to hold that the intermingling of plutonium with soil so that it could not be removed amounted to a form of property damage. In *Pride & Partners v*

---

[127] [2011] QB 86, at [143], quoting Lord Goff in *White v Jones* [1995] 2 AC 207, 259–60.
[128] See above, chapter 1, fn 39.
[129] [2011] QB 86, 105.
[130] See Weston 1999 for a useful discussion as to when someone who has lost computer data can argue that they have suffered a form of damage to property for the purposes of the duty formula discussed here.
[131] *Hunter v Canary Wharf* [1997] AC 655, 676 (per Pill LJ).

Institute of Animal Health (2009), Tugendhat J held that farmers whose pigs became overweight and therefore less valuable because of movement restrictions on animals during an outbreak of foot and mouth disease 'have a real prospect of succeeding in the contention that that is physical damage'.[132]

What about cases of interferences with property that fall short of damaging or destroying it? Consider the **Lost Ring Problem**:

> *Bride* has just been married in a picturesque country house, and is leaning against a wishing well in the house grounds, talking to *Friend*. *Friend* asks to see *Bride*'s wedding ring and *Bride* hands it over. While *Friend* is holding the ring up to the light, *Bridesmaid* rushes excitedly up to *Friend* to get a look at the ring, and is unable to stop herself from crashing into *Friend*, with the result that *Friend* drops the ring and it falls into the well.

Can we say that the ring has been harmed here – even though its fall to the bottom of the well has almost certainly not destroyed or damaged it? We think if the ring is effectively irretrievable then *Bride* could claim that the ring has been harmed,[133] and argue on that basis that *Bridesmaid* owed her a duty to take care not to crash into *Friend* (it being reasonably foreseeable that *Bridesmaid*'s doing this would result in the ring dropping to the bottom of the well). The **Useless T-Shirts Problem** is different:

> *Chancer* manufactures 10,000 T-shirts which he is planning to sell to people attending the opening of the London Olympics. The T-shirts carry the official Olympics logo and say '27 July 2012 – I Was There'. On the day of the opening ceremony, a major accident caused by *Driver*'s carelessness results in *Chancer* being unable to transport the T-shirts to the stall that he has set up outside the Olympic Stadium in Stratford. *Chancer* subsequently tries to sell the T-shirts over the Internet, but no one is interested in buying them.

Here the T-shirts are as useless to *Chancer* as the ring is in Lost Ring. But we do not think *Chancer* can argue that the T-shirts have been harmed as a result of *Driver*'s carelessness. He still has the T-shirts and they are physically unaffected by what *Driver* did.

D. Time of harm

In order to argue that a defendant owed her a duty of care under the duty formula discussed here, a claimant has to show that she had a sufficient interest in an item of property that the defendant harmed *at the time it was harmed*. So it can be very important in certain cases to identify the time at which a given item of property was harmed. For example, consider the **Cracked Vase Problem**:

> *Rich* wants to sell a vase of hers at auction. The day before the auction, all the auction items are on display at the auction house for potential buyers to look at. During the viewing hours, *Clumsy* picks up the vase to look at it, and puts it back down a bit too heavily, with the result that the vase develops an invisible crack at its base. The next day, *Owner* buys the vase and takes it home. Within a week, the crack at the base of the vase spreads and becomes visible and the vase shatters.

---

[132] [2009] EWHC 685 (QB), at [75].

[133] In *The Nicholas H* [1996] AC 211, cargo belonging to the claimant was lost at sea when the ship that was carrying it sank. No one would disagree that in this case the cargo was harmed for the purposes of duty formula under discussion here.

Can *Owner* argue that *Clumsy* owed her a duty of care under the duty formula under discussion here? The answer is no – *Owner* did not have a legal interest in, or possession of, the vase at the time *Clumsy* harmed it. Admittedly, the vase did shatter when it belonged to *Owner*. But that shattering was merely an extension of the initial harm that it suffered in the auction house when *Clumsy* put it back down. And at that time, *Owner* did not have a sufficient interest in the property.

The vase in the above example was initially sound and was subsequently made unsound by *Clumsy*'s rough handling of it. What about a case where an item of property was *always* unsound because it was manufactured in a way that meant that it was doomed to blow up or shatter or fall apart at some point in the future? The duty formula under discussion here will have no application to such a case. The reason is that the property was never harmed by the manufacturer.

Suppose, for example, that *Blower* manufactures window glass and carelessly introduces a contaminant into the molten glass from which he makes his windows. As a result a window pane that is subsequently installed in *Owner*'s house suffers from a flaw that causes it to shatter a couple of years later. *Owner* may be able to point to the shattered window and say 'My property has been damaged by *Blower*'s carelessness'. But appearances deceive: *Blower* has not really harmed *Owner*'s window in this case. The window came into the world in a flawed state, and the shattering is merely an outward manifestation of the internal weakness from which that window always suffered. So *Blower* has not done anything here to make the window worse than it once was.

If *Owner* wants to sue *Blower* in negligence here, it cannot be for the damage suffered by the window, because *Blower* did not really damage the window. Instead, *Owner* will have to sue *Blower* for the *cost of replacing the window* or the *money B wasted on purchasing the window*. This is a form of pure economic loss. The issue of when a claimant can establish that a defendant owed her a duty of care in a pure economic loss case will be discussed below. However, we can briefly anticipate the discussion below by saying here that the fact that it is foreseeable that A's actions will result in B suffering a form of pure economic loss will not be enough to establish that A owed B a duty of care. Usually, it will have to be shown that there existed some kind of special relationship between A and B, based on A's 'assuming a responsibility' to B. In the case we are discussing here, no such special relationship will exist between *Blower* and *Owner*. The result is that *Owner* will have no remedy in negligence against *Blower* for the fact that his window has shattered.

E. Differentiating property

Suppose that *Maker* manufactures beer bottles that suffer from an internal flaw which means that they are liable to shatter if kept in cold conditions. *Owner* buys one of these beer bottles and puts it in his fridge. Two days later, the bottle shatters, spilling beer all over the inside of the fridge and a joint of meat that *Owner* was keeping in the fridge.

If *Owner* wants to sue *Maker* in negligence for the damage to the fridge or the joint of meat, then she should have no problem using the duty formula discussed here to establish that *Maker* owed her a duty of care geared towards protecting those items of property from being harmed. *Maker* has performed a positive act – putting flawed beer bottles into circulation – that has resulted in *Owner*'s fridge and joint of meat being harmed, and it was reasonably foreseeable that *Maker*'s putting flawed beer bottles into circulation would have that kind of effect. So if *Owner* wants to sue *Maker* in negligence for the damage to the fridge or the joint of meat, she will have no problem arguing that *Maker* owed her a duty to take care not to put flawed beer bottles into circulation. The only issue will be whether *Maker* breached that duty: whether he was at fault for the flaw from which the beer bottles suffered.

But what if *Owner* isn't content just to sue for the damage to the fridge or the joint of meat, but wants to sue as well for the *loss of the beer* that spilled all over the fridge when the beer bottle shattered? Can *Owner* establish that *Maker* owed her a duty of care geared towards protecting her from suffering *that* kind of harm? It depends on how we look at the bottle of beer that *Owner* stored in her fridge. Was that *one* item of property – a bottle-containing-beer. Or was it *two* items of property – a bottle, and a quantity of beer?

If it was just one item of property, then *Owner* cannot invoke the duty formula under discussion here to recover damages for the loss of the beer. *Maker*'s positive act in putting flawed beer bottles into circulation harmed *Owner*'s fridge and joint of meat. But it did not harm the other item of property in *Owner*'s fridge – the bottle-containing-beer. That is because that item of property was already damaged, even before *Maker* put it into circulation. Even if we suppose that the bottle-containing-beer was at some point initially sound, but *Maker* did a positive act that resulted in that item of property becoming flawed before it left *Maker*'s factory (for example, by storing the bottle improperly after it rolled off *Maker*'s production line), that postive act harmed *Owner*'s bottle-containing-beer long before it became *Owner*'s property. So *Owner* can use the duty formula under discussion here to establish that *Maker* owed her a duty of care geared towards protecting her fridge or her joint of meat from being harmed; but not in order to establish that *Maker* owed her a duty of care geared towards ensuring that *Owner*'s bottle-containing-beer did not shatter when it was stored in *Owner*'s fridge.

But what if we can say that when *Owner* put the bottle of beer in her fridge, she was putting *two* items of property into the fridge – a bottle, and a quantity of beer? In such a case, *Owner could* use the duty formula under discussion here to launch a negligence claim against *Maker* for the loss of the beer. *Owner* could argue that *Maker*'s positive act of storing beer in a defective bottle has resulted in harm to the beer, and that that beer was harmed when it belonged to *Owner*, in that the beer was perfectly sound up until the moment when the bottle in which it was stored shattered.

So – which is it to be? One item of property, or two?[134] In *Aswan Engineering* v *Lupdine* (1987), Lloyd LJ (with whom Fox LJ agreed) took the 'provisional view'[135] that in this case, the answer is that *Owner* had two items of property – a bottle, and a quantity of beer. So *Owner* would be able to rely on the duty formula under discussion here to sue *Maker* not only for the damage to her fridge and her joint of meat, but also the loss of the beer.[136] It

---

[134] Tettenborn 2000b suggests that if a component part of a chattel can be removed without damaging the other parts of the chattel, the component and the rest-of-the-chattel should be regarded as being two separate items of property. But it is not clear how this test would apply in this case. In theory, the beer could be separated from the bottle without damaging the beer (by pouring it into another container, for example). On the other hand, the beer will spill and be spoiled if it is suddenly deprived of its bottle.

[135] [1987] 1 WLR 1, 21.

[136] In the *Aswan* case itself, the claimants ordered some waterproofing compound from L. L, in turn, ordered some pails from the defendants to store the compound in when shipping it to the claimants. Having obtained the pails from the defendants, L filled them with the compound and L shipped them to the claimants in Kuwait, where they were left in the blazing sun. Eventually the heat caused the plastic pails to collapse and the compound was lost. The claimants sued the defendants in negligence, claiming that the defendants had owed them a duty not to supply L with the pails that they did because it was reasonably foreseeable that doing so would result in the compound sold by L to the claimants being lost. Lloyd and Fox LJJ dismissed the claim on the ground that as the defendants had no idea the pails would be shipped to Kuwait, it was not reasonably foreseeable that the compound sold by L to the claimants would be lost if it was shipped to the claimants in the pails that the defendants supplied to L. Nicholls LJ dismissed the claim on the ground that the manufacturer of a container will not owe a duty of care in manufacturing the container to anyone who loses his or her property as a result of the container being insufficiently sturdy.

may seem quite a trivial question whether or not *Owner* can sue *Maker* for the loss of the beer in this case. But there are other cases that raise the same issue where the stakes will be a lot higher.

For example, suppose that *Maker* manufactures a car and carelessly installs a tyre on the car which is dangerously defective. A year later, *Owner* buys the car from a car dealer. Some time after that, *Owner* is driving the car when the tyre blows out and the car crashes. *Owner* is unharmed, but the car is a write-off. Can *Owner* sue *Maker* in negligence[137] for the loss of her car? Whether *Owner* can use the duty formula under discussion here to establish that *Maker* owed her a duty of care, that was geared towards protecting her car from being damaged, depends on whether we think that *Owner* obtained *one* item of property when she bought the car manufactured by *Maker* (a car), or *more than one* item of property (a car and a set of tyres). If only *one* item of property, then *Maker* did not do anything to harm *Owner*'s car. That car was brought into the world in a flawed state, and the twisted remains of the car lying at the side of the road are merely an extension of that initial flaw. If *more than one* item of property, then we can say that *Maker* did a positive act (installing a defective tyre on the car that was eventually bought by *Owner*) that harmed *Owner*'s car (which was until that moment, perfectly sound) when the tyre on *Owner*'s car blew out. Lloyd LJ's provisional view in *Aswan* was that the second analysis is preferable. If this is right, then *Owner* will be able to argue in this case that *Maker* owed her a duty to take care not to put a defective tyre on the car that she ended up buying, because: (1) his positive act of putting that tyre on the car harmed an item of property (the car) that belonged to her at the time it was harmed (that is, it was perfectly sound up until the tyre blowing out); and (2) it was reasonably foreseeable that putting a defective tyre on the car would result in its being harmed at some point in the future.

Again, suppose that *Builder* constructs a house, and in the course of building that house he instals electrical wiring around the house. The wiring is defective, but the problem is not detected initially, or even by the time *Owner* buys the house a few years later. Some time after *Owner* buys the house, the defective wiring causes a fire to start which results in the house being burned down. *Owner* wants to sue *Builder* in negligence for the loss of her house. Whether she can use the duty formula under discussion here to launch a claim against *Builder* will depend on whether what *Owner* bought when she bought the house was *one* item of property (a house), or *more than one item of property* (a house, and an electrical wiring system that goes with the house). If just one item, then she will not be able to establish that *Builder* did anything to harm the house in this case – the house came into the world in a flawed state, and its charred remains are merely an extension of that initial flaw. If more than one, then *Owner* can rely on the formula under discussion here. She can say that *Builder*'s positive act in wiring the house with defective wiring resulted in a separate item of property – the house – being harmed at the time it belonged to her.

In *Murphy v Brentwood DC* (1990), Lord Keith of Kinkel took the view that in the case we have just described – where the entire house, including the wiring, is built by A – it would be 'unrealistic' to separate out the house from its wiring: 'In that situation the whole package provided by the contractor would ... fall to be regarded as *one* unit rendered unsound as such by a defect in the particular part.'[138] On the other hand, he thought that if the electric wiring had been installed by a third party, *Contractor*, then in that kind of case it could be argued that the house and wiring were separate items of property, so that *Owner* could argue that *Contractor* owed her a duty to take care not to install wiring that

---

[137] B will not be able to sue A under the Consumer Protection Act 1987 for the damage done by the tyre to the car: s 5(2). See below, § 12.5.

[138] [1991] 1 AC 398, 470 (emphasis added).

was defective, because the act of installing such wiring resulted in a separate item of property (the house) being harmed at a time when it belonged to *Owner*.[139]

In the same case, Lord Bridge of Harwich took a different approach, drawing a distinction between a case where:

> some part of a complex structure . . . does not perform its proper function in sustaining the other parts [and a case where] some distinct item incorporated in the structure . . . positively malfunctions so as to inflict positive damage on the structure in which it is incorporated.[140]

In the first type of case, one could not say that there were two separate items of property, one (defective item) harming the other (previously sound item). There is just one piece of property that was brought into the world in a defective state and is now falling apart under its own flaws. But in the second type of case, a claimant could argue that a previously sound item of property belonging to her ('the structure') has been harmed by defects in a 'distinct item' of property for which the defendant is responsible. It was not clear on which side of the line Lord Bridge would have thought our example fell. He said that:

> if a defective central heating boiler explodes and damages a house or a defective electrical installation sets the house on fire, I see no reason to doubt that the owner of the house, if he can prove that the damage was due to . . . negligence . . . can recover damages . . . But the position in law is entirely different where, by reason of the inadequacy of the foundations of the building to support the weight of the superstructure, differential settlement and consequent cracking occurs.[141]

But it is not clear whether Lord Bridge's reference to an 'electrical installation' was meant to cover the case of electrical wiring that is inside the walls of a building.[142]

F. Normally

We said at the start of this section that if A has harmed an item of property P by doing some positive act, and B can show that: (1) she had a sufficient interest in P at the time it was harmed, and (2) it was reasonably foreseeable that A's actions would result in property like P being harmed, then the courts will *normally* find that A owed B a duty of care not to act as he did. The same exceptions to the usual practice of finding a duty of care when physical injury is foreseeable also apply in this area. That is, even if (1) and (2) are shown to be true, A will still *not* be found to have owed B a duty of care if: (i) B was happy for A to do what he did, despite the dangers for P; (ii) it was reasonable for A to do what he did; or (iii) it would be contrary to the public interest to find that A owed B a duty of care.

(iii) will be rarely made out, but probably underlies the decision of the House of Lords in *The Nicholas H* (1996). In that case, the eponymous ship, which was carrying the claimant's cargo, developed a crack in its hull while it was travelling from South America

---

[139] ibid: '[In such a case] it might not be stretching ordinary principles too far to hold the electrical subcontractor liable for the damage.'

[140] [1991] 1 AC 398, 478.

[141] ibid.

[142] For another case raising this kind of problem, see *Bellefield Computer Services Ltd v E Turner & Sons Ltd* [2000] BLR 97 (noted, Duncan Wallace 2000). A wall separating a storage area within a building from the rest of the building was badly constructed with the result that when a fire broke out in the storage area, it spread to the rest of the building. It was held that this was a case of one item of property – a building divided up into different areas by a wall – suffering from a defect from the moment of its creation, with the defect manifesting itself in eventual fire damage. It was not a case of a sound item of property – the area of the building outside the storage area – being damaged because another item of property – the wall separating the storage area from the rest of the building – was defective.

to Italy. The ship anchored off Puerto Rico and was inspected by the defendant classification society. The defendants told the shipowners that they would be willing to pass *The Nicholas H* as seaworthy – and thus allow it to continue on its way – if the shipowners temporarily repaired its hull and then repaired it properly as soon as possible after it discharged its cargo. The temporary repairs were done and *The Nicholas H* went on its way. However, it sank a week later when the temporary repairs failed. The claimant's cargo, which was worth $6,200,000, was lost. The claimant could recover only $500,000 from the shipowner by way of compensation for the loss of his cargo due to a limitation clause in the contract between the claimant and the shipowner.

The claimant sued the defendants for the balance of his loss, claiming that they had been negligent in allowing *The Nicholas H* to proceed on its way. The House of Lords dismissed the claim, holding that the defendants had not owed the claimant a duty of care not to approve the ship as seaworthy when it was not. This was so even though it had been perfectly foreseeable that the claimant's cargo would be harmed if the defendants approved the *Nicholas H* as seaworthy when it was not. So why did the House of Lords not give effect to the duty formula under discussion here?[143] The reason was that the House of Lords thought it would be contrary to the public interest to rule that a classification society will owe the owners of cargo aboard a ship a duty to take care not to say that a ship is seaworthy when it is not. Lord Steyn, giving the leading judgment, gave two reasons why such a ruling would be contrary to the public interest.

First, classification societies act in the general public interest in certifying whether or not ships are seaworthy – their doing so helps to save lives, ships and cargo at sea. If classification societies could be sued in negligence when their surveyors carelessly passed as seaworthy ships that were not seaworthy, then they would not – Lord Steyn thought – be able to carry out their functions as efficiently. They would be exposed to a wide number of claims; their surveyors would be overly inclined to label ships as unseaworthy if there was any doubt on the matter; classification societies' staff and resources would be tied up in dealing with claims made against them instead of being used for the main task of classifying ships.[144]

Secondly, Lord Steyn thought that if classification societies could be sued in negligence when their surveyors carelessly passed as seaworthy ships that were not seaworthy, then they would, before passing a ship as seaworthy, demand that the shipowner agree to indemnify them against any negligence liability they might incur as a result of passing the ship as seaworthy. So, in the end, any liabilities incurred by the classification societies in negligence would be passed on to shipowners – thus bypassing the limitations of liability that shipowners insert into their contracts of carriage with cargo owners. As a result, shipowners would no longer be able to predict for insurance purposes the extent of the liabilities they would incur if their ships sank and merchant shipping would as a result be disrupted.

---

[143] Lord Lloyd, dissenting, thought that a duty of care should have been found: 'All that is required is a straightforward application of *Donoghue* v *Stevenson*': [1996] 1 AC 211, 230. It seems likely that had anyone on board the *Nicholas H* been drowned when it sank, the House of Lords would not have hesitated to find that the defendants owed the people on board the *Nicholas H* a duty to take care not to approve the ship as being seaworthy when it was not, on the basis that it was reasonably foreseeable when the *Nicholas H* was in dock that those on board on the *Nicholas H* would suffer some kind of physical injury if the defendants approved it as being seaworthy when it was not. But of course, that duty of care would have been geared towards protecting people on board the *Nicholas H* from being killed or injured, and could not be prayed in aid of the claimants' case here for damages for the loss of their cargo.

[144] For much the same reason, it has been held that the Civil Aviation Authority will *not* owe the owner of an aircraft a duty of care not to certify an aircraft as being fit to fly when it is not: *Philcox* v *Civil Aviation Authority, The Times*, 8 June 1995.

6.10 PURE ECONOMIC LOSS (1): *HEDLEY BYRNE* – THE BASIC PRINCIPLE

Until 1964, it was thought that a claimant could not sue a defendant in *negligence* if a defendant's positive act resulted in the claimant suffering pure economic loss – that is, economic loss not resulting from the claimant's being injured (physically or mentally), or the claimant's property being harmed.[145]

In a long series of cases[146] decided both before and after the House of Lords' decision in *Donoghue* v *Stevenson* (1932), the courts made it clear that the mere fact that it was reasonably foreseeable that the defendant's conduct would result in a claimant suffering some form of pure economic loss would *not* be enough to ground a duty of care, owed by the defendant to the claimant. The reasons why in this context foreseeability of harm is not enough to give rise to a duty of care were well set out by Lord Denning MR in the 'relational' economic loss case of *Spartan Steel & Co Ltd* v *Martin* (1973).

A 'relational' economic loss case is one where a defendant has carelessly harmed a third party's person or property and the claimant has suffered pure economic loss as a result of his relationship with that third party's person or property. So it was in the *Spartan Steel* case: the defendants had carelessly cut through a power supply line that fed power to, among others, the claimants' factory. The claimants' power was cut off for about 14 hours. The claimants wanted to sue the defendants for the profits they could have made had they been allowed to work during those 14 hours. But to do that, they had to show that the defendants owed them a duty of care not to cut off their power supply, that was geared towards protecting them from suffering an interruption to their business activities.[147] The Court of Appeal held that no such duty of care had existed in this case. Lord Denning MR explained:

> the cutting of the supply of electricity . . . is a hazard we all run . . . [W]hen it does happen, it affects a multitude of persons: not as a rule by way of physical damage to them or their property, but by putting them to inconvenience, and sometimes to economic loss. The supply is usually restored in a few hours, so the economic loss is not very large. Such a hazard is regarded by most people as a thing they must put up with – without seeking compensation from anyone. Some there are who who instal a stand-by system. Others seek refuge by taking out an insurance policy against breakdown in the supply. But most people are content to take the risk on themselves. When the supply is cut off, they do not go running round to their solicitor. They do not try to find out whether it was anyone's fault. They just put up with it. They try to make up the economic loss by doing more work next day. This is a healthy attitude which the law should encourage . . . [Another] consideration

---

[145] Actions for pure economic loss had long been available where the defendant committed the tort of *deceit* in relation to the claimant (by deliberately inducing the claimant to act in a particular way by telling the claimant a lie when the defendant knew what he was saying was a lie, or didn't care whether it was true or not), or where the defendant committed the tort of *intentional infliction of harm using unlawful means* or the tort of *conspiracy* in relation to the claimant. These torts were (and are) known as the *economic* torts precisely because they can form the basis of a claim for pure economic loss. The economic torts are discussed below, chapter 24. A claim in negligence for pure economic loss *was* allowed in the odd case of *Morrison Steamship Co* v *Greystoke Castle* [1947] AC 265, but that case remained an isolated precedent until 1964. The decision of the House of Lords in the *Greystoke Castle* case is examined below, § 6.13(G).

[146] See above, § 5.3, fn 30.

[147] The claimants could establish that the defendants owed them an identical duty of care that was geared towards protecting them from having their property harmed as a result of their power being cut off. This was because the defendants' act in cutting off the claimants' power supply *did* cause harm to some 'melts' that were being processed by the claimants at the time the power went off, and it was reasonably foreseeable that cutting off the power supply would cause people like the claimants to suffer that kind of property damage. But that duty of care could not be relied on by the claimants to sue for the quite independent loss of profits from their not being able to do any work for 14 hours.

is this: if claims for economic loss were permitted for this particular hazard, there would be no end of claims. Some might be genuine, but many might be inflated, or even false. A machine might not have been in use anyway, but it would be easy to put it down to the cut in supply. It would be well-nigh impossible to check the claims . . . Rather than expose claimants to such temptation and defendants to such hard labour – on comparatively small claims – it is better to disallow economic loss altogether, at any rate where it stands alone, independent of any physical damage.[148]

So mere foreseeability of harm could not, in this context, ground a duty of care because: (1) a claimant's interest in not suffering pure economic loss was generally not *important* enough to justify subjecting the defendant to a duty of care; and (2) there was a *floodgates* fear that if foreseeability of pure economic loss was enough to ground a duty of care, the courts would be flooded with claimants arguing that a defendant was liable for some pure economic loss the claimant had suffered because it was foreseeable the defendant's actions would have that effect.

While everyone acknowledged foreseeability of pure economic loss was not enough to give rise to a duty of care, it seemed until 1964 that in pure economic loss cases, there was nothing else that could give rise to a duty of care either. In *Candler v Crane, Christmas & Co* (1951), Denning LJ suggested that accountants who were drawing up accounts for a company would not only owe a contractual duty to the company to draw up those accounts with reasonable skill and care, but also a duty in negligence to any claimant who they knew would be shown the accounts and who would rely on those accounts in a particular transaction.[149] But that suggestion was rejected by the other two members of the Court of Appeal in the *Candler* case, who reaffirmed the general rule that there was no liability in negligence for pure economic loss.

But then along came the great case of *Hedley Byrne & Co Ltd v Heller* (1964). Hedley Byrne, a firm of advertising agents, wanted to find out whether a company called Easipower Ltd was creditworthy or not before they placed some advertising orders on Easipower's behalf. Hedley Byrne were personally liable for the cost of these advertising orders and were therefore understandably concerned to know whether they could recoup the cost of placing those orders from Easipower. Hedley Byrne's bankers approached Heller & Partners, Easipower's bankers, for a reference as to Easipower's creditworthiness. Heller gave Easipower a favourable reference, on the strength of which Hedley Byrne placed a number of advertising orders on Easipower's behalf. Soon afterwards, Easipower went into liquidation and Hedley Byrne were unable to recover from Easipower the money they had laid out on Easipower's behalf in placing those advertising orders.

Hedley Byrne sued Heller, claiming that Heller had owed them a duty to take care that it did not mislead them as to Easipower's creditworthiness and that Heller breached that duty when it supplied them with a positive reference as to Easipower's creditworthiness. The House of Lords dismissed Hedley Byrne's claim on the ground that Heller's advice to Hedley Byrne as to Easipower's creditworthiness had been given 'without responsibility'.[150] But the House of Lords made clear that had Heller not done this, it *would* have owed Hedley Byrne a duty to take care not to mislead them as to Easipower's creditworthiness.

But why would Heller have owed Hedley Byrne a duty of care? Their Lordships came up with a number of different explanations. Lord *Reid*: Heller would have 'accepted a responsibility' for the accuracy of their advice or would have 'accepted a relationship' with

---

[148] [1973] 1 QB 27, 38–39.
[149] [1951] 2 KB 165, 179–184.
[150] [1964] AC 465, 492, 504, 511, 532–3, 539–40.

Hedley Byrne which required them to take care in advising Hedley Byrne.[151] Lord *Morris*: Heller would have 'assumed a responsibility' to tender Hedley Byrne 'deliberate advice'.[152] Lord *Morris* (with the agreement of Lord *Hodson*): Heller would have known or ought to have known that their advice would be relied upon by Hedley Byrne.[153] Lord *Hodson*: there would have existed a 'sufficiently close'[154] or 'special'[155] relationship between Heller and Hedley Byrne which would have given rise to a duty of care owed by Heller to Hedley Byrne. Lord *Devlin*: there would have existed a 'special relationship' between Heller and Hedley Byrne that was 'equivalent to contract'. In other words, Heller would have 'assumed a responsibility' towards Hedley Byrne in circumstances where, if Heller had been paid by Hedley Byrne to assume that responsibility, there would have existed a contract between Hedley Byrne and Heller.[156] Lord *Pearce*: there would have existed a 'special relationship' between Heller and Hedley Byrne which gave rise to an 'assumption that care as well as honesty' was demanded when Heller advised Hedley Byrne.[157]

Given the vagueness and variety of these statements it is understandable that there has been a great deal of debate as to when exactly one person will owe another a duty of care under the decision in *Hedley Byrne*. Subsequent caselaw establishes that Lords Morris and Hodson's view that if A knows or ought to know that B will rely on some advice of his, A will owe B a duty of care in rendering that advice is too wide to be acceptable.[158] Something more is required before A will be found to have owed B a duty of care. But what is that 'something more'? The speeches of Lords Reid, Devlin and Morris in *Hedley Byrne* suggest that it needs to be shown that A 'assumed a responsibility' towards B for the quality of his advice. But when will A be held to have done this? There are essentially two schools of thought on this issue.

(1) *'Assumption of responsibility' is an empty concept.* According to this school of thought, the concept of an 'assumption of responsibility' is essentially meaningless. In other words, the courts will be free to find that A 'assumed a responsibility' towards B for the quality of his advice *whenever* they *want* to find that A owed B a duty of care in giving that advice.

This was the line taken by Lord Griffiths in the case of *Smith* v *Eric S Bush* (1990):

> I do not think ... assumption of responsibility is a helpful or realistic test of liability [under *Hedley Byrne*] ... The phrase 'assumption of responsibility' can only have any real meaning if it is understood as referring to the circumstances in which the law will deem the maker of the statement to have assumed responsibility to the person who acts upon the advice.[159]

In *Phelps* v *Hillingdon LBC* (2001), Lord Slynn made essentially the same point: 'The phrase ["assumption of responsibility"] means simply that the law recognises that there is a duty of care. It is not so much that responsibility is assumed as that it is recognised or imposed by law.'[160]

(2) *Assumption of responsibility' is not an empty concept.* According to this second school of thought, the concept of an 'assumption of responsibility' is meaningful. In other words,

---

[151] [1964] AC 465, 486.
[152] [1964] AC 465, 494.
[153] [1964] AC 465, 503, 514.
[154] [1964] AC 465, 509.
[155] [1964] AC 465, 511.
[156] [1964] AC 465, 528–9, 530.
[157] [1964] AC 465, 539.
[158] See, in particular, the decision of the House of Lords in *Williams* v *Natural Life Health Foods Ltd* [1998] 1 WLR 830, discussed below.
[159] [1990] 1 AC 831, 862.
[160] [2001] 2 AC 619, 654. See also the judgment of Lord Roskill in *Caparo Industries plc* v *Dickman* [1990] 2 AC 605 at 629; Stapleton 1998, 64–5; Barker 1993.

it is only possible to say truthfully that someone has 'assumed a responsibility' to another in *certain definable circumstances*. Of course, the courts may have in the past found that a defendant 'assumed a responsibility' to a claimant outside those circumstances, but in those cases the courts were guilty of abusing the concept – in those cases the courts wanted to find that the defendant owed the claimant a duty of care for such-and-such a reason and they simply *said* that the defendant 'assumed a responsibility' to the claimant in order to provide themselves with some legal justification for their finding that the defendant owed the claimant a duty of care.[161]

Lord Steyn took this view of the concept of an 'assumption of responsibility' in *Williams* v *Natural Life Health Foods Ltd* (1998): 'There was, and is, no better rationalisation for [this] head of tort liability than assumption of responsibility . . . There is nothing fictional about this species of liability in tort.'[162] Lord Bingham took the same view in *Customs and Excise Commissioners* v *Barclays Bank plc* (2007) when he remarked that 'there are cases in which one party can *accurately* be said to have assumed responsibility for what is said . . . to another';[163] as did Lord Hoffmann in the same case when he said that:

> In . . . cases in which the loss has been caused by the claimant's reliance on information provided by the defendant, it is critical to decide whether the defendant (rather than someone else) assumed responsibility for the accuracy of the information to the claimant (rather than to someone else) . . .[164]

We prefer the second view, not least because it seems that in *Hedley Byrne*, Lords Reid, Devlin and Morris must have had *something* in mind when they talked of a defendant owing a claimant a duty of care if he 'assumed a responsibility' to her. We would go further and say that if A takes on the job of advising B on a particular matter, A will 'assume a responsibility' to B for the quality of his advice if and only if *he indicates to B that she can safely rely on his advice*. If this is right then we can say that the House of Lords' decision in *Hedley Byrne* establishes that: If A takes on the job of advising B on a particular matter and he indicates to B that B can safely rely on that advice, then A will owe B a duty to take care that he does not give B any incorrect advice on that matter. Let us call this the *basic principle* in *Hedley Byrne*.[165] We can now look at a number of different kinds of situations to see this principle in action.

A. Advice given 'without responsibility'

The decision of the House of Lords in *Hedley Byrne* makes it clear that if A takes on the job of advising B on a particular matter but makes it clear that his advice is given 'without responsibility', he will normally not owe B a duty of care in giving that advice. By making it clear that his advice is given 'without responsibility', he is making it clear to B that his advice cannot be safely relied on.

---

[161] See Lord Goff's judgment in *White* v *Jones* [1995] 2 AC 207 for a particularly transparent example of this happening.

[162] [1998] 1 WLR 830, 837. See also the judgment of Lord Browne-Wilkinson in *White* v *Jones* [1995] 2 AC 207, at 273–4.

[163] [2007] 1 AC 181, at [4] (emphasis added).

[164] [2007] 1 AC 181, at [35].

[165] It is worth noting that this basic principle cannot explain the House of Lords' finding in *Smith* v *Eric S Bush* [1990] 1 AC 831 that a duty of care was owed in that case: see below, § 6.13. It is hardly surprising, then, that Lord Griffiths should have poured scorn in that case on the idea that an assumption of responsibility was a prerequisite to a duty of care being owed under *Hedley Byrne*: had he found that an assumption of responsibility *was* required, he would not have been able to rely on the decision of the House of Lords in *Hedley Byrne* as authority for the view that a duty of care was owed in *Smith* v *Eric S Bush*.

It was necessary to say in the above paragraph that A will not *normally* owe B a duty of care in advising her if he has made it clear to her that his advice is given without responsibility. This is because under s 2(2) of the Unfair Contract Terms Act 1977, if A was acting 'in the course of business' in advising B, and due to his carelessness in advising B she suffered some form of economic loss, A will not be allowed to rely on the fact that he gave his advice 'without responsibility' so as to deny that he owed B a duty of care in advising her, if it would be 'unreasonable' to allow him to rely on that fact to deny that he owed B a duty of care. So it is possible that if A was advising B 'in the course of business' he might still be held to have owed B a duty of care in giving her that advice even if that advice was formally given 'without responsibility'.

B. Advice given directly to advisee knowing that the advice will be relied on

In *Hedley Byrne*, Lord Reid observed that:

> A reasonable man, knowing that he was being trusted or that his skill or judgment were being relied on, would, I think, have three courses open to him. He could keep silent or decline to give the information or advice sought: or he could give an answer with a clear qualification that he accepted no responsibility for it or that it was given without that reflection or inquiry which a careful answer would require: or he could simply answer without any such qualification. If he chooses to adopt the last course he must, I think, be held to have accepted some responsibility for his answer being given carefully, or to have accepted a relationship with the inquirer which requires him to exercise such care as the circumstances require.[166]

It follows from this that if *Anxious* asks *Guru* to advise her on some matter, and *Guru* knows that *Anxious* will rely on whatever he says, then if *Guru* undertakes to advise *Anxious* on that matter, he will owe her a duty of care in giving her that advice. The reason for this is that when he takes on the job of advising *Anxious*, *Guru* will implicitly indicate to *Anxious* that she can safely rely on his advice. *Anxious* will think – and will be entitled to think – that, '*Guru* knew that I would rely on his advice unless I was discouraged from doing so. Given that he knew this, he surely would have discouraged me from relying on his advice if his advice could not be safely relied on. But he did not do this – he gave me his advice and did nothing to discourage me from relying on it. Surely, then, his advice can be safely relied on.'

This was the position in *Welton* v *North Cornwall District Council* (1997). In that case, the claimants owned a guest house which constituted food premises for the purpose of the Food Act 1984 and the Food Safety Act 1990. The claimants were visited by one E, a health inspector. E said that the claimants' kitchen was not up to scratch. He could have closed the claimants' kitchen down – effectively putting their guest house out of business – but instead took it upon himself to advise the claimants as to what they needed to do to their kitchen to bring it up to a satisfactory standard. Acting on this advice, the claimants made numerous alterations to their kitchen, 90 per cent of which – they subsequently discovered – were completely unnecessary. The claimants sued, claiming that E had owed them a duty of care in advising them as to what they needed to do to their kitchen to bring it up to scratch. The Court of Appeal allowed their claim. When E took on the job of advising the claimants as to what they needed to do, he knew that they would rely on whatever he said, and so by undertaking to advise the claimants, he implicitly indicated to them that his advice could be safely relied on.

[166] [1964] AC 465, 486.

It should be noted that in the situation we are considering, *Guru* will be held to have 'assumed a responsibility' to *Anxious*, irrespective of whether or not he *subjectively* wanted to indicate to *Anxious* that she could safely rely on his advice. The duty of care that *Guru* will owe *Anxious* in this situation will arise out of the fact that *Guru* gave *Anxious* the *impression* that his advice could be safely relied upon. So whether or not the courts will find that *Guru* 'assumed a responsibility' to *Anxious* will not depend on whether *Guru intended* to 'assume a responsibility' to *Anxious*, but will instead depend on whether *Guru gave Anxious the impression* that he intended to 'assume a responsibility' to *Anxious*. As Lord Hoffmann observed in *Customs and Excise Commissioners v Barclays Bank plc*:

> The answer [to the question of whether the defendant assumed responsibility to the claimant] does not depend on what the defendant intended but . . . upon what would reasonably be inferred from his conduct against the background of all the circumstances of the case.[167]

C. Advice given on a social occasion

Suppose that *Money* and *Fool* are drinking together in the pub, and *Money* asks *Fool* whether he thinks she should invest her savings on the stock market. *Fool* says, 'Definitely – this is a good time to buy.' *Money* acts on *Fool*'s advice and invests all of her savings in the stock market, and loses most of it when the stock market subsequently crashes. Let us assume that *Fool* was careless in his advice: at the time he talked to *Money* the stock market had reached a record high and there were widespread warnings that a correction in stock market levels was overdue. But did *Fool* owe *Money* a duty of care in advising her whether or not to invest in the stock market? The answer will normally be 'no'. *Fool* did nothing to indicate to *Money* that she could safely rely on his advice – that is, rely on his advice without seeking any further advice from anyone else. The casual context in which *Money* sought *Fool*'s advice meant that he had no reason to think that she would rely on whatever he said, and so *Money* could not have been entitled to infer from the fact that *Fool* gave *Money* his opinion on what she should do that he was indicating to her that she could rely on his advice without consulting anyone else.

So the normal rule is that someone giving advice on a social occasion will not owe a duty of care to the advisee.[168] However, the rule will be displaced if A gives B advice on a social occasion and in doing so explicitly assures B that she *can* safely rely on his advice. In such

---

[167] [2007] 1 AC 181, at [35]. See also [5] (per Lord Bingham): 'it is clear that the assumption of responsibility test is to be applied objectively . . . and is not answered by consideration of what the defendant thought or intended'; and *Henderson v Merrett Syndicates* [1995] 2 AC 145, at 181 (per Lord Goff): 'it must be expected that an objective test will be applied when asking the question whether, in a particular case, responsibility should be held to have been assumed by the defendant . . .'

[168] See *Hedley Byrne & Co Ltd v Heller & Partners Ltd* [1964] AC 465, 482–3 (per Lord Reid); *Howard Marine & Dredging Co v A Ogden (Excavations) Ltd* [1978] QB 574, 592–3 (per Lord Denning MR). The same will be true if John rang Mary out of the blue for her advice without making it clear that he was going to be relying on her advice: *Tidman v Reading Borough Council* [1994] Times LR 592; *Fashion Brokers Ltd v Clarke Hayes* [2000] PNLR 473. Or if the circumstances of John's inquiry were generally such as not to put Mary on warning that John was going to rely on her advice: see *James McNaughton Paper Group Ltd v Hicks Anderson & Co* [1991] 2 QB 113 (held, no liability for an off-the-cuff statement made by accountant as to profitability of a company in the course of negotiations to take over the company). A different result would have been reached if it had been made clear to the accountant that his statement would be relied upon: *Galoo v Bright Grahame Murray* [1994] 1 WLR 1360; *Law Society v KPMG Peat Marwick* [2000] 1 WLR 1921. Puzzlingly, it has been held that a solicitor working for someone selling a house will *not* owe the purchaser of the house a duty of care in answering the purchaser's inquiries even if it is made abundantly clear to him that those answers will be relied upon by the purchaser: *Gran Gelato Ltd v Richcliff (Group) Ltd* [1992] Ch 560 (Nicholls V-C). For criticisms of the decision in *Gran Gelato*, see Reed 1996, 69–73.

a situation, A will owe B a duty of care in advising her. This was the situation in *Chaudhry* v *Prabhakar* (1989). In that case, Chaudhry was thinking of buying a Golf car that her friend Prabhakar had spotted was for sale. Chaudhry obviously wanted to know whether the car was in good condition before buying it. Prabhakar advised her that the car was in good condition and told her that she did not need to get a qualified mechanic to look at it. Chaudhry subsequently bought the car on the strength of this advice. The car subsequently proved to be unroadworthy and Chaudhry sued Prabhakar in negligence for compensation. The Court of Appeal held that Prabhakar had owed Chaudhry a duty of care in advising her as to the condition of the car: he had discouraged her from seeking anyone else's opinion on the condition of the car and had therefore explicitly indicated to her that his advice – that the car was in good condition – could be safely relied on.

D. Advice given by a non-expert

It was suggested by the majority of the Privy Council in *Mutual Life and Citizens' Assurance Co Ltd* v *Evatt* (1971) that if A undertakes to advise B on some matter, A will not owe B a duty of care in giving that advice if A did not hold himself out as being an expert on the matter advised upon. This seems too strong, and the decision in the *Evatt* case – denying that a duty of care was owed by a defendant company advising the claimant investor on whether its sister company's finances were sound – has been criticised by the domestic courts.[169]

The better view, we would submit, is that if A makes it obvious that he is not an expert on the matter on which he is advising B, that is something that should be taken into account in deciding whether or not A indicated to B that his advice could be safely relied on. If A makes it clear to B – or B knows already – that he is not an expert on the matter on which B is seeking A's advice, then the courts will usually find that A did *not* indicate to B that his advice could be safely relied on.

But it would be different if *Anxious* said to *Dabbler*, 'I know you are not a financial expert, but you're more of an expert than me, and I don't trust anyone else to give me good advice, so I'll do whatever you tell me to do – do you think I should invest in the stock market?' If *Dabbler* gives *Anxious* his advice without urging *Anxious* to seek out more opinions, then it will be hard not to find that *Dabbler* – in giving *Anxious* his advice – implicitly indicated to *Anxious* that she could safely rely on his advice. Similarly, it would be different if *Dabbler* said to *Anxious*, 'I'm not a doctor, but even I know that you are as fit as a fiddle. You are going to look stupid if you ask a doctor if you should be concerned about a silly lump on your arm. Take it from me – it's nothing.' In such a case, *Dabbler* will have explicitly indicated to *Anxious* that she could safely rely on his advice as to the state of her health. So in both these alternative scenarios, the courts will – and should – find that *Dabbler* owed *Anxious* a duty of care in advising her, even though *Dabbler* has no expertise (and professes no expertise) in the matter on which he was advising *Anxious*.

E. Advice given in a published work

In *Candler* v *Crane, Christmas & Co* (1951), Denning LJ observed that, 'a scientist or expert . . . is not liable to his readers for careless statements made in his published works.'[170]

---

[169] See *Esso Petroleum Co Ltd* v *Mardon* [1976] QB 801; *Howard Marine & Dredging Co* v *A Ogden (Excavations) Ltd* [1978] QB 574; *Spring* v *Guardian Assurance plc* [1995] 2 AC 296, at 320 (per Lord Goff); *Commissioner of Police of the Metropolis* v *Lennon* [2004] 2 All ER 266.

[170] [1951] 2 KB 164, at 183.

This seems correct, even after the decision of the House of Lords in *Hedley Byrne*. If A writes a textbook or an article, he cannot be taken to have invited his readers to think that the information in that article can be relied upon without seeking further advice.

F. Official registers

Oftentimes, the law will require someone to be officially registered before they are allowed to trade, for example, as a child-minder. If A is in charge of maintaining such an official register, does A invite people looking at the register to think that they can rely on him to have taken care to ensure that C – someone who is on the register – is a fit and proper person to deal with?

The Privy Council said the answer is 'no' in *Yuen Kun Yeu* v *Attorney-General for Hong Kong* (1988). The register in that case was a register of deposit-taking companies. The claimants lost the money they had deposited with a company that was on the register, but had been run fraudulently and with little regard for investors' interests. The claimants sued the defendant – who was in charge of maintaining the register – on the ground that by allowing the company's name to appear on the register, he had represented that people like the claimants could safely rely on him to have taken care to ensure that the company was a fit and proper company to accept deposits. The Privy Council rejected this argument: the existence of the procedure for registering deposit-taking companies did not 'warrant an assumption that all [registered] deposit-taking companies were sound and fully creditworthy'.[171]

G. Advice given by a third party

Suppose that *Money* wants some advice as to whether she should invest in a particular company, *Dodgy* plc. *Money*'s *Friend* asks *Investor*, a self-professed expert on the industry in which *Dodgy* operates, whether it would be a good idea to invest in *Dodgy*. *Investor* assures *Friend*, 'You should buy as many shares as possible. They are working on something at the moment that will quadruple the share price when it's announced.' *Friend* then goes to *Money* and says, 'Take it from me – you won't go wrong if you invest in *Dodgy*.' *Money* then invests a large sum in *Dodgy* and loses all of it when *Dodgy* announces a few months later that it is insolvent. *Money* then finds out from *Friend* that *Investor* was the source of the bad advice to invest in *Dodgy*. *Money* sues *Investor*, claiming that he owed *her* a duty of care in advising *Friend* whether it was a good idea for her to buy shares in *Dodgy*. Her claim will fail. *Investor* did not 'assume a responsibility' to *Money* in giving that advice – he never indicated to *Money* that *she* could safely rely on that advice. There was, in fact, no kind of contact between *Investor* and *Money* that could ground a finding that *Investor* 'assumed a responsibility' to *Money* for the quality of his advice.

That this is correct is confirmed by the decision of the House of Lords in *Williams* v *Natural Life Health Foods Ltd* (1998).[172] Natural Life Health Food Shops Ltd was a company which provided the following service. People who were interested in opening a health food shop could approach Natural Life for an assessment as to how successful the health food shop was likely to be. If, on the basis of that assessment, they were still interested in opening the shop, Natural Life would, for a fee, allow them to open their shop using the Natural Life Health Foods trade name and would advise them as to how to run their shop. The

---

[171] [1988] 1 AC 175, at 197.
[172] Discussed, Armour 1999.

claimants approached Natural Life because they were interested in opening a health food shop in Rugby. The managing director of Natural Life, Richard Mistlin, prepared some reports which predicted that the health food shop the claimants were proposing to open would enjoy a healthy turnover. Even though he prepared the reports, Mistlin never actually had any dealings with the claimants – they dealt with another employee of the company, Ron Padwick. On the strength of Mistlin's reports, the claimants opened a health food shop in Rugby under the Natural Life trade name. However, the shop enjoyed less success than Mistlin's reports indicated it would and the claimants, after trading at a loss for 18 months, were finally forced to close the shop.

The claimants sued Natural Life in negligence. Unfortunately, Natural Life was not worth suing; it was wound up a couple of years after the claimants commenced proceedings against Natural Life. Mistlin, on the other hand, did have substantial assets – so the claimants then tried to sue him in negligence. They argued that he had owed them, and breached, a duty to take care that he did not mislead them as to how successful the Rugby health food shop was likely to be; and that had he not breached this duty, he would have told them that the Rugby health food shop was unlikely to be a success and they would never have invested their money in it.

The House of Lords rejected the claimants' claim. Lord Steyn, giving the only judgment, ruled that Mistlin had not owed the claimants a duty of care in preparing his reports as to how profitable the Rugby health food shop was likely to be under the basic principle in *Hedley Byrne*. While Mistlin *did* take on the job of preparing the reports given to the claimants on the potential profitability of the Rugby health food shop, the lack of contact between Mistlin and the claimants meant that *Mistlin* did not at any point indicate to the claimants that they could safely rely on his advice. In contrast, Natural Life – a separate person from Mistlin – *did* indicate to the claimants that they could safely rely on the advice Natural Life gave them as to how profitable the Rugby health food shop was likely to be. So Natural Life *did* owe the claimants a duty under the basic principle in *Hedley Byrne* to take care that they did not supply the claimants with any incorrect advice as to how profitable the Rugby health food shop was likely to be. However, as has already been observed, this was of little comfort to the claimants as Natural Life was not worth suing.

6.11 PURE ECONOMIC LOSS (2): *HEDLEY BYRNE* – THE EXTENDED PRINCIPLE

It is now well acknowledged that *Hedley Byrne* is not *just* authority in favour of the proposition that someone who takes on the task of advising another on a particular matter will, in certain circumstances, owe that other a duty of care in giving that advice. Certain *dicta* in *Hedley Byrne* suggest that if A has indicated to B[173] that B can safely rely on him to perform a particular task with a certain degree of care and skill and B has so relied on A, A will owe B a duty to perform that task with that degree of care and skill.[174]

---

[173] By 'B' we mean either B or B's agent, acting on B's behalf.

[174] [1964] AC 465, at 502–3 (per Lord Morris): 'it should now be regarded as settled that if someone possessed of a special skill undertakes, quite irrespective of contract, to apply that skill for the assistance of another person who relies upon such skill, a duty of care will arise'; 531 (per Lord Hodson): 'those who hold themselves out as possessing a special skill are under a duty to exercise it with reasonable care'; 531 (per Lord Devlin): 'If a defendant says to a [claimant]: "Let me do this for you; do not waste your money in employing a professional, I will do it for nothing and you can rely on me", I do not think he could escape liability . . .'; 538 (per Lord Pearce): 'if persons holding themselves out in a calling or situation or profession take on a task within that calling or situation or profession, they have a duty of skill and care.'

Many cases, decided before and after *Hedley Byrne*, seem to support this suggestion. (A suggestion which, it should be noted, can not only be relied on in cases where A has performed a *positive act* that has resulted in harm to B, but also in cases where A has *failed to save* B from suffering some kind of harm, when he indicated to B that he could be relied on to act carefully to save B from that harm, and B did so rely.)[175] Most of them deal with the following kind of situation:

(1) A is a professional – that is, he holds himself out as being able to perform a particular task T with a 'professional' degree of care and skill;
(2) as a result, B is led to believe that A can be safely relied on to perform task T with a 'professional' degree of care and skill;
(3) B asks A to perform task T for her;
(4) A knows that B's request is made in the belief that A can be safely relied on to perform task T with a 'professional' degree of care and skill and B knows that A knows this;
(5) A agrees to perform task T for B.

In such a case, B will think – and she will be entitled to think – that, by agreeing to do task T without warning her that she can't expect him to perform that task to his usual high standards, A has indicated to B that she can safely rely on him to perform that task with a 'professional' degree of care and skill. And B will have relied on A to do exactly that by asking him to perform task T. So A's holding himself out to be a professional, and B's asking A to work for her, and A's agreeing to work for B without telling her that she can't trust him to be competent – all combine together to establish that A owes B a duty to perform task T with a 'professional' degree of care and skill under what we can call the *extended principle in Hedley Byrne*.

A lot of cases support the idea that in this kind of situation, a duty of care will be owed. These cases variously hold that:

(1) A doctor will owe his patient a duty to treat his patient with the care and skill that a reasonably competent doctor would exercise in treating a patient.[176]

(2) A dentist will owe his patient a duty to treat that patient with the care and skill that a reasonably competent dentist would exercise in treating a patient.[177]

(3) A vet who treats an animal at the owner's request will owe that owner a duty to treat that animal with the care and skill that a reasonably competent vet would exercise in treating that animal.[178]

(4) A solicitor who handles a case or transaction on behalf of a client will owe that client a duty to handle that case or transaction with the care and skill that a reasonably competent solicitor would exercise in handling that case or transaction.[179]

---

[175] See further, § 7.2, below.
[176] *Pippin* v *Sherrard* (1822) 11 Price 400, 147 ER 512; *Gladwell* v *Steggal* (1839) 5 Bing NC 733, 132 ER 1283; *Barnett* v *Chelsea & Kensington Hospital Management Committee* [1969] 1 QB 428. The concept of a doctor–patient relationship was stretched *very* far by Gage J in *A* v *Leeds Teaching Hospital NHS Trust* [2004] EWHC 644 (QB), holding that the parents of a baby that had died in hospital enjoyed a doctor–patient relationship with the baby's doctor, so that the doctor owed the parents a duty to act towards them with reasonable skill and care – particularly in relation to explaining to them what the baby's post-mortem would involve and whether any of the baby's organs would be retained.
[177] *Edwards* v *Mallan* [1908] 1 KB 1002; *Fish* v *Kapur* [1948] 2 All ER 176.
[178] *Chute Farms* v *Curtis*, The Times, 10 October 1961.
[179] *Nocton* v *Lord Ashburton* [1914] AC 465; *Midland Bank* v *Hett, Stubbs and Kemp* [1979] Ch 383.

(5) A barrister who handles a client's case in court will owe that client a duty to conduct that case in court with the care and skill that a reasonably competent barrister would exercise in conducting that case.[180]

(6) A surveyor will owe a client of his who has asked him to value a house or piece of land that he is thinking of purchasing a duty to survey that house or land with the care and skill that a reasonably competent surveyor would exercise in surveying a house or a piece of land.

(7) An architect will owe a client who has commissioned him to design a building a duty to design that building with the care and skill that a reasonably competent architect would exercise in designing a building.

(8) An architect who has been commissioned by a client to supervise the construction of a building will normally owe that client a duty to supervise the construction work with the care and skill that a reasonably competent architect would exercise in supervising that sort of work.

(9) An engineer who has been engaged to undertake some building work by a client will owe that client a duty to execute that work with the care and skill that a reasonably competent engineer would exercise in doing that sort of work.[181]

(10) An accountant will owe a client who has commissioned him to draw up a set of accounts a duty to draw up those accounts with the care and skill that a reasonably competent accountant would exercise in drawing up a set of accounts;

(11) The referee of a game will owe the participants in the game a duty to referee the game with a reasonable degree of care and skill.[182]

It should be emphasised that if A – implicitly or explicitly – indicates to B that he can be safely relied on to perform a particular task T with a certain degree of care and skill and B did so rely on him, he will *not* owe B a duty to perform that task T with any *more* care and skill than he (objectively) indicated he could be safely relied on to exercise in performing task T.[183]

So – in *Philips* v *William Whiteley Ltd* (1938), the claimant asked the defendants, a firm of jewellers, to pierce her ears. The claimant suffered some ill effects from the operation and sought to recover compensation for those ill effects by suing the defendants in negligence. The court dismissed the claimant's claim: it held that the defendants had owed the claimant a duty to pierce her ears with the skill and care that a reasonably competent jeweller would exercise in piercing someone's ears and that the defendants had not breached that duty. The claimant's claim that the defendant had owed the claimant a more stringent duty of care – a duty to pierce her ears with the skill and care that a reasonably competent surgeon would exercise in piercing someone's ears – was dismissed: the defendants had never indicated to the claimant that they could be safely relied on to pierce her ears with the skill and care that a surgeon would exercise in piercing someone's ears.

Similarly, in *Wilsher* v *Essex Area Health Authority*,[184] the Court of Appeal held that if A treats B, a hospital patient, A will owe B a duty to treat B with the skill and care that a

---

[180] *Arthur J S Hall* v *Simons* [2002] 1 AC 615 (not followed by the High Court of Australia in *D'Orta-Ekenaike* v *Victoria Legal Aid* [2005] HCA 12).

[181] *Congregational Union* v *Harriss and Harriss* [1988] 1 All ER 15; *Ketteman* v *Hansel Properties* [1987] AC 189.

[182] *Vowles* v *Evans* [2003] 1 WLR 1607 (noted, Elvin 2003a).

[183] *Vowles* v *Evans* [2003] 1 WLR 1607, at [28], holding that it is arguable that someone who volunteers to referee a game as a replacement for a referee who has not turned up will not be expected to referee the game with as much skill and care as someone who has been trained to act as a referee: 'the volunteer cannot reasonably be expected to show the skill of one who holds himself out [to be a] referee, or perhaps even to be fully conversant with the [l]aws of the [g]ame.'

[184] [1987] 1 QB 730, reversed on other grounds by the House of Lords: [1988] 1 AC 1074.

reasonably competent person *in A's post* would exercise in treating that patient. It would be unreasonable to take A as indicating that he will exercise any higher degree of care and skill in treating B. So a junior house officer who treats a patient will owe that patient a duty to treat that patient with the skill and care that a reasonably competent junior house officer would exercise in treating a patient; a level of skill and care which would, presumably, be lower than the level of skill and care that a reasonably competent consultant would exercise in treating a patient.[185]

It is worth noting at greater length two cases that seem to lend some support to the suggestion that if A indicates to B that B can safely rely on him to perform a particular task with a certain degree of care and skill and B does so rely on A, then A will owe B a duty to perform that task with that degree of care and skill.

A. *Junior Books Ltd* v *Veitchi Co Ltd* (1983)

Junior Books Ltd engaged Ogilvie Builders Ltd to build a factory for them. The work of laying the floor was contracted out to Veitchi Co Ltd, on the instructions of Junior Books' architect. Veitchi laid the floor of Junior Books' factory but did a poor job of it. Two years after the floor was laid, it began to crack up and needed to be completely replaced. Junior Books sued Veitchi in negligence so as to recover the cost of relaying the floor of their factory. In order to make out their claim, they had to establish that Veitchi, in laying the floor, owed Junior Books a duty to lay the floor with a certain degree of care and skill. The House of Lords held that Veitchi did owe Junior Books such a duty.

The decision in *Junior Books* caused some consternation at the time; it was hard to see what principle underlay the House of Lords' decision and therefore how widely it applied. However, whatever the views were of the Law Lords who decided the case at the time, the decision came to be justified on the basis that Veitchi indicated, in negotiations with Junior Books, that it could be safely relied on to lay the floor of Junior Books' factory with a certain degree of care and skill and Junior Books relied on Veitchi to take such care by causing Veitchi to be nominated as subcontractors by their architect. Viewed in this way, the decision in *Junior Books* was an outgrowth of the *dicta* in *Hedley Byrne* referred to above.[186]

However, the very recent decision of the Court of Appeal in *Robinson* v *Jones (Contractors) Ltd* (2011) has cast the correctness of *Junior Books* into doubt. In *Robinson*, the claimants

---

[185] Of course, one way in which a reasonably competent junior house officer might act negligently would be in failing to seek assistance from a more qualified physician when it ought to have been clear to a reasonably competent junior house officer that such assistance was necessary.

[186] A view taken by Lord Oliver of Aylmerton (*D & F Estates* v *Church Commissioners* [1989] 1 AC 177, 215D: 'the decision of this House in *Junior Books* . . . rests . . . upon the *Hedley Byrne* doctrine of reliance') and Lord Keith of Kinkel (*Murphy* v *Brentwood DC* [1991] 1 AC 398, 466G–H: 'The case would accordingly fall within the principle of *Hedley Byrne* . . . I regard *Junior Books* . . . as being an application of that principle'). See also, to the same effect, Perry 1992, 302–8. In contrast to the facts of *Junior Books*, in *Simaan* v *Pilkington Glass Ltd (No 2)* [1988] QB 758, the claimant contractors were appointed to construct a building in Abu Dhabi (the 'Al-Oteiba building', named after the sheikh who commissioned it). One of the main features of the building was to be a curtain wall, made out of green panels. The job of building the curtain wall was subcontracted to a company named Feal and the claimants instructed Feal to use glass panels manufactured by the defendants in constructing the building. The glass panels proved not to be suitable and the sheikh who commissioned the building refused to pay the claimants the full price due under their contract with the sheikh. The claimants sought to recover their loss from the defendants by suing them in negligence but it was held that the defendants had not owed the claimants a duty to construct the glass panels with reasonable care and skill. The crucial distinction between this case and *Junior Books* is that the defendants did not indicate to the claimants that they could be safely relied upon to do a good job of constructing the glass panels and the defendants had not so relied on them. In fact, the only reason why the claimants instructed Feal to use the defendants' glass panels in constructing the curtain wall was that the building's *architect* wanted the defendants' panels to be used.

agreed to purchase from the defendant a house that the defendant was then constructing. In the contract of sale, the defendant undertook that it would construct the house in 'an efficient and workmanlike manner'. It failed to do so: the gas fires that were installed in the house by the defendant at the claimants' request did not work. The claimants attempted to sue the defendant in negligence, claiming that the defendant had owed the claimants a duty to construct the gas fires with a reasonable degree of care and skill. They based their argument on *Hedley Byrne*, arguing that the defendant had, in the contract of sale that they entered into with the claimant, 'assumed a responsibility' to the claimant.

The Court of Appeal rejected this argument, holding that the only duty of care the defendant had owed the claimant was a *Donoghue* v *Stevenson* style duty to take care not to build the house in such a way that it would be dangerous to live in:[187]

> In the present case I see nothing to suggest that the defendant 'assumed responsibility' to the claimant in the *Hedley Byrne* sense. The parties entered into a normal contract whereby the defendant would complete the construction of a house . . . The defendant's warranties of quality were set out and the claimant's remedies in the event of breach of warranty were also set out. The parties were not in a professional relationship whereby, for example, the claimant was paying the defendant to give advice or to prepare reports or plans upon which the claimant would act.[188]

Burnton LJ went further, condemning the House of Lords' decision in *Junior Books* as 'aberrant, indeed as heretical'.[189]

With respect, it is the decision in *Robinson* that is in danger of being heretical, and aberrant. (Though – unless it is overruled by the Supreme Court – it has now to be followed by every court up to and including the Court of Appeal.) Limiting *Hedley Byrne* style 'assumptions of responsibility' to cases of:

> professional persons . . . [who] give advice, prepare reports, draw up accounts, produce plans and so forth . . . [and who] expect their clients and possibly others to act in reliance upon their work product . . .[190]

threatens to revive the corpse of the Privy Council's decision in *Mutual Life and Citizens' Assurance Co Ltd* v *Evatt* (1971), which – as we have just seen – seemed to suggest that only experts could be held liable under *Hedley Byrne* for negligent misstatement. It is highly likely that the claimants in *Robinson* would not have decided to buy a house from the defendant without having received some strong assurances from the defendant as to the quality of the work that it was putting into constructing that house. It is hard to see why such assurances could not form the basis of a finding that the defendant assumed a responsibility to the claimant under *Hedley Byrne*.

B. *Henderson* v *Merrett Syndicates Ltd* (1995)

This case arose out of the huge losses suffered by names at Lloyd's in the 1990s. Lloyd's was, and is, a major source of insurance policies. If, for example, an American oil company wanted to get insurance against the risk of one of its oil rigs blowing up, it would go to Lloyd's and see if someone at Lloyd's was prepared to insure that risk. Insurance policies would be issued by syndicates of Lloyd's 'names'. Lloyd's was, and is, like a club. If you were

---

[187] [2011] EWCA Civ 9, at [68] and [82] (per Jackson LJ).
[188] [2011] EWCA Civ 9, at [83] (per Jackson LJ).
[189] [2011] EWCA Civ 9, at [92].
[190] [2011] EWCA Civ 9, at [75].

admitted to the club, then you became a 'name' and could join one or more of the syndicates at Lloyd's that issued insurance policies. If you joined a syndicate, then you and your fellow syndicate members shared in the premiums that were paid each year on the insurance policies issued by that syndicate. The downside was that you and your fellow syndicate members would also have to cover the costs of meeting any claims on the insurance policies issued by that syndicate. But the premiums paid on a syndicate's insurance policies usually far outweighed the costs of meeting the claims on a syndicate's insurance policies, so up until the 1990s, a name at Lloyd's could expect to receive a big cheque at the end of each year by virtue of his membership of various syndicates – and for doing absolutely nothing, except agreeing that he or she would be personally liable, without limit, to cover the cost of meeting claims made on his syndicates' insurance policies. But up until the 1990s, the risk that a name at Lloyd's would *lose* money as a result of being a name was regarded as very remote. As a result, the status of being a name at Lloyd's was a much coveted one.

Everything changed in the 1990s. However, the disaster that overtook many Lloyd's names in that decade had its roots in decisions that were made long before the 1990s – in particular, the decision (from 1930 onwards) that Lloyd's would start issuing *unlimited* liability insurance policies to American companies. From 1970 onwards, American companies started facing big claims for asbestos-related diseases from employees who had been exposed to asbestos at work. The bills for meeting those claims would eventually find their way back to Lloyd's, by virtue of the liability insurance policies that Lloyd's syndicates had issued to the American companies that were being sued. At the same time, American companies also began to face a large number of claims for damages for polluting the environment. Again, the costs of meeting those claims would ultimately find their way back to Lloyd's.

By the early 1980s, Lloyd's was in trouble, but the problem was not known to most names. But in 1988, a series of disasters occurred – the Piper Alpha oil platform in the North Sea blew up, the *Exxon Valdez* spilled 500,000 barrels of oil into Alaskan sea waters, and there was a major earthquake in San Francisco. The bills for all these disasters had to be met by Lloyd's syndicates, and various syndicates started making huge yearly losses. These losses had to be met by the names that belonged to those syndicates, and the bills that each name had to pay ran into seven figures in many cases. A lot of names lost their homes.

It was these names who were suing in *Henderson* v *Merrett Syndicates*. They were suing the *managing agents* of their syndicates in negligence. A syndicate's *managing agent* performed a number of functions. First, the managing agent would decide which risks should be insured by the syndicate. Secondly, in the case of risks which were insured by the syndicate, the managing agent would decide whether or not those risks should be reinsured with someone else, so that if a claim was made on an insurance policy issued by the syndicate, the syndicate could recover the costs of meeting that claim by claiming themselves on an insurance policy (against the risk they would have to pay out on their insurance policy) that they had taken out with someone else. Thirdly, the managing agent would decide how to deal with claims against the syndicate – whether to settle those claims, and if so on what terms, and so on.

The claimants in *Henderson* argued that the managing agents of their syndicates had failed to perform these functions competently. In particular, it was argued that the managing agents in *Henderson* had been extremely foolish in both the risks that they chose to insure, and in failing to reinsure those risks with someone else.

The claimants who were suing in *Henderson* fell into two groups: 'direct names' and 'indirect names'. In order to understand the distinction, you have to understand that each

Lloyd's name, when he entered Lloyd's, signed an 'underwriting agency agreement' with an *underwriting agent*, whose job it was to place him with a syndicate. If the underwriting agent placed the name in a syndicate which the underwriting agent managed *himself*, the name was known as a '*direct name*'. In such a case, the name had a contractual relationship – in the form of the underwriting agency agreement – with the managing agent of his syndicate, because his underwriting agent and his managing agent were one and the same person. It was conceded that there was an implied term in every underwriting agency agreement with a Lloyd's name that if that name joined a syndicate that was managed by his underwriting agent, the underwriting agent would administer the affairs of the name's syndicate with a certain degree of care and skill.[191] So 'direct names' could bring a claim for breach of contract against their managing agents (assuming they could prove their managing agents had been careless in administering the affairs of their syndicates). But they wanted to sue their managing agents in *negligence* to take advantage of the fact that the limitation periods for bringing actions in negligence expire later than the limitation periods for bringing actions for breach of contract.[192] In contrast, an '*indirect name*' was a Lloyd's name who joined a syndicate that was managed by someone other than his underwriting agent. An 'indirect name' did not have any contractual relationship with his managing agent. The only way he could sue his managing agent for mismanaging the affairs of his syndicate was by bringing a claim in negligence against the managing agent.

So each claimant in *Henderson* wanted to bring a claim in negligence against the managing agent of his syndicate, and argued that the managing agent of his syndicate owed him a duty under the law of negligence to administer the affairs of the syndicate with a certain degree of care and skill. The House of Lords took the view that *every* claimant in *Henderson* v *Merrett Syndicates Ltd* could establish that the managing agent of his syndicate owed him such a duty.

In the case of claimants who were *direct* names, this is easily explained by reference to the extended principle in *Hedley Byrne*: that if A indicates to B that he can be safely relied on to perform a particular task with a certain degree of care and skill and B does so rely on A, A will owe B a duty to perform that task with that degree of care and skill. When a name became a member of a syndicate which was managed by the name's underwriting agent – thereby becoming a direct name – the agent contracted with the name that he would run the affairs of the name's syndicate with a certain degree of care and skill and thereby indicated to the name that the name could safely rely on him to run the affairs of the syndicate with that degree of care and skill. The direct name would, in turn, rely on his underwriting agent to run the affairs of his syndicate with that degree of care and skill by agreeing to join the underwriting agent's syndicate and by staying on as a member of that syndicate while the underwriting agent administered its affairs.

In the case of the claimants who were *indirect* names, we can again explain the House of Lords' ruling by reference to the extended principle in *Hedley Byrne*. Before an indirect name became a member of a syndicate managed by a particular managing agent, the managing agent would expressly or impliedly indicate to the name, through the name's underwriting agent, that he could be safely relied on to manage the affairs of his syndicate with a certain degree of care and skill. The indirect name would in turn rely on the managing agent to run the affairs of his syndicate with that degree of care and skill by

---

[191] [1995] 2 AC 145, 176.

[192] This is because the time for bringing an action in contract runs from the moment the contract is breached; whereas the time for bringing an action in negligence runs from the moment the defendant's breach of a duty of care owed to the claimant causes the claimant to suffer an actionable loss.

agreeing to join the managing agent's syndicate and by staying on as a member of the syndicate while the managing agent administered its affairs.

So the ruling of the House of Lords in *Henderson* v *Merrett Syndicates Ltd* that the claimant names could establish that the managing agents of their syndicates owed them a duty to administer the affairs of those syndicates with a certain degree of care and skill can be explained by reference to the principle of law examined here. Seen in this way, the decision in *Henderson* v *Merrett Syndicates Ltd* was, like the decision in *Junior Books*, an outgrowth of the *dicta* in *Hedley Byrne* that were referred to above – and that is, indeed, how the Law Lords who decided *Henderson* v *Merrett Syndicates Ltd* viewed their decision.

6.12 PURE ECONOMIC LOSS (3): *HEDLEY BYRNE* – TWO MISCONCEPTIONS

Before concluding our discussion of *Hedley Byrne* we should briefly pause to note and dismiss two common misconceptions about that case.[193] Both arise out of the twin facts that: (1) in *Hedley Byrne* the claimants suffered a form of pure economic loss; and (2) it was in *Hedley Byrne* that the House of Lords first countenanced the possibility that a claimant might be entitled to sue a defendant in negligence for compensation for some form of pure economic loss that she had suffered as a result of the defendant's actions.

(1) *Hedley Byrne only relevant in pure economic loss cases.* The first misconception is that *Hedley Byrne* is only ever relevant in establishing that a duty of care was owed in a case where a claimant has suffered a form of pure economic loss as a result of a defendant's actions. On this view, in cases where a claimant has suffered some other kind of harm – such as physical injury or psychiatric illness – as a result of a defendant's actions or non-actions, the decision in *Hedley Byrne* will be irrelevant to the inquiry as to whether or not the defendant owed the claimant a duty of care. This is nonsense: there is no sign that the Law Lords in *Hedley Byrne* meant their remarks as to when one person will owe another a duty of care to be confined to cases where a defendant has caused another to suffer a form of pure economic loss.[194]

---

[193] A third possible misconception which some students might entertain is that a duty to take care not to mislead others can only exist in a *Hedley Byrne*-type case. This is obviously incorrect. In the right circumstances, the House of Lords' decision in *Donoghue* v *Stevenson* [1932] AC 562 can operate to impose on someone a duty to take care not to mislead someone else. For example, if a blind man asks you if it is safe to cross the road, you will owe him a duty to take care that you do not tell him that it is safe to cross the road when it is not (it being reasonably foreseeable that if you do so, he will suffer some kind of physical injury as a result). See *Haseldine* v *Daw* [1941] 2 KB 343 (discussed below, § 7.1) for an example of a decision which could be explained on the basis that the defendant breached a duty to take care not to mislead someone else which arose under *Donoghue* v *Stevenson*.

[194] For examples of *physical injury* cases where a claimant will be able to invoke *Hedley Byrne* to establish that a defendant owed her a duty of care, see any medical negligence case that involves a failure to treat a patient with reasonable skill and care; also the case of *Swinney* v *Chief Constable of the Northumbria Police* [1997] QB 464, discussed below, § 7.2. For examples of property damage cases where the claimant was allowed to invoke *Hedley Byrne* to establish that the defendant owed her a duty of care see the Canadian case of *Densmore* v *Whitehorse* [1986] 5 WWR 708 and *Stansbie* v *Troman* [1948] 2 KB 48 (both discussed below, § 7.2) and *Bailey* v *HSS Alarms Ltd, The Times*, 20 June 2000 (failure to protect business from being burgled). A *psychiatric illness* case where *Hedley Byrne* could have been used to establish that the defendant owed the claimant a duty of care is *McLoughlin* v *Grovers* [2002] QB 1312, where the claimant developed a psychiatric illness as a result of being wrongfully convicted of robbery and causing grievous bodily harm; he sued his solicitors for compensation for his illness claiming that he would not have been convicted had they conducted his case with reasonable skill and care; held, that the claimant had an arguable claim against the defendants and his claim should not be struck out.

(2) *Recovery for pure economic loss only allowed in Hedley Byrne cases.* The second misconception is that if a claimant has suffered a form of pure economic loss as a result of a defendant's actions, the claimant will *only* be able to establish that the defendant owed her a duty of care not to act as he did if the House of Lords' decision in *Hedley Byrne* covers her case. So if *Hedley Byrne* does not cover the claimant's case, then the defendant will not have owed the claimant a duty of care.[195] This is, again, nonsense: there is no reason to think that the Law Lords in *Hedley Byrne* were seeking to lay down for all time an exhaustive set of rules as to when a duty of care will be owed in a pure economic loss case. As the House of Lords made clear in *Customs and Excise Commissioners* v *Barclays Bank* (2007), to establish that A owed B a duty of care in a case where B has suffered pure economic loss as a result of A's carelessness, it will be sufficient, *but not necessary*, to show that A assumed a responsibility to B not to be careless.[196]

Unfortunately, the misconception that a claimant can only recover in negligence for pure economic loss if *Hedley Byrne* covers her case is now quite widespread and has given rise to the further misconception that *any* pure economic loss case in the law reports in which the courts found that a duty of care was owed is a '*Hedley Byrne* case'.[197] Anyone labouring under this further misconception will find it quite impossible to come up with an intelligible account as to when one person will owe another a duty of care under *Hedley Byrne*. The reason is that while *most* of the pure economic loss cases in the law reports in which the courts have found that a duty of care was owed *are Hedley Byrne* cases, *not all of them are* – some of those cases rest on quite different principles, which we will explore below. So there is no *single* principle underlying all of the pure economic loss cases in the law reports in which the courts have found that a duty of care was owed and any attempt to discover such a principle will be doomed to failure.

6.13 PURE ECONOMIC LOSS (4): SOME DIFFICULT CASES

There are a number of pure economic loss cases where the courts found that the defendant(s) owed the claimant(s) a duty of care, but it is not possible to say that the duty of care was based on a *Hedley Byrne*-style 'assumption of responsibility'.

A. Property surveys

These cases[198] are concerned with the following kind of situation. *Poor* – who was not particularly well-off – wanted to buy a house. She managed to find a fairly cheap house at

---

[195] For an example of this misconception at work, see the Court of Appeal's decision in *Phelps* v *Hillingdon LBC* [1999] 1 WLR 500, where the claimant sued for compensation for the harm done to her prospects as a result of the defendant's failure to diagnose her as being dyslexic while she was at school. As this was regarded in the Court of Appeal as being a pure economic loss case, it was conceded on all sides that the defendant could *only* have owed the claimant a duty of care in treating her if the decision in *Hedley Byrne* applied to the claimant's case: ibid, 513–14. It was found that it did not as the defendant had not 'assumed a responsibility' to the claimant. The claimant in *Phelps* appealed to the House of Lords, and their Lordships found that a duty of care *was* owed to the claimant: [2001] 2 AC 619. For an explanation of the House of Lords' decision in *Phelps*, see below: § 6.14.

[196] [2007] 1 AC 181, at [4] (per Lord Bingham), [52] (per Lord Rodger), [73] (per Lord Walker), and [93] (per Lord Mance).

[197] One of the authors of this book has not been immune to this misconception in the past: see McBride and Hughes 1995. This second misconception seems to have originated in a misreading of some of the speeches in the House of Lords in *Murphy* v *Brentwood DC* [1991] AC 398. Lord Bridge, for instance, stated (at 475) that 'purely economic [losses are] . . . not recoverable in tort in the absence of a special relationship of proximity . . .' and some have misread this as meaning that purely economic losses are not recoverable in tort in the absence of a special relationship of the kind involved in *Hedley Byrne*-type cases.

[198] *Smith* v *Eric S Bush* [1990] 1 AC 831; *Merrett* v *Babb* [2001] QB 1174.

the bottom end of the property market and applied to *Lender* – a bank or building society or local authority – for a loan to help her buy the house. *Lender* appointed *Surveyor* to survey the house for them to check that the house would provide them with adequate security for the loan. *Surveyor* surveyed the house and reported back that it was worth at least as much as the loan for which *Lender* was applying.

Unfortunately, *Lender* failed to survey the house properly and failed to spot some defects in the house which meant that it was worth much less than *Poor* was proposing to pay for it. *Poor* was too poor to afford her own survey, but was reassured that the house was in good condition when *Lender* approved the loan to her – after all, she thought, if *Lender*'s surveyor had spotted any problems with the house, *Lender* would hardly have agreed to loan her the money she needed to buy it. So *Poor* went ahead and purchased the house with the assistance of the loan from *Lender*. She then discovered that the house was worth much less than she agreed to pay for it.

It is now well established that in this sort of situation, *Surveyor* will have owed *Lender* a duty to survey the house with a reasonable degree of care and skill. It is impossible to explain this result by reference to the extended principle in *Hedley Byrne* because the existence of the duty of care owed by *Surveyor* to *Poor* does not depend on *Surveyor*'s having had any contact with *Poor*.[199]

B. References

In *Spring* v *Guardian Assurance plc* (1995), Spring was employed as a sales director and office manager by Corinium Ltd. Corinium sold life assurance policies on behalf of Guardian Assurance, the defendants. When Corinium was taken over by the defendants, Spring was dismissed. Spring attempted to go into business on his own selling life assurance policies for Scottish Amicable. When he approached Scottish Amicable, that company asked the defendants to supply them with a reference for Spring. Scottish Amicable was obliged to do this under the rules of the Life Assurance and Unit Trust Regulatory Organisation (Lautro), of which Scottish Amicable was a member. The defendants supplied Scottish Amicable with a reference for Spring that stated, among other things, that Spring was 'a man of little or no integrity and could not be regarded as honest'. Unsurprisingly, Scottish Amicable

---

[199] This has been made crystal clear by the decision of the Court of Appeal in *Merrett* v *Babb* [2001] QB 1174. In that case, the claimant, Merrett, lost a lot of money purchasing a defective house with the assistance of a loan from a building society. The building society asked a firm of surveyors to value the house for them and an employee of the firm, Babb, valued the house as being worth at least as much as Merrett was wanting to borrow to buy the house. Before Merrett had a chance to sue the firm of surveyors in negligence, they went out of business. So instead she sued Babb – who had substantial assets – claiming that *he* personally had owed her a duty to survey the house with a reasonable degree of care and skill. By the time *Merrett* was decided, the decision of the House of Lords in *Williams* v *Natural Life Health Foods Ltd* [1998] 1 WLR 830 had made it clear that the existence of contact between a defendant and claimant is essential for a duty of care to arise between the defendant and claimant under *Hedley Byrne*. (See also, on this point, *Mills* v *Winchester Diocesan Board of Finance* [1989] Ch 428, *Mariola Marine Corp* v *Lloyd's Register of Shipping* [1990] 1 Lloyd's Rep 547 and *A & J Fabrication (Batley) Ltd* v *Grant Thornton (a firm)* [1999] PNLR 811.) However, there had been absolutely no contact between Merrett and Babb at the time Babb surveyed the house that Merrett ended up purchasing; indeed, she was not even aware of his identity at that time. Despite this, the Court of Appeal still found that Babb *had* owed Merrett a duty of care in valuing the house and the House of Lords refused leave to appeal: [2001] 1 WLR 1859. So the duty of care in *Merrett* v *Babb* and the other survey cases *cannot* be explained by reference to the extended principle in *Hedley Byrne*. Of course, those who have fallen into the trap of thinking that *all* pure economic loss cases where a defendant has been held to have owed a claimant a duty of care are *Hedley Byrne* cases cannot but think that there is some conflict between the decisions in *Williams* v *Natural Life* and *Merrett* v *Babb*. There is, of course, no conflict: the *Williams* case was concerned with when one person will owe another a duty of care under *Hedley Byrne*; the duty of care in *Merrett* v *Babb* arose for some other reason.

declined to allow Spring to sell life assurance policies on its behalf. The same thing happened when Spring approached two other life assurance companies and for the same reason.

Spring sued the defendants in negligence, arguing that the defendants had owed him, and breached, a duty to use reasonable skill and care in supplying his prospective employers with references about him. The House of Lords found that the defendants had owed Spring such a duty of care. Why was this? It is impossible to explain this result on the basis that the defendants owed Spring such a duty under the extended principle in *Hedley Byrne*.[200] The defendants never indicated to Spring that he could safely rely on them to use reasonable skill and care in preparing references about him for prospective employers; and even if they did Spring never did anything in the expectation that they would act in that way. It would have been different if Spring had asked the defendants if he could give his prospective employers their name as a possible source of references and the defendants had agreed that he could. The defendants, by agreeing to supply Spring with a reference, would have implicitly indicated to him that he could safely rely on them to supply his prospective employers with references that were prepared with a reasonable degree of care and skill and Spring would have so relied on them by telling his prospective employers that they could ask the defendants for a reference about him. But this was not the case here. In *Spring*, the references supplied by the defendants were asked for, and supplied, over Spring's head.

C. Diagnosis of special needs

In *Phelps v Hillingdon London Borough Council* (2001), the claimant suffered from (undiagnosed) dyslexia and as a result suffered severe learning difficulties at school. In an attempt to find out what was wrong, the claimant was sent at age 11 to an educational psychologist to be tested. The psychologist failed to notice that the claimant was dyslexic; she reported that the claimant suffered from no specific weaknesses and suggested that the source of the claimant's learning difficulties was a lack of confidence. She recommended that action be taken to boost the claimant's confidence in her abilities. With her dyslexia undiagnosed, the claimant continued to experience learning difficulties and left school at age 16 with no GCSEs.

Shortly after the claimant left school, her parents paid for her to be tested again and this time around the claimant's dyslexia was diagnosed. The claimant sued the defendants, the psychologist's employers, claiming that the psychologist had owed her, and breached, a duty to test her with a reasonable degree of care and skill and that the defendants were vicariously liable in respect of the psychologist's negligence. The House of Lords held that the educational psychologist had indeed owed the claimant a duty to test her with a reasonable degree of skill and care.

It is impossible to explain this result by reference to *Hedley Byrne*. As Stuart-Smith LJ observed when deciding the case in the Court of Appeal:

> [The first instance] judge did not ask himself the question whether [the educational psychologist] had voluntarily assumed responsibility for advising the [claimant] through her parents. [The educational psychologist's] duty was to advise the school and the local authority. Merely because the [claimant] was the object of that advice and the parents were told in effect what the advice was, does not in my judgement amount to such an assumption of responsibility.[201]

---

[200] Admittedly, Lord Goff thought that this *was* a *Hedley Byrne* case ([1995] 2 AC 296, at 316) and Lord Lowry agreed with him (at 325). However, none of the other Law Lords agreed.

[201] [1999] 1 WLR 500, 519. Otton LJ agreed: 'the [claimant] has not shown that [the educational psychologist] assumed responsibility to the [claimant] to prevent her from sustaining such loss or damage as may be recoverable.'

The House of Lords' finding that a duty of care was owed in *Phelps* must have rested on some other basis than that the educational psychologist 'assumed a responsibility' to the claimant.[202]

D. Wills

In *White* v *Jones* (1995),[203] B quarrelled with his two daughters over his deceased wife's will. As a result, he made a will in which he left them nothing. Three months later – in June 1986 – he was reconciled with his daughters and resolved to make a new will under which his two daughters would receive £9,000 each. On 17 July 1986 he instructed the defendant solicitors to draw up a new will in those terms. By 14 September 1986, when B died, the defendant solicitors had still not got around to drawing up B's new will, so the daughters received nothing from B's estate. B's daughters sued the defendant solicitors in negligence, arguing that the defendants had owed them a duty to draw up B's new will with a reasonable degree of care and skill; that the defendants had breached that duty in taking so long over drawing up the will; and that had the defendants not breached that duty, they would have inherited £9,000 each from B's estate. By a bare majority, the House of Lords allowed the daughters' claim.

It is impossible to explain the House of Lords' decision that the defendant solicitors owed B's daughters a duty of care by reference to *Hedley Byrne*. Of course, the defendant solicitors owed B a duty to draw up his will with a reasonable degree of care and skill, as he had asked them to draw up the will, in the full expectation that they would do so competently, and the defendant solicitors had agreed to take on the job. But the defendants never indicated to the *claimants* that they could be relied on and indeed the claimants did not rely on the defendants to draw up the will with a reasonable degree of skill and care; the claimants, for example, did not both go out and buy new cars in the expectation that they would receive £9,000 each under B's will. There was in fact no contact between the defendants and the claimants. So there was no 'assumption of responsibility' by the defendants to the claimants that would have justified a finding that the defendants owed the claimants a duty of care under *Hedley Byrne*.

E. Loss of land rights

In *Ministry of Housing* v *Sharp* (1970), the owner of some land was refused permission to develop his land by the Ministry of Housing, and was awarded £1,828 in compensation. (This would be the equivalent of about £30,000 today.) The refusal of permission to develop the land was later reversed, which meant the Ministry of Housing acquired a charge over the land for the money it had paid the owner, and which was now liable to be repaid. Before the money was repaid, the land was sold to developers. The developers who were buying the land asked the defendants to do a search of the local land charges register and tell them what charges existed over the land. The defendants did not inform the developers of the Ministry of Housing's charge over the land. This meant that when the

---

[202] Perhaps for that reason, Lord Slynn criticised in *Phelps* the idea that 'there has to be an assumption of responsibility by the person concerned. That phrase can be misleading in that it can suggest that the professional person must knowingly and deliberately accept responsibility . . . The phrase means simply that the law recognises that there is a duty of care. It is not so much that responsibility is assumed as that it is recognised or imposed by the law': [2001] 2 AC 619, 654.

[203] Criticised, Weir 1995; also Klar 1998, 317–19.

land was sold to the developers, it came to them free of the Ministry of Housing's charge. The Ministry of Housing sued the defendants in negligence for compensation for the loss of their charge. The Court of Appeal held that the defendants had owed the Ministry a duty of care in responding to the developers' query about land charges. The decision cannot be explained on the basis of *Hedley Byrne* as the defendants never assumed a responsibility to the Ministry of Housing to act carefully in responding to the developers' request for information about what charges existed over the land they were buying.

F. Sterilisation of business

In a number of cases, a local authority or public official has carelessly misused its powers with the result that a business has not been allowed to carry on trading.

In *Harris* v *Evans* (1998), Harris used a mobile telescopic crane to provide bungee jumping facilities to members of the public. Evans was a health and safety inspector who inspected the crane when it was on a site in Devon. Evans recommended to the local council that Harris not be allowed to use the crane until it had been certified as fit to be used for bungee jumping. The council acted on Evans's recommendation and forbade Harris to use his crane until he had obtained such a certificate. It was, in fact, impossible – and also completely unnecessary for the purposes of ensuring the public's health and safety – for Harris to obtain such a certificate, and so Harris found himself unable to offer bungee jumping facilities at the site in Devon. Nor could he do so anywhere else: on Evans's initiative, a neighbouring council warned Harris not to offer bungee jumping facilities at any site within their jurisdiction until he had obtained the right certificate for his crane; and when Harris tried to set up shop at another site, the local council that was in charge of that site forbade Harris from doing so (again, presumably at Evans's instigation). Harris went to court and it was held that Harris need not obtain a certificate saying that his crane was suitable to be used for bungee jumping in order to use the crane. At that stage, Harris had been put out of business for roughly three months.

Harris sued Evans in negligence for compensation for the economic loss he had suffered as a result of Evans's incompetence. The Court of Appeal rejected his claim, holding that Evans had not owed Harris a duty of care. The Court of Appeal held that it would be contrary to the public interest to find that a duty of care was owed in this situation:

> The duty of enforcing authorities, whether inspectors or local authorities, is to have regard to the health and safety of members of the public. If steps which they think should be taken to improve safety would have an adverse economic effect on the business enterprise in question, so be it. A tortious duty which rendered them potentially liable for economic damage to the business enterprise caused by the steps they were recommending to be taken would, in my judgment, be very likely to engender untoward cautiousness and the temptation [to postpone making a decision until further inquiries have been made in the hope of getting more concrete facts].[204]

For much the same reason, the House of Lords denied that a duty of care was owed in *Jain* v *Trent Strategic HA* (2009). That case arose out of s 23(1) of the Registered Homes Act 1984, which made it a criminal offence to carry on a 'nursing home or a mental nursing home' without being registered. The claimants in the *Jain* case ran a nursing home which

---

[204] [1998] 1 WLR 1285, 1298 (per Sir Richard Scott V-C). The passage in square brackets is a quote from Lord Browne-Wilkinson's judgment in *X* v *Bedfordshire CC* [1995] AC 633, 750 to which Scott V-C referred at the end of this passage.

was closed down after the defendant local authority applied to a magistrate to have its registration as a nursing home withdrawn. The hearing lasted 25 minutes, at which the defendant local authority made various misleading allegations about the claimants' nursing home, all of which were designed to convince the magistrate hearing the case that the safety or even lives of residents staying at the nursing home were in danger.[205] The claimants had no chance to rebut these allegations as the hearing was an *ex parte* hearing – which means that only one party to the case (here, the defendant authority) appears in court. Unsurprisingly, the magistrate issued the order that the nursing home's registration be withdrawn, with the result that the claimants' nursing home had to close down with immediate effect.

The claimants applied to have the order set aside, and this was done by the Registered Homes Tribunal, which made some scathing criticisms of the conduct of the defendant authority. By then four months had passed and it proved to be impossible to get the nursing home up and running again. The claimants sued the defendant local authority in negligence. The House of Lords dismissed the claim, finding that it would be contrary to the public interest to find that a duty of care was owed in this case, for precisely the same reason as the Court of Appeal had declined to find a duty of care in the *Harris* case: if local authorities knew that they could be sued if they improperly closed down a nursing home on health and safety grounds, that could have the effect of making local authorities over-cautious in discharging their main function, that of protecting the health and welfare of residents of nursing homes.

While *Harris* and *Jain* were cases where the courts denied that the defendants owed the claimants a duty of care, what is interesting about those cases for our purposes here is that the courts in these cases refused to find a duty of care because they thought it would be contrary to the public interest to find such a duty. That implies that they *would have been willing* to find that a duty of care was owed if such a finding did not have any negative implications for the public interest. The impression is reinforced by the fact that four of the Law Lords who decided *Jain* went out of their way to express their 'regret' that they could not find a way that the claimants could sue the defendants under the law of negligence,[206] and attempted to point out possible arguments that the claimants could make in the European Court of Human Rights if they wanted to pursue a claim that the defendants had infringed their rights under the ECHR in that court.[207]

Given this, it is interesting to note another 'business sterilisation' case where the defendant was not a public body, but a company. This was the Australian case of *Perre* v *Apand Pty Ltd* (1999). That case concerned a set of potato farms located in South Australia. The potatoes grown on these farms would be exported to Western Australia, where the price of potatoes was particularly high. One of the farms was occupied by the Sparnon family. The defendants sold the Sparnons potato seed that the defendants ought to have known was diseased. The potatoes that grew from the seed on the Sparnon farm suffered

---

[205] For example, the defendants alleged that there had been 12 deaths in the claimants' nursing home since February 1998 and seven of those deaths had been reported to the police. (In fact, 11 of those deaths were due to natural causes and six of the seven deaths that had been reported to the police were reported because there was a statutory duty to do so where a resident had died without seeing a doctor in the 14 days before his or her death.)

[206] [2009] 1 AC 853, at [40] (per Lord Scott), [48] (per Baroness Hale), [52] (per Lord Carswell), and [53] (per Lord Neuberger).

[207] [2009] 1 AC 853, [38]–[39] (per Lord Scott), [43]–[45] (per Baroness Hale), [54] (per Lord Neuberger). The claimants could not bring a claim under the Human Rights Act 1998 in this case, as the 1998 Act only came into force on 2 October 2000, some time after the events in this case (which occurred in September 1998).

from a disease called 'bacterial wilt'. Under the Plant Diseases Act 1914, potatoes could not be imported into Western Australia from any farm within 20 km of an outbreak of bacterial wilt for five years. As a result, when bacterial wilt was detected on the Sparnon farm, the claimants – whose farms were based about 3 km from the Sparnon farm – found themselves cut off from the lucrative Western Australia potato market for five years.[208] The claimants sued the defendants in negligence for compensation for their loss of profits. The High Court of Australia allowed the claim. In finding that the defendants had owed the claimants a duty to take care not to sell the Sparnons diseased potato seed, the High Court emphasised the claimants' degree of vulnerability to having their business interfered with if the defendants sold diseased potato seed to one of the claimants' neighbours.[209]

The decision in *Perre* can be compared with the decision of Tugendhat J in *Pride & Partners* v *Institute of Animal Health* (2009), where the claimants were farmers who suffered business losses as a result of an outbreak of foot and mouth disease (FMD) and consequent government-imposed restrictions on the movement of farm animals. The claimants alleged that the FMD virus that was responsible for the outbreak of FMD had escaped from the defendants' laboratories. The claimants cited *Perre* as authority in favour of the proposition that the defendants had owed the claimants a duty to take care not to allow a FMD virus to escape from their laboratories. The defendants conceded that they did owe the claimants such a duty of care, but argued that that duty was geared towards protecting the claimants' animals from being harmed.[210] The defendants denied that they owed the claimants an equivalent duty of care that was geared towards protecting the claimants' businesses from being harmed. Tugendhat J agreed with the defendants. He distinguished the *Perre* case from the *Pride & Partners* case on the basis that the duty of care in *Perre* was only owed to farmers based within 20 km of the Sparnon farm, whereas the suggested duty of care in *Pride & Partners* would have been owed to *every livestock farmer in Britain* whose living was affected by FMD-triggered movement restrictions.[211] Clearly, a finding that the defendants owed a duty of care to the claimants that was geared towards protecting the claimants' businesses would have exposed the defendants to a huge number of claims, and their liability would have spiralled out all proportion to their (supposed) fault in allowing the FMD virus to escape the confines of their laboratory.

Taken together, all of the above cases *may* be taken as indicating that in a 'business sterilisation' case, the UK courts *may* be willing to find that a duty of care was owed if: (i) the defendant has wrecked the claimant's business through a positive and illegitimate act, (ii) the claimant was powerless to protect himself against what the defendant did, (iii)

---

[208] This fact makes *Perre* different from *Jain*, and a weaker case than *Jain* for the imposition of a duty of care: the claimants lost their business in *Jain*, whereas the claimants' business was merely made less profitable in *Perre*. The same distinction marks the difference between the *Jain* case and the case of *Neil Martin Ltd* v *Commissioners for Her Majesty's Revenue and Customs* [2007] EWCA Civ 1041, where the claimant subcontractor sued the defendant tax authorities for failing to give him a tax certificate promptly enough, which certificate would have enabled contractors to pay him without deducting tax. Because deducting tax from payments made to subcontractors and handing that deducted tax over to the government involved a lot of hassle for contractors, the lack of such a tax certificate made contractors less willing to hire the claimant to work for them. The claimant's claim was dismissed on the ground that when Parliament set up the scheme for awarding tax certificates, it imposed a duty on the defendants to award tax certificates to those qualifying for them, *not* a duty to award those certificates promptly. The Court of Appeal held that it was not within their power to do what Parliament had chosen not to, and impose on the defendants via the law of negligence a duty to award the claimant his tax certificate within a reasonable period of time.

[209] (1999) 198 CLR 180, at [10]–[15] (per Gleeson CJ), [38] (per Gaudron J), [50] and [123]–[124] (per McHugh J), [216] (per Gummow J), [296] (per Kirby J).

[210] [2009] EWHC (QB) 685, at [110].

[211] [2009] EWHC (QB) 685, at [115]–[116].

finding that the defendant owed the claimant a duty of care would not expose the defendant to 'liability in an indeterminate amount for an indeterminate time to an indeterminate class'[212] and (iv) finding that the defendant owed the claimant a duty of care not to act as he did would not be contrary to the public interest.[213] Naturally, if the UK courts did find a duty of care was owed in such a case, that finding could not be explained by reference to the extended principle in *Hedley Byrne*.

G. General average

In *Morrison Steamship* v *Greystoke Castle (cargo owners)* (1947), a collision occurred between two ships, the *Cheldale* and the *Greystoke Castle*. It was determined that the *Cheldale* was 25% to blame for the collision. After the collision, the *Greystoke Castle* had to put into port for repairs, and in the course of those repairs, the cargo aboard the *Greystoke Castle* had to be unloaded from the ship and then reloaded. Under the maritime principle of 'general average', when one of the parties in a sea venture has suffered a loss as part of that venture, the other parties are obliged to take on a proportionate share of that loss. So here: the owner of the *Greystoke Castle* incurred expense in unloading and reloading the cargo aboard the *Greystoke Castle*, and under the principle of 'general average' the owners of that cargo had to reimburse the owner for a proportionate share of that expense.

The claimants owned cargo aboard the *Greystoke Castle* and ended up being liable to pay the owner of *Greystoke Castle* about £18,000 as their contribution to the owner's 'general average expenditure' in unloading and reloading cargo aboard the *Greystoke Castle*. The claimants claimed 25% of that amount from the defendants, the owners of the *Cheldale*, as that was how much the owners of the *Cheldale* were to blame for the 'general average contribution' that the claimants had to pay the owner of the *Greystoke Castle*. This was a 'relational economic loss' case: the claimants had suffered pure economic loss as a result of the defendants' damaging property (here, the *Greystoke Castle*) that belonged to someone else. As we have seen, there was and is a long line of authority that denied a duty of care would be owed to a claimant in a 'relational economic loss' case where there was no prior relationship between the defendant and the claimant.[214] Despite this, the House of Lords held by a 3:2 majority that the claimants could sue the defendant here.

About 45 years later, Lord Keith of Kinkel would attempt to limit the decision in the *Greystoke Castle* case by observing in *Murphy* v *Brentwood DC* (1991) that: 'That case, which was decided by a narrow majority, may . . . be regarded as turning on specialties of maritime law concerned in the relationship of joint adventurers at sea.'[215] However, one of the majority speeches took the view that the decision could apply on land, as well as at sea:

> if two lorries A and B are meeting one another on the road, I cannot bring myself to doubt that the driver of lorry A owes a duty to both the owner of lorry B and to the owner of goods carried on lorry B. Those owners are engaged in a common adventure . . . and if lorry A is negligently driven and damages lorry B so severely that whilst no damage is done to the goods in it the goods have to be unloaded for repair of the lorry and then reloaded or carried forward in some other way and the consequent expense is by reason of his contract or otherwise the expense of the goods owner, then in my judgment the goods owner has a direct cause of action to recover such expense.[216]

---

[212] *Ultramares Corporation* v *Touche*, 174 NE 441 (1931), per Cardozo CJ.
[213] For further discussion, see Bagshaw 2009a.
[214] See above, § 5.3, fn 30.
[215] [1991] 1 AC 398, 468.
[216] [1947] AC 265, 280 (per Lord Roche).

Lord Simonds, in the minority, vehemently insisted that on land, at least, in 'relational economic loss' cases there can be no action by someone suffering pure economic loss against a stranger who has caused that loss by harming a third party or property belonging to a third party:

> A and B embark upon a joint adventure on the Great North Road. It is an adventure which cannot be successfully prosecuted unless both of them remain sound in wind and limb. Before it has ended, A is incapacitated by the tortious act of X: the adventure is abandoned and B suffers a loss. No one, I suppose, would contend that B had a right of action against X. I carry it one stage further. A and B, knowing the hazards of their adventure, agree that, if either of them suffers injury, the other will contribute to his loss. Again, A is injured by the tortious act of X. B accordingly pays A his stipulated contribution. Again B has no cause of action against X. This, my Lords, I take to be unquestionably the law of the land . . .[217]

It is still uncertain whether the UK courts would apply the *Greystoke Castle* to such 'joint ventures on land' cases.

6.14 PURE ECONOMIC LOSS (5): EXPLANATION OF THE DIFFICULT CASES

Having set out these exceptions to the normal rule that there is no duty of care in a pure economic loss case absent an 'assumption of responsibility' by the defendant to the claimant, we could simply move on and stop discussing these exceptions. Some students will be tempted to wish that we would do this, and start talking about when A will owe B a duty of care to *save* B from suffering some kind of harm (the topic of the next chapter). But it would be remiss of us not to attempt to explain *why* a duty of care will be owed in the above cases. Such an explanation is needed for two reasons.

First of all, we cannot understand how far these cases go, and what they *actually* tell us about when one person will owe another a duty of care, without an explanation of why a duty of care will be owed in these cases. For example, in *Goodwill v British Pregnancy Advisory Service* (1996), the claimant was a woman who had been made pregnant as a result of having unprotected sex with a man who was supposed to have had a vasectomy performed upon him by the defendants. Counsel for the claimant sought to argue that the House of Lords' decision in *White v Jones* (1995) indicated that the defendants owed the claimant a duty to carry out the vasectomy with a reasonable degree of care and skill. In order to see whether that argument is right or wrong, we have to be able to explain *why* a duty of care will be owed in a *White v Jones*-type situation. Once we can do this, we can see whether that explanation also applies to indicate that a duty of care will also be owed in a *Goodwill*-type case.

Secondly, we won't be able to tell whether or not the courts were right to find that a duty of care was owed in the above cases unless we can first come up with a convincing explanation as to why the courts might have found that a duty of care was owed in these cases. Once we have come up with such an explanation, then we will be in a position to see whether there is *actually* a good reason for finding a duty of care in these cases, or whether the best reason we can come up with for finding a duty of care in such cases is simply not good enough.

In trying to come up with an explanation as to why a duty of care will be owed in the cases set out above, we need to follow certain rules of thumb:[218]

---

[217] [1947] AC 265, 307.
[218] The first two rules are heavily indebted to that part of Ronald Dworkin's theory of law that explains how courts spell out from the decided cases underlying 'principles' that guide their decisions in other cases. See, generally, Dworkin 1986.

(1) Our explanation should fit the decided cases. We should try to avoid coming up with an explanation of why a duty of care was owed in *Spring* v *Guardian Assurance Ltd* (1995) that suggests *Spartan Steel & Co Ltd* v *Martin* (1973) was wrongly decided. Of course, some cases may be wrongly decided. But we should have a prejudice in favour of explanations that do not require us to conclude that the judges have gone wrong in large numbers of cases.

(2) Our explanation should be morally appealing. We should have a prejudice in favour of explanations that do not require us to conclude that a large number of judges are vicious, or mercenaries, or prejudiced, or class warriors. If we have to choose between an explanation of the decision in *White* v *Jones* (1995) which says the ex-barrister Law Lords who decided the case were biased against solicitors, and the explanation of that decision offered below, then we should prefer the explanation offered below.

(3) The judges' own explanations as to how they reached their decisions are no more worthy of respect than anyone else's. The correct explanation as to why a duty of care will be owed in a *Smith* v *Eric S Bush*-type case may be very different from the explanation that any of the judges who decided that case may have offered. Lord Goff, speaking extra-judicially, has characterised the 'judicial act ... as an educated reflex to facts ...'[219] But a judge who experiences a certain reflex to a certain set of facts may not be in the best position to explain *why* he or she experiences that reflex. It depends on the judge's degree of insight and articulacy – and some judges are less insightful and articulate than others.

(4) We should not think that *all* of the above cases can be explained in the *same* way. It is just as likely that *some* of them can be explained in one way, and others can be explained in another way. We should not fall foul of what Lord Goff – speaking extra-judicially on another occasion[220] – called 'the temptation of elegance': of finding *one* rule, *one* principle, *one* idea that can account for *everything*. In fact, the best explanation we can come up with for the above cases is a complex one, where different cases are explained in different ways. Our explanation goes as follows:

A. Severe dependency as a basis for a duty of care

Some of the above cases can be explained on the basis that if A knows that B's future will be ruined if he does a positive act *x*, then A will owe B a duty to take care not to do *x*. This – we would contend – is the best explanation of why a duty of care will be owed in the survey cases, in a *Spring*-type situation, and a *Phelps*-type situation. In each of these cases, the claimant's future was in the defendant's hands,[221] and the defendant knew it, and the defendant ruined their future by doing something positive. In *Smith* v *Eric S Bush* (1990),

---

[219] Goff 1986, 4.
[220] Goff 1983, 174.
[221] The contention that the claimants' future in *Phelps* and so on was in the defendants' hands prompts recall of a story that students may enjoy. Gerry Spence, the great American trial lawyer, customarily tells juries this story in his closing argument, before handing over to the jury the responsibility of doing justice in the case: 'It's a story of a wise old man and a smart-aleck boy who wanted to show up the wise old man as a fool. One day this boy caught a small bird in the forest. The boy had a plan. He brought the bird, cupped between his hands, to the old man. His plan was to say, "Old man, what do I have in my hands?" to which the old man would answer, "You have a bird, my son." Then the boy would say, "Old man, is the bird alive or is it dead?" If the old man said the bird was dead, the boy would open his hands and the bird would fly freely back to the forest. But if the old man said the bird was alive, then the boy would crush the little bird, and crush it, and crush it until it was dead. So the smart-aleck boy sauntered up to the old man and said, "Old man, what do I have in my hands?" And the old man said, "You have a bird, my son." Then the boy said with a malevolent grin, "Old man, is the bird alive or is it dead?" And the old man, with sad eyes, said, "The bird is in your hands, my son."'

and the other survey cases, it was reporting back to the building society that the house the claimant was thinking of buying needed no essential repairs, when it did. In *Spring* (1995), it was telling the claimant's prospective employer that the claimant was 'a man of little or no integrity and could not be regarded as honest'. In *Phelps* (2001), it was reporting back to the claimant's school that the claimant was not dyslexic but was merely suffering from confidence problems.

In each of these cases, the claimant could not afford for the defendant to do what the defendant did, and the defendant knew it. This was literally the case in *Smith v Eric S Bush*, where the claimant was (as the defendant well knew) buying a house at the lower end of the property market and could therefore have been expected by the defendant both to have not enough money to employ his own surveyor, and to be financially ruined if he ended up buying a house that turned out to be worth a lot less than he paid for it, or that needed a lot of money spending on it to make it habitable. This was also the case in *Spring*, where the claimant simply could not get a job in the industry where he made his living without the support of the defendants, as under the rules of life insurance industry, he could not be employed without his employer soliciting a reference from the defendants. And this was obviously the case in *Phelps*, where the claimant's prospects of leaving school with a decent set of qualifications crucially depended on her getting a correct diagnosis of her educational difficulties from the defendant psychologist.

If this explanation of these cases is right, two things follow. *First*, a duty of care should only be owed in a survey case where the surveyor knew that his survey would be relied on by the purchaser,[222] and that the purchaser would suffer a devastating financial loss if the survey turned out to be wrong.[223] Both conditions should be satisfied in a case where the surveyed property is a house, at the bottom end of the market. Neither condition will be satisfied if the surveyed property is a block of offices, or an expensive house: in such a case, the surveyor could expect the purchaser to employ someone to survey the property, and will have no reason to expect that his survey will be relied upon, or reason to think that if he gets his survey wrong, the purchaser will suffer a devastating economic loss.[224] That this is correct has recently been confirmed by the Court of Appeal in *Scullion v Bank of Scotland plc* (2011). In that case, the claimant was an investor who bought a flat, intending to let it out to tenants. He did not bother to have a surveyor assess the flat's capital value and for how much it could realistically expect to be rented out. Instead, he relied on the report on these matters prepared by the defendants for the bank that lent the claimant the money he needed to buy the flat. When the investment turned out to be a bad one, the claimant sued the defendants in negligence, arguing that their report had been carelessly prepared. His

---

[222] *Smith v Eric S Bush* [1990] 1 AC 831, at 865 (per Lord Griffiths): 'The necessary proximity arises from the surveyor's knowledge that the overwhelming probability is that the purchaser will rely upon his valuation . . .'; to the same effect, see *Smith v Eric S Bush* [1990] 1 AC 831, at 844 (per Lord Templeman) and 871–2 (per Lord Jauncey of Tullichettle), and also *Caparo Industries plc v Dickman* [1990] 2 AC 605, at 638–9 (per Lord Oliver of Aylmerton) and 657, 661 (per Lord Jauncey of Tullichettle).

[223] Cf. Hoffmann J in *Morgan Crucible Co v Hill Samuel Co* [1991] Ch 295, at 303: 'the typical plaintiff in a *Smith*-type case is a person of modest means and making the most expensive purchase of his or her life.'

[224] Stapleton 1991 seems to think (at 277–83) that it is hard to understand why a duty of care will be owed in a survey case when a builder of a house will *not* owe a subsequent purchaser of the house a duty to build that house with a reasonable degree of care and skill. In fact, as Stapleton 1995 seems to recognise (at 335–7) there is no contradiction here. The reason why a builder will not owe a subsequent purchaser of a house a duty to build that house with a reasonable degree of care and skill is that the builder – at the time he was building the house – will not *know* that if he does a bad job, a subsequent purchaser will definitely be made drastically worse off as a result. This is because there are ways that a subsequent purchaser of a house can protect herself against the risk that the house will turn out to be no good – for example, by having the house surveyed or by taking out insurance.

claim was dismissed: the defendants had had no reason to think that the claimant would rely on their report, and had therefore not owed the claimant a duty of care.

Secondly, the Court of Appeal was *wrong* to rule in *Kapfunde* v *Abbey National plc* (1999) that the decision of the House of Lords in *Spring* v *Guardian Assurance plc* (1995) had no application to a case where the claimant was sent by her prospective employers for a medical check-up and lost the job that would otherwise have been hers because the doctor told her prospective employers (wrongly) that the claimant was likely to have a higher than average rate of absence from work.[225] The Court of Appeal thought *Spring* had no application in *Kapfunde* because the basis of the duty of care in *Spring* was the prior relationship between the claimant and defendant as employee and employer. In fact, a close reading of *Spring* reveals that the defendant was not technically ever the claimant's employer, because there was no contractual relationship between them.[226]

The true basis of the decision in *Spring*, it is suggested, was identified by Lord Lowry in *Spring* as lying in

> the probability, often amounting to a certainty, of damage to the individual [resulting from a bad reference] which in some cases will be serious and may indeed be irreparable. The entire future prosperity and happiness of someone who is the subject of a damaging reference which is given carelessly but in perfectly good faith may be irretrievably blighted.[227]

Given this, there seems no reason why *Spring* should not extend to:

(1) The set of facts presented in *Kapfunde*.

(2) The set of facts presented in *McKie* v *Swindon College* (2011), where the claimant had enjoyed a number of happy years working at Swindon College and had just been appointed to a job at the University of Bath, when – for no reason anyone could ever fathom – two employees at Swindon egged on Swindon's human resources manager to warn his counterpart at Bath that there had been a number of concerns about the claimant (both in terms of student safety and his relationship with colleagues) while he worked at Swindon. There had not been. The result of the warning was that the claimant was summarily dismissed from his job at Bath. It was held that Swindon College had owed the claimant a duty of care not to ruin unnecessarily his relationship with the University of Bath, and had been put in breach of that duty by the foolish actions of its employees.

(3) The set of facts presented in the Canadian case of *Haskett* v *Trans Union of Canada* (2003), where the claimant was denied credit because the credit reporting agency wrongly reported that the claimant was a bad credit risk. The Ontario Court of Appeal invoked *Spring* as authority for finding that the credit reporting agency had owed the claimant a duty of care in this case, observing that 'Credit is an integral part of everyday life in today's society. Not only people seeking loans, mortgages, insurance or car leases, but those who wish, for example, to rent an apartment or even obtain employment may be the subject of a credit report . . . Without credit, one is unable to conduct any financial transactions over the telephone or on the internet.'[228]

---

[225] Contrast the case of *Everett* v *Griffiths* [1920] 3 KB 163, where it was suggested (at 182) that a doctor examining a patient on behalf of the authorities to determine whether or not the patient should be committed for psychiatric treatment will owe the patient a duty to take care not to diagnose him as in need of treatment when he is not in need.

[226] [1995] 2 AC 296, 315 (per Lord Goff).

[227] [1995] 2 AC 296, 326.

[228] (2003) 224 DLR (4th) 419, at [29].

B. Business sterilisation

It may be that our rationale for the decision of the House of Lords in *Spring* (and *Phelps*, and *Smith* v *Eric S Bush*) also explains why a duty of care *might* be found in a business sterilisation case where (1) the defendant has wrecked the claimant's business through a positive and illegitimate act, (2) the claimant was powerless to protect himself against what the defendant did, (3) finding that the defendant owed the claimant a duty of care would not expose the defendant to 'liability in an indeterminate amount for an indeterminate time to an indeterminate class' and (4) finding that the defendant owed the claimant a duty of care not to act as he did would not be contrary to the public interest. On this view, just as finding a duty of care in *Spring* protects people's significant interests in being allowed to make a living by being employed *by someone else*, finding a duty of care in a 'business sterilisation' case protects people's significant interests in being allowed to make a living through *self-employment*.

If this is right, then a duty of care should only be owed in a 'business sterilisation' case where the claimant is a *real* person who has been deprived of his living by someone else's carelessness. It is noticeable that in all of the 'business sterilisation' cases mentioned above, this condition was satisfied: the claimant was a real person (or a company with a real person as the sole owner) whose living was dependent on his business not being interfered with by the defendant. And it is hard to imagine that the High Court of Australia would have gone out of its way to find a duty of care in *Perre* v *Apand Pty Ltd* (1999) if the claimant had been a multi-national company, one of whose potato farms had become a temporarily less lucrative operation because diseased potato seed had been planted in a neighbouring farm.

One of us has suggested a more limited rationale for finding a duty of care in at least some 'business sterilisation' cases.[229] On this view, having your business made illegal can be treated as a distinct form of damage from pure economic loss, in that a claimant whose business has been made illegal has not just suffered a pure economic loss, but has had his freedom under the law limited. Such an explanation provides a nice fit with the 'business sterilisation' cases, but its moral appeal remains to be established. Is a case where someone is legally not allowed to carry on his business more deserving of the law's intervention than a case where someone is legally allowed to carry on his business, but simply cannot because someone has unlawfully cut off his power supply?

C. Intermeddling

Whether or not the 'business sterilisation' cases can be explained by reference to the same ideas that – we argue – underlie decisions such as the ones in *Smith* v *Eric S Bush* (1991), *Spring* (1995) and *Phelps* (2001), those ideas *cannot* work to explain the decision of the House of Lords that a duty of care was owed in *White* v *Jones* (1995). As the claimants in that case only stood to inherit £9,000 each under their father's will, it can hardly be said that the solicitor who took on the job of drawing up that will knew that the claimants'

---

[229] See Bagshaw 2009a.

future was in his hands when he did so.[230] The best[231] explanation of the decision in *White* v *Jones* that we can come up with goes as follows.

White v *Jones* applies in a case where A wanted to confer a benefit on B, and C undertakes to assist A in conferring that benefit on B,[232] but C's carelessness in assisting A ends up *preventing* A from conferring that benefit on B.[233] In such a case, C will be found to have owed B a duty to be careful in assisting A. The basis of the duty is the fact that B would have had the benefit that A wanted to confer her but for C's intermeddling. As a result, C's unhelpful assistance amounted to a kind of theft, or destruction, of a benefit that – morally, though not legally – belonged to B.

If this is right, then a number of things follow:

(1) *White* v *Jones* will *not* apply in a case where A employs C to convey a parcel of land to B, but due to C's incompetence, the conveyance does not go through, and A subsequently changes his mind and refuses to try again to convey the land to B.[234] In such a case, C's carelessness will not have *prevented* A from conveying the land to B; it will merely have given A a chance to change his mind.

[230] A subtle argument that might be made in favour of thinking that the duty of care in *White* v *Jones* could be based on such an idea goes as follows: 'Had the claimants been left *a house* under the will, the solicitors would have known *in that case* that if they performed the job of drawing up the will badly, the future well-being of the claimants would have been radically impaired, and we could have found that the solicitors owed the claimants a duty of care in that case on the basis of authorities like *Spring* and *Phelps* and *Smith* v *Eric S Bush*. Now – the law would become intolerably uncertain if it said that a solicitor will owe a duty of care in drawing up a will to those who are due to inherit a "large" legacy under the will, but not to those who are due to inherit a "small" legacy. So the only thing we can do in a *White* v *Jones* situation is to say that if A is instructed to draw up a will under which B is due to inherit a legacy, A will owe B a duty to draw up that will with a reasonable degree of care and skill, whatever the size of the legacy B is due to receive under the will.' The problem with this argument is that it rests on an unjustified premise: even if the claimants in *White* v *Jones* had been due to receive a house under their father's will, it is hard to see why the claimants' future well-being would have been radically *impaired* had the solicitors done a bad job of drawing up that will. They would merely have missed out on a large bonus.

[231] Lord Browne-Wilkinson suggested in *White* v *Jones* that the basis of the defendant's duty was the fact that when the defendant took on the job of drawing up the will, he knew that the claimants' future economic welfare was dependent on his doing that job properly: [1995] 2 AC 207, 275. However, that explanation is palpably too wide as the same could be said of many of the 'relational economic loss' cases (see above, § 5.3, fn 30) where a duty of care was denied. Lord Goff suggested that a duty of care needed to be found in *White* v *Jones* because 'practical justice' demanded that the House of Lords close the 'loophole' or 'lacuna' that would otherwise exist in this case, whereby the only person the defendant owed a duty of care to (the father) suffered no loss as a result of the defendant's breach of that duty and therefore could not sue, while the only person who suffered a loss (the claimants) was owed no duty and therefore could not sue: [1995] 2 AC 207, 259. But that presupposes that we should find the defendant liable to *someone* in a *White* v *Jones* case – but why? If the desire is to ensure that the defendant does not 'get away' with being negligent without incurring some kind of sanction from the law, then a complaint to the Law Society should have ensured that 'practical justice' would be done in this case.

[232] The undertaking to assist has to be voluntary, so as to prevent a defendant who is dragooned into a third party's scheme to help the claimant suddenly being fixed with an onerous duty of care to see that he does not screw things up for the claimant. See *Rowley* v *Secretary of State for Work and Pensions* [2007] 1 WLR 2861, holding that the defendant Secretary of State – who had been fixed with a statutory duty to assess, through the Child Support Agency, how much a single mother should be paid in child support maintenance payments – did not owe the claimant (a single mother) a duty to take care not to get the assessment wrong.

[233] In *White* v *Jones*, Lord Mustill (dissenting) thought that some such principle had to underlie the decision in *White* v *Jones* and on that basis condemned the majority decision as going 'far beyond anything so far contemplated by the law of negligence': [1995] 2 AC 207, at 291.

[234] *White* v *Jones* [1995] 2 AC 207, 262 (per Lord Goff). See also *Hemmens* v *Wilson Browne* [1995] Ch 223 (held: no duty owed by firm of solicitors to claimant in drawing up deed under which claimant would have had the right to call on A at any time to pay her £110,000); *Wells* v *First National Commercial Bank* [1998] PNLR 552 (held: bank that agrees to refinance company and, as part of the deal, agrees to pay off some of the company's debts will not owe the debtors a duty to pay off those debts); and *Briscoe* v *Lubrizol* [2000] ICR 694 (held: underwriters of company's health insurance scheme owe no duty of care to employee claiming under that scheme when they assess whether his claim is genuine or not; even if they turn down his claim when it is genuine, that will not prevent the employee obtaining what he is entitled to under the scheme).

(2) *White v Jones* does not just apply in wills cases, but applies in any case where A wants to confer a benefit on B, and is prevented from doing so by C's unhelpful assistance. This was confirmed by the Court of Appeal decision in *Gorham v British Telecommunications plc* (2001). In that case, G, a married man with two young children, wanted to set up a pension which would provide some financial security for his wife and children should he predecease them. He went to Standard Life for some advice and they failed to advise him properly. They advised him to take out a Standard Life pension when in fact G's wife and children would have been far better off had G joined the occupational pension scheme run by his employer, British Telecom. When G died, G's wife and children sued Standard Life claiming that Standard Life had owed them, and breached, a duty to take care that they did not give G bad pensions advice. The Court of Appeal held that Standard Life had owed G's wife and children such a duty of care under *White v Jones*. Rightly so, if we accept the analysis of *White v Jones* advanced here. G wanted to provide his wife and children with as much financial security as possible after he died. Standard Life undertook to assist him in doing that but they in fact prevented him from doing that by giving him bad pensions advice. So – on the analysis of *White v Jones* advanced here – Standard Life owed G's wife and children a duty to take care that they did not give G bad pensions advice.

(3) The Court of Appeal was right to reject counsel for the claimant's argument in *Goodwill v British Pregnancy Advisory Service* (1996) that *White v Jones* indicated that a duty of care was owed to the claimant in that case. In that case, the claimant became pregnant after having sex with M, who was supposed to have been sterilised by the defendants. The Court of Appeal held that *White v Jones* did not apply here because it was hardly realistic to say that, in being sterilised, M was attempting to confer a benefit on women such as the claimant (the benefit of not getting pregnant).[235] It might have been different, though, if the claimant had been M's wife – in such a case, it would have been possible to argue that M wanted to confer a benefit on the claimant in being sterilised. So if the claimant had been M's wife, it might have been possible to argue that the defendants owed the claimant a duty under *White v Jones* to take care that they did not botch M's operation.[236]

D. Expense incurred as a result of property being put in danger

The best explanation we can offer of the House of Lords' decision in the *Greystoke Castle* case is that it is simply the equivalent of *Page v Smith* (1996) in the proprietary context. In *Page v Smith*, it will be recalled,[237] the defendant owed the claimant a duty to take care not to crash into the claimant's car. That duty was geared towards protecting the claimant from suffering a physical injury, but as a result of the defendant's breach of that duty, the claimant did not suffer a physical injury, but a psychiatric illness instead. It was held that the claimant could still sue for that psychiatric illness as it was an 'immediate' consequence of the defendant's breach of duty.[238]

An equivalent analysis can be offered of what happened in the *Greystoke Castle* case. In that case, the owners of the *Cheldale* owed the claimants a duty to take care not to crash into the *Greystoke Castle*. That duty of care was based on the fact that it was reasonably foreseeable that crashing into the *Greystoke Castle* would damage the claimants' cargo aboard the

---

[235] [1996] 1 WLR 1397, 1403.
[236] ibid.
[237] See above § 6.1.
[238] The requirement that the psychiatric illness be an 'immediate' consequence of the defendants' breach of a duty of care geared towards protecting the claimant from physical injury comes from the House of Lords' decision in *Rothwell v Chemical & Insulating Co Ltd* [2008] 1 AC 281: see above, § 6.1.

Greystoke Castle, and was therefore geared towards protecting the claimants' cargo from being damaged. In fact, the breach of that duty of care by the owners of the *Cheldale* did not result in the claimants' cargo being damaged, but the immediate result of that breach was that the claimants suffered a different kind of harm – the pure economic loss of having to contribute to the cost of unloading and reloading that cargo aboard the *Greystoke Castle*. So the House of Lords' decision can be rationalised as saying that it did not matter that the claimants in this case did not suffer the type of harm that the defendants' duty of care was imposed on them in order to avoid – they could still sue for the different, and lesser, harm that the defendants' breach of duty had immediately resulted in the claimants suffering.

But why? Perhaps because it was just a matter of luck that the defendants' negligence did not result in the claimants' cargo being damaged – and so no injustice would have been done to the defendants by holding them liable for the lesser harm that the defendants' negligence did actually cause the claimants to suffer.

On this view, there was no real issue in the *Greystoke Castle* as to whether the defendants owed the claimants a duty of care – the only real issue was whether or not the losses suffered by the claimants as a result of the defendants' breach of the duty that they *did* owe the claimants were actionable. If this is right, then in the hypothetical example provided by Lord Roche in the *Greystoke Castle* – where A carelessly crashes into B's lorry, and C, the owner of goods on board the lorry, has to cover the costs of unloading and reloading those goods aboard the lorry – C might indeed be able to sue A for those costs. A owed C a duty of care not to crash into B's lorry on the basis that it was reasonably foreseeable that doing so would result in damage to C's goods. C's goods were not damaged as a result of A's breach of that duty but the immediate result of A's breach was that C suffered a pure economic loss instead. That lesser loss may be actionable even though it was not the kind of loss that A's duty of care was imposed on him in order to avoid.

By contrast, no action would be available under the *Greystoke Castle* in the hypothetical examples posed by Lord Simonds in that case: where A and B are on a joint venture on the Great North Road, and then due to X's carelessly injuring A, the venture has to be abandoned, and B suffers economic loss as a result. In such a case, B will not be able to sue X for that economic loss because she will not be able to get her claim off first base. Unlike the claimants in the *Greystoke Castle* and the goods owner in Lord Roche's hypothetical example, B will not be able to establish that X breached a duty of care owed to *her* in acting as he did.

In *The Orjula* (1995), the claimant charterers of a ship had to incur expense cleaning the ship when acid leaked out from some drums that had been loaded onto the ship by the defendants. The claimants sued the defendants in negligence, arguing that the defendants should have known that the drums were not secure. The defendants applied to have the action struck out. Mance J declined, holding that it was strongly arguable that the claimants could sue the defendants in negligence in this case.[239] Our analysis of the *Greystoke Castle* supports this view. When the defendants loaded the drums of acid onto the claimants' ship, they owed the claimants a duty to take care not to spill that acid onto the ship because it was reasonably foreseeable that doing so would damage the ship. As a result of the defendants' breach, the ship was not actually damaged, but an immediate consequence of the breach was that the claimants suffered a pure economic loss in trying to save the ship from harm

---

[239] It is also strongly arguable that a claim in restitution could have been made here, on the basis that the defendants – having created a danger to the claimants' ship – owed the claimants a duty to take reasonable steps to alleviate that danger (see below, § 7.3), and the claimants discharged that duty by cleaning the ship of spilled acid themselves: see Moran 1997. A similar explanation can be offered of Lord Bridge's suggestion in *Murphy* v *Brentwood DC* [1991] 1 AC 398, that where A carelessly constructs a dangerously defective building, and the occupier of the building spends money on making the building safe so that it does not threaten the occupier's neighbours or people passing by the building, then that money should be recoverable from A: ibid, 475.

by cleaning up the acid spill. This pure economic loss was actionable, even though it was not the kind of harm that the defendants' duty of care was imposed on them in order to avoid.

E. Interference with intangible property

This leaves the decision of the Court of Appeal in *Ministry of Housing* v *Sharp* (1970) – the hardest case to explain, in our view.

In that case, Lord Denning MR held that the House of Lords' decision in *Hedley Byrne* v *Heller* (1964) indicated that the defendant (who was answering the inquiry as to whether there were any charges over some land some developers were going to purchase) owed the claimant (who had a charge over that land which would be lost if the defendant answered the developers' question in the negative and the developers subsequently bought that land) a duty of care. Counsel for the defendant argued that this was not true – that a duty of care would only be owed in a *Hedley Byrne* situation if the defendant 'assumed a responsibility' to the claimant, and there had been no such 'assumption of responsibility' here. Lord Denning denied that an 'assumption of responsibility' was required for liability to arise under *Hedley Byrne* and held that 'the duty to use due care in a statement arises . . . from the fact that the person making it knows, or ought to know, that others . . . would act on the faith of his statement being accurate.'[240] However, we now know this is not true, as the House of Lords held that mere knowledge that someone would rely on your statement would not be enough to give rise to a duty of care in *Williams* v *Natural Life Health Foods Ltd* (1998).

Salmon LJ seemed to rest his decision that a duty of care was owed in *Ministry of Housing* v *Sharp* (1970) on the basis that it was reasonably foreseeable that a mistake on the part of the defendant would result in the claimants' 'legal rights [being] taken away'.[241] This seems to identify a more satisfactory basis for the decision that a duty of care was owed in *Sharp* than Lord Denning MR's judgment did. However, once you start saying that A will owe B a duty to take care not to do something that will foreseeably interfere with B's legal rights to something, you have a tiger by the tail, as there is no limit to the number of legal rights to something that claimants can argue they have (such as rights to trade, marry, walk down the street, watch TV, go to a football match, and so on) and that could be foreseeably interfered with by a defendant. As McHugh J observed in *Perre* v *Apand Pty Ltd* (1999):

> Nor do I think that this Court should accept that a defendant should owe a duty of care merely because its conduct may defeat or impair 'a precise legal right' of the [claimant] in circumstances where the defendant is in a relationship with the [claimant] and in a position to control the enjoyment of that right . . . To impose duties of care in such situations would extend the liability of defendants, perhaps massively . . . The Perres no doubt had a right to trade, and that is a right that in various circumstances the law will protect, but not by imposing duties of care on others simply because they are in a position to control the enjoyment of the plaintiff's right to trade.[242]

Given this, it would be better to say that it was reasonably foreseeable that a mistake on the part of the defendant would cause the claimants to lose a *proprietary interest* that the claimants had in the land which developers were going to purchase, and it was that which gave rise to a duty of care in *Sharp*. Seen in this way, the decision in *Sharp* is an extension of the rule that if it is reasonably foreseeable that A's actions will result in property that B has a sufficient interest in being harmed, then A will normally owe B a duty to take care not to act in that way – with the rule being extended here to a case where the property was intangible in nature (you can't touch a charge). Whether such an extension is justified or not is another matter.

---

[240] [1970] 2 QB 223, 268.
[241] [1970] 2 QB 223, 280. ·
[242] (1999) 198 CLR 180, at [84]–[85].

This ends our explanation of all the 'difficult cases' that were the subject of the previous section. But you should not think that our explanation is the only one on offer. Other explanations are possible – though in our view, they do not provide as good an explanation of these 'difficult cases' as ours does. But so that you can make up your own mind on this, here is a brief alternative explanation[243] of the above 'difficult cases':

> In cases where A's positive actions have foreseeably resulted in B suffering a form of pure economic loss, the *only* general reason why the courts hesitate to find that A owed B a duty of care not to act as he did is a fear that if they do so, A may be exposed to a multitude of claims, and that his liability will spiral out of all proportion to his fault in acting as he did. So in a 'relational economic loss' case where A has carelessly damaged property belonging to C, and B has suffered economic loss as a result, the reason why the courts will only normally find that A owed C a duty of care in this case is that if they find that A also owed B a duty of care, there may be no end to the number of claims that might be made against A, as more and more people come forward, claiming that they too suffered some form of economic loss as a result of C's property being damaged.
>
> For example, in *Cattle* v *Stockton Waterworks* (1875), Blackburn J justified his refusal to find that the defendants in that case – who had carelessly flooded K's land and disrupted work that the claimant was doing on that land – had owed the claimant a duty of care on the basis that the effect of such a finding would be to allow not only the claimant to sue, but also 'every workman and person employed [by the claimant to work on K's land], who in consequence of [the] stoppage [of that work] made less wages than he would otherwise have done.'[244] Blackburn J acknowledged that this objection to finding a duty of care was 'technical and against the merits, and we would be glad to avoid giving it effect'[245] but felt that he had no alternative but to refuse to find a duty of care in that case. More recently, in *The Mineral Transporter* (1986), Lord Fraser of Tullybelton took the same line, arguing that the rule against a duty of care being owed to a claimant in a 'relational economic loss case' was 'a pragmatic one dictated by necessity'.[246]
>
> It follows that in cases where the courts can find that A owed B a duty to take care not to act in a way that foreseeably caused B to suffer pure economic loss without exposing A to a multitude of claims, they should do so (provided, of course, that there are no other special objections that can be made to finding a duty of care in such a case). This will be the case where A knew or ought to have known that B 'individually, and not merely as a member of an unascertained class, [was] likely to suffer economic loss as a consequence of his negligence . . .'[247] In all of the 'difficult cases' discussed above – and, indeed, in *Hedley Byrne* itself – this requirement is satisfied and as a result, the courts' basic objection to finding a duty of care in a pure economic loss case is removed. In all of the above cases, the defendant knew that the claimant was especially likely to suffer pure economic loss as a result of his actions, and there was no danger that the defendant's actions would cause a wider class of people to suffer pure economic loss.

We think this explanation suffers from the flaw that it is not particularly appealing. It misses the fact that it is often not that important to protect B from suffering pure economic loss at A's hands, because pure economic loss is – viewed in abstraction – not a particularly serious harm that we need to protect people (let alone companies) against suffering. It is only if the pure economic loss that B stands to suffer as a result of A's actions is of a *type* that is particularly serious, that the balance shifts in favour of intervention – and our explanation of the 'difficult cases' set out in this section has been concerned to identify what those types of economic loss might be.

---

[243] See Yap 2009 for an example of this sort of way of thinking about the cases.
[244] (1875) LR 10 QB 453, 457.
[245] ibid.
[246] [1986] AC 1, at 16.
[247] *Caltex Oil Pty Ltd* v *The Dredge 'Willemstaad'* (1976) 136 CLR 529, 555 (per Gibbs J).

Further reading

For an excellent overview of the law on recovery in negligence for pyschiatric illness, see Handford, 'Psychiatric injury in breach of a relationship' (2007) 27 *Legal Studies* 26.

Christian Witting wrote a very stimulating article on why tort law might distinguish between harm to property cases and pure economic loss cases in 'Distinguishing between property damage and pure economic loss in negligence: a personality thesis' (2001) 21 *Legal Studies* 481. Peter Benson wrote the classic article on how we could explain the distinction as based on the fact that in a pure economic loss case, the claimant cannot argue that his rights have been violated: 'The basis for excluding liability for economic loss in tort law' in Owen (ed), *The Philosophical Foundations of Tort Law* (Clarendon Press, 1995) but – as all such articles do – mixed up his 'rights that . . .' (the violation of which can give rise to tort liability) with his 'rights to . . .' (the existence of which is a product of tort law, and does not underlie tort law). Just because you don't have a 'right to' a certain level of business does not mean that you cannot claim that you had a 'right that' a defendant that not carelessly do something that had the effect of damaging your business. See McBride, 'Rights and the basis of tort law' in Nolan and Robertson (eds), *Rights and Private Law* (Hart Publishing, 2012). Stapleton, 'Comparative economic loss: lessons from case-law-focused "middle theory"' (2002) 50 *UCLA Law Review* goes to the opposite extreme of being too wide, but is still on the right lines, and has the signal virtue of being extremely clear and comprehensive (having been written for an American audience which – apparently – pays little attention to issues about the recovery of pure economic loss).

Stevens, '*Hedley Byrne* v *Heller*: judicial creativity and doctrinal possibility' (1964) 27 *Modern Law Review* 121 is an *incredible* article – written just weeks or months after *Hedley Byrne* was decided, and anticipating a huge amount of its future development as a ground of liability. Whittaker, 'The application of the "broad principle of *Hedley Byrne*" as between parties to a contract' (1997) 17 *Legal Studies* 169 is disapproving of a lot of that development, and is more relevant than ever given the recent decision in *Robinson* v *Jones* (2010).

Kit Barker is much more skeptical than we are of the possibility that the notion of an 'assumption of responsibility' can make sense of the scope of liability under *Hedley Byrne*: 'Unreliable assumptions in the law of negligence' (1993) 109 *Law Quarterly Review* 461. He returns to the subject of recovery for economic loss in 'Economic loss and the duty of care: a study in the exercise of legal justification' in Rickett (ed), *Justifying Remedies in the Law of Obligations* (Hart, 2008), but the paper may be too advanced for most students.

Visit **www.mylawchamber.co.uk/mcbride** to access tools to help you develop and test your knowledge of Tort law, including interactive multiple choice questions, practice exam questions with guidance, weblinks, legal newsfeed, additional case summaries, legal updates and tips on answering problem and essay questions.

premium mylawchamber
unrivalled support for legal education

Use **Case Navigator** to read in full some of the key cases referenced in this chapter with commentary and questions:

POWERED BY LexisNexis®

- Barber *v* Somerset County Council
- Hedley Byrne *v* Heller
- Hunter *v* Canary Wharf
- Phelps *v* Hillingdon London Borough Council
- Wainwright *v* Home Office

7 Duty of care – Omissions

7.1   The basics *207*

7.2   Assumption of responsibility *217*

7.3   Creation of danger *222*

7.4   Interference *228*

7.5   Control *231*

7.6   Occupiers *234*

7.7   Landlords *234*

7.8   Employers *235*

7.9   Bailees *237*

7.10 Carriers *237*

7.11 Child carers *238*

Overview

In this chapter we move away from considering when a defendant will owe a claimant a duty of care requiring him *not to do* something, and consider instead when a defendant will owe a claimant a duty of care requiring him *to do* something. For reasons we will explore in section 7.1, it is much rarer for the law to find that a defendant owed a claimant a *positive* duty of care, rather than a *negative* duty of care, and the section headings for this chapter reflect that. Each section, after the introductory section 7.1, picks out one kind of situation where a defendant will owe a claimant a positive duty of care. Sections 7.2 to 7.5 focus on situations where a defendant will owe a claimant a positive duty of care because the defendant has *done something* that makes it 'fair, just and reasonable' to find that he owes the claimant a duty to take positive steps to protect the claimant from being harmed – for example, because the defendant put the claimant in danger of being harmed in the first place (section 7.3) or because the defendant has gotten in the way of a third party protecting the claimant from being harmed (section 7.4). Sections 7.6 to 7.11 are concerned with situations where the defendant's *status* makes it 'fair, just and reasonable' to impose on him a duty of care to look after the claimant – for example, the fact that the defendant is the claimant's employer (section 7.8) or is in possession of the claimant's goods (section 7.9). The most important status giving rise to positive duties of care – that of being an *occupier of land* – is briefly mentioned in this chapter (section 7.6), but is considered in depth in chapter 11.

7.1 THE BASICS

In this chapter, we cross over a fundamental divide in English law – between acts and omissions. It is simply not possible to understand tort law properly without understanding the significance English law attaches to the distinction between acts and omissions. In this context, the significance of the distinction lies in this: while foreseeability of harm may – as we have seen – ground a duty to take care not to act in a particular way, foreseeability of harm is never enough to give rise to a duty of care to come to someone else's assistance. Something more than mere foreseeability of harm must be shown before a duty to save someone else from that harm will arise.

As a result, the rule in English law is that if A is in a position to save B from harm, A will *not* owe B a duty to rescue B unless there is some kind of special relationship between A and B, or there exist some special circumstances that would warrant imposing a duty on A to rescue B.[1] The case of *Sutradhar v Natural Environment Research Council* (2006) provides an example of this rule at work.

That case arose out of what the World Health Organisation has called 'the largest mass poisoning of a population in history.' From the 1970s onwards, the Bangladeshi government – with the assistance of foreign aid from governmental organisations like the UK Overseas Development Agency – had sought to provide drinking water for its citizens by sinking millions of tube wells all over the country, to access underground water supplies. Unfortunately, in many cases the ground in which the tube wells were sunk was contaminated with arsenic, which in turn contaminated the water coming out of those wells. It is estimated that tens of millions of Bangladeshis have suffered arsenic poisoning as a result of drinking water from these tube wells. The claimant in *Sutradhar* was one of them.

The defendants in the *Sutradhar* case were an organisation that had been commissioned by the Overseas Development Agency to do a study on how far the Bangladeshi tube wells (which no one suspected at the time of being anything but a good thing) were standing up to the strain of repeated use. On their visit to Bangladesh to carry out the study, the defendants found that the tube wells they were looking at had not deteriorated at all. So they proposed to use the remaining money allocated for that study to carry out a study of the chemistry of water in the area, so as to see whether the water could support fish farms. In carrying out that study – the results of which were distributed around various Bangladeshi governmental and non-governmental organisations – the defendants failed to test the water they were studying for arsenic. Had they done so, they would have spotted the problem of arsenic contaminating water supplies coming from tube wells, and something could have been done about it. But as it was, everyone continued to think that tube wells were perfectly safe.

The claimant (who lived in the area being tested by the defendants) sued the defendants in negligence, arguing that they had owed him a duty of care in carrying out their study. The House of Lords dismissed the claim as 'hopeless'.[2] The reason was that the defendants had not done anything to make the claimant worse off: they had merely failed to do something that would have saved the claimant from being made ill. As a result, it was not possible to find that the defendants owed the claimant a duty of care – there being no special relationship between them, and no special circumstances attaching to the case that would have made it 'fair, just and reasonable' to find that a duty of care was owed.

The general rule in English law that there is no duty *under the law of negligence*[3] to save others from harm applies just as much to public bodies as it does to private persons.[4]

So, for example, in two of the four cases dealt with in the case of *Capital & Counties plc v Hampshire CC* (1997), firefighters failed to deal effectively with fires that started on the

---

[1] *Yuen Kun Yeu v Attorney-General for Hong Kong* [1988] AC 175, 192; *Stovin v Wise* [1996] AC 923, 931.

[2] [2006] 4 All ER 490, at [2] (per Lord Hoffmann).

[3] It is, of course, different under the Human Rights Act 1998: see above, chapter 3.

[4] See, in addition to the cases cited in the main text, *East Suffolk Rivers Catchment Board v Kent* [1941] AC 74 (river authority that takes on the job of repairing a sea wall owes no duty to repair the wall expeditiously to farmer whose land will be flooded until the sea wall is properly repaired); *Peabody Donation Fund v Sir Lindsay Parkinson & Co Ltd* [1985] AC 210 (local authority which has powers to ensure that houses owned by claimants are being built in conformity to approved designs will not owe claimants a duty to exercise those powers); *Hill v Chief Constable of West Yorkshire* [1989] AC 53 (police authorities do not owe potential victims of criminal on the loose a duty to take reasonable steps to arrest the criminal); *Yuen Kun Yeu v Att-Gen for Hong Kong* [1988] AC 175 and *Davis v Radcliffe* [1990] 1 WLR 821 (banking authorities do not owe depositors with a bank a duty to take reasonable steps to see that the bank's affairs are properly run); *Hussain v Lancaster City Council* [2000] QB 1 (victims of racial harassment by council tenants are not owed duty by council to take reasonable steps to bring harassment to an end); *Van Colle v Chief Constable of Hertfordshire Police* [2009] 1 AC 225 (police do not owe duty of care to protect claimant from being attacked by violent ex-lover, even if they know that the claimant is at risk of attack).

claimants' premises, with the result that the fires destroyed buildings on those premises.[5] The Court of Appeal held that the firefighters had not owed the claimants a duty to take reasonable steps to put the fires out and as a result dismissed the claimants' claims in negligence for compensation for the loss of their buildings. As the Court of Appeal observed, 'In our judgment the fire brigade are not under a common law duty to answer the call for help, and are not under a duty to take care to do so. If, therefore, they fail to turn up, or fail to turn up in time, because they have carelessly misunderstood the message, got lost on the way or run into a tree, they are not liable.'[6]

The House of Lords' decision in *Stovin* v *Wise* (1996) was to the same effect. In that case Stovin was knocked off his motorcycle and severely injured when he was hit by an oncoming car at a junction. The junction was rendered dangerous by a raised bank adjoining it which interfered with Stovin's ability to see the car that hit him and the driver of the car's ability to see Stovin. A claim that the defendant highway authority had owed Stovin a duty to take reasonable steps to flatten the raised bank – which it had the statutory power to do – was rejected by the House of Lords. As the defendant highway authority had not made Stovin worse off in any way but had simply failed to save him from harm, there was no basis for finding that the defendant highway authority had owed Stovin a duty of care.

Stovin v *Wise* was subsequently followed by the House of Lords in *Gorringe* v *Calderdale MBC* (2004). In that case, the claimant driver argued that the defendant highway authority had owed her a duty to warn her to slow down when approaching a curve in the road, and that if it had warned her to do this she would have avoided crashing into a bus with the result that she was severely injured. The House of Lords rejected this argument. Lord Hoffmann strongly endorsed the general rule that there is no duty to rescue in English law, even when a public body is involved: 'Speaking for myself, I find it difficult to envisage a case in which a common law duty can be founded simply upon the failure (however irrational) to provide some benefit which a public authority has [a] power (or a public law duty) to provide.'[7]

The distinction between an act (making someone worse off by doing something positive) and an omission (failing to save someone from harm, or failing to confer a benefit on them by doing nothing) may seem hard to apply in certain cases.[8] Consider, for example, the **Falling Sign Problem**:

> One winter, *Highway Authority* put up a sign by the side of a road to warn drivers of treacherous black ice ahead. The sign was south-facing. Unfortunately, the highway authority did not do enough to secure the sign from being blown over by the strong winds that were common at that time of year.
>
> In Scenario (1), a wind blowing in a south-westerly direction blew the sign over so that it fell into the road, where it lay flat on the road. *Driver* ran over the sign at full speed, lost control of his car, and was severely injured in the ensuing crash.
>
> In Scenario (2), a wind blowing in a north-easterly direction blew the sign over so that it fell backwards and lay flat by the side of the road and was invisible to passing motorists. Unaware of the black ice ahead, *Unlucky* drove onto it at full speed, lost control of his car, and was severely injured in the ensuing crash.

---

[5] The firefighters did, however, owe the claimants a duty to take care not to do something *positive* (such as switching off sprinkler systems) that would make the fires *worse*, and claims in negligence for breach of that duty of care succeeded in the other two cases dealt with in the *Capital & Counties* case.

[6] [1997] QB 1004, 1030.

[7] [2004] 1 WLR 1057, at [32].

[8] See above, § 5.3(C), for another example.

In Falling Sign (1) we are dealing with an 'act' case: *Highway Authority*, through its positive act of putting the sign by the side of the road without securing it from being blown over, made *Driver* worse off than she would have been had the highway authority done nothing.[9] In Falling Sign (2) we are dealing with an 'omission' case: *Highway Authority*, by failing to secure the sign by the side of the road, failed to save *Unlucky* from the danger of crashing on the black ice on the road up ahead.[10]

It may seem paradoxical that whether we are dealing with an 'act' or 'omission' case in the Falling Sign Problem depends on the direction the wind was blowing in that case. But the paradox is more apparent than real. In the first scenario, we are holding *Highway Authority* liable for its positive act in putting up a sign by the side of the road (which was then blown into the middle of the road). In the second scenario, we are not holding *Highway Authority* liable for putting a sign up; we are holding the *Highway Authority* liable for failing to make sure that the sign it put up stayed up (with the result that the sign was not visible when *Unlucky* came driving along).

In *Haseldine* v *Daw* (1941), a firm of engineers was employed by a landlord to maintain a lift in a block of flats owned by the landlord. On one of the firm's monthly visits to maintain the lift, an engineer, having cleaned the lift's machinery, failed to put a component part in the lift's machinery back properly in place. As a result, the next day, when the claimant used the lift, the lift fell to the bottom of the lift shaft, and the claimant was injured.

The Court of Appeal held that the firm of engineers was liable in negligence for the claimant's injuries. This was pretty clearly an act case. A lift that was basically sound in condition (though somewhat worn and battered, the evidence showed) was rendered unsound by the engineer's positive act in removing a component part from the lift's machinery and then failing to replace it properly after he had cleaned it. As it was reasonably foreseeable that this positive act would result in someone like the claimant suffering a physical injury, the engineer was rightly held to have owed a duty of care to the claimant.

But what if *Engineer* had – on his monthly visit – simply failed to spot that there was a problem with the lift that would make it dangerous to use, with the result that *Visitor*, who subsequently used the lift, was injured? Would that be a case of an act, or an omission? If an act, then *Engineer* could be held liable to *Visitor*, based merely on the fact that it was foreseeable that leaving the lift in a dangerous state would result in someone like *Visitor* being injured. If an omission, then *Engineer* could only be held liable to *Visitor* if there was some special relationship between *Engineer* and *Visitor*, or some special circumstances that would warrant imposing a duty on *Engineer* to take positive steps to protect *Visitor* from harm – which requirement would not have been satisfied in the case here.

We think that this scenario is an 'act' case. Presumably, when *Engineer* arrived to inspect the lift, the lift was put out of commission. And when *Engineer* indicated to the landlord at the end of his inspection that *the lift could be used again*, the lift was put back into use. By indicating to the landlord that the lift could be used again, *Engineer* performed a positive act that made *Visitor* worse off than he would have been had *Engineer* done nothing. This is because, if *Engineer* had done nothing and not indicated to the landlord the lift could be used again, the lift would have been permanently out of commission, and *Visitor* could not have used the lift, and would not have been injured as a result of using it.

---

[9] Cf. *Levine* v *Morris* [1970] 1 WLR 71; also *Yetkin* v *Mahmood* [2011] QB 827 (bush planted by defendant authority allowed to grow to such an extent that it obstructed drivers' line of sight, with the result that there was an accident in which the claimant was injured).

[10] Cf. *Gorringe* v *Calderdale MBC* [2004] 1 WLR 1057.

It was different in *Anns* v *Merton LBC* (1978). In that case, a block of flats were constructed on inadequate foundations. The plans for the building – which were deposited with the defendant local authority – specified that the foundations should be at least three foot deep. As it turned out, the building's foundations were shallower than that, by about six inches. The result was that cracks started developing in the building. The claimants were leaseholders of parts of the building. They sued the defendant local authority for failing to exercise its powers under the Public Health Act 1936 to ensure that the building was constructed in accordance with the plans for its construction. This was clearly an 'omission' case. The defendant local authority – by doing nothing – had failed to save the claimants from suffering harm (in this case, the cost of making the building safe). It would have been different, we suggest, if at some stage in the building work, that work could not have continued until the defendants had first issued a certificate, indicating that they were satisfied that the building's foundations were of an adequate depth. Issuing such a certificate would have amounted to a positive act that had the effect of making the claimants worse off, in that had such a certificate not been issued and the defendants had done nothing instead, the building could never have been completed and the claimants would not have had to incur the expense of making it safe.[11]

As it was, *Anns* was an 'omission' case, and the House of Lords created a big exception to the general rule that there is no liability in negligence for failing to save a stranger from harm by finding that the defendant local authority *did* owe the claimants in *Anns* a duty of care, despite the lack of any special relationship existing between the authority and the claimants, or special circumstances that might have warranted finding that the defendant local authority owed the claimants such a duty of care.

The scope of the duty in *Anns* was subsequently cut down by the House of Lords' ruling in *Murphy* v *Brentwood DC* (1991), which held that the duty of care in *Anns* was geared towards protecting people from suffering physical harm as a result of a building falling down, rather than protecting people like the claimants in *Anns* from suffering pure economic loss as a result of having to repair a building that is in danger of falling down. However, it still remains the case, *in theory*, that if – in an *Anns*-type situation – a building falls down and A is physically injured as a result, A can not only sue the builder for his positive act in constructing a dangerous building,[12] but also the relevant local authority for its omission in failing to exercise its powers to stop the builder from constructing a dangerous building. And this is so even though there may have been no special relationship between A and the local authority, or special circumstances that would have warranted the local authority's being subject to such a duty of care. However, we say this remains the case *in theory* because authorities such as *Stovin* v *Wise* (1996) and *Gorringe* v *Calderdale MBC* (2004) make it likely that if such a case ever came to court, *Anns* would be finally and definitively overruled.

Some academics would regret this, and regret the general retrenchment of the law effected in cases like *Stovin* and *Gorringe* in reaffirming the importance of the distinction between acts and omissions. Such academics see no reason why the law should regard acts and omissions so differently. If an act and an omission have the same *consequence* why should they not be regarded as equally culpable, and equally deserving of some legal sanction? Indeed, in some cases, an omission might be regarded as *more* culpable than an act, if we

---

[11] Compare the facts of *The Nicholas H* [1996] AC 211 (discussed above, § 6.9), which was an 'act' case precisely because the ship could not have sailed without a certificate from the defendant society.

[12] See above, § 6.2.

judge such things purely with regard to the consequences of acting and not acting. Consider, for example, the **Trolley Problem**, which was invented by the philosopher Philippa Foot:[13]

A driverless, runaway train is set to go into a tunnel, where there are five people working. They will inevitably be killed if the train is allowed to enter the tunnel. But *Controller* could divert the train into another tunnel, where only one person is working, and who will inevitably be killed if the train were allowed to enter that tunnel.

Most discussions of the Trolley Problem focus on whether it would be permissible to divert the train, and if so, why this is. But another question that could be asked is – Would it be wrong *not* to divert the train, given that if *Controller* fails to do so, five people will die, compared to one who will die if *Controller* does divert the train? Surely in this case, failing to divert the train would be much more culpable than diverting the train? Most people would accept in this case that *if* it is *permissible* for *Controller* to divert the train, then *Controller should* divert the train. Not to do so would be as perverse and as unreasonable as choosing – in a situation where one person, White, is stranded on one rock, and five on another, and you can only go to one rock in your lifeboat before the rising tide drowns everyone – to save White and leave the other five to drown.[14]

So ordinary morality accepts that in certain situations we *do* have duties to save other people from harm. But the fact that we hesitate over whether it *would* be permissible for *Controller* to divert the train even though not doing so will result in a net loss of four lives shows that acts occupy a special place in our moral philosophy. A variation on the Trolley Problem illustrates the point:

A driverless, runaway train is set to go into a tunnel, where there is one person working. He will inevitably be killed if the train is allowed to enter the tunnel. But *Controller* could divert the train into another tunnel, where another solitary individual is working, and who will inevitably be killed if the train were allowed to enter into that tunnel.

Even if we think that it would be permissible to divert the train in our original version of the Trolley Problem, it seems that we would not feel the same way in this variation. We do not think it would be *permissible* for *Controller* to divert the train, so that he would have a *free choice* as to whether or not to divert the train. The reason is that diverting the train involves an act; while not diverting involves an omission. And in a case where an act and an omission would have the *same* negative consequences, the act is more culpable.

The fact that common morality recognises that there is a distinction between acts and omissions does not fully account for the significance of that distinction in the law. For example, we have seen that in our original version of the Trolley Problem, we might well say that *Controller* has a *moral* duty to divert the train. But *Controller* would not have a *legal* duty to divert the train: there is no special relationship between him and the five people who will be killed if he does not divert the train, and no special circumstances either that

---

[13] Foot 1967. The version of the trolley problem supplied in the text was invented by the philosopher Derek Parfit (he calls this version of the trolley problem 'Tunnel'): see Parfit 2011, 219. The reason for preferring 'Tunnel' to Philippa Foot's original formulation of the trolley problem is that it is clearer in 'Tunnel' why the five people will inevitably die unless something is done. (In other versions of the trolley problem, a criminal or mad philosopher has tied five people to the track down which the train or trolley-bus or tram is currently travelling; but this just complicates things.)

[14] Another example from Derek Parfit ('Lifeboat'): see Parfit 2011, 186.

would make it 'fair, just and reasonable' to impose such a duty on *Controller*. Why does law not fully track morality in this situation? The reason can only be that – as a matter of political, rather than personal, morality – it is not legitimate for the State to reinforce *Controller*'s moral duty to act in this case with a legal duty. A number of reasons can be given why it might not be legitimate:

(1) *Intrusiveness*. As Lord Hoffmann pointed out in *Stovin v Wise* (1996), 'it is less of an invasion of an individual's freedom for the law to require him to consider the safety of others in his actions than to impose upon him a duty to rescue or protect.'[15] If A has a duty *not* to do *x*, he is free to do anything but *x*. If A has a duty to do *x*, he is not free to do anything other than *x*. The severe limits on someone's freedom that someone experiences when they are subjected to a duty to do something positive mean that such duties always require very strong justification.

(2) *Certainty*. A concern to avoid uncertainty or lack of clarity in the law may be one of the reasons why the courts have so far been unwilling to recognise the existence of a general 'duty to rescue' in English law.[16]

As Richard Epstein points out:

> Once one decides that . . . an individual is required under some circumstances to act at his own cost for the exclusive benefit of another, then it is very hard to set out in a principled manner the limits of social interference with individual liberty.[17]

He asks, for example: If we admit that someone crossing a bridge has a duty to throw a rope to someone drowning in the waters below, would someone who is asked to donate a very small amount of money to charity to help save a life have a legal duty to make that donation? If a patient needed a life-saving operation which only one surgeon in the world could perform, would that surgeon come under a legal duty to travel to the patient's bedside and perform that operation – assuming of course that someone could be found who would be willing to cover his travel expenses?[18]

Rather than get the law involved in trying to answer these difficult questions, the English courts have preferred to adopt the *simpler, clearer and more certain* position[19] that A is

---

[15] [1996] AC 923, 943.

[16] See Tomlinson 2000 (demonstrating the uncertainty afflicting French law as a result of its recognising a general 'duty to rescue'). The law in Vermont states that a 'person who knows that another is exposed to grave physical harm shall, to the extent that the same can be rendered without danger or peril to himself or without interference with important duties owed to others, give reasonable assistance to the exposed person unless that assistance or care is being provided by others' (12 Vt. Stat. Ann. § 519). It is easy to think up hypothetical situations where it is very uncertain whether someone would have a duty of care under this provision. For example, suppose B has fallen in the street and is bleeding from his head. Some people gather round B and ask him whether he is okay. A, a doctor, comes along. Is B exposed to 'grave physical harm' in this situation? – perhaps he is: perhaps his bleeding will worsen and he will die unless he is given treatment. Is A able to give him that assistance without danger or peril to himself? – perhaps he can't: perhaps B has AIDS and A will expose himself to the risk of infection by treating B's wounds. Is B already being provided with assistance or care by others? – perhaps not, if the people around him are not doing anything effective to help him. Weinrib 1980 suggests (at 268–79) that a general duty to rescue can be recognised without making the law uncertain if it is limited to cases where the potential rescuer could not, or could not easily, *charge* the person in danger for rescuing him. However, this assumes that the law on when someone can charge someone else for rescuing him from danger is relatively clear; but it is not.

[17] Epstein 1973, 198.

[18] Epstein 1973, 198–9. The examples involving the bridge and the life-saving operation are both found in Ames 1908.

[19] See Weinrib 1980, 247: 'No observer would have any difficulty outlining the current state of the law throughout the common-law world regarding the duty to rescue. Except when the person endangered and the potential rescuer are linked in a special relationship, there is no such duty.'

under no duty to attempt to rescue a stranger, B, from a danger if A played no role in creating the danger and is not otherwise responsible for it – and this is so no matter how easy the rescue might be and no matter how serious and imminent the danger B is in.

(3) *Moral crowding out*. Tony Weir observes that, 'The understandable urge to bring legal standards up to those of delicate morality should be resisted, or there would be no room for generosity or for people to go beyond the call of legal duty.'[20] The conservative commentator Dinesh D'Souza explains why this is so important:

> [Suppose] that I am walking down the street, eating a sandwich, when I am approached by a hungry man [who] wants to share my sandwich. Now if I give him the sandwich, I have done a good deed, and I feel good about it. The hungry man is grateful, and even if he cannot repay me for my kindness, possibly he will try to help someone else when he has the chance. So this is a transaction that benefits the giver as well as the receiver. But see what happens [if the law *requires* me to give the hungry man my sandwich]. The government takes my sandwich from me by force. Consequently, I am a reluctant giver. The government then bestows my sandwich upon the hungry man. Instead of showing me gratitude, however, the man feels entitled to this benefit. In other words, the involvement of the [law] has utterly stripped the transaction of its moral value, even though the result is exactly the same.[21]

So compelling people to do the right thing gives people less space to engage in random acts of kindness that may result in them developing positive relationships with people that they do not otherwise know.[22] Of course, this does not mean that the law should be abolished and that everyone should be left free to choose in all circumstances whether or not to do the right thing. But it does mean that people need to be left *some* space to choose whether or not to do the right thing.[23]

(4) *Preserving autonomy*. There is another reason why it is important that there are some areas in people's lives where they are left alone to do what they like, without having to convince any legal official that what they have done or what they are proposing to do is reasonable. If the law required people to act reasonably *all the time*, then people would be deprived of any sense that their lives were genuinely their own. Instead of feeling that they were in some respects authors of their own lives, people would instead feel that they were simply living out their lives along lines that had been pre-programmed according to someone else's dictates. So – in order that people retain some sense of themselves as autonomous beings – there are some areas of people's lives that simply have to remain private and free from legal regulation.

(5) *Deterring rescue*. If the law is going to impose a duty on A to save B from harm, it has to be shown – at the very least – that imposing such a duty on A will actually benefit B. This may not always be the case.[24] Suppose that *Drunk* is drowning in a lake, and *Rambler* walks by and sees *Drunk*'s plight. If *Rambler* knows that he can be sued if he fails to rescue *Drunk*,

---

[20] Weir 2006, 1.

[21] D'Souza 2002, 81–2.

[22] See, further, McBride 2006a, 29–31.

[23] For an identical argument in favour of the law's *not* enforcing all seriously-made promises, see Kimel 2003.

[24] Hyman 2005 investigated whether the absence of a general duty to rescue in American law had an adverse effect on people's willingness to help others out. He counted only 16 examples of bystanders failing to rescue (in the absence of a statutory duty) in the United States between 1994 and 2004. (He combed the accounts in law textbooks, over 100 relevant law review articles, and all newspaper and magazine stories on LexisNexis.) Hyman also sought to measure the relative incidence of voluntary rescue and non-rescue in the United States. Using data from organisations which provide awards for rescues he found that confirmed rescues outnumber non-rescues by about 740:1, and the risk of dying as a result of attempting a voluntary rescue is approximately 70 times higher than the risk of dying as a result of bystanders failing to offer assistance.

that may not encourage him to try to save *Drunk*. It may have the opposite effect, of encouraging *Rambler* to walk on, and not do anything for *Drunk*, for fear that if he does try to help *Drunk*, he will merely bring attention to himself and expose himself to the risk of a lawsuit if anyone is unhappy with how quick or efficient his rescue efforts were. Better to walk on and disappear into the shadows where no one will be able to find him and blame him for what has happened to *Drunk*.

It is not fanciful to suggest that the existence of legally enforceable duties to rescue may actually put people off rescuing others. The need to allay the fears of would-be rescuers that 'no good deed goes unpunished' has led many American states to enact 'Good Samaritan laws' which typically provide that:

> Any person who, in good faith, renders emergency medical care or assistance to an injured person at the scene of an accident or other emergency without the expectation of receiving or intending to receive compensation from such injured person for such service, shall not be liable in civil damages for any act or omission, not constituting gross negligence, in the course of such care or assistance.

However, it is not clear that the existence of such laws would provide sufficient reassurance to would-be rescuers, particularly given that such laws do not apply in cases of 'gross negligence'.

(6) *Unfairness.* In *Stovin* v *Wise* (1996), Lord Hoffmann observed that one argument against the existence of general duties to rescue takes the form of a 'why pick on me?' argument.[25] Two variations on this argument may be identified.

The first is where a large class of people were in a position to help B, but no one did. In this situation, if B suffers harm as a result of the fact that no one would come to his rescue, he will be entitled to sue *any* member of that class for *full* damages for the harm he has suffered. But if B chooses to sue A, a particular member of the class of people who failed to come to B's assistance, A will be entitled to think that it is unfair that he has been picked on to be sued, rather than anyone else who could have helped B. Of course, A could – after he has been held liable in full to B – bring a claim in contribution against everyone else who failed to help B. But this will be scant consolation if those people are untraceable or judgment-proof. In such a case, A will be entitled to think that the law has worked in a completely arbitrary way to fix him with a large part of the bill for what has happened to B. Such arbitrariness is avoided under a system where the mere fact that someone is in a position to save B from harm is not sufficient to give rise to a duty to rescue B.

The second form of the 'why pick on me' argument takes its cue from the fact that it is often not an accident that a particular individual (A) is in a good position to save someone else (B) from harm. A will often be in that position because she has dedicated herself to the job of saving others from harm, and has searched out situations of danger in order to do precisely that. If, having made this effort to put herself in a position to help others in need, A is then fixed with a legally enforceable duty to save those others, A will be entitled to ask 'Why pick on me? – Why subject me to a legal duty and possible legal action if people are unhappy with my efforts to save others from harm, when the law does not touch all those people who have, unlike me, decided to dedicate their lives to pursuing their own self-interest?' Again, the saying, 'No good deed goes unpunished' is apposite here. Were the law to recognise general duties to rescue, such duties would fall disproportionally on public-spirited citizens who have dedicated their lives to saving others from harm. It is not clear why the legal system should inflict a special disadvantage on those kinds of people.

---

[25] [1996] AC 923, 944.

(7) *Public interest*. Chief among the public-spirited defendants who would be most troubled by the existence of general duties to rescue would, of course, be the emergency services. While – we would contend – a desire not to disrupt the activities of the emergency services by exposing them to floods of claims for nonfeasance is *not* the chief reason why such services do not have a general duty under the law of negligence to rescue those in need of their help, the existence of such a desire is undeniable[26] and may tend to stiffen the courts' resolve not to relax the rule that there is no general duty to rescue in cases involving the emergency services.

(8) *Individual responsibility*. In cases where a human being is responsible for A's being in danger of suffering some kind of harm, the courts may be unwilling to recognise that a third party is under a duty to save A from that harm because doing so may end up allowing whoever was primarily responsible for putting A in harm's way to dilute his responsibility for what has happened.

Suppose, first of all, that it was A who put himself in danger of suffering some kind of harm. For example, suppose that *Curious* took some drugs and suffered a bad reaction to them. *Curious*'s *Housemate* failed to call for an ambulance because he was scared of getting into trouble with the authorities. As a result, *Curious* ended up brain-damaged. If we say that *Housemate* owed *Curious* a duty of care in this situation to summon assistance for him, *Curious* will be allowed to sue *Housemate* for compensation for his brain damage, subject to a deduction – for 'contributory negligence'[27] – to take account of the fact that *Curious* is partly responsible for the harm he has suffered. But – it might be argued – *Curious* should not be allowed to sue *Housemate at all* in this situation, because *Curious* is *wholly* to blame for what happened to him.

Suppose, secondly, that it was a third party who put A in danger of suffering some kind of harm. For example, suppose that *Vicious* and *Innocent* were walking home together by a river, and they got into an argument, and *Vicious* pushed *Innocent* into the river. *Innocent* could not swim and soon got into difficulties. *Vicious* called on *Passer-By*, to dive in and drag *Innocent* to shore, but *Passer-By* refused to do so. *Innocent* drowns. If we say that *Passer-By* owed *Innocent* a duty of care in this situation to go to his assistance, then if *Vicious* is held liable in a wrongful death action to compensate *Innocent*'s dependants for the loss of support that they suffered as a result of *Innocent*'s death,[28] *Vicious* will be able to bring a claim in contribution against *Passer-By*, arguing that as *Passer-By* is also liable for *Innocent*'s death, *Passer-By* must contribute his fair share to *Vicious*'s liability in this case. But – it might be argued – *Vicious* should not be allowed to sue *Passer-By at all* in this situation, because *Vicious* is *wholly* to blame for what happened to *Innocent*.

Despite the large number of objections that can be made to the existence of duties to rescue, there are many situations where the law recognises that one person will owe another a duty to take steps to save him from harm. In such situations, the objections to the existence of a duty of care are either attenuated or non-existent. In the following sections of this chapter, we will set out the various situations in which one person will owe another a positive duty to act.

---

[26] See the last part of Lord Keith of Kinkel's judgment in *Hill* v *Chief Constable of West Yorkshire* [1989] AC 53 (quoted above, § 5.1); though it cannot be emphasised too often that that last part of his judgment was *not* the main reason why a duty of care was denied in *Hill*.
[27] See below, § 28.5.
[28] See above, § 1.5, and below, § 34.1.

In setting out these situations, we will not only be drawing on tort cases, but criminal law cases as well. This is because while criminal liability normally only attaches to *acts*, a *wrongful failure to act* will be treated as the equivalent of an act under the criminal law, and criminal lawyers' notions of when a criminal defendant will be under a duty to act are drawn from the law of tort, and the law of negligence in particular.[29] Some academics who specialise in the criminal law are resistant to the idea that the criminal law owes anything to the law of tort. But in cases where the issue is raised whether the defendant was under a duty to act, what other area of law can the criminal lawyers look to, to tell them the answer to this question?

The dependence of this area of the criminal law on the law of tort is made clear by the Corporate Manslaughter and Corporate Homicide Act 2007, which provides that a corporation will commit an offence 'if the way in which its activities are managed or organised – (a) causes a person's death, and (b) amounts to a gross breach of a relevant duty of care owed by the organisation to the deceased'[30] and a 'relevant duty of care' is defined as any of a limited range of 'duties owed by it under the law of *negligence*'.[31] But it is not the relatively recent 2007 Act that tends to provide the richest source of criminal caselaw on when one person will owe another a duty to save that other from harm. It is, rather, the much more well-established offence of *gross negligence manslaughter* that provides that. A defendant will be held to have committed the offence of gross negligence manslaughter if he causes another's death by breaching a duty of care owed to that other and his conduct in breaching that duty of care was so outrageous that it is worthy of punishment.[32] Clearly, in *any* case where a defendant is charged with gross negligence manslaughter for *failing* to assist someone who was in danger of dying, his guilt will crucially depend on whether the courts are willing to find that he owed the deceased a duty of care – and the courts, in deciding that issue, will inevitably have to fall back on the law of negligence's conception of when one person will owe another a duty to save them from harm.[33]

7.2 ASSUMPTION OF RESPONSIBILITY

The first situation where the courts will find that one person will owe another a duty to act should be very familiar to us: it is the situation where A 'assumes a responsibility' to B to protect B's welfare in some way. If A 'assumes a responsibility' to B, the courts have tended to think that it would be *automatically* 'fair, just and reasonable' to find that A owed B a duty of care. As Lord Goff remarked in *Henderson* v *Merrett Syndicates* (1995):

> if a person assumes responsibility to another in respect of certain services, there is no reason why he should not be liable in damages . . . in respect of . . . loss which flows from the neglient performance of those services. It follows that, once the case is identified as falling within the *Hedley Byrne* principle [of 'assumption of responsibility'], there should be no need to embark upon any further enquiry whether it is 'fair, just and reasonable' to impose liability . . .[34]

---

[29] See *R* v *Adomako* [1995] 1 AC 171, at 187 (per Lord Mackay): 'the ordinary principles of the law of negligence apply to ascertain whether or not the defendant has been in breach of a duty of care towards the victim who has died.'

[30] Section 1(1).

[31] Section 2(1) (emphasis added).

[32] *R* v *Adomako* [1995] 1 AC 171.

[33] For general discussion of how the courts determine whether or not a duty of care was owed in a gross negligence manslaughter case, see Herring and Palser 2007.

[34] [1995] 2 AC 145, 181. Whittaker 1997 disagrees, arguing that the extended principle in *Hedley Byrne* undermines the law of contract, which also makes 'assumptions of responsibility' binding, but only if they are made in a deed or if consideration is provided for them.

'Assumption of responsibility' is therefore the *easiest* ground on which to find that A owed B a duty to act.

Such an 'assumption of responsibility' will characteristically take one of two forms. *Either* A will have indicated to B that B can rely on A to look after B's interests with a reasonable degree of care and skill and B will have relied on A to do this. *Or* A will have indicated to B that B can rely on A to take reasonable steps to protect B from some kind of harm and B will have relied on A to do this. It is the first kind of assumption of responsibility that underlies a doctor's duty to treat his patient with a reasonable degree of care and skill. The second type of assumption of responsibility seems to account for the courts' willingness to recognise that a duty of care was owed in the following cases.

In *Stansbie* v *Troman* (1948) – a *Hedley Byrne* case before *Hedley Byrne* – the defendant decorator was working at the claimant's house when the claimant called up to him to tell him that she was going out. As the defendant was in the house, the claimant did not lock the front door. About 90 minutes later, the defendant left the house to look for a roll of wallpaper. He, too, left the front door unlocked. He had some difficulty finding the wallpaper he wanted, and came back to the house about two hours later to find that in his absence the house had been burgled and about £350 worth of valuables had been stolen. The claimant sued the defendant for the loss of these valuables (worth almost £10,000 in today's money). The Court of Appeal held that the defendant had owed the claimant a duty to take reasonable steps to lock up when he left the house empty, as he had – in his contract with the claimant – promised to do that kind of thing for her. In other words, he assumed a responsibility to her to take reasonable steps to see that her house was not burgled when he was left there alone.

In *Welsh* v *Chief Constable of Merseyside Police* (1993), the claimant appeared before a magistrates' court charged with two offences of theft. He was remanded on bail to appear again on 19 August 1987. On 7 August the claimant was due to appear before the Crown Court to be sentenced for committing various criminal offences. Before his case was called, the claimant indicated to the Crown Prosecution Service (CPS) that he did commit the two theft offences for which he was due to appear before the magistrates on 19 August and he wanted the Crown Court to take into account those two offences in sentencing him. The Crown Court took those offences into account and the claimant – believing that the CPS would tell the magistrates that the Crown Court had already dealt with the two theft offences which they were due to try him for – failed to turn up to his hearing before the magistrates on 19 August. The magistrates, knowing nothing of the Crown Court hearing, issued a warrant for the claimant's arrest. The claimant was arrested under the warrant and held in custody for two days until the true facts came to light.

The claimant sued the CPS, claiming that they had owed him a duty to take reasonable steps to alert the magistrates to the fact that he had already been sentenced in the Crown Court for committing the two theft offences for which he was due to be tried in the magistrates' court. Tudor Evans J refused to strike out the claimant's claim, holding that it was strongly arguable that the CPS had owed him such a duty of care. It could be argued that the CPS indicated to the claimant that he could safely rely on them to take reasonable steps to inform the magistrates of what had happened in the Crown Court and that the claimant had relied on the CPS to take such steps by not turning up to his hearing on the 19 August.[35]

---

[35] It is quite clear that if the CPS had *not* indicated to the claimant that they could be safely relied on to take reasonable steps to inform the magistrates of his conviction, they would not have owed him a duty to take any steps to inform the magistrates of his conviction: *Elguzouli-Daf* v *Commissioner of the Police of the Metropolis* [1995] QB 335.

In *Swinney* v *Chief Constable of the Northumbria Police* (1997), the claimant passed on to the police information which indicated that T was involved in the killing of a police officer. The claimant gave the police this information in confidence and made it clear that she did not want T to find out that she had informed on him to the police. As the claimant gave her information to the police, it was written down on a document which named the claimant as the source of the information. This document was then left in an unattended police car which was broken into by criminals. The document was stolen and passed on to T. T then threatened the claimant with violence and arson and the claimant developed a psychiatric illness as a result.

The claimant sued the police, arguing that the police had owed her, and breached, a duty to take reasonable steps to see that T would not find out that she had informed on him. The Court of Appeal refused the police's application to strike out the claim: it thought it was strongly arguable that the police had owed the claimant a duty to take reasonable steps to ensure that T would not find out that she had informed on him. The reason why the Court of Appeal thought it was strongly arguable that the police had owed the claimant such a duty of care was that the police had indicated to her that they could be safely relied on to take reasonable steps to ensure that T would not find out that she had informed on him and the claimant did so rely on the police by giving them her information about T.[36]

We have already seen that if a fire starts in a house, and the fire brigade is summoned to deal with the fire, the fire brigade will not normally owe the householder a duty to take reasonable steps to put out the fire or even a duty to take reasonable care to turn up to the scene of the fire.[37] However, there is a Canadian case called *Densmore* v *Whitehorse* (1986),[38] where a fire brigade was held to owe a duty of care on the basis of an 'assumption of responsibility'. In that case, a fire started in the claimant's house. The claimant rang the fire department and was told a fire engine would be on its way; but none was actually sent and the claimant's house and its contents were destroyed. It was held that the fire department had owed the claimant a duty to take reasonable steps to get a fire engine to her house because she had relied on the fire department to take such steps by not doing anything to save the contents of her house – by, for example, throwing selected items out of the window or carrying them out of the house – while she was waiting for the fire engine to turn up.[39]

A crucial feature of the Yukon Territory Supreme Court's willingness to find a duty of care in *Densmore* was the fact that the claimant had *relied* on the fire department to send a fire engine to her house. This element of reliance will be missing in most fire cases – if your house is burning down, there is very little you yourself will be able to do about it, and so an assurance that a fire engine is on its way will make very little difference to what you do after you receive that assurance. But could a duty to act arise simply in response to the fact that a defendant has *undertaken* or *promised* to do something for the claimant, where that undertaking or promise has *not* induced the claimant to rely on the defendant in any way?

Robert Stevens thinks the answer is 'yes': 'Doctors are entitled to walk past the sick, but if a sign is put up saying "Public Hospital" a duty has been assumed that care will be taken

---

[36] When the case went to trial, the judge (Jackson J) found that the police had indeed owed the claimant a duty to take reasonable steps to see that T did not find out that she had informed on him. However, the claimant's claim was dismissed on the ground that the police had not breached that duty of care. See *Swinney* v *Chief Constable of Northumbria Police (No 2)*, *The Times*, 25 May 1999.

[37] *Capital & Counties plc* v *Hampshire CC* [1997] QB 1004. See above, § 7.1.

[38] Discussed, Bagshaw 1999.

[39] But query whether she should have been confined to suing the defendant fire department for the value of the items she could have saved but for the fire department's misleading assurance: see, ibid.

of those who turn up expecting treatment.'[40] The example is not a good one: those who have turned up expecting treatment might have gone elsewhere but for the sign saying 'Public Hospital'. They have therefore relied on the hospital's general indication to all and sundry that the hospital will take reasonable steps to treat them. A clearer case of non-reliance is presented by the **Unconscious Man Problem**:

> *Doctor*, is on his way to meet his girlfriend for dinner. As he passes by an alleyway, he sees *Drunk*, lying unconscious on the ground. *Doctor* goes to attend to *Drunk*, but after he has taken *Drunk*'s pulse and checked that he is breathing regularly, *Doctor*'s mobile phone goes off. It is *Doctor*'s girlfriend, demanding to know where he is. *Doctor* rushes off to meet his girlfriend without doing anything more to look after *Drunk*. Half an hour later, *Drunk* throws up and chokes on his own vomit and dies because he has not been placed in the right position to stop this happening.

Did *Doctor* owe *Drunk* a duty to take reasonable steps to make him better? Robert Stevens thinks he did: 'the duty of a doctor who assumes responsibility towards a patient [can arise] even though the [patient] is wholly ignorant of the undertaking.'[41] There are some *dicta* which support this position. In *Banbury* v *Bank of Montreal* (1918), Lord Atkinson remarked:

> It is well established that if a doctor proceeded to treat a patient gratuitously, even in a case where the patient was insensible at the time and incapable of employing him, the doctor would be bound to exercise all the professional skill and knowledge he possessed, or professed to possess, and would be guilty of gross negligence if he omitted to do so.[42]

 Lord Morris took the same line in *Hedley Byrne* v *Heller* (1964):

> A medical man may unexpectedly come across an unconscious man, who is a complete stranger to him, and who is in urgent need of skilled attention: if the medical man, following the fine traditions of his profession, proceeds to treat the unconscious man he must exercise reasonable skill and care in doing so.[43]

The decision of the Court of Appeal in *Kent* v *Griffiths* (2001) could also be taken as supporting Stevens' position. In that case, the claimant suffered an asthma attack. Her doctor came to see her and it was decided that she had to be taken to hospital. The doctor rang the London Ambulance Service (LAS) and they told her they would send an ambulance along to take the claimant to hospital. No ambulance had arrived 13 minutes later, so the claimant's husband rang the LAS to be told that the ambulance would be another seven or eight minutes. But still no ambulance came. Twenty-nine minutes after the original call, the claimant's doctor rang the LAS and was told the ambulance would be there in a couple of minutes. It took five more minutes for the ambulance to turn up. The claimant arrived in hospital 46 minutes after the original call, and promptly suffered a respiratory arrest which resulted in her suffering a miscarriage, a change of personality, and

---

[40] Stevens 2007, 11, citing *Barnett* v *Chelsea & Kensington Hospital Management Committee* [1969] 1 QB 428. In that case, three workmen presented themselves to a casualty department, complaining that they were feeling sick. The nurse on duty rang the doctor on call, and he advised that they should go home and consult their own doctors. They were in fact suffering from arsenic poisoning from drinking contaminated tea and one of them died five hours later. There is nothing in the facts of this case that support Stevens' radical position: the nurse and doctor on duty clearly assumed a responsibility to the men to treat them with reasonable skill and care.

[41] Stevens 2007, 12.

[42] [1918] AC 626, 689.

[43] [1964] AC 465, 495.

serious memory impairment. A shameful tale, made worse by the fact that had the LAS gotten the claimant to hospital within a reasonable period of time, the treatment she would have received there would have prevented her suffering a respiratory arrest. The Court of Appeal held that the LAS had owed the claimant a duty to take reasonable steps to get her to hospital reasonably quickly. Lord Woolf MR held that 'The acceptance of the call in this case established the duty of care.'[44]

On the other hand, in *The Ogopogo* (1970), Schroeder JA, in the Ontario Court of Appeal, said that:

> even if a person embarks upon a rescue and does not carry it through, he is not under any liability to the person to whose aid he had come so long as discontinuance of his efforts did not leave the other in a worse condition than when he took charge.[45]

And in *Capital & Counties Plc v Hampshire CC* (1997), Stuart-Smith LJ held that: 'If [a passing doctor] volunteers his assistance [to help the victim of a traffic accident], his only duty as a matter of law is [to take care] not to make the victim's condition worse.'[46]

We prefer Schroeder JA's and Stuart-Smith LJ's view, for this reason. If we find that the mere undertaking to act to help someone else gives rise to a duty of care to make good on that undertaking, the effect will be to penalise those who try to help others. It cannot be right to say that, in Unconscious Man, *Doctor* owed *Drunk* a duty of care to make him better when, if *Doctor* had ignored *Drunk* and not done anything to help him, he would not have owed *Drunk* a duty of care at all. Lords Morris and Atkinson were simply wrong. The better view of *Kent v Griffiths* (2001) is that Lord Woolf MR was *not* saying in that case that a bare undertaking to assist someone else can give rise to a duty of care. Lord Woolf was a liberal judge who was instinctively in favour of finding that the emergency services owe people in need a duty to save them from harm, unless some good reason can be shown why such a duty should not be recognised. For Lord Woolf, the acceptance of the call in *Kent v Griffiths* was not a reason *for* finding that there existed a duty of care in that case; the acceptance of the call meant there was *no* reason why a duty of care should *not* be found in that case:

> An important feature of this case is that there is no question of an ambulance not being available or of a conflict in priorities. Again I recognise that where what is being attacked is the allocation of resources, whether in the provision of sufficient ambulances or sufficient drivers or attendants, different considerations could apply. There then could be issues which are not suited for resolution by the courts. However, once there are available, both in the form of an ambulance and in the form of manpower, the resources to provide an ambulance on which there are no alternative demands, the ambulance service would be acting perversely . . . if it did not make those resources available. Having decided to provide an ambulance an explanation is required to justify a failure to attend within reasonable time.[47]

Lord Woolf's pro-claimant instincts were repudiated by the House of Lords in *Gorringe* v *Calderdale MBC* (2004), where it was emphasised that a duty to act would only be owed in

---

[44] [2001] QB 36, at [49].

[45] [1970] 1 Lloyd's Rep 257, 263. The case was appealed to the Supreme Court of Canada, but the Supreme Court found it unncessary to deal with the issue raised by Schroeder JA's *dictum*: [1971] 2 Lloyd's Rep 410.

[46] [1997] QB 1004, 1035. See also the case of *X and Y v London Borough of Hounslow* [2009] EWCA Civ 286, where it was held that the defendant council had not assumed a responsibility for the safety of the two claimants in that case (both adults with learning disabilities who were bullied and sexually abused by strangers whom they had welcomed into their flat), even though the council's social services department was regularly visiting the claimants, and generally trying to take steps to secure their welfare.

[47] [2001] QB 36, at [47].

special circumstances which provided a positive reason for finding that it would be 'fair, just and reasonable' to find that such a duty of care was owed. However, that does not mean the Court of Appeal was *wrong* to find that a duty of care was owed in *Kent* v *Griffiths*. An alternative, and perfectly sensible, explanation of why a duty of care was owed in that case is set out below.[48]

7.3 CREATION OF DANGER

A number of authorities support the idea that if A knows or ought to know that he has done something to put B in danger of suffering some kind of harm, A *may* owe B a duty to take reasonable steps to protect B from that danger.

This idea will be of no relevance in a case where A has *wrongfully* put B in danger of suffering some kind of harm, and that danger materialises. In such a case, B can sue A for compensation for the harm she has suffered by focusing on A's initial wrong, and will have no need to try to establish that A owed her a duty of care to protect her from the danger he put her in. For example, suppose *Driver One* carelessly runs over *Pedestrian* and as a result she is lying in the middle of the road, unable to move because her legs are broken. *Driver One* sees what has happened but does not do anything to assist *Pedestrian*. She is subsequently run over by another car driven by *Driver Two*. The second impact causes *Pedestrian* to suffer severe brain damage. *Pedestrian* will be able to sue *One* for that brain damage because *One*'s initial act of negligence in running her down contributed to her suffering that brain damage in the sense that, had *One* not run *Pedestrian* down, she would not have been subsequently run over by *Two*. In this case, *Pedestrian* will not need to argue that *having run her down*, *One* owed her a duty to go to her assistance. No doubt he did; but *Pedestrian* will not need to rely on that fact in order to sue *One* for damages for her brain damage.

The duty formula under discussion in this section comes into its own where A has *innocently* put B in danger of suffering some kind of harm, or where A has acted perfectly *reasonably*, but the result of his actions has been to put B in danger of suffering some kind of harm. For example, in the American case of *Hardy* v *Brooks* (1961), the defendant was driving along the highway when a cow wandered into his path. The defendant was unable to avoid crashing into the cow, and the cow died on the spot. The cow's carcass was lying in the middle of the road and posed a clear danger to oncoming traffic. The defendant failed to do anything about this danger, that he had, unwittingly, played a part in creating. He did not try to alert the authorities to try to get them to move the cow out of the road, and did not put up any warning signs to alert oncoming traffic that there was an obstruction up ahead. He simply drove around the cow and proceeded on his way. The claimant subsequently crashed into the cow and was injured. It was held that the defendant had owed the claimant a duty to take reasonable steps to protect the claimant from the danger that he had played a part in creating.

A number of aspects of this duty formula need careful examination.

A. Creating danger

There is clearly a distinction between creating a danger and providing an occasion for danger to arise. For example, if A threatens to kill B, no one would suggest that A's mother

---

[48] See below, § 7.4.

owes B a duty to take reasonable steps to ensure her safety from A because A's mother 'created' the danger B is in by giving birth to A.

But it is difficult to know where to draw the line between conduct that creates a danger and conduct that has merely provided an occasion for danger to arise. On one side of the line – the 'creation of danger' side – lie cases like *Kane* v *New Forest DC* (2002) and *Watson* v *British Board of Boxing Control* (2001). In *Kane*, the defendant council approved the creation of a right of way passing over a main road. There was nothing wrong with that. Unfortunately, the right of way crossed over the main road at a bend in the road, so some motorists would not be able to see a pedestrian using the right of way to cross the road until it was too late. And that is how the claimant ended up being injured. The Court of Appeal held that the defendant council had owed the claimant a duty to take reasonable steps to protect the claimant from the danger created by their approving the creation of a right of way at such a dangerous junction. In *Watson*, Michael Watson spent 40 days in a coma and six years in a wheelchair because he did not receive proper medical attention after a particularly brutal boxing match with Chris Eubank. Watson sued the British Board of Boxing Control (BBBC), which had been involved in putting on and promoting the fight. The Court of Appeal held that the BBBC had owed Watson a duty to take reasonable steps to protect him from the danger that he would suffer lasting injuries as a result of his fight with Eubank by seeing to it that there were adequate medical facilities at ring-side.

On the other side of the line – seemingly – are cases like *Mitchell* v *Glasgow City Council* (2009) and the Canadian case of *Childs* v *Desormeaux* (2006). In *Mitchell*, a 'neighbour from hell' called James Drummond attacked and killed James Mitchell after the defendant council – which rented neighbouring council flats to both Drummond and Mitchell, and which was trying to deal with the problems created by Drummond's anti-social behaviour – informed Drummond in a meeting with him that Mitchell had videoed Drummond threatening him. It was argued that after Drummond became visibly angry and stormed out of the meeting, the defendant council had owed Mitchell a duty to take steps to warn him that he might be in danger. The House of Lords rejected this contention. At least two of their Lordships took the view that the council had not done enough here for it to be correct to say that it had *created* a danger to Mitchell. As Lord Brown observed, 'by threatening a disruptive tenant with eviction a landlord cannot be sensibly said to be creating the risk of personal violence towards others . . .'[49]

In *Childs* v *Desormeaux*, the defendants hosted a New Year's party which was attended by Desmond Desormeaux. The party was a 'bring your own bottle' party. Desormeaux had far too much to drink at the party, and by the time he left, the level of alcohol in his blood was three times the legal limit for drivers. Desormeaux drove home from the party in his drunken state and ended up colliding with another car. One of the passengers in the other car was killed, and the claimant was paralysed. The claimant was obviously entitled to sue Desormeaux in negligence for compensation for her injuries, on the basis that he had owed her a duty to take care not to drive home drunk. The difficult question that the Supreme Court of Canada had to resolve was whether the defendants had owed the claimant a duty to take reasonable steps to stop Desormeaux driving home drunk, on the basis that, by hosting the party at which he got drunk, they had played some part in creating the danger that people like the claimant would be exposed to if Desormeaux drove home drunk. The Canadian Supreme Court ruled that the defendants had not owed the claimant a duty of care in this case:

[49] [2009] 1 AC 874, at [82]. Lord Scott seemed to take much the same view.

Holding a private party at which alcohol is served – the bare facts of this case – is insufficient to implicate the host in the creation of a risk sufficient to give rise to a duty of care to third parties who may be subsequently injured by the conduct of a guest. The host creates a place where people can meet, visit and imbibe alcohol, whether served on the premises or supplied by the guest. All this falls within accepted parameters of non-dangerous conduct. More is required to establish a danger or risk that requires positive action. It might be argued that a host who continues to serve alcohol to a visibly inebriated person knowing that he or she will be driving home has become implicated in the creation or enhancement of a risk sufficient to give rise to a prima facie duty of care to third parties. We need not decide that question here.[50]

What accounts for the difference between *Kane* and *Watson* on the one hand, and *Mitchell* and *Childs* on the other? It is tempting to locate the difference in the fact that in *Mitchell* and *Childs* the ultimate source of the danger to the claimant was the deliberate, voluntary, informed and unreasonable act of a third party (Drummond's attacking Mitchell; Desormeaux's drunk driving), and that kind of act 'breaks the chain of causation' between whatever the defendant has done and the danger to the claimant.[51] However, there are some cases that make it difficult to argue that a defendant cannot be held to have created a danger to a claimant if something has happened to 'break the chain of causation' between the defendant's conduct and the danger the claimant is in.

First, it has been held in both England[52] and Australia,[53] that if it is reasonably foreseeable that a prisoner, A, will attack a fellow prisoner, B, if he is given the chance, the prison authorities will owe B a duty to take reasonable steps to keep A away from B. The existence of this duty of care can be best seen as arising out of the duty formula discussed here – by imprisoning B within the same walls as A, the prison authorities have helped to create a danger that B will be attacked by A. But, it should be noted, it could be argued that there exists a 'break in the chain of causation' between the prison authorities' imprisoning B, and the danger resulting from B's being imprisoned – B's being imprisoned only gives rise to a danger of B being attacked because A has deliberately, voluntarily and unreasonably decided that he wants to attack B.

Secondly, in *R v Evans* (2009), the defendant gave some heroin to her half-sister Carly. Carly injected herself with the heroin and subsequently complained to the defendant that she was feeling hot. The defendant saw that Carly was 'in a mess' – her lips were blue and she had lost colour in her skin – and realised that there was a danger Carly was overdosing on the heroin. Instead of calling for an ambulance, the defendant put her to bed, hoping that she would recover spontaneously. Unfortunately, Carly died during the night. The defendant was charged with gross negligence manslaughter. It was argued that she had owed Carly a duty to call her an ambulance and that the defendant's breach of that duty had contributed to Carly's death and was so outrageous as to be worthy of punishment. A very strong Court of Appeal – five judges – held that the defendant had owed Carly a duty of care in this case, based on the fact that:

> when a person has created or contributed to the creation of a state of affairs which he knows, or ought reasonably to know, has become life threatening, a consequent duty on him to act by taking reasonable steps to save the other's life will normally arise.[54]

---

[50] [2006] 1 SCR 643, at [44].
[51] On the concept of a 'break in the chain of causation', see below, § 9.12.
[52] *Ellis* v *Home Office* [1953] 2 All ER 149.
[53] *New South Wales* v *Budjoso* (2005) 222 ALR 663.
[54] [2009] 1 WLR 1999, at [31].

But, it should be noted, the defendant's act of supplying Carly with heroin only put Carly in danger of dying through an overdose because Carly deliberately, voluntarily and unreasonably injected herself with the heroin, when she knew what the effect of doing this might be on her. Given this, Carly's act would normally be held to have 'broken the chain of causation' between the defendant's supplying her with heroin, and Carly's being in danger of dying from an overdose. However, the Court of Appeal still held that the duty formula under discussion here applied to the defendant in this case.

Perhaps the best that can be said is that there are no iron rules in this area. In a situation where A has done something that has played a part in B being exposed to danger of being harmed either by herself, or a third party, C, the greater the part A has played in B's being put in danger, the more likely the courts are to find that A has 'created a danger' and has a duty to take reasonable steps to protect B from that danger. In *Childs* v *Desormeaux*, the defendants had very little to do with Desormeaux's drunk driving – they merely hosted an event, but were not the ones who supplied the alcohol at that event.[55] Likewise, the defendants in *Mitchell* v *Glasgow City Council*. While their lack of caution in confronting Drummond with the evidence that Mitchell had made a video of him may have played a part in Drummon's subsequently attacking Mitchell, Drummond could well have seized on some other excuse to attack Mitchell, as he had in the past. But in *R* v *Evans*, Carly simply could not have overdosed without the assistance of the defendant. As a result, it was fair to find that the defendant in *Evans* helped to create the danger that Carly would die of a heroin overdose.

B. Further requirements?

In *Mitchell* v *Glasgow City Council* (2009), two of the Law Lords who decided that case seemed to suggest that in a case where A has done something to create a danger that B will be attacked by C, the mere fact that A has created a danger to B will *not* be enough to give rise to a duty of care on A's part to protect B.

---

[55] The lack of any iron rules in this area explains why, when the defendant *did* supply the alcohol and did so on a commercial basis, different courts in different countries have come to different conclusions as to: (1) whether the defendant will owe a duty of care to *road users* who might be injured by the drinker's drunken driving, to stop the drinker driving home; and (2) whether the defendant will owe a duty of care to the *drinker* to see that he gets home safely. In Canada, the courts have answered 'yes' to (1) and (2): *Jordan House Ltd* v *Menow* [1974] SCR 239 (claimant got drunk at defendants' bar and wandered off into the night and was hit by a car; held that the defendants had owed the claimant a duty to arrange for some way to get him home safely) and *Stewart* v *Pettie* [1995] 1 SCR 131 (two couples – the Stewarts and the Petties – went to the defendants' establishment to have something to eat and watch a play; they all had a fair amount to drink and when Stuart Pettie drove them all home, there was an accident in which the Stewarts were injured; held that in principle the defendants might have owed the Stewarts a duty of care to see that they were not injured by Pettie's drunk driving, but on the facts they could not have known that Pettie was not fit to drive). In Australia, the High Court has recently made it clear that a duty of care would only be owed in (2) in very extreme cases: *CAL No 14* v *Motor Accidents Board* (2009) 239 CLR 390 (noted, Guy, Richardson and Hocking 2010). In that case, the claimant had been drinking at the defendant's pub for three hours on his way home from work, and at one point had given the defendant the keys to his motorbike to ensure that he was not tempted to drive home drunk. But he eventually asked for the keys back. The defendant gave them to him and the claimant was injured when he drunkenly fell off the bike driving home. Held, that the defendant had not owed the claimant a duty of care to see that he got home safely, or at least that he did not drive home. For further discussion of 'social host' and 'commercial host' liability for injuries caused by drunkenness, see Orr 1995, Solomon and Payne 1996, Dalphond 2002, Fordham 2010 (at 33–42).

Lord *Hope* remarked that:

> . . . as a general rule . . . a duty to warn another person that he is at risk of loss, injury or damage as the result of the criminal act of a third party will arise only where the person who is said to be under that duty has by his words or conduct assumed responsibility for the safety of the person who is at risk.[56]

Lord *Rodger* seemed to go so far as to say that in the case where A has done something to put B in danger of being harmed by C, there could be no duty to act unless A had acted *wrongfully* in putting B in danger. He noted that in the authorities that had dealt with this kind of case before:

> [The defendant's] act which provides the opportunity for the third party to injure the claimant is itself wrongful . . . that is not enough to make for liability . . . for the harm which a third party subsequently deliberately chooses to inflict. But it is, at least, a start.[57]

If either of these suggestions are taken seriously by the courts in future, the duty formula under discussion here will be effectively *irrelevant* for the purposes of establishing that A owed B a duty to protect her in a case where he had done something to create a danger that she would be harmed by C. This is because if A has already assumed a responsibility for B's safety, then B will be able to base her claim that A owed her a duty to protect her on that, and not the fact that A put her in danger of being injured. And if A has wrongfully put B in danger of being harmed, and that danger materialises and B suffers harm, then B will be able to base her claim for damages for that harm on the wrong that A committed in putting her in danger, and not have to worry about establishing that A owed her a duty to take positive steps to protect her from that danger.

However, we would suggest that the courts should not pay any attention to either of these *dicta* in the *Mitchell* case. They seem to have been thrown out without much thought, or consideration for how they might apply in concrete cases, such as the case where the prison authorities know or ought to know that one of their prisoners is in danger of being attacked by another prisoner.

C. What kind of harm?

All of the cases we have discussed so far have involved a defendant putting a claimant in danger of suffering some kind of physical harm. In *Butchart* v *Home Office* (2006), the defendant prison authorities put the claimant in danger of suffering a psychiatric illness by placing him in the same cell as a prisoner with suicidal tendencies, when they knew or ought to have known that the claimant was in a similarly fragile mental state and there was a real risk he would suffer a mental breakdown (as he did) if his cell mate killed himself. The Court of Appeal held that the prison authorities had owed the claimant a duty to take reasonable steps to monitor the claimant's cellmate to make sure that he did not kill himself.

There is, so far as we know, no tort case where the issue has been addressed as to whether A will owe B a duty to take reasonable steps to protect B's property if A has done something that has put that property in danger of being harmed. (For example, suppose that A is in the park playing with his son, and he attempts to throw a tennis ball to his son. He misses his aim, and the tennis ball falls into a nearby lake. B's dog rushes into the lake to retrieve

---

[56] [2009] 1 AC 874, at [29].
[57] [2009] 1 AC 874, at [58].

the ball and starts to struggle . . .) However, the criminal case of *R* v *Miller* (1983) suggests that creating a foreseeable danger to property *can* give rise to a duty to act.

In that case, the defendant fell asleep in someone else's house while he was still smoking a cigarette. He dropped the lit cigarette onto the mattress on which he was lying. Soon after, the claimant woke up and realised the mattress was on fire. However – because he was very drunk and not thinking straight – he did not attempt to do anything about fire but simply moved to another room to find another place to sleep. The fire subsequently spread to the rest of the house. The defendant was charged with arson under the Criminal Damage Act 1971. He could not be convicted on the basis of his initial act of dropping the lit cigarette. This is because arson is a crime of recklessness, and when the defendant dropped the cigarette he was not aware that that act might result in property being damaged by fire. But if the defendant acted *wrongfully* in *failing to do anything about the fire* when he woke up, then he could be convicted, as he was aware at that stage that if he did not do anything about the fire, property might be damaged by fire. The House of Lords found that the defendant had been under a duty to act in this case, based on the fact that he had (albeit unwittingly) created a foreseeable risk of harm to property by dropping his lit cigarette on the mattress.

D. What sort of steps?

In a case where the duty formula under discussion here applies, and A owes B a duty to take reasonable steps to protect B from some danger that he has created, how much is A actually required to do for B? The question has not been at all well explored, either in the caselaw or in academic articles.

In *E Hobbs (Farms) Ltd* v *Baxenden Chemicals* (1992), it was held that the manufacturer of foam insulation installed in the claimant's farm buildings owed the claimant a duty to *warn* him that the foam was combustible when the manufacturer realised that this was the case: 'a manufacturer's duty of care does not end when the goods are sold. A manufacturer who realises that omitting to warn past customers about something which might result in injury to them must take reasonable steps to attempt to warn them, however lacking in negligence he may have been at the time the goods were sold.'[58]

But in this sort of case, a warning would not have completely protected the claimant against the risk of his farm buildings burning down if the foam insulation caught fire. Could the defendant have been required to do more, and strip the insulation out of the buildings, at the defendant's own expense? We would suggest that it would depend on how far the defendant was at fault for creating the danger to which the claimant's buildings are now exposed. If the defendant was not at fault at all – there was no reason why he should have known about the risk posed by this insulation at the time he installed it – then, we would suggest, a warning is all the defendant has to give the claimant. Once that has been given, the defendant could justifiably claim that he had done enough, and further protection against the risk of fire damage was a matter for the claimant to provide. If the defendant was very culpable for installing such dangerous insulation in the claimant's buildings, then he could be required to do more – but, of course, in such a case, if the risk of fire damage materialised, the claimant would simply be able to sue the defendant for that damage on the basis that he acted negligently in *installing* the insulation, and not worry about arguing that the defendant acted negligently in *failing to remove* the insulation.

---

[58] [1992] 1 Lloyds Rep 54, 65.

In a number of American cases, defendants who have created dangers that claimants will suffer some kind of physical harm *in the future* have been ordered to set up 'medical monitoring funds' which would cover the expense of giving the claimants regular check-ups to ensure that they get medical treatment as soon as their physical condition seems to be deteriorating as a result of what the defendants did.[59] Whether a defendant's duty to take reasonable steps to look after the health of a claimant who he has put in danger of suffering physical harm in the future extends so far as to require him to set up a 'medical monitoring fund' for the claimant would, we suggest, again depend on the circumstances.[60] More specifically, it will depend on how blameworthy the defendant was for putting the claimant in danger of suffering physical harm in future, and how easily the defendant could afford to cover the cost of setting up such a fund.

7.4 INTERFERENCE

A number of cases can be taken as suggesting that if A knows or ought to know that B is in need of help to avoid some harm, and A knows or ought to know that he has done something to put off or prevent someone else helping B, then A will owe B a duty to take reasonable steps to give B the help she needs.

The duty of care that the ambulance service owed the claimant in *Kent v Griffiths* (2001)[61] can be explained on this basis. As Lord Woolf MR observed in that case: 'If wrong information had not been given about the arrival of the ambulance, other means of transport could have been used.'[62] By telling the claimant's doctor and husband that an ambulance was on its way and would be arriving imminently, the ambulance service put them off finding some other way to get the claimant to hospital (for example, in a taxi).[63]

In *Costello v Chief Constable of the Northumbria Police* (1999), the claimant was a woman police officer who was attacked by a prisoner when she took the prisoner down to the cells in a police station. Another officer, H, accompanied the claimant in taking the prisoner down to the cells in order to help her out if there was any trouble. However, when H saw B – a police inspector – standing by the cells, H went back upstairs, assuming that B would assist the claimant if she was attacked by the prisoner. When the claimant was attacked, B – contrary to expectation – stood by and did nothing. The Court of Appeal found that B

---

[59] *Friends for All Children v Lockheed Corporation Inc*, 746 F 2d 816 (1984) (Lockheed ordered to create fund to pay for Vietnamese children – who were involved in a plane crash which was Lockheed's fault – to undergo regular neurological exams to check for any incipient brain disorder caused by the decompression they had experienced in the crash); *Ayers v Jackson*, 525 A 2d 287 (1987) (company that polluted residents' water with carcinogenic chemicals was ordered to create a fund to pay for the residents to undergo regular medical tests in the future to detect whether or not the pollution had caused them to develop cancer); *Potter v Firestone Tire & Rubber Co*, 863 P 2d 795 (1993) (medical monitoring award made against tyre company that dumped hazardous waste next to claimants' land, thus putting them in danger of developing cancer); *Hansen v Mountain Fuel Supply Co*, 858 P 2d 970 (1993) (defendant who exposed contractors to excessive quantities of asbestos dust while they were working for defendant could be ordered to create a fund to pay for contractors' health to be monitored – but only if the contractors were in danger of developing a serious disease as a result of being exposed to the asbestos 'for which a medical test for early detection exists . . . and for which early detection is beneficial, meaning that a treatment exists that can alter the course of the illness' (ibid, at 979)).

[60] So far as we know, John Goldberg and Benjamin Zipursky were the first to suggest (brilliantly) that orders to set up 'medical monitoring funds' could be rationalised as the courts' enforcing a defendant's duty to take reasonable steps to deal with a danger that he had played some part in exposing the claimant to: see Goldberg and Zipursky 2002, 1709–15.

[61] See above, § 7.2.

[62] [2001] QB 36, at [49].

[63] [2001] QB 36, at [17]: 'But for the acceptance of the 999 call the [claimant] would have been driven to the hospital and would have arrived prior to her "arrest".'

had owed the claimant a duty to take reasonable steps to save her from being attacked. The Court of Appeal said that the duty of care arose because B 'assumed a responsibility' to the claimant.[64] However, it seems clear that he did not – B never indicated to the *claimant* that she could rely on him to look after her if she got into trouble. A more satisfactory explanation of the case is that B owed the claimant a duty of care because he indicated to *H* that he would take care of the claimant if she got into trouble, and thereby dissuaded H from sticking around to make sure he would be on hand if anything happened to B.

In *Reeves v Commissioner of Police of the Metropolis* (2000), a man named Martin Lynch was remanded in police custody on charges of credit card fraud; he was also under investigation for handling stolen vehicles. He was known to be a suicide risk, having tried to kill himself twice before while in police custody. This time he succeeded. He took advantage of the fact that the police had left the spyhole into his cell open, and tied a shirt around the metal bars on the outside of his door, over the spyhole, and hanged himself. It was accepted on all sides of the case that the police had owed Lynch a duty to take reasonable steps to see that he did not kill himself. While counsel for the claimant (Lynch's partner) argued that 'The duty . . . arose . . . from the well known fact that custody has a depressive effect on people who are not otherwise suicidal'[65] – which would indicate that the duty in this case arose out of some 'creation of danger' idea – it seems likely that the police would have owed Lynch a duty of care even if their taking him into custody was not the reason why he felt suicidal.[66] Given this, a more satisfactory explanation as to why a duty of care was owed in *Reeves'* case was that, by taking him into custody, the police cut him off from sources of support that might have helped him overcome his suicidal tendencies. Having done this, they owed him a duty to take reasonable steps to stop him committing suicide themselves.

The same idea, that cutting someone off from alternative sources of support gives rise to a duty to act, probably underlies the finding of a duty of care in *Barrett v Ministry of Defence* (1995). In that case, it will be recalled, a soldier got so drunk at a Hawaiian party that had been organised by the defendants at his barracks that he collapsed and later died from choking on his own vomit. The Court of Appeal refused to find that the defendants had owed the soldier a duty of care not to serve him so many drinks that he collapsed. However, it was found at first instance – and not disputed on appeal – that after the soldier collapsed, the defendants had owed the soldier a duty to take reasonable steps to see that he got through the night safely, and had breached that duty by failing to summon a doctor to see him.[67] This duty arose because after the soldier collapsed, the officer in charge of the barracks had the soldier taken to his cabin and put in his bunk. In so doing, the officer cut the soldier off from other sources of support that might have been able to intervene to see that he did not die during the night.

Viewed this way, *Barrett's* case is strongly analogous to the American case of *Zelenko v Gimbel Bros* (1935). In that case, Mary Zelenko collapsed in the defendants' department store. The defendants took her into the store infirmary to look after her, but then failed to do anything for her for six hours. Zelenko died as a result of not being treated quickly enough. While it could not be shown that any particular individual had been dissuaded or prevented from looking after Zelenko as a result of the defendant's taking charge of her, the

---

[64] [1999] 1 All ER 550, 564.

[65] [2000] 1 AC 360, 364.

[66] There is a hint that this was the case in counsel for the defendants' observation in the course of argument that 'The suicidal tendencies of the deceased arose from his concern about his pending criminal trial and his unwillingness to face the possibility of going to prison': [2000] 1 AC 360, 365.

[67] [1995] 1 WLR 1217, 1223.

court was satisfied that it was 'beyond doubt [that if the defendant had left Zelenko alone] some bystander . . . would have summoned an ambulance'[68] and as a result found that the defendant had owed Zelenko a duty to take reasonable steps to give her the medical attention she needed.

In all of the cases we have discussed so far, the defendant either dissuaded or prevented *someone else* from helping someone in need. What about the situation where A has dissuaded or prevented B from *helping themselves*? In such a situation, there will usually be no need to rely on the idea that interference gives rise to a duty to act in order to establish that A owed B a duty of care. In a 'dissuasion' case, it will usually be possible to find that A 'assumed a responsibility' to B, and base a duty to act on that. In a 'prevention' case, it will usually be possible to argue that A had a duty to take care not to stop B helping herself to avoid the danger she was in, on the basis that it was reasonably foreseeable that if he did so, B might suffer physical harm as a result. However, there may be some cases where neither of these analyses will really work to show that a duty of care was owed. And in such cases, recourse to the idea that interference gives rise to a duty to act may be necessary.

For example, in *Mercer v South Eastern & Chatham Railway Companies' Managing Committee* (1922), the claimant was hit by a passing train as he crossed a railway line. The gate to the path over the railway line was usually locked by the defendant when a train was due to come by, but the defendant had on this occasion left the gate unlocked and this had led the claimant to believe that it was safe to cross the railway line. It was held that the defendant had owed the claimant a duty to take reasonable steps to ensure that he locked the gate to the path over the railway line when a train was due to come by.

The finding of a duty of care in this case cannot easily be explained without recourse to the idea that interference gives rise to a duty to act. The defendant did not 'assume a responsibility' to anyone by regularly locking the gate when a train was due to come by: he never indicated to people like the claimant that they could rely on him to take care to do this.[69] And mere foreseeability of physical harm to someone like the claimant could not give rise to a duty on the part of the defendant to take the *positive* step of locking the gate when a train was due to go by.

But it could be argued that the defendant was aware – or ought to have been aware – that his regular custom of locking the gate as a train was due to go by was having the effect of encouraging people like the claimant to think that if the gate was unlocked, they could cross the railway line *without having to worry about whether a train was coming along*. Having encouraged people like the claimant to let their guard down in this way, the defendant owed them a duty to take reasonable steps to protect them from the risk that they might be run down by a train as they crossed the railway line.

While the idea that interference gives rise to a duty to act seems to be well-established in the law, the potential ambit of that duty formula was limited by the first instance decision in *OLL Ltd v Secretary of State for Transport* (1997).[70] In that case, a party of eight children and one teacher got into severe difficulty on a canoeing trip in the sea off Lyme Regis. The coastguard was mobilised but bungled the rescue operation, directing a lifeboat

---

[68] 287 NYS 134, 135 (1935).

[69] For example, the philosopher Immanuel Kant was well-known in his home town of Königsberg for going for a daily walk at exactly the same time every day. So much so, that people would set their watches and clocks according to what time Kant passed their houses. But no one would say that in this case Kant 'assumed a responsibility' to the townsfolk of Königsberg that he would take care to go for a walk at exactly the same time every day. Regularity of behaviour does not give rise to an assumption of responsibility.

[70] Discussed, Bagshaw 1999.

and a Royal Navy helicopter to search for the party in the wrong area. As a result, all the members of the party suffered severe hypothermia and four of the children died. It was claimed in the subsequent litigation that the coastguard had owed the members of the party a duty to take reasonable steps to rescue them.

It was arguable that the idea that interference gives rise to a duty to act applied in this case. It could have been argued that the coastguard prevented the lifeboat crew and the Royal Navy from rescuing the stricken party by giving them wrong directions, and as a result the coastguard owed the party a duty to take reasonable steps to rescue them. However, May J refused to find that a duty of care was owed by the coastguard here, holding that it would be 'artificial'[71] to distinguish between the coastguard and other rescue organisations that were attempting to save the teacher and children at sea. This was a case of one person getting in his own way in attempting to rescue the canoeing party; not a case of someone getting in the way of *someone else* who was trying to rescue the party.[72]

The case of *Poppleton* v *Trustees of the Portsmouth Youth Activities Committee* (2008) might be taken as placing another limit on the idea that interference gives rise to a duty to act. In that case, the defendants ran some indoor climbing premises that were used by the claimant. The claimant attempted to jump from one climbing wall to another. His attempt failed, and he fell to the ground and was severely injured. He sued the defendants, arguing that they had owed him a duty to warn him that the matting at the base of the climbing walls was not very thick and did not offer much protection to falling climbers: had he known this, he would not have attempted to jump from one wall to another. Although it could be said that the defendants lulled the claimant into a false sense of security here by providing safety matting that was not as safe as it might have looked, the Court of Appeal rejected the claim that a duty to warn the claimant was owed by the defendants here as the claimant was still aware that there was *some* risk attached to attempting to jump from one wall to another. So lulling a claimant into a false sense of *relative* security might not be enough to allow a claimant to invoke the idea that interference gives rise to a duty to act.

7.5 CONTROL

It seems to be well established that if A is in control of a dangerous *substance or animal*, and it is reasonably foreseeable that someone like B will be harmed by that substance or animal if A allows it to escape his control, then A will owe B a duty to take reasonable steps to keep that thing or that animal under his control.[73]

What is controversial is what the position is where A is in control of a *human being* and it is foreseeable that someone like B will be harmed if that human being escapes A's control. In a case where B has been harmed by C – who was under A's control – whether or not A

---

[71] [1997] 3 All ER 897, 907.

[72] So in the case of Loraine Whiting – whose estranged husband broke into her house, shot her, and then killed himself, and who then died from loss of blood with the police actively preventing the ambulance services from going into the house because they feared (despite 30 calls from Loraine Whiting telling them that her husband was dead) that the husband might still be in the house waiting to shoot at anyone coming in – the *OLL* decision would seem to prevent interference being used as the basis of an argument that the police owed Loraine Whiting a duty of care to come to her aid, having stopped the ambulance services coming to her assistance. The police and ambulance services should be bundled together into one unit, 'the emergency services', which unit did not owe Loraine Whiting a duty of care because it did not 'assume a responsibility' to her, or put her in danger, or stop anyone else outside 'the emergency services' coming to her assistance.

[73] If the substance or animal escapes A's control without any negligence on his part and B is harmed as a result, B may still be entitled to sue A for compensation under either the rule in *Rylands* v *Fletcher* (see below, chapter 16) or the Animals Act 1971 (see below, chapter 13).

owed B a duty of care to keep C under control seems to depend on how responsible C was for the harm he did B. If he was not at all responsible, A will have owed B a duty of care if it was merely foreseeable that C's escaping A's control would result in B being harmed. If C was responsible for the harm he did B, something more will be required before the courts will find that A owed B a duty of care to keep C under control. In order not to dilute C's responsibility for what he did to B too much, the courts will only find that A owed B a duty of care to control C if B was in *special danger* of being harmed by C if C escaped A's control.

In *Carmarthenshire County Council* v *Lewis* (1955), a four-year-old boy attending nursery school wandered off the school premises and onto the road running alongside the nursery school. The claimant's husband, who was driving along the road, swerved to avoid the boy and crashed into a tree and died. The claimant sued, claiming that the defendant county council – which owned the school – and the teachers at the school had owed her husband, and breached, a duty to take reasonable steps to keep control of the children at the school. The House of Lords agreed that the defendant county council and the teachers at the school had owed the claimant's husband such a duty of care. As the boy was not at all responsible for what happened to the claimant's husband, mere foreseeability that someone like the claimant would be harmed if the boy escaped the defendants' control was enough to give rise to a duty of care to keep the boy under control. And it was, of course, eminently foreseeable that children at the school would wander into the road outside the school and cause accidents if defendants did not keep control of them.[74]

It was different in *Dorset Yacht Co Ltd* v *Home Office* (1970). In that case, seven 'Borstal boys' – young offenders who were in custody – were on a training exercise on Brownsea Island in Poole Harbour. They were under the supervision of three officers. One night the boys escaped, taking advantage of the fact that all three officers had, contrary to instructions, gone to bed. They boarded one of the vessels in the harbour and set sail in it but it collided with the claimant's yacht. They then boarded the claimant's yacht and did further damage to it. The claimant sued the Home Office for compensation, arguing that the officers had owed him a duty to take reasonable steps not to let the boys escape. The House of Lords found that such a duty had been owed to the claimant.

There was no problem showing that it was reasonably foreseeable that someone like the claimant would suffer harm if the boys were allowed to escape the officers' control. This is because it was reasonably foreseeable – very likely or probable – that if the boys were allowed to escape the officers' control, they would commandeer one of the boats in the harbour in an attempt to get off the island and make good their escape, and in so doing would damage the boat. It followed that it was reasonably foreseeable that someone like the claimant – someone who owned a boat in the harbour – would suffer harm if the boys were allowed to escape their officers' control.

However, as the boys were responsible for what happened to the claimant's yacht, foreseeability of harm was not enough to give rise to a duty of care. It had to be shown that the claimant was *especially* at risk of suffering harm if the boys in this case escaped the defendants' control. This requirement of 'special danger' to the claimant was satisfied here because people like the claimant – people who owned boats in the harbour – were at greater risk of suffering harm as a result of the boys' escape than other members of the population such as shopkeepers or owners of bikes on the island. Their boats would be especially valuable

---

[74] See also *Palmer* v *Cornwall County Council* [2009] EWCA Civ 456 (claimant schoolboy was hit in the eye by a large rock thrown by another schoolboy during a lunch break; defendant local authority held liable for failing to have enough staff on the ground supervising children playing at lunchtime to see that this sort of thing did not go on).

to the boys if the boys were allowed to escape – so their boats were especially likely to be targeted by the boys on escape as compared with other items of property such as groceries or bikes. It follows that the result of the case would have been different had the boys, on escaping, robbed a shop on the island.[75] No duty would have been owed to the shopkeeper to take reasonable steps to prevent the boys escaping as there would have been no special risk that the shopkeeper's wares would be targeted by the Borstal boys on escape.

In line with the position taken here in the text, Lord Morris suggested in the case of *Dorset Yacht Co Ltd* v *Home Office* that 'If a person who is in lawful custody has made a threat, accepted as seriously intended, that, if he can escape, he will injure X . . . a duty [will be] owed to X to take reasonable care to prevent escape.'[76] This requirement was not satisfied in *K* v *Secretary of State for the Home Dept* (2002). In that case, M, a Kenyan citizen, was imprisoned for sexual assault and then for burglary. He was detained, awaiting deportation, but was released on order of the Home Secretary. M subsequently raped the claimant. The claimant sued the Home Secretary in negligence, claiming that he had owed her a duty not to release M. The Home Secretary applied to have the action struck out. For the purposes of hearing the striking out claim, it was assumed against the Home Secretary that he had acted unreasonably in ordering M to be released and that it was reasonably foreseeable that if M was released, he would attack someone like the claimant. It made no difference: the Court of Appeal still refused to find that the Home Secretary had owed the claimant a duty not to release M. The special danger requirement was not satisfied here. The claimant was at no greater risk of being attacked by M on release than the rest of the population or the rest of the female population.

'Control' in this context classically means 'physical' control. In *Tarasoff* v *Regents of the University of California* (1976), one of the defendants' psychiatric patients – Prosenjit Poddar – killed the claimants' daughter, Tatiana Tarasoff. Poddar had confided to the defendants in the course of treatment that he was intending to kill Tarasoff. It was held that, in these circumstances, the defendants had owed Tarasoff a duty to warn her of the danger she was in. John Goldberg and Benjamin Zipursky have suggested that the decision can be rationalised on the basis that control of a dangerous person can give rise to a duty to act:

> Although the defendant-therapists in *Tarasoff* did not have custody over the dangerous patient, they had previously ordered his confinement and in any event enjoyed the authority under state law to order confinement of persons posing a danger to themselves or others.[77]

It is not clear whether in the UK, the notion of control giving rise to a duty to act would extend to 'power to control' cases. The closest the UK has come to a *Tarasoff*-type case is *Palmer* v *Tees Health Authority* (1999), where the claimant's four-year-old daughter, Rosie, was kidnapped, sexually assaulted, and murdered by a man called Armstrong. Armstrong was being treated by the defendants for various psychiatric problems as an in-patient, and subsequently as an out-patient. A claim that the defendants had owed Rosie a duty to take reasonable steps to diagnose and treat his tendencies to sexually assault children was dismissed by the Court of Appeal on the basis that Rosie (as opposed to any other child) had not been in special danger of being attacked by Armstrong. The question of whether the defendants would have owed Rosie a duty of care had she been in special danger of being attacked by Armstrong did not therefore arise. We think it is unlikely that such a duty of care would have existed. To base such a duty merely on the power to control someone,

---

[75] [1970] AC 1004, 1070 (per Lord Diplock).
[76] [1970] AC 1004, 1039.
[77] Goldberg and Zipursky 2009, 1240, n 121.

rather than the fact of control, would go too far towards undermining the rule against there being a general duty to rescue people who you are in a position to save from harm.

7.6 OCCUPIERS

The idea that control of a dangerous thing or person may give rise to a positive duty of care to protect other people from that thing or person finds fresh application in the law on occupiers' liability, where someone who is in control of premises that are in a dangerous state may owe people on or near those premises a duty to take reasonable steps to safeguard them from being harmed by the state of those premises.

Some academic lawyers are resistant to the idea that the law on occupiers' liability is part of the law of negligence. It is hard to see why. The occupier of land is subject to duties of care and when he breaches one of those duties, the remedies for his breach are exactly the same as would be awarded against anyone else who breached a duty of care owed to another. However, out of respect for those academics who expect to see the law on 'occupiers' liability' dealt with separately from the law of negligence, we have gathered together the relevant materials on occupiers' liability into a separate chapter in this edition of this textbook. Having said that, students will find it useful to be informed at this stage of the various positive duties of care that an occupier of land will owe to other people:

(1) Under the *Occupiers' Liability Act 1957*, an occupier will normally owe his visitors, and other people lawfully on his land, a duty to take reasonable steps to see that they are reasonably safe for the purposes for which they are on the premises.

(2) Under the *Occupiers' Liability Act 1984*, an occupier will owe a *trespasser* a duty to take reasonable steps to safeguard him or her against a danger arising on his land if: (a) he knows or ought to know of the danger; (b) he knows or ought to know that a trespasser on his land might go into the vicinity of that danger; and (c) that danger is one he could reasonably be expected to do something about.

(3) Under the *general law of negligence*, an occupier will owe a range of positive duties of care to a range of different people. For example, he will owe his neighbours a duty to take reasonable steps to put out any fires on his land that are liable to spread onto his neighbours' land. And he will owe people passing by his land a duty to take reasonable steps to see that any fixtures on his land – for example, a sign or a tree – that overhang the road will not fall on them.

The law on occupiers' liability is dealt with in much more detail in chapter 11, below.

7.7 LANDLORDS

If *Landlord* lets premises to *Tenant* and *Landlord* knows or ought to know that the premises suffer from a defect[78] that *Landlord* is obliged to repair under the contract of tenancy, then s 4 of the Defective Premises Act 1972 provides that *Landlord* will *normally* owe:

---

[78] Defective Premises Act 1972, s 4(2). The Court of Appeal has made it clear that it need not be shown, for the purposes of this requirement, that A had actual knowledge of the existence of the defect or of facts which indicated that the defect existed: it is enough to show that a reasonable man in A's position would have discovered the existence of the defect. See *Sykes* v *Harry* [2001] QB 1014 (leave to appeal refused by the House of Lords: [2002] 1 WLR 2286).

all persons[79] who might reasonably be expected to be affected by defects in the state of the premises a duty to take such care as is reasonable in all the circumstances to see that they are reasonably safe from personal injury or from damage caused to their property by [that] defect.[80]

Under s 4(4) of the 1972 Act, if the contract of tenancy merely gave *Landlord* the *power* to repair the defect, *Landlord* is to be regarded for the purposes of s 4 of the 1972 Act as having a *duty* under the contract of tenancy to repair that defect *unless* the contract of tenancy clearly placed the responsibility for repairing that defect on *Tenant*.

In *McAuley* v *Bristol City Council* (1992), M was a council tenant who fell from an unstable step in her garden and injured her ankle. She sued the council, arguing that she had sustained her injury because the council owed her, and breached, a duty to take care to see that she would not be injured by the unstable step in her garden. The council had not undertaken under the contract of tenancy to repair the unstable step in the garden.[81] However, the Court of Appeal *implied* a term in the tenancy agreement that the council had the power to enter the claimant's garden to inspect and repair any defective structures in the garden. This allowed the Court of Appeal to treat the council, for the purposes of applying s 4 of the 1972 Act, as though it *was* obliged under the contract of tenancy to repair the unstable step in the claimant's garden – and therefore to find that the council did owe the claimant a duty to take care to see that she would not be injured by that step.

It would have been different if *either* the council had expressly provided in the contract of tenancy that the responsibility for repairing defective structures in the claimant's garden fell on the claimant (in which case the council could not have been treated by virtue of s 4(4) of the 1972 Act as having had an obligation under the contract of tenancy to repair the unstable step in the claimant's garden) *or* the council had expressly provided in the contract of tenancy that it had no right to repair defective structures in the claimant's garden (in which case it would have been impossible for the Court of Appeal to have implied a term into the contract of tenancy that the council had the right to enter the claimant's garden to inspect and repair any defective structures there). However, the council did neither of these things.

7.8 EMPLOYERS

It has long been well established that if A employs B, A will *normally* owe B a duty to take reasonable steps to see that she is not killed or physically injured in working for him. So A will *normally* owe B a duty to take reasonable steps to ensure: (1) that B's fellow employees are competent and are therefore not likely to act in ways which would unreasonably endanger B's health and safety; (2) that B's place of work is reasonably safe to enter and work in; (3) that B and B's fellow employees will do their work in a way that will not unreasonably endanger B's health and safety; and (4) that B is provided with the necessary plant and equipment to enable her to do her work without unreasonably endangering her health and safety and that that plant and equipment is reasonably safe to use.

This duty will rarely be displaced on the grounds that *volenti non fit injuria*. For example, the mere fact that B goes to work every day knowing that her workplace is not a reasonably safe place to work in does not establish that she is willing to work for A in a place of work

---

[79] Including the tenant(s) of the let premises: *McAuley* v *Bristol City Council* [1992] 1 QB 134; *Sykes* v *Harry* [2001] QB 1014, at [21].

[80] Section 4(1).

[81] So no claim for breach of contract was available to the claimant.

that is not reasonably safe for her to work in.[82] In such a case – where B's only alternative to turning up for work is to quit her job and seek alternative employment on an uncertain job market – it cannot be said that B *willingly* chooses to work for A in a dangerous workplace when she continues to turn up for work in the knowledge that her workplace is not a reasonably safe place to work in.[83] Similarly, if A warned B before employing her that her future place of work would not be reasonably safe to work in and B agreed to work for A on that basis, B cannot be said to have *willingly* chosen to work for A in a dangerous workplace if her only reason for taking such a risk with her life or health was that she needed a job. So, in the case just described, A, having employed B, will – despite his warning to B – still owe B a duty to take reasonable steps to ensure that B's workplace is reasonably safe for her to work in.

How far does the duty that A will owe B to take reasonable steps to see that she will not be killed or injured working for him go? For example, suppose that A employs B to do a particular kind of work and it becomes clear that B is very likely to suffer injury if she is made to carry on doing that kind of work. No doubt in such a case it would be good practice for A to reassign B to some other kind of work which is less dangerous. But what if there is no other work available? Will A owe B a duty to dismiss her? For a long time, the courts took the view that A could not owe B such a duty.[84] However, in *Coxall v Goodyear GB Ltd* (2003), Simon Brown LJ took the view that if the risk that B will be injured if she carries on working for A is serious enough then A may well owe B a duty to dismiss her.[85]

So far we have discussed the duty an employer will owe his employee to see that she is not *killed or injured* while working for him. Will he also owe her a duty to take reasonable steps to see that she will not suffer *other kinds of harm*? The decision of the House of Lords in *Frost v Chief Constable of South Yorkshire* (1999) seems to establish that an employer will not owe his employees a *general* duty to take reasonable steps to see that they do not suffer any kind of *psychiatric illness* in working for him.[86] However, we have already seen that it is well established that if it is reasonably foreseeable that an employee will suffer a nervous breakdown if she is made to do a certain kind of work without any kind of assistance or counselling, then the employer will owe his employee a duty to take reasonable steps to see that she gets that assistance or counselling.[87] Furthermore, the House of Lords has held that it is strongly arguable that if A employs B and A knows or ought to know that B is being harassed to such an extent by her fellow employees that there is a danger she will suffer a breakdown, A will owe B a duty to take reasonable steps to stop the harassment.[88]

---

[82] *McCafferty v Metropolitan Police District Receiver* [1977] 1 WLR 1073.

[83] *Smith v Baker* [1891] AC 325.

[84] See *Withers v Perry Chain Co Ltd* [1961] 1 WLR 1314, at 1317 (per Sellers LJ): 'I cannot believe that the common law requires employers to refuse to employ a person who is willing to work for them simply because they think that it is not in the person's best interests to do the work. That would be imposing a restriction on the freedom of the individual which I think is foreign to the whole spirit of the common law of our country.'

[85] [2003] 1 WLR 536, at [29]. In *Barber v Somerset County Council* [2004] 1 WLR 1089, Lord Rodger of Earlsferry took much the same view, acknowledging that in cases where an employee would be exposed to a substantial risk of injury if he carried on working, his employer might owe him a duty to sack him: ibid, at [30].

[86] See also *French v Chief Constable of Sussex Police* [2006] EWCA Civ 312 (no duty to give police officers adequate training in running operations involving firearms even if it was foreseeable – which it was not – that failure to do so would result in police officers who were involved in a wrongful shooting suffering psychiatric illnesses as a result of being subjected to criminal and disciplinary proceedings).

[87] See above, § 6.6.

[88] *Waters v Commissioner of Police of the Metropolis* [2000] 1 WLR 1607 (held that it was strongly arguable that this principle applied in the case where the defendant commissioner occupied a status analogous to an employer in relation to the claimant policewoman, who suffered a breakdown as a result of being subjected to severe harassment from her fellow police officers for reporting that she had been raped by a fellow police officer).

Turning to harms to property and economic harms, it seems that an employer will not owe an employee a duty to take reasonable steps to see that her property is not harmed while she is working for him;[89] neither will he owe her a duty to take reasonable steps to see that she does not suffer some kind of pure economic loss in working for him.[90]

7.9 BAILEES

If A holds B's goods on a bailment for B, A (who is known as a 'bailee') will owe B (who is known as a 'bailor') a duty to take reasonable steps to safeguard those goods from being destroyed, damaged or stolen.

Some academics are resistant to regarding the breach of this duty of care as *negligence*. Unlike those academics who dislike the idea that the law on occupiers' liability is part of the law on negligence, these academics have a point.

First, s 2(2) of the Torts (Interference with Goods) Act 1977 provides that 'An action lies in conversion for loss or destruction of goods which a bailee has allowed to happen in breach of his duty to his bailor'. It seems, then, that conversion (another tort entirely) and not negligence is the appropriate course of action when goods are lost or destroyed as a result of a bailee's breach of the duty of care he owes the bailee.

Secondly, in the recent case of *Yearworth* v *North Bristol NHS Trust* (2010) – where the defendants were being sued for failing to take reasonable steps to preserve sperm deposited with them by the claimants, who were undergoing treatment for cancer and might have been made infertile by that treatment – the Court of Appeal expressed itself 'strongly attracted' to the idea that the liability of a bailee who has failed to safeguard goods that have been bailed to him arises neither in contract, nor in tort, but is '*sui generis*' and 'where the gratuitous bailee has extended, and broken, a particular promise to his bailor, for example that the chattel will be stored in a particular place or in a particular way, the measure of damages may be more akin to that referable to breach of contract rather than to tort.'[91]

In light of all this, we will defer a detailed discussion of the law of bailment to our chapter on 'Torts to Things'.[92]

7.10 CARRIERS

If A gives B a lift in his car, A will normally owe B a duty under the Occupiers' Liability Act 1957 to take reasonable steps to ensure that the condition of his car is such that B will be reasonably safe in taking a lift in his car. This is because the law on occupiers' liability does not just cover occupiers of land but anyone 'occupying or having control over any fixed or moveable structure, including any vessel, vehicle or aircraft'.[93] But A will, in any case, owe B a more general duty to take reasonable steps to ensure that B will not be killed or injured in taking a lift in his car.

For example, in *Jebson* v *Ministry of Defence* (2000), the claimant was a soldier who went to Portsmouth with some fellow soldiers for a night out. Anticipating that the claimant

---

[89] *Deyong* v *Shenburn* [1946] KB 227 (no duty to prevent theft of clothes from dressing room). However, if an employee's property is destroyed or damaged while she is working in her employer's factory, she may be able to bring a claim in negligence against her employer under the Occupiers' Liability Act 1957. See below, § 11.2.

[90] *Reid* v *Rush & Tompkins Group plc* [1990] 1 WLR 212 (no duty to advise employee of advisability of taking out insurance when working for defendant abroad).

[91] [2010] QB 1, at [48] ((h) and (i)).

[92] See below, § 17.5.

[93] Occupiers' Liability Act 1957, s 1(3)(a).

and his companions would be in no condition to get back to their barracks after their night out, the defendants – the claimant's employer – sent a lorry to take them back home. The claimant – who was considerably the worse for wear after his night out – attempted to climb onto the roof of the lorry as it took him back to barracks. Unfortunately for the claimant, he failed in his attempt and fell off the lorry and into the road, suffering various injuries in the process. He claimed that the defendants had owed him a duty to take reasonable steps to ensure that he would not suffer any kind of injury in travelling in their lorry and that they had breached that duty in failing to have someone in the back of the lorry to supervise him and his companions and to make sure that they did not – in their drunken state – try to climb out of the lorry while it was travelling along. The Court of Appeal allowed the claimant's claim.

7.11 CHILD CARERS

Cases involving children seem to bring out the judges' most protective instincts. The courts will readily find that people involved with looking after children will owe those children a range of positive duties of care:[94]

A. Parents

Paradoxically, our opening statement is *least* true in cases involving those closest to a child: his or her parents. In cases involving parents, the courts have been wary of finding that parents owe their children duties of care, for fear of fostering litigation between family members, and intruding into difficult issues about what constitutes 'good parenting' and 'bad parenting'.[95]

Having said that, it seems clear that a parent will owe her child any duty of care that she would owe someone who was not her child. So a parent who is driving a car with her child in the back seat will owe the child a duty to take care not to drive dangerously.[96] She will also owe him a duty to take reasonable steps to feed him. So in *R v Gibbins and Proctor* (1919), a father who had starved his child with the aim of killing her was convicted of murder on the ground that his failure to feed the child was a wrongful omission. In *Surtees v The Royal Borough of Kingston upon Thames* (1991), Stocker LJ was prepared to accept that a parent who is looking after their child *for a particular period of time* will owe the child a duty 'to take such care as in all the circumstances was reasonable to ensure that the [child is] not exposed to unnecessary risk of injury, the standard of care being that of a careful parent in the prevailing circumstances.'[97]

In *XA v YA* (2010), Mrs Justice Thirlwall was doubtful whether it would be 'fair, just and reasonable' to find that a mother owed her son a duty to take reasonable steps to protect him from being continually assaulted by his father, for two reasons: (i) in such a case, the mother would probably be the subject of domestic violence as well, and it would be unfair to burden her with a duty of care when she was in such a vulnerable state; and (ii) it would not be desirable to get the civil courts involved in second-guessing a mother's decisions as to how best to protect her child from being harmed by an abusive partner.[98] And in *Barrett*

---

[94] See, generally, Bagshaw 2001.
[95] For an extended discussion of how far parents should be held to owe their children legally enforceable duties to raise them properly, see Shmueli 2010.
[96] *Barrett v Enfield LBC* [1998] QB 367, 377; *XA v YA* [2010] EWHC 1983, at [140].
[97] [1991] 2 FLR 559, 569.
[98] [2010] EWHC 1983 (QB), at [143].

v *Enfield LBC* (1998), Lord Woolf MR held that a parent would *not* owe a child a duty to make decisions about his or her future with a reasonable degree of care and skill:

> parents are daily making decisions with regard to their children's future and it seems to me that it would be wholly inappropriate that those decisions, even if they could be shown to be wrong, should be ones which give rise to a liability in damages.[99]

B. Teachers

It seems well established that a teacher will owe the students in his charge a duty to take reasonable steps to see that those students do not come to any harm while on the school premises.[100] As Lord Clyde observed in *Phelps* v *Hillingdon London Borough Council* (2001):

> [there] is no question that a teacher owes a duty of care for the physical safety of a child attending school under the charge of that teacher. The teacher has a duty to take reasonable care that the child does not come to any harm through any danger which may arise during the course of the child's attendance at the school.[101]

It also seems to be accepted that if a student has 'special needs' or suffers from learning difficulties, his teachers will owe him a duty to take reasonable steps to ensure that that student is not disadvantaged as a result of the fact that he suffers from those special needs or learning difficulties. So in *X* v *Bedfordshire County Council* (1995), Lord Browne-Wilkinson held – with the agreement of the other Law Lords deciding the case – that if 'it comes to the attention of [a] headmaster that a pupil is under-performing, he does owe a duty to take such steps as a reasonable teacher would consider appropriate to try to deal with such under-performance'.[102] In the *Phelps* case, the House of Lords refused to strike out a number of claims which were premised on the basis that the teachers of a student who suffers from special needs or learning difficulties will owe him a duty to take reasonable steps to ensure that that student is not disadvantaged from the fact that he suffers from those special needs or learning difficulties. The House of Lords held it was *arguable* that the teacher of a student who suffers from special needs or learning difficulties would owe him such a duty of care. Lord Nicholls – with the agreement of Lord Jauncey of Tullichettle – went further and held that 'a teacher [*will*] owe a duty of care to a child with learning difficulties . . . A teacher must exercise due skill and care to respond appropriately to the manifest problems of such a child, including informing the head-teacher or others about the child's problems and carrying out any instructions he is given.'[103]

The cases do not go so far as to say that the teachers of a *normal* student will owe him a duty to teach him with reasonable skill and care. Lord Nicholls held that the teachers of a normal student would owe him such a duty of care in *Phelps*[104] but only one of the other six Law Lords who decided *Phelps* indicated that he agreed with Lord Nicholls on this point.

[99] [1998] QB 367, 377.
[100] The duty does not extend to seeing that the child does not come to any harm off the school premises: *Bradford-Smart* v *West Sussex County Council* [2002] EWCA Civ 7 (discussed, Elvin 2003b).
[101] [2001] 2 AC 619, 670. See also *Van Oppen* v *Clerk to Bedford Charity Trustees* [1990] 1 WLR 235, at 250 (per Balcombe LJ). The same is true of educational authorities: see *New South Wales* v *Lepore* (2003) 212 CLR 511.
[102] [1995] 2 AC 633, 766.
[103] [2001] 2 AC 619, 667.
[104] ibid.

C. Social services

In *Barrett* v *Enfield LBC* (2001), the claimant had been taken into care by a local authority when he was 10 months old. He stayed in care until he was 18 years old. In that time – the claimant alleged – he was placed with two foster families, and was moved into six different homes in 12 years. The claimant further alleged that the authority made no proper attempt to have someone adopt him, or to reunite him with his mother. The claimant sued the authority in negligence, claiming that they had owed him a duty to raise him with a reasonable degree of care and skill, and that he had developed psychological problems as a result of the authority's breaching that duty of care. The House of Lords unanimously held that it was *arguable* that the defendant local authority had owed the claimant a duty of care once they had taken him into care.

Given the endorsement that the decision in *Barrett* subsequently received from the House of Lords in *Gorringe* v *Calderdale MBC* (2004),[105] it may be that there is no longer any doubt that a local authority will owe a duty of care to someone in the position of the claimant in *Barrett*. This is so even though, as we have seen, a parent would not owe a child a duty of care of the type contended for in *Barrett*. The House of Lords did not think that this was an insuperable objection to the claimant's claim in *Barrett*: they thought that it should be easier to sue a *substitute* parent – like the social services in *Barrett* – than an *actual* parent. Lord Hutton suggested in *Barrett* that this was partly because some of the decisions that the local authority had to make were very different from those that a natural parent would normally have to make and partly because the local authority employs expert staff and advisers to assist it in making decisions about the future of the children in its care.[106]

It was at least arguable in *Barrett* that the social services had assumed a responsibility to the claimant in that case, and that the social services' duty of care to the claimant could be explained on that basis.[107] No such explanation can be offered of the decision of the Court of Appeal in *D* v *East Berkshire Community NHS Trust* (2004), which held that if a local authority receives reports that a child is being abused or neglected and the authority decides to investigate those reports, the authority will owe the child in question a duty to investigate the reports with a reasonable degree of care and skill.[108]

The decision of the Court of Appeal is very hard to reconcile with the starting point of this chapter – that a defendant will not have owed a claimant a duty to save her from harm unless there existed some special relationship between them, or some special circumstances that would make it 'fair, just and reasonable' to find that the defendant owed the claimant a duty to act. It is difficult to see what is the 'special relationship' or what are the 'special circumstances' that give rise to a duty of care in a *D* v *East Berkshire*-type situation, where a local authority has received reports that a child is in danger of abuse or neglect, and it decides to investigate those reports.

It may be that the existence of a duty of care in a *D*-type case can be justified on the basis that the local authority's investigation may put off anyone else from taking steps to protect at-risk children. However, the decision in *D* v *East Berkshire* might also be a classic example

---

[105] [2004] 1 WLR 1057, at [39] (per Lord Hoffmann), [73] (per Lord Scott), [100] (per Lord Brown).

[106] [2001] 2 AC 550, 587–588.

[107] This was Lord Hoffmann's explanation of *Barrett* in *Gorringe* v *Calderdale MBC* [2004] 1 WLR 1057, at [39]. The one difficulty with it is the lack of reliance (in the sense of doing something different that he would not otherwise have done) by the claimant on his carers.

[108] The position in New Zealand is the same: see *Attorney-General* v *Prince* [1998] 1 NZLR 262 (NZCA) and *B* v *Attorney-General* [2003] 4 All ER 833 (PC).

of the dangers involved in making the right decision but for the wrong reasons.[109] This timeline will illustrate the point:

> 1995: The House of Lords is asked in *X* v *Bedfordshire CC* to decide whether a local authority owes a duty of care to children who have been reported to it as being in danger of being abused or neglected. The House of Lords says 'no' but comes up with the *wrong reason* to support its decision. Instead of focusing on the lack of any 'special relationship' between the local authority and the at-risk children to explain why there is no duty in this case, the House of Lords instead says that it is important on grounds of *public policy* to find that there is no duty of care in this kind of case, because if a local authority could be sued for failing to act on reports that children were being abused, then it would become excessively cautious and overactive in investigating and acting on allegations of child abuse.[110]
>
> 1998: The Human Rights Act 1998 (HRA) was enacted. Under the HRA, for the first time, claimants would be allowed to sue public bodies in a UK court for violating their 'rights' under the European Convention on Human Rights (ECHR). One such right is the right under Article 3 of the ECHR not to 'be subjected to torture or to inhuman or degrading treatment or punishment'.
>
> 2000: The HRA comes into force.
>
> 2001: The European Court of Human Rights rules in *Z* v *United Kingdom* (which was the same case as *X* v *Bedfordshire CC*, but taken to the European Court of Human Rights) that a local authority that fails to take a child into care when it knows or ought to know that the child is at risk of being abused or neglected may be found to have violated the child's rights under Article 3 of the ECHR.
>
> 2004: The Court of Appeal rules in *D* v *East Berkshire Community NHS Trust* that the stated basis for refusing to find a duty of care in an *X* v *Bedfordshire CC*-type case – a desire to allow local authorities to make decisions about taking children into care free from the fear that their decisions might result in their being sued – no longer applies as a local authority in an *X* v *Bedfordshire CC*-type case can now be sued for a culpable failure to protect an at-risk child under the HRA. Given this, there is no longer any objection to finding that a duty of care is owed in an *X* v *Bedfordshire CC*-type case, and so it should now be recognised that a duty of care *will* be owed in that type of case.

It is interesting to note that in the conjoined appeals *Van Colle* v *Chief Constable of Hertfordshire Police, Smith* v *Chief Constable of Sussex Police* (2009), the House of Lords was faced – in relation to the police's liability in negligence for failing to protect someone from being killed – with *exactly* the same argument that convinced the Court of Appeal to recognise that a duty of care was owed in *D* v *East Berkshire Community NHS Trust* (2004). That is:

(1) In *Hill* v *Chief Constable of West Yorkshire Police* (1989), the House of Lords refused to find that the police owed a duty of care to a victim of crime because they thought it was important to ensure that police investigations were not distorted or impeded by a fear that if the investigation went wrong, the police could be sued in negligence.

---

[109] For other examples, see below, §§ 23.1, 24.6.

[110] [1995] 2 AC 633, 650. This fear seems not to have been unfounded. After the 'Baby P' scandal, where a child was killed in his family home, despite being the subject of regular visits by the social services, the resulting opprobrium towards social workers generally triggered a huge increase in the number of applications to court by local authorities to take 'at risk' children into care.

(2) But the police can now be sued under the Human Rights Act 1998 if they fail to take reasonable steps to protect a specific individual who they know is very likely to be attacked by someone else.[111]

(3) Given this, there is now no point in refusing to recognise that a duty of care is owed in a case where the police know that a named individual is in danger of being attacked, and so the courts should find that the police owe that individual a duty of care to protect him.

However, the majority of the House of Lords refused to accept this line of reasoning. They took the view that the common law 'should be allowed to stand on its own feet side by side with the alternative remedy [under the Human Rights Act 1998]'[112] and said they found it difficult to understand why the common law should be developed to provide a remedy in a situation which was now covered by the Human Rights Act 1998.[113] The same points could be made in objection to the decision in *D* v *East Berkshire Community NHS Trust* (2004).

Further reading

For more detailed expositions of the law in this area, see **Bagshaw, 'The duties of care of emergency service providers' [1999]** *Lloyd's Maritime and Commercial Law Quarterly* **71**, and **Fordham, 'Saving us from ourselves – the duty of care in negligence to prevent self-inflicted harm' (2010) 18** *Torts Law Journal* **22**, brilliantly synthesising the UK, Australian and Canadian authorities on when (if ever) defendants will owe claimants a duty of care to protect them from: (i) killing themselves; (ii) drunkenly injuring themselves; (iii) injuring themselves while engaging in dangerous sports; and (iv) gambling their money away.

Most academic writing in this area is hostile to the current law, arguing that negligence law should be more expansive in holding people (particularly public bodies) liable for omissions. **Donal Nolan's 'The liability of public authorities for failure to confer benefits' (2011) 127** *Law Quarterly Review* **260** is representative of mainstream academic opinion: puzzled by the decision of the House of Lords in *Gorringe* v *Calderdale MBC* (2004), and eager to find some ways of limiting it.

Tom Cornford's *Towards a Public Law of Tort* **(Ashgate, 2008)** proposes that the law of negligence should be reformed to give effect to a principle ('Principle I') that a claimant who suffers harm as a result of a public authority's unreasonable failure to treat the claimant in the way that the law requires should be entitled to sue that public authority for compensation. The proposal assumes that negligence law is fundamentally about compensating for loss rather than vindicating rights. In **David Howarth's** casenote **'Poisoned wells: "proximity" and "assumption of responsibility" in negligence' (2005a) 64** *Cambridge Law Journal* **23**, the former LibDem MP is acute (and disapproving) in pointing out that the common law regards decent public services as not something we have a *right* to; but he does not pursue that insight and instead concludes that decisions against holding public bodies liable for omissions are just a matter of 'policy' (boring). What gives us a right to decent public services? Those who pay for those services might think they had a right to decent public services. But would we be happy with a law that said that taxpayers have a right to be protected by the police, but non-taxpayers must go hang? And how much of an individual

---

[111] As a result of the decision of the European Court of Human Rights in *Osman* v *UK* [1999] FLR 193: see above, § 3.1.
[112] [2009] 1 AC 225, at [82] (per Lord Hope).
[113] [2009] 1 AC 225, at [81] (per Lord Hope), [139] (per Lord Brown).

taxpayer's money actually goes into the pocket of a policeman who is in a position to save that taxpayer from a beating?

In its 2008 Consultation Paper *Administrative Redress: Public Bodies and the Citizen*, the Law Commission proposed that a public authority should be held liable for harm caused or not averted as a result of the authority acting unlawfully but only if the authority was seriously at fault in acting (or not acting) as it did. The effect of the proposal would have been to radically expand public bodies' liability for failing to prevent harm, and radically contract their liabilities for causing others to suffer harm. The paper was widely criticised and was withdrawn.

Academics gave a generally warmer welcome to the decision of the New South Wales Court of Appeal in *Lowns* v *Woods* (1996), holding a GP liable for failing to come to the assistance of a boy having an epileptic fit: see **Williams, 'Medical Samaritans: is there a duty to treat?' (2001) 21** *Oxford Journal of Legal Studies* **393, Gray and Edelman, 'Developing the law of omissions: a common law duty to rescue?' (1998) 6** *Torts Law Journal* **240,** and **Haberfield, '*Lowns* v *Woods* and the duty to rescue' (1998) 6** *Tort Law Review* **56**.

Visit **www.mylawchamber.co.uk/mcbride** to access tools to help you develop and test your knowledge of Tort law, including interactive multiple choice questions, practice exam

questions with guidance, weblinks, legal newsfeed, additional case summaries, legal updates and tips on answering problem and essay questions.

Use **Case Navigator** to read in full some of the key cases referenced in this chapter with commentary and questions:

- D *v* East Berkshire Community NHS Trust
- Hedley Byrne *v* Heller
- Mitchell *v* Glasgow City Council
- Phelps *v* Hillingdon London Borough Council
- Sutradhar *v* Natural Environment Research Council

8 Breach of duty

8.1   The basics *244*

8.2   Objectivity *248*

8.3   Balancing *252*

8.4   Common practice *256*

8.5   Public powers *258*

8.6   Breach through others *260*

8.7   Proof *267*

Overview

In this chapter we will be looking at when a defendant can be said to have *breached* a duty of care that he owed to a claimant. In section 8.1 we make the point that there is no general rule that can be applied to determine this issue: whether or not a defendant is held to have breached a duty of care not only depends on the facts of the case, but what type of duty he owed and the status of the defendant and the claimant. In the following sections, we provide the reader with an overview of the particular rules that are relevant to the inquiry as to whether or not a duty of care was breached. Sections 8.2 to 8.4 examine when pleas such as 'I did my best!' or 'It would have cost too much to do that!' or 'Everyone else would have done the same as me!' will be relevant (in the first and third case, not usually) to the inquiry as to whether a defendant breached a duty of care owed to a claimant. Section 8.5 is a difficult section, dealing with when a public body will be held to have breached a duty of care because it has failed to exercise a statutory power that has been vested in it. Section 8.6 looks at situations when a defendant can be held to have breached a duty of care because *someone else* was careless. Finally, section 8.7 is a procedural section, dealing with who has the burden of proof in a dispute as to whether a duty of care has been breached.

8.1 THE BASICS

We have now finished discussing when one person will owe another a duty of care. In this chapter, we turn to the issue of when a duty of care will be held to have been breached. It is an obvious point, but one which is often overlooked by students, that a duty of care is not a duty to *ensure* that something happens or does not happen. The fact that A has crashed his car into B's car does not necessarily mean that A breached the duty of care that he owed B to *take care* not to crash into B's car. To show that A breached this duty of care we have to establish that . . . And at this point the law gets very difficult.

Most people would say that we have to establish that A's driving failed to come up to the standards of a *reasonable* driver, and more generally that we establish whether or not a defendant has breached a duty of care owed to a claimant by seeing whether the defendant failed to do what a *reasonable person* would have done, in the circumstances. Such formulations do emphasise an important point about duties of care. In most situations where it is alleged that a defendant breached a duty of care owed to the claimant, it is not enough for a defendant to say 'I did my best!' So, in the case we are considering, A cannot argue that he took care not to crash into B's car by merely saying he did his best not to crash into B's car. The duty of care that drivers owe other drivers requires drivers to live up to an *objective* standard of care in their driving, one which makes no allowances for the individual idiosyncrasies of a particular driver.

But at the same time, saying that we determine whether A breached the duty of care he owed B not to crash into B's car by seeing whether A's driving came up to the standards of a reasonable driver leaves too much open. How do we determine what those standards are? Suppose that A crashed into the back of B's car because his attention was momentarily distracted by a picture of a half naked model on a billboard beside the road, and he failed to spot that B had unexpectedly braked in front of him. Would a *reasonable* driver's attention have been distracted in this way? How can we tell? If it could be established that 75% of male drivers would have taken their eye off the road when faced with such a distraction, would that show that a *reasonable* driver would have taken his or her eye off the road? Or do we follow the American judge Learned Hand's line that –

> in most cases reasonable prudence is in fact common prudence; but strictly speaking it is never its measure . . . Courts must in the end say what is required; there are precautions so imperative that even their universal disregard will not excuse their omission.[1]

The truth is – it is not possible to come up with any single rule, or standard, by which to determine whether a given defendant has breached a duty of care owed to a claimant. Many people have tried to come up with some such rule or standard. For example, the same American judge we have just quoted came up with a very famous formula for determining whether or not a failure to take a certain precaution meant that a defendant had breached a duty of care. In the case of *United States* v *Carroll Towing Co* (1947), the issue came up as to whether the owner of a barge that was tied up at a pier should have had someone on the barge during normal business hours to look after the barge if (as happened) it became untied from its moorings. Learned Hand J said:

> Since there are occasions when every vessel will break from her moorings, and since, if she does, she becomes a menace to those about her; the owner's duty, as in other similar situations, to provide against resulting injuries is a function of three variables: (1) The probability that she will break away; (2) the gravity of the resulting injury, if she does; (3) the burden of adequate precautions. Possibly it serves to bring this notion into relief to state it in algebraic terms: if the probability be called P; the injury, L; and the burden, B; liability depends upon whether B is less than L multiplied by P: i.e., whether $B < PL$.[2]

Learned Hand J applied the formula to find that the barge owner in the *Carroll Towing* case should have had someone on board during normal business hours: the cost of taking such a precaution was outweighed by the *magnitude of the risk* of something going wrong if someone was not on board at such a time. (Where the magnitude of the risk is assessed by multiplying the probability of something going wrong by the harm that will be done if something goes wrong.)

However, as we will see, the 'Hand Formula' for determining whether someone has breached a duty of care owed to another may not always apply.[3] Consider the **Defective Car Problem**:

---

[1] *The TJ Hooper*, 60 F 2d 737 (1932).
[2] 159 F 2d 169, 173 (1947).
[3] Richard Wright is the most vocal critic of the Hand Formula: see Wright 1995 and Wright 2003. See also Zipursky 2007.

Designers at *Deadly*, a car company, have alerted *Deadly* to the fact that *Deadly*'s flagship car, the 'Legend', suffers from a design flaw which means that every thousand times the car is driven at over 90 mph, the brakes will fail. *Deadly* has commissioned a study which says that: (i) letting existing users of the car know about this dangerous feature without offering to recall the cars and repair them will cost *Deadly* £100m in lost sales due to damage to its reputation; (ii) recalling existing models of the car and repairing the defect will cost £45m; (iii) redesigning future models of the car to eliminate this defect will shave £25m off A's profits on future sales of the car; (iv) if the company does nothing for the next five years (at which point the Legend will be superseded by a new model), then it is likely that, on average, five people will be killed or injured each year as a result of the Legend's brakes being defective, and the losses resulting from each death or injury will come to, on average, £1m per death.

The Hand Formula would indicate that *Deadly* will *not* breach the duty of care it owes current and future owners of the Legend if it does *nothing* here. The cost of protecting current and future owners of the Legend from its design flaw is £70m (the cost of implementing recall-and-repair measures while redesigning future versions of the Legend). At the same time, the magnitude of the risk of harm to which people are exposed if nothing is done about this design flaw can be valued at £25m. We arrive at this figure by multiplying the number of deaths and injuries that are likely to occur over the next five years (at which point the Legend would be withdrawn from production anyway) by the cost of those deaths and injuries. The cost of precautions here exceeds the magnitude of the risk (by a factor of 2.8) – so according to the Hand Formula, *Deadly* need do nothing here to protect current and future owners of the Legend from its brakes going wrong.

However, it is very likely that *Deadly* would be held to have acted negligently if it did nothing in this situation. It is also very likely that if *Deadly* calculated that it should do nothing in this situation because the worst that could happen was that it would have to pay out £30m over the next five years for failing to rectify a problem that would cost £75m to sort out,[4] *Deadly* would be held liable to pay exemplary (or punitive) damages to the victims of its negligence, on the basis that not only had it acted negligently in failing to rectify the defect, it had acted so outrageously in failing to rectify the defect that its conduct was worthy of punishment.

Given that it is not possible to come up with a *single* rule, or standard, that we can employ to determine whether or not a given defendant has breached a duty of care that he owed to a claimant, the way we will proceed in this chapter is to set out a number of *different* rules that will govern this enquiry, but in relation to each rule explain the exceptions that exist to those rules (and, in some cases, the exceptions that exist to the exceptions). Those rules and their exceptions are briefly set out below:

(1) *Objectivity*. The *rule* is – as we have already seen – that the fact that a defendant did his or her personal best to avoid something happening will not necessarily mean that he or she did not breach a duty of care owed to the claimant. The standard of care that a defendant is expected to exercise in the interests of a claimant is *objective*. The *exceptions* to this rule are too complicated to set out here, but are set out in the next section.

---

[4] Something that Ford is alleged to have done in the famous 'Ford Pinto case' (*Grimshaw* v *Ford Motor Co*, 119 Cal App 3d 757 (1981)), where – it is claimed – Ford decided against repairing a defect in the protection around the fuel tank in its Pinto range of cars on the ground that the repairs would cost more than it would have to pay out if the inadequate protection resulted in an accident. For a measured view of the Ford Pinto case, see Schwartz 1991.

(2) *Balancing*. The *rule* is laid out in the Hand Formula. If A owed B a duty to take reasonable steps to avoid X happening, and failed to take a given precaution P to avoid X happening, we determine whether A's failure to take precaution P put him in breach of the duty of care that he owed B by *balancing* the *cost* of taking precaution P against the *magnitude* of the *foreseeable* risk that X would happen if precaution P were not taken.

A possible *exception* to this rule is where the magnitude of the foreseeable risk that X would happen if precaution P were not taken was *very serious*. As the Defective Car Problem shows, in such a case balancing the cost of taking precaution P against the magnitude of the risk that X would happen if that precaution were not taken may be inappropriate, and the courts may refuse to excuse A's failure to take precaution P on cost grounds. A possible *exception to this exception* is where taking precaution P would have *social costs* – that is, costs to society at large. In such a case, it might be that failing to take precaution P could be justified on grounds of the social cost involved in taking that precaution, even if the risk that X would happen if that precaution were not taken was relatively serious.

(3) *Common practice*. The *rule* is that pleading 'everyone (or most people) would have done the same as me' does not work to establish that you have not breached a duty of care owed to someone else. So the fact that 75% of male motorists would have taken their eyes off the road to look at a poster of a half naked model will not excuse a defendant who ran into the claimant's car because his attention was distracted by such a poster.

The *exception* is where a professional is under a duty to exercise a reasonable degree of care and skill in looking after a client's interests. In such a case, the courts will normally allow the professional to plead that he did exercise such care and skill in looking after the client's interests by showing that there is a significant body of opinion within his profession that would regard it as proper for him to treat his client in the way he did. (This is known as the '*Bolam* test' for professional negligence, after the case of *Bolam v Friern Hospital Management Committee* (1957), in which it was first set out.)

However, there is an *exception to the exception* (known as the '*Bolitho* exception', after the case of *Bolitho v City and Hackney Health Authority* (1998)) where the courts regard the 'significant body of opinion' as being plainly wrong-headed or irrational.

(4) *Public powers*. The *rule* is that a public body ('PB') that has a statutory power ('SP') will breach a duty of care that it owes someone else if it fails to exercise SP when exercising that power would have helped it discharge that duty of care, and it has not done anything else to discharge its duty of care. There are two *exceptions* to this rule.

The first arises when, in the circumstances in which PB found itself, it was authorised by Parliament *not* to exercise SP. In such a case, the courts *cannot* find that PB acted unlawfully by failing to exercise SP as doing so would be contrary to Parliament's intentions in endowing PB with that power. So the courts cannot find that the failure to exercise SP put PB in breach of its duty of care.

The second arises when exercising SP for the purpose of discharging its duty of care would have put PB in breach of one of the *public law duties* governing how SP is to be exercised.[5] In such a case, the courts cannot find that PB acted unlawfully by failing to exercise power SP as doing so would put PB in the impossible position of being condemned to act unlawfully whatever it did with SP. So PB's failure to exercise SP cannot be said to have put PB in breach of its duty of care.

---

[5] For a brief list of these public law duties, see above, § 2.6.

(5) *Personal fault*. The *rule* is that in determining whether a defendant breached a duty of care owed to a claimant, we look at the defendant's *own* conduct and see whether *that* conduct fell short of the standard of care that the defendant was expected to live up to. There are two *exceptions* to this rule.

First of all, in the case where A owed B a *non-delegable duty of care* to take reasonable steps to avoid X happening, and A gave the job of avoiding X happening to C, if C failed to take reasonable steps to avoid X happening, then A will be held to have breached the duty of care *he* owed B to take reasonable steps to avoid X happening.

Secondly, as a company does not do anything itself, but instead operates through people who work for it, in determining whether a company has breached a duty of care, we look at the conduct of the people whose conduct can be fairly *attributed* to the company.

(6) *Proof*. The *rule* is that the burden of proving that a defendant has breached a duty of care owed to the claimant falls on the claimant. The burden of proof shifts to the defendant in a case where the maxim '*res ipsa loquitur*' ('the thing speaks for itself') applies. If what has happened to the claimant was unlikely to have happened had the defendant taken care, what has happened to the claimant will count as evidence that the defendant has breached his duty of care, and the burden of proof will then fall on the defendant to show that, in fact, he did *not* breach his duty of care and that what happened to the claimant has some other explanation.

We will now look at each of these rules and their exceptions in much more detail.

8.2 OBJECTIVITY

A. The rule

That a defendant cannot claim to have discharged a duty of care that he owed the claimant by merely saying 'I did my best' has been established in English law ever since the case of *Vaughan* v *Menlove* (1837).

In that case, the defendant constructed near the claimant's property a hay-rick (a pile of hay that has been left out in the sun to dry). The hay-rick spontaneously ignited in the sunshine, and the fire spread to the claimant's land, and the claimant's house burned down as a result. The claimant sued the defendant, claiming that the defendant had acted negligently either in the way he constructed the hay-rick, or in choosing to locate it so close to the claimant's land. The defendant was held liable at first instance, but argued that the case should be tried again to determine 'whether he had acted bona fide to the best of his judgment' on the ground that 'if he had, he ought not to be responsible for the misfortune of not possessing the highest order of intelligence.'[6] The Court of Common Pleas dismissed the application, on the ground that whether 'the Defendant had acted honestly and bona fide to the best of his own judgment' was irrelevant to the case. Inquiring into such matters:

> would leave so vague a line as to afford no rule at all, the degree of judgment belonging to each individual being infinitely various ... Instead, therefore of saying that the liability in negligence should be co-extensive with each individual, which would be as variable as the length of the foot of each individual, we ought rather to adhere to the rule which requires in all cases a regard to caution such as a man of ordinary prudence would observe.[7]

---

[6] (1837) 3 Bing NC 468, 471; 132 ER 490, 492.
[7] (1837) 3 Bing NC 468, 475; 132 ER 490, 493 (per Tindal CJ).

The court's justification for adopting an objective approach to questions of whether a defendant has breached a duty of care owed to a claimant found a strong echo in the decision of the Court of Appeal in *Nettleship* v *Weston* (1971), almost 150 years later. In that case, the claimant agreed to give a friend's wife, the defendant, some driving lessons. During the third lesson, the defendant panicked while taking the car round a corner, failed to straighten up the car, and it mounted the pavement and struck a lamp-post. The claimant's knee was injured in the collision, and he sued the defendant in negligence. Lord Denning MR held that the defendant owed *other road users* a duty to take care to drive 'in as good a manner as a driver of skill, experience and care, who is sound . . . in limb, who makes no errors of judgment, had good eyesight and hearing, and is free from any infirmity'.[8] He went on to hold that the *same* duty of care was owed to the claimant instructor – the fact that he got into the car, knowing that the defendant was only capable of driving to the standard of a learner driver, made no difference:

> The driver owes a duty of care to every passenger in the car, just as he does to every pedestrian on the road: and he must attain the *same* standard of care in respect of each. If the driver were to be excused according to the knowledge of the passenger, it would result in *endless confusion and injustice*. One of the passengers may know that the learner driver is a mere novice. Another passenger may believe him to be entirely competent . . . Is the one passenger to recover and the other not? Rather than embark on such inquiries, the law holds that the driver must attain the same standard of care for passengers as for pedestrians.[9]

Applying that standard of care to the facts of *Nettleship* v *Weston*, the Court of Appeal found the defendant liable in negligence for the claimant's injury.

B. Justifications for the rule

The cases justify holding people to an *objective* standard of care – a standard of care that makes no allowances for a particular defendant's incapacity to meet that standard – on *practical* grounds. As Megaw LJ observed in *Nettleship* v *Weston*:

> if [a] doctrine of varying standards were to be accepted as part of the law . . . it could not logically be confined to the duty of care owed by learner drivers. There is no reason in logic why it should not operate in a much wider sphere. The disadvantages of the resulting unpredictability, uncertainty and, indeed, impossibility of arriving at fair and consistent decisions outweighs the advantages. The certainty of a general standard is preferable to the vagaries of a fluctuating standard.[10]

However, more *principled* justifications for the objective standard of care may be also offered.

(1) In a case where *Professional* has voluntarily assumed a responsibility to *Client*, it is *fair* to hold *Professional* to the standard of care that *Professional* indicated to *Client* that she could be expected to live up to when she assumed a responsibility to *Client*. If *Professional* has persuaded *Client* to allow her to work for him by holding herself out as having the expertise of a consultant, she cannot complain at then being expected to treat *Client*

---

[8] [1971] 2 QB 691, 699.
[9] [1971] 2 QB 691, 700. The High Court of Australia originally disagreed with this, holding in *Cook* v *Cook* (1986) 162 CLR 376 that a lesser duty of care would be owed to a passenger who knew the driver was inexperienced. However, the High Court reversed that position in *Imbree* v *McNeilly* (2008) 82 AJLR 1374 (noted, Allen 2009) and adopted *Nettleship* v *Weston* as good law in Australia.
[10] [1971] 2 QB 691, 707.

with the degree of care and skill that a reasonable consultant would apply in working for *Client*.[11]

(2) In a case where *Inexpert* and *Expert* simultaneously owe each other duties of care – for example, in the case where *Inexpert* and *Expert* are both driving in each other's vicinity – it might be thought *unfair* if *Inexpert* owed *Expert* a lesser degree of care than *Expert* owed *Inexpert*. Holding that *Expert* owes *Inexpert* more than *Inexpert* owes *Expert* would seem to punish *Expert* for his expertise, and reward *Inexpert* for her inexperience.

(3) In a case where *Inexpert* and *Other People* each owe A a duty of care, it might be thought *unfair* if *Inexpert* owed A a lesser duty of care than *Other People* did. Holding that *Other People* are subject to a more stringent duty of care than *Inexpert* might be thought to punish *Other People* for not being *Inexpert*, and reward *Inexpert* for not being like *Other People*.

(4) In a case where *Dangerous* could avoid exposing anyone to danger by simply doing *nothing*, if *Dangerous* chooses to put other people at risk of harm by *acting*, it is *not unfair* to require *Dangerous* to take a great deal of care to ensure that his choice to act does not result in those other people suffering harm, even if *Dangerous* is incapable of meeting that standard of care. If *Dangerous* had not wanted to be subjected to such a demanding standard of care, he could have avoided it by simply *not acting*.

Holding a defendant to an objective standard of care is hardest to justify in a *principled* way in a situation where none of the above four factors apply. That is: in a case where a defendant owes a claimant a duty of care that: (1) has not been voluntarily assumed; (2) is not matched by a corresponding duty of care that the claimant owes the defendant; (3) is only owed to the claimant by the defendant and not by other people; and (4) does not arise out of a defendant's choice to act in a way that has put the claimant in danger of being harmed. As it happens, in at least two situations where (1)–(4) are true, the courts do *not* apply an objective standard of care to the defendant, and require him instead to do his best with what he has to protect the claimant from harm. But before we get on to those situations, we will first look at how the objective standard of care is applied in practice.

C. Application of the rule

The objective standard of care takes no account of the defendant's personal circumstances, but it is not *inhumane*. It does *not* require a defendant to demonstrate *superhuman* levels of care for the claimant. Two features of the way the objective standard of care is applied demonstrate this.

First, it is well-known that people tend to react sub-optimally in emergencies and other stressful situations. It would be unreasonable to require people in such situations to do whatever a reasonable person would do in the cool light of day, and the objective standard of care is tempered to take that into account. For example, in *Surtees v Kingston-upon-Thames Borough Council* (1991), Sir Nicolas Browne-Wilkinson V-C warned that the courts:

> should be wary in its approach to holding parents in breach of a duty of care owed to their children ... The studied calm of the Royal Courts of Justice, concentrating on one point at a time, is light years away from the circumstances prevailing in the average home. The mother is looking after a

---

[11] See *Wilsher v Essex Area Health Authority* [1987] 1 QB 730 (if A treats B, a hospital patient, A will owe B a duty to treat B with the skill and care that a reasonably competent person in A's *post* would exercise in treating the patient).

fast moving toddler at the same time as cooking a meal, answering the telephone, looking after the other children and doing all the other things that the average mother has to cope with simultaneously, or in quick succession, in the normal household. We should be slow to characterise as negligent the care which ordinary loving mothers are able to give individual children, given the rough-and-tumble of home life.[12]

Similarly, in *Wilsher v Essex Area Health Authority* (1987), Mustill LJ held that, in considering whether or not a doctor or a nurse had failed in his or her duty to treat a patient with the degree of care and skill that a reasonably competent doctor or nurse occupying the same post would exercise in treating a patient:

> full allowance must be made for the fact that certain aspects of the treatment may have [had] to be carried out in what [one may call] 'battle conditions.' An emergency may overburden the available resources, and, if an individual is forced by circumstances to do too many things at once, the fact that he does one of them incorrectly should not lightly be taken as negligence.[13]

The same point applies where a player in a game makes, in the heat of the moment, an error of judgment with the result that another player is injured. It would be unreasonable for the law to expect people playing games to avoid making any such errors. Given this, a player will only be held to have breached a duty of care not to injure other players in the game if he made a mistake that demonstrated a *wanton or reckless disregard* for another player's safety.[14]

Secondly, if the defendant is not responsible for what his body is doing – in the sense that his body is beyond his control or it is very difficult for him to control what is body is doing – he will not be found to have breached an objective standard of care merely because he has failed to bring his body under control. For example, in *Mansfield v Weetabix* (1998), the defendant was a driver who was unaware that he suffered from malignant insulinoma – a condition which meant that, if he did not eat properly, his brain would be starved of the quantities of glucose necessary for it to function properly. One day, the defendant set out on a 40-mile journey without eating properly and, as a result, his driving became more and more erratic, culminating in his driving off the road and into the claimants' shop. The claimants sued the defendant, claiming that he had breached the duty he owed them to take care not to drive dangerously. The Court of Appeal dismissed the claim.[15] The defendant's malignant insulinoma meant that he could not have helped driving the way he did. Of course, it would have been different if the defendant had been aware of his condition and gone out driving without taking care to eat properly. His failure to take reasonable steps to ensure that his driving would not be affected by his condition would have put him in

---

[12] [1991] 2 FLR 559, 583–4. See also *Carmarthenshire County Council v Lewis* [1955] AC 549 (held, teacher did not breach duty of care not to allow child to escape into the road outside the school merely because her attention was momentarily distracted by the need to bandage up another child's wounds).

[13] [1987] 1 QB 730, 749. To the same effect, in relation to soldiers conducting peace-keeping operations, see *Bici v Ministry of Defence* [2004] EWHC 786, at [46].

[14] See *Wooldridge v Sumner* [1963] 2 QB 43 (spectator injured when defendant rode his horse too fast); *Condon v Basi* [1985] 1 WLR 866 (footballer injured as a result of foul tackle by defendant); *Caldwell v Fitzgerald* [2001] EWCA Civ 1054 (jockey injured in race as a result of actions of two other jockeys); *Blake v Galloway* [2004] EWCA Civ 814 (claimant struck in eye by piece of bark thrown at him by defendant in course of good natured horseplay). See also *Orchard v Lee* [2009] EWCA Civ 295, where the claimant was a teacher who was injured when a 13-year-old schoolboy who was playing tag ran into her: held that as the boy was playing 'within a play area, not breaking any rules . . . [and] not acting to any significant degree beyond the norms of the game', he was not liable.

[15] In so doing, they disapproved Neill J's judgment in *Roberts v Ramsbottom* [1980] 1 All ER 7, which suggested that a driver who drove his car dangerously due to the fact that he suffered some personal failing would be held to have breached the duty he owed others to take care not to drive dangerously if, at the time he was driving, he enjoyed some *limited* control of the car.

breach of the duty he owed to all those on or near the roads used by him – including the claimants – to take care not to drive dangerously.

D. Exceptions to the rule

There are two principal exceptions to the objective standard of care.

(1) *Assumption of responsibility.* In a case where A owes B a duty of care arising out of an 'assumption of responsibility' by A to B, A's duty of care will only require her to live up to the standard of care that she indicated to B she could be relied upon to apply in dealing with B. Sometimes this works against A, if she holds herself out to B as being capable of working for B to a higher standard of care than A is in fact capable. But if A has made it clear to B that B cannot expect very much of her, but B has – notwithstanding that – still put her trust in A, all A will have to do is live up to that very modest standard of care.

(2) *Duties to act.* We said above that the objective standard of care was hard to justify in a *principled* way in a situation where a defendant owes a claimant a duty of care that: (a) has not been voluntarily assumed; (b) is not matched by a corresponding duty of care that the claimant owes the defendant; (c) is only owed by the defendant and not by other people; and (d) does not arise out of a defendant's choice to act in a way that has put the claimant in danger of being harmed. But we also said that in at least two situations where (a) – (d) are true, all the defendant would be required to do for the claimant was *his best*, given his circumstances.

The first situation is where a landowner owes his neighbours a duty to take reasonable steps to deal with a naturally-occurring hazard (such as a fire) arising on his land. The duty of care owed by the landowner in this case will be 'measured' in the sense that all it requires the landowner to do is to do *his best* to deal with the hazard, given his circumstances:

> [L]ess must be expected of the infirm than of the able-bodied: the owner of a small property where a hazard arises which threatens a neighbour with substantial interests should not have to do as much as one with larger interests of his own at stake and greater resources to protect them: if the small owner does what he can ... he may be held to have done his duty: he should not be held liable unless it is clearly proved that he could, and reasonably in his individual circumstances should, have done more.[16]

The same sort of reasoning applies in the case where a prisoner is in police custody, with the result that the police owe him a duty to take reasonable steps to protect him from killing himself. That duty of care will only require the police to do their best, with the resources that they have, to save the prisoner from killing himself.[17]

8.3 BALANCING

A. The rule

In a case where A owes B a duty to take reasonable steps to avoid X happening, and has failed to take a precaution P against X happening, *the rule* is that we determine whether A's

---

[16] *Goldman v Hargrave* [1967] AC 645, 663 (per Lord Wilberforce). If dealing with the hazard effectively was beyond the landowner, given his resources, he may still be held to have breached the duty of care that he owed his neighbours to take reasonable steps to deal with the hazard if he did not warn his neighbours of the danger and invite them to join with him in dealing with it: see *Holbeck Hall Hotel Ltd* v *Scarborough BC* [2000] QB 836.

[17] *Knight* v *Home Office* [1990] 3 All ER 237.

failure to take precaution P has put him in breach of the duty of care he owed B by balancing the *cost* of taking precaution P against the *magnitude of the foreseeable risk* that X would happen if precaution P were not taken. (The magnitude of the foreseeable risk is given by multiplying the probability that X would happen if precaution P were not taken by the extent of harm B would suffer if X happened – with the probability and extent of harm being assessed according to what a reasonable person in A's position would have assessed them as being at the time A failed to take precaution P.)

	Magnitude of foreseeable risk	
Cost of precaution	*High*	*Low*
High	*Miller* v *Jackson* (1977) (negligence)	*Bolton* v *Stone* (1951) (no negligence) *Latimer* v *AEC* (1953) (no negligence) *Tomlinson* v *Congleton BC* (2004) (no negligence)
Low	*Paris* v *Stepney BC* (1951) (negligence)	*Scout Association* v *Barnes* (2010) (negligence) *Harris* v *Perry* (2009) (no negligence)

The above table, and the cases below, demonstrate this rule in action.

(1) *High risk-low cost.* Where there is a high degree of foreseeable risk to the claimant if a given precaution is not taken, and it would not cost very much to take that precaution, it would be negligent not to take that precaution. This was the case in *Paris* v *Stepney BC* (1951), where the defendant employers failed to provide the claimant with goggles to protect his one remaining good eye while he removed a bolt on a rusty vehicle. While the probability that doing such 'bolt work' would result (as happened) in a chip of metal flying up and damaging the claimant's one remaining good eye was low, the seriousness of the harm that would result from that eye being damaged was such that the magnitude of the foreseeable risk of harm that the claimant would be exposed to if he were not given goggles was very high. Given that it would not have been very expensive to supply the claimant with goggles, the House of Lords held that defendants had breached the duty of care they owed the claimant to see that he would be reasonably safe in working for them by failing to provide him with goggles.[18]

(2) *Low risk-high cost.* Where things are the other way around, and it would cost a lot of money to eliminate a risk of harm to the claimant that is of a low magnitude, it will not be negligent to allow the risk to stand and not do anything about it. This was the case in *Bolton* v *Stone* (1951) (not negligent on the part of a cricket club not to do anything about the very small risk that someone might be hit by a cricket ball flying out of the ground given the cost involved in reducing that risk, either by putting higher fences around the ground or by stopping playing cricket at the ground altogether), *Latimer* v *AEC* (1953) (where an

---

[18] See also *Hudson* v *Ridge Manufacturing Co Ltd* [1957] 2 QB 348 (negligent not to take more serious action than merely reprimanding an employee who had a long history of playing dangerous pranks on his fellow employees).

employer was held not to have been negligent in merely spreading sawdust over an oil spill at work to make the floor less slippery; eliminating the remaining possibility that someone might have slipped on the oil would have cost too much relative to the risk posed by the oil now that it had sawdust scattered over it), and *Tomlinson v Congleton BC* (2004) (not negligent to fail to protect people who disregarded 'no swimming' signs around a lake in a public park from the small risks of harm to which they exposed themselves by swimming in the lake given that the only way to stop those people endangering themselves would have been to destroy the beaches around the lake and turn them into swamp-land, thereby discouraging anyone from going near the lake).

(3) *Low risk-low cost.* Cases where the magnitude of the risk of harm R that the claimant would have been exposed to if the defendant did not take a particular precaution P was low, but the cost of taking that precaution would also have been low, are marginal. An assessment of whether the defendant's failure to take precaution P was negligent will depend on a fine assessment of the magnitude of the risk R and the cost of precaution P. It is no surprise, then, to find that in a recent 'low risk-low cost' case – *The Scout Association v Barnes* (2010) – the Court of Appeal divided 2:1 on whether to find that the defendant had acted negligently.

In that case, a group of boy scouts played a game known as 'Objects in the Dark', where *n* scouts run about a hall in the dark, each trying to find and pick up one of *n-1* blocks of wood. The unlucky scout who has been unable to pick up a block of wood is eliminated from the game, and the game starts again with one less scout and one less block of wood, until the final round where there are only two scouts left, searching in the dark for one block of wood. The claimant fell over a bench near a wall while playing this game and was injured. It was found that the risks associated with playing this game in the dark (as opposed to in the light) were quite small – no one in the claimant's scout group had ever been injured before playing this game. But at the same time, the cost involved in playing the game in the light rather than in the dark was not that great. Playing the game in the dark added some spice of excitement to the game, but it was not essential to the playing of the game (which was called 'Grab' if played in the light). Jackson LJ found that it had *not* been negligent to play the game in the dark:

> Obviously the risks of this particular game were increased by turning off the main lights. But I do not see how it could possibly be said that these increased risks outweighed the social benefits of the activity. Children and teenagers have played games with an element of risk, including games in the dark, since time immemorial. The game played by the claimant and his fellow scouts . . . was much safer than many games which children might play, if left to their own devices . . . It was a game which has been played on many occasions before and since that date without mishap.[19]

Smith and Ward LJJ disagreed, preferring to trust the judgment of the first instance judge who had taken a different view of the relative balance of risk and cost in this case. He had asked himself: 'Is the benefit of added fun worth the added risk? [and] decided it was not worth it. Scouting would not lose much of its value if the game was not to be played in the dark.'[20]

In another low risk-low cost case, *Harris v Perry* (2009), the Court of Appeal found for the defendant. In that case, the claimant was a child who suffered very serious head injuries when he was hit by another child doing a somersault on a bouncy castle on which they were both playing. The defendants were a husband and wife who had had triplets. They had put the bouncy castle up in their back garden for children to play in as part of a birthday party

---

[19] [2010] EWCA Civ 1476, at [32].
[20] [2010] EWCA Civ 1476, at [59] (per Ward LJ).

they were holding for the triplets. The wife stood in front of the bouncy castle and an inflatable bungee run, keeping an eye on what was happening on both inflatables. The accident to the claimant happened while the wife's attention was distracted helping a child on the bungee run. It was held that the defendants had not been negligent in not having someone spend all the time watching what was happening on the bouncy castle. Although the cost involved in having someone supervise the bouncy castle full time might not have been that high, it was still not unreasonable to have someone look after both inflatables at the same time given that the magnitude of the foreseeable risk of a child's being injured on the bouncy castle was very low. (Even though injury might have been quite probable, the extent of the injury that a child would foreseeably suffer as a result of playing on a bouncy castle was not serious.)

B. The exception to the rule

A possible exception to the above balancing approach to determining whether it is negligent not to take a given precaution against a particular risk is in *high risk-high cost* cases: where it would cost a lot to guard against a risk of a high degree of magnitude. In such a case, it might be improper for a defendant not to do anything about the risk on the ground that it would cost too much to deal with it. Allowing a defendant to ignore such a risk on grounds of cost would – it could be argued – violate the *separateness of persons*: the idea that harming A, or exposing A to a serious risk of harm, cannot be justified simply by reference to the benefit *B* will obtain from harming A or exposing A to a serious risk of harm.

A case which supports the idea that balancing is not allowed in *high risk-high cost* cases, and that in such a case it would be negligent not to guard against the possibility of the claimant being injured no matter how expensive it might be to guard against that possibility, is *Miller* v *Jackson* (1977). In that case, the claimants lived so near to a cricket ground that it was very likely that a ball hit out of the ground might end up flying into their house; and it was quite common for cricket balls to be hit out of the ground. So the magnitude of the risk of harm to which the claimants were exposed as a result of living next to the cricket ground was very high. But the cost of averting that risk – essentially, closing down the cricket ground – would also have been very high, in terms of loss of enjoyment for the cricketers and their spectators. It was for this reason that Lord Denning MR refused to find that the cricket club was doing anything wrong in continuing to play cricket on their ground:

> There is a contest here between the interest of the public at large; and the interest of a private individual. The *public* interest lies in protecting the environment by preserving our playing fields in the face of mounting development, and by enabling our youth to enjoy all the benefits of outdoor games, such as cricket and football. The *private* interest lies in securing the privacy of his home and garden without intrusion or interference by anyone . . . As between their conflicting interests, I am of [the] opinion that the public interest should prevail over the private interest. The cricket club should not be driven out.[21]

But the other two judges in the Court of Appeal disagreed: no matter how great the cost might have been of closing down the cricket club, that could not justify exposing the claimants to such a high degree of risk: 'The risk of injury to person and property is so great that on each occasion when a ball comes over the fence and causes damage to the [claimants], the defendants are guilty of negligence.'[22]

[21] [1977] 1 QB 966, 981–2.
[22] [1977] 1 QB 966, 985 (per Geoffrey Lane LJ).

C. Section 1 of the Compensation Act 2006

This section provides that –

> A court considering a claim in negligence or breach of statutory duty may, in determining whether the defendant should have taken particular steps to meet a standard of care (whether by taking precautions against a risk or otherwise), have regard to whether a requirement to take those steps might –
>
> (a) prevent a desirable activity from being undertaken at all, to a particular extent or in a particular way, or
> (b) discourage persons from undertaking functions in connection with a desirable activity.

In so far as this section applies to cases that are *high risk-low cost*, or *low risk-high cost*, or *low risk-low cost*, it merely restates the balancing approach that is already employed in the common law to determine whether a failure to take a given precaution was negligent.[23] But it might also be taken as saying that the courts should *also* adopt a balancing approach in a *high risk-high cost* situation, where averting a high risk of harm to a claimant would involve a substantial social cost. Of course, if the section does apply to *high risk-high cost* situations, it merely says that in such situations the courts '*may . . . have regard to*' the social cost involved in guarding against the risk of harm to the claimant. So a court that *chose* not to take that sort of cost into account in a *Miller* v *Jackson* type case would not violate s 1 of the 2006 Act. However, s 1 does strengthen the arm of future Lord Dennings who think that exposing individuals to even quite severe risks of harm might be justified in the name of the public interest.

Could s 1 also be used to justify adopting a balancing approach in *high risk-high cost* situations where only *private* interests are at stake? For example, going back to the Defective Car Problem, could *Deadly* invoke s 1 to say that it would not be negligent to do nothing about the serious risks of harm posed by the design of the 'Legend', on the basis that taking the necessary precautions to deal effectively with those risks might prevent a 'desirable activity' – their manufacturing cars – being undertaken at all, or to as great an extent as it would be if they did not have to take those precautions? It seems unlikely that the courts would extend s 1 so far, and would only apply it – if at all – in *high risk-high cost* situations where guarding against a particular risk would genuinely impact on the public interest.[24]

8.4 COMMON PRACTICE

A. The rule

The rule in this area is so well-established, there is no real authority to demonstrate it:[25] the fact that people generally might be expected to act in a particular way does not, of and in

---

[23] *The Scout Association* v *Barnes* [2010] EWCA Civ 1476, at [34] (per Jackson LJ): '[The] principle . . . enshrined in section 1 of the Compensation Act 2006 . . . has always been part of the common law'; *Uren* v *Corporate Leisure* [2011] EWCA Civ 66, at [13] (per Smith LJ): 'section 1 of the Compensation Act 2006 [does] not add anything to the common law position.'

[24] An example of such a situation would be a *Tomlinson*-type situation where it is clear that people will not pay any attention to signs around a public lake telling them it is dangerous to swim there and there is a very high risk that swimming in the lake will cause an individual swimmer to contract Weil's Disease (a possibly fatal disease contracted by contact with animal urine in water), but each individual swimmer discounts this risk as 'not going to happen to me' and the only way of effectively stopping swimmers running such a risk would be to turn the beaches around the lake into swampland, thus ruining a valuable public amenity.

[25] Though see the quote of Learned Hand J, above, at fn 1.

itself, establish that acting in that way is a reasonable thing to do. So a defendant cannot argue that he or she discharged a duty of care owed to a claimant merely by showing that everyone else or most people could have been expected to act in the same way that he or she did.

B. The exception to the rule

There is an exception to the above rule in cases where A owes B a duty to perform some task with the skill and care that a reasonably competent professional would have exercised in performing that task. As a general rule, in judging whether or not A's performance was up to scratch, the courts will allow themselves to be guided by the opinion of professionals in the field. The general rule traces its origin to the direction of McNair J in *Bolam* v *Friern Hospital Management Committee* (1957):

> A doctor is not guilty of negligence if he has acted in accordance with a practice accepted as proper by a responsible body of medical men skilled in that particular art . . . Putting it the other way round, a doctor is not negligent, if he is acting in accordance with such a practice, merely because there is a body of opinion that takes a contrary view.[26]

The general rule is, as a result, known as the '*Bolam* test for negligence'. The case of *Maynard* v *West Midlands Regional Health Authority* (1984) illustrates the test in action. In treating the claimant, the defendants subjected the claimant to a diagnostic procedure called a mediastinoscopy which damaged the claimant's vocal cords. The claimant sued the defendants, claiming that they had breached the duty they owed her to treat her with a professional degree of skill and care. The claim failed: the defendants could show that a substantial body of medical opinion would have supported the claimant's being subjected to a mediastinoscopy given her condition.

C. An exception to the exception

In *Bolitho* v *City and Hackney Health Authority* (1998), the House of Lords ruled:

> the court is not bound to hold that a defendant doctor escapes liability for negligent treatment or diagnosis just because he leads evidence from a number of medical experts who are genuinely of [the] opinion that the defendant's medical treatment or diagnosis accorded with sound medical practice . . . the court has to be satisfied that the exponents of the body of opinion relied upon can demonstrate that such opinion has a logical basis. In particular in cases involving . . . the weighing of risks against benefits, the judge . . . will need to be satisfied that, in forming their views, the experts have directed their minds to the question of comparative risks and benefits and have reached a defensible conclusion on the matter.[27]

So in a case where the court is convinced that a particular body of opinion within a profession as to how a professional should conduct himself is not 'responsible, reasonable and respectable'[28] because that body of opinion is 'not capable of withstanding logical analysis',[29] a defendant will *not* be allowed to rely on that body of opinion to establish that he discharged the duty of care that he owed the claimant as a professional.

---

[26] [1957] 1 WLR 582, 587.
[27] [1998] AC 232, 241–2 (per Lord Browne-Wilkinson).
[28] [1998] AC 232, 241.
[29] [1998] AC 232, 243.

The pre-*Bolitho* case of *Edward Wong Finance Co Ltd* v *Johnson Stokes & Master* (1984) demonstrates this exception to the *Bolam* test at work.[30] In that case, the claimants agreed to lend a company $1,355,000 to enable it to purchase a factory in Hong Kong. The loan was to be secured by, among other things, a mortgage of the factory. The defendant firm of solicitors acted for the claimants in the transaction. The factory was already subject to a mortgage which would have to be cleared by the time it was purchased. The defendant firm of solicitors followed the practice – usual in Hong Kong at the time – of forwarding to the sellers the purchase price in return for the sellers' giving them undertakings that they would apply the purchase price to clear the existing mortgage on the factory. The sellers did no such thing and absconded with the purchase money, leaving the claimants with a greatly reduced security for the money they had lent the company to purchase the factory. The claimants sued the defendant firm of solicitors in negligence. They won: it was held that the defendant firm had breached the duty of care it owed the claimants in relation to how it handled the purchase and mortgage of the factory. Given that the defendant firm could easily have secured the claimants' interests by paying off the existing mortgagee rather than relying on the sellers of the factory to do so, the defendant firm could not establish that it handled the purchase and mortgage of the factory with the skill and care that a reasonably competent solicitor would have handled it. The fact that most solicitors in Hong Kong would have acted – and would have thought it proper to act – in the same way as the defendants did was irrelevant.

In an excellent survey of the caselaw on when a body of opinion within the medical profession will fall foul of *Bolitho*,[31] Rachael Mulheron has identified six grounds on which the courts might find that a particular body of opinion is 'not capable of withstanding logical analysis':[32] (1) if the body of 'opinion has overlooked that a "clear precaution" to avoid the adverse outcome for the patient was available'; (2) if the body of opinion has failed to weigh 'the comparative risks and benefits of the chosen course of conduct'; (3) if the body of opinion contravenes 'community expectations of [what amounts to] acceptable medical practice'; (4) if the body of opinion 'cannot be correct when taken in the context of the whole factual evidence'; (5) if the body of opinion 'is not internally consistent' – for example, because it says that it would be both improper and proper to conduct a certain procedure; and (6) if the body of opinion is directed at whether performing a particular procedure would involve a *gross* or *wanton* lack of care on the part of the doctor performing it.[33]

8.5 PUBLIC POWERS

A. The rule

The rule is that a public body's failure to exercise a statutory power with which it has been vested will put it in breach of a duty of care that it owes someone if exercising that power

---

[30] See also *Lloyds Bank Ltd* v *E B Savory and Co* [1933] AC 201 and *G & K Landenbau (UK) Ltd* v *Crawley & De Reya* [1978] 1 WLR 266.

[31] Mulheron 2010.

[32] ibid, 620–35.

[33] A seventh (actually, the second in her list) factor identified by Mulheron (ibid, 623) – that the court will be *unwilling* to apply *Bolitho* to override a body of medical opinion if that body of opinion is directed at balancing conflicting demands on a doctor or a hospital's resources – is omitted from the above list as this factor identifies a situation where the courts will *not* apply the *Bolitho* exception to the *Bolam* test, rather than a situation where the courts *will* apply *Bolitho*.

would have helped the public body discharge that duty, and it has done nothing else to discharge that duty.

The Court of Appeal's decision in *Connor v Surrey County Council* (2011) illustrates the rule at work. In that case, the claimant was employed by the defendant council as the head teacher of a maintained school. She was subjected to a long running campaign of harassment by some members of the school's governing body, who were determined to turn the school into a faith school, and agitated for the claimant's replacement on the ground that the parents of the school 'no longer [had] confidence in [the claimant] to educate our children in a way that respects and values our faith, culture and heritage' and that the claimant was 'contemptuous of the parents and has as little to do with them as possible' and 'dresses in a way that is inappropriate to our community's values'. The defendants did very little to defend the claimant from these completely groundless accusations, which had the effect of wearing away the claimant's mental health. In particular, the defendants failed to exercise their powers under the School Standards and Framework Act 1998 to replace the school's governing body with an Interim Executive Board – something which would have had the effect of depriving the claimant's tormentors of the platform from which they were harassing the claimant.

After enduring three years of abuse with little protection from the defendants, the claimant's health finally broke down and she left her position as headmistress in September 2005, never to return. She sued the defendants in negligence. It was conceded that the defendants 'owed the claimant a duty of care to take reasonable steps to safeguard her health, including her mental health, in the course of her employment with them.'[34] The only issue was whether the defendants had breached that duty of care. The Court of Appeal found that the defendants' failure to exercise its statutory powers under the 1998 Act had put the defendants in breach of the duty of care that they owed the claimant. Dismissing the governing body would have helped protect the claimant's mental health, and the defendants had not taken any effective alternative steps to protect the claimant from the abuse she was suffering from certain of the governors of her school.

B. Exceptions to the rule

The decision in *Connor* also establishes two exceptions to the above rule.

(1) *Statutory authority*. The first arises out of the fact that 'public bodies' acts or omissions which are authorised by Parliament generally cannot, though they cause injury, sound in damages recoverable by private law cause of action.'[35] So if a public body is authorised by Parliament not to exercise a particular power in the circumstances in which it finds itself, then the body's failure to exercise that power cannot put the public body in breach of a duty of care that it owed someone else. To find otherwise would result in the courts saying that the failure to exercise the power was both lawful (because authorised by Parliament) and unlawful (because of the existence of the duty of care). This exception did not help the defendants in *Connor* because the defendants were *not* authorised by Parliament to stand aside and not exercise their powers under the 1998 Act to replace the governing body in a situation where 'there has been a serious breakdown in the way the school is managed or governed which is prejudicing, or likely to prejudice [the standards of performance of

---

[34] [2011] QB 429, at [52].
[35] [2011] QB 429, at [82] (per Laws LJ).

pupils at the school].'[36] The Court of Appeal found that such a situation had arisen at the claimant's school long before she was forced to leave her post on grounds of ill-health.

(2) *Violation of public law*. The second exception was set out by Laws LJ in his judgment in *Connor*:

> the law will in an appropriate case require the duty-ower to fulfil his existing private law duty by the exercise of a public law discretion, *but only if that may be done consistently with the duty-ower's full performance of his public law obligations . . .*[37] [in particular, the requirement] that a discretion, apparently conferred in unfettered terms, must nevertheless by exercised only for the purposes for which the statute has provided it.[38]

The reason for this exception is that the 'demands of a private law duty of care cannot justify, far less require, action (or inaction) by a public authority which would be unlawful in public law terms'[39] Again, this exception did not assist the defendants in *Connor* because replacing the governing body in order to protect the mental health of the claimant headmistress would have been perfectly consistent with the purpose for which the defendants were granted the power to replace the governing body – that is, to protect the pupils of the claimant's school from receiving a substandard education. But the exception *would* apply in the **Suicidal Prisoner Problem**:

> *Husband* and *Wife* are both arrested for being drunk and disorderly contrary to s 91 of the Criminal Justice Act 1967. They are subsequently locked up in separate cells in a nearby police station, to give them a chance to sober up. *Husband*, in his drunken state, starts loudly threatening that if he and *Wife* are not released immediately, he will kill himself. The police on duty could have given *Husband* and *Wife* a caution for being drunk and disorderly and released them both, but they chose not to. *Husband* subsequently kills himself in his cell by ramming his head against a wall.

Can we say that the police breached the duty of care that they owed *Husband* to take reasonable steps to save him from killing himself by failing to caution *Husband* and *Wife* and then release them? The answer must be 'no' as it would have been improper (and therefore unlawful in a public law sense) to release *Husband* from custody with a caution purely for the purpose of averting a threat that *Husband* or a third party would kill himself if *Husband* were not released from custody.

8.6 BREACH THROUGH OTHERS

A. The rule

As a general rule, a defendant who owes a claimant a duty of care can only be held to have breached that duty of care if he *personally* failed to live up to the standard of care required of him by that duty. For example, in *Gwilliam v West Hertfordshire Hospitals NHS Trust* (2003), a hospital organised a fund-raising fair within its grounds. As one of the activities laid on at the fair, the hospital hired a 'splat wall' from a firm called 'Club Entertainments'.

---

[36] [2011] QB 429, at [111].
[37] [2011] QB 429, at [106] (emphasis added).
[38] [2011] QB 429, at [108].
[39] [2011] QB 429, at [107].

Someone using the splat wall would don a Velcro suit, bounce on a trampoline and then launch themselves from there at a wall, to which they would stick. Unfortunately, the splat wall in *Gwilliam* was not properly set up by the Club Entertainments staff that provided the wall, and Ethel Gwilliam's foot got stuck in the trampoline as she tried to jump off it, with the result that she was permanently disabled. She sued the hospital for compensation, claiming that it had breached the duty of care that it owed her as a visitor to its premises under s 2(2) of the Occupiers' Liability Act 1957 to 'take such care as in all the circumstances of the case is reasonable' to see that she would be 'reasonably safe in using the premises for the purposes for which [she was] invited or permitted . . . to be there.' Her claim failed: the *hospital* had personally taken such care. Club Entertainments seemed like a reputable company, and there was no reason to think that the staff had not set up the trampoline properly.[40] The fact that *Club Entertainments* had not taken care to see that Gwilliam would be safe in using their trampoline had no effect on whether the hospital had breached its duty of care to her.

B. The first exception to the rule: non-delegable duties

The first exception to the above rule arises out of the existence of *non-delegable* duties. A non-delegable duty works as follows. If A owes B a duty to take reasonable steps to see that X does not happen, and A gives the job of seeing that X does not happen to C, if A's duty is *non-delegable*, then if C fails to take reasonable steps to see that X does not happen, then A will be held to have breached the duty of care that A owed B.

The duty of care that an occupier owes his visitors under the Occupiers' Liability Act 1957 is *delegable*. This is made clear by s 2(4)(b) of the Act, which provides that:

> where damage is caused to a visitor by a danger due to the faulty execution of any work . . . by an independent contractor employed by the occupier, the occupier is *not* to be treated without more as answerable for the danger if in all the circumstances *he* had acted reasonably in entrusting the work to an independent contractor and had taken such steps (if any) as *he* reasonably ought in order to satisfy himself that the contractor was competent and that the work had been properly done.[41]

So the fact that Club Entertainments failed to take reasonable steps to ensure the safety of Ethel Gwilliam did not put the hospital in *Gwilliam* in breach of the duty of care that it owed her under s 2(2) of the 1957 Act.

The following duties of care *are* non-delegable:

(1) *Employment.* The most important example of a non-delegable duty of care is the duty an employer owes his employees to see that they are not killed or injured in working for him.[42] So if *Boss* gives *Foreman* the job of supervising the work done by *Boss*'s employees, to see that they will be reasonably safe in doing that work, and *Foreman* fails to give *New Boy* adequate instructions as to how to use a particular machine, with the result that *New Boy* is injured, *New Boy* will be able to sue *Boss* in negligence for breaching the duty of care that *Boss* owed *New Boy* as his employee to take care to see that *New Boy*

---

[40] It was argued the hospital's duty of care to Gwilliam required it to check that Club Entertainments had adequate liability insurance. This aspect of the case is discussed in detail in § 11.2(A)(9), below.

[41] Emphasis added.

[42] *Wilsons & Clyde Coal Co Ltd* v *English* [1938] AC 57; *McDermid* v *Nash Dredging & Reclamation Co Ltd* [1987] 1 AC 906.

would be reasonably safe in working for him. *Foreman's* lack of care will have put *Boss* in breach of *his* duty of care.[43]

(2) *Bailment*. If A hands over some goods to B to look after for her, B is said to hold those goods on a bailment for A (with B being referred to as the 'bailee' of those goods, and A the 'bailor'), and as a result B will owe A a duty to take reasonable steps to protect the goods from being lost, damaged or stolen. That duty of care is non-delegable. So if B subsequently gives the goods to C to look after, and C fails to take reasonable steps to protect the goods, then C's carelessness will put B in breach of the duty of care that she owed A.

For example, in *Morris v C W Martin & Sons Ltd* (1966), the claimant gave her fur coat to a firm of furriers to be cleaned. The furriers sent the coat to the defendant cleaners. The defendants were bailees of the coat for the claimant and as such they owed her a duty to take reasonable steps to safeguard the coat. Unfortunately, the defendants gave the job of looking after the coat to one of their employees, who promptly stole it. Lord Denning MR held[44] that the employee's theft of the coat put the defendants in breach of the duty of care that they owed the claimant to safeguard her coat and accordingly held the defendants liable to the claimant for the loss of her coat.[45] The fact that it was the employee *who had been given the job* of looking after the coat who stole it was crucial to the finding that the defendants had breached the duty of care that they owed the claimant. Had it been some other employee who stole the coat, the defendants would not have been held liable unless they, or the employee who was given the job of looking after the coat, were personally at fault for the occurrence of the theft.[46]

---

[43] But note that this is only so because *Foreman* was *given the job* of seeing that employees like *New Boy* would be reasonably safe in working for *Boss*. See *Davie v New Merton Board Mills Ltd* [1959] AC 604 (employee injured by defective tool unable to sue employer on ground that manufacturer's negligence in manufacturing tool put employer in breach of non-delegable duty of care that he owed employee because employer never gave manufacturer the job of ensuring that employees would be safe; note, however, employee would now be able to sue employer under s 1 of the Employers' Liability (Defective Equipment) Act 1969); and *O'Reilly v National Rail & Tramway Appliances Ltd* [1966] 1 All ER 499 (employee injured as a result of fellow employees' negligence in handling live shell that was in a pile of scrap metal being processed by employees unable to sue employer on ground that employees' negligence put employer in breach of the non-delegable duty of care that he owed employee because employees were not given the job of ensuring employee's safety).

[44] [1966] 1 QB 716, 725, 728.

[45] Note that there is some dispute as to whether the true basis of the defendants' liability in this case was that: (a) the defendants' employee put them in breach of the non-delegable duty that they owed the claimant to safeguard her coat; or (b) the defendants were vicariously liable in respect of the tort committed by their employee (the tort of conversion) when the employee stole the coat. Lord Denning MR's judgment supports view (a). Diplock LJ's judgment in the same case supports view (b). Salmon LJ's judgment straddles both views. In *Lister v Hesley Hall Ltd* [2002] 1 AC 215 it was assumed without any debate that *Morris v C W Martin* was a vicarious liability case: ibid, at [19] (per Lord Steyn), [46] (per Lord Clyde), [57] (per Lord Hobhouse), [75]–[76] (per Lord Millett). In *Dubai Aluminium Co Ltd v Salaam* [2003] 2 AC 366, Lord Millett once again assumed without debate that *Morris* was a vicarious liability case (at [129]). Lord Nicholls was less dogmatic (at [29]), noting that there was some debate over the basis of liability in *Morris*. However, he thought it unnecessary to express his views on the issue. The High Court of Australia was divided in *New South Wales v Lepore* (2003) 212 CLR 511 over the issue of how best to analyse the basis of liability in *Morris*. Gleeson CJ (at [48]) and Kirby P (at [312]) held that *Morris* was a vicarious liability case; Kirby P going so far as to deride alternative explanations of the case as 'feeble' (ibid). However, Gaudron J (at [127]) and McHugh J (at [147], [161]) both viewed the defendants' liability in *Morris* as resting on the fact that their employee had put them in breach of a non-delegable duty of care that they owed the claimant. Tony Weir is in no doubt that the latter analysis is correct, pointing out that the defendants would have been just as liable in *Morris* to the claimant had they given her fur coat to an independent contractor to look after, which he then stole: Weir 2006, 112. (Had that happened, of course, there would have been no possibility of the defendants being held vicariously liable for the tort committed by the contractor in stealing the coat because one cannot ever be held vicariously liable in respect of torts committed by one's independent contractors: see below, § 37.1.) This seems to us the clinching argument and establishes that the liability in *Morris* is more satisfactorily viewed as arising out of the fact that the defendants' employee's actions put them in breach of the non-delegable duty of care that they owed the claimant to safeguard her coat.

[46] [1966] 1 QB 716, 740–1, per Salmon LJ.

(3) *Extra-hazardous activities*. We have already seen that if A is going to engage in some activity that creates a danger for B, A will owe B a duty to take reasonable steps to see that that danger does not materialise.[47] In *Honeywill & Stein* v *Larkin Bros* (1934), the Court of Appeal held that if A's activity was *extra-hazardous* in nature, the duty of care that A owed B to take reasonable steps to see that B was not harmed by that activity would be non-delegable in nature.

So in *Honeywill & Stein* itself, Honeywill & Stein (H&S) had some photographs taken of the inside of a cinema where they had installed some equipment. At the time, taking the photographs involved setting off magnesium flashes. The work of taking the photographs was delegated to Larkin Bros (LB). Due to LB's carelessness in setting off the magnesium flashes, a fire started and the cinema was damaged. The Court of Appeal held that H&S were liable to the cinema owners for the fire damage. Because taking the photographs was an ultra-hazardous activity, the duty of care that H&S had owed the cinema owners to see that the cinema was not damaged by that activity was non-delegable, and H&S had been put in breach of that duty through LB's carelessness.

The decision in *Honeywill & Stein* was severely criticised by the Court of Appeal in *Biffa Waste Services* v *Maschinenfabrik* (2009)[48] on the grounds that the decision was unsupported by authority, and it was very difficult to tell when an activity should be classified as 'ultra-hazardous'.[49] The Court of Appeal made it clear that it would have liked to overrule *Honeywill & Stein* if it could, but as the Court of Appeal is bound by its own decisions, all it could say was that:

> the doctrine enunciated in . . . *Honeywill* . . . is so unsatisfactory that its application should be kept as narrow as possible. It should be applied only to activities that are exceptionally dangerous whatever precautions are taken.[50]

(4) *Educational authorities*. As we have seen, an educational authority will owe children at a school under its control a duty to take reasonable steps to see that they do not come to any physical harm while they are at school.[51] The High Court of Australia has held in *New South Wales* v *Lepore* (2003) that that duty of care is non-delegable in nature[52] and there is no reason to think that an English court would come to any other conclusion if the question arose here.

(5) *Assumption of responsibility*. There are numerous authorities that seem to indicate that if A owes B a duty of care under the extended principle in *Hedley Byrne* because she has 'assumed a responsibility' to B to do some work with a reasonable degree of care and skill, or to take reasonable steps to see that X does not happen, that duty of care will be non-delegable in nature.

For example, in *Cassidy* v *Ministry of Health* (1951), Lord Denning MR said that:

> when hospital authorities undertake to treat a patient, and themselves select and appoint . . . the professional men and women who are to give the treatment, then they are responsible for the negligence of those persons in failing to give proper treatment, no matter whether they are doctors, surgeons, nurses or anyone else.[53]

---

[47] See above, § 7.3.
[48] Noted, Stanton 2009.
[49] [2009] QB 725, at [70]–[75].
[50] [2009] QB 725, at [78].
[51] See above, § 7.11.
[52] Callinan J dissented on this point: (2003) 212 CLR 511, at [340].
[53] [1951] 2 KB 343, 362. See also *Gold* v *Essex County Council* [1942] 2 KB 293, at 301–2 (per Lord Greene MR).

Similarly, it was held in *Philips* v *William Whiteley Ltd* (1938) that the defendant firm of jewellers in that case owed the claimant a non-delegable duty to pierce her ears with the degree of care and skill that a reasonably competent jeweller would exercise in piercing someone's ears. The defendants had summoned an employee of another firm to perform the operation but, fortunately for the defendants, the employee in question pierced the claimant's ears with the requisite degree of care and skill and did not therefore put the defendants in breach of the duty of care that they owed the claimant.

It may be that the decision in *Lloyd* v *Grace, Smith & Co* (1912) can also be explained on this basis.[54] The claimant in that case consulted a firm of solicitors with a view to increasing the income she received from her investments. Her affairs were entrusted to the care of the firm's managing clerk, who used his position to defraud the claimant of two cottages that she owned. The firm was held liable for the loss suffered by the claimant. The case is often viewed as one where the firm was held vicariously liable in respect of the managing clerk's deceit.[55] However, it is possible to argue that the true basis of the firm's liability in this case was that the firm owed a non-delegable duty to the claimant to handle her affairs with a reasonable degree of care and skill and that the managing clerk – who was given the job of handling the claimant's affairs – put the firm in breach of that duty of care when, far from handling her affairs with a reasonable degree of care and skill, he defrauded her of her cottages.[56]

Students often ask whether there is any test by which we can determine whether a given duty of care is delegable or non-delegable. John Murphy has argued that far from being just *one* category of situation where a duty of care will be non-delegable in nature, 'assumption of responsibility' is the keystone concept underlying *all* non-delegable duties of care. In other words, in all cases where a duty of care is non-delegable, the duty is non-delegable because it is based on an 'assumption of responsibility' by the defendant to the claimant.[57] The Court of Appeal's disapproval of *Honeywill & Stein* in *Biffa Waste Services* could be taken to have strengthened Murphy's thesis, as the duty of care that arises out of a defendant's choice to engage in an 'ultra-hazardous' activity cannot be said to have been 'assumed' to those potentially affected by that activity. But we have our doubts as to whether the duty of care that an employer owes his employees is based on an 'assumption of responsibility' to them (in the sense that an employer who makes it clear to his employees that he is indifferent to their safety will *still* owe them a duty to take reasonable steps to see

---

[54] Other difficult cases that might also be explained on this basis are *Rogers* v *Night Riders* [1983] RTR 324 (minicab firm that responded to the claimant's call for a mini-cab held liable for defective door on mini-cab that caused claimant injury; maybe the mini-cab firm could be said to have 'assumed a responsibility' to the claimant to take reasonable steps to see that the mini-cab they recommended was safe to travel in, and had been put in breach of the resulting duty of care by the driver's failure to check that the car was safe to travel in?) and *Photo Production* v *Securicor* [1980] AC 827. In *Photo Production*, the defendant security company in that case was employed to patrol the claimants' factory at night to see that it was not burned down or broken into during the night. The job of patrolling the factory was given to one of the defendants' security guards who, one night, deliberately started a fire in the factory with the result that the factory burned down. The defendant security company was held *prima facie* liable for the fire damage. (In fact, there was an exclusion clause in the contract between the defendants and the claimants that absolved the defendants of liability.) There are *dicta* in the case (ibid, at 846 (per Lord Wilberforce) and 852 (per Lord Salmon) which indicate that the source of the defendants' *prima facie* liability in this case was that they were vicariously liable for the tort committed by their employee in starting the fire. However, it is possible to argue that the real source of the defendants' liability in this case was that their employee's lack of care put them in breach of a non-delegable duty of care that they owed the claimants: see *New South Wales* v *Lepore* (2003) 212 CLR 511, at [146]–[148] (per McHugh J).

[55] *Lister* v *Hesley Hall Ltd* [2002] 1 AC 215, at [19] (per Lord Steyn), [73] (per Lord Millett).

[56] See *New South Wales* v *Lepore* (2003) 212 CLR 511, at [127] (per Gaudron J).

[57] Murphy 2007a, 379–90.

that they are safe working for them). Moreover, if Murphy's thesis were correct, it is hard to understand why the duty of care that an occupier owes his visitors under the Occupiers' Liability Act 1957 is delegable, rather than non-delegable, as that duty has as much claim as an employer's duty to his employees to be based on an 'assumption of responsibility' by the occupier to his visitors.

C. The second exception to the rule: companies and other artificial legal persons

A company is an artificial legal person. As such, as Lord Diplock remarked in *Tesco Supermarkets Ltd* v *Natrass* (1972), 'it is incapable itself of doing any physical act or being in a state of mind'.[58] If a company is to act, then, it can only do so through natural persons – people who are, of course, capable of performing physical actions. This creates a problem when we want to determine whether or not a *company* breached a duty of care that it owed to someone else.[59] *Whose* actions should we look at in order to determine whether or not that duty of care was breached? The facts of the *Tesco Supermarkets* case illustrate the problem.

In that case, a customer at a Tesco store was charged 3s 11d for a packet of washing powder when posters in the window of the store advertised that brand of washing powder as being on special offer at 2s 11d per packet. The general manager of the store, one Mr Clement, was at fault for this: he had failed to take reasonable steps to ensure that the store was stocked with some packets with the lower price on them. Tesco was charged with committing an offence under s 11(2) of the Trade Descriptions Act 1968 which provided that:

> if any person offering to supply any goods gives . . . any indication likely to be taken as an indication that the goods are being offered at a price less than that at which they are in fact being offered he shall, subject to the provisions of this Act, be guilty of an offence.

In their defence, Tesco sought to rely on s 24(1) of the Act which provided that:

> In any proceedings for an offence under this Act . . . it shall be a defence for the person charged to prove – (a) that the commission of the offence was due . . . to the act or default of another person and (b) that he took all reasonable precautions and exercised all due diligence to avoid the commission of such an offence by himself or any person under his control.

Tesco could establish that (a) was true – the offence was committed because of Mr Clement's 'default'. Could it establish that (b) was true – that *it* took all reasonable care to ensure that its goods were not sold at a price higher than the advertised price? Clearly, *Mr Clement* did not take such care – but did that mean that *Tesco*, Mr Clement's employer, did not take such care? More generally, whose actions should be looked at to determine whether Tesco took reasonable care to ensure that its goods were not sold at a price higher than the advertised price?

In the *Tesco Supermarkets* case, the House of Lords adopted the *traditional rule* for determining such issues – according to which, one determines what a company has done

---

[58] [1972] AC 153, 198.

[59] Of course, this issue only comes up if we want to establish whether a company is *personally* liable to compensate a claimant for some loss that he or she has suffered. If it is not personally liable to pay such compensation it may still be *vicariously* liable to pay such compensation if one of its employees caused the claimant to suffer the loss in question by committing the tort and there was a sufficiently close connection between what the employee was employed to do and the tort committed by the employee: see below, § 37.2.

by looking at the actions of those who represent the company's *'directing mind or will'*.[60] By this yardstick, Tesco *had* taken reasonable care to ensure that its good were not sold at a price higher than the advertised price. Mr Clement, the House of Lords held, did not 'function as the directing mind or will of the company. He was . . . being directed.'[61]

The traditional rule – that we determine what a company did by looking at what those who represent the company's 'directing mind or will' did – came under challenge in the 1990s, when it was suggested that *how* we ascertain what a company did depends very much on the *nature and purpose* of the legal rule that requires us to find out what that company did. The first hint of a challenge to the traditional rule came in the case of *Re Supply of Ready Mixed Concrete (No 2)* (1995), where four companies which were engaged in the supply of ready mixed concrete entered into agreements with each other which fixed the prices at which they would supply ready mixed concrete to customers and determined what share each company would enjoy of the market for ready mixed concrete in the area in which the four companies operated. These agreements were unlawful under s 35(1) of the Restrictive Trade Practices Act 1976 and the Director General of Fair Trading obtained injunctions against the four companies, requiring them not to enter into or give effect to any such agreements in future.

After the injunctions were obtained, employees of the four companies, without the knowledge of the management of those companies and contrary to their express instructions, started to operate a new agreement to fix prices and allocate work among the four companies. The Director General claimed that the companies had breached the injunctions and were therefore in contempt of court. In defence, the companies claimed that they had not entered into or given effect to any unlawful price fixing and work allocation agreement. The House of Lords dismissed the companies' claim on the basis that what the companies' employees did, the companies did. So if the companies' employees entered into and gave effect to an unlawful price fixing and work allocation agreement among themselves, the companies entered into and gave effect to such an agreement among themselves in breach of the injunction against them. This was so even though there was no way the companies' employees could be said to have represented the 'directing mind or will' of the companies.

In a subsequent Privy Council case, *Meridian Global Funds Management Asia Ltd* v *Securities Commission* (1995), Lord Hoffmann – giving the only judgment – endorsed the result in *Re Supply of Ready Mixed Concrete (No 2)* (1995) and sought to reconcile it with the decision in the *Tesco Supermarkets* case by arguing that in applying a legal rule that required the courts to determine what a company did, the courts should adopt the approach to finding out what that company did that the creators of the legal rule in question intended them to adopt for the purposes of applying that rule:

---

[60] The traditional rule traces its origin to the judgment of Viscount Haldane LC in *Lennard's Carrying Co Ltd* v *Asiatic Petroleum Co Ltd* [1915] AC 705, 713: 'My Lords, a corporation is an abstraction. It has no mind of its own any more than it has a body of its own; its active and directing will must consequently be sought in the person of somebody who for some purposes may be called an agent, but who is really the directing mind and will of the corporation, the very ego and centre of the personality of the corporation.' Denning LJ found a characteristically colourful way to express the principle in *Bolton (Engineering) Co Ltd* v *Graham & Sons Ltd* [1957] 1 QB 159, 172: 'A company may in many ways be likened to a human body. It has a brain and a nerve centre which controls what it does. It also has hands which hold the tools and act in accordance with directions from the centre. Some of the people in the company are mere servants or agents who are nothing more than hands to do the work and cannot be said to represent the mind or will. Others are directors and managers who represent the directing mind or will of the company, and control what it does. The state of mind of these managers is the state of mind of the company and is treated by the law as such. So you will find that in cases where the law requires personal fault as a condition of liability in tort, the fault of the manager will be the personal fault of the company.'
[61] [1972] AC 153, 180 (per Lord Morris).

This is always a matter of interpretation: given that [the rule in question] was intended to apply to a company, how was it intended to apply? Whose act . . . was *for this purpose* intended to count as the act . . . of the company? One finds the answer to this question by applying the usual canons of interpretation, taking into account the language of the rule (if it is a statute) and its content and policy.[62]

So, in Lord Hoffmann's view, the *Tesco Supermarkets* case was decided the way it was because those who created the defence contained in s 24(1) of the Trade Descriptions Act 1968 did not intend the courts to treat Tesco as having failed to take care to ensure that its goods were not sold at a price higher than the advertised price if one of the Tesco store managers did not take such care. On the other hand, Lord Hoffmann argued, *Re Supply of Ready Mixed Concrete (No 2)* was decided the way it was because an injunction against a company, requiring it not to enter into or give effect to unlawful price fixing and work allocation agreements with other companies, would be of little use if a company that was subject to such an injunction could not be held liable for breaching that injunction if its employees set up and operated an unlawful price fixing and work allocation agreement without the knowledge of the company's management.

However, Lord Hoffmann's approach is difficult to apply in the context that we are concerned with here – determining whether a company has breached a duty of care that it owes to someone else. The reason is that the sort of duties of care we are concerned with in this book are not targeted specifically at companies, and so the creators of those duties of care – usually judges, sometimes legislatures – will have had *no* intentions as to what approach we should adopt in determining whether a company has breached that duty of care. Moreover, since the decision in *Meridian Global Funds*, both the Court of Appeal and the House of Lords have taken the position that the 'directing mind or will' approach to determining what a company did should be adopted unless there is a good reason why a different approach should be adopted (such as that Parliament intended that a different approach should be adopted in the context of determining whether a company committed a particular statutory offence).[63]

So to sum up: in every case where an artificial legal person owed someone else a duty we are confronted with the problem – Whose actions should we look at to determine whether or not that person breached that duty? In the case of companies that problem is solved, we suggest, by adopting the 'directing mind or will' principle according to which we ascertain what a company did at a particular time by looking at what those who represented that company's 'directing mind or will' at that time did. The same approach should be adopted in relation to artificial legal persons that are not companies, such as local authorities.

8.7 PROOF

A. The rule

The general rule is that it is up to the claimant in a negligence case to prove that the defendant breached a duty of care owed to her. So, for example, in *Knight* v *Fellick* (1977),

---

[62] [1995] 2 AC 500, 507.
[63] See *Attorney-General's Reference (No 2 of 1999)* [2000] QB 796, 814, 816: 'the primary "directing mind and will" rule still applies though it is not determinative in all cases' and *Stone & Rolls Ltd* v *Moore Stephens* [2009] 1 AC 1391 (company cannot sue for losses resulting from auditor's negligent failure to detect the company sole director's misappropriations of company funds as the company – through the director, as its 'directing mind and will' – was party to the illegal acts that resulted in those losses occurring). For a full survey of the authorities, see Ferran 2011.

the claimant was run down by the defendant driver. The claimant was so badly injured in the accident that she had no memory of how it happened. The claimant sued the defendant in negligence for compensation but her claim failed: she could not prove that the defendant was driving without due care and attention at the time he hit the claimant.

B. *Res ipsa loquitur*

The burden of proof shifts to the defendant – who will then have to show that he did *not* breach a duty of care owed to the claimant – if the facts of the case are such that the most natural explanation of what happened is that the defendant was careless.[64] In such a case the facts of the case will indicate (*'res ipsa loquitur'* means *'the thing speaks for itself'*) that the defendant breached his duty of care, and it will be up to the defendant to show that he was not, in fact, careless.

So a *res ipsa loquitur* argument would have been available to the claimant in *Knight* had the accident happened in broad daylight: one would not usually expect a driver to run someone down when visibility is perfect unless the driver was careless in some way. Unfortunately for the claimant in *Knight*, the accident happened at night, on a road which had no lighting, and the claimant was wearing dark clothes at the time. So the fact that the claimant had been run down did not, of and itself, indicate that the defendant had been careless in running her down.

Res ipsa loquitur has been applied to help establish that the defendant breached a duty of care owed to the claimant in the following types of cases: (1) the defendant performed a minor operation on the claimant's hand and after the operation was over the claimant lost the use of his hand;[65] (2) the claimant was working in the defendant's factory and an electrical panel fell on his head;[66] (3) the claimant was injured when a coach driven by the defendant suddenly veered across the road into the claimant's path;[67] (4) the defendant cleaned a suit belonging to the claimant and the claimant suddenly developed dermatitis on wearing the suit again.[68] A plea of *res ipsa loquitur* was not allowed in the case where a door on a moving train operated by the defendant suddenly opens and the claimant falls out.[69] The fact that the door opened suddenly did not of itself indicate that the defendant was careless in operating the train: the door could just as well have opened because of the fault of another passenger.

C. Exceptions to the rule

The law on *res ipsa loquitur* does not create a genuine exception to the rule as to burden of proof set out above: the burden of proving carelessness still starts with the claimant, who

---

[64] The requirements that had to be satisfied before a *res ipsa loquitur* argument could be made in favour of the view that the defendant had breached a duty of care owed to the claimant were first set out by Erle CJ in *Scott* v *London and St Katherine Docks Company* (1865) 3 H & C 595, 601; 159 ER 665, 667: 'where the thing [which caused the accident complained of] is shewn to be under the management of the defendant . . . and the accident is such as in the ordinary course of things does not happen if those who have the management use proper care, it affords reasonable evidence, in the absence of explanation by the defendants, that the accident arose from want of care.'

[65] *Cassidy* v *Ministry of Health* [1951] 2 KB 343.

[66] *Bennett* v *Chemical Construction* (GB) Ltd [1971] 1 WLR 1571.

[67] *Ng Chun Pui* v *Lee Chuen Tat* [1988] RTR 298 (note that no finding of negligence was ultimately made in this case – even though it looked at first as if the defendant had been careless in driving the coach, he had an explanation for his driving into the claimant's lane: he was trying to avoid a car that had cut in front of him).

[68] *Mayne* v *Silvermere Cleaners* [1939] 1 All ER 693.

[69] *Easson* v *London and North Eastern Railway Company* [1944] 1 KB 421.

is then allowed to shift it onto the defendant by pleading *res ipsa loquitur*. But there are a couple of genuine exceptions to the rule as to burden of proof as to carelessness in a negligence case:

(1) *Bailment.* If A holds goods on a bailment for B and those goods are lost, damaged, or stolen, it will be presumed – unless A can prove otherwise – that A breached the duty of care that he owed B to take reasonable steps to safeguard those goods.[70]

(2) *Criminal conviction.* If A owed B a duty of care and has been convicted of a criminal offence which A could not have committed had he fulfilled the duty of care that he owed B, in any civil proceedings between A and B it will be conclusively presumed – unless A can prove otherwise – that A breached the duty of care that he owed B.[71]

Further reading

The law on breach of duty of care does not excite academics very much. Except for adherents to the law and economics school, who think that the 'Hand Formula' for determining whether or not a duty of care has been breached indicates a commitment on the part of the judges to maximising economic efficiency (the idea being that you only have to take a precaution against a given risk if taking that precaution can be justified on cost-benefit grounds). For more, see **Posner, 'A theory of negligence' (1972) 1 *Journal of Legal Studies* 29**; and for responses to Posner, see **Wright, 'Hand, Posner and the myth of the "Hand Formula" ' (2003) 4 *Theoretical Inquiries in Law* 145** and **Zipursky, 'Sleight of Hand' (2007) 48 *William and Mary Law Review* 1999**.

Of course, legal economists – and many tort lawyers who have nothing to do with law and economics – see 'fault' as being the foundational concept in the law of negligence, and 'duty' as something that could easily be dispensed with. On this view, liability in negligence is justified on the basis that the defendant was *at fault* for the harm suffered by the claimant. For a lecture delivered from within that kind of world view see **Tunc, 'Tort law and the moral law' (1972) 30 *Cambridge Law Journal* 247**. One problem with this view is that in requiring people to live up to an objective standard of care, the law of negligence frequently holds people liable for harms for which they were *not* personally to blame. For an explanation as to why it might be *not unfair* to hold someone liable for the outcome of their actions even though they were not personally to blame for those outcomes, see **Honoré, 'Responsibility and luck: the moral basis of strict liability' (1988) 104 *Law Quarterly Review* 530**.

Mayo Moran criticises the objective standard of care as potentially discriminatory in her monograph *Rethinking the Reasonable Person* (OUP, 2003). The book is too long and complex for students to be reasonably expected to read it, but it is well-reviewed from a tort lawyer's perspective by **Richard Mullender in 'The reasonable person, the pursuit of justice, and negligence law' (2005) 68 *Modern Law Review* 681**. Moran's 'The reasonable person: a conceptual biography in comparative perspective' (2010) 14 *Lewis & Clark Law Review* 1233 also supplies a good summary of her views on the objective standard care in tort law at 1238–49.

For an excellent exploration of whether negligence law asks too much of us, see **Mullender, 'Negligence law and the concept of community' (2008) 16 *Tort Law Review* 85**.

[70] *Houghland v R R Low (Luxury Coaches) Ltd* [1962] 1 QB 694; *Port Swettenham Authority v T W Wu & Co* [1979] AC 580.
[71] Civil Evidence Act 1968, s 11. On which, see *Stupple v Royal Insurance Co Ltd* [1971] 1 QB 50.

Visit **www.mylawchamber.co.uk/mcbride** to access tools to help you develop and test your knowledge of Tort law, including interactive multiple choice questions, practice exam questions with guidance, weblinks, legal newsfeed, additional case summaries, legal updates and tips on answering problem and essay questions.

Use **Case Navigator** to read in full some of the key cases referenced in this chapter with commentary and questions:

• Tomlinson *v* Congleton Borough Council

9 Causation

9.1   The basics *271*

9.2   The 'but for' test *275*

9.3   Divisible and indivisible harm *279*

9.4   Evidential difficulties (1): the standard approach *281*

9.5   Evidential difficulties (2): the *Fairchild* exception *285*

9.6   Evidential difficulties (3): loss of a chance cases *291*

9.7   *Gregg* v *Scott* *296*

9.8   Overdetermination *300*

9.9   Another solution to overdetermination? *303*

9.10 Coincidences *305*

9.11 Coincidental overdetermination *309*

9.12 Break in the chain of causation *311*

9.13 Alternative approaches to causation *317*

9.14 Fact and policy *325*

Overview

In this chapter, we look at the law on when a tort can be said to have *caused* harm to the victim of a tort. The main focus will be on the law of negligence – both because the victim of a breach of a duty of care will have to prove that the breach has caused her loss if she is going to be allowed to sue the person who breached that duty, and because negligence cases tend to give rise to the most difficult causation issues. But the rules and principles laid out in this chapter apply to all torts. After introducing those rules and principles in section 9.1, we explain in sections 9.2 to 9.9 how the basic test for causation (asking whether the claimant would have suffered the harm she has suffered but for the defendant's tort) works, both in theory and in practice. Sections 9.2 and 9.3 lay out the basic test. Sections 9.4 to 9.5 discuss how the test works in a situation where it is uncertain whether or not the claimant would have suffered a particular harm but for the defendant's tort. Sections 9.6 to 9.7 discuss whether, in these situations of uncertainty, a claimant could alternatively sue on the basis that the defendant's tort caused her to suffer the harm of losing a *chance* of gaining a benefit or avoiding a harm. Sections 9.8 to 9.9 discuss how we should handle cases of overdetermination, when the presence of other factors means that a harm suffered by a claimant would have been suffered anyway, even if the defendant had not committed his tort. Sections 9.10 to 9.12 discuss exceptions to the basic 'but for' test of causation. Sections 9.13 and 9.14 are more theoretical: section 9.13 discusses whether there is a superior basic test for causation than the 'but for' test, and section 9.14 discusses the relevance of findings of fact and considerations of policy in determining what caused what.

9.1 THE BASICS

The victim of a breach of a duty of care will not be able to sue in negligence unless she can show that the breach *caused* her to suffer an *actionable* loss. This chapter is about causation; the next chapter is about actionability. However, it is important for the student reader to remember that the law on causation and actionability is not just relevant to the law on negligence. It is relevant in *every* case where the victim of a tort – *any* tort – wants to sue for compensatory damages. In such a case, he will always have to show that the commission of that tort *caused* him to suffer some kind of *actionable* loss. If it did not, then compensatory damages will simply not be available.[1] And the law on causation is not just relevant in cases where the victim of a tort wants to sue for compensatory damages. It is also relevant to:

(1) Wrongful death claims, where the dependants of the victim of a tort will only be allowed to sue under the Fatal Accidents Act 1976 if they can show that that tort *caused* the death of the victim of the tort.[2]

(2) Cases where a claimant wants to bring a claim for compensation under some liability rule which entitles him to sue for compensation for losses *caused* by a certain event (for example, the manufacture of a dangerously defective product, under the Consumer Protection Act 1987).

(3) Cases where a defendant is being prosecuted under the criminal law for *causing* some harm (for example, in a murder case, where the prosecution has to show that the defendant caused another's death).

Whatever the context, the rules and principles of the law of causation remain the same.[3] The basic starting point is the 'but for' test – would *x* have happened but for what A did? If *x* would have happened anyway, that would normally count against finding that what A did caused *x* to happen. If *x* would not have happened at all, that would normally count in favour of finding that what A did caused *x* to happen. But the 'but for' test is notoriously inadequate as a test for determining causation issues. Sometimes it produces paradoxical results, indicating that *no one* caused *x* to happen, when we know someone must have. Sometimes it is overbroad: it will indicate that A caused *x* to happen, when such a finding will seem counter-intuitive to ordinary people. As an example of a paradox produced by the 'but for' test, consider the **Water Bottle Problem**:

> The night before *Traveller* is due to make a trip into the desert, her camel is loaded up with provisions, including a very large and very full water bottle. During the night, *Malice* empties the water bottle and fills it with poison, so that the next day, when *Traveller* needs to have a drink from the water bottle, she will drink the poison, and die. A couple of hours later (and unaware of what *Malice* has done), *Envy* makes a tiny hole in the bottom of the water bottle, so that the contents of the water bottle start dribbling out of the hole. *Envy*'s plan is that the water bottle will still seem fairly full in the morning, when *Traveller* starts out on her journey, but by the time she needs a drink, the bottle will be completely empty, and *Traveller* will die of dehydration. The next morning, *Traveller* gets up, checks her camel, sees nothing wrong with the water bottle, and rides out into the desert. By the time she needs a drink, the water bottle is empty. *Traveller* dies of dehydration in the desert.

Who caused *Traveller*'s death here? If we apply the 'but for' test we reach a paradoxical conclusion. Looking at *Malice* first, *Malice* can argue that had he not done what he did,

---

[1] Though some other form of damages such as nominal damages (see below, chapter 27) or gain-based damages (see below, chapter 31) might be.
[2] See below, § 34.1.
[3] Though some would question whether that is true: see the discussion of Lord Hoffmann's views below, § 9.13.

Traveller would have died in exactly the same manner and at exactly the same time as she actually did. *Malice*'s replacing *Traveller*'s water with poison turned out to have zero effect on how *Traveller* died. Turning to *Envy*, *Envy* can argue that had she not done what she did, *Traveller* would have died a lot more quickly than she actually did. *Traveller* would have dropped down dead from being poisoned as soon as she had a drink from the water bottle. As a result of what *Envy* did, *Traveller* instead got a chance to live for a few more days before finally collapsing from dehydration. So rather than causing *Traveller*'s death, *Envy* actually saved *Traveller*'s life.

So applying the 'but for' test in this context produces the paradoxical conclusion that *neither Malice nor Envy* caused *Traveller*'s death. The conclusion seems[4] paradoxical because we know that had *Malice* and *Envy* not messed around with *Traveller*'s water bottle, she would not now be lying dead in the desert.

Here are two situations where applying the 'but for' test seems to produce a 'false positive' result (in other words, the 'but for' test indicates that someone's actions caused something to happen, when our intuitions tell us that such a finding is incorrect):

> (1) *Footballer* scores a last-minute winner in an important World Cup game. *Gambler* had a bet that the game would end in a draw, and is so angered at losing his bet that later on that evening, he gets into a fight in a pub, and ends up stabbing *Drinker*. No ordinary person would say that *Footballer*'s scoring a last-minute goal caused *Drinker* to be stabbed, even though *Drinker* would not have been stabbed 'but for' *Footballer*'s last-minute winner.
>
> (2) *Happy* puts on a new dress to go to a party. At that party, *Drunk* carelessly spills wine over the dress, and it is permanently stained. No ordinary person would say that *Happy*'s wearing her new dress to the party caused the dress to end up with a wine stain on it, even though that would not have happened 'but for' *Happy*'s wearing the dress to the party.

In cases where application of the 'but for' test produces paradoxical results, or 'false positives', the 'but for' test needs to be modified or supplemented by additional tests for causation. The main additional tests that the courts use are the *break in the chain of causation* test and the *material increase in risk* test.

The *break in the chain of causation* test is what we have to appeal to in order to explain why *Footballer*'s scoring a last-minute winner did not cause *Drinker* to be stabbed. In between *Footballer*'s scoring a last-minute winner and *Drinker*'s being stabbed, something else happened that contributed to *Drinker*'s being stabbed: *Gambler* lost his temper, got into a fight, and got out a knife. Because *Gambler*'s actions were *deliberate* (he was in control of what he was doing), *voluntary* (he was not acting under pressure), *informed* (he knew what the effects of his actions would be) and *unreasonable* (it was stupid of him to do what he did), they amount to what lawyers call a *novus actus interveniens* – a new and intervening act, that has the effect of breaking the chain of causation between *Footballer*'s goal and *Drinker*'s being stabbed.

We cannot use the break in the chain of causation test to explain why *Happy*'s wearing her new dress to the party did not cause it to end up stained. While *Drunk*'s carelessness in spilling the wine over *Happy*'s new dress undoubtedly contributed to its being stained, the fact that *Drunk* was not acting *deliberately* in spilling wine over the dress means that what *Drunk* did, did not break the chain of causation between *Happy*'s wearing her new dress to

---

[4] We will suggest later on that this conclusion may not be as paradoxical as it seems: see below, § 9.13.

the party and its ending up stained. (It would have been different if *Lecher* intentionally spilled wine all over *Happy*'s dress to encourage her to get out of it.)

Instead, we explain why *Happy*'s wearing her new dress to the party did *not* cause it to end up being stained by reference to the *material increase in risk* test – wearing a new dress to a party does not materially increase the risk that it will end up being stained. Of course, *Happy*'s dress would not have been at *any* risk of being stained if she had left it in her wardrobe. But *Happy* did not increase the risk to the dress of its being stained to any *substantial* extent by taking it out of the wardrobe and putting it on. (It would have been different if *Happy* was going to a Bugsy Malone theme party where it was contemplated that the guests would have a big custard pie fight: in that case, one could say that *Happy* did cause any damage that her clothes sustained in the fight by choosing to wear those clothes to the party.)

But even these tests need modification and supplementation where *they* threaten to produce undesirable conclusions. This is particularly the case where the application of tests like the break in the chain of causation test and the material increase in risk test would mean that a breach of a particular duty of care would *never* give rise to a liability to pay compensatory damages to the victim of the breach, because the defendant breaching the duty of care could *always* rely on these tests to say that his breach did not cause the victim of the breach to suffer any loss, and thereby escape any kind of sanction for his breach.

For example, we have seen that if the police take someone into custody who they know or ought to know is suicidal, then they will have a duty to take reasonable steps to see that he does not kill himself.[5] If they breach that duty, and their prisoner takes advantage of their breach to kill himself, they could always argue – if they were sued for damages – that they are not liable because the prisoner's *deliberate, voluntary, informed* and *unreasonable* decision to kill himself broke the chain of causation between their breach and his death. If such an argument were successful, then the police's duty of care to suicidal inmates would become meaningless – they would be free to breach it with impunity. In order to avoid this result, the House of Lords ruled in *Reeves v Commissioner of Police of the Metropolis* (2000) that in this kind of case, the police would not be allowed to rely on the 'break in the chain of causation' test to say that their negligence did not cause the death of someone who killed themselves in custody.

Three more points need to be made about the law of causation before we can move on to look at it in more detail:

(1) It is possible for more than one person to cause something to happen. For example, suppose *Driver One* carelessly runs into *Pedestrian* while she is crossing the road. *Pedestrian* flies through the air onto the opposite side of the road, where she is run over for a second time by *Driver Two*, who is too busy arguing with his wife to pay any attention to the drama playing out in front of him. In this second collision, *Pedestrian* suffers serious spinal injuries that mean she will be paralysed for life. In this situation, *both One and Two*'s careless driving has caused *Pedestrian*'s paralysis. Had *One* not been driving badly, *Pedestrian* would not have been run over by *Two* and been paralysed; and *Two*'s bad driving did not break the chain of causation between *One*'s bad driving and *Pedestrian*'s paralysis because *Two* was not *deliberately* driving badly. Had *Two* not been driving badly, *Pedestrian* would obviously not have been run over by *Two* and been paralysed.

[5] See above, § 7.4.

(2) Academics try to express the distinction between the 'but for' test for causation and tests that are designed to modify or supplement the 'but for' test by saying that the 'but for' test is concerned with *factual causation*, while tests like the 'break in the chain of causation' test and the 'material increase in risk' test are concerned with *legal causation*. We are not fans of this distinction, for three reasons.

First, it does not seem right to say that issues such as 'Was there a break in the chain of causation between what the defendant did and the outcome of his actions?' and 'Did the defendant's actions materially increase the risk that this outcome would occur?' have *no bearing* on the issue of whether the defendant's actions *in fact* caused a particular outcome to occur. It is not only lawyers who might be expected to be attentive to such issues in trying to determine who was responsible for something that has happened.

Secondly, saying that there is a distinction between issues of *factual* causation and *legal* causation does not seem to contribute anything to our understanding of the law. How is our understanding of the law enhanced by saying that the 'but for' test is concerned with *factual* causation and other tests for causation are concerned with *legal* causation? In fact, the use of such language could well get in the way of our understanding what lawyers are doing when they deal with causation issues. It suggests that lawyers are prone to *lying* about causation issues – refusing to find *in law* that the defendant's actions caused a particular outcome when *in fact* the defendant's actions *did* cause that outcome.

Thirdly, once one starts down the road of saying that there is a relative disconnect between the *law* on causation and ordinary people's views on causation, there is literally no limit on how many rules or principles one could see as being rules about *legal* causation. All the rules and principles set out in the next chapter (on 'Actionability') could be recharacterised as rules and principles that say 'There is no liability in this kind of case because the defendant's actions were not a *legal* cause of the loss suffered by the claimant.' A concept that can be abused so easily has nothing to recommend it.

(3) The presentation of the law on causation in this chapter is pretty conventional – it corresponds with the way most lawyers approach causation issues. However, some academics think that the conventional approach to causation should be abandoned. They think that asking, 'Would this have happened but for what the defendant did?' is the wrong place to start. We continue to think that the best way for students to get a good working understanding of the law of causation is to adopt the conventional approach to the law on causation set out in this chapter. But in deference to the critics of the conventional approach, and in order to deepen students' understandings of the law on causation, one of the sections towards the end of this chapter is devoted to alternative approaches to the law on causation.

9.2 THE 'BUT FOR' TEST

According to the 'but for' test for causation, if we want to see whether A's tort caused B to suffer some kind of loss, we must first ask whether that loss would not have occurred 'but for' A's committing that tort.

In *Barnett v Chelsea & Kensington Hospital Committee* (1969), three nightwatchmen presented themselves at a hospital casualty department, complaining that they had started vomiting after drinking some tea. The casualty officer on duty told the men to go to bed and call their own doctors. The men followed his advice and five hours later one of them died from arsenic poisoning. It was held that the casualty officer's failure to treat the man who died (in breach of the duty of care he owed him to treat him with a reasonable degree of care and skill) did not cause his death; he would have died anyway, even if he had been treated by the casualty officer.

In *McWilliams* v *Sir William Arrol & Co* (1962), the claimant's husband was working for the defendant, his employer, on a steel lattice tower when he fell to his death. It was found that the defendant's failure to provide the husband with a safety belt (in breach of his duty under s 36(2) of the Factories Act 1937) did not cause the husband's death. If the defendant had supplied the husband with a safety belt he would not have worn it so it could not be said that but for the defendant's failure to supply the husband with a safety belt, the husband would not have fallen to his death.[6]

In *Jobling* v *Associated Dairies Ltd* (1982), the claimant was employed by the defendants in their butchers' shop. In 1973 he slipped on the floor of the shop because the defendants had failed (in breach of their duty under the Offices, Shops and Railway Premises Act 1973) to keep the floor free from slippery substances. The claimant suffered a back injury which was somewhat disabling. In 1976 the claimant's back became completely disabled because he developed a condition called myelopathy. The myelopathy was completely unconnected with the claimant's accident in 1973. It was held that while the defendants' failure to keep the floor of their shop free from slippery substances had caused the claimant's disablement between 1973 and 1976, that failure had not caused any of the claimant's disablement after 1976. If the defendants had kept the floor of their shop free from slippery substances, the claimant would still have been completely disabled from 1976 onwards.

In *Calvert* v *William Hill Ltd* (2008), the claimant lost about £2m, gambling money with the defendants, using a special telephone betting account that they had set up for him. The claimant had asked the defendants to close the account down, so as to put a brake on his gambling habit. However, the claimant's instruction was never acted on, with the result that when the gambling bug next hit him and he picked up the phone and rang the defendants, they continued to accept his bets. It was found that the defendants had 'assumed a responsibility' to the claimant to close the account down, and as a result, they owed him a duty of care from then on not to accept bets on that account. However, at first instance, Briggs J found that had the defendants not breached this duty of care, the claimant would still have suffered the same loss in any case, except perhaps at a slower rate:

> had [the claimant] been excluded from telephone betting by [the defendants] . . . he would have sought other avenues for large scale betting, whether on the telephone or on the internet, and would have continued his gambling, albeit on a lesser daily scale than that in which he indulged with [the defendants] . . . even if deprived of the opportunity to pursue his telephone gambling with [the defendants] . . . the claimant would ultimately have ruined himself financially, albeit at a slower rate because of the reduced scale of gambling which would have been available to him.[7]

It is important to note that in a tort case, the question we ask in applying the 'but for' test is – Would B have suffered the loss she did 'but for' A's *tort*? Tortfeasors are not held

---

[6] It might have been different if the defendant had owed the claimant's husband a duty not only to supply him with a safety belt but *also* to take steps to ensure that he wore it. In that case, it could have been argued that had the defendant supplied the claimant's husband with a safety belt *and* taken steps to ensure that he wore it, the claimant's husband would have worn a safety belt while he was working and would not have fallen to his death. It could therefore have been argued that the defendant's breach of the duty he owed the claimant's husband to supply the claimant's husband with a safety belt *and* to take steps to ensure that he wore it caused the claimant's husband to die. See, for example, *Nolan* v *Dental Manufacturing Co Ltd* [1958] 1 WLR 936.

[7] [2008] EWHC 454 (Ch), at [203]. The Court of Appeal decided the case on slightly different grounds, which are dealt with below, § 9.8.

liable in tort for the losses caused by their bare acts or omissions, but for the losses caused by their *wrongs*.

The difficulty this sometimes creates in applying the 'but for' test is illustrated by the case of *The Empire Jamaica* (1957). In that case, the defendants' ship collided with, and damaged, the claimants' ship. At the time of the accident, the defendants' ship was sailing in breach of regulations that said that the first and second mate of the ship should be certified: in fact only the first mate on the defendants' ship was certified. Did the defendants' breach of regulations cause the accident? Applying the 'but for' test to this question produces an ambiguous answer. This is because there were two ways the defendants could have complied with the regulations that they breached.

The first way of complying with the regulations was to ensure that when the ship sailed, the first and second mates on the ship were certified. The defendants failed to do this, but this failure did *not* cause the accident that damaged the claimants' ship according to the 'but for' test. The accident would still have happened, even if the second mate on the defendants' ship was certified. However, the second way of complying with the regulations was not to allow the defendants' ship to sail at all, given that the second mate on board was not yet certified. Again, the defendants failed to do this. Now – we can say that the accident which damaged the claimants' ship would not have happened but for this failure. Had the defendants' ship not sailed at all, it would never have been in a position to collide with the claimants' ship.

So – whether we say that the claimants' ship would not have been damaged but for the defendants' breach of regulations depends on how we characterise that breach. Do we say that the defendants' breach consisted in their sailing their ship without having a certified second mate on board? Or do we say that the defendants' breach simply consisted in their sailing their ship? It seems that the approach we should adopt in cases like this is to characterise the defendants' breach in the way that is most favourable to the defendants. This is what the House of Lords did in *The Empire Jamaica* case – they characterised the defendants' breach as consisting in their sailing their ship without having a certified second mate on board and consequently found that the defendants' breach of regulations did not cause the accident in which the claimant's ship was damaged.

Consider, in light of this, the **Learner Driver Problem**:

Learner is learning to drive. One day, he goes out driving in his car without having a qualified driver sitting beside him in the car. While *Learner* is driving along – *and driving perfectly carefully* – *Child* suddenly runs out into the middle of the road without looking to see if there is any oncoming traffic and is hit by *Learner*'s car. The accident happened so suddenly that there was nothing *Learner* – or any other driver, however careful and experienced – could have done to avoid it. *Child* is injured as a result of the accident and wants to sue *Learner* in negligence for compensation for her injuries.

Can she do so? There is no problem in finding that *Learner* owed someone like *Child* a duty not to go out driving without having a qualified driver sitting beside him. This is because it was reasonably foreseeable that if he did this, someone like *Child* – a nearby pedestrian – would be injured.[8] But *Learner* could have complied with this duty in one of two ways:

(1) *Learner* could have stayed at home and not gone out driving (in which case, *Child* would not have been injured).

---

[8] See above, § 6.2.

(2) *Learner* could have gone out driving with a qualified driver sitting beside him (in which case, *Child* would still have been injured because the qualified driver would not have been able to do anything to avoid the accident, any more than *Learner* could have done).

So this gives us two different ways of characterising *Learner's* breach of the duty that he owed *Child* in this case. We can say that *Learner* breached that duty by: (1) going out driving; or (2) going out driving without having a qualified driver sitting beside him. Characterising *Learner's* breach in the way that is most favourable to him, we will say that *Learner's* breach of duty to *Child* consisted in his going out driving without having a qualified driver sitting beside him – and consequently find that *Learner's* breach of duty did *not* cause *Child's* injuries. Had *Learner* gone out driving with a qualified driver sitting beside him, *Child* would still have been injured in the way she was.

The case of *Lumba v Secretary of State for the Home Department* (2011) demonstrates the above principles in action. In that case, the claimants were held by the Supreme Court to have been falsely imprisoned. They had been detained by the Home Office under the Immigration Act 1971 pursuant to a policy that the Home Office was not entitled to pursue because it was a *secret* policy that did not accord with the Home Office's *official* policy on when it would detain people like the defendants.[9] However, it was conceded that even under the Home Office's official policy, the claimants would have been eligible to be detained. It followed that there were two ways the Home Office could have avoided falsely imprisoning the claimants:

(1) It could have let the claimants go.
(2) It could have applied its official policy to the claimants and detained them under that policy.

Characterising the Home Office's wrong in the way that was most favourable to it, we can say that their wrong in this case involved a failure to apply its official policy to the claimants' case. But that wrong caused the claimants no harm: had the official policy been applied, the claimants still would have been detained. Given this, the Supreme Court found that the claimants in *Lumba* were not entitled to sue for compensation for the fact that they had been falsely imprisoned by the Home Office.[10]

The point that defendants are held liable in tort for the losses caused by their *wrongs*, not their bare acts or omissions, helps solve a problem that puzzles Michael Moore, a well-known writer on causation issues. He cannot understand how any defendant could be said to have caused another person's loss through an omission, when 'omissions . . . are literally no things at all.'[11] He argues that in cases where A is held liable in tort for failing to save B from suffering some kind of harm, A's liability is 'non-causal in nature': 'we should be upfront about it. [A is] liable in such cases because [he] failed to prevent harm, not because [he] caused harm.'[12] This is the sort of confusion academics fall into when they cease to make wrongdoing the central focus of tort law, and start to think of it as a system for allocating responsibility for loss. In the sort of case Moore is talking about, A is held liable not for a bare failure to prevent harm, but because he has done something wrong when, had he not done wrong, B would not have suffered the harm for which she is seeking

---

[9] This aspect of the *Lumba* case is discussed in more detail above, § 2.6.
[10] [2011] 2 WLR 671, at [95] (per Lord Dyson).
[11] Moore 2009, 129.
[12] Moore 2009, 142.

damages. While it may make no sense to think of a bare omission as causing harm,[13] a *wrong* that involves a failure to act can perfectly well be said to have caused harm, in the case where had that wrong not occurred, the harm would not have been suffered.

9.3 DIVISIBLE AND INDIVISIBLE HARM

A *divisible* harm is a harm that may be suffered to a greater or lesser extent. An *indivisible* harm is one that does not vary in extent. An example of a divisible harm is a disease affecting the proper functioning of the lungs such as asbestosis or silicosis. An example of an indivisible harm is death or the loss of a hand.

The significance of the distinction between divisible and indivisible harms when considering causation questions is twofold. First, it is much easier to establish some causal link between the defendant's tort and the harm suffered by the claimant where the harm is divisible. Secondly, where a causal link is established between the defendant's tort and the harm suffered by the claimant, the claimant will usually be entitled to full compensation from the defendant for that harm where the harm is indivisible, but may only obtain partial compensation where the harm is divisible. These two propositions are illustrated by two decisions of the House of Lords: *Bonnington Castings* v *Wardlaw* (1956) and *McGhee* v *National Coal Board* (1973).

Bonnington was a divisible harm case. The claimant was suffering from pneumoconiosis – a form of lung disease. In the claimant's case he had developed the disease from inhaling silica dust at work. Some of the dust he inhaled he should have been protected from inhaling by his employer. The rest of the dust the employer could do nothing about. The House of Lords held that the employer's negligence in failing to protect the claimant from silica dust had made a 'material contribution' to his lung disease. The fact that the claimant's lung disease was a divisible harm allowed them to reach that conclusion. It seemed obvious that the claimant's lung disease would not have been as bad as it was had his employer protected him from inhaling silica dust at work.

Given that the claimant's employer was being held liable in this case on the basis that his negligence had made the claimant's lung disease *worse*, it would seem to follow that he should only have been held liable to compensate the claimant for the *extent* to which he had made the claimant's lung disease worse. However, this did not happen in *Bonnington*: the claimant's employer was held liable for *all* of the claimant's lung disease.[14] This was because the House of Lords was not asked in *Bonnington* to decide what the extent of the claimant's employer's liability should be – just whether the claimant's employer was liable. Had they been, it is generally acknowledged that the claimant's employer should only have been liable for that proportion of the claimant's lung disease that was attributable to the employer's negligence.[15]

The courts have adopted this approach to assessment of damages in other divisible harm cases since *Bonnington*. For example, in *Holtby* v *Brigham & Cowan (Hull) Ltd* (2000), the

---

[13] So it is almost certain that right at this moment, a baby is dying in the Third World who could have been saved had you chosen to live your life differently. But no one in their right mind would say that your choice to live your life in the way you do has *caused* that baby's death.

[14] This feature of *Bonnington* may be why some judges regard that case as an exception to the normal 'but for' test for causation rather than an application of it (in the sense that the claimant's employer ended up being held liable for harm that would have been suffered anyway, even if the employer had not been negligent): see, for example, *Sienkiewicz* v *Greif (UK) Ltd* [2011] UKSC 10, at [17] (per Lord Phillips).

[15] See Bailey 2010, 174; *Sienkiewicz* v *Greif (UK) Ltd* [2011] UKSC 10, at [176] (per Lord Brown).

claimant developed asbestosis after working for a number of different employers, including the defendants. It was found that the defendants' negligence had caused the claimant's asbestosis to be 75% worse than it would otherwise have been. Accordingly, the defendants were held liable to pay the claimant compensation for 75% of his asbestosis. (This sum was assessed by figuring out what sum would fully compensate the claimant for his asbestosis, and then knocking 25% off this figure.)

The harm suffered in *McGhee v National Coal Board* (1973)[16] was an example of an indivisible harm.[17] The claimant in that case had developed dermatitis as a result of being employed by the defendants to clean out some brick kilns. This was hot and dirty work which exposed the claimant to clouds of abrasive brick dust. The defendants (in breach of the duty of care they owed the claimant as his employers) failed to provide the claimant with any on-site washing facilities which would allow him to wash off the brick dust as soon as he knocked off work. Instead, the claimant had to cycle home and wash there. After some days of working in the brick kilns, the claimant was found to be suffering from dermatitis. Because the harm suffered by the claimant in this case was indivisible, he could not sue the defendants on the basis that their negligence in failing to provide him with washing facilities had made his dermatitis worse than it would otherwise have been. Instead, he was forced to argue that he would not have suffered dermatitis *at all* had the defendants not been negligent.

Unfortunately, it was impossible for the claimant to show this. There was no evidence that he could point to, to show that the defendants' negligence in failing to provide him with washing facilities was a crucial factor in his developing dermatitis. Given how much brick dust the claimant was exposed to at work, and for how long, the claimant's dermatitis might still have developed even if the claimant had been allowed to wash off the abrasive brick dust at the end of his shift. Despite this, the House of Lords still felt itself able to find that the defendants' negligence *had* caused the claimant's dermatitis, on the basis that the defendants' negligence had materially increased the *risk* that the claimant would develop dermatitis in working for them. Once the House of Lords had made its finding that the

---

[16] Discussed, Hope 2003.

[17] For another example, see *Bailey v Ministry of Defence* [2009] 1 WLR 1052, where the claimant was in a weakened state post-surgery, was given a drink, vomited, inhaled some of the vomit and suffered brain damage as a result. The claimant's weakened state was a consequence both of the claimant's having pancreatitis but also the lack of care that she had received from the defendants while staying at their hospital. If you keep your eye on the brain damage, the harm suffered by the claimant was clearly indivisible – it was not possible to argue that 'had the defendants not been negligent, the claimant would still have suffered brain damage, just not as bad'. But some confusion was caused in the case by focusing on the claimant's weakened state, and the argument that 'had the defendants not been negligent, the claimant would still have been weakened, just not as bad.' Even if that were true, that would only be relevant to whether the defendants' negligence caused the *whole* of the claimant's brain damage (the idea being that had the defendants not been negligent, the claimant might still have vomited and inhaled her vomit when given the drink), not to whether it in fact caused *part* of the brain damage. The Court of Appeal reached the right conclusion, finding the defendants liable for the *whole* of the brain damage on the ground that their negligence had contributed to that brain damage being suffered. In the subsequent case of *Dickins v O2 Plc* [2008] EWCA Civ 1144 – which was a psychiatric illness case, resulting from a vulnerable employee not getting enough support at work – the Court of Appeal indicated that in future psychiatric illnesses should usually be regarded as indivisible harms as it will not usually be possible to argue 'had the defendants not been negligent, the claimant would still have suffered a psychiatric illness, just not as bad.' The decision in *Dickins* reverses a trend that had begun with *Rahman v Arearose Ltd* [2001] QB 351 of attempting to treat psychiatric illnesses as divisible harms. In *Rahman*, the victim of an assault developed a psychiatric illness as a result, in part because of the fact of the assault and in part because when his doctors tried to repair the damage that he suffered to his eye in the assault, they negligently blinded him in that eye. Weir 2001 was not impressed at the Court of Appeal's finding that the claimant's psychiatric illness could be split into two, with one part being caused by the assault and the other by the negligent blinding.

defendants' negligence had caused the claimant to suffer the indivisible harm of developing dermatitis, the claimant was allowed to sue the defendants for *full* compensation for this harm and not just a proportion of that harm.

We will discuss later whether the modern day Supreme Court would decide *McGhee* the same way today.[18] For the time being, all we need to note is how much harder it was for the claimant to establish a causal link between his harm and the defendants' negligence in *McGhee* than it was in *Bonnington*; and note that a finding of a causal link opened the door to full compensation in *McGhee* but should have only led to an award of partial compensation in *Bonnington*. The difference between the two cases rests on the difference between divisible and indivisible harm.

9.4 EVIDENTIAL DIFFICULTIES (1): THE STANDARD APPROACH

As the *McGhee* case shows, applying the 'but for' test often gives rise to evidential difficulties because what the test requires us to do is engage in a *counterfactual* inquiry, where we try to imagine what the world would be like had something *not* happened that *did* happen. All of us will have had the experience of thinking, 'What would have happened had I not . . .' ('. . . gone to that party where I met my wife', '. . . missed that appointment for a job interview', '. . . had that argument with my friend') and being left completely uncertain what the answer is. The courts are faced with the same difficulty. It can often be very difficult to tell what would have happened to the victim of a tort had that tort not been committed.

In physical injury cases, the standard approach that the courts adopt to resolve these evidential difficulties is to ask is it *more likely than not* that the claimant would not have suffered a particular injury but for the defendant's tort? If the claimant can show that the *probability* that she would *not* have suffered a given injury had the defendant not committed his tort is *greater* than 50%, then the courts will decide the case on the basis that the claimant would *not* have suffered that injury but for the defendant's tort. If she can do this, the courts will say that the claimant has established *on the balance of probabilities* that she would not have suffered the injury but for the defendant's tort.

So, for example, in *Chester v Afshar* (2005),[19] Chester was suffering from back pain. She consulted the defendant doctor, Afshar, who recommended that she have an operation to remove three discs from her back. Unfortunately, he failed to warn her that there was a very small risk (1–2%) that she would suffer nerve damage in her back as a result of the operation. Chester agreed that Afshar could operate on her and three days later, on 21 November 1994, Afshar carried out the operation. Although Afshar carried out the operation with all due care and skill, Chester suffered nerve damage and was partially paralysed as a result of the operation. Chester sued Afshar in negligence for compensation for the harm she had suffered.

There was no doubt in this case that Afshar breached the duty he owed Chester, as her doctor, to treat her with reasonable skill and care. Afshar should have told Chester of the risk of nerve damage associated with the operation he was proposing to carry out on her. But was it the case that Chester would not have been paralysed but for Afshar's breach of the duty of care that he owed her? To answer that question, we have to think about what would have happened had Afshar told Chester about the risk of nerve damage associated

---

[18] See below, § 9.5.
[19] Noted, Stevens 2005.

with the operation. It was established that had he done this, Chester would have taken a few days to think over whether she should go ahead with the operation. As a result, the operation would probably have taken place on something like the 25 November 1994. Had the operation been carried out *then*, it was more likely than not (in fact, it was 98–99% likely) that the operation would have passed off without incident, and Chester would not have suffered any nerve damage or paralysis in her back. So, on the balance of probabilities, Chester would not have been paralysed had Afshar not breached the duty of care that he owed her. Given this, the House of Lords accepted that the 'but for' test for causation was satisfied in Chester's case.

It was different in *Hotson* v *East Berkshire HA* (1987) and *Wilsher* v *Essex AHA* (1988). In *Hotson*, the claimant fell when climbing a tree and one of his hips sustained an acute traumatic fracture. He was taken to hospital but the defendants (in breach of the duty of care they owed him) failed to diagnose his injury and sent him home. After five days the claimant was taken back to the hospital and this time his injury was correctly diagnosed. As things turned out, the hip fracture resulted in the claimant being permanently disabled. The claimant claimed that the defendants' breach of the duty of care they owed him when he first went to the hospital caused him to be permanently disabled. It was impossible to tell with any certainty whether or not the claimant would have been permanently disabled even if the defendants had correctly diagnosed and treated his injury when he first went to the hospital. If the claimant's fall had damaged a certain proportion – call it x% – of the blood vessels in his hip then the claimant would have been permanently disabled whatever the defendants had done when he first went to hospital. If the fall had damaged less than x% of the blood vessels in his hip then the defendants would have been able to prevent the claimant becoming permanently disabled had they acted promptly when the claimant first went to hospital. No one could tell with any degree of certainty what proportion of blood vessels in the claimant's hip were damaged by his fall and therefore no one could tell with any degree of certainty whether or not the claimant would have been permanently disabled even if the defendants had treated his injuries when he first came to the hospital.

The courts in *Hotson* resolved this uncertainty by asking – Was it more likely than not that the claimant's fall damaged *less than* x% of the blood vessels in his hip? If the answer was 'yes' then they would have held that the claimant would *not* have become permanently disabled but for the defendants' negligence. But if the answer was 'no' then the courts would have held that the claimant was doomed to become permanently disabled even if his hip had received impeccable treatment when he first went to hospital. As things turned out, the answer was 'no'. It was found that the probability that the claimant's fall damaged less than x% of the blood vessels in his hip was only 25%. It was therefore more likely than not that the claimant's fall damaged at least x% of the blood vessels in his hip and therefore more likely than not that the defendants' negligence made no difference to the claimant's becoming permanently disabled. The claimant's claim for damages therefore failed: he could not show that the defendants' negligence caused him to become permanently disabled.

In *Wilsher*, the claimant was a baby that was born prematurely. Shortly after he was born, he developed a serious eye condition called retrolental fibroplasia (RLF for short) and was blinded as a result. The claimant was exposed to excess oxygen by the defendants' employees when he was in hospital, being looked after in an incubator. This excess oxygen may have caused him to develop RLF. However, the claimant also suffered from four medical conditions that could also have accounted for his developing RLF. Given this, he could not show that it was more likely than not that he would not have developed RLF but for the defendants' employees' breaching the duty of care they owed him to treat him with reasonable skill and care. As a result, the House of Lords dismissed the claimant's claim in negligence against the defendants for compensation for the fact that he was blind: he could not show that the defendants' employees' negligence had caused him to go blind.

It is fashionable nowadays to express the 'more likely than not' rule in terms of 'doubling the risk'. That is, the courts ask: 'Did the defendant's tort more than double the risk that the claimant would suffer the harm that he did?' If so, it is more likely than not that the defendant's tort caused the claimant to suffer that harm. An example drawn from Lord Mackay's judgment in the *Hotson* case will make this clear. In talking about the *McGhee* case, Lord Mackay presented the following hypothetical:

> say that it was established that of 100 people working under the same conditions as the [claimant] and without facilities for washing at the end of their shift 70 contracted dermatitis: of 100 people working in the same conditions as the [claimant] when washing facilities were provided for them at the end of the shift 30 contracted dermatitis.[20]

In this hypothetical, the nature of the work done by the claimant in *McGhee* meant he had a 30% risk of contracting dermatitis. However, the failure to provide him with washing facilities raised that risk of contracting dermatitis to 70% – more than doubling the risk that the claimant would contract dermatitis. Now that the claimant *has* contracted dermatitis, we can say that there was a 3 in 7 chance that it was due to his being exposed to brick dust while at work and a 4 in 7 chance that it was due to the lack of washing facilities. It was therefore more likely than not that it was the failure to provide washing facilities that caused the claimant to develop dermatitis.

While it did not disapprove of the use of statistical information like this to resolve evidential difficulties over causation, the Supreme Court in *Sienkiewicz v Greif (UK) Ltd* (2011)[21] counselled caution over the use of such statistics as a way of proving whether or not a given event caused a particular outcome. Lord Rodger, in particular, emphasised:

> the point made by *Phipson on Evidence*, 17th edn (2010), para 34.27, that, unless a special rule applies, 'Where there is [statistical] evidence of association [between a particular event and a particular outcome], the court should not proceed to find a causal relationship without further, non-statistical evidence.' In other words, since, by its very nature, the statistical evidence does not deal with the individual case, something more will be required before the court will be able to reach a conclusion, on the balance of probability, as to what happened in that case. For example, where there is a strong [statistical] association between a drug and some condition which could have been caused in some other way, that evidence along with evidence that the claimant developed the condition immediately after taking the drug may well be enough to allow the judge to conclude, on the balance of probability, that it was the drug that caused the claimant's condition.[22]

Lady Hale agreed with Lord Rodger, arguing that 'the existence of a stastically significant association between factor X and disease Y does not prove that in the individual case it is more likely than not that factor X caused disease Y.'[23] For example, just because there is (let's suppose) a statistically significant association between going to the opera and developing gout, that does not mean that going to the opera causes gout. The association of gout with

---

[20] [1987] AC 750, 786.
[21] The official citation of this case is [2011] UKSC 10. From now on, we will simply refer to this case as 'Sienkiewicz'.
[22] *Sienkiewicz*, at [163].
[23] *Sienkiewicz*, at [172].

opera-going (if there is one) is due to the fact that opera-goers are likely to drink more than people who do not go to the opera, and has nothing to do with their attending the opera.

Lords Mance and Kerr took a slightly softer line than Lord Rodger and Lady Hale, holding that statistical information can only be relied upon as the *sole* source of evidence as to whether a defendant's tort caused a claimant harm in 'the rarest of cases'.[24] On the other hand, Lords Phillips and Dyson thought that there was no fundamental reason why the courts should not rely on statistical information to establish that the defendant's tort had caused the claimant to suffer a particular harm, on the basis that the defendant's tort 'doubled the risk' of the claimant suffering that harm.[25] However, Lord Phillips counselled that in cases where statistics indicate that the probability that the defendant's tort caused the claimant harm only slightly exceeded the probability that something else did, such statistics should probably not be relied on. They would provide a 'tenuous basis' for concluding that the defendant's tort caused the harm because 'the balance of . . . probability is a very fine one . . . [and] the [statistical] data may not be reliable.'[26]

Despite these disagreements over whether statistical information could be used in a case where we have *no doubt* that event X and event Y have occurred and we want to know whether event X *caused* event Y to happen, *all* of the Supreme Court Justices who expressed a view on this issue were hostile to the use of *general* statistical information to establish that *a particular event actually happened*. So, for example, they considered the hypothetical situation of 'a town in which there were only two cab companies, one with three blue cabs and the other with one yellow cab.'[27] Assuming that a claimant has been knocked down by a cab whose colour has not been observed, the Supreme Court Justices in *Sienkiewicz* agreed that the fact that there was a 75% probability that a blue cab knocked the claimant down, did not provide a sufficient basis for finding that a blue cab *did* knock the claimant down.[28] (However, statistical information *specific* to the claimant's situation *might* still be relevant. For example, if someone saw the claimant being knocked down by a blue cab, and two out of the three drivers employed by the blue cab company were observed an hour beforehand drunkenly staggering out of a pub and getting into their respective cabs, that *might* be taken as evidence that the blue cab that knocked down the claimant was being driven by a drunk driver.)

The standard ('more likely than not', or 'doubling the risk') approach to resolving evidential difficulties can be productive of injustice. Consider the **Two Hunters Problem**, which is based on a real case, the Canadian case of *Cook* v *Lewis* (1951):

Shooter One and *Shooter Two* are both out hunting with shot guns. They simultaneously hear some rustling in the bushes and simultaneously fire in the direction of the noise. *Beater* was hit in the leg by one of the shots, but forensic analysis is unable to tell from whose gun the shot was fired.

---

[24] *Sienkiewicz*, at [192] (per Lord Mance). See also [205] (per Lord Kerr): 'the use of [statistical] data to seek to establish any specific proposition in an individual case requires to be treated with great caution.'

[25] *Sienkiewicz*, at [78], [90]–[93] (per Lord Phillips) and at [222] (per Lord Dyson). The only other Supreme Court Justice to sit in the *Sienkiewicz* case – Lord Brown – expressed no view on these issues.

[26] *Sienkiewicz*, at [83].

[27] *Sienkiewicz*, at [95].

[28] *Sienkiewicz*, at [96] (per Lord Phillips), [156] (per Lord Rodger), [171] (per Lady Hale), [216]–[217] (per Lord Dyson).

In this case, both *One* and *Two* have clearly been negligent in relation to *Beater*. They each owed him a duty to take care not to fire their guns in the way they did – as it was reasonably foreseeable that doing so would result in physical injury to someone like *Beater* – and they each breached that duty of care. But if we apply the 'more likely than not' rule to *Beater's* case, he will not be able to sue *either One or Two* for compensation for his wound. The reason is that he will only be able to show that it is 50% likely that *One* shot him, and 50% likely that *Two* shot him. He will not be able to reach the magic figure of 51% in relation to either of them. In *Cook* v *Lewis* itself, the Supreme Court of Canada thought that such a result would be very unfair, and ended up finding that, in the case we are considering, *both One and Two* would be liable *in full* to compensate C for his injury.[29] In the case of *Fairchild* v *Glenhaven Funeral Services Ltd* (2003), the House of Lords indicated that it agreed with this solution.[30]

9.5 EVIDENTIAL DIFFICULTIES (2): THE *FAIRCHILD* EXCEPTION

The decision of the House of Lords in *Fairchild* v *Glenhaven Funeral Services* (2003)[31] is a good example of the maxim, 'The road to hell is paved with good intentions'. *Fairchild* actually concerned three cases. In each of them, an employee (C) was

> employed at different times and for differing periods by both A and B . . . A and B were both subject to a duty to take reasonable care to prevent C inhaling asbestos dust because of the known risk that asbestos dust (if inhaled) might cause a [form of cancer called] mesothelioma . . . [Both] A and B [breached] that duty . . . during the periods of C's employment by each of them with the result that during both periods C inhaled excessive quantities of asbestos dust.[32]

C subsequently developed mesothelioma and sought to recover damages from either A or B for his mesothelioma. Mesothelioma is a cancer that is always fatal in those who contract it. It is also a cancer about which we know very little. It is associated with exposure to asbestos dust: the more asbestos dust you inhale, the higher your risks of developing mesothelioma. But we do not know how asbestos dust causes mesothelioma to develop. So if C inhales a particular quantity of asbestos dust while working for A, we cannot say how probable it is that *that* exposure to asbestos dust will result in C developing mesothelioma. It might be 0% – C may already be doomed to develop mesothelioma because of the asbestos dust he has already inhaled while working for other people, or from the general atmosphere. It might be 100% – the asbestos dust that C inhaled while working for A might have doomed C to develop mesothelioma (either all by itself or in combination with other dust that C had already inhaled). We just don't know.[33]

Given this, in the cases dealt with in *Fairchild*, C could not rely on the standard ('more likely than not', or 'doubling the risk') approach to resolving evidential difficulties about causation to determine *whose* negligence caused him to develop mesothelioma. It was impossible to say whether it was more likely than not that C developed mesothelioma because of A's negligence or B's negligence. Despite this, the House of Lords held in *Fairchild* that C *would* be entitled to sue *both* A *and* B for compensation for his

---

[29] To the same effect, see the American case of *Summers* v *Tice*, 199 P 2d 1 (1948).
[30] [2003] 1 AC 32, at [39] (per Lord Nicholls), [169] (per Lord Rodger).
[31] The case is reported at [2003] 1 AC 32, and we will henceforth refer to it as '*Fairchild*'.
[32] *Fairchild*, at [2] (per Lord Bingham).
[33] See, further, Stapleton 2002b, 280–1, 299.

mesothelioma. Why was this? Two arguments seem to have led the House of Lords to reach this conclusion:

(1) *The fairness argument* goes as follows. If we applied the standard approach to resolving evidential difficulties about causation to cases such as C's, then it seems that employees who worked for *one* bad employer and contracted mesothelioma as a result would be much better off than employees who worked for *two or more* bad employers and contracted mesothelioma as a result. An employee who worked for *one* bad employer would have no problem establishing that it was his employer's negligence that triggered his mesothelioma and would therefore have no problem obtaining full compensation for his mesothelioma from that employer. An employee who worked for two or more bad employers would find it very difficult to establish which of his employers' negligence caused his mesothelioma and would therefore find it very difficult to identify anyone whom he was entitled to sue for compensation for his mesothelioma. This is unfair: why should an employee who worked for one bad employer be in a much better position to obtain compensation for his mesothelioma than an employee who worked for two or more bad employers?[34] To avoid this unfairness, we have to waive the normal rules on causation in the case where an employee who has contracted mesothelioma worked for two or more employers and allow the employee to sue his employers for compensation for his mesothelioma even though we cannot establish *which* of his employers' negligence caused that mesothelioma to develop.[35]

(2) *The sanction argument* goes as follows. If we do not allow C to sue A and B for compensation for his mesothelioma in this sort of case, then the duties that employers owe their employees to take reasonable steps to see that they do not inhale asbestos dust will become essentially empty. An employer will know that if he breaches that duty and one of his employees subsequently develops mesothelioma, he will not be held liable so long as he can show that that employee was also exposed to asbestos dust during the course of his working life while working for someone else.[36] We have to ensure that employers do not feel free to breach the duties of care that they owe their employees – and so in this sort of case we have to make it clear that an employer who has negligently exposed an employee to asbestos dust will be held liable to pay that employee compensation if the employee

---

[34] *Fairchild*, at [36]: '[Holding that C could not obtain compensation for his mesothelioma] would be deeply offensive to instinctive notions of what . . . fairness demands' (per Lord Nicholls).

[35] It could be argued against this that it is unfair to hold a negligent employer liable for mesothelioma developed by a claimant when it was more likely than not that his negligence did not cause that mesothelioma to develop. However, their Lordships were able to overcome this objection, arguing that if they had a choice between being unfair to an innocent claimant and being unfair to a negligent employer, they would rather be unfair to the wrongdoing employer: *Fairchild*, at [33] (per Lord Bingham), [39]–[42] (per Lord Nicholls), [155] (per Lord Rodger).

[36] *Fairchild*, at [33]: 'Were the law [not to allow C's claim in the kind of case we are considering], an employer exposing his employee to asbestos dust could obtain complete immunity against mesothelioma . . . claims by employing only those who had previously been exposed to excessive quantities of asbestos dust. Such a result would reflect no credit on the law' (per Lord Bingham); at [62]: 'a rule requiring proof of a link between the defendant's asbestos and the claimant's disease would, with the arbitrary exception of single-employer cases, empty the duty of content. If liability depends upon proof that the conduct of the defendant was a necessary condition of the injury, it cannot effectively exist' (per Lord Hoffmann); at [155]: 'if the law did [here] impose a standard of proof that no [one claiming compensation for mesothelioma] could ever satisfy, then, so far as the civil law is concerned, employers could with impunity negligently expose their workmen to the risk of . . . mesothelioma. The substantive duty of care would be emptied of all practical content so far as victims are concerned' (per Lord Rodger).

subsequently develops mesothelioma and this is so even if it cannot be shown that it was the employer's negligence that caused the employee to develop his mesothelioma, because the employee was also exposed to asbestos dust while working for other people.[37]

In holding in *Fairchild* that C could sue *both* A *and* B in negligence for compensation for his mesothelioma, the House of Lords left two questions unanswered:

(1) *The extent of liability question.* For how much are A and B liable? Are they each liable *in full* to compensate C for his mesothelioma – so that C can then recover full compensation from *either* A *or* B? (Lawyers call this 'liability *in solidum*'.) Or are A and B each liable only to compensate C for a *proportion* (or what lawyers call an '*aliquot* share') of C's mesothelioma – so that C will have to sue *both* A *and* B if he wants to recover full compensation for his mesothelioma?

(2) *The single wrongful exposure question.* Does the *Fairchild* exception to the standard approach to resolving evidential difficulties in causation (the 'more likely than not' – or 'doubling the risk' – approach) also apply in cases where *only* one employer has wrongfully exposed C to mesothelioma, and C's mesothelioma might also be due to asbestos dust that he has been innocently exposed to (for example, from the general atmosphere) or that he has exposed himself to (for example, by doing some DIY work at home)?

The House of Lords got the chance to answer these questions in the subsequent case of *Barker v Corus UK Ltd* (2006).[38] In that case, the House of Lords said:

(1) *In response to the extent of liability question.* In a case where A and B have each wrongfully exposed C to asbestos dust, and C has subsequently developed mesothelioma, A and B will each be liable only to compensate C for a proportion of his mesothelioma, with their proportionate shares being assessed according to how much each of them did to expose C to the risk of developing mesothelioma.[39]

(2) *In response to the single wrongful exposure question.* In a 'single wrongful exposure' case, the *Fairchild* exception will apply, and C will be entitled to sue an employer who has wrongfully exposed him to asbestos dust for damages, even though C's mesothelioma

---

[37] This argument is actually quite weak in this context. This is for two reasons. First, the argument's success in this context depends on a verbal sleight of hand. The argument only works in this context if one says that the duty of care that C's employers owed him, and breached, was a duty to take reasonable steps to see that he did not inhale asbestos dust – the argument being that if C were not allowed to sue A and B here, then employers generally would be left free to breach this duty of care. But if one characterises the duty of care that C's employers owed him, and breached, in wider terms – as a duty to take reasonable steps to see that he did not come to any physical harm in working for him – then not allowing C to sue *in this situation* would not mean that employers generally would be free to breach this wider duty of care. Secondly, even if *Fairchild* had gone the other way, employers would hardly have had *carte blanche* to expose their employees to excessive amounts of asbestos dust. An employer acting in this way would be: (1) subject to criminal sanctions; and (2) held liable to an employee who contracted asbestosis after working for him (the idea being that the employer's negligence in exposing the employee to asbestos will have either caused the employee to develop asbestosis or made the asbestosis 'worse' – in which case the employer will be held liable to compensate the employee for that 'part' of the asbestosis which is attributable to the employer's negligence).

[38] This case is reported at [2006] 2 AC 572, and is referred to below as '*Barker*'.

[39] See *Barker*, at [48] (per Lord Hoffmann): 'The damages which would have been awarded against a defendant who actually caused the disease must be apportioned to the defendants according to their contributions to the risk. It may be that the most practical method of apportionment will be according to the time of exposure for which each defendant is responsible, but allowance may have to be made for the intensity of exposure and the type of asbestos.'

might be attributable to asbestos dust that C has been innocently exposed to, or that C has exposed himself to.[40]

The House of Lords' answer to the 'extent of liability' question was severely criticised by trades unions and MPs who represented the interests of employees who had developed mesothelioma as a result of being exposed to asbestos dust at work. The reason is that the House of Lords' decision in *Barker* made it much harder for employees in mesothelioma cases to recover *full* compensation for their mesothelioma. To recover full compensation, they would have to sue *all* of their employers who had exposed them to asbestos, and hope that those employers were still in existence and still worth suing.

The then Labour government immediately responded to this criticism by enacting s 3 of the Compensation Act 2006. This provides that if: (1) C has contracted mesothelioma as a result of being exposed to asbestos dust, and (2) A is liable under *Fairchild* to compensate C for the fact that he has contracted mesothelioma, then (3) A will be liable to compensate C *in full* for his mesothelioma, though the damages payable may be reduced for any contributory negligence on C's part.

Unfortunately, at least two of the Law Lords who decided *Barker* had answered the 'single wrongful exposure' question in the affirmative *because* they thought that an employer who had wrongfully exposed an employee to asbestos dust would *only* be liable to compensate that employee for a proportion of the mesothelioma that he had subsequently developed.[41] So suppose C has developed mesothelioma after having been exposed to asbestos dust: (1) for two weeks while working for A; and (2) for six months while doing DIY work in his house. Two of the Law Lords who decided *Barker* thought it would not be unfair to hold A liable to pay damages to C here *because* A's liability would be limited to take account of the extent to which he had increased the risk that C would develop mesothelioma.

So s 3 of the Compensation Act 2006 made it unclear again what the answer was to the 'single wrongful exposure' question. Would the courts hold that there was liability in a single wrongful exposure case such as the one we have just been discussing if they knew that the effect of holding A liable to pay C damages was that A would be held liable *in full* to compensate C for his mesothelioma – and this is so even though A only exposed C to asbestos for two weeks, and C was exposed to asbestos from other sources for six months?

The Supreme Court supplied the answer in the case of *Sienkiewicz v Greif (UK) Ltd* (2011), holding that the *Fairchild* exception to the standard approach for resolving evidential uncertainties *did* apply in single wrongful exposure cases. This was so even though applying the *Fairchild* exception in such cases – in conjunction with s 3 of the Compensation Act 2006 – could have the 'draconian' effect of holding an employer liable in full for a claimant's mesothelioma when he was 'responsible for only a small proportion of the overall exposure of [the] claimant to asbestos dust'.[42] In such a case, the only way an employer could moderate his liability would be either: (1) to show that the amount of asbestos to which he exposed the claimant was so small that it exposed the claimant to an 'insignificant'

---

[40] *Barker*, at [16]–[17] (per Lord Hoffmann), [59] (per Lord Scott), [97]–[99] and [101] (per Lord Rodger), [117] (per Lord Walker), [128] (per Baroness Hale).

[41] *Barker*, at [117] (per Lord Walker), [128] (per Baroness Hale). See also Lord Rodger at [101], holding that *in solidum* liability should *not* apply where there is a single wrongful exposure and self-exposure to asbestos dust. Also see Lord Brown in *Sienkiewicz*, at [182]: 'It is to my mind quite clear that the preparedness of the majority of the court in *Barker* to extend the reach of the *Fairchild* principle [to cases of single wrongful exposures] was specifically dependent on their being aliquot liability only.'

[42] *Sienkiewicz*, at [58] (per Lord Phillips); also at [184] (per Lord Brown).

or '*de minimis*' risk of developing mesothelioma (in which case the employer would not be liable at all);[43] or (2) to show that the claimant culpably exposed himself to asbestos dust (in which case the damages payable to the claimant would be reduced for contributory negligence).[44]

The facts of *Sienkiewicz* itself illustrate the point. In that case, Enid Costello was wrongfully exposed to a moderate amount of asbestos dust over 18 years while working for the defendant employers. She subsequently developed mesothelioma, and died. Her daughter brought a wrongful death claim under the Fatal Accidents Act 1976, alleging that the defendants' negligence had caused her mother's death. The judge at first instance found that everyone runs a risk of developing mesothelioma from breathing air that has asbestos dust in it. He quantified that risk in Costello's case as being 24 cases per million.[45] He found that the asbestos dust that the defendants had wrongfully exposed Costello to increased the risk that she would develop mesothelioma to 28.39 cases per million. This represented an increase in risk of 18%. As this increase in risk was not insignificant or *de minimis*, the Supreme Court held the defendants liable *in full* to compensate the claimant for the losses flowing from Costello's death.

As Lord Brown observed, *Sienkiewicz* was a very different case from the sort of case that the House of Lords was considering in *Fairchild*.[46] Because *Sienkiewicz* was a case where there was only one wrongful exposure, it was not a case where the *fairness argument* demanded that the defendants be held liable for the deceased's mesothelioma.[47] But in *Sienkiewicz*, the Supreme Court identified a new basis for the *Fairchild* exception to the standard ('more likely than not', or 'doubling the risk') approach to resolving cases of evidential uncertainty about causation. This we can call the '*rock of uncertainty*'[48] argument. According to this argument, the reason why the standard approach to resolving evidential difficulties about causation was not applied in *Fairchild* (and the claimants' claims in that case dismissed) was because in mesothelioma cases, it is impossible at the moment to say with any certainty what is the probability that a claimant developed mesothelioma because of a given exposure. It is to prevent claimants' cases foundering on this impossibility that the *Fairchild* exception was developed (or so the Supreme Court claimed in *Sienkiewicz*). Given this, the Supreme Court thought that there was no logical reason why the *Fairchild* exception should not also apply in a case like *Sienkiewicz*: the 'rock of uncertainty' posed just as much of an obstacle to bringing a claim in *Sienkiewicz* as it did in *Fairchild*.[49]

While confirming that *Fairchild* applied in a single wrongful exposure case like *Sienkiewicz*, the Supreme Court was very keen to place a limit on the scope of *Fairchild*. Lord Brown seemed to suggest that the *Fairchild* exception to the standard approach to resolving evidential difficulties about causation *only* applied in mesothelioma cases. He

---

[43] *Sienkiewicz*, at [107] (per Lord Phillips), [176] (per Lord Brown).

[44] Compensation Act 2006, s 3(3)(b).

[45] This is higher than the normal risk we all run of developing mesothelioma from the environment because the area where Costello lived had high levels of asbestos in the air (probably due to undetected torts – though this was not a point that anyone made an issue of in *Sienkiewicz*).

[46] *Sienkiewicz*, at [178].

[47] Though the *sanction argument* might still apply: not applying *Fairchild* to a single wrongful exposure case might allow defendants to expose claimants to small, but still unacceptable, levels of asbestos and escape liability for mesothelioma on the basis that other, environmental, factors could have caused the mesothelioma.

[48] The phrase is from *Fairchild*, at [7] (per Lord Bingham). The phrase appears 15 times in the Supreme Court judgments in *Sienkiewicz*.

[49] *Sienkiewicz*, at [106] (per Lord Phillips), [141]–[142] and [160] (per Lord Rodger), [167] (per Lady Hale), [184] (per Lord Brown), [189] (per Lord Mance), [200] and [203] (per Lord Kerr), [208] and [212] (per Lord Dyson).

remarked that, 'Mesothelioma cases are in a category all their own'[50] and that 'Save only for mesothelioma cases, claimants should henceforth expect little flexibility from the courts in their approach to causation.'[51] The general emphasis placed in *Sienkiewicz* on the *Fairchild* exception having been created to assist claimants who – because of our general level of scientific ignorance about the links between asbestos dust and mesothelioma – were simply unable to satisfy the standard approach to resolving evidential uncertainties about causation also seems to support the idea that the *Fairchild* exception only applies in mesothelioma cases; and will only apply in such cases so long as we remain ignorant as to how asbestos dust triggers mesothelioma.[52]

Having said that, there is *one* non-mesothelioma case where we think *Fairchild* would *still* apply after the decision of the Supreme Court in *Sienkiewicz*. That is the kind of case presented by the Two Hunters Problem:[53] where two or more people have committed a wrong in relation to the claimant, and we know that the claimant has suffered harm as a result of one of those wrongs, but the probability that a particular wrong caused the claimant to suffer that harm is 50% or less. Applying the standard approach to resolving evidential uncertainties about causation would result in the claimant *not* being able to sue *anyone* for compensation for the harm he has suffered when the *sanction argument* and the *fairness argument* that underlay the original decision in *Fairchild* indicate that this would be unsatisfactory.

Some support for the idea that the claimant would be allowed to sue for compensation in the Two Hunters Problem is provided by Lord Phillips' judgment in *Sienkiewicz*. In para [105] of his judgment, he said:

> even if one could postulate with confidence … the extent of the contribution of a defendant to the victim's exposure to asbestos … there would still be justification for the application of the *Fairchild* rule where *all the exposure was wrongful.* Imagine four defendants each of whom had contributed 25% to the victim's exposure so that there was a 25% likelihood in the case of each defendant that he had caused the disease. The considerations of fairness that had moved the House in *Fairchild* would justify holding each of the defendants liable, notwithstanding the impossibility of proving causation on the balance of probability.[54]

Were each of the defendants to be held liable in this case, s 3 of the Compensation Act 2006 (assuming it was still in force) would kick in to make each of the defendants liable *in full* for the claimant's mesothelioma. However, s 3 only applies to mesothelioma cases. In any other case where *Fairchild* applies, the House of Lords' decision in *Barker v Corus (UK) Ltd* remains good law. So in the Two Hunters Problem itself, we could expect the courts to hold *both One and Two* liable to pay damages to *Beater* (who has been shot either by *One*'s gun or *Two*'s gun, but we cannot tell which). But *Barker* would apply to limit *One* and *Two*'s liability so that they would each only be held liable for 50% of the harm suffered by *Beater*.

Beyond the sort of non-mesothelioma case presented by the Two Hunters Problem, *Sienkiewicz* makes it unsafe to go. The Supreme Court decision in *Sienkiewicz* makes it highly unlikely that *Fairchild* would ever be applied in a case like *Wilsher v Essex AHA* (1988), where a baby that had been delivered prematurely was blinded, possibly by a single

---

[50] *Sienkiewicz*, at [174].

[51] *Sienkiewicz*, at [187]. See also [189] (per Lord Mance: '[we should learn] the lesson of caution that history may teach in relation to future invitations to depart from conventional principles of causation.')

[52] That the *Fairchild* exception may disappear as our knowledge of how mesothelioma is triggered develops was explicitly contemplated by Lord Phillips (at [103]), Lord Rodger (at [142]), and Lord Dyson (at [208]).

[53] See above, § 9.4.

[54] Emphasis added.

wrongful exposure to excess oxygen but also possibly because of a range of other, innocent, factors. Unlike in the Two Hunters Problem or the situation contemplated by Lord Phillips above, a range of different agents[55] might have caused the harm in *Wilsher*, and only one of those agents was wrongful. While the *rock of uncertainty* argument might apply in a *Wilsher*-type scenario – it may be impossible to tell with any certainty what the probabilities were that a given agent caused the baby's blindness – the House of Lords made it clear in *Sienkiewicz* that the *rock of uncertainty* argument will only be allowed to subvert the normal causation requirements in mesothelioma cases.

Similarly, it seems unlikely that *McGhee v National Coal Board* (1973) would be decided the same way today. (Though there is nothing in the judgments in *Sienkiewicz* that would allow us to say that it has been overruled.) *McGhee* was – like *Wilsher* – another case of a single wrongful exposure (to brick dust that the defendants should have allowed the claimant to wash off at work before going home). It was uncertain whether *that* exposure (as opposed to the (non-wrongful) exposure to brick dust at work) had caused the claimant to suffer the harm (dermatitis) for which he sought compensation. Unlike in *Wilsher*, the claimant was allowed to sue for damages in *McGhee*. Lord Brown made it clear in *Sienkiewicz* that he thought *McGhee* was 'undoubtedly a problematic case'.[56] Lord Phillips took much the same view, describing *McGhee* as a 'puzzling case' on the ground that:

> no other workman had ever contracted dermatitis at the defendants' brick kiln, so one wonders what the basis was for finding that the lack of shower facilities was potentially causative. Had there been [statistical] evidence, it seems unlikely that this would have demonstrated that the extra ten or fifteen minutes that, on the evidence, the pursuer took to cycle home doubled his risk of contracting dermatitis, or came anywhere near doing so.[57]

Plainly Lord Phillips thought that in *McGhee*, recovery could only be justified on the presentation of statistical evidence that supported the inference that it was more likely than not the claimant would not have suffered dermatitis had he been provided with washing facilities.

9.6 EVIDENTIAL DIFFICULTIES (3): LOSS OF A CHANCE CASES

So far, we have been looking at how the courts handle cases where a claimant wants to sue for compensation for a *physical injury* that she claims the defendant's tort has caused her to suffer, and it is uncertain whether or not the claimant would not have suffered that injury but for the defendant's tort. The courts adopt a quite different approach in economic loss cases, where the claimant is suing for compensation for some form of economic loss that she claims the defendant's tort has caused her to suffer. Suppose, for example, that *Applicant* wants to sue for compensation for the fact that she did not get a job as a skiing instructor which, she claims, she would have obtained but for *Defendant*'s tort.

Not getting a job is a form of economic loss. In *Applicant*'s case, the economic loss could be pure (which would be the case where *Applicant* didn't get the job because *Defendant* gave her an unfairly bad reference) or the economic loss could be consequent on physical injury (which would be the case where *Applicant* didn't get the job because *Defendant*

---

[55] In both *Fairchild* and *Barker*, *Wilsher* was distinguished on the basis that the harm in that case might have been caused by different agents, operating in *different* ways on the baby: see *Fairchild*, at [22] (per Lord Bingham), [118] (per Lord Hutton), [170] (per Lord Rodger); and *Barker*, at [23] (per Lord Hoffmann).

[56] *Sienkiewicz*, at [177].

[57] *Sienkiewicz*, at [92].

negligently injured her so badly that she could no longer be considered for a job as a skiing instructor). It doesn't matter. In either case, the courts do *not*: (a) require *Applicant* to show that it was at least 51% likely that she would have gotten the job as a skiing instructor but for *Defendant*'s tort, and if *Applicant* can show this, (b) hold that *Defendant*'s tort *caused* *Applicant* not to get the job as a skiing instructor. Instead, the courts simply find out what (if any) was the *chance* that *Applicant* would have gotten the job as a skiing instructor had *Defendant* not committed his tort, and if there was a chance that *Applicant* would have gotten the job but for *Defendant*'s tort, they will award *Applicant* compensation for the loss of that chance of getting the job.[58]

Why do the courts do this? Why don't they adopt the 'all or nothing' approach that they adopt in physical injury cases, and say that the *only* thing *Applicant* can sue for is the loss of the job, and she can sue for that, *in full*, if she can show that it was at least 51% likely that she would have gotten the job but for *Defendant*'s tort? The reason they do not, it seems, is that adopting such an approach would either *overcompensate* or *undercompensate* *Applicant*. If all *Defendant*'s tort deprived *Applicant* of was the *chance* of getting a job, then why should she get damages assessed on the basis that *Applicant* would *certainly* have gotten the job but for *Defendant*'s tort if the chance that she would have gotten the job was still only 55%, or 60%, or 70%? And if *Defendant*'s tort *did* deprive *Applicant* of the chance of getting a job, why should she not get damages for the loss of that chance even if the chance she would have gotten the job was only 45%, or 30%, or even 15%?

But then the question must be asked – So why don't the courts adopt the same approach in physical injury cases? Instead of adopting an 'all or nothing' approach, and saying that in a physical injury case the *only* thing a claimant can sue for is compensation for that injury, and she can sue for that, *in full*, if she can show that it was at least 51% likely that she would not have suffered that injury but for the defendant's tort – why can't the claimant simply sue for the chance (however big or small the chance might have been) that she would not have suffered that injury but for the defendant's tort, and recover damages designed precisely to compensate her simply for the loss of that chance? There are two large obstacles in the way of the claimant's making a claim for damages for loss of a chance in the context of a physical injury case.

A. Proof

In the case where *Applicant* is applying for a job as a skiing instructor, it is easy to see why we might say that *Applicant* has a *chance* of getting the job. The reason is that whether she gets the job or not is down to the decision of the employer, and human beings enjoy free will. There is always a chance that the decision *could* go your way when you apply for a job.

In the case where a claimant wants to sue for damages for the loss of a chance of avoiding a physical injury, it is much more difficult for the claimant to show that the defendant's tort deprived her of a *genuine chance* of avoiding that injury. This is an obstacle the claimant in *Hotson* was not able to overcome. In that case, it will be recalled, the

---

[58] See, for example, *Brown v Ministry of Defence* [2006] EWCA Civ 546, holding that first instance judge erred in awarding claimant 100% compensation for loss of pension rights that she would have earned had she worked continuously for 22 years in the army, on basis that it was probable she would have served those 22 years. He should instead have awarded her damages tailored to compensate her for the chance that she would have earned the pension payable after 22 years' service. (The Court of Appeal assessed that chance as being 30% and therefore ordered she be awarded damages equal to 30% of the pension she would have obtained had she retired after 22 years' service.)

claimant fell out of a tree and suffered a hip fracture which resulted in him eventually becoming permanently disabled. The House of Lords found that it was 75% likely that when the claimant fell out of the tree, he damaged so many blood vessels in his hip that he was doomed to become disabled, no matter how well he was treated by the defendant. But this not only means it was more likely than not that the defendant's failure to treat him properly did not make any difference to his becoming disabled. It *also* means that it was more likely than not the defendant's failure to treat the claimant properly did not *even* deprive him of a chance of avoiding disability: it was more likely than not that the claimant had *no chance* of avoiding disability when he was first seen by the defendant.

Students who have trouble appreciating this point should consider the **Lottery Ticket Problem**:

> *Friend* went to a birthday party for *Ungrateful* at her house and included inside her birthday card a ticket for the National Lottery draw that was due to take the place the same evening as *Ungrateful*'s party. *Friend* could not remember what numbers he had picked for the ticket. *Ungrateful* accepted the card and saw the ticket (without noting the numbers), but quickly put both the card and ticket aside and did not even bother to watch the National Lottery draw being made to see if she had won. *Friend* was so angry that *Ungrateful* did not seem at all excited by his present that, when her back was turned, he ripped up the ticket and threw the pieces of the ticket away. Due to a computer breakdown, there is no record of where the winning tickets for the draw on the evening of *Ungrateful*'s birthday were bought, and indeed there is no record of whether there was any winning ticket for that draw.

Did *Friend* deprive *Ungrateful* of a chance of winning the National Lottery when he ripped her ticket up? Most students will be tempted to say 'Yes – though it was a very small chance.' The temptation should be resisted. Either *Friend* picked the winning numbers or he did not. If he did, *Ungrateful* won the Lottery. If he did not, *Ungrateful could not have won* the Lottery with the ticket *Friend* gave her. Which is it – was *Ungrateful* a winner, or a loser? The only way of resolving that question is through consulting the balance of probabilities. And when we do this, we will obviously conclude that it is more likely than not that *Ungrateful could not have won* the National Lottery with the ticket *Friend* gave her.[59]

It was the same with the claimant in *Hotson*. He could not prove, on the balance of probabilities, that when he was wheeled into the defendant's hospital, that he had *any* chance of avoiding permanent disability. As a result, it was simply not possible to make a claim for damages for loss of a chance of avoiding disability in *Hotson*.[60] However, there do seem to be cases where the courts are willing to accept that Nature gives everyone a genuine chance of avoiding harm. For example, if A negligently dislocates B's knee, the courts recognise that in such a case we can say B has a *chance*, but no more than a *chance*, of

---

[59] The chance that *Friend* actually came up with the winning numbers for the weekend National Lottery draw was 1 in 14 million.

[60] Though some academics do insist that damages for loss of a chance could have been awarded in *Hotson*: see Peel 2003b, 627, and references contained therein. An amazing number of academics argue that the fact that the House of Lords awarded the claimant in *Hotson nothing* means that *Hotson* is authority for the proposition that damages for loss of a chance of avoiding physical injury cannot be claimed in negligence: see Porat and Stein 2003, 679; Weir 2004, 214–15. As the majority of the Court of Appeal recognised in *Gregg* v *Scott* [2002] EWCA Civ 1471 (at [39], per Latham LJ and at [78], per Mance LJ) this is incorrect – the facts of the case in *Hotson* were such that the claimant simply could not bring a claim for loss of a chance against the defendants. See, to the same effect, Reece 1996; also Hill 1991. Fleming 1997 puts the point quite well (at 69): '[A] 25% probability that there was a chance [of avoiding injury cannot] be conflated into a 25% chance [of avoiding injury].'

developing arthritis in his knee in the future as a result of what A has done. The courts do not approach that kind of case on the basis that B is either inevitably doomed to develop arthritis, or is inevitably fated to get better with proper treatment – and ask B to establish, on the balance of probabilities, which it is going to be in his case.

B. Type of loss

The second big obstacle in the way of a claimant suing for damages for loss of a chance of avoiding injury[61] is the fact that the courts seem to regard a loss of a chance of avoiding physical injury as *economic* in nature. It is understandable that the courts should have taken such a position. A loss of a chance of avoiding physical injury is not to be equated with a physical injury. There is a big difference between having your leg broken, and losing a chance to avoid having your leg broken. But if a loss of a chance of avoiding physical injury is not a physical injury, what kind of loss is it? Because chances are economically valuable – for example, people are willing to pay good money to enhance their chances of avoiding injury by buying expensive safety equipment – it seems only natural to regard the loss of a chance of avoiding physical injury as an economic loss.[62]

But this has an important implication. Because they seem to think of losses of a chance of avoiding physical injury as being economic in nature, the courts tend to only allow claims for such losses of a chance to be made in cases where claims for economic loss can be made. There is no problem where the loss of a chance is consequent on a physical injury, or harm to property – in such cases, it has long been recognised that damages for economic loss flowing from the physical injury or harm to property may be recoverable. So where A's tort physically injures B, and as a result, B's chances of avoiding some further injury (such as arthritis) in the future are diminished, B may be able to recover damages for the loss of those chances.[63] Similarly, where A's tort damages B's property, and as a result, B's chances of selling that property for a good price in future are diminished, B can recover damages for the loss of those chances.[64]

But where B is suing A for damages for a *pure* loss of a chance, that seems to count in the eyes of the courts as a pure economic loss and – as we have seen – damages for pure economic loss are only recoverable in negligence where the duty of care that A owed B, and breached, was geared towards protecting B from suffering some form of pure economic

---

[61] To save words, the term 'avoiding physical injury' here and below should be taken as including the case where a claimant loses the chance to recover from some physical injury.

[62] Though compensation for the loss of a chance of avoiding physical injury would not just be limited to the economic consequences of being injured, but would include damages for the loss of a chance of avoiding the pain and suffering consequent on being injured.

[63] To save words, we are of course assuming that B is the victim of A's tort, and that B's physical injury is an actionable consequence of A's tort. The same applies to the immediately following sentence about harm to property.

[64] See *Blue Circle Industries plc* v *Ministry of Defence* [1999] Ch 289. The claimants owned land next to land owned by the Atomic Weapons Establishment (AWE). The claimants were in negotiations to sell the land for about £10.5m to a third party when it was discovered that the land was contaminated with nuclear waste from the AWE's land. The third party broke off negotiations and the claimants set about cleaning up their land. The property market collapsed in the meantime and once the claimants' land was cleaned up and marketable again, it was only worth £5m. The claimants sued the defendants for damages, claiming that the defendants had committed a tort in contaminating their land. The trial judge found that there was a 75% chance that had the defendants not committed their tort, the third party would have bought the claimants' land for £10.5m and therefore that there was a 75% chance that but for the defendants' tort, the claimants would have been £5.5m better off than they were. Consequently, he awarded the claimants 75% of £5.5m as compensation for the fact that the defendants' tort deprived the claimants of the chance of selling their land for £5.5m more than they ended up obtaining for it.

loss. The idea that damages for a pure loss of a chance will only be available in negligence where the defendant assumed some responsibility for the claimant's financial welfare seems to explain the cases quite well. In particular, it explains the difference between *Allied Maples Group Ltd* v *Simmons & Simmons* (1995) on the one hand, and *Gregg* v *Scott* (2005) and *Rothwell* v *Chemical & Insulating Co Ltd* (2008) on the other. The defendants in the *Allied Maples* case owed the claimants a duty of care to protect their financial welfare. They were very different from the defendants in *Rothwell* (employers) and *Gregg* v *Scott* (doctors), who owed the claimants in their respective cases a duty of care to protect the claimants' physical well-being, not their financial welfare.

In the *Allied Maples* case, the claimants bought the share capital of K, a subsidiary of G, in order to acquire leases held by K. The claimants' solicitors – the defendants – conducted the negotiations with G over the terms of the share deal. The defendants negligently failed to tell the claimants that the terms of the share deal did not protect them against the risk that they would have to meet any liabilities incurred by K's subsidiaries. The claimants successfully argued that had they been told this, there was a chance they would have successfully renegotiated the deal with G to obtain such protection. As a result, they were allowed to sue the defendants for damages to compensate them for the fact that they lost that chance to renegotiate the deal with G as a result of the defendants' negligence.

In *Rothwell*, the claimants were negligently exposed to asbestos fibres by the defendant employers, but were not allowed to sue the defendants for damages to compensate them for the chance that they might develop asbestos-related diseases in the future as a result of the defendants' negligence. It was crucial to the Court of Appeal's reasoning in this case that the defendants' negligence had not so far caused the claimants to suffer any kind of physical injury.[65] So the claimants had lost a *pure* chance of avoiding developing an asbestos-related disease in the future as a result of the defendants' negligence, and the Court of Appeal ruled that damages could not be recovered for the loss of that chance. A similar claim for a *pure* loss of a chance – of recovering permanently from cancer – was dismissed in *Gregg* v *Scott*. In that case, the claimant's doctor negligently failed to spot that the claimant was presenting with symptoms of cancer. As a result, his treatment was delayed by eight months. The claimant wanted to sue for the loss of a chance of going into permanent remission that – he claimed – that eight month delay in treatment had cost him. A 3:2 majority in the House of Lords dismissed the claim.

Gregg v *Scott* is a case where the facts are hard to understand, and the judgments in the House of Lords are even harder to assimilate. By way of a postcript – or appendix – to this section, we will do our best in the following section to make the House of Lords' decision in *Gregg* v *Scott* easy to understand for readers who want, or need, to know what was said in that case. But the normal student reader need not worry unduly about reading the following section. Most readers should aim to skip forwards to the section on 'Overdetermination'. After they have read and mastered the remainder of this chapter, from 'Overdetermination' onwards, they can then come back to the section on '*Gregg* v *Scott*' – but only if they have the time and inclination to do so.

---

[65] The claimants had developed what are called 'pleural plaques' – small, smooth plates – on their lungs as a result of being exposed to the asbestos fibres, but both the Court of Appeal and, subsequently, the House of Lords ([2008] 1 AC 281) ruled that these were not serious enough to count as a physical injury. The Scottish Parliament responded to the decision in *Rothwell* by passing the Damages (Asbestos-related Conditions) (Scotland) Act 2009, which provides that 'Asbestos-related pleural plaques are a personal injury which is not negligible' and that 'Accordingly, they constitute actionable harm for the purposes of an action of damages for personal injuries' (ss 1(1) and 1(2), respectively).

9.7 GREGG V SCOTT[66]

In order to understand the facts of *Gregg* v *Scott* (2005), it is first necessary to understand some points of terminology relating to the treatment of cancer patients. Someone suffers from cancer if they have at least one malignant tumour in their body. A cancer patient is said to go into remission if all the malignant tumours that were in their body have been killed. A cancer patient who is in remission is said to have suffered a relapse if a new malignant tumour is detected in their body. This new tumour will almost always have developed from a cancer cell that was secreted by one of the tumours that were formerly in the cancer patient's body. A cancer cell can take years to develop into a tumour, so a cancer patient who is in remission can suffer a relapse some years after they went into remission. A cancer patient is said to be 'cured' if they have been in remission for 10 years. The reason for this is that if a cancer patient has been in remission for 10 years it is unlikely that they are still carrying any cancer cells that were secreted by the tumours that were in their body 10 years ago: if they were, one would expect the cancer cells to have developed into tumours by now, thus causing the patient to suffer a relapse.

Now we can make sense of the facts of *Gregg* v *Scott*. In 1994, the claimant developed a lump under his left arm. He consulted his doctor, the defendant, and the defendant told him not to worry about it. Had the defendant treated the claimant with a reasonable degree of skill and care, he would have referred the claimant to hospital, where they would have discovered the lump was cancerous, and treatment of the lump would have started in April 1995. Had the lump been treated at that stage there was a 42% chance that the claimant's cancer would have been 'cured'. However, the lump went untreated and the claimant's cancer spread. A year later, the claimant consulted another doctor, the cancer was detected and treatment started in January 1996. However, because the cancer was more advanced, the treatment that the claimant underwent was much more intensive, and his chances of being 'cured' were now only 25%. The claimant did go into remission after treatment commenced, but he subsequently suffered two relapses. However, he went into remission after the second relapse, and by the time the House of Lords heard the claimant's claim for damages against the defendant – that is, in May 2004 – he had been in remission for six years.

The claimant could not establish that had the defendant doctor not been negligent he would have been 'cured'. Had the defendant doctor not been negligent, and treatment of the claimant's cancer commenced in April 1995, it was still more likely than not at that stage that the claimant's cancer would not have been 'cured'. So, on the balance of probabilities, the claimant's cancer would not have been 'cured' even if the defendant doctor had not been negligent. Instead, then, of suing the defendant doctor for damages for the fact that he had not been 'cured', the claimant sought to sue the defendant for damages to compensate him for the fact that, as a result of the defendant doctor's negligence, his chances of being 'cured' had gone down by 17 percentage points from 42% to 25%.

By a majority of 3:2, the House of Lords dismissed the claimant's claim for damages. Only Lord Nicholls was in favour of allowing the claimant to make a claim for a 'pure' loss of a chance of being cured. He advanced three basic arguments in favour of his position:

(1) *The sanction argument.* If claims for the loss of a chance of being cured cannot be brought under English law, then a doctor who is presented with a patient with a very poor chance of being cured will have no incentive to treat the patient properly.[67] If he fails to

---

[66] Reported at [2005] 2 AC 176; referred to below as '*Gregg*'.
[67] *Gregg*, at [4].

treat the patient properly and the patient's condition worsens, he will always be able to argue that he should not be held liable to the patient because it was more likely than not that the patient's condition would have got just as bad had he treated the patient with a reasonable degree of care and skill.

(2) *The fairness argument.* If claims for the loss of a chance of being cured are not allowed in English law, then the law will unfairly discriminate between different kinds of patients.[68] For example, suppose that *Patient One* and *Patient Two* both independently consult *Doctor* because they have been feeling unwell. In fact, both of them are – without knowing it – HIV+. *One*'s condition is more advanced than *Two*'s and he has only a 45% chance of avoiding developing AIDS, even if he receives proper treatment. *Two*, on the other hand, has a 55% chance of avoiding developing AIDS, if she receives proper treatment. Unfortunately, neither of them receive proper treatment because *Doctor* negligently fails to diagnose that they are HIV+. *One* and *Two* both subsequently develop AIDS.

In this situation, *Two* will be able to claim full compensation from *Doctor* for the fact that she has developed AIDS.[69] She will be able to argue that it was more likely than not that had *Doctor* not been negligent she would not have developed AIDS and so *Doctor*'s negligence caused her to develop AIDS. In contrast, *One* will not be able to argue that *Doctor*'s negligence caused him to develop AIDS because it was more likely than not that he would still have developed AIDS even if *Doctor* had treated him properly. Now – if *One* is *not* allowed here to sue *Doctor* for damages for the fact that as a result of her negligence he lost a 45% chance of avoiding developing AIDS, then the result is that *Two* will be allowed to sue for compensation for the fact that she has developed AIDS, and *One* will not be allowed to sue for anything. And this is so even though the difference between *One* and *Two*'s chances of avoiding developing AIDS with proper treatment was only 10%.

(3) *The argument from authority.* The law already allows claims for pure losses of a chance in other contexts.[70] For example, if a court throws out A's claim for damages because his solicitor negligently failed to file the claim in time, A will be able to sue his solicitor in negligence for compensation for the loss of the chance that he might have won his case. So why not allow a claim for the pure loss of a chance here? Why should doctors be treated more favourably than solicitors?

Lord Hoffmann and Baroness Hale advanced the following arguments against awarding damages for the pure loss of a chance of being cured:

(1) *The Hotson*[71] *problem.* In cases such as *Gregg* v *Scott*, it may well be that the claimant never had a chance of being cured, and if this is the case it would be inappropriate to award him damages on the basis that his doctor's negligence deprived him of a chance of being 'cured'.[72] The statisticians tell us that of 100 patients presenting with a lump like the claimant's in *Gregg* v *Scott*, 42 will be 'cured' if they are treated immediately. One way of interpreting this statistic is to say that each of those 100 patients has a 42% chance of being 'cured'. If this is right, then it would be correct to say that the claimant in *Gregg* v *Scott* had a 42% chance of being 'cured' when he saw the defendant doctor. But there is a different

---

[68] *Gregg*, at [3].

[69] Though the courts will reduce the compensation somewhat to take account of the possibility that *Two* would have developed AIDS anyway even if *Doctor* had not been negligent.

[70] *Gregg*, at [15]–[19].

[71] See above, § 9.6.

[72] *Gregg*, at [79]–[81] (per Lord Hoffmann).

way of reading the statistics. It may be that of 100 patients presenting with a lump like the claimant's in *Gregg* v *Scott*, the varying genetic make-ups of the 100 patients mean that 42 of them are certain to be 'cured' so long as the lump is treated immediately, and 58 of them have no chance of being 'cured' no matter how much treatment they receive. If this is right, then it was more likely than not that the claimant in *Gregg* v *Scott* had *no chance* of being 'cured' and it would therefore be inappropriate to award him damages on the basis that he did have a chance of being cured.

(2) *Administrative difficulties.* Even if this problem could be overcome, and the claimant in *Gregg* v *Scott* did genuinely have a chance of being 'cured' when he saw the defendant doctor – though it is hard to know how that could be established – allowing claimants to bring claims for the pure loss of a chance of being cured would create a number of administrative difficulties.

First, the number of claims that could be brought against doctors would be hugely increased, with 'enormous consequences for insurance companies and the National Health Service'.[73] Doctors would, in effect, become liable to pay damages to their patients every time it was established that they had failed to treat their patients with reasonable skill and care. This is because in every such case the doctor's patient would be able to argue that his or her doctor's negligence had diminished his or her chances of being cured and that he or she was therefore entitled to compensation for the loss of that chance of being cured.[74]

Secondly, personal injury claims arising out of medical negligence would become much more complicated to process. In the case we were just discussing above, if *One* were allowed to sue *Doctor* for the fact that her negligence deprived him of a chance of avoiding developing AIDS, the law could no longer justifiably hold *Doctor* liable to compensate *Two in full* for the fact that she had developed AIDS based only on the fact that *Two* had a 55% chance of avoiding developing AIDS with proper treatment when she saw *Doctor*. *Two* would instead be confined to suing *Doctor* for the loss of the 55% chance of avoiding AIDS that she was deprived of as a result of *Doctor*'s negligence. So all personal injury claims arising out of medical negligence would become loss of a chance claims, involving 'expert evidence [that] would have to be far more complex than it is at present. Negotiations and trials would be a great deal more difficult. Recovery would be much less predictable . . .'[75]

(3) *Lord Nicholls' arguments.* Finally, none of Lord Nicholls's arguments in favour of allowing recovery for a pure loss of a chance in *Gregg* v *Scott* stand up.

First, as to the sanction argument, it is not necessary to allow claims for a pure loss of a chance of being cured to be made against doctors in order to encourage them to treat patients who have poor prospects of recovering properly. The doctor's natural desire to do his or her best for his or her patients, the General Medical Council, and the criminal law provide sufficient encouragement.[76]

Secondly, as to the fairness argument, any unfairness in the way the law currently treats patients in terms of the remedies they are provided with when their doctors let them down is justified on the grounds of the administrative difficulties, described above, that would arise under any other remedial regime.

---

[73] *Gregg*, at [90] (per Lord Hoffmann).
[74] *Gregg*, at [215] (per Baroness Hale).
[75] *Gregg*, at [225] (per Baroness Hale).
[76] *Gregg*, at [217] (per Baroness Hale).

Thirdly, as to the argument from authority, there may be a difference between a case like *Gregg* v *Scott* and cases where the law currently allows claims for a pure loss of a chance to be made.[77] A pure loss of a chance may count in the law's eyes as a form of pure economic loss and is thus only claimable in cases where A has hired B to safeguard or promote his economic welfare, which is not the case in a medical negligence case.

As to the other two judges who decided *Gregg* v *Scott*:

(1) *Lord Hope* would have allowed the claimant's claim for damages, not on the ground that it was a claim for a pure loss of a chance, but on the basis that the defendant doctor's negligence had caused the claimant to suffer a physical injury – the spreading of his cancer. The claimant, Lord Hope argued, was entitled to be compensated for this injury, and such compensation would include a sum for the chance that, because of the spread in the cancer, the claimant's cancer would not be cured in future. (In the same way, if A has tortiously caused B to suffer a hip injury, A will not only be held liable to compensate B for the hip injury, but also for the chance that B will develop arthritis in the future as a result of the hip injury.) The problem with this approach is that it assumes that the defendant's negligence caused the claimant's cancer to spread – but, on the balance of probabilities, it is far from clear that the claimant's cancer would not have spread in any case, even if the defendant had not been negligent.

(2) *Lord Phillips MR* indicated that he would be willing to allow a claim for damages for a loss of a chance in a case – such as the case, discussed above, where *One* develops AIDS after his HIV+ status is not diagnosed by *Doctor* – where a patient has suffered an 'adverse outcome' and there was a chance that it could have been avoided had the patient been treated with a reasonable degree of care and skill by his or her doctor.[78] However, it was not clear whether the claimant in *Gregg* v *Scott* had suffered an 'adverse outcome' – which in this case would mean *not being cured*. Given that at the time of the House of Lords' hearing, the claimant had been in remission for six years, and the fact that the official definition of being cured of cancer is being in remission for ten years, there was every chance that the claimant would in fact finally be cured. So Lord Phillips concluded that *Gregg* v *Scott* was simply not an appropriate case in which damages for the loss of a chance of avoiding an 'adverse outcome' could be awarded.

Lord Phillips' judgment means that there was a technical majority in *Gregg* v *Scott* in favour of allowing a claim for damages for the loss of a chance of getting better to be made in the case where a patient who had a 40% chance of avoiding developing AIDS with prompt diagnosis and proper treatment subsequently developed AIDS when his case was not properly handled by his doctors. However, in reality, *Gregg* v *Scott* has been interpreted as effectively ruling out – for the time being – claims for loss of a chance of getting better being made against a negligent doctor. As Lord Neuberger MR observed in the Court of Appeal in *Wright* v *Cambridge Medical Group* (2011):

> I accept that the reasoning of the House of Lords [in *Gregg* v *Scott*] ... does not conclusively shut out ... this court from applying a loss of a chance approach ... However, certainty and consistency are of great importance in this difficult area and, while the question would be appropriate for reconsideration by the Supreme Court, I consider that, at this level, we should probably not expand the loss of a chance doctrine into the realm of clinical negligence.[79]

[77] *Gregg*, at [218]–[220] (per Baroness Hale).
[78] *Gregg*, at [190].
[79] [2011] EWCA Civ 669, at [84].

9.8 OVERDETERMINATION

We can say that a loss or event is *overdetermined* if a defendant's tort would have been sufficient to bring about that loss or event, but that loss or event would have happened anyway even if the defendant had never committed his tort. Consider, for example, the **Double Poison Problem**:

> *Husband* and *Wife* are deeply unhappy; *Wife* because she loves another man, and *Husband* because *Wife* does not love him anymore. *Husband* decides to kill himself and puts a cyanide pill in a cup of coffee that he has made for himself. While his back is turned, *Wife* – who is unaware of what *Husband* has done – puts some poison in *Husband*'s coffee cup. The poison has the side effect of neutralising the cyanide in the coffee. *Husband* subsequently drinks the coffee and drops down dead.

Did *Wife*'s putting poison in *Husband*'s coffee cause his death? If we apply the but for test, we run into a problem. Had *Wife* not put poison in *Husband*'s coffee, *Husband* would have died from poison anyway. *Husband*'s death is overdetermined in this situation. *Wife*'s putting poison in *Husband*'s coffee would have been sufficient to bring about *Husband*'s death. But *Husband* would still have died from poisoning had *Wife* not put poison in his coffee. So does this mean that *Wife*'s putting poison in *Husband*'s coffee did *not* cause his death? The conclusion is counter-intuitive. It was, after all, *Wife*'s poison that flooded *Husband*'s system when he drank the coffee. So we would say in this situation that *Wife* caused *Husband*'s death. At the same time, we would *not* say that *Wife* caused any of the *losses* (for example, to *Husband*'s dependants) flowing from *Husband*'s death, as those losses would have been suffered anyway, even if *Wife* had never poisoned *Husband*.

In the **Double Poison Problem Reversed**, we would *not* say that *Wife* caused *either* *Husband*'s death, *or* any of the losses flowing from *Husband*'s death:

> *Husband* and *Wife* are deeply unhappy; *Wife* because she loves another man, and *Husband* because *Wife* does not love him anymore. *Husband* decides to kill himself, but *Wife* is unaware of this decision. *Wife* presents *Husband* with a cup of coffee that she has secretly laced with poison. *Husband* thanks her for the cup of coffee, and secretly puts a cyanide pill in the cup, which has the side effect of neutralising the poison that *Wife* put in the cup. *Husband* then drinks the coffee and drops down dead.

In these situations, there does not seem to be any problem with saying that *Wife* did not cause the losses flowing from *Husband*'s death. But consider the **Two Fires Problem**:

> A and B both negligently start fires at an equal distance from C's house. The fires spread at an equal pace and engulf C's house at exactly the same time.

In this case, if we apply the 'but for' test, we will end up saying that neither A nor B's negligence caused C's house to burn down: had A not been negligent, C's house would still have burned down as a result of B's negligence; and had B not been negligent, C's house would still have burned down as a result of A's negligence. But in this situation, it would be unjust to allow both A and B to escape being held liable for what has happened to C's house. A variant on the Two Fires Problem is the **Three References Problem**:

A, B and C are each requested by D – a former student of theirs – to write a reference for him for a job that he is applying for. A, B and C each mix D up with E, a student who had a history of drug use and petty theft. A, B and C each write a bad reference for D, who had an excellent record as a student. D does not get the job.

Again, if we apply the 'but for' test, we will end up saying that none of A, B or C caused D to lose the chance of getting the job for which he was applying: had A not been negligent, B and C's bad references would have put paid to D's chances; had B not been negligent, A and C's bad references would have ensured D didn't get the job; and C not been negligent, A and B's bad references would have crushed D's hopes. Again, it would be unjust to apply the 'but for' test to allow each of A, B and C to rely on the other two's negligence to each escape liability for what has happened to D here.

It might be suggested that although *Fairchild* v *Glenhaven Funeral Services Ltd* (2003) was *not* a case of overdetermination,[80] we could invoke that case as authority for finding the wrongdoers liable for the harms suffered by the claimants in cases like Two Fires and Three References. After all the same sort of arguments about fairness and the need to sanction wrongdoing that might motivate us to find liability in cases like Two Fires and Three References also underlay the House of Lords' decision in *Fairchild*. However, there are two problems with this.

First of all, the decision of the Supreme Court in *Sienkiewicz* v *Greif (UK) Ltd* (2011) has made it clear that *Fairchild* is intended to help claimants in certain cases – predominantly mesothelioma cases – where *evidential* difficulties get in the way of their suing a defendant for compensation.[81] However, the problem the claimants face in making out causation in overdetermination cases are more *conceptual or philosophical*, than evidential.

Secondly, the House of Lords' decision in *Barker* v *Corus (UK) Ltd* (2006) will apply to any non-mesothelioma case where *Fairchild* applies to limit a defendant's liability to a proportion of the harm suffered by the claimant. However, it is not clear that in an overdetermination case like the Two Fires Problem, C should be forced to sue A *and* B in order to recover *full* compensation for the loss of her house.

Most writers on causation would reject the suggestion that we should invoke *Fairchild* in overdetermination cases like Two Fires or Three References. They would argue instead that recovery in cases like these is justified on the basis that the wrongdoers in these cases *have* caused harm to the claimant. Some support this argument by adopting a qualified form of the 'but for' test for causation, according to which A will have caused C to suffer some kind of harm if that harm would not have been suffered *in the way it was* but for A's actions. So in Two Fires, *both* A *and* B caused C's house to burn down because it would not have burned down *in the way it did* had A and B not lit their fires. Others argue that causation is established in cases like Two Fires and Three References by adopting the 'NESS' test for causation, which we will discuss in detail later on.[82] On this test, A *and* B *and* C caused D not to get a job in Three References because there is a set of circumstances in which A's failing to give D a good reference would have been sufficient to produce the result that D did not get his job, and the same could be said of B and C.

---

[80] It was *not* the case in *Fairchild* that had one of the defendants not been negligent, the claimant would have contracted mesothelioma anyway as a result of one of the other defendants' negligence. The claimant might well not have contracted mesothelioma at all. The problem in *Fairchild* was not knowing *whose* negligence caused the claimant's mesothelioma.

[81] See above, § 9.5.

[82] See below, § 9.13(A).

We do not need to get involved in the debates (which tend to be interminable, anyway) as to which of these approaches to overdetermination cases should be preferred. What is important is that *everyone agrees* that in overdetermination cases like Two Fires and Three References, the wrongdoers involved should each be held liable, and held liable *in full*, for the harm suffered by the claimant. If this is right, then it would be dangerous to apply *Fairchild* – and, by necessary implication, *Barker* – to these kinds of overdetermination cases. Instead we should simply say that in cases like Two Fires and Three References a causal link *will* be found between a wrongdoer's conduct and the harm suffered by the claimant, even though that harm would have been suffered anyway as a result of the conduct of other wrongdoers.

In the situations we have looked at so far, had the defendant not done what he did, the same harm would have occurred anyway, *at the same time* as it occurred in real life. But the problem of overdetermination also arises when, had the defendant not done what he did, the same harm would have occurred *a bit later* than it did in real life. We have already seen a couple of examples of this: *Jobling* v *Associated Dairies Ltd* (1982) and *Calvert* v *William Hill Ltd* (2008).[83] In *Jobling* the claimant suffered from a condition that would have disabled his back three years after it was disabled due to the defendants' tort. The claimant was only allowed to sue for damages for three years' worth of disability, on the basis that after that time, the defendants' tort did not cause any of the losses flowing from the claimant's disability as those losses would have happened anyway. In *Calvert*, the claimant was allowed to use a telephone gambling account with the defendants that should have been disabled. He was not allowed at first instance to sue for any of the losses that he suffered using that telephone account as those losses would have eventually been suffered anyway, even if the account had been disabled.

While these decisions seem unexceptionable, problems again rear their head when a third party's wrong would have eventually caused the claimant to suffer the same losses that he has suffered as a result of the defendant's tort. In *Baker* v *Willoughby* (1970), the defendant negligently ran over the claimant. As a result of the accident the claimant suffered fairly severe injury to his left leg and ankle. The accident occurred in 1964. The claimant sued the defendant so as to be compensated for the fact that the defendant's negligence had caused him to lose the use of his left leg. In 1967 – before the claimant's case against the defendant had been tried – the claimant was shot in the left leg during an armed robbery and the claimant's left leg had to be amputated immediately.

If we apply the 'but for' test to determine the respective liabilities of the defendant and the armed robbers for the claimant's loss of the use of his left leg, we reach a paradoxical conclusion. Had the defendant not committed his tort, the claimant would have had the use of his left leg for three years, before it was shot in the armed robbery and amputated. So the defendant should be liable to pay damages for the loss of the use of the claimant's left leg for three years. Turning to the armed robbers, had they not shot the defendant's leg, he would have carried around a useless leg for the rest of his life. So it is hard to see that the armed robbers caused the defendant any loss – according to the 'but for' test – by shooting his left leg. (In fact, they may have benefited him by saving him years of pain and strain in trying to get around on a left leg that was so severely damaged.)

So if we apply the 'but for' test to this situation, we will end up concluding that the claimant should be able to recover from the defendant damages for the loss of his leg for three years *and that is it*. Nothing else will be recoverable, even though in 1964, the claimant

---

[83] See above, § 9.2.

had a perfectly sound left leg, and since then he has not been able to use his left leg and that will be the case until he dies. Applying the 'but for' test in this situation would therefore result in the claimant being severely undercompensated. He would get nothing for the fact that from 1967 to the end of his life, he would have to manage without a left leg.

To avoid this paradox, the House of Lords in *Baker* awarded damages against the defendant on the basis that the defendant's negligence had caused the claimant to lose the use of his left leg *for the rest of his life*. So the defendant was not just liable for the loss of the use of the claimant's left leg from 1964 to 1967, but from 1967 onwards as well – even though, had the defendants not committed their tort, the claimant would still have lost the use of his left leg from 1967 onwards. No injustice was done to the defendant by the House of Lords in so holding. It was just a matter of luck that the claimant was shot in the armed robbery, and there is no reason why the claimant's bad luck (where it is due to someone else's wrong) should turn into good luck for the defendant, in terms of reducing his liability from a liability to compensate the claimant for the loss of the use of his left leg for the rest of his life into a liability just to compensate the claimant for the loss of the use of his left leg before it was shot.

The table below sums up how the courts handle cases of overdetermination:

Unrelated event . . .	. . . was innocent	. . . was wrongful
. . . would have produced same harm same time or before	No Damages (Double Poison Problem)	Both Wrongdoers Caused Harm (Two Fires Problem; Three References Problem)
. . . would have produced same harm later	Damages Reduced (*Jobling*; *Calvert*)	Original Wrongdoer Held Fully Liable (*Baker*)

To see how the table works, let us apply it to the Water Bottle Problem, where *Traveller* died in the desert after *Malice* poisoned *Traveller*'s water bottle, and *Envy* ensured that it was empty before *Traveller* could have a drink from it. As we saw above,[84] applying the 'but for' test to this situation suggests that neither *Malice* nor *Envy* caused *Traveller*'s death: had *Malice* not done what he did, *Traveller* would have died in exactly the same way and at exactly the same time as she did in real life; and had *Envy* not done what she did, *Traveller* would have died a lot sooner than she did in real life. However, as both *Malice* and *Envy* are wrongdoers, the courts will find that *both Malice and Envy* caused *Traveller*'s death in this situation.

9.9 ANOTHER SOLUTION TO OVERDETERMINATION?

In *Cook* v *Lewis* (1951), Rand J suggested that each of the hunters who shot in the direction of the claimant in that case should be held liable because their negligence in shooting had destroyed the claimant's ability to sue the person who had actually shot him:

> What, then, the culpable actor has done by his initial negligent act is, first, to have set in motion a dangerous force which embraces the injured person within the scope of its probable mischief; and next, in conjunction with circumstances which he must be held to contemplate, to have made more difficult if not impossible the means of proving the damaging results of his own act or the

[84] § 9.1.

similar results of the act of another. He has violated not only the victim's substantive right to security, but he has also culpably impaired the latter's remedial right of establishing liability.[85]

Cook v *Lewis* was not an overdetermination case – it was an evidential uncertainty case – but some people think that Rand J's idea that a claimant can sue a defendant not for injuring her, but for depriving her of the right to sue someone else for damages, can be applied to solve overdetermination problems where two wrongdoers have each done something that was independently sufficient to cause a claimant to suffer a particular loss for which the claimant wants to sue.

For example, in the Two Fires Problem – where A and B each negligently start fires that engulf C's house – we could straightforwardly say that because the loss of C's house is overdetermined by A and B's negligence C cannot sue either A or B for the fire damage to his house. However, had A not been negligent, C would have had a perfectly good claim against B for the fire damage to his house – so C can sue A in negligence for compensation for the fact that he does not now have a right to sue B for that fire damage. And – on the same basis – C can sue B in negligence for the fact that, had B not been negligent, C would now have a perfectly good claim against A for the fire damage to his house.

In *Wright* v *Cambridge Medical Group* (2011), the Court of Appeal endorsed the idea that overdetermination problems could be solved by allowing a claimant to sue a defendant for depriving him of the right to sue a third party for damages. In *Wright*, the Court of Appeal considered what the position would be in the **Two Negligent Doctors Problem**:

> *Ill* presents herself at *GP*'s surgery, complaining that her leg hurts. She is in fact suffering from a deep vein thrombosis (a blood clot) in her leg, but *GP* tells her not to worry, and that the pain will probably go away if she just rests her leg for a couple of days. *GP* had no reasonable basis for making that diagnosis, and should have referred *Ill* to a hospital, where she could have been seen by *Consultant*. In fact, *Ill*'s leg pains do not go away, and two days later she suffers severe brain damage when the thrombosis in her leg travels to her brain. There is evidence that even if *GP* had referred *Ill* to *Consultant* when she first presented herself at *GP*'s surgery, *Consultant* would have culpably failed to diagnose *Ill*'s deep vein thrombosis (DVT), as he was at the time telling all his patients that their problems were 'all in your mind' and that 99% of medical problems could be solved through prayer and meditation.

If *Ill* tries to sue *GP* for compensation for her brain damage, he might try to argue that his negligence in treating her did not cause her brain damage because even if he had referred her to *Consultant*, her DVT would have still gone undiagnosed, and she would have still suffered her brain damage. In *Wright*, both Lord Neuberger MR and Elias LJ thought that *Ill* would still be entitled to sue *GP*, not for her brain damage, but for the fact that had *GP* referred her to *Consultant*, she would then have been entitled to sue *Consultant* for substantial damages for failing to diagnose her DVT properly.[86] So *Ill* could sue *GP* for the fact that his negligence resulted in her suffering an economic loss – the loss of the money she would have been able to recover from *Consultant* had she been referred to him, and had he failed to treat her properly.

Elegant though this may seem as a solution to the problem of overdetermination, as a matter of legal principle, it is untenable. This is for three reasons.[87]

---

[85] [1951] SCR 830, 832.
[86] [2011] EWCA Civ 669, at [58] (per Lord Neuberger MR) and at [98] (per Elias LJ).
[87] Noting the first two reasons, see Nolan 2009, 177.

(1) A claim for losing the right to sue someone for damages is a claim for economic loss, and damages for pure economic loss are not ordinarily available in cases like Two Negligent Doctors or Two Fires. A claim for pure economic loss could not normally be made in Two Fires as there is no kind of special relationship between the claimant and the defendants. There is a special relationship in Two Negligent Doctors, but it is one that is geared towards protecting *Ill* from physical injury, not pure economic loss.

(2) In a lot of overdetermination cases, the loss of a right to sue someone for damages will count as being an unforeseeable consequence of a defendant's negligence, and will therefore be non-actionable as too remote. For example, in Two Fires it will not – in the ordinary course of things – have been reasonably foreseeable that A's negligently starting a fire near C's house would result in C suffering the loss of 'being unable to sue B for damages for the fire damage to his home'. So that loss will be too remote a consequence of A's negligence for it to be actionable.[88]

(3) This 'solution' to problems of overdetermination has the potential in certain cases to plunge the law into unsolvable paradoxes akin to the paradox of Protagoras.[89] For example, suppose that in Two Fires, C sues A for compensation for depriving C of the right to sue B for the fire damage to his house. If C does this, it is not clear why A cannot argue: 'You can't sue me. My negligence in starting a fire has caused you no effective loss, as you can still sue B for depriving you of the right to sue *me* for the fire damage to your house.' But if C sues B for compensation for depriving C of the right to sue *A* for the fire damage to his house, it seems that B could make a similar reply to C's claim. So C cannot sue either A or B because each can rely on the fact that C can sue the other to deny that he is liable to C. The fact that each is liable to C is a reason why neither can be liable to C. The only way for the law to avoid becoming trapped by this paradox in cases like Two Fires[90] is to reject outright the suggestion that in overdetermination cases, it might be possible for a claimant to sue a defendant for depriving him of the right to sue a third party in tort.

9.10 COINCIDENCES

Consider the **Healed Victim Problem**:

> *Driver* negligently runs over *Unlucky* and she suffers various injuries to her head and chest as a result. She spends a month in hospital being treated for her injuries and is largely healed of those injuries by the time she leaves hospital. As *Unlucky* is walking out of the hospital front door, she is hit by a car that is being negligently driven by *Careless*. Her leg is broken in the collision.

Has *Driver*'s tort caused *Unlucky* to suffer a broken leg in this case? Most people would instinctively say 'no', even though *Unlucky*'s leg would not have been broken had *Driver* not negligently run her over. Most people would say that it is just a *coincidence* that *Unlucky* broke a leg leaving the hospital where she was being treated for the injuries she sustained

---

[88] See below, § 10.2.

[89] Protagoras, a famous lawyer, took on a pupil, Euathlus, on the understanding that E would pay P for his instruction once E won his first case. Before E had won any case, P sued for his fee, arguing that if his claim was turned down on the basis that E had not yet won his first case, E should be ordered to pay up anyway as he would – by definition – have just won his first case. E argued in response that if he were ordered to pay up then he would – by definition – still not have won his first case, and so should not be ordered to pay up.

[90] The paradox does not arise in Two Negligent Doctors as there is only one possible defendant (*GP*) who can be sued by *Ill* in that situation.

as a result of being run over by *Driver*. They would say the same thing in the **Careless-Careful Driver Problem**:

> *Driver*, angered by an argument that he has had with his wife, drives very fast to a junction. But he quickly realises how irresponsible he is being and as he approaches the junction, he slows down and keeps a proper look out for nearby traffic and pedestrians. *Teen* tries to cross the road at the junction and steps out right in front of *Driver*'s car, which she has not seen because she is distracted by a conversation she is having on her mobile phone. *Driver* is unable to avoid *Teen* and runs into her, breaking her leg.

Let's assume that *Driver* committed a tort (negligence) in relation to *Teen* by driving very fast to the junction: it was reasonably foreseeable that doing so might result in someone waiting at the junction being injured,[91] and so *Driver* owed *Teen* a duty to take care not to drive very fast up to the junction. Now – if *Driver* had not committed this tort, it seems very likely that *Teen* would not have been injured in the way she was. Had *Driver* not driven so fast up to the junction, his car would not have been in the wrong place at the wrong time when *Teen* stepped out into the road. His car would have been some way away from *Teen*, and *Driver* would have had time to brake and stop the car before he collided with *Teen*. Despite this, most people would feel unease about saying that *Driver*'s negligence caused *Teen*'s injuries in this case. It is just a *coincidence*, they would say, that *Driver*'s negligence resulted in his car being in the exact place it needed to be to hit *Teen* when she unthinkingly walked out into the middle of the road.

These examples have been carefully constructed so that we cannot say in either case that there was a break in the chain of causation between *Driver*'s torts and the broken legs suffered by *Unlucky* and *Teen*. *Careless*'s negligent driving in Healed Victim, and *Teen*'s carelessness in stepping out onto the road in Careless-Careful Driver, are not sufficiently serious as acts to break the chain of causation between what *Driver* did and what happened to *Unlucky*/*Teen*.[92] Instead, what makes the broken leg a *coincidental result* of *Driver*'s wrong in each of the above cases is that *Driver*'s wrong did not *materially increase the risk* that *Unlucky*/*Teen* would suffer a broken leg in the way she did. In Healed Victim, *Driver*'s running over *Unlucky* did not materially increase the risk that she would be run over again in leaving the hospital, after having made a full recovery from the injuries she suffered as a result of being hit by *Driver*. In Careless-Careful Driver, *Driver*'s driving fast up to the junction did not materially increase the risk that *Teen* would be hit by *Driver*'s car once *Driver* had slowed the car down and started keeping a proper look out for nearby people and traffic.

In *Carslogie Steamship Co Ltd v Royal Norwegian Government* (1952), the claimants' ship, the *Heimgar*, was damaged in a collision with the *Carslogie*, which was owned by the defendants. The collision occurred because of the defendants' negligence. The *Heimgar* was on its way to port to have the damage it had suffered in the collision with the *Carslogie* repaired permanently when it was involved in a violent storm which rendered the *Heimgar* unseaworthy. The *Heimgar* limped into port where it spent 30 days having both the storm damage and the damage done in the collision with the *Carslogie* repaired simultaneously. If the *Heimgar* had not suffered any storm damage it would have taken ten days to repair

---

[91] There was a real risk, for example, that *Driver* might lose control of the car when he was driving at such a speed and end up ploughing into pedestrians who were waiting to cross the road at the junction.

[92] See below, § 9.12.

the damage done in the collision with the *Carslogie*. It was held that the defendants' negligence did not cause the *Heimgar* to suffer the storm damage which resulted in its being detained in port for 30 days. In previous editions of this book, we explained this result by saying that the storm broke the chain of causation between the defendants' negligence and the storm damage. It now seems to us that a better explanation is that the defendants' negligence did not materially increase the risk that the *Heimgar* would suffer storm damage on its way to be repaired. It was just a coincidence that a violent storm broke out over the path the *Heimgar* was taking to port, to be repaired.

We have already mentioned *Chester* v *Afshar* (2005), as an example of a situation where the courts applied a balance of probability test to determine whether the claimant (Chester) would have suffered paralysis had the defendant (Afshar) not breached the duty of care he owed her as his patient in failing to inform her that there was a 1–2% risk that the operation he was proposing to perform on her back would result in her being paralysed.[93] It was found that had Chester been told this she probably would have delayed having the operation, as she considered her options, but having done so she probably would gone ahead with the operation. But the probability that she would *not* have been paralysed as a result of having that later operation was 98–99%. So it was (overwhelmingly) more likely than not that had Afshar informed Chester of the risks associated with her operation, that she would not have been paralysed.

The but for test indicates, then, that Afshar's negligence caused Chester's paralysis. But it was just a coincidence that Afshar's negligence had this effect. Afshar's negligence in failing to disclose to Chester that there was a risk of paralysis associated with her operation did not materially increase the risk that when she went under the knife, she would end up paralysed. The risk was always the same, whatever Afshar said or didn't say to Chester. It was just Afshar's bad luck that the one time (we can suppose) he did not tell his patient that there was a risk of paralysis associated with her operation, that that risk materialised. Given this, we cannot say that Afshar's negligence caused her paralysis.[94]

Despite this, the House of Lords held – by a 3:2 majority – that Afshar *should* be held liable to compensate Chester for her paralysis. The majority so ruled because they were concerned that, if Afshar were not held liable, then every time a doctor advised a patient to have an operation and failed – in breach of the duty of care he owed the patient – to inform her of the risks associated with the operation, his breach of duty would go unsanctioned by tort law. If the patient agreed to have the operation and suffered harm as a result, even though the operation was carried out impeccably, the doctor could argue that he should not be held liable for that harm because his breach of duty in failing to inform the patient of the risks associated with that operation had not caused the harm suffered by the patient. The doctor's duty to inform his patient of the risks associated with a particular operation would then become empty – the doctor would be free to breach that duty with impunity.

In order, then, to vindicate the patient's 'right to know', the majority felt[95] that it was necessary to create a special exception to the rules on causation in *Chester* v *Afshar* and hold that: (1) if a doctor wrongfully failed to inform a patient of a risk associated with an operation that it was proposed the patient undergo; and (2) had the patient been informed of this risk, she would probably have either refused to undergo the operation or delayed

---

[93] See above, § 9.4.

[94] [2005] 1 AC 134, at [13]–[22] (per Lord Steyn); [30]–[32] (per Lord Hoffmann); and [61] and [81] (per Lord Hope).

[95] [2005] 1 AC 134, at [22]–[24] (per Lord Steyn); [56] and [87] (per Lord Hope); and [101] (per Lord Walker).

having the operation so as to think it over whether she should undergo it;[96] and (3) in the course of the operation, this risk materialised with the result that the patient suffered harm; then (4) the doctor should be held liable in negligence to compensate the patient for that harm.[97]

In dissent, Lord Hoffmann held that if (1), (2) and (3) were established, then there might be a case for awarding the patient a 'modest solatium'[98] to compensate her for the fact that her right to know the risks associated with her operation so as to make an informed decision whether or not to undergo the operation had been violated. However, he failed to see why the compensation payable to a patient whose 'right to know' had been violated should depend on whether the risk which the patient was not informed of had materialised, and how much harm had been suffered by the patient as a result of that risk's materalising.[99] Lord Bingham also dissented. He dismissed the majority's justification for allowing Chester's claim on the ground that 'in the current legal and social climate' few doctors would 'consciously or deliberately violate' a patient's 'right to be appropriately warned' of the risks associated with her operation. He saw no reason why 'the law should seek to reinforce that right by providing for the payment of very large damages by a defendant whose violation of that right is not shown' to have caused the claimant to suffer the injury for which she is seeking compensation.[100]

The case of *Wright* v *Cambridge Medical Group* (2011) illustrates how tricky it can be, to apply the idea that a tort does not cause a particular outcome that would not have happened but for that tort being committed if the tort did not materially increase the risk of that outcome occurring – and serves as a salutary warning to students who might be tempted to apply this idea promiscuously in answering problem questions. In *Wright*, when the claimant was a baby she developed an infection in her hip. She was taken to see the defendant doctor on a Wednesday, and he negligently failed to refer her to a hospital for further examination. Her condition grew worse, and a different doctor referred her to hospital on the Friday. Unfortunately, the hospital failed to treat the claimant's condition properly, with the result that her hip became permanently damaged. The Court of Appeal held that the claimant could sue the defendant doctor for damages: had he referred her to hospital on the Wednesday, it was more likely than not that she would have been properly treated and avoided permanent damage to her hip. Elias LJ dissented on the ground that had the claimant been treated properly in hospital on the Friday, she would have avoided any permanent damage to her hip. So, he argued, the negligent delay in referring the

---

[96] There is an issue as to whether this requirement has to be satisfied in order for an award of damages to be made under *Chester* v *Afshar* [2005] 1 AC 134. The argument is that if the object of such an award of damages is to vindicate a patient's 'right to know' such damages should be available even if telling the patient of the risks associated with her operation would have had no effect on the timing of her operation. However, of the majority judges, both Lord Steyn (ibid, at [19]) and Lord Hope (at [61] and [81]) attached importance to the fact that had Chester been told of the risk of nerve damage associated with her operation, her operation probably would not have gone ahead when it did. In light of this, it seemed to us correct to say that damages will only be awarded to a patient under *Chester* v *Afshar* if requirement (2) is satisfied.

[97] It is crucial that the *very* risk that the doctor was under a duty to warn the patient about materialise. So there would be no recovery in a case where *Patient* was not advised by *Doctor* that there was a 2% risk of her being paralysed as a result of her operation, and *Patient* went ahead with the operation, and it went perfectly well, but as she left the hospital, she was run over by *Driver*. Although the *Doctor*'s failure to warn *Patient* of the risk of paralysis might have been a but for cause of her being run over – had he warned *Patient*, she might have taken a couple of days before agreeing to the operation, and never encountered *Driver* on the way out of hospital – the risk that *Doctor* was under a duty to warn *Patient* about did not materialise in this case.

[98] [2005] 1 AC 134, at [34].

[99] [2005] 1 AC 134, at [35].

[100] [2005] 1 AC 134, at [9].

claimant to the hospital did not materially increase the risk that she would end up suffering permanent damage to her hip, and could not therefore be said to have caused her to suffer that damage.[101] However, as Smith LJ pointed out, this argument was incorrect. The delay in referring the claimant to hospital *did* materially increase the risk that the claimant would suffer permanent damage to her hip as it shortened the period that was available to the hospital to diagnose and treat the claimant's hip problem and correct any initial incorrect diagnosis and treatment of that problem.[102]

9.11 COINCIDENTAL OVERDETERMINATION

And now for something completely mind-bending – the **Disabled-Blind Footballer Problem**:

> *Fool* negligently injures *Star*, a Premier League footballer, so that *Star* can never play Premiership-level football again. *Star* announces his retirement from football, and in order to get away from the press, he takes a holiday on an island in South East Asia. While there, he is bitten by an insect and contracts a very rare disease that causes him to go blind.

Can *Star* sue *Fool* in this situation for the money he would have made if he had been allowed to continue plying his trade as a Premiership footballer? Applying the but for test, it seems clear that *Fool*'s tort has caused *Star* to suffer a significant loss of earnings. Had *Fool* not committed his tort, *Star* would never have been injured – and, in addition, *Star* would never have taken the holiday that resulted in him becoming blind. So one *cannot* say in this situation that had *Fool* not committed his tort, *Star* would have gone blind *anyway* and would *in any case* have been prevented from carrying on playing Premiership football. The Disabled-Blind Footballer Problem is different, then, from the case of *Jobling* v *Associated Dairies Ltd* (1982), where it could be said that had the defendant not done what he did, the claimant's back would have become disabled anyway.

What is going on here, in Disabled-Blind Footballer, is that *Fool*'s tort has resulted in a coincidental event occurring that has *reinforced* the effect of *Fool*'s tort. Before *Star* was bitten by the insect, there was only one reason why he could not play football at Premiership level anymore – the injury he had received from *Fool*. After *Star* was bitten, there were two reasons – the injury he had received from *Fool*, and the fact that he was blind. The question is whether this should make any difference to *Fool*'s liability. Should *Star*'s bad luck in being bitten by the insect turn into good luck for *Fool* (the fact that *Star* is now blind means that he can no longer sue *Fool* for his loss of earnings from not being able to play Premiership football anymore) and double bad luck for *Star* (the insect bite has not only blinded *Star* but has also deprived *Star* of the right he would otherwise have enjoyed to sue *Fool*)? It is hard to see why *Star*'s being made blind should have an adverse effect on his right to sue *Fool*. *Star* is, after all, not suing to be compensated for the consequences of his bad luck in being bitten and made blind (in which case, *Fool* could argue that he did not cause those consequences because they are merely coincidental results of his negligence), but to be compensated for the consequences of *Fool*'s negligence in injuring him.

In Disabled-Blind Footballer, *Star* is not to blame for the fact that he has been bitten by an insect. But what if he was? What if he was warned not to stray into an area where insects that could make some blind through their bites were common, but he was so depressed by

[101] [2011] EWCA Civ 669, at [106].
[102] [2011] EWCA Civ 669, at [131].

his being forced into retirement that he paid no attention to the warnings and courted the danger posed by the insects? There is some authority in the shape of a couple of judgments in the House of Lords' decision in *Gray* v *Thames Trains Ltd* (2009) which suggest that if *Star* was *to blame* for the subsequent event that reinforced the effects of *Fool*'s tort, then the damages that *Star* can sue *Fool* for will be reduced, even if that subsequent event *would not have happened* but for *Fool*'s tort.

In *Gray*'s case, the claimant was a passenger on a train that de-railed due to the defendants' negligence. In the ensuing crash, the claimant suffered various injuries and subsequently developed post-traumatic stress disorder (PTSD). As a result of those injuries and PTSD, the claimant was no longer able to work. The PTSD caused the claimant's personality to change for the worse, and he ended up stabbing a stranger to death. The claimant pleaded guilty to manslaughter on grounds of diminished responsibility, and was ordered to be detained in hospital under the Mental Health Act 1983. The issue in *Gray*'s case was whether the claimant could sue for damages to compensate him for the money he would have earned had the defendants not been negligent during the period that he would, in real life, be spending detained in hospital. The House of Lords ruled that the claimant's claim for damages for these earnings must fail.

Before the claimant committed manslaughter, he had a perfectly good claim for the money he would have earned over the course of his working life had he never been injured and never suffered PTSD as a result of the defendants' negligence. But the claimant's committing manslaughter reinforced the effect of the defendants' negligence. Now – and for the duration of the claimant's time in hospital – there were two reasons, and not one, why the claimant's earning capacity was reduced: first, because his injuries and PTSD meant he could not work, and second, because he was detained in hospital.

Both Lords Hoffmann and Rodger took the view that in this case, the fact that the claimant had reinforced the effect of the defendants' negligence on his earning capacity by doing something that had resulted in his being detained in hospital meant that the claimant could not sue for damages for the loss of earning capacity that he experienced during his time in hospital:

> [In *Jobling*, the] fact that [the claimant] would in any event have been disabled from earning could not be disregarded. Likewise in this case, in assessing the damages for the effect of the stress disorder upon Mr Gray's earning capacity, the fact that he would have been unable to earn anything after arrest because he had committed manslaughter cannot be disregarded.[103]

> even if the court were satisfied that the claimant would have continued to lose earnings after 19 August 2001 [the date of the manslaughter], due to the PTSD brought on by the accident, it would be highly artificial to ignore the fact that, by committing manslaughter, the claimant had created a new set of circumstances which actually made it impossible for him to work and to earn after that date. Why should the defendants pay damages on the basis that, but for his PTSD, the claimant would have been able to work after 19 August, when, as the court knows, because of the manslaughter, at all material times after that date he was actually in some form of lawful detention which prevented him from working?[104]

These *dicta* seem to suggest that in cases like Disabled-Blind Footballer, the damages payable to the claimant *will* be reduced if the claimant was to blame for a subsequent event that reinforced the effect of the defendants' negligence on the claimant; but, we would

---

[103] [2009] 1 AC 1339, at [49] (per Lord Hoffmann).
[104] [2009] 1 AC 1339, at [75] (per Lord Rodger).

submit, the damages payable to the claimant should remain *unaffected* if the claimant was *not to blame* for that subsequent event occurring.

9.12 BREAK IN THE CHAIN OF CAUSATION

Where *Victim* would not have suffered *Harm* but for *Defendant*'s tort, *Defendant*'s tort will still not be held to have caused *Harm* to occur if something happened *after Defendant*'s tort that also contributed to *Harm* occurring and that was *sufficiently serious* to 'break the chain of causation' between *Defendant*'s tort and *Harm* occurring.

As a working hypothesis, we will suggest that the only sort of event that can break a chain of causation is a *positive act* that is *deliberate, voluntary, informed* and *unreasonable*. (Such an act is often referred to in the case law as a '*novus actus interveniens*'.) You need all five (as well as showing that the positive act contributed to the harm suffered by the claimant) to establish a break in the chain of causation between the defendant's tort and the harm suffered by the claimant. The following cases seem to support the idea that *positive acts* will break a chain of causation if, and only if, they are *deliberate* (that is, the act was done intentionally . . .), *voluntary* (. . . not under pressure or mental incapacity . . .), *informed* (. . . knowing the consequences of acting in that way . . .) and *unreasonable*.

In *Haynes* v *Harwood* (1935), the defendant left some horses unattended in a street. The horses bolted and the claimant, a policeman, dashed out and attempted to stop the horses. He was injured in doing so. It was held that the defendant's negligence in leaving the horses unattended in the street had caused the claimant to be injured. True, the claimant was only injured as a result of the defendant's negligence because he deliberately ran out and attempted to stop the defendant's horses bolting. However, it had been reasonable for the claimant to do this.

In *Hyett* v *Great Western Railway Company* (1948), a fire broke out in a train wagon which had been left by the defendants – the wagon's owner – in a railway siding. The fire broke out because of the defendants' negligence in leaving a number of leaking paraffin drums in the wagon. The claimant – who was employed to do work on the wagons in the railway siding – saw the fire and tried to deal with it. While a friend of his went for assistance, the claimant attempted to remove a number of the paraffin drums from the wagon. While he was doing so one of the drums exploded and the claimant was injured. It was held that the defendants' negligence had caused the claimant to be injured. While the claimant was only injured as a result of the defendants' negligence because he deliberately chose to try to remove some of the paraffin drums in the wagon, as it was reasonable for the claimant to do this, this deliberate act of his did not break the chain of causation between the defendants' negligence and his being injured.

In *Lagden* v *O'Connor* (2004), the claimant's car was damaged as a result of the defendant's negligence and needed to be repaired. While his car was out of action, the claimant hired a replacement car. The claimant could not afford to hire a car from a normal car hire firm at what is called the 'spot' hire rate for hiring a replacement car ('on the spot', as it were). Instead he hired a car from a credit hire company called Helphire which – crucially – did not charge him anything upfront for the hire of the car. Instead, Helphire allowed him to hire the car on credit – the idea being that when the claimant succeeded in his claim against the defendant, the damages payable to the claimant would cover the cost of renting a car from Helphire, and the defendant would be able to pay off his debt to Helphire out of that portion of the damages. The claimant ended up owing £659 to Helphire for the hire of their car; and he sought to recover that sum from the defendant.

Now – a normal car hire firm would have charged the claimant a lot less to use one of their cars for an equivalent period of time. Helphire's rates were a lot higher because they were hiring their cars out on credit and their hire charges included charges designed to cover the cost of helping the claimant to sue the defendant for damages and the cost of taking out an insurance policy to pay off the claimant's debt to Helphire should his claim against the defendant fail. A majority of the House of Lords held that the claimant *was* allowed to recover damages from the defendant to cover the cost of renting a car from Helphire. The fact that he had chosen to rent a car from Helphire rather than a normal car hire firm did not break the chain of causation between the defendant's negligence and the claimant's owing Helphire £659 for the use of one of their cars. This is because – given the claimant's impecuniosity – the claimant had acted quite reasonably in hiring a replacement car from Helphire rather than a normal car hire firm, despite the fact that Helphire's rental charges were a lot higher than a normal car hire firm's would have been.[105]

Of course, it would have been different if the claimant had been rich enough to afford to hire a replacement car from a normal car hire company. Had this been the case, his decision to hire a replacement car from Helphire would have been unreasonable and would have broken the chain of causation between the defendant's negligence and the claimant's owing Helphire £659 for the use of one of their cars.[106]

In *Knightley* v *Johns* (1982), the defendant drove his car dangerously down a tunnel, in breach of the duty of care he owed other users of the tunnel. As a result, the car overturned near the exit to the tunnel. The police turned up but failed to close the entrance to the tunnel to oncoming traffic. A police inspector at the exit to the tunnel realised the omission and told the claimant – a police constable on a motorcycle – to ride through the tunnel to the entrance and close off the entrance to oncoming traffic. The claimant did so, travelling against the traffic coming through the tunnel, and was hit by a car as he came round a bend in the tunnel.

It was held that the defendant's dangerous driving did not cause the claimant's accident, even though the accident would not have happened but for the defendant's dangerous driving. The defendant's dangerous driving only resulted in the claimant being injured because the police inspector deliberately and unreasonably instructed the claimant to ride back through the tunnel against the flow of the traffic. Given this, the defendant's dangerous driving did not cause the claimant's injury – the police inspector's instruction broke the chain of causation between the defendant's dangerous driving and the claimant's accident. It would have been different, of course, if the inspector's instruction had been a reasonable one to give: in that case, the giving of the instruction would not have broken the chain of causation between the defendant's dangerous driving and the claimant's accident.

---

[105] It was suggested in *The Liesbosch* [1933] AC 449 that damages could not be recovered by the victim of a tort in respect of economic losses incurred by him because of his impecuniosity. However, this was not followed by the House of Lords in *Lagden* v *O'Connor*, and quite rightly too.

[106] This was the majority's explanation of the House of Lords' decision in *Dimond* v *Lovell* [2002] 1 AC 384. The facts in *Dimond* were identical to those in *Lagden* v *O'Connor* except for the fact that the claimant in *Dimond* 'could have found the money needed to hire a replacement car until she was reimbursed by [the defendant in that case] or his insurers' (*Lagden* v *O'Connor* [2004] 1 AC 1067, at [5], per Lord Nicholls). It was held in *Dimond* that the defendant could not recover anything from the defendant for the cost of hiring a replacement car from a credit hire company because her credit agreement with the credit hire company was not binding under the Consumer Credit Act 1974. However, three of the Law Lords in *Dimond* went on to observe that even if the agreement had been binding, the claimant would *not* have been entitled to sue the defendant for more than whatever a normal car hire firm would have charged her to hire a replacement car from them.

In *The Oropesa* (1943), two steam vessels, *The Manchester Regiment* and *The Oropesa* collided. The collision was, in part, due to the negligence of the defendants, who were in charge of *The Oropesa*. Although *The Manchester Regiment* was badly damaged in the collision, its master thought it could be salved and set out in a boat with 16 men to go to *The Oropesa* and to discuss what could be done to rescue *The Manchester Regiment*. Before the boat could reach *The Oropesa* it capsized in rough weather and nine of the men in the boat were drowned. It was held that the collision between *The Manchester Regiment* and *The Oropesa* had caused the death of the nine men in the boat. While the defendants' negligence only resulted in the nine men dying because the master of *The Manchester Regiment* voluntarily set out to sea with those nine men – and seven more – the master acted reasonably in doing so and therefore his voluntarily setting out to sea did not break the chain of causation between the negligence of the defendants and the men's deaths.

In *Wieland v Cyril Lord Carpets Ltd* (1969), the claimant was injured in a traffic accident caused by the defendant's negligence. She was taken to hospital where a collar was fitted to her neck. The collar made it difficult for the claimant to move her head and as a result she was unable to use her bifocal glasses with her normal skill. The result was that shortly afterwards, when she was descending some stairs with the assistance of her son, she became confused as to the position of the stairs and fell. Her ankles were damaged in the fall. It was held that the defendant's negligence had caused the damage to the claimant's ankles. Admittedly, the defendant's negligence only resulted in the claimant's ankles being fractured because: (1) the hospital put a collar on the claimant which made it difficult for the claimant to use her bifocals; and (2) the claimant chose to walk down a flight of steps while it was difficult for her to use her bifocals. However, it was obviously reasonable for the hospital to do (1) and it was reasonable for the claimant to do (2) given that she walked down the stairs with the assistance of her son and so there was no break in the chain of causation between the defendant's negligence and the claimant's ankles being fractured.

It was different in *McKew v Holland & Hannen & Cubitts (Scotland) Ltd* (1969). In that case, the claimant was employed by the defendants. The claimant suffered certain injuries as a result of the defendants' negligence. The claimant's injuries meant, among other things, that his left leg was prone to give way suddenly. A few days later the claimant and a few members of his family inspected a flat which he was thinking of renting. On leaving the flat, the claimant, unassisted, walked down some steep stairs which had no handrail. The claimant's left leg suddenly gave way and he fell down the stairs with the result that he fractured one of his ankles. The House of Lords held that the defendants' negligence did not cause the claimant's ankle fracture. The defendants' negligence only resulted in the claimant suffering an ankle fracture because the claimant chose to walk down a steep staircase which had no handrail without any assistance. This was an unreasonable thing to do and so the claimant's decision to walk down the staircase without any assistance broke the chain of causation between the defendants' negligence and the claimant's ankle fracture.

In *Lynch v Knight* (1861) – a defamation case – the defendant warned the claimant's husband that the claimant was a 'notorious liar', that she took 'delight in causing disturbances' wherever she went and that her behaviour could be attributed to one Dr Casserley who 'all but seduced' the claimant. The claimant's husband reacted to these words by divorcing the claimant. The claimant sued the defendant in slander for compensation for the fact that her husband had divorced her. It was admitted that the defendant's words amounted to slander, but it was held that the husband's decision to divorce the claimant had broken the chain of causation between the defendant's words and the break-up of the claimant's marriage: it had not been reasonable for the claimant's husband to react to the defendant's words in the way he did.

A number of points need to be made about the law on what sort of events will break a chain of causation.

A. Omissions

It is clear that an omission – however wrongful, deliberate, voluntary, informed and unreasonable – will *not* break a chain of causation. Suppose, for example, that *Malice* pushes *Drunk* into a lake, where *Drunk* starts drowning. *Bystander* could very easily save *Drunk's* life, but does not do so. If *Drunk* drowns, *Malice* will not be able to say that *Bystander's* failure to save *Drunk's* life broke the chain of causation between his pushing *Drunk* into the lake and *Drunk's* death through drowning. This will be so even if *Bystander* was under a legal duty to save *Drunk's* life – as would be the case if *Bystander* were *Drunk's* bodyguard.

However, the fact that omissions do not break chains of causation does not mean that a claimant will be able to sue if she *allows* a defendant's tort to cause her some kind of harm that the claimant could easily have avoided. In such a case, the claimant might be barred from suing for that harm, not because the defendant's tort did not cause her that harm, but because the claimant was under a *duty to mitigate* the harm she suffered as a result of the defendant's tort.[107] For example, in *McAuley* v *London Transport Executive* (1958), the claimant suffered an accident at work as a result of the defendants' negligence. The claimant's left wrist was cut in the accident. The claimant was taken to hospital but he refused to have an operation on his wrist that would have gone some way towards restoring the claimant's left hand and wrist to full working order. Without an operation, the condition of the claimant's left wrist deteriorated and he lost the use of his left hand. In this case, the defendants' negligence caused the claimant to lose the use of his left hand: the claimant's failure to agree to the operation that would have saved his hand did not break the chain of causation between the defendants' negligence and the claimant's losing the use of his left hand. However, the claimant was still barred from suing for compensation for the loss of the use of his left hand: he only lost the use of his left hand because he failed to mitigate the losses suffered by him as a result of the defendants' negligence.

B. Natural events

It is often contended that a *natural* event that is *unforeseeable* – such as an earthquake – can have the effect of breaking the chain of causation between a defendant's tort and a harm suffered by a claimant.[108] Such a rule, it is argued, explains the lack of causation in the **Lightning Problem:**

> *Thug* stabs *Unlucky*. As *Unlucky* is being taken to hospital in an ambulance, the ambulance is struck by lightning and *Unlucky* is electrocuted to death.

Thug has not caused *Unlucky's* death in this case, it is argued, because the lightning strike that contributed to *Unlucky's* death broke the chain of causation between *Unlucky's*

---

[107] See below, § 10.6.
[108] Hart and Honoré 1985.

stabbing and *Unlucky*'s death. However, such a case could easily be explained away as an example of a *coincidence*: *Thug*'s stabbing *Unlucky* did not materially increase the risk that he would die from electrocution. Given this, it is submitted there is no need for the hypothesis that unforeseeable natural events break chains of causation: all examples of such cases can be explained on the basis that the harm suffered by the claimant is merely a coincidental result of the defendant's actions.

C. Foreseeability

It is clear that the foreseeability of someone's acting in a particular way is *not* relevant – of and itself – to the issue of whether that someone's act has had the effect of breaking a chain of causation. No one contends that an unforeseeable act cannot have the effect of breaking a chain of causation. (For example, if *Distracted* carelessly sets a house on fire, and *Strange* is burned because he walks into the house while it is ablaze because he is curious to see what it feels like to be in a burning building, *Distracted* has not caused *Strange*'s burns.) So academics who contend that the foreseeability of an act *is* relevant to the issue of whether that act has broken a chain of causation must be taken to be arguing that a foreseeable act will *never* break a chain of causation. That is plainly not true. If *Curious* wants to take heroin and injects himself with a needle full of heroin that *Supplier* has supplied him with, and *Curious* dies of overdosing on the heroin, *Supplier* has not caused *Curious*'s death.[109] The fact that it was foreseeable that *Curious* would take the heroin that *Supplier* gave him does not prevent *Curious*'s deliberate, voluntary, informed and unreasonable act of taking the heroin from breaking the chain of causation between *Supplier*'s giving *Curious* the heroin and *Curious*'s death.

D. Medical expenditure

If A tortiously injures B and B opts to have her injuries privately treated, can A argue that B's decision to 'go private' broke the chain of causation between his tort and B's medical expenditure, as B's injuries could have been treated on the National Health Service? The answer is 'no'. Section 2(4) of the Law Reform (Personal Injuries) Act 1948 provides that in 'an action for damages for personal injuries . . . there shall be disregarded, in determining the reasonableness of any expenses, the possibility of avoiding those expenses or part of them by taking advantage of facilities available under the National Health Service . . .'

E. Exceptions

There are a number of occasions where the courts will *not* find that a deliberate, voluntary, informed and unreasonable act broke a chain of causation. To save words below, let us called a deliberate, voluntary, informed and unreasonable act a 'DIVU' act.[110] The main situation in which the courts will refuse to give effect to the idea that DIVU acts break chains of causation is where doing so would deprive a defendant's duty of care of any force.

---

[109] *R v Kennedy* [2008] 1 AC 269.

[110] Students who over-estimate the popularity of this textbook among tort law academics should be warned that if they use the term 'DIVU act' in their essays or problem answers, their teachers and examiners will probably not know what they are talking about.

For example, in *Stansbie* v *Troman* (1948),[111] the defendant decorator owed the claimant a duty to take reasonable steps to lock up her house if he went out, as he had 'assumed a responsibility' to the claimant to do so whenever she was away from the house. The defendant breached this duty of care by leaving the house unlocked for two hours while he went shopping for some wallpaper. A thief took advantage of the defendant's negligence to steal some valuables from the claimant's house. If the defendant were allowed to say in this case that the thief's DIVU act of stealing from the claimant broke the chain of causation between the defendant's negligence in leaving the house unlocked and the claimant's losing her valuables, then the defendant's duty of care would become meaningless. He would be free to leave the house open all day to thieves, safe in the knowledge that he could never be held liable for any thefts resulting from his negligence: he would always be able to plead that the thieves' DIVU acts in stealing from the claimant broke the chain of causation between his negligence and her losses.

In *Reeves* v *Commissioner of Police of the Metropolis* (2000), a man named Lynch hanged himself while in the defendants' custody. Lynch was known to be a suicide risk and the defendant police force therefore owed him a duty to take reasonable steps to ensure that he did not commit suicide.[112] The defendant police force breached this duty. Lynch – who was of sound mind and knew what he was doing – took advantage of the defendants' negligence to hang himself. The claimant brought a wrongful death action against the defendants, claiming that their negligence had caused Lynch's death and that the defendants were therefore liable to compensate her for the loss of support that she and her child by Lynch suffered as a result of Lynch's death. It was argued that the defendants' negligence had not caused Lynch's death: there was a break in the chain of causation between the defendants' negligence and Lynch's death because Lynch performed a DIVU act in hanging himself.[113]

The House of Lords refused to find that the defendants' negligence had not caused Lynch's death:

> [If] the law [has imposed] a duty [on someone] to guard against loss caused by the free, deliberate and informed act of a human being ... [it] would make nonsense of the existence of this duty if the law were to hold that the occurrence of the very act which ought to have been prevented negatived [the existence of a] causal connection between the breach of duty and the loss.'[114]

In other words, if the normal rules on when there will be a break in the chain of causation were applied in this case, then the defendants could never have been held liable for breaching the duty of care they owed Lynch to take reasonable steps to see that he did not kill himself. If Lynch took advantage of their breach of duty to kill himself, the defendants would always be able to argue that their breach did not cause Lynch's death because his DIVU act in killing himself broke the chain of causation between their breach and Lynch's death.[115]

Another example of a situation where the courts will refuse to give effect to the idea that DIVU acts break chains of causation is provided by the criminal law case of *Environment Agency* v *Empress Car Co (Abertilly) Ltd* (1999). In that case, the defendant company owned

---

[111] Discussed above, § 7.2.

[112] See above, § 7.4.

[113] Had it been shown that Lynch was acting under some pressure or depression in hanging himself, such an argument would have immediately failed: *Pigney* v *Pointer's Transport Services Ltd* [1957] 1 WLR 1121; *Kirkham* v *Chief Constable of the Greater Manchester Police* [1990] 2 QB 283; *Corr* v *IBC Vehicles Ltd* [2008] 1 AC 884.

[114] [2000] 1 AC 360, at 367 (per Lord Hoffmann).

[115] It is for this reason B will be held liable for A's brain damage in the Unfortunate Rock Star Problem: see above, § 4.1.

a diesel tank in a yard that drained directly into a river. Diesel was taken from the tank by turning a tap. When the tap was turned on, diesel would flow down a pipe into another tank. On 20 March 1995, someone unknown turned the tap on, the diesel started flowing, filled up the other tank and overflowed into the yard. The diesel then drained away into the river. The defendant company was charged with committing an offence under s 85(1) of the Water Resources Act 1991 which says that a defendant will commit an offence if 'he causes . . . any poisonous, noxious or polluting matter . . . to enter any controlled waters.'

The defendants argued that they had not caused the diesel to enter the river. The DIVU act of the unknown person who had turned the tap on had broken the chain of causation between whatever they did and the diesel polluting the river. The House of Lords held that this argument did not work. As a matter 'of statutory construction, having regard to the policy of the Act'[116] it was intended that people like the defendants should be held responsible for an escape of polluting matter from their land into controlled waters where that escape was the result of the defendants doing something on their land that played a part in the escape, and where the escape was not also attributable to a natural event or an intervention of a third party that was wholly unexpected and abnormal.

9.13 ALTERNATIVE APPROACHES TO CAUSATION

We have now said enough to give the reader a good working knowledge of how the courts will approach cases where they have to decide whether a defendant's tort caused a claimant to suffer some kind of harm. However, there are a number of people who disagree with the approach we have adopted to presenting the law on causation in this chapter. In this section, we will take a look at their views.

A. Richard Wright

Richard Wright is an American academic who argues that what he calls the 'NESS test' provides a superior basic test of causation to the 'but for' test.[117] The NESS test says that event X causes event Y if event X is a **N**ecessary **E**lement in a **S**et of circumstances that were **S**ufficient to bring about event Y.

What seems to make the NESS test superior to the 'but for' test, is that – unlike the 'but for' test – the NESS test can handle cases of overdetermination. For example, consider again the **Two Fires Problem**:

A and B both negligently start fires at an equal distance from C's house. The fires spread at an equal pace and engulf C's house at exactly the same time.

As we have seen, the 'but for' test suggests that neither A's negligence nor B's negligence caused C's house to be destroyed: had A not been negligent, C's house would still have been destroyed by the fire negligently started by B; had B not been negligent, A's negligence would still have resulted in C's house being destroyed. The NESS test avoids such a seemingly paradoxical conclusion.

Under the NESS test, we ask whether A's negligence was a necessary element in a set of circumstances that was sufficient to bring about the damage to C's house that actually happened in this case. The answer is 'yes' – the set of circumstances 'A negligently started a

[116] [1999] 2 AC 22, 32 (per Lord Hoffmann).
[117] See, most recently, Wright 2011a.

fire, the fire spread, the fire reached C's house, C's house was sound and intact at the time the fire reached the house' describes a set of circumstances that are sufficient to produce the result 'C's house burns down' and A's negligently starting the fire is a necessary element of that set. So we conclude under the NESS test that A's negligence was a cause of C's house burning down. But the NESS test also allows us to say that B's negligence was a cause of C's house burning down. B's negligence also forms a necessary part of a set of circumstances ('B negligently started a fire, the fire spread, the fire reached C's house, C's house was sound and intact at the time the fire reached the house') that were sufficient to produce the result 'C's house burns down'. So both A's negligence and B's negligence caused C's house to burn down under the NESS test.

The NESS test also produces a positive finding that A caused B's death in the **Murder on the Orient Express Problem:**[118]

> *Tycoon* is stabbed in his sleep by 13 people, including *Butler*. Each of the 13 only stabs *Tycoon* once and no stab affects a vital organ. *Tycoon* dies of blood loss from his 13 stab wounds.

The 'but for' test tends to suggest that *Butler* did not cause *Tycoon*'s death here: had *Butler* not stabbed *Tycoon*, *Tycoon* would still have died of blood loss from the 12 other stab wounds he received. The NESS test reaches an opposite conclusion. Assume that six stab wounds were the bare minimum number of stab wounds *Tycoon* would have had to suffer to die of loss of blood in the way he did. Given this, we can describe a set of circumstances, which include as a necessary part *Butler*'s stabbing *Tycoon*, that were sufficient to give rise to *Tycoon*'s dying through loss of blood: '*Butler* stabbed *Tycoon*, *Tycoon* received five other stab wounds'. As a result, we can say – under the NESS test – that *Butler*'s stabbing *Tycoon* was a cause of *Tycoon*'s death. (The same would be true of any of the other 12 people who stabbed *Tycoon*: under the NESS test, each of them caused *Tycoon*'s death because their stabbing *Tycoon* was sufficient (in conjunction with five other people stabbing *Tycoon*) to bring about *Tycoon*'s death.)

In applying the NESS test, two things are very important: (1) you have to accurately describe the event the causes of which you are asking about; and (2) a set of circumstances can only count as having been sufficient to bring about a particular event if *every single element* of that set *actually existed* to bring about that event.

The **Julius Caesar Problem** illustrates point (1):

> On the 15th March 44 BC, Julius Caesar was attacked in the Roman Senate by over 60 Roman notables who had decided to kill him. He was stabbed 23 times, including by his close friend Brutus. According to the historian Suetonius, only the second stab wound, to Caesar's chest, was lethal.

Did Brutus cause Caesar's death by stabbing him? The answer is 'no'. While the stab wound inflicted by Brutus may have been sufficient – along with an unspecified number of the other stab wounds inflicted on Caesar – to bring about Caesar's death through loss of blood, Caesar did not die of loss of blood. He died from the injury to his chest triggered by the second stab wound that he suffered. If Brutus did not inflict that second stab wound, he did not cause Caesar's death.

---

[118] This problem is named after the famous Agatha Christie novel *Murder on the Orient Express* where an American businessman is stabbed to death while sleeping on the Orient Express.

The Double Poison Problem and the Double Poison Problem Reversed illustrate point (2). In the Double Poison Problem,[119] *Husband* poisons a cup of coffee so that he can kill himself. Before he can drink the coffee, *Wife* poisons it in order to kill *Husband*. *Wife's* poison has the side effect of neutralising the poison *Husband* has put in the cup. *Husband* subsequently drinks the coffee and drops down dead. The NESS test has no problem reaching the conclusion that *Wife* caused *Husband's* death here. *Wife's* putting poison in *Husband's* coffee cup formed a necessary part of a set of circumstances ('*Wife* put poison in *Husband's* coffee cup, *Husband* drank the coffee, the poison was still active at the time the coffee touched *Husband's* lips') that were sufficient to bring about *Husband's* death.

In the Double Poison Problem Reversed, *Wife* poisoned *Husband's* cup of coffee first, and *Husband* slipped some poison into his coffee second, with the side effect that it neutralised *Wife's* poison. *Husband* then drank the coffee and died. In this case, the NESS test indicates that *Wife* did *not* cause *Husband's* death. We *can* envisage a set of circumstances where *Wife's* putting poison in *Husband's* coffee *would* have been sufficient to bring about *Husband's* death: '*Wife* put poison in *Husband's* coffee cup, *Husband* drank the coffee, the poison was still active at the time the coffee touched *Husband's* lips'. However, the third element in that set of circumstances did not exist in this case: the poison was no longer active at the time the coffee touched *Husband's* lips.

So should we adopt the NESS test as our basic test for causation? We think people should be cautious about adopting the NESS test for the following reasons.

(1) Richard Wright argues that the NESS test 'captures the essence of causation and gives it a comprehensive specification and meaning.'[120] While the NESS test may be better than the but for test of causation at handling problems of overdetermination, it shares with the but for test of causation a basic flaw that should make anyone doubt whether *either* test is an adequate basic test of causation. The flaw is this: under the NESS test (as well as the but for test) a huge range of circumstances count as causes of any particular event. Any list of the set of circumstances that were sufficient to bring about the event of your reading this book at this particular moment would include: 'the universe coming into existence', 'the Earth settling into a stable orbit around the Sun'; 'trees growing on the surface of the Earth'; 'human beings coming into existence'; 'Julius Caesar being stabbed on 15th March 44 BC' – all these things count as causes of your reading this book at this particular moment under the NESS test.[121] But there is something odd about any view of causation which counts such a huge range of events, stretching back over unimaginably huge periods of time, as causes of your reading this book at this particular moment in time. The same point could be made in the context of the case where A throws a stone at B's window, shattering it. The presence of the window is a necessary element in the set of circumstances sufficient to bring about the consequence of the window being shattered. But would anyone normally argue that the existence of the window was a cause of its being shattered?

(2) It may be questioned whether the NESS test *is* actually better at handling problems of overdetermination than the 'but for' test. The issue is this: In a case like the Two Fires

---

[119] See above, § 9.8.

[120] Wright 2011a, text at fn 202.

[121] Julius Caesar's being stabbed counts as a cause under the NESS test as had Julius Caesar not been assassinated, history would have been so different that you, the writers of this book, and this book itself would almost certainly not have come into existence but for that event. So Julius Caesar *had* to die for you to read this book at this particular time.

Problem,[122] is it *obvious* that *each* of A *and* B have caused C's house to burn down? Or is it the case that it is not at all obvious that each of A and B have caused C's house to burn down, but we do not wish to *say* that *neither* of them caused C's house to burn down because doing so would produce results that are unacceptable or paradoxical? If it is obvious that each of A and B have caused C's house to burn down, then the NESS test is superior to the 'but for' test – it, unlike the 'but for' test, identifies who has caused C's house to burn down. If it is not at all obvious that *each* of A *and* B have caused C's house to burn down in the Two Fires Problem, then the 'but for' test is better than the NESS test[123] – it identifies the Two Fires Problem as a genuinely problematic case for the law on causation, while the NESS test just waves the problem away.

Richard Wright argues that if we say that *neither* A *nor* B *caused* C's house to burn down then we must say that C's house burning down was an 'unexplained miracle'.[124] But this is too quick. We can perfectly well explain why C's house burned down: 'A negligently started a fire some way away from C's house and B independently did the same thing. The two fires converged on C's house and it burned down.' The real issue is whether we can honestly reduce *that* explanation down to the formula: 'A and B each caused C's house to burn down.' Or would it be more *accurate* to say that while *neither* A *nor* B *caused* C's house to burn down (as the but for test indicates), each *played a part in*, or was *involved in*, or had *something to do with* C's house burning down?

The point becomes extremely pressing when we consider the Water Bottle Problem.[125] Richard Wright argues that under the NESS test the Water Bottle Problem is not a problem at all.[126] *Malice* (who put poison in *Traveller*'s water bottle) did not cause *Traveller*'s death in this case as *Malice*'s poisoning *Traveller*'s water bottle was not a necessary element in a set of circumstances that would have been sufficient to bring about *Traveller*'s death *from dehydration*.[127] But the NESS test tells us that *Envy* (who put a hole in the bottom of *Traveller*'s water bottle, which was by then filled with poison) *did* cause *Traveller*'s death here as we can describe a set of circumstances ('*Envy* put a hole in the bottom of *Traveller*'s water bottle, *Traveller* did not notice the hole when she inspected her water bottle, by the time *Traveller* wanted a drink the contents of her water bottle had completely dribbled out of the hole that *Envy* put in the water bottle') which include what *Envy* did and which would have been sufficient to bring about *Traveller*'s death from dehydration.

What do you think? Do you think it is *easy* to say here that *Envy*, and not *Malice*, caused *Traveller*'s death in this situation? Our view is that it is not easy at all, and the 'but for' test works better than the NESS test in that it makes clear that this is a situation that is genuinely problematic for the law on causation. In our view, it is not possible confidently to explain what happened here as '*Envy*, and not *Malice*, caused *Traveller*'s death'. And we see no reason why we cannot say that while neither *Envy* nor *Malice* caused *Traveller*'s death, each of them *played a part in*, or *was involved in*, or had *something to do with*, *Traveller*'s death.

---

[122] See above, § 9.8.
[123] And is better than a modified form of 'but for' test under which A can only be said to have caused event X to occur if event X would not have occurred *in the way it did* had A not done what he did.
[124] Wright 2011a, text at n 92.
[125] See above, § 9.1.
[126] See Wright 2011a, text at n 88.
[127] It would be different if the poison had been so foul smelling that as soon as A lifted the water bottle to his lips, he would have known something was up and would not have drunk the water.

B. Lord Hoffmann

Lord Hoffmann delivered a lecture at Oxford on 'Causation' in May 2005 that was subsequently published in the *Law Quarterly Review*.[128] In that lecture, he argued that there is no *one* approach to questions of causation that should be applied across the board to all cases where we have to determine whether A's actions caused B to suffer some kind of harm. What approach should be adopted in any given case is a matter for the law to decide. Once one has ascertained 'what causal connection the law requires . . . one then decides, as a question of fact, whether the claimant has satisfied the requirements of the law. There is, in my opinion, nothing more to be said.'[129]

The trouble with this *non-essentialist* approach to the law on causation is that it seems to leave it up to the judges to determine what rules on causation they will adopt in particular types of case. (Assuming, of course, that Parliament has not pre-empted their decision by dictating what rules they should adopt in a particular type of case.) This raises the possibility that the judges may adopt rules on causation that are counter-intuitive or bear no relation to the way ordinary people think about the notion of causation. For example, if Lord Hoffmann is right what is there to stop the judges adopting a rule that says that if 'A does *x* with the object of producing effect Y, and Y occurs after A has done *x*, A's doing *x* will have caused Y to happen'? Such a rule seems counter-intuitive. How can A's intention – a mental state – in doing *x* have any effect on whether A's doing *x* caused Y to happen? And, unsurprisingly, the application of such a counter-intuitive rule would produce odd results – for example, that *Wife* caused *Husband*'s death by poisoning his coffee in *both* the Double Poison Problem (right) *and* the Double Poison Problem Reversed (wrong). Lord Hoffmann's non-essentialist approach to causation opens the door to the judges falling into these kinds of errors.

It may be that Lord Hoffmann would deny that this is the case and argue that by 'causal connection' he meant *valid* causal connection – so in a case where A is alleged to have caused B to suffer some kind of harm, A *cannot* be held liable for that harm if a finding that A caused B to suffer that harm would, for example, violate some natural law (for example, that something you do now cannot cause the death of someone who is already dead). But if one concedes that, then the question arises – What counts as a valid causal connection? Can we validly say that A's doing *x* caused B harm if there is only a coincidental connection between A's doing *x* and the harm suffered by B? Can we validly say that A's doing *x* caused B harm if that harm would have been suffered anyway (and in exactly the way it was suffered, and at the exact same time too) had A not done *x*? On these sorts of questions it is far from true that there is 'nothing more to be said.'

C. Jane Stapleton

In 2008, Jane Stapleton published an article – 'Choosing What We Mean by "Causation" in the Law'[130] – that was clearly intended to make a fresh start[131] at addressing the question of when we can say that A caused B to suffer some kind of harm.

---

[128] Hoffmann 2005.

[129] ibid, 603.

[130] Stapleton 2008.

[131] The abstract of the article says that it presents 'a radical new account of "causation" in the Law' and in fn 18 of the article, Stapleton 'happily recant[s] any of my earlier ideas [on causation] that are inconsistent with the approach outlined in this paper' (ibid, 441).

Stapleton argues that lawyers should adopt a very wide definition of causation, according to which a 'factor' should be said to have caused a 'phenomenon' to occur if application of the NESS test indicates that that factor was 'involved' in the occurrence of that phenomenon.[132] How is this position different from Richard Wright's? Well, Richard Wright only advances the NESS test as an account of what he calls 'natural causation' and what some lawyers might call 'factual causation' or 'cause in fact'. He would not object to lawyers supplementing this account of causation with doctrines that 'deliberate, voluntary, informed and unreasonable acts break chains of causation' or 'events that are a merely coincidental effect of a defendant's conduct were not caused by that conduct', which doctrines may result in a lawyer saying that A's conduct was a cause *in fact* of some harm that B has suffered but was not a cause *in law*.

Jane Stapleton *does* object to this. She wants to reshape the law on causation so that the NESS test is the *exclusive* test for causation. What then will happen to the areas of law dealt with in sections 9.10 ('Coincidences') and 9.12 ('Break in the chain of causation') of this book? They will no longer have anything to do with the law on causation, but will rather become part of the law on 'the scope of liability for consequences' – that is, how far a defendant will be held liable for the consequences of his actions. In terms of the scheme of this book, Stapleton wants sections 9.10 and 9.12 of this book to appear in the next chapter ('Actionability'), not this one.

Why does Stapleton want to do this? She argues that we need to adopt a very wide account of causation for two reasons. First, there are many different reasons why lawyers might be interested in determining whether A has caused B to suffer some kind of harm, and we need a very wide account of causation 'to accommodate smoothly all the many diverse enquiries'[133] lawyers might be engaging in when they ask whether A has caused B to suffer harm. Secondly, employing 'involvement' – as defined by Stapleton – as *the* criterion for determining whether A has caused B to suffer some kind of harm means that our inquiry into whether A has caused B to suffer some kind of harm will be 'untainted by normative interrogations and controversies'. Those 'normative concerns' should be dealt with elsewhere in the law, where they can be seen for what they are 'and evaluated accordingly.'[134]

What should we make of this? We think Jane Stapleton's views should be rejected, for a number of different reasons.

(1) Lord Hoffmann would observe that it is far from clear why lawyers should adopt *one* account of causation that will apply *across the board* to *all* cases where lawyers have reason to ask: 'Did A cause B to suffer some kind of harm here?' Doing so could be productive of great injustice. For example, in *R v Kennedy* (2008), K prepared a syringe of heroin, handed it to an acquaintance, B, who injected himself with the heroin and handed the syringe back to K. K left the room. B subsequently overdosed and died. K was charged with manslaughter. K's guilt turned on whether he had *caused* B to die by giving him the syringe. Jane Stapleton would say that he did. The House of Lords held that he did not – B's deliberate, voluntary,

---

[132] Stapleton is less direct than we are here, distinguishing (at 436) three different forms of 'involvement' in the occurrence of a phenomenon: 'necessity, duplicate necessity and contribution'. After some discussion of each of these forms of involvement, Stapleton winds up (at 444) saying that 'modern lawyers are fortunate to have an algorithm broad enough to identify all [three] forms of involvement when operated in the light of sufficient data including evidence of behaviour and our knowledge of the physical laws of nature: this is the 'NESS' algorithm . . .'.

[133] Stapleton 2008, 445.

[134] Stapleton 2008, 446.

informed and unreasonable act in injecting himself with the heroin broke the chain of causation between K's giving B the heroin and B dying. Stapleton would argue that some other rule or doctrine should accommodate the House of Lords' 'normative concern' not to find defendants criminally liable for outcomes that were the more immediate consequence of other people's deliberate, voluntary, informed and unreasonable acts. But what other rule or doctrine is there, in this context? If the House of Lords had found that K had caused B's death by giving him the syringe, K would have to have been found guilty.

(2) If we confine Stapleton's proposals to the realm of tort law – as the case of *R* v *Kennedy* seems to indicate we have to – it is far from clear why tort lawyers should adopt an account of causation that is as wide as Stapleton's is. Stapleton argues that such a wide account needs to be adopted in order to meet the 'wide needs of the Law'.[135] But this seems to have things backwards. Surely we should first of all identify why *tort lawyers* need to determine whether A has caused B to suffer some kind of harm[136] and then, in the light of that, determine what rules tort lawyers should adopt to determine whether A has caused B to suffer that harm. After all, if our *only* concern – in presenting tort lawyers with an account of causation – is to allow tort lawyers maximum room to let their 'normative concerns' as to who should and should not be held liable for some harm a claimant has suffered roam free, why should we have a law on causation at all? Why not say that the question of whether a tortfeasor should be held liable for a harm suffered by a claimant should rest completely on normative considerations and should be unaffected by humdrum factual inquiries into whether the tortfeasor's tort was actually *involved* in the claimant's suffering that harm?

(3) Stapleton seems, in her article on 'Choosing What We Mean by "Causation" in the Law', to be trying to do for the law on causation what Lord Wilberforce attempted – in *Anns* v *Merton LBC* (1978) – to do for the law on when one person will owe another a duty of care.[137] Just as Lord Wilberforce suggested in *Anns* that a defendant should be held to have owed a claimant a duty of care if it was foreseeable that the defendant's conduct would result in harm to the claimant and there are no public policy considerations that militate against the defendant being held to have owed the claimant a duty of care, Jane Stapleton is proposing that in a case where A has committed a tort and B has suffered some kind of harm, A should be held liable for that harm if A's tort was 'involved' in B's suffering that harm and there are no public policy considerations that militate against A's being held liable for that harm. Adopting such a stance on causation would make tort law significantly more pro-claimant than it is at the moment.

The point can be illustrated by another article that Jane Stapleton wrote, on the House of Lords' decision in *Chester* v *Afshar* (2005).[138] Stapleton regards the finding of liability in *Chester* v *Afshar* as entirely orthodox on the basis that Afshar's negligence in failing to inform Chester of the risk of paralysis associated with her operation was 'historically involved' in Chester's being paralysed as a result of the operation and there was no convincing reason why Afshar should *not* be held liable to compensate Chester for that paralysis.[139] But the reasoning of the majority of the House of Lords in *Chester* v *Afshar* was quite different. Their starting point was that Afshar's negligence did *not* cause Chester's paralysis, but there was a positive reason why Afshar should *still* be held liable for that

[135] Stapleton 2008, 473.
[136] A question we will address at length below, in § 28.7.
[137] For discussion of the *Anns* test for when one person will owe another a duty of care, see above, § 5.2.
[138] Stapleton 2006b.
[139] ibid, 437.

paralysis which justified setting aside the normal rules on causation in this case. And the dissenting judges in *Chester* v *Afshar* – Lords Hoffmann and Bingham – did not dissent on the ground that they thought there *was* a good reason why the claimant's claim should be *dismissed*; they dissented on the ground that they could *not* see a good reason why the claimant's claim should be *allowed*. Had the House of Lords adopted Jane Stapleton's starting point – that once 'historical involvement' is established, the claimant should win unless there is a good reason why she should not – Chester could have been expected to win her case much more easily than she did.

It is not clear that the pro-claimant tendencies inherent in Jane Stapleton's proposals for the law on causation will have any happier consequences for tort law than did the pro-claimant tendencies inherent in Lord Wilberforce's *Anns* test. Certainly, we need better reasons for making it easier for claimants to sue in tort than Jane Stapleton has offered so far.

D. Roderick Bagshaw

In a very recent paper,[140] Roderick Bagshaw has started to sketch out a very different view of causation than any we have looked at so far. On this view, instead of seeking to trace out *lines* of causation between different events, we should instead see events as carrying with them *fields of influence* on subsequent events. The stronger the influence event A has on a subsequent event B, the greater its *causal potency*, and the more likely we are to say that event A was *a cause* of event B occurring.

To take an example given by Bagshaw:

> Suppose that Trevor is walking up a stony beach when he decides to pick up a stone and throw it through Claire's window. He then does this. Did the presence on the beach of the stone he threw 'cause' the breaking of the window?[141]

Both Richard Wright and Jane Stapleton would apply the NESS test here to say that the presence of the stone on the beach *was* a cause of the breaking of the window (though Wright would say that it was a cause 'in fact' and Stapleton would say it was a cause full stop). Bagshaw disagrees, appealing to the relative 'causal potency' of the presence of the stone on the beach:

> The stone's 'inert presence' on the beach [was] clearly not wholly irrelevant to the breaking of the window. It was, after all, only by being present on the beach that *that* stone (eventually) came to strike the window. But . . . the mere presence of the stone is a very *weak* 'cause' when set alongside Trevor's choice [to throw the stone through the window].[142]

In another example considered by Bagshaw, he imagines a pond full of fish, and that 50 units of poison need to be introduced into the pond to kill all the fish. Suppose that A carelessly spills 40 units of poison into the pond, B carelessly spills 30 units of poison into the pond, and C carelessly spills 10 units of poison into the pond. All the fish die. Who caused their death? The NESS test tells us that *each* of A, B and C caused the death of the fish. We can construct a set of circumstances which was sufficient to bring about the death of the fish, and which actually occurred, where each of A, B and C's putting poison in the

---

[140] Bagshaw 2011a.
[141] ibid, text at n 41.
[142] ibid.

pond was a necessary element of that set of circumstances.[143] But on Roderick Bagshaw's approach, this is too crude an answer.

If A, B and C *simultaneously* spilled the poison in the pond, on a 'causal potency' approach, we would say that 'A was more *causally involved* in killing the fish than B, who was *more involved* than C.'[144] But despite the different levels of influence that A, B and C's spillages had on the subsequent death of the fish, we would probably still say that each of them caused the death of the fish as their *degree of contribution* was relatively strong in each case. But it might be different if A and B spilled their poison into the pond *first* and then C only spilled his poison into the pond later (but before the poison spilled by A and B into the pond had begun to do its work). In such a case, C's spilling the poison into the pond had very little influence on what happened later. The fish were already doomed by the time C came along. While C's spilling the poison into the pond will have had a physiological influence on some of the fish – it is hard to imagine that some of the fish did not absorb some of the molecules of poison spilled by C[145] – the degree of influence that C's spillage had on what happened to the fish was so weak that we might well, in this case, say that C did *not* cause the death of the fish.

Unsurprisingly, we would contend that this 'analogue' account of causation (where an event only counts as a cause of a subsequent event if it has a *strong* influence on that subsequent event occurring) has a lot going for it, and may well give a better account of how we intuitively think about causation than more traditional 'digital' accounts of causation (which attempt to provide us with tests that can give a simple yes/no answer to whether an event was a cause of a subsequent event). However, it must be questioned whether such an account of causation can be successfully employed in a *legal* context, where understandable importance is placed on the law's being clear and predictable in its application.

9.14 FACT AND POLICY

We will conclude our discussion of the law on causation by considering the issue of how far inquiries into causation are simply inquiries into matters of fact, and how far those inquiries are affected by policy considerations. As so often, the truth lies in between two opposing extremes.

The first extreme view is that in a case where A has committed a tort and B has suffered some kind of harm, our conclusion as to whether A's tort caused B to suffer that harm will *always* turn on policy considerations.[146] This seems too extreme. If A punches B in the face, breaking B's nose in the process, our conclusion that A's battery caused B to suffer a broken nose does not seem to rest on any considerations of public policy. One way of rescuing this *policy-based* view of causation might be to argue that public policy considerations account for why we are content to find that it was *A's tort* that caused B's nose to break in the above case, instead of focusing our attention on A's upbringing, or his genetic make-up, or anything B might have done to provoke B into hitting him. It might be argued that the

---

[143] For example: A puts 20 units of poison in the pond, B puts 20 units of poison in the pond, C puts 10 units of poison in the pond. This actually happened: the fact that A *also* put *another* 30 units of poison in the pond, and B *also* put *another* 10 units of poison in the pond is irrelevant under the NESS test.

[144] Bagshaw 2011a, text at n 42.

[145] A point acknowledged in Bagshaw 2011a, text at n 29.

[146] Clarkson, Keating and Cunningham 2010 (a criminal law text and materials book) sums up this view (at 103) in the following way: 'There are no underlying *general* principles of causation. Judges simply resort to considerations of "policy" to determine whether a particular defendant caused the specified harm.'

reason why we do this is that we do not want to make it *too easy* for tortfeasors to escape liability for the consequences of their actions, by blaming their upbringing or their genetic makeup or the victim of the tort for what they did. But it might equally be argued that the reason why we do not allow tortfeasors to do this is that, *as a matter of fact*, those factors do not prevent us from finding that A's tort caused B's nose to break. In any explanation of why B's nose broke, A's punching B in the face will loom very large; so large that whatever the chain of events leading up to the punch, the punch will still remain *a* cause of B's nose breaking.

The second extreme view is that in a case where A has committed a tort and B has suffered some kind of harm, if we ask whether A's tort caused B to suffer that harm, we are always asking a question of fact. Allan Beever takes this extreme view, arguing that:

> to say that causation is, even in part, a normative or policy matter is to imply that our judgments or preferences for deciding liability determine the fundamental nature of the universe; as if, were human beings not to exist, or were even just law to be abolished, the fundamental nature of the universe would change. This is, of course, nonsense.[147]

Beever is right to point out that questions of causation are relevant to scientific inquiries into 'the fundamental nature of the universe' and that it is nonsense to suggest that the scientists' approach to questions of causation might be affected by public policy considerations. But Beever goes too far in denying that causation is not '*even in part*, a normative or policy matter' (emphasis added). It seems undeniable that public policy considerations do play *a role* in the courts' deliberations as to whether or not A's tort caused B to suffer some kind of harm.

In taking this view, we do not go so far as Jane Stapleton, who – as we have seen – argues that any part of the law of causation that does not involve the basic and straightforward application of the 'but for' test, or NESS test, of causation rests on public policy considerations. We do not accept, for example, that the law on what amounts to a *novus actus interveniens* rests on public policy considerations.[148] But it seems obvious that the courts *do* monitor the outcomes of the application of what Lord Hoffmann calls 'the standard criteria'[149] for determining what was a cause of what, and will adjust those outcomes if they consider them to be contrary to the public interest.

So in a case where A allows B to kill herself, or even encourages B to kill herself, we would *normally* say that B and only B caused her own death. But where A was under a duty to take reasonable steps to save B from killing herself and application of the normal rules on causation would allow A to breach that duty of care with impunity, the courts will refuse to apply the normal rules and will find that A's breach of duty *did* cause B's death.[150] In a case where A, B and C each employed D to work for them for five years, and they each exposed D to excessive quantities of asbestos while he worked for them, and D subsequently developed mesothelioma, we would *normally* find that *none* of A, B or C could be said

---

[147] Beever 2007, 413.
[148] See above, § 9.12. In support of Stapleton's analysis of that aspect of the law on causation, see Lord Bingham in *Corr* v *IBC Vehicles Ltd* [2008] 1 AC 884, at [15]: 'the rationale of the principle that a *novus actus interveniens* breaks the chain of causation is fairness.' *Against* her analysis, see Lord Bingham (!) in *R* v *Kennedy* [2008] 1 AC 269, at [14]: 'The criminal law generally assumes the existence of free will . . . generally speaking, informed adults of sound mind are treated as autonomous beings able to make their own decisions how they will act . . . Thus D is not to be treated as causing V to act in a certain way if V makes a voluntary and informed decision to act in that way rather than another.'
[149] Hoffmann 2005.
[150] See above, § 9.12.

to have caused D's mesothelioma. However, the courts will instead find that *each* of A, B and C caused D's mesothelioma so as to ensure that an employer's duty of care not to expose his employees to dangerous substances such as asbestos is not rendered nugatory, and in order to ensure that D gets the compensation that we know is due to him from someone.[151]

It seems, then, that inquiries into causation are neither exclusively a matter of fact nor exclusively a matter of policy. They are, at base, inquiries into questions of fact – but the courts will adjust the outcome of those inquiries where they threaten to work injustice, or harm the public interest.

Further reading

We think we have summed up the various academic views about causation well enough above, but for those interested in reading those views at first hand, see: **Stapleton, 'Choosing what we mean by "causation" in the law' (2008) 73** *Missouri Law Review* **433**; Hoffmann, 'Causation' (2005) 121 *Law Quarterly Review* 592; Wright, 'The NESS account of natural causation: a response to criticisms' and Bagshaw, 'Causing the behaviour of others and other causal mixtures', both in Richard Goldberg (ed), *Perspectives on Causation* (Hart Publishing, 2011). The *Perspectives on Causation* book is the result of a special conference on causation in Aberdeen and is well worth looking at as it represents the current state of the art in academic thinking about causation.

Elsewhere, **Sandy Steel and David Ibbetson's article 'More grief on uncertain causation in tort' (2011) 70** *Cambridge Law Journal* **451** provides a very good and readable summary of the state of the law after the Supreme Court's decision in *Sienkiewicz*, and **Stephen Bailey's 'Causation in negligence: what is a material contribution?' (2010) 30** *Legal Studies* **167** helps sort out a lot of the confusions implicit in the cases' attempting to resolve causation issues by asking whether the defendant's actions materially contributed to the harm suffered by the claimant.

Visit **www.mylawchamber.co.uk/mcbride** to access tools to help you develop and test your knowledge of Tort law, including interactive multiple choice questions, practice exam

questions with guidance, weblinks, legal newsfeed, additional case summaries, legal updates and tips on answering problem and essay questions.

Use **Case Navigator** to read in full some of the key cases referenced in this chapter with commentary and questions:

- Chester *v* Afshar
- Fairchild *v* Glenhaven Funeral Services Ltd
- Gregg *v* Scott
- Sienkiewicz *v* Greif (UK) Ltd

---

[151] See above, § 9.5.

10 Actionability

10.1 The basics *328*

10.2 Remoteness of damage *331*

10.3 Scope of duty *339*

10.4 The *SAAMCO* principle *342*

10.5 Wrongful pregnancy/birth *346*

10.6 Mitigation *350*

10.7 No double recovery *353*

10.8 Public policy *353*

Overview

In this chapter we look at the rules that govern what losses that have been caused by a tort are actionable – in other words, compensable through a claim for compensatory damages by the victim of the tort. Although this chapter follows hard on a number of chapters on the law of negligence, the principles in this chapter apply to *any* tort claim. The principles are laid out briefly in section 10.1, and then in much more detail in the subsequent sections. Section 10.2 lays out the general rule that losses that were not a reasonably foreseeable consequence of that tort are too remote a consequence of that tort to be actionable; and explains when the courts make exceptions to that rule. Section 10.3 deals with when a loss will be held to be non-actionable on the ground that it is the wrong kind of loss – not the kind of loss that the law was hoping to protect the victim of a tort from when it imposed a duty on the defendant not to do what he did. Section 10.4 deals with the *SAAMCO* principle, which governs when losses arising out of the breach of a *Hedley Byrne* duty of care will be non-actionable on the ground that they are the wrong kind of loss. The complicated rules on what losses can be sued for when someone becomes pregnant or gives birth due to another's wrong are dealt with in Section 10.5. Sections 10.6 and 10.7 are technical sections explaining when someone will be barred from suing for a loss either because it was easily avoidable or because they have already been compensated for it. Finally, if all else fails, a defendant might try to plead that a claimant cannot sue for a loss because it would be contrary to 'public policy' to allow recovery for that loss: section 10.8 deals with that type of plea.

10.1 THE BASICS

Many academics would name this chapter 'Remoteness of Damage', and discuss in this chapter when a claimant will be prevented from suing a defendant in tort for compensation for a loss that the claimant has suffered on the ground that that loss was a *remote* consequence of the defendant's tort. However, the law on remoteness of damage is only one aspect of a more fundamental area of tort law: the law on when a loss that a defendant's tort has caused a claimant to suffer will be *actionable*. That is the concern of this chapter. Again, it should be emphasised that this chapter (despite its location in this textbook) is relevant to *all* cases where the victim of a tort wants to sue for compensatory damages – not just negligence cases.

The law on actionability will be briefly laid out here:

(1) *Remoteness*. Some losses that are suffered by the victim of a tort will be non-actionable because they are too remote a consequence of that tort being committed. There are

different rules for determining whether or not a loss is 'too remote', depending on what sort of tort has been committed.

The normal rule in *negligence* cases is that unforeseeable losses are too remote to be actionable. But there are exceptions. For example, if A negligently injures B, and B is entitled to sue A in negligence for that physical injury, then B will *also* be entitled to sue A for any economic losses or psychiatric illnesses flowing from that physical injury, no matter how unforeseeable those losses or illnesses might have been.

The rule that unforeseeable losses are too remote to be actionable applies to all *non-intentional torts* – that is, torts which can be committed by a defendant without his having any intention to injure someone else, or some form of very culpable intent. Though, again, there may be an exception where someone commits a non-intentional tort *intentionally* – for example, where someone intentionally breaches a duty of care, or trespasses on someone's land, or defames someone's reputation. There are *dicta* in the cases suggesting that the remoteness rule that applies to *intentional torts* will also apply in cases where someone has intentionally committed a non-intentional tort.

The remoteness rule that applies to intentional torts says that *any* losses suffered by the victim of an intentional tort as a *direct* consequence of that tort being committed will not be too remote to be actionable, no matter how unforeseeable they were.

(2) *Scope of duty.* Some losses will be non-actionable because they fall outside the 'scope of the duty' that the defendant owed the claimant. The best example of this is actually a case about breach of statutory duty rather than negligence. In *Gorris v Scott* (1874), the claimant's sheep were transported to a foreign port on the defendant's ship. Under the Contagious Diseases (Animals) Act 1869, the defendant had a statutory duty to ship the claimant's sheep in pens. However, he did not bother doing this. As a result, the claimant's sheep were swept out to sea when a wave crashed onto the defendant's ship; had they been placed in pens at the time, the sheep would have been perfectly safe. The claimant sued the defendant for compensation for the loss of his sheep but his claim was dismissed. The reason was that the duty that the defendant owed the claimant was imposed on him *not* in order to stop the claimant's sheep from drowning but in order to help ensure that if some of the claimant's sheep contracted some kind of disease mid-voyage, the disease would not spread to the rest of the claimant's sheep; if the claimant's sheep were kept separated in pens the sheep in one pen would not be able to pass on any disease they were suffering from to the sheep in the other pens. So the loss suffered by the claimant in this case fell outside the 'scope of the duty' that the defendant had owed the claimant. In other words, the loss suffered by the claimant in this case was non-actionable because it was the *wrong kind of loss*.

The idea that a loss may be non-actionable because it is the wrong kind of loss applies in negligence cases, and indeed in all cases where someone is suing in tort for compensatory damages. We saw an examples of this idea applying in a (hypothetical) negligence case when we considered the **Forgetful Investor Problem**:

One morning, *Commuter* reads something in the newspapers that makes her think that she needs to sell all her shares in *Dodgy* plc. She then takes a train to work, resolving that once she gets into work, she will call her broker and have him sell her shares. Unfortunately, due to the carelessness of the *Train Driver*, *Commuter*'s train de-rails. *Commuter* is unharmed, but is so shaken by the accident that she completely forgets to sell her shares in *Dodgy*. By the time she remembers, the value of shares in *Dodgy* has plummeted.

In this case, the loss suffered by *Commuter* as a result of *Train Driver*'s negligence is the wrong kind of loss. The duty that *Train Driver* owed *Commuter* was imposed on him in order to help ensure that *Commuter* did not suffer some kind of physical injury, not in order to help ensure that *Commuter* was not distracted from some business that she had to do when she got into work.

It is because losses will be non-actionable if they fall outside the 'scope of the duty' that the defendant owed the claimant that in negligence cases, a claimant has to be quite selective about what sort of duty of care she will claim the defendant owed her. As we have already observed:[1] it is not enough for a claimant to show that the defendant owed her, and breached, a duty of care. The claimant has to show that the defendant owed her, and breached, a duty of care that was geared towards saving her from suffering the kind of harm for which she wants damages.

(3) *Other reasons.* Finally, there are a whole host of losses that a claimant might have suffered as a result of a defendant's tort that are non-actionable not because they are too remote, or because they are the wrong kind of loss, but for some other reason.

Sometimes considerations of *public policy* dictate that a claimant should not be able to sue for a particular loss. Public policy concerns can explain the result in *Gray v Thames Trains Ltd* (2009), which was discussed above.[2] In that case, the defendants' negligence resulted in the claimant suffering a psychiatric disorder that resulted in him killing a stranger. He pleaded guilty to manslaughter on the grounds of diminished responsibility and was ordered to be detained in hospital under the Mental Health Act 1983. Had the defendants not been negligent, the claimant would have been working and earning good money during the period that, in real life, he was going to be detained in hospital because of his manslaughter conviction. The House of Lords held that the claimant could not sue for the money that, but for the defendants' negligence, he would have earned during the span of time he was going to be locked up in hospital. To allow him to do so would have been to allow him to evade one of the normal, and intended, consequences of detaining someone under the criminal justice system, which is to hit the detainee in the pocket by preventing them earning the money they would have been able to earn had they obeyed the law and remained at liberty.

Other times, the courts will hold that a particular loss is non-actionable because allowing a claim for that loss would *bring the law into disrepute*. This was the reason why the House of Lords ruled in *McFarlane v Tayside Health Board* (2000) that in a case where a doctor's negligence resulted in a claimant having a baby that she would not otherwise have had, the claimant will not be allowed to sue for the cost of bringing up that baby. To rule otherwise would have sent out a message that the courts regarded having a baby as a harm rather than a benefit, and would have required the courts to make unacceptable distinctions between rich families (that could afford to have their child privately educated and would then seek to recover that cost from the defendant whose negligence was responsible for that child being born in the first place) and poor families (that could never afford to have their child privately educated and so could not then put themselves in a position to claim damages for that kind of loss).

---

[1] See above, § 5.1.
[2] See above, § 9.11.

10.2 REMOTENESS OF DAMAGE

Suppose A has committed a tort in relation to B and B has suffered some kind of loss as a result. *Normally* that loss will count as a remote consequence of A's tort if it was *not* reasonably foreseeable at the time A committed his tort that someone like B would suffer *that kind of loss* as a result of A's committing that tort. Let's call this the *foreseeability test* for determining whether a loss suffered by the victim of a tort was a remote consequence of that tort.

The foreseeability test may seem straightforward to apply, but it is not. The reason is that in cases where the courts have applied the foreseeability test to determine whether a loss suffered by a claimant was a remote consequence of a defendant's tort, they have emphasised that neither 'the precise *manner* [in] which the injury occurred nor its *extent* [have] to be foreseeable.'[3] So what does have to be foreseen? In *Jolley* v *Sutton LBC* (2000), Lord Hoffmann observed that

> what must have been [foreseeable] is not the precise injury that occurred but injury of a given description. The foreseeability is not as to the particulars but the genus. And the description is formulated by reference to the nature of the risk which ought to have been foreseen.[4]

But the courts enjoy a great deal of leeway in determining *how to describe* what type of injury could have been reasonably foreseen would result from the defendant's tort.

In *Jolley* v *Sutton LBC* itself, a council owned a piece of amenity land near a block of flats. A boat had been left lying on this land for about two years. The boat was in a poor condition and anyone playing about on the boat was liable to put a foot through the rotten timbers of the boat and suffer an injury. Given this – and given the fact that children playing on the amenity land were liable to clamber onto the boat and run the risk of being injured – the council owed children going onto the amenity land a duty under the Occupiers' Liability Act 1957 to take reasonable steps to remove the boat from the land. The council breached this duty when they did nothing about the boat for two years. In that time, the claimant and a friend of his – two 14-year-old children – saw the boat and decided to repair it; they had a wild dream that if they did this, they would one day be able to go sailing in it. They used a car jack to elevate one side of the boat and, crawling underneath, repaired some of the holes in the hull of the boat. Unfortunately, one day when the claimant was working under the boat, the car jack gave way and the boat fell on the claimant's back, causing him severe spinal injuries. The claimant sued the council for damages. The case turned on whether the claimant's injuries were a remote consequence of the council's admitted negligence under the foreseeability test.

Now whether or not you think that the foreseeability test was satisfied here will depend a great deal on how you describe what kind of loss it was reasonably foreseeable might be suffered if the council left the boat on its land. If we say that the type of loss was simply 'Physical injury from meddling with the boat', then the foreseeability test was plainly satisfied here: the claimant suffered that kind of loss here as a result of the council's breach of the duty of care it owed him. However, if we say that it was only reasonably foreseeable that leaving the boat on the council land would result in 'Physical injury from the boat's rotting floorboards giving way' then the foreseeability test was not satisfied in *Jolley*: the claimant did *not* suffer that kind of loss as a result of the council's breach of the duty of care it owed him. The trial judge and the House of Lords adopted the first description of

---

[3] *Jolley* v *Sutton LBC* [2000] 1 WLR 1082, 1090 (per Lord Steyn).
[4] [2000] 1 WLR 1082, 1091.

what kind of loss it was reasonably foreseeable might be suffered as a result of the council's negligence in leaving the boat on its land, and allowed the claimant's claim for damages. In contrast, the Court of Appeal adopted the second description of what kind of loss it was reasonably foreseeable would be suffered if the council left the boat on its land, and as a result dismissed the claimant's claim for damages.[5] What accounts for the difference?

At a formal level, we determine whether it was reasonably foreseeable that a defendant's tort would result in a claimant suffering a particular type of loss by asking whether at the time the defendant acted, there was a 'real risk' that the claimant would suffer that kind of loss as a result of the defendant's conduct. A risk that a reasonable person would have brushed off as 'fantastic or far-fetched' will not satisfy this requirement.[6] It may be that the trial judge and the House of Lords thought that a reasonable person in the position of the defendant council would have recognised that if they left the boat on their land, there was a real risk that a child like the claimant could be injured in more ways as a result of being attracted to the boat than by simply putting his leg through a rotting floorboard; whereas the Court of Appeal may have been less imaginative in its approach to the question of what risks of injury a reasonable person in the position of the council could have foreseen.

However, it may be that the *only* real risk in this situation was that a child like the claimant would put his foot through a rotting floorboard in clambering over the boat, but sympathy for the claimant and the fact that the council was a 'deep pockets' defendant may have led the trial judge and the House of Lords to describe *that* risk in relatively wide terms – 'It was reasonably foreseeable that someone like the claimant would suffer physical injury from meddling with the boat' – so as to enable the claimant's injury to slip under the foreseeability test.

Something like this seems to have happened in *Hughes v Lord Advocate* (1963), where the defendants opened a manhole in the street in order to work on some telephone cables, about nine feet under the road. A paraffin lamp provided them some illumination in doing their work. The area around the manhole was covered by a tent. The defendants went for a 15 minute tea break at 5 pm. They left the manhole open and the tent around the manhole unattended. The claimant – another child, this time eight years old – took advantage of the defendants' absence to enter the tent and see what was inside. The defendants had owed the claimant a duty of care not to leave the tent unattended because it was reasonably foreseeable that someone like the claimant would be attracted into the tent, and might fall into the hole, or be burned by the paraffin lamp being knocked over, or some combination of these events. What *actually* happened was something that could not have been foreseen. The claimant stumbled over the lamp, knocking it into the hole. The lamp broke, and paraffin vapour escaping from the lamp ignited through contact with the lamp flame, creating an explosion that threw the claimant into the hole, where he was severely burned.

The House of Lords held that it did not matter that the *manner* in which the claimant was injured was unforeseeable. Instead, they adopted a wide definition of the kind of risk of harm that it could be foreseen the claimant was exposed to in this case – 'It was reasonably foreseeable that leaving the tent unattended would result in a child like the claimant suffering burns from playing about in the tent' – which allowed the injuries that the claimant did suffer in this case to slip under the foreseeability test.

[5] [1998] 1 WLR 1546.
[6] *The Wagon Mound (No 2)* [1967] 1 AC 617, 641–2 (per Lord Reid).

Lord Reid held that it was enough that 'The accident was caused by a known source of danger'[7] (the lamp). Lord Jenkins thought that distinguishing between injuries due to burning (foreseeable) and injuries due to explosion (unforeseeable) involved drawing a 'distinction ... [that] is too fine to warrant acceptance.'[8] He thought that what was reasonably foreseeable in this case was 'a danger of fire of some kind' and so the claimant's injuries fell within the range of injuries that were reasonably foreseeable consequences of the defendants' leaving the tent unattended. Lord Morris held that:

> it could reasonably have been foreseen that a boy who played in and about the canvas shelter and played with things that were thereabouts might get hurt and might in some way burn himself. That is just what happened. The [claimant] did burn himself, though his burns were more grave than would have been expected. The fact that the features or developments of an accident may not reasonably have been foreseen does not mean that the accident itself was not foreseeable. The [claimant] was ... injured as a result of the type or kind of accident or occurrence that could reasonably have been foreseen.[9]

Lord Guest agreed that it would be wrong in this case to say that the accident here was of a type that was not reasonably foreseeable: 'An explosion is only one way in which burning can be caused. Burning can also be caused by the contact between liquid paraffin and a naked flame. In the one case paraffin vapour and in the other case liquid paraffin is ignited by fire. I cannot see that these are two different types of accident.'[10] Lord Pearce also took the view that the fact that the claimant's burns were caused by an explosion was irrelevant: 'The resulting damage, though severe, was not greater than or different in kind from that which might have been produced had the lamp spilled and produced a more normal conflagration in the hole.'[11]

In other cases not involving children, the courts have not been so expansive in defining the type of loss that it was reasonably foreseeable a claimant might suffer as a result of a defendant's tort.

In *Doughty* v *Turner Manufacturing Co* (1964), the defendants' factory contained two cauldrons full of molten liquid; the defendants' employees would dip metal parts into the cauldron to heat them up. Each cauldron had an asbestos cover that would sit on top of the cauldron, to conserve its heat. The claimant was injured when one of the asbestos covers was carelessly knocked into the cauldron on which it was sitting: the molten liquid unexpectedly reacted with the asbestos and exploded, and the claimant – who was standing nearby – was severely burned as a result. The Court of Appeal was doubtful whether anyone had been negligent in this case (given that it was unforeseeable that knocking the asbestos cover into the cauldron would result in an explosion) but held that even if negligence were made out, the claimant would still not be able to recover for his injuries as it was not reasonably foreseeable that knocking the asbestos cover into the cauldron would result in the claimant suffering the kind of injury that he did. While it was reasonably foreseeable that knocking the asbestos cover into the cauldron might result in the claimant being burned from molten liquid splashing on him, 'it would be quite unrealistic to describe this accident as a variant of the perils from splashing.'[12]

---

[7] [1963] AC 837, 847.
[8] [1963] AC 837, 850.
[9] [1963] AC 837, 852.
[10] [1963] AC 837, 856.
[11] [1963] AC 837, 858.
[12] [1964] 1 QB 518, 527 (per Lord Pearce).

In *Tremain* v *Pike* (1969), the claimant worked for the defendant on a farm that had a rat infestation. He contracted Weil's Disease from handling hay on which the rats had urinated. The judge trying the claimant's claim for damages was – like the Court of Appeal in *Doughty* – doubtful whether the defendant had been negligent in failing to take steps to control the rat infestation on the farm. But the judge went on to say that even if negligence could be established, the claimant could still not sue for damages for contracting Weil's Disease as Weil's Disease did not fall within the class of injuries that it was reasonably foreseeable the claimant might suffer as a result of a rat infestation:

> The kind of damage suffered here was a disease contracted by contact with rats' urine. This, in my view, was entirely different in kind from the effect of a rat bite, or food poisoning by the consumption of food or drink contaminated by rats. I do not accept that all illness or infection arising from an infestation of rats should be regarded as of the same kind.[13]

It should be clear from the above cases that the foreseeability test for remoteness of damage is not a self-executing test. Judges enjoy some freedom of manoeuvre in characterising what type of harm was a reasonably foreseeable consequence of the defendant's tort. This, and the fact that any finding as to whether the foreseeability test is satisfied in a given case will always turn on a detailed scrutiny of the facts of that case,[14] means that cases like those we have discussed above provide very limited guidance as to whether the foreseeability test will be satisfied in a particular case. As Lord Steyn observed in the *Jolley* case: '[In] this corner of the law the results of decided cases are inevitably very fact-sensitive. Both counsel nevertheless at times invited your Lordships to compare the facts of the present case with the facts of other decided cases. That is a sterile exercise.'[15]

We will now turn to note a number of exceptions that exist to the foreseeability test for remoteness of damage.

[13] [1969] 1 WLR 1556, 1561 (per Payne J).
[14] An example of a situation where this was true is provided by the *Wagon Mound* litigation. The litigation arose out of a fire that started when the defendants negligently allowed a lot of oil to spill into Sydney Harbour. The oil spread and drifted close to the first claimants' wharf, where the first claimants were doing some welding work on a ship called the *Corrimal*, which belonged to the second claimants. A piece of molten metal from the welding work dropped into the oil and set it on fire. The wharf and the *Corrimal* suffered severe fire damage. The first claimants sued the defendants in negligence for compensation for the fire damage done to their wharf in *Overseas Tankship (UK) Ltd* v *Morts Dock & Engineering Co Ltd, The Wagon Mound* [1961] AC 388. Their claim failed because it was held that it was not reasonably foreseeable at the time that if the defendants spilled any oil into the harbour it would ignite and set the first claimants' wharf on fire. (Why then did the defendants owe the first claimants a duty to take care that they did not spill any oil into the harbour? The reason is that it *was* reasonably foreseeable that if the defendants spilled any oil into the harbour it would spread and foul the first claimants' wharf.) When the second claimants subsequently sued the defendants for compensation for the fire damage done to the *Corrimal* (in *Overseas Tankship (UK) Ltd* v *Miller Steamship Co Pty, The Wagon Mound (No 2)* [1967] 1 AC 617) they introduced a lot of scientific evidence to show that it *was* reasonably foreseeable at the time the defendants spilled the oil into Sydney Harbour that it could ignite and start a fire. As a result, they convinced the courts that the fire damage to the *Corrimal* was a reasonably foreseeable consequence of the nuisance the defendants created by spilling oil into Sydney Harbour. Why didn't the first claimants press this evidence on the courts in the original *Wagon Mound* case? Two reasons can be given. First, they did not think that they had to: they assumed that if they showed that the defendants were negligent, the defendants would be held liable for *all* the losses that were a *direct* result of the defendants' negligence, however unforeseeable. This was the rule laid down by the Court of Appeal in *Re Polemis* [1921] 3 KB 560. This rule was, however, overturned in the first *Wagon Mound* case, with the Privy Council ruling that a negligent defendant could not be held liable for a loss suffered by a claimant if that loss was not a reasonably foreseeable consequence of the defendant's negligence. Secondly, it would have harmed the first claimants' claim for compensation if they had admitted that it was reasonably foreseeable that the oil that the defendants spilled into Sydney Harbour could ignite. If it *was* reasonably foreseeable, then the first claimants would have been partly to blame for the fire damage done to their wharf, having carried on doing welding work on the *Corrimal* while oil was lapping around their wharf. And if the first claimants were partly to blame for the fire damage done to their wharf, the damages payable to compensate them for that fire damage would have been reduced on the grounds of contributory negligence.
[15] [2000] 1 WLR 1082, 1089.

A. The eggshell skull rule[16]

This rule (otherwise known as the '*thin skull rule*') says that if it was foreseeable that A would suffer some kind of physical injury as a result of B's tort, but because A has a pre-existing condition, A suffers a much worse injury as a result of B's tort, that much worse injury will *not* count as a remote consequence of B's tort.

In *Smith* v *Leech Brain* (1962), the defendant employed the claimant's husband to work with molten metal. Due to the defendant's failure to take adequate measures to protect the claimant's husband, he was struck on the lip by a piece of molten metal. The ensuing burn caused the tissues in the husband's lip to turn cancerous and the husband eventually died from the cancer. The claimant brought a wrongful death action against the defendant. It was held that the husband's death was not a remote consequence of the defendant's negligence. It had been reasonably foreseeable that the husband would suffer some kind of physical injury as a result of the defendant's negligence, and he ended up suffering a much worse injury because he had a pre-existing condition.

The same rule applies to cases where the victim of a tort has what is sometimes called an 'eggshell personality' and develops a very serious psychiatric illness as a result of that tort being committed when only a much less serious psychiatric illness was foreseeable. In such a case the very serious psychiatric illness will *not* count as a remote consequence of the defendant's tort.

For example, in *Brice* v *Brown* (1984), the claimant was involved in a car accident that was caused by the defendants' negligence. The claimant had suffered from a hysterical personality disorder from early childhood and developed a severe mental illness as a result of the accident. Stuart Smith J held that the claimant's illness was not a remote consequence of the defendants' negligence even though it had not been reasonably foreseeable that the claimant would suffer a psychiatric illness as severe as the one she developed as a result of the accident in which she was involved. It was enough that it had been reasonably foreseeable that the claimant would develop *a* psychiatric illness as a result of the accident.[17]

B. Economic loss consequent on physical injury

A rule analogous to the eggshell skull rule says that if A has committed a tort in relation to B, and B has suffered some kind of physical injury as a result, if B can recover compensation for the physical injury that she has suffered as a result of A's tort, B will be able to sue A for compensation in respect of *any* loss of income or other economic losses flowing from that injury whether or not those economic losses were a foreseeable consequence of A's tort. Scrutton LJ made the point graphically in *The Arpad*:

> In the cases of claims in tort, damages are constantly given for consequences of which the defendant had no notice. You negligently run down a shabby-looking man in the street, and he turns out to be a millionaire engaged in a very profitable business which the accident disables him from carrying on [you will be held liable for the economic loss so caused].[18]

---

[16] For an excellent discussion, see Stigglebout 2009.

[17] It should be noted that nowadays, under the House of Lords' ruling in *Page* v *Smith* [1996] AC 155 (discussed above, § 6.1, and below) the claimant would not even need to show that it was reasonably foreseeable that she would suffer a psychiatric illness as a result of being involved in the accident: it would be enough for her to show that it was reasonably foreseeable that she would suffer some kind of physical injury as a result.

[18] [1934] P 189, 202. To the same effect, see *Smith* v *London and South Western Railway Co.* (1870) LR 6 CP 14, 22–3 (per Blackburn J).

The same rule does not apply in property damage cases. *However*, if you negligently damage someone else's property, you must compensate them for the full value of that property, no matter how unforeseeable it might have been that that property would be worth that much. As Scrutton LJ went on to observe in *The Arpad*, if 'you negligently and ignorantly injure the favourite for the Derby'[19] you have to compensate the owner of *that* horse for the damage done to *that* horse, even though you may have had 'no notice' of its value at the time it was injured. Consider, for example, the **Hollywood Dog Problem**:

> *Trainer* owns a dog that is used in a lot of TV series and films because it is so well-trained. *Trainer* earns about £3m a year from allowing his dog to be used in this way. One day, *Unlucky* carelessly runs the dog down in the street as it is crossing the road.

In this case, *Trainer* might not be able to sue directly for the loss of the £3m a year income resulting from his dog's death: that economic loss was an unforeseeable consequence of the dog being killed. But what he can do is sue for damages to compensate him for the loss of his dog, and those damages will equal the value of the dog. Given that the dog was capable of producing an income stream of £3m a year, that value will have been considerable, and would have run into millions of pounds.

C. *Page* v *Smith* (1996)[20]

In this case, the defendant negligently ran into the claimant's car while the claimant was in it. As a result,[21] the claimant developed chronic fatigue syndrome (CFS).[22] The House of Lords held, by a bare majority, that the claimant's CFS was *not* a remote consequence of the defendant's negligence. Two of the Law Lords who made up the majority in *Page* v *Smith* held that it was reasonably foreseeable at the time the defendant negligently ran into the claimant's car that if he did so the claimant would develop a psychiatric illness as a result.[23] But they *also* expressed their agreement with the opinion of Lord Lloyd, the third member of the majority, and *he* said that the claimant would be entitled to recover for his psychiatric illness even if it was *not* reasonably foreseeable at the time the defendant crashed into the claimant's car that the claimant would suffer a psychiatric illness as a result.[24]

Lord Lloyd's view is hard to justify. He seemed to take the view that even if the claimant's psychiatric illness was not a reasonably foreseeable consequence of the defendant's negligence, the claimant's psychiatric illness would *not* count as a remote consequence of the defendant's negligence under the foreseeability test because psychiatric illness counts as a form of physical injury[25] and it *was* reasonably foreseeable that the claimant would suffer

---

[19] [1934] P 189, 202–3.

[20] For discussion, see Bailey and Nolan 2010.

[21] It was found in *Page* v *Smith (No 2)* [1996] 1 WLR 855 that the claimant's CFS was indeed attributable to his being involved in the crash.

[22] The collision was quite trivial but the claimant – having suffered from CFS in the past – was liable to develop CFS again as a result of incidents such as these.

[23] [1996] AC 155, 170 (per Lord Ackner), 181–2 (per Lord Browne-Wilkinson).

[24] Though he too thought that at the time the defendant crashed into the claimant's car, it was reasonably foreseeable that the claimant would develop a psychiatric illness as a result: [1996] AC 155, at 197. The two dissenting Law Lords in *Page* v *Smith* thought that the crash had not been serious enough as to make it reasonably foreseeable that the claimant would suffer a psychiatric illness as a result: [1996] AC 155, at 169–70 (per Lord Keith of Kinkel), 180 (per Lord Jauncey of Tullichettle).

[25] [1996] AC 155, at 197: 'There is no justification for regarding physical and psychiatric injury as "different kinds of damage".'

that kind of loss if the defendant crashed into the claimant's car.[26] However, it is hard to see why we should treat psychiatric illnesses and physical injuries as being the same kind of loss in this context when in almost every other context we recognise that there is a distinction between them.[27] Perhaps recognising this, the courts have made it clear that *Page* v *Smith* will only apply in cases where a claimant's psychiatric illness was triggered by the experience of being almost injured by a defendant's negligence.[28]

D. Intentional torts

The foreseeability test for determining whether the loss suffered by the victim of a tort was a remote consequence of that tort does not seem to apply to cases where someone commits an *intentional* tort.

An intentional tort is *not* a tort that is committed intentionally. An intentional tort is a tort that can *only* be committed intentionally – that is, by someone who knows what he or she is doing. So the torts we have looked at so far – negligence, assault, battery, and false imprisonment – are examples of *non-intentional torts*. All these torts can be committed unintentionally or inadvertently.[29] So are private nuisance and defamation. In contrast, malicious falsehood is an example of an intentional tort: it can only be committed intentionally – by *maliciously* making a false statement about someone to a third party which results in that someone suffering loss. Other examples of intentional torts are: the intentional infliction of harm using unlawful means, conspiracy, deceit and malicious prosecution.

The cases indicate that the foreseeability test applies to determine what losses are a remote consequence of a defendant's tort when the tort that the defendant has committed is a non-intentional one.[30] But a different remoteness rule applies where the defendant's tort is an intentional one. This remoteness rule goes as follows. If A has committed an intentional tort in relation to B and B has suffered some kind of loss as a result, that loss

---

[26] That was after all the main reason why the defendant owed the claimant a duty to take care not to run into his car in the first place.

[27] See above, § 6.4.

[28] See above, § 6.1. Though see *Essa* v *Laing* [2004] EWCA Civ 2, where the defendant committed the statutory tort of racial discrimination (discussed below, § 22.6) in relation to the claimant and the claimant suffered a psychiatric illness as a result. Held, on the basis of *Page* v *Smith*, that the claimant could sue for damages in respect of his psychiatric illness even if it was not a foreseeable consequence of the defendant's tort: it was enough that it was reasonably foreseeable that the claimant would suffer distress as a result of the defendant's tort. Rix LJ dissented on this point. Also see *Donachie* v *Chief Constable of Greater Manchester* [2004] EWCA Civ 405, where *Page* v *Smith* was applied to allow a claimant police officer to sue for the hypertension that he had suffered as a result of being made by the defendants to make nine trips to a suspect's car to attach a tagging device to the underside of the car (the tagging device was faulty and it took nine trips to make it work). It was held that the defendants had owed the claimant a duty of care not to make him make so many trips to the car because it was reasonably foreseeable that he would suffer some kind of physical injury at the hands of the suspect if he were made to do so. It was held that the claimant could sue for the psychiatric illness that he had suffered as a result of the defendants' breach of this duty of care even though it was not foreseeable that he would suffer such an illness as a result of the defendants' breach; it was enough that it was reasonably foreseeable that the claimant would suffer some kind of physical injury as a result of the defendants' carelessness.

[29] Though of course they can also be committed intentionally. See above, § 4.2, for a discussion of whether the tort of negligence can be committed intentionally.

[30] See *Overseas Tankship (UK) Ltd* v *Morts Dock & Engineering Co Ltd, The Wagon Mound* [1961] AC 388 (negligence); *Overseas Tankship (UK) Ltd* v *Miller Steamship Co Pty, The Wagon Mound (No 2)* [1967] 1 AC 617 (nuisance); *Slipper* v *British Broadcasting Corpn* [1991] 1 QB 283 (libel).

will *not* have been a remote consequence of A's tort if it was a *direct*[31] consequence of A's tort.[32] So A may be held liable to compensate B for the loss she has suffered even if it was *not* reasonably foreseeable at the time A committed his tort that B would suffer that kind of loss as a result. Why is this? Why do the courts treat people who commit unintentional torts more favourably than they do people who commit intentional torts?

The reason must be that the courts recognise that people can commit non-intentional torts quite innocently, and accordingly attempt to ensure that the liability of someone who commits a non-intentional tort does not get out of all proportion to his fault for committing that tort. In contrast, someone who commits an intentional tort will always be very wicked and there is no reason why we should try to put a limit on such a person's liabilities. Accordingly, someone who commits an intentional tort will be held liable for all the losses that were suffered by the victim of his tort as a direct result of that tort being committed – however unforeseeable those losses were.

Of course, if A has *deliberately* committed a non-intentional tort, it is hard to see why the courts should treat him any more indulgently than it does people who commit intentional torts. Given this, there is a strong case for saying that the remoteness rule which applies to people who commit intentional torts should also be applied to people who deliberately commit non-intentional torts.[33] Under this approach, if A has deliberately committed a non-intentional tort in relation to B and B has suffered some kind of loss as a direct result of A's committing that tort, that loss would not be a remote consequence of A's tort – even if it was not reasonably foreseeable that B would suffer that kind of loss when A committed his tort.

There is some authority in favour of the view that the remoteness rule that applies to people who commit intentional torts should also be applied to people who intentionally commit non-intentional torts. Lord Nicholls indicated he thought that a defendant who intentionally converted another's goods should be held liable for all the losses suffered by that other as a direct result of the defendant's act of conversion in *Kuwait Airways Corpn* v *Iraqi Airways Co (Nos 4 & 5)*:

> as the law now stands, the tort of conversion may cause hardship for innocent persons. This suggests that foreseeability, as the more restrictive test [for remoteness of damage], is appropriate for those who act in good faith. Liability remains strict, but liability for consequential loss is confined to types of damages which can be expected to arise from the wrongful conduct . . .
>
> Persons who knowingly convert another's goods stand differently. Such persons are acting dishonestly. I can see no good reason why the remoteness test of 'directly and naturally' applied in cases of deceit should not apply in cases of conversion where the defendant acted dishonestly.[34]

---

[31] 'Direct' here probably means 'without the intervention of any other cause'. So the fire damage that resulted from the defendant's parking his car without authority in the claimants' car park in *Mayfair Ltd* v *Pears* [1987] 1 NZLR 459 (discussed below, § 14.6, fn 50) was not a direct consequence of the defendant's intentional trespass on the claimants' land: the defendant's trespass only resulted in the claimants' car park suffering fire damage because the car caught on fire.

[32] *Doyle* v *Olby (Ironmongers) Ltd* [1969] 2 QB 158 and *Smith New Court* v *Scrimgeour Vickers (Asset Management) Ltd* [1997] AC 254 confirm that this is the position in relation to the tort of deceit. Lord Lindley confirmed that this is the position in regard to conspiracy in *Quinn* v *Leathem* [1901] AC 495, 527.

[33] See Gordley 1998.

[34] [2002] 2 AC 883, at [103]–[104]. The New Zealand Court of Appeal held in *Mayfair Ltd* v *Pears* [1987] 1 NZLR 459 that a defendant who intentionally trespasses on another's land should be held liable for all the losses suffered by that other as a direct result of the defendant's trespass. See also Pill LJ's judgment in *Essa* v *Laing* [2004] EWCA Civ 2, discussed below.

E. Statutory torts

In *Essa* v *Laing* (2004), the Court of Appeal held that if A has committed a tort by breaching a statutory duty owed to B and B has suffered some kind of loss as a result, the foreseeability test will *not* necessarily apply to determine whether the loss suffered by B was a remote consequence of A's tort. To see whether the test will apply or not, one simply has to interpret the Act or Regulations that created the statutory duty breached by A.[35]

In *Essa*, the defendant committed a tort under the Race Relations Act 1976 by racially abusing the claimant. The claimant developed a psychiatric illness as a result of the abuse he had suffered. Pill and Clarke LJJ held that – given the language of, and policy underlying, the 1976 Act – the foreseeability test should *not* be applied to determine whether the claimant's psychiatric illness was a remote consequence of the defendant's tort. It seems that Pill LJ might have taken a different view had the defendant's tort been committed unintentionally,[36] whereas Clarke LJ took the view that the foreseeability test should *never* apply in race discrimination cases. The third judge in the *Essa* case – Rix LJ – thought that the foreseeability test should apply in race discrimination cases: there was no reason to adopt a more relaxed remoteness rule given that a tort can be committed under the 1976 Act even if one has no intention of doing so.[37]

In the subsequent case of *Jones* v *Ruth* (2011), the Court of Appeal had to decide what remoteness rule would apply in cases where a defendant harassed a claimant, contrary to the Protection from Harassment Act 1997. The Court held that in such a case, the claimant could recover for harm suffered as a result of the harassment even if it was not foreseeable. In reaching this conclusion, Patten LJ placed stress on two factors: (a) there was nothing in the provisions of the 1997 Act that suggested that damage had to be foreseeable before it would be actionable under the Act; and (b) harassment is a form of 'deliberate conduct of a kind which the defendant knows or ought to know will amount to harassment of the claimant.'[38]

10.3 SCOPE OF DUTY

We said above that the reason why the courts have adopted the foreseeability test for remoteness of damage in non-intentional tort cases is to help ensure that a tortfeasor's liability does not get out of all proportion to his fault. As Viscount Simonds observed in *The Wagon Mound* (1961) (the first tort case to adopt the foreseeability test for remoteness of damage):

> it does not seem consonant with current ideas of justice or morality that for an act of negligence, however slight or venial, which results in some trivial foreseeable damage the actor should be liable for all consequences however unforeseeable and however grave, so long as they can be said to be 'direct'. It is a principle of civil liability . . . that a man must be considered to be responsible for the probable consequences of his act. To demand more of him is too harsh a rule . . .[39]

---

[35] [2004] EWCA Civ 2, at [46], [48] (per Clarke LJ).
[36] [2004] EWCA Civ 2, at [39].
[37] [2004] EWCA Civ 2, at [98], [105]. Rix LJ was unenthusiastic (at [106]) about the idea that the foreseeability test should apply in cases of non-intentional racial discrimination but not in cases of intentional race discrimination.
[38] [2011] EWCA Civ 804, at [32].
[39] [1961] AC 388, 423.

However, Viscount Simonds' judgment identified an *additional* reason why, in a negligence case at least, a defendant's liability should be limited to the reasonably foreseeable consequences of his actions:

> Just as . . . there is no such thing as negligence in the air, so there is no such thing as liability in the air. Suppose an action brought by A for damage caused by the carelessness (a neutral word) of B, for example, a fire caused by the careless spillage of oil. It may, of course, become relevant to know what duty B owed to A, but the only liability that is in question is the liability for damage by fire. It is vain to isolate the liability from its context and to say that B is or is not liable, and then to ask for what damage he is liable . . . If . . . B liability's (culpability) depends on the reasonable foreseeability of the consequent damage, how is that to be determined except by the foreseeability of the damage which in fact happened – the damage in suit?[40]

Some find these words of Viscount Simonds hard to understand. But they seem to suggest that loss suffered as a result of a breach of a duty of care is not actionable unless that duty of care was imposed in order to help ensure that the claimant would not suffer that kind of loss. So it is useless for A to establish that B owed him a duty of care not to do *x* because it was reasonably foreseeable that B's doing *x* would cause A to suffer one kind of loss, if A actually suffered a quite different loss as a result of B's breach. A must show that B's duty of care not to do *x* was imposed on her because it was reasonably foreseeable that B's doing *x* would cause A to suffer the kind of loss that she *actually* suffered. But A will not be able to do this if it was, in fact, *not* reasonably foreseeable that B's actions would result in A suffering *that kind of loss*. In such a case, the loss suffered by A will be outside the scope of whatever duty of care B did owe A, and therefore non-actionable.[41]

We have already seen, in looking at the law of negligence, plenty of examples of this principle, that a loss will be non-actionable if the duty of care that the defendant owed the claimant, and breached, was not geared towards protecting the claimant from suffering that kind of loss:

First, if A carelessly causes B to be crushed to death, but before she dies she does not suffer any physical injury, but simply pure distress, the distress is not actionable: *Hicks* v *Chief Constable of South Yorkshire* (1992). The duty of care A will have owed B, and breached, in this case was imposed on A to help ensure she did not suffer physical injury, not to help her avoid being distressed.

Secondly, if A carelessly shuts off the power to B's factory, and the power cut has two independent effects – damaging some products B was processing at the time of the power cut, and preventing B doing any further work – the damage to the products will be actionable, but not the pure economic loss resulting from B's not being able to do any more work: *Spartan Steel & Co Ltd* v *Martin* (1973). The duty of care A will have owed B in this case was imposed on A in order to help ensure his property was not harmed, not in order to prevent B's business being interfered with.

Thirdly, if A carelessly constructs a dangerously defective building, and B – a subsequent occupier of the building – has to spend money having the building made safe, B will not be able to sue A in negligence for compensation for the money he has spent if there is no *Hedley Byrne*-type relationship between A and B: *D & F Estates* v *Church Commissioners* (1989), *Murphy* v *Brentwood DC* (1991). In the absence of an 'assumption of responsibility'

---

[40] [1961] AC 388, 425.

[41] See, to the same effect, Lord Hoffmann in *Jolley* v *Sutton LBC* [2000] 1 WLR 1082, 1091: 'unless the injury [suffered by the claimant] is of a description which was reasonably foreseeable, it is (according to taste) "outside the scope of the duty" or "too remote".' See also Machin 1954 and Stauch 2001, both of whom advance 'scope of duty'-type arguments in favour of a foreseeability test of remoteness in negligence.

by A to B for the quality of his building work, the only duty of care A will have owed B, and breached, (a duty to take care not to construct a dangerously defective building, arising under *Donoghue v Stevenson*) in this situation will have been imposed on A to help ensure that B's person and property was not harmed from A's building falling down, not in order to help ensure that B would not have to spend money making A's building safe.[42]

Fourthly, if A carelessly exposes B to excessive quantities of asbestos dust, but B has not yet suffered any physical ill effects from this, B will not be allowed to sue A for the chance that he might develop an asbestos-related disease in the future: *Rothwell v Chemical & Insulating Co Ltd* (2006, CA). The duty of care A will have owed B in this case (to take reasonable steps to see that B's place of work is a safe place to work in) was imposed on A to help ensure that B did not suffer physical injury, not in order to maximise B's chances of avoiding physical injury in the future.

Now – suppose that A's breach of a duty of care that he owes B results in B suffering some kind of loss L that A's duty of care *was* designed to help ensure that B did not suffer. In suing A for compensation for loss L, B will *also* be entitled to sue A for compensation for *any consequential losses* flowing from loss L, so long as those losses are not too remote a consequence of A's negligence. This is so even if those consequential losses are of a different type from loss L.

For example, if *Driver* negligently runs over *Pedestrian*, and *Pedestrian's* knee is dislocated as a result, *Pedestrian* will not only be entitled to sue for the physical injury he has suffered as a result of *Driver's* negligence, but also the chance that because his knee has been dislocated, he might develop arthritis in the future. The fact that a loss of a chance of avoiding physical injury in future is a very different kind of loss from actual physical injury does not matter in this context: because, in this case, the loss of a chance of avoiding an arthritic knee in future flows from the injury to *Pedestrian's* knee, the loss of that chance can be sued for as part of *Pedestrian's* claim to be compensated for the injury to his knee.

In *Attia v British Gas* (1988), the defendants were installing some central heating in the claimant's home. In the course of so doing, they negligently started a fire. It took fireman four hours to get the fire under control, and the house and its contents suffered extensive damage. While the fire was blazing away, the claimant came home and saw what was happening. She claimed to have developed a psychiatric illness as a result of the shock of seeing her house going up in flames. The Court of Appeal held that so long as the claimant's psychiatric illness was a reasonably foreseeable consequence of the defendants' negligence, it was actionable. The decision can be supported on the basis that the defendants had owed

---

[42] The position taken by the House of Lords in *Murphy* and *D & F Estates* is not without its critics (see, for example, Cooke 1991; Fleming 1997, 59–60) and it is clear that in other common law jurisdictions B *would* be entitled to sue A in negligence for compensation for the cost of making the building safe, even in the absence of a special relationship between them: see *Bryan v Moloney* (1995) 182 CLR 609 (Australia); *Winnipeg Condominium Corporation No 36 v Bird Construction Co. Ltd* [1995] 1 SCR 85 (Canada). It may be that the criticism of the House of Lords' stance rests on a false premise. The critics say that in the situation we are considering B *ought* to be able to sue A for the money she has spent on making the building safe; *therefore* she ought to be able to sue A in *negligence*. But this assumes that the *only* cause of action available to B in this situation is a claim in negligence. There is no reason to think that this is true. See Moran 1997 for an interesting argument that B would be able to bring a claim in *restitution* against A to recover the money she has spent in making the building safe to live in; also Stevens 2007, 30–1. There are a number of American cases which support Moran's argument: see *City of New York v Keene Corp*, 505 NYS 2d 782 (1986) (aff'd, 513 NYS 2d 1004 (1987)) (claimants allowed to sue defendants in restitution for cost of removing potentially toxic asbestos which defendants had installed in claimants' schools); *Adams-Araphoe School District No 28-J v Celotex Corp*, 637 F Supp 1207 (1986) (ditto); *Drayton Public School District No 19 v WR Grace & Co*, 728 F Supp 1410 (1989) (ditto); *City of New York v Lead Industries Ass'n, Inc*, 644 NYS 2d 919 (1996) (claimants allowed to sue manufacturers of potentially toxic paint in restitution for cost of removing paint from their city buildings).

the claimant a duty to take care not to set her house on fire, which duty was geared towards protecting the claimant's house and possessions from being damaged. The defendants' breach of this duty caused exactly the type of loss that the duty of care was designed to avoid – damage to the house and contents. In suing for compensation for the damage to the house and contents, the claimant could also recover for any non-remote consequential losses flowing from that damage. Provided the claimant's psychiatric illness was reasonably foreseeable, it counted as a non-remote consequential loss flowing from the damage done to her house and contents, and would therefore be actionable.

The principle of non-actionability under discussion here does not just apply in negligence cases, but across the board in all tort cases. We have already seen its application in a breach of statutory duty case, *Gorris v Scott* (1874), where the claimant was not allowed to sue for the loss of his sheep that resulted from the defendant's breach of statutory duty to keep them in pens while they were being transported by ship, because that duty was imposed on the defendant to stop disease spreading among the sheep, not to stop them being drowned. As the defendant's breach had resulted in the sheep drowning, and not becoming diseased, then the claimant's loss was non-actionable.

Another example of the same principle at work in the context of a breach of statutory duty is provided by the case of *Nicholls v F Austin (Leyton) Ltd* (1946), where the claimant was hit and injured by a piece of wood flying out of a piece of machinery that had been inadequately fenced, in breach of s 14(1) of the Factories Act 1937. It was held that the claimant could not sue her employer for damages because s 14(1) was designed to prevent the claimant coming into contact with dangerous machinery, not to prevent her being hit by something that had been ejected from a machine.

10.4 THE *SAAMCO* PRINCIPLE

The '*SAAMCO* principle' is an off-shoot of the idea, discussed in the previous section, that a loss will not be actionable if it falls outside the 'scope of the duty' that the defendant owed the claimant, and breached. The principle was introduced into the law in the case of *South Australia Asset Management Corp v York Montague Ltd* (1997)[43] – hence, '*SAAMCO*'. The principle affects how much A can sue B for by way of damages if A breaches a *Hedley Byrne*-type duty of care that A owed to B because he 'assumed a responsibility' to B.

The *SAAMCO* principle has been described as being 'easier to formulate than to apply'.[44] This is not true: the *SAAMCO* principle is *both* extremely difficult to formulate *and* extremely difficult to apply.[45] The basic idea behind it seems to go like this.[46] If A has 'assumed a responsibility' to B in performing some task, and as a result A owes B a duty of care in performing that task, B will only be able to sue for compensation for a loss caused

---

[43] Noted, O'Sullivan 1997a. The case is otherwise known as *Banque Bruxelles Lambert SA v Eagle Star Insurance Ltd*.

[44] *Nykredit Plc v Edward Erdman Ltd* [1997] 1 WLR 1627, 1631 (per Lord Nicholls).

[45] A couple of cases illustrate the difficulties that the courts have experienced in applying the *SAAMCO* principle. See *Platform Home Loans v Oyston Shipways Ltd* [2000] 2 AC 190 (discussed below, § 28.5(E)), where the House of Lords reversed a unanimous Court of Appeal's application of the *SAAMCO* principle, but not without dissent from one Law Lord (Lord Cooke); also *Aneco Reinsurance Underwriting Ltd v Johnson & Higgins Ltd* [2001] UKHL 51 where neither the House of Lords nor the Court of Appeal below could reach a unanimous decision as to how the *SAAMCO* principle applied in that case.

[46] For more detailed treatments of the *SAAMCO* principle and how it operates, see Dugdale 2000, Evans 2001, Peel 2003a; Butler 2003. The originator of the *SAAMCO* principle talks about it extra-judicially at Hoffmann 2005, 596.

by A's breach if A's 'assumption of responsibility' to B was designed to safeguard B from suffering that kind of loss.

In the *South Australia* case, Lord Hoffmann – the originator of the *SAAMCO* principle – gave an example of a situation where the principle would bite:

> A mountaineer about to undertake a difficult climb is concerned about the fitness of his knee. He goes to a doctor who negligently makes a superficial examination and pronounces the knee fit. The climber goes on the expedition, which he would not have undertaken if the doctor had told him the true state of his knee. He suffers an injury which is an entirely foreseeable consequence of mountaineering but has nothing to do with his knee.[47]

In this case, the doctor will have 'assumed a responsibility' to inspect the climber's knee properly, and will as a result have owed the climber a duty of care under *Hedley Byrne* to inspect the knee with a reasonable degree of care and skill. The climber has been injured (let's assume in an avalanche that he was caught up in) as result of the doctor's breach of this duty of care, in the sense that had the doctor inspected the knee properly, he would have told the climber that his knee was knackered, and the climber would have abandoned his plans to go mountaineering. But the injury suffered by the climber in this case was unrelated to the reason why the doctor 'assumed a responsibility' to the climber in the first place. The doctor 'assumed a responsibility' to the climber to safeguard the climber from suffering a knee-related injury while climbing. But the injury the climber suffered here was not knee-related, and therefore non-actionable under the *SAAMCO* principle.[48]

The *South Australia* case itself was concerned with the following kind of situation. *Customer* applies to *Bank* for a loan of £200,000 and offers certain properties – call them 'security properties' – as security for the loan. *Bank* gets *Surveyor* to value them and *Surveyor* values the properties as being worth £220,000. In fact, *Surveyor* failed to value the security properties with a professional degree of care and skill, thereby breaching the duty of care he owed *Bank* in valuing the properties. The security properties were in fact worth only £180,000. Unaware of this, *Bank* lends *Customer* the £200,000 requested. Come the time for repayment, *Customer* defaults on the loan. *Bank* then seeks to get his money back by selling the security properties but – due to a fall in the market – the properties are now worth only £110,000. So *Bank* makes a net loss of £90,000 on the loan – the difference between the value of the loan and what he has managed to claw back by selling the security properties.

Bank discovers that *Surveyor* was negligent in valuing the security properties and he sues *Surveyor* for compensation for the £90,000 he lost on the loan to *Customer*. *Bank* argues that if *Surveyor* had not been negligent, *Surveyor* would have told *Bank* that the security properties were worth only £180,000 and so *Bank* would not have loaned *Customer*

---

[47] [1997] AC 191, 213.

[48] There is another way of getting to this result. If we characterise the duty of care the doctor owed the climber in this case as a duty to take care not to tell the climber that his knee was sound when it was not, there were two ways the doctor could have discharged that duty: (1) he could have told the climber that his knee was not sound (in which case, the climber would not have gone on the expedition and would not have been injured); or (2) the doctor could have treated the knee and made it sound, before passing the climber as fit to climb (in which case, the climber would still have gone on the expedition and would still have been injured). Characterising the doctor's breach in the way that is most favourable to him (see above, § 9.2) we say that the doctor breached his duty to the climber in this case by failing to make his knee sound – and consequently find that the doctor's breach did *not* cause the climber to be injured, as that injury would still have been as it was even if the doctor had not breached his duty to the climber. Having said that, it is not possible to explain all instances of the application of the *SAAMCO* principle as resting on such reasoning: in a lot of the cases covered by *SAAMCO* there is only one way of characterising the defendant's breach of his duty of care.

anything – *Customer* would have been unable to offer him sufficient security for the loan. It follows that had *Surveyor* not been negligent, *Bank* would not have lost £90,000. However, *Bank* will only be able to sue *Surveyor* for *£40,000* in damages under the *SAAMCO* principle. Why is this? The reason is *Surveyor's* 'assumption of responsibility' to *Bank* was designed to safeguard *Bank* from suffering loss *as a result of lending money to Customer on inadequate security.*

Now – how much of the loss suffered by *Bank* here is suffered *because it lent money to Customer on inadequate security?* Well, the fact that *Bank* was willing to lend *Customer* £200,000 on security that was valued at £220,000 shows that it thought that security *worth that much* was adequate security for the loan. Had *Bank* lent *Customer* £200,000 on security worth that much, that security would have been worth £150,000 when the time came for *Customer* to repay. (We assume here that the security would have declined in value by £70,000 as a result of a fall in the market, just like the security properties that *Customer* actually offered to *Bank* as security for *Bank's* loan to him.) So had *Bank* lent money to *Customer* on adequate security, it would still have lost £50,000 on his loan to *Customer*. It follows that of the £90,000 loss suffered by *Bank* in this case, only £40,000 of that loss was suffered by it as a result of its lending money to *Customer on inadequate security*. So, under the *SAAMCO* principle, *Bank* will only be able to sue *Surveyor* for compensation for that £40,000 loss.[49]

A pre-*SAAMCO* case which can, in its result, be seen as giving effect to the *SAAMCO* principle is Caparo Industries plc v Dickman (1990). In that case, Caparo Industries plc were a company that held shares in Fidelity plc. Touche Ross, the defendants, audited Fidelity's accounts before they were circulated to Fidelity's shareholders. Touche Ross stated that the company's accounts gave a 'true and fair' representation of the company's financial position. This was not correct and Touche Ross should have known it. The accounts showed that Fidelity enjoyed a pre-tax profit of £1.3m. The true position was that Fidelity had suffered a loss of over £400,000. Caparo launched a takeover bid for Fidelity, relying on the fact that Touche Ross had given the company's accounts their seal of approval. The takeover bid was successful but when Caparo took a closer look at the books it discovered that it had paid too much for Fidelity.

Caparo sued Touche Ross in negligence, arguing that Touche had owed them, as one of Fidelity's shareholders, a duty of care in auditing the accounts. Had Touche not breached that duty of care, Caparo argued, Touche would have uncovered the truth about Fidelity's financial position and as a result Caparo would not have taken over Fidelity or Caparo would have paid a much smaller price for Fidelity. Caparo's claim for compensation was dismissed. It was conceded that Touche *had* owed Caparo a duty of care in auditing Fidelity's accounts – but Touche had only owed Caparo that duty *in their capacity as shareholders*. The loss that Caparo suffered as a result of Touche's negligence was suffered by Caparo in a quite different capacity – in their capacity as corporate raiders. Given this, Caparo could not sue Touche for compensation for the loss, by analogy to the rule that if

---

[49] It would have been different if the fall in the property market had been more modest: say the security properties were actually worth £170,000 when *Customer* defaulted, having been originally worth £180,000. In that case, *Bank's* loss on the loan would have come to £30,000 and the loss it would have suffered had it lent *Bank* £200,000 on adequate security (that is, security worth £220,000) would have been £0 – the security properties would have declined in value from £220,000 to £210,000 but that would still have afforded enough security to allow *Bank* to get back all the money that it loaned *Customer*. So *all* of the £30,000 loss suffered by *Bank* in this scenario would have been attributable to the fact that it loaned *Customer* money on inadequate security and *Surveyor* would therefore be liable to compensate *Bank in full* for the loss suffered by it as a result of *Surveyor's* negligence.

A commits a tort in relation to B and C suffers some kind of loss as a result, C will not normally be entitled to sue A for compensation for that loss. Touche committed a tort in relation to Caparo *qua* shareholders in auditing Fidelity's accounts but it was Caparo *qua* corporate raiders who suffered a loss as a result.

Nowadays, Caparo's claim for compensation could be dismissed by reference to the *SAAMCO* principle. When Touche 'assumed a responsibility' to Caparo and the other shareholders in Fidelity when auditing Fidelity's accounts, Touche did so in order to help Caparo and the other shareholders in Fidelity decide whether to reward or punish Fidelity's board of directors for their performance over the previous financial year. Touche's did *not* 'assume a responsibility' to Caparo in order to help ensure that Caparo did not bid too much for Fidelity on taking it over. So any losses suffered by Caparo in bidding too much for Fidelity were non-actionable under the *SAAMCO* principle.[50]

In light of this, let's now consider the **Misdiagnosed Patient Problem**:

> *Patient* visits *Doctor*, complaining of headaches. *Doctor* sends *Patient* for some scans and tells *Patient* that, sadly, her headaches are being caused by an inoperable and cancerous brain tumour. He tells her that she has, at most, six months to live. *Patient* reacts to this news by quitting her job and spending all her savings (£100,000) on holidays and extravagant parties for her friends. Six months later, *Patient* is still extremely healthy. Puzzled, *Patient* goes back to *Doctor* for another check-up. *Doctor* apologises and says that due to his mixing up *Patient*'s scans with *Another Patient*'s, he gave *Patient* the wrong diagnosis. He tells *Patient* that she is in fact completely healthy and that her headaches were probably due to watching too much television.

While *Patient* has suffered a considerable loss here as a result of *Doctor*'s breach of the duty of care he owed *Patient* to treat her with a reasonable degree of care and skill, it is strongly arguable that *Patient*'s loss is non-actionable under the *SAAMCO* principle. *Doctor* 'assumed a responsibility' to *Patient* in order to help *Patient* get better, not in order to help *Patient* decide how to spend her savings.[51]

A comparison can be drawn with the case of *Stevens* v *Bermondsey & Southwark Group Hospital Management Committee* (1963). In that case, the defendant's negligent diagnosis of the extent of the injuries suffered by the claimant as a result of a third party's negligence caused the claimant to settle his claim for damages against the third party for £125, when he would have been entitled to sue for much more. The claimant sued the defendant for the extra amount he would have demanded from the third party had the defendant not been negligent. It was held that the claimant's claim failed. The *SAAMCO* principle

---

[50] See also *Reeman* v *Department of Transport* [1997] 2 Lloyd's Rep 648, where the claimant bought a boat which had been certified as being seaworthy by the defendant. In fact, the boat was not seaworthy and was, as a result, practically valueless. The claimant's action for damages was dismissed: the defendant had been employed to determine whether or not it would be safe for people to travel on the boat, not to ensure that the claimant did not make a bad bargain in buying a boat. The *Caparo* case was distinguished in *Morgan Crucible Co plc* v *Hill Samuel & Co Ltd* [1991] Ch 295 where, it was claimed, the defendant representatives of a company made various representations to the claimants, who were thinking of taking over the company, as to the financial health of the company with the object of persuading the claimants to increase their bid for the company. The claimants subsequently discovered that they had bid too much for the company and sued for compensation. It was held that if these facts were made out, the claimants had an arguable claim against the defendants.

[51] In *Hedley Byrne & Co Ltd* v *Heller* [1964] AC 465, Lord Devlin suggested (at 517) that it would be 'nonsense' for the law not to give a remedy in the case where a doctor negligently advises a patient 'that he cannot safely pursue his occupation when in fact he can and he loses his livelihood'. (Our thanks to Sandy Steel for bringing this *dictum* to our attention.) Such a case would not, we think, be caught by the *SAAMCO* principle as the whole point of consulting the doctor here is to determine whether it would be a good idea for the patient to carry on working as he does, and the doctor's advice deprives him of the opportunity to carry on working when it would in fact be a good idea to carry on.

explains the result. The defendant 'assumed a responsibility' to the claimant in this case to help the claimant get better, not in order to help him determine how much he should sue a third party for by way of compensation for his injuries.

A more difficult case is presented by the **Second Misdiagnosed Patient Problem**:[52]

Patient visits Doctor, complaining of headaches. Doctor sends Patient for some scans and tells Patient that, sadly, her headaches are being caused by an inoperable and cancerous brain tumour. He tells her that she has, at most, six months to live. Patient does some research on the Internet and discovers that there is a group of doctors in the United States working on cures for the type of brain tumour that Doctor has diagnosed her as having. She requests Doctor to send her scans to the American doctors, and the doctors tell Patient that they are willing to treat her. Patient pays a deposit for her treatment, and travels to the United States at great expense. The American doctors examine Patient and tell her that she is perfectly healthy; Patient cannot recover the deposit for her treatment.

In this case, it is much more difficult to tell whether the economic losses suffered by *Patient* as a result of *Doctor*'s misdiagnosis are non-actionable under the *SAAMCO* principle. *Doctor* 'assumed a responsibility' to *Patient* to help *Patient* get better, and *Patient*'s expenses here have been incurred in an attempt to get better. But it is likely that a claim for these expenses will still fail under the *SAAMCO* principle. *Doctor* did not 'assume a responsibility' to *Patient* in order to save her money from consulting alternative doctors to obtain the treatment she needed. *Doctor*'s reasons for 'assuming a responsibility' to *Patient* were purely non-pecuniary in nature: they were to help *Patient* get better, and she is not physically in worse shape as a result of *Doctor*'s misdiagnosis.

10.5 WRONGFUL PREGNANCY/BIRTH

Suppose *Doctor* committed a tort in relation to *Mother* and *Mother* ended up giving birth to a child that she would not otherwise have had. This simple sentence covers a number of different situations:

(1) *Wrongful pregnancy.* *Mother* did not want to become pregnant, and *Doctor* 'assumed a responsibility' to *Mother* for sterilising her or her permanent partner. *Doctor* carelessly failed to carry out the sterilisation operation properly, with the result that *Mother* became pregnant and carried her baby *Son* to term.

(2) *Wrongful birth (1).* *Mother* becomes pregnant accidentally but *Doctor* fails to spot that she is pregnant in time for her to have an abortion, which she probably would have had, had she been told about her pregnancy in time.[53] *Mother* carries her baby *Son* to term.

(3) *Wrongful birth (2).* *Mother* becomes pregnant intentionally but does not want to have a disabled baby. *Doctor* fails to spot that the baby in *Mother*'s womb is disabled. Had *Mother* been told this, she probably would have had an abortion.[54] *Mother* carries her baby *Son* to term.

---

[52] We are grateful to Kirsty Mills for suggesting this variation.

[53] Section 1(1)(a) of the Abortion Act 1967 allows an abortion to be performed if the pregnancy 'has not exceeded its twenty fourth week and . . . continuance of the pregnancy would involve risk, greater than if the pregnancy were terminated, of injury to the physical or mental health of the pregnant woman . . .'

[54] Section 1(1)(d) of the Abortion Act 1967 allows an abortion to be performed 'if there is a serious risk that if the child were born it would suffer from such physical or mental abnormalities as to be seriously handicapped'.

It seems to be well established that in all of these situations, *Mother* will be entitled to sue *Doctor* for compensation in respect of the inconvenience that she suffered in the run-up to giving birth, the pain and suffering that she went through in labour, any economic losses that she suffered before giving birth as a result of taking time off work, having to spend money on new clothes to fit her as she grew larger, and so on.[55]

But if *Mother* attempts to sue *Doctor* for compensation in respect of the money she is going to have to spend on bringing up *Son*, she will usually find that that loss is regarded as being automatically non-actionable by the courts.[56] In order to understand *when* this loss will be held to be non-actionable, we have to distinguish between the case where *Son* is healthy and the case where *Son* is born disabled.

A. Healthy child

The House of Lords ruled in *McFarlane* v *Tayside Health Board* (2000)[57] that if *Mother* and *Son* are both healthy then the cost of bringing up *Son* will be automatically non-actionable.[58] In a subsequent case – *Rees* v *Darlington Memorial Hospital NHS Trust* (2004)[59] – the House of Lords placed a 'gloss' on the ruling in *McFarlane*, holding that while *Mother* would not be entitled to sue *Doctor* for damages representing the cost of bringing up *Son*, *Mother would* be entitled to sue *Doctor* for a fixed sum of £15,000 to compensate her for the disruption to her life that bringing up *Son* will involve.

Two issues arise out of this: (1) Why is *Mother not* allowed to sue *Doctor* for the cost of bringing up *Son*? (2) Why *is Mother* allowed to sue *Doctor* for a fixed sum of £15,000 to compensate her for the disruption to her life that bringing up *Son* will involve?

(1) On the first issue, a number of reasons were advanced by the Law Lords in both *McFarlane* and *Rees* as to why the cost of bringing up *Son* should be held to be non-actionable.

First, it would be wrong, in assessing the damages payable to *Mother* to disregard the benefits *Mother* would reap from bringing up *Son*. These benefits must be taken as *at least equalling* the cost of rearing *Son* – either because thinking anything else would be morally

---

[55] *McFarlane* v *Tayside Health Board* [2000] 2 AC 59, 74 (per Lord Slynn), 81 (per Lord Steyn), 87 (per Lord Hope), 102 (per Lord Clyde). It is unclear why, in either of the *wrongful birth* situations, B will be entitled to sue A for compensation in respect of these losses – it could be argued (particularly in the case of the second wrongful birth situation) that she willingly took the risk that she would suffer these losses when she became pregnant. See, on this, Mason 2002, 50.

[56] The cost of bringing up B's child will be regarded as actionable in Australia: *Cattanach* v *Melchior* (2003) 215 CLR 1 (noted, Cane 2004).

[57] Reported in [2000] 2 AC 59. (We will refer to it below as '*McFarlane*').

[58] For criticisms of this ruling, see Hoyano 2002. An attempt to get round this ruling was made in *Greenfield* v *Irwin* [2001] 1 WLR 113, where the claimant – who had given birth to a baby that she would not have had but for the defendants' negligence – did not sue the defendants for the cost of bringing up the baby, but rather sued to be compensated for the loss of income she had experienced as a result of giving up work to look after the baby full time. The claim was dismissed on the ground that if it were allowed, a coach and horses would be driven through the House of Lords' ruling in *McFarlane*. Another attempt to get round *McFarlane* was made in *Rees* v *Darlington Memorial Hospital NHS Trust* [2004] 1 AC 309, where a woman who was near-blind decided that she would be incapable of bringing up a baby properly and as a result had the defendants perform a sterilisation operation on her. The defendants performed the operation incompetently and the claimant subsequently conceived, and gave birth to, a healthy baby boy. It was argued that while the claimant's boy was perfectly healthy, the fact that the *claimant* was disabled meant that *McFarlane* did not apply, and that the claimant should at the very least be allowed to recover the *extra* cost of bringing up the boy that was attributable to the fact that *she* was disabled. The House of Lords rejected this claim by 4:3, holding that *McFarlane* applies across the board to *all* cases where someone gives birth to a healthy child as a result of another's negligence.

[59] Reported in [2004] 1 AC 309. (Henceforth, '*Rees*'.)

offensive[60] or because the only fair way of taking these benefits into account is to *assume* that they at least equal the cost of bringing up *Son*.[61] Given this, it must be taken that the benefits of bringing up *Son* at least equal the costs and therefore no claim can be made for the cost of bringing up *Son*.

Secondly, to make *Doctor* liable for the cost of bringing up *Son* would impose on *Doctor* a liability far out of proportion to his fault in either causing *Mother* to become pregnant or failing to bring her pregnancy to an end.[62]

Thirdly, if *Doctor* were required to compensate *Mother* for the cost of bringing up *Son*, the funds would in all probability come out of the hard-pressed coffers of the National Health Service; and the general public would think it wrong for that money to be used to subsidise the upbringing of *Son*, as opposed to using it to treat patients.[63]

Fourthly, were *Mother* to be compensated for the cost of bringing up her child, then the amount payable to *Mother* would depend on how rich she is – the richer she is, the more she could be expected to spend on bringing up *Son* and therefore the greater the damages that would be payable to *Mother*. It would be 'unseemly' for the law to allow *Mother*'s award to depend on how rich or poor she is.[64]

(2) Moving on to the second issue, why will *Mother* be allowed to sue *Doctor* for a fixed sum of £15,000 in the situation we are considering? The House of Lords divided 4:2 in *Rees* over the issue of whether *Mother* should be allowed to make such a claim against *Doctor*.[65] The majority thought that it would be wrong if the law did nothing to compensate *Mother* for the 'loss of autonomy' that she had suffered as a result of giving birth to a child.[66] They thought that awarding *Mother* £15,000 would afford her some compensation for this 'loss of autonomy'.[67]

Lords *Steyn* and *Hope* criticised the majority ruling on this issue. Lord *Steyn* took the view that the courts simply did not have the power to make awards designed to compensate individuals for intangible fancies such as 'loss of autonomy' – let alone to rule that such awards would be fixed across the board at £15,000, whatever the circumstances of a claimant who gave birth to an unwanted healthy baby as a result of someone else's negligence.[68] Lord *Hope* said he could not understand why the majority was proposing to compensate for the 'loss of autonomy' suffered by a claimant who gave birth to an unwanted healthy baby as a result of someone's negligence through the award of a *fixed* sum of £15,000. If such an award is meant to be compensatory, then why should such a claimant not be entitled to say, 'The value of *my* loss of autonomy comes to much more than £15,000, and so I should be awarded much more than the fixed sum the majority in *Rees* said I should be given.'[69]

---

[60] *McFarlane*, at 82 (per Lord Steyn), 111 (per Lord Millett); *Rees*, at [28] (per Lord Steyn), [112] (per Lord Millett).

[61] *McFarlane*, at 97 (per Lord Hope); *Rees*, at [51] (per Lord Hope), [138] (per Lord Scott).

[62] *McFarlane*, at 91 (per Lord Hope); *Rees*, at [16] (per Lord Nicholls).

[63] *Rees*, at [6] (per Lord Bingham).

[64] *McFarlane*, at 82 (per Lord Steyn).

[65] Lord Hutton, sitting in *Rees*, did not express an opinion on the issue.

[66] *Rees*, at [8] (per Lord Bingham), [17] (per Lord Nicholls), [123] (per Lord Millett); [148] (per Lord Scott).

[67] Though Lord Bingham took the view that the award of £15,000 is not designed to *compensate* B for any loss that she has suffered: *Rees*, at [8]. For a possible alternative explanation of the nature of this award, see below, § 32.2(G).

[68] *Rees*, at [45].

[69] *Rees*, at [71]–[73].

B. Disabled child

Let's now consider what the position is if, in the situation we are considering, *Son* is *disabled*. The House of Lords' decision in *McFarlane* did not deal with that issue at all – it was purely concerned with what the position would be if *Son* were healthy.

After *McFarlane* was decided, the Court of Appeal ruled in *Parkinson* v *St James and Seacroft University Hospital NHS Trust* (2002)[70] that if, in the situation we are considering, *Son* was disabled, *Mother* would be entitled to sue *Doctor* for the *extra cost of raising Son that is attributable to the fact he was born disabled*. So, on this view, the normal costs of raising *Son*, that *Mother* would have incurred whether or not *Son* was disabled, would still be non-actionable. But any *extra* expenses that *Mother* would have to incur in raising *Son* because he is disabled would be actionable.

In *Rees*, the House of Lords found themselves split on the issue of what the position should be in the case where *Son* is disabled. Lords Steyn, Hope and Hutton took the view that *Parkinson* was correctly decided.[71] Lords Bingham and Nicholls took the view that *Parkinson* was wrongly decided and that in the situation we are considering, *Doctor*'s liability to *Mother* should not depend on whether *Son* was born healthy or disabled. In *both* cases, *Mother* should not be allowed to claim *anything* for the cost of bringing up the child: instead, all she will be entitled to sue *Doctor* for (in addition to damages for the pain of pregnancy and so on) is a fixed sum of £15,000 to compensate her for her 'loss of autonomy'.[72]

Lord Scott took the view that we may have to distinguish between: (1) the case where *Doctor* was employed to stop *Mother* becoming pregnant, or continuing with her pregnancy, because she was fearful that any baby she had would be disabled; and (2) the case where *Doctor* was employed to stop *Mother* becoming pregnant because she did not want to have another baby. He thought that the Court of Appeal's ruling in *Parkinson* should only be allowed to apply in case (1). So he thought that if (2) were true, *Mother* should not be allowed to sue for *anything* in respect of the cost of her disabled *Son*.[73]

As the issue of whether *Parkinson* was rightly decided did not arise for decision in *Rees*, Lord Millett preferred to leave the question 'open'.[74] He went on to observe that while in 'strict logic', a claimant who gave birth to a disabled child should not be allowed to claim anything for the cost of bringing up the child,[75] he himself did not think that the Court of Appeal's ruling in *Parkinson* was 'morally offensive'. At the same time, he expressed himself fearful that allowing *Mother* to sue for the extra cost of bringing up *Son* that was attributable to the fact that *Son* was born disabled might 'prove difficult to achieve without introducing nice distinctions and unacceptable refinements of a kind which tend to bring the law into disrepute'.[76]

What a mess! However, as *Parkinson* was not overruled in *Rees*,[77] *Parkinson* will remain binding on all courts up to and including the Court of Appeal until the House of Lords

---

[70] Reported at [2002] QB 266. (Henceforth, '*Parkinson*'.)

[71] *Rees*, at [35] (per Lord Steyn), [57] (per Lord Hope), [91] (per Lord Hutton).

[72] *Rees*, at [9] (per Lord Bingham), [18] (per Lord Nicholls).

[73] *Rees*, at [145].

[74] *Rees*, at [112].

[75] Because – following the logic underlying Lord Millett's judgments in *McFarlane* and *Rees* on the issue of whether a claim for the cost of bringing up a healthy child should be allowed – if one did allow such a claim to be made in the case where a claimant gave birth to a disabled child, one *would* be saying that bringing up a disabled child *is* more trouble than it is worth; which can hardly be right.

[76] *Rees*, at [112].

[77] Nor could it have been as the correctness of the Court of Appeal's ruling in *Parkinson* was not at issue in *Rees*.

readdresses the issue of whether *Parkinson* was correctly decided. As this is not likely to happen any time soon, we can safely assume that for the foreseeable future, the Court of Appeal's decision in *Parkinson* will determine how much a claimant is entitled to sue a defendant for in a disabled child case. So in the situation we are considering – where *Mother* has given birth to a disabled *Son* because of *Doctor*'s negligence – *Mother* will be entitled to sue *Doctor* for compensation in respect of any extra expenses that she will have to incur in raising *Son* because he is disabled.[78] This ruling gives rise to a couple of complications that need to be addressed.

First of all, what is the difference between a disabled child and a healthy child? Suppose, for example, that due to *Doctor*'s negligence, *Mother* gives birth to a baby *Girl*. As *Girl* grows up, it becomes clear that she is short-sighted and will need to wear glasses. Will *Mother* be able to sue *Doctor* for the cost of providing those glasses? It depends on whether *Girl* counts as being 'disabled' or not: if she is a 'healthy' child, then *Mother* will not be able to recover *any* of the costs of raising *Girl*, including the cost of providing her with spectacles. In the *Parkinson* case, Hale LJ suggested that a child will be held to be disabled if 'he is blind, deaf or dumb or suffers from mental disorder of any kind or is substantially and permanently handicapped by illness, injury or congenital deformity . . .'[79] On this definition, *Girl* would probably not count as being disabled and so *Mother* would not be able to sue *Doctor* for the cost of providing her with glasses.

Secondly, what is the position in the following case? *Doctor* negligently performs a vasectomy on *Husband*. Thinking (incorrectly) that the operation has been a success, *Wife* and *Husband* have unprotected sex. As a result *Wife* becomes pregnant. She decides to carry the child to term but six months into her pregnancy, she is involved in a car accident due to the negligence of *Driver*. *Wife* survives the car accident but her doctors tell her that, as a result of the accident, her baby is liable to be severely brain-damaged when he is born. Nevertheless *Wife* decides to carry on with the pregnancy and three months later she gives birth to *Girl*, who suffers from severe brain damage.[80] Will *Doctor* be liable for the extra cost that *Wife* will have to incur in raising *Girl* that is attributable to the fact that she has been born brain-damaged? One would have thought not, but in *Parkinson* the Court of Appeal held that *Doctor* *would* be liable so long as *Driver*'s negligence did not break the chain of causation between *Doctor*'s negligence and *Wife*'s giving birth to *Girl*.[81] As *Driver*'s negligence will not have had that effect, *Doctor* will be liable.[82]

10.6 MITIGATION

Suppose that A has committed a tort in relation to B and B has suffered some kind of loss as a result. That loss will be non-actionable if B could have done something after A

---

[78] Though this point was not addressed by any of the Law Lords in *Rees*, it is presumably the case that *Mother* would *also* be entitled to sue *Doctor* for a fixed sum of £15,000 to compensate her for the 'loss of autonomy' suffered by her as a result of *Doctor*'s negligence.

[79] *Parkinson*, at [91] (quoting s 17(11) of the Children Act 1989).

[80] In this situation, the driver will be liable to compensate *Girl* for the fact that she was born disabled under the Congenital Disabilities (Civil Liability) Act 1976: see below, § 35.2.

[81] *Parkinson*, at [53] (per Brooke LJ) and [92] (per Hale LJ).

[82] *Driver*'s negligence was not a *novus actus interveniens* because it was not deliberate. Could it be argued that *Wife*'s failure to have an abortion when she was told that *Girl* would be born severely brain-damaged broke the chain of causation between *Doctor*'s negligence and *Wife*'s giving birth to *Girl*? No – it must be remembered that omissions do not break chains of causation (see above, § 9.12). Could it be argued, alternatively, that *Wife* is barred from suing *Doctor* for the extra cost of raising *Girl* that is attributable to the fact that she has been born with brain damage because by failing to have an abortion she failed to mitigate the losses suffered by her as a result of *Doctor*'s negligence? The answer is 'no' – see below, § 10.6.

committed his tort to avoid suffering that loss but she *unreasonably* failed to do so. B has a 'duty to mitigate'[83] the losses suffered by her as a result of A's tort and will be barred from suing A for damages in respect of any losses that she has only suffered as a result of A's tort because she breached that 'duty'.[84]

We have already seen an example of this principle at work in the case of the workman who unreasonably refused to have an operation which would have saved his left hand, the hand having been originally injured by the defendants' negligence.[85] He was not allowed to sue the defendants for compensation in respect of the loss of his left hand because the loss of that hand was attributable to his failure to mitigate the losses suffered by him as a result of the defendants' negligence. Let's now look at how the duty to mitigate applies in a couple of concrete situations:

A. Avoidable births

What is the position in the following case? Suppose *Husband* and *Wife* asked *Surgeon* to carry out a vasectomy on *Husband* so that *Husband* and *Wife* could have sexual relations without using contraceptives. *Surgeon* performed the operation but (in breach of the duty of care he owed *Wife* and *Husband*) he failed to carry it out properly and the operation was as a result ineffective. Thinking, however, that the operation had been a success, *Wife* and *Husband* began to have unprotected sexual intercourse and *Wife* eventually became pregnant. Nine months later, *Wife* gave birth, experiencing a lot of pain and suffering in doing so. *Wife* also had to take time off work during the pregnancy and spent money on new clothes that would fit her in the latter stages of her pregnancy. Suppose she wants to sue *Surgeon* for damages in respect of these forms of economic loss and the pain and suffering experienced by her in labour, arguing that *Surgeon*'s negligence caused her to suffer these forms of loss.

Could *Surgeon* argue that *Wife* is barred from suing him for damages in respect of these losses on the ground that she could have avoided these losses by having an abortion? Obviously, the answer is 'no'. It cannot be argued that *Wife* acted *unreasonably* in not having an abortion – so it cannot be said that her failure to have an abortion put her in breach of her 'duty to mitigate' the losses suffered by her as a result of *Surgeon*'s negligence. Astonishingly, in *Emeh* v *Kensington Area Health Authority* (1985), Park J, at first instance, took the opposite line and suggested that in the case we are considering, *Wife might* be barred from suing *Surgeon* for damages in respect of the losses that her pregnancy caused her to suffer on the ground that she could have avoided those losses by having an abortion. Fortunately, good sense has prevailed in the courts: Park J's views have been firmly rejected by both the Court of Appeal in *Emeh*'s case and by the House of Lords in *McFarlane* v *Tayside Health Board* (2000).[86]

---

[83] This is, of course, not a real duty – B cannot be compelled to mitigate the losses suffered by her as a result of A's tort or sued if she fails to mitigate those losses.

[84] It seems, in light of the decision of the Privy Council in *Geest plc* v *Lansiquot* [2002] 1 WLR 3111, that the burden of proving that B has breached this 'duty' will fall on A. So if B has suffered some kind of loss as a result of A's tort that she could have avoided, B will still be able to claim compensation for that loss unless A can show that B acted *unreasonably* in failing to avoid that loss. In an earlier case, the Privy Council took the opposite view, holding that in the situation just described, B would not be able to claim compensation for the loss that she has suffered unless *she* could show that she acted *reasonably* in failing to avoid that loss: *Selvanayagam* v *University of West Indies* [1983] 1 WLR 585. There is something to be said for the position taken by the Privy Council in *Selvanayagam*: it will surely be easier for B to demonstrate that she acted reasonably in failing to avoid the loss in question than it will be for A to show that B acted unreasonably in failing to avoid that loss.

[85] See above, § 9.12(A).

[86] *McFarlane*, 74 (per Lord Slynn), 81 (per Lord Steyn), 104 (per Lord Clyde), 112–13 (per Lord Millett).

Having said that, in the case of *Richardson v LRC Products Ltd* (2000), Ian Kennedy J suggested that if *Wife* was warned by *Surgeon* that *Husband*'s vasectomy had been unsuccessful the day after *Husband* impregnated her, then *Wife* might be barred from suing *Surgeon* for damages in respect of the losses suffered by her as a result of her pregnancy if she failed to bring that pregnancy to a halt by taking a 'morning-after' pill. In such a case he thought it could be said that *Wife* had failed to mitigate the losses suffered by her as a result of *Surgeon*'s negligence.[87]

B. *White* v *Jones* (1995)[88]

An unusual case which raised a 'duty to mitigate' point – though it was not argued as such in the case – was *Gorham v British Telecommunications plc* (2000).[89] That case, it will be recalled, concerned a man, G, who was given some bad pensions advice by the defendants. As a result, the claimants, G's wife and two young children, were left worse off after G's death then they would have been had the defendants advised G properly. Had the defendants advised G properly, G would have joined his employer's pension scheme, instead of taking out a pension plan with the defendants. And had G joined his employer's pension scheme, the claimants would have obtained a lump sum on his death.

The claimants sued the defendants for compensation and it was held that the defendants had owed them a duty of care in advising G under the principle in *White v Jones* and that the defendants had breached that duty of care. However, it was held that the claimants could not sue for the lump sum that they would have received on G's death had he been properly advised by the defendants. The reason was that some time after being badly advised by the claimants, G discovered that his employer's pension scheme was superior to the pension plan that he had taken out with the defendants, but he then failed to join his employer's pension scheme. Had he done so, the claimants would have received the lump sum on G's death that they were suing the defendants for not receiving. In other words, G failed to mitigate the loss that the defendants' negligence caused the claimants to suffer on G's death.

It is not surprising that G's failure to mitigate the claimants' loss should have been held against the claimants. If the principle in *White v Jones* is (as we contend)[90] concerned with situations where A has been *prevented* by B's actions from conferring a benefit on C no action should be available to C under *White v Jones* if B's actions did not actually *prevent* A from conferring that benefit on C.

---

[87] The case actually concerned a claim under the Consumer Protection Act 1987: a married couple claimed that the wife had become pregnant as a result of their using a defective condom which split while they were making love. Ian Kennedy J rejected the claim that the condom was defective but held that even if it were, the claimants still had no case because the wife – knowing that the condom had split – could have easily avoided suffering any loss as a result by taking a 'morning-after' pill. The decision is not easy to reconcile with the views expressed by the Court of Appeal in *Emeh* and the House of Lords in *McFarlane*. Is there a distinction between taking a 'morning-after' pill and having an abortion? Munby J thought there was in *R (Smeaton) v Secretary of State for Health* [2002] EWHC 610 (Admin) (*not* a tort case), ruling that the 'morning-after' pill was not an abortifacient under the Abortion Act 1967.

[88] For a straightforward *White v Jones* case which raised a duty to mitigate point, see *Walker v Medlicott & Son* [1999] 1 WLR 727, where the defendant firm of solicitors failed to draft a will properly with the result that the claimant was not left a house in the will which the testatrix had intended to leave to the claimant; the claimant's claim for compensation was dismissed because he could have applied to have the will rectified under s 20(1) of the Administration of Justice Act 1982 and so had failed to mitigate the loss suffered by him as a result of the defendants' negligence.

[89] Discussed above, § 6.14.

[90] See above, § 6.10.

10.7 NO DOUBLE RECOVERY

The principle against double recovery (the victim of a tort recovering twice for the same loss) applies in a number of different contexts to make a loss suffered by the victim of a tort non-actionable:

(1) *Compensation from another tortfeasor.* If *Defendant One* and *Defendant Two* are both liable in tort to compensate *Victim* for some loss that she has suffered, and *Victim* has recovered *full* compensation for that loss from *One, Victim* cannot – of course – subsequently sue *Two* for compensation for that loss. The effect of *One's* payment is to make *Victim's* loss non-actionable with regard to *Two. One* will, however, be entitled to bring a claim in contribution against *Two* under the Civil Liability (Contribution) Act 1978, requiring *Two* to pay him a 'just and equitable'[91] sum as a contribution towards *One's* compensation payment to *Two.*

(2) *Legal costs.*[92] It is well-established that in a case where *Defendant* has committed a tort in relation to *Victim, Victim* will *not* be able to sue *Defendant* for damages in respect of the legal costs that she has incurred in bringing a claim in tort against *Defendant,* even though *Defendant's* tort undoubtedly caused *Victim* to incur those costs and those costs were an obviously non-remote consequence of *Defendant's* tort. This is because the law already provides *Victim* with a way of recovering those costs from *Defendant* – through an action for costs, under the Civil Procedure Rules – and does not want that mechanism for recovering costs to be subverted by a claim for costs being made under cover of a claim for damages in tort.

(3) *Damage to property.* In a case where *Defendant* has tortiously damaged *Owner's* property, *Owner* will be entitled, as of right, to compensation for that damage, assessed on either a 'cost of repair' or 'cost of replacement' basis. Whether *Owner* gets 'cost of repair' damages or 'cost of replacement' damages will depend on which sum is more reasonable, under the circumstances.[93] But the fact that *Owner* has a right to sue *Defendant* for compensation for the damage to his property on either a 'cost of repair' or 'cost of replacement' basis, means that *Owner cannot* sue *Defendant* for the *actual* costs that he has incurred either repairing or replacing the damaged property. If he could, he would then recover the cost of repairing or replacing his property from *Defendant* twice over – once as compensation for the damage to his property, and once as compensation for the consequential loss that he has suffered as a result of his property being damaged.

10.8 PUBLIC POLICY

There are a residual number of cases where losses suffered by the victim of a tort will be regarded as non-actionable because it would be contrary to public policy to allow recovery for those losses.

A. Losses associated with a divorce

In *Pritchard v J H Cobden Ltd* (1988), the claimant suffered some brain damage in a road traffic accident caused by the defendant's negligence. The brain damage had the effect of

---

[91] Section 2(1).
[92] See, generally, Merrett 2009.
[93] See below, § 28.3(C).

changing the claimant's personality for the worse. As a result, the claimant's marriage broke down and his wife divorced him. The claimant sued the defendant, seeking to be compensated for the economic loss that he had suffered when his assets were divided up between him and his wife in the divorce. The Court of Appeal held that this loss was not actionable, on the ground that it would be contrary to public policy to allow the claimant to recover for this loss.

There were a number of reasons why this was so. First, allowing this sort of claim could lead to abuse. Suppose *Husband* and *Wife* were a married couple who were going to divorce when *Husband* was involved in an accident negligently caused by *Driver*. If the sort of claim made by the claimant in *Pritchard* were allowed, *Husband* and *Wife* could easily collude with each other and claim that, when they divorced each other, they did so because of the effects of the accident. *Husband* would then be allowed to recover from *Driver*, and split with *Wife*, the value of the assets that he lost in the divorce.

Secondly, allowing this sort of claim could undermine marriages. Suppose that *Husband* was happily married to *Wife* when he was involved in an accident that was negligently caused by *Driver*, and that the injuries sustained by *Husband* in the accident had a damaging effect on his personality. If the sort of claim made by the claimant in *Pritchard* were allowed then *Husband* would know that if *Wife* divorced him because of his change in personality he would suffer no financial prejudice whatsoever: he would be able to claim the value of any assets he lost in the divorce. He would then have less incentive to try and moderate the effect of the accident on his personality for the sake of preserving his marriage.

Thirdly, if this sort of claim were allowed, then in the case we have just been considering – where *Husband* was happily married to *Wife* when he was negligently injured by *Driver* – if *Wife* wanted to divorce *Husband* because of the effect that his injuries have had on his personality, *Driver* would be entitled to be represented in any proceedings dealing with how *Husband* and *Wife*'s assets should be divided. This is because such proceedings would have an effect on *Driver*'s legal liabilities. So the divorce court dealing with *Husband* and *Wife*'s divorce would have to have regard not only to their interests, but also to *Driver*'s interests, in deciding how *Husband* and *Wife*'s assets should be divided between them.

B. Illegality

We will talk in a subsequent chapter about the defence of illegality (otherwise known as the defence of *ex turpi causa non oritur actio* – no action will arise from a shameful cause).[94] This defence may be available in a case where *Defendant* has committed a tort in relation to *Crook*, and either *Defendant*'s tort or the losses suffered by *Crook* as a result of that tort are closely related to a serious criminal offence that *Crook* has committed. In such a case, *Crook* may be barred from suing *Defendant* for damages on grounds of public policy.

We have already come across one example of this in the case of *Gray* v *Thames Trains Ltd* (2009). In that case, the defendants' negligence resulted in the claimant suffering a psychiatric illness that meant both: (a) that the claimant could not work anymore, and (b) that the claimant committed a manslaughter. It was held that public policy required that the claimant could not sue for compensation for (a) in respect of the period he was detained in hospital because of (b).

---

[94] See below, § 26.11.

Lord Brown thought that a 'consistency principle' required that the claimant's action for damages for loss of earnings during his period of detention be struck out: 'the integrity of the justice system depends upon its consistency. The law cannot at one and the same time incarcerate someone for his criminality and compensate him civilly for the financial consequences [of the incarceration].'[95] While not adopting Lord Brown's language in *Gray*'s case, Lord Hoffmann's judgment certainly endorsed a version of Lord Brown's 'consistency principle'. He saw this principle as giving effect to a 'special rule of public policy' which:

> In its narrower and more specific form . . . says that you cannot recover for damage which flows from loss of liberty, a fine or other punishment lawfully imposed upon you in consequence of your own unlawful act. In such a case it is the law which, as a matter of penal policy, causes the damage and it would be inconsistent for the law to require you to be compensated for that damage.[96]

But, as Lord Hoffmann observed, this 'special rule of public policy' ranges more widely than just to bar claims in cases like *Gray*. In some cases, a 'wider form' of this rule applies to make a loss suffered by the victim of a tort non-actionable. This 'wider form' of the rule says that 'you cannot recover compensation for loss which you have suffered in consequence of your own criminal act.'[97]

An example where this 'wider form' of Lord Hoffmann's 'special rule of public policy' applied is provided by the case of *Meah v McCreamer (No 2)* (1986). That case concerned yet another situation where the victim of a tort suffered a personality change. (In *Meah*'s case, the claimant suffered head injuries in a car accident brought about by the defendant's negligence.) The claimant's injuries caused his personality to change for the worse. Before the accident, he had been involved in various scrapes with the law but did not have a history of being violent. After the accident, he developed a tendency to attack women. As a result, he sexually assaulted two women and was sent to prison.

In the first *Meah v McCreamer* case (1985), the claimant sued the defendant for compensation for the fact that he had been sent to prison and Woolf J allowed his claim, awarding the claimant £45,500 in damages. We can safely say that Woolf J should not have done this: such a claim would be dismissed nowadays,[98] as inconsistent with Lord Brown's 'consistency principle' and Lord Hoffmann's 'narrower' formulation of his 'special rule of public policy'.

Woolf J's decision in the first *Meah v McCreamer* case caused something of a public outcry, which had the useful side effect of letting the two women who had been attacked by the claimant know that the claimant now had some money and was worth suing. Accordingly, they sued the claimant in tort for compensation in respect of the harm they had suffered when he attacked them and between them they obtained £17,000 in damages.[99] The claimant then sued the defendant again in *Meah v McCreamer (No 2)*, arguing that the defendant was liable to compensate him for the damages he had had to pay out to the women he had attacked.

---

[95] [2009] 1 AC 1339, at [93].
[96] [2009] 1 AC 1339, at [29].
[97] ibid.
[98] As it was in *Clunis v Camden and Islington HA* [1998] QB 978, where the claimant – who had a history of mental disorder – stabbed Jonathan Zito to death at a tube station and was convicted of manslaughter on grounds of diminished responsibility, and detained in hospital under the Mental Health Act 1983. He sued the defendant health authority for damages for the fact that he had been detained, claiming that had the defendant health authority taken greater care of his mental health, he would never have ended up stabbing Jonathan Zito.
[99] *W v Meah, D v Meah* [1986] 1 All ER 935.

This time round, Woolf J – perhaps wary of the outcry that had attended his first decision[100] – dismissed the claimant's claim. He held that it would be contrary to public policy to allow the claimant to sue the defendant for the £17,000 he had had to pay in damages to the victims of his sexual assaults.[101] Woolf J did not say much in support of his finding on this issue, remarking only that it would be 'distasteful' to allow the claimant to sue.[102] However, it can be inferred from other parts of his judgment that he was concerned that if the claimant's claim was allowed here, then the defendant's liability to the claimant might become unlimited in nature – with the defendant being held liable for any harm caused by the claimant's personality disorder.

Other cases where a claimant has been barred from suing a defendant on grounds of illegality, or Lord Hoffmann's 'wider' version of his 'special rule of public policy', will be discussed below, in the chapter on 'Defences'.[103] But it is worth noting here that the public policy rule discussed here may not just apply in cases where a loss suffered by the victim of a tort is associated with their engaging in some illegal conduct. Merely immoral conduct might be enough to make the loss they have suffered non-actionable on grounds of public policy. Consider the **Injured Prostitute Problem**:

> *Belle* works as a high-class prostitute. One day, she is attacked by *Client*, and is so severely disfigured as a result of the attack that she can no longer work as a prostitute. Instead, she gets a job as a secretary, which pays a lot less than she earned as a prostitute.

In this country, it is not illegal to work as a prostitute, but it is likely that any claim for loss of earnings that *Belle* makes against *Client* will be struck out as contrary to public policy.

Further reading

On remoteness, see **Stauch, 'Risk and remoteness of damage in negligence' (2001) 64** *Modern Law Review* **191**. On *McFarlane* and *Rees*, see **Hoyano, 'Misconceptions about wrongful conception' (2002) 65** *Modern Law Review* **883; Bagshaw, 'Children as actionable damage' (2004) 15** *King's College Law Journal* **117; and Priaulx,** *The Harm Paradox: Tort Law and the Unwanted Child in an Era of Choice* (Routledge, 2007).

---

[100] In *Meah* v *McCreamer (No 2)* [1986] 1 All ER 943, Woolf J attempted (at 951) to justify his decision in the first *Meah* v *McCreamer* case on the ground that the claimant had a wife and child who had suffered a loss of support as a result of the claimant's being locked up. So allowing the claimant to recover compensation for his being imprisoned would help him support his wife and child while he was in prison. (Dependants of the victim of a tort who have suffered a loss of support as a result of that tort are entitled to sue the tortfeasor for compensation in respect of the loss of support that they have experienced, but only if the tort caused the victim of the tort to die: see below, § 34.1.)

[101] He also found that the payout to the victims of the claimants' sexual assaults was a remote consequence of the defendant's negligence ([1986] 1 All ER 943, 950) but that finding is impossible to reconcile with his decision in *Meah* v *McCreamer* [1985] 1 All ER 367. If, in that case, the claimant's imprisonment was *not* a remote consequence of the defendant's negligence then the claimant's being sued for damages for the things he did which got him imprisoned could not have been a remote consequence of the defendant's negligence either.

[102] [1986] 1 All ER 943, 950.

[103] See § 26.11, below.

Visit **www.mylawchamber.co.uk/mcbride** to
access tools to help you develop and test your
knowledge of Tort law, including interactive
multiple choice questions, practice exam
questions with guidance, weblinks, legal newsfeed, additional case summaries, legal
updates and tips on answering problem and essay questions.

premium
mylawchamber
unrivalled support for legal education

Use **Case Navigator** to read in full some of the key cases referenced
in this chapter with commentary and questions:

• Caparo Industries *v* Dickman

11 Occupiers' liability

11.1 The basics *358*
11.2 Occupiers' Liability Act 1957 *360*
11.3 Occupiers' Liability Act 1984 *366*

11.4 Warnings, disclaimers, exclusions *370*
11.5 Liability under the general law of negligence *376*

Overview

In this chapter, we look at a particular topic within the law of negligence – that of the liability of occupiers of land. (Though as we will see, this liability can also extend to other occupiers, such as occupiers of boats or cars.) The two most important statutes affecting occupiers' liability are the Occupiers' Liability Act 1957 (which defines what duties of care an occupier owes his visitors and other people lawfully on his land in relation to dangerous features of that land), and the Occupiers' Liability Act 1984 (which defines what duties of care an occupier owes trespassers on his land in relation to dangerous features of that land). These are discussed in sections 11.2 and 11.3 respectively. Section 11.4 discusses an area of the law on occupiers' liability that often confuses students – that is, the distinction between, and the significance for the law on occupiers' liability of: (1) warning someone on your land of a danger; (2) telling someone entering your land that you don't accept any responsibility for their safety; (3) and limiting how much someone on your land can sue you for if they are injured as a result of your negligence. Section 11.5 sets out what duties of care an occupier will owe various people, not under the 1957 Act or the 1984 Act, but under the general law of negligence.

11.1 THE BASICS

The law has long taken the view that the occupation of land gives rise to positive duties of care to protect the interests of other people who might be affected by hazards arising on that land. In this chapter, we will split up the liabilities incurred by an occupier who fails to protect someone from a hazard arising on that land according to whether they arise –

(1) *Under the Occupiers' Liability Act 1957* ('OLA 1957') – under which an occupier will owe his visitors, and other people lawfully on his land (though not by virtue of using a right of way over his land), a duty to take reasonable steps to see that they are reasonably safe for the purposes for which they are on the land.

(2) *Under the Occupiers' Liability Act 1984* ('OLA 1984') – under which an occupier will owe trespassers on his land (and those using a right of way over the land) a duty to take reasonable steps to protect them against dangerous features of his land when: (i) he knows or ought to know about the dangerous feature; and (ii) he knows or ought to know a trespasser (or someone using a right of way) might come into the vicinity of that dangerous feature; and (iii) he can reasonably be expected to offer some protection against that danger.

(3) *Under the general law of negligence* – under which an occupier will owe a variety of people a range of duties of care: (i) to his visitors, a new duty – only recently established – to take reasonable steps to protect them against being harmed by fellow visitors; (ii) to his neighbours, a duty to take reasonable steps to abate hazards arising on his land that threaten to damage his neighbours' land; (iii) to people passing by his land, a duty to take reasonable steps to avoid their being injured as a result of any fixtures on his land falling into the road outside his land.

An important issue is how far an occupier of land can escape owing someone else a duty of care under one of these heads by making it clear that he does not want to be subject to that duty. We can call this the *disclaimer issue*. Another important issue is how far an occupier of land who has breached one of the duties of care set out above can escape being held liable for the harm resulting to a claimant from his breach by pointing to a contract or notice which says that anyone harmed as a result of the occupier's negligence cannot sue the occupier, or can only sue the occupier for a limited amount of money. We can call this the *exclusion of liability issue*. A third important issue is how far an occupier of land can claim that he has discharged the duty of care that he owed a claimant to protect the claimant against some risk of harm by giving the claimant a warning about that danger. We can call this the *warning issue*. These issues will be discussed in much more detail in section 11.4, but briefly –

(1) So far as the *disclaimer issue* is concerned, an occupier of land is in theory free to avoid owing visitors (and other people lawfully on his land) a duty of care under OLA 1957 by notifying them that he does not want to be subject to that duty. However, in the case of occupiers of business premises, their ability to do this is limited by the Unfair Contract Terms Act 1977 ('UCTA'), s 2(1) of which prevents a business avoiding liability in negligence (which includes liability under OLA 1957) for *death or personal injury* by reference to a contract term or notice, and s 2(2) of which only allows a business to avoid liability in negligence for *other forms of loss* (such as property damage) if it would be reasonable to do so.

An occupier of land is not, even in theory, free to disclaim the duty of care that he owes trespassers (and people using rights of way over his land) by notifying them that he accepts no responsibility for their safety. So – and this is subject to some more complicated points about the disclaimability of duties of care under OLA 1984 that we will make in section 11.4, below – so far as the disclaimer issue is concerned, if you are going onto domestic premises, having had it made clear to you that the occupier of the premises accepts no responsibility for your safety, you get much more protection under the law if you are a trespasser than if you are a visitor. Which is puzzling – and highlights one of perennial dangers of law-making through legislation: legislators failing to think through the implications of their legislation.

(2) So far as the *exclusion of liability issue* is concerned, an occupier of land is in theory free to exclude or limit liability for harm caused by an admitted breach of a duty of care by reference to a contract term or notice *so long as* the claimant is bound by that term or notice. It may be difficult to establish that where the claimant is a trespasser, and therefore not someone with whom the occupier had any prior dealings. Even if the claimant is a visitor who entered the premises on the understanding that if he was harmed on the premises, he could not sue the occupier, or only sue the occupier for a limited amount in damages, he will not be bound by that term or notice if s 2 of UCTA applies to his case.

(3) So far as the *warning issue* is concerned, an occupier of land can rely on the fact that he warned the claimant about a particular danger, for the purposes of showing that he did take care to protect the claimant against that danger, if it was reasonable for the occupier to think that the warning was *sufficient* to protect the claimant against that danger. If the claimant was a child, a warning may not have been sufficient as children are well-known for disregarding warnings. But if the claimant was an adult, and the warning enabled the claimant to avoid the danger that was warned of, then a warning will usually have been sufficient to discharge the occupier's duty to take reasonable steps to protect the claimant against that danger. In such a case – where the occupier's warning allowed the claimant to be reasonably safe – as the effect of the warning is not to allow the occupier to *avoid* liability, but to establish that there is nothing for which he can be held liable (because he has done nothing wrong), s 2 of UCTA *does not place any limit* on the ability of the occupier to rely on that warning to defeat the claimant's claim against him.

11.2 OCCUPIERS' LIABILITY ACT 1957

A. Establishing a duty under the Act

Nine points need to be borne in mind, in considering whether or not a defendant owed a claimant a duty of care under the 1957 Act.

(1) *The common duty of care.* Section 2 of OLA 1957 provides that:

(1) An occupier of premises owes the same duty, the 'common duty of care', to all his visitors, except in so far as he is free to and does extend, restrict, modify or exclude his duty to any visitor or visitors by agreement or otherwise.

(2) The common duty of care is a duty to take such care as in all the circumstances of the case is reasonable to see that the visitor will be reasonably safe in using the premises for the purposes for which he is invited or permitted to be there.

(2) *Premises.* Section 1(3) of OLA 1957 provides that the 'common duty of care' will extend not just to occupiers of land, but also any person 'occupying or having control over any fixed or moveable structure, including any vessel, vehicle or aircraft.' But for the purposes of the discussion below, we will disregard this point and focus on the 'common duty of care' that an occupier of land will owe other people under OLA 1957.

(3) *Occupier.* The term 'occupier' is not defined in OLA 1957, but in *Wheat v E Lacon & Co Ltd* (1966), Lord Denning suggested that:

. . . wherever a person has a sufficient degree of control over premises that he ought to realise that any failure on his part to use care may result in injury to a person coming lawfully there, then he is an 'occupier' . . . In order to be an occupier it is not necessary for a person to have entire control over the premises. He need not have exclusive occupation. Two or more people may be 'occupiers'.[1]

We can distinguish four situations: (a) where *Owner* – or no one[2] – lives in the house owned by *Owner*; (b) where *Owner* has leased the house he owns to *Tenant*; (c) where *Owner* is not living in the house he owns, but is permitting *Licensee* to live there on a casual

---

[1] [1966] AC 552, 577.
[2] See *Harris v Birkenhead Corporation* [1976] 1 WLR 279 (an abandoned house which was compulsorily purchased by the defendant local authority was occupied by the defendant local authority even though it never took possession of the house).

basis; (d) where *Owner* is not living in the house he owns because *Contractor* is currently doing work renovating the house. *Owner* will be an occupier of the house in (a) and (c) because he has control over the house. He will not be an occupier of the house in (b) because *Tenant* will have control over the house; so *Tenant* will be the occupier of the house in (b). In (d), *Owner* will be an occupier of the house because he has control over it; but *Contractor* might *also* be an occupier, depending on how much control he has over who comes into the house.

In *Wheat* v *E Lacon & Co Ltd*, the defendants owned a pub which was run by a manager. The defendants allowed the manager to use the first floor of the pub as his private accommodation. A guest of the manager fell down some stairs on the first floor of the pub and was killed. It was held that at the time of the accident the first floor of the pub was occupied by the defendants and that the defendants therefore owed the deceased a duty to take care to see that he was reasonably safe for the purposes for which he was on the first floor.

In *Ribee* v *Norrie* (2001), the defendant owned a hostel which contained a number of bedrooms which various people would rent from him. A fire started in the sitting room of the hostel which was set aside for the communal use of those using the hostel. The fire damaged a house adjoining the hostel. Whether the defendant was liable for the fire damage turned on whether he occupied the sitting room where the fire started. The court held that he did – he exercised a sufficient degree of control over the sitting room. As Ward LJ remarked, 'he had full power to regulate how that part of the hostel was to be used or not used as the case may be'.[3]

(4) *Visitor.* Not everyone who goes onto someone's premises does so as the occupier's 'visitor'. If B enters premises occupied by A, B will do so as A's 'visitor' if: (i) B was *invited* or *permitted* to enter those premises by A; or (ii) B was invited or permitted to enter those premises by someone who had the ostensible authority to issue such an invitation or permission on A's behalf.[4]

(5) *Estoppel.* It will generally not be difficult to establish whether (i) or (ii), above, are true.[5] But even if they are not, A may still be prevented (or estopped) from denying that B entered his premises as his 'visitor' if he (or someone with ostensible authority to act on his behalf) reasonably led B to *believe* that A had invited or permitted her to be on those premises. As Lord Oaksey observed in *Edwards* v *Railway Executive* (1952):

> in considering the question whether a licence can be inferred, the state of mind of the suggested licensee must be considered. The circumstances must be such that the suggested licensee could have thought and did think that he was not trespassing but was on the property in question by the leave and licence of its owner.[6]

In that case, the claimant was a child who had been injured on a railway line. For many years, children had gone onto the defendant railway company's land in order to toboggan down an embankment. The House of Lords held that the claimant could not argue that when he had entered the defendant's land for that purpose, he had done so as a visitor. The defendant railway company had done nothing to lead children like the claimant to believe

---

[3] (2001) 33 HLR 777, at [20].
[4] For a discussion of the concept of 'ostensible authority' in this context, see *Ferguson* v *Welsh* [1987] 1 WLR 1553, 1563 (per Lord Goff).
[5] Though see the extraordinary facts of *R* v *Collins* [1973] QB 100, where the defendant climbed up to the window of a young lady's bedroom and she invited him in for sex, in the mistaken belief that he was her boyfriend.
[6] [1952] AC 737, 748.

that they were permitted to come onto the land for the purpose of playing on it. In coming to this conclusion, the House of Lords emphasised that the defendant company had done its best to stop children from coming onto its land to play – it put a fence around its land and whenever it discovered that children had breached a hole in it, the defendant company sought to repair the fence.

In contrast, in *Lowery* v *Walker* (1911), members of the public had for about 35 years taken a short cut across the defendant's field to get to a railway station. In all that time, the defendant never started legal proceedings to try and get people to stop crossing his field. The House of Lords found that by acting in this way the defendant had led members of the public to believe that they were permitted to cross his land to access the railway station and could not therefore now argue that they were trespassing on his land when they cut across his land for that purpose.

(6) *Ceasing to be a visitor*. A claimant who enters a defendant's premises as a visitor may cease to be a visitor if he goes beyond the bounds within which he is permitted (or has been led to believe he is permitted) to be there. As Scrutton LJ famously observed in *The Calgarth* (1927): 'when you invite a person into your house to use the staircase, you do not invite him to slide down the bannisters.'[7]

Until very recently, this *dictum* had always been interpreted as meaning that as *Guest* slid down the bannisters in *Host*'s house, *Guest* would no longer be a visitor, but a trespasser. So at the moment he was sliding down the bannister, he would no longer be protected by OLA 1957 against (for example) the risk of being cut by a splinter of wood sticking out of the bannister, but he might be protected instead by OLA 1984 (which governs the duties of care an occupier owes trespassers). However, in *Harvey* v *Plymouth City Council* (2010), Carnwarth LJ (with whom the other two members of the Court of Appeal agreed) entertained the novel proposition that as *Guest* was sliding down the bannisters, he might still be a visitor, but would not be protected by OLA 1957's 'common duty of care', which only requires an occupier to take steps to see that a visitor is reasonably safe 'for the purposes for which he is invited or permitted to be there'.[8] We think this suggestion is dangerous, as it threatens to consign *Guest* to a legal limbo: neither protected by OLA 1957 (because he is a visitor, but not protected by the 'common duty of care' in sliding down the bannisters) nor by OLA 1984 (because he is a visitor, and not a trespasser). The safest view is that in the situation we are considering, *Guest* is a trespasser at the moment he is sliding down the bannisters.

In the *Harvey* case, the claimant was injured when drunkenly running about in the dark on a piece of council land adjoining and overlooking a supermarket car park: he tripped over the chain link fence at the boundary of the land and fell about 18 feet into the car park below. He suffered brain damage as a result of the fall. The Court of Appeal found that the defendant council had not owed the claimant a 'common duty of care' under OLA 1957 as he was drunkenly running about. The land had been used for a long time – without any objection from the council – by teenagers wanting somewhere to hang out or fool around with each other. The Court of Appeal held that such teenagers 'had every reason to think that they were there with the licence of the owners' and were therefore 'visitors' for the purpose of OLA 1957.[9] However, no one using the land could have thought that the council

---

[7] [1927] P 93, 110.
[8] [2010] EWCA Civ 860, at [22].
[9] [2010] EWCA Civ 860, at [18].

was permitting people to use it for activities that carried an 'obvious risk of accident'.[10] So, by drunkenly running about in the dark, the claimant ceased to be a visitor for the purposes of OLA 1957.[11]

(7) *Persons lawfully on the premises.* Section 2(6) of OLA 1957 provides that the 'common duty of care' that an occupier of premises owes his visitors will also be owed to someone who enters the premises 'in the exercise of a right conferred by law'. There is, however, an important exception to this. Section 1(4) of OLA 1957 provides that 'a person entering any premises in exercise of rights conferred by . . . the Countryside and Rights of Way Act 2000, or . . . the National Parks and Access to the Countryside Act 1949' will not be protected by OLA 1957; such a person comes under OLA 1984.

(8) *State of the premises.* Although section 1(1) of OLA 1957 provides that OLA 1957 'regulate[s] the duty which an occupier of premises owes to his visitors in respect of dangers due to the state of the premises *or to things done or omitted to be done on them*',[12] it is now generally accepted that the duties of care imposed on occupiers by both OLA 1957 and OLA 1984 are duties to protect people from being harmed as a result of the *state of the premises* being in a dangerous condition.[13]

The key case – although it deals with OLA 1984, rather than OLA 1957 – is *Tomlinson v Congleton BC* (2004). In that case, it may be recalled, the claimant was injured when he went swimming in a lake on the defendant council's land. He had no permission to go swimming in the lake and so was trespassing on the council's land when he went into the lake. The claimant sued the council for compensation under OLA 1984 but his claim was dismissed: the claimant had not been harmed as a result of the state of the council's premises being in a dangerous condition. As Lord Hoffmann observed of the lake in the *Tomlinson* case:

> There was nothing special about [the lake]; there were no hidden dangers. It was shallow in some places and deep in others, but that is the nature of lakes. Nor was the council doing or permitting anything to be done which created a danger to persons who came to the lake. No power boats or jet skis threatened the safety of either lawful windsurfers or unlawful swimmers.[14]

Could the claimant have argued that the lake *itself* was a dangerous feature of the land on which it was located and that he had therefore been injured because the council's land had a dangerous feature? Not on the facts of *Tomlinson*, where the claimant was a mature adult: the mere existence of the lake did not pose any kind of danger to *him*.[15] However, it might have been different if the claimant in *Tomlinson* had been a *small child* who fell into the lake and was injured.

---

[10] [2010] EWCA Civ 860, at [27].

[11] [2010] EWCA Civ 860, at [28]. Note that Carnwarth LJ's conclusion on this point is in line with the traditional reading of Scrutton LJ's *dictum* in *The Calgarth*, and inconsistent with his suggestion (at [22]) that a visitor who exceeds the bounds for which he is permitted to be on another's premises might remain a visitor, but will not be protected by the 'common duty of care'.

[12] Emphasis added.

[13] *Fairchild* v *Glenhaven Funeral Services Ltd* [2002] 1 WLR 1052 (CA), at [109]–[133]; *Everett* v *Comojo (UK) Ltd* [2011] EWCA Civ 13, at [33] ('the relationship between the parties already carries with it an established duty, under the Occupiers' Liability Act 1957, in relation to *the condition of the premises*' (emphasis added)).

[14] [2004] 1 AC 46, at [26].

[15] See *Donoghue* v *Folkestone Properties Ltd* [2003] QB 1008, at [36]: 'An expanse of water, be it a lake, pond, river or the sea, does not normally pose any danger to a person on land'; also *Baldacchino* v *West Wittering Council* [2008] EWHC 3386 (QB), holding (at [70]) that no danger due to the state of the premises existed in case where claimant dived into the sea off the defendants' beach from a navigation beacon at a time when (unknown to the claimant) the tide was going out and the waters around the beacon were becoming shallow.

The decision of the Court of Appeal in *Keown* v *Coventry Healthcare NHS Trust* (2006) makes it clear that in such a case the lake *itself* would have counted as a dangerous feature of the land – with regard to the child – if the child was unaware of the danger of drowning that it was incurring by going near the lake. So if the child in our imagined case was too young to appreciate the danger posed by going near the lake on the council's land, the council would have owed the child a duty to take reasonable steps to protect him from that danger.[16] In the *Keown* case itself, the claimant was a child who was injured when he fell from a fire escape attached to the defendants' accommodation block; the claimant had been climbing the fire escape to impress his friends. The Court of Appeal held that the defendants had not owed the claimant a duty under the 1984 Act to take reasonable steps to protect him from the danger of falling from the fire escape. As the claimant well knew how dangerous it was to climb the fire escape, the mere presence of the fire escape did not pose any danger to *him*; it was what he chose to do on the fire escape that put him in danger.

(9) *Property*. So far we have been assuming that an occupier's duty under OLA 1957 will be to take reasonable steps to protect visitors on his land from being physically injured. However, s 1(3) of OLA 1957 makes it clear that the 'common duty of care' extends to taking reasonable steps to see that *property* that is lawfully on the premises is not damaged or destroyed as a result of the occupier's premises being in a dangerous condition, which duty will be owed to whoever happens to own the property at the time it is on the premises (whether the owner is a visitor or not).

B. Establishing a breach of a duty under the Act

All of the principles set out in chapter 8 of this book will be relevant to the inquiry as to whether an occupier of premises breached the 'common duty of care' he owed a visitor. However, OLA 1957 makes a number of specific points about when we can find this 'common duty of care' has been breached, which we will consider below.

(1) *Children*. Section 2(3)(a) provides that an occupier 'must be prepared for children to be less careful than adults'. So an occupier must do more to protect children from dangers on his land than he might have to do to protect adults: while a warning might be enough for an adult, fencing-off a danger might be necessary for a child. At the same time, children do normally come with adults (in the form of their parents, or carers) in tow, and if an occupier can expect a child to be accompanied by an adult who can protect them from harm, a warning to the adult might be enough to protect the child. So – in *Phipps* v *Rochester Corporation* (1955),[17] a boy fell into an unprotected trench that had been dug across some grassland for the purpose of laying a sewer. It was held that the defendant occupiers of the land had not breached the duty of care they owed the boy in doing nothing to protect children from falling into the trench: they could have reasonably expected the boy to have his parents with him and to protect him from this danger. However, note the date of the case: what might have been reasonable to expect in 1955 may be very different nowadays.[18]

---

[16] If the child had been allowed to come onto the council's land then the said duty would have been owed under OLA 1957; if he had not been, then the duty would have been owed under OLA 1984 (assuming of course that all the other conditions required for a duty to have been owed under the 1984 Act were satisfied in this case).

[17] [1955] 1 QB 450.

[18] Having said that, see *Bourne Leisure Ltd* v *Marsden* [2009] EWCA Civ 671, where the owners of a caravan site were *not* held liable for the drowning of a two year old in a pond on the caravan site based on their failure to warn the parents of the boy of the presence of the pond as it would have been obvious to the parents that it would be dangerous to let a two-year-old boy wander around the site unaccompanied.

(2) *Known risks*. An occupier will not be under a duty to take special steps to protect a visitor against a risk that the visitor knows about and can easily avoid given that he or she knows about it. Two provisions in OLA 1957 reflect this point. First, s 2(3)(b) provides that:

> an occupier may expect that a person, in the exercise of his calling, will appreciate and guard against any special risks ordinarily incident to it, so far as the occupier leaves him free to do so.

Secondly, s 2(4)(a) provides that:

> where damage is caused to a visitor by a danger of which he had been warned by the occupier, the warning is not to be treated without more as absolving the occupier from liability, unless in all the circumstances it was enough to enable the visitor to be reasonably safe . . .

(3) *Accepted risks*. Section 2(5) provides that the 'common duty of care' does not require an occupier to protect a visitor against 'risks willingly accepted as his by the visitor'. The maxim *volenti non fit injuria* will apply in such a case.

For example, in *Simms* v *Leigh Rugby Football Club* (1969), the defendant rugby club's ground had a concrete barrier running around the pitch, seven feet from the touchline, in order to keep the spectators from going onto the pitch. It was held that S, a rugby player who played on the defendant rugby club's ground, took the risk that he would be injured by being thrown against this concrete barrier when he stepped onto the pitch – the existence and location of the barrier being permitted under the byelaws of the game, as laid down by the Rugby Football League. So the defendant rugby club did not owe S a duty to take care to ensure that he was not injured by being thrown against the concrete barrier around the pitch.

But *scienter* is not *volens* (knowing is not willing), and it is clear that when a visitor enters premises in the knowledge that she might be harmed in a particular way, she will not be held to have willingly taken the risk that she would be harmed in that way if she had no choice but to enter premises. For example, in *Burnett* v *British Waterways Board* (1973), B was employed to work on a barge which was being towed into the defendant's lock. B was injured when the rope towing the barge snapped and hit B. Even though B knew this might happen, it was not held that he had willingly taken the risk of being injured in this way. This is because B had no choice but to stay on the barge as it was towed into the defendant's lock.

(4) *Independent contractors*. We have already seen that the 'common duty of care' that an occupier of premises owes his visitors is *delegable*.[19] That is, an occupier can only be held to have breached that duty of care if he *personally* failed to take reasonable steps to see that his visitors would be reasonably safe for the purposes for which they were on his premises. Section 2(4)(b) makes this clear:

> where damage is caused to a visitor by a danger due to the faulty execution of any work of construction, maintenance or repair by an independent contractor employed by the occupier, the occupier is not to be treated without more as answerable for the danger if in all the circumstances *he had acted reasonably* in entrusting the work to an independent contractor and had taken such steps (if any) as *he reasonably ought* in order to satisfy himself that the contractor was competent and that the work had been properly done.[20]

In *Gwilliam* v *West Hertfordshire Hospitals NHS Trust* (2003), the Court of Appeal suggested that an occupier might not have done as much as he reasonably ought in order to satisfy himself that the contractor was *competent* if he had not taken reasonable steps to reassure

---

[19] See above, § 8.6(B).
[20] Emphasis added.

himself that the contractor carried *liability insurance*: the idea being that if a contractor did not carry liability insurance, that might raise a question mark over whether the contractor was actually that reputable, and therefore competent.[21] Sedley LJ dissented on this point in *Gwilliam*, observing that there is a big difference between reassuring yourself that a contractor is competent, and reassuring yourself that a contractor will be worth suing if he proves to be incompetent.[22]

Since *Gwilliam*, the Court of Appeal has twice said that it prefers Sedley LJ's reasoning on this point.[23] However, there may be one way of saving the majority's reasoning in *Gwilliam*. Going back to a point made much earlier in this book,[24] the need to carry liability insurance will place a substantial constraint on *Insured*'s behaviour: *Insured*'s *Insurer* will be in a strong position to dictate to *Insured* how he should conduct himself by holding over *Insured* the threat that if he does not do what *Insurer* tells him to do, his liability insurance will be withdrawn. So requiring a contractor to carry liability insurance may be a good way of ensuring that his work is 'properly done', by effectively subcontracting the job of ensuring that the contractor is competent to his liability insurer, who will have a substantial incentive (in the form of wanting to avoid having to pay out on the contractor's liability insurance policy) to ensure that the contractor performs his duties properly.

C. Wrong kind of loss

Even if *Occupier*'s breach of the 'common duty of care' that he owes to *Visitor* has caused *Visitor* injury, *Visitor* will be barred from suing *Occupier* for damages if the injury *Visitor* has suffered is the 'wrong kind of loss' – not the sort of injury the *Occupier* was supposed to be guarding against when he breached the 'common duty of care' that he owed *Visitor*.

The case of *Darby* v *National Trust* (2001) makes the point. In that case, the claimant's husband drowned swimming in a pond maintained by the defendants. The defendants breached the 'common duty of care' that they owed the husband under OLA 1957 in failing to warn him of the risk that he might contract Weil's Disease in swimming in the pond. Had they done so, the husband probably would not have gone swimming, and not have drowned. However, the husband's *drowning* was the 'wrong kind of loss' to ground a claim for damages against the defendants here. *That* sort of harm – having nothing to do with Weil's Disease – was not the sort of harm that the defendants were duty-bound to protect the claimant's husband against suffering.

11.3 OCCUPIERS' LIABILITY ACT 1984

A. Antecedents to the Act

Until 1984, the law drew a big distinction between an occupier's liability to his visitors and an occupier's liability to trespassers on his land. Reasonable care had to be taken to protect visitors from injury to their persons or property. In contrast, an occupier would only owe a trespasser a duty to take reasonable steps to protect them from harm when 'common humanity' demanded it.[25] This may have been acceptable when an adult was *deliberately*

[21] [2003] QB 443, at [15] (per Lord Woolf CJ).
[22] [2003] QB 443, at [56].
[23] *Naylor* v *Payling* [2004] EWCA Civ 560; *Glaister* v *Appleby-in-Westmorland Town Council* [2009] EWCA Civ 1325.
[24] See above, § 1.14.
[25] *British Railway Board* v *Herrington* [1972] AC 877.

trespassing on someone else's land, but less so when a child went onto someone else's land to play, or a hiker lost his way and ended up trespassing on someone else's land. So OLA 1984 was passed in order to enhance the protection available to trespassers.

B. Establishing a duty under the Act

The following points should be borne in mind in determining whether a defendant owed a claimant a duty of care under the 1984 Act.

(1) *The basic rule* underlying OLA 1984 is that an occupier of premises will owe a duty:

> to persons other than his visitors in respect of any risk of their suffering injury on the premises by reason of any danger due to the state of the premises or to things done or omitted to be done on them[26] . . . if –
>
> (a) he is aware of the danger or has reasonable grounds to believe that it exists;
> (b) he knows or has reasonable grounds to believe that . . . [someone who is not his visitor] may come into the vicinity of the danger; and
> (c) the risk is one against which . . . he may reasonably be expected to offer [someone is not his visitor] some protection.[27]

If (a)–(c) are satisfied in relation to a particular danger, the occupier will owe someone who is not his visitor a duty to take reasonable steps to see that that someone 'does not suffer injury on the premises by reason of the danger concerned.'[28]

(2) *State of the premises.* As has already been observed, this duty is a duty to protect trespassers from being injured as a result of an occupier's premises being in a dangerous state.[29]

(3) *Protected persons.* The duty owed under OLA 1984 is to 'persons other than [the occupier's] visitors'. This does not just include trespassers but also, by virtue of s 1(4) of OLA 1957, 'a person entering any premises in exercise of rights conferred by . . . the Countryside and Rights of Way Act 2000, or . . . the National Parks and Access to the Countryside Act 1949' (who is defined not to be a 'visitor' for the purposes of OLA 1957).

   However, OLA 1984 makes various special provisions for the case where *Rambler* crosses land occupied by *Owner* using a right of way created by the Countryside and Rights of Way Act 2000. First, *Owner* will not owe *Rambler* a duty to protect her against a risk:

> resulting from the existence of any natural feature of the landscape, or any river, stream, ditch or pond whether or not a natural feature, or . . . a risk [that she will suffer injury] when passing over, under or through any wall, fence or gate, except by proper use of the gate or of a stile[30]

unless she has intentionally or recklessly created that risk.[31]

   Secondly, if Owner *does* owe *Rambler* a duty of care under OLA 1984, the courts must, in determining whether that duty has been breached, have regard to the fact that the existence of the right of way under the 2000 Act being used by *Rambler* ought not to place an undue burden on *Owner*, and the importance of maintaining the character of the countryside.[32]

---

[26] Section 1(1)(a).
[27] Section 1(3).
[28] Section 1(4).
[29] See above, § 11.2(A)(8), above.
[30] Section 1(6A).
[31] Section 1(6C)
[32] Section 1A.

(4) *Public highway*. Someone crossing land using a public highway will not be protected either by OLA 1957,[33] or by OLA 1984.[34] However, someone who is injured as a result of the public highway being in a dangerous condition may be able to sue the highway authority that it is in charge of its maintenance under s 41 of the Highways Act 1980.[35]

(5) *Property*. The duty of care (if any) owed by an occupier of premises to someone on those premises who is not his visitor is a duty to take reasonable steps to protect them from being physically harmed by some dangerous feature of the premises: it does not require the occupier to take reasonable steps to see that anyone's property is not destroyed or damaged by that dangerous feature.

(6) *The importance of time*. An occupier of premises will only owe someone who is not his visitor a duty to take reasonable steps to protect them against a dangerous feature on his land if he knows or ought to know that people who are not his visitors may come into the vicinity of that dangerous feature. In *Donoghue* v *Folkestone Properties* (2003), the Court of Appeal held that whether this requirement was satisfied would depend on the *time* at which the claimant went onto the premises: it has to be shown that at *that* time, it was reasonably foreseeable that people who were not the occupier's visitors would come into the vicinity of the dangerous feature that ended up harming the claimant.

In that case, the claimant dived into the defendant council's harbour in the middle of winter. He hit his head on a submerged gridbed and was severely injured. He sued the council for compensation claiming that it had owed him a duty under the 1984 Act to take reasonable steps to see that he did not injure himself on the submerged gridbed.[36] The claimant's claim was dismissed on the ground that at the time the claimant dived into the harbour – the *middle of winter* – the defendants had no reason to think that anyone would try to dive into the harbour. So they had no reason to think at the relevant time that anyone would go anywhere near the submerged gridbed. It would have been different if the diver had executed his dive in the middle of *summer*. At *that* time of year it would have been reasonably foreseeable that trespassers *would* go near the submerged gridbed (by jumping into the harbour at a spot over the gridbed) and so the council in *Donoghue* would have come under a duty to provide trespassers with some protection against that danger by, for example, posting up warning signs telling people not to jump into the harbour.

(7) *Accepted risks*. Section 1(6) of OLA 1984 mirrors s 2(5) of OLA 1957 in that it provides that no duty is owed under OLA 1984 'to any person in respect of risks willingly accepted by that person'. This provision was applied in *Ratcliff* v *McConnell* (1999), where the claimant was a student, R, who suffered serious injuries when he dived into his college's swimming pool at the shallow end. The pool was locked up for the winter and so when R used the swimming pool he did not do so as a visitor. R sued the college's governors, seeking to recover compensation for his injuries under OLA 1984. The Court of Appeal dismissed his claim, holding that when he dived into the swimming pool he willingly took the risk that he would be killed or injured as a result. He knew when he made his dive that there was a risk that the swimming pool would be too shallow to dive in but he nevertheless went ahead with his dive.

---

[33] *McGeown* v *Northern Ireland Housing Executive* [1995] 1 AC 233.
[34] Section 1(7).
[35] Discussed below, § 22.4.
[36] The claimant brought his claim under the 1984 Act because he was a trespasser when he dived into the harbour.

C. The boundary between OLA 1957 and OLA 1984

It can sometimes be a difficult question which Act to apply to determine whether an occupier of premises owed a claimant a duty to protect them against a dangerous feature of those premises. Consider, for example, the **Slippery Floor Problem**:

> Host held a dinner party at her house. She told all her guests they could go anywhere in the house, except into the kitchen. Guest – suspecting that Host had prohibited her guests from going into the kitchen to prevent them discovering that she had not actually cooked the dinner herself but was instead serving takeaway food – walked into the kitchen and promptly slipped on the floor and suffered a severe spinal injury. Host had in fact told everyone not to go into the kitchen because she had had to clean up some food that she had spilled on the floor and as a result the floor was extremely slippery.

Suppose *Guest* wants to sue *Host* for compensation for his injury. But which OLA applies to determine whether or not a duty of care was owed in this case? The argument for thinking that we must look to OLA 1957 is that we want to know whether *Host* owed *Guest* a duty to take reasonable steps to *stop* him going into her kitchen, as by the time he was in the kitchen it would have been too late to save him from harm. That duty – to stop *Guest* going into the kitchen – must have been owed to *Guest before* he went into *Host*'s kitchen and *at that stage*, *Guest* was a visitor.[37] So we should look to OLA 1957 to determine whether *Host* owed *Guest* a duty to take reasonable steps to stop him going into her kitchen. The logic of this argument seems impeccable, but a majority of the House of Lords ruled in *Tomlinson v Congleton BC* (2004) that we should in fact look at OLA *1984* to determine whether *Host* owed *Guest* a duty to take reasonable steps to stop him going into her kitchen.[38] On this view, the 1984 Act not only determines when you have a duty to protect a *trespasser* on your land from some danger arising on your premises but also when you have a duty to take reasonable steps to stop a *visitor* of yours from entering a dangerous area of your land which she is not permitted to enter.

D. The difference between OLA 1957 and OLA 1984

It may be questioned whether – claims for property damage aside (which can be brought under OLA 1957, but not under OLA 1984) – the extent of protection afforded by OLA 1957 to visitors is any more extensive than the protection afforded by OLA 1984 to non-visitors. If it is not, it is hard to see why we have separate Occupiers' Liability Acts. Test it this way. Imagine that a *Visitor* is injured on premises occupied by *Owner* as a result of those premises having a dangerous *Feature*, but

(1) *Owner* did not know, and had no reason to know, about *Feature*; or
(2) *Owner* did know about *Feature* but had no reason to suppose someone like *Visitor* would go anywhere near it; *or*
(3) Owner did know about *Feature* but it would have been unreasonable to expect him to do anything to protect *Visitor* against being harmed by *Feature*.

---

[37] Of course, as soon as he entered the kitchen, he became a trespasser: see § 11.2(A)(6), above.

[38] Applying the Act, the question of whether *Host* did owe *Guest* such a duty under the 1984 Act will largely turn on whether *Guest* knew or ought to have known that despite her prohibition someone like *Guest* would attempt to enter the kitchen. If this condition is satisfied, then the courts may well find that *Guest* owed *Host* a duty to take reasonable steps to stop him going into the kitchen.

If any of (1), (2) or (3) were established, would *Visitor* be able to sue *Owner* for compensation under OLA 1957? If the answer is 'no' then *Visitor* would be *no better off* than a *Trespasser* who wanted to sue *Owner* for compensation for being injured by *Feature* and who would only be able to sue under OLA 1984 if none of (1), (2) or (3) were true in his case. We think the answer is 'no'. Given this, the only possible explanation as to why we have separate Occupiers' Liability Acts is ideological – that people would be uncomfortable with the idea that the law affords the same protection to visitors as it does to non-visitors. But (cases of property damage aside) it seems that the differences between OLA 1957 and OLA 1984 are more apparent than real.

11.4 WARNINGS, DISCLAIMERS, EXCLUSIONS

Suppose that *Hurt* has been injured as a result of some dangerous *Feature* of land occupied by *Owner*. In this section, we are concerned with three different arguments *Owner* might make if *Hurt* sues him for damages under OLA 1957 or OLA 1984: (1) 'I warned *Hurt* about *Feature*'; (2) 'I told *Hurt* I did not accept any responsibility for his safety'; (3) '*Hurt* agreed that if he was injured on my land, he would not sue me'.

By making argument (1), *Owner* is saying that he is not liable to *Hurt* because he did not do anything wrong to *Hurt*. While he did owe *Hurt* a duty of care to protect him from being harmed by *Feature*, he did not breach that duty because by warning *Hurt* about *Feature*, he took reasonable steps to protect *Hurt* from being harmed by *Feature*.

By making argument (2), *Owner* is again saying that he is not liable to *Hurt* because he did not do anything wrong to *Hurt*. But on this occasion – unlike with argument (1) – *Owner* is saying that he did not do anything wrong to *Hurt* because he did *not* owe *Hurt* a duty of care to protect him from being harmed by *Feature*. In effect, *Owner* is arguing here that by telling *Hurt* that he did not accept any responsibility for his safety, he effectively *disclaimed* any duty of care that he might otherwise have owed *Hurt*.

By making argument (3), *Owner* is conceding that he did something wrong to *Hurt* and *Hurt* was injured as a result, but is saying that *Hurt* still cannot sue him because *Hurt* agreed that he would not sue him if he was injured. In effect, *Owner* is arguing here that *Hurt*'s agreement not to sue has effectively *excluded* the liability that *Owner* would otherwise have incurred to *Hurt* under OLA 1957 or OLA 1984.

We will now look at how far an occupier of land can rely on each of these arguments to defeat a claim for damages that is being made against him under OLA 1957 or OLA 1984.

A. Warnings

OLA 1957 makes it clear that in a case where *Visitor* has been harmed by a dangerous feature of premises occupied by *Owner*, *Owner can* rely on the fact that he warned *Visitor* of that danger to establish that he discharged 'the common duty of care' that he owed *Visitor* to see that *Visitor* would be reasonably safe in using those premises, *so long as Owner*'s warning 'was enough to enable the [claimant] to be reasonably safe'.[39] Section 1(5) of OLA 1984 says something slightly different:

> Any duty owed [under OLA 1984] in respect of a risk may, in an appropriate case, be discharged by taking such steps as are reasonable in all the circumstances of the case to give warning of the danger concerned or to discourage persons from incurring the risk.

[39] Section 2(4)(a).

The difference in language may reflect the fact that a trespasser who has been warned of a danger can always walk away from it, back the way he came. In contrast, a visitor might have no choice but to incur a danger, even if they have been warned of it. (For example, a babysitter might be warned that the staircase at the top of which the child she is looking after is sleeping is dangerous; but that warning will not enable her to be reasonably safe if the child starts crying and needs attention.)[40] So a warning to a trespasser always enables the trespasser to be reasonably safe; whereas this is not necessarily so with a warning given to a visitor.

So long as a warning given by the occupier *was* enough to enable the claimant to be safe, and reasonable efforts were made to bring that warning to the claimant's attention, the occupier will be able to argue that he discharged the duty of care that he owed the claimant to see that the claimant would be safe on his land, whether the duty was owed under OLA 1957 or OLA 1984. There is nothing in the Unfair Contract Terms Act ('UCTA') 1977 that would prevent the occupier relying on the fact that such a warning has been given to defeat the claimant's claim against him: in such a case, the occupier is not trying to avoid being held liable to the claimant. There is no liability to avoid: he is simply not liable.

B. Disclaimers of duty to visitors

Section 2(1) of OLA 1957 says that:

> An occupier of premises owes the same duty, the 'common duty of care', to all his visitors, except in so far as he is free to and does extend, restrict, modify or exclude his duty to any visitor or visitors by agreement or otherwise.

This suggests that an occupier can disclaim the 'common duty of care' that he would otherwise owe a visitor under OLA 1957. The Act says the occupier can do this 'by agreement or otherwise'. The '. . . or otherwise' is an implicit reference to the Court of Appeal's decision in *Ashdown* v *Samuel Williams Ltd* (1957), which said that merely notifying a visitor that you were not accepting any responsibility for their safety would be effective to disclaim the duty of care that you might otherwise owe them as an occupier of land. There is no need to show that the visitor *agreed* to this, or that there was a contract between the visitor and the occupier which specified that the occupier would not owe the visitor a duty of care. It is, however, worth noting the facts which led the Court of Appeal in *Ashdown* to find that no duty of care was owed to the claimant in that case:

> The [claimant] saw this notice [which said that 'This property is private property. Every person . . . whilst on the said property is there entirely at his own risk . . .']; she read the first few lines of it; she knew that she went on the . . . defendants' premises at her own risk . . . We are, I think, bound to hold that she entered upon the premises by licence from the . . . defendants, and on the conditions contained in the notice.[41]

This suggests that for a notice to work to disclaim the 'common duty of care' that the occupier of land would otherwise owe a visitor: (1) the visitor has to see the notice; (2) the visitor has to understand it; and (3) the visitor has to be entering on the occupier's land by virtue of being invited or permitted to come onto the land, rather than entering the land

---

[40] See, for example, *The Intruder Detection and Surveillance Fire & Security Ltd* v *Fulton* [2008] EWCA Civ 1009 (warning to employee who had to go upstairs to fit a security system that the stairs and landing at the top of the stairs had no protective bannister did not enable the employee to be reasonably safe).

[41] [1957] 1 QB 409, 418 (per Singleton LJ).

by right. If any of these conditions are not made out (for example, if the visitor is a child it is unlikely that conditions (1) or (2) will be made out), it is arguable that the notice will not work to release the occupier from the 'common duty of care' that he would otherwise owe the visitor under OLA 1957.

Even if these hurdles can be overcome, an occupier may still be prevented by UCTA 1977 from relying on an agreement or notice to argue that he did not owe a visitor a 'common duty of care'. The basic provision is set out in s 2 of UCTA 1977:

> (1) A person cannot by reference to any contract term or to a notice . . . exclude or restrict his liability for death or personal injury resulting from negligence.
> (2) In the case of other loss or damage, a person cannot so exclude or restrict his liability for negligence except in so far as the term satisfies the requirement of reasonableness.

That this provision applies to a disclaimer of a duty under OLA 1957 is a result of a combination of s 1(1) of UCTA 1977 (which provides that '"negligence" means the breach [among other things] . . . of the common duty of care imposed by the Occupiers' Liability Act') and s 13(1) of UCTA 1977 (which provides that s 2 of UCTA 1977 'also prevent[s] excluding or restricting liability by reference to terms and notices which exclude or restrict the relevant obligation or duty').

Section 2 of UCTA 1977 only applies to attempts to exclude 'business liability' (s 1(3)) which is defined as:

> liability for breach of obligations or duties arising –
>
> (a) from things done or to be done by a person in the course of a business . . . ; or
> (b) from the occupation of premises used for business purposes of the occupier . . .

Section 1(3) of UCTA 1977 goes on to say that:

> [the] liability of an occupier of premises for breach of an obligation or duty towards a person obtaining access to the premises for recreational or educational purposes . . . is not a business liability of the occupier unless granting that person such access for the purposes concerned falls within the business purposes of the occupier.

So, for example, suppose *Eagle* is a law firm that allowed a group of students, including *Unlucky*, to tour its offices. Prominently displayed at the entrance to *Eagle*'s offices is a sign that says 'We accept no responsibility for anyone's safety on the premises'. All the students, including *Unlucky*, saw this sign when they walked through the entrance. *Unlucky* and some other students got into a lift along with *Caterer*, who comes in every day to supply *Eagle*'s employees with sandwiches for lunch. Due to *Eagle*'s fault in failing to have the lift checked regularly, the lift was defective and underwent a free fall for 10 floors, with the result that *Unlucky* and *Caterer* were injured. Both try to sue *Eagle* for damages under OLA 1957.

So far as *Unlucky* is concerned, *Eagle* will probably be able to deny that it owed *Unlucky* a 'common duty of care' under OLA 1957. It will argue that its notice effectively disclaimed that duty of care, and that s 2(1) of UCTA 1977 does not prevent it relying on that notice to say that it did not owe *Unlucky* a 'common duty of care' as the liability that it would otherwise have incurred to *Unlucky* had it owed him such a duty of care was not a 'business liability'. This is because *Unlucky* was allowed onto the premises for 'educational purposes' and allowing students like *Unlucky* into *Eagle*'s offices for 'educational purposes' did not further *Eagle*'s business. In contrast, *Caterer* will be able to sue *Eagle*. If *Eagle* attempts to argue that the notice at its entrance meant that it did not owe him a 'common duty of care' under OLA 1957, *Caterer* can counter by arguing that s 2(1) operates to prevent it making that argument as it amounts to an attempt to exclude their being held liable for 'death or personal injury resulting from negligence.' Their liability in this case counts as a 'business liability' because the premises on which *Caterer* was harmed were used for the business purposes of the defendant, and he was not accessing the premises for 'educational or recreational purposes'.

Clearly, what counts as a 'business' for the purpose of UCTA 1977 has a big impact on how far s 2 of UCTA 1977 operates to prevent occupiers of land disclaiming the 'common duty of care' that they would otherwise owe visitors to that land. Section 14 of UCTA 1977 provides that ' "business" includes a profession and the activities of any government department or local or public authority'. A charity that ran a shop to raise money for the charity would clearly be using the shop for 'business purposes' and would therefore be caught by 2 of UCTA 1977 if it attempted to disclaim the 'common duty of care' it would otherwise owe people visiting that shop. In contrast, it is not clear that a motor-racing club that held races on a field rented out for that purpose could be said to be acting in the course of business in running those races.[42] If it charged for admission to watch the races, and used the money to cover the cost of renting the land, then perhaps; but even so, it could be argued that the purpose for which it is occupying the field is not business, but pleasure.

C. Disclaimers of duty to trespassers

While OLA 1957 does hold out the possibility that the 'common duty of care' imposed by it on occupiers might be disclaimed 'by agreement or otherwise', there is no similar provision in OLA 1984. If conditions (a)–(c) in s 1(3) of OLA 1984 are made out in respect of a dangerous feature on the occupier's land, then the occupier *will* owe someone who is not a visitor a duty to take reasonable steps 'to see that he does not suffer injury on the premises by reason of the danger concerned' (s 1(4)).

However, in the case where *Owner* has a prominent notice on land occupied by him saying 'Trespassers enter at their own risk', two strategies might be open to *Owner* to allow him to rely on that notice to say that he is not liable to *Trespasser*, who has been injured on *Owner*'s land as a result of that land having a dangerous *Feature*.

(1) Section 1(3)(b) provides that *Owner* will only have owed *Trespasser* a duty of care under OLA 1984 if he knew or ought to have known that people like *Trespasser* were liable to come into the vicinity of *Feature*. *Owner* might try to argue that his notice meant that it was reasonable for him to think that no one like *Trespasser* would come anywhere near *Feature* – because anyone like *Trespasser* would be put off by the notice from even attempting to come onto *Owner*'s land. This is quite a weak argument, as not many people would be intimidated by a 'Trespassers enter at their own risk' notice into not going onto someone else's land.

(2) Section 1(6) provides that 'No duty is owed [under OLA 1984] to any person in respect of risks willingly accepted as his by that person . . .'. *Owner* might try to argue that if

---

[42] In *White* v *Blackmore* [1972] 2 QB 651, a motor-racing enthusiast was killed at an event put on by the defendant club. It was held that the club had effectively disclaimed the 'common duty of care' it would otherwise have owed him under OLA 1957 because it had made it clear in notices at the entrance and in the programme setting out the day's events that motor-racing was dangerous and no responsibility was accepted for the safety of people attending the event. However, this was before UCTA 1977 was enacted.

Trespasser saw his notice, he willingly accepted all and any risks of being injured that he would run by going onto *Owner*'s land, including the risk of being harmed by *Feature* – with the result that *Owner* would not have owed *Trespasser* a duty to protect him from being harmed by *Feature*. This is a more promising argument, but is vulnerable to the objection that it will not work in a case where *Trespasser* was injured by *Feature* in a way that he could not possibly have anticipated when he saw the notice 'Trespassers enter at their own risk'.[43]

If *Owner can* make an argument for saying that his notice meant that he did not owe *Trespasser* a duty to protect him against being harmed by *Feature*, it seems there is nothing in UCTA 1977 to stop him denying that he owed *Trespasser* a duty of care under OLA 1984. This is because 'negligence', as defined in s 1(1) of UCTA 1977, includes breach 'of the common duty of care imposed by the Occupiers' Liability Act 1957' but does not mention breach of the duty of care imposed by OLA 1984. However, this is probably an oversight (UCTA 1977 came before OLA 1984, and when OLA 1984 was enacted, probably no one thought to update UCTA 1977 to cover OLA 1984), and it is likely that some way would be found to ensure that an occupier of business premises would not be allowed to disclaim the duty of care he would otherwise owe a non-visitor to those premises under OLA 1984 if allowing him to disclaim that duty would result in him not being held liable for that non-visitor's being killed or injured.[44]

D. Exclusions

Subject to statutory provisions preventing him from doing so, a claimant can contract away his right to sue a defendant for damages if X happens so long as: (1) he has reasonably given the defendant the impression that he has agreed not to sue the defendant if X happens; and (2) he has received something in return – some *consideration* – for agreeing to do this. In light of this, let's consider the **Electrocuted Couple Problem**:

> *Husband* and *Wife* go to a rock concert put on by Promoter, planning to buy tickets on the door. At the entrance to the concert, where tickets are being sold for £50 per person, there are prominent signs saying 'No liability accepted for any harm suffered by anyone on the premises'. *Husband* thinks the price of the tickets is too high, so he decides to get into the concert some other way, which he does by going through a side door which is unlocked. *Wife* pays £50 for a ticket. *Husband* and *Wife* reunite inside the concert hall and both suffer electrocution burns as a result of stepping on a live cable that is, because of the fault of *Promoter*, insufficiently insulated.

Subject to the provisions of UCTA 1977, we can say that *Wife* is bound by the notice saying 'No liability accepted . . .'. It was reasonably brought to her attention that *Promoter* was only willing to allow her to enter the concert hall on condition that she agreed not to sue *Promoter* if she suffered any kind of harm in the hall, and by buying a ticket, she reasonably gave the impression she was agreeing to that condition. If she did not want to agree to it, she need not have bought a ticket. And *Wife* has obtained something in return – some

---

[43] For example, if *Trespasser* was injured by a man-trap, or developed cancer as a result of being exposed to radiation from some illegally obtained uranium that *Owner* had left lying around his property.

[44] Where some other loss was suffered by the non-visitor, OLA 1984 would not apply to protect the non-visitor from that kind of harm: see above, § 11.2.

consideration – for agreeing to waive her rights to sue *Promoter* for damages under OLA 1957, by being allowed into the concert hall.

In contrast, it is much tougher to say that *Husband* is bound by the notice saying 'No liability accepted . . .'. He did not buy a ticket, and so did not give the impression that he was agreeing to this condition. And even if he did, he did not obtain anything in return for agreeing to that condition. So it seems that – subject to the provisions of UCTA 1977 – *Promoter* can rely on the *exclusion clause* in the notice at the entrance to defeat *Wife's* claim for damages under OLA 1957, but cannot use it against *Husband*, who will be suing *Promoter* under OLA 1984. However, there seems to be something wrong with this conclusion. Why should *Husband* benefit from his illegal act of sneaking into the concert hall? However, UCTA 1977 comes to the rescue here and kicks in to ensure that, in the end, *Husband* and *Wife* will be treated equally in this case. If *Promoter* tries to rely on the exclusion clause in the notice at the entrance to defeat *Wife's* claim for damages under OLA 1957, *Wife* can invoke s 2(1) of UCTA 1977 to prevent him from doing this: *Promoter* will not be allowed to rely on an exclusion clause to exclude his liability for 'death or personal injury resulting from negligence'.

Are there any cases that would not have such a happy outcome? – Where a trespasser (who will *not* normally be bound by an exclusion clause that an occupier wants people coming onto his land to agree to) will be better off than a visitor (who will be bound, subject to the provisions of UCTA 1977, by an exclusion clause that an occupier wants people coming onto his land to agree to if the visitor reasonably gives the impression of acceding to that desire, and receives something (usually access to the land) in return for that)? Suppose – in the situation we were considering in the previous section – that when *Unlucky* visited *Eagle's* premises, he was faced with a notice saying 'No liability accepted for any harm suffered by anyone on the premises.' He gains entrance to the premises, and ends up sharing a lift with *Thief*, who has entered the premises through a side door (but knows all about the notice at the entrance to *Eagle's* premises having cased the joint many times before) and plans to steal some industrial secrets from a partner's computer. Due to *Eagle's* fault, the lift free-falls for 10 floors and both *Unlucky* and *Thief* are injured.

In this case, *Eagle* might be able to say – in response to *Unlucky's* claim for damages under OLA 1957 – that the notice at the entrance effectively excluded the liability they would otherwise have incurred under OLA 1957 to *Unlucky*. By walking through the entrance where the notice was prominently displayed, he reasonably gave the impression that he was agreeing to waive the rights to sue for damages that he would otherwise have had against *Eagle* under OLA 1957, and he obtained something in return for agreeing to do that (access to *Eagle's* premises). And s 2(1) of UCTA 1977 will not operate to prevent *Eagle* making that argument, as the liability they are excluding in this case is not a 'business' liability.

In contrast, it is hard to see how *Eagle* could argue that their notice is binding on *Thief*, who will be attempting to sue *Eagle* for damages under OLA 1984. He did not give the impression of agreeing to waive whatever rights he might have had to sue *Eagle* under OLA 1984, and even if he did, he did not receive anything in return. So it seems that *Thief* will be better off than *Unlucky* in this situation. This seems wrong, but there does not seem to be any fault in the reasoning leading up to this conclusion. In order to avoid reaching this conclusion, we need to argue that the law includes some equitable principle of estoppel which says that you are prevented (or 'estopped') from advancing any arguments in court that would allow you to profit from your illegal act. But it is not clear that such a principle exists in English law.

11.5 LIABILITY UNDER THE GENERAL LAW OF NEGLIGENCE

That concludes our discussion of occupiers' liability under OLA 1957 and OLA 1984. We now turn to situations where an occupier will be held liable to a claimant under the general law of negligence.

A. Liability to visitors

An occupier will, of course, owe people on his land a normal *Donoghue v Stevenson*-type duty to take care not to do something *positive* that would put them in unreasonable danger of being killed or injured.[45] However, so far as *omissions* were concerned, it was thought until recently that the Occupiers' Liability Act 1957 was the only basis on which an occupier could be found to owe a visitor a *positive* duty to act to save that visitor from harm. That has now proved to be incorrect.

In *Everett* v *Comojo (UK) Ltd* (2011), the claimants were drinking at a nightclub, the Met Bar in the Metropolitan Hotel in London. A member of the club, SB, was aggrieved at the discourteous way in which, in his opinion, the claimants had treated their waitress. He took it on himself to remonstrate with them, more than once. Things gradually got out of control, and the claimants ended up being stabbed by an associate of SB's. Instead of suing the associate for damages, the claimants sued the defendant owners of the Met Bar. Their claim was dismissed: there was no evidence that the defendants had failed to take care to protect the claimants from being injured in the way they were. However, the importance of the case is that the Court of Appeal held that the defendants *had* owed the claimants a duty of care under the general law of negligence to protect them from being injured by a third party on the defendants' premises. Smith LJ held (with the agreement of the other two members of the court):

> I regard it as relevant that the relationship between the parties already carries with it an established duty, under the Occupiers' Liability Act 1957, in relation to the condition of the premises . . . It would be surprising if management could be liable to a guest who tripped over a worn carpet and yet escape liability for injuries inflicted by a fellow guest who was a foreseeable danger – for example in that he had previously been excluded on account of his violent behaviour and who on this occasion had been allowed in carrying an offensive weapon.[46]

Smith LJ's reasoning is hard to understand. If Parliament has legislated in the form of OLA 1957 to impose on occupiers a duty to take reasonable steps to protect visitors from dangerous features of the premises they occupy, it is hard to see how that warrants the common law imposing a duty on occupiers to protect visitors against risks from the activities of third parties on those premises. Parliament's failure to impose such a duty of care on occupiers in OLA 1957 is far more likely to indicate that Parliament did *not* want occupiers to be subject to such a duty of care, than it indicates that Parliament was happy for the courts to develop such a duty of care in parallel to the 'common duty of care' imposed by OLA 1957.

Be that as it may, *Everett* (unless and until it is overruled by the Supreme Court – which is turning out to be quite a common expression in this edition of this textbook) at its *narrowest* stands for the proposition that an occupier will owe his visitors a duty under the

---

[45] *Slater v Clay Cross Co Ltd* [1956] 2 QB 264, 269 (per Lord Denning MR) (example of occupier driving a car down the drive and meeting someone coming the other way).

[46] [2011] EWCA Civ 13, at [33].

common law to take care to protect them from being attacked by a third party and at its *widest* stands for the proposition that an occupier will owe his visitors a duty under the common law to take care to see that they are not injured by third parties engaging in unreasonably dangerous activities on his premises. It is uncertain at the moment just how far *Everett* goes.[47]

B. Liability to trespassers

Section 1(1) of OLA 1984 provides that OLA 1984 'shall have effect, in place of the rules of the common law, to determine' whether any duty is owed by an occupier of premises to non-visitors 'in respect of any risk of their suffering injury on the premises by reason of any danger due to the state of the premises . . .'. So OLA 1984 leaves space for the common law to determine what duties of care occupiers owe trespassers in respect of risks of harm that do *not* result from dangers due to the state of the premises.

As usual, an occupier will owe trespassers a *Donoghue* v *Stevenson*-style duty not to do a positive act that will create a foreseeable risk of a trespasser being injured, or his property being damaged.[48] So far as risks of harm that trespassers are exposed to as a result of the activities of third parties, the 'duty of common humanity' that occupiers owed trespassers before 1984 *may* still apply to determine whether an occupier owes a trespasser a duty to protect him or her against such a risk. The phrase 'duty of common humanity' comes from the case of *British Railways Board* v *Herrington* (1972), where – pre-OLA 1984 – the defendant railway company was held liable to compensate a child who had been electrocuted while walking over the defendants' railway line, which the child had access to because the defendants had allowed a fence separating the railway from a nearby meadow to fall into a dilapidated condition. But the danger there was created by the occupier[49] and situations where 'common humanity' would require an occupier to protect a trespasser against a risk of harm created by the activities of a third party may be few and far between – even assuming that the phrase 'duty of common humanity' was ever intended to apply outside cases where a trespasser was endangered by the state of the premises on which he was trespassing.

C. Liability to neighbours

An occupier of premises will owe a neighbour a duty to take reasonable steps to eliminate a dangerous situation that has arisen on his land if he knows or ought to know of that

---

[47] Para [36] of Smith LJ's judgment (which starts 'The common duty of care is an extremely flexible concept, adaptable to the very wide range of circumstances to which it has to be applied. It can be applied to the static condition of the premises and to activities on the premises . . . I think that it is appropriate . . . that it [surely not the very duty of care imposed by s 2 of OLA 1957, but rather the principles applicable to that duty] should govern the relationship between the managers of a hotel or night club and their guests in relation to the actions of third parties on the premises' and which finishes 'In a nightclub where outbreaks of violence are not uncommon, liability might well attach if a guest is injured in an outbreak of violence and there is no one on hand to control the outbreak . . . On the other hand, in a respectable members-only club, where violence is virtually unheard of . . . the duty on management may be no higher than that staff be trained to look out for any sign of trouble and to alert security staff') seems to start with the wide view and then finish with the narrow view.

[48] *Revill* v *Newbery* [1996] QB 567 (duty not to fire a gun through a hole in an shed door that a trespasser was standing behind, while trying to break into the shed).

[49] Indeed, given the facts, the House of Lords had no need to invoke a 'duty of common humanity' to explain why the claimant was owed a duty of care in this case: a *Donoghue* v *Stevenson*-style duty to take care not to run electricity down the defendants' line while someone might be on it would have sufficed; as would have a duty of care to avert the foreseeable danger to people like the claimant that the defendants created by running electricity down their line.

danger, and it is reasonably foreseeable that that danger threatens to damage his neighbour's land.

For example, in *Goldman* v *Hargrave* (1967), lightning struck a redgum tree on the defendant's land and set it on fire. The defendant cut down the tree but then did not do enough to put out the fire. The fire spread onto the claimant's land, causing much damage. The claimant successfully sued the defendant in negligence for compensation for the damage done to his land.[50] The Privy Council held that the defendant had owed the claimant a duty to take reasonable steps to put out the fire on his land, and that the defendant had breached that duty.[51] Decisions of the Privy Council are, of course, not binding on the English courts but the House of Lords has indicated that the decision in *Goldman* v *Hargrave* was correct.[52]

It is more uncertain whether A will owe a duty to his neighbour B to take reasonable steps to prevent his premises *becoming* a source of danger to B's land. The question was raised in *Smith* v *Littlewoods* (1987). The defendants purchased a cinema: they intended to knock it down and redevelop the land. For a few months the cinema was left unattended and unlocked. Vandals broke into the cinema and set it on fire. The fire spread to and damaged the claimants' premises. The claimants sued the defendants: they argued that the defendants had owed them a duty to take reasonable steps to keep the cinema secure, so as to prevent the cinema becoming a source of danger to their premises. The House of Lords dismissed the claimants' claim on the ground that it had not been reasonably foreseeable that the claimants' premises would be harmed if the defendants' cinema was not kept secure.[53]

In the course of deciding the case, Lords Brandon and Griffiths indicated that in the situation we are considering, A *will* owe B a duty to take reasonable steps to prevent his premises *becoming* a source of danger to B's land.[54] In contrast, Lord Goff thought that an occupier of land will *not* owe his neighbours a duty to take proactive steps to prevent his land *becoming* a source of danger to his neighbours' land: he will only owe his neighbours a duty of care in a *Goldman* v *Hargrave*-type situation where a danger *has* arisen on his land and he knows or ought to know of its existence.[55] Lord Mackay steered a middle path

---

[50] The claimant could have alternatively sued the defendant in *private nuisance* for compensation for the damage done to his land (see below, § 15.9(C)) and, indeed, it is customary nowadays for claims for damage done to land as a result of dangerous situations arising on neighbouring land to be brought in private nuisance rather than negligence (see, for example, *Leakey* v *National Trust for Places of Historic Interest or Natural Beauty* [1980] QB 485 and *Holbeck Hall Hotel Ltd* v *Scarborough BC* [2000] QB 836). Where the neighbour has suffered personal injury as a result of the defendant's failure to deal effectively with a fire arising on the defendant's land, a claim in private nuisance will be unavailable as claims for private nuisance do not cover personal injuries (see below, § 15.12). So in such a case, the neighbour would have to sue in negligence under *Goldman* v *Hargrave* [1967] 1 AC 645, but such a claim may be thrown out on the basis that the claimant's personal injury is the 'wrong kind of loss' to be sued for in negligence. That is, a court might find that the duty of care arising under *Goldman* v *Hargrave* was imposed on the defendant to protect his neighbour's land from being damaged, not in order to protect his neighbour from being injured.

[51] Had the fire been intentionally or carelessly started by the defendant, the claimant would have been entitled to sue the defendant for compensation for the damage done to his land without having to prove that the defendant was at all careless in allowing the fire to spread: see below, § 16.6(B).

[52] *Stovin* v *Wise* [1996] AC 923, 930 (per Lord Nicholls), 944 (per Lord Hoffmann).

[53] [1987] AC 241, at 250 (per Lord Brandon), 251 (per Lord Griffiths), 258–59 (per Lord Mackay).

[54] [1987] AC 241, at 250: '[the defendants] owed to the [claimants] a duty to exercise reasonable care to ensure that the cinema . . . did not become . . . a source of danger to neighbouring buildings owned or occupied by the claimants' (per Lord Brandon); 'the duty of care owed [by the defendants] was a duty to take reasonable care that the condition of the premises they occupied was not a source of danger to neighbouring property' (per Lord Griffiths).

[55] [1987] AC 241, at 272–4, 277–9.

between these two extremes. He thought that if A occupies some premises and it is reasonably foreseeable that if those premises are not kept secure vandals will break into A's premises and start a fire which is liable to spread to B's land, then A *will* owe B a duty to take reasonable steps to keep his premises secure, thereby preventing them becoming a source of danger to B's land.[56] But Lord Mackay thought things would be different in the case where it is reasonably foreseeable that if A's premises are not kept secure, thieves will break into A's premises and use those premises to gain access to B's land and steal property from B.[57] While he did not go so far as to say that *no* duty of care would be owed in this situation,[58] he plainly thought this case more difficult than the 'fire' case just discussed. Puzzlingly, the fifth judge to decide *Smith* v *Littlewoods* – Lord Keith of Kinkel – expressed agreement with the judgments of Lord Mackay *and* Lord Goff, despite the clear differences between them.

So *Smith* v *Littlewoods* did not finally resolve the issue of whether an occupier of premises will owe his neighbours a duty to take reasonable steps to prevent his property becoming a source of danger to his neighbours' land. The most that can be said in light of the decisions in that case is that there was a clear majority in favour of the proposition that such an occupier *will* owe his neighbours a duty to take reasonable steps to keep his premises secure *if* it is reasonably foreseeable that if he does not vandals will break in and start a fire which is liable to spread to his neighbours' land.

D. Liability to passers-by

The area of law we have just discussed overlaps with the law of private nuisance, which area of law helps to determine the rights and duties that neighbours owe each other. We now turn to an area of law which overlaps with the law on *public* nuisance, which helps (in part) prevent people's use of highways being unreasonably interfered with.

If *Owner* occupies premises that adjoin a highway, and there is some *Fixture* attached to those premises – such as a sign or a tree – which is liable to fall into the highway if it falls into disrepair, *Owner* will owe a duty to people using the highway next to his premises to take reasonable steps to see that *Fixture* does not fall into the highway and injure them. So if *Fixture* is in an obviously dangerous condition, *Owner* will have a duty to take reasonable steps to repair it or take it down.[59] And even if *Fixture* looks perfectly sound, *Owner* will have a duty from time to time to have an expert look at it to see that it does not suffer from any latent defects which mean that it is a danger to passers-by.[60]

---

[56] [1987] AC 241, at 258.

[57] [1987] AC 241, at 268.

[58] He did think that if A came back home to find a thief boring a hole through one of his walls to gain access to B's house, then A would owe B a duty to take reasonable steps to stop the thief gaining access to B's house in this way: [1987] AC 241, at 265. However, this result can easily be justified by reference to *Goldman* v *Hargrave*. In the case considered here a danger *will* have arisen on A's land which A knows about and therefore A will owe those of his neighbours who will be affected by that danger a duty to take reasonable steps to deal with it.

[59] *Tarry* v *Ashton* (1876) 1 QBD 314. The duty is non-delegable in nature. That is, if A employs someone else to repair the fixture, and that person fails to take reasonable steps to repair it properly, then A will be held to have breached his duty to take reasonable steps to repair the fixture: ibid. See above, § 8.6.

[60] *Caminer* v *Northern and London Investment Trust* [1951] AC 88 (held: occupiers not liable in negligence for injuries caused as a result of an elm tree falling into a road from their premises because the tree was apparently healthy; and, while the occupiers had failed to get anyone in to inspect the tree, even if they had, no action would have been taken to repair the tree or take it down because inspection by an expert would not have revealed that there was a problem with the tree).

If *Owner* breaches the duty he owes people passing by his property to take care to see that *Fixture* does not fall into the highway, and as a result of his breach *Fixture* does fall into the highway, and *Passer-By* is injured, he can be sued in negligence, but alternatively *Passer-By* could sue him for damages in public nuisance on the basis that *Owner* has adopted or continued a state of affairs that unreasonably interferes with the highway, and *Passer-By* has suffered special damage as a result.[61]

Visit **www.mylawchamber.co.uk/mcbride** to access tools to help you develop and test your knowledge of Tort law, including interactive multiple choice questions, practice exam questions with guidance, weblinks, legal newsfeed, additional case summaries, legal updates and tips on answering problem and essay questions.

Use **Case Navigator** to read in full some of the key cases referenced in this chapter with commentary and questions:

- Tomlinson *v* Congleton Borough Council

---

[61] See below, chapter 23.

12 Product liability

12.1 The basics *381*

12.2 Product *383*

12.3 Defect *384*

12.4 Defendants *387*

12.5 Damage *388*

12.6 Defences *390*

12.7 Remedies *393*

12.8 Discussion *394*

Overview

In this chapter, we finally move away from the law of negligence and discuss one area of law where *strict liability* prevails – that is, an area of law which makes a defendant liable for harm suffered by a claimant regardless of whether the defendant was at fault for the claimant suffering that harm. The area of law we are concerned with in this chapter is dominated by the Consumer Protection Act 1987 which makes a producer of a product (and other peripheral parties) strictly liable if that product turns out to be defective and a claimant suffers physical injury or damage to their property as a result. Section 12.1 explains the background of the 1987 Act. Sections 12.2 to 12.7 set out various different aspects of the liability regime created by the 1987 Act. Section 12.8 discusses whether producers of defective products should be held strictly liable for the harm done by those products.

12.1 THE BASICS

In this chapter, and for the first time in this book, we start to move outside tort law – if we conceive of tort law as being part of the law of wrongs. In this chapter we are not concerned with a defendant being held liable for *doing something wrong*; we are concerned instead with a defendant being liable because *something has gone wrong*. More specifically, this chapter is about when a defendant can be held liable to a claimant for harm suffered by that claimant because a product has turned out to be dangerously defective in some way.

Before 1987, such a claimant only had two avenues of recourse. First, if he had bought the product from someone, he could sue the *Seller* of the product *in contract*. *Seller* would be held *strictly liable* under s 14 of the Sale of Goods Act 1979 if the product was not of satisfactory quality, or not fit for the purpose for which the claimant indicated to the seller he wanted the product. In such a case, *Seller* would be liable to compensate the claimant for *any and all* foreseeable losses that the claimant suffered as a result of the product being no good, including the cost of replacing the product and any pure economic losses that the claimant would not have incurred had the product not been defective.

Secondly, the claimant could sue the *Manufacturer* of the product *in negligence*. *Manufacturer* would only be held liable for the product being defective if he was *at fault* for its being defective, *and* if it was reasonably foreseeable that someone like the claimant would suffer harm to their person or other property belonging to them if the product was defective. If this were the case, the claimant would only be able to sue *Manufacturer* for compensation for any foreseeable physical injury, or damage to other property belonging to him, that he had suffered as a result of the product being defective. The claimant would *not* be entitled to sue *Manufacturer* for the cost of replacing the product, and would *not* be entitled to sue *Manufacturer* for compensation for any pure economic losses that he would not have incurred had the product not been defective.

The Consumer Protection Act 1987 gave claimants who had suffered harm as a result of a product being dangerously defective a third avenue of recourse, and one which combines elements from the first two avenues. Section 2 of the 1987 Act lays out the basic liability rule created by the Act. It provides that:

(1) Subject to the following provisions of this Part, where any damage is caused wholly or partly by a defect in a product, every person to whom subsection (2) applies shall be liable for the damage.

(2) This subsection applies to –

(a) the producer of the product;

(b) any person who, by putting his name on the product or using a trade mark or other distinguishing mark in relation to the product, has held himself out to be the producer of the product;

(c) any person who has imported the product into a member State [of the European Union] from a place outside the member States in order, in the course of any business of his, to supply it to another.

As with a claim in contract under s 14 of the Sale of Goods Act 1979, liability under the 1987 Act is *strict*: a defendant who is sued under the 1987 Act will not be able to defend the claim by simply saying, 'I wasn't at fault for the product being defective!' or 'I wasn't at fault for what happened to the claimant!'. As with a claim in negligence, a defendant can only be held liable under the 1987 Act to compensate a claimant for physical injury or harm to other property belonging to the claimant that has been suffered as a result of a product being dangerously defective.

The 1987 Act has a European origin. It was passed to give effect to Council Directive 85/374/EEC ('the Directive') which required each Member State of the European Union to take steps to ensure that under their national laws the producer of a defective product would be held liable on a 'no-fault' basis for the damage done by that product – that is, would be held liable without the necessity of showing that the producer was at fault for the existence of the defect in the product in question. On its face, the object of the Directive was to harmonise the laws on product liability across the European Union because 'existing divergences may distort competition and affect the movement of goods within the [European Union's] common market'.[1] The idea was that producers of products in a particular country might gain an unfair competitive advantage if they were subject to products liability rules that were less harsh than those applied to producers of similar products in other countries within the European Union.[2] The Directive has signally failed to achieve this objective for three reasons.

---

[1] Preamble to Council Directive 85/374/EEC.

[2] For this reason, the European Court of Justice has ruled that the Directive is a 'maximum harmonisation' directive – that is, national governments are not allowed to give effect to a products liability regime which is *stricter* than that contemplated by the Directive.

First, the Directive sought to harmonise only the laws on when the producer of a defective product would be held liable in respect of damage done by that product to people or property 'intended for private use or consumption'.[3] National laws on when the manufacturer of a defective product would be held liable in respect of damage done by that product to *commercial property* were left untouched by the Directive.

Secondly, European Union governments did not have to implement *all* aspects of the Directive; they had some latitude to pick and choose which parts of the Directive they would implement. For example, the Directive provides that the producer of a defective product should not be held liable as a result of that product being defective if 'the state of scientific and technical knowledge at the time when he put the product into circulation was not such as to enable the existence of the defect to be discovered'.[4] However, national governments were allowed, in implementing the Directive, to choose whether or not to implement this particular provision.[5] Again, Article 16(1) of the Directive gave national governments the option of introducing a cap of not less than 70 million Euros on 'a producer's total liability for damage resulting from a death or personal injury and caused by identical items with the same defect'.[6]

Thirdly, the Directive did nothing to harmonise the remedies that would be available if someone was killed or injured as a result of a product being defective; for instance, the Directive did nothing to harmonise the law on whether – if someone was killed as a result of a product being defective – the deceased's dependants would be able to bring an action for damages in respect of the loss of support suffered by them as a result of the deceased's death.

Given this, it may be suspected that the real reason for the 1985 Directive was *not* to harmonise the law on products liability across the European Union, but that the Directive was a 'health and safety' measure, designed to enhance the level of protection from injury and damage to property enjoyed by 'citizens' of the European Union. Whatever the objectives that were sought to be achieved by adopting the 1985 Directive, as the Consumer Protection Act 1987 was enacted in order to implement that Directive the courts are required to take the Directive into account in interpreting the provisions of the 1987 Act and to interpret those provisions in such a way as will give effect to the Directive and promote its objectives.[7] It is to the provisions of the 1987 Act that we now turn.

12.2 PRODUCT

Section 1(2) of the 1987 Act provides that ' "product" means any goods or electricity and includes a product which is comprised in another product, whether by virtue of being a component part or raw material or otherwise'. So the term 'product' covers not only *manufactured products* (like cars, radios and computers)[8] but also *natural products* (like coal, flowers and animals).

There is some debate over whether body parts and blood count as 'products' under the Act. It seems likely that they do – 'goods' is defined in the Act as including 'substances',[9]

---

[3] Art 9.
[4] Art 7(e). This is known as the 'development risks defence'. On which, see below, § 12.6(5).
[5] Art 15(1)(b). All of the member states of the EU, except for Finland and Luxembourg, chose to adopt some form of 'development risks defence' in implementing the Directive.
[6] Only Germany, Portugal and Spain took up this option.
[7] Consumer Protection Act 1987, s 1(1).
[8] But not buildings: s 46(3).
[9] Section 45(1).

which would cover body parts and blood products; and Article 2 of the Directive defines the term 'product' as covering 'all moveables', which again would cover body parts and blood products. Indeed, it was conceded in the important case of *A v National Blood Authority* (2001) that contaminated blood did count as a 'product' under the Act.[10]

Opinion is more divided on the issue of whether an inaccurate map or some faulty software will count as a defective product under the 1987 Act.[11] The problem is that the map or software *qua* physical item will not be deficient in any respect. It is the information *on* the map or *in* the software that is deficient and that information does not seem to count as a 'substance' or a 'moveable'. This question has yet to be settled by the courts. It would seem an arbitrary result if, for example, an inaccurate map was not counted as being a defective product under the 1987 Act while, for example, a faulty pair of boots was regarded as defective under the Act: the danger posed by each to a mountaineer is the same. However, it may be that the language of the 1987 Act and the Directive will leave the courts with little choice but to reach such a conclusion.

12.3 DEFECT

Section 3 of the 1987 Act sets out when a product will count as being defective under the Act. Section 3 follows the Directive[12] in adopting a *legitimate expectations test* for determining whether a given product is defective: 'there is a defect in a product . . . if the safety of the product is not such as persons generally are entitled to expect.' The test is unhelpfully vague. There seems no right answer to the question of how safe we are entitled to expect products to be. However, the very limited caselaw on s 3 seems to have taken the *legitimate expectations test* as setting a *limit* on when a product will be regarded as defective under the Act. That is, the fact that a product has feature X or lacks feature Y *cannot* mean that it is defective for the purposes of s 3 *if* people *generally expect* the product to have feature X or people generally would not expect that product to have feature Y. But if people generally had *no expectations* as to whether a particular product would have feature X or lack feature Y, then the courts seem to have taken the view that they should find that the presence of feature X or the absence of feature Y in a product rendered the product defective if it would be consistent with the policy of the Act (and the underlying Directive) to make such a finding.

The case of *A v National Blood Authority* (2001) illustrates the point. That was a 'feature X' case. The claimants in that case were all infected with the hepatitis C virus as a result of receiving blood transfusions containing blood donated by people who had hepatitis C. At the time the claimants were infected, no test existed to detect whether a given bag of blood contained the hepatitis C virus. The claimants sued the National Blood Authority (the NBA) for compensation under the 1987 Act, claiming that the blood that they were given was defective under the 1987 Act because it was contaminated with hepatitis C. The NBA could not rely on the *legitimate expectations test* to argue that the blood received by the claimants was *not* defective because at the relevant time people generally were not aware that there was a risk that someone receiving a blood transfusion might contract hepatitis C.[13] Nor could they argue that the blood received by the claimants was not defective

---

[10] [2001] 3 All ER 289, at [17]. Blood and other human body parts and tissues are not generally regarded as 'products' under American products liability laws.

[11] See, generally, Whittaker 1989. For a negative view, see Stapleton 1994a, 333–4.

[12] See Art 6(1).

[13] [2001] 3 All ER 289, at [65].

because it would have been *very difficult* for the NBA to avoid giving the claimants contaminated blood.[14] The policy of the Act (and underlying Directive) demanded that defendants in the position of the NBA be held *strictly* liable for the harm caused by their products being contaminated in some way. If a defendant like the NBA could argue that a contaminated product was not defective because it was not its fault the product was contaminated, then liability under the 1987 Act for harm caused by contaminated products would no longer be strict, but fault-based. Given this, Burton J had no hesitation in finding that the contaminated blood given to the claimants in the *A* case was defective.

It was different in *Tesco Stores Ltd* v *Pollard* (2006). As in the *A* case, the Court of Appeal in *Pollard* was dealing with what Burton J called in *A*, a 'non-standard product . . . different from the norm which the producer intended for use by the public.'[15] Others would categorise this case as a *manufacturing defect* case – the product in *Pollard* did not conform to its intended design. The product was a bottle of dishwasher powder. The bottle top was fitted with a child-resistant lock, but there was some evidence that it was not as strong as it was intended to be. The claimant in *Pollard* was a 13-month-old child who had managed to unscrew the top of the bottle and was made sick by eating some of the powder inside the bottle. This was a 'feature Y' case – the claim was that the bottle was defective because the bottle top was not as child-resistant as it was supposed to be. The Court of Appeal rejected this claim. It applied the *legitimate expectations test* to find that people generally expected child-resistant locks to make the 'bottle . . . more difficult to open than if it had an ordinary screwtop.'[16] The lock in this case – though weaker than it was supposed to be – satisfied this expectation. So people generally did not expect the child-resistant lock in *Pollard* to be stronger than it actually was. The fact that the manufacturers of the bottle had expected, and wanted, it to be stronger was irrelevant. To hold that the lock's failure to live up to the manufacturer's standards meant it was defective would mean that 'every producer of a product whose use causes injury effectively warrants to the general public that the product fulfils its design standards . . . It is quite impossible to get such a result out of the terms of the 1987 Act.'[17]

So far we have been concerned with 'non-standard' products: products that have some feature X that they were not supposed to have, and products that lack some feature Y that they were supposed to have. But what about 'standard products' – that is, products that are exactly the way they are supposed to be? Consider the following couple of examples:

Customer is served a cup of coffee at her table at a restaurant. A passer-by accidentally knocks into *Customer*'s table and the coffee is spilled all over *Customer*'s lap, scalding her. The coffee was served at exactly the temperature it was supposed to be served at. *Customer* argues that the coffee was defective because it was served at too hot a temperature.

Husband tried to microwave a meal for himself. He misread the cooking instructions on the microwaveable meal, and thought that the time for cooking the meal in an oven was the time for cooking it in a microwave. Accordingly, he set the meal to be microwaved on full power for 30 minutes. After 20 minutes, the microwave blew up. *Husband* claims: (i) the microwaveable meal was defective because the cooking instructions on the meal were not clear enough; and (ii) the microwave was defective because there was no warning on the face of the microwave against using it for so long on ordinary meals.

---

[14] [2001] 3 All ER 289, at [63].
[15] [2001] 3 All ER 289, at [65].
[16] [2006] EWCA Civ 393, at [18].
[17] [2006] EWCA Civ 393, at [17].

The first case is commonly referred to as a *design defect* case – it is argued that the product in question was defective because it should have been designed to a higher safety standard. The second case is commonly referred to as a *marketing defect* case – it is argued that the products in this case were defective because they did not carry a warning against some danger that harmed the claimant.

In both of these cases, it is not clear that the *legitimate expectations test* indicates that the products in these examples were *not* defective. It is not clear that persons generally positively expect coffee served in a restaurant to be served at a temperature that is sufficient to scald someone if it is knocked over them. And it is not clear that persons generally do not expect to be warned of the dangers of over-microwaving meals. So whether the products in these examples are defective or not will depend on whether the policy of the 1987 Act (and underlying Directive) demands that the courts should find that these products are defective.

So far as 'standard products' are concerned, we think – and the courts seem to agree – that the policy of the Act does *not* demand that a manufacturer of a product should be invariably held liable for harm resulting from the fact that the product in its *intended* state has some dangerous feature X or lacks some safety feature Y. It is not in the public interest for the law to encourage manufacturers to ensure that their products in their *intended* state have no features that might cause another harm, and are overloaded with expensive safety features.

Instead, it seems, a 'standard product' will only be adjudged to be defective under the Act if *in retrospect* it would have been desirable for the product not to have some dangerous feature X or to have some safety feature Y given the costs and benefits involved in removing, or installing, that feature.

For example, in *B (a child)* v *McDonald's Restaurants Ltd* (2002), the claimants sued McDonald's for compensation under the 1987 Act when they were scalded by McDonald's coffee that was spilled on them. The coffee would not have scalded the claimants so badly had it been served at 55°C rather than the 90°C that it was actually served at. However, Field J refused to find that the coffee was defective under the Act. He held that the costs involved in serving the coffee at this lower temperature – in the shape of a loss in custom – outweighed the benefits:

> coffee served at between 55°C and 60°C would not have been acceptable to McDonald's customers. Indeed, on the evidence, I find that the public want to be able to buy . . . coffee served hot, that is to say at a temperature of at least 65°C [the temperature at which coffee will cause a severe burn if spilled on skin] even though they know . . . that there is a risk of a scalding injury if the drink is spilled.[18]

Again, in *Worsley* v *Tambrands* (2000), the claimant claimed that a box of tampons was defective under the 1987 Act because it carried a full warning of the danger of suffering 'toxic shock syndrome' ('TSS') from using tampons in a leaflet inside the box, but the box itself only carried a direction to consult the leaflet and did not reproduce the warning in the leaflet. So if the leaflet was thrown away, the box on its own would not do enough to alert users that their use of tampons might result in their suffering TSS. Ebsworth J rejected the claimant's argument:

> TSS is a rare but potentially very serious condition which may be life threatening, but it is necessary to balance the rarity and the gravity. That balance is reasonably, properly and safely struck by the dual system of a risk warning on the box and a full explanation in the leaflet if the former is clearly visible and the latter is both legible and full.[19]

---

[18] [2002] EWHC 490, at [33].
[19] [2000] PIQR 95, 102.

The sort of cost–benefit analysis that the courts engage in, in determining whether a 'standard product' is defective under the 1987 Act, might tempt the reader into thinking that a 'standard product' will only be defective under the 1987 Act if the manufacturer of that product could be held liable in *negligence* for the harm done by that product. That would be a mistake; as is shown by the case of *Abouzaid v Mothercare (UK) Ltd* (2001).

In that case, the claimant was injured when he attempted to fit a sleeping bag onto a pushchair. The sleeping bag was to be attached to the pushchair by passing two elasticated straps attached to the sleeping bag around the back of the pushchair and buckling them together. Unfortunately, the claimant let go of one of the elasticated straps and the buckle at the end of the strap hit him in the eye. He sued the defendants who marketed the sleeping bag under their name for compensation in negligence and under the 1987 Act. The claim in *negligence* was dismissed on the ground that at the time the sleeping bag was manufactured, it was not foreseeable that marketing a sleeping bag with that kind of design would result in injury to someone like the claimant.[20] But the sleeping bag *was* held to be defective under the 1987 Act. The sleeping bag could have been designed to a higher safety standard, either by making the straps attached to the sleeping bag non-elasticated or by having one continuous elasticated strap stretch from one side of the sleeping bag to the other. And, *in retrospect*, it would have been desirable to design the sleeping bag to such a higher safety standard: it would have been quite easy to make the sleeping bag safer to use at no added cost.

So the availability of a claim in negligence against the manufacturer of a 'standard product' depends on what was foreseeable at the time the product was manufactured. The inquiry into whether a 'standard product' is defective under the 1987 Act is not so constrained: it purely depends on whether, given what we know now, it would have been better for the product to have been designed or marketed in a different way.

12.4 DEFENDANTS

As we have seen, where a defective product causes a claimant damage (as defined in the Act) the claimant will normally be able to sue the following people for compensation: (a) the producer of the product; (b) anyone who held themselves out as being the producer of the product; and (c) anyone who imported the product into the EU.

Section 1(2) of the 1987 Act explains who will be the 'producer' of a product. If the product was manufactured, the 'producer' of that product will be the person who manufactured it. If the product in question was not manufactured but was instead 'won or abstracted' – say the product in question was coal – 'the person who won or abstracted it' will be the producer of the product.[21] The 1987 Act goes on to specify that 'in the case of a product which has not been manufactured, won or abstracted but essential characteristics of which are attributable to an industrial or other process having been carried out (for example, in relation to agricultural produce), the person who carried out that process' will be the 'producer' of that product.

---

[20] See above, § 6.2.

[21] What is the position if John dies and a surgeon, Wendy, takes out his heart for transplantation purposes and the heart is given to Fred in a heart transplant operation? If the heart proves to be defective (say, for example, it is cancerous), who will count as being the 'producer' of the heart? Stapleton 1994a suggests (at 310–11) that John will be the producer because he 'manufactured' the heart. However, this seems unreal: a heart is not a manufactured product but a natural product. The better view is that Wendy is the producer because she 'won or abstracted' the heart.

Sometimes it is difficult for a claimant to identify who (a), (b) or (c), above, are for the purposes of suing them under the 1987 Act. To help such a claimant identify who (a), (b) or (c) are, the Act gives claimants the option of suing the *supplier* of a defective product. Under s 2(3) of the Act, the supplier of a product will be held liable for the damage suffered by a claimant as a result of a product being defective if he does not identify within a reasonable period of time of being requested to do so either: (i) who (a), (b) and (c) are, in relation to that product; or (ii) who supplied the defective product to him. In this way, a claimant who wants to sue for compensation under the 1987 Act can chase up a chain of supply, threatening each person in the chain that they will be held liable unless they identify who is the next highest person in the chain, until he eventual arrives at the producer of the product that harmed him.

In any given case, there may be more than one defective product that has harmed a claimant, and therefore two sets of defendants who can be sued under the 1987 Act for the harm that has been suffered by the claimant. For example, consider the following case:

> *Pedestrian* is run over by a car driven by *Driver* when one of the car's tyres explodes, and *Driver* loses control of the car. The tyre was manufactured by *Rubber*, and was fitted on the car by its manufacturer, *Automobile*. The tyre suffered from a tiny flaw which meant that when heated to a high temperature, it was liable to explode.

In this case *both* the tyre *and* the car are defective. They are both 'non-standard products' in that that neither the tyre nor the car are operating in the way they were designed to operate. So *Pedestrian* will be able to sue both *Automobile* and *Rubber* for the harm that he has suffered here.

12.5 DAMAGE

The sort of damage that can be sued for under the 1987 Act is defined in s 5(1) of the Act: ' "damage" means death or personal injury or any loss of or damage to any property (including land).'

Personal injury is defined by the Act as including 'any disease and any other impairment of a person's physical *or mental condition*.'[22] The reference to 'mental condition' suggests that claimants can bring claims for psychiatric illnesses caused by defective products under the 1987 Act in circumstances where it would be impossible to bring a claim in negligence. For example, suppose that in the case we were just considering, *Bystander* witnessed *Pedestrian* being run over and was so shocked by the sight that she developed a psychiatric illness. In such a case, she could not bring a claim in negligence against anyone who was at fault for *Pedestrian*'s being run over;[23] but she might be able to sue *Automobile* and *Rubber* for compensation for her psychiatric illness under the 1987 Act.

The Act places three limits on when a claimant can sue for compensation in respect of damage to property that has occurred as a result of a product being defective:

(1) *Auto-destruction*. Section 5(2) of the 1987 Act provides that:

> A person shall not be liable in respect of any defect in a product for the loss of or any damage to the product itself or for the loss of or any damage to the whole or any part of any product which has been supplied with the product in question comprised in it.

---

[22] Section 45(1) (emphasis added).
[23] See above, § 6.4.

So, in the case we have been considering, suppose that as a result of one of the tyres on *Driver*'s car exploding, not only is *Pedestrian* run over, but *Driver*'s car slams into a lamp-post and is a complete write-off. In this case, *Driver* will not be entitled to sue *Rubber* for the loss of his car because the car came with *Rubber*'s defective tyre installed as part of the car. And *Driver* will not be entitled to sue *Automobile* for the loss of his car because his claim against *Automobile* will be based on the argument that the car manufactured by *Automobile* was defective, and s 5(2) prevents him suing for the damage that the car did to itself as a result of being defective.

Two points about this should be noted. The first is that the law of negligence is a bit more generous to claimants in allowing them to sue for compensation where a product has been damaged because part of that product was defective. So long as the defective part of the product and the rest of the product can be viewed as two separate items of property, the law of negligence allows the owner of the product to sue whoever was at fault for the defective part of the product being defective for the damage done to the rest of the product.[24] So if, in the above case, *Rubber* was at fault for not detecting that its tyre was defective, and the defective tyre is viewed as a separate item of property from the rest of the car, then *Driver* would be able to sue *Rubber* in negligence for the damage done to the rest of the car as a result of *Rubber*'s tyre being defective.

Secondly, *Rubber* cannot be sued for the damage done to the car here because the car was supplied with their tyre as part of the car. It follows that if the car was supplied to *Driver* with a different set of tyres, and *Driver* had the tyres replaced with tyres manufactured by *Rubber*, then *Rubber* could be held liable for the damage done to the car as a result of one of their tyres exploding.

(2) *Damage to commercial property.* Section 5(3) of the 1987 Act provides that a claim for compensation cannot be brought under the Act in respect of damage to property that: (1) is not 'ordinarily intended for private use, occupation or consumption; *and* (2) is not in fact 'intended by the person suffering the loss or damage mainly for his own private use, occupation or consumption.'

Both (1) *and* (2) have to be satisfied before a claim for compensation for property damage can be ruled inadmissible under s 5(3). So, for example, in the case where *Driver*'s car slams into a lamp-post because one of its tyres blows out, the council that owns the lamp-post could not sue *Rubber* or *Automobile* for the damage done to the lamppost. Lamp-posts are not ordinarily intended for private use, and this particular lamp-post was not in fact intended for private use. It would be different if the lamp-post that *Driver*'s car slammed into was a feature of someone's driveway – in that case, a claim could be made for the damage to the lamp-post under the 1987 Act as that particular lamp-post was intended for private use.

(3) *Trivial damage to property.* Section 5(4) of the 1987 Act provides that:

> No damages shall be awarded to any person by virtue of this [Act] in respect of any loss or damage to any property if the amount which would fall to be awarded to that person . . . does not exceed £275.

There is a question – that has not been resolved – as to how this provision applies in a case where a defective toaster causes a small fire in a kitchen which damages curtains worth £200, and damage to the paintwork in the kitchen that will cost £250 to repair. Is the claim

---

[24] For much more discussion of this point, see above, § 6.9(E).

for compensation for this damage to property knocked out on the ground that the damages payable in respect of *each* item of damaged property do not exceed £250? Or can we aggregate the claims for damage to property here and say that the total claim for damage to property comes to £450, and is therefore unaffected by s 5(4)?

The question is one that is more likely to exercise law students and their examiners than anyone in the real world. In the real world, the owner of the toaster would claim on their household insurance, and their insurer would either write off the loss, or would make a claim for the damage (under the law on subrogation) against the manufacturer of the toaster and that claim would be settled as not worth the trouble of disputing. But, for what it is worth, we think that the language of the Act (and the Directive) indicates that you cannot aggregate the claims for property damage here, and each claim will be struck out as falling short of the s 5(4) threshold. The main reason for taking this view is that both the Act and the Directive talk of claims for compensation in respect of 'any property' (the Act) or 'any item of property' (the Directive)[25] – and the use of the word 'any' here would seem to indicate that the £275 threshold is meant to apply in respect of *each* item of property that has been damaged as a result of a defective product.

12.6 DEFENCES

Defendants who would normally be held liable under s 2(1) of the 1987 Act for damage caused by a defective product may be able to take advantage of one of the range of defences set out in s 4(1) of the Act:

(1) *That the defect was attributable to compliance with any requirement imposed by or under any enactment or with any Community obligation.*[26]

(2) *That he did not put the product into circulation.*[27] So say *Automobile* manufactures a car which is then stolen from their factory before it is shipped out. The car is then sold to *Driver* who is injured because the car suffers from some flaw. *Driver* will not be able to sue *Automobile* for damages under the 1987 Act because *Automobile* did not put the car into circulation.

(3) *That he did not supply the product to another in the course of business and he did not produce, brand or import it with a view to profit.*[28] So if *Helpful* bakes some cakes for a school fair and *Father*, having bought them at the fair, is poisoned by them, *Father* will not be entitled to sue *Helpful* for damages under the 1987 Act: *Helpful* did not supply the cakes to the fair organisers in the course of a business of hers and she did not supply those cakes for profit. It would be different if the poisonous cakes were donated by a nearby *Bakery*. As *Bakery* produced those cakes in the course of business, it will not be able to take advantage of this defence if *Father* tries to sue it.

(4) *That the defect did not exist in the product at the time he supplied the product to someone else.*[29] Go back to the case where *Driver's* car spins out of control because one of the tyres that was fitted to the car after *Driver* bought it exploded. If *Driver* attempts to sue *Automobile* under the 1987 Act for any injuries he suffered as a result of his car crashing,

---

[25] Art 9(b).
[26] Section 4(1)(a); Art 7(d).
[27] Section 4(1)(b); Art 7(a).
[28] Section 4(1)(c); Art 7(c).
[29] Section 4(1)(d); Art 7(b).

arguing 'Your car was defective!', Automobile will be entitled to reply, 'It wasn't defective when it left our factory; it was made defective afterwards because you fitted it with dodgy tyres.'

(5) *That the state of scientific and technical knowledge at the time when he put the product into circulation was not such as to enable the existence of the defect to be discovered.*[30] The classic case where this defence – known as the 'development risks defence' – will be available is where A puts into circulation some drug that has a dangerous side-effect which no one[31] could have known about at the time the drug was marketed. Those who have suffered harm as a result of the drug's having that side effect will not be able to sue A for compensation under the 1987 Act.

It is now clear from the decision in *A v National Blood Authority* (2001) that the defence may also be available in a manufacturing defect case, where a product is defective because it does not conform to its intended design. Suppose, for example, that *Genius* manufactures computer chips, and one of the millions of chips that came off its assembly line suffered from a microscopic flaw which meant that it did not function properly when installed in a light airplane, with the result that the airplane crashed and *Pilot* was injured. *Genius might* be able to take advantage of the 'development risks defence' if it can show that the state of scientific and technical knowledge at the time it manufactured the defective chip meant that it was simply not possible to identify that chip as being defective.

However, in the *A* case, Burton J placed one very important limit on the availability of the defence in a manufacturing defect case. He held that A will not be able to take advantage of the defence if *he was aware at the time he manufactured the product that there was a risk that it might not conform to its intended design in the way it did.*[32] This limit severely curtails the availability of the development risks defence in manufacturing defect cases. For example, in the case we have been considering, *Genius* will almost certainly have been aware that there was a risk that one of its chips might suffer from a microscopic flaw. If he was – and he did not arrogantly think that there was absolutely no possibility of any of his chips being defective – then he will not be able to take advantage of the 'development risks defence' to defeat *Pilot*'s claim for damages against him under the 1987 Act.

Burton J's limit on the applicability of the development risks defence also meant that it was unavailable to the defendants in the *A* case. They sought to argue that the defence was available to them because the state of scientific and technical knowledge at the time the claimants contracted hepatitis C was not such as to enable them to detect which of their bags of blood were contaminated with hepatitis C. Burton J held that even if this were true,

---

[30] Art 7(e). The equivalent provision in the 1987 Act – s 4(1)(e) – might appear to be somewhat narrower. That provides that someone who is sued in respect of a defect in a product under the Act will have a defence if the 'state of scientific and technical knowledge at the relevant time was not such that a *producer or producers of products of the same description as the product in question might be expected to have discovered the defect . . .*' (emphasis added). This led the European Commission to bring an action against the UK, claiming that the UK had failed in s 4(1)(e) correctly to implement the Directive. However, the European Court of Justice expressed itself content with the wording of s 4(1)(e), holding that 'there is nothing . . . to suggest that the courts in the United Kingdom, if called upon to interpret s 4(1)(e), would not do so in light of the wording and purpose of the Directive so as to achieve the result it has in view': *European Commission v UK* [1997] All ER (EC) 481, at [33].

[31] If, at the time A put the drug into circulation, an academic had published a paper in Manchuria revealing that the drug had this side effect, that – it seems – would not be enough to deprive A of the development risks defence: see the opinion of the Advocate-General in [1997] All ER (EC) 481, at [24]. It has to be shown that the state of *accessible* scientific and technical knowledge at the time the drug was circulated was not such as to allow the existence of the side-effect to be discovered: ibid, at [23].

[32] [2001] 3 All ER 289, at [74].

the defence was unavailable because the defendants were aware at the time the claimants contracted hepatitis C that there was a risk that the blood supplied by them to people like the claimants might be contaminated with hepatitis C.

(6) *That the defect – (i) constituted a defect in a product ('the subsequent product') in which the product in question was comprised; and (ii) was wholly attributable to the design of the subsequent product or to compliance by the producer of the product in question with instructions given by the producer of the subsequent product.*[33] It is often said that this defence will cover the case where, say, a lorry manufacturer fits tyres on one of his lorries which are completely unsuitable for that lorry with the result that when the lorry is driven the tyres blow out and an accident is caused. It is said that the tyre manufacturer will be able to take advantage of this defence if he is sued by the people involved in the accident under the 1987 Act. But it is difficult to see how he could be sued in any case by the people involved in the accident: surely his tyres were never defective?

It is worth mentioning two defences that are *not* available to a defendant who is sued for damages under the 1987 Act:

(1) *Voluntary assumption of risk.* Suppose that *Vain* goes to her *Doctor* for some botox injections into her face. *Doctor* warns her against having the operaton, telling her that he has heard 'on the grapevine' that there are some stocks of botox that are infected with flesh eating viruses. *Vain* insists on going ahead with the operation. If the botox injected into *Vain*'s face *is* contaminated with flesh eating viruses and *Vain* suffers horribly as a result then *Vain* will be entitled to sue the *Manufacturer* of the botox for compensation under the 1987 Act. It will be no defence for *Manufacturer* to say that *Vain* voluntarily took the risk that she would be infected with flesh-eating viruses when she had her injections.

(2) *More good than harm.* As we will see,[34] there is some authority that a negligent defendant might be able to take advantage of an 'I did more good than harm' defence, in the case where he was negligent in the course of saving a claimant or the claimant's property from harm, and had he not been negligent, the claimant would have been even better off than the defendant made her. But no such defence is available to an action under the 1987 Act. So suppose that *Ill* is admitted to hospital in desperate need of a heart transplant. A donor heart is tracked down and is transplanted into *Ill*. Unfortunately, and unknown to everyone, the heart is cancerous and *Ill* develops cancer as a result of the heart transplant operation. *Ill* wants to sue the 'producers' of the heart for compensation. It seems likely that her claim will succeed: the heart was defective under the 1987 Act (it was cancerous) and *Ill* suffered actionable damage as a result of the heart being defective (she developed cancer). The producers of the heart will not be able to defeat *Ill*'s claim for compensation by pointing out that her having the heart transplant operation did her more good than harm – that is, had she not had the operation, she would be dead by now.

It is also worth mentioning that under s 11A of the Limitation Act 1980, a defendant cannot be held liable for damage caused by a defective product unless he is sued for that damage within ten years of the product going into circulation. This gives effect to Art 11 of the Directive.[35] This does not, of course, mean that a claimant who has suffered relevant

---

[33] Section 4(1)(f); Art 7(f).
[34] See below, § 26.13.
[35] On the interpretation of which, see the Supreme Court decision in *O'Byrne* v *Aventis Pasteur MSD Ltd* [2010] 1 WLR 1412.

damage as a result of a product being defective will have ten years from the date the product was to put into circulation to bring a claim for that damage under the 1987 Act. He will have to bring his claim within three years of the date he first suffered that damage, or the date he could have been reasonably expected to realise he had suffered 'significant damage' and to identify the person responsible for that damage.[36]

12.7 REMEDIES

A number of different points need to be made here about the remedies that will be made available under the 1987 Act when someone suffers some relevant damage as a result of a product being defective.

(1) *Consumers and third parties.* Although the title of the 1987 Act is the *Consumer Protection Act*, the Act operates to protect *anyone* who has suffered actionable 'damage' as a result of a product being defective. So in the example we were considering – where *Pedestrian* is run over by a car (manufactured by *Automobile*) that is spinning out of control because one of its tyres (manufactured by *Rubber*) has exploded – *Pedestrian* will be entitled to sue *Automobile* and *Rubber* for compensation for his injuries even though no one would say that he is a 'consumer'.

(2) *Range of liability.* Having said that, the 1987 Act is completely silent on the issue of whether any limits should be drawn on the range of third parties who will be entitled to sue for damages under the 1987 Act.

Suppose, for example, that in the above example, *Pedestrian*'s injuries had an adverse effect on his personality with the result that he eventually raped *Victim*. Will *Victim* be able to sue *Automobile* and *Rubber* for damages under the 1987 Act to compensate her for the fact that she was raped by *Pedestrian*? There is nothing in the Act to guide us one way or the other on this issue.

Suppose, alternatively, that *Pedestrian* was so severely injured that his *Wife* had to give up her job and look after *Pedestrian*. She was eventually so worn down by the strain of looking after *Pedestrian* that she suffered a nervous breakdown. If she sued *Automoble* or *Rubber* in negligence for compensation for her breakdown, she would lose: she would not be able to establish that either owed her a duty of care in manufacturing the tyre.[37] But could she instead sue *Automobile* and *Rubber* for compensation for her breakdown under the 1987 Act? Again, there is nothing in the Act to give us any guidance on this issue.

(3) *Fatal accidents.* Section 6(1) of the 1987 Act provides that any 'damage for which a person is liable under [the Act] shall be deemed to have been caused . . . for the purposes of the Fatal Accidents Act 1976, by that person's wrongful act, neglect or default'. So, if – in the situation we have been considering – *Pedestrian* has been killed as a result of the car spinning out of control, and had he not been killed but merely injured, he would have been entitled to sue *Automobile* and *Rubber* for damages under the 1987 Act, *Pedestrian*'s dependants may be entitled to sue those producers for damages under the Fatal Accidents Act 1976. Whether they will or not depends on who they are and what sort of loss they have suffered as a result of *Pedestrian*'s death.

---

[36] Limitation Act 1980, s 11A(4).
[37] See above, § 6.4.

(4) *Exclusion/limitation clauses.* Section 7 of the 1987 Act makes it impossible for a defendant to exclude or limit his liability under the 1987 Act. It provides that the 'liability of a person [under this Act] to a person who has suffered damage caused wholly or partly by a defect in a product, or to a dependant or relative of such a person, shall not be limited or excluded by any contract term . . .'.

(5) *Remoteness of damage.* The 1987 Act leaves it completely open what rules on remoteness of damage will apply to claims under the Act. Presumably, the same rules that apply in a negligence case[38] will also apply to a claim under the 1987 Act. It would be strange if the law were to treat a negligent defendant less harshly than someone who was held strictly liable under the 1987 Act for the harm caused by a malfunctioning product. 'Strict' liability means liability without having to prove fault; it does not mean 'unlimited' liability or 'oppressively harsh' liability.

(6) *Contributory negligence.* If a claimant was partly to blame for the damage she suffered as a result of a product being defective – for example, she should have known the product was defective but carried on using it regardless – then the damages payable to the claimant may be reduced on the ground of *contributory negligence.* This is the effect of s 6(4) of the 1987 Act, which provides that where:

> any damage is caused partly by a defect in a product and partly by the fault of the person suffering the damage, the Law Reform (Contributory Negligence) Act 1945 and section 5 of the Fatal Accidents Act 1976 (contributory negligence) shall have effect as if the defect were the fault of every person liable by virtue of [this Act] for the damage caused by the defect.

12.8 DISCUSSION

It seems to us that five arguments can be made in favour of the strict liability regime created by the 1987 Act. None of these arguments is capable of justifying *all* of the features of the 1987 Act. So they only provide a rough, and not detailed, justification of the 1987 Act. Moreover, some of these arguments – if taken to their limit – suggest that we should extend strict liability to other areas of life (such as driving on the road) where strict liability is not currently the rule. So even if these arguments roughly justify the 1987 Act, they are not necessarily given effect to by other areas of the law.

(1) *Proof problems.* The first argument in favour of the 1987 Act focuses on how difficult it can be for a consumer who has been injured by a defective product to prove that the defect was due to a manufacturer's negligence. So a strict products liability regime may be justified as the most efficient way of delivering compensation to all the claimants who should, in principle, be entitled to sue for compensation in negligence for the product-related harms they have suffered, but would find it very difficult to make out a claim were they confined to suing in negligence. Of course, such a regime also makes liable some manufacturers – such as the sleeping bag manufacturer in *Abouzaid* (2001) – who could not have been sued for compensation under the law of negligence. But given the choice between allowing an injustice to be done to many consumers (who should be allowed to sue under negligence, but cannot obtain an effective remedy under that area of law) and doing an injustice to some manufacturers, the latter option may be preferable.

(2) *Fletcher's argument.* However, it may be that a strict products liability regime is not unjust at all. This thought underlies the next two arguments in favour of strict liability for

---

[38] For which, see above, § 10.2.

harms caused by defective products. The first such argument was made by George Fletcher in a very famous 1972 article called 'Fairness and utility in tort theory'.[39]

Fletcher argued that holding a defendant liable in tort to pay compensation to a claimant was justified where the defendant's actions exposed the claimant to a non-reciprocal risk of harm. In such a case, the defendant could justly be held liable if that risk materialised, even if he was not at fault either for exposing the claimant to a risk of harm in the first place, or the fact that that risk materialised. The fact that the defendant had exposed the claimant to a risk of harm that was not matched by any risk of harm that the claimant exposed the defendant to made it only fair that if that risk materialised, the defendant should bear the consequences. (Where the risk is reciprocal – for example, where the defendant and claimant are each driving on the same road – the only thing the defendant has to do for the claimant (and vice versa) is to take care to see that that risk does not materialise.)

This argument could be adapted to support the strict products liability regime created by the 1987 Act. The risk of harm from a product being defective that manufacturers of products expose ordinary people to is not matched by any risk of harm that ordinary people expose manufacturers to. So if that risk materialises, it is only fair that the consequences of that risk materialising should be borne by the manufacturer.

(3) *Keating's argument.* Just over a quarter of a century after Fletcher published his article, another American academic, Greg Keating, made a slightly different argument in favour of strict liability that may apply to justify the 1987 Act.[40]

Keating's argument distinguishes between what he called the 'world of acts' and the 'world of activities'. In the world of acts, whether or not you suffer harm at another's hands is a matter of pure chance. But in the world of activities, risks of harm are predictable. If you continuously repeat the same activity it becomes possible to predict how likely it is that your activity is going to result in harm to someone else. And if you can predict that, then if the law holds you liable on a strict liability basis when your activity results in harm to someone else, that is not such a burden on you. You can predict how often you will be held liable and for how much, and take out insurance to cover yourself against that liability. In contrast, if someone who is harmed by your activity can only sue if you were at fault for their being harmed, they will sometimes go without a remedy, and have to bear the burden of the harm they have suffered without any support from anyone else.

So, Keating argues, in the world of activities, strict liability provides a more satisfactory way of striking the right balance between the competing demands of security (which demands that someone who has been injured always have a remedy for that injury) and the demands of freedom (which demands that people be allowed to go about their business without being held liable to anyone):

> In the world of activities . . . the choice between strict liability and negligence is a choice between a grave disruption of security and a more modest disruption of liberty. Activity liability [which means here strict liability for harms regularly associated with a particular activity] strikes a more favorable balance between the competing claims of liberty and security than negligence liability does, because activity liability disrupts the liberty of injurers less than negligence impairs the security of victims. Enterprise liability thus secures more favorable conditions than negligence liability for citizens concerned to pursue their conceptions of the good over complete lives.[41]

[39] Fletcher 1972.
[40] Keating 1997.
[41] ibid, 1355.

The application of this argument to the 1987 Act should be pretty obvious. A manufacturer of computer chips can predict how many per million of the chips that roll off its production line will turn out to be flawed. Holding the manufacturer liable for the harm done by the flawed chips will be less burdensome for it than a negligence liability regime would be for those harmed as a result of the manufacturer's chips being defective.

(4) *Deterrence*. A fourth argument in favour of a strict products liability regime is that the existence of such a regime encourages manufacturers to do as much as they can to improve the safety of their products; the idea being that under a strict liability regime, they know that they are much less likely to 'get away' with producing unsafe products than they would be under a negligence liability regime. Whether strict products liability does actually encourage better safety standards among manufacturers has been the subject of recent debate.[42] The most that can be said is that the jury is still out on the question.

(5) *Making externalities internal*. The fifth and final argument in favour of a strict products liability regime is an economic one. The argument starts from the uncontroversial premise that only products that are beneficial to society should enjoy a market. A product will be beneficial if the benefits attached to its production outweigh the costs. The best way of ensuring that only beneficial products survive in the marketplace is to ensure that the price of a product reflects its real cost. If people are willing to buy a product at a price that exceeds its real cost, then that shows – almost by definition – that the benefits of that product outweigh its costs. But frequently the price of a product does not reflect its real costs. A given product may impose external costs on society which the manufacturer of the product never has to take into account in pricing that product.[43] Strict liability for harms caused by defective products is one way of ensuring that some of the externalities associated with the production of a particular product are brought home to the manufacturer, so that the price of that product will more closely reflect the real costs associated with that product.

All of these arguments seem to us to be good ones, and to put it beyond doubt that the broad effect of the 1987 Act is amply justified. (Details of the Act can, of course, be criticised.) We are more doubtful that liability under the 1987 Act or some other strict product liability regime can be justified as an example of compensation for wrongdoing, as some theorists have recently tried to argue. The most prominent such theorist is Richard Epstein, who argues[44] that if a defendant causes some harm to a claimant's person or property, then the defendant has presumptively done something wrong to the claimant: 'entering into the space of another creates the prima facie case of liability for what happens thereafter.'[45] John Goldberg and Benjamin Zipursky have also argued that:

> the case for the imposition of liability on manufacturers for product-related injuries more or less on the terms set by the current law is no different from the case for the recognition of tort law in many other instantiations. There are many reasons to have a law that . . . permits victims to respond to those who have wronged them through the courts, and deems a commercial seller that injures someone through the sale of a dangerously defective product to have committed . . . a wrong.[46]

---

[42] See Polinsky and Shavell 2010 and Goldberg and Zipursky 2010b.

[43] For example, if burgers or chips were priced to reflect the real cost to society of their consumption, they might well become luxury items.

[44] The classic article is Epstein 1973.

[45] Epstein 2010, text at n 32.

[46] Goldberg and Zipursky 2010b, at 1944.

Robert Stevens has taken a similar line, arguing that:

> a producer's duty is . . . to refrain from manufacturing defective products which cause harm[;] the fact that the manufacturer took all care in manufacturing the product does not excuse. It is not meaningless to describe the claim of a person harmed by a defective product as based upon a tort, although the manufacturer is without blame in any moral sense.[47]

All such arguments, we think, rest on a linguistic mistake: that of thinking that because we all have a right *to* bodily integrity (for example), it follows that when someone else violates our bodily integrity, they have violated our rights, and done something wrong to us.[48] The mistake is to forget that we only have a right *to* bodily integrity insofar as the law grants us rights against other people *that* they not violate our bodily integrity in various ways. And there is no reason to think that the law gives us rights against other people that *unqualifiedly* demand, as Epstein puts it, 'forbearance against physical interference with [our] person and property'.[49] Given this, we have no reason to think that a manufacturer of a defective product that has harmed a claimant's person or property has done anything legally wrong to that claimant.[50] It follows that liability under the 1987 Act is better seen as an example of 'compensation without wrongdoing' rather than as a standard example of a wrongdoer being held liable to compensate the victim of his wrong.

Further reading

Students should be careful in reading any academic literature on the Consumer Protection Act 1987 that was written at the time the Act was passed. A lot of the criticisms made of the Act at that time – for example, that it was too weak to have any real impact on the law, or that the 'development risks defence'meant that a manufacturer would effectively have a 'no fault' defence to being sued under the Act – have proved to be completely unjustified. It is safer to stick to literature written after the decision in *A* v *National Blood Authority* (2001), such as **Howells and Mildred, 'Infected blood: defect and discoverability' (2002) 65** *Modern Law Review* **95**; Shears, 'The EU Product Liability Directive – twenty years on' [2007] *Journal of Business Law* 884; and **Fairgrieve and Howells, 'Rethinking product liability: a missing element in the European Commission's third review of the Product Liability Directive' (2007) 70** *Modern Law Review* **962**. A collection of essays edited by Duncan Fairgrieve and published as *Product Liability in Comparative Perspective* (Cambridge University Press, 2005) contains many interesting papers, in particular **Howells, 'Defect in English law – lessons for the harmonisation of European product liability'; Mildred, 'The development risks defence';** and **Stapleton, 'Bugs in Anglo-American product liability'**. On justifications of strict liability generally, **George Fletcher's 'Fairness and utility in tort theory' (1972) 85** *Harvard Law Review* **537** is a classic and well worth reading.

Visit **www.mylawchamber.co.uk/mcbride** to access tools to help you develop and test your knowledge of Tort law, including interactive multiple choice questions, practice exam questions with guidance, weblinks, legal newsfeed, additional case summaries, legal updates and tips on answering problem and essay questions.

premium
mylawchamber
unrivalled support for legal education

---

[47] Stevens 2007, at 99.

[48] See above, § 1.2.

[49] Epstein 2010, text at n 31.

[50] The fact that s 6(1) of the Consumer Protection Act 1987 explicitly creates a fiction that someone who has been killed by a defective product has been the victim of a wrong, so as to bring his case within the Fatal Accidents Act 1976, only strengthens this point.

13 Liability for animals

13.1 The basics *398*

13.2 Section 2(2) *399*

13.3 Defences *404*

Overview

The last chapter dealt with situations where a defendant would be held strictly liable for harm caused by a dangerously defective product. This chapter is concerned with situations where a defendant will be held strictly liable for harm caused by dangerous animals. Section 13.1 sets out the basic liability rules that apply in this area of law. Section 13.2 discusses how those rules are interpreted. And section 13.3 looks at the defences that might be available to a defendant who is sued under those rules.

13.1 THE BASICS

As we have seen, if A is in control of a dangerous thing and it escapes his control due to his carelessness, and B suffers foreseeable harm as a result, B may be entitled to sue A in negligence for compensation for that harm.[1]

However, the common law went further in cases where someone was in control of a dangerous animal. Under the common law, the keeper of an animal which had a tendency to do harm was held liable for any damage that the animal caused – whether the keeper was at fault for that harm or not – so long as the keeper knew that that animal had a tendency to do harm.[2] Animals were divided by species into two classes. If an animal belonged to a *dangerous species*, it would be conclusively presumed to have a tendency to do harm, its keeper would be conclusively presumed to know that it had a tendency to do harm,[3] and its keeper would be held liable for any damage that it caused. If, on the other hand, the animal which caused harm belonged to a species that was by nature harmless or generally tamed or domesticated, then its keeper would only be held liable for the harm under the above liability rule if it could be specifically proved that the animal had a tendency to do such harm and that its keeper knew that it had a tendency to do such harm.

The Animals Act 1971 abolished these common law rules[4] and replaced them with the following set of liability rules:

(1) *Liability of the keeper of an animal belonging to a dangerous species.* Section 2(1) of the 1971 Act provides that the keeper of an animal which belongs to a dangerous species is liable for the damage that it causes unless a relevant defence applies.

---

[1] See above, § 7.5.

[2] In this context 'harm' covers both personal injury and property damage.

[3] Thus for the purposes of the common law, elephants were treated as wild and dangerous, even if individual elephants were docile and tame: *Behrens* v *Bertram Mills Circus Ltd* [1957] 2 QB 1.

[4] Section 1 of the Animals Act 1971 provides that the 'provisions . . . of this Act replace . . . the rules of the common law imposing a strict liability . . . for damage done by an animal on the ground that the animal is regarded as ferae naturae or that its vicious or mischievous propensities are known or presumed to be known.'

Section 6(3) of the 1971 Act provides that 'a person is a keeper of an animal if – (a) he owns the animal or has it in his possession; or (b) he is the head of a household of which a member under the age of sixteen owns the animal or has it in his possession'. Section 6(4) of the 1971 Act qualifies this by providing that someone who takes an animal into his possession 'for the purpose of preventing it from causing damage or of restoring it to its owner' will not thereby become a keeper of that animal. Section 6(3) goes on to provide that:

> if at any time an animal ceases to be owned by or to be in the possession of a person, any person who immediately before that time was a keeper thereof by virtue of the preceding provisions of this subsection [will continue] to be a keeper of the animal until another person becomes a keeper thereof by virtue of those provisions.

For the purposes of applying s 2(1) of the 1971 Act, an animal belongs to a dangerous species if two conditions are met. The conditions are that the species is not commonly domesticated in the British Isles and that fully grown animals of that species have characteristics making it likely that they will cause severe damage, or that if they cause damage it is likely to be severe.

(2) *Liability of the keeper of an animal that does not belong to a dangerous species.* Section 2(2) of the 1971 Act provides that the keeper of an animal which does not belong to a dangerous species will be liable for damage that has been caused by that animal if three conditions are satisfied and no relevant defence applies. The three conditions, as set out in the Act are as follows:

(a) the damage [was] of a kind which the animal, unless restrained, was likely to cause or which, if caused by the animal, was likely to be severe; and

(b) the likelihood of the damage or of its being severe was due to characteristics of the animal which are not normally found in animals of the same species or are not normally so found except at particular times or in particular circumstances; and

(c) those characteristics were known to that keeper or were at any time known to a person who at that time had charge of the animal as that keeper's servant or, where that keeper is the head of a household, were known to another keeper of the animal who is a member of that household and under the age of sixteen.

Section 2(2) is the most difficult section in the Act to interpret and apply, and is discussed in detail in the following section.

(3) *Liability of the keeper of a dog that has killed or injured livestock.* Section 3 of the 1971 Act provides that the keeper of a dog is liable for damage it causes by killing or injuring livestock unless a relevant defence applies.

(4) *Liability of person in possession of livestock for the damage done by that livestock.* Section 4 of the 1971 Act provides that the possessor of livestock is liable for certain types of damage and expenses caused by that livestock straying onto land in the ownership or occupation of another person unless a relevant defence applies.[5]

13.2 SECTION 2(2)[6]

Several judges have complained about the difficulty of interpreting s 2(2) of the 1971 Act, which (very roughly speaking) makes the keeper of an animal that does not belong to a

---

[5] This provision replaces the old common law rules on liability for cattle trespass and is discussed below, § 16.6(C).
[6] See, generally, Compton and Hand 2009.

dangerous species strictly liable for harm caused by the animal's having a dangerous and uncommon characteristic which the keeper knows about. Section 2(2) has been described by Lord Denning MR as 'very cumbrously worded',[7] by Ormrod LJ as 'remarkably opaque',[8] and by Slade LJ as 'somewhat tortuous'.[9]

As the authorities stand at the moment, it seems that for s 2(2) to apply to make the keeper (K) of an animal (A) liable for some harm (harm H) caused by A, four conditions[10] need to be satisfied:

(1) *The Causation Condition.* Harm H must have been caused by A having some characteristic C.[11]

(2) *The Dangerous Characteristic Condition.* The fact that A had that characteristic C must have meant that it was likely to cause harm H, or if it caused harm H, the harm it caused was likely to be severe.

(3) *The Uncommon Charateristic Condition.* It must be shown either (i) that it is never normal for animals of the same species as A to have characteristic C; or (ii) that it is only normal for animals of the same species as A to have characteristic C 'at particular times or in particular circumstances'.

(4) *The Knowledge Condition.* K – or someone who had charge of A as K's servant, or someone under 16 who was a member of K's household and was also a keeper of A – must have known that A had characteristic C.

A claimant wanting to sue a defendant under s 2(2) must frame their case in a way that satisfies *all* of these conditions. So in a case where the harm suffered by the claimant, and the characteristics of the animal that caused that harm, can be described in a variety of different ways, the claimant must be careful to describe the harm that she has suffered and the relevant characteristic that caused that harm in a way that satisfies all of the above four conditions.

We will now look at a number of cases to see how the courts have applied and interpreted these different conditions. The first case is *Mirvahedy* v *Henley* (2003), still the only case from the UK's final court of appeal on how s 2(2) should be interpreted. In that case, the claimant was severely injured when a horse belonging to the defendants ran into his car as he drove it along the A380. The horse had been kept in a field – along with two other horses owned by the defendants – and all three horses had been scared, for some unknown reason, into bolting out of the field and running towards the A380. The horse's bolting was the characteristic that had caused the harm to the claimant in *Mirvahedy*. The issue that divided the House of Lords in *Mirvahedy* was whether the horse's bolting satisfied the *Uncommon Characteristic Condition* given that it was completely normal for the horse to bolt in the circumstances in which it found itself (that of being subjected to a severe fright). The House of Lords ruled by 3:2 that the *Uncommon Characteristic Condition* was satisfied

---

[7] *Cummings* v *Grainger* [1977] QB 397, 404.

[8] [1977] QB 397, 407.

[9] *Curtis* v *Betts* [1990] 1 WLR 459, 462.

[10] It should be emphasised that the language we use to describe these conditions is ours, and is used simply to try and help readers understand how s 2(2) applies. Students should not in their written work or their exams assume that the people reading their work will automatically understand what phrases such as 'the causation condition' or 'the dangerous characteristic condition' refer to, and should not therefore use those phrases without some accompanying explanation of what those phrases refer to.

[11] *Curtis* v *Betts* [1990] 1 WLR 459.

in this case because it was only normal for horses to have the characteristic of bolting 'at particular times or in particular circumstances'.[12]

One point which was left unaddressed by the House of Lords was the fact that the accident in *Mirvahedy* occurred shortly after midnight. So the defendants in *Mirvahedy* were unaware that their horse had bolted from its field at the time it was bolting. Does this mean the *Knowledge Condition* was not satisfied in *Mirvahedy*? It seems to have been assumed that the *Knowledge Condition was* satisfied in *Mirvahedy*. The only way of rationalising this is to assume that in a case where an animal A has caused harm H because it had a characteristic C that was *uncommon* but *not abnormal* – because it is normal for animals of the same species as A to have characteristic C in the situation that A found itself in – the *Knowledge Condition* will be satisfied by showing that A's keeper (or some other relevant individual) knew that it is normal for animals of the same species as A to have characteristic C in the situation in which A found itself.[13] If this is right, then the *Knowledge Condition* could have been satisfied in *Mirvahedy* merely by showing that the defendants knew that it is normal for horses to bolt when they are subjected to a severe fright.[14] But it must be remembered that this way of satisfying the *Knowledge Condition only* applies where an animal A has caused harm as a result of its acquiring a characteristic that was *uncommon but not abnormal* in that animals of the same species as A normally do not have that characteristic, but tend to acquire it in the situation in which A found itself. Where – as in the case of *McKenny* v *Foster* (2008), discussed below – an animal suddenly and unexpectedly acquires a dangerous characteristic that is wholly abnormal for its species to have, actual knowledge of the fact that that particular animal has acquired that characteristic will be required before the *Knowledge Condition* is satisfied.

Mirvahedy opened the door to keepers of animals – in particular, horses – being held liable for harm caused as a result of those animals acting entirely normally.[15] Since *Mirvahedy*, the courts have struggled properly to apply s 2(2) to the claims that have come

---

[12] In so ruling, the House of Lords followed the approach of the Court of Appeal in *Cummings* v *Grainger* [1977] QB 397 and *Curtis* v *Betts* [1990] 1 WLR 459, and rejected the opinions of Lloyd and Oliver LJJ in *Breeden* v *Lampard*, 21 March 1985, unreported.

[13] In support of this view, see Hale LJ's judgment in the Court of Appeal in *Mirvahedy* v *Henley* [2002] QB 769, at [31]: 'in the case of an animal who only has such a tendency in particular circumstances or at particular times, it might be thought that the keeper must know, not only of the tendency but also that the particular time or particular circumstances currently exist: for example that his bitch has just had pups or his dog was guarding his territory. Applied to this case, the keeper would have to know, not only that horses can behave in this way if frightened or panicked, but also that these horses had been frightened or panicked. Some of the above quotations from the Law Commission's Report and from Hansard might be thought to support that view. However, the Act does not. Section 2(2)(c) merely requires knowledge of the 'characteristics', and not both characteristics and circumstances. In any event, if the rationale for the strict liability is the greater vigilance needed and the greater opportunity to insure brought by that knowledge then those can be employed whether or not the particular circumstances are known to exist at the time.'

[14] See, for example, *Welsh* v *Stokes* [2008] 1 WLR 1224, where the defendants were held liable under s 2(2) for the head injuries suffered by the claimant – a trainee working at the defendants' stables – when the horse she was riding on reared up, causing her to fall off the horse, and then fell on her. It was held that the characteristic that had caused the harm was the characteristic of 'rearing up when being ridden by an unconfident rider'. This characteristic was not abnormal but it was uncommon as it would only usually manifest itself 'at particular times or in particular circumstances' (such as when the horse was made to go somewhere it did not want to go). The Court of Appeal held that the *Knowledge Condition* would be satisfied in this case merely by showing that the defendants knew that it was normal for horses to 'rear up when being ridden by an unconfident rider' when they are made to go somewhere they do not want to go.

[15] Though – as has already been noted (above, fn 12) – the door was already ajar as a result of the Court of Appeal's decisions in *Cummings* v *Grainger* [1977] QB 397 and *Curtis* v *Betts* [1990] 1 WLR 459, the decision in *Mirvahedy* does seem to have provoked much more litigation against animal owners than those earlier decisions did.

through the door that *Mirvahedy* opened. For example, in *Clark* v *Bowlt* (2006), the claimant was injured driving past two horses on a highway. As his car passed one of the horses, the horse moved into the path of the car, damaging the car and causing the claimant whiplash injuries. The claimant sued the horse's rider (who had been seriously injured in the accident) for compensation under s 2(2). The first instance judge got into a muddle by focusing on the horse's characteristic of being *heavy* to find that the *Dangerous Characteristic Condition* was satisfied (on the basis that the horse's weight meant that if the horse hit the car, any damage it did was likely to be severe), and then focused on the horse's characteristic of *asserting an inclination to go otherwise than as directed* to find that the *Uncommon Characteristic Condition* was satisfied (on the basis that it is only normal for horses to assert such an inclination 'at particular times or in particular circumstances'). In reversing the first instance judge's decision, the Court of Appeal emphasised that in applying s 2(2), the *same* characteristic has to be focused on in order to see whether all of the conditions set out above for liability to arise under s 2(2) are satisfied. And whether one focused on the horse's *weight* in *Clark* or its *wilfulness*, not all of these conditions were satisfied. If we focus on the *weight*, the *Uncommon Characteristic Condition* was not satisfied as it is normal for horses to be heavy, and not just 'at particular times or in particular circumstances'. If we focus on the *wilfulness*, the *Dangerous Characteristic Condition* was not satisfied as the horse in *Clark*'s asserting an inclination to go otherwise than as directed did not mean that it was likely to do harm, or that any harm that it did do was likely to be severe.

McKenny v *Foster* (2008) was another case where the characteristic that led an animal to cause the claimant harm could be described in a couple of different ways, but neither way could satisfy all of the conditions needed for s 2(2) to apply. In that case, the claimant was injured when a cow escaped from the field where it was being kept by the defendants and wandered onto the A614 where it collided with the claimant's car. It was claimed that the cow had become so agitated as a result of being separated from its calf that it scaled a six-barred livestock gate and leapt across a twelve-foot cattle grid. There were two ways of describing the characteristic of the cow that caused the accident in this case: the cow's *agitation* at being separated from her calf, and the cow's *extreme agitation* at being separated from her calf that enabled her to perform near miracles such as leaping across a twelve-foot cattle grid. Unfortunately for the claimant, neither characteristic could give rise to a claim under s 2(2) of the Animals Act 1971. If we focus on the cow's *agitation*, that did not satisfy the *Dangerous Characteristic Condition* – the cow's agitation did not mean that it was likely to do harm, or that any harm it did was likely to be severe. If we focus on the cow's *extreme agitation*, that satisfied the *Dangerous Characteristic Condition* (in that her extreme agitation made it likely for her to do harm) and the *Uncommon Characteristic Condition* (in that it is never normal for cows to get as agitated as the cow in *McKenny* was), but it did not satisfy the *Knowledge Condition* (in that the defendants were not aware of the cow's state of extreme agitation).[16]

In *Freeman* v *Higher Park Farm* (2008), the claimant went for a ride on a horse owned by the defendants. She was thrown off the horse and injured when the horse bucked

---

[16] It is important that it was wholly abnormal for the cow to be in a state of extreme agitation, and it could not be said that cows generally become extremely agitated 'at particular times or in particular circumstances'. Were the cow's state of extreme agitation to be uncommon but not abnormal, the *Knowledge Condition* could have been satisfied by showing that the defendants in *McKenny* knew that cows generally tend to become extremely agitated in the circumstances in which the cow in *McKenny* found itself. See above, text at fn 14. It is also important that this was the first time the cow in *McKenny* had become extremely agitated in this way. Had the defendants known that the cow had the characteristic of 'becoming extremely agitated when separated from her calf' then a claim under s 2(2) could have been brought on the basis that *that* conditional characteristic had caused the harm, was dangerous, was uncommon, and was known.

(kicked out backwards with its hindlegs) as she attempted to make it canter. Her claim for compensation under s 2(2) of the 1971 Act was thrown out by the Court of Appeal. The relevant characteristic that the court focused on in determining whether s 2(2) applied was the horse's *bucking*. It was held that this characteristic fulfilled the *Dangerous Characteristic Condition* on the ground that if the horse's bucking caused harm, that harm was likely to be severe. However, the claim failed at the next fence: the *Uncommon Characteristic Condition*. It could not be said that it is not normal for a horse to have a tendency to buck in the way that the horse in *Freeman* did.[17] So the only way to satisfy the *Uncommon Characteristic Condition* in *Freeman* was to show that horses normally only have a tendency to buck 'at particular times or in particular circumstances'. The Court of Appeal held that not enough evidence had been provided as to when horses generally tend to buck for it to be possible to say that bucking is something that horses only tend to do 'at particular times or in particular circumstances'.

The post-*Mirvahedy* cases on interpreting s 2(2) make it hard to provide any kind of principled explanation as to why certain defendants (such as the defendants in *Mirvahedy*) are held liable under s 2(2), while others (such as the defendants in *McKenny*) are not. In cases where a keeper has chosen to keep under his control an animal that is abnormally dangerous then there is little problem with holding him strictly liable for the harm done by that animal's abnormally dangerous tendencies.[18] But *Mirvahedy* extends the scope of liability under s 2(2) to cases where a keeper is in control of an animal A which he knows belongs to a species that is only liable to do harm *in a certain situation S*, and which does do harm in situation S. It is hard to see why the keeper of A should be held liable for the harm done by A in situation S if he had no reason to know that situation S had arisen,[19] or he did know that situation S had arisen but had no opportunity to prevent A doing harm in that situation.[20]

---

[17] Whether a given characteristic counts as 'normal' was said by the Court of Appeal in *Welsh* v *Stokes* [2008] 1 WLR 1224 (at [42] and [59]) to depend on whether it falls outside the range of characteristics that we might expect a typical animal of the same species to exhibit.

[18] See above, § 12.8, for possible explanations of the keeper's liability in such a case.

[19] In the 2007–8 Parliamentary Session, a Private Members' Bill was introduced that would have amended s 2(2) of the Animals Act 1971 to say that where harm was caused as a result of an animal having a 'conditional characteristic' (that is, one 'that is shared by animals of that species generally, but only in particular circumstances'), the keeper of that animal would not be held liable for that harm if he could show that 'there was no particular reason to expect that those circumstances would arise' at the time the harm was caused. The Bill, and reaction to it, revealed something of a town–country divide: it was advanced by the MP for Preseli Pembrokeshire (country) and opposed by the MP for Hendon (town). The Bill was backed by 26 votes to one in its second reading in the House of Commons, but as fewer than 40 MPs were present to vote on it, the Bill was lost. (In the subsequent 2010 General Election, the MP for Hendon lost his seat; the MP for Preseli Pembrokeshire increased his majority.) In March 2009 the Department for Environment, Food and Rural Affairs launched a consultation with the intention of changing s 2(2)(b) in the same way by using a Legislative Reform Order, as opposed to ordinary legislation. The results of the consultation, however, were mixed: a majority favoured clarification of the Act, but only a minority supported the government's proposed wording. As a result the government has delayed taking further action.

[20] Consider Lord Scott's example in *Mirvahedy* v *Henley* [2003] 2 AC 491, at [115], of a police horse that is jabbed in the side by a protestor and kicks out and injures an innocent bystander. (Though it may be questioned whether the characteristic 'kicking out' fulfils the *Dangerous Characteristic Condition* as *merely* 'kicking out' is not liable to do harm and any harm done by *merely* 'kicking out' is not liable to be severe. The point is difficult to appreciate because we associate 'kicking out' with *another* characteristic that horses have, that of having a *powerful kick*. Having a powerful kick definitely does satisfy the *Dangerous Chacteristic Condition* – in that if a horse gives you a powerful kick, the harm it does is likely to be severe – but will not satisfy the *Uncommon Characteristic Condition* in that it is normal for horses to have a powerful kick, and not just 'at particular times or in particular circumstances'. However, it may be possible to attribute some other harm-causing characteristic to the horse in this case – such as 'being so shocked as to kick out automatically and with great power' – that will tick all the boxes needed for a claim to be brought under s 2(2).)

The expansion of liability under s 2(2) of the 1971 Act brought about by the House of Lords' decision in *Mirvahedy* has resulted in the range of defences available to claims under the 1971 Act becoming of greater importance. We will now consider these defences.

13.3 DEFENCES

There are a number of defences open to someone who is sued under the 1971 Act.

(1) *Wholly at fault*. If B sues A for compensation for harm suffered by her under any of the liability rules set out above, A will have a defence to B's claim if B was wholly at fault for the fact that she suffered that harm.[21]

(2) *Voluntary assumption of risk*. If B has been harmed by an animal and seeks to sue A for compensation for that harm under ss 2(1) or 2(2) of the 1971 Act, A will have a defence to B's claim if B voluntarily took the risk that she would be harmed by that animal.[22]

(3) *Trespass*. A will also have a defence if: (i) the animal in question harmed B while she was trespassing on premises on which that animal was kept; *and* (ii) *either* that animal was *not* kept on the premises for the protection of persons or property, *or* that animal *was* kept on the premises for the protection of persons or property and the keeping of the animal on those premises for that purpose was not unreasonable.[23]

The question whether a trespasser on someone else's premises who is injured by an animal might be able to sue the occupier of the premises (rather than the animal's keeper) under the Occupiers' Liability Act 1984 is not straightforward, and depends on the scope of that Act.[24]

(4) *Straying livestock*. Suppose livestock belonging to B strayed onto land belonging to someone else and was attacked there by a dog. If B sues A – the dog's keeper – for compensation for the damage done to her livestock by the dog under s 3 of the 1971 Act, A will have a defence to B's claim if: (i) the dog belonged to the occupier of the land on which the livestock was attacked; *or* (ii) the dog was authorised to be on the land on which the livestock was attacked.[25] .

If an animal has caused B to suffer some kind of harm, and B seeks to sue A – the keeper of that animal – for compensation for that harm under the Animals Act 1971, it seems that the fact that the animal acted in the way it did because of the malicious act of a stranger or an Act of God will afford A *no defence* to B's claim. Consequently, the potential liability of the keeper of a dangerous animal is wider than the potential liability of the keeper of an inanimate dangerous thing.[26]

Visit **www.mylawchamber.co.uk/mcbride** to access tools to help you develop and test your knowledge of Tort law, including interactive multiple choice questions, practice exam questions with guidance, weblinks, legal newsfeed, additional case summaries, legal updates and tips on answering problem and essay questions.

premium
my**law**chamber
unrivalled support for legal education

---

[21] Animals Act 1971, s 5(1). The defence of contributory negligence also applies: s 10.

[22] Section 5(2). See *Freeman* v *Higher Park Farm* [2008] EWCA Civ 1185 (claimant was told repeatedly about horse's tendency to buck when required to canter, and repeatedly said that she was happy to ride the horse).

[23] Animals Act 1971, s 5(3). In *Cummings* v *Grainger* [1975] 1 WLR 1330, O'Connor J thought that it was unreasonable for a scrap metal dealer to keep an untrained Alsatian with a known propensity to attack black people as protection for his yard, but the Court of Appeal disagreed: [1977] QB 397. It is worth noting, however, that the case arose before the Guard Dogs Act 1975 made it unlawful to keep an uncontrolled guard dog.

[24] On which see above, chapter 11.

[25] Animals Act 1971, s 5(4).

[26] On which see below, chapter 16.

14 Trespass to land

14.1 The basics *405*

14.2 Conduct requirements *406*

14.3 Intention and fault *408*

14.4 Defences *409*

14.5 Title to sue *411*

14.6 Remedies *413*

Overview

The last ten chapters have been spent either looking at the law on negligence, or areas of strict liability that supplement the scope of liability under the law of negligence. In this chapter we move away from negligence completely and back to an area of law first explored in chapter 2 – the tort of trespass. This time round, we are looking at the law relating to the tort of trespass *to land*. But many of the same ideas that we came across in chapter 2 reoccur here, in particular the idea that the defendant must have *directly* interfered with the claimant's interests – here, in land. Sections 14.2 and 14.3 set out the requirements that have to be fulfilled for someone to commit the tort of trespass to land. Section 14.4 explains when someone who has fulfilled those requirements might still have a defence to being sued for trespass. Section 14.5 explains who will be able to sue when land has been trespassed on, and section 14.6 explains what remedies will be available to a claimant who is entitled to sue a defendant for trespass to land.

14.1 THE BASICS

The tort of trespass to land provides someone who is in possession of a plot of land with a claim if someone else intrudes into that plot by, for example, marching onto it in person, or by throwing or placing something on it, always assuming that the intruder has no lawful justification for acting in this way.[1] Putting the matter in more precise terms: (1) A will commit the tort of trespass to land in relation to B if he crosses the boundary onto land possessed by B[2] when he has no lawful justification for doing so; and (2) A will also commit the tort of trespass to land in relation to B if he causes some object or matter to move directly onto land possessed by B when he has no lawful justification for doing so.

The language of *intruding* might make it sound as if trespasses to land have to be intentional, but this is not the case. No doubt many trespasses *are* intentional, but the key question is whether the crossing of the boundary onto B's land was a *direct* result of A's actions. As we will see, this means that where B has ended up on A's land he will be able to establish that he has not committed trespass to land where he can show that: (i) this was only an *indirect* consequence of his actions; or (ii) this was not a consequence of any of his *actions* at all; or (iii) he had a lawful justification for crossing onto B's land. Under the next three headings we explore these propositions in more detail, before turning to justifications for trespassing, who can sue, and remedies.

---

[1] *Bocardo SA v Star Energy UK Onshore Ltd* [2011] 1 AC 380 at [6] (per Lord Hope): 'a trespass occurs when there is an unjustified intrusion by one party upon land which is in the possession of another.'

[2] The degree of connection that has to be established between B and the land is discussed in detail below, § 14.5.

14.2 CONDUCT REQUIREMENTS

In order to discuss what a defendant needs to have *done* in order to commit the tort of trespass to land, we need to distinguish cases where a defendant is alleged to have committed the tort: (a) by physically moving onto the claimant's land; (b) by causing an inanimate object to go onto the claimant's land; and (c) by causing an animal to go onto the claimant's land.

A. Physical movement

A defendant will not be held to have 'crossed' the boundary of the claimant's land unless he had sufficient control over his own movements for the action which took his body across the boundary to be attributed to him. In *Smith* v *Stone* (1647), the defendant pleaded that he had been carried across the boundary onto the claimant's land by the force and violence of others. Roll J held that this meant that the defendant had *not* committed the tort of trespass to land in relation to the claimant. The same judge later held that the defendant would have been liable if he had crossed the boundary under duress. It might be different, however, if a threat caused A to leap across the boundary of B's land in an instinctive panic.[3]

B. Inanimate objects

With regard to the case where A has caused some object or matter to move directly onto land possessed by B, it is orthodox to distinguish between the movement of such a thing across the boundary which is a *direct* result of A's actions (and thus within the scope of the tort) and a movement which is an *indirect* consequence of A's behaviour (and thus outside the tort).

The primary factor which the courts will use when trying to identify this distinction is the degree to which A's actions can be said to have *controlled* the crossing of the boundary by the object or matter. Thus where A has placed or thrown or fired an object across the boundary onto land B possesses A will have committed trespass to land in relation to B. But where A has released some substance into the atmosphere which has then emanated across the boundary (for instance, where A's operations release acid fumes which then drift on the breeze across the boundary) A will not have committed trespass to land, though B will still gain redress if he can establish that A committed the tort of private nuisance in acting as he did.[4] Similarly, if A loses control of a vehicle that he is driving so that it leaves the road and crosses onto land possessed by B this crossing is likely to be considered an *indirect* consequence of A's actions.[5]

The distinction between crossings which are a *direct* result of the defendant's actions and those which are *indirect* consequence of the defendant's actions is *not* the same as the distinction between crossings which are *intentional* and those which are *unintended*. In some circumstances, the connection between A's behaviour and an unintended crossing will be so close that A will be unable to deny that the crossing was a *direct* result of his behaviour. For instance, if Brian hits a golf ball towards land possessed by Chloe with the intention that it should stop just before the boundary then if, despite his intention, it bounces across the boundary it is unlikely that he will be able to claim that the crossing was

---

[3] *Braithwaite* v *South Durham Steel Co Ltd* [1958] 1 WLR 986.
[4] For the tort of private nuisance, see below, chapter 15.
[5] Thus A will not be liable in relation to B for trespass to land, but may be liable for the tort of negligence. The situation would be different if A *chose* to drive off the highway and onto B's land in order to avoid colliding with another vehicle or a pedestrian, though here A may be able to rely on the defence of necessity.

merely an *indirect* consequence of his behaviour. The outcome might be different, however, if the ball was caught by a sudden gust of wind or deflected off a passing seagull. Similarly, if a lorry driver attempts to manoeuvre his lorry under a narrow bridge, but misjudges the width of his load so that it collides with the side of the bridge, this collision would certainly be a *direct* consequence of the driver's actions even though it was not *intended*.[6]

A landowner is not generally treated as having sufficient control over the plants, trees and natural features of his land so as to make him liable for trespass if they cross onto B's land as a result of ordinary natural processes. Thus where the roots or branches of a tree on A's land gradually grow so that they cross onto B's land no trespass will be committed but A may be guilty of committing the tort of private nuisance by encroachment.[7]

C. Animals

The law on when A will commit a trespass to land in relation to B if his animals cross over onto land possessed by B is complicated. The problem is caused by the fact that animals behave less predictably than inanimate objects, so it is harder to say when their behaviour is a *direct* consequence of a person's action.

In some circumstances it is not necessary to determine whether an animal's keeper has committed trespass to land when his animal intrudes on land in another's possession because some other tort will apply. For example, the possessor of livestock which strays onto another's land is strictly liable for *damage* done by that livestock to the land or that other's property which is on the land.[8] (Although this liability is based on a statutory provision that replaced the common law wrong known as 'cattle trespass'[9] it is best understood as part of the law relating to the keeping of dangerous things[10] rather than part of the law on when someone will commit the tort of trespass to land.) Further, the Animals Act 1971 also makes the keepers of *dangerous* animals liable for the damage that such animals cause[11] and consequently it will not usually be necessary to determine whether the keeper is also liable for having committed trespass to land through the intrusion of such an animal.

In practice, then, the situations where it is most important to consider whether A has committed trespass to land as a result of an animal crossing onto land possessed by B are those involving animals which are neither 'livestock' nor 'dangerous animals'. In *Buckle* v *Holmes* (1926) – where the defendant's cat strayed onto the claimant's property and killed the claimant's pigeons and poultry – the Court of Appeal held that where an animal did not fall within either the class of livestock or the class of dangerous animals, and was of a

---

[6] In *Conarken Group Ltd* v *Network Rail Infrastructure Ltd* [2010] EWHC 1852 (TCC), Akenhead J held that an owner of a bridge could sue for trespass in circumstances similar to these. But he did not consider how far the later consequences of an initial collision can be described as 'direct'. In the case the load on the lorry which had initially collided with one side of the bridge subsequently struck a vehicle which was travelling in the opposite direction, and this vehicle then struck the other side of the bridge. We think that the difficulty of determining whether the collision with the other side of the bridge was also a *direct* consequence of the lorry driver's actions helps to explain why incidents like this commonly give rise to claims in the tort of negligence, rather than trespass. The Court of Appeal subsequently upheld the conclusions that Akenhead J had reached as to the appropriate measure of damages, but did not re-consider his opinion as to the scope of the tort of trespass to land: [2011] EWCA Civ 644.

[7] *Lemmon* v *Webb* [1895] AC 1. See below, § 15.6.

[8] Animals Act 1971, s 4. A claim can also be brought for expenses reasonably incurred in keeping the livestock and ascertaining the owner.

[9] Section 1(1)(c).

[10] See below, § 16.6(C).

[11] Section 2. Which animals are considered 'dangerous' is discussed above, § 13.2.

class not generally confined and unlikely to cause substantial damage on straying, such as dogs and cats, the owner of the animal would not commit the tort of trespass to land whenever the animal strayed onto someone else's land.[12] But while this rule clearly applies to a dog or cat acting of its own volition, equally clearly it would be a tort for A to *send* such an animal onto B's land.

In *League Against Cruel Sports* v *Scott* (1986), Park J held that the master of a hunt would be liable for trespass to land if 'he either intended that the hounds should enter the land or by negligence he failed to prevent them from doing so'.[13] In so far as this makes a huntsman liable for *sending* hounds onto another's land it is uncontroversial. But the suggestion that a huntsman is liable for trespass if he negligently allows the hounds to stray is not easy to reconcile with *Buckle* v *Holmes* (1926), which was not drawn to Park J's attention.[14] Our view is that an owner of a pet dog will not commit the tort of trespass to land if he negligently fails to prevent it from straying onto someone else's land,[15] but that Park J was correct to state that if such straying frequently happened and the owner was apparently indifferent to it, this might give rise to an inference that the owner intended the dog to cross the boundary.[16]

14.3 INTENTION AND FAULT

Suppose A at some time crossed the boundary onto land possessed by B. In order to establish that A committed the tort of trespass to land in so doing, B does *not* have to prove: (i) that when A crossed the boundary he intended to trespass on land possessed by B; *or* (ii) that when A crossed the boundary, he knew or ought to have known that there was a risk he would be trespassing on land possessed by B. Indeed, A will have committed the tort of trespass to land in relation to B even if, when he crossed the boundary onto land possessed by B, he honestly believed that he was remaining on land where he was permitted to be. An honest mistake by A is not a defence to the tort of trespass to land.

We have already seen that it has been held that A cannot commit the tort of battery in relation to B unless he directly applied force to B *intentionally* or *carelessly*.[17] It has been argued that a similar rule should apply with regard to the tort of trespass to land. Such a similar rule would mean that A would only commit the tort of trespass to land in relation to B if his movement – by which he crossed the boundary of B's land – was *intentional* or

---

[12] In *Tutton* v *A D Walter Ltd* [1986] QB 61 the judge refused to treat unwanted straying bees as trespassers for the purpose of deciding whether a landowner owed their owner a duty to take care not to harm them. Suppose A, a beekeeper, released bees which strayed onto B's land and A knew they were likely to do this when he released the bees. Will A have committed the tort of trespass to land in relation to B? The doctrine expounded in *Buckle* v *Holmes* indicates that the answer is 'no'. We think it *would* be trespass to land, however, to put bees through B's letterbox, or otherwise send them onto B's property.

[13] [1986] QB 240, 251–2.

[14] In a subsequent passage Park J confined his opinion to the case '[w]here a master of staghounds takes out a pack of hounds and deliberately sets them in pursuit of a stag or hind, knowing that there is a real risk that in the pursuit hounds may enter or cross prohibited land'. This makes the case far closer to that of the golfer who hits balls towards the claimant's land with the intention that they should stop just before the boundary. It must be doubtful whether Park J intended to hold that a master of hounds would be liable for trespass if he negligently lost control of the dogs but they then strayed to a place that he would not have expected them to go. In such a case it would be difficult to argue that the crossing of the boundary to such a place was a sufficiently *direct* consequence of the master's behaviour to constitute trespass to land by the master.

[15] The owner might, however, be liable for any consequential damage, in the tort of negligence, or under Animals Act 1971, ss 2, 3 or 8.

[16] *League Against Cruel Sports* v *Scott* [1986] QB 240, 252.

[17] See above, § 2.3, discussing the result of the decision in *Fowler* v *Lanning* [1959] 1 QB 426.

careless.[18] It has not, however, been authoritatively settled that this is the law. The main reason why the point remains unsettled is that a defendant will not be held to have 'crossed' unless he had sufficient control over his own movements for the action which took his body across the boundary to be attributed to him. This means that even without a similar rule defendants will not usually be held liable for movements which were not intentional or careless.[19]

14.4 DEFENCES

If A has crossed the boundary of B's land, there are many different ways in which A could establish that he had a lawful justification for crossing that boundary. We will not attempt to catalogue them here. A may, for instance, seek to establish that, in acting as he did, he was merely making lawful use of a highway[20] or private right of way, or that he had a licence to enter, or that statute[21] or common law[22] conferred on him a power to enter.[23] Here we will discuss only two instances where A might be able to establish that he had a lawful justification or excuse for crossing the boundary of B's land.

(1) *Licence (consent).* Suppose A enters B's land. A will not commit the tort of trespass to land in so doing if B has licensed him to enter. A may commit the tort of trespass to land, however, if he either exceeds the terms of the licence[24] or fails to leave within a reasonable time after the licence is withdrawn. Sometimes a contract will restrict B's power to withdraw a licence. But it is important to distinguish between cases where the withdrawal is wrongful (a breach of contract) but still effective and those where the withdrawal is ineffective.[25] If the withdrawal is effective, then A must leave B's land within a reasonable

---

[18] In *Conarken Group Ltd* v *Network Rail Infrastructure Ltd* [2010] EWHC 1852 (TCC), Akenhead J confirmed that a trespass to land does not have to be intentional, but can be negligent. Some passages in his judgment also imply, however, that he thought that there could be no liability unless the trespass was intentional or negligent. See, for example, at [65]: 'If Y in an effective state of automatism, say, a blackout from an unknown medical condition, drives his or her car onto someone else's land, that would be unintentional and non-negligent and no trespass.' Douglas 2011 argues that a defendant should only be held to have committed trespass to land if he 'intended to make physical contact' with the land (that the claimant possessed).

[19] What sort of case might involve a non-intentional and non-negligent trespass? Suppose that *Driver* owns a garage the back wall of which is against the boundary of *Gardener's* land. Each night *Driver* parks his car by reversing it slowly into his garage and gently touching the rear wall. He does not realise that the rear wall is actually not fixed and that each time he touches it he moves it a millimetre into *Gardener's* property. Eventually *Gardener* notices that the wall has moved into his land.

[20] The public's right to use a highway is limited: In *DPP* v *Jones* [1999] 2 AC 240 the majority held that the public's right was not limited to passing, repassing and ancillary uses, and accepted that *at least some* other reasonable, peaceful and non-obstructive uses were lawful (at 257, per Lord Irvine; 281, per Lord Clyde; and 286–7, per Lord Hutton).

[21] For example, police officers have statutory powers under ss 17 and 18 of the Police and Criminal Evidence Act 1984 to enter premises in order to make an arrest and to search after making an arrest.

[22] For example, the common law confers powers to enter premises in order to reclaim wrongfully taken personal property, in order to abate a nuisance (though sometimes notice may be required), and in order to preserve person or property from immediate danger.

[23] Where a person who is authorised by law to enter for a particular purpose afterwards abuses that authority he may be treated as a trespasser *ab initio*, that is, he may be treated as if the initial entry was unlawful. The doctrine is associated with *The Six Carpenters' Case* (1610) 8 Co Rep 146a, 77 ER 695. Although Lord Denning MR thought in *Chic Fashions Ltd* v *Jones* [1968] 2 QB 299 that the doctrine should be interred with the bones of the old forms of action, he later used the doctrine in *Cinnamond* v *BAA* [1980] 1 WLR 582.

[24] The picturesque illustration commonly given is that a person licensed to walk down the stairs becomes a trespasser if he slides down the bannisters.

[25] A textbook on tort is not the appropriate place to explore when licences cannot be revoked and when they will bind third parties. The interested reader should consult a standard textbook on land law.

period of time – if he does not, then he will commit the tort of trespass to land in relation to B. If, on the other hand, the withdrawal is ineffective, A will *not* commit the tort of trespass to land if he stays on B's land.

(2) Necessity. In *Esso Petroleum* v *Southport Corporation* (1953), the defendant shipowners dumped some oil from their ship into the sea when their ship ran aground. The defendants dumped the oil because they feared that the ship would break its back and the crew would be endangered if they did not. The oil washed up onto the claimants' foreshore. The claimants sued the defendants, claiming that they had committed the tort of trespass to land in dumping the oil.

Devlin J thought that the defendants could rely on the defence of *necessity* to justify their dumping the oil.[26] He also held, however, that the defendants would not be permitted to rely on the defence if the predicament was a result of their own negligence.[27] The defence is available only in cases of *immediate* danger or emergency. So in *Southwark LBC* v *Williams* (1971), the Court of Appeal held that the defence did not stretch to cover the case of homeless people who made an orderly entry into empty property:

> Lord Hale said that 'if a person, being under necessity for want of victuals, or clothes, shall upon that account clandestinely, and animo furandi, steal another man's food, it is felony . . .': Hale, *Pleas of the Crown*, i. 54. The reason is because, if hunger were once allowed to be an excuse for stealing, it would open a way through which all kinds of disorder and lawlessness would pass. So here. If homelessness were once admitted as a defence to trespass, no one's house could be safe. Necessity would open a door which no man could shut. It would not be only those in extreme need who would enter. There would be others who would imagine that they were in need, or would invent a need, so as to gain entry. Each man would say his need was greater than the next man's. The plea would be an excuse for all sorts of wrongdoing. So the courts must, for the sake of law and order, take a firm stand. They must refuse to admit the plea of necessity to the hungry and the homeless: and trust that their distress will be relieved by the charitable and the good.[28]

The fact that in some circumstances necessity seems to make the defendant's decision to cause harm to the claimant justifiable does not mean that the defendant should necessarily be free from an obligation to pay compensation for the harm that he has caused. For instance, in the American case of *Vincent* v *Lake Erie Transportation Co* (1910), the defendant's boat was moored at the claimant's dock when a severe storm arose. The crew acted to prevent the boat from getting away from the dock and being lost, but with the result that the vessel was repeatedly thrown against the dock and damaged it. A majority of the Supreme Court of Minnesota held that the claimant was entitled to compensation for the damage done. One explanation for such an outcome is that there is an *incomplete* privilege to perform an act which would otherwise be a tort in a situation of necessity – that is, the act may be performed and the claimant cannot resist or prevent this, but liability is still imposed for any *material* harm done.[29] An alternative explanation is that while the

---

[26] [1953] 2 All ER 1204. This judgment was reversed by the Court of Appeal but restored by the House of Lords: [1956] AC 218. See also *Cope* v *Sharpe* (No 2) [1912] 1 KB 496.

[27] *Esso Petroleum* v *Southport Corporation* [1953] 2 All ER 1204, 1210. See also *Rigby* v *Chief Constable of Northamptonshire* [1985] 1 WLR 1242.

[28] [1971] 1 Ch 734, 744 (per Lord Denning MR). See also *Monsanto* v *Tilly* [2000] Env LR 313.

[29] Bohlen 1926, 313; also Stevens 2007, 104. The reference to 'material' harm is intended to denote that the claimant cannot recover *simply* for the 'invasion of the right'. See also *Burmah Oil* v *Lord Advocate* [1965] AC 75, where the House of Lords treated a situation where oil installations were destroyed in wartime to prevent them falling into enemy hands as one where the acts were performed in the lawful exercise of the Royal prerogative but there was nonetheless an obligation to pay compensation.

availability of a defence of necessity meant that the defendant could not be held liable to compensate the claimant in *tort* for the damage done to the dock, the defendant could still be held liable in *restitution* for the damage done to the dock.[30]

14.5 TITLE TO SUE

B will be able to sue someone for trespassing on a particular piece of land if she was in *possession* of the land at the time of the alleged trespass.[31] But it is important to note that possession of land is a legal concept, and is *not* synonymous with simple physical occupation. So if B's mother-in-law visits for a week then she will not take *possession* of the spare bedroom even if she physically occupies it.

In *J A Pye (Oxford) Ltd* v *Graham* (2003), Lord Browne-Wilkinson confirmed that 'there are two elements necessary for legal possession: (1) a sufficient degree of physical custody and control ('factual possession'); (2) an intention to exercise such custody and control on one's own behalf and for one's own benefit ('intention to possess').'[32] Except in the case of *joint* possessors, only one person can be in possession of a piece of land at any one time,[33] and, while the necessary degree of 'physical custody and control' will vary somewhat in accordance with the nature of the land concerned, what is looked for is *dealing* with the land in the same way that 'an occupying owner might have been expected to deal with it'.[34]

An owner of land will generally be deemed to be in *possession* in the absence of evidence to the contrary. Where the owner has granted a lease, however, and the tenant has moved onto the premises, it will be the tenant who has exclusive possession and can sue for trespass.[35] Whether a licensee (someone with permission to be on land but not with an

---

[30] See Weinrib 1995, 196–203.

[31] Although the rule is that the claimant must be in possession *at the time of* the trespass, if a person who is entitled to possession *enters* land, and thereby gains possession, the law will treat him as if he was in possession from the date when he became entitled to enter *and* will allow him to sue someone who has trespassed after that time. This doctrine is known as *trespass by relation*. See, for example, *Ocean Accident & Guarantee Corp* v *Ilford Gas Co* [1905] 2 KB 493.

[32] [2003] 1 AC 419, at [40].

[33] It is possible, however, to *split* land so that, for instance, one person possesses the surface and another person possesses the subsoil. Furthermore, the holders of certain rights over land known as *profits à prendre* can also sue for trespass to land. Thus a holder of a right to herbage, a liberty of hunting or a fishery can sue for a trespass to the land which damages the right. This rule has been applied in a modern context to hold that the company which 'owned' a genetically-modified crop being grown on another's land was entitled to sue third parties for trespass to land: *Monsanto* v *Tilly* [2000] Env LR 313. By contrast, a person entitled to an easement, such as a right of way, will *not* be able to claim that A committed the tort of trespass to land in relation to her if A interfered with that right; but she may be able to claim that A committed the tort of private nuisance in relation to her in so acting: see below, § 15.7.

[34] *Powell* v *McFarlane* (1977) 38 P & CR 452, 471 (per Slade J), *approved* by the House of Lords in *J A Pye (Oxford) Ltd* v *Graham* [2003] 1 AC 419, [41] (per Lord Browne-Wilkinson).

[35] Nonetheless, a reversioner can sue where there is a trespass to land which causes either: (a) damage to the property which the reversioner will in time gain the right to possess; or (b) injury of such a permanent nature as to be necessarily prejudicial to the reversion: *Mayfair Property Co* v *Johnston* [1894] 1 Ch 508 (trespass by foundations of wall); *Jones* v *Llanrwst UDC* [1911] 1 Ch 393 (trespass by deposit of faecal matter on riverbank). The right of a reversioner to bring an immediate action is useful because the reversioner might be more willing to take the risks of litigation than a tenant with a time-limited interest and there are occasions when it is desirable for a claim in trespass to be brought sooner rather than later, for instance when it is better for repairs to be effected immediately. Technically, the claim made by the reversioner in such cases is not identical to a claim for trespass to land since the reversioner will allege that the defendant has injured his reversion rather than his land.

interest in the land) is treated as being in possession for the purposes of suing a third party for trespass[36] depends on the terms of the licence.[37]

Where B is in possession of land, A cannot successfully defend an action for trespass to land on the basis that someone else has a title superior to B's,[38] unless A can establish that *he* has a superior title, or that he crossed the boundary with the permission of the person with a superior title.[39] This means that B can usually safely sue if *in fact* she is in possession, even if as a matter *of law* she has no title or formal interest in the land.

One question that has attracted some attention is how far B can claim to be in possession of the airspace above his property so as to be able to object to A's crossing that airspace or placing something in it. The original principle was often said to be that 'the man who has land has everything above it, or is entitled at all events to object to anything else being put over it'.[40] Thus possessors of land have successfully objected to, for instance, overhanging signs[41] and cranes.[42] Modern cases have suggested, however, that passing over land at a height at which there can be no interference with the ordinary use of that land is not a trespass, and that all members of the public have an equal right to use this airspace.[43] Thus the modern principle seems to be that the possessor of the surface's interest only extends to superjacent airspace which must be controlled if the possessor is to be able reasonably to enjoy the land and put it to purposeful use.[44] Even if the modern principle represents the law, it is merely a presumption, since often in a multi-storey building one owner's rooms on a higher floor will protrude over the rooms owned by another on the ground floor.[45]

Just as the tort of trespass to land can be committed by intruding into the airspace immediately above B's land, it can also be committed by intruding into the ground beneath it.[46] In *Bocardo SA* v *Star Energy UK Onshore Ltd* (2010) – where the claimants were complaining that the defendants' oil pipelines had crossed the boundary of their land roughly 1,000 feet below the surface of the claimants' land – the UK Supreme Court held

---

[36] Where the licensor throws the licensee off the land, or tries to do so, the question is generally whether the licensee has become a trespasser (after failing to leave) and not whether the licensee can sue *for* trespass to land. The question often arises where the licensee sues for a trespass to the person committed in throwing him off the land and the licensor relies on the justification of using reasonable force to expel a trespasser.

[37] In *Hill* v *Tupper* (1863) 2 H & C 121, 159 ER 51 the claimant was granted the 'sole and exclusive right or liberty' to put pleasure boats on the Basingstoke Canal, but this was held to be insufficient. By contrast in *Manchester Airport plc* v *Dutton* [2000] QB 133, the claimant was granted the right to enter and occupy the land concerned and this was held to be sufficient to allow it to obtain an order for possession against third parties who were squatting, partly on the basis that if the claimant had already entered under such a licence then it would have had sufficient possession to seek such an order. This strongly suggests that the claimant, although a licensee, would have had sufficient possession to sue for trespass. *Manchester Airport plc* v *Dutton* [2000] QB 133 was distinguished in *Countryside Residential (North Thames) Ltd* v *Tugwell* [2000] 34 EG 87, where a claimant seeking an order for possession against protesters who were camping on the site only had a licence to enter and carry out investigatory work and not one which granted 'effective control over the land'.

[38] This defence is commonly referred to as the defence of *ius tertii*.

[39] *Nicholls* v *Ely Beet Sugar Factory* [1931] 2 Ch 84, 86.

[40] *Wandsworth Board of Works* v *United Telephone Co Ltd* (1884) 13 QBD 904, 919 (per Bowen LJ). This doctrine is often presented in Latin as *cujus est solum ejus est usque ad coelum*.

[41] *Kelsen* v *Imperial Tobacco Co* [1957] 2 QB 334.

[42] *Anchor Brewhouse Developments Ltd* v *Berkley House Ltd* [1987] 2 EGLR 173.

[43] *Bernstein* v *Skyviews* [1978] QB 479. Cited with approval by the Supreme Court in *Bocardo SA* v *Star Energy UK Onshore Ltd* [2011] 1 AC 380, [26]. An overflight by a civil aircraft at a reasonable height is immune from liability under the Civil Aviation Act 1982, s 76(1).

[44] *Bernstein* v *Skyviews* [1978] QB 479. See also Gray 1991.

[45] *Corbett* v *Hill* (1870) LR 9 Eq 671. In *Ramzan* v *Brookwide Ltd* [2011] EWCA Civ 985, the trespass was to a 'flying freehold': the claimant owned a store room on the first floor of a building while the defendants owned the ground floor and the ground which supported the building.

[46] For instance, by foundations or mining. As has already been observed, encroaching tree roots are treated as a form of private nuisance.

that the modern principle that applies to delimit landowner's rights to the airspace above the land did *not* apply in cases to delimit a landowner's rights to what was below his land. So the claimants could establish here that the defendants had trespassed on their land, even though the trespass was occurring at a depth that could have no effect on the claimants' ordinary enjoyment of their land.[47]

14.6 REMEDIES

The normal remedy in a trespass to land case, at least where the trespass is not on-going,[48] will be compensatory damages – damages designed to compensate the victim of the trespass for the losses resulting from the trespass. As we have seen, the rule in negligence cases is that if A breaches a duty of care owed to B, B will only be allowed to claim compensatory damages for the reasonably foreseeable losses suffered by her as a result of A's breach.[49] Given that trespass is a tort that can be committed by A without his being any more blameworthy than a defendant in a negligence case, we would expect the same rule to apply in a case where A has trespassed on B's land.

But what if A *deliberately* trespassed on B's land? For instance, consider the **Exploding Car Problem**:

> *Cheap* does not like paying to park. Consequently he sneaks his car into the underground car park possessed by *Busyco Ltd* without their permission, and ignores the notices that say that parking is only for their staff and clients. While *Cheap's* car is in the underground car park it explodes – without any fault on *Cheap's* part – and causes severe damage to the building.

On such facts, it is obvious that *Cheap* has committed the tort of trespass to land in relation to *Busyco*, but how far should *Cheap* be held liable for the *consequences* of his trespass? It is a matter of dispute what rule will be applied to determine whether *Cheap* is liable for the damage done to *Busyco's* car park. On one view, the normal rule set out above will apply to determine the scope of *Cheap's* liability in this case and *Cheap* will only be held liable if he intended the car to explode or it was reasonably foreseeable that the car might cause this kind of damage when he parked it in the car park. On another view, *Cheap* will be held liable for the damage done to the car park *if* it was a direct result of his trespass, even if that kind of damage (damage by explosion) was unintended and unforeseeable; the fact that *Cheap* is a deliberate wrongdoer makes us inclined to hold him liable for *all* the losses directly suffered by *Busyco* as a result of his wrong.[50] Whichever view one takes, it is clear that whether *Cheap* will be held liable for the fire damage done to *Busyco's* car park will

---

[47] [2011] 1 AC 380, at [27] (per Lord Hope).

[48] Where the trespass is on-going, or regularly repeated, the claimant will normally be entitled to obtain an injunction against the defendant. Injunctions are discussed in more detail below, § 15.12, and chapter 33.

[49] See above, § 10.2.

[50] This was the view preferred by the New Zealand Court of Appeal in *Mayfair Ltd* v *Pears* [1987] 1 NZLR 459, from which our hypothetical example is drawn. (The court went on to find that the fire damage caused by the car bursting into flames in that case was *not* a *direct* result of the defendant's parking his car in the claimant's building. Consequently, it held that – in the absence of proof that the car's bursting into flames was intended or reasonably foreseeable at the time the defendant parked his car – the defendant could not be held liable for the fire damage suffered by the claimant.) Some support for the New Zealand Court of Appeal's approach comes from Lord Nicholls's judgment in *Kuwait Airways Corpn* v *Iraqi Airways Co (Nos 4 & 5)* [2002] 2 AC 883. Lord Nicholls suggested that while the normal rule is that someone who converts another's goods should only be liable for the reasonably foreseeable consequences of his conversion, if A knowingly converts B's goods, A should be held liable for *all* the losses suffered by B that were a direct consequence of A's conversion: ibid, at [103]–[104]. There is no reason to think that he would apply a different rule if A knowingly trespassed on B's land.

depend a great deal on what his state of mind was when he parked his car there. But his state of mind at the time he parked his car is *not* relevant to the issue of whether he committed the tort of trespass to land in relation to *Busyco* when he parked his car; he did.

In a case where A has trespassed on B's land without causing B to suffer any kind of loss, B will still be entitled to sue A for nominal damages: trespass to land is a tort that is actionable *per se*.[51] But it is also clear that even if A's trespass has not caused B to suffer any loss, B may be entitled to sue A for damages designed to make A pay B a reasonable sum for the use he has made of her land.[52] Such damages are increasingly referred to as 'user damages' in the caselaw,[53] though we have given them a different title below.[54] The fact that there is no established label for this measure of damages is indicative of the fact that it is not clear *why* such damages can be claimed by B. Some argue that they are really compensatory damages – designed to compensate B for what she could have charged A for the privilege of using her land.[55] Others argue that these damages are designed to 'substitute' for the right that A has violated by trespassing on B's land.[56] We argue below that they are gain-based, and are designed to make A pay a reasonable sum for the freedom he has been allowed to enjoy as a result of trespassing on B's land.[57]

Further reading

In the case of *Bocardo SA* v *Star Energy UK Onshore Ltd* (2010) Lord Hope made two references to an article discussing when the owner of the surface should be able to sue for trespass as a result of activities underground, though he did not eventually adopt its author's preferred solution: **J.G. Sprankling, 'Owning the center of the Earth' (2008) 55** *UCLA Law Review* **979**. In **B. Depoorter, 'Fair Trespass' (2011) 111** *Columbia Law Review* **1090**, the author discusses whether a special 'public interest' defence to trespass to land should be developed which might assist investigative journalists, among others.

Visit **www.mylawchamber.co.uk/mcbride** to access tools to help you develop and test your knowledge of Tort law, including interactive multiple choice questions, practice exam questions with guidance, weblinks, legal newsfeed, additional case summaries, legal updates and tips on answering problem and essay questions.

premium
my**law**chamber
unrivalled support for legal education

---

[51] See above, § 1.6(B), and below, § 27.1.
[52] For much more detailed discussion of this aspect of the law, see below, § 31.3.
[53] *Bocardo SA* v *Star Energy UK Onshore Ltd* [2011] 1 AC 380, at [74] (per Lord Brown), [118] and [125] (per Lord Clarke).
[54] See below, § 31.1.
[55] See Sharpe and Waddams 1982.
[56] See Stevens 2007, 59f.
[57] See below, § 31.3.

15 Private nuisance

15.1 The basics *415*

15.2 Ways of committing the tort *416*

15.3 Emanation cases (1): establishing an interference *419*

15.4 Emanation cases (2): reasonable interferences *422*

15.5 Emanation cases (3): establishing an unreasonable interference *429*

15.6 Encroachment cases *434*

15.7 Obstruction cases *435*

15.8 Affront cases *438*

15.9 Responsibility *440*

15.10 Defences *446*

15.11 Title to sue *448*

15.12 Remedies *454*

15.13 Peculiar forms of the tort *464*

Overview

In this chapter we consider the tort of private nuisance, a tort which protects interests in land. There are many ways in which a state of affairs can impede someone's ability to use and enjoy their land, and many ways in which you can be responsible for a state of affairs, and as a result there are many ways of committing the tort. The chapter explains why there are so many ways in section 15.2, and is then divided (sections 15.3 to 15.8) in accordance with the four main ways in which a state of affairs can bring about problems for another's use and enjoyment of land: emanation; encroachment; obstruction and affront. Section 15.9 discusses when someone will be responsible for a particular state of affairs that interferes with someone's ability to use and enjoy their land. Section 15.10 deals with some prominent defences, and then section 15.11 summarises who can bring a claim for private nuisance. Section 15.12 presents the law relating to the two main remedies for nuisance – injunctions and damages – and the final section 15.13 briefly mentions some peculiar forms of the tort of private nuisance.

15.1 THE BASICS

The tort of private nuisance is a tort which protects interests in, or associated with, land. Thus it is the tort which a claimant who owns a house will invoke if his use and enjoyment of the house is destroyed by the loud noises made by a neighbouring factory, or his paintwork is repeatedly chipped by fragments blasted out by a nearby quarry, or his private right of way to gain access to the house is regularly blocked by piles of rubble dumped by a local builder. As we will see in the next section, there are many ways of committing the tort. But it can, to some extent, be summarised:

> A will have committed the tort of private nuisance in relation to B if he has created, authorised, adopted or continued a state of affairs that has unreasonably interfered, or is unreasonably interfering, with either the use and enjoyment of land in which B has a sufficient interest, or some right associated with that land.

Some elements of this definition require careful elaboration. For example, in section 15.11 we will describe the rules which determine who will be able to sue for a private nuisance: in summary, those with a sufficient interest in land, those actually enjoying exclusive possession of land, and those who actually enjoy various legal rights associated with land, such as private rights of way. Similarly, in section 15.9 we will set out what must be shown in order to demonstrate that a defendant is responsible for a state of affairs, either because he has *created* it, or because he has *authorised* it, or because he has *continued* or *adopted* it. At the core of the tort, however, is a requirement that the state of affairs should bring about an *unreasonable* interference.

What makes an interference into an *unreasonable* interference? We answer this in detail in sections 15.4 and 15.5. But at this stage it is worth making three basic points. First, an interference does not have to involve any risk of injury to a person or physical damage to property in order to be unreasonable. So a loud noise, or a bad smell, or a bright reflected light, can be an unreasonable interference, even if there is no risk of it injuring anyone or damaging anything.

Secondly, where an interference does not cause physical damage then the question whether it is unreasonable will depend on the nature of the locality where the events take place: in some localities more noise is reasonable than in others.

Thirdly, what is reasonable in a particular locality depends on a notion of reciprocity, or 'give-and-take': nobody should be able to complain about insubstantial interferences, or about the effects of houses being used as houses in an ordinary and convenient way, but beyond such easy propositions it is not straightforward to settle how many noisy parties, smoky bonfires, or smelly brewery-cleansings should be tolerated before it can be said that a neighbour has gone beyond ordinary 'give and take' and committed the tort of private nuisance.

15.2 WAYS OF COMMITTING THE TORT

There are several ways of committing the tort of private nuisance. (This is true even if we disregard for the time being some peculiar forms of the tort.)[1] The reason why there are so many ways of committing the tort is that within the scope of the tort: (1) there are different ways in which a defendant can be responsible for a state of affairs; (2) there are different ways in which a state of affairs can have an effect on land in which a claimant has a sufficient interest; and (3) there are different kinds of effects that are, or may be, regarded as being harmful for the purposes of the tort of private nuisance.

As we have seen, to establish that a defendant has committed the tort of private nuisance in relation to a claimant, it has to be shown that –

> The defendant created, authorised, adopted or continued a state of affairs that has unreasonably interfered, or is unreasonably interfering, with either the use and enjoyment of land in which the claimant has a sufficient interest, or some right associated with that land.

This summary already incorporates the first important factor: (1) the different ways in which a defendant can be responsible for a state of affairs which interfered, or is interfering, with the claimant's land,[2] or some right associated with that land. The summary refers to three different ways of establishing a defendant's responsibility for a state of affairs: (a) creating; (b) authorising; and (c) adopting or continuing.

---

[1] For which, see § 15.13, below.
[2] We use the phrase 'the claimant's land' here and below as shorthand here for 'land in which the claimant has a sufficient interest'.

Let's now turn to the other two important factors: (2) the different ways in which a state of affairs can have an effect on land in which a claimant has a sufficient interest; and (3) the different kinds of effects that are, or may be, regarded as being harmful for the purposes of the tort of private nuisance.

With regard to (3), the different effects that are *sometimes* treated as being harmful for the purposes of the tort of private nuisance are: (a) *violation of the boundaries* of the claimant's land; (b) *physical damage* to the claimant's land; (c) *reduction of the amenity value* of the claimant's land; (d) *interference with some right* associated with the claimant's land, such as a right to have water or light come onto the land, or a private right of way. But it is important to note the word '*sometimes*': we will see below that (a) (violating the boundaries of the claimant's land) is not *always* treated as harmful.

With regard to (2), the different ways in which a state of affairs can have an effect that amounts to a private nuisance *include*: (a) something (such as smoke, smells, noise or electromagnetic waves) *emanating* onto the claimant's land; (b) something (such as branches, tree roots or a leaning wall) *encroaching* onto the claimant's land; (c) something (such as water, air, light or TV signals) being *obstructed* from coming onto the claimant's land; (d) something (such as drug dealing or prostitution) happening near the claimant's land that offends or *affronts* the claimant and makes him unhappy to live where he does.

We can sum all this up in the table below, which shows us some of the different things we have to attend to in considering whether a given defendant has committed the tort of private nuisance in relation to a claimant:

Defendant	Claimant	
Connection	*How*	*Effect*
Create	Emanation	Violation of boundaries
Authorise	Encroachment	Physical damage to land
Adopt or Continue	Obstruction	Reduction of amenity value
	Affront	Interference with associated right

Combinations of elements from each of the above three columns create various different ways of committing the tort of private nuisance. For example: *creating* a state of affairs in which there is an *emanation* onto the claimant's land that *physically damages* the land (which would be the case where smoke emitted from the defendant's factory damages trees on the claimant's land). Or: *adopting or continuing* a state of affairs in which there is an *encroachment* onto the claimant's land that *violates the boundaries* of the claimant's land (which would be the case where roots from a tree on the defendant's land grow so that they intrude onto the claimant's land and the defendant knows or ought to know that this is happening and does nothing about the problem).

In theory, there are 48 different possible combinations that we could put together from the above menu of options. However, some combinations do not exist. For example:

(1) The *effect* of violation of the boundaries of a claimant's land is only usually sufficient to constitute a private nuisance[3] when the violation involves a physical intrusion of some permanence (such as tree roots or a leaning wall). Clearly such a physical intrusion cannot

---

[3] Indeed, as we will see below, mere violation of the boundaries may only be sufficient to confer on the claimant a right to *abate* the nuisance; the claimant may only be able to make a claim for substantial damages if the encroachment has caused some further damage.

be brought about by an *affront* or by *obstructing* something from coming onto the claimant's land. Indeed tort lawyers tend to use the word *encroaching* to describe *how* a state of affairs can have such an effect. Thus where there is a physical intrusion of some permanence, which can be a private nuisance merely because the boundaries of the claimant's land have been violated, such as where the roots of the defendant's tree have grown so that they have crossed over into the claimant's soil, such an intrusion would always be described by tort lawyers as an *encroachment* rather than an *emanation*.

(2) As we will see,[4] where a claim is based on something intangible, like a noise or a smell, affecting a claimant on his or her land it will not be enough for the claimant merely to assert that there has been a *violation of the boundaries* of his or her land. Moreover, no tort lawyer is ever likely to describe something like noise or smells as *encroaching* on a claimant's land.

(3) As we will see,[5] obstructing something from coming onto the claimant's land can *only* ever amount to a nuisance if that obstruction interferes with some right associated with that land.

(4) A state of affairs that affronts the claimant will only ever reduce the amenity value of the claimant's land: it won't result in the claimant's land being physically damaged, or its boundaries violated.

If we modify the above table to get rid of all the combinations that don't exist, we end up with this:

Defendant	Claimant
Create Authorise Adopt or Continue	Emanation resulting in physical damage to land
	Emanation resulting in reduction of amenity value of land
	Encroachment (violation of boundaries sufficient, though it may also cause physical damage)
	Obstruction that interferes with right associated with land
	Affront resulting in reduction of amenity value of land

Combining the various options in the different columns in the above table now gives us 15 different ways in which someone can commit the tort of private nuisance.[6] What really matters, however, is not exactly *how many* different ways there are of committing the tort,[7]

---

[4] See below, § 15.4.

[5] See below, § 15.7.

[6] In *Hunter v Canary Wharf* [1997] AC 655, Lord Lloyd remarked (at 695) that 'Private nuisances are of three kinds. They are (1) nuisance by encroachment on a neighbour's land; (2) nuisance by direct physical injury to a neighbour's land; and (3) nuisance by interference with a neighbour's quiet enjoyment of land.' If this were right, then combining that with the three different ways of being responsible for a private nuisance, would give us only nine ways of committing the tort. But there are some problems with Lord Lloyd's statement. (1) It misses out cases of private nuisance which involve interfering with a right associated with land. (2) It fails to observe that cases where a defendant *directly* damages a claimant's land are more likely to be treated as trespass to land cases (where the defendant damages the land by going onto the land or by throwing something onto the land) than private nuisance cases, and that where private nuisance deals with physical damage it is usually concerned with *indirect* damage to the claimant's land. (3) It fails to distinguish between cases where the quiet enjoyment of land is interfered with by: (i) an emanation onto the claimant's land, and (ii) by the claimant being affronted by something going on near his land.

[7] It should be re-emphasised that there are also some peculiar forms of the tort of private nuisance, which we will deal with at the end of this chapter and which have the effect of expanding the number of ways that the tort can be committed. And, to keep things simple, we have also omitted from the above list of possible ways of committing the tort of private nuisance some well-recognised ways of committing the tort, such as withdrawing support from the claimant's land. These will also be briefly mentioned below, § 15.7.

but remembering that when we consider whether a defendant has committed the tort of private nuisance in relation to a claimant we must assess all the *possible* combinations of: (1) the different ways in which a defendant can be responsible for a state of affairs which interfered, or is interfering, with the claimant's land, or some right associated with that land, (2) the different ways in which a state of affairs can have an effect on land in which a claimant has a sufficient interest; and (3) the different effects that are, or might be, regarded as being harmful for the purposes of the tort of private nuisance.

In the rest of this chapter we start by dividing our discussion in line with the different ways *how* a state of affairs for which the defendant is responsible can have an effect on the claimant's land, or on a right associated with land. Thus in sections 15.3 to 15.5 we present the law governing situations where a state of affairs has led to an *emanation* onto the claimant's land, and then in the following three sections we deal with the other ways in which a state of affairs can have an effect: *encroachment, obstruction* and *affront*. In section 15.9 we turn to the different ways in which a defendant can be responsible for a state of affairs: *creating, authorising* and *continuing or adopting*. Thereafter we discuss who can sue for private nuisance (section 15.11) and what remedies they can obtain (section 15.12), followed by a summary of some unusual forms of the tort (section 15.13).

15.3 EMANATION CASES (1): ESTABLISHING AN INTERFERENCE

As we have seen, in a case where something has emanated onto the claimant's land, the claimant has *two* ways of establishing that the emanation has caused 'harm' with respect to her use and enjoyment of land: (1) establishing that the emanation has reduced the amenity value of the land; (2) establishing that the emanation has physically damaged the land.

A. Reduction of amenity value

What is the 'amenity value' of land? Essentially, it means the day-to-day usefulness of the land. So, for example, an emanation will reduce the amenity value of an ordinary house if it makes the house less useful by doing something like making it harder to sleep there (because of loud noise at night) or harder to relax there (because of nauseating smells).

Usually an on-going reduction in amenity value will reduce the price for which the claimant could sell her land. But it is sometimes important to distinguish between a reduction in amenity value and such a reduction in the price. This will be important when, for example, an emanation was temporary or a claimant will obtain an injunction ordering the defendant to stop some activity which had been causing an emanation: in such circumstances the price for which the land could be sold may return to its previous level but the claimant may nonetheless be able to obtain a remedy for having suffered a loss of amenity value in the period during which the interference lasted. What this shows is that amenity value can be measured in terms of time: loss of amenity value can be for one day, or for one month, of for one year.

In the leading case of *St Helen's Smelting* v *Tipping* (1865) Lord Westbury LC referred to emanations which produce 'sensible personal discomfort' rather than those which reduce the amenity value of land. But there are two reasons why we think it is better to avoid this phrase. The first reason is that although emanations *very often* make land less useful because they cause discomfort to those who are using the land this is not the only way in which an emanation can reduce the day-to-day usefulness of land. For example, if the emanation of electromagnetic waves means that mobile telephones and computers cannot be used on the claimant's land then this will reduce the amenity value even though no one will suffer any discomfort. The second reason is that the phrase 'sensible personal discomfort' has sometimes led people to mistakenly think that the amount of damages that a defendant will be liable to pay for committing a private nuisance will depend on *how many people* suffered discomfort. This is a mistake. In *Hunter v Canary Wharf* (1997) Lord Hoffmann made clear that the damages that a claimant can recover for private nuisance by an emanation which reduces amenity value 'may be affected by the size, commodiousness and value of his property but cannot be increased merely because more people are in occupation and therefore suffer greater collective discomfort'.[8]

Can a claimant argue that an emanation reduces the amenity value of her land *even if* she uses the land in a way which means that *she* is not inconvenienced? For instance, if A's factory emits nauseating smells on *weekdays* which drift into B's neighbouring cottage, then can B argue that these smells reduce the amenity value of her land *even if* B only uses the cottage at weekends? We think that the answer is 'yes': the day-to-day usefulness of B's cottage is reduced by the smells *even if* B happens not to want to use it on weekdays. The fact that B suffers no 'consequential loss' will, perhaps, affect the amount of damages she might be able to claim from A in this case.[9] But if she seeks a remedy to prevent any future unreasonable interference with her *right* to use and enjoy the land, A will not be able to claim that he is not committing a tort simply because B is personally not put out as a result of the smells coming from B's factory.[10]

A claimant can also argue that an emanation is reducing the amenity value of the land even if she never *personally* uses the land, but instead permits others to use it. So, in the above example, B might be able to sue A even if she never visits the cottage and uses it by renting it out to holidaymakers. The fact that the holidaymakers would have been subjected to the nauseous smell, and not B, would not prevent B from making a claim. B can still claim because the nauseous smell has reduced the usefulness of her land, as a holiday cottage. Thus in *Andreae* v *Selfridge & Co Ltd* (1938), where a defendant's building operations unreasonably interfered with the amenity value of land used by the claimant as a hotel, the claimant did not have to establish that she had been *personally* disturbed by the noise or dust in order to recover damages covering the consequential loss of business. Indeed, it would not have mattered if the claimant had been a company, and thus incapable of being woken up at night or choked with dust.

B. Physical damage to land

Land includes things which are *attached* to the land – buildings, fences, trees, shrubs – and it will count as having been physically damaged if it undergoes 'a physical change which renders [it] less useful or less valuable.'[11] Obvious examples of emanations causing physical damage would include debris blasted from a defendant's quarry breaking roof tiles and smashing windows, or acid smuts from a defendant's chemical works killing trees and shrubs. Less obvious examples include emanations which end up resting on the claimant's

---

[8] [1997] AC 655, 706–7.
[9] We discuss the question whether the use that a claimant makes of his land will affect the damages that he can receive below, at § 15.12. In *Dobson v Thames Water Utilities Ltd* [2009] 3 All ER 319, Waller LJ stated (at [34]) that he was 'unable to see how there can be any damages beyond perhaps the nominal' in a situation where a claimant has not been inconvenienced at all.
[10] *Price v Hilditch* [1930] 1 Ch 500, 509; *Nicholls v Ely Beet Sugar Factory Ltd (No 2)* [1936] Ch 343.
[11] *Hunter v Canary Wharf* [1997] AC 655, 676 (per Pill LJ).

land, or become intermingled with it, and will reduce its usefulness or value unless they are cleaned away. Thus, in *Hunter* v *Canary Wharf* (1997), the Court of Appeal held that the deposit of excessive dust on a carpet could amount to physical damage to the carpet, and there is no reason to think that a deposit of mud or oil on a paved area of land would be treated any differently. Similarly, in *Blue Circle Industries* v *Ministry of Defence* (1999) the Court of Appeal was willing to hold that the intermingling of plutonium with soil so that it could not be removed amounted to a form of property damage.

If an emanation only causes damage to personal property that was present *on* the claimant's land but *not attached* to it, such as vehicles, animals or clothes, should this be treated as involving a 'reduction in the amenity value of land' or 'physical damage to land'? This question is raised by the **Dog Whistle Problem**:

> *Barker* uses his land for breeding pedigree dogs. *Grinder* operates machinery on neighbouring land which emits a high-pitched whistle. The whistle is too high-pitched for *Barker* to hear but it drives the dogs on his land into such a frenzy that they sometimes injure themselves.

We think that it cannot be said that the Dog Whistle Problem involves physical damage *to land*, and that *Barker* would have to claim that the emanation of the whistle reduces the amenity of his land by restricting his ability to use it for the purposes of dog breeding. (We discuss below the separate question whether a claimant who has established that a defendant has committed private nuisance in relation to him or her can obtain damages which compensate for damage done to personal property.)[12]

C. Personal injury

The decision in *Hunter* v *Canary Wharf* (1997) and subsequent decisions have made it clear that a claimant cannot sue in private nuisance for physical injuries that he or she suffers as a result of an emanation onto her land.[13] Consider, for example, the **Blinded Gardener Problem**:

> An accident occurs one day in A's factory with the result that A's factory emits some acid smoke which drifts across B's land. Unfortunately, B is standing in her back garden admiring her flowers when the smoke comes across her land, and she is permanently blinded by it. As a result, B is unable to enjoy the view of her garden, or do any more gardening, which used to be her favourite hobby.

There is no doubt that in this situation B has suffered an interference with the way *she* uses and enjoys her land. But A is not liable to her in private nuisance because he has not made *the land* less useful. B's land remains just as useful for creating a beautiful garden even though *B* is not able any more to use the land for that purpose.[14]

---

[12] See below, § 15.12.

[13] [1997] AC 655, 696 (per Lord Lloyd), 707 (per Lord Hoffmann). In *Transco plc* v *Stockport Metropolitan Borough Council* [2004] 2 AC 1, a majority of the House of Lords held that damages for personal injuries could not be recovered under the rule in *Rylands* v *Fletcher* (discussed in chapter 16, below) because this was the rule in private nuisance: see [9] (per Lord Bingham), [35] (per Lord Hoffmann), [52] (per Lord Hobhouse).

[14] In light of this, it is questionable whether Lawton J was correct to hold in *British Celanese Ltd* v *A H Hunt (Capacitors) Ltd* [1969] 1 WLR 959 that an isolated escape of metal foils from the defendant's land, which blew into the claimant's factory and shorted out its power supply for 12 minutes, could amount to a private nuisance. Such a short interruption to the claimant's power supply could hardly be said to have reduced the amenity value of the land. However, some temporary damage was done to the claimant's machines as a result of the power cut, and that sort of harm *might* have been capable of being counted as damage to the claimant's land.

Not allowing claimants to sue in private nuisance for physical injuries has its advantages and disadvantages. If damages for physical injuries could be recovered in private nuisance then the anomalous situation would arise that a person would find it easier to recover damages for physical injury if she was injured in her garden – as in the Blinded Gardener Problem – than if she were injured in the street, or at work. Further, because only a claimant with an interest in land can sue in private nuisance,[15] a second anomaly would then arise. A landowner who was injured in her garden by an emanation would be able to sue the creator of that emanation in private nuisance for damages in respect of her injury without having to prove that the creator of the emanation acted carelessly; on the other hand, if the landowner's infant son (who would not have an interest in the land affected by the emanation) were injured by the same emanation, he would have to prove carelessness on the part of the creator of the emanation before he could sue for damages (in the tort of negligence) in respect of his injuries. One possible solution to the second anomaly would be to let those without interests in land sue in private nuisance. But the House of Lords rejected this solution in *Hunter* v *Canary Wharf* (1997), and ruled that it was inconsistent with the *function* of the tort which is to protect interests in land. The preferred solution to both anomalies was to deny that anyone could sue in private nuisance for compensation in respect of personal injuries.

It may be worth noting, however, that not allowing claimants to recover for physical injuries in private nuisance cases has the effect of *creating* an anomaly in the law. If foul-smelling acidic smoke coming from A's land drifts across land belonging to B, B will find it easier to sue A for the bad smell carried by the smoke than she will if the smoke physically burns her nostrils. If the bad smell reduces the amenity value of B's land then she will be able to sue A in private nuisance for compensation for that without having to prove carelessness on A's part. On the other hand, carelessness must be established on A's part before B will be able to sue him for compensation in respect of the harm to her nostrils. The impression given is that the law attaches greater importance to protecting people's land from being made less useful than it does to protecting people's persons from being injured.

15.4 EMANATION CASES (2): REASONABLE INTERFERENCES

In a case where a claimant can show that an emanation onto her land has either (1) reduced the amenity value of that land or (2) physically damaged the land, that emanation will only amount to a nuisance if the interference with the use and enjoyment of land that the claimant has experienced, or is experiencing, is *unreasonable*. Not all interferences which result from an emanation are unreasonable. Nobody can expect that every noise, smell or vibration coming onto their land will amount to a tort. Ordinary social living requires a degree of 'give and take'. Your neighbours have to put up with your singing in the shower; you, in turn, have to put up with their wailing baby.

The following three rules are particularly helpful in identifying interferences that are *not unreasonable* and therefore not actionable under the law on private nuisance:

(1) An interference will *not* be unreasonable if it is *insubstantial*, in particular, if an ordinary occupier of land in the locality would regard the interference as tolerable.

(2) An interference will *not* be unreasonable if it *results from acts 'necessary for the common and ordinary use and occupation of land and houses', so long as these acts are 'conveniently done'*.[16]

---

[15] See below, § 15.11.

[16] These phrases originally come from the judgment of Bramwell B in *Bamford* v *Turnley* (1862) 3 B & S 66, 122 ER 27.

(3) An interference will *not* be unreasonable if it *results from the 'reasonable user' of land.*[17]

Although we will discuss each of these rules in turn it will probably be apparent already that there is a degree of overlap between them: some people will argue that a teenager practising the drums for half an hour each evening is 'tolerable', others that such music practice is 'necessary for the common and ordinary use and occupation of land and houses', and still others that it is a 'reasonable user' of land. But any overlap causes no difficulties, because if any of the three rules is applicable then the claimant will be unable to establish that the interference is unreasonable. This highlights, however, that these three rules all focus on what does *not* amount to an unreasonable interference; so after discussing each of them we will still have to consider what factors determine whether other interferences *are* unreasonable.

A. Insubstantial interferences

An interference will only be unreasonable if it would be regarded as unreasonable by an ordinary occupier of land in the locality.

(1) *Hypersensitive claimants.* Ordinary occupiers are generally contrasted with hypersensitive claimants. So if an interference could only be regarded as substantial from the perspective of a hypersensitive occupier then it will not be unreasonable.[18] According to the leading case, for an interference to be actionable it must be '[an] inconvenience materially interfering with the ordinary comfort . . . of human existence, not merely according to elegant or dainty modes of living, but according to plain and sober and simple notions among the English people'.[19]

The same rule applies to interference with 'delicate trades' as to interference with 'dainty modes of living'. Thus in *Robinson* v *Kilvert* (1889), the claimant complained that brown paper he had been storing had been damaged by the defendant's over-heating of the room below. The court held that there had not been an unreasonable interference because the heat could only have had a detrimental effect on an 'exceptionally delicate trade'.

It is important, however, to distinguish the test for liability from the question of the *extent* of a defendant's liability once the tort of private nuisance has been established. This distinction means that once it has been established that a defendant is responsible for a state of affairs which led to an emanation which would have unreasonably interfered even with a *reasonably robust* trade, a claimant can claim even though she actually operates a delicate trade.[20] Thus in *McKinnon Industries* v *Walker* (1951), the Privy Council held that the claimant could obtain a remedy for the noxious fumes and sulphur dioxide emitted from the defendant's factory. The fumes would have damaged any reasonably robust

---

[17] In the phrase 'reasonable user' the word 'user' does not refer to the *person* who is using the land. Instead in this phrase the word 'user' means 'use', so a 'reasonable user of land' is a 'reasonable use of land'. Today, only lawyers use the word 'user' in this way.

[18] In *Network Rail Infrastructure Ltd* v *CJ Morris* [2004] EWCA Civ 172, the Court of Appeal suggested that it was no longer necessary to determine whether particular uses were hypersensitive since this issue had been subsumed in the more general question whether the defendant's behaviour was 'reasonable between neighbours'. We believe that the court was wrong to say this since the general question is far too loose for lawyers to use in a predictable and consistent manner. Sub-rules have developed to foster predictability and consistency, and the *insubstantial interference* rule is one of these sub-rules which is used when deciding whether an interference for which the defendant is responsible is an *unreasonable* interference.

[19] *Walter* v *Selfe* (1851) 4 De G & Sm 315, 322, 64 ER 849, 852 (per Knight Bruce VC).

[20] Of course, any claim for damages for past losses will be subject to the rules relating to 'remoteness of damage'. See below, § 15.12.

neighbouring trade so it did not matter that what had actually been interfered with was the claimant's delicate trade as an orchid grower.

(2) *Nature of locality*. The nature of the locality is important when the interference causes a reduction in amenity value rather than physical damage to the land. The effect on the claimant's land was identified as a significant distinction in this context by the House of Lords in *St Helen's Smelting* v *Tipping* (1865). In that case Lord Westbury LC suggested that where there was an interference with personal sensibilities by, for instance, noise or smell, the question whether the interference was unreasonable would have to be judged taking into account the nature of the locality, while there would be no need to consider the nature of the locality if the interference resulted in material injury to the property.

Unfortunately, the *St Helen's* case left some loose ends. First, Lord Westbury LC at one point talks about 'material injury to property' being the condition for ignoring the locality, but later talks about 'sensible injury to the *value* of property' being the condition.[21] If the latter were right, then the distinction would virtually disappear, because most interferences with ordinary sensibilities will cause at least a temporary reduction in land value. Nobody is likely to pay as much for a bad-smelling house or for one with a noisy factory next door. This suggests that the distinction should be between interferences which cause physical damage and interferences which reduce amenity value. The degree of noise, smell and the like which one should tolerate as part of the social rules of 'give and take' may vary with locality, but there is no *locality* where it is reasonable to do things which will physically damage the reasonably robust land of others.[22] Lords Hoffmann and Cooke both mentioned *St Helen's Smelting* and the locality rule in *Hunter* v *Canary Wharf* (1997), and both expressed the key distinction as being between interferences causing 'material injury to the property' and those causing 'sensible personal discomfort'.[23] Lord Lloyd used a similar distinction, though he did not expressly link it to *St Helen's*.[24]

The second issue raised by Lord Westbury's distinction is that there are difficulties in identifying and classifying localities. The famously quotable observations on locality, such as that of Byles J, during argument in *Hole* v *Barlow* (1858), that a 'swine-style might not be considered a nuisance in Bethnal Green: but it certainly would be so in Grosvenor Square'[25] do not subdivide localities in any detail. *Gaunt* v *Fynney* (1870) provides a fairly typical example of the 'broad brush' sometimes used by the judiciary in classifying localities: in this case Lord Selborne went no further than categorising Leek, Staffordshire, as a 'manufacturing town'.[26] Some cases, however, have adopted much finer distinctions. For example, in *Adams* v *Ursell* (1913) the evidence suggested that most of Silver Street was 'in the lowest district of Dursley . . . but that the [claimant's] house and others near it were of a much better character.'[27] In these circumstances Swinfen Eady J granted an injunction against the defendant preventing him from operating a fried fish shop in a building

---

[21] (1865) 11 HLC 642, at 650–1.

[22] There may, however, be *occasions* when it is reasonable to do things which may cause physical damage to the reasonably robust land of others. One example may be occasions where it is reasonable to take steps against a 'common enemy', discussed below, § 15.5(E).

[23] [1997] AC 655, 705 (per Lord Hoffmann), 712 (per Lord Cooke). Consistently with our previous view we would prefer to talk of interferences which 'reduce the amenity value of land' rather than interferences which cause 'sensible personal discomfort'.

[24] [1997] AC 655, 695.

[25] (1858) 4 CB NS 334, 340; 140 ER 1113, 1116.

[26] (1872–3) LR 8 Ch App 8, at 11 and 12.

[27] [1913] 1 Ch 269, 270.

adjoining the claimant's, but refused to extend the injunction so as to prevent him from opening such a shop elsewhere on the street.

Joanne Conaghan and Wade Mansell have argued that the locality principle conceals judicial prejudice and is an essentially class-based exercise.[28] We think, however, that it is necessary to reflect carefully on what this criticism means. It is certainly true that the locality principle has been used to protect the well-heeled from fish and chip shops,[29] but it has also been used to protect blue-collar residential districts from industrial noise.[30] The core of the criticism is probably that the locality principle tends to lead to inhabitants of working-class housing areas having to put up with greater degrees of interference than inhabitants of more expensive areas. There is a risk here, however, of treating the social reality that the locality principle reflects as if it is a *consequence* of the principle.[31] Furthermore, it is worth noting that the locality principle applies equally to both claimants and defendants. Thus if it is established that *Fryer* cannot use his property as a fish and chip shop because of the locality, then equally *Fryer* is protected against others carrying on activities similar to fish frying which might reduce the amenity value of *his* land. Likewise, if it is found that in a particular locality it is reasonable for *Boxer* to interfere with *Dreamer's* use and enjoyment of her land by using his land for light industry, then it will be equally reasonable for *Dreamer* to interfere with other people's use and enjoyment of *their land* by using *her* land for light industry. Thus while the locality principle means that there are inequalities between owners of property situated in different places, at the same time all owners in a particular locality have equal opportunities and restrictions on their use and enjoyment of land.[32]

B. Interferences arising from acts that are necessary for the common and ordinary use of land, and conveniently done

Even a *substantial* disturbance will not amount to an unreasonable interference if it results from ordinary use of a house as a *house*. An example of this is provided by the case of *Southwark London Borough Council v Tanner* (2001). The claimants in this case were tenants who lived in old houses with inadequate soundproofing and they could hear everything their neighbours did, 'their coming and going, their cooking and cleaning, their quarrels and their love-making.'[33] Lord Millett accepted that '[life] in these conditions must be intolerable'.[34] But the House of Lords unanimously found that this sort of interference did not amount to an actionable private nuisance. Despite the 'intolerable' effect of their everyday noises it was not unreasonable for the claimants' neighbours to make such noises – the interference resulted from those neighbours' reasonable, common and ordinary use of their property.

---

[28] Conaghan and Mansell 1999, 137.

[29] *Adams* v *Ursell* [1913] 1 Ch 269.

[30] *Halsey* v *Esso Petroleum* [1961] 1 WLR 683.

[31] To put the same point another way – housing is more affordable in such localities *because* they are areas which are understood to be noisy, etc, rather than the law allowing such areas to be subjected to additional noise, etc, because that is where the affordable housing is.

[32] The significance of this formal 'equality of opportunities and restrictions' should not be exaggerated. For example, in *Barr* v *Biffa Waste Services Ltd* [2011] EWHC 1003 (TCC) Coulson J ruled that a locality on the outskirts of Ware, Hertfordshire, was one where a large waste tip was appropriately located. Clearly the residents of the estate who were regularly subjected to the smell of rotting rubbish might attach little value to their 'equal opportunity' to open waste tips.

[33] [2001] 1 AC 1, 7.

[34] [2001] 1 AC 1, 18.

Lord Millett expressly stated that there could be no liability if the acts causing the interference were *necessary for the common and ordinary use and occupation of land* and *conveniently done*.[35] But the test of necessity is weak here: *common and ordinary* is the phrase which governs. Babies, televisions and washing machines are not strictly *necessary* for occupation of land as a house, but they are all part of *common and ordinary occupation*, and they will not ordinarily be treated as involving unreasonable interference.

Conveniently done is an important qualification, however. The point seems to be that to avoid potential liability babies, televisions and washing machines must not be arranged so as to expose neighbours to substantial noise where it would be equally convenient to arrange them otherwise. Thus, if there was nowhere in his house that a defendant could put the washing machine without it disturbing his neighbours then the noise caused by the washing machine (at least at times of day when washing machines are commonly used) would not amount to an unreasonable interference with the neighbours' use and enjoyment of their land, but if it disturbed the neighbours only because he chose to put it in an alcove where the wall between the houses was particularly thin then the interference so caused might be unreasonable.

C. Interferences arising from the reasonable user of land

The rule that an interference with land will not be unreasonable if it arises from the reasonable user of land is potentially relevant in a far broader range of cases than the two we have already discussed. There is considerable scope for argument, however, as to what will count as a 'reasonable user'.

(1) *Reasonable user and reasonable care.* It is important to note that saying that a defendant will not be liable for interference resulting from a 'reasonable user' is *not* the same as saying that a defendant cannot be liable if he has taken 'reasonable care' to reduce the interference he is causing to a minimum.[36] If a defendant has failed to take reasonable care to minimise the interference then this will usually prevent him from demonstrating that the interference stems from a reasonable user of land. But taking reasonable care to minimise interference does not establish that the defendant's activities involved a reasonable user of land.

Suppose, for example, *Industrialist* operates a chemical factory that emits clouds of acidic gas. The gas emanates to the garden of a nearby cottage which is owned by *Restful*, who uses it as a weekend retreat. There the gas causes a nauseous smell and damages the shrubs. In such a case it can be concluded that the operation of *Industrialist*'s chemical works is unreasonably interfering with *Restful*'s use and enjoyment of her land without there being any need to investigate whether the chemical works are being carelessly operated or not: *Restful* should not be expected to have to put up with nauseous smells and damaged shrubs as part of ordinary 'give and take' regardless of how much *Industrialist* has invested in limiting the emanations from his factory.[37] No doubt if the chemical works are

---

[35] [2001] 1 AC 1, 21.

[36] In *Cambridge Water Co Ltd v Eastern Counties Leather plc* [1994] 2 AC 264 at 299, Lord Goff stated that 'if the user is reasonable, the defendant will not be liable for consequent harm to his neighbour's enjoyment of his land; but if the user is not reasonable, the defendant will be liable, even though he may have exercised reasonable care and skill to avoid it.'

[37] We discuss below how far the question may be influenced by the fact that *Industrialist* has obtained planning permission for his factory and may have permits 'authorising' such emissions.

emitting the acidic gas because *Industrialist* is operating them in a careless[38] manner that would make it easy for *Restful* to show that the interference is unreasonable. But, to put the point firmly, it is *not necessary* for her to show careless operation in order to establish unreasonable interference.[39]

This example suggests that unreasonableness in private nuisance is different from unreasonableness in negligence. Some commentators, however, think that the way we have presented the difference is misleading. They think that even if *Industrialist* has taken all reasonable precautions to minimise the emission of acidic gas he may still be *careless* in a special way in such a case: his failure to exercise reasonable care is not in his *operation* of the chemical works but in his decision to *locate* it in such a place that it can interfere with *Restful*'s use and enjoyment of her cottage.

We think that this view does not prove that unreasonableness in private nuisance requires *carelessness*. As before, if *Industrialist* has *unreasonably* chosen to locate his factory in a place where it is likely to cause substantial interferences with the ability of others to use and enjoy their land then this will make it easier for *Restful* to show that the interference is not a result of a 'reasonable user' of land. But, we think that *Restful* can demonstrate that the factory is causing an unreasonable interference even if there is evidence that it is located in by far the most sensible place for it, and is being operated so as to minimise interference. We think that even if everyone agrees that such chemical factories are valuable for society, and that this one has been located where it will interfere with the smallest number of people to the least extent, it can still be said that the interference that it causes – a nauseous smell and physical damage to the shrubs – is unreasonable.

How can this be? How can what seems valuable and sensible be castigated as unreasonable and wrong? The answer we think is that the chemical works and its location is valuable and sensible *from the perspective of society as a whole*, but is unreasonable *from the perspective of Restful*, who has had her garden made unpleasant and her shrubs damaged. *Restful* can quite fairly argue that what is valuable and sensible *from the perspective of society as a whole* is not the same as what a neighbouring property owner must put up with by way of 'give and take', and it is unreasonable to expect her to put up with *all* the consequences of the chemical factory without any redress.[40]

One way of thinking about what the common law is doing in this area is to think of *Industrialist* and *Restful* as having *equal* rights to use and enjoy their land.[41] If both have

---

[38] It is worth noting that there is some ambiguity even in the word 'careless' in this context. Thus in the tort of negligence carelessness often refers to the degree of risk being created, while here one may just mean that *Industrialist* is not meeting the standards of comparable chemical works operators.

[39] For instance, in *Dennis v Ministry of Defence* [2003] EWHC 793, it was found that the circuit flying of Harrier jump-jets from RAF Wittering caused a private nuisance to Mr Dennis, a neighbouring landowner, but it was not suggested that the jets were being flown carelessly or that the Ministry of Defence had carelessly chosen to train its pilots in an inappropriate way.

[40] The argument in this paragraph demonstrates why we would not want to adopt Conor Gearty's suggestion that *all* cases involving physical damage to land should be dealt with by the tort of negligence (or under the rule in *Rylands v Fletcher*, discussed below, chapter 16) rather than in private nuisance: see Gearty 1989. In contrast to Gearty, Lee 2003 argues that the label 'unreasonable' is 'unnecessary and misleading' in situations where a court is considering whether an interference which has caused physical damage to land is actionable because all that the court is really considering is whether strict liability should apply to a particular *activity*. But we do not believe that all that courts do in such cases is classify *activities*. For instance, they may also have to consider if an activity, although ordinary, was *conveniently done*, and whether the damage was merely trivial or a result of hypersensitivity.

[41] A defendant and a claimant will not have equal rights in *all* private nuisance cases. We argue below (§ 15.9(A)) that a defendant may be held liable even if he has no right to use the land where he creates the nuisance. We have merely chosen an example where a defendant and a claimant have equal rights in order to illustrate the necessity for compromise.

bought their land then surely they both have *equal* rights to exploit it for uses which are ordinary in the locality. But if *Industrialist* is allowed to argue that the importance of his chemical factory for society as a whole means that he should be able to continue operating in such a way as to render *Restful's* land far less valuable for *her* ordinary purposes then he will not be respecting her *equal* right.

Similarly, everyone would agree that *Industrialist* should not be permitted to seize *Restful's* cottage and evict her without redress merely because it would be valuable and sensible to extend the chemical factory onto the land occupied by the cottage. Seizing the cottage would clearly be a tort, even if *Restful's* land was by far the best place in the country to locate a new chemical factory. But if seizing the cottage would clearly be a tort then how can doing physical damage to it, or reducing its amenity to a substantial degree, be more acceptable? From this perspective, private nuisance exists to cover the situation where *Industrialist* has not seized the cottage directly but is responsible for a state of affairs that is causing an emanation that is indirectly causing damage to it or substantially reducing the extent to which it can be used and enjoyed.

(2) Reasonable user, ordinary use and uses which do not cause unreasonable interference. The third rule – that an interference will not be unreasonable if it results from the 'reasonable user' of land – was formulated as an extension of the second rule, that an interference will not be unreasonable if it results from acts 'necessary for the common and ordinary use and occupation of land and houses', so long as these acts are 'conveniently done'. The primary reason for extending this second rule was to exclude from the scope of the tort the consequences of *other* uses of land – beyond use as a house – that are *wholly ordinary* in a particular locality. Where a use of land is *wholly ordinary* in a particular locality then the interference that it causes can easily be treated as one which ought to be tolerated in accordance with the general principle of 'give and take'. For example, if *Framer* and *Glazier* lease adjoining units in an industrial estate neither ought to be able to complain about daily disturbance caused by the noise of hammering, use of power tools and delivery lorries: the noises from such wholly ordinary activities on an industrial estate are clearly to be tolerated as part of 'give and take'.

Some courts, however, invoke the third rule even in cases that do not seem to involve uses of land that are *wholly ordinary* in a particular locality. We think that in many of these cases the courts have stated that a defendant's use of land was a 'reasonable user' only *after* concluding that the interference it caused went no further than what the claimant ought to tolerate as part of 'give and take' in the locality. In other words, we do not think that in these cases the judges applied the third rule in order to decide that the interference was reasonable; instead each judge's statement that a defendant's use of land was reasonable expressed a conclusion that the defendant had not committed a tort. Our main reason for thinking this is that courts seem to decide whether defendants who promote powerboat racing on their lake, or motor-racing at their circuits, are using their land reasonably by considering the nature of the *interference* that these activities cause rather than attempting any general assessment of the reasonableness of the activities concerned.

A very different view of the third rule was adopted in the case of *Barr v Biffa Waste Services Ltd* (2011). In this case Coulson J seems to have concluded that a large waste tip, which was being operated in accordance with permits, was a 'reasonable user of land' because 'the large scale tipping of waste as landfill is a necessity of modern society, and the best (perhaps the only) way in which non-recyclable waste can be disposed of without causing significant harm to the environment'.[42] We think that this approach tends to confuse: (i) what is valuable and sensible *from the perspective of society as a whole*, and (ii) what neighbouring property owners ought to put up with, by way of 'give and take' without any redress, and we have explained above, using the case of *Industrialist* and *Restful*, that these are different things. In other cases judges have acted consistently with our point of view. For example, in *Dennis* v *Ministry of Defence* (2003) it was found that the noise caused by the circuit flying of Harrier jump-jets from RAF Wittering caused a private nuisance to Mr Dennis, a neighbouring landowner, even though training RAF pilots might be thought to be a wholly reasonable use of land from the perspective of society as a whole.

15.5 EMANATION CASES (3): ESTABLISHING AN UNREASONABLE INTERFERENCE

So far we have established that an interference caused by an emanation will *not* be unreasonable if it is: (1) insubstantial; or (2) caused by acts 'necessary for the common and ordinary use and occupation of land and houses', so long as these acts are 'conveniently done', or (3) caused by a use of land that is wholly ordinary in the locality.

But what if an interference *is* substantial and is *not* caused by an wholly ordinary use of land? How will a court decide if the interference is unreasonable? We think that there are four helpful guidelines:

(1) In assessing whether an interference is unreasonable a court will ignore any amplification of the degree of interference caused by the hypersensitivity of the claimant.

(2) In assessing whether an interference that reduces the amenity value of land is unreasonable a court will consider the nature of the locality.

(3) In assessing whether an interference that reduces the amenity value of land is unreasonable a court will measure the significance of the interference by considering matters such as the time, duration, regularity and intensity of the interference.

(4) In assessing whether an interference that reduces the amenity value of land is unreasonable a court will consider the reasons for the interference, in particular whether the interference results from malice, negligence, or pursuit of a legitimate purpose.

These guidelines are important so we will say something about each of them in turn, before setting out a special rule on when an interference will be unreasonable, which applies to cases where the defendant interferes with the claimant's land in defending his land against a 'common enemy' that threatens both their properties.

A. Hypersensitivity

We noted above that a court will decide that an interference is *insubstantial* if it could only be regarded as intolerable by a hypersensitive occupier.[43] Consistently with this, when a court is assessing the significance of an interference in order to determine whether it is unreasonable it will adopt the perspective of a reasonably robust occupier in the locality, and will leave out of account any additional effects which derive from the claimant's

---

[42] [2011] EWHC 1003 (TCC), at [360].
[43] Cases regularly cited in support of this proposition include *Walter* v *Selfe* (1851) 4 De G & Sm 315; 64 ER 849 and *Robinson* v *Kilvert* (1889).

sensitivity. In practice this means that if a claimant advances a claim based on the noise or smell emanating from a defendant's premises but there is no record of complaints from the claimant's near neighbours, who were probably subject to the same noise or smell, then the claimant will find it difficult to demonstrate that the interference was unreasonable.

B. Nature of locality

We noted above that when an interference causes a reduction in amenity value, but not when it causes physical damage, a court will consider the nature of the locality when addressing the questions whether the interference was insubstantial or resulted from a 'reasonable user'.[44] For similar reasons the nature of the locality is important when considering whether the interference caused by an emanation is unreasonable.

One suggestion that has gathered some momentum is that in classifying localities reference should be made to the opinions of planning authorities. The orthodox view, however, is that *planning permission cannot authorise a private nuisance.*[45] Private nuisance is a matter of private right, and Parliament has not granted planning authorities the power to remove private rights. Thus in *Wheeler v JJ Saunders Ltd* (1996), a case involving 'swine-styles' in the Mendips (a range of limestone hills in the South of England), Peter Gibson LJ stated, 'The court should be slow to acquiesce in the extinction of private rights without compensation as a result of administrative decisions which cannot be appealed and are difficult to challenge.'[46] This view was also supported by Lord Hoffmann in *Hunter v Canary Wharf* (1997): 'It would, I think, be wrong to allow the private rights of third parties to be taken away by a permission granted by the planning authority to the developer. The Court of Appeal rejected such an argument in this case and the point has not been pursued in your Lordships' House.'[47]

This orthodox view had to be reconfirmed in *Wheeler* and *Hunter* because doubt had been cast on it by the case of *Gillingham BC v Medway (Chatham) Dock Co Ltd* (1993). This case involved unusual facts in that the council that was presently claiming that a dockyard was a nuisance had previously authorised the development. The case is now taken to stand for the principle that while a grant of planning permission cannot directly authorise a nuisance, it may nonetheless have the effect of changing the character of the neighbourhood or locality. Thus *Gillingham* suggests that the decisions of planning authorities may help to define the nature of a locality for the purposes of deciding whether an interference is unreasonable. If this is correct, then, for example, if planning permission were given for the development of an industrial park on a greenfield site, a neighbour would no longer be able to claim on the basis that the level of noise was inappropriate for an undeveloped field, but would have to show instead that the level of noise was inappropriate for an industrial park. Lord Cooke felt it necessary to apply the *Gillingham* principle to explain why an interference with television reception was not actionable in *Hunter v Canary Wharf* (1997).[48] But none of the other Law Lords used this approach.

---

[44] *St Helen's Smelting v Tipping* (1865).

[45] There are some special statutory exceptions. For example, s 158 of the Planning Act 2008 provides that an order granting development consent, which is a type of order used for nationally significant infrastructure projects, confers statutory authority to carry out the development concerned.

[46] [1996] Ch 19, 35.

[47] [1997] AC 655, 710. Similarly Lord Cooke said at 722: 'compliance with planning controls is not itself a defence to a nuisance action.'

[48] [1997] AC 655, 722.

Although the *Gillingham* principle does not suggest that planning authorities can authorise a nuisance, it may still be open to criticism because it allows an administrative decision *indirectly* to redefine and reduce private rights without compensation. If administrative decisions like this are sometimes made without all the interested parties being represented, can be based on incomplete information, and are difficult for third parties to challenge, then it can be argued that allowing them to redefine private rights is equally objectionable whether the effect is indirect or direct. But even if this fundamental criticism of the *Gillingham* principle is not accepted, two limits on its scope must always be borne in mind.

First, it seems that planning permission is only likely to 'change the nature of the locality' when it is permission relating to a major development. As Lord Cooke suggested in *Hunter* v *Canary Wharf* (1997), the principle only applies to a 'strategic planning decision affected by considerations of public interest.'[49] This suggests that a routine grant of small-scale planning permission will not trigger the principle.

Secondly, it is important to remember what planning permission actually permits. If *Hobbyist* applies for permission to build an extension on the back of his house in the suburbs, the planning authority will not consider how much noise *Hobbyist* is going to make in the extension if he decides to practise his electric guitar in there, nor what pungency of smell *Hobbyist* is going to emit if he uses the extension for making fibreglass sculptures. In simple terms, if *Hobbyist* gets planning permission for building a particular structure, that does not mean that the planning authority regards it as reasonable in the locality for *Hobbyist* to do whatever he may choose to do in the structure.

So far we have presented the orthodox view of the effect of planning permission. However, in the case of *Barr* v *Biffa Waste Services Ltd* (2011), Coulson J distinguished between the effect of planning permission and the effect of a detailed environmental permit. In this case the defendants operated a large waste tip and had to comply with terms specified in permits granted by the Environment Agency. The claimants, who owned houses on an estate adjacent to the tip, claimed the smells emanating from the waste tip constituted a private nuisance, and argued that their claims could succeed even without showing that the defendants had broken the terms of their permits or failed to take reasonable care to limit emissions. Coulson J rejected that argument: 'An activity should not be permitted by one set of specific rules (derived from detailed legislation), yet at the same time give rise to a liability to a third party by reference to the much more general set of principles to be derived from the common law.'[50] In other words, Coulson J held that a defendant could not commit the tort of private nuisance if its actions complied with a detailed permit from the Environment Agency. To reach this conclusion he distinguished the cases which have established the orthodox view of the effect of planning permission: these cases concerned forms of planning permission which granted a general permission to develop land, as opposed to permits which sought to regulate in detail activities to take place on the land.

We explained above that the concept of 'reasonable user' in the tort of private nuisance requires a distinction to be drawn between (1) what is valuable and sensible *from the perspective of society as a whole* and (2) what neighbouring property owners ought to put up with, by way of 'give and take' without any redress. We think that when negotiating and enforcing permits the Environment Agency is primarily concerned with what is valuable

---

[49] [1997] AC 655, 722.
[50] [2011] EWHC 1003 (TCC), at [347].

and sensible *from the perspective of society as a whole*, and that consequently Coulson J was wrong to treat it as effectively having the power to redefine the private law rights of landowners. No doubt properly-regulated waste tips have to be put somewhere. But if the best location for such a tip is alongside a housing estate, and it is inevitable that this will mean that emanating smells will substantially reduce the amenity value of some neighbouring homes, then the operators of the tip should be obliged to provide redress for this.

C. Time, duration, regularity, intensity

The third rule is largely a matter of common sense. The magnitude of an interference is clearly an important factor when assessing whether it is unreasonable, and this can only be assessed by considering the time, duration, regularity and intensity of the interference in question.

Thus night-time noise which interferes with sleep is far more likely to be held a nuisance than day-time noise. The unreasonableness of interfering with sleep was a major consideration in the case of *Rushmer* v *Polsue & Alferi* (1906), where a disgruntled resident persuaded North J to close down the printing presses of Fleet Street at night. When dawn breaks and when night begins are clearly matters of degree. In *Metropolitan Properties Ltd* v *Jones* (1939), Goddard LJ held that an electric motor which started at 8 am was a nuisance since 'after [that] hour an elderly gentleman is quite entitled to stay in bed, if he wants to, and have a restful time'.[51] On the other hand, in the case of *Vanderpant* v *Mayfair Hotel* (1930), the judge only granted an injunction against a hotel's noise-making between 10 pm and 8 am. Locality will also be a relevant factor: in agricultural areas no doubt the day begins rather earlier than it does in localities specialising in the accommodation of students.

On regularity, even the most innocent of noises may become a nuisance if it is repeated too often. Thus in the case of *Soltau* v *De Held* (1851), the claimant succeeded in obtaining an injunction against a Roman Catholic church in Clapham which rang its chapel bell at 5 am and 6.45 am every morning, its steeple bell at 8.45 am, 6.45 pm and 7.15 pm every day, with occasional additional peals of all its bells at weekends.

D. Malice, negligence, and pursuit of a legitimate purpose

When considering whether an interference is unreasonable courts take into account *why* the interference is being caused.

An important, and disputed, question is whether, if A reduces the amenity value of B's land *maliciously*, this will be sufficient to make the interference unreasonable.

In *Christie* v *Davey* (1893), the defendant was unfortunate enough to live next door to a 'musical family' in Brixton.[52] Their musical activities disturbed his concentration and he responded by knocking on a party wall, beating on trays, whistling, shrieking and imitating what was being played. North J decided that this alternative symphony was an unreasonable interference and granted an injunction, stating that 'what was done by the Defendant was

---

[51] [1939] 2 All ER 202, 204.
[52] Mrs Christie was a teacher of music and singing; her daughter was a medallist at the Royal Academy of Music and gave lessons on violin and piano; her lodger was also a medallist in music; and her son was in the habit of playing the cello in the kitchen up until 11 at night. Only Mr Christie was not musical. As North J observed, Mr Christie 'perhaps fortunately for himself, is very deaf' ([1893] 1 Ch 316, 324).

done only for the purpose of annoyance and in my opinion it was not a legitimate use of the Defendant's house to use it for the purpose of vexing and annoying his neighbours.'[53] It may be useful to compare this case with the *Southwark* case where a comparable degree of disturbance was not actionable because it was a product of ordinary domestic living.

A similar conclusion to that in *Christie* was reached in *Hollywood Silver Fox Farm Ltd* v *Emmett* (1936). In that case the claimant bred silver foxes and put up a sign advertising this fact. The defendant was developing one of his fields as plots for bungalows and took the view that people were less likely to buy a bungalow plot if they knew it was a mere 29 yards from where foxes were being bred. When the claimant refused to remove the sign the defendant carried out a threat to shoot with 'black powder' to frighten the foxes and disturb their breeding. Macnaghten J held that this firing had amounted to a nuisance, emphasising the use of bird-scaring cartridges and that the defendant's intention in firing the cartridges was to alarm and disturb the foxes. It is worth noting that in this case the defendant's malice meant that the interference was found to be unreasonable *even though* the claimant's activity, breeding silver foxes, was arguably *hypersensitive*.[54]

The difficulty facing the suggestion that malice *is* sufficient to establish that an interference is unreasonable is that it seems to be inconsistent with the decision of the House of Lords in *Bradford Corporation* v *Pickles* (1895). In this case it was alleged that Pickles had interfered with the groundwater percolating under his land principally because he wanted to force the Corporation, which used the water for its waterworks, to buy his land for an inflated price. In deciding the case against the Corporation their Lordships treated the question whether Pickles was malicious as irrelevant. Lord Watson, for instance, said that 'No use of property, which would be legal if due to a proper motive, can become illegal because it is prompted by a motive which is improper or even malicious.'[55]

It can be argued, however, that *Bradford* v *Pickles* can be distinguished from *Christie* and *Hollywood Silver Fox* because the *Bradford* case involved interference by *obstruction* of something coming onto the claimant's land, while *Christie* and *Hollywood Silver Fox* involved interference by the *emanation* of noise.[56] As we will see, in an *obstruction* case a claimant can only sue if she can show that she has a *right* to receive the benefit that has been obstructed,[57] and the claimants in *Bradford* v *Pickles* could not establish that they had a *right* to the water which the defendant obstructed.[58] Instead, the law treated the defendant as having an absolute right to obstruct the water. Thus it did not matter that the defendant had acted maliciously in obstructing the water. If the claimants had no right to receive the water, they had no claim in private nuisance. So the House of Lords' broad statements about malice in *Bradford* v *Pickles* can be seen as being limited to situations where A prevents something going onto B's land which B had no right to receive. *By contrast*, in an *emanation* case the lawfulness of the defendant's activity can only be ascertained by considering whether the claimant should be expected to tolerate such interference, and obviously the fact that an interference is not a consequence of a 'reasonable user' of land

---

[53] [1893] 1 Ch 316, 326–7.

[54] The defendant's barrister argued that 'the shooting would have caused no alarm to the animals which are usually to be found on farms in Kent': [1936] 2 KB 468, 474.

[55] [1895] AC 587, 598.

[56] See Taggart 2002, 189.

[57] See, further, below, § 15.7.

[58] See, similarly, Stevens 2007, 22: 'it was held that the claimants had no (property) right to the percolating water. Without a right exigible against the rest of the world to the percolating water, no tort was committed when the supply was cut.'

– but rather a consequence of the defendant seeking to injure the claimant[59] – is *highly* relevant to the question whether the emanation involves an *unreasonable* interference. There is no reason why a claimant should be expected to put up with an interference created by a malicious emanation onto her land.

The courts' strict approach to malicious emanations can be usefully contrasted with their tolerant approach to emanations caused by a defendant pursuing the sort of project that many reasonable property owners will want to pursue. Thus the courts have held that the temporary disturbances associated with building works are not a nuisance, provided that the works are carried on with reasonable care and skill. In *Andreae* v *Selfridge & Co Ltd* (1938), the claimant's hotel on Wigmore Street, London, was affected by a major development by Selfridges. Lord Greene MR stated that reasonable care required restricting the hours of work, and 'using proper scientific means of avoiding inconvenience',[60] but that it was not unreasonable to use pneumatic hammers for six days to break up reinforced concrete.

E. Common enemy

Some situations arise so often that the courts have developed special rules to determine whether an interference arising out of them will be unreasonable or not. For example, in *Arscott* v *The Coal Authority* (2004)[61] the Court of Appeal confirmed that it is not tortious for an owner or occupier of land to take convenient steps to protect her land against a 'common enemy', for instance flooding, even if the reasonably foreseeable consequence of these steps is to displace the problem onto a neighbour's land.[62] This rule is subject to three exceptions. First, a defendant is not permitted to protect her land by altering an established watercourse. Secondly, the rule only permits a defendant to take steps in *anticipation* of a threat from a 'common enemy' and does not permit a defendant to cure a problem that has *already* arisen on her land by exporting the misfortune.[63] Thirdly, while a court will not seek to weigh up whether each and every protective measure was necessary and proportionate, it may still find that the defendant's actions were unreasonable if the protective measures were clearly excessive and the harm to the claimant was caused by their excess.

15.6 ENCROACHMENT CASES

Not much needs to be said about such cases. If branches or tree roots cross onto the claimant's land, lawyers tend to refer to such cases as involving 'encroachments', rather than 'emanations'. The most significant difference between 'encroachment' cases and

---

[59] Stevens 2007 suggests (at 23) that malice is relevant only because it demonstrates that a defendant's actions are 'pointless', or 'without social value'. We do not agree. The decision in *Hollywood Silver Fox* did not turn on whether there was greater 'social value' in fox-breeding or bungalow-development. It turned on the *unreasonableness* of intentionally reducing the amenity value of the claimant's land when it was not *necessary* for the defendant to do so in order to use his own land in a common and ordinary way.

[60] [1938] Ch 1.

[61] [2004] EWCA Civ 892. The defendants were held not liable for raising the level of a playing field situated on a flood plain in order to protect it from flooding even though raising the field caused a flood to affect the claimants' houses more severely than it might otherwise have done.

[62] The parties in the *Arscott* case were content to treat the 'common enemy' rule as existing independently of the question whether the defendant had *unreasonably* interfered with the use and enjoyment of land in which B has a sufficient interest. We believe, however, that the 'common enemy' situation is merely one where the courts have developed clear guidance as to what is reasonable; a view apparently shared by Laws LJ: [2004] EWCA Civ 892, at [40].

[63] *Whalley* v *Lancashire and Yorkshire Railway Co* (1884) 13 QBD 131.

'emanation' cases is that it seems that all encroachments which violate the boundaries of a claimant's land *automatically* amount to an unreasonable interference with the claimant's use and enjoyment of land. (Though of course, in practice, many occupiers of land tolerate overhanging branches and straying roots.) This is not to say that a claimant will be automatically entitled to *sue* a defendant from whose land branches or roots are encroaching onto the claimant's land: the claimant will also need to show that the defendant is *responsible* for that encroachment, which is an issue we deal with below.[64] Moreover, the authority of *Lemmon* v *Webb* (1895) suggests that although any encroachment by branches or roots is a private nuisance which a claimant is entitled to *abate* by cutting off the offending protuberances, he will only be able to make a claim for damages if the encroachment has caused further damage.[65]

15.7 OBSTRUCTION CASES

We have already seen that the law on private nuisance not only protects a claimant from having the use and enjoyment of his land unreasonably interfered with, but also from unreasonable interferences with rights associated with his land. In obstruction cases – where a claimant is complaining that something has been obstructed from coming onto his land – the claimant will *only* be allowed to sue in private nuisance if the obstruction unreasonably interferes with some right that is associated with his land. If this condition is *not* satisfied, it will not matter that the obstruction is reducing the claimant's use and enjoyment of his land, or even causing physical damage: the claimant will not be allowed to sue.

Bradford v *Pickles* (1895) and *Hunter* v *Canary Wharf* (1997) are examples of obstruction cases where the claimant could *not* show that the obstruction interfered with some right associated with his land. In *Bradford* v *Pickles*, the defendant stopped water that was percolating under his land through undefined channels from continuing on its way into the claimants' reservoirs. It was unclear why the defendant did this: he may have been acting out of pure malice towards the claimants. More likely, he was trying to persuade the claimants either to buy his land, or pay him a fee for allowing the water to continue on its way under his land uninterrupted. The claimants sued the defendant, but their claim failed. As the water was flowing through undefined channels under the defendant's land, the claimants had no right to receive that water, and could not therefore complain of its obstruction – whatever the defendant's reason for stopping it was.

In *Hunter* v *Canary Wharf*, one of the complaints was that the building of the Canary Wharf Tower interfered with the claimants' television reception because it stood between their homes and the Crystal Palace transmitter. In *Bridlington Relay Ltd* v *Yorkshire Electricity Board* (1965), Buckley J had suggested that interference with television reception could not constitute a legal nuisance because it was interference with a purely recreational facility, as opposed to interference with the health or physical comfort or well-being of the claimants. In *Hunter* the House of Lords expressed doubt as to whether such reasoning was still convincing in the light of the increased social importance of television.[66] The majority held, however, that interference with television reception merely by building on one's own land was not actionable, because – just as a landowner has no right to a beautiful view that he currently enjoys from his land by looking across a neighbour's undeveloped fields – a

[64] See § 15.9.
[65] If a tree is protected by a 'tree preservation order' then the right to abate may be limited: see *Perrin* v *Northampton Borough Council* [2008] 1 WLR 1307.
[66] [1997] AC 655, at 684–5 (per Lord Goff), 708 (per Lord Hoffmann), 722 (per Lord Cooke).

landowner has no right to receive TV signals that would otherwise come across a neighbour's land onto his land.[67]

So when will a claimant be able to establish that she enjoys some right associated with her land to have something cross a neighbour's land without obstruction? Generally speaking, English land law is very cautious about holding that B has a right against her neighbour A that A allow some benefit to pass over, across or through A's land. In particular, English land law is reluctant to recognise such obligations where they cannot be precisely defined. Saying that A must not unreasonably interfere with the passage of a river which flows in a defined channel over or under A's land is one thing, but it is quite another thing to say that A must not unreasonably interfere with wind that would otherwise travel onto B's land and power B's wind turbine, or water percolating under A's land through undefined channels, or invisible electromagnetic signals that B depends on receiving for business or leisure pursuits. Alongside the problem of defining such obligations with precision is the further difficulty that such benefits could easily be obstructed by activities that the law would not want to discourage. Thus almost any building might interfere with wind, groundwater and electromagnetic signals.

The ancients thought that there were only four elements: earth, air, fire and water. The classification – with the substitution of the word 'light' for 'fire' – provides a useful way of thinking about what rights are associated with a given parcel of land.

(1) Starting with *light*, a landowner may acquire through grant or prescription (as a result of having enjoyed light coming to windows in his building for a certain period of time without interruption or dispute from a neighbour) a right to freedom from such an obstruction of light as would interfere with the ordinary occupations of life.[68]

Acquiring a right to light coming through your windows is one thing, but you cannot acquire by prescription a right to receive photons coming onto your land from a beautiful landscape which can be seen from your land. So if you want to acquire such a right, you must go to whoever is in a position to obstruct your view and get them to enter into a *restrictive covenant* under which they agree not to build on their land in a way that would obstruct your view. In the absence of such a covenant, there is no right to sue someone who interferes with a beautiful view. In the United States some courts have been willing to draw a distinction between obstructing a view (which is not usually actionable) and positively creating an ugly sight (which can be treated as analogous to an emanation). But English law has not adopted this distinction. So there is no right either to receive a beautiful view, or not to have an ugly view foisted on you.[69] And as we have just seen, there is no right to receive TV signals either.

(2) So far as *air* is concerned, there is no *general* right to receive air or wind that would, but for an obstruction, have come onto your land.[70] But where air flows across a defendant's

---

[67] [1997] AC 655, at 685 (per Lord Goff), 699 (per Lord Lloyd), 709 (per Lord Hoffmann), 726–7 (per Lord Hope). Because *Hunter* was an obstruction case, it does not decide whether an *emanation* of electromagnetic waves *onto* B's land which interferes with B's television reception can be actionable.

[68] *Colls* v *Home & Colonial Stores Ltd* [1904] AC 179.

[69] This was clearly stated by Lord Blackburn in *Dalton* v *Angus* (1881) 6 App Cas 740, 824, where he commended the reasoning that Lord Hardwicke LC used in *Attorney-General* v *Doughty* (1752) 2 Ves Sen 453, 28 ER 290 to explain this rule: 'I know of no general rule of common law, which warrants that, or says, that building to stop another's prospect is a nuisance. Was that the case, there could be no great towns; and I must grant injunctions to all the new buildings in this town [London].'

[70] *Chastey* v *Ackland* [1895] 2 Ch 389, 402 (per Lindley LJ): 'no one has a right to prevent his neighbour from building on his own land, although the consequence may be to diminish or alter the flow of air over it on to land adjoining. So to diminish a flow of air is not actionable as a nuisance.'

land to a defined aperture in the claimant's building, like a ventilator, he can acquire a right to that flow of air, by establishing that he has acquired an *easement*.[71] The word 'easement' is more commonly associated with rights of way over other people's land. And the rule that allows a claimant to sue a defendant who has *unreasonably* interfered with a flow of air to a defined aperture where the claimant had acquired an easement is simply a particular instance of the general rule that if A unreasonably interferes with B's ability to exercise her rights protected by an easement then B can sue A for having committed the tort of private nuisance. Thus if A *unreasonably* interferes with a private right of way that his neighbour, B, has over A's land, then B will be able to sue A in private nuisance for that interference.

(3) Turning to *water*, an owner of land adjacent to a river or stream has a natural right to receive the regular flow of the stream, but this is subject to the rights of owners upstream to use the water for their domestic purposes and cattle.[72] Thus a downstream owner can make a claim in private nuisance against an upstream owner who substantially diminishes the flow of water by taking it for other purposes, or against anyone who pollutes the water. But – as *Bradford* v *Pickles* (1895) shows – there is no right to receive water that flows in undefined channels underneath your neighbour's land.

(4) What about *earth*? For simplicity, we have been talking so far in this section of cases where a claimant wants to sue in private nuisance because some benefit has been *obstructed* from coming onto his land. But a claimant might want to sue in private nuisance because a defendant has *withdrawn* some benefit that the defendant's land would otherwise have provided for the claimant's land. The same principles apply to such cases as apply to obstruction cases: the claimant must establish a right to that withdrawn benefit before she can sue in private nuisance for its withdrawal. So if *Digger* has done some excavations on his land, which has had the effect of withdrawing the support that buildings on *Neighbour*'s land previously enjoyed, *Neighbour* will not be able to sue *Digger* in private nuisance unless she can establish a right to that support. Under English law, *Neighbour* will not automatically enjoy such a right. The common law recognises a natural right to the support of land in its undeveloped state. But if *Neighbour* wants a right to support for a *building*, she must enter into an agreement with *Digger* which will give her what is called an *easement of support*, or acquire such a right by prescription. This means that in the absence of such an easement *Digger* will be permitted to excavate on his own land even if the result is that a building on *Neighbour*'s land collapses.[73]

We have stated that in cases of obstruction or withdrawal the claimant will not be allowed to sue in private nuisance unless she can show that the obstruction or withdrawal interfered with some right associated with her land. Must the claimant also go further and show that

---

[71] *Cable* v *Bryant* [1908] 1 Ch 259.

[72] *Miner* v *Gilmour* (1858) 12 Moore PC 131, 156 (per Lord Kingsdown); *John Young & Co* v *Bankier Distillery Co* [1893] AC 691, 698 (per Lord Macnaghten): 'A riparian proprietor is entitled to have the water of the stream, on the banks of which his property lies, flow down as it has been accustomed to flow down to his property, subject to the ordinary use of the flowing water by upper proprietors, and to such further use, if any, on their part in connection with their property as may be reasonable under the circumstances. Every riparian proprietor is thus entitled to the water of his stream, in its natural flow, without sensible diminution or increase and without sensible alteration in its character or quality.'

[73] *Dalton* v *Angus* (1881) 6 App Cas 740, 804 (per Lord Penzance): 'It is the law, I believe I may say without question, that at any time within twenty years after the house is built the owner of the adjacent soil may with perfect legality dig that soil away, and allow his neighbour's house, if supported by it, to fall in ruins to the ground.' See also *Ray* v *Fairway Motors (Barnstaple) Ltd* (1969) 20 P & CR 261. Similarly, a landowner can extract percolating groundwater from beneath his own land even if this drains water from beneath another's land and causes damage: *Popplewell* v *Hodkinson* (1869) LR 4 Ex 248; *Langbrook Properties Ltd* v *Surrey CC* [1970] 1 WLR 161.

the interference was *unreasonable*? The answer to this requires attention to two things. First, often the right on which the claimant bases her claim will be *defined* in such a way that any interference with it will *by definition* be unreasonable. For example, we noted above that the right to light that a claimant can acquire is a right to enough light for the ordinary occupations of life. Thus any interference with this will involve depriving the claimant of sufficient light to use her property for ordinary purposes and will be *by definition* unreasonable. The second element in the answer is that it will make a difference whether the purpose of the claim is (1) to establish whether the claimant has the right that she claims to have or (2) to obtain compensation for an interference with the right. Where the purpose of the claim is the latter the courts will apply the rule that they do not deal with *trivial* interferences, so a claimant will have to demonstrate more than a *technical* interference with her rights.

Everything we have said so far has indicated that in obstruction and withdrawal cases, the claimant will not be allowed to sue in private nuisance unless she can show that the obstruction or withdrawal violated some right associated with her land. However, before we leave this topic, we should note two *expressions of opinion* in *Hunter* v *Canary Wharf* (1997) which are inconsistent with this view. Lord Cooke took the view that the *real* reason why no claim for interference with TV signals could be brought in that case was the idea that neighbours must simply be expected to put up with such interferences under the 'principle of reasonable user, of give and take.'[74] But, he also stated that: 'The malicious erection of a structure for the purpose of interfering with television reception should be actionable in nuisance on the principle of such well-known cases as *Christie* v *Davey* . . . and *Hollywood Silver Fox Farm Ltd* v *Emmett*'[75] And Lord Hope might be taken to have provided some support for Lord Cooke's position when he observed that the Canary Wharf Tower 'is a very large building and its cladding is made of stainless steel. But it is not suggested that it was designed in that way maliciously in order to interfere with the [claimants'] television reception.'[76] These *dicta* seem to suggest an obstruction or withdrawal case might still give rise to a right to sue in nuisance even if the claimant had no right to the obstructed or withdrawn benefit so long as the obstruction or withdrawal was *malicious* and interfered with the claimant's use and enjoyment of land. However, the majority of the House of Lords in *Hunter* v *Canary Wharf* did not express any support for this position, which is – in any case – flat contrary to the House of Lords' decision in *Bradford* v *Pickles* (1895).

15.8 AFFRONT CASES

English law has made only tentative moves towards accepting that *affront* can amount to an actionable nuisance. Within this category the interference with the use and enjoyment of the claimant's land is caused by the mental disturbance – the affront – that comes from knowledge that nearby land is being used for a particular purpose, rather than by any emanation, encroachment or obstruction. In England this form of claim has been used principally against brothels, pornographic cinemas and sex shops.

For example, in *Laws* v *Florinplace* (1981), ten residents of an area of Pimlico, London – which (it was claimed) enjoyed an attractive village atmosphere – sought an injunction to close down the 'Victoria Sex and Video Centre'. Vinelott J held that even if the defendant

---

[74] [1997] AC 655, 720.
[75] [1997] AC 655, 721.
[76] [1997] AC 655, 726.

changed the business's name and altered its signs and displays, it was still arguable that the 'profound repugnance' caused to the claimants by knowledge of nearby trade in hard pornography could amount to sufficient interference with the use and enjoyment of their land for the purposes of the tort of private nuisance.[77]

In practice, claims such as the one brought in *Laws* are rare because a claimant must demonstrate *not only* that he has suffered interference by affront *but also* that the interference was unreasonable when judged from the perspective of ordinary people. This limits the number of claims that can be brought for nuisance by affront because it will be difficult to persuade a court that it is *unreasonable* for a defendant to carry on a *lawful* business[78] which causes no interference more severe than making people living nearby feel uncomfortable about the fact that such activities are going on near where they live. A court should also feel concerns about allowing the majority in a locality to use such an ill-defined area of law to impose its *moral* views on others.

A doctrine similar to nuisance by affront may explain a group of cases in which extreme dangers, such as warehouses of gunpowder, were held to be nuisances before they had caused any physical harm.[79] It might be said that in such cases there was an *immediate* nuisance from the fear and anxiety caused to people living in the vicinity.[80] There is a tension, however, between this explanation and the rule that a claimant can only obtain an injunction to restrain an *anticipated* tort when such a tort is 'highly probable' and 'imminent',[81] since a claimant might become fearful or anxious even when a risk is 'improbable' or 'remote'. It might also be objected that this sort of reasoning could allow a claimant to establish a tort where there was no rational basis for any fear or anxiety.[82] Indeed, in *Birmingham Development Co Ltd v Tyler* (2008)[83] the Court of Appeal held that a defendant had not committed the tort of private nuisance by allowing a wall on its land to remain in such a condition that the claimant was advised to stop working on its own land because of the risk of the wall collapsing: the Court held that the claimant's claim for private nuisance could only have succeeded if the fear of an imminent collapse was 'well-founded', and this meant that there must have been *actual* danger. In the particular case later investigations had revealed that the section of the wall that had caused concern was actually not likely to collapse.

---

[77] See also *Thompson-Schwab v Costaki* [1956] 1 WLR 335, where the Court of Appeal did not accept that the defendants could only be liable for using a house as a venue for prostitution if their activity had a *physical* effect on the claimant's enjoyment of his neighbouring house. In the United States 'nuisance by affront' has also been relied on against undertakers.

[78] In *Laws v Florinplace* [1981] 1 All ER 659, 668, Vinelott J treated it as relevant to whether to grant an interim injunction that the defendant's business was 'at least near the boundary of the criminal law' and thought that at a full trial of the action it would be necessary to decide whether the business was lawful or not.

[79] *R v Lister* (1856–7) 7 Dears & B 209, 169 ER 979; *Hepburn v Lordan* (1865) 2 H & M 345, 71 ER 497; *R v Chilworth Gunpowder Co* (1888) 4 TLR 557.

[80] In *R v Lister* (1856–7) 7 Dears & B 209, 227, 169 ER 979, 987, Lord Campbell CJ stated that, 'the well-founded apprehension of danger which would alarm men of steady nerves and reasonable courage, passing through the street in which the house stands, or residing in adjoining houses, is enough to show that something has been done which the law ought to prevent'. It is unclear whether a series of claims in the nineteenth century against smallpox hospitals and asylums are best explained as 'nuisance by anxiety', 'nuisance by affront', or both.

[81] The Court of Appeal in *Hooper v Rogers* [1975] Ch 43 treated this rule as requiring no more than that the degree of probability was sufficient to make an injunction just, and the application was not premature, but even this softened version of the rule seems more stringent than the approach taken in the gunpowder factory cases.

[82] The nuisance claim against the operators of a smallpox hospital which gave rise to the appeal in *Metropolitan Asylum District Managers v Hill* (1881) 6 App Cas 193 is often mentioned in this context. Although the claimants' evidence included allegations as to the emanation of smells from the morgue and of a disproportionate infection rate in the vicinity of the hospital it seems that many of the fears were exaggerated.

[83] *Birmingham Development Co Ltd v Tyler* [2008] EWCA Civ 859.

15.9 RESPONSIBILITY

The reader should now have a good understanding of what kind of interference a claimant has to establish that he is suffering, or he has suffered, in order to bring a claim in private nuisance. But if the claimant wants to sue a particular defendant for that interference, he has to show that the defendant was *responsible* for it – by showing that the defendant created, authorised, adopted or continued the state of affairs that brought about the interference.

A. Creating

If A *creates* a state of affairs that brings about an unreasonable interference with B's use and enjoyment of his land then it seems straightforward that A should be liable. Thus if *Amber* creates a bonfire on which she burns old tyres, and the thick smoke emanates onto *Brian*'s land, and fills his house with choking, pungent, smoke, *Amber* will be responsible for the interference, and hence liable for committing private nuisance in relation to *Brian*.

Does it matter *where Amber* creates the bonfire? It is sometimes asserted that private nuisance is a tort committed between *neighbours*. And this might be read as suggesting that only a neighbouring *landowner* can be held liable in nuisance, and not someone who creates an unreasonable interference but not on her own land. In *Hussain v Lancaster City Council* (2000), the Court of Appeal relied on a thesis that Professor Newark was 'prepared . . . to nail . . . to the doors of the Law Courts and to defend against all comers'. The thesis states: 'the term "nuisance" is properly applied only to such *actionable user of land* as interferes with the enjoyment by the claimant of rights in land.'[84] Unfortunately, the Court of Appeal took this to mean that the essence of private nuisance required that 'the defendant's use *of the defendant's land* interferes with the claimant's enjoyment of the claimant's land.'[85] Thus the Court rejected the claim in *Hussain* because the harassment of the claimants by the tenants of the defendant did not involve the tenants using their own premises. Rather the tenants were carrying out the harassment from the street and from open ground over which they had no rights.

But what the Court of Appeal said in *Hussain* is not orthodoxy. Indeed, in our opinion, it is nonsense. There are plenty of cases to suggest that a defendant can be held liable for creating a state of affairs that unreasonably interferes with another's land even if he does not own or have a tenancy over the land that he creates it on. Thus a defendant can be liable if he creates the interference on a highway, or on land that he does not own but merely occupies or uses.[86] Quite apart from these cases, there is no reason in principle to make a

---

[84] Newark 1949, 489 (emphasis added). This thesis was approved by Lord Goff in *Hunter* v *Canary Wharf* (1997) but in that case the focus was on the second part of the thesis – that the interference had to be with rights in land.

[85] [2000] QB 1, 23 (emphasis added). It will not have escaped the notice of the observant reader that Professor Newark only insists that nuisance must involve *user of land*, and not that it must involve *the defendant's use of the defendant's land*.

[86] Cases suggesting that the defendant does not have to possess or own the land that he creates the nuisance from include: *Halsey* v *Esso Petroleum* [1961] 1 WLR 683 (nuisance created from highway); *Hall* v *Beckenham Corp* [1949] 1 KB 716 (nuisance created from public park); *Bernstein* v *Skyviews* [1978] QB 479 (nuisance created from air). There is also a series of cases supporting the view that picketing can be a private nuisance, at least if it involves obstruction, violence, intimidation, molestation or threats (*J Lyons & Sons* v *Wilkins* [1899] 1 Ch 255, 267, 271–2; *Hubbard* v *Pitt* [1976] QB 142, 177, 183, 189; *Thomas* v *NUM (South Wales Area)* [1986] Ch 20, 65), and none of these suggests that the pickets must be using their own land in order to commit the tort. For *dicta* pointing the other way, see *Esso Petroleum* v *Southport Corp* [1954] 2 QB 182, 196–7 (per Denning LJ), [1956] AC 218, 242 (per Lord Radcliffe), suggesting that private nuisance cannot be committed from the sea.

claimant's degree of protection turn on the status of the person who creates the interference. A landowner deserves protection from an over-noisy neighbour regardless of whether that neighbour is owner, tenant, lodger or squatter. As Sir Christopher Staughton has pointed out,[87] it is not self-evident why a defendant who plays his stereo loudly at home may commit the tort of private nuisance in relation to his neighbour but a defendant who plays his car stereo loudly while parked outside his neighbour's house will not. Furthermore, acceptance of the Court of Appeal's opinion in *Hussain* would lead to an undesirable distinction between this tort and the tort of trespass to land. Clearly a defendant can commit trespass to land without using his own land.[88]

Someone can *create* a nuisance even if he or she did not *intend* to bring about the state of affairs that amounted to a nuisance. In *R* v *Moore* (1832), a gunmaker possessed land that he encouraged his customers to use for shooting at pigeons. Some of the pigeons were not brought down by his customers and a nuisance resulted from the large number of people who gathered outside his premises to shoot at the strays. In response to the argument that the gunmaker had not committed nuisance because he had not invited this crowd, Littledale J asserted that 'If the experience of mankind must lead any one to expect the result, he will be answerable for it.'[89]

B. Authorising

A1 can commit the tort of private nuisance by *authorising* A2 to create a state of affairs that causes an unreasonable interference with B's land. This principle plays an important role in determining when liability will attach to owners of land who are not in occupation of land, for instance because they have leased that land to someone else, when a state of affairs on that land causes a nuisance.

In *Hussain* v *Lancaster City Council* (2000), Malazam Hussain and his partner Linda Livingstone had bought a shop on the Ryelands estate in Lancaster. Thereafter they were subjected to over 2,000 racist attacks. Their claim listed several hundred attacks on their property (including use of petrol bombs), assaults and thefts, and named 106 alleged culprits. Many of these alleged culprits were tenants of Lancaster City Council on the Ryelands estate. Importantly, the council had power to evict these tenants from their homes if they were causing a nuisance to their neighbours, but it had not done so. The claimants' case was that in these circumstances the council was liable for the state of affairs being created by its tenants.

One difficulty with the claim was that it sought to make the council liable for the racist attacks even though it was clearly not the council which was carrying them out. When can a landlord be held responsible for a state of affairs resulting from the deliberate misbehaviour of its tenants? The answer given by English law, found in cases such as *Rich* v *Basterfield* (1847), is that a landlord is *only* liable for a state of affairs created by his *tenants* if he has *authorised* the creation of such a state of affairs. Thus in *Southwark London Borough Council* v *Tanner* (2001), Lord Millett expressed the general rule when he said:

---

[87] *Lippiatt* v *South Gloucestershire CC* [2000] QB 51, 65.

[88] The inconvenience of the distinction can best be appreciated by remembering that it is a trespass to land to throw something directly onto B's land, and a private nuisance to release something so that it indirectly drifts onto B's land and causes an unreasonable interference. If the Court of Appeal's view was confirmed then B would seek, whenever A created an emanation from land other than his own land, to argue that the emanation was *direct* (and thus a trespass to land).

[89] (1832) 3 B & Ad 184, 110 ER 68. Although *R* v *Moore* was a case of public nuisance the same principle has been applied in cases of private nuisance, for example, *Walker* v *Brewster* (1867) LR 5 Eq 25 ('assemblage of idle and dissolute persons' outside a house used by defendant for twice weekly fêtes with fireworks).

The person or persons directly responsible for the activities in question are liable; but so too is anyone who authorised them. Landlords have been held liable for nuisances committed on this basis. It is not enough for them to be aware of the nuisance and to take no steps to prevent it.[90]

What will suffice for authorising? Lord Millett clearly asserts that knowing about a problem and taking no steps to solve it is insufficient. But a distinction should be drawn between 'taking no steps to prevent' a nuisance – which is *not* an instance of 'authorising' – and granting a lease for a purpose which will *inevitably* lead to a nuisance. In the latter situation it could obviously be said that the landlord had authorised the nuisance. But what if the landlord only knew when the lease was granted that the tenant was *very likely* to create a nuisance? In *Smith* v *Scott* (1973), Pennycuick V-C stated that it might be sufficient if the nuisance was 'virtually certain' to result from the purposes for which the property was let.[91] But subsequently, in *Tetley* v *Chitty* (1986), Medway Borough Council was held liable for the noise nuisance caused by go-karts when they had leased land with (at least) implied permission to use it as a go-kart track. In that case, McNeill J pointed out that there was some inconsistency in the previous cases as to what degree of knowledge or foresight a claimant would have to prove that the landlord had, and seemed attracted by the possibility that proving mere reasonable foreseeability of nuisance might be enough. We think, however, that there is a significant gulf between foreseeing that something might possibly happen and *authorising* it. Even if judges in future follow the generous view of McNeill J, this will not be enough to help claimants in the same position as those in *Hussain*: it would have been difficult to prove that when Lancaster City Council granted tenancies to the alleged culprits it ought reasonably to have foreseen that they would pursue a campaign of racial persecution.

C. Adopting or continuing

Hussain can be contrasted with the case of *Lippiatt* v *South Gloucestershire CC* (2000), where a group of travellers allegedly set up camp on land belonging to the council and used that camp as a 'launching pad' for a series of damaging invasions of a neighbouring farmer's property. In this case the Court of Appeal held that the council was arguably liable for the nuisance resulting from the state of affairs on its land. A crucial distinction from *Hussain* is that in *Lippiatt* the travellers were *not* tenants of the council, and consequently the council continued to occupy the land. Orthodoxy holds that the responsibility of an *occupier of land* for a state of affairs which he did not create goes beyond responsibility for what he authorised, and extends to any state of affairs that he continued or adopted.[92] So what must B prove in order to establish that A continued or adopted a state of affairs arising on land occupied by him?

In *Sedleigh-Denfield* v *O'Callaghan* (1940), the defendants owned and occupied land on which there was a drainage ditch. Middlesex County Council decided to use this ditch to drain water from a new residential development and substituted a culvert[93] for the ditch. The County Council's action was both lawless – it did not obtain permission from the

---

[90] [2001] 1 AC 1, 22.
[91] [1973] Ch 314, 321. He stated that such a degree of 'high probability' was necessary in order to infer that the nuisance was impliedly authorised.
[92] For criticism of this area of the law, see Bright 2001, arguing that a landowner should only be held liable for actions of people on his land if he authorised or encouraged those actions.
[93] In less obscure language, a fifteen-inch pipe.

owners – and incompetent – it failed to take the sensible precaution of putting in a grid to prevent the culvert becoming blocked. Three years later the culvert did block, and water which could not escape down it instead flooded the claimant's property. The House of Lords found that the defendant occupiers of the land were liable even though the state of affairs which led to the flood had been created by the trespassing and incompetent County Council.

Viscount Maugham stated that an occupier in such a situation would be liable if he had 'continued' or 'adopted' the nuisance, and explained that

> an occupier of land 'continues' a nuisance if, with knowledge or presumed knowledge of its existence, he fails to take any reasonable means to bring it to an end, though with ample time to do so. He 'adopts' it if he makes use of the erection, building, bank or artificial contrivance which constitutes the nuisance.[94]

On the facts, Viscount Maugham found that the defendants had both 'continued' and 'adopted' the nuisance. The other Law Lords did not draw such a stern distinction between 'continuing' and 'adopting'. They did, however, stress the importance of 'knowledge' or 'presumed knowledge' of the nuisance or the potential for nuisance before the occupier could be liable on this basis. In fact, although the language of 'continuing' and 'adopting' is regularly used, cases like *Sedeligh-Denfield* show that the relevant doctrine often makes defendant occupiers liable for 'failing to prevent' a nuisance from arising on their land *as well as* for 'failing to eliminate' a state of affairs that is *already* causing problems.

In *Sedleigh-Denfield* the potential for interference with the claimant's land could have been easily and cheaply rectified by the defendants' putting a grid in front of the pipe's orifice. Moreover, the defendants might well have been able to obtain the cost of installing the grid from the County Council. More difficult questions are raised, however, where it will be costly for the occupier to remove the potential for nuisance, and where those costs may not be recoverable from a third party, for instance because the potential for nuisance has been caused by an unidentified malefactor or by natural forces.

These more difficult questions had to be addressed by the Court of Appeal in *Leakey* v *National Trust* (1980). In this case the defendants owned and occupied a cone-shaped hill in Somerset called Burrow Mump. The claimants lived in converted cottages beneath the Mump. In 1976 the hot summer and wet autumn caused a crack which made it likely that the Mump would collapse onto the claimants' houses. Stabilising the Mump was likely to prove expensive and consequently the National Trust denied that it was responsible for a state of affairs created by the wondrous workings of nature. The Court of Appeal, however, held that the National Trust, as a landowner in occupation,[95] was responsible. Megaw LJ (with whom Cumming-Bruce LJ agreed) held that the *Sedleigh-Denfield* principle applied to a potential nuisance caused by the workings of nature,[96] and that if the defendant knew or ought to have known of the potential for nuisance, it was obliged to take reasonable steps to eliminate the problem. Importantly, however, the Court of Appeal also said that in judging whether particular steps were reasonably required, the defendant's capacity to find the money would be relevant; and alongside this could be considered the claimants' capacity to protect themselves from damage by erecting a barrier or providing funds for agreed works. While the occupier's duty to act reasonably is clearly subjective to this extent,

---

[94] [1940] AC 880, 894.
[95] In fact there were some doubts as to whether the National Trust really occupied the Mump, but for the purposes of the litigation it conceded that it did: [1980] QB 485, 509.
[96] [1980] QB 485, 517–24.

Megaw LJ stressed that he did not envisage that it would be necessary to assess the wealth of the parties in anything other than an impressionistic manner.[97]

We will call the duty which an occupier must comply with, if he is to avoid being found responsible for 'continuing' or 'adopting' a state of affairs on his land, a 'measured duty of care'. We have added the word 'measured' to the usual phrase – 'duty of care' – in order to highlight that it is a *special form* of duty of care, one which takes account of: (1) the occupier's capacity to find the money, or other resources, needed to obviate the problems, and (2) the potential victim's capacity to take steps to protect himself from the problems.

The nature of the occupier's measured duty of care with regard to problems resulting from natural forces was further explored in *Holbeck Hall Hotel Ltd* v *Scarborough Borough Council* (2000). In that case, a cliff on land belonging to the defendant council gave way and as a consequence a hotel on neighbouring land belonging to the claimant was destroyed. The case was particularly difficult because while the defendant ought to have foreseen some minor slips causing damage to the claimant's rose garden and lawn, there was no reason why it ought to have foreseen such an exceptional event as the massive slip which destroyed the hotel. In these circumstances, the Court of Appeal held that an occupier which failed to meet the measured duty to take reasonable steps to prevent a nuisance from occurring on its land should only be liable to the extent of the damage that ought to have been foreseen.[98] Further, the Court of Appeal suggested that in such a situation, where the hazard was a result of the forces of nature and the defendant would have gained little benefit from preserving its own land against the hazard, the defendant might well have fulfilled the measured duty to act reasonably by doing no more than informing the claimants of the risk and sharing information relating to it.

The case of *Marcic* v *Thames Water Utilities Ltd* (2004) raised the question whether a public authority responsible for sewers is responsible for flooding incidents caused by the inadequate capacity of those sewers. The Court of Appeal held that the defendants were 'in no more favourable position than a landowner on whose property a hazard accumulates by the act of a trespasser or of nature', that they ought to have known of the hazard, and that consequently, following cases such as *Sedleigh-Denfield* and *Leakey*, they would be liable unless they took reasonable steps to avoid problems arising.[99] The House of Lords, however, disagreed because such a common law duty would conflict with the statutory scheme under the Water Industry Act 1991 for enforcing the statutory obligations of 'sewerage undertakers' and controlling their prices. Lord Hoffmann, in particular, doubted whether a claimant could determine the level of service that a public utility provider must provide by invoking the common law occupier's duty not to 'continue' a state of affairs on his land which might lead to a nuisance, because a judge would not be able to determine what 'reasonable steps' ought to be taken.[100]

The expansion of the rule that an occupier will be held to have continued a nuisance if he ought to have known of a state of affairs causing interference and has failed to take

---

[97] [1980] QB 485, 526–7. In *Abbahall* v *Smee* [2003] 1 WLR 1472, in circumstances where defendant and claimant occupied different floors of a building beneath a leaking roof, and the defendant sought to argue that because of her relative poverty she should not have to contribute towards the repairs, the Court of Appeal held that such an approach would be 'unjust to the point of absurdity' (at [57]) and that the costs should normally be divided in proportion to the benefit that each party would gain from the work (at [41]). The problems which may arise where a nuisance causes consequential damage while the parties are squabbling about contributions have not yet been addressed by the courts.

[98] This contrasts with the usual rule of remoteness of damage (see above, § 10.2) that a defendant is liable for all damage of the same *type* as ought to have been foreseen, regardless of the *extent*.

[99] [2002] QB 929, at [84].

[100] [2004] 2 AC 42, at [63]–[64], [70].

reasonable steps to deal with it has led to some tension between the law of torts and established principles of land law. In particular, it is a basic principle of land law that a person whose land is subject to an easement is not obliged to undertake any repairs to the land so as to facilitate continued enjoyment of the easement, but instead the beneficiary of the easement has a right to enter the land to carry out works necessary to protect his right.[101] It seems that in light of the development of wider liability for failing to prevent nuisances this principle of land law can no longer be treated as an exhaustive summary of the law, at least when a failure to repair the land will lead to physical damage to the claimant's land.[102]

Given that the question whether an occupier will be liable for a state of affairs he did not create is answered by considering whether he has fulfilled a measured duty of care, it is sometimes suggested that this group of cases properly forms part of the tort of negligence.[103] We would reject this suggestion. It is important to note that such a suggestion is not merely one about the appropriate distribution of topics within textbooks. If the *Sedleigh-Denfield* doctrine were to be treated as *only* part of the tort of negligence then this would make it difficult for a claimant to bring an action when a defendant occupier had failed to deal with a state of affairs which merely had the effect of reducing the amenity value of the claimant's land.[104] Why? Because the tort of negligence imposes duties to take reasonable care not to cause *physical damage* to property, while *amenity damage* does not require any *physical* change to property. We think that the true position is that a breach of the measured duty can lead to a claim for continuing a private nuisance, but that there is also a parallel duty of care breach of which will amount to the tort of negligence.[105]

So far we have discussed when occupiers will be held to have 'continued' or 'adopted' a state of affairs existing on land which they occupy. The case of *LE Jones (Insurance Brokers) Ltd v Portsmouth City Council* (2003) raised the question whether anyone *other than the occupier* might be held liable for a private nuisance if he did not take steps to abate a problematic state of affairs. The case involved damage caused by a tree which was situated on land vested in the highway authority but which the defendant council had agreed to maintain. Dyson LJ stated that

> the basis for the liability of an occupier for a nuisance on his land is not his occupation as such. Rather, it is that, by virtue of his occupation, an occupier usually has it in his power to take the measures that are necessary to prevent or eliminate the nuisance. He has sufficient control over the hazard which constitutes the nuisance for it to be reasonable to make him liable for the foreseeable consequences of his failure to exercise that control so as to remove the hazard.[106]

---

[101] *Jones v Pritchard* [1908] 1 Ch 630, 637–8.

[102] *Bradburn v Lindsay* [1983] 2 All ER 408.

[103] This view is advanced by Gearty 1989, who writes of *Sedleigh-Denfield* (at 237): 'This was negligence pure and simple, confused by an ill-fitting and woolly disguise of nuisance.' See also Weir 1998a, 102–3: 'that the defendant's liability in nuisance [in *Sedleigh-Denfield*] [was] affected by considerations relevant in the tort of negligence seems beyond doubt.'

[104] An example of such a case might be an occupier failing to deal with regular noisy trespassers, or with smelly rotting rubbish tipped onto his land by trespassers. In such a case the type of damage suffered by the claimant would not normally give rise to a claim in the tort of negligence but could give rise to a claim in private nuisance.

[105] See above, § 11.5(C). The scope of the negligence duty may be important. Compensation for personal injuries can never be recovered in the tort of private nuisance (see below, § 15.12), but can of course sometimes be recovered in the tort of negligence. Although Megaw LJ expressed the opinion that if an occupier breached a *Goldman* v *Hargrave*-type duty of care owed to his neighbour and his neighbour suffered a personal injury as a result, then the neighbour should be able to sue the occupier for damages in negligence (see *Leakey* v *National Trust* [1980] QB 485, at 523) there is currently no binding authority as to whether 'personal injury' suffered as a result of the breach of a *Goldman* v *Hargrave*-type duty of care will count as the 'right kind of loss' to be actionable in negligence.

[106] [2003] 1 WLR 427, at [11].

Dyson LJ's test, which focuses instead on *control* over the *hazard*, rather than *occupation* of the land, has the potential to catch not just occupiers, but also independent contractors managing hazards on land on behalf of occupiers, and possibly also non-occupiers, such as public officials, which have power to intervene and deal with hazards. Indeed, Dyson LJ's test might require reassessment of the orthodox rule, discussed in the previous section, that a landlord is only responsible for a nuisance created by his tenant if he has *authorised* the tenant to act in such a way as to create a nuisance: if *a capacity to control* is sufficient to impose a measured duty of care then landlords, who are of course *not* usually in occupation, may be liable for more than what they expressly or impliedly authorise. Consequently, we suspect that the courts will be very cautious about extending liability beyond those in occupation,[107] and, in the interests of simplicity, we have continued to use the phrase 'occupiers' to describe those who may be found to have adopted or continued a private nuisance.

15.10 DEFENCES

It is appropriate at this point to mention four defences that may prevent a defendant from being held liable under the law of private nuisance for a state of affairs that unreasonably interferes with the claimant's land.

A. Necessity

In the case of *Southport Corporation* v *Esso Petroleum Ltd* (1953), a tanker got into difficulties and, fearing for the ship and the safety of his crew, the captain discharged his cargo of oil to make the tanker lighter. The oil polluted the claimant's beach. At first instance Devlin J suggested *obiter* that it would be a defence to create a nuisance in order to save human life, but that he was unwilling to hold that one could damage another's property in order to save one's own property without providing compensation.[108] The Court of Appeal split on the defence of necessity. Singleton LJ suggested that there was a defence of necessity to claims for creating a nuisance, and that the defendant could rely on it unless he was negligent in creating the necessity.[109] Denning LJ also suggested that there was a defence of necessity, but it was for the defendant to prove that the necessity was unavoidable.[110] In the House of Lords[111] the decision concentrated on the pleadings, but Lord Radcliffe suggested *obiter* that there was a defence of necessity in nuisance, unless it was the defendant's carelessness which brought about the necessity.[112]

One reason for the divergence in judicial opinion is that where the necessity was brought about by circumstances for which neither party was responsible the principal issue is which of two innocents should bear the cost. Had the ship been caught in freak weather which itself led to the spillage of the oil, the defendant would probably have been held not to have *created* the pollution. Should we treat the case differently if the defendant responds reasonably to freak weather and was not at fault in exposing himself to the risk in the first

---

[107] Many of the principles applied, for instance that which relates contributions to the cost of dealing with the state of affairs to the degree of benefit that claimant and defendant will gain from the state of affairs being dealt with, are difficult to apply to defendants who are not occupiers.

[108] [1953] 3 WLR 773.

[109] [1954] 2 QB 182, 194.

[110] [1954] 2 QB 182, 197. Strictly speaking, Denning LJ only discussed *public* nuisance, but his reasoning on necessity, which relied on a parallel with the tort of trespass to land, can be applied equally to *private* nuisance.

[111] [1956] AC 218.

[112] [1956] AC 218, 242.

place? Whatever the final judicial answer to this question, it is already clear that the courts will not countenance the development of a wide defence of necessity. In *Andreae v Selfridge & Co Ltd* (1936), Bennett J was scathing about a plea that it was necessary for builders to create severe disturbance in order to complete their work swiftly. He referred to a line from *Paradise Lost*: 'So spake the Fiend, and with necessity, the tyrant's plea, excused his devilish deeds.'[113]

B. Statutory authority

A defendant will not be liable if he can demonstrate that a statute authorised him to do what would otherwise amount to an actionable nuisance. In each case care must be taken to establish precisely what Parliament intended. In some cases it has been found that Parliament intended to authorise the defendant to conduct an activity *in a way that paid reasonable regard and care to the interests of others*, and did not intend to permit the defendant to cause any nuisance beyond that which would be an *inevitable* consequence of conducting the activity.[114] In other cases, however, it has been found that Parliament *assumed* that the authorised activity could be conducted somewhere and under some circumstances without creating a nuisance, and did not intend to permit the defendant to cause any nuisance whatsoever.[115]

C. Act of third party

There seems little doubt that a defendant will avoid liability if he can prove that any unreasonable interference arising on his land was caused by a wholly unpredictable act of a trespasser. Where, however, a state of affairs created by a trespasser does not immediately cause an unreasonable interference but may do so in future, or causes an interference over an extended period, an occupier of land may be held liable for 'continuing' the state of affairs if he knew or ought to have known of it and failed to take reasonable steps to rectify the situation.[116]

Further, where the trespasser's intervention was not wholly unpredictable a landowner may be held liable in negligence for failing to take reasonable precautions against the intervention. The question of how predictable an intervention must be before the landowner will be under a duty to take reasonable steps to prevent it is difficult to answer with confidence. The decision of the House of Lords in *Smith v Littlewoods Organisation Ltd* (1987) provides no single clear answer.

Lord Mackay LC stated that a landowner would only have had a duty to take reasonable steps to prevent a trespasser acting in some way if it was reasonably foreseeable that if he failed to take such steps then damage to the claimant would be probable, and that to establish that damage was probable it would be necessary to consider carefully both how likely the trespasser's intervention was and how likely it was that such an intervention would cause damage to the claimant.[117]

By contrast, Lord Goff argued that a landowner would only owe his neighbour a duty to take reasonable steps to prevent a trespasser causing harm to his neighbour if: (1) the

---

[113] [1936] 2 All ER 1413, 1422.
[114] See, for example, *Allen v Gulf Oil* [1981] AC 1001.
[115] See, for example, *Metropolitan Asylum District Managers v Hill* (1881) 6 App Cas 193.
[116] *Sedleigh-Denfield v O'Callaghan* [1940] AC 880.
[117] [1987] 1 AC 241, 261.

landowner had assumed a responsibility to his neighbour; *or* (2) the landowner was responsible for controlling the trespasser in question;[118] *or* (3) the landowner had negligently caused or permitted the creation of a source of danger which it was reasonably foreseeable that a trespasser might 'spark off';[119] *or* (4) the landowner knew or ought to have known that the trespasser in question had created a fire risk.[120]

In *Mitchell v Glasgow City Council* (2009) Lord Hope and Lord Rodger both stated that they agreed with Lord Goff's approach, as opposed to Lord Mackay's.[121]

D. Act of God

A defendant will avoid liability in private nuisance if he can prove that any unreasonable interference was caused by a wholly unpredictable and uncontrollable natural force. In *Sedleigh-Denfield* v *O'Callaghan* (1940), Lord Maugham stressed that the defendants had not tried to argue that the rainfall which caused the flood was so heavy as to give rise to a defence of 'Act of God'. He suggested that such a defence would, in any case, only have been available if the rain had been 'so exceptional in amount that no reasonable man could have anticipated it'.[122] A defendant may be liable if the force of nature was reasonably foreseeable, or if the state of affairs created by the force did not *immediately* lead to the interference. In the latter situation, if the defendant is an occupier, then he will be liable if he fails to take reasonable steps to deal with a known risk, or one that he ought to have known about.[123]

15.11 TITLE TO SUE

The decision of the House of Lords in *Hunter* v *Canary Wharf* (1997) made it clear that in a case where a defendant created, authorised, adopted or continued a state of affairs that resulted in an unreasonable interference with the use and enjoyment of land, a claimant could only succeed in establishing that the tort of private nuisance had been committed in relation to her if she had a sufficient interest in that land. Similarly, if the claimant's claim alleged an unreasonable interference with a right associated with land then it could only succeed if the claimant enjoyed the relevant right.

Four questions require further attention. First, what counts as a sufficient interest *in land*? Secondly, if A is responsible for a state of affairs that has unreasonably interfered with the use and enjoyment of a particular piece of land and B wants to sue A on the basis that because of this A has committed the tort of private nuisance in relation to her, does B have to *prove* that she *has* a sufficient interest in the land in question, and will B be barred from suing A if A can prove that B did *not* have a sufficient interest in the land? Thirdly, would the law be better if a wider class of people could sue for private nuisance? Fourthly, might Article 8 of the ECHR compel the courts to reform this part of the law?

---

[118] [1987] 1 AC 241, 272.

[119] [1987] 1 AC 241, 273–4. Lord Goff's example is the storage of a quantity of fireworks in an unlocked garden shed.

[120] [1987] 1 AC 241, 274. Here the duty seems to be parallel to the measured duty of care that is considered in cases of *continuing* a private nuisance.

[121] [2009] 1 AC 874, [20]–[21] and [56].

[122] [1940] AC 880, 886.

[123] This is another situation where the relevant duty is the measured duty of an occupier to take reasonable steps to prevent conditions on his land causing nuisance to his neighbour. *Goldman* v *Hargrave* [1967] AC 645 provides a good example of a state of affairs created by an uncontrollable force of nature (red gum set alight by lightning) only causing harm to a neighbour after the occupier had a reasonable opportunity to abate the risk.

A. Sufficient interests in land[124]

English land law draws a distinction between interests *in land* and *personal* interests. The main distinction between these is that interests *in land* can bind third parties while *personal* interests generally do not. A person with a fee simple in possession over Greenacre obviously has a sufficient interest *in land* while a person who has purchased a ticket from the owner of Greenacre entitling him to visit Greenacre Hall for a guided tour has only a *personal* (contractual) interest. Consequently, if Greenacre Hall is blighted by intolerable noise created by *Drummer*, the person with a fee simple in possession can sue for private nuisance but the visitor on the guided tour cannot.

In *Hunter v Canary Wharf* (1997) Lord Goff summarised who will be held to have a sufficient interest in land:

> [A]n action in private nuisance will only lie at the suit of a person who has a right to the land affected. Ordinarily, such a person can only sue if he has the right to exclusive possession of the land, such as a freeholder or tenant in possession, or even a licensee with exclusive possession. Exceptionally, however . . . this category may include a person in actual possession who has no right to be there; and in any event a reversioner can sue in so far as his reversionary interest is affected. But a mere licensee on the land has no right to sue.[125]

We will explain the exception mentioned by Lord Goff in the next section. At this stage we want to emphasise that both freeholders and tenants in possession can sue. So, if Greenacre Hall has an owner-occupier, *Lord Greenacre*, then he will be able to sue for private nuisance if Greenacre Hall is affected by unreasonable noise created by *Drummer*, or intolerable smells created by *Stinker*, or the like. But if *Lord Greenacre* has leased the Hall to *Renter*, who is in possession, then *Renter* will be able to sue for private nuisance if the Hall is affected by unreasonable noise created by *Drummer*, or intolerable smells created by *Stinker*, or the like. The fact that *Renter* can sue does not mean that *Lord Greenacre* cannot: *Lord Greenacre* will have the status of 'reversioner' (that is, the person who will take back Greenacre Hall at the end of the tenancy), and a reversioner may also sue if a private nuisance has any effect on *his own* interest in land.[126] This might be the case if, for instance, the noise created by *Drummer* was sufficiently loud to damage the windows, *Renter* was not obliged to repair them, and the building would deteriorate if they were not repaired immediately. In these circumstances the noise would have damaged the reversioner's – *Lord Greenacre*'s – interest in the land.

The interests of two classes of persons are particularly difficult to classify: (1) licensees, and (2) the spouses and children of people with interests in land. With regard to licensees, if the licence grants exclusive possession then Lord Goff suggests that the licensee will have a 'right to the land affected' and will be able to sue. We have no doubt that such a licensee will be able to sue, but would attribute that to the *de facto* possession rule discussed in the next section. With regard to family members, it is clear that they will not be treated as having interests *in land* if they merely occupy the house as a home.[127] Thus if *Lord Greenacre* is the owner-occupier, but allows his adult sons, *Feckless* and *Fretful*, to live in the

---

[124] We will not attempt to list *all* the interests which may qualify as sufficient interests *in land*. The interested reader should consult a standard textbook on land law.

[125] [1997] AC 655, at 692. Later in his speech, at 694, Lord Goff held that the court should not alter the law presented in this summary.

[126] If, for instance, the noise is sufficiently loud to damage the windows, the tenant is not obliged to repair them, and the building will deteriorate if they are not repaired immediately, then the noise damages the reversioner's interest in the land.

[127] *Hunter v Canary Wharf Ltd* [1997] AC 655.

attic of the East Wing of Greenacre Hall, then his sons will be unable to bring a claim against *Drummer* if he creates intolerable noise.

B. Proof issues

A person who *in fact* enjoys or asserts exclusive possession over a piece of land will not be required to *prove* that he has a *right* to that possession in order to sue a defendant in private nuisance for unreasonably interfering with the use and enjoyment of that land. Moreover, the defendant will only be permitted to rely on the fact that the possessor has *no* right to possess the land in question[128] if either the defendant has the right to possession of that land, or the defendant created the nuisance with the authority of the person with the right to possession. This rule has several consequences.

First, a person enjoying exclusive possession *in fact* (often called '*de facto* possession'), but who has a defective title, will still be able to sue.[129] Secondly, a licensee enjoying exclusive possession may be able to sue without having to convince the court that a licence granting exclusive possession creates an interest *in land*. Thirdly, a person asserting exclusive possession over something which cannot be owned as land, but which clearly is not personal property, may be able to sue.[130]

Because most[131] of those who qualify as having a title to sue in private nuisance under the first rule (on the ground that they have a sufficient interest *in the land* being interfered with) will also qualify under the second rule (on the ground that they enjoy exclusive possession *in fact* of the land interfered with), it might be thought to be a sensible simplification to treat the law as simply saying that a person who enjoys exclusive possession *in fact* of a piece of land can sue in private nuisance. Such a simplification is harmless as long as three points are borne in mind. First, by way of exception to the simplification, a reversioner (who is not in exclusive possession *in fact* of the land) can sue for interference with *his own* interest in land. Secondly, a defendant will have a good defence if he can prove that *he* has the right to possession of the land in question or is acting with the authority of the person with that right. Thirdly, it may be necessary to investigate *interests* rather than *possession* when deciding what remedy to grant. In particular, if a court wanted to award damages compensating for *future* interferences in lieu of an injunction[132] it would be important to ascertain who would suffer those future interferences.[133]

C. Evaluation of the law

In ruling that a claimant has to have a sufficient interest in land to sue in private nuisance, the House of Lords overruled in part the decision of the Court of Appeal in *Khorasandjian* v *Bush* (1993), which allowed a claimant who was living in her parents' home to bring

---

[128] This is often referred to as the defence of *ius tertii*.

[129] See, for example, *Pemberton* v *Southwark London Borough Council* [2000] 1 WLR 1672. In *Metropolitan Properties Ltd* v *Jones* [1939] 2 All ER 202 the claimant, Jones, had been a tenant of the flat affected by the nuisance, but he had assigned the tenancy (and hence the right to occupy) to a person called Storer, before returning to live in the flat when Storer disappeared, leaving him (Jones) still liable for the rent. Lord Hoffmann suggested in *Hunter* v *Canary Wharf Ltd* [1997] AC 655, at 704, that Jones should have been allowed to sue on the basis of his possession *in fact*.

[130] In *Foster* v *Warblington UDC* [1906] 1 KB 648 the claimant sued for the pollution of oyster ponds on the foreshore.

[131] The obvious exception is a reversioner.

[132] For this remedy see below, § 15.12(A)(2).

[133] The fact that someone *presently* enjoys exclusive possession does not mean that such possession is likely to continue in the future.

a private nuisance claim against a defendant who was continually pestering her with telephone calls. Such a claimant would now have a remedy under the Protection from Harassment Act 1997.[134] However, other claimants who might have been protected under the ruling in *Khorasandjian* may not be so lucky.

For example, the claimants in *Dobson v Thames Water Utilities Ltd* (2009) alleged that the way in which the Mogden Sewage Treatment Works had been operated had led to private nuisance by emanation of odours and proliferation of mosquitoes. Many of the 1,300 claimants had sufficient interests in land, but many others, who had suffered just as much discomfort as a result of the odours and mosquitoes, were children living with their parents, residents of old peoples' homes, and others who did not have sufficient interests in land or exclusive possession *in fact*. In the particular case these claimants without sufficient interests in land sought damages under the Human Rights Act 1998. But this avenue would not have been available if the defendant had been a private company, as opposed to a 'public authority'. If the defendant had been a private company then the claimants without sufficient interests in land could only have recovered compensation if they could have established that the defendant had committed the tort of negligence in relation to them, and had thereby caused them personal injuries.

Can it be satisfactory that an owner-occupier can sue for the stench of a sewage works while his children cannot, unless they can establish both personal injury and negligence? The majority in *Hunter v Canary Wharf* (1997) insisted that the distinction between the *function* of the tort of private nuisance and the *function* of the tort of negligence explained the differences between the two torts[135] and explained why claims in private nuisance could only be brought by someone with a sufficient interest in the land affected by a private nuisance. The House of Lords argued, in summary, that private nuisance protects a claimant's interests in land, while negligence protects the personal safety of all persons regardless of whether they have interests in land. So if those without interests in land were allowed to sue in private nuisance that would 'transform it from a tort to land into a tort to the person'[136] and blur the distinction between the two torts.

This transformation would also conflict with the way a majority of their Lordships thought that damages should be assessed for *past* harm[137] in private nuisance cases. Lords Lloyd, Hoffmann and Hope all insisted that the appropriate measure of damages for an interference with the use and enjoyment of land in cases not involving physical damage to the land is the diminution in the amenity value of the land caused by the nuisance.[138] This amenity value is an amount relative to the land, not relative to how many people live on it. Lord Hoffmann said, 'Damages for nuisance recoverable by the possessor or occupier may be affected by the size, commodiousness and value of his property but cannot be increased merely because more people are in occupation and therefore suffer greater discomfort.'[139]

---

[134] See below, § 20.2.

[135] Lord Hope pointed out one difference ([1997] AC 655, at 724), that 'the tort of nuisance is a tort of strict liability in the sense that it is no defence to say that the defendant took all reasonable care to prevent it' and Lord Hoffmann noted another ([1997] AC 655, at 707), that 'the law of negligence gives no remedy for discomfort or distress which does not result in bodily or psychiatric illness'.

[136] [1997] AC 655, 693.

[137] Damages may be claimed for *past* harm. Further, where an injunction is claimed, a court may decide to award damages for anticipated *future* harm *in lieu* of an injunction. For more details, see chapter 33, below.

[138] [1997] AC 655, 696 (per Lord Lloyd), 706 (per Lord Hoffmann), 724 (per Lord Hope).

[139] Thus both Lord Hoffmann ([1997] AC 655, at 706) and Lord Lloyd ([1997] AC 655, at 698–9) expressly disapproved of the suggestion in *Bone v Seale* [1975] 1 WLR 797 that damages for private nuisance by smell might be assessed by drawing an analogy with awards in personal injury cases for loss of the sense of smell. Lord Hope's views were less clear.

Their Lordships also treated both the weight of the 'transformation' argument and the persuasiveness of the damages point as reinforced by the symmetry which would consequently exist between the three different effects that a private nuisance can have on someone's land: physically damaging the land, reducing its amenity value, and encroaching on its boundaries. Where the private nuisance has the effect of encroaching on the boundaries to land, or physically damaging the land, it seems obvious that the person who should be able to sue is the person with the interest in the land. Equally, it seems obvious that if that person claims damages in an encroachment or a physical damage case then these should be calculated to compensate him for the diminution in the value of his interest in the land. Thus there is a degree of consistency in holding that where the private nuisance reduces amenity value *only* those with sufficient interests in the land should be able to sue, and that *all* they can sue for is reduction of the amenity value *of the land*.

Lord Goff provided two additional practical reasons why liability in private nuisance should only extend to those with sufficient interests in land. First, he pointed out that potential claimants often reach compromises with potential defendants, for instance by permitting the nuisance to continue for a fixed period in exchange for payment. Lord Goff feared that the likelihood of such sensible arrangements would be reduced if potential defendants had to identify and deal with not just those with sufficient interests in the land but all the occupiers of each property affected by their activities.[140] Secondly, he suggested that if the class of those able to claim in private nuisance extended beyond the clear limit of those with sufficient interests in land it would prove impossible to find any other easily definable limit. Thus he raised the awkward cases of lodgers, au pairs, resident nurses, and employees.[141]

Of the Law Lords who heard the *Hunter* case, only Lord Cooke rejected the traditional rule. His dissent urged that there was no *logical* reason why those who had actually been enjoying the amenities of a home should be unable to sue for an unreasonable interference with those amenities and that consequently a judicial determination of the issue depended on a policy choice.[142] In approaching this choice he expressed a preference for utility and justice over symmetry and tidiness,[143] discounted Lord Goff's concerns about sensible compromises and au pairs,[144] and concluded, 'occupation of the property as a home is, to me, an acceptable criterion, consistent with the traditional concern for the sanctity of family life and the Englishman's home'.[145] A tolerable paraphrase of Lord Cooke's reasoning might be that in modern society a domestic house, a home, is more than just a piece of investment property. No doubt if the home is invaded by noxious fumes or bad vibrations the owner's investment is harmed, and only the owner should be able to claim for that damage *to the investment*. But equally without doubt other occupants of the home will have suffered – their lives will have been rendered less restful and fulfilling – and, so far as they are concerned, they should be compensated for their loss. In doctrinal terms, Lord Cooke might be said to have been arguing that the interest that the tort of private nuisance should protect is not merely an interest in land but a wider 'interest in a home'.

Some academics, such as Janet O'Sullivan,[146] have expressed a preference for Lord Cooke's view. We think, however, that Lord Cooke was unfair to the majority when he

---

[140] [1997] AC 655, 692–693.
[141] [1997] AC 655, 693.
[142] [1997] AC 655, 711.
[143] ibid.
[144] [1997] AC 655, 718.
[145] ibid.
[146] O'Sullivan 1997b.

portrayed the divergence as turning on whether one prefers symmetry and tidiness or utility and justice. We think that the majority was motivated by the need to set down clearly who is protected by the law on private nuisance and for what harm damages can be recovered. Clarity on these issues is not merely a matter of 'tidiness'; it is important for settling disputes and also important for those who want, in advance of any dispute, to negotiate permission to develop and use land in ways which may inconvenience neighbours. Moreover, it is important to remember that many private nuisance claims do not involve interference with 'homes' but with land used for various business purposes and it is unclear whether Lord Cooke would have also supported allowing those without *interests in land* to claim in such cases.[147] On the other hand, we also think that the majority's treatment of 'homes' as simply *investments in property* fails to reflect the way in which most members of our society value 'homes'. The question of who is protected by the law on private nuisance is part of a more general dispute in the law of torts between the desire to draw bright lines which will allow people to plan around the law and the desire to decide each case on its individual merits. There are no easy answers to the question of how to balance these two desires. In the area under discussion, it would be very helpful to have more evidence about whether those who carry out activities which *may* create a nuisance generally *try* to negotiate in advance, or not, before deciding whether the balance struck by the majority is preferable to the balance struck by Lord Cooke.[148]

D. Article 8 of the ECHR

Article 8 of the European Convention on Human Rights (ECHR) provides that 'Everyone has the right to respect for his private and family life, his home and his correspondence', and the European Court of Human Rights has held that this right *can* be violated by 'homes' being exposed to extreme noise or environmental pollution.[149] Moreover, the Court has held that even when the State has not created the noise or pollution it may nonetheless be responsible for the violation if it has failed properly to regulate private industry.[150]

We saw in chapter 2 that several lawyers have argued that s 6 of the Human Rights Act 1998 obliges the English courts to develop the common law so as to make it compatible with the ECHR.[151] Such reasoning has been used to support the argument that the courts should extend the tort of private nuisance so that *all* those who reside in a 'home' can sue (regardless of whether they have a sufficient interest in the land) and damages should be available for any 'distress' they suffer as a result of such nuisances.[152] Three problems with this argument are worth mentioning here.

First, although the English courts are obliged to act compatibly with the ECHR, the cases before the European Court of Human Rights have *not* established that a failure by a State

---

[147] Some academics have argued that private nuisance should protect interests in land beyond 'use as a home', such as a cricket club's recreational interest in a public park where it regularly plays: Wightman 1998.

[148] If such negotiating in advance is very rare we think this would strengthen the case for accepting Lord Cooke's views.

[149] Interference with a person's 'home' by noise or pollution will not always be a violation of Article 8. An interference can be justified under Art 8.2 if it is prescribed by law and necessary in a democratic society.

[150] *Powell & Rayner* v *United Kingdom* (1990) 12 EHRR 355; *Lopez Ostra* v *Spain* (1995) 20 EHRR 277; *Guerra* v *Italy* (1998) 26 EHRR 357; *Hatton* v *United Kingdom* (2003) 37 EHRR 28.

[151] See, for example, Hunt 1998.

[152] In *McKenna* v *British Aluminum, The Times*, 25 April 2002, Neuberger J thought that it was arguable that the English courts would accept this argument.

to create *private law actions* for children and other non-owners to bring against polluters is incompatible with Article 8. The cases have established that a failure of the State to prevent such pollution by *regulation* is incompatible with Article 8, but that is not the same as saying that such regulation must be by the provision of private law actions.

Secondly, in *Dobson* v *Thames Water Utilities Ltd* (2009) the Court of Appeal held that where a child lived with his parents in a house affected by a private nuisance created by a public authority the fact that the child's parents had obtained damages for the private nuisance would be highly relevant to the question whether it was necessary to award the child damages as 'just satisfaction' for a violation of his right under Article 8. What the court seems to have had in mind is that in many cases if the parents had obtained compensation for the reduction in amenity value of the house then no further award of damages to the child under Article 8 would be necessary. If this is correct then it tends to undermine the argument that it is necessary to extend a private law claim to such children, since the private law claims that their parents can bring may be sufficient to prevent the sort of pollution that will violate Article 8.

Thirdly, extending the tort of private nuisance may not be required because to do so would actually provide children and non-owners with *far more* protection than Article 8 requires. As we have seen, the tort of private nuisance allows the owner of a house in a luxurious residential district to sue when the premises are subjected to the smell of frying fish,[153] but it seems highly unlikely that the European Court of Human Rights would regard such an owner's children as victims of a human rights violation.[154]

15.12 REMEDIES

There are two kinds of remedies that a claimant in a private nuisance case may be seeking: (1) an *injunction* to prevent *future* unreasonable interferences with the use and enjoyment of his land, or a right associated with that land; and (2) *damages* to compensate for *past* unreasonable interferences with the use and enjoyment of his land, or a right associated with that land. But in some cases where a claimant seeks an injunction the court may refuse this and *instead* award (3) damages *in lieu of an injunction*, which will be calculated to compensate for *future* unreasonable interferences. (We will discuss (3) (damages *in lieu of an injunction*) in the section dealing with injunctions.)

A. Injunction

In a case where a claimant can establish that he is currently suffering an unreasonable interference with the use and enjoyment of his land, or some right associated with that land, and that the defendant is responsible for creating the state of affairs that is bringing about the interference, the claimant will normally be entitled to obtain an injunction requiring the defendant to cease doing whatever is bringing about the nuisance. Such an injunction is commonly called a *prohibitory* injunction, for the obvious reason that it prohibits the defendant from continuing to do whatever is bringing about the nuisance.

---

[153] *Adams* v *Ursell* [1913] 1 Ch 269.

[154] In *Dennis* v *Ministry of Defence* [2003] EWHC 793 (QB), Buckley J held that the amount he was awarding a landowner for private nuisance caused by noise was sufficient to amount to 'just satisfaction' of the claim by the landowner and *his wife* that their rights under Art 8 had been infringed. It seems, however, that he reached this conclusion after using the wrong method to assess damages for private nuisance, and without considering whether the amounts would always coincide. See further, Bagshaw 2004a, 41.

(1) *Types of injunction.* A *prohibitory injunction* is the type of injunction that is most commonly sought in cases of private nuisance, and our discussion will focus on them. But for the sake of completeness we should mention three other types of injunction.

First, if a state of affairs is on the verge of causing significant damage to a claimant, and the circumstances are such that if it does cause such damage the defendant will have committed the tort of private nuisance in relation to the claimant, a court may sometimes order a defendant to do something which will prevent the state of affairs from causing serious damage. Such an injunction is commonly called a *mandatory injunction*, and the power to grant them is 'exercised sparingly and with caution'.[155]

Secondly, a court can also grant an injunction to a claimant who can establish that the defendant is about to commit the tort of private nuisance in relation to him. Such an injunction is commonly called a *quia timet injunction*, because the Latin phrase 'quia timet' – 'because he fears' – formerly featured in the pleading. Such an injunction will usually *prohibit* a defendant from committing the tort that it is established that he was about to commit.

Thirdly, a court can grant an *interim injunction* to a claimant *before* any trial of the claimant's claim. The purpose of such an injunction is usually to make sure that a trial will not be *pointless*, for example, because the claimant will have already suffered irreparable damage in the meantime. The precise circumstances in which interim injunctions will be awarded are discussed below, in chapter 33.

(2) *Damages in lieu of a prohibitory injunction.* The courts will not *always* award an injunction in a case where B can establish that she is the continuing victim of a private nuisance for which A is responsible. The courts may refuse to award B an injunction but at the same time award B damages *in lieu of* (instead of) an injunction.[156] But the courts will exercise this power to *refuse* an injunction and award damages *in lieu* only in 'very exceptional circumstances'.[157]

The effect of refusing to grant an injunction in a case where a continuing private nuisance has been established will be to leave the defendant *in effect* free to continue committing the tort. We say '*in effect* free', rather than simply 'free', because refusing an injunction does not mean that it is not a *wrong* for the defendant to continue committing private nuisance in relation to the claimant: it will remain *wrongful*, and as a result it may be appropriate to make the defendant pay damages – *in lieu of injunction* – in advance. Such damages are, in effect, a reasonable sum for the privilege of being allowed to commit that tort. If the court decides to award damages in lieu of an injunction it will assess how much should be paid by way of damages in lieu by asking: How much would a reasonable person in the claimant's shoes charge the defendant for the privilege of being allowed to commit the tort complained of?[158] The figure the court comes up with will be the amount it awards by way of damages in lieu.

So suppose the court is dealing with a claim by *Lord Greenacre*, the owner-occupier of Greenacre Hall, against *Racetrack*, for private nuisance by the creation of noise, and has decided to deny *Lord Greenacre*'s application for an injunction and to award him damages

---

[155] *Morris* v *Redland Bricks Ltd* [1970] AC 652, 665 (per Lord Upjohn).

[156] The Chancery Amendment Act 1858, better known as Lord Cairns's Act, allowed the Court of Chancery to award damages in lieu of an injunction. This statute has been repealed, but s 50 of the Senior Courts Act 1981 preserves the court's jurisdiction to award damages in lieu of an injunction.

[157] *Watson* v *Croft Promosport Ltd* [2009] EWCA Civ 15, [44] (per Sir Andrew Morritt).

[158] *Jaggard* v *Sawyer* [1995] 1 WLR 269.

in lieu of an injunction instead. In determining how much *Racetrack* should pay by way of damages in lieu, the court will take into account how much *Lord Greenacre* stands to lose if *Racetrack* is allowed to continue making the noise which it is a private nuisance to make *and* how much money *Racetrack* will make if he is allowed to commit the tort.[159] A reasonable man in *Lord Greenacre*'s shoes would take both matters into account in determining how much to charge *Racetrack* for the privilege of being allowed to commit the tort.[160]

So an award of damages in lieu of an injunction in this case would in effect amount to a forced sale of *Lord Greenacre*'s rights to be free of a private nuisance against *Racetrack*. Consequently, the courts have traditionally been cautious about using their power to award damages in lieu of injunctions. In the leading case of *Shelfer* v *City of London Electric Lighting Co* (1895), A.L. Smith LJ stated:

> In my opinion it may be stated as a good working rule that – (1) If the injury to the claimant's legal rights is small, (2) And is one which is capable of being estimated in money, (3) And is one which can be adequately compensated by a small money payment, (4) And the case is one in which it would be oppressive to the defendant to grant an injunction: – then damages in substitution for an injunction may be given.[161]

A.L. Smith LJ then went on to suggest that regardless of the four factors, a defendant who had acted in reckless disregard of the claimant's rights would be unable to ask the court to award damages in lieu of an injunction.[162]

In *Jaggard* v *Sawyer* (1995), the Court of Appeal treated A.L. Smith LJ's list of four factors as having 'stood the test of time'.[163] Indeed, Lord Bingham MR favoured a narrow interpretation of the fourth factor and said, 'It is important to bear in mind that the test is one of oppression, and the court should not slide into application of a general balance of convenience test.'[164] Millett LJ did not doubt the utility of A.L. Smith LJ's four factors, but he also observed that they were not to be treated as an *exhaustive* list of the situations when it would be appropriate to award damages in lieu of an injunction.[165] Most probably he was referring here to the fact that injunctions to prevent people committing torts were originally awarded by the Court of Equity, and therefore general equitable principles still apply today to determine whether an injunction can be granted. These principles mean that an injunction may be refused if a claimant waits an unreasonably long time before seeking one, or is sought by a claimant who has behaved badly towards the defendant.

It is worth drawing attention to the fact that A.L. Smith LJ's four factors do not make any reference to the question whether awarding an injunction will be contrary to the

---

[159] *Carr-Saunders* v *Dick McNeil Associates Ltd* [1986] 1 WLR 922.

[160] In *Tamares Ltd* v *Fairpoint Properties Ltd (No 2)* [2007] 1 WLR 2167, Gabriel Moss QC held that where a court refused to grant a party an injunction to protect its right to light against a development on neighbouring land the owner of the right should normally be awarded some part of the likely profit from the development, but not so much as would have been likely to prevent the development from taking place (at [22]). In the particular case he awarded the claimant £50,000, which was slightly less than a third of the developer's expected profit and considerably *more* than the claimant's loss of amenity (assessed at no more than £3,030).

[161] [1895] 1 Ch 287, 322–3.

[162] ibid, 323. In *Ketley* v *Gooden* (1996) 73 P & CR 305, the Court of Appeal awarded damages in lieu of an injunction despite the fact that the defendant had recklessly disregarded the claimant's rights because of delay by the claimant in starting proceedings and the minor nature of the damage.

[163] [1995] 1 WLR 269, 287 (per Millett LJ). In *Regan* v *Paul Properties Ltd* [2007] Ch 135, the Court of Appeal held that the same approach – based on *Shelfer* – applied in 'right to light' cases.

[164] [1995] 1 WLR 269, 283.

[165] [1995] 1 WLR 269, 287.

public interest. The question whether the claimant should be able to obtain an injunction which might close down an enterprise operating in the public interest is controversial. In *Shelfer*, Lindley LJ expressed the strong view that,

> the Court has always protested against the notion that it ought to allow a wrong to continue simply because the wrongdoer is able and willing to pay for the injury he may inflict. Neither has the circumstance that the wrongdoer is in some sense a public benefactor (eg, a gas or water company or a sewer authority) ever been considered a sufficient reason for refusing to protect by injunction an individual whose rights are being persistently infringed.[166]

Thus the court was willing to grant an injunction against the Bankside power station in London. Similarly, in *Manchester Corporation* v *Farnworth* (1930), an injunction was granted closing one of Manchester's main power stations.

A contrasting view was adopted by the majority of the Court of Appeal in *Miller* v *Jackson* (1977). The action in *Miller* was brought by owners of a new house bordering a cricket field in County Durham seeking an injunction ordering the village cricket club not to conduct games without first taking adequate steps to prevent balls being struck out of the ground. Such an order would effectively have prevented cricket being played, since the club had already erected a 15-foot-high chain-link fence (they could not build a higher one because of the wind) and even that was insufficient to prevent half a dozen balls a season escaping onto the new estate.[167]

A majority of the Court of Appeal found that the club's activities amounted to a private nuisance, with Lord Denning MR dissenting. But when it came to considering the appropriate remedy Cumming-Bruce LJ joined Lord Denning MR to form a majority in favour of taking into account the interests of the public generally when deciding whether to grant an injunction. Cumming-Bruce LJ said,

> a court of equity must seek to strike a fair balance between the right of the claimants to have quiet enjoyment of their house and garden without exposure to cricket balls occasionally falling like thunderbolts from the heavens and the opportunity of the inhabitants of the village in which they live to continue to enjoy the manly sport which constitutes a summer recreation for adults and young persons, including one would hope and expect the [claimants'] son.[168]

Striking this balance, the injunction was refused. The trial judge had awarded £174.14 for past damages as well as granting an injunction. The Court of Appeal substituted an award of £400 to cover both past and future loss.

This decision understandably attracted criticism from those who shared the views expressed by Lindley LJ in *Shelfer*. When a similar point arose four years later, in *Kennaway* v *Thompson* (1981), the Court of Appeal returned to the orthodox view. In that case, the claimant owned a house next to a lake. A motor boat racing club frequently held races on the adjoining lake, and the noise disturbed the claimant's enjoyment of her house. She brought a claim against the club in private nuisance for an injunction and damages. The trial judge held that the races organised by the club on the lake were so frequent that they amounted to a nuisance but denied an injunction on the ground that it was in the public

---

[166] [1895] 1 Ch 287, 315–16.
[167] The club had offered to take other measures, such as putting a net over the Jacksons' garden, or fitting their windows with shutters and unbreakable glass, but those offers were rejected by the Jacksons on the ground that they were measures which would not prevent the nuisance in the garden but would merely limit the resulting damage.
[168] [1977] QB 966, 988.

interest for the club to be allowed to carry on with its activities. On appeal, the Court of Appeal reversed the trial judge and granted the claimant an injunction.

Lawton LJ said:

> We are of the opinion that there is nothing in *Miller* v *Jackson*, binding on us, which qualifies what was decided in *Shelfer*. Any decisions before *Shelfer's* case (and there were some at first instance . . .) which give support to the proposition that the public interest should prevail over the private interest must be read subject to *Shelfer's* case.[169]

The Court of Appeal therefore held that the trial judge should have granted an injunction restricting the noise made by the motor boat racing club. Importantly, however, the Court of Appeal in *Kennaway* stressed that any injunction should be carefully drafted to deal only with the nuisance, and should not outlaw the whole activity. The injunction which the court drafted recognised that while motor boat racing every weekend from March to November was a nuisance, a reasonable inhabitant of a lakeside house could be expected to tolerate some motor boat racing. The injunction thus allowed the club each year to have one three-day international event, two two-day national events and three one-day club events, with a further rule that no boat emitting more than 75 decibels was to be used at any event.

In the United States, the American Law Institute's Restatement 2d of Torts, §936(1) advocates an approach somewhere between those adopted in *Miller* and *Kennaway*. Thus the Institute recommends determining the appropriate remedy by taking into account a list of factors including the nature of the claimant's interest, the relative adequacy of damages and injunction, the relative hardship involved in granting or refusing an injunction and the effects on the interest of third parties and the public generally.

In England, however, it seems that in almost all cases since *Kennaway* the courts have reverted to applying *Shelfer*. For instance, in *Elliott* v *London Borough of Islington* (1991), a case involving private nuisance by encroaching tree roots, Lord Donaldson MR said,

> I would only be echoing the authorities, and in particular *Shelfer's* case, if I say that it is not the function of the courts to licence breaches of the rights of citizens. Compulsory purchase under statute is a well-known concept and is subject to well-known protections, but it is not for the courts to add to that burden on the citizen a system whereby, as in this case, they will grant, for a fee [ie damages in lieu of injunction] payable to the claimant, a compulsory lease of land to accommodate the roots of this tree in addition to putting up with the nuisance it creates.[170]

And again, in *Watson* v *Croft Promosport Ltd* (2009), a case involving the noise from a rural motor-racing circuit being used for events where members of the public could drive fast cars,[171] the Court of Appeal applied *Shelfer*. In this case, however, Sir Andrew Morritt held that 'in a marginal case where the damage to the claimant is minimal' it is legitimate, consistently with *Shelfer*, to take into account the effect on the public interest of awarding an injunction; but he also emphasised that the public interest could not negate the requirements under *Shelfer* that an injunction should only be refused 'in exceptional circumstances' *and* when it would be 'oppressive' to grant one.[172]

---

[169] [1981] QB 88, 93.
[170] [1991] 1 EGLR 167, 168.
[171] The claimants in the *Watson* case did not seek to prevent the circuit from holding car and motorcycle racing fixtures.
[172] [2009] 3 All ER 249, at [51].

While the modern cases suggest that damages will only rarely be awarded *in lieu* of a prohibitory injunction, and that invocation of the public interest will not *on its own* be sufficient to prevent an injunction being granted, *where* there is a risk that an injunction will harm the public interest it is common for the injunction to be *suspended* for a period sufficient to give the defendant time to make alternative arrangements.

(3) *Declarations and undertakings.* Damages in lieu are not the only alternative to awarding an injunction. In situations where there is no doubt that the defendant will voluntarily comply with the law as soon as it has been clarified the court may choose to make a declaration rather than granting an injunction. Similarly, the defendant may volunteer to give a formal undertaking that he will behave in a particular way rather than the court having to order him to do so.

(4) *Eliminating the need for an injunction.* One other situation where a court might refuse an injunction is where future damage can reasonably be eliminated by the defendant providing the victim of his tort with some form of protection. The best illustration of this is the unusual New Zealand case of *Bank of New Zealand* v *Greenwood* (1984). In that case, the defendant had built a shopping centre with a glass-roofed walkway. Unfortunately, the angle of the glass roof was such that it reflected the glare of the sun in the windows of the Bank of New Zealand, to the discomfort of staff and customers. The judge found that this amounted to a private nuisance, but that the defendant did not have to alter the roof, which would have cost the defendant $20,000. Instead, the defendant could provide 'venetian blinds' for the Bank.

The precise nature of this remedy is not easy to classify. Hardie Boys J insisted that he was not awarding damages in lieu of an injunction, but was merely pointing out a way in which the defendant could leave the claimant without a claim. It is probably best to treat the case as exemplifying a principle that an injunction can be refused when the defendant has offered to provide the victim of his tort with a reasonable way of eliminating future damage and the victim of his tort has refused this offer. This principle will only be applied, however, where it would be wholly unreasonable for the victim to reject the offer and insist on an injunction. In *Elliott* v *London Borough of Islington* (1991), the owners of a tree with encroaching roots offered to rebuild the claimant's wall on a pre-cast concrete bar raised above the ground, so that the roots could pass underneath it without causing any damage.[173] This solution, however, would not have eliminated the private nuisance by encroachment, but merely reduced its effects, and the Court of Appeal held that Elliott was still entitled to an injunction.

B. Damages

An injunction is the obvious remedy to seek in order to prevent a private nuisance from continuing into the future. But often a claimant will *also* want damages to compensate for past losses. The question of what measure of damages ought to be awarded to a claimant in a private nuisance case raises a number of difficult issues, such as what to do about claimants who use their property in ways which mean they are not inconvenienced by nuisances, unforeseeable losses, and consequential damage to personal property. We will

---

[173] Lord Donaldson MR described this as 'the arborial equivalent of a cat-flap' ([1991] 1 EGLR 167, 168).

deal with each of these in turn, but will start by dealing with simple cases of physical damage to property and loss of amenity.

(1) *Simple property damage cases.* In a simple case of private nuisance causing physical damage to the land itself, or to a building on the land, the most obvious measure of damages will be either (a) the cost of repair, or (b) the diminution in capital value of the land or building. Thus if *Blaster*'s private nuisance in relation to *Graham*, the owner-occupier of a neighbouring house, causes damage to the slates on *Graham*'s roof, then the obvious measure of damages will be the cost of replacing the slates.

(2) *Simple loss of amenity cases.* In a simple case of private nuisance causing a loss of amenity, that is, a loss of usefulness, the measure of damages will reflect the (a) the usefulness of the land, (b) the degree to which it was rendered less useful, and (c) the time for which it was rendered less useful.

For example, if *Graham* is again the owner-occupier of a house, *Hector* is the owner-occupier of an office-building, and *Ian* is the owner-occupier of a horse paddock, where he keeps his horse, and all three have to stop using their land for a year because of the emanation of clouds of poisonous dust from demolition work being carried out in a reckless manner by *Jerry* on the neighbouring land that he owns, then, assuming that each can demonstrate that *Jerry* has committed the tort of private nuisance in relation to him, *Graham* will obtain damages calculated on the basis of the loss of a year's use of a house, *Hector* will obtain damages calculated on the basis of the loss of a year's use of an office-building, and *Ian* will obtain damages calculated on the basis of the loss of a year's use of a horse paddock. In each case the obvious starting point for assessing an appropriate award of damages will be either (a) what it would have cost to rent a house like *Graham*'s, an office-building like *Hector*'s, and a horse paddock like *Ian*'s for a year, or (b) what each reasonably paid to rent replacement premises during the year.

Importantly, the basic measure of damages in a loss of amenity case is a reflection of the amenity value of the *land* and *not* of the distress felt by those occupying the land. We have already quoted Lord Hoffmann's statement, in *Hunter* v *Canary Wharf* (1997) to the effect that amenity value 'may be affected by the size, commodiousness and value of his property but cannot be increased merely because more people are in occupation and therefore suffer greater collective discomfort'.[174] At this stage it is appropriate also to quote longer passages from the reasoning of three of the Law Lords who heard this case:

> The effect of smoke from a neighbouring factory is to reduce the value of the land. There may be no diminution in the market value. But there will certainly be loss of amenity value so long as the nuisance lasts . . . the reduction in amenity value is the same whether the land is occupied by the family man or the bachelor.[175]

> In the case of nuisances 'productive of sensible personal discomfort,' the action is not for causing discomfort to the person but, as in the case of the first category, for causing injury to the land. True it is that the land has not suffered 'sensible' injury, but its utility has been diminished by the existence of the nuisance. It is for an unlawful threat to the utility of his land that the possessor or occupier is entitled to an injunction and it is for the diminution in such utility that he is entitled to compensation.
>
> I cannot therefore agree with Stephenson LJ in *Bone* v *Seale* [1975] 1 WLR 797, 803–804 when he said that damages in an action for nuisance caused by smells from a pig farm should be fixed

---

[174] [1997] AC 655, 706–7.
[175] [1997] AC 655, 696 (per Lord Lloyd).

by analogy with damages for loss of amenity in an action for personal injury. In that case it was said that 'efforts to prove diminution in the value of the property as a result of this persistent smell over the years failed.' . . . But diminution in capital value is not the only measure of loss. It seems to me that the value of a right to occupy a house which smells of pig must be less than the value of the occupation of an equivalent house which does not. In the case of a transitory nuisance, the capital value of the property will seldom be reduced. But the owner or occupier is entitled to compensation for the diminution in the amenity value of the property during the period for which the nuisance persisted. To some extent this involves placing a value upon intangibles. But estates agents do this all the time.[176]

The effect [of the nuisance] on [the claimants'] interest in land will . . . provide the measure of his damages, if reimbursement for the effects of the nuisance is what is being claimed . . . The cost of repairs or other remedial works is of course recoverable, if the [claimant] has [been] required to incur that expenditure. Diminution in the value of the [claimants'] interest, whether as owner or occupier, because the capital or letting value of the land has been affected is another relevant head of damages. When the nuisance has resulted only in loss of amenity, the measure of damages must in principle be the same. I do not see how an assessment of the damages appropriate for claims for personal injury . . . can be the right measure . . . At best it is no more than a guide to the true measure of liability, which is the extent to which the nuisance has impeded the comfortable enjoyment of the [claimant's] property.[177]

All three Law Lords make clear that loss of amenity value is something quantified by focusing on the loss of usefulness of the claimant's land, and not by focusing on the distress and suffering of the claimant. Thus, where *Florence* and *Flora* are owner-occupiers of identical, neighbouring terraced houses, and *Stinker* committed private nuisance in relation to each of them by regularly subjecting their houses equally to the strong smell of solvents from his paint-mixing business while he was waiting for a new odour-extraction system to be delivered, we would expect *Florence* and *Flora* to each be awarded the same amount by way of damages, and it would make no difference if *Florence* lives in her house on her own while *Flora* shares her house with her mother, her sister, and three children.

(3) *Claimants who do not suffer any interference.* A difficult question arises where a particular claimant uses her premises in such a way that she does not suffer any interference with her use and enjoyment of them. Consider the **Two Flats Problem**:

Constance lives in a house that has three floors, and that has been split into three flats, with one flat on each floor. *Constance* owns the top floor flat. *Drummer* owns the middle floor flat. *Flyer* owns the ground floor flat. *Drummer* acquires a drum kit, which he practises on incessantly, going on even until 4 am. *Constance* is very disturbed by *Drummer's* drumming – she cannot sleep, her work suffers, and she feels herself unable to invite anyone to visit her flat because conversation is frequently impossible because of the sound of *Drummer's* drumming. *Flyer* is not disturbed at all by the sound of *Drummer's* drumming because she never stays in her flat. Instead, she spends all her time at the university at which she teaches, teaching and writing and living in accommodation provided by the university. She has no inclination to visit her flat – she owns it purely for investment purposes – and no inclination to let it out to anyone else. In fact, she would not even be aware that *Drummer* is drumming all the time in his flat if it were not the fact that *Constance* complained to *Flyer* about it, and asked whether *Flyer* had any ideas what they could do about it.

---

[176] [1997] AC 655, 706 (per Lord Hoffmann).
[177] [1997] AC 655, 724–5 (per Lord Hope).

In this case, both *Constance* and *Flyer* appear to be the victims of a private nuisance for which *Drummer* is responsible. His drumming is unreasonably interfering with the amenity value of both *Constance*'s flat and *Flyer*'s flat; neither of their flats is currently very useful as a flat. As a result, there is no doubt that both *Constance* and *Flyer* could – either jointly or individually – obtain an injunction, requiring *Drummer* to moderate his drumming in future. But what could *Constance* and *Flyer* sue *Drummer* for by way of *damages*, for the nuisance he has created *in the past* through excessive drumming?

On the basis of the statement above – that loss of amenity value is something quantified by focusing on the loss of usefulness of a claimant's land, and not by focusing on the distress and suffering of the claimant – we might think that in Two Flats both *Constance and Flyer* will be entitled to sue *Drummer* for substantial damages. As we said: neither of their flats is currently very useful as a flat. Except – if we look more closely then it seems that *Flyer* is actually using her flat in such a way that *Drummer*'s behaviour is not reducing her ability to use and enjoy it *in this way* at all. *Should* we award *Flyer* substantial damages[178] in these circumstances?

We think that the answer is 'no': *Flyer* should *not* be awarded substantial damages.[179] But, this does not mean that damages for loss of amenity are *actually* for distress and suffering, and not for loss of usefulness of land; rather, it reflects the fact that a claimant can only recover damages for an interference with the usefulness of land if she was actually *using* the land in a way which was interfered with. Thus the conclusion that *Flyer* should receive no compensation for *past* loss is no more controversial that concluding that a person who has paved over their garden should receive no compensation from a defendant who is responsible for a private nuisance that would typically damage plants and shrubs.

For the sake of completeness we should consider what the outcome would be if we changed the facts of the Two Flats Problem, so that *Flyer* actually *did* commonly reside in her flat, but because of *Drummer*'s drumming she swiftly moved to another flat, which she inherited a few years ago and kept because she *anticipated* it might be useful if she ever had problems with her neighbours. In these circumstances we think that *Flyer* would be entitled to a substantial award of damages, similar to the award made to *Constance*. The fact that *Constance* has experienced the noise as disturbance and distress, while *Flyer* has only suffered the hassle of having to move to a different flat that she had available to her, does not mean that they should receive different amounts: both *Constance* and *Flyer* have suffered identical interferences with the usefulness of their flats.

(4) *Unforeseeable losses*. The rule on remoteness of damage that applies to negligence cases – that losses that are an unforeseeable consequence of a tort being committed will normally be too remote to be actionable – will also apply in private nuisance cases. Consider, for example, the **Chemical Vats Problem:**

---

[178] If we do not award substantial damages then it may be the case that we cannot award nominal damages instead: it seems that private nuisance is not a tort that is actionable *per se* unless the nuisance takes the form of an interference with the right to light, or some other right associated with the claimant's land. See *Nicholls v Ely Beet Sugar Factory Ltd (No 2)* [1936] 1 Ch 343, 348–9.

[179] This was also the view of Waller LJ in *Dobson v Thames Water Utilities Ltd* [2009] 3 All ER 319, [34].

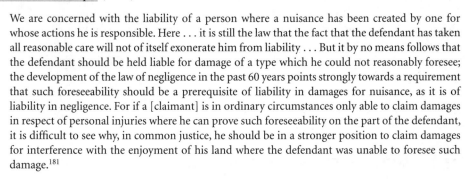

An experiment goes wrong in *Advance*'s laboratory and results in some acid smoke coming from *Advance*'s land and drifting across *Beatnik*'s land. It is perfectly foreseeable that the acid smoke would damage any trees or shrubs on *Beatnik*'s land, but there are no such things on *Beatnik*'s land. Instead – and unknown to *Advance* – *Beatnik* has some vats of chemicals on her land that are exposed to the open air. She uses these vats for dyeing clothes. The acid smoke reacts with the chemicals to cause an explosion which results in a twenty foot deep crater opening up on *Beatnik*'s land where the chemical vats used to be.

It seems very unlikely that *Beatnik* would be entitled to sue for the damage to her land here. The decision of the Privy Council in *The Wagon Mound (No 2)* (1967) purported to make foreseeability 'a necessary element in determining damages in . . . all cases of nuisance . . .'[180] and this position was endorsed by the House of Lords in *Cambridge Water Co v Eastern Counties Leather plc* (1994):

> We are concerned with the liability of a person where a nuisance has been created by one for whose actions he is responsible. Here . . . it is still the law that the fact that the defendant has taken all reasonable care will not of itself exonerate him from liability . . . But it by no means follows that the defendant should be held liable for damage of a type which he could not reasonably foresee; the development of the law of negligence in the past 60 years points strongly towards a requirement that such foreseeability should be a prerequisite of liability in damages for nuisance, as it is of liability in negligence. For if a [claimant] is in ordinary circumstances only able to claim damages in respect of personal injuries where he can prove such foreseeability on the part of the defendant, it is difficult to see why, in common justice, he should be in a stronger position to claim damages for interference with the enjoyment of his land where the defendant was unable to foresee such damage.[181]

(5) *Consequential damages (1): damage to personal property.* The ordinary rule in tort law is that a claimant who can establish that he has been the victim of a tort committed by a defendant can recover compensatory damages for any consequential losses resulting from the tort provided that they are not too remote and not the wrong kind of loss.[182] Thus if *Blaster* commits the tort of private nuisance in relation to *Hotelier* by using such powerful explosives to excavate that *Hotelier*'s hotel is regularly shaken, and most of the guests who had been staying there leave in protest, *Hotelier* is likely to be able to recover for the loss of profits associated with the early departure of the guests.

What is the position, however, if the consequential damage involves physical damage to *personal property*, as opposed to damage to the land itself, or buildings on the land? For example, what would be the position if *Blaster*'s activities cause vases to fall off shelves and mantelpieces in *Hotelier*'s hotel and smash on the floor? There are certainly some cases where claimants appear to have been awarded damages in a private nuisance claim for physical harm done to their personal property. For example, in *Halsey* v *Esso Petroleum* (1961) the claimant occupied a terraced house in Fulham and successfully brought a claim against the defendants, who operated a large oil distributing depot in the vicinity, for, among other things, the damage which acid smuts emanating from the defendants' chimney had done to his washing and the paintwork of his car.

In *Hunter* v *Canary Wharf* (1997), Lord Hoffmann said that if a claimant's land was flooded with water coming from the defendant's land, in addition to recovering damages

---

[180] [1967] AC 617, 640.
[181] [1994] 2 AC 264, 300 (per Lord Goff of Chieveley).
[182] See above, ch 10.

for the 'injury to his land' from the flooding, the claimant may be able to recover 'damages for consequential loss' such as 'damages for chattels or livestock lost as a result [of the flood].'[183] This suggests that damages for harm to property on land but not *attached* to the land can be recovered *provided that* the damage to the personal property is a consequence of the land itself being damaged or its amenity value being reduced. We think that this condition would be satisfied in the case of the vibrations from *Blaster*'s activities causing *Hotelier*'s vases to be smashed. But in any case where the condition is not satisfied, or the owner of the personal property does not have title to sue for private nuisance, then any claim for damage to personal property will have to be brought as a claim in *negligence*.

(6) *Consequential damages (2): personal injuries.* We noted above, when we discussed the Blinded Gardener Problem that the decision in *Hunter v Canary Wharf* (1997) made it clear that a claimant cannot sue in private nuisance for personal injuries that he or she suffers as a result of an emanation onto her land, or any other form of private nuisance.[184] Thus if *Tapster* committed private nuisance in relation to *Snorer* by creating a state of affairs that led to the flooding of *Snorer*'s basement flat, and *Snorer* only awoke after inhaling such a quantity of water that she had to be hospitalised, *Snorer* would be able to recover compensation for: (a) any physical damage caused to her flat by the flooding; (b) the loss of ability to use her flat while it was flooded; (c) any consequential damage to her personal property in the flat; but not for (d) her personal injury. To recover compensation for (d), *Snorer* would have to demonstrate that *Tapster* had committed some other tort in relation to her, such as the tort of *negligence*.

15.13 PECULIAR FORMS OF THE TORT

There are some other torts that are treated as forms of private nuisance though they do not fit within the definition of what committing the tort of private nuisance involves that was advanced at the start of this chapter. For example: the tort of organising a rival market within six and a half miles of a franchise or statutory market;[185] or the tort of organising a ferry service which rivals that of a person with a franchise right to operate a ferry. Such torts have often developed their own esoteric rules, such as that making the distance of six and a half miles significant, and consequently can claim to be treated as independent torts rather than forms of private nuisance. We think that it is likely, however, that a judge asked to resolve any uncertainty about the rules applying to these torts would draw strong analogies with the tort of private nuisance.

---

[183] [1997] AC 655, 706.

[184] [1997] AC 655, 696 (per Lord Lloyd), 707 (per Lord Hoffmann). In *Transco plc v Stockport Metropolitan Borough Council* [2004] 2 AC 1, a majority of the House of Lords held that damages for personal injuries could not be recovered under the rule in *Rylands v Fletcher* (discussed in Chapter 16, below) because this was the rule in private nuisance: see [9] (per Lord Bingham), [35] (per Lord Hoffmann), [52] (per Lord Hobhouse).

[185] *Tamworth BC v Fazeley Town Council* (1978) 77 LGR 238; *Sevenoaks DC v Vinson Ltd* [1984] Ch 211; *Stoke-on-Trent City Council v W & J Wass Ltd* [1988] 1 WLR 1406.

Further reading

Anyone eager to explore the law in more detail should start with **John Murphy, *The Law of Nuisance* (OUP, 2010)**.

The story behind the leading case of *St Helen's Smelting* v *Tipping* (1865) is revealed by **Brian Simpson** in **'Victorian judges and the problems of social cost: *Tipping* v *St Helen's Smelting Company* (1865)'**, chapter 7 in his book *Leading Cases in the Common Law* (Clarendon Press, 1995).

A classic, and highly influential, account of the proper scope of the tort of private nuisance can be found in **F.H. Newark, 'The boundaries of nuisance' (1949) 65 *Law Quarterly Review* 480**.

An interesting, and accessible, account of the law from an economic perspective is provided in **A.I. Ogus and G.M. Richardson, 'Economics and the environment: a study of private nuisance' (1977) 36 *Cambridge Law Journal* 284**.

Maria Lee has written several interesting and important articles about private nuisance, and we think **'What is private nuisance?' (2003) 119 *Law Quarterly Review* 298** and **'Safety, regulation and tort: fault in context' (2011) 74 *Modern Law Review* 555**, in particular, present significant arguments that are not adopted by our chapter.

Two important recent essays considering private nuisance from the perspective of rights-based accounts of the law can be found in **Donal Nolan and Andrew Robertson (eds), *Rights and Private Law* (Hart, 2011): chapter 16 by Donal Nolan, '"A tort against land": private nuisance as a property tort'** and **chapter 17 by Richard W. Wright, 'Private nuisance: a window on substantive justice'**.

16 The rule in *Rylands* v *Fletcher*

16.1 The basics *466*

16.2 Rationale *468*

16.3 Scope of liability *471*

16.4 Strict liability? *477*

16.5 Remedies *479*

16.6 Analogous liability rules *480*

Overview

Some judges and academics think that the topic of this chapter – the rule in *Rylands* v *Fletcher* (which – very roughly makes a landowner liable if he has brought a dangerous thing onto his land, or stored it on his land, in the course of using his land in a non-natural way, and the thing has escaped from his land and caused a reasonably foreseeable kind of damage) is an offshoot of the law on private nuisance. So it is appropriate for us to discuss this rule in the chapter immediately following our discussion of private nuisance. Section 16.2 discusses various views as to why this rule exists in English law, including the view that it is closely related to the tort of private nuisance. Section 16.3 sets out the requirements that have to be satisfied for someone to be held liable under this rule. Section 16.4 discusses the question of whether the rule can be fairly said to be one of *strict liability*. Section 16.5 outlines the remedies that a claimant can obtain under the rule, while section 16.6 tries to help the reader see the rule in *Rylands* v *Fletcher* in context by setting out some other liability rules that seem to work in the same way as the rule in *Rylands* v *Fletcher*.

16.1 THE BASICS

In the 1860s John Rylands was the leading textile manufacturer in England. He arranged for contractors to build a reservoir to provide water for the steam engines that powered the looms in one of his mills. The reservoir was built over old mine shafts which had been filled with earth, but one of these plugs of earth gave way and water escaped from the reservoir into the mine workings. It flowed through some abandoned mine workings and flooded a mine worked by Thomas Fletcher.

In the Court of Exchequer Martin B found that Rylands was not liable to compensate Fletcher for the flooding to his mine.[1] He stated that 'the making of a pond for holding water is a nuisance to no one'.[2] This must be correct: a pond does not *in itself* interfere unreasonably with the interests of neighbours. But Martin B went on to say that even when the water in a pond escaped the owner of the land on which it was built should not be liable, because 'To hold the defendants liable would . . . make them insurers against the consequences of a lawful act upon their own land when they had no reason to believe or suspect that any damage was likely to ensue.'[3] As it was not reasonably foreseeable that

---

[1] *Rylands* v *Fletcher* (1865) 3 H & C 774; 159 ER 737.
[2] (1865) 3 H & C 774, 792; 159 ER 737, 745.
[3] (1865) 3 H & C 774, 793; 159 ER 737, 745.

building a reservoir on Rylands' land would result in Fletcher suffering any harm, it could not be argued that Rylands owed Fletcher a duty not to build a reservoir on his land. So it was not possible to argue that Rylands committed any kind of wrong – let alone a tort – in building the reservoir on his land.

On appeal, however, the Court of Exchequer Chamber decided the case in favour of the claimant, Fletcher. Blackburn J said,

> We think the rule of law is, that the person who, for his own purposes, brings on his land and collects and keeps there anything likely to do mischief if it escapes, must keep it in at his peril; and if he does not do so, is *prima facie* answerable for all the damage which is the natural consequence of its escape. He can excuse himself by showing that the escape was owing to the claimant's default; or perhaps that the escape was the consequence of *vis major*, or the act of God.

He went on to explain the justice of this rule:

> It seems but reasonable and just that the neighbour who has brought something onto his own property (which was not naturally there), harmless to others so long as it is confined to his own property, but which he knows will be mischievous if it gets on his neighbour's, should be obliged to make good the damage which ensues if he does not succeed in confining it to his own property.[4]

In the House of Lords Lord Cairns LC quoted the rule and the explanation for it then stated, 'I must say I entirely concur.'[5] Lord Cranworth similarly supported Blackburn J's exposition of the law.[6] However, Lord Cairns LC suggested that the rule of liability formulated by Blackburn J would *only* apply to someone who had in the course of a *non-natural use* of his land brought onto or stored on his land something which was liable to do damage if it escaped.[7] This limit on the application of the rule in *Rylands* v *Fletcher* – as originally formulated by Blackburn J – has been followed ever since; though, as we will see, different views have been expressed as to what will count as a *non-natural use*.

Almost 150 years on, lawyers continue to debate the scope of the rule in *Rylands* v *Fletcher*. However, the decision of the House of Lords in *Transco plc* v *Stockport Metropolitan Borough Council* (2004)[8] seems to establish that the rule applies where A has brought onto, or kept on, some land an *exceptionally dangerous or mischievous thing in extraordinary or unusual circumstances*. Let's call such a thing 'T' and the land which the thing was brought onto, or kept on, 'Blackacre'. The rule in *Rylands* v *Fletcher* – as interpreted by the House of Lords in *Transco* – says that if:

(1) T *escapes* from Blackacre and
(2) T consequently *damages B's land*[9] and
(3) the kind of damage that T causes is a kind that was a reasonably foreseeable consequence of such an escape, then

---

[4] (1866) LR 1 Ex 265, 279–80.
[5] (1868) LR 3 HL 330, 340.
[6] Three Law Lords heard the appeal in *Rylands* v *Fletcher* but there is some mystery as to who the third Law Lord was. See, generally, Heuston 1970.
[7] (1868) LR 3 HL 330, 339.
[8] Noted, Bagshaw 2004b. We will refer to this case (reported at [2004] 2 AC 1) hereafter as '*Transco*'.
[9] When we use the phrase 'B's land' in this context we intend the word 'land' to include not just the earth itself but also things attached to it, such as buildings, which count as real property. The statement that the land must be 'B's' is shorthand for the fact that in order to claim B must have a particular relationship with the land. The precise nature of that necessary relationship is discussed below, § 16.3(B). At this stage, an adequate summary is that the land will count as 'B's land' if B has a legally-recognised interest in the land, and in certain circumstances it may be sufficient that B has exclusive possession of the land.

(4) B will be entitled to sue A for compensation for that damage unless

(5) A can raise a *defence* to B's claim.[10]

Importantly, in order to sue A for compensation under the rule in *Rylands* v *Fletcher*, B will *not* have to prove that A was at fault for the fact that T escaped from Blackacre.

16.2 RATIONALE

Lord Hoffmann has observed that 'it is tempting to see, beneath the surface of the rule, a policy of requiring the costs of a commercial enterprise to be internalised; to require the entrepreneur to provide, by insurance or otherwise, for the risks to others which his enterprise creates.'[11] But in most contexts English law has rejected this policy and has insisted that entrepreneurs (and others) should only be liable for damage caused by their *wrongs*.

Can it be said that liability under the rule in *Rylands* v *Fletcher* involves some sort of *wrong*? On this, Carleton Kemp Allen has observed, it is very hard to see how a defendant who has (without fault on his part) failed to ensure that a dangerous thing on his land stays on his land has done anything wrong to a claimant whose land has been damaged by that escape:

> It is often said that in respect of peculiarly dangerous things, there is a 'duty' irrespective of negligence or wilful aggression, to 'insure' neighbours and others against damage. This use of the term 'duty' is unfortunate . . . There is of course a duty of careful management of any material thing, whether it belong to the family of '*Rylands* v *Fletcher* objects' or not; but it is difficult to see that there is any 'duty' to prevent a dangerous thing escaping through causes which have nothing to do with the maintainer's fault . . . The true situation seems to be that he who maintains for his own advantage a peculiarly dangerous thing in proximity to others, necessarily imposes upon those others a risk of injury . . . greater than is to be reasonably expected in the ordinary circumstances of social life, and it is therefore just and expedient that he himself should bear the risk of making good any damage to others which results from the maintenance of the object. This is certainly a liability; but it is a confusion of ideas to [say that it arises out of the breach of] a duty.[12]

Thus, a defendant's liability under the rule in *Rylands* v *Fletcher* is not based on any sense that the defendant committed a wrong: quoting Lord Hoffmann again, 'with hindsight, *Rylands* v *Fletcher* can be seen as an isolated victory for the internalisers. The following century saw a steady refusal to treat it as laying down any broad principle of liability.'[13]

Given that this was an *isolated* victory, and the policy beneath the rule has been rejected in most contexts,[14] we might ask why the House of Lords has resisted calls to abolish the rule. One explanation is simply that to overturn a case which has been part of English law for so long is 'too radical a step' for judges to take.[15] A second explanation, however, is that

---

[10] This statement of the rule is based on the formulation of Lord Bingham in *Transco*, at [11].

[11] *Transco*, at [29].

[12] Allen 1931, 193–4. See also Holmes 1873, 653; Wright 1961, 86; Restatement Torts 2d (1965) §4 Comment b; Cane 1998, 165; Waddams 1998, 124–5.

[13] *Transco*, at [29]. Oliphant 2005 suggests (at 118) that although the facts of *Rylands* v *Fletcher* provided an ideal testing ground for a fledgling theory of enterprise liability, an examination of the judgments gives 'no reason to believe that ideas of loss-distribution, deterrence, etc, were in the minds of the judges who participated in the decision'.

[14] For example, if B brings a peculiarly dangerous thing onto his land, and, without any fault on his part, the thing escapes from his control and injures A, who is a lawful visitor to B's land, then B is not liable to A: the cost of A's injuries are not 'internalised' to B's business: *Read* v *J Lyons & Co Ltd* [1947] AC 156.

[15] *Transco*, at [43] (per Lord Hoffmann).

the fairness of liability without the need to prove fault where a defendant has created an extraordinary risk still appeals to some judges.[16]

The combination of the refusal to abolish the rule in *Rylands* v *Fletcher* with the 'refusal to treat it as laying down any broad principle of liability' has led to the rule being restricted within narrow limits. These limits, however, have proved difficult to define with any precision. The High Court of Australia castigated them as so uncertain that 'the practical application of the rule in a case involving damage caused by the escape of a substance is likely to degenerate into an essentially unprincipled and *ad hoc* subjective determination'.[17] One of the principal aims of the speeches in the House of Lords in *Transco* was to 'restate [the rule] so as to achieve as much certainty and clarity as attainable'.[18]

The House of Lords sought in *Transco* to achieve such certainty and clarity by seeing the rule in *Rylands* v *Fletcher* as 'a sub-species of nuisance',[19] 'an aspect of the law of private nuisance'[20] or 'a species, or special case, of nuisance'.[21] In seeing the rule in *Rylands* v *Fletcher* in this way, the House of Lords in *Transco* was following in the footsteps of Lord Macmillan in *Read* v *J Lyons & Co Ltd* (1947), who took the view that *Rylands* was part of the law concerning 'the mutual duties of adjoining or neighbouring landowners'[22] and Lord Goff in *Cambridge Water Co* v *Eastern Counties Leather plc* (1994), who regarded the rule in *Rylands* v *Fletcher* as having an 'historical connection with the law on nuisance' and stated that 'the rule in *Rylands* v *Fletcher* was essentially concerned with an extension of the law of nuisance to cases of isolated escape.'[23] In reaching this conclusion, Lord Goff was heavily influenced by Professor F H Newark's article, 'The Boundaries of Nuisance', in which Newark argued that:

> those who decided [*Rylands* v *Fletcher*] were quite unconscious of any revolutionary or reactionary principles implicit in the decision. They thought of it as calling for no more than a restatement of settled principles, and Lord Cairns went so far as to describe those principles as 'extremely simple'. And in fact the main principle involved was extremely simple, being no more than the principle that negligence is not an element in the tort of nuisance.[24]

If it is correct to say that the rule in *Rylands* v *Fletcher* is part of the law on private nuisance, then such a classification will determine who can be liable, who can claim, and what types of damage can be claimed for under the rule: the answers to these questions will be the same as the answers which have been established in the tort of private nuisance.[25] The association with private nuisance might also explain why a *Rylands*-type defendant is held liable under the rule in *Rylands* v *Fletcher*: he is held liable because he has unreasonably interfered with the use and enjoyment of land in which the claimant has a sufficient interest. Unfortunately, we think that this classification is misguided,[26] and for three reasons:

---

[16] For instance, *Transco*, at [6] (per Lord Bingham) and [110] (per Lord Walker). Nolan 2005 (at 449) remains unconvinced: '[T]he best way forward appears to be abolition.'

[17] *Burnie Port Authority* v *General Jones Pty Ltd* (1994) 179 CLR 520, 540 (per Mason CJ, Deane, Dawson, Toohey and Gaudron JJ).

[18] *Transco*, at [8] (per Lord Bingham).

[19] *Transco*, at [9] (per Lord Bingham).

[20] *Transco*, at [52] (per Lord Hobhouse).

[21] *Transco*, at [92] (per Lord Walker).

[22] *Read* v *J Lyons & Co Ltd* [1947] AC 156, 173 (per Lord Macmillan).

[23] [1994] 2 AC 264, 304.

[24] Newark 1949, 487.

[25] In the previous chapter we explained how the House of Lords in *Hunter* v *Canary Wharf* (1997) provided clear, if controversial, answers to the questions who could bring a claim for private nuisance and what kinds of damage they could claim compensation for: see above, §§ 15.11–15.12.

[26] We are not alone in believing this classification to have been misguided. See Murphy 2004 and Nolan 2005.

(1) Private nuisance is a tort. In contrast, liability under the rule in *Rylands* v *Fletcher* does not arise in response to someone's committing a tort: a defendant does not have to commit any kind of legal *wrong* in order to be held liable under the rule in *Rylands* v *Fletcher*.

(2) The original rationale behind *Rylands* – internalisation of costs to commercial enterprises – provides no justification for distinguishing between costs from damage to neighbouring land and costs from other types of damage, for instance personal injuries. Instead this rationale suggests that the rule has more in common with the other liability rules discussed at the end of this chapter, most of which cover types of damage beyond damage to neighbouring land.

(3) The reasons provided by the House of Lords in *Transco* for preserving the rule in *Rylands* v *Fletcher* provide no justification for limiting its operation to compensating for damage to land. For example, Lord Bingham observed in *Transco* that 'there is . . . a category of case, however small it might be, in which it seems just to impose liability even in the absence of fault' going on to cite the 'tragedy at Aberfan' as one such case.[27] In Aberfan, in 1966, a huge heap of waste and debris from a nearby colliery slid down a hill and buried a school at the bottom of the hill in mud and rubble, killing 116 children and 28 adults. The implication of classifying the rule in *Rylands* v *Fletcher* as a sub-species of private nuisance is that the owners of the school would be able to sue the owners of the slag heap for compensation for the damage to the school buildings on a strict liability basis, while the families of the deceased would have to prove that the owners of the slag heap were at fault for its falling on the school. It is hard to see that anyone would regard this as 'just'.

Are there other possible justifications for preserving the rule in *Rylands* v *Fletcher*? One possibility is that although liability under the rule does not depend on *proof* of fault, most of the defendants who are held liable by it were *at fault*, so the rule in *Rylands* is justified because it prevents defendants who have wrongfully caused significant disasters from avoiding liability because of the difficulties of proving their fault. This sort of reasoning seems to be behind Lord Walker's observation in *Transco* that the rule in *Rylands* v *Fletcher* can play a useful role in cases such as the *Transco* case given the practical difficulties sometimes involved in 'bringing a claim in negligence, perhaps against a powerful corporate opponent.'[28] But clearly this rationale can only stand if it is true that: (a) most of the defendants who have been held liable under the rule in *Rylands* v *Fletcher* were at fault, and (b) without the rule in *Rylands* v *Fletcher* a significant number of them would have escaped liability because of the difficulties of proving their fault. We do not know of any statistics that establish whether these two propositions are true. Moreover, this rationale is wholly inconsistent with the classification of the rule in *Rylands* v *Fletcher* as an aspect of the law on private nuisance. The effect of this classification is that people who suffer physical injuries as a result of an escape of a dangerous thing from a defendant's land are forced to prove negligence against that defendant, and only those claimants whose *land* is damaged avoid the burden of having to prove fault. If we were concerned about the 'practical implications . . . of [being forced to bring] a claim in negligence'[29] then why would we single out cases of damage to *land* (where the person who is really funding the claim may well be the claimant's property insurer).

---

[27] *Transco*, at [6].
[28] *Transco*, at [110].
[29] ibid.

Unfortunately, it seems that the error involved in classifying the rule in *Rylands* v *Fletcher* as part of the law on private nuisance is too firmly woven into the speeches of a majority of their Lordships in *Transco* for any court below the Supreme Court to ignore it. Consequently in the next section we will assume that this erroneous classification is an unshakeable element of the current law on the scope of liability under the rule in *Rylands* v *Fletcher*.

16.3 SCOPE OF LIABILITY

There are a number of issues that need to be dealt with under this heading:

A. Who can be held liable under the rule?

The proposition that *Rylands* is part of the law concerning 'the mutual duties of adjoining or neighbouring landowners'[30] might be taken to mean that only *an owner* of land from which a dangerous thing escapes can be held liable. Weighing against this suggestion, however, are several cases where defendants who neither owned the land, nor were tenants of it, were held liable.[31] These cases suggest that liability can attach to any *occupier* of land from which the dangerous thing escaped.[32] Some *dicta* seem to go further and suggest that the person responsible for storing or collecting the mischievous substance can be liable regardless of his relation to the land.[33] Our view, consistent with our view as to who can be liable in private nuisance,[34] is that it is these *dicta* which correctly express the law.

B. Who can claim under the rule?

The conclusion that liability under *Rylands* arises out of the law on private nuisance means that the question of who can claim under the rule should be answered in line with the way that the House of Lords answered the question who can sue in private nuisance in *Hunter* v *Canary Wharf Ltd* (1997).[35] Thus to sue under *Rylands*[36] a claimant must have a legally-recognised interest in the land[37] or must be in exclusive possession of the land,[38] and

---

[30] *Read* v *J Lyons & Co Ltd* [1947] AC 156, 173 (per Lord Macmillan).

[31] *Eastern & South African Telegraph Co* v *Cape Town Tramways Co* [1902] AC 381; *West* v *Bristol Tramways Co* [1908] 2 KB 14; *Charing Cross Electricity Supply Co* v *Hydraulic Power Co* [1914] 3 KB 772; *Rainham Chemical Works Ltd* v *Belvedere Fish Guano Co Ltd* [1921] 2 AC 465; *Shiffman* v *Order of St John* [1936] 1 All ER 557.

[32] In *Transco*, at [11], Lord Bingham's restatement uses the phrase 'occupier of land' to refer to the potential defendant.

[33] In *Rainham Chemical Works* v *Belvedere Fish Guano Co Ltd* [1921] 2 AC 465, Lord Sumner said (at 479) 'they cannot escape any liability which otherwise attaches to them on *storing it* [explosives] there merely because they have no tenancy or independent occupation' (emphasis added). In *Powell* v *Fall* (1880) 5 QBD 597 the escape was from the highway.

[34] See above, § 15.9.

[35] Discussed above, § 15.11.

[36] This would have caused problems for the claimant in *Eastern & South African Telegraph Co* v *Cape Town Tramways Co* [1902] AC 381 because it was claiming for damage done to its submarine cable.

[37] Such as a fee simple in possession, a tenancy, or a reversionary interest. A more detailed presentation of what interests in land the law recognises is to be found in the chapter on the tort of private nuisance, above, § 15.11.

[38] Exclusive possession will be sufficient *unless* the defendant has the right to possess the land, or acted with the authority of the person with the right to possess. But exclusive possession is not necessary because, for instance, a reversioner may be able to sue. Unfortunately, in *Transco*, [9] and [11], Lord Bingham seems to have over-simplified when he stated that the claimant only had to be an 'occupier' of the land.

such a claimant can only sue for physical harm caused to the land, harm to its amenity value and consequential damage to chattels, not for personal injuries.[39]

A claimant cannot therefore rely on *Rylands* to recover compensation for pure economic losses that he has suffered as a result of a dangerous thing's escaping onto a third party's land. In *Cattle* v *Stockton Waterworks Co* (1875), Blackburn J was clear that in the *Rylands* case a claim could not have been made 'by every workman and person employed in the mine, who in consequence of its stoppage made less wages than he would otherwise have done'.[40] This should not be taken to mean, however, that *all* economic losses are irrecoverable under the rule in *Rylands* v *Fletcher*. Compensation for any diminution in the amenity value of land and compensation for economic losses *consequential on* physical damage to the claimant's land may be recovered under the rule in *Rylands* v *Fletcher*.[41]

C. An exceptionally dangerous or mischievous thing

Blackburn J spoke of the rule in *Rylands* v *Fletcher* as covering 'anything likely to do mischief if it escapes'. For a time, however, courts seemed to insist that this meant that the rule only extended to things which were 'inherently dangerous'. Thus in *Hale* v *Jennings Bros* (1938), the Court of Appeal discussed whether a fairground 'chair-o-plane' was inherently dangerous, and concluded that it was because it was intended for use by 'ignorant people' who would be unaware of the dangers of fooling about in flying chairs.

It is difficult to disagree, however, with Professor Stallybrass who exhaustively examined the cases and concluded that a condition of 'inherent dangerousness' was unhelpful because 'just as there is nothing which is at all times and in all circumstances dangerous so it seems that there is scarcely anything which is in all circumstances safe.'[42]

In *Transco*, Lord Bingham reasserted the importance of the 'dangerousness' condition. He said that:

> It must be shown that the defendant has done something which he recognised, or judged by the standards appropriate at the relevant place and time, he ought reasonably to have recognised, as giving rise to an exceptionally high risk of danger or mischief if there should be an escape, however unlikely an escape may have been thought to be.[43]

Moreover, he stated that he did not think that 'the mischief or danger test should be at all easily satisfied'.[44] However, while Lords Hoffmann and Walker agreed with Lord Bingham that 'creation of an exceptional risk' was a relevant factor in the application of the rule, they both treated the matter as more relevant to the requirement of 'an extraordinary use of land'.[45]

D. Extraordinary use

The rule in *Rylands* v *Fletcher* as originally formulated by Blackburn J applied only to cases where someone brought onto land or kept on land something 'which was not naturally

---

[39] A majority in *Transco* expressly states that claims cannot be brought for personal injuries under the rule in *Rylands* v *Fletcher*: see [9] (Lord Bingham), [35] (Lord Hoffmann), and [52] (Lord Hobhouse).

[40] (1875) LR 10 QB 453, 457.

[41] The claimants' claim in *Cambridge Water Co* v *Eastern Counties Leather* [1994] 2 AC 264 (discussed below) was a claim to be compensated for economic loss suffered by them as a result of their land suffering some kind of physical damage.

[42] Stallybrass 1929, 387.

[43] *Transco*, at [10].

[44] ibid.

[45] *Transco*, at [49] (per Lord Hoffmann), [103] (per Lord Walker).

there'. As we have seen, in the House of Lords, Lord Cairns LC built on this statement and drew a distinction between defendants who use their land 'for any purpose for which it might in the ordinary course of the enjoyment of land be used ... what I may term the natural user of land' and those who 'not stopping at the natural use of their close, had desired to use it for any purpose which I may term a non-natural use'.[46] So Lord Cairns LC seemed to think: (i) that liability under the rule in *Rylands* v *Fletcher* was limited to cases where someone used his land in a 'non-natural' way; *and* (ii) that someone would use his land in a 'non-natural' way if he used it in an *extraordinary* way.

The early cases do not provide any clear answer as to the original meaning of 'non-natural user'. Since the House of Lords upheld the decision in favour of Fletcher their Lordships must have concluded that a reservoir was a sufficiently non-natural use of land. Moreover, the reasoning in Blackburn J's judgment suggested that the rule would also cover straying cattle and an escape of sewage.[47] Other early cases treated the rule as covering poisonous yew trees,[48] creosote,[49] and large quantities of electricity.[50] In *Wilson* v *Waddell* (1876), however, Lord Blackburn (as he had by then become) stated that use of land for ordinary mining operations was a natural use.

In *Rickards* v *Lothian* (1919) the Privy Council held that an escape of water from ordinary plumbing[51] did not fall within the scope of the rule in *Rylands* v *Fletcher*. Lord Moulton said:

> It is not every use to which land is put that brings into play that [rule]. It must be some special use bringing with it increased danger to others, and must not merely be the ordinary use of land or such a use as is proper for the general benefit of the community.[52]

The last portion of this statement – 'not merely ... such a use as is proper for the general benefit of the community' – can be interpreted to suggest that only *improper* uses of land should fall within the scope of the rule in *Rylands* v *Fletcher*. By adopting such an interpretation those who disliked the rule in *Rylands* v *Fletcher* could severely restrict its scope. Thus in *Read* v *J Lyons & Co* (1947), two members of the House of Lords suggested that use of land for a munitions factory in wartime might not be a 'non-natural user',[53] and in *Cambridge Water* v *Eastern Counties Leather* (1994), the trial judge held that the use of chemical solvents by a tannery in an industrial village was not a non-natural user given the benefits for local employment.

---

[46] (1868) LR 3 HL 330, 339.

[47] In *Smeaton* v *Ilford Corp* [1954] Ch 450, Upjohn J stated that 'To collect into a sewer a large volume of sewage, inherently noxious and dangerous and bound to cause great damage if not properly contained, cannot be described, in my judgment, as a natural use of land' (ibid, 472).

[48] *Crowhurst* v *Amersham Burial Board* (1878) 4 CPD 5. The rule does not, apparently, cover thistles which are 'the natural growth of the soil': *Giles* v *Walker* (1890) 24 QBD 656, 657.

[49] *West* v *Bristol Tramways Co* [1908] 2 KB 14.

[50] *Eastern & South African Telegraph Co* v *Cape Town Tramways Co* [1902] AC 381.

[51] The line is not easy to draw between ordinary and extraordinary plumbing but it seems to lie somewhere between *Western Engraving Co* v *Film Laboratories Ltd* [1936] 1 All ER 106, where the Court of Appeal held that the use of large quantities of water for film-washing was a non-natural user, and *Peters* v *Prince of Wales Theatre* [1943] KB 73 where a differently constituted Court of Appeal suggested that connection of water to a sprinkler system in a theatre was an ordinary and usual user. In *Transco* [2004] 2 AC 1 a water pipe carrying sufficient water for 66 flats was treated as 'entirely normal and routine' (at [13]) and thus not an 'extraordinary use', though Lord Bingham complicated the matter somewhat by stating that in his opinion the volume of water in a domestic plumbing system was also insufficient to amount to a sufficiently dangerous thing (at [10]).

[52] [1913] AC 263, 280.

[53] In the earlier case of *Rainham Chemical Works* v *Belvedere Fish Guano Co Ltd* [1921] 2 AC 465, the House of Lords had shown no hesitation in finding that making munitions during the First World War was 'certainly not the common and ordinary use of the land': ibid, 471 (per Lord Buckmaster).

Shortly before the judgment of the House of Lords in *Cambridge Water* we could have described the meaning of 'non-natural user' as having shifted from 'not naturally there' to 'improper', via 'extraordinary'. But in his judgment in that case Lord Goff spoke against any broad reading of Lord Moulton's phrase. Four points made by Lord Goff in this part of his judgment are worth particular attention.

First, he made clear that in his opinion 'the storage of substantial quantities of chemicals on industrial premises should be regarded as an almost classic case of non-natural use'.[54] Secondly, he stated that the creation of employment could not be sufficient of itself to establish that a particular use of land was 'natural or ordinary'.[55] Thirdly, he suggested that because in the same case the House of Lords was deciding that there could be no liability under the rule in *Rylands* v *Fletcher* for unforeseeable consequences of escapes, it would be less necessary *in future* to interpret the phrase 'non-natural user' narrowly in order to limit the scope of liability.[56] Fourthly, he thought that the historic relationship between the rule in *Rylands* v *Fletcher* and the tort of private nuisance meant that in future the concept of 'non-natural user' might develop alongside the concept of 'reasonable user' in private nuisance.[57] The fourth point is particularly important because it suggests that the main activities which should be excluded from the scope of 'non-natural user' are those which create risks which are generally accepted as part of ordinary social give-and-take.

In *Transco*, Lord Bingham confirmed that a defendant's use of land does not have to be 'unreasonable' or 'improper' in order to fall within the scope of the rule:

> I think it is clear that ordinary user is a preferable test to natural user, making it clear that the rule in *Rylands* v *Fletcher* is engaged only where the defendant's use is shown to be extraordinary and unusual. This is not a test to be inflexibly applied: a use may be extraordinary and unusual at one time or in one place but not so at another time or in another place . . . I also doubt whether a test of reasonable user is helpful, since a user may well be quite out of the ordinary but not unreasonable, as was that of *Rylands*, *Rainham Chemical Works* or the tannery in *Cambridge Water*. Again, as it seems to me, the question is whether the defendant has done something out of the ordinary in the place and at the time when he does it. In answering that question, I respectfully think that little help is gained (and unnecessary confusion perhaps caused) by considering whether the use is proper for the general benefit of the community.[58]

While Lord Bingham cast doubt on the utility of tests which asked whether particular uses were unreasonable or improper he offered little guidance on how to draw the line between the ordinary and extraordinary. Indeed Lord Hoffmann seemed to regard a test based around 'ordinary uses of land' as 'rather vague'.[59] He offered 'a use creating an increased risk' as the 'converse' of 'natural use',[60] stated that 'the criterion of exceptional risk must be taken seriously',[61] and, contentiously, asserted that a 'useful guide in deciding whether the risk has been created by a "non-natural" user of land is . . . to ask whether the damage which eventuated was something against which the [claimant] occupier could reasonably be expected to have insured himself'.[62]

---

[54] [1994] 2 AC 264, 309.
[55] ibid.
[56] ibid.
[57] [1994] 2 AC 264, 299.
[58] *Transco*, at [11]. Lord Scott agreed with Lord Bingham's judgment. Lord Walker expressly commended Lord Bingham's discussion of this requirement, but also commended the different approach of Lord Hoffmann!
[59] *Transco*, at [37].
[60] *Transco*, at [44].
[61] *Transco*, at [49].
[62] *Transco*, at [46].

An approach which distinguishes between ordinary and extraordinary uses of land in terms of the degree of risk posed to neighbours in the event of an escape seems as easy to apply and attractive as any. Thus we think that Akenhead J was correct, in *Harooni* v *Rustins* (2011), to distinguish between occupiers who might have a small amount of some highly inflammable substance on their property, like a tankful of petrol or a bottle of turpentine, and those who have a wholly unusual amount, like the paint warehouse in the case he was considering.[63] But we cannot offer any support for Lord Hoffmann's extraordinary proposition about insurability. It seems to us that insurability of the claimant's property is *irrelevant* to the correct classification of the defendant's activity. When a property owner insures a terraced house against destruction such insurance generally does not distinguish between a car swerving into the front wall or the local fireworks factory exploding, but that surely cannot make the local fireworks factory into an ordinary use of land in the locality?

Furthermore, in many situations, as Lord Hoffmann noted,[64] *both* the person responsible for the activity *and* the neighbouring property owners will be insured. In such circumstances it is doubtful whether leaving losses with the property owners will be economically efficient.[65] Moreover, as Lord Hobhouse pointed out, the issue is not solely about efficiency but also about whether it is fair to make potential claimants pay the insurance premiums which cover the risk of damage as a result of such incidents. Lord Hoffmann's argument that most property losses should be dealt with by self-insurance rather than by claims against those responsible for the activity looks remarkably like an argument *against* internalisation of costs to the activity, and thus an argument against the existence of *Rylands* v *Fletcher* liability, rather than a criterion for determining *when* costs should be internalised.

It is worth briefly making two further points about the 'extraordinary use' requirement. First, where statute has authorised a particular use of land that use will be considered as 'natural and ordinary' unless there has been negligence.[66] Secondly, Blackburn J's original formulation of the rule stated that the collection of the dangerous thing had to be 'for his own purposes'. A court would be unlikely to use this phrase to protect a defendant whose activity was intended to benefit the public generally, but might use it to protect a defendant whose activity was intended to benefit both himself and the claimant. In such circumstances, however, there is often an overlap with the defence of consent.

---

[63] [2011] EWHC 1632 (TCC), at [66]–[68]. In this case the defendant was storing 200,000 litres of flammable products, including 25,000 litres of highly flammable products, and Akenhead J considered that this was a non-natural use. The defendant was, however, not liable since these products had not caused the burning down of the claimant's warehouse.

[64] *Transco*, at [39].

[65] Leaving the potential claimant to bear the loss might be efficient if *either*: (a) the claimant was better placed to avoid the harm caused by an escape than the defendant to prevent the escape; *or* (b) the claimant was better placed to evaluate and insure against the risk of his suffering loss as a result of an escape from the defendant's land and *only* he carried insurance to guard against that loss. Neither of these conditions is likely to be satisfied. One might think that by leaving the loss with the potential claimant at least the legal costs of determining whether the defendant is liable will be saved. But because a *negligence* claim can certainly be brought when a careless escape has caused personal injury or damage to personal property, and probably *can* be brought if a careless escape has caused damage to land, the costs saved by preventing claims under the rule in *Rylands* v *Fletcher* where land has been damaged by an escape will be small. To spell the point out, the costs saved in not pursuing a claim under the rule in *Rylands* v *Fletcher* will often be spent instead determining whether there is a good claim in negligence.

[66] *Transco*, at [89] (per Lord Scott). Lord Hoffmann, at [30]–[31], agreed that statutory authority for a particular use of land would prevent liability being imposed under the rule in *Rylands* v *Fletcher*, but did not state that this was because the statutory authority would make the use into a 'natural' one.

E. Escape

In *Read* v *J Lyons & Co* (1947), the claimant was an inspector at a munitions factory who was injured by an exploding shell. The House of Lords held that the rule in *Rylands* v *Fletcher* did not apply in these circumstances because the explosive had not escaped from the defendant's premises, but merely from its control. An escape from the defendant's land was treated as logically necessary because, in the words of Lord Macmillan, 'the doctrine of *Rylands* v *Fletcher*, as I understand it, derives from a conception of mutual duties of adjoining or neighbouring landowners, and its cogenors are trespass and [private] nuisance'.[67] A requirement of an escape from the defendant's premises ensures that the *Rylands* rule does not become entangled with the rules concerning the liability of an occupier to his or her visitors.

Transco involved an escape of water from one part of the defendant's premises to another part of the premises where it threatened to damage a gas pipe which the claimant had a right to run across the defendant's premises. Lord Scott was adamant that even if the claimant's right to run the pipeline across the defendant's land was a proprietary right, an easement, the claimant still could not sue the defendant because there had been no escape from the defendant's land.[68]

F. Reasonable foreseeability

Suppose A brought a dangerous thing, T, onto his land in the course of an extraordinary use of his land and T then escaped off A's land with the result that B suffered some kind of damage to his land. In *Rylands* v *Fletcher*, Blackburn J seemed to be of the opinion that B would be entitled to sue A for compensation for the harm suffered by her so long as her suffering that harm was a 'natural' consequence of T's escaping from A's land.[69] However, the House of Lords made it clear in *Cambridge Water Co* v *Eastern Counties Leather* (1994) that, in the case we are considering, B will *only* be entitled to sue A under the rule in *Rylands* v *Fletcher* for compensation for the harm that she suffered as a result of T's escaping from A's land if it was *reasonably foreseeable* that someone like B would suffer *that kind of harm* if T escaped from A's land.

The facts of the *Cambridge Water* case illustrate the point. The defendants ran a tanning business that used large quantities of chemicals. Some of these chemicals got spilled from time to time on the defendants' factory floor and they seeped through the factory floor and into the ground beneath the defendants' factory. The chemicals then flowed along impermeable strata until they reached a borehole owned by the claimants which was located over a mile away from the defendants' factory. The claimants used this borehole to obtain water which they would then supply to nearby residents. The chemicals from the defendants' factory contaminated this borehole with the result that the claimants were forbidden to extract any more water from the borehole.[70] The claimants sued the defendants under the rule in *Rylands* v *Fletcher* for compensation for the costs incurred by

---

[67] [1947] AC 156, 173.
[68] *Transco*, at [78]–[80].
[69] (1866) LR 1 Ex 265, 279–80.
[70] The water may have been drinkable despite the contamination, but it fell foul of legislation that had been introduced pursuant to an EC Directive, banning the supply of water which contained even the slightest traces of the kind of chemicals that had contaminated the claimants' borehole.

them in creating a new borehole.[71] The House of Lords dismissed this claim on the ground that no one could have foreseen that the claimants' borehole would be contaminated if the chemicals that the defendants used escaped from their land.

It should be noted that in the case we are considering, B will not have to show that it was reasonably foreseeable that T *would escape* from A's land in order to bring a claim under the rule in *Rylands* v *Fletcher*. All B will have to show is that it was reasonably foreseeable that *if* T escaped, someone like her would suffer the kind of harm for which she wants compensation. So suppose that A kept some chemicals on his land. Suppose further that A used elaborate precautions to ensure that the chemicals would not escape from his land and as a result it was not reasonably foreseeable that the chemicals would escape from his land. Suppose further that the chemicals – against all expectation – managed to escape and damaged B's neighbouring land.

In such a case, the fact that it was not reasonably foreseeable that the chemicals would escape from A's land would not be fatal to a claim by B under the rule in *Rylands* v *Fletcher*. All B would have to show – for the purposes of satisfying the requirement of reasonable foreseeability of damage under the rule in *Rylands* v *Fletcher* – is that it was reasonably foreseeable that someone like her would suffer damage to her land *if* the chemicals escaped from A's land.[72]

16.4 STRICT LIABILITY?

The decision of the House of Lords in *Cambridge Water* did nothing, then, to undermine the strictness of liability under the rule in *Rylands* v *Fletcher*. A defendant who has taken so many precautions to stop an escape from his land that escape is unforeseeable will still be held liable if an escape occurs and causes foreseeable damage to neighbouring land.

Some students find this hard to understand because they associate 'strict' liability with a harsh, unyielding liability regime. So the fact that a claimant cannot sue under *Rylands* v *Fletcher* for losses suffered as a result of an escape from the defendant's land where those losses were an unforeseeable consequence of the escape tends to make students think that liability under the rule in *Rylands* v *Fletcher* is not as harsh or as unyielding as a strict liability regime ought to be.

However, all strict liability means is – the defendant can be held liable without the claimant having to prove that the defendant was at fault for what happened to the claimant. Given that a defendant in a negligence case will only be held liable for the reasonably foreseeable consequences of his actions,[73] it would be paradoxical if a defendant who might be blameless for something escaping from his land were held liable under the rule in *Rylands* v *Fletcher* for harms caused by that escape that were *not* reasonably foreseeable. It is only those who are *very much to blame* for what happened to a claimant who can be justly held liable for *all* the consequences of their actions, no matter how unforeseeable.[74]

---

[71] This claim did not fall foul of the rule in *Cattle* v *Stockton Waterworks* (1875) LR 10 QB 453 that compensation for pure economic loss may not be recovered under the rule in *Rylands* v *Fletcher*. The economic loss for which the claimants wanted to be compensated in *Cambridge Water* was consequential on the claimant's property (their borehole) being damaged.

[72] However, B's claim under the rule in *Rylands* v *Fletcher* for compensation for the damage suffered may still be defeated if a defence is available to A. On which, see the next section.

[73] See above, § 10.2.

[74] ibid.

Strict liability is not absolute liability. Absolute liability exists when a defendant is held liable for some harm that a claimant has suffered even though it was *impossible* for the defendant to prevent that harm occurring to the claimant. Strict liability occupies the terrain between fault-based liability and absolute liability: under a strict liability regime a defendant can be held liable without proof of fault, but will not be held liable if harm was impossible to prevent. So the notion of strict liability allows – indeed, demands – that a defendant not be held liable if it was impossible for him to prevent the harm to the claimant.

The fact that liability under *Rylands* v *Fletcher* is strict, and not absolute, is reflected in the fact that a defendant who is being sued under the rule in *Rylands* v *Fletcher* may be able to take advantage of a number of different defences, the first three of which are roughly centred round the idea of 'impossibility of avoiding harm':

(1) *Act of a stranger*. A will have a defence to B's claim for compensation under the rule in *Rylands* v *Fletcher* if the escape from A's land resulted from the act of a person whom A could not control.[75] It seems to be assumed that a landowner has a sufficient degree of control over the anticipated activities[76] of independent contractors who he engages to bring the dangerous thing onto his premises or to store it there.[77] A defendant will not be liable, however, for an escape resulting from the deliberate and malicious act of a stranger, unless such an act ought to have been anticipated and guarded against. So in *Perry* v *Kendricks Transport Ltd* (1956), a couple of boys threw a lighted match into the petrol tank of a motor coach that was standing on the defendants' land. The coach blew up and the claimant, who was standing outside the defendants' land at the time of the explosion, was injured. The defendants were not held liable to compensate the claimant for his injuries under the rule in *Rylands* v *Fletcher*.[78]

(2) *Act of God*. A will have a defence to B's claim for compensation under the rule in *Rylands* v *Fletcher* if the escape from his land resulted from a wholly extraordinary natural event.[79]

(3) *Fault of the claimant*. A will have a defence to B's claim for compensation under the rule in *Rylands* v *Fletcher* if B was wholly at fault for the fact that she suffered the harm for which she is seeking compensation.[80]

(4) *Volenti*. A will have a defence to B's claim for compensation under the rule in *Rylands* v *Fletcher* if B consented to the dangerous thing being accumulated or stored by A, provided

---

[75] *Box* v *Jubb* (1879) 4 Ex D 76; *Rickards* v *Lothian* [1913] AC 263; *Perry* v *Kendricks Transport Ltd* [1956] 1 WLR 85.

[76] Where the independent contractor behaves in a wholly unanticipated way A may be able to avoid liability. This has certainly been the position in the analogous cases involving fire. See below, § 16.5.

[77] In *Rylands* v *Fletcher* itself the escape seems to have been caused by the carelessness of the independent contractors who built the reservoir.

[78] It is now clear that the claimant's claim under the rule in *Rylands* v *Fletcher* should also have failed because the rule does not apply in personal injury cases: see above, § 16.3(B).

[79] *Nichols* v *Marsland* (1876) 2 Ex D 1, where a rainstorm was said to have been the heaviest in human memory. A different heavy storm was judged insufficiently unusual in *Greenock Corporation* v *Caledonian Railway Co* [1917] AC 556. In *Transco*, at [59], Lord Hobhouse stated that the phrase 'Acts of God' was 'used to describe those events which involved no human agency and which it was not realistically possible for a human to guard against: an accident which the defendant can show is due to natural causes, directly and exclusively, without human intervention and could not have been prevented by any amount of foresight, pains and care, reasonably to be expected of him'.

[80] *Rylands* v *Fletcher* (1868) LR 1 Ex 265, 280.

that the dangerous thing did not escape as a result of A's negligence. The thinking behind this is that if B has consented to the dangerous thing being accumulated or stored by A then he must have also accepted the risk of suffering harm if there is an escape, since if a dangerous thing is accumulated or stored there is always a possibility of an escape. But by consenting to the accumulation or storage of the dangerous thing B will not have indicated any willingness to accept the risk of the thing escaping as a result B's negligence. Thus where B stores the dangerous thing negligently A's consent to him storing it will be vitiated, unless, perhaps A has made clear that he is even content to accept the risks of negligent storage.

One example of a case where the defence applied is *Peters v Prince of Wales Theatre* (1943). In this case, the defendants owned a theatre, and a shop formed part of the theatre building. The claimants leased the shop from the defendants, knowing that a sprinkler system was installed in the theatre building, including in the shop. Due to a severe frost, the sprinkler system burst (without the defendants being in any way at fault for this) and water poured all over the claimants' shop, damaging the goods they had for sale there. The claimants sued the defendants for compensation under the rule in *Rylands v Fletcher*, but the claim was dismissed on the basis that the claimants had been happy to rent the shop knowing that there was a risk that their goods might be damaged by the sprinkler system breaking down. An analogy was drawn with the rule that if A has granted possession of a parcel of land to B, and it is contemplated at the time of the grant that A will continue to use adjoining property for a particular purpose, B will not be able to complain that A's using the adjoining premises for that purpose will amount to a nuisance.[81]

The rule that negligence will vitiate A's consent to a dangerous thing being stored was applied in *Colour Quest Ltd v Total Downstream UK PLC* (2009), which dealt with claims arising from explosions at the Buncefield Oil Storage Depot. In this case, simplifying to an extent, Total accepted that, if certain points were decided against it, then it would be liable under the rule in *Rylands v Fletcher* for the damage that the explosions had caused to owners of land beyond the boundaries of the Depot. But Total argued that it should not be held liable for damage to the property of other oil companies which was within the boundaries of the Depot because these claimants had consented to the storage of oil in large quantities. David Steel J held that Total could not rely on this defence because the explosions had been caused by negligence that it was responsible for, and the other oil companies had not consented to *negligent* storage of oil.[82]

16.5 REMEDIES

We have already noted that the consequences of treating liability under the rule in *Rylands v Fletcher* as an off-shoot of the tort of private nuisance include it becoming the law that a claimant can only claim under this rule if she has suffered damage to her land (including buildings) and cannot claim compensation for personal injuries or *pure* economic losses.[83] Where a defendant is liable under the rule in *Rylands v Fletcher* for physical damage to a

---

[81] *Vanderpant v Mayfair Hotel Co Ltd* [1930] 1 Ch 138, 162–3; *Thomas v Lewis* [1937] 1 All ER 137.

[82] [2009] EWHC 540 (Comm), at [405]–[406]. The Court of Appeal dealt with an appeal against part of David Steel J's decision in *Shell UK Ltd v Total UK Ltd* [2011] 1 QB 86, but his conclusion as to the scope of the defence of volenti under *Rylands v Fletcher* was not challenged.

[83] See above, § 16.3(B). We expect that the rules as to when a claimant can obtain compensation for consequential damage to chattels will be the same as those which apply in the tort of private nuisance: for an account of these rules the reader should refer back to § 15.12.

building the remedy that the claimant is most likely to obtain will be compensatory damages, and these will be calculated so as to provide *either* (1A) the cost of repair *or* (1B) the diminution in capital value of the land or building, and, in either case, also (2) redress for *consequential* economic losses.

The reader will recall that in cases of private nuisance claimants often also obtain *injunctions*, usually ordering the defendant not to continue to commit private nuisance. Can a claimant obtain an injunction in a case covered by the rule in *Rylands* v *Fletcher*? In practice this question is rarely likely to arise because the rule is most often relied on where there has been a *one-off* escape of a dangerous thing. But perhaps we should focus on two situations: (1) where a defendant is storing a dangerous thing on his land in such a way that an escape seems imminent, and (2) where a dangerous thing is continuing to escape from the defendant's land and the defendant is not taking steps to prevent this. We think that a court would have the power to grant an injunction in both of these situations,[84] but doubt whether such an injunction would really be granted under the rule in *Rylands* v *Fletcher*, as opposed to being to prevent negligence or a continuing public or private nuisance.[85]

16.6 ANALOGOUS LIABILITY RULES

There are a number of liability rules that are analogous to the rule in *Rylands* v *Fletcher*, in that they make a defendant strictly liable for harm done by a dangerous thing under his control. The existence of these rules supplies one reason for retaining the rule in *Rylands* v *Fletcher*: abolishing the rule would put landowners who bring onto, or store on, their land something that is liable to do damage if it escapes in a better position that people who fall under the liability rules dealt with below. It is not clear whether such a concession to landowners would be justified.

A. Animals

We have already seen that the keeper of an animal that belongs to a dangerous species, or that – to the keeper's knowledge – has an uncommon characteristic that means it is likely to do harm (or any harm it does is likely to be severe), may be held strictly liable for the harm done by that animal if it escapes his control.[86]

B. Fire

It is commonly believed that the ancient common law made an occupier of premises *absolutely* liable for *any* damage caused by fire escaping from those premises. This stern rule was altered by statute and s 86 of the Fire Prevention (Metropolis) Act 1774 now states that no action can be brought on the basis of this ancient common law rule 'against any person in whose house, chamber, stable, barn or other building, or on whose estate any fire shall . . . accidentally begin'. But the interpretation and application of this provision is not

---

[84] See *Attorney-General* v *Cory Brothers & Co* [1921] AC 521.
[85] Why does it matter what tort such an injunction would aim to prevent? Our answer is that it matters because injunctions order people to comply with their legal duties – not to commit *wrongs* – while the rule in *Rylands* v *Fletcher*, as we have explained above (see § 16.2), imposes liability even when the defendant has not broken any duty that he owed to the claimant.
[86] See above, chapter 13.

straightforward. In order to explain the current pattern of an occupier's liability for the spread of fire it may be helpful to distinguish three types of situation.

(1) In the first situation, *a fire is negligently started on A's property and then spreads to B's property*. It has been held that the 1774 Act does not protect the occupier from liability when the fire has been started 'negligently' rather than 'accidentally'.[87] Importantly, this exception to the Act applies even when the negligence was not the negligence of the occupier or his employee but of a guest or independent contractor. Thus a claimant who wishes to sue the occupier for damage done by a fire negligently started by a guest or independent contractor will be able to sue the occupier under the ancient common law rule and not have to rely on the tort of negligence.[88]

The 1774 Act *will* protect the occupier from being sued under the ancient common law rule, however, if the fire was started by the negligence of a *stranger*. In this context 'a "stranger" is anyone who in lighting a fire . . . acts contrary to anything which the occupier could anticipate that he would do'.[89] In rare circumstances a guest or independent contractor may become a 'stranger' for the purposes of this rule 'if his conduct in lighting a fire is so alien to your invitation that he should *qua* the fire be regarded as a trespasser'.[90] By way of illustration, in *Ribee* v *Norrie* (2001), the defendant owned a hostel and rented out bedrooms in it to various people. A fire started in the hostel's sitting room, probably as a result of a tenant dropping a smouldering cigarette onto the settee. The fire spread and damaged the adjoining house which belonged to the claimant. The defendant was held liable for the fire damage done to the claimant's house. He was held to have been in occupation of the hostel's sitting room when the fire started. The fire was negligently started in the sitting room by a tenant who had permission from the defendant to use the sitting room. Finally, the tenant's conduct was not 'so alien' that he could '*qua* the fire be regarded as a trespasser' because the defendant could reasonably have anticipated that a tenant using the sitting room 'might inadvertently drop a smouldering cigarette onto the settee eventually setting it on fire'.[91]

(2) In the second situation, *a fire is deliberately started on A's property and then spreads to B's property*. Liability in this type of situation depends on the *type* of fire involved and *why it spread*.

The *type* of fire involved is relevant because it has been held that some deliberately lit fires involve the 'extraordinary use' of land and potentially fall within the ambit of the rule in *Rylands* v *Fletcher*. In such cases, a claimant will not have to rely on the ancient common law rule regarding fire in order to sue, and will therefore not be affected by the 1774 Act. In such a case, the occupier may be held liable for the escape of a deliberately lit fire from his premises even if the fire spread from its original location accidentally. But lighting an ordinary domestic fire in a fireplace is not an 'extraordinary use', so there will be no liability for the accidental escape of such a fire.[92]

The reasons *why the fire spread* are relevant because where a fire was started deliberately, but then it spread from its original location because of the *negligence* of the occupier, his employee, his guest or his independent contractor, it has been held that the 1774 Act does

---

[87] *Balfour* v *Barty-King* [1957] 1 QB 496.
[88] The claimant can, of course, seek to sue the guest or the contractor in negligence.
[89] *H & N Emmanuel Ltd* v *GLC* [1971] 2 All ER 835, 839 (per Lord Denning MR).
[90] ibid.
[91] (2001) 33 HLR 777, at [26] (per Ward LJ).
[92] *Sochacki* v *Sas* [1947] 1 All ER 344; *J Doltis Ltd* v *Issac Braithwaite & Sons (Engineers) Ltd* [1957] 1 Lloyd's Rep 522; *Johnson* v *BJW Property Developments Ltd* [2002] 3 All ER 574, at [31].

not protect the occupier against being held liable under the ancient common law rule regarding damage done by fire.[93] Again, the occupier's liability does not stretch to cover liability for the negligence of a 'stranger'.[94]

(3) In the third situation, *natural forces or a stranger start a fire on A's property and it then spreads to B's property*. In this situation, it seems that the 1774 Act will prevent A being held liable for the damage to B's premises *unless* the claim can be brought under the rule in *Rylands v Fletcher* or the rule in *Goldman v Hargrave*.[95] In such a case, B will not have to rely on the ancient common law rule regarding damage done by fire in order to sue A, and the 1774 Act will not therefore apply to him.

In order to show that the rule in *Rylands* applies in this kind of situation, it would have to be shown that the fire started on the occupier's premises because he used those premises in an extraordinary way. This requirement would probably be satisfied if the occupier stored large quantities of inflammable chemicals on his land which accidentally caught fire.[96] But the 'extraordinary use' requirement will probably not be satisfied if what happened was that A parked his car on his land and the petrol in the tank accidentally caught fire.[97] *Goldman v Hargrave*[98] may assist a neighbour in claiming against an occupier for damage caused by the spread of a natural fire from his land if he failed to take reasonable steps to stop the fire spreading onto the neighbour's property. Whether the occupier will be held to have taken such reasonable steps will depend on factors such as his interests and resources, and the relative interests and resources of anyone imperilled by the fire.[99]

We should finally consider how far that remnant of the ancient common law rule relating to the escape of fire which has survived the 1774 statute is 'analogous to the rule in *Rylands v Fletcher*' since this may determine questions such as who can claim and what types of damage they can claim for under that ancient rule.[100] From one perspective this remnant is analogous to the rule in *Rylands* because it makes an occupier liable for escapes of fire which were the consequence of the negligence of a guest or independent contractor. But two distinctions may also be worth mentioning. First, under the remnant the occupier will

---

[93] *H & N Emmanuel Ltd v GLC* [1971] 2 All ER 835. This seems to be the opinion of Lord Denning MR (ibid, at 838; though he later evinces a reluctance to classify the liability rule at 839) and also the opinion of Phillimore LJ (at 842). See also *Johnson v BJW Property Developments Ltd* [2002] 3 All ER 574.

[94] *H & N Emmanuel Ltd v GLC* [1971] 2 All ER 835, 838–9 (per Lord Denning MR).

[95] *Goldman v Hargrave* [1967] 1 AC 645. See above, §§ 11.5, 15.8.

[96] In *Mason v Levy Auto Parts* [1967] 2 QB 530, MacKenna J found that the storage of a large number of motor spares coated in oil or wrapped in waxed paper was a non-natural user of land. Similarly, in *LMS International Ltd v Styrene Packaging and Insulation Ltd* [2005] EWHC 2065 (TCC) HHJ Peter Coulson QC held that the use in the defendant's factory of several tonnes of inflammable expanded polystyrene beads, pentane, and hot-wire cutting machines, amounted to a non-natural use of land. The fact that it is not the inflammable material which escaped in these cases but a fire is not legally important. In cases of explosion courts have similarly not treated it as important whether the explosive chemicals *themselves* escaped (as opposed to mere shockwaves). See, for example, *Rainham Chemical Works Ltd v Belvedere Fish Guano Co Ltd* [1921] 2 AC 465.

[97] Admittedly, in *Musgrove v Pandelis* [1919] 2 KB 43, the Court of Appeal held that a motor car and its petrol tank were a 'dangerous thing' to which the rule in *Rylands v Fletcher* could apply, but paid less attention to the question whether storage of a car in a garage was an extraordinary user. The better view, which accords with the opinion of Romer LJ in *Collingwood v Home & Colonial Stores Ltd* [1936] 3 All ER 200, 209, must be that parking a car in a garage attached to residential property is not an extraordinary use of land. Indeed in *Transco*, [107] Lord Walker used the *Musgrove* case to illustrate how the 'extraordinary use' test changes though time. It might still be arguable that to park a petrol tanker on land is an 'extraordinary user': see *Perry v Kendricks Transport Ltd* [1956] 1 WLR 85.

[98] *Goldman v Hargrave* [1967] AC 645.

[99] See above, § 8.2.

[100] For these matters under the rule in *Rylands v Fletcher* see above, § 16.3.

avoid liability if he can prove that the escape was 'accidental', in the sense of not involving negligence. This is a broader defence than any available under the rule in *Rylands*.[101] Secondly, it is not clear that the ancient common law rule *only* protects neighbours against damage to their land.[102] One of the best known ancient authorities for the rule involves a claim for damage to chattels[103] and more recent judgments have also assumed that such claims were possible.[104]

C. Cattle trespass

Under s 4 of the Animals Act 1971, if livestock[105] belonging[106] to any person strays[107] onto land in the ownership or occupation of another, the person to whom the livestock belongs is liable for any damage[108] caused by the livestock to the land and property on it and for expenses reasonably incurred in impounding the livestock,[109] tracing who owns it and keeping it pending return. There is no defence covering escapes of livestock caused by malicious strangers or Acts of God. However, s 5(1) of the 1971 Act provides that a 'person [will not be] liable under [s 4] for any damage which is due wholly to the fault of the person suffering it'.[110]

Someone who has suffered harm as a result of straying livestock may not have to rely on s 4 of the Animals Act 1971 to obtain compensation for that harm: he may be entitled to bring a claim in tort for such compensation. So if A *sends* livestock onto B's land, he will commit the tort of trespass to land and B will be entitled to sue A in trespass for compensation for the harm caused by the livestock while it was on her land. Again, if A *carelessly* allows livestock to stray when it is reasonably foreseeable that they will do harm to B if they are allowed to stray, A will commit the tort of negligence and if B suffers foreseeable harm as a result of the livestock straying, B will be entitled to sue A in negligence for damages sufficient to compensate her for that harm.[111]

D. Escape of water from the mains

Where an escape of water, however caused,[112] from a pipe vested in a water undertaker causes loss or damage, the undertaker shall be liable for the loss or damage.[113]

---

[101] For defences under the rule in *Rylands v Fletcher* see above, § 16.4.

[102] See above, § 16.3, for the limits on who can sue and for what under the rule in *Rylands v Fletcher*.

[103] *Beaulieu v Finglam* (1401) YB 2 Hen IV fo 18, pl 6.

[104] *Sochacki v Sas* [1947] 1 All ER 344, 345: 'If I happen to be on somebody else's land at a time when a fire spreads to that land and my motor car or property is destroyed, I have just as much right against the person who improperly allows the fire to escape from his land as the owner of the land on which I happen to be' (per Lord Goddard CJ).

[105] This is broadly defined in s 11. It includes cattle, horses, sheep, pigs and poultry.

[106] Animals Act 1971, s 4(2): 'For the purposes of this section any livestock belongs to the person in whose possession it is.'

[107] There is no liability where livestock strays from a highway which it was being driven along or across: Animals Act 1971, s 5(5), following the common law rule in *Tillett v Ward* (1882) 10 QBD 17. There could be liability in negligence if the drovers were careless, or under s 2 of the Animals Act 1971 if the livestock in question was known to have an unusual and dangerous tendency.

[108] Not limited to damage to land.

[109] See Animals Act 1971, s 7.

[110] Damages can also be reduced for contributory negligence: s 10.

[111] In this context the tort of negligence will straightforwardly allow B to claim for personal injury or property damage.

[112] There is an exception where the escape was due wholly to the fault of the person who sustained the loss or damage: Water Industry Act 1991, s 209(2).

[113] Water Industry Act 1991, s 209(1). There are some exceptions to this liability in s 209(3) and (6). Claims are not limited to claims for damage to land.

E. Nuclear installations

The licensee of a nuclear installation is liable for injuries to persons and damage to the property of others caused by occurrences involving nuclear matter or the escape of ionising radiation.[114] Licensees cannot escape liability by showing that the occurrence was the result of an Act of God or of an uncontrollable third party, though there is a defence for incidents caused by 'hostile action in the course of armed conflict'.[115] The courts, however, have defined the forms of damage covered by the statutory liability narrowly,[116] and some claimants seeking to rely on it have been unable to prove causation.[117]

Further reading

So many articles have been written about *Rylands* v *Fletcher* that some scholars feel that it is necessary to provide an excuse for adding to the library: see, for example, **Ken Oliphant**, '*Rylands* v *Fletcher* and the Emergence of Enterprise Liability in the Common Law' in **H. Koziol and B. Steininger (eds)**, *European Tort Law* 2004 (Springer, 2005).

From the clutch of articles written in the aftermath of the *Transco* case we would recommend Oliphant's piece, and also **D.P. Nolan, 'The Distinctiveness of *Rylands* v *Fletcher*' (2005) 121** *Law Quarterly Review* 421, and **J. Murphy, 'The Merits of *Rylands* v *Fletcher*' (2004) 24** *Oxford Journal of Legal Studies* 643.

For those more interested in the story behind the leading case the best accounts are **A.W.B. Simpson, 'Bursting reservoirs: the historical context of *Rylands* v *Fletcher*' (1984) 13** *Journal of Legal Studies* 209 (a revised version appears as chapter 8 in his book *Leading Cases in the Common Law* (Clarendon Press, 1995)) and **K.S. Abraham '*Rylands* v *Fletcher*: tort law's conscience' in R.L. Rabin and S. Sugarman (eds),** *Torts Stories* (West Law School, 2003).

[114] Nuclear Installations Act 1965, ss 7 and 12. Thus for there to be liability under the Act there does not have to be an escape from the land occupied by the licensee.

[115] Nuclear Installations Act 1965, s 13(4).

[116] In *Merlin* v *BNFL* [1990] 2 QB 557, Gatehouse J held that a fall in the value of a house as a result of radioactive contamination was not 'damage' to property, and suggested *obiter* that 'the presence of alpha-emitting radionuclides in the human airways or digestive system or even in the bloodstream merely increases the risk of cancer to which everyone is exposed from both natural and artificial radioactive sources. They do not *per se* amount to injury' (ibid, 572–3).

[117] *Reay* v *BNFL*, *Hope* v *BNFL* [1994] PIQR P171.

17 Torts to things

17.1 The basics *485*

17.2 Some key concepts *487*

17.3 Conversion *494*

17.4 Trespass to goods *500*

17.5 Bailment *503*

17.6 Remedies *504*

Overview

In the last three chapters we have been looking at torts and liability rules that help protect people's interests in land. In this chapter the focus moves away from land. We will be looking at a number of torts that are committed by interfering with, or failing to protect, things that amount to property, and which you can touch, but which are not land. The key concepts that underlie these torts are set out in section 17.2. Having laid out these concepts, in section 17.3 we look at the most difficult and least well-understood tort in this chapter (and maybe the whole book): the tort of conversion. This can be very roughly defined as intentionally doing something in relation to a thing that has the effect of excluding other people with a better title to that thing from possessing it. Much easier is the tort of trespass to goods, which is dealt with in section 17.4: this is the tort of directly and unjustifiably interfering with goods in someone else's possession. Section 17.5 is the long-promised section on bailment, and explains when someone will hold another's goods on a bailment for them and the duty of care to protect the goods from coming to harm that such a bailment will give rise to. Section 17.6 sets out what remedies will be available when someone commits a tort by interfering with, or failing to protect, a thing.

17.1 THE BASICS

This chapter aims, among other things, to answer questions such as:

(1) If *Dealer* is in possession of your car, are you entitled to sue him, and if so for what?

(2) If *Dealer* came into possession of your car and he subsequently sold it to *Buyer*, are you entitled to sue either *Dealer* or *Buyer*, and if so for what?

(3) If *Warden* clamps your car, are you entitled to sue *Warden* and if so for what?

(4) If you park your car in a car park and the car is subsequently stolen from the car park due to the fault of the car park *Attendant*, are you entitled to sue *Attendant* and if so for what?

English law actually finds it most difficult to answer question (1). This is so even though the answer to question (1) seems obvious: of course you should be entitled to sue *Dealer* to get your car back. Unfortunately, English law cannot give such a simple answer because it does not have the equivalent of what Roman lawyers called the action of *vindicatio*, which entitled a claimant to ask a court to force the defendant to hand over property to which the claimant had a better title. Remedies under English law are usually only made available in a case where the claimant can establish that she has been the victim of a *wrong*. So if a claimant wants to sue a defendant who has her property, it isn't enough for her to say, 'He's got my property! Make him give it back!' She has to argue, 'He has done something wrong in retaining my property! Give me a remedy for the wrong that has been done to me!'[1]

This feature of English law is highlighted very nicely in a passage from Lord Denning MR's judgment in *Miller v Jackson* (1977). Considering what the position would be if someone hit a cricket ball into a neighbour's back garden, he observed:

> If one or two of the players went round and asked the householder if they could go into the garden to find it, the householder could deny them access . . . If the cricketers said: 'It's a new ball. It cost us over £6,' the householder could say: 'That is your lookout. You ought not to have put it there.' Of course, if the householder picked up the ball himself and gave it to his son to play with he would be liable . . . But otherwise he would not be liable at all.[2]

It is only at the point that the householder *picks the ball up and gives it to his son* that English law could say that he has done anything wrong in relation to the ball, and allow the cricketers some sort of remedy for the fact that they have not got their ball back. The wrong committed by the householder in picking the ball up and giving it to his son is called *conversion* – which we can very roughly define here as acting inconsistently with the cricketers' superior rights over the cricket ball. And the remedy for that wrong was that the householder would be liable to pay the cricketers the value of the ball – unless, in the meantime, the cricketers somehow recovered the ball (perhaps as a result of the householder's son giving it back to them), in which case they would only be allowed to sue for compensation for the actual losses suffered by them as a result of the householder's giving his son, and not them, the ball.

So English law's answer to question (1) is – you can sue *Dealer*, but only if he has done something in relation to your car that is inconsistent with your rights over your car. So you can't sue *Dealer* just because he happens to be in possession of your car. You have to put him in the wrong, by doing something like demanding that he hand the car over to you, and establishing that he has refused to comply with that demand. And – as the above passage in *Miller v Jackson* shows – sometimes a demand and refusal will not be enough to establish that the person refusing is doing anything wrong in making that refusal. But if he *does* do something wrong by refusing to hand over your car, you can then sue him. But your remedy will not usually be an order that *Dealer* hand over your car. That will be the remedy – known as 'specific restitution of goods' – if the car is unique (say it was once owned by Marilyn Monroe and is a collectors' item). But if the car is not unique, your remedy will usually be an order that the *Dealer either* give you your car *or* give you its monetary value.

Holding *Dealer* liable for acting inconsistently with your rights over your car is unobjectionable where he *still has your car*. But by making *Dealer*'s liability in (1) arise from his having done something inconsistent with your rights over your car, the courts have opened the door to holding *both Dealer and Buyer* liable in (2).[3] For *Dealer* has acted inconsistently with your rights by handing over your car to *Buyer* and *Buyer* has acted inconsistently with your rights by taking possession of your car. Both, it seems, have committed the tort of conversion. But each may have acted in complete good faith in handing over, and in taking, the car. And if they did act in complete good faith, then it is rough on *Dealer* to hold him liable for the value of the car, if he sold it to *Buyer* at a special

[1] See Birks 2000a, 3–6.
[2] [1977] 1 QB 966, 978.
[3] See Birks 2000a, 6–7; Weir 2004, 483–6; Douglas 2009, 218.

discount, or if he took the money that he earned from the sale and spent it on a special holiday. And it is rough on *Buyer* to hold him liable for the value of the car, if he no longer has it and has no means of recovering it – because, for example, he gave the car to his daughter as a birthday present, and she subsequently crashed it and damaged it so badly that the car had to be written off. This rough justice is a consequence of the *formalism* of English law, which dictates that if you can sue for the value of your car in (1) because *Dealer* has acted inconsistently with your rights by refusing to hand it over to you, then you must also be able to sue for the value of your car in (2) because both *Dealer* and *Buyer* have acted inconsistently with your rights by respectively handing over, and taking delivery of, the car.

Turning to question (3), *Warden* may have had some *lawful justification or excuse* for clamping your car; in which case, she cannot have committed a tort in so doing. If she did not have a lawful justification or excuse for clamping your car, then one would have thought that she has – like *Dealer* or *Buyer* in (2) – committed the tort of conversion, as she has acted inconsistently with your rights over the car by clamping it. However, clamping a car does not amount to conversion – it amounts to a different tort to property, *trespass to goods*; a tort which is committed by directly applying force to another's goods when you had no lawful justification or excuse for doing so. Why is clamping a car trespass and not conversion? It just isn't, seems to be the only answer we can give.

More technicalities are raised by question (4), where you want to sue *Attendant* for failing to protect your car from being stolen. As all *Attendant* is guilty of here is an omission – a failure to act – you will need to show that there exists some kind of special relationship between you and *Attendant* that would warrant imposing on him a positive duty to protect your car from being stolen. One way of doing this is to show that *Attendant* held your car as a *bailee* for you. If the car – when it was parked in the car park – was held on a *bailment* then *Attendant* will have owed you a duty to take reasonable steps to protect your car from being destroyed, damaged or stolen. But for a bailment to exist, it has to be shown that *Attendant* took *possession* of your car when you parked the car in the car park. And it has been held that those in charge of a car park do not take possession of cars that are parked in the car park.[4] So no bailment will exist here, and you will have to find some other basis for suing *Attendant* for failing to protect your car.

The *formalism* and *technicalities* that characterise this area of law mean that it is only ever studied in advanced courses on tort law; it is regarded as too difficult for students studying tort law for the first time. This is a pity as the law on torts to things frequently gives rise to disputes that are likely to come to court and the less well understood this area of law is, the more likely it is that, in time, judicial decisions dealing with this area of law will reduce the law on torts to things into a disordered and chaotic shambles.

17.2 SOME KEY CONCEPTS

In order to understand this area of law, we have to first come to grips with some basic concepts, the first of which could not be more basic – the concept of 'property'.

A. Property

Section 436(1) of the Insolvency Act 1986 illustrates just how many different things can amount to property under English law:

---

[4] *Ashby* v *Tolhurst* [1937] 2 KB 242.

'property' includes money, goods, things in action, land and every description of property wherever situated and also obligations and every description of interest, whether present or future or vested or contingent, arising out of, or incidental to, property.[5]

We are concerned in this chapter with the first two items of property on the list – money and goods: items of property that are not land but which you can touch.[6] The next chapter is concerned with torts to *intangible property*. 'Things in action' (otherwise known as 'choses in action') – basically, rights to sue someone else – are examples of items of *intangible property*. For example, the right to sue someone for money that they owe you is regarded as an item of property because it can be sold to someone else (for example, a debt collection agency).[7] Because you cannot physically touch that right, that right to sue amounts to a piece of intangible property. However, some rights to sue take a documentary form. An example is a cheque – a piece of paper that, in the right circumstances, will give the holder of the cheque a right to draw on the bank account of the person who drew up the cheque for the amount of money stated on the cheque. Where a right to sue takes a documentary form, interfering with the document that represents that right to sue may amount to one of the torts considered in this chapter.

Almost anything that can be touched is capable of amounting to a piece of tangible property that can be owned or traded. The most important exception to this is ourselves – our bodies, and the parts of our bodies. While philosophers like to talk of us 'owning ourselves', and acquiring ownership of other things through our basic ownership of our own bodies, the traditional position of English law was that bodies and body parts could not amount to property. This is still the position where living bodies and body parts are concerned – they are protected by the law of trespass to the person and negligence, not by the law on conversion and trespass to goods.[8] However, where dead bodies, or body parts or fluids that have been removed from someone were concerned, the position of English law used to be that a dead body or a removed body part or fluid *would* amount to property *if* work had been done on it, either to preserve it or alter it.[9] This exception to the general rule that bodies and body parts/fluids cannot amount to property has been radically expanded by the decision of the Court of Appeal in *Yearworth v North Bristol NHS Trust* (2010).[10]

The claimants in that case were male cancer patients who deposited sperm with the defendant sperm bank before they underwent chemotherapy, the idea being that if the chemotherapy rendered a patient sterile, he could still have children using his donated

---

[5] Thanks to Robert Stevens for bringing this provision to our attention.

[6] So 'goods' does not include 'documents stored in electronic form'. The result is that the action of wiping files on a computer hard drive will not – of and in itself – be covered by any of the torts covered in this Chapter. See *Thunder Air Ltd v Hilmarsson* [2008] EWHC 355, at [28]–[29] (per Patten J).

[7] Law of Property Act 1925, s 136.

[8] Though Keren-Paz 2010b argues that it would be 'poetic justice' for a client who has sex with a woman who has been forced into working as a prostitute to be held liable for converting her body; having treated the woman's body like a tradeable piece of property, he should not be allowed to argue that her body was not in fact a piece of property.

[9] *Dobson v North Tyneside Health Authority* [1997] 1 WLR 596; *R v Kelly* [1999] QB 621; *In Re Organ Retention Litigation* [2005] QB 506, at [148] and [161]. See, generally, Matthews 1983, 196–221. Nwabueze 2007 criticises English law for taking the position that there is (usually) no tort of interference with a dead body, approvingly citing section 868 of the US Second Restatement Torts, which says that 'One who intentionally, recklessly or negligently removes, withholds, mutilates or operates upon a body of a dead person or prevents its proper interment or cremation is subject to liability to a member of the family of the deceased who is entitled to the disposition of the body.'

[10] Discussed, Lee 2009, Harmon and Laurie 2010.

sperm and artificial fertilisation techniques. The donated sperm was preserved by freezing it. Unfortunately, and due to the defendant's carelessness, the sperm thawed out and became useless. The claimants sued, arguing that the donated sperm was property that belonged to them, and that they were entitled to damages for the damage done to the sperm and the consequential distress and psychiatric illnesses they had suffered as a result of knowing that they could not have any more children. The Court of Appeal allowed the claimants' claims.

The Court of Appeal could have easily found that the donated sperm amounted to property on the basis that work had been done on it to preserve it. However, the Court of Appeal thought that the rule that dead bodies or body parts/fluids would amount to property if work had been done on them was 'not entirely logical'.[11] Instead, the Court of Appeal held that the donated sperm amounted to property belonging to the claimants because:

> By their bodies, they alone generated and ejaculated the sperm . . . The sole object of their ejaculation of the sperm was that, in certain events, it might later be used for their benefit . . . [the] sperm [could not] be stored or continue to be stored without their subsisting consent [under the terms of the Human Fertilisation and Embryology Act 1990] . . . no person, whether human or corporate, other than each man [who supplied the sperm had] any *rights* in relation to the sperm which he . . . produced.[12]

The Court's finding that the donated sperm was property that belonged to the claimants seems to have rested on two facts: (a) the sperm was produced by the claimants; and (b) after it left their body, they intended to, and did, retain control over how it was disposed of.

It is not clear how far *Yearworth* goes – would it, for example, allow *Rock Star* to sue *Fan* for collecting some of his hair from the floor of the barber shop where *Rock Star*'s hair has been cut, and selling that hair on eBay? But *Yearworth* would not – we think – have assisted the claimant in the very famous American case of *Moore* v *Regents of University of California* (1990).[13]

In that case, the claimant's spleen was removed at the UCLA Medical Center in the course of treating him for hairy-cell leukemia. Cancerous cells were extracted from the spleen that were then replicated in huge quantities for other doctors to experiment on in coming up with treatments for cancer. Experimenters would have to pay for these cells, and the cell-line developed from the claimant's spleen became the basis of a $3 billion dollar industry. The claimant wanted to sue for some of that money, so he argued that the doctors at UCLA had committed the tort of conversion in relation to him by using his spleen to produce a cell-line without his consent. The claim was dismissed on the ground that the claimant had no rights over the spleen once it had been extracted from his body. We think that even after *Yearworth*, the same decision would be reached here. While the spleen was produced by the claimant, the claimant did not intend to retain control over the spleen after it was extracted from his body. (Though it might be different if the claimant knew how lucrative the market was for good cell-lines and made it clear before his operation that he wanted to keep his spleen after it had been taken from his body.)

B. Ownership

We have been brought up since we were children to think that the key question in relation to any item of property is – Who does it belong to? In fact, English law is not so much

---

[11] [2010] QB 1, at [45](d).
[12] [2010] QB 1, at [45](f).
[13] Discussed Harris 1986, 75–84.

concerned with questions of ownership. In any dispute between a claimant and a defendant that involves a particular item of property, English law prefers to focus on the question: who has the *better title* to this item of property? So if A is in possession of a car which is then taken from him by B, B will be presumed to have done something wrong in depriving A of possession of the car. (This is where we get the saying that 'Posession is nine tenths of the law.') Because A was in possession of the car, and B was not, it will be presumed that A had a better title to the car than B did. Of course, this may not be true. If A was in possession and B had an *immediate right* to possess the car, then B may not have done anything wrong in taking the car away from A; though the law may still find that B did something wrong, so as to discourage B from taking the law into his own hands to recover his car. And if A was in possession and B had an immediate right to possess the car, and C stole the car, then both A and B can sue C for conversion, on the basis that both A and B had a better title to the car than C did.

C. Possession

So the issue of who was in possession of an item of property that has been interfered with is far more important to the law than abstract questions as to who, ultimately, owned that item of property. But when can a claimant say that she was in possession of an item of property at the time it was interfered with? The basic answer is – if she *acquired* possession before the property was interfered with, and did not *lose* possession in between acquiring possession and the property being interfered with.

(1) *Acquiring possession.* A will acquire possession of an item of property if: (a) she takes *control* of that item of property with (b) the *intention* of preventing others from taking control of that item of property.

Someone will take control of an item of property if he takes as much control over that item of property as the nature of that item of property will admit. So, for example, in *Young v Hichens* (1844), the claimant was fishing for pilchards and had almost encircled a shoal of pilchards with his nets when the defendant rowed through a gap in the nets and prevented the claimant from capturing the pilchards. The claimant sued the defendant, claiming that he had been in possession of the pilchards and that the defendant had disturbed his possession of the pilchards. The claim was rejected: at no time did the claimant have the pilchards completely under his control.

In contrast, in *The Tubantia* (1924), the claimants attempted to salvage the cargo of a Dutch steamship which had been sunk in the First World War and lay under 100 feet of water. The claimants located the steamship in April 1922 and spent as many days exploring the ship and salvaging its cargo as the weather permitted until November 1922 when it became impracticable to continue exploring the ship during the winter. The claimants marked the location of the ship and returned in April 1923. They then spent about 25 days exploring the ship and salvaging the cargo until July 1923 when the defendants – encouraged by rumours that the ship had been carrying treasure at the time it was sunk – started to send divers down to the ship in an attempt to locate the treasure and take it for themselves. The claimants sued the defendants, claiming that they had possession of the ship and that the defendants were acting unlawfully in disrupting their possession of the ship. The claimants' claim was allowed: they had taken as much control over the Dutch steamship as the nature of the thing and its location allowed.

Someone who takes control of an item of property will not acquire possession of that item of property unless he intends, in taking control of that item of property, to prevent other people from taking control of that item of property. If he lacks this intention, he is said to have 'custody' of the item of property in question, not 'possession'. So, for example, if *Owner* asks *Jeweller* to value a ring for her, when *Owner* gives *Jeweller* the ring, he will acquire custody but not possession of the ring.[14] When *Jeweller* takes control of the ring to inspect it he does not intend, in taking control of the ring, to prevent other people from taking control of it. Again, it is often said that employees only have custody of their work tools – they do not possess their work tools. When an employee takes control of some tools that he has been given to work with, he does not intend, in taking control of those tools, to prevent other people from taking control of those tools.[15] Of course, if an employee steals some work tools and takes them home he will acquire possession of those tools – he will have taken control of those tools with the intention of preventing other people from taking control of those tools.

(2) *Losing possession*. If A has acquired possession of an item of property, A will then lose possession of that item of property if: (a) someone else takes possession of that item of property; or (b) A intentionally abandons that item of property.

So A does *not* have to *retain control* of an item of property in order to retain possession of that item of property. For example, if *Householder* goes on holiday he retains possession of all the items of property in his house even though he does not have physical control over them while he is gone. Obviously, though, if someone breaks into *Householder*'s house while he is gone and steals some items of property from the house, *Householder* will lose possession of those items of property – someone else (the burglar) will have taken possession of those items of property. Again, suppose *Householder* employs *Oddjob* to perform some task for him and gives *Oddjob* the tools she will need to do the job. *Householder* will retain possession of the tools even after he has given them to *Oddjob* – and this is so even though *Householder* will not physically control the tools once he gives them to *Oddjob*. This is because when *Householder* gives the tools to *Oddjob*, *Oddjob* will merely acquire custody of the tools: she will not possess them.

D. Immediate right to possess

Subject to certain exceptions, only someone who is in possession of goods is entitled to sue a defendant in *trespass* for interfering with those goods. The rule for the tort of conversion is different – both the person who was in possession of the goods at the time they were converted, and anyone who had an *immediate right to possess* those goods at that time, will be entitled to sue for conversion.

A will have an *immediate right* to possess goods in B's possession if A *currently* has a right to call on B to hand over those goods to her. For example, in *Gordon v Harper* (1796), *Landlord* leased a fully furnished flat to *Tenant*. *Tenant* owed some money and *Sheriff* – thinking that the furniture in the flat belonged to *Tenant* – seized it and sold it in execution

---

[14] *Armory v Delamirie* (1721) 1 Stra 505, 93 ER 664.

[15] While this works to explain the rule that an employee only has custody of his work tools and does not possess them, the rule, it should be noted, has its origins in the definition of the now defunct crime of larceny. Someone would commit the offence of larceny if he removed goods from the possession of their owner. Under this definition, an employee who had possession of his work tools would not commit the offence of larceny if he absconded with them – by definition, if he had possession of his work tools he would not remove them from the possession of their owner (his employer) if he absconded with them. In order to ensure that employees who absconded with their employer's tools *did* commit the offence of larceny in so doing, the idea grew up that employees did not possess their work tools – they only had custody of them.

of the debt. *Landlord* sued *Sheriff* in conversion. He lost: *Landlord* could not establish that at the time *Sheriff* seized and sold the furniture in the flat, *Landlord* had a right to call on *Tenant* to hand over possession of the furniture to him.[16] At the expiry of the lease, he would have acquired such a right but the lease had not expired at the time *Sheriff* seized and sold the furniture in question. *Tenant*, on the other hand, being in possession of the furniture at the time it was seized and sold, could have sued *Sheriff* in conversion for selling the furniture.

Let's now look at a few categories of situations in which someone *may* have an immediate right to possess an item of property.

(1) *Theft*. If *Thief* steals a watch from *Owner*, *Owner* will acquire an immediate right to possess that watch.

(2) *Evidence*. Suppose that *Fence* was in possession of stolen goods and that those goods were seized by the police in pursuit of a criminal investigation.[17] Suppose further that the true owner of the goods is untraceable and the police no longer have any statutory authority to retain those goods. In this situation, *Fence* will have an immediate right to possess the goods in question.[18] So if *Fence* demands that the police give him back the goods and the police refuse to do so, they will commit the tort of conversion.[19] It seems that this will be the case even if *Fence* actually stole the goods in question.[20]

(3) *Lost property*. If *Smeagol* has found a ring on your land which has been lost by a third party, *you* will have an immediate right to possess that ring if: (a) *Smeagol* is your employee and he found the ring in the course of his employment;[21] *or* (b) *Smeagol* is a trespasser on your land;[22] *or* (c) the ring was buried on your land;[23] *or* (d) you have 'manifested an intention to exercise control over [your] land and the things which may be upon it or in it'.[24] If none of (a)–(d) are made out, you will have no right to possess the item of property found by *Smeagol* and he may keep it until, of course, the rightful owner turns up and claims the ring in question.[25]

(4) *Bailment*. If A holds B's property as a bailee, B will have an immediate right to possess that property if the bailment on which A holds B's property is a bailment *at will* – that is, if B has reserved the right to reclaim her property from A at any time.

---

[16] However, the law protects *Landlord* by allowing him an independent action for damage to his 'reversionary interest' in the chattels sold by *Sheriff*: see Tettenborn 1994, Green 2010, and *HSBC Rail (UK) Ltd* v *Network Rail Infrastructure Ltd* [2006] 1 WLR 643.

[17] Section 19 of the Police and Criminal Evidence Act 1984 grants the police a statutory power to do this: see below, § 17.3(B)(6).

[18] It must be emphasised that this will only be the case if the police remain in custody of the goods and the true owner of the goods cannot be traced. If the police have exercised a statutory power to transfer the stolen goods to a third party, then *Fence* will no longer have any rights over the goods: *Buckley* v *Gross* (1863) 3 B & S 566, 122 ER 213. Similarly, if the stolen goods are still in the custody of the police, but the true owner can be identified, then *Fence* will have no right to demand that the goods be returned to him.

[19] *Costello* v *Chief Constable of Derbyshire Constabulary* [2001] 1 WLR 1437.

[20] ibid, at [31].

[21] *City of London Corporation* v *Appleyard* [1963] 1 WLR 982; *Parker* v *British Airways Board* [1982] QB 1004, 1017.

[22] *Hibbert* v *McKiernan* [1948] 2 KB 142; *Parker* v *British Airways Board* [1982] QB 1004, 1017.

[23] *Waverley Borough Council* v *Fletcher* [1996] QB 334.

[24] *Parker* v *British Airways Board* [1982] QB 1004, 1018.

[25] Of course, if *Smeagol* takes the ring with the intention of keeping it for himself, that will be conversion – *Smeagol* is only allowed to take the ring if his intention in so doing is to restore it to its rightful owner: see below, § 17.3(A)(1).

If A holds B's property on a fixed-term bailment, B will normally only acquire a right to call on A to hand over possession of the property once the fixed term has elapsed. But if A misuses B's property before the term has elapsed, B may immediately acquire a right at that stage to call on A to hand over possession of the property. So, for example, suppose *Car-Hire* rented out a car to *Hirer* for six months. Two months later, *Hirer* gave the car away to *Third Party*. In such a case, *Car-Hire* will probably be able to establish that when *Hirer* gave the car away, *Car-Hire* acquired an immediate right to possess the car. As a result, *Car-Hire* will probably be able to establish that *Hirer* and *Third Party* both committed the tort of conversion in relation to *Car-Hire* when *Hirer* gave the car away to *Third Party* and *Third Party* took possession of the car.

(5) *Trusts.* Suppose A holds an item of property on trust for B. Will B have an immediate right to possess that item of property? If the property is held *solely* on trust for B then B will have a right – under the decision in *Saunders* v *Vautier* (1841) – to call on A to hand over the property to her.[26] One would have thought, then, that if A held the trust property solely on trust for B and then disposed of that property to C in breach of trust, B would be able to sue both A and C in conversion – and indeed one case held exactly that.[27]

However, if the law *did* say this, then the rule in Equity that a bona fide purchaser of trust property disposed of in breach of trust cannot be sued for the value of that property[28] would be subverted.[29] A claim in conversion would lie against the bona fide purchaser. In order to prevent this happening, the Court of Appeal has ruled in *MCC Proceeds Inc* v *Lehman Bros International (Europe)* (1998) that if trust property which is held solely on trust for B is disposed of in breach of trust, a claim in conversion will *not* lie either against the trustee disposing of the property or the recipient of the property. While B might have an immediate right to possess the trust property, that right, being *equitable* in nature, is not sufficient to allow B to bring a claim in conversion. What has to be established is that B had an immediate right to possess the trust property *under the common law* – and this B cannot do, as she merely had an equitable interest in the trust property.

E. Wrongful interference with goods

In 1977, the law governing the remedies for a 'wrongful interference with goods' was amended by the Torts (Interference with Goods) Act 1977. Section 1 of the Act made it clear that by 'wrongful interference with goods', it meant conversion, trespass to goods, 'negligence so far as it results in damage to goods or to an interest in goods' and 'any other tort so far as it results in damage to goods or to an interest in goods'. It did *not* create a new tort of 'wrongful interference with goods' – it simply reformed the law on what remedies would be available for the above nominate torts. Despite this, in *Kuwait Airways Corpn* v *Iraqi Airways Co (Nos 4 & 5)* (2002), Lord Nicholls said this:

---

[26] If A holds the property on trust for B and C, then B will only acquire a right to demand that A hand over the property to her if C agrees that she can do so. So B will not have an *immediate* right to demand possession of the property.

[27] *International Factors* v *Rodriguez* [1979] 1 QB 751.

[28] See *Pilcher* v *Rawlins* (1872) LR 7 Ch App 259.

[29] Though Tettenborn 1996 questions whether this is true (at 40–1). He argues that the real reason for maintaining that the beneficiary under a trust cannot bring a claim for conversion when the property is misappropriated is that to allow such a claim would expand the liabilities of: (1) innocent donees of trust property; (2) people who innocently assist a trustee to dispose of trust property; *and* (3) trustees who innocently commit a breach of trust by disposing of trust property to another.

The aim of the law, in respect of the wrongful interference with goods, is to provide a just remedy. Despite its proprietary base, *this tort* does not stand apart and command awards of damages measured by some special and artificial standard of its own. The fundamental object of an award of damages in respect of *this tort*, as with all wrongs, is to award just compensation for loss suffered.[30]

The 'tort' that Lord Nicholls is referring to as 'this tort' does not exist. There are only the torts that we are going to discuss in the next two sections. (We have already discussed situations where a claimant can sue in negligence for damage to her goods, or goods in which she has an interest.)[31]

17.3 CONVERSION

We begin by discussing the tort of conversion. The tort is a difficult one to understand because there is no good general definition of when someone will commit the tort. As Lord Nicholls observed in the *Kuwait Airways* case: 'Conversion of goods can occur in so many different circumstances that framing a precise definition of universal application is well nigh impossible.'[32] We will proceed by first of all identifying six typical ways in which the tort might be committed; we will then identify nine situations where someone who is being sued for doing something that would normally amount to conversion will be able to establish that they had a lawful justification or excuse for what they did.

A. Modes of conversion

As we have just said, there seem to be at least[33] six ways of committing the tort of conversion.

(1) *Taking possession.* The first way of committing the tort is to take possession of goods that are in another's possession, with the intention of keeping them.[34] So, for example, suppose *Thief* steals some jewellery from *Rich*, and then hands the jewellery over to *Buyer*. In this case, both *Thief* and *Buyer* will have committed the tort of conversion in relation to *Rich* – *Thief* in stealing the jewellery from *Rich* and *Buyer* in taking possession of the stolen jewellery with the intention of keeping it. *Buyer*, it should be noted, will have committed the tort of conversion in this situation even if he bought the jewellery from *Thief* in perfect good faith and had no idea it was stolen.

It is essential to show – for the purpose of showing that a defendant has committed the tort of conversion under this head – that the defendant *took possession* of the claimant's goods *with the intention of keeping them*.[35] For example, in *Tear* v *Freebody* (1858), the claimant unlawfully erected a building and the defendant was given the job of tearing the

---

[30] [2002] 2 AC 883, at [67] (emphasis added).

[31] See above, § 6.8.

[32] [2002] 2 AC 883, at [39]. See also Bramwell LJ in *Hiort* v *The London and North Western Railway Company* (1879) 4 Ex D 188, 194: 'I have frequently stated that I never did understand with precision what was a conversion . . . I find it impossible to give an exhaustive description as to what was or was not a conversion.'

[33] There may well be other ways of committing this tort. However, a student reader of this book need not be troubled with these.

[34] The expression 'keeping' here covers both the situation where A took possession of the goods with the intention of keeping them for himself and the situation where A took possession of the goods with the intention of giving them to a third party.

[35] See Lord Nicholls in *Kuwait Airways Corpn* v *Iraqi Airways Co* (Nos 4 & 5) [2002] 2 AC 883, at [42]: 'To constitute conversion detention . . . must be accompanied by an intention to keep the goods.' So someone who picks up a wallet in the street will not commit the tort of conversion if he picks it up with the object of restoring it to its rightful owner: *Isaack* v *Clark* (1615) 2 Bulstr 306, 312; 80 ER 1143, 1148.

building down. The defendant did so and then took the bricks and so on out of which the building was made to a stone yard, intending to retain them until he was paid for the work he had done in tearing down the building. The defendant was not entitled to do this. It was held that the defendant committed the tort of conversion in taking possession of the bricks.

In contrast, in *Club Cruise Entertainment* v *Department of Transport* (2008), a health and safety officer issued a notice detaining in port a ship in which there had been an outbreak of the norovirus. It was held that while the officer had no authority to issue this notice, he had not committed the tort of conversion in detaining the ship in port as he had not at any stage taken possession of the ship. Again, in *Fouldes* v *Willoughby* (1841), the defendant operated a ferry that ran between Birkenhead and Liverpool. The claimant took two horses on board the ferry, which the defendant refused to carry. The claimant refused to take the horses off the ferry so the defendant took hold of them and led them off the ferry and onto the shore where the defendant's brother took charge of them. The claimant stayed on the ferry which took him to Liverpool where he sent for the horses. The horses were never returned to him. The claimant sued the defendant, claiming that in taking the horses off the ferry he had committed the tort of conversion. The court doubted whether this was true: when the defendant took the horses off the ferry, he had no intention of keeping them.

(2) *Refusal to hand over goods*. Another way of committing the tort of conversion is by refusing to hand over goods in your possession that someone else has an immediate right to possess when they have been demanded from you.[36]

For example, in *Howard E Perry* v *British Railways Board* (1980), the members of the Iron and Steel Trades Confederation went on strike. In order to support this strike, the employees of the British Railways Board (BRB) were instructed by their union – the National Union of Railwaymen (NUR) – not to assist in the transport of any steel. The claimants had some 500 tonnes of steel located at various depots owned by the BRB which the BRB could not transport because of the action of the NUR. The claimants asked the BRB if they could collect the steel themselves and transport it by road but the BRB refused because it feared that if it agreed it would be subjected to further industrial action by the NUR. The claimants sued the BRB, claiming that it had committed the tort of conversion in refusing to hand over the steel to them. The claimants succeeded in their claim: the BRB had no lawful justification or excuse for refusing to hand over the claimants' steel to the claimants.

In order to show that A has committed the tort of conversion in relation to B under this head, it is essential to show that A *refused* to give B's property back to him. Merely showing that A failed to return B's property to him when he was supposed to is not enough. B must

---

[36] *Marcq* v *Christie's* [2004] QB 286, at [33]. A couple of authorities may be interpreted as contradicting this. In *Miller* v *Jackson* [1977] QB 966, at 978, Lord Denning MR remarked that it is not conversion to refuse to give back a cricket ball that has been hit into your back garden. However, this may be explained on the basis that if a cricket ball is hit into your back garden, you are legally entitled to refuse to give it back, so as to encourage people not to hit cricket balls onto your property. In *British Economical Lamp Co* v *Empire Mile End (Limited)* (1913) 29 TLR 386, the claimants hired out some electrical lamps to the tenants of a theatre which was owned by the defendants. When the tenants moved out of the theatre, they left the lamps behind. At the end of the period for which the lamps had been hired out, the claimants demanded their lamps back from the defendants. The defendants refused to hand over the lamps or to allow the claimants to come onto their land to remove the lamps themselves. It was held that the defendants did not commit the tort of conversion in refusing to allow the claimants to get their lamps back. This case *is* very difficult to reconcile with the position taken here and we are forced to suggest that it was wrongly decided.

have demanded the property back and A must have refused to give it back or to allow B to get it back herself.[37]

(3) *Delivery into hands of third party*. The third way of committing the tort of conversion is by intentionally doing something that resulted in goods in someone else's possession, or that someone has an immediate right to possess, being delivered[38] into the hands of a third party.

So, for example, *Chancer* will commit the tort of conversion if he pledges[39] *Owner's* property to *Pawn Store* when he has no lawful justification or excuse for doing so.[40] Similarly, if *Shop* gives *Agent* some goods to deliver to *Buyer* and *Agent* gives it to *Lucky* instead, *Agent* will normally be held to have committed the tort of conversion in relation to *Buyer*.

In order to make out that A has converted B's property under this head it is not necessary to show that A *physically* handed over B's property to a third party – but it must be shown that a third party obtained possession of B's property as a result of something A did.

In *Ashby* v *Tolhurst* (1937), a thief stole the claimant's car from a private parking ground which was supervised by an attendant. It was claimed that the attendant had committed the tort of conversion in allowing the thief to get away with the car. The claim was rejected. The thief did not obtain possession of the car as a result of anything the attendant did; all the attendant did was allow the thief to make good his escape once he had obtained possession of the claimant's car.

In contrast, in *Moorgate Mercantile Co Ltd* v *Finch and Read* (1962), the hirer of a car under a hire-purchase agreement lent his car to the defendant who, unknown to the hirer, used the car to smuggle watches into the country. When the defendant's activities were discovered, the car was forfeited and sold by the Customs and Excise authorities. The owners of the car argued that the defendant had committed the tort of conversion. The Court of Appeal agreed: Customs and Excise had obtained possession of the claimant's car as a result of what the defendant did – that is, smuggling watches in the claimant's car.

Similarly, in *R H Willis & Son* v *British Car Auctions Ltd* (1978), the claimants leased a car to one David Croucher under a hire-purchase agreement under which he would become the owner of the car after making a certain number of hire payments. Before Croucher had made enough hire payments to become owner of the car, he took the car to the defendant firm of car auctioneers and asked them to auction it for him. The minimum he was willing to accept for the car was £450. Unfortunately, at auction the highest bid was merely £400. The car was withdrawn but after the auction was over the auctioneers persuaded Croucher to sell the car to the highest bidder for £400 by agreeing to reduce their

---

[37] *Barclays Mercantile Finance Ltd* v *Sibec Developments Ltd* [1992] 1 WLR 1253, 1258 (per Millett J); also *Kuwait Airways Corpn* v *Iraqi Airways Co (Nos 4 & 5)* [2002] 2 AC 883, at [37] (per Lord Nicholls): 'mere unauthorised possession or detention is not an act of conversion. Demand and refusal to deliver up are required . . .'.

[38] It seems that for A to have committed the tort of conversion under this head, it is essential that his actions must have resulted in B's goods being *delivered* into the hands of a third party. So if A sells, or attempts to sell, B's goods to C, that will not *of itself* amount to conversion: it is only when the goods are actually handed over to C that the tort will have been committed. See, on this, *Lancashire Waggon Co* v *Fitzhugh* (1861) 6 H & N 502, 158 ER 206; *Consolidated Company* v *Curtis & Son* [1892] 1 QB 495, 498; *Marcq* v *Christie's* [2004] QB 286, at [19]. *A fortiori*, if A goes about insisting that B's goods belong to A, that will not amount to conversion: see Torts (Interference with Goods) Act 1977, s 11(3) ('Denial of title is not of itself conversion').

[39] A will pledge B's property to C if he transfers possession of that property to C as security for a debt owed by A to C.

[40] *Pawn Store* will also be held to have converted *Owner's* property by accepting it as a pledge. See s 11(2) of the Torts (Interference with Goods) Act 1977, which provides that '[receipt] of goods by way of pledge is conversion if delivery of the goods is conversion'.

commission on the sale. The claimants sued the defendants, claiming that they had committed the tort of conversion in acting as they did. (Croucher was not worth suing as he was bankrupt.) The defendants were held liable: the Court of Appeal held that the claimants' car had been delivered into a third party's hands as a result of the actions of the defendants in reducing their commission on the sale.

(4) *Use*. The fourth way of committing the tort of conversion is by using goods that are in someone else's possession, or which someone else has an immediate right to possess.[41] This has long been well acknowledged. As far back as 1591 it was observed: '[no] law compelleth him that finds a thing to keep it safely . . . but if a man findeth a thing and useth it, he is answerable, for it is conversion.'[42] Rolle's *Abridgement* took the same view: '[if] a man takes my horse and rides it and then redelivers it to me nevertheless I may have an action against him, for this is a conversion . . .'[43]

(5) *Destruction*. The fifth way of converting goods in someone else's possession, or which someone else has an immediate right to possess is by *intentionally* doing something that results in those goods being *destroyed*. Destruction is crucial – merely damaging someone else's goods does not amount to conversion. This can create difficulty because it is sometimes difficult to tell whether a given item of property has been damaged or destroyed. If a plank of wood is sawn in two that seems to be a case of damage rather than destruction.[44] But if a cask of wine is watered, that seems to be a case of destruction.[45]

(6) *Bailment*. Section 2(2) of the Torts (Interference with Goods) Act 1977 provides that: 'An action lies in conversion for loss or destruction of goods which a bailee has allowed to happen in breach of his duty to his bailor . . .'.

B. Defences

Now that we have looked at the different ways in which someone might commit the tort of conversion, we will look at a number of situations in which someone will be able to argue that they had a lawful justification or excuse for doing something that would normally amount to conversion of another's property.

(1) *Consent*. This is an obvious point which requires little amplification: a claimant cannot argue that a defendant committed the tort of conversion by interfering with property in her possession or which she had an immediate right to possess if she consented to the property being interfered with in the way it was.

(2) *Inquiry into title*. We have already seen that if A is in possession of goods that B has an immediate right to possess, A may commit the tort of conversion if he refuses to hand those goods over to B when they are demanded from him. But A will not commit the tort of conversion in so acting if it is reasonable for him to delay handing over the goods to B so that he can first look into whether B is the right person to hand the goods over to, and if he has refused to hand over the goods to B in order to inquire into B's title to the goods.

---

[41] There seems to be an exception in the case where a bailee uses property which he holds on a bailment for another without denying the bailor's right to the return of the property: *McKenna & Armistead Pty Ltd* v *Excavations Pty Ltd* (1957) 57 SR (NSW) 483.

[42] *Mulgrave v Ogden* (1591) Cro Eliz 219, 78 ER 475.

[43] Rolle, *Abridgement*, Action sur Case, p 5.

[44] *Simmons v Lillystone* (1853) 8 Ex 431, 155 ER 1417.

[45] *Richardson v Atkinson* (1723) 1 Stra 576, 93 ER 710.

For example, in *Clayton* v *Le Roy* (1911), *Owner* bought a watch from *Jeweller*. A few years later the watch was stolen. *Owner* asked *Jeweller* to keep an eye out for it. The watch went through a few people's hands before it was purchased by *Innocent*. *Innocent* sent the watch to *Jeweller* to be valued. *Jeweller* recognised the watch as being the one which had been stolen from *Owner*. He wrote to both *Owner* and *Innocent* informing them of the position and asking them what they wanted him to do. A few days later a representative of *Owner's* solicitors went to *Jeweller's* shop and demanded that he hand over the watch. *Jeweller* refused, and it was held rightly so: 'a man does not act unlawfully in refusing to deliver up property immediately upon demand made. He is entitled to take adequate time to inquire into the rights of the claimant.'[46]

It had always been thought that this principle did not apply in an *Armory* v *Delamirie* (1721) type situation where B gave goods to A to look after, or to look at, and B then demanded them back from A. In that situation, it had been always thought, that A had to give the goods back and could not say 'I must wait to inquire into whether you are really entitled to these goods.'[47] However, in *Spencer* v *S Franses Ltd* (2011), Thirlwall J held that if A was put on notice[48] that B might *not* be entitled to the goods that B has asked A to look after, or to look at, then A might be legally entitled to retain the goods for a reasonable time to see if B is the right person to whom to hand the goods.[49]

(3) *Animals Act 1971*. This authorises the occupier of land in certain cases to detain or destroy animals which trespass on his land. For example, s 7 gives the occupier of land powers to detain livestock trespassing on his land, and eventually to sell the livestock if no one has claimed it back. Section 9 allows an occupier of land to kill someone else's dog on his land if the dog was worrying the occupier's livestock and killing the dog was the only reasonable means of protecting the livestock.

(4) *Distress damage feasant*. If an *inanimate* item of property belonging to A is on B's land without permission and is causing damage to B's land or disrupting the operation of B's business on that land, B will be allowed: (a) to take steps to move that item of property so that it no longer causes any damage or disruption, and then (b) to detain it until B fairly compensates him for the damage or disruption caused by the presence of that item of property on his land.[50] This remedy is known as 'distress damage feasant'.[51]

(5) *Recaption*. If B is in possession of an item of property that rightly belongs to A, then A may be allowed to seize the item of property in question and take it into his possession. This will be the case, for example, if *Thief* steals *Owner's* goods and *Owner* arrests him while they are still on his person – *Owner* will be entitled to seize the goods and take them

---

[46] [1911] 2 KB 1031, 1051 (per Fletcher Moulton LJ).

[47] See *China Pacific SA* v *Food Corporation of India, The Winson* [1982] AC 939.

[48] [2011] EWHC 1269, at [295]: what is required is 'actual knowledge of facts indicating that the bailor is not in fact the owner.'

[49] [2011] EWHC 1269, at [300]. (But on the facts of the case – where the claimant gave the defendant some embroideries, asking the defendant to investigate their history – too much time (six years) had elapsed after the embroideries were entrusted to the defendant to make it reasonable for the defendant to withhold the embroideries from the claimant on the basis that it was doubtful whether the claimant was really entitled to the embroideries.)

[50] See, for example, *The Ambergate, Nottingham and Boston and Eastern Junction Railway Company* v *The Midland Railway Company* (1853) 2 E & B 793, 118 ER 964.

[51] The remedy of distress damage feasant also used to be available when an animal of B's strayed onto A's land and caused damage or destruction: see, for example, *Sorrell* v *Paget* [1950] 1 KB 252. But s 7(1) of the Animals Act 1971 provided that the 'right to seize any animal by way of distress damage feasant is hereby abolished'.

back into her possession.[52] What if a watch that rightly belongs to *Jeweller* is on *Landowner*'s land? When will *Jeweller* be allowed to go onto *Landowner*'s land and seize the watch and take it back into her possession? The position is unclear. If *Landowner* stole the watch from *Jeweller*, *Jeweller* will be allowed to go onto *Landowner*'s land and reclaim it.[53] But where *Landowner* came by the watch innocently, the position is far more uncertain. In *Anthony* v *Haney* (1832), Tindal CJ suggested in some *obiter dicta* that in such a case, *Jeweller* will only be entitled to go onto *Landowner*'s land and reclaim the watch if: (a) the watch ended up on *Landowner*'s land by accident; *or* (b) someone stole the watch from *Jeweller*; or (c) *Jeweller* has already asked *Landowner* to return the watch to her and *Landowner* has wrongfully refused to comply with that demand.

(6) *The Police and Criminal Evidence Act 1984.* Section 19 of the 1984 Act gives a constable who is lawfully on any premises the power to seize goods that he reasonably thinks have been obtained through the commission of an offence, or that he reasonably thinks amount to evidence relevant to some offence, if he reasonably thinks it is necessary to do so to prevent the goods 'being concealed, lost, damaged or destroyed'.

(7) *Returning goods.* If A has B's goods and B has an immediate right to possess those goods, A will of course do no wrong if he returns the goods to B. What if A gives the goods to a third party, C, with instructions to return them to B? A will be allowed to do this so long as it is *reasonable* to give the goods to C for the purpose of returning them to B.

In *Elvin & Powell Ltd* v *Plummer Roddis Ltd* (1934), a conman approached the claimants – a firm of coat makers – and ordered about £350 worth of coats, asking them to be delivered to the defendants' shop. The coats were sent and the conman sent a telegram to the defendants in the claimant company's name, saying 'Goods despatched to your branch in error. Sending van to collect.' When the coats arrived at the defendants' shop, the conman turned up in a van and took the coats from them. He then disappeared. The claimants sued the defendants, claiming that they had committed the tort of conversion in handing the coats over to the conman. The claim was rejected – the defendants had only handed the coats to the conman because they wanted to return them to the claimants and it had been reasonable for them to hand the coats over to the conman for the purpose of returning them to the claimants.

This defence was not available to the defendants in *Hiort* v *Bott* (1874). In that case, the claimants mistakenly sent the defendants an invoice for barley together with a delivery order. The defendants had not in fact ordered any barley from the claimants but the invoice stated that the defendants had ordered the barley through one G. The defendants got in touch with G. He said there had been a mistake and asked them to endorse the delivery order to him so that he could have the barley delivered to the customer who actually ordered it. This the defendants did. G then used the delivery order to obtain the barley himself and absconded with it. The claimants sued the defendants, claiming that the defendants, in endorsing the delivery order, had committed the tort of conversion. The court agreed: the defendants had delivered the barley into G's hands without the claimants' consent and they had no lawful justification or excuse for doing so. They could not argue that they had delivered the barley into G's hands in order to return it to the claimants as the barley was already in the claimants' hands at the time they signed the delivery order.

---

[52] *Whatford* v *Carty, The Times*, 29 October 1960.
[53] *Patrick* v *Colerick* (1838) 3 M & W 483, 150 ER 1235.

(8) *The principle in Hollins v Fowler*. In *Hollins* v *Fowler* (1875), Blackburn J argued:

> I cannot find it anywhere distinctly laid down, but I submit to your Lordships that on principle, one who deals with goods at the request of the person who has the actual custody of them, in the bona fide belief that the custodier is the true owner, or has the authority of the true owner, should be excused for what he does if the act is of such a nature as would be excused if done by the authority of the person in possession ... Thus a warehouseman with whom goods had been deposited is guilty of no conversion by keeping them, or restoring them to the person who deposited them with him, though that person turns out to have had no authority from the true owner.[54]

So if *Thief* steals *Owner's* dog and, pretending to *Pound* that the dog is his, asks *Pound* to look after the dog over the weekend, *Pound* will not commit the tort of conversion in relation to *Owner* if *Pound* gives the dog back to *Thief* at the end of the weekend.[55] Again, suppose *Thief* steals *Owner's* painting and, pretending that the painting is his, hands it over to *Agent* so that she can find a buyer for it. If *Agent* cannot find a buyer and hands the painting back to *Thief*, she will not commit the tort of conversion in relation to *Owner* in so doing.[56]

(9) *Common currency*. In the interests of ensuring the smooth running of the economy, the law provides that someone who accepts stolen money paid over to him as common currency will not be liable for conversion: 'Conversion does not lie for money, taken and received as currency ...'[57] So if *Thief* steals some money out of *Owner's* wallet he will commit the tort of conversion. But if *Thief* takes that money and uses it to pay for some goods in *Supermarket* using that money, *Supermarket* will not commit the tort of conversion in accepting that money.

17.4 TRESPASS TO GOODS

A will have committed the tort of trespass to goods in relation to B if: (1) he directly interfered with goods in B's possession; (2) he did so intentionally or carelessly;[58] *and* (3) he had no lawful justification or excuse for acting as he did. Only three points need to be made about this tort.

---

[54] (1875) LR 7 HL 757, 766–7.

[55] What would be the position if *Thief* instructed *Pound* at the end of the weekend to give the dog to *Third Party*? Would *Pound* commit the tort of conversion in relation to *Owner* if she handed the dog over to *Third Party*? The Privy Council's decision in *Maynegrain Pty Ltd* v *Compafina Bank* (1984) 58 ALJR 389 could be read as suggesting that the answer is 'no'. However, that case may rest on technicalities of the law of agency which do not apply in *Pound's* case.

[56] *Marcq* v *Christie's* [2004] QB 286. There is an issue as to whether *Hollins* v *Fowler* goes even further and says that if *Agent* found a *Buyer* for the painting, she would not be liable for conversion if she sold and delivered the painting to *Buyer*. According to the terms of the principle in *Hollins* v *Fowler*, she should not be liable, but that may be pushing the principle too far.

[57] *Lipkin Gorman* v *Karpnale Ltd* [1991] 2 AC 548, 559 (per Lord Templeman). For similar reasons, the law provides that a bank that accepts a stolen cheque will not be liable in conversion so long as it acted in good faith and without negligence in accepting the cheque: Cheques Act 1957, s 4.

[58] This seems to follow from *Fowler* v *Lanning* [1959] 1 QB 426. See *National Coal Board* v *J E Evans & Co (Cardiff) Ltd* [1951] 2 KB 861, where the defendant contractors struck an underground cable belonging to the claimants when digging a trench on land belonging to the local county council. The claimants sued the defendants, claiming that they had committed the tort of trespass to goods in damaging the cable. Held: no trespass, even though the defendants had directly interfered with the claimants' cable – they had not intended to damage the cable and had not carelessly damaged the cable as they did not know and had no reason to know it was under the land on which they were digging.

A. The requirement of direct interference

It is easier to provide illustrations of situations in which someone's goods[59] will be directly interfered with than it is to define what directly interfering with someone's goods involves. So if *Sadist* beats *Gran's* cat, he will directly interfere with it;[60] but he will not if he kills the cat by laying down some poison which the cat eats. *Warden* will directly interfere with *Driver's* car if he places a wheel clamp on it;[61] but he will not if he locks the entrance to the land on which the car is parked, so that the car cannot be driven away.[62] If *Chancer* gets on *Rich's* horse and rides away on it, she will directly interfere with the horse; but she will not if her dog escapes her control, runs up to the horse and makes it run away by barking at it.

B. Lawful justification or excuse

Suppose A has directly interfered with B's goods. Not much more needs to be said here, in addition to what has been said in the previous section, on the issue of when A will be able to establish that he had a lawful justification or excuse for interfering with B's goods. Only three situations where a defendant might try to set up a defence to a claimant's action for trespass to goods need to be mentioned here.

(1) *Wheel clamping.* The question of when wheel-clamping someone's car that has been parked on your land will amount to a trespass has exercised the courts in the past,[63] but cl 54 of the Protection of Freedoms Bill 2011 that is (at the time of writing) currently before Parliament will (if enacted into law) render the question irrelevant by providing that:

(1) A person commits an offence who, without lawful authority –
(a) immobilises a vehicle . . .
intending to prevent . . . the removal of the vehicle by a person otherwise entitled to remove it.

(2) The express or implied consent . . . of a person otherwise entitled to remove the vehicle to the immobilisation, movement or restriction concerned is not lawful authority for the purposes of subsection (1).

(2) *Divorce.* In a situation where *Wife* and *Husband's* marriage is in the process of breaking down, and *Wife* fears that *Husband* will not fully disclose the extent of his assets to the courts, so as to minimise the amount of support (known as ancillary relief) that he will be ordered to pay *Wife* on divorce, the question of whether *Wife* will commit a trespass to goods by copying bank statements or letters addressed to *Husband* that reveal the true state of his finances has been recently addressed by the Court of Appeal.

In *White v Withers* (2009), the Court of Appeal divided on the issue. Ward LJ held that *Wife* would commit the tort of trespass to goods in so acting, though, depending on the facts

---

[59] For the sake of convenience, in this chapter when goods are referred to as 'someone's goods' or some equivalent expression is used, what is meant is *not* that those goods belong to that someone but that that someone is in possession of those goods.
[60] *Slater* v *Swann* (1730) 2 Stra 872, 93 ER 906.
[61] *Arthur* v *Anker* [1997] QB 564; *Vine* v *Waltham Forest LBC* [2000] 1 WLR 2383.
[62] *Hartley* v *Moxham* (1842) 3 QB 701, 114 ER 675.
[63] See *Arthur* v *Anker* [1997] QB 564 (not trespass so long as driver voluntarily took risk that car might be clamped) and *Vine* v *Waltham Forest LBC* [2000] 1 WLR 2383 (driver who parked car and did not see sign warning that vehicles might be clamped because it was obscured did not voluntarily take risk that it might be clamped).

of the case, the damages payable to *Husband* might turn out to be nominal.[64] Wilson LJ suggested that *Wife* would not commit the tort of trespass to goods, so long as she did not use force to obtain the documents, did not retain the originals, and had reasonable grounds for believing that her *Husband* would not in subsequent divorce proceedings disclose the true state of his finances.[65] Sedley LJ expressed some sympathy for Wilson LJ's position:

> if a choice has to be made between the sanctity of property and the value of privacy on the one hand and the doing of justice between spouses on the other, the law is in a position to choose the latter.[66]

In the subsequent case of *Imerman* v *Tchenguiz* (2011), the Court of Appeal strongly approved the position taken by Ward LJ in *White* v *Withers* (2009).[67] The Court of Appeal held that the need for *Wife* and her lawyers to be able to obtain a accurate picture of *Husband*'s finances in order to prevent *Husband* cheating *Wife* out of her due in any matrimonial proceedings between them did *not* justify interfering with his property:

> The tort of trespass to chattels has been known to our law since the Middle Ages . . . yet no hint of any defences of the kind now being suggested is to be found anywhere in the books. Self-help has a narrow and jealously policed role to play, for example, in the form of the right in certain circumstances to abate a nuisance, but it is far too late to suggest that self-help should be extended into the territory we are here concerned with.[68]

(3) *Trivial touching.* In *White* v *Withers* (2009), Ward LJ suggested that it was arguable that a trivial touching of another's goods that was 'acceptable in the ordinary conduct of daily life'[69] would not amount to a trespass to goods.[70] Even if it did, such a trespass would not give rise to a claim for anything more than nominal damages and a claim for such damages could be struck out as an abuse of process.[71]

C. The requirement of possession

As we have said, A will commit the tort of trespass to goods in relation to B if he directly interferes with goods in B's *possession* when he has no lawful justification or excuse for doing so. But it is not always necessary for B to show that goods that have been interfered with were in her possession before she can sue for a trespass to them.

(1) *Trust.* If *Trustee* held goods on trust for *Beneficiary* and *Beneficiary* was in possession of them at the time *Third Party*, without lawful justification or excuse, directly interfered with them, *Third Party* will have committed the tort of trespass to goods in relation to *Trustee* as well as *Beneficiary*.[72]

(2) *Death.* If A, without lawful justification or excuse, directly interfered with a deceased's goods, A will have committed the tort of trespass to goods in relation to the deceased's executors or administrators even if they had not taken possession of the goods at the time A interfered with them.[73]

---

[64] [2009] EWCA Civ 1122, at [58].
[65] [2009] EWCA Civ 1122, at [83].
[66] [2009] EWCA Civ 1122, at [73].
[67] [2010] EWCA Civ 908, at [105].
[68] [2011] EWCA Civ 908, at [117].
[69] Quoting Robert Goff LJ in *Collins* v *Wilcock* [1984] 1 WLR 1172, 1178.
[70] [2009] EWCA Civ 1122, at [59]–[61].
[71] [2009] EWCA Civ 1122, at [61]. Sedley LJ seemed to agree at [72].
[72] *White* v *Morris* (1852) 11 CB 1015, 138 ER 778; *Barker* v *Furlong* [1891] 2 Ch 172.
[73] *Tharpe* v *Stallwood* (1843) 5 M & G 760, 134 ER 766.

(3) *Franchise*. If B is the owner of a franchise (as will be the case, for example, if B has the right to the goods on a shipwreck), A will commit the tort of trespass to goods in relation to B if he, without lawful justification or excuse, directly interferes with the goods covered by that franchise – and this is so even if B has not yet taken possession of those goods.[74]

(4) *Theft*. In *White* v *Withers* (2009), Ward LJ considered what the position would be if *Wife* took financial documents that belonged to *Husband* and handed them over to her *Solicitor* to look at. Would *Solicitor* commit the tort of trespass to goods in relation to *Husband* by touching the documents? Ward LJ was uneasy with the idea that *Husband* could not bring a claim against *Solicitor* for trespass to goods merely because *Husband* was not in possession of the stolen documents at the time they were handed over to *Solicitor*. He thought that if *Solicitor* took the documents knowing that they had been stolen, then his 'taking possession and handling the documents may be as trespassory as' *Wife*'s.[75] But he expressed no concluded view on the issue.

17.5 BAILMENT

In *TRM Copy Centres (UK) Ltd* v *Lanwall Services Ltd* (2009), the House of Lords held that:

> bailment . . . embraces all situations in which possession of goods is given by one person to another upon the condition that they shall be restored to the person by whom possession has been given, or dealt with as he directs upon expiry of the agreed period of possession . . .[76]

While it is arguable that a bailment exists in *any* situation where A is voluntarily in possession of B's goods,[77] it is true that the *central case* of a bailment is the case where A has been *entrusted* with B's goods.[78] And that is the case we will focus on in this section. Two such cases can be distinguished:

(1) *Simple bailment*. In this case *Owner* entrusts *Bailee* with goods that belong to her. *Bailee* will hold the goods on a bailment for *Owner*, and will normally owe *Owner* a duty to take reasonable steps to ensure that those goods are not lost, stolen, destroyed, or damaged. If the goods come to some harm while in *Bailee*'s hands, the burden of proof will be on *Bailee* to show that they were not harmed as a result of his neglect.[79] If he cannot show this, he will be held to have breached the duty of care that he owed *Owner*, and will be held liable accordingly.[80]

(2) *Sub-bailment*. In this case *Owner* entrusts *Bailee* with goods that belong to her, and then *Bailee* hands the goods over to *Sub-Bailee*, for *Sub* to look after them. In this situation, *Owner* will be able to sue *Bailee* if her goods come to some harm due to *Sub*'s neglect of them. The duty of care *Bailee* will owe *Owner* is non-delegable.[81] So if *Sub* – having been entrusted with the task of looking after *Owner*'s goods – fails to protect them properly, *Sub* will put *Bailee* in breach of the duty of care he owed *Owner*, and will be held liable

---

[74] *Bailiffs of Dunwich* v *Sterry* (1831) 1 B & Ad 831, 109 ER 995.

[75] [2009] EWCA Civ 1122, at [49].

[76] [2009] 1 WLR 1375, at [10] (per Lord Hope).

[77] There is an exception where C hands goods over to A to look after them and then sells the goods to B while they are still in A's possession. In such a case, A will only hold those goods on a bailment for B if he attorns to B (that is, if he acknowledges that he holds those goods on a bailment for B).

[78] So it is debatable whether a thief who has stolen *Owner*'s goods will hold those goods on a bailment for *Owner*.

[79] See above, § 8.7.

[80] See below, § 17.6.

[81] See above, § 8.6(B)(2).

accordingly. *Bailee* will then be able to sue *Sub* on the basis that *Sub* was holding *Owner's* goods on a bailment for *Bailee*, and therefore owed *Bailee* a duty to take reasonable steps to look after them, which duty he breached. Even if *Owner* never sues *Bailee*, *Bailee* will still be entitled to sue *Sub* for substantial damages for the harm done to *Owner's* goods, which damages will then be held on trust for *Owner*.[82]

Where things get complicated is if *Owner* wants to sue *Sub* *directly* for the harm done to her goods. If *Sub* carelessly did something positive that foreseeably resulted in *Owner's* goods being harmed, then *Owner* can simply sue *Sub* under the general law of negligence, arguing that *Sub* owed her, as the owner of the goods, a duty to take care not to act as he did.[83]

But let's suppose that *Sub* merely *failed to protect Owner's* goods from being harmed. In such a case, *Owner* will only be able to sue *Sub* if he owed her a positive duty to protect her goods from being harmed. Probably the only way *Owner* will be able to do this is if she can establish that when *Sub* received her goods from *Bailee*, he not only held them on a bailment for *Bailee*, but *also* for *Owner*. If *Owner* can show this, then she may be able to argue that *Sub* owed her a duty to take reasonable steps to protect her goods from being harmed. So *Owner* will have to establish two things: (a) that *Sub* held *Owner's* goods on a bailment for her; and (b) that the terms of that bailment required *Sub* to take reasonable steps to protect *Owner's* goods from coming to harm.

So far as (a) is concerned, the cases are pretty clear that *Sub* will have held *Owner's* goods on a bailment for her if and only if, when he received her goods from *Bailee*, he was aware that those goods did not belong to *Bailee*.[84] So far as (b) is concerned, if *Sub* held *Owner's* goods on a bailment for *Owner*, he will have owed *Owner* a duty to take reasonable steps to protect those goods from being harmed unless he: (i) made it clear to *Bailee* that he was not willing to be subject to such a duty when he accepted the goods from *Bailee*; and (ii) *Owner* authorised *Bailee* to entrust the goods to someone like *Sub* on the terms on which *Bailee* entrusted those goods to *Sub*.[85]

17.6 REMEDIES

The law on what remedies will be available when someone commits a tort to a thing is very complex. Perhaps the best way of approaching it is by considering a series of examples of situations where such a tort has been committed.

> (1) *Thief* steals *Owner's* car, who then sells it to *Gullible* for £4,000 (a fair price). *Gullible* drives the car for six months and then sells it to *Innocent* for £3,000 (a fair price). *Innocent* subsequently crashes the car and it is written-off.

In this situation, *Thief*, *Gullible* and *Innocent* have all committed the tort of conversion in relation to *Owner*. *Thief* has done so twice – first by stealing *Owner's* car, and then by handing it over to *Gullible*. *Gullible* has also converted *Owner's* car twice – first by accepting the car from *Thief* and then by handing it over to *Innocent*. *Innocent* has only converted the car once – by accepting it from *Gullible*. *Innocent's* crashing the car does not amount to conversion as he did not do that intentionally.

---

[82] *The Winkfield* [1902] P 42, 61.
[83] See above, § 6.9.
[84] *The Pioneer Container* [1994] 2 AC 324, 342 (per Lord Goff); *Marcq v Christie's* [2003] 3 WLR 980, at [49]–[50].
[85] *Morris v CW Martin Ltd* [1966] 1 WLR 716, 729 (per Lord Denning MR); *The Pioneer Container* [1994] 2 AC 324.

As *Owner's* car is irrecoverable, the only remedy *Owner* can pursue is that of damages. The normal rule in conversion cases is that if the claimant has not recovered the property that has been converted, he can sue *anyone* who has converted that property for *market value* damages equal to the value of the property at the time it was converted and *consequential* damages for any further losses he has suffered as a result of having his property converted. Lord Nicholls attempted in *Kuwait Airways Corpn* v *Iraqi Airways Co (Nos 4 & 5)* (2002) to argue that *market value damages* are really compensatory in nature:

> The fundamental object of an award of damages in respect of this tort, as with all wrongs, is to award just compensation for loss suffered. Normally ('prima facie') the measure of damages is the market value of the goods at the time the defendant expropriated them. This is the general rule, because generally this measure represents the amount of the basic loss suffered by the defendant. He has been dispossessed of his goods by the defendant. Depending on the circumstances some other measure, yielding a higher or lower amount, may be appropriate.[86]

It is debatable whether this is true.[87] For example, in the case we are considering *Gullible* could argue that he has not really done anything to add to the loss suffered by *Owner* as a result of having his car stolen by *Thief* – so why should he be liable to pay *Owner* either £4,000 (the value of the car at the time *Gullible* received it from *Thief*) or £3,000 (the value of the car at the time *Gullible* passed it on to *Innocent*)? However, Lord Nicholls argued in the *Kuwait Airways* case that *Gullible's* liability to pay market value damages to *Owner* is really compensatory because his wrong in converting *Owner's* car lies in his *not giving the car back to Owner*: 'By definition, each person in a series of conversions wrongfully excludes the owner from possession of his goods. This is the basis on which each is liable to the owner.'[88] And had *Gullible* given the car back to *Owner*, either at the time he received it from *Thief* or at the time he passed it on to *Innocent*, *Owner* would have received an asset worth £4,000 or £3,000 respectively.

Whatever the basis of a converter's liability to pay the victim of his tort market value damages (in a case where the converted property has not been restored to the claimant), it is clear that in this case, *Owner* will be entitled to sue:

(i)   *Thief* for £4,000 (the value of the car at the time it was stolen, or handed over to *Gullible*); or

(ii) *Gullible* for £4,000 (the value of the car at the time *Gullible* received it) or £3,000 (the value of the car at the time *Gullible* handed it over to *Innocent*); or

(iii) *Innocent* for £3,000 (the value of the car at the time *Innocent* received it).

If *Owner* sues *Thief* and recovers £4,000, his title to sue *Gullible* and *Innocent* for conversion will then be extinguished. The idea is that by recovering £4,000 from *Thief*, *Owner's* title to the car subsequently received by *Gullible* and *Innocent* is retrospectively extinguished.[89]

(2) The same as (1), except when *Gullible* received the car from *Thief*, he improved it and sold it to *Innocent* for £6,000 (a fair price).

In this situation, if *Owner* is allowed to sue *Gullible* for *market value damages* equal to the value of *Owner's* car at the time it was sold to *Innocent* (£6,000), this would be unfair on

---

[86] [2002] 2 AC 883, at [67].
[87] For a full discussion of the basis of the right to sue for the price of the goods in conversion cases, see Tettenborn 1993.
[88] [2002] 2 AC 883, at [82].
[89] Torts (Interference with Goods) Act 1977, s 5.

Gullible. He will not receive any return for the work he did improving *Owner*'s car. To avoid this happening, s 6 of the Torts (Interference with Goods) Act 1977 provides that the damages payable to *Owner* in respect of *Gullible*'s converting *Owner*'s car by handing it over to *Innocent* will be reduced to £4,000.

> (3) *Chancer* goes for a ride on *Rich*'s horse, without *Rich*'s permission. *Chancer* returns the horse safely to its stable, without anyone having missed the horse and without having harmed the horse in any way. His actions have, however, been filmed on a CCTV camera, and *Rich* subsequently sees the footage.

In this situation, *Chancer* has converted *Rich*'s horse by using it, but as *Rich* still has the horse, he cannot sue *Chancer* for the value of the horse.[90] If *Rich* had suffered a loss as a result of *Chancer* converting his horse, he could sue for that – but there seems to be no loss here. However, the law does not leave *Rich* without a remedy in this situation. *Rich* will be entitled to sue *Chancer* for a reasonable sum for the use he has made of his horse. This remedy will be discussed in much more detail in subsequent chapters.[91]

> (4) *Supplier* rents a machine to *Factory* for a year. After the year is up, *Supplier* demands the return of the machine, but *Factory* continues to use it.

Here, there is no doubt that *Factory* has converted *Supplier*'s machine by refusing to give back the machine when it was demanded. But what is *Supplier*'s remedy? *Supplier* might want the courts to order *Factory* to give back the machine. (This remedy is known as *specific restitution of goods.*) The power to make such an order is now given to the courts by s 3(2)(a) of the Torts (Interference with Goods) Act 1977; however the courts will not exercise this power in cases where the property that has been converted 'is an ordinary article of commerce and of no special value or interest, and not alleged to be of any special value to the [claimant], and where damages would fully compensate.'[92] So in this case, it is unlikely that the courts would order that *Factory* hand over the machine to *Supplier*. Instead, the courts will probably exercise their powers under s 3(2)(b) of the 1977 Act to order that *Factory either* give the machine back *or* pay *Supplier* damages equal to the value of the machine at the time *Factory* converted it.

An important difference between these two options is that if *Factory* gives the machine back, it will still be liable to pay *Supplier* a reasonable sum for the use it made of *Supplier*'s machine after the lease of the machine expired, in the same way that *Chancer* was liable to pay *Rich* a reasonable sum for the use he made of *Rich*'s horse in (3). By contrast, if *Factory* pays *Supplier* damages equal to the value of the machine at the time they converted it, that will – by virtue of s 5 of the 1977 Act – have the effect of retrospectively extinguishing *Supplier*'s title to the machine. Which means, in turn, that *Supplier* will have no basis for suing *Factory* for a reasonable sum for the use it made of the machine after it refused to give it back to *Supplier*. The machine will be treated as though it belonged to *Factory*, and not *Supplier*, when *Factory* carried on using it.[93]

---

[90] See *BBMB Finance (Hong Kong) Ltd* v *Eda Holdings Ltd* [1990] 1 WLR 409.

[91] See below, § 31.3; also § 32.2.

[92] *Whiteley Limited* v *Hilt* [1918] 2 KB 808, 819 (per Swinfen Eady J). See also *IBL Ltd* v *Coussens* [1991] 2 All ER 133, 137 (per Neill LJ) and *Tanks and Vessels Industries Ltd* v *Devon Cider Company Ltd* [2009] EWHC 1360 (Ch), [55]–[56]. Specific restitution of goods was ordered in relation to a quantity of steel in *Howard E Perry & Co Ltd* v *British Railways Board* [1980] 1 WLR 1375, at a time when widespread industrial action meant that steel was hard to obtain.

[93] *Tanks and Vessels Industries Ltd* v *Devon Cider Company Ltd* [2009] EWHC 1360 (Ch).

Many students will think it outrageous that *Factory* will in this situation be able to keep *Supplier*'s machine so long as it is willing to give *Supplier* what the machine was worth at the time it first converted it by refusing to hand it over. This seems to allow *Factory* to compulsorily purchase *Supplier*'s machine. However, if *Factory* behaved in a particularly outrageous manner in refusing to give back *Supplier*'s machine, it may be liable to pay *Supplier* aggravated and exemplary damages.[94] So a blatant disregard for *Supplier*'s rights will attract some kind of sanction from the courts.

> (5) *Widow* deposits a number of boxes at *Storage* company's warehouse. Due to *Storage*'s fault, a fire breaks out and *Widow*'s boxes are burned to a crisp. *Widow* is distraught because the boxes contained all of her late husband's effects.

In this case, *Storage* has breached the duty of care that it owed *Widow* as a bailee of her boxes to take reasonable steps to protect those boxes from coming to any harm. In *Yearworth* v *North Bristol NHS Trust* (2010), the Court of Appeal held that the rules governing the assessment of damages in a case where a bailee has breached the duty of care that he owed his bailor are '*sui generis*'[95] and 'more akin [to the rules relating] to breach of contract rather than to tort.'[96] The major difference between the rules for assessing damages in breach of contract cases, as opposed to tort cases, is that the rule on remoteness of damage in breach of contract cases is that a loss suffered as a result of a breach of contract will count as too remote to be recoverable if it was not reasonably foreseeable that kind of loss might be suffered as a result of the contract being breached *at the time the contract was entered into*. So in the case we are looking at here, *Widow* will not be able to recover for her distress at the loss of her late husband's effects if it was not foreseeable at the time she deposited the boxes at *Storage* that she would suffer that kind of distress if the boxes were lost.

Further reading

The areas of law dealt with in this chapter are so thick with complication and confusion that only the most confident academics dare to write about them. Numbered among these intrepid souls are **Peter Birks ('Personal property: proprietary rights and remedies' (2000) 11 *King's College Law Journal* 1)**, Andrew Tettenborn **('Damages in conversion – the exception or the anomaly?' (1993) 52 *Cambridge Law Journal* 128**, and **'Trust property and conversion: an equitable confusion' (1996) 55 *Cambridge Law Journal* 36)**, Sarah Green **('Understanding the wrongful interference actions' (2010) 74 *Conveyancer and Property Lawyer* 15)**, Simon Douglas **('The nature of conversion' (2009) 68 *Cambridge Law Journal* 198)**, and Graham McBain **('Modernising and codifying the law of bailment' [2008] *Journal of Business Law* 1)**.

Visit **www.mylawchamber.co.uk/mcbride** to access tools to help you develop and test your knowledge of Tort law, including interactive multiple choice questions, practice exam questions with guidance, weblinks, legal newsfeed, additional case summaries, legal updates and tips on answering problem and essay questions.

premium
mylawchamber
unrivalled support for legal education

---

[94] Discussed below, chapters 29–30.
[95] [2010] QB 1, at [48](h).
[96] [2010] QB 1, at [48](i).

18 Torts to intangible property

18.1 The basics *508*

18.2 Intellectual property *511*

18.3 Goodwill *513*

18.4 Contractual rights *516*

18.5 Virtual property *519*

Overview

Having looked, in the previous chapter, at when interfering with a tangible thing would amount to a tort, we explain in this chapter when interfering with property that cannot be touched will, and will not, amount to a tort. Tort law's roots in the need to protect people from trespassory touchings and breakings means this area of law is still developing (and some would say, still ill-developed). So far, what protection tort law gives to people against interferences with intangibles has focused on protecting the accoutrements of business, such as intellectual property rights (section 18.2) and the goodwill attached to a business' name and products (section 18.3). Attempts to expand the tort of conversion to cover unauthorised disposals of other people's contractual rights have been firmly rebuffed, and they are discussed in section 18.4. Section 18.5 deals with a topic that is destined eventually to become 'hot': how far the law should protect resources that have been acquired in the course of, and exist only within, a computer game.

18.1 THE BASICS

This chapter is about: (1) when someone can say of something that cannot be touched, 'Legally, that's mine!'; (2) what rights such a person will have; and (3) what remedies the law will make available when those rights are violated.

Someone who can say of something that cannot be touched, 'Legally, that's mine!' will normally enjoy two basic rights against everyone else in the world. The first is a right that other people not culpably destroy or damage, or otherwise interfere with the owner's use and enjoyment, of the thing that is his. Let's call this kind of right a *use right*. The second is a right that other people not exploit that thing without the owner's permission. Let's call this kind of right an *exclusivity right*. Exclusivity rights are hugely important, because if you have the right to stop someone exploiting something without your permission, then you can make money licensing them to exploit that thing.

This is quite abstract, so let's put some flesh on these bones with a concrete example. In 2004, Cameron and Tyler Winklevoss sued Mark Zuckerberg, the creator of Facebook, claiming that he had stolen their idea of creating an exclusive social network for Harvard University students. (The Winklevosses had originally approached Zuckerberg to ask him to work on creating the social network.) One way they could have tried to make out their claim against Zuckerberg would have been to argue that, legally, the idea of creating an exclusive social network for Harvard students belonged to them. If that had been the case, they could have argued that they had an exclusivity right that Zuckerberg not use their idea without their permission, thus opening the door to charging Zuckerberg a licence fee for using their idea, or suing him for damages for exploiting their idea without their permission. Unfortunately for the Winklevosses, you cannot own a mere idea. So they could not argue that their idea for creating an exclusive social network for Harvard students legally belonged to them. Instead, they were forced to bring a breach of contract claim against Zuckerberg instead, which was settled for $65m.

So if ideas – of and in themselves – cannot be legally owned,[1] what sort of *intangibles* can be owned? Songs, films, the contents of books, and other original forms of expression, when put in permanent form, are the subject of *copyright* – with the result that no one else is allowed to copy them. (So if another tort textbook writer plagiarised chunks of this book, he or she would be sued for breach of copyright by our publishers, who hold the copyright on this book.) Someone who has *patented* a new idea for an invention will have a right that no one else exploit that idea (even if they came up with it themselves, quite independently). The law provides similar protections against properly *registered designs* and *trade marks* being exploited by other people. Copyrights, patents, registered designs and trade marks make up the stuff of intellectual property law, which is the primary body of law within tort law[2] that is concerned with recognising and protecting people's property in intangibles. But the law on passing off also belongs to this area of tort law. The law on *passing off* recognises people as owning the goodwill that attaches to their name or business, and protects those people from others damaging or exploiting that goodwill.[3] The law of tort already goes some way – through the tort of *inducing a breach of contract* – towards protecting people from having their contractual rights interfered with by other people. We deal with the tort of inducing a breach of contract in chapter 24, but in section 4 of this chapter, we look at whether the law of *conversion* (which we discussed in the previous chapter)[4] should be extended to protect people from having their contractual rights interfered with or devalued by others. The final section of this chapter discusses whether the law of tort should get involved with protecting *virtual property* – that is, resources that are acquired and exist within the confines of a computer game that creates a virtual world for players to move around in – from being interfered with by other people.

But before we get into the details of the areas of law dealt with in this chapter, it is worth asking – for the sake of evaluating and discussing these areas of law – why the law should ever get into the business of recognising people as owning intangibles? For example, when they were starting out in the music business, Paul McCartney and John Lennon thought that songs didn't belong to anyone. They thought that songs just floated around in the ether and were simply written down by people like Lennon and McCartney who had the talent to 'hear' them. As a result, they thought song writers had no more right to say that

---

[1] You also cannot own a gap in the market which you have spotted and worked hard to develop and fill. If someone else sees how well you are doing, and decides to muscle in on your territory, you have no recourse: *Cadbury Schweppes Pty Ltd* v *Pub Squash Co Pty Ltd* [1981] RPC 429 (held, no tort committed by defendant who marketed a sports drink aimed at the same kind of consumer as the claimant's sports drink).

[2] Though in one of those inter-jurisdictional classificatory disputes that bedevils the law of tort, some might say intellectual property law belongs to equity and not tort law. (On the relationship between tort law and equity, see above, § 1.9.)

[3] In *Inland Revenue Commissioners* v *Muller & Co's Margarine Ltd* [1901] AC 217, Lord Macnaghten recognised (at 223) that the goodwill attached to someone's name or business was a form of property that someone could own: 'It is very difficult . . . to say that goodwill is not property. Goodwill is bought and sold every day. It may be acquired, I think, in any of the different ways in which property is usually acquired. When a man has got it he may keep it as his own. He may vindicate his exclusive right to it if necessary by process of law. He may dispose of it if he will – of course under the conditions attaching to property of that nature.'

[4] See above, § 17.3.

those songs were 'theirs' than anyone else did. Why does the law not take the same position and say that songs, and other intangibles, belong to no one? A number of different arguments have traditionally been made in favour of the view that the law should recognise people as having use rights and exclusivity rights over certain intangibles.

A. Moral arguments

The moral argument in favour of the law's recognising that people own certain intangibles comes from John Locke's *labour theory* of property, as set out in his 1698 work *Two Treatises of Government*. According to this theory, you own something if it is the product of your labour. So if you have worked long hours writing a book or a song, or producing a film or a drug, you are entitled to say that book/song/film/drug belongs to you. The argument is intuitively appealing, but one limit to, and one flaw in, the argument should be noted.

The limit is that the theory only applies where no one has a prior, or better, claim to the thing that you have produced. For example, if you take someone else's block of marble and turn it into a statue, you cannot argue that the statue belongs to you. Locke himself was careful to confine his labour theory of property to cases where someone removed something 'out of the state that Nature hath provided and left it in' – with the result that 'he hath mixed his labour with it, and joined to it something that is his own, and thereby makes it his property.'[5] That is, a case where the thing that is being made your own is something that was originally unowned.

The flaw in the theory is that many people's work may have gone into producing a given work. Certainly, this book would have been impossible to produce without the earlier efforts of previous tort textbook writers, the efforts of those producing the law reports, the efforts of those producing the technologies that we have made use of in writing this book, the efforts of our parents in bringing us up and so on. If the labour theory of property were correct, it is not clear why any of those should not be able to claim a share of this book.[6]

However, there is no doubt that the labour theory of property has great intuitive appeal in today's society – for example, the fact that song writing came so easily to Lennon and McCartney may account for why they initially did not think their songs could belong to them – and could be used as the basis of an alternative, *civil recourse*, theory as to why the law should recognise certain intangibles as being owned by individuals. The idea behind this theory is that if *Worker* feels intuitively on the basis of something like a labour theory of property that *Resource* belongs to him, *Worker* will feel aggrieved if *Interferer* fails to respect the rights *Worker* thinks he has over *Resource*, and might well feel entitled as a result to take counter-measures against *Interferer*. Given this, and in the interests of social peace, it might be wise for the law to give *Worker* what he thinks is his due, recognise that he legally owns *Resource* and give him a peaceful way of dealing with anyone like *Interferer* who might try to damage or exploit *Resource*.

So, for example, in 2005, a Chinese gamer called Qiu Chengwei won a 'dragon sword' in the course of playing *Legend of Mir 3*. He lent the sword – which only existed virtually, as

---

[5] *Two Treatises of Government*, Second Essay, Part V ('On Property'), section 26.
[6] John Rawls pursued this point in his *Theory of Justice* (1971) to argue that all property is initially held in common until distributed according to his principles of justice (where, so far as property goes, unequal distributions are only to be tolerated where they make the worst off under those distributions better off than they would have been under a more equal distribution).

part of the game – to a fellow *Legend* player called Zhu Caoyuan. Chengwei then discovered that Caoyuan had auctioned off the sword on eBay to a third gamer for almost £500. The Chinese police told Chengwei that they could not do anything as virtual property was not protected under Chinese law. Chengwei then exercised his own individual brand of justice by stabbing and killing Caoyuan. Caoyuan might never have died had Chinese law done more to recognise and uphold the rights that Chengwei intuitively felt he had in this case.

B. Utilitarian arguments

Utilitarian arguments for recognising that people own certain intangibles assert that we are all better off as a result of giving people use rights and exclusivity rights over some intangibles.

In the context of something like land, such utilitarian arguments focus on the dangers of land being *over-exploited* if it is not owned privately. (Such an argument is known as a '*tragedy of the commons*' argument. The idea is that when no one has exclusive control over property, then it is liable to get used up and wasted as everyone piles in to use it and no one takes responsibility for ensuring the property is conserved. A point borne out by the state of shared kitchens in student residences and fishing stocks under the EU's Common Fisheries Policy.) Such dangers of over-exploitation in the absence of individual ownership of an intangible are few and far between. It could be argued, though, that the legal protection given to registered designs and trade marks, as well as the law on passing off are justified on this basis. If all restaurants were free to kit themselves out with a McDonald's style set of 'golden arches' on their roof, we would not know where to go for a genuine Big Mac.

In the context of intangibles, utilitarian arguments for the private ownership of intangibles focus much more on the *stimulus to creativity* created by the prospect of obtaining use rights and exclusivity rights over one's productions, which can then be exploited to make a lot of money for the rights holder. Some have questioned the *stimulus to creativity* argument in the context of works that are cheap to produce and are labours of love. For example, the authors of this textbook are certainly not writing it for the royalties they earn from it, but to benefit their students and (we hope) other people's students. But there is no doubt that in the case of products that are very expensive to produce – such as films or new medicines – it would make no economic sense to attempt to produce such works if one could not recoup one's investment by exploiting the use rights and exclusivity rights that the law will give the producer over that product.

At the same time, utilitarian arguments are vulnerable to objections that recognising ownership over intangibles ends up doing more harm than good, particularly in *stifling innovation*. In particular, it is argued that the patent system can be too easily abused by *Patent Trolls* who think of an invention, patent it, do nothing to produce or market the invention, but simply sit back and wait for an honest *Inventor* to come along with the same idea who does want to produce the invention. The *Troll* will then charge *Inventor* a fee for the privilege of being allowed to go ahead and produce and market the invention. And if *Inventor* will not agree to the *Troll*'s demands, the invention is never produced.

18.2 INTELLECTUAL PROPERTY

English law recognises and protects a variety of different forms of intellectual property:

(1) *Copyright*. The law on copyright protects people who have created an 'original literary, dramatic, musical or artistic' work, or a sound recording, film or broadcast,[7] from having their efforts exploited by others copying that work.

Someone who creates a work that can be protected by copyright will automatically own the copyright over that work (though they may have agreed to assign the copyright to a third party, such as the publisher of that work), and other people will be required under the Copyright, Designs and Patents Act 1988 not to infringe the copyright in that work. It is not possible to summarise the various ways in which someone can infringe another's copyright in some kind of work: the interested reader should consult ss 16–76 of the 1988 Act and specialist works on intellectual property law. But *very roughly* if B owns the copyright in some kind of work, A will infringe that copyright if: (1) he makes a copy of that work without B's consent; *or* (2) he reproduces that work in any material form without B's consent; *or* (3) he issues copies of that work without B's consent; *or* (4) he rents or lends the work to the public without B's consent; *or* (5) he performs, shows or plays the work in public without B's consent.

If A infringes B's copyright in some kind of work, A will commit a tort: s 96 of the 1988 Act provides that an 'infringement of copyright is actionable by the copyright owner' and that in 'an action for infringement of copyright all such relief by way of damages, injunctions, accounts or otherwise is available to the claimant as is available in respect of the infringement of any other property right'. However, if A has infringed B's copyright in a work when he 'did not know, and had no reason to believe, that copyright subsisted in [that] work', B will be barred from suing him for compensatory damages in respect of any losses suffered by her as a result of A's infringing her copyright.[8]

(2) *Patent*. A patent gives someone who has had an idea for a new invention a monopoly over the development and exploitation of that invention. If B takes out a patent over an invention, A will owe B a statutory duty under the Patents Act 1977 not to infringe B's patent, in the ways specified under s 60 of the 1977 Act. If A breaches this duty he will commit a tort: s 61 of the Patents Act 1977 provides that 'civil proceedings may be brought in the court by the proprietor of a patent in respect of any act alleged to infringe the patent.' However, if A infringes B's patent when he 'was not aware, and had no reasonable grounds for supposing that [B's] patent existed', B will be barred from suing A for damages in respect of any loss suffered by her as a result of A's infringement of her patent or damages in respect of any profit made by A in infringing B's patent.[9]

(3) *Registered design*. So long as the design or appearance of *Product X* is novel and distinctive, the *Producer* of *Product X* can protect himself from other people's marketing products similar to *Product X* with the same, or a similar, design or appearance by registering the design of *Product X* under the Registered Designs Act 1949.[10] While the 1949

---

[7] Copyright, Designs and Patents Act 1988, s 1(1). The Supreme Court held in *Lucasfilm Ltd* v *Ainsworth* [2011] UKSC 39 that a mould of an Imperial Stormtrooper's helmet from the *Star Wars* films did not qualify as an 'artistic work' and was therefore not protected by copyright; the defendant owner of the mould was therefore free to produce copies of the helmet for sale to *Star Wars* enthusiasts.

[8] Copyright, Designs and Patents Act 1988, s 97(1).

[9] Patents Act 1977, s 62(1).

[10] Any 'aspect of the shape or configuration (whether internal or external) of the whole or part' of a product so long as it is not 'commonplace' may also be protected by a design right, even if unregistered, under s 213 of the Copyright, Designs and Patents Act 1988. Infringement of a design right will be treated in the same way as any other property tort (s 229), subject to a defence to being sued for compensatory damages where the defendant did not know, and had no reason to know, that the design to which the action against him relates was protected by a design right: s 233.

Act does not say expressly that infringement of a registered design will amount to a tort, s 7 of the Act gives the owner of a registered design 'the exclusive right to use the design' and s 9 assumes that damages will be payable by anyone who infringes that right, unless the infringer can establish that he did not know and had no reason to know that the design in question was registered.

(4) *Trade marks.* Trade marks protect any distinctive logos or words under which goods and services are marketed. A defendant will infringe a *Producer's* registered trade mark if the defendant markets goods or services similar to the *Producer's* under a sign that is similar to the registered trade mark.[11] The infringement of a claimant's registered trade mark will amount to a tort: s 14(2) of the Trade Marks Act 1994 provides that 'In an action for infringement all such relief by way of damages, injunctions, accounts or otherwise is available to [the claimant] as is available in respect of the infringement of any other property right.' Unlike with patents and design rights, a defendant cannot rely on an 'I had no reason to know this sign infringed someone else's trade mark' to defeat an action against him for compensatory damages.

Compensatory damages are not the only form of damages that may be sued for by someone whose intellectual property has been infringed. Equally important, if not more so, are disgorgement damages – damages designed to strip the defendant of the gain he has made from infringing the claimant's intellectual property rights. We discuss disgorgement damages in more detail in the chapter on 'Gain-Based Damages' later in this book,[12] but for the time being we can say that disgorgement damages may be awarded against someone who infringes another's copyright[13] or trade mark.[14] In the case where a defendant has infringed another's patent, disgorgement damages may be awarded if the defendant knew or ought to have known of the existence of the patent at the time he infringed it.[15]

18.3 GOODWILL

The tort of passing off protects the goodwill attached to someone's name or business from being exploited or damaged by another.

A. Exploitation of goodwill

The first form of the tort is committed if A *exploits* the *goodwill* attached to B's name or business when he was not entitled to do so. What is 'goodwill'? Lord Macnaghten supplied a definition in *Inland Revenue Commissioners* v *Muller & Co's Margarine Ltd* (1901), observing that goodwill 'is a thing very easy to describe, very difficult to define. It is the benefit and advantage of the good name, reputation, and connection of a business. It is the attractive force which brings in custom.'[16]

---

[11] Trade Marks Act 1994, s 10.

[12] See chapter 31.

[13] Copyright, Designs and Patents Act 1988, s 96(2). It is not thought that s 97(1) of the 1988 Act affects this point. That subsection provides that: 'Where in action for infringement of copyright it is shown that at the time of the infringement the defendant did not know, and had no reason to believe, that copyright subsists in the work to which the action relates, the claimant is not entitled to damages against him, but without prejudice to any other remedy.' It is thought that the reference to *damages* in this section is a reference to *compensatory* damages.

[14] Trade Marks Act 1994, s 14(2).

[15] Patents Act 1977, s 62(1).

[16] [1901] AC 217, 223–4.

So A will commit this form of the tort if he markets his goods or services in such a way as to create a substantial risk that people will purchase those goods or services in the belief that they are B's goods or services.[17] If he does this he will mislead people into thinking that his goods or services are supplied by B and in so doing appropriate the goodwill attached to B's name or business.[18] This is what happened in *Reddaway* v *Banham* (1896). The claimant had for some years made belting and sold it as 'Camel Hair Belting'. As a result, the name 'Camel Hair Belting' was used in the trade to refer to the belts manufactured by the claimant. The defendant began to manufacture belts made of the yarn of camel's hair and stamped the words 'Camel Hair Belting' on them. He was held to have committed the tort of passing off – in stamping 'Camel Hair Belting' on his belts he had created a substantial risk that people would purchase his belts in the belief that they were manufactured by the claimant.

Similarly, in *Reckitt & Colman Products Ltd* v *Borden Inc* (1990), the House of Lords held that Borden would commit the tort of passing off if it sold its lemon juice in lemon-shaped bottles. Reckitt & Colman had been selling its Jif lemon juice in lemon-shaped bottles for 30 years and as a result consumers tended to think that lemon-shaped bottles contained Jif lemon juice. There was therefore a substantial risk that if Borden sold *its* lemon juice in lemon-shaped bottles, consumers would purchase Borden's lemon juice in the belief that it was Jif lemon juice. Borden could not, it was found, eliminate this risk by labelling its lemon-shaped bottles to make it clear that they did not contain Jif lemon juice; the House of Lords found that, when selecting a lemon juice from a range of bottles of lemon juice on sale in a supermarket, shoppers tended not to look at the labels on the bottles of lemon juice in making their choice. So Borden's labelling its lemon-shaped bottles to make it clear that they did not contain Jif lemon juice would not eliminate the risk that shoppers would purchase Borden's lemon juice in the belief that it was Jif lemon juice.

It should be emphasised that this form of the tort may *also* be committed in situations *outside* the sort of situation we have just been considering. To establish that A committed this form of the tort it does *not* have to be established that he marketed his goods or services in such a way as to create a substantial risk that his customers would think those goods or services were B's. It merely has to be shown that A exploited the goodwill attached to B's name or business when he was not entitled to do so.

So it has been held that if A markets his goods or services in such a way as to mislead people into thinking that they are of the *same quality* as B's goods or services, he will

---

[17] See, in addition to the cases cited in the text, *Parker-Knoll Ltd* v *Knoll International Ltd* [1962] RPC 265 (held it would be passing off to market furniture under the name 'Knoll International' because doing so would create a substantial risk that people would purchase that furniture in the belief that it was marketed by Parker-Knoll); *Norman Kark Publications Ltd* v *Odhams Press* [1962] 1 WLR 380 (held the defendants would not commit the tort of passing off in relation to the claimants – the publishers of a magazine called *Today* – if they published a magazine called *Today, the New John Bull*; there was no substantial risk that people would be confused into purchasing the defendants' magazine in the mistaken belief that it was the claimants'); *Alain Bernardin et Compagnie* v *Pavilion Properties Ltd* [1967] RPC 581 (held the defendants did not commit the tort of passing off in relation to the claimants when they opened a nightclub in London called 'The Crazy Horse Saloon'; while the claimants ran an identically named nightclub in Paris, the Paris nightclub was not so well known that people in London were liable to go the defendants' nightclub in London in the mistaken belief that it was run by the claimants).

[18] Note that it is essential to show that A appropriated the goodwill specifically attached to B's name or business. If B has spotted a gap in the market and moved to fill it, A will do nothing wrong if he copies B's example and attempts to corner that part of the market himself: while it is wrong for A to appropriate the goodwill that is specifically attached to B's products, there is nothing wrong in A's borrowing B's good ideas. See n 1, above; also Cane 1996, 80–1.

commit the tort of passing off[19] – if A markets his goods by making people think that his goods are as good as B's when they are not, A will exploit the goodwill attached to the products marketed by B when he is not entitled to do so. It has also been held that a charity will commit the tort of passing off if it solicits donations under a name which is liable to make people think that they are donating money to a quite different, and well-established, charity.[20] It has further been held that a radio station committed the tort of passing off in relation to Eddie Irvine, the Formula One driver, when it misled potential advertisers on the station into thinking that Irvine was a fan of the station, thereby exploiting the goodwill associated with Eddie Irvine's name when it was not entitled to do so.[21]

It should also be noted that this form of the tort can be committed quite innocently.[22] Suppose, for example, *Nerd* opened a DVD shop in Bristol and decided to call it 'Videodrome' after the famous David Cronenberg film of that name. Suppose further that *Buff* had already had the same idea and had run for a number of years a well-regarded DVD shop in London, also called 'Videodrome'. In this situation *Nerd* may well have committed the tort of passing off in relation to *Buff* – and this is so even if *Nerd* had no idea *Buff*'s shop existed and had no intention, in naming his shop 'Videodrome', of exploiting any of the goodwill that had become attached to *Buff*'s shop.

B. Endangering goodwill

The second form of the tort of passing off is committed if A markets his goods or services in such a way as to create a danger that the goodwill attached to B's name or business will be unjustifiably damaged.

This is what happened in *Associated Newspaper plc* v *Insert Media Ltd* (1991). In that case, the defendant inserted advertising material into the claimant's newspapers without the claimant's consent. The Court of Appeal held that the defendant, in so acting, had committed the tort of passing off. There was a substantial risk that people would think that the defendant's advertising material was inserted with the claimant's consent. There was therefore a substantial risk that people would associate the defendant's advertising material with the claimant and would hold it against the claimant if the advertising material proved to be dishonest or inaccurate.

---

[19] See *J Bollinger* v *Costa Brava Wine Co* [1960] 1 Ch 262 (held that the defendants committed the tort of passing off in relation to the claimant champagne manufacturers when they sold wine made in Spain or from grapes produced in Spain as 'champagne' or as 'Spanish champagne', thereby appropriating the goodwill attached to the claimants' business when they were not entitled to do so – the defendants' wine not being as good as genuine champagne); also *Erven Warnink Besloten Vennootschap* v *J Townend & Sons (Hull) Ltd* [1979] AC 731 (held that it was passing off for the defendants to manufacture a mixture of dried egg powder and Cyprus sherry under the name 'Keeling's Old English Advocaat'; if the defendants marketed their product under this name, they would appropriate the goodwill attached to genuine advocaat when they were not entitled to do so – genuine advocaat, which is made out of brandy, egg yolks and sugar, being far superior to the defendants' product).

[20] See *British Diabetic Association* v *Diabetic Society Ltd* [1995] 4 All ER 812 (held that it would be passing off for a charity to solicit contributions under the name 'The Diabetic Society' because there was a substantial risk that people would make donations to the charity in the belief that they were donating money to the quite distinct British Diabetic Association).

[21] *Irvine* v *Talksport Ltd* [2002] 1 WLR 2355.

[22] It used to be a matter of debate whether someone who innocently committed the tort of passing off could be held liable to pay anything more than nominal damages to the victim of his tort, with the House of Lords reserving its position on the issue in *Marengo* v *Daily Sketch and Sunday Graphic* (1948) 65 RPC 242. However, in *Gillette UK Ltd* v *Edenwest Ltd* [1994] RPC 279, Blackburne J held that no special rule existed for defendants who innocently committed the tort of passing off: they would be held liable to pay damages to the victims of their torts in the same way as any other tortfeasors.

Similarly, in *Mirage Studios* v *Counter-Feat Clothing Company Ltd* (1991), the claimants were owners of copyright in the Teenage Mutant Ninja Turtles. A major part of the claimants' income came from licensing other people to use images of the Teenage Mutant Ninja Turtles on products manufactured by those people. The defendants sought to cash in on the craze for the Teenage Mutant Ninja Turtles by drawing pictures of humanoid turtles and licensing various garment manufacturers to use those pictures on T-shirts and jogging clothes. It was held that the defendants had committed the tort of passing off in so acting. There was a substantial risk that people would mistake the defendants' drawings for images of the Teenage Mutant Ninja Turtles and would think that the claimants – the owners of the Teenage Mutant Ninja Turtle image – had licensed the use of those drawings on the items of clothing on which they appeared. There was therefore a substantial risk that people would associate the claimants with the items of clothing on which the defendants' drawings appeared and would therefore hold it against the claimants if those items of clothing proved to be of poor quality.

Again, in *Clark* v *Associated Newspapers Ltd* (1998), the *Evening Standard* was held to have committed the tort of passing off when it published a weekly column called 'The Secret Diary of Alan Clark MP'. The column was written in the same manner as Alan Clark's published diaries and amounted to a witty and exaggerated weekly fantasy as to what Alan Clark might have written in his diary that week. Although it was made clear that the diary entries were written by Peter Bradshaw, an *Evening Standard* journalist, it was held that there was a substantial risk that people would think that the diary entries were written by Alan Clark and that people would think less well of Alan Clark as a result.

C. Remedies

Where the tort of passing off has been committed, the claimant will be entitled in the normal way to sue the person who has committed that tort for compensatory damages. As an alternative, the claimant could sue the defendant for disgorgement damages, designed to strip the defendant of whatever gain he made by exploiting the goodwill attached to the claimant's name or business. We will discuss how such damages are assessed when we discuss 'Gain-Based Damages' generally in chapter 31 of this book.[23] An injunction may also be applied for where the tort is continually being committed.

18.4 CONTRACTUAL RIGHTS

As we will see below, in chapter 24, in a case where A is contractually obliged to do something for B, the law protects B against a third party *persuading* A to breach his contract with B. Such persuasion will amount to a tort: the tort of inducing a breach of contract. However, the existence of that tort was of no assistance to the claimants in *OBG Ltd* v *Allan* (2008).

In that case, the claimant company ('OBG') got into severe financial difficulties. In order to protect his interests, one of OBG's creditors – who thought he had a charge over OBG's assets – had some receivers go in and take over OBG's business. The receivers tried to raise money to pay off OBG's debts by selling off its assets, and settling various debts that were owed to OBG for much less than the paper value of those debts. It was discovered too late that the receivers' appointment had been invalid because the creditor who had sent the

---

[23] See below, § 31.2.

receivers in did not in fact have a charge over OBG's assets. OBG was then taken over by liquidators who sued the receivers for – they claimed – wrongfully interfering with the contractual rights that OBG had against people who owed it money. It was argued that the receivers had been too lax in settling the debts that were owed to OBG, and had demanded too little in return for settling those debts.

But what sort of wrong had been committed here? Clearly not the tort of inducing a breach of contract as no breach – but rather partial performance – had been induced by the receivers' actions. So OBG's liquidators argued that the receivers had committed the tort of conversion in relation to OBG's contractual rights against its debtors. This was a novel claim, as conversion traditionally only applied to cases where a defendant interfered with a tangible thing that the claimant possessed, or had an immediate right to possess. So the issue faced by the House of Lords was whether the tort of conversion should be extended to cover cases where a defendant interfered with a contractual right that the claimant had against a third party.

The House of Lords rejected the invitation to extend the tort of conversion in this way by a majority of 3:2. The majority held that the tort of conversion only covered interferences with tangible property, and did not extend to interferences with intangible property, such as a contractual right.

The minority (Lord Nicholls and Baroness Hale) made two basic arguments in favour of the view that the law of conversion should extend to interferences with contractual rights. The first argument was that if an action for conversion could not be brought here, then the paradoxical result would arise that the receivers *could* be sued in conversion for selling off OBG's physical assets, but could *not* be sued in conversion for throwing away for a song the debts that it was owed – when those debts comprised up to 70%[24] of OBG's assets.[25] The second argument was that extending the tort of conversion to cover the sort of facts presented in *OBG* would involve a 'modest but principled extension of the scope of the tort'.[26] Lord Nicholls' main argument for thinking that allowing a claim for conversion in a case like *OBG* would represent a 'modest' development of the law is that the law already allows a claimant to sue a defendant for interfering with a contractual right of his where that right is embodied in documentary form.[27] The classic example of this, Lord Nicholls argued, is the case where a defendant is sued in conversion for the face value of a cheque that he has misapplied. In such a case, Lord Nicholls argued, the defendant is effectively being held liable in conversion for misappropriating the right to draw on the bank account against which the cheque was drawn. Lord Nicholls saw no reason why the law of conversion should provide a remedy when someone appropriates a contractual right that is embodied in documentary form, but should not when the right interfered with is disembodied – and extending the scope of conversion to cover interference with the second kind of right would not, he thought, represent a radical development given that the tort of conversion already protects people against interference with the first kind of right.

---

[24] A figure arrived at by Goymour 2011, 68, presumably on the basis of the figures in Lord Nicholls' judgment ([2008] 1 AC 1, at [211]–[212]) where the debts owed to OBG were said to be worth £1,820,000 (and settled for £753,000) and the land, plant and equipment owned by OBG and sold by the receivers were worth £244,000. OBG had some other assets, such as cash in the bank, which make the sums come out right.

[25] [2008] 1 AC 1, at [221] (per Lord Nicholls): 'Why should [the receivers] be liable strictly in respect of their unauthorised dealings with some parts of the company's property but not others? This distinction makes no sense'; and [311] (per Baroness Hale): 'it makes no sense that the defendants should be strictly liable for what was lost on the tangible assets but not for what was lost on the intangibles.'

[26] [2008] 1 AC 1, at [233] (per Lord Nicholls).

[27] [2008] 1 AC 1, at [225]–[233].

The majority (Lords Hoffmann, Walker and Brown) roundly rejected the minority's arguments. The majority were agreed that extending the tort of conversion to interferences with forms of intangible property such as contractual rights would represent a dramatic change in the law. Lord Hoffmann remarked scathingly, 'As for authority for such a change, it hardly needs to be said that in English law there is none.'[28] Lord Walker thought that Lord Nicholls' views 'involved too drastic a reshaping of this area of the law of tort'.[29] And Lord Brown thought that the minority's position involved 'no less than the proposed severance of any link whatever between the tort of conversion and the wrongful taking of physical possession of property (whether a chattel or document) having a real and ascertainable value.'[30]

The majority's criticism of the minority was basically constitutional in nature: the minority were trying to bring about a radical change in the law when the judicial role is simply to apply and clarify the law. But four other criticisms can also be made of the minority's position.

(1) Conversion is – as currently defined – an intensely physical tort. It is involves *taking possession* of, or *refusing to deliver* up, or *delivering into the hands* of a third party, or *using*, or *destroying* an *asset* in someone else's *possession*, or which someone else has an immediate right to *possess*. All the italicised expressions in the previous sentence demonstrate the real world, physical, nature of conversion. Given this, it is hard to see how the tort would be defined, or what its bounds would be, if it covered interferences with intangible property. A whole new definition of the tort would need to be created, and with that would come the threat of the tort swallowing up other areas of law that govern interferences with intangible property, such as the law on inducing a breach of contract, the law on third party liability for assisting a trustee to commit a breach of trust, and the law on intellectual property.[31]

(2) Lord Nicholls' 'If cheques, why not debts?' argument does not stand up. As Amy Goymour has painstakingly explained,[32] when D is held liable to C in conversion for the face value of a cheque that he has misapplied and which was either (a) drawn on C's bank account or (b) drawn in C's favour, it is often very difficult to say that D is really being held liable in such a case for misappropriating a right of C's. Where the cheque was (a) drawn on C's bank account, the cheque represented not a right of C's to draw on his bank account but (if anything) a right that someone else had to draw on C's bank account. Where the cheque was (b) drawn in C's favour, if the cheque was a gift to C, it will confer 'no right on [C to be paid the sum on the cheque], but merely a power to be paid the relevant sum.'[33] The cheque cases can be more easily explained: (i) as straightforward conversion cases where C sues D for the actual loss he has suffered as a result of D's misappropriating a physical asset (the paper cheque) which was in C's possession or which C had an immediate right to possess;[34] or (ii) as disguised unjust enrichment cases where C is allowed to sue D for money that D has unjustly obtained at C's expense (even though that money never technically belonged to C).[35]

---

[28] [2008] 1 AC 1, at [100].
[29] [2008] 1 AC 1, at [271].
[30] [2008] 1 AC 1, at [321].
[31] See Goymour 2011, at 80.
[32] Goymour 2011, at 74 and 77.
[33] Goymour 2011, at 77.
[34] Goymour 2011, at 74–75, and 77.
[35] Lord Hoffmann's analysis at [2008] 1 AC 1, [103]–[104]; and ultimately Goymour 2011's as well, at 83–6.

(3) We have seen that under the law on intellectual property, someone who innocently infringes another's copyright or patent or trade mark cannot be sued for compensatory damages.[36] If the minority's position in *OBG* had been adopted, no such defence of innocent infringement would be available to someone who converted another's contractual rights. It is not clear why a contractual right (such as a right to be paid a debt, as in *OBG*) should be given greater protection than a right in relation to intellectual property.

(4) If it were thought desirable or important to allow some remedy to OBG for having their rights to sue for money owed to it thrown away by their receivers, it was not necessary to reform the law of conversion to do it. The law on the liability of receivers could have been reformed instead, perhaps by analogy to the law on the liability of administrators of an estate who transfer assets to the wrong person. This is an important point as the liquidators of OBG are currently taking their case to the European Court of Human Rights, arguing that the decision of the House of Lords in *OBG* means that UK law has failed properly to protect OBG's rights under Article 1 of the First Protocol to the European Convention on Human Rights, which provides that:

> Every natural or legal person is entitled to the peaceful enjoyment of his possessions. No one shall be deprived of his possessions except in the public interest and subject to the conditions provided for by law and by the general principles of international law.

Should the ECtHR find against the UK in the case of *OBG Ltd* v *United Kingdom*, that does not necessarily mean that the minority's approach in *OBG* to the law on conversion must be adopted.

18.5 VIRTUAL PROPERTY

With computer games becoming more and more popular forms of entertainment, it is worth noting that English law currently provides gamers with no protection against 'virtual property' being damaged or stolen by hackers or being otherwise interfered with. The phrase 'virtual property'[37] refers to a resource which exists within a computer game[38] – such as a weapon or a currency traded within that game – and which has been purchased, won, or developed by the person playing the game. The effort and real world money that can be expended on acquiring virtual property[39] has led people to ask whether the law should take any steps to protect such property from being interfered with after it has been acquired.[40]

---

[36] See above, § 18.2.

[37] A popular misnomer which we perpetuate here: if 'virtual property' is unprotected from being interfered with, it is hard to see how it counts as 'property'. For this reason, Nelson 2010 prefers the term 'virtual resource'.

[38] Examples of such games are: *World of Warcraft* (a fantasy wizard and orcs type game), *Ultima Online* (ditto), *EverQuest* (ditto), *Eve Online* (a science fiction game), and *Second Life* (an alternative version of our world).

[39] For example, the currency used in *Second Life* is known as the 'Linden dollar'. Linden dollars can be bought or sold for real life currency on currency exchanges. At the time of writing, the total amount of Linden dollars held by the players of Second Life comes to the equivalent of 30 million US dollars, and rising rapidly. That's a lot of money to be holding without any individual rights to sue if that money is stolen or wiped out by hackers. *New Scientist* also reported in 2009 that it was estimated that US citizens would spend $620m that year on acquiring virtual property; and in Asia, $5 *billion* would be spent on virtual property in one year alone. Countries such as South Korea and China have responded to this huge investment in virtual property in their countries by taking steps to give virtual property holders legal rights over that property that are enforceable in real life.

[40] The question is confined to cases where virtual property is stolen or destroyed as a result of people – usually computer hackers – doing things in the real world. Where virtual property is stolen or destroyed within the game, as a result of what another player has done, no one really contends that that 'virtual tort' should amount to a real tort. (It is presumed, if one player can loot another player's property within the game, then it was within the rules of the game to do that sort of thing.)

The most commonly made argument for saying that the law should get involved with protecting virtual property is a Lockean argument that in cases where virtual property has been acquired by a gamer through his expending time and skill on acquiring that property, that property should be regarded as 'his'.[41] However, it has been pointed out that the Lockean argument cannot apply here as a gamer who expends time and effort in acquiring virtual property is doing so by expending that time and effort on a game that belongs to its developers.[42] So the developers of a game have a better claim to anything that exists within the game than anyone playing that game could have, in the same way that the owner of a block of marble has a better claim to the statue that has been carved out of the block than the carver does. And the developers of games tend to make it clear in their End User Licence Agreement that they retain all and any rights they have over things that exist within the game.

Richard Bartle – the co-creator of the first ever virtual world computer game ('Multi-User Dungeon', or 'MUD') – has also argued, on utilitarian grounds, that the law should not get involved in protecting virtual property from outside interference.[43] The existence of such protection would, he argues, damage what is valuable about virtual world games. Bartle's objections are twofold.

First, once legally enforceable user rights attach to virtual property that has been acquired within a game, the ability of the developers of the game to change and improve the game will be radically diminished as such changes and improvements may well have negative effects for gamers who hold virtual property within the game. Such gamers could well argue that these negative effects violate their use rights.

Secondly, once legally enforceable exclusivity rights attach to virtual property, virtual property will become easily tradeable. The commodification of virtual property that exists within a computer game will, Bartle argues, damage both the virtuality and the point of the game. Virtuality will be damaged because the real world – in the shape of how rich people are in real life – will start determining who is asset-rich in the virtual world of the computer game. The point of the game will be damaged as the point of many such games is to acquire prestige and status by going on a journey within the game. The significance of acquiring such prestige and status will be lost for gamers if they know that others can acquire it simply by flexing their credit card.

Given these arguments, we think those responsible for shaping this area of the law should be very cautious about developing legally enforceable rights in relation to virtual property.

---

[41] See, for example, Lastowka and Hunter 2004.
[42] See Nelson 2010, at 290–1.
[43] Bartle 2004.

Further reading

We have only faintly skimmed the surface of intellectual property law in this chapter. Those wishing to read more about it should consult one of the many excellent textbooks available on that subject. However, the details of intellectual property law can be quite dry, and readers might want to look elsewhere for insights into the battles around intellectual property law, particularly over film piracy and drug development. For such readers, we can warmly recommend: **James Bessen and Michael J. Meurer's** *Patent Failure* **(Princeton, 2009),** **Marcia Angell's** *The Truth About Drug Companies* **(Random House, 2005), Lawrence Lessig's** *Free Culture* **(Penguin, 2005), and Michael Heller's** *The Gridlock Economy* **(Basic Books, 2008)**. Sir Hugh Laddie's 'The insatiable appetite for intellectual property rights' (2008) 61 *Current Legal Problems* 401 is an entertaining tour of the more egregious abuses of intellectual property law in recent years. **Sarah Worthington** carefully examines the value of intellectual property law in **'Art, law and creativity' (2009) 62** *Current Legal Problems* **168. Henry C. Mitchell** is worth reading on the moral arguments for intellectual property law in his ***The Intellectual Commons*** (Lexington Books, 2005).

19 Defamation

19.1 The basics *522*

19.2 What is defamatory? *530*

19.3 Reference to the claimant *535*

19.4 Publication to a third party *538*

19.5 Title to sue *543*

19.6 Consent *546*

19.7 Justification *547*

19.8 Honest (or fair) comment *549*

19.9 Absolute privilege *555*

19.10 Qualified privilege *557*

19.11 *Reynolds* privilege *562*

19.12 Other defences *568*

19.13 Remedies *570*

19.14 Options for reform *572*

Overview

In this chapter, we look at the law on defamation – the area of tort law concerned with protecting and vindicating people's reputations. Section 19.1 provides an overview of this area of the law, and explains why many people think this area of the law is in need of reform. Sections 19.2 to 19.5 set out the basic elements that need to be established for a claimant to sue a defendant in defamation. Sections 19.6 to 19.12 set out the various defences that might be raised by a defendant who is being sued for defamation. Section 19.13 deals with the remedies that are available to a claimant who is able to sue someone else for defamation. Section 19.14 considers various options for reforming the law in order to mitigate the negative impact it has on people's rights to freedom of expression.

19.1 THE BASICS

Some torts are very unsocial in nature. The trespass torts and the tort of invasion of privacy (which we will be discussing in a couple of chapters' time) are based on, and give effect to, a right 'to be left alone'. By contrast, defamation is a social tort. It seeks to protect the valuable relationships we have with other people from being interfered with by third parties telling damaging lies about us. At the same time, defamation is a tort that constantly threatens to work in an anti-social way. There are two reasons for this.

First, defaming other people is something that is very easy to do, and something we do all the time. Whenever you say something negative about someone else, you defame them; and very few of us adhere to the maxim, 'If you can't say something nice about someone, say nothing.'[1] Secondly, it is very often very important that people be allowed to say negative things about other people. We need to be able to tell other people that their politicians are corrupt; that their role models have feet of clay; that their prospective employees are incompetent or dishonest; that their friends and lovers are disloyal; that the medicine they are taking has dangerous side effects; that the hotel they are planning to stay at is horrible.

---

[1] A maxim that was given a very human twist by President Theodore Roosevelt's daughter, Alice Roosevelt Longworth: 'If you haven't got anything nice to say about anybody, come sit next to me.'

So if the law of defamation were allowed unbounded sway over our lives, it would make tortfeasors of all of us, and severely limit our abilities to tell each other what we need to know. But it does not. The courts have long limited the reach of the law of defamation by allowing defendants who are sued for defamation a variety of defences: principally, *justification* ('What I said was substantially true'); *honest comment* (formerly known as 'fair comment') ('I was only expressing my honest opinion on a matter of public interest'); and *privilege* ('What I said is protected under the law from being the object of a defamation claim, either because of *where* I said it (in court, in Parliament) or because of the person *to whom* I said it (because had what I said been true, it would have been my duty to tell her, or it would have been to our mutual advantage for me to tell her) or because of *how* I said it (because I acted responsibly in saying what I said, and what I said was on a matter of public interest)').

Despite this, critics continue to claim that the law of defamation is in dire need of reform. Taking their cue from Article 10 of the European Convention of Human Rights which provides that,

1. Everyone has the right to freedom of expression. This right shall include freedom to hold opinions and to receive and impart information and ideas without interference by public authority and regardless of frontiers . . .

2. The exercise of these freedoms, since it carries with it duties and responsibilities, may be subject to such formalities, conditions, restrictions or penalties as are prescribed by law and are necessary in a democratic society . . . for the protection of the reputation or rights of others . . .

critics argue that the law on defamation exercises an unacceptable 'chilling effect' on freedom of expression, not only here, but across the world. The main charges laid against the law of defamation run as follows:

(1) *Ease of suit*. It is argued, first, that it is just too easy to sue someone else for defamation in England and Wales. All a claimant has to do is show that the defendant made a statement to a third party that might lead a reasonable person to think less well of the claimant. Of course, the claimant might not win his case: the defendant may be able to take advantage of one of the defences available to people like him. But that is not the point. If A is thinking of saying something critical about B, the fact that it would be so easy for B to respond to A's attack by suing him for defamation might well lead A to censor himself and avoid saying anything critical about B. No one could blame A for preferring a quiet life to the possibility of years of litigation, even if those years of litigation ended in success for A.

(2) *Abuses of the right to sue*. We began by saying that the law of defamation protected our relationships with other people from being damaged by third parties telling damaging lies about us. However, claims for defamation are not always brought with the intention of preserving the claimant's status in the eyes of other people.

In some cases, the claimant has not suffered any serious harm as a result of the defendant's words, but still brings a claim with the twin object of punishing the defendant for daring to say something negative about the claimant, and warning other people not to take similar liberties. If the defendant's words were published in permanent form (and therefore amounted to a *libel*), the law makes it very easy for the claimant to bring such a punitive claim against the defendant: in a libel case, the claimant can sue even if the defendant's words caused him no loss at all.

In other cases, the claimant is not even a human being. The claimant is a company, or some other organisation enjoying legal personality. The law of defamation allows 'artifical legal persons' to sue in defamation to protect their business reputation. However, there is evidence that the law of defamation is now being abused by companies (particularly drug companies)[2] and other organisations to suppress criticism of the company or organisation's activities. Particularly worrying is the case of *British Chiropractic Association* v *Singh* (2011), where an article in the *Guardian* newspaper criticised the claimant association for associating itself with claims that chiropractic (manipulation of the spine) could cure a range of childhood illnesses. The claimant association chose to sue the *writer* of the article, but *not* the *Guardian*, for libel. As the Court of Appeal commented:

> **11.** It is now nearly two years since the publication of the offending article. It seems unlikely that anyone would dare repeat the opinions expressed by Dr Singh for fear of a writ. Accordingly this litigation has almost certainly had a chilling effect on public debate which might otherwise have assisted potential patients to make informed choices about the possible use of chiropractic . . .
>
> **12.** By proceeding against Dr Singh, and not the *Guardian*, and by rejecting the offer made by the *Guardian* to publish an appropriate article refuting Dr Singh's contentions, or putting them in a proper perspective, the unhappy impression has been created that this is an endeavour by the BCA to silence one of its critics . . .[3]

Although – as we will see – the claim in the *Singh* case was dismissed (the defendant, it was held, could take advantage of the defence of honest comment),[4] the Court of Appeal felt itself unable to dismiss the claim simply on the basis that it amounted to an abuse of the right to sue: 'if that is where the current law of defamation takes us, we must apply it.'[5]

(3) *Forum shopping/Libel tourism.* The courts will strike out claims for defamation as an abuse of process if they do not think that they have been brought with the serious intention of vindicating the claimant's reputation *in England*.[6] In order to satisfy this requirement, the claimant will have to show that there has been a substantial publication of material defaming the claimant in England.[7] However, the advent of the Internet has made this requirement much easier to satisfy. Defamatory statements that have been posted on the Internet from anywhere in the world are automatically available to view in England. Books that have been printed somewhere else in the world may be ordered by people living in England via Amazon or other book websites.

So a claimant who has been libelled by a defendant in the United States may no longer have to look to the US courts for a remedy. Instead, he may be able to bring a claim in England, on the basis that there has been a substantial publication of the defendant's statement in England.[8] The key advantage to suing in England, as opposed to the United States, is this: in 1964, the US Supreme Court ruled in a case called *New York Times* v *Sullivan* that the constitutional guarantees for freedom of expression contained in the First Amendment to the US Constitution required that a public figure not be allowed to sue a defendant for defamation unless the defendant made his statement maliciously; that is, knowing that his statement was not true. Public figures suing for defamation in England

---

[2] See 'Anger at bid to silence heart op whistleblower' *Daily Mail*, 26 February 2009; and 'Danish scientist sued by drug firm under British libel laws to counterclaim' *The Guardian*, 16 February 2010.

[3] [2011] 1 WLR 133.

[4] Discussed below, § 19.8.

[5] [2011] 1 WLR 133, at [12].

[6] 'England' is used here and below as shorthand for 'England and Wales'.

[7] *Jameel (Yousef)* v *Dow Jones & Co* [2005] QB 946.

[8] Though there is *no* presumption that a statement posted on the Internet has been substantially published in England: *Al-Amoudi* v *Brisard* [2007] 1 WLR 113.

are not subject to the same disability: they may be able to sue a defendant in England for defamation even if the defendant honestly believed what he was saying about them was true. So a public figure in the United States who wants to sue for defamation will now try to 'forum shop' and look to bring her claim in England, rather than in the United States. However, if he or she is allowed to do this, the law of defamation will not only have a negative impact on freedom of speech in England; it will also impact on freedom of speech in the United States.

It was the case of *Bin Mahfouz* v *Ehrenfeld* (2005) that first alerted law makers on both sides of the Atlantic to the dangers posed by the law of defamation for freedom of speech in the United States. The subject of that case was a book by the American academic Rachel Ehrenfeld called *Funding Evil*. The book alleged that the Saudi businessman Khalid bin Mahfouz and his family were some of the principal financial supporters of international terrorism. *Funding Evil* was published in the United States, but 23 copies of the book found their way to England via book websites such as Amazon. Excerpts from the book were also available on the American TV network ABC's website and could thus be viewed in England. Bin Mahfouz sued for libel in the English courts. Ehrenfeld refused to contest the claim on the basis that it subverted the rights to freedom of expression that she enjoyed under the American Constitution. Eady J accepted the claimant's assurances that his reputation in England was important to him, and that he was not 'forum shopping' or engaging in 'libel tourism' by bringing a claim in England.[9] In Ehrenfeld's absence, Eady J found that she was liable to pay bin Mahfouz £10,000 in damages,[10] as well as £30,000 in solicitors' costs.

Having obtained judgment in his favour in a UK court, bin Mahfouz would have hoped to enforce the judgment through the US courts, which will normally enforce the judgments of English courts. Ehrenfeld attempted to obtain a declaration from the New York courts that the English court's judgment in her case was not enforceable in New York. Her application was dismissed on the ground that there was no basis for the court to make such a declaration.[11] However, a number of different states reacted to the *Ehrenfeld* decision by passing legislation that protected US citizens from having foreign defamation judgments enforced against them at state level. At federal level, the United States government has now passed the SPEECH Act 2010,[12] which provides that:

> a domestic [US] court shall not recognize or enforce a foreign judgment for defamation unless the domestic court determines that – (A) the defamation law applied in the foreign court's adjudication provided at least as much protection for freedom of speech . . . as would be provided by the first amendment to the Constitution of the United States . . . ; or (B) . . . the party opposing recognition or enforcement of [the] foreign judgment would have been found liable for defamation by a domestic court applying the first amendment to the Constitution of the United States . . .[13]

There are two significant controls on the ability of defamation claimants to engage in 'forum shopping' (or what is often called 'libel tourism'). The first we have already mentioned: the claimant has to show that there has been a substantial publication of defamatory material in England, giving him a legitimate interest in seeking to vindicate his

[9] [2005] EWHC 1156, at [39].

[10] This was the maximum Eady J could have awarded bin Mahfouz in summarily allowing his claim against Ehrenfeld: Defamation Act 1996, s 9(1)(c).

[11] Which is *not* to say bin Mahfouz *would* have been able to recover his money had he brought a claim in New York to enforce Eady J's judgment. However, this never happened: bin Mahfouz died in 2009 of a heart attack.

[12] The complete title of the Act is the Securing and Protecting our Enduring and Established Constitutional Heritage Act 2010.

[13] § 4102(a).

reputation in England. If there has been no such substantial publication, his claim may be struck out on the ground that it amounts to an *abuse of process*.[14]

The second control arises where the claimant seeks to sue for defamation a defendant who lives outside the European Union. In such a case, the courts may decline to hear the claimant's case on the ground of *forum non conveniens* – in other words, on the basis that another jurisdiction provides a more appropriate forum for the claimant's case to be heard.[15] However, it is not clear whether this control adds anything to the first control. In other words, if a claimant has shown that a substantial publication of defamatory material has occurred within England, it is not clear whether the courts will *ever* decline to hear the claimant's case on the basis that there is another jurisdiction that provides a more appropriate forum for the case to be heard.

The key case is *Berezovsky* v *Michaels* (2000).[16] In that case, *Forbes* magazine published an article suggesting that Boris Berezovsky – the Russian businessman and politician – was little better than a Mafia gangster. Berezovsky tried to sue the American publishers of *Forbes* for defamation in the English courts. Almost 800,000 copies of the offending magazine were sold in the United States, as opposed to almost 2,000 in England. Despite this, the majority of the House of Lords held that the English courts were the most appropriate forum in which to hear Berezovsky's claim for defamation, on the ground that there had been a substantial publication in England and Berezovsky's connections with England were more substantial than his connections with the United States.[17] Lord Hoffmann dissented:

> The common sense of the matter is that [Berezovsky] wants the verdict of an English court that he has been acquitted of the allegations in the article, for use wherever in the world his business may take him. He does not want to sue in the United States because he considers that *New York Times* v *Sullivan* (1964) . . . makes it too likely that he will lose. He does not want to sue in Russia for the unusual reason that other people might think it was too likely that he would win . . . because [success] might be attributed to his corrupt influence over the Russian judiciary . . . The [claimants] are forum shoppers in the most literal sense. They have weighed up the advantages to them of the various jurisdictions that might be available and decided that England is the best place in which to vindicate their international reputations. They want English law, English judicial integrity and the international publicity which would attend success in an English libel action.[18]

(4) *Wealth*. The law of defamation, it is argued, only benefits the very wealthy, who can afford the substantial costs of bringing a defamation claim, and can afford to take the risk of being held liable for the other party's costs if they lose their claim. If this is right, then the law of defamation operates in asymmetric fashion. The *benefits* of having a law of defamation – in terms of being able to vindicate one's reputation – are mainly reserved for the very wealthy. On the other hand, the *costs* of having a law of defamation – in terms of chilling effects on freedom of expression, as well as increases in the price of newspapers –

---

[14] Discussed further below, § 19.4(10).

[15] If the claimant is suing a defendant *who lives in the European Union* for committing a tort in England, the courts here cannot decline to hear the case on the ground of *forum non conveniens* (though they may still strike it out as an abuse of process): *Shevill* v *Presse Alliance* [1995] 2 AC 18, [1996] AC 959.

[16] See also *King* v *Lewis* [2004] EWCA Civ 1329 (statements were posted on a California-based website accusing an American boxing promoter of being anti-semitic because he accused a New York-based lawyer who was conducting litigation against the promoter in New York of being a 'shyster lawyer' and otherwise showed disrespect towards this lawyer at Yom Kippur; held, the English courts were the most appropriate forum to hear the promoter's claim for defamation!).

[17] [2000] 1 WLR 1004, 1015 (per Lord Steyn). Lord Nolan remarked (at 1017) that 'This case is solely concerned with the [claimants'] reputations in England. They seek to have their reputations judged by English standards. The Court of Appeal thought that for this purpose England was the natural forum, and I agree with them.'

[18] [2000] 1 WLR 1004, 1024.

are borne by all of us. Why, it may be asked, should we *all* pay for an area of law that only the very wealthy really benefit from?

Two counter-arguments can be made to this. It could be argued, first, that we have no interest in reading untrue stories in the newspapers. So we all benefit from the check that the law of defamation puts on newspapers that might otherwise be tempted to rush into print with untrue and damaging stories. Secondly, it could be argued that the existence of conditional fee agreements (otherwise known as 'no win, no fee' agreements) do provide some access to justice for individuals who cannot afford legal representation out of their own pocket. So it is not true to say that it is only the very wealthy who can take advantage of the law of defamation.

Whether these counter-arguments work is a very difficult question. In relation to the first, it is not at all clear whether the public would be better or worse informed by a press operating under no constraints from the law of defamation. An unchecked press would give the public access to more information than it has at the moment – but it is uncertain what the quality of that information would be. In the absence of any evidence one way or the other, it is hard to say whether the law of defamation does help to ensure that the public is better informed than it would be in the absence of such a law.

In relation to the second argument, two points need to be borne in mind. First, a law firm will only take on a client on a conditional fee basis if there is a more than 50% chance of their winning their case. A lot of defamation cases are not so clear that either side can be confident that they have a more than 50% chance of winning, and so the possibility of entering into a conditional fee agreement will not assist a claimant who is not very well off in a lot of defamation cases.

Secondly, it could be argued that while conditional fee agreements help more people to benefit from the law of defamation, they also increase the costs attached to having a law of defamation, in the form of the chilling effect that that area of the law has on freedom of expression. This is because (at the time of writing) under a conditional fee agreement, a law firm that successfully represents a claimant on a conditional fee basis will not only recover its costs from the other side but also a success fee (otherwise known as an 'uplift') of up to 100% of those costs to compensate it for all the times it represents a claimant on a conditional fee basis but loses. The losing side will also have to cover the cost of the claimant's taking out 'ATE insurance' (or 'after the event insurance'), which would have protected the claimant in the event that he had lost by covering his liability to pay the defendant's costs. So conditional fee agreements can have the effect of more than doubling the costs to a defendant of losing a defamation case, thereby substantially increasing the incentives defendants already have to avoid doing or saying anything that might result in their being sued for defamation.

The European Court of Human Rights has now ruled – in *MGN Ltd* v *United Kingdom* (2011) – that making Mirror Group Newspapers (MGN) pay Naomi Campbell's lawyers a 100% success fee after MGN were held liable to Campbell for invading her privacy amounted to a 'disproportionate' interference with MGN's freedom of expression, violating its rights under Article 10 of the European Convention of Human Rights. This aspect of UK law is likely to change very soon, as the UK government is proposing – in Part 2 of the Legal Aid, Sentencing and Punishment of Offenders Bill – to implement Jackson LJ's recommendation in his report on *Civil Litigation Costs* (2009) that in tort cases losing defendants should no longer be liable to pay any 'uplift' in the winning law firm's fees. Instead, any 'success fee' agreed between a law firm and its client should come out of the client's damages, and should not exceed 25% of the client's damages. The government also proposes to prevent successful claimants recovering the costs of taking out ATE insurance in all but clinical negligence cases.

While such reforms may decrease the chilling effect that conditional fee agreements have on freedom of expression in defamation cases, they are likely to make it much harder for ordinary claimants who have been unjustly defamed to obtain a remedy under the law of defamation. In a case where the damages that a claimant stands to recover by suing in defamation will be quite low: (1) any law firm that is thinking about taking the claimant's case on will probably conclude that it is not worth their while to do so as the 'success fee' they stand to recover if they win will be too low; and (2) the claimant may well be discouraged in any case from seeking legal representation to help him win the case because some of the already modest damages he stands to recover if he wins will go to his lawyers, and not into his pocket. As a panel of 11 academics specialising in the field of tort law (including one of us) recently observed of the Jackson Report:

> In our view, implementing the core changes proposed by the Jackson Report creates a serious risk that claimants with genuine grievances will not be able to find a lawyer willing to take their case, especially claimants whose cases might need to go to trial. This . . . constitutes an unacceptable threat to access to justice . . . Though the empirical data that are publicly available are woefully deficient, the Report's own figures . . . testify to the risk that as many as one in five claims [in tort, not just in defamation] that are currently settled out of court would not, post Jackson reform, be pursued through lack of legal representation, and that the figure could rise to four out of five claims that currently go to trial.[19]

It seems, then, that the only way to make remedies in defamation readily accessible to ordinary claimants – other than through huge increases in publicly funded legal aid schemes, which is never going to happen[20] – is through cost regimes that markedly increase the chilling effects that the law of defamation has on freedom of expression. Given this, it seems there may be no way of making remedies in defamation accessible to ordinary people at acceptable cost.

(5) *Vindication.* It is questionable how much even those who are wealthy enough to be able to take advantage of the law of defamation actually benefit from its existence. The main difficulty arises out of one of the features of the law of defamation that makes it so easy to bring a claim under it – in order to sue a defendant successfully in defamation, a claimant does not actually have to prove that what the defendant said about him was untrue. All the claimant has to do, to launch his claim, is show that the defendant said somthing derogatory about him – and then it is up to the defendant, if she wishes, to defend the claim by showing that what she said about the defendant was true. So if a claimant wins a defamation case, that is not because a court has found that what the defendant said about the claimant was untrue; it is because it has not been proven, to the court's satisfaction, that what the defendant said about the claimant was true. So winning a defamation claim just means the allegations about the claimant were – in Scottish legal terms – 'not proven'. But 'not proven' does not provide much satisfaction to a claimant who wants to be able to say he was 'not guilty'.

---

[19] Oliphant 2011, para 6.14.

[20] The European Court of Human Rights' decision in *Steel and Morris* v *UK* (2005) 41 EHRR 22 (to the effect that, in the famous *McLibel* case, the defendants' rights to freedom of expression under Art 10 of the European Convention on Human Rights were violated as a result of their not being given sufficient publicly-funded assistance to equalise the 'inequality of arms' between them and the corporate claimants in that case) seems to have been completely ignored by the UK government.

What vindication for his reputation a claimant can get from winning a defamation claim tends to rest on the size of the damages he is awarded. The more unfounded the allegation, the greater the damages – or so the thinking goes. However, such thinking tends to inflate the amount of damages awarded in defamation cases, which again enhances its chilling effect on freedom of expression. Moreover, vindicating people's reputations through awards of damages tends to mean that defendants in defamation cases are held *strictly liable* to pay substantial amounts of money to successful claimants. If damages are being awarded in defamation cases simply to mark the fact that the claimant's reputation has been unjustly traduced, then it is irrelevant whether the defendant was at fault or not for damaging the claimant's reputation. But this can create injustices in cases where a defendant innocently and perfectly reasonably said something that had the effect of making the claimant look bad. In such cases, a defendant can now make an 'offer to make amends' to the claimant and thereby avert a defamation claim.[21] But the offer must be adequate, and include an offer to compensate the claimant. So even the option of making an 'offer to make amends' involves the defendant being made monetarily worse off for acting perfectly reasonably.

The charge sheet against the law of defamation is a heavy one and it is one that has now impelled the UK government to attempt to reform it. In March 2011, the government published a Defamation Bill that will form the basis of a Defamation Act that will probably be passed into law in mid-2012. However, the most striking feature of the Defamation Bill, in its current form, is its timidity – there are very few provisions in the Bill that could seriously be said to bring about fundamental change in the law of defamation.

For example, clause 1 of the Bill seeks to deal with the 'ease of suit' problem posed by the law of defamation by providing that 'A statement is not defamatory unless its publication has caused or is likely to cause substantial harm to the reputation of the claimant.' However, as we will see, it may be argued that the courts have already incorporated a requirement of serious harm into their definition of what is defamatory. Clause 7 seeks to deal with the problem of 'forum shopping' (or 'libel tourism') by providing that in a case where the defendant does not live in the European Union, a British court will not 'have jurisdiction to hear [the claimant's case] unless the court is satisfied that, of all the places in which the statement complained of has been published, England and Wales is clearly the most appropriate place in which to bring an action in respect of the statement.' However, this is much the same standard as the one the courts apply already in determining whether they should decline to hear a defamation case on the ground of *forum non conveniens*. It is not at all clear, for example, that *Berezovsky* v *Michaels* (2000) would have been decided differently had clause 7 been in force at the time.[22]

We will note the various 'reforms' to the law of defamation proposed by the Defamation Bill in the relevant sections below, in which we look at the law of defamation in detail.

---

[21] Defamation Act 1996, s 2. See below, § 19.12.

[22] In the Consultation Paper accompanying the Bill, the government expresses the view (at [85]) that the emphasis in clause 7 on '*all* the places where the statement . . . has been published' (emphasis added) will 'overcome the problem of courts readily accepting jurisdiction simply because a claimant frames their claim so as to focus on damage which has occurred in this jurisdiction only. This would mean that, for example, if a statement was published 100,000 times in Australia and only 5,000 times in England that would be a good basis on which to conclude that the most appropriate jurisdiction in which to bring an action in respect of the statement was Australia rather than England.' In this example, there are 20 publications in Australia for every one in England. But in *Berezovsky* there were *400* publications in the US for every one in England, and yet the House of Lords still accepted jurisdiction.

19.2 WHAT IS DEFAMATORY?

In order to sue a defendant in defamation, a claimant has to show three things. He has to show that:

(1) the defendant *published* to a third party . . .
(2) . . . a statement that *referred to* the claimant . . .
(3) . . . and that that statement was *defamatory* of the claimant.

The third requirement is the most fundamental, and yet the most ill-defined.[23] In future, the definition laid down by Tugendhat J in *Thornton v Telegraph Media Group Ltd* (2010) is likely to be accepted as providing the *core* definition of what is defamatory. On this definition, a statement will be defamatory if it 'substantially affects in an adverse manner the attitude of other people towards him, or has a tendency to do so.'[24] Tugendhat J also observed that the word 'attitude' in this definition 'makes clear that it is the actions of right-thinking persons that must be likely to be affected (so that they treat the claimant unfavourably, or less favourably than they would otherwise have done) not just their thoughts or opinions.'[25] Putting these two statements together, we arrive at the following *core* definition of when a statement will be defamatory of a claimant:

> A statement will be defamatory of a claimant if it substantially affects in an adverse manner the way the claimant is treated by right-thinking persons, or has a tendency to do so.

The emphasis in this definition on the claimant being able to show that the treatment he has received (or is likely to receive) from right-thinking person has been *substantially* affected in an adverse manner is mirrored by clause 1 of the Defamation Bill, which currently provides that 'A statement is not defamatory unless its publication has caused or is likely to cause substantial harm to the reputation of the claimant.'

The courts and the government have both moved to incorporate a requirement of 'substantial affect' or 'substantial harm' into the definition of what is defamatory in order to protect people's rights of freedom of speech under Article 10 of the European Convention on Human Rights. Allowing claims to be made in defamation for trivial slights (such as calling a claimant 'hideously ugly'[26] or the 'worst tennis player in the world'[27]) amounts to a disproportionate interference with freedom of expression: the harm done by allowing such claims outweighs the good. However, this new requirement of 'substantial affect' or 'substantial harm' is not free from difficulties, and is likely to add to the cost and complexity of defamation trials. For example, consider the review of an actress' performance in a TV series that gave rise to a defamation claim in *Cornwell v Myskow* (1987): 'she can't sing, her bum is too big and she has the sort of stage presence that jams lavatories.' The claimant successfully argued that this was defamatory. Whether nowadays a court would say that the above statement was liable to 'substantially affect' the way she was treated by right-thinking people is anyone's guess.

The core definition as to when a statement will be defamatory of a claimant that is set out above is not exhaustive. *All* of the following points need to be borne in mind in considering whether or not a given statement is defamatory.

---

[23] See *Berkoff v Burchill* [1996] 4 All ER 1008, 1019: 'Defamation has never been satisfactorily defined. All attempted definitions are illustrative. None of them is exhaustive' (per Millett LJ).
[24] [2010] EWHC 1414 (QB), at [95].
[25] [2010] EWHC 1414 (QB), at [91].
[26] *Berkoff v Burchill* [1996] 4 All ER 1008.
[27] *Dee v Telegraph Media Group Ltd* [2010] EWHC 924 (QB).

(1) *Ridicule*. It has long been accepted that a statement that exposes a claimant to ridicule by right-thinking people will be defamatory.[28] For example, in *Berkoff* v *Burchill* (1996), the majority of the Court of Appeal accepted that the journalist Julie Burchill's calling the writer-director-actor Steven Berkoff 'hideously ugly' *might* have been defamatory on the basis that it might have made 'him an object of ridicule.'[29] Millett LJ dissented on the ground that 'It is one thing to ridicule a man; it is another to expose him to ridicule.'[30] He thought that Burchill had stayed on the right side of that divide in saying what she did about Berkoff.

(2) *Procedure*. The case of *Berkoff* v *Burchill* illustrates an important point of procedure that has to be borne in mind in reading defamation cases. Ever since Fox's Libel Act 1792 allowed civil claims to be brought for defamation, parties to a defamation case have had a right to have their case heard by a jury. In a case where a jury is to be used to hear the claim, it is for the jury to decide whether the words complained of *were* defamatory; the judge can only decide whether the words complained of *were capable of being* defamatory. That was the issue at stake in *Berkoff* v *Burchill*: whether calling Steven Berkoff 'hideously ugly' was *capable* of defaming him. The majority accepted that it was; but it was then for a jury to decide whether Julie Burchill's statement was *actually* defamatory. This point of procedure is increasingly becoming of merely historical importance. Most defamation claims are now heard by judges, and under clause 8 of the Defamation Bill, rights to have a defamation case decided by a jury will be abolished.

(3) *Abusive words*. It is often said that words of abuse are not defamatory if they are uttered and heard as such.[31] As Lord Atkin observed in *Sim* v *Stretch* (1936): 'exhibitions of bad manners or discourtesy are [not to be] placed on the same level as attacks on character.'[32] The reason is presumably that if a right-thinking person heard A being abused by B, he would realise that B's words are being uttered in anger and would therefore not take them seriously.[33] A right-thinking person would not then be led to treat A any less well because of B's words.

(4) *Offensive words*. An offensive statement about B will not be defamatory *per se*. For example, it is offensive to be labelled the 'world's worst tennis player'[34] or as being 'hideously ugly', or to be misquoted as disparaging a couple of celebrity vegetarians.[35] But the mere fact that someone has said something offensive about you does not bring your case within the law of defamation.[36]

(5) *Business/professional defamation*. It has long been accepted that a statement casting aspersions on the way a business is run will be defamatory of the business if the effect or

---

[28] *Parmiter* v *Coupland* (1840) 6 M & W 105, 108; 151 ER 340, 341–2.

[29] [1996] 4 All ER 1008, at 1018 (per Neill LJ); also at 1021 (per Phillips LJ).

[30] [1996] 4 All ER 1008, at 1020.

[31] *Penfold* v *Westcote* (1806) 2 B & P (NR) 335, 127 ER 656; *Fields* v *Davis* [1955] CLY 1543.

[32] *Sim* v *Stretch* [1936] 2 All ER 1237, 1242.

[33] For the same reason, Handley and Davis 2001 argue that 'words are not defamatory if they are spoken in a context where it is clear that they are in jest'. It is not clear whether the English courts would accept this. If they did not, comedians' freedom of expression would be seriously interfered with: almost all satirical depictions of public figures would be defamatory and *prima facie* actionable.

[34] *Dee* v *Telegraph Media Group Ltd* [2010] EWHC 924 (QB).

[35] *Ecclestone* v *Telegraph Media Group Ltd* [2009] EWHC 2779 (QB).

[36] Though see *Youssoupoff* v *MGM Pictures Ltd* (1934) 50 TLR 581 (discussed, Treiger-Bar-Am 2000), where it was held that it would be defamatory to suggest in a film about the life and death of the Russian monk Rasputin that the claimant had been *raped* by Rasputin, even though it is hard to imagine right-thinking people doing anything but treating the claimant with sympathy on hearing such a statement.

likely effect of that statement is to harm that business' credit or custom.[37] Likewise, it has also long been accepted that it is defamatory to cast aspersions on someone's skill or competence in practising a particular trade that is their profession.[38] However, applying these rules has given rise to difficulty.

First, in the case of a business, the law draws a distinction between: (1) damaging a business by casting aspersions on the quality of its goods or services; and (2) damaging a business by casting aspersions on the way it is run. Only (2) is capable of giving rise to an action for defamation.[39] A business that suffers (1) will only be able to sue if they can show the defendant's words amounted to *malicious falsehood*.[40] However, in a case where a defendant has criticised a business' goods or services as being no good, it is often difficult to determine whether the defendant's criticism carries with it a criticism of the way the business is run; after all, if the business was run well, its goods or services would normally be good.

The same difficulty afflicts cases of professional defamation. In *Drummond-Jackson* v *BMA* (1970), the *British Medical Journal* published a serious scientific paper casting doubt on the safety of a particular method of administering anaesthetic during dental procedures that had been developed by the claimant. The claimant sued for defamation. Lord Denning MR wanted to dismiss the claim on the ground that the paper merely criticised the claimant's *technique*, not him *personally*. However, the majority disagreed:

> A professional man's technique is at least relatively permanent, and it belongs to him: it may be considered to be an essential part of his professional activity and of him as a professional man. In the case of a dentist it may be said: if he uses a bad technique, he is a bad dentist and a person needing dental treatment should not go to him.[41]

It is not, however, defamatory to say of a professional person that they carry on their trade in one way rather than another if it would be legitimate for them to carry on their trade in either of those ways; so it is not defamatory to say that McBride & Bagshaw's *Tort Law* provides readers with a broad overview of the law of tort, even if the authors of that work are aiming to produce something more substantial.[42]

(6) *Bane and antidote.* In determining whether a particular statement is defamatory, regard must be paid to the context in which the statement was published, and in particular anything that was said together with the statement to neutralise or counter-act any adverse effect that it might otherwise have had.

For example, in *Charleston* v *News Group Newspapers Ltd* (1995), the *News of the World* published an article on a pornographic computer game which had superimposed the faces of the claimants – two stars of the television series *Neighbours* – on the bodies of two persons engaged in various sexual activities. The article had as its headline 'Strewth! What's Harold up to with our Madge?' and the article carried two large stills from the computer game. The text of the article made it clear that the claimants' faces had been used without their knowledge or consent.

The claimants sued the owners of the *News of the World*, claiming that the photographs and the headlines were defamatory – the claimants claimed that a right-thinking person

[37] *South Hetton Coal Company Ltd* v *North-Eastern News Association Ltd* [1894] 1 QB 133.
[38] *Drummond-Jackson* v *British Medical Association* [1970] 1 WLR 688, 698–9: 'words may be defamatory of a . . . professional man . . . if they impute lack of qualification, knowledge, skill, capacity, judgment or efficiency in the conduct of his . . . professional activity' (per Lord Pearson).
[39] *South Hetton Coal Company Ltd* v *North-Eastern News Association Ltd* [1894] 1 QB 133, 139.
[40] For discussion of this tort, see below, § 24.9.
[41] *Drummond-Jackson* v *British Medical Association* [1970] 1 WLR 688, 698 (per Lord Pearson).
[42] *Thornton* v *Telegraph Media Group Ltd* [2010] EWHC 1414 (QB) (not defamatory to say of a writer that she does not write to the standards of a professional journalist).

who looked at the photographs and the headlines would have thought that the claimants had willingly participated in the production of the pornographic computer game in question and would therefore think less well of the claimants as a result. The House of Lords dismissed the claimants' claim: a right-thinking person who saw the headline and photographs complained of would also have read the article below the headlines and the photographs and would have realised that the claimants had nothing to do with the production of the computer game in question.

(7) *The repetition rule.* Suppose *Gossip* said to *Ear*, '*Rumour* thinks/*Rumour* told me that *Jerry* is a thief'. In such a case, it will be *conclusively presumed* that a right-thinking person who heard or read *Gossip's* statement would have concluded that *Jerry was* a thief. This rule of law is known as the 'repetition rule'.

The repetition rule applies even if it would have been clear to a right-thinking person who heard or read *Gossip's* statement that *Gossip* was not necessarily endorsing *Rumour's* opinion of *Jerry* – as would be the case if *Gossip* qualified his statement by saying that 'Of course, I have no way of knowing myself whether or not *Jerry* is a thief, but . . .'[43] It follows that *Gossip's* statement in the above case *will* be defamatory of *Jerry* – it will be conclusively presumed that a right-thinking person who heard or read *Gossip's* statement would have concluded from it that *Jerry* was a thief and would as a result have thought less well of *Jerry*.

A similar rule applies if *Accuser* said to *Ear*, 'I think *Jerry* is a thief'. Again, it will be conclusively presumed that a right-thinking person who heard or read *Accuser's* statement would have concluded from it that *Jerry* was a thief and would therefore have thought less well of *Jerry*. It will therefore be conclusively presumed that *Accuser's* statement was defamatory of *Jerry* – and this is so even if a right-thinking person who heard or read *Accuser's* statement could actually have been expected to think, 'Well, *Accuser* thinks *Jerry* is a thief, but his opinion is not necessarily correct and I should wait to make up my own mind about *Jerry* instead of just blindly going along with *Accuser's* opinions.'

Similarly, if *Suspicious* said to *Ear*, 'I have reasonable grounds to suspect *Jerry* of being a thief', it will be conclusively presumed that a right-thinking person who heard or read *Suspicious's* statement would have concluded from it that there *were* reasonable grounds to suspect *Jerry* of being a thief and would have thought less well of *Jerry* as a result.[44] So, again, it will be conclusively presumed that *Suspicious's* statement was defamatory of *Jerry* – and this is so even if a right-thinking person who heard or read *Suspicious's* statement could actually have been expected to think, 'Well, *Suspicious* may think he has reasonable grounds to believe that *Jerry* is a thief – but what does he know? I should make up my own mind and judge *Jerry* on the evidence presented to me.'

(8) *Community standards.* In judging how a right-thinking person would react to a given statement about someone, one must take into account the current state of public opinion. So, for example, suppose A tells B that C is a practising homosexual. Is that defamatory? Forty years ago, the answer would have been 'yes' – the state of public opinion at that time was such that a right-thinking person would have tended to think less well of someone if it were alleged that he was having homosexual sex.[45] Nowadays, people generally think

---

[43] *Stern* v *Piper* [1997] QB 123.

[44] *Shah* v *Standard Chartered Bank* [1999] QB 241.

[45] In *R* v *Bishop* [1975] QB 274, the Court of Appeal expressed the view (at 281) that if A said that B was a homosexual 'a submission that [A's] words were incapable of a defamatory meaning would be bound to fail and a jury would generally be likely to find them defamatory.' Also Dworkin 1977, at 240: 'No doubt most Americans and Englishmen think that homosexuality, prostitution, and the publication of pornography are immoral.'

there is nothing wrong with people of the same sex having sex and, given this, it is difficult to say that a right-thinking person would nowadays think less well of someone if it was alleged that he was a practising homosexual. This creates a problem for C in the situation we are discussing. If C wants to sue A so as to establish publicly that he is in fact heterosexual, the courts may rule that A's allegation was not defamatory and thereby prevent C from suing A for defamation.

It follows from what has just been said that if *Prim* has higher standards of behaviour than the general public and *Journo* accuses *Prim* of engaging in conduct that is inconsistent with those high standards, *Prim* will find it difficult to show that *Journo*'s words were defamatory for the purpose of suing *Journo* for defamation. So, for example, suppose *Prim* is a teetotaller but *Journo* wrote that he saw *Prim* drinking a pint of lager in a pub at the weekend. *Journo*'s statement will not be defamatory of *Prim* – a right-thinking person who read *Journo*'s statement about *Prim* would not think any the worse of *Prim* as a result. However, it would be different if *Prim* was well known to be a mentor working for Alcoholics Anonymous to help other alcoholics avoid drinking. In such a case, a right-thinking person who read *Journo*'s statement would tend to think that *Prim* was a hypocrite and would tend to think less well of *Prim* as a result. On these facts, then, a case could be made out for thinking that *Journo*'s statement was defamatory of *Prim*.

(9) *Innuendo.* The last example we have been considering – where *Journo* has said that he saw *Prim* drinking a pint of lager in a pub, but *Prim* works as a mentor for Alcoholics Anonymous – is an example of a statement that is defamatory because it gives rise to an *innuendo* that is defamatory of *Prim*. A genuine innuendo case is where a defendant makes a statement that is innocent on its face, but would make a right-thinking person *who was possessed of certain special knowledge* think less well of the claimant. So *Journo*'s statement that he saw *Prim* drinking in a pub is totally innocent on its face, but would still make a right-thinking person think less well of *Prim* if *she knew that Prim worked as a mentor for Alcoholics Anonymous.*

In an innuendo case, the claimant can only sue the defendant if she can establish that the defendant's statement was published to one or more people who were actually possessed of the special knowledge that would make a right-thinking person who heard or read the claimant's statement think less well of the claimant. So, to take a well-known example, suppose that A said to B that he saw C coming out of a particular house the other day. Suppose further that that house happened to be a brothel. So a right-thinking person who knew the house in question was a brothel would, on hearing A's statement, tend to think less well of C as a person – he would tend to think that C used prostitutes. C will only be able to sue A for what he said to B if B *knew* that the house A said he saw C was coming out of was a brothel. Note that, so far as C is concerned, that is *all* he has to show in order to sue A for defamation. He does *not* have to show that B concluded from A's statement that C used prostitutes. He does not even have to show that B believed A's statement. All he has to show is that B had the knowledge that would make a right-thinking person who heard or read A's statement think less well of C.

In *Cassidy* v *Daily Mirror Newspapers Ltd* (1929), the *Daily Mirror* published a photograph of one Cassidy with a lady companion. The caption accompanying the photograph informed the reader that Cassidy and his companion had announced their engagement. In fact, Cassidy was married to the claimant. The claimant successfully sued the *Daily Mirror* for libel. A right-thinking person who knew (i) the claimant and (ii) that she purported to be Cassidy's wife, would conclude on the basis of the *Daily Mirror*'s caption that the claimant was not Cassidy's wife at all and was therefore a liar. But because a right-thinking person would only think less well of the claimant as a result of the caption in the *Daily Mirror* if he knew (i) and (ii), the claimant had to show that at least one person who knew (i) and (ii) had seen the caption. The claimant was able to do this, and could therefore sue the *Daily Mirror* for defamation on the basis that its caption gave rise to an innuendo that was defamatory of her.

(10) *The single meaning rule.* Some statements are ambiguous. Suppose that A tells B that C 'made D an offer he couldn't refuse' in order to persuade D not to accept a job that one of C's clients wanted. A's statement might be taken as implying that: (i) C threatened to kill D if he took the job. But it might equally well be taken as implying that: (ii) C made D a really generous offer of alternative employment that meant D would have been crazy to accept the original job offer.

In defamation cases, the courts will not accept that statements are ambiguous in this kind of way. They are committed to the idea that *every statement has a single meaning* in the mind of a right-thinking person.[46] So if C sues A for defamation in the case we are discussing, the task of the judge or jury deciding C's case is to discover what *single meaning* a right-thinking person would have given to A's statement. Would a right-thinking person have taken A as saying (i) or (ii)? Of course, determining the answer to this question is impossible – a right-thinking person would have been uncertain what A's words meant. One might as well toss a coin to see which single meaning a right-thinking person would have ascribed to A's words. Even the courts acknowledge that the 'single meaning rule' is 'highly artificial',[47] 'the product of an accident of history resulting in a fiction that assumes that the reasonable man will understand a particular statement in only one way.'[48] However, it seems that the courts are stuck with the rule: it is too well-established to be swept away by the judges. They have, however, refused to extend it to other torts,[49] such as the tort of malicious falsehood.[50]

19.3 REFERENCE TO THE CLAIMANT

Sometimes a statement is obviously defamatory, but there is an issue over whether the statement can be said to refer to the claimant. Two classes of statement need to be distinguished in this context.

A. Statements not intended to refer to the claimant

This sort of statement will be defamatory of the claimant if:

(a) a right-thinking person who *knew of the claimant and her circumstances* would have, on hearing or reading the statement in question, thought that it referred to the claimant and would, as a result, have tended to think less well of the claimant; *and*

(b) the statement in question was published to one or more people *who thought that it referred to the claimant.*

If (a) *and* (b) are true then the statement in question will be defamatory of B even though it was not intended specifically to refer to B.

[46] *Slim* v *Daily Telegraph* [1968] 2 QB 157, 172 (per Diplock LJ).
[47] *Bonnick* v *Morris* [2003] 1 AC 300, at [21] (per Lord Nicholls).
[48] *Ajinomoto Sweeteners SAS* v *Asda Stores Ltd* [2011] QB 497, at [40] (per Rimer LJ).
[49] *Ajinomoto Sweeteners SAS* v *Asda Stores Ltd* [2011] QB 497.
[50] Discussed below, § 24.9.

The question of whether a statement that was not intended specifically to refer to the claimant is defamatory of the claimant tends to come up in two contexts: (1) *mistaken identity* cases; and (2) *defamation of a class* cases.

(1) *Mistaken identity cases.* In *E Hulton & Co* v *Jones* (1910), the *Sunday Chronicle* carried an article describing a motor festival at Dieppe. The article featured various figures who attended the festival including one 'Artemus Jones'. He was described as being a 'churchwarden at Peckham'. The article alleged that while he was at the festival he had consorted with a woman who was not his wife and that he was, in general, 'the life and soul of a gay little band that haunts the Casino and turns night into day, besides betraying a most unholy delight in the society of female butterflies'.

The claimant was a barrister called Artemus Jones. He sued the defendants, the publishers of the *Sunday Chronicle*, for libel. His claim was successful. It was found that friends of the claimant had seen the article in question and thought it referred to the claimant. Moreover, it was found that a right-thinking person who knew the claimant would have thought, on reading the article, that it referred to him and would have tended as a result to think less well of him as a person. The fact that the claimant was a barrister and not a churchwarden at Peckham did not affect the issue. No doubt the fact that the claimant and the person referred to in the article shared such a distinctive name as Artemus Jones played a large part in the finding that a right-thinking person who knew the claimant would have thought on reading the article in question that it referred to him.

In *Newstead* v *London Express Newspaper Limited* (1940), the *Daily Express* published an account of a trial for bigamy, referring to the accused as 'Harold Newstead, thirty-year-old Camberwell man'. The claimant – who was called Harold Newstead and who worked in Camberwell and was aged about 30 – sued the publishers of the *Daily Express* for libel. His claim succeeded. It was found that some acquaintances of the claimant had read the account in the *Daily Express* and thought that it referred to the claimant. Moreover, it was found that a right-thinking person who knew the claimant would have – on reading the report of the trial – thought that the report referred to the claimant and would therefore have thought less well of the claimant as a person.

It might have been different if the name of the prisoner who was accused of bigamy had been 'John Smith' and the prisoner had simply been described as 'John Smith, a 30-year-old London man'.[51] In such a case, if another John Smith who came from London and was about thirty years old had sued the publishers of the *Daily Express* for libel, he would *not* have been able to establish that a right-thinking person who knew him would, on reading the report in the *Daily Express*, have thought that the report referred to the claimant and would therefore have tended to think less well of him: such a right-thinking person would have had no reason to identify the claimant with the prisoner named in the report in the *Daily Express* even though their names, ages and residences coincided.

In *Morgan* v *Odhams Press Ltd* (1971), the claimant took into his house a kennel girl who was helping a journalist with his inquiries into the activities of a dog doping gang. The claimant spent six days with the girl in his flat and in that period a few acquaintances of the claimant met him in the company of the girl. After the six days were up, the girl in question went to stay with the journalist she was helping. The journalist published his story about the dog doping gang in a Sunday newspaper and the story included a photograph of the kennel girl who had helped him break the story. The next day, *The Sun* published a

---

[51] [1940] 1 KB 377, 391 (per MacKinnon LJ).

story claiming that the kennel girl in question had been kidnapped by members of the gang.

The claimant successfully sued *The Sun* for libel. It was found that a right-thinking person who saw the kennel girl with the claimant during the six days that she spent with the claimant would, on reading the story in *The Sun*, think that the claimant was one of the dog doping gang who had kidnapped the girl and would therefore think less well of the claimant. It was also found that people who had seen the kennel girl with the claimant during the six days that she spent with the claimant had thought the story in *The Sun* referred to him.

(2) *Defamation of a class.* Suppose we wrote in this book, 'All law students are dishonest'. Could you sue us for libel? The answer is 'no'. No court would find that a right-thinking person who read the above statement would think that it applied to you, and would have tended as a result to think less well of you.[52] Why is this? The answer is that generalisations always admit of exceptions and a right-thinking person who read the above statement would not think that it applied *without exception* to *all* law students, including you.[53]

It would be different if we said that, 'All the clerks who work at the Supreme Court are extremely lazy.' There are very few such clerks (one or two per Supreme Court Justice) – so our statement could be taken by a right-thinking person as applying to every single clerk employed at the Supreme Court, without exception.

In *Knupffer* v *London Express Newspaper Ltd* (1944), the *Daily Express* carried an article during the Second World War which accused members of the 'Young Russia' party of being willing to help Hitler by building up a pro-German movement within the Soviet Union. The claimant was the head of the British branch of the 'Young Russia' party. A number of people read the article and thought it referred to or reflected on the claimant. The claimant sued the publishers of the *Daily Express* for libel. His claim was dismissed by the House of Lords: a right-thinking person who read the *Daily Express* article would not have thought it referred to the claimant in particular. The accusations against members of the 'Young Russia' party contained in the *Daily Express* article were far too generalised to make it reasonable to think that they applied to the claimant in particular.

In contrast, in *Riches* v *News Group Newspapers Ltd* (1986), the *News of the World* published a letter from a man who was holding his son and a woman hostage at gun point. The letter made various allegations against 'the Banbury CID' – including an allegation that members of the Banbury CID had raped his wife. Ten members of the Banbury CID sued the publishers of the *News of the World* for libel and were awarded substantial damages at first instance. The Court of Appeal held that the damages awarded to the claimants should be reassessed but did not question the propriety of awarding each of the claimants something by way of damages. Clearly, the Court of Appeal agreed with the court of first instance that the letter published in the *News of the World* was defamatory of *each* of the claimants. A right-thinking person who read the letter published in the *News of the World* would have thought that the allegations contained in the letter applied to *each and every* member of the Banbury CID – he would not have simply thought that those allegations

---

[52] *Eastwood* v *Holmes* (1858) 1 F & F 347, 349, 175 ER 758, 759: '[If] a man wrote that all lawyers were thieves, no particular lawyer could sue him unless there was something to point to the particular individual' (per Willes J).

[53] See Lord Atkin's remarks in *Knupffer* v *London Express Newspaper Ltd* [1944] AC 116, 122: 'The reason why a libel published of a large or indeterminate number of persons described by some general name generally fails to be actionable is the difficulty of establishing that the claimant was, in fact, included in the defamatory statement, for the habit of making unfounded generalisations is ingrained in ill-educated or vulgar minds, or the words are occasionally intended to be a facetious exaggeration.'

merely amounted to sweeping generalisations which did not necessarily apply to each and every member of the Banbury CID.

B. Statements intended to refer to the claimant

Sometimes a defendant will make a statement that is intended to refer to the claimant, but does not specifically identify the claimant as the person being referred to. An example of the sort of statement we have in mind here is provided by a Rod Liddle article in *The Sunday Times* on 22 January 2006, describing a visit to Goodison Park to watch his team Millwall play Everton:

> My abiding memory of the Millwall midweek FA Cup replay at Everton was . . . of an incalculably dense, porky little Hitler of a Merseyside copper yapping out orders from astride his horse: 'Come on, keep up, keep up. Shut your mouth. Don't answer back. Do as you're . . . told.' And so on, interminably, throughout the duration of our five mile forced march from the football ground to Liverpool Lime Street station (where, incidentally, most of us did not want to go).'

Would the policeman who *actually did* escort the Millwall fans from Goodison Park to the railway station on horseback be entitled to sue Rod Liddle for defamation on the basis that Rod Liddle intended to describe *him* as being a 'dense, porky little Hitler of a Merseyside copper'? Or would the policeman have to show – in line with the approach adopted in cases where a statement was *not* intended to refer specifically to the claimant – that: (1) a right-thinking person *who knew the claimant and knew of his circumstances* would have thought that the description 'dense, porky little Hitler of a Merseyside copper' applied to the claimant and would have thought less well of the claimant as a result; and (2) the article was published to one or more people who thought that it referred to the claimant?

So far as we know, the question has not really been addressed by the courts. However, we think in principle that the policeman that Rod Liddle intended to refer to in his article should have been able to sue for defamation (subject to defences, of course) without having to establish that (1) and (2) were true. The fact that a claimant has not been referred to by name by the defendant should not prevent him suing for defamation where he was the very person that the defendant was intending to refer to.[54]

19.4 PUBLICATION TO A THIRD PARTY

If B wants to sue A for defamation, B will have to show that A *published* a statement that was defamatory of him to a *third party*. So, obviously, if A said *to B*, 'You are a liar and a cheat', B will not be able to sue A for defamation: A's statement was not published to a third party.

This simple requirement of publication to a third party conceals a host of difficulties, which we will now explore.

(1) *Spouses*. If A tells his wife, 'B is a liar and a cheat', B will not be able to sue A for defamation. The reason is that the courts will *not* find that A's statement in this case was published to a *third party*.[55] The courts' attitude is a throwback to the days when a husband

---

[54] In *Jameel (Yousef) v Dow Jones & Co Inc* [2005] QB 946, the Court of Appeal said at [45] that: 'Where a common name is included in an article, the name itself will not suffice to identify any individual who bears that name.' However, it is submitted that this *dictum* is intended to apply only in cases where the article was *not* specifically intended to refer to the claimant.

[55] *Wennhak v Morgan* (1888) 20 QBD 635. The same rule will apply, of course, if a wife tells her husband something that is defamatory of another.

and wife were regarded as having a common identity. While we have, of course, abandoned the idea that a husband and wife share a common identity, the courts still seem to think that someone who makes a defamatory statement to his or her spouse does not publish that statement to a third party.

(2) *Secretaries*. If A dictates a letter to his secretary saying that 'B is a liar and a cheat', B may be able to sue A even if the letter is never sent. A will have published the defamatory statements contained in the letter to a third party, namely his secretary. But if A's secretary hands back the letter to A for checking, B will not be able to sue *the secretary*. The reason is that the re-publication to A of something that A has already told his secretary will not be regarded as a publication to a third party.[56] It would be different, of course, if the secretary showed or sent the letter to someone other than A or B – in that case, B may well be able to sue the secretary for libel.

(3) *Misunderstanding*. It seems to be generally acknowledged that if A made a statement to C that was defamatory of B, A will not be held to have published that statement to a third party if C did not understand what A said because, for example, he was deaf or illiterate.

(4) *Private notes*. Suppose that A wrote down on a piece of paper 'B is a liar and a cheat' and locked the piece of paper in a desk drawer. Suppose further that C, a burglar, subsequently broke into the desk drawer and read the piece of paper. B will not be able to sue A for libel.[57] A did not publish the defamatory material to C: he did not show C the piece of paper or allow him to read it.

(5) *Unintended recipients*. If A sent a letter to B that said 'You are a liar and a cheat' and C opened the letter and read it, the courts will not hold that A published the letter to C *unless* it was *reasonably foreseeable* when A sent the letter that it would be opened and read by someone like C.

In *Pullman* v *Hill & Co* (1891), the defendant sent a letter to the claimants at their firm which claimed that they had obtained money under false pretences. The letter was opened by a clerk in the claimants' firm and was read by him and two other clerks. It was held that the defendant had published his defamatory letter about the claimants to the clerks because it was reasonably foreseeable that they would open and read the letter; it being normal practice for the clerks in a firm to open and read all the correspondence addressed to the firm.

Similarly, in *Theaker* v *Richardson* (1962), the defendant sent a letter to the claimant, a member of the local council, which accused her of shoplifting, of running a brothel, of being a prostitute and of having committed various acts of dishonesty in her position as a council member. The claimant's husband opened the letter and read it. The claimant sued the defendant for libel. A jury found for the claimant, holding that the defendant had published his letter to the claimant's husband – it had been reasonably foreseeable when the defendant sent his letter to the claimant that the claimant's husband would read the letter. The Court of Appeal declined to set aside the jury's verdict.[58]

In contrast, in *Huth* v *Huth* (1915), the defendant sent a letter to his estranged wife which, the claimants claimed, was defamatory of them. The claimants were the defendant's

---

[56] *Eglantine Inn Ltd* v *Smith* [1948] NI 29, 33.
[57] *Pullman* v *Hill & Co* [1891] 1 QB 524, 527.
[58] Note that the old-fashioned view that husbands and wives share a common identity does not extend to cases where A makes a defamatory remark about B to B's husband. In such a case, the courts will hold that the remark *has* been published to a *third party*. They will not regard A's remark as having just been made to B.

children – they claimed the defendant's letter suggested that they were illegitimate. In order to sue the defendant they had to show that the defendant had published the letter to someone other than his wife. (The fact that the defendant published the letter to his wife was not, of course, enough to allow the claimants to sue the defendant – as we have already seen, if someone publishes a defamatory statement to his wife, that statement will not be regarded as having been published to a third party.) In fact, the butler in the house where the defendant's wife was staying when she received the letter had opened and read the letter before he handed it over to the defendant's wife. The Court of Appeal held that the defendant had not published his letter to the butler as it was not reasonably foreseeable that the butler would open and read his letter. The claimants could not therefore show that the defendant had published his letter to anyone other than his wife and their claims were dismissed.

(6) *Shops*. If a shop sells a newspaper or a book containing a defamatory statement, it seems that the shop will not be held to have published that statement to the person buying the book unless it knew or ought to have known that the newspaper or book in question contained a defamatory statement.[59] Such a shop would, in any case, be covered by the defence of 'innocent dissemination'.[60] But *dicta* of Eady J in two recent cases[61] seem to indicate that the shop would not need to take advantage of such a defence as it could not be held in the first place to have published the defamatory statement to the purchaser of the book or newspaper.

(7) *Internet search engines*. In the second of those two cases – *Metropolitan International Schools Ltd* v *Designtechnica Corporation* (2009) – Eady J held that a company (such as Google) that administers an internet search engine will not publish to someone using that engine any defamatory statements that the searcher comes across in using that search engine. This is so even if the company knows that conducting a particular search will bring up results that contain defamatory statements about a claimant. The reason is that the company is not responsible for those statements coming up in response to a particular search: they have no control over what results will be yielded by a particular search.

(8) *Platforms*. It is different if A posted the statement 'B is a liar and a cheat' on an electronic bulletin board or website that was maintained by C. In such a case, the courts will hold that C – as well as A – published that statement to whoever accessed the bulletin board or website and read A's statement (though C may be able to take advantage of the defence, discussed below, of 'innocent dissemination').[62]

What is the position if A posted the statement 'B is a liar and a cheat' on some premises which were owned or run by C? In such a case, the courts will hold that C – as well as A – published the statement to the people who read it *if* there is some evidence that C *approved* of the posting up of that statement.[63] Similarly, it is suggested, if A said that 'B is a liar and

---

[59] *Emmens v Pottle* (1885) 16 QBD 354, 357 (per Lord Esher MR).

[60] Discussed below, § 19.12.

[61] *Bunt* v *Tilley* [2007] 1 WLR 1243, at [21]–[23]; *Metropolitan International Schools Ltd* v *Designtechnica Corporation* [2009] EWHC 1765 (QB), at [49].

[62] *Godfrey v Demon Internet Limited* [2001] QB 201.

[63] See *Byrne v Deane* [1937] 1 KB 818. A poem suggesting that the claimant had told the authorities about some illegal gambling machines in a golf club run by the defendants (with the result that the machines were removed) was posted up on the walls of the golf club. The poem was held to have been published by the defendants to whoever read the poem because there was some sign that they approved of its being posted up – the defendants had had the power to take the poem down, but none of them had. However, no claim could be made against the defendants because the poem was held not to be defamatory because a right-thinking person who read the poem would think the claimant was to be congratulated on upholding the law.

a cheat' in the course of a meeting held on premises owned or run by C, C – as well as A – will be held to have published that statement to the people who attended the meeting if there is some evidence that he approved of the making of that statement.

(9) *Printers*. We saw above that a shop that sells a book or newspaper that contains a defamatory statement will not be held to have published that statement to the purchaser of the book or newspaper if they did not know, and had no reason to know, that the book or newspaper in question contained a defamatory statement. The rule seems to be different for the printer of the book or newspaper: the printer will be held to have published to the reader of the book or newspaper any defamatory statements in the book or newspapers whatever the printer's level of knowledge about those statements.[64]

(10) *Abuse of process*. The courts reserve the power to strike out a claim in defamation if they take the view that the claimant has no legitimate interest in bringing that claim. This will be the case, the Court of Appeal laid down in the key case of *Jameel (Yousef)* v *Dow Jones & Co Inc* (2005) if the defamatory publications that have occurred in England do not amount to a 'real and substantial tort'.[65] Where those publications have caused minimal damage to the claimant's reputation, the courts will strike out the claimant's claim for damages on the basis that 'the game [of suing for defamation] will not be worth the candle' in terms of the cost of litigating the case and tying up the courts' time in hearing the case.[66]

This was the basis on which the Court of Appeal struck out the claim in the *Jameel (Yousef)* case. In that case, the *Wall Street Journal* (WSJ) published an article about a list – known as the 'Golden Chain' – of 20 people who provided financial backing for Al-Qaeda in its early years. The article was posted up on the WSJ's American website and a hyperlink was inserted into the Internet version of the article which allowed people reading the article on the Internet to see the 'Golden Chain' list. The fourth name on the list was 'Yousif Jameel'.

Yousef Jameel – a Saudi businessman – sued the *Wall Street Journal* for defamation in England. It was accepted that the name 'Yousif Jameel' referred to the claimant, but the defendants argued that Yousef Jameel's claim should be struck out because he had suffered no loss in England as a result of the existence of the hyperlink on the WSJ's American website. Only five people based in England had accessed the hyperlink: two of them had no idea who Yousef Jameel was, and the other three were all close associates of the claimant and did not therefore think any the worse of the claimant as a result of seeing the name 'Yousif Jameel' on the 'Golden Chain' document.

The Court of Appeal held that the claim should be struck out as an abuse of process. Allowing the claim to continue would not be worthwhile, either in terms of repairing any damage to the claimant's reputation in England (as that was minimal) or in terms of ensuring that the WSJ would not repeat the defamatory allegation about the claimant in England (as the WSJ had already removed the offending article from its website).

The subsequent case of *Mardas* v *New York Times Co* (2008) also involved someone who did not live in England trying to sue an American publisher for defamation in the English courts. The *New York Times* (NYT) and the *International Herald Tribune* (IHT) had alleged – on the death of the Maharishi Mahesh Yogi – that the reason why the Beatles had fallen out with the Maharishi was that the claimant (who was known at the time as 'Magic Alex'

---

[64] However the printer may be able to take advantage of the defence of innocent dissemination: see below, § 19.12(A).

[65] [2005] QB 946, at [70].

[66] [2005] QB 946, at [57], quoting Eady J in *Schellenberg* v *British Broadcasting Corp* [2000] EMLR 296, 318–9.

for the inventions he was working on) may have fabricated stories of the Maharishi making sexual advances on women staying at the ashram in India where the Maharishi and the Beatles and various other guests were staying. The claimant sued in defamation. He argued that the NYT's defamatory remarks about him had been published in England both via its website and in some hard copies of the NYT that had been sold in England. It was estimated at first instance that four people had accessed the defamatory story about the claimant via the NYT website, and that 117 copies of the NYT containing that story had been sold in England. The defamatory story about the claimant did not make the printed version of the IHT but could be found on its website. It was estimated that 27 people from England had accessed the story about the claimant on the IHT website.

Despite these paltry numbers (which were disputed), Eady J declined to strike out the claimant's claim, holding that the question 'whether there has been a real and substantial tort within the jurisdiction . . . cannot depend on a numbers game.'[67] He then went on to say that 'a few dozen [people accessing a defamatory story from within England via the Internet] is enough to found a cause of action here, although the damages would be likely to be modest.'[68] The fact that the claimant had lived in England for many years (before moving to Greece) and had two children still living in England convinced Eady J that the claimant had a legitimate interest in seeking to protect his reputation within England.

In *Wallis* v *Meredith* (2011), the defendant was sacked from his job with the claimant's firm and entered into communications with the claimant's solicitor, seeking compensation for the fact that he had been (in his eyes) wrongfully dismissed. In one letter to the claimant's solicitor, he complained that 'two burly men with East European accents' had come to his front door, threatening him and telling 'me to "phone the man who you have offended and say 'sorry'. You have 24 hours".' The claimant launched proceedings for defamation against the defendant, arguing that the defendant was suggesting that the claimant had tried to intimidate the defendant. The claimant's lawyers could not establish that the defendant had made this suggestion to anyone other than the claimant's solicitor, and as a result the claim for defamation was struck out as an abuse of process:

> the publication relied on is as numerically minimal as it could get, and was to the claimants' professional agent, who was acting in respect of a commercial dispute with [the defendant]. It does not seem to me that the claimants require vindication in respect of such a publication to a solicitor who has been busily engaged in stating that the allegation is false . . .[69]

(11) *The multiple publication rule.* Under s 4A of the Limitation Act 1980, a claimant who wishes to sue a defendant for publishing a defamatory statement about him has to bring his claim within one year of the moment he was first entitled to sue for that publication. (As we will see in the next section, where the publication was in permanent form – and thus *libel* – the claimant is entitled to sue from the moment of publication. Where the publication is in impermanent form – and thus *slander* – the claimant is normally only entitled to sue from the moment the publication first causes him harm.)

Under the 'multiple publication rule', *every* time a defamatory statement is published, a fresh cause of action arises and the claimant has a year from the moment that cause of action arose to bring a claim. The rule goes back to the case of *The Duke of Brunswick* v *Harmer* (1849), where the claimant was allowed in 1848 to sue a newspaper in defamation for an article that it had published in 1830, by the simple device of having one of his

---

[67] [2008] EWHC 3135 (QB), at [15].
[68] [2008] EWHC 3135 (QB), at [31].
[69] [2011] EWHC 75 (QB), at [60].

employees purchase a back copy of the newspaper and look at the article in question. It was held that the publication to the employee constituted a fresh tort, for which the claimant could sue within the limitation period for suing for defamation.[70]

This rule creates difficulties for newspapers that maintain online archives. Application of the rule means that a newspaper could be sued in defamation within a year of someone accessing a defamatory article in an online archive, no matter how old the article might be. (Though it should be noted that if the article defames someone who is now dead, no claim for defamation can be brought by the deceased's estate.)[71] The government proposes to deal with this problem in clause 6 of the Defamation Bill, sweeping away the 'multiple publication rule' in favour of a 'single publication rule' under which a claimant has one year to sue in defamation from the date of the *first* publication of a defamatory statement by a defendant, even if the statement has subsequently been re-published by the defendant in a form 'which is substantially the same.'

19.5 TITLE TO SUE

Two points need to be made under this heading.

A. Legal personality

Not everyone who is recognised in law as being a person will have a right to sue in defamation.

If the claimant is a *natural person* then there is no problem: a flesh-and-blood person may bring an action for defamation against someone else. The case of *South Hetton Coal Company Ltd* v *North-Eastern News Association Ltd* (1894) establishes that a *company* may be able to sue a defendant for libel or slander if the defendant publishes to another a statement that is defamatory of the company – but only if the statement in question has a tendency to damage the company's trading interests. Section 10(1) of the Trade Union and Labour Relations (Consolidation) Act 1992 provides that a 'trade union is not a body corporate' – so a *trade union* does not enjoy sufficient personality to bring an action for libel or slander in respect of a statement that is defamatory of the trade union.[72]

If A publishes a statement to another that is defamatory of a *public body* – such as a local authority – the public body in question will *not* be entitled to sue A for defamation. This was established by the House of Lords' decision in *Derbyshire County Council* v *Times Newspapers Ltd* (1993). In that case, *The Sunday Times* printed a couple of articles which alleged that Derbyshire County Council had acted improperly in investing funds in its superannuation fund. Derbyshire County Council sued *The Sunday Times* for libel but its claim was dismissed by the House of Lords on the ground that an action for libel could not be maintained by a public body.

The House of Lords admitted that a public body could have a legitimate interest in bringing an action for libel or slander if it were the subject of a defamatory statement. As Lord Keith of Kinkel observed, the making of a defamatory statement about a public body 'might make it more difficult [for the body] to borrow or to attract suitable staff and thus

---

[70] The claim would nowadays be dismissed, either on the basis that the claimant had consented to his employee seeing the defamatory article (see below, § 19.6) or on the basis that the claim amounted to an abuse of process.

[71] Law Reform (Miscellaneous Provisions) Act 1934, s 1(1).

[72] *EETPU* v *Times Newspapers Ltd* [1980] 3 WLR 98. A trade union used to enjoy sufficient legal personality to bring an action for libel or slander: *National Union of General and Municipal Workers* v *Gillian* [1946] KB 81.

affect adversely the efficient carrying out of its functions'.[73] However, the House of Lords felt that freedom of speech would be unreasonably infringed if the law did not assure people that they could criticise public bodies without fear of being made subject to actions for libel or slander as a result. Lord Keith remarked, 'it is of the highest public importance that a democratically elected governmental body, or indeed any governmental body, should be open to *uninhibited* public criticism. The threat of a civil action for [libel or slander] must inevitably have an inhibiting effect on freedom of speech'.[74]

The House of Lords did *not* go further in the *Derbyshire* case and say that a *politician* would have no right to sue for libel or slander if he felt that some criticism of his conduct in office was defamatory. Indeed, the House of Lords made it clear that if a defendant's criticism of a public body reflected badly on the people running the affairs of that body, those people might well be able to sue the defendant for libel or slander.[75] No doubt this can be explained on the basis that politicians have more of an interest in vindicating their reputation than public bodies do – a politician, after all, has a life inside and outside politics which can be seriously affected by the publication of a defamatory statement about him – and this warrants giving politicians a higher degree of protection from being defamed than the House of Lords was willing to afford to public bodies.

It is now clear that the *Derbyshire* decision extends to *political parties* and that a political party that feels that it has been defamed by some statement made by someone else will not be able to bring an action for libel or slander in respect of that statement;[76] though, of course, if the statement simultaneously defamed a member of that party, he or she might be able to sue for libel or slander.

B. Libel and slander

The law draws a distinction between defamation cases where a claimant is suing for *libel* and cases where a claimant is suing for *slander*. Very roughly speaking, libel involves defaming someone else by publishing a statement to another in *permanent* form. Slander involves defaming someone else by publishing a statement to another in *impermanent* form. In a libel case, the claimant does not have to prove that he has suffered any loss in order to sue the defendant. In a slander case, the claimant normally does have to prove that the defendant's publication caused him loss; if he cannot, his claim for defamation will be dismissed.

So, for example, if A *says* to C, 'B is a liar and a cheat' then that is slander. However, if A sends C a letter saying, 'B is a liar and a cheat', then that is libel. If A dictates a letter to his secretary saying, 'B is a liar and a cheat', that is slander. But if the letter is read out to a third party, that – it seems – will be libel.[77] It is submitted that if A records himself saying, 'B is a liar and a cheat' and then plays the recording back to C, that is libel: A's statement will have been published in a permanent form because it could be replayed.[78]

---

[73] [1993] AC 534, 547.

[74] ibid.

[75] [1993] AC 534, 550.

[76] *Goldsmith v Bhoyrul* [1998] QB 459.

[77] *Forrester v Tyrell* (1893) 9 TLR 257. However, in *Osborn v Thomas Boulter & Son* [1930] 2 KB 226, Scrutton and Slesser LJJ both thought that reading out a defamatory letter to a third party would amount to slander. Greer LJ disagreed.

[78] Though see the discussion in *Youssoupoff v Metro-Goldwyn-Mayer Pictures Ltd* (1934) 50 TLR 581 as to whether the tort – if any – committed in playing a film which contained a defamatory statement in its soundtrack would be slander or libel. The Court of Appeal expressed no firm view on the issue – merely saying (at 587) that the statement would be libellous if it served to amplify or explain the visual images presented in the film.

Some statutes provide that certain statements are to be treated as having been published in permanent form. So s 166 of the Broadcasting Act 1990 provides that for 'the purposes of the law on libel and slander . . . the publication of words in the course of any programme included in a programme service shall be treated as publication in permanent form'. So if A gives a speech in a public hall in which he makes various defamatory allegations about B, that will be slander. But if A makes the same speech on television, that will be libel. Similarly, s 4 of the Theatres Act 1968 provides that, subject to one exception, for 'the purposes of the law on libel and slander . . . the publication of words in the course of a performance of a play shall . . . be treated as publication in permanent form'. Section 7 of the 1968 Act makes it clear that this rule will not 'apply in relation to a performance of a play given on a domestic occasion in a private dwelling'.

A claimant will not always be prevented from suing a defendant for slander if she cannot prove that the defendant's publication caused her loss. There are four cases where the courts will presume that slander has caused a claimant loss, and will not require the claimant to prove loss as a precondition of allowing her to sue. Loss will be presumed where the defendant's slander suggested: (1) that the claimant had committed a serious criminal offence; or (2) that the claimant had a communicable disease;[79] or (3) that the claimant was no good at her job;[80] or (4) that the claimant was unchaste or had committed adultery.[81] It should be noted that in each of these cases, the claimant would find it very difficult to prove that the defendant's slander caused her to suffer loss. This is because the tendency of each of these statements would be to encourage people to 'shun and avoid' the claimant – but it would be very hard for the claimant to demonstrate that but for the defendant's statement, certain people would not have shunned and avoided the claimant. It should also be noted that the government proposes to repeal the presumption of loss in situations (2) and (4) in its Repeals Bill.[82]

The courts have addressed the issue of whether the rule that libel victims do not have to prove that they have suffered any loss before they can sue for libel is compatible with Article 10 of the European Convention on Human Rights.

In *Jameel (Yousef)* v *Dow Jones & Co Inc* (2005), the Court of Appeal held that the fact that an *individual* could sue for libel without having to prove that the libel had caused him any loss was not incompatible with Article 10 of the ECHR:

> We believe that circumstances in which a claimant launches defamation proceedings in respect of a limited circulation which has caused his reputation no actual damage will be very rare. We reject the suggestion that the fear of such suits will have a chilling effect on the media.[83]

Moreover, the Court of Appeal made it clear that in such cases they had the power to strike out the claim as an abuse of process. As we have just seen,[84] this is what happened in the *Jameel (Yousef)* case: the claimant's claim was struck out on the ground that the damage done to the claimant's reputation by the defendant's publication was minimal and that allowing the case to continue would serve very little point at great expense.

In *Jameel (Mohammed)* v *Wall Street Journal Europe SPRL* (2007), the House of Lords examined whether a *company* that was the victim of a libel should be able to sue in

---

[79] *Bloodworth* v *Gray* (1844) 7 Man & Gr 334, 135 ER 140.
[80] Defamation Act 1952, s 2.
[81] Slander of Women Act 1891, s 1.
[82] See para [6] of the consultation document issued along with the Defamation Bill.
[83] [2005] QB 946, at [39].
[84] See above, § 19.4(10).

defamation without having to prove that the libel had caused it any loss. The House of Lords ruled that allowing the company to sue without proving that it had suffered any loss was not incompatible with Article 10. The majority of their Lordships in the *Jameel (Mohammed)* case thought that if A said that company C was run in a corrupt fashion, requiring C to prove that it had actually suffered loss as a result of A's statement might be too much to ask. Because the natural tendency of A's statement would be to cause people to 'shun and avoid' C's goods or services, C might find it very difficult to show that certain people who would otherwise have done business with C were put off doing business with C because of A's statement.[85]

19.6 CONSENT

We will now begin to look at the various defences that might be available to a defendant who is being sued for defamation. The first defence is the rarest, but also the most obvious. If a claimant has consented to a defendant's publishing a defamatory statement about him, he cannot subsequently turn round and sue the defendant for defamation on the basis of that publication.[86]

For example, in *Chapman* v *Lord Ellesmere* (1932), a stewards' inquiry held by the Jockey Club found that a horse trained by the claimant was doped when it ran a particular race. The Jockey Club disqualified the horse and 'warned' the claimant off the course where the horse ran. The Jockey Club's decision was published in the *Racing Calendar*, the Jockey Club's official journal. The claimant sued, claiming the publication was defamatory of him. The claimant's claim was dismissed – he had consented to that publication. He was held to have consented to the publication because when he obtained a trainer's licence, he agreed to abide by the rules of the Jockey Club, and one of these rules specified that a decision of the Jockey Club could be published in the *Racing Calendar* if the Jockey Club thought it fit to do so.

Let's now consider the **Desperate Academic Problem:**

> *Academic* – a specialist in the law of defamation and a well-respected member of the Law Faculty at Maxbrook University – had run up some very serious debts, due to his having a gambling problem. Using his knowledge of the law on defamation, he hit on an idea as to how he could get himself out of financial trouble. One day, he told *Student*, whose father was the editor of the *Daily Herald*, that for many years he had been accepting bribes from students, in return for which he would allow them to see in advance the questions they would be asked in their end of year Law exams. *Student* told his father this, and the *Daily Herald* ran an exclusive the next day explaining that *Academic* was corrupt. In fact, *Academic* had never accepted a bribe in his life, and had never allowed any students advance sight of their end of year exam papers. Can *Academic* sue the *Daily Herald* in defamation?

There seems something wrong about allowing *Academic* to sue in this case. He has, after all, entrapped the *Daily Herald* into defaming him. But it is not clear whether the *Daily Herald* could take advantage of any established defence in this case. The most promising defence is consent – *Academic* did *want* the *Daily Herald* to print this story (so that he could then

---

[85] [2007] 1 AC 359, at [26] (per Lord Bingham), [97] (per Lord Hope), and at [121] (per Lord Scott).
[86] In *Carrie* v *Tolkien* [2009] EWHC 29 (QB), the claimant was barred from suing a defendant for posting a defamatory statement about the claimant on the claimant's own website. As the claimant could have easily taken the statement down, it was held that the claimant had consented to the publication of the statement by knowingly leaving the statement up on the website.

sue them for thousands of pounds in damages, thereby digging himself out of his financial hole). However, *Academic* did not *agree* that the *Daily Herald* could print the story about him – and agreement may be necessary to raise a defence of consent to a claim in defamation.

19.7 JUSTIFICATION[87]

Suppose A has published to another a statement that was defamatory of B because a right-thinking person who read or heard A's statement would have thought that x was true of B and would as a result have tended to think less well of B. In such a case, A will have a defence if B sues him for libel or slander if he can prove that x *was* true of B. If A can prove this, we currently say that A has a defence of *justification* to B's claim. The government proposes to abolish this defence in clause 3 of the Defamation Bill and replace it with a new defence of 'truth'. However, this new defence will be indistinguishable from the defence of justification, and so everything said below will be relevant to the new defence of 'truth' if it enters the statute books.

In order to raise this defence (of justification, or 'truth'), it will *not* be enough for A to show that his words were *literally* true – he will have to show that the impression a right-thinking person would have gained of B from A's words was a correct one. So suppose A wrote a letter in which he remarked, 'I have heard B is a liar and a cheat'. B sues A for defamation and A wants to raise a defence of justification to B's claim, it will not be enough for A to prove that *he had actually heard* that B is a liar and a cheat and so the statement in his letter was literally true. Under the repetition rule,[88] it will be conclusively presumed that a right-thinking person who heard or read A's statement would have thought on the basis of it that B *is* a liar and a cheat – given this, if A wants to raise a defence of justification to B's claim, he will have to prove that B *is* a liar and a cheat.

Sometimes there will be some dispute as to what impression a right-thinking person would have gained from hearing or reading a given statement. In *Lewis v Daily Telegraph Ltd* (1964), the defendants, the *Daily Mail* and the *Daily Telegraph*, both published frontpage reports which alleged that the Fraud Squad was inquiring into the affairs of the claimant, Rubber Improvement Ltd. The claimant sued both newspapers for libel. It was admitted that the reports were defamatory: a right-thinking person who read the reports would have tended to think less well of the claimant as a result. The defendants sought to rely on a defence of justification to defeat the claimant's claim. The issue was: what would the defendants have to prove to raise such a defence? This turned on what impression of the claimant would have been gained by a right-thinking person who heard about or read the reports in the newspapers. The claimant argued that a right-thinking person who heard about or read the reports in question would have concluded from them that the claimant had operated in a dishonest or fraudulent manner – so the defendants would have to prove that the claimant *had* conducted its affairs in a dishonest way if they wanted to rely on a defence of justification to defeat the claimant's claim.

The House of Lords disagreed. At best, a right-thinking person would have concluded from the stories in the defendants' newspapers that the claimant had conducted its affairs in such a way as to give rise to a *suspicion* that it was guilty of some dishonest or fraudulent conduct. As Lord Reid observed – if someone, on reading the stories in the defendants' newspapers had observed 'Oh, if the fraud squad are after these people you can take it they are guilty' a right-thinking person would have rounded on him.

[87] See, generally, Descheemaeker 2011.
[88] See above, § 19.2(7).

with such remarks as – 'Be fair. This is not a police state. No doubt their affairs are in a mess or the police would not be interested. But that could be because [someone] has been very stupid or careless. We really must not jump to conclusions. The police are fair and know their job and we shall know soon enough if there is anything in it. Wait till we see if they [bring charges]. I wouldn't trust [the people involved in this company] until this thing is cleared up, but it is another thing to condemn [them] unheard.'[89]

So, in order to establish a defence of justification to the claimant's claim, the defendants did *not* have to show that the claimant had operated its affairs in a dishonest or fraudulent manner; at best, the defendants were required to show that the claimant had operated its affairs in such a way as to give rise to a suspicion that it had acted dishonestly or fraudulently in the way it operated.

In *Wakley* v *Cooke and Healey* (1849), the claimant, a former journalist, was a coroner in Middlesex. The defendants published an article in the *Medical Times* which contained an attack on the claimant. The article observed, 'There can be no court of justice unpolluted which this libellous journalist [meaning the claimant] . . . is allowed to disgrace with his presidentship.' The claimant sued the defendants for libel. It was held that a right-thinking person would gather from this statement that the claimant had been in the habit of libelling others when he was a journalist. So the defendants could not raise a defence of justification to the claimant's claim by showing that the claimant had on *one* occasion been found to have libelled someone else as a journalist; they would have to show that the claimant had on *many* occasions libelled other people when working as a journalist. As the defendants could not show this, the claimant's claim was allowed.

A few more points may be made about the defence of justification:

(1) *Substantial justification.* If A has published a statement to another that is defamatory of B, A does not have to prove – for the purpose of raising a defence of justification to any claim B might bring against him for libel or slander – that *every word* of what he said was correct; it is enough if he can show that what he said was *substantially correct*.

So in *Alexander* v *The North Eastern Railway Company* (1865), the defendant railway company reported that the claimant had been convicted of what would now be known as 'fare-dodging' and sentenced either to pay a fine of £9 or serve three weeks' imprisonment. In fact the claimant had actually been sentenced either to pay a fine of £1 or to serve two weeks' imprisonment. The claimant sued the defendants for libel. His claim was dismissed: while the defendants' report was inaccurate in its details, it was at the same time substantially correct – the claimant *had* been convicted of fare-dodging and had been sentenced either to pay a fine or spend time in jail.

(2) *Partial justification.* Section 5 of the Defamation Act 1952 provides that:

In an action for libel or slander in respect of words containing two or more distinct charges against the claimant, a defence of justification shall not fail by reason only that the truth of every charge is not proved if the words not proved to be true do not materially injure the claimant's reputation having regard to the truth of the remaining charges.[90]

---

[89] [1964] AC 234, 259–60.
[90] The government proposes to repeal this provision (Defamation Bill clause 3(4)) and replace it with the following, substantially identical, provision: 'If [in a case where a claim for defamation is brought in relation to a statement which conveys two or more distinct imputations] one or more of the imputations is not shown to be substantially true, the defence under this section does not fail if, having regard to the imputations which are shown to be substantially true, the imputations which are not shown to be substantially true do not materially injure the claimant's reputation' (Defamation Bill clause 3(3)).

So suppose A said to someone else, 'B is a rapist and a thief'. Suppose further that B sues A for defamation for saying that he is, one, a rapist, and two, a thief. Suppose finally that A can prove that B is a rapist, but cannot prove that B is a thief. In such a case, A will not only have a defence of justification to B's claim against her for saying that he is a rapist; A will *also* have a defence of justification under s 5 of the 1952 Act in respect of B's claim against him for saying that A is a thief. Now that it has been established that B is a rapist, A's statement that B is a thief could hardly further injure B's reputation in the eyes of ordinary, reasonable people – B's reputation in those people's eyes will have gone about as low as it possibly could go.

But suppose B simply chooses to ignore A's statement that he is a rapist, and sues A for defamation just for saying that he is a thief? In this case, A will not be able to raise a defence of justification by showing that B is a rapist.[91] However, if B leaves A's claim that he is a rapist unchallenged, he is not likely to be awarded much by way of damages to compensate him for the harm done by A's statement that he is a thief. The courts will take the view that a rapist does not have much of a reputation to lose and therefore suffers little harm if he is unjustly accused of being a thief.[92]

(3) *Criminal conviction.* Suppose A told C, 'B is an arsonist'. In such a case, if B has been convicted for burning down someone's house, A will *normally* be able to raise a defence of justification to any claim for defamation that B might bring against A. A will *not* have to prove that B was rightly convicted of arson: the conviction will be treated in court as conclusive evidence that B *is* an arsonist.[93] *However*, if A made her allegation about B 'with malice' and B's conviction for arson counts as 'spent' under the Rehabilitation of Offenders Act 1974, then A will *not* be able to rely on B's conviction, or what B did to earn that conviction, to raise a defence of justification to B's claim for defamation.[94]

19.8 HONEST (OR FAIR) COMMENT

English law has long taken the view that people should be free to express their views on matters of public interest. The defence of 'honest comment' (which was originally known as the defence of 'fair comment' but was renamed by the Supreme Court in *Joseph* v *Spiller* (2010))[95] exists to protect this freedom from being undermined by the law of defamation.

A defendant who is being sued in defamation for making a statement S can take advantage of this defence if:

(1) S was, on its face, a statement of *opinion* rather than fact;
(2) S was on a matter of *public interest*;
(3) the defendant must, in making statement S, have 'explicitly or implicitly indicate[d], at least in general terms, the facts on which it [was] based';[96]

---

[91] *Polly Peck (Holdings) plc* v *Trelford* [1986] 1 QB 1000.
[92] See *Grobbelaar* v *News Group Newspapers Ltd* [2002] 1 WLR 3024 (£1 awarded in damages to Bruce Grobbelaar, the ex-Liverpool and Southampton goalkeeper, who – it was found – was justifiably accused by the defendant of taking bribes to 'throw' football matches but unjustifiably accused of acting on those bribes and actually throwing football matches).
[93] Civil Evidence Act 1968, s 13(1): 'In any action for libel or slander in which the question whether the claimant did or did not commit a criminal offence is relevant to an issue arising in the action, proof that at the time when that issue falls to be determined, he stands convicted of that offence shall be conclusive evidence that he committed that offence . . .'
[94] Rehabilitation of Offenders Act 1974, ss 4(1), 8.
[95] *Joseph* v *Spiller* [2011] 1 AC 852, at [117]; also [130].
[96] *Joseph* v *Spiller* [2011] 1 AC 852, at [105].

(4) those facts must have been true (or, at least, enough of those facts that would be sufficient to support statement S must have been true);
(5) the defendant honestly believed statement S to be true when he made it.[97]

The government proposes to replace the defence of honest (or fair) comment with one of 'honest opinion'. The new defence will still require elements (1), (2) and (5) to be made out. But requirement (3) will no longer apply, and a different version of (4) – set out below – will have to be satisfied. We will now look at each of the elements of the defence of honest comment in turn, bearing in mind that everything we say below (except in relation to requirements (3) and (4)) will apply equally to the new proposed defence of honest opinion.

A. Opinion, not fact

The defence of honest comment can only apply to a statement that was, on its face, a statement of opinion, as opposed to a statement of fact. However, the distinction between what is a statement of opinion and what is a statement of fact is very hard to draw. Consider the **Dramatic Detective Problem:**

> *Detective* was called in to investigate the murder of *Rich*. After two days, *Detective* thought he had cracked the case. He summoned the 12 principal suspects into the study of *Rich*'s manor house and summed up the conversations he had had with the suspects over the past two days. He then concluded, 'I now have no doubt as to who the murderer is. Everything I have heard points to one, irrefutable, conclusion: that it was you, *Sue Rich*, it was you who killed your uncle when he threatened to reveal to the world that your fiancé was his secret love child, with the result that everyone would know you and your fiancé were in fact first cousins, and marriage between you would have become a practical impossibility.'

Assuming *Detective* has got it wrong (the butler did it), could he raise a defence of honest comment to *Sue Rich*'s claim for defamation, arguing that his statement that she murdered her uncle was, on its face, merely a statement of opinion, rather than a statement of fact? The question is a very difficult one.

The most obvious examples of statements that, on their face, are statements of opinion rather than statements of fact are *value judgments*. A value judgment involves deciding whether something is good or bad in some way or other. So the defence of honest comment classically protects journalists reviewing plays or books or restaurants, telling their readers whether they are any good or not. The defence also applied to an article damning the newpaper proprietor Lord Beaverbrook under the headline, 'Lower than Kemsley'. When Viscount Kemsley, the then owner of *The Sunday Times*, sued the author of the article – Michael Foot – for defamation, arguing that the headline suggested that Kemsley ran his newspapers in a dishonourable way, the House of Lords held that the headline was covered by the defence of honest (then 'fair') comment.[98] A statement that A is dishonourable, or has acted in a dishonourable way, obviously involves a value judgment and is, on its face, a statement of opinion.[99] The defence also covers defendants who comment adversely on

---

[97] *Tse Wai Chun v Cheng* [2001] EMLR 777, at [41] (per Lord Nicholls, in the Hong Kong Court of Final Appeal); *Joseph v Spiller* [2011] 1 AC 852, at [67]–[69] and [108].
[98] *Kemsley v Foot* [1952] AC 354.
[99] See also *Joseph v Spiller* [2011] 1 AC 852, at [88], disapproving the suggestion that 'To say that "A is a disgrace to human nature" is an allegation of fact, but if the words were "A murdered his father and is therefore a disgrace to human nature", the latter words are plainly a comment on the former.' The defence of honest comment would not be available for the first statement, not because it is a statement of fact rather than opinion, but because it fails the third requirement, set out above and discussed below, for the defence to be made out: that some indication be given as to the factual basis of the statement.

someone else's competence: for example, saying that a doctor is 'a quack of the rankest species'.[100] It should also cover a case where a defendant disparages a medicine or course of medical treatment as useless.[101]

Another kind of statement that is traditionally treated in English law (particularly in the law of contract) as being a statement of opinion rather than fact is a *prediction* about what will happen in the future. So a newspaper's statement that an MP's constituents *would* be furious to discover that she had criticised reforms to the system for reimbursing MPs' expenses was held to be a statement of opinion, rather than fact.[102] A statement that a band could not be relied upon to fulfil its contracts would also count as a statement of opinion:[103] such a statement is a prediction as to what the band would do in future.

Neither of the preceding two paragraphs would assist *Detective* in his argument that his statement that *Sue Rich* murdered her uncle was a statement of opinion, rather than a statement of fact. Such a statement does not involve either a value judgment, or a prediction about the future. This kind of statement, rather, involves an *inference of fact* (that *Sue Rich* is guilty of murder) from other facts (the conversations *Detective* has had with the suspects in *Rich*'s murder). Whether, and when, an inference of fact will amount to a statement of opinion is a very controversial question. In *Joseph* v *Spiller* (2010), the Supreme Court seemed to take the view that an inference of fact will not be covered by the defence of honest comment: someone who says that he thinks A is guilty of fraud because A has been charged with fraud will not be able to plead honest comment if he is subsequently sued by A.[104]

However, there seems to be an exception (which the Supreme Court acknowledged existed) where the fact being inferred is a fact about someone else's motivations. A statement that 'A acted as he did because he . . .' will – it seems – be treated as a statement of opinion, rather than a statement of fact, even though 'the state of a man's mind is as much a fact as the state of his digestion.'[105] So in *Hunt* v *Star Newspaper Co Ltd* (1908), a newspaper story alleging that the claimant returning officer had acted in a biased way in conducting an election was held to be capable of being covered by the defence of honest (then, 'fair') comment. In *Jeyaretnam* v *Goh Chok Tong* (1989), the leader of the Singaporean Workers' Party (WP) was invited to speak at a party conference held by the Singapore Democratic Party. After giving his speech, the leader of the WP left the hall, followed by a large number of his supporters. The defendant newspaper ran a story claiming that the leader of the WP was trying to show the leader of the SDP 'who is boss' by acting in this way. It was held that this inference as to the motives for the leader of the WP's leaving the hall (he was in fact on his way to a dinner engagement) amounted to a statement of opinion capable of being protected by the defence of honest comment.

The Court of Appeal's judgment in *British Chiropractic Association* v *Singh* (2010) seems to have created a further exception to the general rule that inferences of fact are not capable of amounting to statements of opinion. In that case, the defendant wrote an article in the *Guardian* about chiropractic medicine, in the course of which he remarked:

> The British Chiropractic Association claims that their members can help treat children with colic, sleeping and feeding problems, frequent ear infections, asthma and prolonged crying, even

[100] *Dakhyl* v *Labouchere* [1908] 2 KB 325n.
[101] Compare *British Chiropractic Association* v *Singh* [2011] 1 WLR 133 ('not a jot of evidence' for the efficacy of chiropractic (manipulation of the spine) to help 'children with colic, sleeping and feeding problems, frequent ear infections, asthma and prolonged crying').
[102] *Lait* v *Evening Standard* [2010] EWHC 3239 (QB).
[103] *Joseph* v *Spiller* [2011] 1 AC 852.
[104] ibid, at [114].
[105] *Edgington* v *Fitzmaurice* (1885) 29 Ch D 459, 483 (per Bowen LJ).

though there is not a jot of evidence. This organisation is the respectable face of the chiropractic profession and yet it happily promotes bogus treatments.

The Court of Appeal held that the statement that there is 'not a jot of evidence' for the efficacy of chiropractic (manipulation of the spine) in treating the children's conditions listed was one of opinion, rather than fact. The Court of Appeal argued that such a conclusion amounted to a 'value judgment'.[106] With respect, that cannot be right – anymore than a statement that the Earth revolves around the Sun involves a 'value judgment'. Judgment is, of course, required to answer the question of whether there is any valid proof that chiropractic helps with the listed conditions – but the judgment required is not a value judgment, but a scientific judgment. However, the Court of Appeal's decision to treat the above passage as a statement of opinion rather than fact can be defended on the basis that it is not for the courts to determine whether or not there is a 'jot of evidence' to support the view that chiropractic helps treat the above children's conditions – but that is what they might have ended up doing if the above passage had been treated as a statement of fact and the author invited to justify it, or find himself liable to the British Chiropractic Association for defamation.[107]

It is not clear how far the Court of Appeal's decision in the *Singh* case goes. For example, in *Irving* v *Penguin Books & Lipstadt* (2000), the historical author David Irving sued Deborah Lipstadt and her publisher in defamation. The focus of his claim was Lipstadt's book *Denying the Holocaust*, which made a number of damaging allegations about Irving. Chief among these allegations was that Irving consistently distorted the historical record to make it conform to his agenda, which is to deny that the Holocaust happened. In that case, the defendants argued that their claims about Irving were justified, and the judge deciding the case undertook – in the words of the Court of Appeal in the *Singh* case – 'the role of historian or investigative journalist' in order to determine whether that was the case.[108] In a 333 page judgment, the judge found that Lipstadt's allegations about Irving were justified. However, it may be questioned – in light of the *Singh* decision – whether the courts should get involved in adjudicating where the truth lies in such academic disputes, and it might be thought that the wiser course in the *Irving* case would have been to hold that the defendants could take advantage of a defence of honest comment and dismiss Irving's claim for defamation on that basis.

Returning now to the Dramatic Detective Problem, it seems unlikely that *Detective* would be able to raise a defence of honest comment to *Sue Rich*'s claim against him for defamation. The inference of fact that *Detective* has drawn in this case does not go to *Sue Rich*'s motives; nor does it involve the sort of exercise of scientific or historical judgment that the courts would be ill-placed and unwilling to second-guess.

B. Public interest

The defence of honest comment only operates to protect people who utter defamatory opinions on matters of *public interest*. So what counts as a matter of public interest? In *London Artists Ltd* v *Littler* (1969), Lord Denning MR suggested that whenever 'a matter is such as to affect people at large, so that they may be legitimately interested in, or concerned,

---

[106] [2011] 1 WLR 133, at [26].

[107] See, in particular, the Court of Appeal's judgment at [23]: 'the material words . . . are in our judgment expressions of opinion. The opinion may be mistaken, but to allow the party which has been denounced on the basis of it to compel its author to prove in court what he has asserted by way of argument is to invite the court to become an Orwellian ministry of truth.'

[108] [2010] EWCA Civ 350, at [22].

at what is going on; or what may happen to them or to others; then it is a matter of public interest on which everyone is entitled to make [honest] comment.'[109]

C. Indication of facts

The Supreme Court's decision in *Joseph* v *Spiller* (2011) has made it clear that for a defence of honest comment to be available to a defendant who has expressed a critical comment on some matter of public interest, the defendant must have identified

> at least the general nature of the facts that have led him to make the criticism. If he states that a barrister is 'a disgrace to his profession' he should make it clear whether this is because he does not deal honestly with the court, or does not read his papers thoroughly, or refuses to accept legally aided work, or is constantly late for court, or wears dirty collars and bands.[110]

The object of this requirement is to ensure that the concession to free speech embodied by the honest comment defence is not abused. The honest comment defence exists to allow people freely to express their opinions on matters of public interest. If people do not make it clear, at least in general terms, what the basis of their opinions are, their opinions will become 'wholly unfocused'[111] and consequently the expression of those opinions will become less valuable and not worth protecting.

How much a defendant needs to say by way of indicating the facts that have led him to say what he did will depend on the circumstances. Where the defendant is commenting on facts that are already in the public domain – such as the production of a play, or the conduct of a well-known public figure – almost nothing need be said explicitly to indicate the basis of the defendant's comment. The basis of the comment will be obvious from the context. For example, when Michael Foot said that Lord Beaverbrook was 'Lower than Kemsley', the House of Lords held in *Kemsley* v *Foot* (1951) that Foot could take advantage of the defence of honest (then, 'fair') comment to defeat Viscount Kemsley's claim against him for defamation. Foot did not lose the defence because he had not gone out of his way to explain that Viscount Kemsley was a newspaper proprietor and that the way Kemsley ran his newspapers had given rise to Foot's comment. All that was already obvious.

In contrast, where the facts giving rise to the defendant's comment are less well-known, some general indication of what those facts are will need to be given by the defendant if he is to take advantage of the defence of honest comment.

As we have already observed, the Defamation Bill does not require a defendant who wishes to take advantage of the defence of 'honest opinion' to have indicated, in his comment, the rough nature of the facts on which he was commenting. But a defendant may find it hard to establish that his statement was a statement of opinion, and not a statement of fact, if he does not expressly indicate that his statement is based on certain facts. So, for example, if you call someone a 'racist' without indicating why you are doing so, you may find that your statement is held to be a statement of fact, rather than opinion.[112]

D. Truth of facts

A defendant who wishes to rely on the defence of honest comment will need to show that the facts that led him to make his comment were either true, or were protected by privilege.

---

[109] [1969] 2 QB 375, 391.
[110] [2011] 1 AC 852, at [103].
[111] [2011] 1 AC 852, at [101].
[112] *Telnikoff* v *Matusevitch* [1992] 2 AC 343.

So if a newspaper publishes a defamatory story about A, and other newspapers comment adversely on A's character in light of the first newspaper's 'scoop', the other newspapers' adverse criticisms of A's character will only be covered by the defence of honest comment if either the original story about A was true, or the original story was privileged for some reason.[113]

The requirement that the facts that led a defendant to make an adverse comment about the claimant must be true (if they are not privileged) is qualified by s 6 of the Defamation Act 1952:

> In an action for libel or slander in respect of words consisting partly in expressions of opinion, a defence of fair comment shall not fail by reason only that the truth of every allegation of fact is not proved if the expression of opinion is fair comment having regard to whether such of the facts alleged or referred to in the words complained of are proved.

What this means is this. Suppose A says of B, 'I think B is a disgrace as a human being – despite all his wealth, he has never done anything to assist his estranged wife and child or his destitute mother.' Suppose further that B sues A for defamation. Suppose finally that while B does nothing to support his destitute mother, he does actually help to support his wife and child. If A can show that, had she known the true facts, she would honestly still have thought that B was a disgrace as a human being, A will be able to raise a defence of honest comment to defeat B's claim. How can A show that, had she known the true facts, she would honestly still have thought that B was a disgrace as a human being? One way is for A to show that an honest person who knew the true facts *could* still have come to the conclusion that B was a disgrace as a human being.[114]

Under the Defamation Bill, this area of law will be subtly altered. Section 6 of the Defamation Act 1952 will be repealed, and its place taken by a requirement that it be shown –

> that an honest person could have held the opinion on the basis of –
>
> (a) a fact which existed at the time the statement complained of was published;
> (b) a privileged statement which was published before the statement complained of.

The big difference between this requirement and the (roughly) equivalent requirement for the defence of honest comment is that it does not have to be shown that *any* of the facts *on which the defendant made his comment* were true or protected by privilege.

Suppose that A – on hearing that B had beaten up his wife – said that 'B is a disgrace as a human being'. If B had not in fact beaten up his wife, A could not take advantage of the defence of honest comment. But the Defamation Bill will allow A to take advantage of the defence of honest opinion if A can establish that before A said 'B is a disgrace as a human being', B did something (or someone said something about B that was protected by privilege) that would allow an honest person to reach that conclusion. And it will not matter if A was completely unaware of what B had done (or what someone has said about B) at the time he made his comment.

In *Joseph* v *Spiller* (2011) it was suggested that the Supreme Court adopt a very similar rule in relation to the defence of honest comment, but the Supreme Court rejected this on

---

[113] See below, §§ 19.9–19.10, for a discussion of the variety of situations in which a defamatory statement will be held to be privileged.

[114] Of course, even if A can defeat B's claim for defamation for calling him a disgrace as a human being, it will still be open to B to sue A for defamation in respect of her allegation that B has never supported his estranged wife and child. As this is a statement of fact, not opinion, the defence of honest comment will not protect A from being sued in respect of this allegation.

the basis that it would 'radically alter the nature of the defence' without doing anything to simplify the complexity of defamation trials.[115] It is slightly surprising to see the government going where the Supreme Court feared to tread.

E. Honesty

The defence of honest comment will not be available to a defendant who has *maliciously* expressed an opinion on a matter of public interest. It used to be thought that this meant the defence would not be available if the defendant had acted with an *improper purpose* in expressing the opinion. It is now clear that this is no longer the case.[116] In the context of the defence of honest comment, it does not matter if the defendant said what he did out of spite or ill-will. All that is required is that the defendant honestly believed that what he was saying was true when he said it.

19.9 ABSOLUTE PRIVILEGE

If A has published a statement to C that is defamatory of B, B will *not* be entitled to sue A for libel or slander if the statement in question was *privileged*. Certain statements will *always* be privileged – such statements are said to be *absolutely privileged*. Other statements will only be privileged provided that certain conditions are met – these statements are said to be protected by *qualified privilege*. In this section, we will look at what sort of statements will be absolutely privileged; the following two sections are concerned with statements that will be protected by qualified privilege.

The reason why some statements are protected by absolute privilege is that there are occasions where the law places such a high priority on people being able to say what they want without *any* fear of being sued that it assures such people that what they say will *always* be privileged.

So, for example, the law places such a high priority on MPs and members of the House of Lords being allowed to say what they want to say in Parliament without fear of being sued that it assures MPs and members of the House of Lords that what they say on the floor of the House of Commons or the House of Lords will always be privileged.[117] So if A is an MP he will be able to say what he wants about B on the floor of the House of Commons without fear of being sued by B for defamation – and this is so even if A knowingly tells complete lies about B: he cannot be sued.

The following statements will also always be privileged:

(1) *Statements made in reports, papers and proceedings ordered to be published by Parliament.*[118]

---

[115] [2011] 1 AC 852, at [110]–[111].

[116] *Tse Wai Chun v Cheng* [2001] EMLR 777, at [41] (per Lord Nicholls, in the Hong Kong Court of Final Appeal); *Joseph v Spiller* [2011] 1 AC 852, at [67]–[69] and [108].

[117] This follows from Art 9 of the Bill of Rights 1688 which states that 'the freedom of speech and debates or proceedings in Parliament ought not to be impeached or questioned in any court or place out of Parliament'. An exception to this rule was created by s 13 of the Defamation Act 1996 which provides that where 'the conduct of a person in or in relation to proceedings in Parliament is in issue during defamation proceedings, he may waive for the purpose of those proceedings, so far as concerns him, the protection of any enactment or rule of law which prevents proceedings in Parliament being impeached or questioned in any court or place out of Parliament'.

[118] Parliamentary Papers Act 1840, s 1.

(2) Statements made in the course of judicial or quasi-judicial proceedings by anyone involved in those proceedings. However, statements made in the course of judicial or quasi-judicial proceedings which have no relevance to those proceedings may not be privileged.[119] A court-martial will count as a 'judicial or quasi-judicial' proceeding;[120] as will disciplinary proceedings held by the Law Society.[121] So statements made in the course of either will be absolutely privileged. However, the holding of an industrial conciliation procedure will not count as a 'judicial or quasi-judicial' proceeding[122] and neither will an investigation by the European Commission into alleged breaches of European competition law.[123]

(3) Statements made by a witness to his solicitor in preparing his testimony for court.[124] While it is certain that such statements will always be privileged, it is uncertain whether other kinds of statements that a client may make to his solicitor will always be privileged. The House of Lords left the matter open in *Minter* v *Priest* (1930). There does not seem to be any reason why they should be: there does not seem to be any reason why the law should go further than it currently does to ensure that a client will be able to talk to his solicitor free from the fear that he might be sued as a result of what he says to his solicitor.

(4) Statements made in the course of being questioned by someone investigating a crime; statements made at the request of someone investigating a crime.[125] It is unclear whether a statement that is *spontaneously* made to the authorities for the purpose of encouraging them to start an investigation will be absolutely privileged. In *Hasselblad (GB) Ltd* v *Orbinson* (1985), the Court of Appeal thought that a letter sent to the European Commission complaining that a particular firm was engaging in anti-competitive practices would be protected by absolute privilege; their reason for so holding was that it was extremely important that people should be able to report these sorts of practices to the European Commission free from fear that their doing so would result in their being sued. However, in *Mahon* v *Rahn (No 2)* (2000), Brooke LJ refused to decide whether an informant who spontaneously told the authorities that a particular investment adviser was guilty of fraud would always be able to claim that his statement to the authorities was privileged, preferring to leave the task of deciding that question to another day.[126]

(5) Statements made in a report prepared by an expert which may be used in later criminal proceedings.[127]

(6) Statements made by an investigator to someone else in the course of investigating a crime.[128]

(7) Statements made to an investigator who is investigating a crime, or for the purpose of encouraging an investigator to investigate a crime.[129]

(8) Statements made by one officer of state to another for the purpose of discharging some official business. There is some authority in favour of the view that such statements

---

[119] *Seaman* v *Netherclift* (1876) 2 CPD 53, 56.
[120] *Dawkins* v *Lord Rokeby* (1875) LR 7 HL 744.
[121] *Addis* v *Crocker* [1961] 1 QB 11.
[122] *Tadd* v *Eastwood* [1985] ICR 132.
[123] *Hasselblad (GB) Ltd* v *Orbinson* [1985] QB 475.
[124] *Watson* v *M'Ewan* [1905] AC 480; *Evans* v *London Hospital Medical College (University of London)* [1981] 1 WLR 184, 191. See below, § 26.6.
[125] *Mahon* v *Rahn (No 2)* [2000] 1 WLR 2150.
[126] ibid, at [195].
[127] *X* v *Bedfordshire County Council* [1995] 2 AC 633, 755G. See below, § 26.6.
[128] *Taylor* v *Director of the Serious Fraud Office* [1999] 2 AC 177. See below, § 26.6.
[129] *Westcott* v *Westcott* [2009] QB 407. See below, § 26.6.

will always be privileged. In *Chatterton v Secretary of State for India in Council* (1895), the claimant, a captain in the Indian Army, sued the Secretary of State for India for libel; he claimed the Secretary of State had, in a letter to his Under-Secretary of State, claimed that the Commander-in-Chief of the Indian Army had recommended that the claimant be put on half-pay on the grounds that keeping him as a full-time member of the Indian Army would be extremely undesirable. The claimant claimed that the Commander-in-Chief had made no such recommendation and that the Secretary of State had lied in his letter to the Under-Secretary of State so as to induce the Under-Secretary of State to besmirch the claimant's reputation in Parliament where questions were to be asked about the Secretary of State's treatment of the claimant. The claimant's claim against the Secretary of State was dismissed on the ground that his letter to the Under-Secretary of State was absolutely privileged. However, it is uncertain whether the same principle applies to statements made by one civil servant to another[130] or by one officer in the army to another.[131]

(9) *Statements made in an internal memorandum circulated within a foreign embassy.*[132]

(10) *Statements made in a fair and accurate and contemporaneous report of proceedings in public before a UK court or the European Court of Justice or the European Court of Human Rights or any international criminal tribunal.* Section 14(1) of the Defamation Act 1996 provides that such statements will always be privileged. Section 14(2) provides that a 'report of proceedings which by an order of the court, or as a consequence of any statutory provision, is required to be postponed shall be treated as published contemporaneously if it is published as soon as practicable after publication is permitted'.

19.10 QUALIFIED PRIVILEGE

A statement which is protected by *qualified privilege* will be privileged so long as it was *not made maliciously*. For the purposes of this area of the law, A will be held to have acted maliciously in making a statement about B if: (1) he knew that that statement was untrue when he made it; *or* (2) when he made that statement, he did not care whether it was true or not; *or* (3) he made that statement for some improper or illegitimate reason.[133] The following kinds of statements will be protected by qualified privilege:

(1) *Statements attracting qualified privilege under the duty-interest test.* The traditional rule was that if A has made a statement to C, that statement would be protected by qualified privilege if, *had the information contained in that statement been correct*, A would have had a moral or legal duty to pass that information on to C and C would have had an interest in receiving that information.

In *Watt v Longsdon* (1930), the claimant was the managing director of the Morocco branch of the Scottish Petroleum Company. The manager of the Morocco branch wrote to the defendant, a director of Scottish Petroleum, accusing the claimant of being drunk, dishonest and immoral. The defendant showed the letter to the chairman of the board and also the claimant's wife. The claimant sued the defendant for defamation in respect of both publications of the letter.

The allegations contained in the letter were untrue so the defendant could not defeat the claimant's action by raising a defence of justification. However, the publication to the

---

[130] Henn-Collins J thought not in *Szalatnay-Stacho v Fink* [1946] 1 All ER 303.
[131] The Court of Queen's Bench thought it would in *Dawkins v Lord Paulet* (1869) LR 5 QB 94.
[132] *Fayed v Al-Tajir* [1988] 1 QB 712.
[133] *Horrocks v Lowe* [1975] AC 135. See also Mitchell 1999.

chairman of the board was held to be privileged. *Had the information contained in the letter been correct*, the defendant would obviously have had a duty to show the letter to the chairman of the board and the chairman of the board would have had an interest in seeing the letter. This established that the publication to the chairman of the board was protected by qualified privilege and, as the defendant had not been acting maliciously in showing the letter in question to the chairman of the board, the publication of that letter to the chairman of the board was privileged.

It was different with the publication to the claimant's wife. Obviously, had the allegations in the letter been true, the claimant's wife would have had an interest in seeing the letter. However, the defendant could *not* establish that had the allegations in the letter been true, he would have had a *duty* to show that letter to the claimant's wife. The Court of Appeal refused to be drawn on the question – If A has found out that B's husband has been cheating on her and generally engaging in disreputable activities, when will A have a duty to tell B of this fact? However, the Court of Appeal thought that the nature of the defendant's relationship with the claimant's wife was not such as to make it his place to tell the claimant's wife of what her husband was supposed to have been getting up to.

Such was the position with what is called the 'duty-interest' test for qualified privilege until the decision of the Court of Appeal in *Clift* v *Slough Borough Council* (2010). In that case, the claimant – Jane Clift – felt victimised by a council employee to whom she had been trying to make a complaint about a couple who had abused and threatened her in a council park. The claimant – outraged at the employee's indifference to the abuse she had suffered – contacted an administrator in the office of the council's Chief Executive to say that she felt so 'affronted and so filled with anger' at the way the council employee had treated her that 'I would have physically attacked her if she had been anywhere near her.' This was enough to get the claimant's name entered on a 'Violent Persons Register' that the council maintained; which register was subsequently circulated to numerous council employees and council 'partner organisations'.

The claimant sued the council for defamation. The council's attempt to argue that its warning employees and partner organisations that the claimant was on the Violent Persons Register was protected by qualified privilege under the duty-interest test was upheld in part and dismissed in part at first instance. It was held that the council's warning employees who were likely to come into contact with the claimant was protected by qualified privilege as they would have an interest in knowing the claimant was violent. However, the council had gone too far in warning other employees and organisations that were never likely to come into contact with the claimant: they had no interest in knowing whether the claimant was violent or not, and so the warnings to them could not be protected by qualified privilege under the duty-interest test.

So far, so good. The council appealed. The Court of Appeal said that the issue of whether the warning to what was referred to as the 'supernumerary employees' (to save words, we will refer to them as 'SE' for short) was protected by qualified privilege under the duty-interest test was a 'puzzling question'.[134] With respect, it was not. It was as obvious as a punch in the face that the publication to the SE could *not* be protected by qualified privilege under the duty-interest test as the SE had no interest in knowing whether or not the claimant was violent. However, as the council was a *public body* – and therefore bound by the Human Rights Act 1998 – the Court of Appeal thought that it could resolve the issue of whether the council's warning to the SE was protected by qualified privilege by asking

---

[134] [2011] 1 WLR 1774, at [24].

whether giving such a warning violated the claimant's Article 8 rights under the European Convention on Human Rights 'to her private and family life, [her] home and [her] correspondence'.

The Court of Appeal thought that the council *had* violated the claimant's Article 8 rights by warning the SE that the claimant was a violent person. By defaming her, they had interfered with her private life,[135] and such interference could not be justified under Article 8(2) of the ECHR. This was because while the warning to the SE may have served a legitimate purpose – that of protecting those connected with the council from violence – it did so in a disproportionate way as the SE were not likely to come into contact with the claimant.[136] So the council had acted unlawfully under the Human Rights Act 1998 in warning the SE, and could not therefore argue that it had a duty to give that warning.[137]

The Court of Appeal's decision in *Clift* is disastrous. Four criticisms can be made of it. First, and most fundamentally, it radically changes the duty-interest test (in so far as it applies to a public body) from one that rests on a hypothetical question ('*Had* the claimant been violent, would the council have had a duty to warn the SE of that fact, and did the SE have an interest in knowing that fact?') into one that rests on a real question ('Given the facts of this case as they actually were, did the council act unlawfully under the Human Rights Act 1998 in warning the SE that the claimant was violent?'). The difference this makes is well-illustrated by the following remarks of Ward LJ:

> *Ill-considered* and indiscriminate disclosure is bound to be disproportionate and no plea of administrative difficulty *in verifying the information* and limiting publication to those who truly have the need to know or those reasonably thought to be at risk can outweigh the substantial interference with the right to protect reputations.[138]

The italicised words refer to things that, traditionally, were *never* regarded as relevant to the issue of whether a publication was protected under the duty-interest test. Whether the defendant acted in undue haste in giving a third party some damaging information about the claimant was never relevant under the duty-interest test, because that test traditionally asked: *Had the information been true*, would the defendant have had a duty to tell the third party, and would the third party have had an interest in knowing it? So whether the defendant acted hastily or not in telling the third party never came into it. But it does now – so far as public bodies are concerned.

This takes us on to the second criticism of the *Clift* decision, which is that as the Human Rights Act 1998 only applies to public bodies, it is only against public bodies that one can invoke the 1998 Act to say that the duty-interest is not satisfied. But it seems profoundly unsatisfactory for one form of the duty-interest test to apply to public bodies and a quite different form (the traditional form) to apply to private persons. In order to avoid this happening, there will be calls for the approach to *Clift* to be applied to private persons as well – that is, for a private person's publication to be deprived of protection under the duty-interest test if that publication cannot be justified under Article 8(2) of the ECHR. But it is hard to see how Article 8(2) could ever apply to a publication by a private person given that it begins by saying: 'There shall be no interference *by a public authority* with the exercise of this right . . .'.[139]

---

[135] [2011] 1 WLR 1774, at [32].
[136] [2011] 1 WLR 1774, at [35].
[137] [2011] 1 WLR 1774, at [36].
[138] [2011] 1 WLR 1774, at [35] (our emphasis).
[139] Our emphasis.

The third criticism of the *Clift* decision is that Article 8(2) of the ECHR is relatively narrow, and requiring a public body to establish that a given publication is justified under Article 8(2) before it can claim that the publication is protected under the duty-interest test may be asking too much. Article 8(2) provides that a public authority's interfering with someone's 'private and family life' can only be justified if it is necessary

> in the interests of national security, public safety or the economic well-being of the country, for the prevention of disorder or crime, for the protection of health or morals, or for the protection of the rights and freedoms of others.

Suppose that, within a particular council, *Manager* reports to *Superior* that he has noticed that the quality of *Secretary*'s typing seems to be deteriorating. Such a report would have attracted qualified privilege under the traditional duty-interest test. After *Clift*, it is not so clear. The report does not seem to fall under any of the situations listed in Article 8(2) as warranting an interference with *Secretary*'s private life.

The fourth criticism of *Clift* is that it makes it difficult to know what effect it has on all the other situations where a statement will attract qualified privilege. If a statement that falls into one of the categories below is made by a public body and cannot be justified under Article 8(2), will it be protected by qualified privilege or not? It is very difficult to tell. We will not mention *Clift* again in going through the other sorts of statements that are protected by qualified privilege; but it should always be borne in mind that the effect of *Clift* may be that a statement that falls into one of the categories below will *not* be protected by qualified privilege if it is made by a public body and cannot be justified under Article 8(2).

(2) *Statements attracting qualified privilege under the common interest test.* If A has made a statement to C, that statement will be protected by qualified privilege if it served A's interests to make that statement to C and it served C's interests to hear it.

For example, in *Watt* v *Longsdon* (1930), the claimant *also* sued the defendant for libel in respect of a letter that the defendant wrote to the manager of the Morocco branch of Scottish Petroleum in which the defendant voiced his own suspicions about the claimant and asked the manager to obtain confirmation of the allegations contained in the manager's letter. The Court of Appeal held that the defendant's letter was protected by qualified privilege. This was because the defendant and the manager had a common interest in protecting the interests of Scottish Petroleum and this shared interest of the defendant and the manager's was served by the defendant's writing his letter to the manager and the manager's receiving it and acting on it. And as the defendant had not acted maliciously in writing to the manager, the letter was privileged.

Similarly, in *Hunt* v *Great Northern Railway Company* (1891), the claimant worked as a guard for the defendant railway company. The defendants sacked the claimant on the ground that he had been guilty of gross neglect of duty. The defendants inserted a notice in the monthly circular which was distributed to the defendants' employees saying that the claimant had been guilty of gross neglect of duty and had been sacked as a result. The claimant sued the defendants for libel but his case was dismissed on the ground that the statement in the monthly circular was privileged. It was protected by qualified privilege, the court held, because the publication of the statement in the monthly circular served the interests of both the defendants and the people to whom the statement was published to, the defendants' employees – in both cases, because publication of the statement let the defendants' employees know that they would be sacked if they were guilty of gross neglect of duty. And as the defendants had not acted maliciously in publishing the statement in their monthly circular – they had not, for example, published the statement in order to make the claimant unemployable or published it in the knowledge that the claimant had not been guilty of a gross neglect of duty – that statement was privileged.

Lord Denning MR thought that what we might call the common interest test could be used to establish that statements made by an employer to his secretary in dictating a letter will be protected by qualified privilege. He argued in *Bryanston Finance* v *de Vries* (1975) that as the employer and the secretary would both have an interest in getting the letter dictated by the employer written, any statements made to the secretary by the employer in dictating the letter would be protected by a qualified privilege. Such statements would therefore be privileged so long as the employer did not act maliciously in publishing them to his secretary. However, neither of the two other members of the Court of Appeal in *Bryanston Finance* agreed with Lord Denning MR on this point. They both thought the statements made in dictation would only be privileged if the publication to the intended recipient of the letter would also be privileged.

(3) *Statements attracting qualified privilege under the* Reynolds *test for qualified privilege.* These kinds of statements will be discussed in the following section.

(4) *Statements attracting qualified privilege because made in self-defence.* It is well established that if someone attacks or criticises A verbally or in print, then any statements made by A in order to rebut that attack or criticism will be protected by qualified privilege.

So in *Osborn* v *Thomas Boulter & Son* (1930), the claimant – a publican – wrote to the defendants to complain about the quality of their beer. The defendants wrote back suggesting that the source of the claimant's problems with their beer was that he watered it down once it was delivered to him. The claimant sued the defendants for slander on the basis that the defendants' letter had been published not only to the claimant but also to the defendants' secretary when it was dictated to her. His claim was dismissed on the ground that the defendants' rebuttal of the claimant's attack on the quality of their beer was protected by qualified privilege and the defendants had not acted maliciously in making the allegations that they did.

In *Watts* v *Times Newspapers Ltd* (1997), *The Sunday Times* published a story which accused the claimant, Nigel Watts, of plagiarism. However, they accompanied the story with a photograph of a quite different Nigel Watts, a property developer. This Nigel Watts complained and *The Sunday Times* printed an apology in its next edition which was dictated by Nigel Watts's solicitors, Schilling & Lom. The apology repeated the original defamatory story about the claimant. The claimant sued *The Sunday Times* for libel, claiming that the apology was defamatory of him. It was held that *The Sunday Times* could not claim that their apology was privileged as they were not publishing it to rebut an attack on themselves. *The Sunday Times* then sought to make a claim in contribution against Schilling & Lom on the ground that, having dictated the terms of the apology, they were also liable to pay damages to the claimant in respect of the publication of the apology. This claim was dismissed; it was held that, vis-à-vis Schilling & Lom, the apology was privileged as it had been dictated in order to rebut the attack which *The Sunday Times* had inadvertently made on their client.

(5) *Statements attracting qualified privilege under the Defamation Act 1996.* The 1996 Act confers qualified privilege on a wide range of statements made on a matter of public concern or interest.[140] The Act splits these statements into two groups.

---

[140] Section 15(3) of the Defamation Act 1996 provides that the 1996 Act does not confer qualified privilege on matter published 'to the public, or a section of the public, . . . which is not of public concern and the publication of which [was] not for the public benefit'.

First, the Act provides that certain statements on matters of public concern or interest will be protected by qualified privilege *'without explanation or contradiction'.* These include: (1) statements made in a fair and accurate report of proceedings in public of a legislature or a court or a public inquiry or an international organisation or an international conference located anywhere in the world; and (2) statements made in a fair and accurate copy of or extract from any matter published by a government or a legislature or an international organisation or an international conference located anywhere in the world.[141] Such statements will be privileged so long as the person who published it did not act maliciously in doing so.[142]

Secondly, the 1996 Act provides that certain other statements on matters of public concern or interest will be protected by qualified privilege *'subject to explanation or contradiction'.* What this means is that if A, a newspaper, has published such a statement and the statement in question is defamatory of B, A will *not* be able to claim – if B sues it for defamation – that the statement was privileged if: (1) A acted maliciously in publishing that statement;[143] *or* (2) A refused or neglected to publish in a suitable manner a 'reasonable letter or statement by way of explanation or contradiction' of the statement published by A when it was requested to do so by B.[144]

The 1996 Act provides that statements that will be protected by qualified privilege 'subject to explanation or contradiction' include:[145] (1) statements made in a fair and accurate report of proceedings at any lawful meeting held in the EU on a matter of public concern;[146] (2) statements made in a fair and accurate copy of or extract from matter issued by any member state of the EU or by any organisation performing governmental functions in a member state of the EU[147] or by the European Commission; (3) statements made in a fair and accurate report of proceedings at any general meeting of a UK public company; (4) statements made in a fair and accurate copy of or extract from any document circulated to the members of a UK public company by its board or its auditors; (5) statements made in a fair and accurate report of any decision or finding made by an organisation concerned to promote a trade or a profession or a business or a game or a charitable object or general interest in art or science or religion or learning.

19.11 *REYNOLDS* PRIVILEGE

This is such an important form of qualified privilege that it deserves its own section. '*Reynolds* privilege' is a form of qualified privilege named after the House of Lords' decision in *Reynolds* v *Times Newspapers Ltd* (2001), which established that statements made in an article published in a newspaper will be protected by qualified privilege if: (1) the article was on a matter of public concern or interest *and* (2) the newspaper acted responsibly in going ahead and publishing the article when they did and in the form that they did.[148] Such statements are said to be protected under the *Reynolds* test for qualified privilege.

---

[141] For a full list, see Part I of Sch 1 of the Defamation Act 1996.
[142] Section 15(1).
[143] ibid.
[144] Section 15(2).
[145] For a full list, see Part II of Sch I of the Defamation Act 1996.
[146] The House of Lords has held that a report which fairly and accurately summarises the contents of a press release issued to accompany a press conference will be protected by qualified privilege under this head: *McCartan Turkington Breen* v *Times Newspapers Ltd* [2001] 2 AC 277.
[147] Defined in the Act as including 'police functions': Sch 1, Part II, para. 9(2).
[148] See *Jameel (Mohammed)* v *Wall Street Europe SPRL* [2007] 1 AC 359, at [31]–[32] (per Lord Bingham), [55] (per Lord Hoffmann), [107] (per Lord Hope), [137] (per Lord Scott).

Such is the theoretical importance of *Reynolds* privilege in protecting newspapers from being sued for defamation that the government proposes in clause 2 of its Defamation Bill to put this form of privilege on a statutory footing, in the shape of a defence of 'Responsible publication on [a] matter of public interest'. However, this 'new' defence will operate in exactly the same way as *Reynolds* privilege, and everything said below about *Reynolds* privilege will equally apply to the defence of 'responsible publication on a matter of public interest'.

In the *Reynolds* case, Lord Nicholls provided a list of ten factors which could be taken into account in determining whether a newspaper acted responsibly in publishing a particular article about someone when they did and in the form that they did:[149]

1. The seriousness of the [allegations made in the article]. The more serious the charge, the more the public is misinformed and the individual harmed, if [the allegations in the report were] untrue. 2. The nature of the information [in the article], and the extent to which the subject matter is a matter of public concern. 3. The source of the information. Some informants have no direct knowledge of the events. Some have their own axes to grind, or are being paid for their stories. 4. The steps taken to verify the information. 5. The status of the information. [The allegations made in the article] may already have been the subject of an investigation which commands respect. 6. The urgency of the matter. News is often a perishable commodity. 7. Whether comment was sought from the [subject of the article]. He may have information others do not possess or have not disclosed. [However, an] approach . . . will not always be necessary. 8. Whether the article contained the gist of the [subject of the article's] side of the story. 9. The tone of the article. A newspaper can often raise queries or call for an investigation. It need not adopt allegations as statements of fact. 10. The circumstances of the publication, including the timing.[150]

In the *Reynolds* case itself, *The Sunday Times* published an article which dealt with the resignation of Albert Reynolds, the Irish prime minister. The article alleged that Reynolds had deliberately and dishonestly misled the Irish Dáil on a particular matter and that Reynolds had been forced to resign when his colleagues found out about Reynolds's misconduct. In fact, this was not true: Reynolds never misled the Dáil and he resigned for other reasons. Reynolds sued *The Sunday Times* for libel and *The Sunday Times* claimed in its defence that its article was privileged. The House of Lords held that the article was not privileged. While there was no doubt that the article was on a matter of public concern and interest,[151] the House of Lords found that *The Sunday Times* did *not* act responsibly in publishing the article in the form that it did. The reason for this was that the article was unjustifiably one-sided in its presentation of the reasons why Reynolds resigned. No account was given of Reynolds's explanation of why he had resigned which Reynolds presented to the Irish Dáil on the day he resigned when, in fairness, one would have expected such an account to have been given. Indeed, the coverage of the story behind Reynolds's resignation had been much more balanced in the Irish editions of *The Sunday Times* and this must have counted against *The Sunday Times* in the eyes of the House of

---

[149] Clause 2(2) of the Defamation Bill sets out a non-exhaustive list of eight factors that ought to be taken into account. Comparing the (a)–(h) list in the Defamation Bill with Lord Nicholls' factors: (a) = 2. (b) = 1. (c) = 2. (d) = 3 and 5. (e) = 7 and 8. (f) = 4. (g) = 10. (h) = 9.

[150] [2001] 2 AC 127, 205. The decision of the Court of Appeal in *Loutchansky* v *Times Newspapers Ltd* [2002] QB 321 makes it clear that, in judging whether a newspaper acted responsibly in publishing a particular article when it did and in the form that it did, one should only take into account the information available to the newspaper at the time it published the article.

[151] As Reynolds was one of the architects of the Northern Ireland peace process, the reasons for his resignation were of public concern and interest in the UK.

Lords in determining whether *The Sunday Times* acted responsibly in publishing its article about Reynolds's resignation in the form that it did.

Five points need to be made about the *Reynolds* test for qualified privilege:

A. Rationale

Let's say that A is the editor of the *Daily Herald* and one of his reporters has come to him with a damaging story about B, a famous politician. The story is clearly on a matter of the public interest – it is alleged that B has been taking bribes – but it is not 100% certain that the story is correct. So there is a risk that if A publishes the story, B might sue his newspaper for defamation and the newspaper will be unable to make out a defence of justification to defeat her claim. In formulating the *Reynolds* test, the House of Lords tried to provide A with some reassurance that he could safely go ahead and publish the story about B even though he was uncertain whether a defence of justification could be made out if the story went to court. The House of Lords essentially promised A, 'So long as you handle the story about B *responsibly*, then your newspaper will be immune from being sued successfully by B; and this is so even if the story about B turns out to be untrue.' In making this promise, the House of Lords was concerned to ensure that the law on defamation did not have a 'chilling' effect on legitimate freedom of expression by deterring editors like A from publishing stories like the story about B because they could not be 100% certain they were correct. Of course, if it turned out that B was *not* taking bribes, the effect of the House of Lords' ruling in *Reynolds* would have been to encourage A to publish an untrue story about B that unjustifiably besmirched her reputation. But the House of Lords thought that the risk of this happening was a price worth paying to ensure that other *true* but damaging stories on matters of the public interest were not suppressed by newspaper editors because they could not be certain that they would be able to prove that they were true in court.

B. Application

In *Jameel (Mohammed) v Wall Street Europe SPRL* (2007), the House of Lords expressed concern that the *Reynolds* test was being applied too restrictively by the lower courts – that is, the courts of first instance and the Court of Appeal – and that the protection that it was intended to afford newspapers' freedom of speech was thereby being undermined. The House of Lords has now made it clear that while it is for the courts to decide whether a newspaper acted responsibly in handling a particular story in the way it did, the courts have to give newspapers some latitude in determining this issue. In particular, Lord Nicholls' list of factors that should be taken into account in determining whether a newspaper acted responsibly in handling a particular story should *not* be regarded as a series of hurdles *all* of which have to be cleared before the courts will find that the newspaper acted responsibly in handling that story.[152] Lord Hoffmann suggested that the newspapers' Code of Practice, as ratified by the Press Complaints Commission, could provide 'valuable guidance' as to whether a newspaper had acted responsibly in handling a particular story.[153] Lord Bingham went further and urged that in applying the *Reynolds* test, the courts should adopt something akin to the *Bolam* test for determining whether a professional acted negligently:[154]

---

[152] [2007] 1 AC 359, at [33] (per Lord Bingham) and at [56] (per Lord Hoffmann).
[153] [2007] 1 AC 359, at [55].
[154] See above, § 8.4(B).

editorial decisions and judgments made at the time, without the knowledge of falsity which is a benefit of hindsight, are [not] irrelevant. Weight should ordinarily be given to the professional judgment of an editor or journalist in the absence of some indication that it was made in a casual, cavalier, slipshod or careless manner.[155]

In the *Jameel (Mohammed)* case itself, the *Wall Street Journal Europe* (WSJE) published a story that suggested that the Saudi Arabian banking authorities were monitoring bank accounts held by, among others, Mohammed Jameel and the Abdul Latif Jameel Company, to ensure that they were not used 'wittingly or unwittingly' to help fund terrorist activities carried out by Al-Qaeda. Both Mohammed Jameel and the Abdul Latif Jameel Company sued the WSJE in defamation. The WSJE argued that the article in question was protected by qualified privilege under the *Reynolds* test. The Court of Appeal ruled that the *Reynolds* test was not satisfied in this case because the WSJE had not given Mohammed Jameel 24 hours to respond to the allegations in the article before publishing them. The House of Lords overruled the Court of Appeal, holding that it had adopted far too fussy an approach to the issue of whether the WSJE had acted responsibly in publishing its article. Looking at all the circumstances of the case, they held that the WSJE's article was plainly an example of the 'sort of neutral, investigative journalism which *Reynolds* privilege exists to protect'.[156]

Sadly, if the decision of the Court of Appeal in *Flood* v *Times Newspapers Ltd* (2011) is anything to go by, it seems that the lower courts are continuing to adopt an over-fussy approach to what does and what does not count as 'responsible journalism', thus undermining the attempts the House of Lords made in *Reynolds* and in *Jameel (Mohammed)* to prevent the law of defamation having a chilling effect on editor's decisions as to what to put in their newspapers.

In the *Flood* case, a serving police officer sued *The Times* in defamation for printing a story alleging that he was under investigation for taking bribes from Russian exiles; the bribes were being paid, it was claimed, to obtain inside information as to what attempts the Russian government was making to extradite these exiles back to Russia. The claimant argued that the story suggested that there were reasonable grounds for suspecting that he had been abusing his position as a police officer. In fact, there were no such grounds and the claimant was cleared. So no defence of justification could be raised to defeat the claimant's claim. *The Times* sought, instead, to argue that the story was subject to qualified privilege under the *Reynolds* test.

The Court of Appeal dismissed this argument, holding that *The Times'* story about the claimant did not amount to 'responsible journalism'. Lord Neuberger MR went through Lord Nicholls' list of factors that should be taken into account in judging whether a given piece of journalism amounts to 'responsible journalism' and observed:

> When one turns to the 'steps taken to verify the information', the journalists *do not seem to have done much* to satisfy themselves that the allegations were true . . . As to urgency, there was no reason for rushing to publish, *so far as I can see.*[157]

Moore-Bick LJ held that:

> *In my view*, responsible journalism requires a recognition of the importance of ensuring that persons against whom serious allegations of crime or professional misconduct are made are not forced to respond to them before an investigation has been properly carried out and charges have been made . . . If the details of such allegations are made public [prematurely], they are capable of

---

[155] [2007] 1 AC 359, at [33]. To the same effect, see [51] (per Lord Hoffmann).
[156] [2007] 1 AC 359, at [35] (per Lord Bingham).
[157] [2011] 1 WLR 153, at [73]–[74] (emphasis added).

causing a great deal of harm to the individual concerned, since many people are inclined to assume that there is 'no smoke without fire'.[158]

He acknowledged that a different view might be taken in relation to a police investigation into misconduct by a police officer. The police have a long history of sweeping such allegations of misconduct under the carpet, and responsible journalism might require making the allegations and the investigation into them public before the investigation is over so as to put pressure on the police to investigate those allegations properly. However, Moore-Bick LJ dismissed that argument:

> The judge [at first instance, who accepted that *The Times* article was an example of responsible journalism] accepted that part of the public interest in publishing the story lay in prompting the police to pursue an investigation that they would or might otherwise abandon. However, *I am unable* to accept that. If that had been the purpose of the article, it would *surely* have been written in a way that would have placed *greater emphasis* on the allegations and the failure of the police to pursue an investigation. In fact the police were pursuing an investigation . . .[159]

Moses LJ held that the story had so many unsubstantiated and unwarranted details that it went beyond the bounds of 'responsible journalism':

> Of course, the details in *The Times* article added spice to the story; of course, those details might make it more likely that a reader would notice the article. Editors know how to attract the attention and interest of their readers and the courts must defer to their judgement of how best to achieve that result . . . *But non sequitur that it can be left to them to judge whether publication of the impugned details is of public interest. That is for the courts* . . .[160]

All of the italicised expressions in the above four quotes are, in our view, inconsistent with the tenor of the House of Lords' decision in *Jameel (Mohammed)* (from which – very unusually – no relevant sections were quoted in the *Flood* case) and the rationale of the *Reynolds* test for qualified privilege. Editors can have no confidence that their decisions to publish a story will be protected under the *Reynolds* test for qualified privilege if judges persist in refusing to find that a story does not count as responsible journalism merely because: the story contains some details that the judge would not have included in the story if he had been an editor; or the story does not contain, or does not make strongly enough, the sort of points the judge would have wanted to see it make; or the journalists handling the story have not done as much work on the story as the judge would have wanted them to do. The *Reynolds* test simply will not work to reassure editors and journalists that they can go about their work free from the fear that they will be held liable for defamation unless they are given *far* more latitude in how they handle stories than a decision like the one in *Flood* gives them.

C. Reportage

Reportage is a 'fancy word'[161] for 'the neutral reporting without adoption or embellishment or subscribing to any belief in its truth of attributed allegations of both sides of a political and possibly some other kind of dispute'.[162]

An example of *reportage* is provided by the case of *Roberts* v *Gable* (2008), where the defendant newspaper *Searchlight* – which exposes the activities of parties on the far right

---

[158] [2011] 1 WLR 153, at [104] (emphasis added).
[159] [2011] 1 WLR 153, at [106] (emphasis added).
[160] [2011] 1 WLR 153, at [118] (emphasis added).
[161] *Roberts* v *Gable* [2008] QB 502, at [34] (per Ward LJ).
[162] [2008] QB 502, at [53] (per Ward LJ).

wing of British politics – published a story reporting that there had been a falling out in the aftermath of a London BNP (British National Party) rally with the claimants and two other individuals accusing each other of stealing the money collected at the rally. *Searchlight* did not take any sides in this dispute – its only desire was to report the fact that members of the BNP were feuding among themselves.

The claimants sued the defendant newspaper for libel, claiming that (under the repetition rule)[163] its article alleged that they *had* stolen the money collected at the BNP London rally. *Searchlight* claimed that the article was protected by qualified privilege under the *Reynolds* test. One problem with that claim was that *Searchlight* had not attempted to give the claimants an opportunity to respond to their article; nor had it attempted to find out the truth of what happened in the aftermath of the London BNP rally. However, the Court of Appeal held that this did not matter: *reportage* would be protected under the *Reynolds* test without there being any 'need to take steps to ensure the accuracy of the published information'.[164] So long as: (1) it was in the public interest to report the *fact* of the dispute being reported on; *and* (2) the newspaper reporting on the dispute reported it in a 'fair, disinterested and neutral way' without adopting any of the allegations made in that dispute as its own;[165] *and* (3) the newspaper acted responsibly in publishing the information about the fact of the dispute, *then* (4) the newspaper's report would be protected by qualified privilege under the *Reynolds* test.

Clause 2(3) of the Defamation Bill specifically provides for the case of reportage, stipulating that 'A defendant is to be treated as having acted responsibly in publishing a statement if the statement was published as part of an accurate and impartial account of a dispute between the claimant and another person.'

D. Scope

There is no reason to think that the category of statements that are protected by qualified privilege under the *Reynolds* test covers only statements made in articles published in newspapers. *Reynolds* privilege is also capable of protecting statements made in speeches, books, television documentaries or news programmes.[166] It may also apply to statements made in articles that have been posted in a newspaper archive on the Internet.[167]

E. Relationship with the duty-interest test

One issue which divides the courts and affects the language in which they discuss the *Reynolds* test is the relationship between the *Reynolds* test for qualified privilege and the duty-interest test for qualified privilege, discussed above.[168]

---

[163] See above, § 19–2(7).

[164] [2008] QB 502, at [61](2) (per Ward LJ).

[165] [2008] QB 502, at [61](5).

[166] *Seaga v Harper* [2009] 1 AC 1, at [11]: 'their Lordships . . . can see no valid reason why [*Reynolds* privilege] should not extend to publications made by any person who publishes material of public interest in any medium, so long as the conditions framed by Lord Nicholls as being applicable to "responsible journalism" are satisfied.'

[167] *Loutchansky v Times Newspapers Ltd (Nos 2–5)* [2002] QB 783. The Court of Appeal held that a newspaper could not claim to have acted responsibly when it placed a defamatory article originally published in its print edition in an archive on the Internet without qualifying the article in any way to make it clear that its accuracy had been challenged. See, to the same effect, *Flood v Times Newspapers Ltd* [2011] 1 WLR 153, holding that any *Reynolds* privilege attaching to an article on a newspaper Internet archive will be lost if reasonable steps are not taken to revise it when it becomes clear that the article is misleading.

[168] See above, § 19.10(1).

On one view, the *Reynolds* test for qualified privilege is an outgrowth of, or application of, the duty-interest test. On this view, a newspaper that published an article on a matter of the public interest and that acted responsibly in publishing that article when it did and in the way it did can argue that it had a duty to publish that article and that its readers had an interest in reading it, and that is why the article is protected by qualified privilege. On another view, the *Reynolds* test for qualified privilege is completely independent of the duty-interest test and stands on its own two feet.

In the *Jameel (Mohammed)* case, the House of Lords split 3:2 over this issue, with three Law Lords taking the view that the *Reynolds* test is an outgrowth of the duty-interest test,[169] while Lord Hoffmann and Baroness Hale took the view that the *Reynolds* test is a 'different jurisprudential creature' from the duty-interest test.[170] Our own view, for what it is worth, is that the *Reynolds* test *cannot* and *should not* be seen as an outgrowth of the duty-interest test for qualified privilege.

The *Reynolds* test *cannot* be seen as an outgrowth of the duty-interest test for qualified privilege because when we apply the latter test to determine whether a statement made by A to B is protected by qualified privilege we ask – *Had the statement been true*, would A have had a duty to make it to B, and did B have an interest in hearing that statement? We do *not* engage in this kind of exercise when we ask whether an article was protected by qualified privilege under the *Reynolds* test.[171] We do *not* ask: If the article *had* been true, would the newspaper have had a duty to publish the article, and would the newspaper's readers have had an interest in reading it?[172]

The *Reynolds* test for qualified privilege *should not* be seen as an outgrowth of the duty-interest test because asking whether a newspaper had a *duty* to publish a particular article and asking whether its readers had an *interest* in reading that article can – in the hands of a press-hostile judge – result in the bar for an article being protected by qualified privilege under *Reynolds* being set forbiddingly high.[173]

19.12 OTHER DEFENCES

There are two more defences that we should mention, both designed to protect someone who has been involved in the publication of a defamatory statement about the claimant to another, but whose culpability in the matter is very low:

A. Innocent dissemination

Section 1(1) of the Defamation Act 1996 provides that if A has published to another a statement which was defamatory of B, A will have a defence to any claim for damages B

---

[169] *Jameel (Mohammed)* v *Wall Street Europe SPRL* [2007] 1 AC 359, at [30] (per Lord Bingham); [107] (per Lord Hope); and at [130], [135] and [137] (per Lord Scott).

[170] [2007] 1 AC 359, at [46] (per Lord Hoffmann), and at [146] (per Baroness Hale), quoting *Loutchansky* v *Times Newspapers Ltd* (Nos 2–5) [2002] QB 783, at 806.

[171] See *Kearns* v *General Council of the Bar* [2003] 1 WLR 1357.

[172] Even if we did ask this, the answer would always be 'no' because it will not be true that each and every one of the newspaper's readers had an interest in reading the article. This is a further reason why the *Reynolds* test for privilege cannot be seen as an outgrowth of the duty-interest test.

[173] Normally, it is only publishers of small specialist journals who could claim qualified privilege for their articles under the duty-interest test or the common interest test (on the basis that *all* of their readers will have been interested in what those articles had to say), but even they can fail on occasion to show that distribution has been limited to those interested in the subject matter of the journal: *Trumm* v *Norman* [2008] EWHC 116 (QB), *Brady* v *Norman* [2008] EWHC 2481 (QB) (defamatory statements in monthly magazine of ASLEF trade union not protected by qualified privilege because circulation not limited to ASLEF members).

might bring against A if: (1) A was not the 'author, editor or publisher' of the statement in question; (2) A took reasonable care in relation to its publication; *and* (3) A did not know, and had no reason to believe, that what he did would cause or contribute to the publication of a defamatory statement.[174]

So the 'author, editor or publisher' of a defamatory statement will *not* be able to take advantage of the defence set out in s 1(1) of the 1996 Act. Section 1(2) makes it clear that the term 'author', as used in s 1(1) of the 1996 Act,

> means the originator of the statement [in question], but does not include a person who did not intend that his statement be published at all . . . 'editor' means a person having editorial or equivalent responsibility for the content of the statement [in question] or the decision to publish it . . . [and] 'publisher' means a commercial publisher, that is, a person whose business is issuing material to the public, or a section of the public, who issues material containing the statement [in question] in the course of that business.

Section 1(4) of the 1996 Act provides that an employee or agent of someone who was the 'author, editor or publisher' of a defamatory statement according to the above definition will *also* be held to have been the 'author, editor or publisher' of the statement in question if he was 'responsible for the content of the statement in question or the decision to publish it'.[175]

For the avoidance of doubt, s 1(3) goes on to provide that a person:

> shall not be considered the author, editor or publisher of a statement if he is only involved – (a) in printing, producing, distributing or selling printed material containing the statement; (b) in processing, making copies of, distributing, exhibiting or selling a film or sound recording . . . containing the statement; (c) in processing, making copies of, distributing or selling any electronic medium in or on which the statement is recorded, or in operating or providing any equipment, system or service by means of which the statement is retrieved, copied, distributed or made available in electronic form; (d) as the broadcaster of a live programme containing the statement in circumstances in which he has no effective control over the maker of the statement; (e) as the operator of or provider of access to a communications system by means of which the statement is transmitted, or made available, by a person over whom he has no effective control.

In *Godfrey* v *Demon Internet Ltd* (2001), the defendant was a company that ran an electronic bulletin board on the Internet. Someone posted a message on the Internet which was defamatory of the claimant and the message ended up on the defendant's bulletin board where it was accessed by various people. The claimant complained about the message to the defendant but even after he had done so the defendant failed to remove the message from its bulletin board. The claimant sued the defendant for libel on the ground that it had published the message on its bulletin board to other people. The defendant sought to take advantage of the defence set out in s 1(1) of the 1996 Act to defeat the claimant's claim. It was held that the defendant could not take advantage of this defence.

---

[174] It should be remembered that a statement can still be defamatory *even if it is true*. So suppose a bookseller sold a book which contained damaging allegations about A and A wants to sue the bookseller for libel. If we want to know whether the bookseller can take advantage of the defence set out in s 1(1) of the 1996 Act we ask – did the bookseller know, or have reason to know, that the book sold by him contained damaging allegations about A? If so, he will not be able to take advantage of the defence set out in s 1(1) of the 1996 Act. It will not matter whether or *not* the bookseller in question knew, or had reason to know, that the allegations in question were *untrue* – even if he did not know, and had no reason to know, that those allegations were untrue, he will still *not* be able to take advantage of the defence set out in s 1(1) of the 1996 Act if he knew, or ought to have known, that the book contained those allegations.

[175] Section 1(4).

Admittedly, the defendant was *not* the 'author, editor or publisher' of the message complained of – that was made clear by s 1(3) of the 1996 Act. However, the defendant could not show that in running its bulletin board it was unaware it was contributing to the publication of a statement that was defamatory of the claimant. The claimant *did* draw the defendant's attention to the presence of the message on its bulletin board and it was obviously defamatory of the claimant. From that moment onwards, the defendant was aware that it was contributing to the publication of a statement that was defamatory of the claimant in running its bulletin board without removing the message complained of by the claimant. Given this, s 1(1) of the 1996 Act did not operate to protect the defendant from being sued for libel in respect of any publications to third parties of the message on the defendant's bulletin board that took place after the presence of that message on the defendant's bulletin board was brought to the defendant's attention.

B. Offer to make amends

Suppose A has published to another a statement that was defamatory of B and B wants to sue A for libel or slander. If A cannot take advantage of one of the defences set out above to defeat B's claim, he may still be able to prevent B from suing him for libel or slander by making an 'offer to make amends' to B under s 2 of the Defamation Act 1996.

Section 2 of the Defamation Act 1996 provides that if A wants to make an 'offer to make amends' to B he *must* offer

(a) to make a suitable correction of the statement complained of and a sufficient apology to [B], (b) to publish the correction and apology in a manner that is reasonable and practicable in the circumstances, and (c) to pay [B] such compensation (if any), and such costs, as may be agreed or determined to be payable.[176]

If A only offers to do one or two of these things, then his offer will not amount to an 'offer to make amends' and will have no effect on B's right to sue A for libel or slander.

If A does make an 'offer to make amends' to B and B *accepts* the offer, B will be barred from suing A for defamation.[177] If B does *not* accept the offer, B will *still* be barred from suing A for defamation *unless*, when A published the statement which was defamatory of B: (1) he knew or had reason to believe that that statement referred to B or was likely to be understood as referring to B *and* (2) he knew or had reason to believe that the statement in question was *both* false *and* defamatory of B.[178] If (1) and (2) are true then A's 'offer to make amends' will have no effect on B's right to sue A for defamation.

19.13 REMEDIES

There are two remedies that successful claimants in defamation cases are entitled to obtain: an injunction requiring the defendant not to repeat the statement that gave rise to the claim in defamation; and damages.

Damages in defamation cases perform a vindicatory and compensatory function. The compensatory function is performed by an award that is designed to compensate the

---

[176] If B accepts A's offer but then they find themselves unable to agree on what should be paid to B by way of compensation, the courts will decide for them: Defamation Act 1996, s 3(5).

[177] Section 3(2).

[178] Section 4. *Milne* v *Express Newspapers Ltd* [2005] 1 WLR 772 makes it clear that (2) will only be true if A acted *recklessly* in publishing the statement in question. Merely showing that a reasonable person in A's position would have realised that that statement was untrue and/or defamatory will not be enough.

claimant for the reasonably foreseeable[179] losses that the defendant's statement caused the claimant to suffer. But damages can also be awarded in defamation cases with a view to 'send[ing] out a signal to people that there was no truth at all in the [defendant's] allegation':[180]

> In actions of defamation . . . [n]ot merely can [a claimant] recover the estimated sum of his past and future losses, but, in case the libel, driven underground, emerges from its lurking place at some future date, he must be able to point to a sum awarded by a jury sufficient to convince a bystander of the baselessness of the charge.[181]

> [the jury] should be asked to ensure that any award they make is proportionate to the damage which the plaintiff has suffered and is a sum which it is necessary to award him to provide adequate compensation and to re-establish his reputation.[182]

In a defamation case where a defence of justification has been pleaded and has been rejected in a reasoned judgment by a judge, the vindicatory element of any damages to be awarded to the claimant *may* be reduced to take account of the fact that the judge's judgment may go some of the way towards vindicating the claimant's reputation. But –

> The effect of such an earlier judgment depends on all the circumstances . . . there are . . . cases where the judgment will provide no or no significant or reasonable vindication. They will perhaps arise where the justification has been struck out for some technical reason in circumstances where, in truth, no consideration whatever has been given to the merits.[183]

In a case where a claimant is regarded as having little reputation to lose, an award of damages designed to vindicate the claimant's reputation will tend to reflect this, with claimants being awarded as little as £1 or one penny to make it clear of what little worth the claimant's reputation was even before he was defamed.[184] In such cases, the damages awarded to the claimant are known as 'contemptuous' or 'derisory' damages. So, for example, in *Reynolds* v *Times Newspapers Ltd* (2001), Albert Reynolds was successful in his claim against *The Sunday Times* for giving a one-sided and misleading account of the reasons why he resigned as the Irish prime minister. But he was only awarded one penny by way of damages to reflect the general disrespect in which he was held by the time his case was heard.[185]

The damages awarded to a claimant may also include a punitive element, as well as a compensatory element and a vindicatory element. Exemplary (or punitive) damages may be awarded against a defendant in a defamation case where: (1) his conduct in defaming the claimant is so outrageous as to be worthy of punishment; (2) he defamed the claimant with a view to making a gain for himself or someone else; and (3) an award of damages that did not include a punitive element would not be sufficient to punish the defendant for his behaviour.[186]

---

[179] *Slipper* v *BBC* [1991] 1 QB 283; *McManus* v *Beckham* [2002] 1 WLR 2982.
[180] Per Gray J, quoted in *Purnell* v *BusinessF1 Magazine Ltd* [2008] 1 WLR 1, at [7].
[181] *Broome* v *Cassell & Co Ltd* [1972] AC 1027, 1071 (per Lord Hailsham LC).
[182] *Rantzen* v *Mirror Group Newspapers (1986) Ltd* [1994] QB 670, 696.
[183] *Purnell* v *BusinessF1 Magazine Ltd* [2008] 1 WLR 1, at [29]–[30] (per Laws LJ).
[184] *Plato Films Ltd* v *Speidel* [1961] AC 1090.
[185] See also *Grobbelaar* v *News Group Newspapers* [2002] 1 WLR 3024 (£1 awarded in damages to Bruce Grobbelaar, the ex-Liverpool and Southampton goalkeeper, who – it was found – was justifiably accused by the defendant of taking bribes to 'throw' football matches but unjustifiably accused of acting on those bribes and actually throwing football matches).
[186] The requirements that have to be satisfied before an award of exemplary damages may be made against a defendant are discussed in much more detail below: chapter 30.

These different features of awards of damages in defamation cases mean that such awards tend to be 'highly subjective'.[187] In the past, the subjectivity of such awards has been added to by the fact that claimants in defamation had a qualified[188] right to have a jury hear their case and determine the size of the damages that should be awarded them. Juries tend to put a high value on reputation and have in the past awarded damages for loss of reputation which are far in excess of the damages that someone could hope to recover for a broken leg or the loss of an eye. To take some examples from previous cases: Lord Aldington was awarded £1.5m by a jury when he sued the authors of a pamphlet which suggested that he had participated in a war crime at the end of the Second World War;[189] the wife of the Yorkshire Ripper was awarded £600,000 by a jury when *Private Eye* published a story which suggested that she had known of her husband's guilt before he was arrested;[190] Esther Rantzen was awarded £250,000 by a jury when the *Daily Mirror* suggested that she had knowingly shielded a child abuser from prosecution;[191] and Elton John was awarded £350,000 by a jury when the *Daily Mirror* accused him of being bulimic.[192]

It was doubtful whether awards of this size were compatible with Article 10 of the European Convention on Human Rights: they seemed to go well beyond what was necessary to achieve the legitimate aim of compensating the claimant, vindicating his reputation and – where necessary – punishing the defendant for his behaviour.[193] As a result, both Parliament and the courts acted to bring jury awards of damages in defamation cases under control.[194] But now a much simpler solution to the problem of excessive jury awards is in the offing: under clause 8 of the Defamation Bill defamation claimants' rights to have their cases heard by a jury will be done away with altogether.

19.14 OPTIONS FOR REFORM

As we have seen, the Defamation Bill – as presently drafted – represents a bit of a damp squib in terms of reforming the law of defamation. While it does make some substantive changes at the margin of the law – notably, abolishing the right to a jury trial in defamation cases, and abolishing the 'multiple publication rule' – there is nothing in the Defamation Bill that will make a big difference to the law of defamation. Below we consider the merits of some more radical changes to the law.

(1) *Abolition.* Why not abolish the law of defamation? Tony Weir is the most forceful critic of the tort, calling it 'a blot on the lawscape',[195] 'the most difficult of all torts . . . certainly

---

[187] *Broome* v *Cassell & Co Ltd* [1972] AC 1027, 1071 (per Lord Hailsham LC).
[188] Section 69(1) of the Senior Courts Act 1981 provides that a jury trial should not be allowed if 'the court is of the opinion that the trial [will require] any prolonged examination of documents or accounts or any scientific or local investigation which cannot conveniently be made with a jury'.
[189] *Watts* v *Aldington, The Times,* 16 December 1993.
[190] *Sutcliffe* v *Pressdram Ltd* [1991] 1 QB 153.
[191] *Rantzen* v *MGN (1986) Ltd* [1994] QB 670.
[192] *John* v *MGN Ltd* [1997] QB 586. Admittedly, a large proportion of this award (£275,000) was made up of exemplary damages, damages designed to punish the *Daily Mirror* for the way it acted in publishing the story about Elton John.
[193] The award in the *Aldington* case was held by the European Court of Human Rights to violate the defendants' right to freedom of expression under Art 10 of the ECHR in *Tolstoy Miloslavsky* v *United Kingdom* (1995) 20 EHRR 442; as was the award of £40,000 damages against the two impecunious defendants in the *McLibel* case, whose distribution of leaflets defaming McDonald's had not been established to have caused McDonald's any loss at all (*Steel and Morris* v *UK* (2005) 41 EHRR 22).
[194] See the Courts and Legal Services Act 1990, s 8 (giving the Court of Appeal the power to set aside excessive jury awards) and *John* v *MGN Ltd* [1997] QB 586, 611–16 (on what guidance trial judges should give juries in deciding how much to award a defamation claimant).
[195] Weir 2006, 190.

the oddest . . . odd at the very core.'[196] However, it could be argued that the social nature of the tort of defamation, in that it protects the valuable relationships we have with other people from being unjustly damaged by other people, makes the tort (at least potentially) an important guarantor of our well-being. As the European Court of Human Rights recognised in *Pfeifer* v *Austria* (2007), 'a person's reputation . . . forms part of his or her personal identity and psychological integrity'.[197] Given this, it is now increasingly accepted that damaging someone's reputation will violate their rights under Article 8 of the European Convention on Human Rights 'to respect for [their] private and family life . . .' .[198] If this is right, then the UK would violate its obligations under the ECHR to uphold people's Article 8 rights if it did not protect people's reputations from being damaged.

(2) *Declaration of falsity*. Under s 9 of the Defamation Act 1996, the courts have the power – in giving summary judgment[199] in favour of a claimant in a defamation case – to declare that the defamatory statement complained of by the claimant was false. However, there seems to be no official power to grant such a remedy in a case that goes to trial. (Though it would always be open to a judge in his judgment to make it clear that he thought the statement complained of by the claimant was false.) As we have seen, the result is that an action for defamation is not that effective a means of vindicating a claimant's reputation. Just because a defendant has not been able to justify his allegations about the claimant does not mean they were not true. Adding the power to make an official declaration that the defendant's allegations about the claimant were false to the courts' armoury of remedies in a defamation case would provide the courts with a way of effectively vindicating the reputation of a claimant who has brought a claim for defamation. Moreover, the possibility of making an official declaration of falsity would take the pressure off courts and juries to include a vindicatory element in the damages they award to defamation claimants, thus reducing both the overall level of damages awards in defamation cases and their chilling effect on freedom of expression.

However, a declaration of falsity will not be a remedy that all claimants can pursue. It is much harder to prove a negative than a positive. In a case where A has said of B, 'B has been unfaithful to his wife', it will be almost impossible to establish that A's claim is positively false – unless, of course, B's movements have been continually monitored since he married his wife. In this sort of case, the only way to vindicate B's reputation will be through an award of damages (possibly combined with a strongly reasoned rejection of any defence of justification that A might offer to B's claim for defamation).

(3) *Liability of distributors*. Suppose A has written a book that obviously makes defamatory allegations about B. Suppose further that C, a bookseller, is considering whether to stock and sell copies of A's book. C may well think,

> Well – if I do stock and sell copies of A's book and the allegations in the book prove to be incorrect, I could well be sued for libel by B. In such a case, I will be held to have published the allegations in the book to the people who buy it,[200] and section 1 of the Defamation Act 1996 will not protect me because that only applies to people who unwittingly distribute material that is defamatory –

---

[196] Weir 2004, 519.

[197] (2007) 48 EHRR 175, at [35].

[198] *In Re Guardian News and Media Ltd* [2010] 2 AC 697, at [37]–[42] (per Lord Rodger); *Clift* v *Slough Borough Council* [2010] EWCA Civ 1484, at [32] (per Ward LJ).

[199] Under s 8, summary judgment is to be given if 'it appears to the court that there is no defence to the claim which has a realistic prospect of success, and there is no other reason why the claim should be tried.'

[200] See above, § 19.4(6).

and I won't fall into that category. I can't be sure that the allegations in A's book are correct so I will definitely be taking a risk of being sued for libel by B if I stock and sell copies of A's book. All in all, it might be best if I did not stock A's book.

Now – if all booksellers react in the same way as C, A will be unable to find a market for his book – and this is so even if all the allegations contained in the book are correct. This is hardly satisfactory.

Similarly, suppose A has posted a message on an electronic bulletin board that is run by C. The message is obviously defamatory of B. B complains to C about the message and requests C to take it down. Again, C may well think,

> If I don't agree to B's request and the allegations made in A's message prove to be untrue, I could well be sued for libel by B. I won't be protected by section 1 of the Defamation Act 1996 because that only protects people who unwittingly distribute defamatory material – and I won't fall into this category of protected defendants if I keep A's message on the bulletin board now that my attention has been drawn to it and its defamatory nature. I have no idea whether the allegations contained in A's message are true or not so I will definitely be taking a risk of being sued for libel by B if I don't take A's message down. Given this, it might be better if I withdrew A's message from the bulletin board.

If C does think in this way, A's message will be withdrawn from C's bulletin board even if the allegations contained in that message were true. Again, this is hardly satisfactory.

In both these cases, the law on libel operates to 'chill' legitimate expression. In the first case, A's book will be rendered unmarketable by the law of libel even though it is perfectly accurate in what it says about B. In the second case, C will be encouraged by the law on libel to 'censor' A's message even though it is perfectly accurate in what it says about B. What can be done to ensure that the law on libel does not have this effect? Probably the most satisfactory solution would be to change the law so that it comes into line with Lord Denning MR's (unsuccessful) suggestion in *Goldsmith* v *Sperrings* (1977):

> Common sense and fairness require that no subordinate distributor – from top to bottom – should be held liable for a libel contained in it unless he knew or ought to have known that the newspaper or periodical contained a libel on the [claimant] himself; that is to say, that it contained a libel on the [claimant] which could not be justified or excused . . .[201]

If the law were changed in this way then, in the first case described above, booksellers could stock A's book confident in the knowledge that if the allegations in A's book proved to be untrue and they were sued for libel by B, they would have a defence to B's claim based on the fact that they did not know and had no reason to know that A's allegations were untrue. Similarly, in the second case described above, C could refuse to withdraw A's message from the bulletin board, confident in the knowledge that if the allegations contained in that message proved to be untrue and B sued her for libel, she would have a defence to B's claim based on the fact that she did not know and had no reason to know that the allegations in A's message were untrue.

---

[201] [1977] 1 WLR 478, 487. The other two judges deciding the case declined to accept that Lord Denning's statement of the law was correct (on the ground that the point had not been argued before them) and it seems to have been assumed ever since that Lord Denning was wrong on this point. See, for example, *Metropolitan International Schools Ltd* v *Designtechnica Corporation* [2009] EWHC 1765 (QB), at [70] (per Eady J, arguing that even if there were still a common law defence of innocent dissemination (which was the subject of Lord Denning's *dictum* above), 'It would almost certainly not be available to a defendant who has had it drawn to his attention that the words are defamatory or, at least, arguably so').

(4) *Companies.* The social nature of the tort of defamation makes it doubtful whether companies should *ever* be allowed to take advantage of it. The justification for having a tort of defamation – that the preservation of the intimate relationships we have with other people is an important component of our well-being – simply does not translate across to a case where a company is complaining that its reputation is being damaged by imputations as to how it is run. Of course, if such imputations reflect personally on the people running the company, then they could have an action in their own names; but it is hard to see why the company *itself* should be able to sue.

Despite this, companies are still allowed to sue in defamation for statements that have 'a tendency to damage it in the way of its business'[202] and where those statements are made in permanent form, they are allowed to sue without having to prove that they have suffered any loss. As we have seen, the courts – both here and in Strasbourg – have refused to find that allowing companies to take advantage of the law of defamation in this way violates people's rights to freedom of expression under Art 10 of the European Convention on Human Rights.[203]

However, there is increasing concern that companies are attempting to use the law of defamation to suppress legitimate criticism of their products or activities.[204] One creative way of ensuring that companies do not take unfair advantage of the law of defamation to limit other people's freedom of speech would be to bar companies above a particular size (whether measured by capital value, or number of employees) from suing in defamation at all. For example, under the Australian Uniform Defamation Laws (a catch-all term for an identical set of provisions that were adopted by all Australian states to govern claims for defamation), a company is not allowed to bring a claim for defamation unless it has fewer than ten employees (and is not a subsidiary of a larger company) or is a non-profit organisation. This approach has been criticised as arbitrary – why ten employees? why not 20? or 30? – but it does ensure that most small businesses are able to obtain satisfactory redress through the courts when a defendant's unjustified allegations threaten to put them out of business, while at the same time forcing companies like McDonald's and Shell to rely on their public relations departments to combat any unjustified criticism of their activities.

(5) *Honest comment on matters of private interest.* As we have seen, a defendant will only be entitled to take advantage of the defence of 'honest comment' (to become the defence of 'honest opinion' under clause 4 of the Defamation Bill) if his comment was on a matter of public interest. If it was not (for example: 'I think this is a terrible business plan'), then the defendant will be forced to rely on some other defence, such as justification, to defeat a claim against him for defamation. It is arguable that this is unfair. As the European Court of Human Rights observed in *Lingens v Austria* (1986) (where a journalist was sued for making aspersions about the conduct of the then Austrian chancellor and was required under Austrian law to prove that his comments were justified, or face being prosecuted for them):

> a careful distinction needs to be made between facts and value judgments. The existence of facts can be demonstrated, whereas the truth of value judgments is not susceptible to proof . . . As regards value judgments [a requirement that a defendant prove that they are justified] is impossible of fulfilment and it infringes freedom of opinion itself, which is a fundamental part of the the right secured by Article 10 . . .[205]

---

[202] *Derbyshire County Council v Times Newspapers Ltd* [1993] AC 534, at 547 (per Lord Keith of Kinkel).

[203] See above, § 19.5. Also *Steel and Morris v UK* (2005) 41 EHRR 22 (holding (at [94]) that allowing a company to sue for defamation without having to prove what was said about it was false was not incompatible with Art 10).

[204] See above, § 19.1.

[205] (1986) 8 EHRR 407, at [46].

In *Joseph* v *Spiller* (2011), the Supreme Court expressed itself open-minded on the issue of whether the defence of honest comment should apply in cases where the comment was not on a matter of public interest.[206] The government has invited submissions on the issue before presenting a final draft of its Defamation Bill to Parliament.

(6) *New York Times v Sullivan* (1964). As we have seen, in the United States, a politician – like any other public figure – will not be able to sue a defendant in defamation unless the defendant acted maliciously in saying what he did.[207]

Most judicial discussion as to whether England should adopt what is called the *Sullivan* position with regard to public figures has focused on whether politicians should be disabled from suing for non-malicious allegations about them; the idea being that if we do not adopt *Sullivan* in relation to political figures, we can hardly apply it to any other public figures. As is well known, the House of Lords declined to adopt the *Sullivan* position in relation to politicians in *Reynolds* v *Times Newspapers Ltd* (2001), preferring to adopt the position that politicians would be able to sue a newspaper in defamation for publishing a defamatory and untrue story about them unless the story was on a matter of public interest, and was responsibly handled. Their Lordships advanced a number of reasons for taking this position.

Lord Nicholls observed that if statements about political figures were protected by qualified privilege, a politician whose reputation had been unjustly sullied by a newspaper acting in good faith would have no means of clearing his name – he would be barred from suing the newspaper for libel.[208] Lord Nicholls did not think that this was satisfactory:

> Once besmirched by an unfounded allegation in a national newspaper, a reputation can be damaged for ever, especially if there is no opportunity to vindicate one's reputation. When this happens, society as well as the individual is the loser . . . It is in the public interest that the reputation of public figures should not be debased falsely. In the political field, in order to make an informed choice, the electorate needs to be able to identify the good as well as the bad.[209]

Lords Nicholls and Cooke both observed that if statements about politicians were automatically protected by qualified privilege, one could have no confidence that newspapers – especially the tabloid press – would act responsibly in using this new won freedom to make statements about politicians free from the fear that they would be sued as a result of what they said.[210] They did not elaborate on this point but they must have feared that the press would use this freedom to print damaging stories about political figures based on the slenderest of materials and to print damaging stories about politicians which were of no conceivable public interest.

Lords Cooke and Steyn observed that if political speech were protected by qualified privilege, a politician who was defamed by a story in a newspaper would find it very difficult to establish that the newspaper acted maliciously in publishing that story.[211] This is for two reasons. First, malice is in itself a difficult thing to prove. Secondly, English law does not compel journalists to prove their sources for a story – thus making it very difficult for a claimant to show that a story had no source and was simply made up. Given these difficulties of proving malice, politicians would have very little protection against being

---

[206] [2011] 1 AC 852, at [113].
[207] See above, § 19.1(3).
[208] [2001] 2 AC 127, 201.
[209] [2001] 2 AC 127, 201.
[210] [2001] 2 AC 127, 201–2 (per Lord Nicholls), 219 (per Lord Cooke).
[211] [2001] 2 AC 127, 210 (per Lord Steyn), 219–20 (per Lord Cooke).

defamed if political speech were protected by qualified privilege – such speech would be *de facto* absolutely privileged; a politician who was defamed by a particular story would in effect find it impossible to sue for libel in respect of that story.

Finally, Lord Steyn advanced another argument against holding that all statements about politicians are protected by qualified privilege. He thought that such a rule might violate the European Convention on Human Rights, under which the resolution of competing rights and interests – such as the right to freedom of speech and the interest in preserving one's reputation undamaged – is to be done on a case-by-case basis rather than by laying down general rules which apply in a wide variety of cases.[212]

While the law of defamation does not protect political speech *as such*, it does protect *some* statements about political figures. In particular, statements that amount to fair comment on a matter of public interest and statements that are protected by the *Reynolds* test for qualified privilege are protected under UK law. Given this, *in theory* most forms of political speech will be protected under the law in the United Kingdom and those forms of political speech which will not be protected – malicious speech, tittle-tattle and the publication of irresponsible and untrue stories about politicians – are perhaps not worthy of protection. However, *in practice* the law on defamation can still have the effect of chilling legitimate political speech if an editor is encouraged to 'sit on' a damaging story about a politician because he simply does not have any confidence that the courts will find that he acted responsibly in handling that story and consequently hold that that story was protected by qualified privilege.

As we have seen,[213] the House of Lords attempted in *Jameel (Mohammed)* v *Wall Street Journal SPRL* (2007) to reassure editors in this regard and tried to ensure that the courts would in future adopt a more 'journalist friendly' approach to determining whether a story was handled in a responsible fashion than they have in the past. However, the subsequent decision of the Court of Appeal in *Flood* v *Times Newspapers Ltd* (2011) seems to show that the House of Lords' pleas have fallen on deaf ears, and that the lower courts are incapable of embracing properly the liberalisation of defamation of law that the House of Lords' decision in *Reynolds* was intended to effect.[214] Given this, it may be that the only way to ensure that the law of defamation does not have the effect of chilling legitimate speech about politicians is to adopt a modified *Sullivan* position in relation to politicians and rule that all speech about politicians (other than speech about their private lives that clearly has no bearing on the public interest) is protected by qualified privilege.

---

[212] [2001] 2 AC 127, 211.

[213] See above, § 19.11.

[214] Though to be fair to Tugendhat J, who was the first instance judge in the *Flood* case, he was very happy to find that the article in that case was an example of responsible journalism: [2009] EWHC 2375 (QB).

Further reading

Those wanting to explore further the case for reforming the law of defamation may be interested to read:

Barendt, 'Libel and freedom of speech in English law' [1993] *Public Law* 449;

Barendt, 'What is the point of libel law?' [1999] *Current Legal Problems* 110;

Loveland, 'Political libels – whose right is it anyway?' (2000) 53 *Current Legal Problems* 333;

Coad, '*Reynolds* and public interest – what about truth and human rights?' (2007) 18 *Entertainment Law Review* 75;

Coad, '*Reynolds*, *Flood* and the King's new clothes' (2011) 22 *Entertainment Law Review* 1; and

Howarth, 'The cost of libel actions: a skeptical note' (2011) 70 *Cambridge Law Journal* 397.

It might also be worth checking out the Libel Reform Campaign website at **www.libelreform. org** and their report on the law of defamation and its impact on freedom of speech. Also Google 'Ben Goldacre libel' to access online material on how the law of defamation has been used to try to suppress scientific criticism and analysis. **Tony Weir**'s attacks on the law of defamation in his little book on tort law (*An Introduction to Tort Law*, 2nd edn (Clarendon Press, 2006), chapter 12) and/or his casebook (*A Casebook on Tort*, 10th edn (Sweet & Maxwell, 2004), 519–23) are not to be missed.

Paul Mitchell's *The Making of the Modern Law of Defamation* (Hart Publishing, 2005) tells us how we got where we are today.

The colourful nature of defamation cases means that they have always attracted interest from journalists and non-specialist publishers, and that interest has resulted in some interesting books: **Adam Raphael's** *My Learned Friends* (Virgin Books, 1989) (an account of the Jeffrey Archer libel action and other libel cases); **Alan Watkins'** *A Slight Case of Libel* (Duckworth, 1990) (an account of Michael Meacher's libel action against Watkins and his newspaper, *The Observer*, for accusing Meacher of exaggerating his working-class background; Meacher lost); **John Vidal's** *McLibel: Burger Culture on Trial* (Pan Books, 1997); and **Dominic Carman's** *No Ordinary Man: A Life of George Carman* (Hodder & Stoughton, 2002) (a biography of the famous libel lawyer, by his son).

Visit **www.mylawchamber.co.uk/mcbride** to access tools to help you develop and test your knowledge of Tort law, including interactive multiple choice questions, practice exam

questions with guidance, weblinks, legal newsfeed, additional case summaries, legal updates and tips on answering problem and essay questions.

Use **Case Navigator** to read in full some of the key cases referenced in this chapter with commentary and questions:

• Jameel *v* Wall Street Journal Europe SPRL

20 Harassment

20.1 The basics *579*

20.2 Protection from Harassment Act
1997 *580*

20.3 Equality Act 2010 *585*

Overview

This chapter and the next look at a couple of relatively novel areas of tort liability. This chapter is concerned with liability in tort for harassing someone else. After introducing this area of law in section 20.1, we look at the major statute in this area – the Protection from Harassment Act 1997 – in section 20.2. However, this statute has now been supplemented by provisions in the new Equality Act 2010, and those provisions are the subject of section 20.3.

20.1 THE BASICS

Until 1997, English law did not make it a tort – of and in itself – to harass someone else. Of course, someone who harassed someone else might commit another tort in the course of so doing. For example, harassing someone by constantly threatening them with imminent violence would amount to an assault; harassing someone with the result that they suffered a nervous breakdown would result in one committing the tort in *Wilkinson* v *Downton* (or, nowadays, negligence); harassing someone by continually calling them at home would amount to a private nuisance (so long as the person being called had an interest in the home where the calls were received).[1] But harassment *per se* did not amount to a tort. However, things are very different nowadays. We now have not one, but two sets of statutory provisions that make it a tort to harass someone else.

Section 1(1) of the Protection from Harassment Act 1997 provides that 'A person must not pursue a course of conduct – (a) which amounts to harassment of another, and (b) which he knows or ought to know amounts to harassment of the other.' That breach of this provision will amount to a tort is made clear by s 3(1) of the 1997 Act, which provides that an 'actual or apprehended breach . . . may be the subject of a claim in civil proceedings by the person who is or may be the victim of the course of conduct in question.'

The protection against being harassed provided by the 1997 Act has now been added to by the Equality Act 2010. The structure of this Act is quite complex. Part 2 of the Act lays out various forms of 'prohibited conduct'. Included in Part 2 of the Act is s 26, which defines a form of 'prohibited conduct' that it calls 'harassment'. Someone (A) will 'harass' someone else (B) if he engages in any of three specific forms of conduct, *and* that conduct has the purpose or effect of violating B's dignity, or has the purpose or effect of creating an 'intimidating, hostile, degrading, humiliating or offensive environment for B'. The three

---

[1] *Hunter* v *Canary Wharf Ltd* [1997] AC 655, disapproving *Khorasandjian* v *Bush* [1993] 1 QB 727 (which had ruled that an interest in the premises where the calls were received was not necessary to bring a claim in private nuisance against a defendant who was harassing you by continually calling you at home).

specific forms of conduct that might amount to 'harassment' under the 2010 Act are: (i) engaging in 'unwanted conduct' related to a 'protected characteristic'; (ii) engaging in 'unwanted conduct' of a 'sexual nature'; and (iii) treating someone less favourably because they have submitted to or rejected 'unwanted conduct' of a 'sexual nature or that is related to gender reassignment or sex'.

Parts 3–7 of the Act define who is not allowed to engage in the 'prohibited conduct' laid out in Part 2, and in what ways. So Part 3 deals with service providers; Part 4, people who deal with, or have an interest in, premises; Part 5, employers; Part 6, education providers; and Part 7, associations. So, for example, ss 101(4) and 102(3) of the Act (which belong to Part 7 of the Act) provide that an association must not 'harass' a member of the association, or someone seeking to be a member of the association, or an associate member of the association, or a guest of the association, or someone seeking to be a guest of the association.

Part 9 of the Act sets out what happens if a defendant breaches a provision laid out in Parts 3–7 of the Act, that required the defendant not to engage in conduct that is 'prohibited' under Part 2 of the Act. Section 119(2) of the Act provides that a defendant who 'harasses' someone else contrary to a provision in Parts 3, 4, 6 or 7 of the Act can be sued in tort in the county court by the victim of that harassment. That leaves workplace harassment (governed by Part 5 of the Act), which will be dealt with by an employment tribunal. Section 124(2) provides that in a case where a defendant violates a provision under Part 5 of the Act not to engage in conduct that is 'prohibited' under Part 2 of the Act, the tribunal may order the defendant to pay compensation to the victim of that conduct.

The next section will deal with the Protection from Harassment Act 1997. The third and final section will take a more detailed look at the Equality Act 2010.

20.2 PROTECTION FROM HARASSMENT ACT 1997

(1) *The basic provision*. Section 1(1) of the 1997 Act provides that:

A person must not pursue a course of conduct –

(a) which amounts to harassment of another, and
(b) which he knows or ought to know amounts to harassment of another.

Section 1(4) provides someone who engages in such a conduct with a defence if that conduct:

(a) ... was pursued for the purpose of preventing and detecting crime,
(b) ... was pursued under any enactment or rule of law or to comply with any condition or requirement imposed by any person under any enactment, or
(c) ... was reasonable [in the circumstances].

(2) *A crime and a tort*. Someone who violates s 1 of the 1997 Act will commit a crime (s 2) and a tort (s 3). This is unusual. Normally, the sort of crimes which make up the core of the criminal law involve committing a tort *with* the sort of *mens rea* (or fault element) that makes committing that tort worthy of punishment.[2] Not so here: anyone who commits the tort of harassment created by the 1997 Act will also commit a crime; no added fault element need be established for the crime of harassment to have been committed. This creates a difficulty for the courts. In interpreting the 1997 Act for the purposes of deciding

---

[2] See above, § 1.11.

whether a claimant can sue a defendant in tort for harassment, the courts have to keep one eye out for the fact that their decision will also have implications for whether people can be criminally punished for acting in the way the defendant did.

(3) *Threshold of seriousness.* It is for this reason that the courts have decided that a defendant's conduct has to pass a threshold of seriousness before he will be held to have committed the tort of harassment under the 1997 Act. Lord Nicholls held in *Majrowski* v *St Guy's and St Thomas's NHS Trust* (2007) that this threshold of seriousness would only be passed if the defendant's conduct was 'offensive and unacceptable':

> ... irritations, annoyances, even a measure of upset, arise at times in everybody's day-to-day dealings with other people. Courts are well able to recognise the boundary between conduct which is unattractive, even unreasonable, and conduct which is oppressive and unacceptable. To cross the boundary from the regrettable to the unacceptable the gravity of the misconduct must be of an order which would sustain criminal liability under s 2.[3]

This suggests that whether a defendant's conduct is regarded as 'offensive and unacceptable' should be determined according to whether it is worthy of punishment. But in the subsequent case of *Veakins* v *Kier Islington* (2009), the Court of Appeal made it clear that whether a defendant's conduct was 'offensive and unacceptable' should be decided independently of whether it was the sort of conduct that a prosecutor might want to prosecute.[4]

(4) *Alarm and distress.* Section 7(2) of the 1997 Act provides that 'References to harassing a person include alarming the person or causing the person distress.' The use of the word 'include' here seems to suggest that a defendant can be held liable under the 1997 Act for harassing someone even if his conduct did not cause the claimant to suffer alarm or distress. If you said that the people at the dinner *included* 'Andy and Mary', that would suggest that there were *more* people at the party than just Andy and Mary. Likewise, saying that 'References to harassing a person *include* alarming the person or causing the person distress' would suggest that there are more ways of harassing someone than just alarming them or causing them distress. In the previous edition of this book, we suggested that this was right: that there was no reason why A's treatment of B should not be held to amount to harassment just because B was merely annoyed or bored by A's treatment of her. (Though such treatment may not cross the threshold of seriousness required for it to amount to harassment under the 1997 Act.)

University of Oxford v *Broughton* (2008) *could* be taken as adopting a different view. In that case, the University of Oxford was seeking an injunction to prevent animal rights demonstrators (who have a long history of campaigning around the University because some members of the University carry out experiments on animals as part of their research) disrupting graduation ceremonies at the University's Sheldonian Theatre by standing outside the Theatre and chanting slogans. Treacy J denied the injunction on the basis that there was no evidence that people attending the graduation ceremonies were 'alarmed, distressed, threatened or frightened' by the demonstrators' chanting.[5]

The decision *could* be taken as holding that: (1) a defendant's treatment of a claimant *cannot* be held to amount to harassment unless it 'alarmed, distressed, threatened or frightened' the claimant. But – equally – Treacy J's judgment could be taken as holding that: (2) *in this case*, the defendants' behaviour did not cross the threshold of seriousness

---

[3] [2007] 1 AC 224, at [30].
[4] [2009] EWCA Civ 1288, at [15].
[5] [2008] EWHC 75 (QB), at [33].

required to amount to harassment, though *in another case* the defendant's conduct might cross the threshold of seriousness even if it did not 'alarm, distress, threaten or frighten' the claimant; or (3) *in this case*, the judge thought that granting an injunction against the defendants' chanting slogans would be an unacceptable restriction on their freedom of speech, given the lack of serious impact their speech was having on people attending the graduation ceremonies.

In support of reading (1) is the fact that Treacy J held that:

> In my judgment the claimants have failed to adduce evidence capable of showing that on balance these protests are sufficiently distressing or alarming as to amount to harassment. Not only is there an absence of evidence to show alarm, fear or distress, but the demeanour of those present at the ceremony did not appear to bear out the assertion that they were people undergoing harassment.[6]

This passage strongly links the idea of being alarmed and distressed with the idea of being harassed. Against reading (1), and in favour of either reading (2) or (3) is that immediately after saying this, Treacy J indicated that he thought it would be right to grant an injunction stopping the sustained chanting of slogans outside a workplace or examination hall where the noise of the chanting would intrude on 'persons attempting to achieve sustained intellectual concentration'.[7] This suggests that chanting slogans might amount to harassment even if the only effect of the chanting would be severe annoyance on the part of the people whose work was disrupted by it.

Rather than requiring that the defendant's treatment of the claimant *cause* her alarm or distress, Lord Phillips MR suggested in *Thomas v News Group Newspapers* (2001) that it had to be shown that the defendant's treatment of the claimant was 'calculated' to cause the claimant alarm or distress.[8] While this *dictum* has received subsequent endorsement,[9] this does not seem right. First, s 1(1) of the 1997 Act provides that someone can be held liable for harassment if he merely 'ought' to have known that his conduct amounted to harassment. A requirement that his conduct must have been 'calculated' to cause alarm or distress undermines this aspect of s 1(1). Secondly, if we take the example of stalking – which the 1997 Act was originally targeted at – it does not seem correct to say that stalking is always 'calculated' to cause alarm or distress. If *Dumped* starts following around his *Ex* everywhere, he might do so in the belief that she will eventually realise how much she loves him, and the fact that she might find his conduct alarming or distressing might never enter his head. But *Dumped*'s conduct here would undoubtedly amount to 'harassment', even if well-intentioned.

(5) *Course of conduct.* One of the key – and most difficult – requirements for establishing liability under the 1997 Act is that it has to be shown that the defendant engaged in a *course of conduct* that amounted to harassment of the claimant. This makes it obvious that a one-off act cannot amount to harassment under the 1997 Act.[10] (As we will see, the position is quite different under the Equality Act 2010.) But where a defendant has done X, and later on Y, when will his doing X and Y be held to amount to a *course of conduct*?

---

[6] [2008] EWHC 75 (QB), at [36].
[7] [2008] EWHC 75 (QB), at [37].
[8] [2001] EWCA Civ 1233, at [30].
[9] *R v Curtis* [2010] 1 WLR 2770, at [29].
[10] Though see *Kelly v DPP* [2003] Crim LR 43, where it was held that leaving three messages on someone's answering machine – all of which were listened to on the same occasion – could amount to a 'course of conduct' under the 1997 Act.

The fact that X and Y are the same, or similar, forms of behaviour will not suffice to turn doing X and doing Y into a course of conduct. For example, in *R v Hills* (2001), it was held that hitting one's live-in girlfriend once in April and then again in October could not be said to amount to a 'course of conduct'. And in *R v Curtis* (2010), the Court of Appeal held that the defendant's hitting, or threatening to hit, his live-in girlfriend on six different occasions in a nine month period of co-habitation did not amount to a 'course of conduct'.[11] So what will turn two or more separate actions into a course of conduct? The cases provide very little guidance on this issue, but it might be suggested that doing X, and later on Y, amounts to a 'course of conduct' if X and Y were each done with the intention of achieving a particular goal that was not achieved by doing X alone.

So if *Unhappy* is co-habiting with *Miserable*, and *Unhappy* starts screaming at *Miserable* one day with the sole object of making her feel bad that day, and then he does the same thing a month later, that is not a 'course of conduct'. The first screaming fit achieved its goal, and there is therefore no connection between the first and second screaming fits, even though each fit was aimed at the same goal. But if *Unhappy* starts screaming at *Miserable* one day with the object of making her so miserable that she will leave him – thus allowing him move in the new object of his affections – and, when he does not initially achieve this goal, he starts screaming at her again a week later in order to give her some more encouragement to leave him, his two screaming fits will amount to a 'course of conduct'. Similarly, if *Unhappy* resolves to make *Miserable*'s life a living hell, and starts screaming at her each day to make that day miserable for her. In such a case, each individual screaming fit is not undertaken for the sole purpose of making *Miserable* sad for the day – but for a concurrent, wider, purpose of making *Miserable* sad for a very long time: something which one isolated screaming fit is not enough to achieve. So in this case, again, the screaming fits, taken together, will amount to a 'course of conduct'.

In *Iqbal* v *Dean Manson Solicitors* (2011), the Court of Appeal emphasised that not every element in a 'course of conduct' need be experienced as harassment for that 'course of conduct' to amount to harassment. This is right: if *Dumped* rings *Ex* to ask her how things are going for her, she may think nothing of that call. But if he then rings her the following day to ask exactly the same question, the first phone call may then become part of a 'course of conduct' that amounts to harassment. (Whether it does – we would suggest – depends on what *Dumped*'s intentions were in ringing up *Ex* the first time. If the first call was just a friendly call, but it made *Dumped* so obsessed with speaking to *Ex* that he could not help calling the next day, the two calls will not form part of a 'course of conduct'. But if, before the first call, *Dumped* resolved to call *Ex* every day until she agreed to take him back, then obviously the two calls will amount to a 'course of conduct'.)

(6) *Scope of liability*. *Jones* v *Ruth* (2011) is now the leading case on the scope of a defendant's liability to pay damages to a claimant under the 1997 Act. The Court of Appeal ruled in that case that damages will be payable to the victim of harassment even in respect of harms that were not a foreseeable consequence of that harassment. The decision was based in part on the fact that foreseeability of harm is not mentioned in the Act as placing a limit on a defendant's liability to pay damages under the Act; but the fact that harassment involves some form of deliberate conduct also must have played a part in the Court's

---

[11] *Pratt* v *DPP* [2001] EWHC 483 (Admin) (holding that losing one's temper with one's wife once at Christmas and subsequently in March amounted to a 'course of conduct') always looked wrong and the result (though nothing said in the decision) in *Curtis* seems to confirm that it was wrong.

decision to adopt a rule on remoteness of damage for harassment cases that usually applies in fraud cases or other cases of deliberate malfeasance.

(7) *Defences.* As we have seen,[12] a defendant who has engaged in a course of conduct that amounts (as he knows or ought to know) to harassment may have a defence under s 1(4) to being sued for harassment. The question of when a newspaper that had run a campaign targeted at a particular individual could take advantage of the defence of 'reasonable conduct' under s 1(4)(c) was considered by the Court of Appeal in *Thomas* v *News Group Newspapers Ltd* (2001). Lord Phillips MR explained that a newspaper would only be held to have acted unreasonably in running a series of articles criticising a particular individual if the campaign amounted 'to an abuse of the freedom of the press which the pressing social needs of a democratic society require should be curbed'.[13]

As a test for determining when a newspaper will be held to have acted unreasonably in running a campaign against a particular individual, this is unsatisfactory: it is likely to have a 'chilling' effect on newspapers' legitimately exercising their right to freedom of expression. This is because the test is so vague that a newspaper which is thinking of running a campaign against an individual will find it hard to know whether it will or will not be held liable under the 1997 Act if it runs the campaign. As a result, it may well choose to 'pull' the campaign rather than run it and take the risk of being sued (or prosecuted) under the 1997 Act. It would have been more satisfactory if the Court of Appeal in *Thomas* had adopted the test set out in the second American Restatement of Torts for determining when the infliction of severe emotional distress will be tortious, and ruled that a newspaper which ran a series of articles targeted at a particular individual could only be held to have acted unreasonably in so doing if its running that campaign was so 'extreme and outrageous' that it went beyond 'all possible bounds of decency . . . and [was] utterly intolerable in a civilized society'.[14] (Which test would probably have been satisfied in the *Thomas* case anyway, given the newspaper's concession in that case that the articles were aggressive and inflammatory, and the Court of Appeal's finding that the articles were probably racist.)

(8) *Companies as defendants.* The defendant in the *Thomas* case was a company – News Group Newspapers Ltd. There is no problem with a company being sued personally under the 1997 Act, or on the basis that it is vicariously liable for an employee's committing the tort of harassment under the 1997 Act.

For a company to be held *personally* liable under the 1997 Act, it has to be shown that *the company* engaged in a course of conduct which it knew or ought to have known amounted to harassment. This creates a problem (already encountered earlier in this book)[15] about – whose acts should we look at in order to determine what the company did? In *Ferguson* v *British Gas* (2010), the Court of Appeal held that the traditional answer – we look at the actions of those who are the company's 'directing mind or will' – was not meant by Parliament to apply in the context of the 1997 Act. Instead, a company will be held to have engaged in a course of conduct that amounted to harassment if someone employed to act on behalf of the company (at whatever level) engaged, on behalf of the company, in a course of conduct that amounted to harassment.

---

[12] Above, § 20.2(1).
[13] [2001] EWCA Civ 1233, at [50]. It was conceded in *Thomas* that this test would be satisfied if a newspaper campaign was calculated to stir up racial hatred.
[14] Rest 2d, Torts, §46, Comment *d.*
[15] See above, § 8.6(C).

So far as *vicarious liability* is concerned, in *Majrowski* v *Guy's and St Thomas's NHS Trust* (2007), the House of Lords confirmed that, unless Parliament provides otherwise, the principle that an employer will be vicariously liable in respect of an employee's torts that were committed in the course of his employment applies just as much to statutory torts as it does to common law torts, such as negligence or assault. So an employer will be held vicariously liable if one of his employees commits the tort of harassment in relation to someone else in the course of his or her employment.[16]

(9) *Companies as claimants.* Section 7(2) of the 1997 Act makes it clear that only a natural person, and not a company, can claim to be a victim of harassment: 'References to a person, in the context of the harassment of a person, are references to a person who is an individual.' So in *Daiichi Pharmaceuticals UK Ltd* v *Stop Huntingdon Animal Cruelty* (2004), it was held that the claimant company could not seek an injunction against people attempting to disrupt the running of its business on the basis that *it* was the victim of harassment.

However, subsequent cases have made it clear that if a defendant is committing a breach of s 1(1A) of the 1997 Act by harassing two or more people (such as company employees), with the object of inducing the company not to do something that it is required to do or to do something that it is under no obligation to do, the company can seek to obtain an injunction against the defendant under s 3A of the 1997 Act.[17] Moreover, if a defendant has been convicted under the Act of harassing a particular individual or group of individuals, a company that was affected by the harassment can ask the courts to impose a restraining order on the defendant, for the company's protection, under s 5 of the 1997 Act, requiring the defendant not to re-offend.[18]

20.3 EQUALITY ACT 2010

A. Significance

Although the provisions on harassment in the Equality Act 2010 have a narrower focus than those in the Protection from Harassment Act 1997 – the 2010 Act only applies to certain defendants, while the 1997 Act applies to everyone – a critical advantage that the 2010 Act has over the 1997 Act is that under the 2010 Act, there is no requirement that a defendant have engaged in a 'course of conduct' before he will be found liable for harassment. So one-off acts involving unwelcome sexual conduct or suggestions might be actionable as harassment under the 2010 Act when they would not be under the 1997 Act.

B. The definition of harassment

Section 26 of the 2010 Act offers a two-part definition of when we can say that A has harassed B.

(1) The *first* part requires it to be shown that A has engaged in any of three different types of 'unwanted conduct':

---

[16] On when someone can be said to have committed a tort in the course of his or her employment, see below, §§ 37.5–37.6.
[17] *SmithKline Beecham* v *Avery* [2009] EWHC 1488 (QB). Note that breach of s 1(1A) will not give rise to a right to sue for damages (s 3 of the 1997 Act only applies to an actual or apprehended breach of s 1(1) of the Act: s 3(1)).
[18] *R* v *Buxton* [2011] 1 WLR 857.

(a) UC(1): unwanted conduct related to a 'relevant protected characteristic' (that is, age, disability, gender reassignment, race, religion or belief, sex, or sexual orientation);[19]

(b) UC(2): unwanted conduct of a sexual nature;[20]

(c) UC(3): unwanted conduct 'of a sexual nature or that is related to gender reassignment or sex' that results in A treating B less favourably because B rejected, or submitted to, that conduct.[21]

(2) The *second* part requires it to be shown that A's conduct had 'the purpose or effect' of:

(a) P/E(1): violating B's dignity; or

(b) P/E(2): creating 'an intimidating, hostile, degrading, humiliating or offensive environment for B.'[22]

If we separate out situations where A acted with purpose P(1) or P(2), and situations where A's actions had the effect of E(1) or E(2), that gives us four different situations where the *second* part will be satisfied. Combine that with the three different situations in which the *first* part will be satisfied, and we end up with no less than 12 different ways in which one person can harass another under the 2010 Act.[23]

C. Potential defendants

Having defined what amounts to harassment under the 2010 Act, Parts 3–7 of the Act set out (among other things) when someone will be required not to harass someone else under the Act:

(1) *Service-providers*. First up are service-providers (who are 'concerned with the provision of a service to the public or a section of the public (for payment or not)'.[24] Section 29(3) provides that a service-provider must not harass 'a person requiring the service' or 'a person to whom the service-provider provides the service'. Various provisions ensure that 'unwanted conduct' related to someone's being under 18, religion or belief, or sexual orientation will *not* amount to harassment for the purposes of this section.[25]

(2) *People exercising public functions*. Section 29(6) provides that 'A person must not, in exercise of a public function . . . do anything that constitutes harassment.' Again, 'unwanted conduct' related to someone's being under 18, religion or belief, or sexual orientation will not amount to harassment for the purposes of this section.[26]

(3) *People disposing of or managing premises*. Section 33(3) of the Act provides that 'A person who has the right to dispose of premises' (such as a landlord) must not 'in connection with anything done in relation to their occupation or disposal, harass' the

---

[19] Sections 26(1)(a) and (5).

[20] Section 26(2).

[21] Section 26(3).

[22] Section 26(1)(b).

[23] If we separate out the different protected characteristics listed under (1)(a) and the different forms of 'unwanted conduct' that can amount to harassment under (1)(c), we end up with 12 different situations where the *first* part of the 2010 Act's definition of harassment will be satisfied. Combining that with the four different situations where the *second* part will be satisfied gives us no less than 48 different ways one person can harass another under the 2010 Act.

[24] Section 29(1).

[25] Sections 28(1)(a), and 29(8).

[26] ibid.

occupier of those premises or someone applying for those premises. 'Unwanted conduct' related to age, religion or belief, or sexual orientation will *not* amount to harassment for the purposes of this section.[27] The same applies to someone who manages premises.[28]

(4) *Employers*. Employers are required not to harass their employees, or people who have applied to the employer for employment under s 40(1) of the 2010 Act.[29] Similar provisions apply to partnerships,[30] barristers,[31] qualification bodies,[32] trade organisations,[33] and local authorities.[34]

Unlike these other bodies, an *Employer* comes under a special duty – under s 40(2) of the 2010 Act – to take reasonable steps to ensure that *Employee* is not subjected to harassment by a third party in the course of *Employee*'s employment. (Which duty kicks in once *Employer* knows *Employee* has been subjected to such harassment on at least two occasions.)[35] This provision has created some disquiet among employers – who argue that such a duty places too onerous a burden on them to protect their employees from harassment – and is currently under review by the present government.

Employers are also under a duty – under s 108(2) – not to harass ex-employees if the harassment 'arises out of and is closely connected' to the fact that the ex-employee used to be employed by the employer.

(5) *Education-providers*. Under s 85(3), the body in charge of a school must not harass a pupil of the school, or someone who has applied to be a pupil of the school. 'Unwanted conduct' in relation to someone's age, gender reassignment, religion or belief, or sexual orientation will *not* count as harassment for the purposes of this section.[36] A similar provision applies to a body in charge of an institution of higher education, though without the saving proviso as to what will not count as harassment on the part of a school.[37]

(6) *Associations*. The relevant sections governing when associations are not allowed to harass someone have already been set out above.[38]

D. Remedies

As has already been explained above,[39] anyone who is the victim of harassment in breach of any of the duties set out above (other than in (4), above) may sue the person who breached

---

[27] Sections 32(1)(a), and 33(6).

[28] Section 35(2).

[29] Section 109(1) provides that anything done by an employee in the course of his employment is to be treated 'as also done by the employer'. So if an employee (A) harasses a fellow employee (B) in the course of A's employment by C, C will be held to have harassed B.

[30] Section 44(3) (firm not allowed to harass partner in relation to his position as partner, or to harass someone applying for position as partner).

[31] Section 47(3) (not allowed to harass pupil or tenant, or someone who has applied for pupillage or tenancy).

[32] Section 53(3) (not allowed to use their powers to confer that qualification to harass someone holding the qualification or applying for the qualification).

[33] Section 57(3) (not allowed to use their powers to determine membership of the organisation to harass a member or someone applying to become a member).

[34] Section 58(2) (not allowed to harass member of local authority in relation to his carrying out official business of the authority).

[35] Section 40(3).

[36] Sections 84(a), and 85(10).

[37] Section 91(5).

[38] See above, § 20.1.

[39] ibid.

that duty not to harass in tort, in the county court. Where someone suffers harassment in the workplace in breach of a duty set out in (4) above, the victim may seek redress in an employment tribunal, which will be empowered to grant him or her compensation as well as to make a declaration of rights and 'an appropriate recommendation'.[40]

---

[40] Section 124(2).

21 Invasion of privacy

21.1 The basics *589*

21.2 Wrongful disclosure of private information *591*

21.3 Private information *594*

21.4 Freedom of expression *605*

21.5 Striking the balance *611*

21.6 Fault elements *613*

21.7 Wrongfully obtaining access to private information *614*

21.8 Remedies *617*

21.9 Cases not involving wrongful disclosure or access *621*

Overview

In this chapter, we look at two situations where a claimant can sue a defendant in tort for invading his privacy: where the defendant has wrongfully disclosed private information about the claimant and where the defendant has wrongfully obtained access to private information about the claimant. We start with the former, since more cases have discussed it, and consequently it is easier to give an account of its key features. The latter is more difficult to describe because it has been developed so recently, and consequently many elements are uncertain. The remaining sections of the chapter discuss the remedies available for these torts – in particular, the special rules relating to injunctions – and the question of whether further torts should be developed to protect additional dimensions of privacy.

21.1 THE BASICS

English law recognises privacy as a value which underpins various rules of tort law (for instance, parts of the torts of trespass to land, private nuisance, defamation, and malicious falsehood). However, English law has not elevated the protection of privacy to the status of a legal principle from which judges can directly derive conditions of tortious liability.[1] To put the same point another way, English law has *not* recognised a *general* 'over-arching, all-embracing cause of action for "invasion of privacy"'.[2]

During the last two decades, however, and partly under the influence of the Human Rights Act 1998, the judges have developed a civil wrong which deals with a *specific* form of invasion of privacy, disclosing private information, and most of this chapter deals with this new civil wrong. More recently still the judges have gone further and started to develop another civil wrong to deal with a second *specific* form of invasion of privacy, wrongfully obtaining access to private information. In the penultimate section of this chapter we will

---

[1] In *Wainwright* v *Home Office* [2004] 2 AC 406, Lord Hoffmann suggested (at [31]–[33]) that English law should not give effect to a general principle such as 'the unjustified invasion of another's privacy is always actionable' because the detailed attention of a legislator would often be necessary in order to fashion conditions of liability and appropriate defences in the very different areas where the value of privacy might be invoked. He mentioned regulation of the use of images recorded by CCTV cameras as an example of an area where detailed legislation would be more appropriate than a judicial attempt to derive a solution from a broad principle.

[2] *Campbell* v *MGN Ltd* [2004] 2 AC 457, at [11] (per Lord Nicholls).

try to describe the key features of this developing wrong, which may allow the courts to impose liability on those who listen to other people's voicemail messages without consent. Then in the final section of this chapter we will discuss how far English law recognises civil wrongs which can deal with other specific forms of invasion of privacy, such as spying on people or drawing attention to them, and whether further innovations to deal with such matters should be encouraged.

The *tort of wrongful disclosure of private information* is regularly used to prevent newspapers from publishing salacious information about the sex lives of professional footballers and other celebrities. But its potential scope is wider than this, and it has also been invoked by other people who have attracted the attention of the media, such as victims of crime, people who suffer from unusual illnesses, and the children of famous parents. We will refer to this new civil wrong as the *tort of wrongful disclosure of private information*, though it is also common to see judges refer to it as *misuse of private information*.[3] In summary, the tort will be committed where:

(1) A discloses information about B to C
(2) that B reasonably expects to remain private,
(3) A knows, or ought to know this, and
(4) the circumstances are *not* such that A's being left free to disclose the information to C is more important than protecting B's interest in the information remaining private.

Thus if *Tabloid* publishes salacious details about a sexual encounter between *Rocker* and *Groupie* it is very likely that *Tabloid* will commit the tort of wrongful disclosure of private information in relation to *Rocker*. (Indeed, if *Groupie* is not the source of the information that *Tabloid* publishes then it is very likely that *Tabloid* will commit the tort of wrongful disclosure of private information in relation to *Groupie* as well.) We cannot say for certain that *Tabloid* will commit the tort in this situation without investigating the facts in more detail since in some circumstances *Tabloid* will be able to establish: (a) that the information is not private at all (perhaps because it has already been widely published by others); or (b) that publishing the information serves some public interest that is more important than the protection of *Rocker's* (and perhaps *Groupie's*) privacy. An example of such a public interest justification for publication would be if the story goes no further than necessary to correct a false impression that *Rocker* has conveyed to the public.

When we discuss the details of the law, below, we will see that in real life matters are often more complicated than this simple scenario, because where information is not just about a claimant but also about someone else – for instance, a member of his family – the court must also take into account any interest that this other person may have in the information remaining private. For example, if *Rocker* is married and has young children, then the court will not be able to decide whether *Tabloid's* publication is a tort until it has considered the effect of the publication on *Rocker's* wife and children. Where a court finds that the tort has been committed it can award damages, and may also grant an injunction prohibiting further publication of the private information, unless that would be a futile gesture. In practice, however, many of the cases dealt with by the courts involve claims for injunctions in advance of any widespread publication, where the claimant's aim is to prevent publication of private information rather than to seek redress afterwards.

---

[3] *Murray v Express Newspapers plc* [2009] Ch 481, at [24](ii) (per Sir Anthony Clarke MR) 'the essence of the tort is better encapsulated now as misuse of private information'.

The *tort of wrongfully obtaining access to private information* has been developed so recently that it is difficult to describe its scope with any certainty. So far the courts have said that A will commit this tort in relation to B if he intentionally obtains information by secretly looking at a document or copying it, knowing that B reasonably expects this information to be private, and the circumstances are not such that A's interest in obtaining the information is more important than the B's interest in it remaining private. Thus *Rocker*'s wife may commit the tort in relation to *Rocker* if she sneaks into his office and makes copies of financial documents that he has always kept hidden from her. It seems likely that the tort will extend beyond this to apply in a wider range of situations. For example, we expect that it will cover intentionally obtaining information by secretly listening to recordings of private messages or conversations, or copying them. It is also possible, though this is far less clear, that it will be stretched to cover eavesdropping and surveillance. The remedies that a court can award where this tort has been committed are likely to be the same as those for *wrongful disclosure*, except that courts may also make mandatory orders to return or destroy copies of private documents.

21.2 WRONGFUL DISCLOSURE OF PRIVATE INFORMATION

The case of *Campbell v MGN* (2004)[4] concerned the publication in the *Daily Mirror* of the information that Naomi Campbell was a drug addict, was seeking treatment through Narcotics Anonymous, some details of her treatment, and a photograph of her at a place where a Narcotics Anonymous meeting took place. She conceded that the *Daily Mirror* was entitled to disclose some of this information to the world, in particular that she was a drug addict and was seeking treatment. But she contended that the defendant had committed a tort in relation to her by publishing the other details and the photograph. The House of Lords unanimously confirmed that someone (A) will commit a tort[5] in relation to someone else (B) if he unjustifiably discloses to a third person (C) information which A knows or ought to know is private information about B. By a bare majority of three to two the House of Lords held that the *Daily Mirror* had committed this tort in publishing the details of Naomi Campbell's treatment and the photograph.

A. The independence of the new tort

Most of the judges involved in developing this new tort *said* that they were not actually creating a new tort but were *extending* the long-established equitable wrong of breach of confidence. But we think that it is artificial to pretend that all that has happened is that breach of confidence 'has evolved'. The traditional features of breach of confidence are no longer decisive in cases involving the wrongful disclosure of *private* information. For instance, the 'cause of action has now firmly shaken off the limiting constraint of the need for an initial confidential relationship'[6] and the narrow limits on the defences to the equitable wrong do not apply in cases protecting privacy.[7] Moreover, when judges are asked

---

[4] Reported at [2004] 2 AC 457; and referred to henceforth as '*Campbell*'.
[5] Strictly speaking only one of their Lordships refers to the wrong as a 'tort' (Lord Nicholls at [14]). But in the next subsection we explain why we think that the wrong should be acknowledged as a tort. Any reader who does not accept this explanation can instead treat the first part of this chapter as dealing with *part of* an equitable wrong for pragmatic reasons. See above, § 1.9.
[6] *Campbell*, at [14] (per Lord Nicholls).
[7] *Theakston v MGN* [2002] EMLR 137, at [66].

to settle disputes about features of the new wrong they are generally referred to human rights law and analogies with torts like libel and slander rather than to any principles developed by the Courts of Equity. Thus we think that it makes sense to treat the civil wrong committed by the *Daily Mirror* in *Campbell* as a *new and independent tort* – the tort of wrongful disclosure of private information.[8]

One advantage of treating wrongful disclosure of private information as an independent tort is that it avoids confusion with the *original* form of the equitable wrong of breach of confidence, which continues to exist. The *original* form of breach of confidence deals with situations where abstract information, which need not be private information – such as a trade secret – is disclosed to someone on the condition that it will remain confidential.[9] Some lawyers might argue, however, that treating the two wrongs as *independent* tends to exaggerate the differences between them. Indeed in *Imerman v Tchenguiz* (2011) the Court of Appeal stated that 'the law should be developed consistently and coherently in both privacy and "old fashioned confidence" cases, even if they sometimes have different features.'[10] Moreover, in practice cases often arise where claimants rely on both wrongs simultaneously. This makes it important to consider how judges treat cases where the information that the defendant has disclosed is arguably both private information within the scope of the new tort *and* information that the defendant was told or discovered in the course of a confidential relationship with the claimant. The answer is that in such cases a claimant gains an advantage by demonstrating that a duty of confidence in the *original* form attaches to the information since: (i) if the information is *also* private the original duty of confidence will add weight to the claim that it is appropriate to restrict a defendant's right to free expression,[11] and (ii) if the information is *not* private then the claimant will only be able to win if she can demonstrate a duty of confidence in the original form.

B. Article 8 of the ECHR

The most important influence on the development of the new tort has been and remains the right to privacy contained in Article 8 of the European Convention on Human Rights (ECHR). Although s 6 of the Human Rights Act 1998 does not impose a duty on *private individuals* to act compatibly with Convention rights,[12] it does impose such a duty on public authorities, including the courts. Further, the European Court of Human Rights has held that to comply with Article 8, States must do more than merely ensure that public

---

[8] Although the majority of the House of Lords in *Campbell* refused to treat wrongful disclosure of private information as an independent tort – and this refusal will have significant practical consequences, particularly in the field of remedies – two subsequent Court of Appeal decisions have referred to 'the rechristening of the tort as misuse of private information' as if Lord Nicholls's opinion (*Campbell*, at [14]) on this point was orthodox: *McKennitt v Ash* [2008] QB 73, at [8], *Lord Browne of Madingley v Associated Newspapers Ltd* [2008] QB 103, at [21]–[22].

[9] In *Douglas v Hello! Ltd (No 3)* [2008] 1 AC 1, a majority of the House of Lords accepted that a private event could be organised in such a way as to make the information that would be disclosed by a *photographic* image of the event into a commercial secret, which could be protected by the wrong of breach of confidence, and this could clearly cover what a particular person *looked like during the event*. The protection provided by this aspect of the wrong of breach of confidence is *separate* from the duty not to publish photographic images which disclose *private* information. The latter duty is discussed below, § 21.2.

[10] *Imerman v Tchenguiz* [2011] 2 WLR 592, at [67]. This case is discussed in detail below, § 21.7.

[11] For instance, when considering the unauthorised publication of Prince Charles's travel journals the Court of Appeal stated that '[b]oth the nature of the information and of the relationship of confidence under which it was received weigh heavily in the balance in favour of Prince Charles': *HRH Prince of Wales v Associated Newspapers Ltd* [2008] Ch 57, at [71].

[12] See above, § 3.3.

authorities avoid acting so as to violate privacy *themselves*: States must also assist private individuals who want to preserve their privacy against other private individuals. As the Court expressed the point in *Von Hannover* v *Germany* (2005):

> although the object of Article 8 is essentially that of protecting the individual against arbitrary interference by the public authorities, it does not merely compel the State to abstain from such interference: in addition to this primarily negative undertaking, there may be positive obligations inherent in an effective respect for private or family life. These obligations may involve the adoption of measures designed to secure respect for private life even in the sphere of the relations of individuals between themselves.[13]

Clearly one way of assisting private individuals to preserve their privacy against other private individuals is by recognising a new tort, and this is what the English courts have done. Indeed they have modelled the new tort on the assumption that 'the values underlying Articles 8 and 10 are not confined to disputes between individuals and public authorities'.[14] It is important to note, however, that the new tort is *limited* to protecting claimants against *wrongful disclosure of private information* in situations where the balance between Articles 8 and 10 means that such protection is justifiable:[15] the courts have *not* simply made *all* behaviour what would amount to a violation of Article 8 if done by a State into a tort if done by a private individual. This point needs emphasis because Article 8 protects privacy in many contexts well beyond the boundaries of the new tort. For example, Article 8 has been relied on to compel States to recognise the new genders of those who have undergone gender-reassignment[16] and to prohibit States from retaining DNA samples taken from innocent people.[17]

C. The structure of the new tort

The new tort has an unusual structure because it exists at the meeting point of *two* human rights: *Teller's* disclosure to *Reporter* of private information about *Striker may* infringe *Striker's* right to privacy, but a restriction on *Teller* making such a disclosure *may* infringe the right to free expression of *Teller*, *Reporter* and the public generally.[18] Neither of these human rights is pre-eminent, so 'the proportionality of interfering with one has to be balanced against the proportionality of restricting the other'.[19]

The term 'balancing' is shorthand for a more complex process, and one which requires an 'intense focus' on the particular facts of the case.[20] In order to impose tort liability only when that is appropriate given the competing rights at stake, the court is likely to find it convenient to proceed by asking the following questions:

---

[13] (2005) 40 EHRR 1, at [57].
[14] *Campbell*, at [18] (per Lord Nicholls). Article 10 is, of course, the provision which defines the right to free expression in the ECHR. See also at [50] (per Lord Hoffmann), 'I can see no logical ground for saying that a person should have less protection against a private individual than he would have against the state for the publication of personal information for which there is no justification.'
[15] The degree of correspondence is strong. Buxton LJ expressed the relationship as follows in *McKennitt* v *Ash* [2008] QB 73, at [11]: 'Those articles are now not merely of persuasive or parallel effect but . . . are the very content of the domestic tort that the English court has to enforce.'
[16] *Goodwin* v *United Kingdom* (2002) 35 EHRR 18.
[17] *S and Marper* v *United Kingdom* (2008) 48 EHRR 50.
[18] It is important to remember that both *publisher* and *recipient* have a right to free expression.
[19] *Campbell*, at [140] (per Baroness Hale). See also [113] (per Lord Hope) and [167] (per Lord Carswell).
[20] *Re S (A Child) (Identification: Restrictions on Publication)* [2005] 1 AC 593, at [17] (per Lord Steyn).

(1) Is the information about B which A has disclosed to C sufficiently *private* to come within the potential ambit of the tort?

(2) If the information is sufficiently private, how important is it to protect this aspect of B's privacy?

(3) Was A's disclosure of the information to C *expression* within the ambit of Article 10?

(4) If so, how important is it not to restrict this sort of expression?[21]

(5) Using the answers to (2) and (4), will making A liable amount to a *proportionate* restriction on A's and C's freedom of expression in order to protect B's privacy *or* will not holding A liable constitute a *proportionate* limit on the protection of B's privacy in order preserve freedom of expression?

It *may* also sometimes be necessary to ask a further question:

(6) Did A know, or ought A to have known, that the information was sufficiently private?

We have expressed these six steps in the terms that will be appropriate if a court is dealing with a case where the information has already been published. In practice, however, cases are often brought to try to *prevent* widespread publication, and consequently a court will often have to amend questions (1) and (3) so that they ask about possible future disclosure. For example, question (1) will become: (1) Is the information about B which A *is about to* disclose to C sufficiently *private* to come within the potential ambit of the tort? Moreover, in a case brought before widespread publication, question (6) – about what the defendant knew or ought to have known – will become irrelevant: if a pre-publication claim is successful then this will mean – unless the defendant is unaware of the proceedings[22] – that the defendant *knows* that the information is private *before* publication.

In many cases, of course, it will not be necessary to go through all these steps. Often it will be obvious that *if* the information about B is sufficiently *private* to come within the potential ambit of the tort – question (1) – then B ought to win the case, since no significant value associated with free expression will be served by disclosing the information to C. (Indeed, media organisations sometimes make no attempt to establish a justification for publishing the information *but* still refuse to concede the case because they want to report that they have been 'gagged'.) And in other cases it will be obvious that *if* the information about B advances the public interest in the way that A claims then A ought to win the case because of the importance of freedom to express such information.

21.3 PRIVATE INFORMATION

What sorts of information are sufficiently private to come within the ambit of the tort?

A. The reasonable expectation test

The basic test is whether B had a 'reasonable expectation of privacy' in relation to the information that A disclosed to C.[23] Some simple points can be made about this test.

---

[21] Importance must be assessed considering the interests of both *publisher* and *recipient*.

[22] In some circumstances a claim can be brought against an unidentified person; for example, where the claimants do not know who has been offering to provide private information to the newspapers: *X & Y v Persons Unknown* [2006] EWHC 2783 (QB).

[23] *Campbell*, at [21] (per Lord Nicholls), [85] (per Lord Hope), [134] (per Baroness Hale).

(1) *A reasonable expectation of privacy is not inconsistent with limited disclosure.* People can have a 'reasonable expectation of privacy' with regard to information even if it is not totally secret: what matters is whether they can reasonably expect to retain some control over its dissemination.[24] Thus, when *Poorly* goes to *Doctor* and describes his symptoms he will be aware that medical professionals usually record such information and sometimes share it with colleagues and assistants, but it would nonetheless usually be reasonable for *Poorly* to expect to retain control over whether the information is disclosed to his wife, his employer, or a journalist. In practice most[25] cases are likely to involve information which the claimant has permitted someone else to discover or has disclosed to a limited circle of family, friends or colleagues. Thus the relevant expectation is as to whether B ought to be able to control in what circumstances, if ever, the information will be released more widely.

(2) *A reasonable expectation of privacy cannot exist where information is already 'in the public domain'.* Where information has already been widely or indiscriminately disclosed B will usually be unable to claim that she has a reasonable expectation of controlling its further publication. In cases where B seeks to prevent further publication of information that would normally be private but which has become widely known, the judge will consider if any useful purpose could be served by preventing further publication.[26] Identifying the point at which prevention will be pointless is not straightforward. In *KGM v News Group Newspapers Ltd* (2010), Eady J suggested that the point could certainly be reached *before* information had been 'widely published in a newspaper', but that the mere availability of information on the internet would not necessarily establish that it was in 'the public domain'.[27]

Where private information is *available* to the public, but not straightforward to access and not widely known, it is unlikely to be held to be 'in the public domain'. For example, in *KGM v News Group Newspapers Ltd* (2010) the fact that the relevant information could be found in the claimant's daughter's wedding certificate, and this document was available to the public, did not mean that it was no longer *private* information: there is a gulf between information in an obscure 'public record' and information which is in the 'public domain', so it may be reasonable for people to expect that *some* information in public records will not be published on the front pages of tabloid newspapers.

While most information will be 'in the public domain' if it has previously been widely or indiscriminately published, the Court of Appeal has suggested that the position may be different with regard to the information in a photograph. In *Douglas* v *Hello! Ltd (No 3)* (2006) the Court of Appeal explained:

> In so far as a photograph does more than convey information and intrudes on privacy by enabling the viewer to focus on intimate personal detail, there will be a fresh intrusion of privacy when each

---

[24] In *Campbell*, at [51], Lord Hoffmann said that the new tort 'focuses upon the protection of human autonomy and dignity – *the right to control the dissemination of information about one's private life* and the right to the esteem and respect of other people' (emphasis added).

[25] Exceptional cases can be imagined; for instance, where *Snapper* takes a photograph of *Tripper* falling over in the street and sells it to *Tabloid* this may disclose information that *nobody* previously *knew*: exactly what *Tripper* looks like when he's falling over.

[26] In *Browne of Madingley (Lord)* v *Associated Newspapers Ltd* [2008] QB 103, at [61], the Court of Appeal identified 'an important distinction between information which is made available to a person's circle of friends or work colleagues and information which is widely published in a newspaper.' The Court cited Lord Goff's opinion in *Att-Gen* v *Guardian Newspapers (No 2)* [1990] 1 AC 109, 282, that the key question is whether the information has become 'so generally accessible that, in all the circumstances, it cannot be regarded as confidential'.

[27] [2010] EWHC 3145 (QB), at [22] and [30]. Eady J's judgment was upheld on appeal without further discussion of this point: [2011] EWCA Civ 808.

additional viewer sees the photograph and even when one who has seen a previous publication of the photograph is confronted by a fresh publication of it. To take an example, if a film star were photographed, with the aid of a telephoto lens, lying naked by her private swimming pool, we question whether widespread publication of the photograph by a popular newspaper would provide a defence to a legal challenge to repeated publication on the ground that the information was in the public domain.[28]

This said, when a photograph or film has been widely published on the internet so many copies of it may be available that it would be pointless for a court to grant an injunction prohibiting further publication: for example, Eady J ruled that an injunction before trial would be futile in *Mosley v News Group Newspapers Ltd* (2008), where edited footage of a sado-masochistic sex session involving the claimant had been viewed on the internet more than 1.4 million times before the injunction was sought.[29]

(3) *'The law of privacy is not intended for the protection of the unduly sensitive'.*[30] 'The question is what a reasonable person of ordinary sensibilities would feel if she was placed in the same position as the claimant and faced with the same publicity'.[31] So a claim cannot be based on the publication by *Tabloid* of information about *Diva* that a reasonable person would not be worried about maintaining any degree of control over. For example, if *Diva* is inexplicably sensitive about other people finding out the date of her birthday this will not mean that *Tabloid* will commit a tort if it discloses the date to its readers.

The ordinary sensibilities rule is qualified to an extent, however, by the further rule that the reasonableness of the expectation of privacy as to information about a particular feature is judged from the perspective of people who share the same feature. Thus in *Campbell* the question whether it was reasonable for Naomi Campbell to expect that the details of her treatment should be kept private was assessed from the perspective of a reasonable drug addict receiving treatment.[32]

(4) *Problems with the reasonable expectation test.* One problem with the reasonable expectation test is that it is unclear what the *nature* of the expectation must be. It is difficult to conclude that it must be a *factual* expectation because very few celebrities could claim that they *in fact expect* tabloid newspapers not to publish salacious details obtained from former lovers or photographs of them in embarrassing poses. Thus it seems that when judges ask about whether B had a 'reasonable expectation of privacy' they are really asking whether B *ought to be able to* expect privacy. But this, of course, is often a controversial question. It also raises a second problem, which is that reasonable people have different views as to what should remain private. For example, if *Hedonist* puts photographs of himself at a party up on his Facebook page, having set the privacy setting so that only his friends can see them, then is it reasonable for him to expect that the photographs will not be shown to a prospective employer, or published in a newspaper when he publishes a novel two years later? Similarly, in the New Zealand case of *Andrews v Television New Zealand Ltd* (2009) the claimants were involved in a car accident in which their car left the road, and some months later the defendant broadcast film of them while they were trapped in the vehicle awaiting rescue as part of a television series called 'Fire Fighters':

---

[28] *Douglas v Hello! Ltd (No 3)* [2006] QB 125, at [105].
[29] [2008] EWHC 687 (QB). This reference is to the judgment in the claimant's unsuccessful claim for an interim injunction. His subsequent claim for damages is discussed below at § 21.8.
[30] *Campbell*, at [94] (per Lord Hope).
[31] *Campbell*, at [99] (per Lord Hope).
[32] *Campbell*, at [98] (per Lord Hope), [136] (per Baroness Hale).

would an English court have held that they could reasonably expect such pictures not to be published?[33] We do not think that there is any easy solution to the problems caused by uncertain and inconsistent expectations. But it is important to avoid complacently assuming that the reasonable expectation test is easy to apply.

B. Factors relevant to whether a claimant can establish a reasonable expectation

An analysis of the cases suggests that courts treat the following six factors as relevant when considering whether a claimant had a 'reasonable expectation of privacy':

(1) *The nature of the information.* Certain types of information, for example information relating to sexuality or health,[34] can be straightforwardly classified as private as a result of their *private nature*.

(2) *The form in which the information was kept.* Certain ways of storing information, such as in a private diary or a confidential file, add weight to a claimant's assertion that it was reasonable for him to expect that the contents would not be generally published.

(3) *The relationship between the claimant and the person who discloses the information.* There is clearly a stronger expectation that information discovered in the course of a relationship will be kept private when the parties are priest and penitent, or doctor and patient, than when they are storekeeper and customer, or journalist and celebrity.[35] In other words, the *nature of the relationship* which led to B holding information about A can affect whether A has a reasonable expectation of privacy with respect to that information.

(4) *How the information was obtained.* If the information had to be obtained by subterfuge or trickery this will add weight to the argument that it was private.[36]

(5) *The claimant's previous behaviour.* A claimant's previous behaviour may indicate that he has waived any right to keep information about some aspect of his life private, and a claimant cannot reasonably expect people to refrain from publishing information about him if he has led them to believe that he is content for such information to be published.[37]

---

[33] The judge, Allan J, held that the claimants could establish that they had a reasonable expectation of privacy, but eventually gave judgment for the defendants because of another point.

[34] The category of 'sexuality' includes information about a person's gender identification, sexual orientation and sexual life: *PG v United Kingdom* [2001] ECHR 546, at [56]. The category 'health' includes 'information about a person's health and treatment for ill-health', *Campbell* at [145] (per Baroness Hale), though *trivial matters* will not be protected: ibid, at [157] (per Baroness Hale), 'the privacy interest in the fact that a public figure has a cold or a broken leg is unlikely to be strong enough to justify restricting the press's freedom to report it'.

[35] For example, in *McKennitt v Ash* [2008] QB 73 at [14]–[18], [24], the Court of Appeal thought that the relevant information *might* have been private in *nature* anyway, but held that the conclusion that it should be protected from disclosure became irresistible once account was taken of the fact that the information had only become available to the defendant in the course of a close friendship between herself and the claimant.

[36] Lord Hoffmann suggested, in *Campbell* at [75], that it might be a violation of privacy to publish a photograph obtained by intrusion because to do so demonstrated that apparently private space was not inviolate.

[37] The Court of Appeal in *McKennitt v Ash* [2008] QB 73, at [35]–[36] suggested that *Woodward v Hutchins* [1977] 1 WLR 760 might be a rare example of such a doctrine being applied: Bridge LJ, at 765, explained the outcome of that case as turning on the principle that 'those who seek and welcome publicity of every kind bearing upon their private lives so long as it shows them in a favourable light are in no position to complain of the invasion of their privacy by publicity that shows them in an unfavourable light'. But in *McKennitt* Buxton LJ described as 'cruelly insensitive' (at [54]) the suggestion that Loreena McKennitt's controlled disclosures about the effect on her of her fiancé's drowning prevented a claim based on the defendant's publication of a detailed description of her pitifully grief-stricken reaction.

More often, however, a claimant's previous disclosures about some aspect of his life may establish that it is in the public interest for further information about the same aspect of his life to be published.

(6) *The likely consequences of the disclosure.*[38] Privacy is closely linked with autonomy and liberty. Thus information is more likely to be classified as private if its disclosure would be likely to restrict a person's ability to live the life that he chooses. For example, the European Court of Human Rights has emphasised that one of the reasons why information that a person is HIV-positive is private is that publication of such information 'may dramatically affect his or her private and family life, as well as the individual's social and employment situation, by exposing that person to opprobrium and the risk of ostracism.'[39]

Real cases usually require a combination of these factors to be assessed, and it is often difficult to identify any particular factor as *decisive*. Thus a claimant's reasonable expectation is often established by 'an interdependent amalgam of circumstances'.[40] For instance, when considering whether the Prince of Wales had a reasonable expectation of privacy with respect to a journal recording his impressions on a visit to Hong Kong, the Court of Appeal stated, 'It is not easy in this case, as in many others, when concluding that information is private to identify the extent to which this is because of the nature of the information, the form in which it is conveyed and the fact that the person disclosing it was in a confidential relationship with the person to whom it relates.'[41]

C. The substantial offence test

Because of the difficulty of applying the reasonable expectation test in borderline cases some judges have advocated the use of a test based on a reasonable person's reaction to the publication. For instance, in *Campbell* Lord Hope stated that 'the broad test is whether disclosure of the information about the individual ("A") would give substantial offence to A, assuming that A was placed in similar circumstances and was a person of ordinary sensibilities'.[42] This echoes a suggestion made by Gleeson CJ in the High Court of Australia that a 'useful practical test' is whether the 'disclosure or observation of information or conduct would be highly offensive to a reasonable person of ordinary sensibilities'.[43]

Other judges, however, have criticised this test. For instance, in *Campbell* Lord Nicholls was concerned that the 'highly offensive' test raised the threshold of liability higher than the 'reasonable expectation' test, and that a person's reaction to a publication might reflect factors relevant to the later stages of an inquiry into whether a defendant could be held liable for disclosing private information (for instance, whether the publication was justified by free speech values) and not just whether the information was potentially private.[44] A further problem with a test based on a reasonable person's reaction to the publication is that such a test is unlikely to work when the information is about someone who does not

---

[38] This factor is more likely to be significant when weighing the *importance* of respecting the claimant's expectation of privacy (see below, § 21.3(G)). But on occasion the likely consequences may establish the expectation, for example, where a defendant publishes which branch of a supermarket a celebrity claimant shops in each Thursday night or that the claimant has won the lottery.

[39] *Z v Finland* (1997) 25 EHRR 371, at [95]–[96]; *Armonienė v Lithuania* (2009) 48 EHRR 53, at [40].

[40] *HRH Prince of Wales v Associated Newspapers Ltd* [2008] Ch 57, at [36] (per Lord Phillips CJ).

[41] ibid.

[42] *Campbell*, at [92].

[43] *Australian Broadcasting Corporation v Lenah Game Meats Pty Ltd* (2001) 208 CLR 199, at [42].

[44] *Campbell*, at [22]. See also [135] (per Baroness Hale).

understand the significance of privacy, such as a disturbed adult[45] or a very young child.[46] These criticisms mean that the substantial offence test is not a reliable guide to the sorts of information potentially protected by the tort, though some judges may continue to use it *alongside* the reasonable expectation test.

D. Applications of the reasonable expectation test

We will now describe how the basic test has been applied in some specific contexts.

(1) *Sexual information.* In *TSE* v *News Group Newspapers Ltd* (2011) Tugendhat J stated that

> For decades both the English Courts and the ECHR have recognised a reasonable expectation of privacy in relation to sexual relationships; sexual conduct being '*an essentially private manifestation of the human personality*'[47]

and granted an injunction prohibiting the defendant from publishing the fact that two claimants had been involved in an adulterous affair.

By contrast, in *Donald* v *Ntuli* (2011) the Court of Appeal upheld Eady J's decision that the *mere fact* that the defendant had had a sexual relationship with the claimant was probably not private information, particularly since the relationship had not been wholly clandestine, but that the claimant could reasonably expect that the defendant would not disclose 'any intimate, personal or sexually explicit details about the relationship'.[48] And in *Goodwin* v *News Group Newspapers Ltd* (2011) Tugendhat J held that neither party to an affair between the then Sir Fred Goodwin, the former Chief Executive of the Royal Bank of Scotland, and another senior employee of the bank was likely to establish that they had a reasonable expectation of privacy with regard to the *bare* fact of their relationship. This was largely because they ought to have expected their work colleagues to want to know about such a relationship *and* the wider public to want to know of it because of the important role Sir Fred played in public life.[49] Thus it seems that sexual information – particularly the 'salacious details' of any encounter – will generally be private information, but that on occasion a claimant will be unable to establish that he or she could reasonably expect no publicity to be given to the bare fact of a sexual relationship.

(2) *Relationship cases.* One person can be told, or otherwise learn, information about another in the course of lots of different types of relationship; such as in the course of employment, friendship, a casual sexual relationship, or a marriage or civil partnership. We noted in the previous section that the nature of such a relationship will be an important factor when deciding whether one party can reasonably expect the other not to publish

---

[45] In *T* v *BBC* [2007] EWHC 1683 (QB) the claimant was an 18 year old who was incapable of giving informed consent, and whose reactions to appearing in a television documentary were likely to be unpredictable and inconsistent, but on balance negative.

[46] In *Murray* v *Express Newspapers plc* [2009] Ch 481 the claimant, the son of the author J.K. Rowling, was two years old at the time of the relevant publication.

[47] *TSE* v *News Group Newspapers Ltd* [2011] EWHC 1308 (QB), at [24]. The quoted words, which the judge put in italics, are from the European Court of Human Rights' judgment in *Dudgeon* v *UK* (1981) 4 EHRR 149, at [52] and [60].

[48] English law seems to have changed on this issue: Five years earlier the Court of Appeal observed, in *Douglas* v *Hello! Ltd (No 3)* [2006] QB 125, at [73], that 'to date the English courts appear to have taken a less generous view of the protection that the individual can reasonably expect in respect of his or her sexual activities than has the Strasbourg court'.

[49] *Goodwin* v *News Group Newspapers Ltd* [2011] EWHC 1437 (QB), at [102]–[104].

information about the relationship, or learned in the course of it. At one end of the spectrum of relationships are those where the expectation is easiest to establish, such as marriages and civil partnerships. Relationships where there is an express contractual agreement not to publish any information are also likely to be at the protective end of the spectrum. In *Campbell* v *Frisbee* (2003), the Court of Appeal stated that it was at least arguable 'that a duty of confidentiality that has been expressly assumed under contract carries more weight, when balanced against the restriction of the right of freedom of expression, than a duty of confidentiality that is not buttressed by express agreement'.[50] At the less protective end of the spectrum are relationships which are more transitory or less exclusive. In such circumstances a person may still be able to establish a reasonable expectation of privacy, but such a conclusion will tend to depend on the *nature of the information* rather than the *nature of the relationship*.

The interplay between the nature of the relationship and the nature of the information can be seen in *Lord Browne of Madingley* v *Associated Newspapers Ltd* (2008). Here the claim was brought by Lord Browne, the group chief executive of BP plc, to restrain the defendants from publishing information received from Jeff Chevalier, who had been Lord Browne's homosexual partner for four years. Eady J, at first instance, held that the relationship was such that Lord Browne was entitled to expect that any comments he made to Jeff Chevalier about his business colleagues, and the content of conversations at dinner parties and the like, would remain private. But Eady J concluded, and the Court of Appeal upheld this, that Lord Browne could not expect the fact that he had provided Jeff Chevalier with assistance from BP plc's staff and resources, or the mere fact of the relationship, or the fact that he had discussed BP plc's business with his lover, to remain private.

(3) *Photographs.* If a person goes to a public place then she clearly accepts that other people will be able to look at her and thereby obtain certain information about her. But a photograph taken of the person may capture more information than even a careful observer would perceive, will preserve that information in a potentially permanent form, and can be used to communicate more information more efficiently than mere words easily could. For instance, if *Husband* wanted to let *Friend* know about a dress that *Wife* wore to a child's birthday party (in order to criticise her for choosing to wear such a dress) then showing *Friend* a photograph of *Wife* wearing the dress would communicate more information about the dress more quickly and more convincingly than trying to describe it verbally.

If observers can see a person at a particular moment then how can she claim to have a reasonable expectation of privacy as to what would appear on a photograph taken at that moment? In *Campbell* Lord Hoffmann suggested that:

> The famous and even the not so famous who go out in public must accept that they may be photographed without their consent, just as they may be observed by others without their consent.[51]

But he thought that they could nonetheless object to some photographs taken in public being made available to the world at large.[52] He pointed to the case of *Peck* v *United Kingdom* (2003), where it was held that a person walking in the street with a knife could

---

[50] [2003] ICR 141, at [22].

[51] *Campbell*, at [73]. In *Murray* v *Express Newspapers plc* [2007] EWHC 1908 (Ch), at [37], Patten J stated that 'A photograph taken by a member of the public which remains the property of that person and is at most shown to family and friends does not infringe any right of privacy because it does not lead to any real public exposure of the events portrayed.' Although Patten J's judgment was overturned on appeal, [2009] Ch 481, this opinion was not discussed by the Court of Appeal.

[52] *Campbell*, at [74]–[75]. See also at [122] (per Lord Hope).

not object to being filmed by CCTV but could object to that film being broadcast on television.

So which photographs of people in public places is there a duty not to publish? In *Campbell* the House of Lords clearly suggested that it was not reasonable for a person to expect an innocuous photograph taken in public not to be published. This is because the information contained in such an image is unlikely to be the sort of information that a reasonable person would be worried about maintaining any degree of control over. Baroness Hale, for instance, stated that there was nothing essentially private about what Naomi Campbell 'looks like if and when she pops out to the shops for a bottle of milk'.[53] But where a photograph contains information that a reasonable person would want to maintain control over – for instance what the person looks like when in extreme distress or when eating messy food – then publication of a photograph of such an event might violate the person's privacy even though looking at the person during the event would not. Lord Hoffmann stated that:

> the widespread publication of a photograph of someone which reveals him to be in a situation of humiliation or severe embarrassment, even if taken in a public place, may be an infringement of the privacy of his personal information.[54]

The European Court of Human Rights, however, has expressed a different view as to whether the publication of innocuous photographs taken in public can breach Article 8. In *Von Hannover* v *Germany* (2005), the Court held that Germany had violated Article 8 by permitting the publication in German magazines of photographs showing Princess Caroline of Monaco in the course of everyday activities such as visiting a market and riding a bicycle. An influential factor was that Princess Caroline had been subject to near-continuous observation by press photographers and it is easy to see how the innocuous nature of each photograph, judged individually, did not reflect the effect of such a campaign on her privacy. The Court's response was to treat the publication of *each* photograph, no matter how innocuous, as potentially violating Article 8: 'In the present case there is no doubt that the publication by various German magazines of photos of the applicant in her daily life either on her own or with other people falls within the scope of her private life.'[55]

In *Murray* v *Express Newspapers plc* (2007) and (2009), the English courts had to confront the apparent inconsistency between *Campbell* and *Von Hannover* when faced with a claim arising from a photographic agency supplying a newspaper with a photograph taken in public of David, the 19-month-old son of the author J.K. Rowling, being pushed in his pushchair by his parents. At first instance Patten J struck out David's claim as unarguable on the basis that even after *Von Hannover* 'there remains an area of innocuous conduct in a public place which does not raise a reasonable expectation of privacy.'[56] The Court of Appeal, however, restored David's claim because they thought that it was arguable that he had a reasonable expectation that he would 'not be targeted in order to obtain

---

[53] *Campbell*, at [154]. This was applied in *John* v *Associated Newspapers Ltd* [2006] EWHC 1611 (QB), when Eady J refused to grant an interim injunction to prevent the defendant from publishing a photograph of Sir Elton John in the street, wearing a tracksuit and baseball cap, opening his front gate.

[54] *Campbell*, at [76].

[55] (2005) 40 EHRR 1, at [53].

[56] [2007] EWHC 1908 (Ch), at [68]. A similar claim, involving a photograph of the 18-month-old twins of a television personality was rejected by the New Zealand Court of Appeal: *Hosking* v *Runting* [2005] 1 NZLR 1. In New Zealand, however, the publication of private facts is only actionable when 'the publicity given to those private facts . . . would be considered highly offensive to an objective and reasonable person.'

photographs in a public place for publication which the person who took or procured the taking of the photographs knew would be objected to on behalf of the child.'[57]

We agree with the conclusion that photographs of the children of famous people should not usually be published. But it is necessary to make three points about the Court of Appeal's reasoning in *Murray* (2009).

First, it is not easy to understand how the fact that a person is 'targeted' can transform an image of an ordinary occurrence in a public place into '*private information*'. Where the only way in which a defendant can obtain a photograph is by lying in wait and then taking it surreptitiously this tends to emphasise that the subject (or his parents) was not consenting to publication, but a lack of consent cannot in itself be enough to establish a reasonable expectation of privacy.

Secondly, the Court of Appeal thought that a child of famous parents should have the same entitlement to privacy as a child of 'ordinary parents', and then reasoned from the premise that 'a child of "ordinary" parents could reasonably expect that the press would not target him and publish photographs of him.'[58] We agree that the law should protect *all* children against publication of private information, but think that reference to the expectations of 'ordinary' parents is unhelpful here because such 'ordinary' parents would not expect their toddlers to be targeted by the paparazzi principally because the photographs would be *of no interest* to newspaper readers.

Thirdly, we think that the Court of Appeal could have provided a convincing explanation for the conclusion that publication of mundane photographs of *all* children should be treated differently from photographs of adults by focusing on the different likely *consequences*. For instance, it might be thought that most adult celebrities are *capable of coping* with the irritation of photographs being published of them performing mundane tasks in public. (This does not, of course, in itself determine that they *ought* to be expected to cope with such behaviour without redress, particularly when the marketability of such innocuous photographs generates conditions in which a person may be subjected to continuous surveillance.) But, by contrast, the effects on *any* child's life of the widespread publication of mundane photographs would be much more severe.

What if a photograph is taken of someone in a private place? Clearly such photographs will often contain information that a reasonable person might want to maintain control over and will thus infringe the subject's reasonable expectation of privacy. But, in *Campbell*, Lord Hoffmann went further than the other Lords and stated that:

> the publication of a photograph taken by intrusion into a private place (for example, by a long distance lens) may in itself be [an infringement of the privacy of personal information], even if there is nothing embarrassing about the picture itself.[59]

No doubt most people would describe being spied on in a private place with a long-distance lens as an invasion of privacy regardless of whether the spy obtained and then published any information that a reasonable person would want to maintain control over. But this demonstrates that the essence of such a violation is not the publication of the information obtained. Thus we think that Lord Hoffmann's example involves intrusion – a different form of invasion of privacy from wrongful disclosure of private information – and the law would be more coherent if it treated it separately.[60]

---

[57] [2009] Ch 481, at [57].
[58] [2009] Ch 481, at [46].
[59] *Campbell*, at [76].
[60] We discuss whether the courts should develop a tort of invasion of privacy *by intrusion* below, § 21.9(A).

E. Iniquity

The case law governing the 'old-fashioned' wrong of breach of confidence took the view that there could be no protection for 'iniquity'.[61] But it seems that a claimant can reasonably expect *some* 'iniquitous behaviour' to remain private, and that consequently a defendant will have to justify publishing such information.

Thus in *Campbell* (2004) Lord Hoffmann said that 'use of drugs' was a matter in respect of which 'even a public figure would ordinarily be entitled to privacy'.[62] And in *CC* v *AB* (2006),[63] and several subsequent cases,[64] it has been held that there is no general rule that an adulterer cannot obtain an injunction to restrain the publication of matters relating to his adulterous relationship. In *Mosley* v *News Group Newspapers Ltd* (2008), a case involving sado-masochistic sex, Eady J questioned whether the 'iniquity' exception could ever be applied 'to sexual activity, fetishist or otherwise, conducted between consenting adults in private'.[65] By contrast, in *X* v *Y* (2004) Mummery LJ held that a person's sexual activity in a transport café lavatory 'did not take place in his private life nor was it within the scope of application of the right to respect for it'[66] apparently because it amounted to a criminal offence.

Even where a person's behaviour is so iniquitous that he could have no immediate expectation of privacy with regard to it the experience of other jurisdictions warns against the stark position that such a person can *never*, even after the passage of time, develop a right to prevent further publication of details of his behaviour.[67] With the passage of time a person's legitimate interest in maintaining the benefit of successful rehabilitation may come to outweigh any possible public benefit to be gained by further publication, and in such circumstances a person may reasonably expect his past iniquities not to be re-published. The question whether a claimant who had been convicted of forging a will more than twenty years previously could reasonably expect this fact to be kept private in future was raised in *KJO* v *XIM* (2011), but Eady J left it unanswered since the matter was not suitable for summary judgment.

F. Companies

Should a company be able to sue for invasion of privacy if, for instance, information about its private operations is published? The simplest way of answering this question would be to say 'yes' – tort law applies the same rules to claimants whether they are human beings or artificial legal persons.[68] But if we look deeper then it seems that many of the reasons for creating a privacy tort, such as protecting human dignity and facilitating love, friendship and community, do not apply to artificial legal persons.

---

[61] *Gartside* v *Outram* (1857) 26 LJ Ch 113.

[62] *Campbell*, at [36].

[63] [2006] EWHC 3083 (QB), at [30].

[64] See, for example, *ETK* v *News Group Newspapers Ltd* [2011] EWCA Civ 439.

[65] *Mosley* v *News Group Newspapers Ltd* [2008] EWHC 1777 (QB), at [106].

[66] [2004] EWCA Civ 662, at [53]. See also [69]–[71] (per Dyson LJ). Brooke LJ dissented on this point.

[67] *Melvin* v *Reid*, 121 Cal App 285 (1931), is a famous example from California: the claimant had been a prostitute and had been acquitted of shooting her pimp and lover in 1918, but had subsequently married and been accepted into 'respectable society'. She successfully sued when her past was revealed in a popular movie. (The movie, called 'The Red Kimona' on its credits, but 'The Red Kimomo' on posters, was successful in the United States but banned by the British Board of Film Censors.)

[68] The 'old-fashioned' wrong of breach of confidence clearly protects the interests of companies in preserving their industrial secrets and the like.

In *R* v *Broadcasting Standards Commission, ex p BBC* (2001), the Court of Appeal held that the Commission was entitled to uphold a complaint by Dixons (a company) that the BBC had infringed its privacy unjustifiably by carrying out covert filming in one of its stores. Lord Woolf MR pointed out that companies could engage in private activities which should be protected from unwarranted intrusion, such as board meetings. But both he and Hale LJ drew attention to the fact that Article 8 of the ECHR did not refer to a 'right to privacy' in general but only to a 'right to respect for his private and family life, his home and correspondence'. Thus the fact that Dixons succeeded in this case may not be a good guide to the scope of the new tort because its development has been strongly tied to Article 8.

Extending the new tort to protect companies would also be inconsistent with the opinion of three members of the High Court of Australia who expressly held in *Australian Broadcasting Corporation* v *Lenah Game Meats* (2001) that Australia's emergent tort of invasion of privacy was for 'the benefit of natural, not artificial, persons'.[69] Similarly, companies are not protected under the United States Rest 2d, Torts, §652I: 'an action for invasion of privacy can be maintained only by a living individual whose privacy is invaded'.[70]

By contrast, others have argued that companies should be able to sue for invasions of privacy because they can sue for libel and slander, and allowing them to sue for invasions of privacy will prevent them from seeking to distort other torts to prevent unwanted publications about their private activities. A further reason for allowing companies to sue may be that their interests in keeping information from being published will often be hard to separate from the privacy interests of their employees and clients. For instance, in *Green Corns Ltd* v *Claverley Group Ltd* (2005), a claimant company sought to prevent the defendant from publishing the addresses of properties being used by the claimant company to house disturbed children and their carers and the weight of the privacy claim was treated as an aggregation of the weight of the claims that could have been brought by the company, the children and the carers.

G. Measuring the importance of protecting privacy

The importance of protecting people against the disclosure of particular private information can be measured by reflecting on the reasons which are commonly given for such protection: to protect human dignity[71] and personality,[72] and to facilitate the formation of *special* relationships such as love, friendship and community.[73] Generally, the significance of an affront to dignity and personality can be measured by considering how *intimate* the information was. Similarly, it can be assessed how far *control* over the distribution of such information is important in forming particular *special relationships*. An alternative approach, which can be used alongside the first, ranks the importance of privacy interests

---

[69] (2001) 208 CLR 199, at [132].

[70] American Law Institute (1965), emphasis added. It seems that the protection offered by Art 8 of the ECHR does *not* end with an individual's death: see *Plon* v *France* (58148/00), 18 May 2004, unreported.

[71] See, for example, Bloustein 1964, 1003, 'The man who is compelled to live every minute of his life among others and whose every need and thought, desire, fancy or gratification is subject to public scrutiny, has been deprived of his individuality and human dignity.'

[72] *Von Hannover* v *Germany* (2005) 40 EHRR 1, at [50]: 'the guarantee afforded by Article 8 of the Convention is primarily intended to ensure the development, without outside interference, of the personality of each individual in his relations with other human beings.'

[73] See, for example, Fried 1968; also Feldman 1997.

by estimating the *intensity of the offence* that a reasonable person in the claimant's position might be expected to suffer on the publication of such information. And a further relevant factor is the likelihood that the publication will cause *other significant harm* to the claimant beyond distress. For example, in *Campbell* the majority in the House of Lords attached particular weight to the fact that publication of the details of Naomi Campbell's treatment might cause *harm* by disrupting her treatment.[74]

Where the publication of the information will have effects on the private and family lives of people other than the immediate claimant these effects must be considered by the judge when measuring the importance of preserving privacy. Thus in *ETK v News Group Newspapers Ltd* (2011) where the anonymous claimant, a man who worked in the entertainment industry, sought to prevent publication of the fact that he had been involved in an adulterous affair with *X*, a woman who worked in the entertainment industry, the Court of Appeal held that the judge should have given weight to the privacy interests of the claimant's wife and children and *X*, as well as the claimant's interest.[75] Indeed, Ward LJ suggested that the factor which 'tipped the balance' and made it appropriate to grant an injunction was the interests of the children in avoiding 'playground ridicule' and in the preservation of the stability of the marriage while their parents pursued a reconciliation.[76]

21.4 FREEDOM OF EXPRESSION

A. What counts as expression?

Although it is *logical* to ask whether the defendant's disclosure of the information amounted to 'expression' within the ambit of Article 10 we might expect it to be rare for the answer to be 'no'.

One unusual situation where the defendant's behaviour may not count as 'expression' is where the disclosure is *unintentional*, such as where *Medic* permits *Tabloid* to obtain private information about *Starlet* by forgetfully leaving *Starlet*'s medical records on a train. But this example raises the awkward question of what is meant by 'disclosure' in the context of the new tort: all the cases considered so far in England have involved deliberate publication so the courts have not provided any guidance as to whether the tort covers accidental or careless disclosures.[77]

ASG v GSA (2009) raised the question whether a person could rely on her free expression rights to resist an injunction prohibiting publication where there was evidence that she was actually seeking to blackmail the claimant into paying her *not* to publish the story.[78] In that case the Court of Appeal granted a temporary injunction without reaching a final conclusion on the point, but in a subsequent case at first instance Sharp J accepted that 'the expression rights of blackmailers are extremely weak (if they are engaged at all).'[79]

---

[74] *Campbell*, at [98] and [119] (per Lord Hope), [130] and [165] (per Baroness Hale), [169] (per Lord Carswell).
[75] [2011] EWCA Civ 439, at [14].
[76] [2011] EWCA Civ 439, at [17]–[22].
[77] A parallel could be drawn with the legal rules on what counts as 'publication' for the purposes of the tort of defamation (see above, § 19.4). But these rules might be thought only to be tolerable from a free expression perspective because of the existence of the special statutory defence for 'innocent dissemination' and the 'offer to make amends' procedure (see above, § 19.12), and these provisions do not extend to liability for invasion of privacy.
[78] *ASG v GSA* [2009] EWCA Civ 1574, at [26].
[79] *DFT v TFD* [2010] EWHC 2335 (QB), at [23].

B. Measuring the importance of preserving freedom of expression

Some types of expression are more important to protect than others. Thus in *Campbell* Baroness Hale said:

> There are undoubtedly different types of speech, just as there are different types of private information, some of which are more deserving of protection in a democratic society than others. Top of the list is political speech. The free exchange of information and ideas on matters relevant to the organisation of the economic, social and political life of the country is crucial to any democracy ... This includes revealing information about public figures, especially those in elective office, which would otherwise be private but is relevant to their participation in public life. Intellectual and educational speech and expression are also important in a democracy, not least because they enable the development of the individuals' potential to play a full part in society and in our democratic life. Artistic speech and expression is important for similar reasons, in fostering both individual originality and creativity and the free-thinking and dynamic society we so much value.[80]

Expression which is not political, intellectual, educational or artistic, such as mere gossip, is still protected to an extent, because it may play an important role in preserving social networks and in making newspapers financially viable. But it will be far easier to justify a restriction on the publication of mere gossip[81] to protect privacy than a restriction on political debate.

(1) *Public interest.* An influential factor in measuring the importance of preserving free expression is whether it was in the public interest for the information to be disclosed to the people to whom the defendant disclosed it. But 'public interest' is obviously a broad concept which cannot be *defined* with any precision. Indeed judges usually avoid attempting definitions: in *A v B* (2003) the Court of Appeal simply stated that 'in the majority of situations whether the public interest is involved or not will be obvious' and that where it is not obvious the factor is 'unlikely to be decisive'.[82]

The Press Complaints Commission's Code of Practice (2011) provides a more helpful catalogue of aspects of the public interest which are regularly raised:

1. The public interest includes, but is not confined to:
   - (i)   Detecting or exposing crime or serious impropriety.
   - (ii) Protecting public health and safety.
   - (iii) Preventing the public from being misled by an action or statement of an individual or organisation.

2. There is a public interest in freedom of expression itself.

The recognition of a public interest in the *exposure of crime* has encouraged some defendants to put forward ingenious arguments about the scope of the criminal law. For example, in *CDE v MGN Ltd* (2010) the claimants, a man who often appeared on television and his wife, sought an injunction to prevent the *Sunday Mirror* from publishing

---

[80] *Campbell*, at [148].

[81] In *Von Hannover* v *Germany* (2005) 40 EHRR 1, the European Court of Human Rights treated (at [65]) the preservation of freedom to publish photographs of Princess Caroline of Monaco's daily activities as relatively unimportant when 'the sole purpose was to satisfy the curiosity of a particular readership regarding the details of the applicant's private life, [and the photographs] cannot be deemed to contribute to any debate of general interest to society despite the applicant being known to the public'.

[82] [2003] QB 195, at [11](viii).

the details of a relationship between the man and another woman that was conducted by means of telephone, texts, emails and tweets. The defendants apparently argued that their story would expose a crime, since by sending intimate images of himself by email the male claimant may have committed the offence of *improper use of a public electronic communications network* under s 127 of the Communications Act 2003. Eady J, however, was unimpressed and noted that even if a crime had technically been committed 'it would not follow that the public interest in exposing this would be such as to justify the infringement of their privacy involved in newspaper exposure'.[83] In support he referred to his own judgment in *Mosley* v *News Group Newspapers Ltd* (2008), where he had held that it would not be logical to recognise a public interest in *exposing* a crime if it was so minor that it would not be in the public interest for there to be a prosecution.[84]

The aspect of *Mosley* v *News Group Newspapers Ltd* (2008) that caused most controversy was the judge's refusal to treat the case as one where the defendant could rely on the public interest in exposing 'serious impropriety'. The defendants argued that it was in the public interest to expose the claimant's participation in a sado-masochistic sex session because his behaviour was 'immoral, depraved and to an extent adulterous'.[85] Eady J, however, held that a belief that such behaviour was 'depraved' did not justify telling the world that someone had behaved in that way. He drew an important distinction:

> Everyone is naturally entitled to espouse moral or religious beliefs to the effect that certain types of sexual behaviour are wrong or demeaning to those participating. That does not mean that they are entitled to hound those who practise them or to detract from their right to live life as they choose.[86]

This opinion was not shared by Paul Dacre, Editor-in-Chief, of the *Daily Mail*:

> Since time immemorial public shaming has been a vital element in defending the parameters of what are considered acceptable standards of social behaviour, helping ensure that citizens – rich and poor – adhere to them for the good of the greater community. For hundreds of years, the press has played a vital role in that process. It has the freedom to identify those who have offended public standards of decency – the very standards its readers believe in – and hold the transgressors up to public condemnation.[87]

No doubt different views can be held as to whether 'public shaming' by tabloid newspapers ever advances the public interest. We expect, however, that other judges will follow the approach of Eady J and hold that 'the fact . . . that someone's tastes are unconventional or "perverted", does not give the media *carte blanche*.'[88]

(2) *Public figures.* In *A* v *B* (2003), Lord Woolf CJ suggested that public figures must accept a greater degree of disclosure of information than ordinary individuals even when that disclosure is not justified by the public interest:

---

[83] [2010] EWHC 3308 (QB), at [46].

[84] [2008] EWHC 1777 (QB), at [117]: 'It would hardly be appropriate to clutter up the courts with cases of spanking between consenting adults taking place in private property and without disturbing the neighbours. That would plainly not be in the public interest. It would not be logical, therefore, to pray in aid the public interest when seeking to justify hidden cameras and worldwide coverage.'

[85] [2008] EWHC 1777 (QB), at [124]. The defendants also argued that their publication was in the public interest because the sex session had a 'Nazi theme', but Eady J held that it was simply untrue that the session had any such theme.

[86] [2008] EWHC 1777 (QB), at [127].

[87] Paul Dacre, Speech to the Society of Editors, 9 November 2008.

[88] [2008] EWHC 1777 (QB), at [128].

because of his public position [a public figure] must expect and accept that his actions will be more closely scrutinised by the media . . . Whether you have courted publicity or not you may be a legitimate subject of public attention. If you have courted public attention then you have less ground to object to the intrusion which follows. In many of these situations it would be overstating the position to say that there is a public interest in the information being published. It would be more accurate to say that the public have an understandable and so a legitimate interest in being told the information.[89]

In *Campbell* the Court of Appeal analysed this passage and insisted that Lord Woolf CJ was not intending to say that once a person was identified as a legitimate subject of public attention then *any information of any type* about that person could be published. While it is clearly not the law that all public figures must expect the details of their private lives to be published, two narrower propositions made by Lord Woolf CJ must be assessed: that the public will have 'an understandable and so legitimate interest' where: (a) the information contradicts or clarifies information that the claimant has published about the same aspect of his life; or (b) the information is about disreputable behaviour and the claimant is 'a role model whose conduct could well be emulated by others'.

With regard to (a), subsequent cases have confirmed Lord Woolf CJ's statement in *A v B* (2003) that, 'where a public figure chooses to make untrue pronouncements about his or her private life, the press will normally be entitled to put the record straight.'[90] This is also listed as a category of public interest in the Press Complaints Commission's Code of Practice (2011).

But with regard to (b), there are two grounds for doubting the fairness of any rule which suggests that there is a special public interest in learning about the disreputable behaviour of 'role models'.

First, such a rule would be harsh when applied to persons who have never *projected* themselves as positive 'role models' for others. For example, in *A v B*, Lord Woolf CJ suggested that *all* footballers were 'role models' whether they liked this or not. Where a person has *chosen* to enter a particular sphere of life where he might expect to be treated as a 'role model', for instance by becoming a vicar or a teacher, *perhaps* he can be fairly taken to have consented to information about particular aspects of his life being published. But where a person has become a 'role model' unintentionally, for instance by saving a drowning dog or making a scientific discovery, a consequential diminution of his privacy seems harder to justify.

Secondly, the logic behind the rule is opaque: If 'role models' can influence young people then why should the law make it easier for the public to learn about their disreputable behaviour? In *Campbell* the Court of Appeal stated that it did 'not see why it should necessarily be in the public interest that an individual who has been adopted as a role model, without seeking this distinction, should be demonstrated to have feet of clay'.[91] The force of such criticisms,[92] coupled with the approach adopted by the European Court

---

[89] [2003] QB 195, at [11](xii).
[90] [2003] QB 195, at [43]. See, for example, *Campbell*, at [58] (per Lord Hoffmann).
[91] [2003] QB 633, at [41]. See also *Campbell*, at [151] (per Baroness Hale).
[92] Lord Justice Stephen Sedley was particularly cutting about this line of reasoning in his 2006 Blackstone Lecture 'Sex, Lies and Video-surveillance': 'As for the customary claim, which the court seems to have accepted, that the revelations served the high purpose of exposing the flaws in a young persons' role model, one has to wonder what our moral custodians imagine goes on in young people's minds. Possibly – just possibly – a certain number of boys want to grow up playing football like Garry Flitcroft. Is the revelation in the family's Sunday paper that he has been sleeping with a lap dancer going to make them switch to, let us say, Wayne Rooney as their preferred role model? Or is it conceivably going to suggest to them that the great thing about being a professional footballer, or any other kind of media star, is that you can sleep with just about anyone?'

of Human Rights in *Von Hannover* (2005), which we discuss in the next section, has fortunately led to the disappearance of the 'role model doctrine' from recent judicial accounts of the tort.

(3) *Contribution to a debate of general interest.* We have already mentioned that *Von Hannover v Germany* (2005) arose out of the publication in German magazines of photographs of Princess Caroline of Monaco depicting her in the course of ordinary tasks like going shopping and playing tennis. The German courts had concluded that such publications were not wrongful because the public has a legitimate interest in being allowed to judge whether the personal behaviour of a 'figure of contemporary society *par excellence*' ('*absolute Person der Zeitgeschichte*') convincingly tallies with his behaviour during official engagements. But the European Court of Human Rights held that the application of this doctrine to the case of Princess Caroline had left her with insufficient protection for her right to privacy when 'the interest of the general public and the press is based solely on her membership of a reigning family whereas she herself does not exercise any official functions'.[93] The Court insisted that 'the public does not have a legitimate interest in knowing where the applicant is and how she behaves generally in her private life even if she appears in places that cannot always be described as secluded and despite the fact that she is well known to the public'[94] and suggested that 'the decisive factor in balancing the protection of private life against freedom of expression should lie in the contribution that the published photos and articles make to a debate of general interest.'[95] Subsequent English cases, such as *Mosley v News Group Newspapers* (2008) have echoed this final phrase, and elevated whether a publication made a 'contribution to a debate of public interest' into a pivotal issue.[96] Unsurprisingly, Eady J concluded in that case that the many thousands of people who watched the edited footage of the claimant's sado-masochistic encounter on the defendant's website were not 'prompted by a desire to participate in a "debate of general interest" of the kind contemplated in *Von Hannover*.'[97]

(4) *Autobiography.* In some cases the person who wishes to publish the information argues that the court should attach weight to her freedom 'to tell her story'. This freedom will be given substantial weight where disclosure is important for self-development or to preserve reputation, perhaps by 'setting the record straight'. But the freedom will be given significantly less weight if it seems that the defendant is primarily interested in being paid, either for telling a story or for remaining silent, or wants to disclose information to inflict pain by way of revenge.[98] The weight accorded to the freedom will also vary according to how far the defendant's story is *about* the defendant. Thus the Court of Appeal in *McKennitt v Ash* (2008) held that the freedom had to give way to the claimant's privacy interest where the story to be told involved mainly private facts about the claimant's life that the defendant

---

[93] *Von Hannover*, at [72].
[94] *Von Hannover*, at [77].
[95] *Von Hannover*, at [76].
[96] [2008] EWHC 1777 (QB), at [131].
[97] [2008] EWHC 1777 (QB), at [132].
[98] In *CC v AB* [2006] EWHC 3083 (QB), at [35]–[36], Eady J drew a distinction between a husband disclosing that his wife had been involved in an adulterous affair with the defendant when 'discussing his wife's adultery with a close friend, or with members of the family, or (if he needed to do so) with a family doctor, counsellor or social worker, or with his lawyers' and selling the information to the tabloids for money or revenge. In *Donald v Ntuli* [2011] 1 WLR 294 the Court of Appeal regarded the defendant's claim that she needed to tell the story of her relationship with Howard Donald, a member of 'Take That', for reasons of self-development and personal autonomy as 'an ex post facto dignification', at [23].

had learnt or observed while in a relationship with the claimant rather than genuinely 'shared' experiences'.[99]

(5) *Errors.* How should a court approach a case where the reason that a defendant thought that it was justifiable to publish private information was based on an error of fact? Consider, for example, the **Deceptive Appearances Problem**:

> Tabloid received an anonymous tip-off that Politico, a government minister who had made speeches extolling the virtue of 'traditional marriage and monogamy', regularly invited a prostitute to his family home while his wife was away. To confirm the story Tabloid employed a photographer to wait outside Politico's family home, and this photographer later took pictures of Politico's wife leaving the house in the early evening and a younger woman arriving an hour later. The younger woman was also photographed leaving the house at midnight, and Tabloid's inquiries establish that she is eighteen years old and employed by an 'escort agency'. Tabloid then published a story under the headline 'Politico's Teenage Vice Girl Shame' which accused Politico of making use of the sexual services of a teenage prostitute. Tabloid believed that it was in the public interest to expose Politico's hypocrisy. But when he read the story Politico called a press conference and disclosed that the younger woman is in fact his daughter, and that she visited him while his wife, her mother, was away because his wife strongly disapproves of her job.

No doubt *Politico* could sue *Tabloid* for libel in this situation. But his prompt rebuttal of *Tabloid's* accusation may mean that his reputation has not been significantly damaged. Nonetheless, *Politico*, his wife, and daughter, may all be distressed by the way in which *Tabloid* has revealed aspects of their family affairs that they could reasonably expect to remain private. So if *Politico* sues *Tabloid* for wrongful disclosure of private information how will a court deal with *Tabloid's* claim that it was in the public interest to disclose the information in order to expose hypocrisy?

In *Mosley* v *News Group Newspapers* (2008) Eady J was clear that the defendants could not avoid liability for publishing private information about the claimant's participation in a sado-masochistic sex session merely by establishing that they honestly believed that the events had a Nazi-theme and involved mockery of victims of the Holocaust. Indeed he held that 'the public interest is to be determined solely by the court *ex post facto*',[100] and that consequently his finding that there was no Nazi-theme or mockery was decisive. He acknowledged, however, that in the tort of libel the doctrine associated with *Reynolds* v *Times Newspapers Ltd* (2001) allows a defendant to avoid liability for publishing a *false* and *defamatory* story on a matter of public interest if the error was consistent with 'responsible journalism',[101] and that there was an argument for drawing an analogy between libel and the wrongful disclosure tort. In *Mosley* (2008) it was unnecessary to reach a final view on this matter since Eady J found that the defendants' judgment about the nature of the sex session 'was not based on enquiries or analysis consistent with "responsible journalism"' but 'made in a manner that could be characterised, at least, as "casual" and "cavalier"'.[102]

Returning to the Deceptive Appearances Problem, we can see that it requires a decision as to whether a defendant can rely on an aspect of the public interest when he has made an error, but an error that is consistent with 'responsible journalism'. The most convincing

---

[99] [2008] QB 73, at [50]–[52], relying on findings reported at [31]–[32].
[100] [2008] EWHC 1777 (QB), at [171].
[101] We discuss this doctrine above, at § 19.11.
[102] [2008] EWHC 1777 (QB), at [170]. The terms 'casual' and 'cavalier' are quoted from the account of the *libel* defence in *Jameel (Mohammed)* v *Wall Street Journal Sprl* [2007] 1 AC 359, at [33] (per Lord Bingham).

argument against allowing this invokes the impossibility of restoring privacy: where false defamatory material has been published about *Politico* – the province of libel – his reputation can be restored by general recognition that it was false, but nothing can undo the fact that after *Tabloid's* story many people will know private details about his family life. On balance, however, we think that this concern can be addressed by ensuring that the relevant standard of 'responsible journalism' reflects the risk of irreparable damage to privacy: responsible journalists should take special care before acting in a way that will permanently destroy privacy. Thus we would encourage the courts to develop a doctrine analogous to that associated with *Reynolds*, but which recognises the fragility of privacy. But this said, we think that *Tabloid* would struggle to establish that its error was consistent with 'responsible journalism' if it had made no attempt before publication to confirm the story with *Politico*.[103]

21.5 STRIKING THE BALANCE

Suppose that A has disclosed to C information about B that is sufficiently private *potentially* to attract the protection of the tort considered here. How will the courts strike the balance between the desire, on the one hand, to protect B's privacy and the desire, on the other hand, not to limit disproportionately A's freedom of expression? It is hard to give any useful *general* guidance on this issue: there must always be an 'intense focus' on the particular facts of the case.[104] However, two points can be made.

(1) *The dual perspective approach.* In deciding which right is to prevail in this case – A's right to freedom of expression or B's right to privacy – a court must take account of the fact that *neither* right should be subjected to a disproportionate restriction. So if the court is considering making A liable – thus restricting A's freedom of expression in order to protect B's privacy – it must ask if the restriction it is considering imposing on A's right to freedom of expression is rational, fair, not arbitrary and the minimum restriction necessary to protect B's right to privacy. In order to decide whether this is the case it will often be helpful for the court *also* to consider the case from the converse perspective; that is, to consider – if B's privacy is *denied* protection in order to protect A's right to freedom of expression, will this restriction on the protection of B's right to privacy be rational, fair, not arbitrary and the minimum restriction necessary to protect A's right to freedom of expression? The reason for this is that since one right must prevail, and neither right should be subject to any disproportionate restriction, the court will *only* be able to hold A *liable* if doing so amounts to a proportionate restriction on A's right to freedom of expression in order to protect B's privacy; while, at the same time, it will *only* be able to hold that A is *not* liable if turning down B's claim amounts to a proportionate limit on the protection of B's right to privacy in order to protect A's right to freedom of expression. Adopting a dual perspective approach allows the court to compare the *relative merits* of these two possible conclusions.[105]

---

[103] In *Mosley v United Kingdom* [2011] ECHR 774, the European Court of Human Rights ruled that it was not necessary for the United Kingdom to enact a law requiring newspapers to inform the subjects of their stories about them in advance of publication. Max Mosley, who had successfully obtained compensation from News Group Newspapers Ltd for having disclosed private information about his participation in a sado-masochistic sex session, argued that such prior notification was required so that if the publication was unjustifiable an injunction could be sought before irreparable damage was done.

[104] *Re S (A Child) (Identification: Restrictions on Publication)* [2005] 1 AC 593, at [17] (per Lord Steyn).

[105] A summary of the dual perspective approach is set out by Baroness Hale in *Campbell*, at [141], and it also seems to have been the approach used by Lord Hope, at [105], with the agreement of Lord Carswell, at [167]. Some subsequent cases have used the label 'parallel analysis' to refer to the same approach.

(2) *Practical reality*. In striking a balance between protecting people's privacy and people's rights to freedom of expression, the courts must be careful to ensure that they are not devising standards which real journalists cannot be reasonably expected to meet. For instance, a real journalist cannot be expected to produce a justification for every choice of phrasing or supporting detail. In *Campbell* all of their Lordships recognised:

> the importance of allowing a proper degree of journalistic margin to the press to deal with a legitimate story in its own way, without imposing unnecessary shackles on its freedom to publish detail and photographs which add colour and conviction.[106]

Thus a judge setting the balance must be careful not to hold a defendant liable merely because he or she would have presented the story in a different way, and must take account of the advantages which come with detailed argument and hindsight.

Having made these points, let's consider a concrete example, the **Drunken Student Problem**, so as to get a better 'feel' for how the courts will strike a balance between people's rights to freedom of expression and people's interests in having their privacy protected:

> *Student* gets so drunk celebrating the end of her exams that she collapses in the street and has to be treated by paramedics. The incident is recorded by CCTV cameras belonging to *University*, and *University* later uses the images in a video it shows to other students to warn them about the dangers of binge drinking. *Watcher*, one of the students who are shown the video, recognises *Student* as the daughter of *Rocker*, a famous musician with a reputation for 'hard living'. *Watcher* tells *Tabloid* that images of *Rocker's* daughter are being used by *University* to warn of the dangers of binge drinking, and *Tabloid* publishes this story under the headline 'Your Dad Will be so Proud'.

Here, *Student* may want to bring claims for wrongful disclosure of private information against *University*,[107] *Watcher* and *Tabloid*.

To claim against *University* it will be necessary for *Student* to establish that the images contain information about her that a reasonable person would want to retain control over. Since she is apparently recognisable it is likely that the images will convey what she looked like during a distressing and humiliating episode which is something that a reasonable person would want to retain control over, at least to the extent of preventing a record of it being released to a wide audience. However, her willingness to expose this information about herself to those present in a public street will diminish her ability to claim that her interest in maintaining control over the information is very weighty.

To claim against *Watcher* and *Tabloid* it will be necessary for *Student* to establish that the information about her that they publish – that she collapsed as a result of consuming too much alcohol, was filmed in these circumstances, and images of her are being shown to others as a warning – are private facts that a reasonable person would expect not to be published to the general public. To establish such a reasonable expectation *Student* may argue that (i) the information was in part about her need for medical treatment, and (ii) the fact that her father is a celebrity should not mean that she is entitled to less protection for her privacy than a child of ordinary parents. And against *Watcher* she may be able to

---

[106] *Campbell*, at [169] (per Lord Carswell). Lord Nicholls and Lord Hoffmann thought that this factor was decisive in favour of the defendants, but the majority disagreed.

[107] If *University* is a public authority within the Human Rights Act 1998 *Student* could claim against it under that statute and thereby seek to circumvent the limits on the new tort. In this example we assume that it is a *private* institution.

rely on an additional argument based on the relationship between students in the same institution: it may be the case that students in an institution generally recognise that it is not appropriate to tell stories about each other's disreputable behaviour to outsiders. But again, the weight of her claim will be reduced by her willingness to expose this information about herself to those present in a public street.

From the point of view of expression *University* may seek to argue that the violation of *Student*'s privacy is proportionate to the public interest in expressing an important social message in a graphic and effective manner. The court will want to investigate, however, whether it was *necessary* to violate *Student*'s privacy in order to express this message effectively, or whether it was merely *convenient* to do so. In this context it will consider whether the same scene could have been equally well-presented using actors or by disguising *Student*'s identity.[108] On balance it seems unlikely that *University* will be able to justify using the images.

Tabloid may argue that its story contributed to more than one 'debate of general interest', such as those about how to reduce binge-drinking and about whether children of parents famous for their 'hard-living' are more likely than other children to behave in irresponsible ways. No doubt such debates can be pursued without giving publicity to the specific incident involving *Student*, but *Tabloid* is likely to argue that specific examples attract the attention of their readers. In *Goodwin v News Group Newspapers* (2011) Tugendhat J quoted from a speech of Lord Rodger:

> stories about particular individuals are simply much more attractive to readers than stories about unidentified people. It is just human nature. . . . A requirement to report it in some austere, abstract form, devoid of much of its human interest, could well mean that the report would not be read and the information would not be passed on. Ultimately, such an approach could threaten the viability of newspapers and magazines, which can only inform the public if they attract enough readers and make enough money to survive.[109]

In practice we think that the most important factor in determining the weight of *Tabloid*'s free expression arguments is whether it appears to the judge that the story did contribute to any such debate, as opposed to being mere gossip satisfying curiosity about the life of a child of a celebrity. We would expect the weight of *Watcher*'s free expression arguments to be no greater than the weight of *Tabloid*'s, unless *Watcher* had some reason for thinking that *Tabloid* would use the information in some other way. Indeed, *Watcher*'s case may be weaker than *Tabloid*'s from the perspective of free expression if it turns out, for example, that she had no desire to contribute to any debate and simply wanted to be paid for supplying a story.

21.6 FAULT ELEMENTS

Where a claim is brought against a publisher who has obtained the information *indirectly* the question may arise whether the publisher *knew or ought to have known* that the material

---

[108] In *Peck v United Kingdom* (2003) 13 BHRC 669, the European Court of Human Rights held that a local authority's disclosure to the media of CCTV footage showing the applicant in a public place with a large knife in order to increase the effectiveness of a new CCTV system 'pursued the legitimate aim of public safety, the prevention of disorder and crime and the protection of the rights of others' (at [67]), but interfered with the applicant's privacy to a disproportionate extent because no attempt was made to secure his consent and too little was done to ensure that his identity was properly masked (at [85] and [87]). Similarly, in *T v BBC* [2007] EWHC 1683 (QB), while Eady J recognised that there was a genuine public interest in the subject of adoption and that the BBC's proposed documentary intended to deal with the subject in a serious and informative way, he doubted whether it was necessary to *identify* T, a vulnerable young adult, when portraying her final meeting with her child.

[109] [2011] EWHC 1437, at [110], quoting from *In re Guardian News and Media Ltd* [2010] 2 AC 697, at [63] (per Lord Rodger).

it was publishing violated the subject's reasonable expectation of privacy.[110] Thus where A provides information about B to C, a newspaper, and C publishes this information, it will be C's knowledge which is in issue if B sues C.[111]

It seems, however, that the courts may define what a *media defendant* 'ought to know' so widely that the requirement will be rendered nugatory. In the *Campbell* case, the Court of Appeal held that 'the media can fairly be expected to identify confidential information about an individual's private life which, absent good reason, it will be offensive to publish'.[112] This suggests that a *professional* publisher will not be able to defend itself by relying on a misunderstanding as to what sorts of information the law potentially protects. But the court did not expressly consider the difficult situations which might arise where a defendant, professional or otherwise, is misled as to the nature of the relationship between A and B or the circumstances in which a photograph was obtained. Consider, for example, the **Unreliable Paparazzi Problem**:

Actress has recently had a baby and has told the world that she will abandon her celebrity lifestyle and concentrate on caring for her child. *Snapper* photographs her in St Tropez carrying suitcases and without her baby, and sells the picture to *Tabloid*, explaining that 'it was a hotel, and she looked like she was on holiday'. This explanation is untrue, and the picture was actually taken as *Actress* was arriving at a private retreat that specialises in treating those suffering from post-natal depression. *Tabloid* publishes the picture under the headline: 'Normal service resumed: *Actress* off on holiday without her baby'. *Actress* is extremely distressed by the publication of the photograph, particularly since many of her celebrity acquaintances will recognise the private retreat.

Some people might argue that it would be harsh to hold *Tabloid* liable in this situation, unless there was some reason why they should have been sceptical about *Snapper*'s explanation and realised that the photograph communicated private information. Others, however, might argue that a professional media organisation must take responsibility for what it publishes, and *Actress*'s right to privacy should not be diminished just because *Tabloid* has been misled by *Snapper*. On balance, we would support allowing *Tabloid* to avoid liability if it could demonstrate that it had acted consistently with standards of 'responsible journalism'.

21.7 WRONGFULLY OBTAINING ACCESS TO PRIVATE INFORMATION

In *Imerman* v *Tchenguiz* (2011) the claimant, Vivian Imerman, shared the office premises of his two brothers-in-law, Robert and Vincent Tchenguiz, and used the computer system which served the offices for his personal and business purposes. The claimant's wife, Elizabeth, petitioned for divorce in December 2008, and in January and February 2009 her brothers, Robert and Vincent, accessed the server which supported the computer system and made electronic copies of emails and other documents stored by the claimant. The brothers primarily did this because they were worried that the claimant would conceal his assets to reduce what their sister would receive as a result of the divorce. The brothers later sent printed copies of the documents to their solicitor, and some were subsequently sent on to the solicitors who were handling the divorce for their sister, the claimant's wife. The claimant

---

[110] *Campbell*, at [85] (per Lord Hope), [134] (per Baroness Hale).
[111] Of course, if B only sues A then C's knowledge will be irrelevant.
[112] *Campbell* v *MGN Ltd* [2003] QB 633, at [68].

sought the return of the documents, and injunctions prohibiting the brothers from disclosing, copying or using any information contained in them. The Court of Appeal granted the injunctions, and held, in a judgment delivered by Lord Neuberger MR, that A would commit a wrong[113] in relation to B if she intentionally and secretly obtained information in respect of which she must have appreciated that B had an expectation of privacy.[114]

The reasoning that persuaded the Court of Appeal to recognise this new wrong proceeds like this: (1) If there is information about B that A would be under a duty not to disclose if she *accidentally* came to learn it, then (2) A will commit a wrong if she intentionally and secretly *obtains* it.[115] As a result – because this new wrong is based on what information it would be wrongful for A to disclose if she discovered it accidentally – some crucial elements of this new wrong will be the same as those of the tort of *wrongful disclosure of private information*. For example, the new tort will only protect information which a claimant *reasonably expects* to remain private. Moreover, we expect that the courts will use 'the dual perspective approach' to determine whether some countervailing interest makes it justifiable to disappoint that expectation. Five elements of the Court of Appeal's definition of the tort in *Imerman* (2011) require further discussion.

(1) *Intention*. The wrong is said to require the *intentional* acquisition of information. Thus if *Daydreamer* accidentally opens mail that has been erroneously delivered to his house instead of his neighbour's he may be under a duty not to publish what he sees, but he will not have committed the tort of *wrongfully obtaining access to private information*. You will recall that when we discussed the tort of *wrongful disclosure of private information* we said that all the cases so far had involved *intentional* disclosure and that consequently it was not clear whether the tort could be committed by carelessly leaving a confidential document in a public place. So it may still turn out to be the case that both torts require intentional behaviour.

(2) *Secretly*. In our opinion the Court of Appeal should not have incorporated *secrecy* into the definition: we think that the brothers' behaviour in *Imerman* (2011) would still have been wrongful if they had *openly* copied the documents from the server (after taking steps to prevent the claimant from deleting them).

(3) *Obtained information*. If a defendant copies documents, reads another person's correspondence, or listens to another person's voice-mail then it is obvious that he has 'obtained information', and in such situations we can then proceed to ask whether the claimant had a reasonable expectation of privacy with regard to that information. But what if a defendant simply requires the claimant to undress in front of him, as two prison officers required *Alan* to do in Wainwright v Home Office (2004)?[116]

Technically, it might be said that the prison officers 'obtained information'; what *Alan* looked like naked. But it is doubtful if the prison officers remembered this information for more than an instant, and they also did not obtain it secretly. Indeed it is not clear that their intention was to obtain such information – rather, their goal was to check that *Alan* was not smuggling any contraband into the prison. We can see, however, that if 'obtained information' is read broadly then the new tort will be capable of covering a wide range of

---

[113] The Court of Appeal referred to this wrong as 'breach of confidence', and stated that 'the normal equitable rules apply': [2011] 2 WLR 592, at [74]. But we have argued above, at § 21.1, that there are good reasons for treating wrongfully disclosing private information as an independent tort, and similar reasons mean we are also inclined to treat wrongfully obtaining access to private information as a tort.

[114] [2011] 2 WLR 592, at [68].

[115] ibid.

[116] Discussed above, § 6.4.

forms of intrusion: perhaps, taking photographs of people on private property using a long-range lens, as well as simple copying of private documents. Nothing in the judgment in the *Imerman* case suggests that the Court of Appeal intended 'obtained information' to be read broadly, but, equally, nothing in the judgment suggests that it was intended to be read narrowly.

(4) *Expectation of privacy.* In our discussion of the parallel requirement of a 'reasonable expectation of privacy' in the tort of *wrongful disclosure of private information* we noted that a claim can be made on the basis that the claimant reasonably expected that the fact would not be *generally* published, even if he did expect that it might be published to some more limited class of people. We expect that the approach taken by the courts will be *similar* when considering whether the tort of wrongfully obtaining access has been committed, and that consequently courts will have to take account of *why* the defendant was obtaining access to the information: thus if information about allegations that *Tantrum*'s wife has made against him is held on the police computer *Tantrum* will be able to establish that he reasonably expects *Constable* not to obtain access to this information in order to satisfy his curiosity, even if he cannot claim that he reasonably expects *Constable* not to obtain access to the same information when it is relevant to his inquiries.

(5) *Absence of justification.* We stated above that we expect the courts to use 'the dual perspective approach' to determine whether any countervailing interest makes it justifiable to disappoint the claimant's 'reasonable expectation of privacy'. Often the relevant countervailing interest will be the interest of some audience in learning the information which the defendant obtains access to. For example, if *Sleuth* believes that *Politico* has misled his constituents about what clubs he was a member of while at University, and copies private documents of *Politico* which confirm this, perhaps the diary he kept while a student, then *Sleuth* will argue that he has not committed the tort of wrongfully obtaining access to private information in relation to *Politico* because of the interest of the constituents in learning the truth. As we mentioned above, in *Imerman* (2011) the brothers copied the claimant's documents because they feared he might conceal his assets to reduce what their sister would receive as a result of the divorce. But, since the divorce process had not reached the stage at which the claimant was obliged to disclose his assets the court held that there was no justification for the copying at the time when it took place.

What if there were grounds for *Sleuth* to *suspect* that *Politico* had lied but the copied documents confirmed his previous statements? You will recall that when we discussed the parallel defence to claims for wrongful disclosure of private information we noted that the courts have held that their task is to decide *ex post facto* – with the benefit of hindsight – whether the publication sufficiently advanced the public interest: so should the question be whether the public interest was sufficiently advanced by the defendant *obtaining access*? Consider, for example, the **Concerned Sister Problem**:

Two years ago *Brother* successfully completed a drug rehabilitation programme and stopped using heroin. *Sister* thinks that *Brother* has recently started to behave erratically, and is concerned that he may be using heroin again. One day she sees *Brother* arguing with *Friend* in the street, and this increases her anxiety since *Friend* regularly used heroin with *Brother* before *Brother* kicked the habit. *Sister* knows where *Brother* has written down a list of his passwords, so she looks at this list and logs in to his email account. She reads some messages passing between *Brother* and *Friend*, and discovers that *Brother* is gay, but does not want his family to know. *Friend*, who is also gay, has been counselling him.

If the justification test is applied with the benefit of hindsight then it seems that *Sister* will have no defence: she had no justification for obtaining access to information about either her *Brother*'s or *Friend*'s sexuality. (Moreover, although she did not intend to obtain access to information about *Brother*'s sexuality it will be difficult for her to argue that she did not intend to obtain access to any information that he could reasonably expect her not to look at – the contents of his communications with *Friend*.) But when we discussed the Deceptive Appearances Problem[117] we argued that the courts should develop a doctrine allowing a defendant in a case of wrongful disclosure to avoid liability if the disclosure would have been justifiable had the circumstances been as he mistakenly believed, provided that the mistake was consistent with 'responsible journalism'. Consistently, we think that in Concerned Sister it would be appropriate for the court to ask: (a) if *Sister* would have had a sufficient justification for reading *Brother*'s e-mails if *Brother* had been taking heroin; and (b) whether her conclusion that he might be taking heroin was reached after what was a 'reasonable investigation' in the circumstances. Of course the *answers* to these questions are difficult to predict. But assuming that *Brother* is an adult, and is unlikely to do serious harm to anyone except himself by taking heroin, then the answer to question (a) might be 'no'.

21.8 REMEDIES

In this section we consider the remedies that can be granted when either the tort of wrongful disclosure of private information or the tort of wrongfully obtaining access to private information has been committed, or is about to be committed, or has allegedly been committed. As we have seen, however, the tort of wrongfully obtaining access to private information has only developed very recently. As a result almost all the cases concerning remedies involve the tort of wrongful disclosure. We expect, however, that because the torts are so closely related to one another there will be very few differences, if any, between the remedies available.

A. Damages

(1) *Compensatory and aggravated damages*. Where a defendant has wrongfully disclosed private information or wrongfully obtained access to it the claimant will normally be entitled to claim compensatory damages. But how are such damages calculated? In *Mosley v News Group Newspapers Ltd* (2008) Eady J noted that whatever sum he awarded could not *restore* the claimant's privacy in any meaningful sense: 'Accordingly, it seems to me that the only realistic course is to select a figure which marks the fact that an unlawful intrusion has taken place while affording some degree of *solatium* to the injured party'.[118] He eventually awarded £60,000. Two factors clearly influenced this figure. First, the award was increased because the defendants aggravated the wrong by persisting in their claim that the sex session had a 'Nazi theme'. Secondly, the award was apparently reduced because the claimant was *himself* responsible to some extent for the embarrassment and distress he suffered: Eady J did not expressly confirm that he had reduced the claimant's award to reflect the extent to which 'a casual observer' would have regarded the claimant's behaviour 'as reckless and almost self-destructive'. But he said that: 'It could be thought unreasonable to absolve him of all responsibility for placing himself and his family in the predicament in

---

[117] Above, at § 21.4(B)(5).
[118] [2008] EWHC 1777 (QB), at [231].

which they now find themselves. It is part and parcel of human dignity that one must take at least some responsibility for one's own actions.'[119]

(2) *Gain-based damages*. In chapter 31 we clarify what we mean by 'gain-based damages' and explain when they are available in tort law. We note there that because the tort of wrongful disclosure of private information has its origins in the equitable wrong of breach of confidence this makes it likely that disgorgement damages will be available as a remedy that can be obtained against defendants who commit the tort. Indeed, in *Douglas v Hello! Ltd (No 3)* (2006), the Court of Appeal accepted that if the defendants in that case had made a profit from publishing unauthorised photographs of the claimants' wedding celebrations, then the claimants would have been entitled to sue the defendants for a sum equal to that profit.[120]

(3) *Exemplary damages*. In *Mosley v News Group Newspapers Ltd* (2008) Eady J held that exemplary damages could not be awarded for a *wrongful disclosure of private information*, even if a defendant had committed the wrong deliberately after calculating that by doing so he would make a profit in excess of what he might have to pay by way of compensatory damages.[121] He based this conclusion on three arguments: (1) the wrong is an equitable wrong – breach of confidence – and therefore authorities which say that exemplary damages can be awarded in cases of tort are not directly applicable; (2) the wrong has directly incorporated elements from the European Convention on Human Rights, particularly Articles 8 and 10, and consequently it would be odd to graft onto it an approach to measuring damages which is not used by the Strasbourg court; (3) the possibility of an award of exemplary damages is not necessary in a democratic society, and would 'chill' free speech to a disproportionate extent.[122]

We disagree with all three of these arguments: (1) we have argued above that *wrongful disclosure* should be treated as an independent tort, and in any case we do not think that it is sensible to make the availability of a measure of damages turn on something as irrelevant as whether a cause of action was historically developed by the Courts of Equity; (2) the Strasbourg Court is concerned with awarding 'just satisfaction' to injured parties against States, and not with deciding what measures are necessary *within* a State to ensure that private bodies respect the law and victims feel they have received sufficient recourse; (3) many States which have signed the European Convention have decided that it is necessary to impose *criminal penalties* for invasions of privacy, and provided that awards of exemplary damages are set at an appropriate level and only imposed when calculating contempt for the law has been *clearly* demonstrated, we cannot see why their availability will have an unjustifiable effect on free expression.[123] Thus we hope that in future Eady J's conclusion on this point will be reconsidered.

B. Injunctions

In chapter 33 we discuss the different types of injunction that are potentially available, and set out the tests which determine when they will be granted. With regard to cases of *wrongful disclosure of private information*, if a claimant successfully proves at trial that the defendant

[119] [2008] EWHC 1777 (QB), at [226].
[120] [2006] QB 125, at [249].
[121] This is one of the situations when exemplary damages *can* usually be awarded in tort law: see, below, at § 30.2.
[122] [2008] EWHC 1777 (QB), at [172]–[197].
[123] For further discussion of the utility of exemplary damages and when they should be awarded, see chapter 30.

has committed this tort then a court will grant an injunction prohibiting him from committing it again, unless this would be pointless, either because the information is now in the public domain or there is no prospect of the defendant committing the tort in the future.

More often, however, a claimant seeks an injunction *before* widespread disclosure of private information has taken place. In such situations the claimant will usually seek an *interim* injunction requiring the defendant not to disclose the information before trial (or before a further order of the court). Four issues relating to injunctions in cases involving wrongful disclosure require further discussion.

(1) *Freedom of expression.* Because an injunction which prohibits disclosure will usually prohibit *expression* courts must be particularly cautious before granting such an order. Indeed in s 12(3) of the Human Rights Act 1998, Parliament stated that:

No . . . relief [affecting the exercise of the Convention right to freedom of expression] is to be granted so as to restrain publication before trial unless the court is satisfied that the applicant is likely to establish that publication should not be allowed.

It was held in *Cream Holdings Ltd v Banerjee* (2005) that this means that an interim injunction which prohibits expression should usually only be granted where a claimant can demonstrate that he is more likely than not to establish at trial both that the defendant is liable and that a *final* injunction is appropriate. Moreover, to make this judgment a court must reach a provisional view on disputes of fact and questions of law. This makes it more difficult for a claimant to obtain an interim injunction that will restrict expression than to obtain one which will restrict commission of some tort that does not involve expression.

(2) *Effect on third parties.* Where an interim injunction has been granted against a defendant, a third party will commit contempt of court if it knows this and nonetheless publishes information that thwarts the purpose of the injunction. This is commonly called the *Spycatcher* doctrine, because this was the name of the book which gave rise to the litigation which established it.[124] In practice this means that a claimant who has obtained an interim injunction against an individual defendant will commonly serve this on a range of news organisations so as to prevent them from disclosing the information concerned.

While the *Spycatcher* doctrine will protect a claimant *until* trial, once he obtains a *final* injunction a third party cannot commit contempt of court by thwarting the purpose of an *interim* injunction.[125] Of course, once a *final* injunction has been granted a news organisations may be *aware of the risk* that publishing particular information will be a tort. But in some circumstances the possibility of a tort claim may be insufficient to prevent them from yielding to temptation; certainly such a prospect is likely to be less of a deterrent than the threat of proceedings for contempt of court. In circumstances such as these, provided that a court considers that the step is necessary and proportionate in order to protect a claimant's privacy, it can grant an injunction *contra mundum* (that is, against the world), prohibiting *everyone* from disclosing the private information in future.[126]

---

[124] See *Attorney-General v Newspaper Publishing Plc* [1988] Ch 333 and *Attorney-General v Times Newspapers Ltd* [1992] 1 AC 191.
[125] *Jockey Club v Buffham* [2003] QB 462. This doctrine will be re-considered in a case to be argued before the Court of Appeal in 2011.
[126] *OPQ v BJM* [2011] EWHC 1059 (QB).

(3) *Anonymity*. When a court has decided that an interim injunction should be granted prohibiting disclosure of private facts it may also need to restrict how the case should be reported, since otherwise the way in which it is reported might undermine the injunction.

For example, if *Striker* obtained an injunction prohibiting his former lover *Dancer* from revealing that he takes Viagra to deal with erectile dysfunction then it would not make sense to allow the press to report that *Striker* had obtained an injunction against *Dancer* prohibiting her from revealing that he 'has a medical condition that he wants to remain private': such a report would attract unwanted attention to *Striker's* health, and lead to speculation about what sort of medical condition he might be willing to go to court to hide.

In cases of disclosure of private information such restrictions on reporting are often achieved by granting an *anonymised injunction*. Such an injunction will prohibit the party that it is granted against from revealing who has obtained the interim injunction, and will bind third parties because of the *Spycatcher* doctrine that we discussed above. Such an order, however, is a far more serious matter than an ordinary interim injunction since it will impinge on the principle of *open justice*, a fundamental constitutional principle that helps to ensure the integrity and legitimacy of the legal system.

In *H v News Group Newspapers Ltd* (2011) the Court of Appeal held that what a judge must do in such a case is: (a) decide whether it is *necessary* to place some restriction on the free reporting of legal proceedings in order to protect a claimant's privacy, and if the answer is 'yes', then (b) decide what is the least restrictive way of protecting the claimant's privacy.[127] The Court of Appeal suggested that *usually* if a claimant is granted anonymity then it will be possible for the judge to include more detail in her judgment about why an interim injunction is being granted, and that will usually involve less of a restriction on *open justice* than allowing the claimant to be named but limiting what details about the claim can be reported.[128]

It has sometimes been suggested that *all* anonymised injunctions in cases of wrongful disclosure of private information are pointless because *anonymous* websites and users of Twitter, and the like, can reveal the name of the claimant with impunity. Three points can be made in response to this suggestion. First, the claimant's name can *only* be published with *impunity* so long as the person publishing it succeeds in remaining *anonymous*: there is a risk of punishment for contempt of court, or a claim in tort by the claimant, if the publisher's identity is discovered. Secondly, anonymous websites, Twitter, and the like, are *currently* read by less people than read newspapers, listen to the radio or watch television news. Thus a claimant may think that there is still a *sufficient* reason for obtaining an interim injunction *even if* his identity is 'an open secret' in cyberspace. Thirdly, in some cases it has emerged that the person most prominently 'identified' by anonymous websites was not actually the person who obtained the injunction. This may mean that people attach less credence to such 'identifications' than they would attach to reports by traditional news organisations. In combination these help to explain, at least in part, why celebrities, and others, think that it is still worthwhile to obtain *anonymised* injunctions.

Most discussion and controversy has surrounded applications for anonymous *interim* injunctions. What if a claimant succeeds in a claim at trial and wants an anonymous *final* injunction? It seems clear that a court can grant such an injunction where it is necessary and proportionate to do so. But, as we noted above, *final* injunctions do not currently bind *third parties*. Of course, any third party who reveals a claimant's identity after a *final*

---

[127] [2011] 1 WLR 1645, at [21]–[22].
[128] [2011] 1 WLR 1645, at [25].

injunction has been granted may be liable for committing the tort of *wrongful disclosure of private information*. But if a claimant wishes to secure a *final* injunction prohibiting *third parties* from revealing his identity he will have to seek an injunction *contra mundum*.

(4) *Super-injunctions*. The label 'super-injunction' is appropriately used for an *interim* injunction which prohibits the party against which it is obtained from disclosing to others that a claim has been made and an *interim* injunction obtained. Thus if *Striker* makes a claim of wrongful disclosure of private information against *Dancer* and obtains a *super-injunction* against her, then she will be prohibited from telling others that *Striker* has made a claim against her and obtained an injunction.

It seems to be generally agreed that *super-injunctions* are a legitimate *interim* remedy when they are granted for a short period in order to prevent accomplices, or the like, from being 'tipped off'. For example, if there is strong evidence that *Dancer* has supplied copies of intimate photographs of *Striker* to an *unknown agent*, who has instructions to send them to an overseas news agency if *Striker* applies for an injunction against *Dancer*, then there might be a strong case for prohibiting *Dancer* from disclosing to anyone the fact that *Striker* has made such an application. But greater controversy surrounds the granting of *super-injunctions* simply in order to prevent speculation about what private information might be being protected. For example, it is easy to imagine that if *Dancer* revealed that 'a well-known footballer' had obtained an interim injunction against her then this might prompt a frenzy of speculation, which might well indirectly lead to revelation of the identity of the claimant and the private information.

Because *super-injunctions* involve a very significant restriction on *open justice* – indeed they permit the workings of the justice system to be wholly hidden from public view, at least temporarily – a Committee, chaired by Lord Neuberger MR, was asked to consider them.[129] This Committee concluded that there might be some situations beyond prevention of 'tipping-off' when it would be appropriate to grant a *super-injunction*, but that such an injunction should 'only be granted following intense scrutiny by the court in the individual case, and only when it is strictly necessary as a means to ensure that justice is done.'[130]

21.9 CASES NOT INVOLVING WRONGFUL DISCLOSURE OR ACCESS

We have already mentioned that some aspects of privacy may be protected by torts dealt with elsewhere in the book (for instance, by the torts of trespass to land, private nuisance, defamation, harassment and malicious falsehood). But these and the two torts discussed above do not between them provide comprehensive protection for privacy. For example, a *Star* footballer may feel that his privacy is invaded when: (1) *Star*'s meal in a restaurant is disturbed by fans seeking autographs; (2) a *Bore* who occupies the seat next to *Star* on an aeroplane insists on recounting at great length to *Star* the details of *Bore*'s own athletic shortcomings; and (3) a popular comedienne amuses her television audience by confessing that *Star* is the regular subject of her sexual fantasies. Should the English law of torts attempt to deal with any forms of invasion of privacy *other than* intentionally obtaining access to and disclosing private information?

In the United States of America a fourfold division of forms of invasion of privacy is commonly used: (1) unreasonable intrusion into private situations; (2) unreasonable

---

[129] *Report of the Committee on Super-Injunctions: Super-Injunctions, Anonymised Injunctions and Open Justice* (20 May 2011).
[130] ibid, at 2.38.

publication of private facts; (3) publicity unreasonably placing the claimant in a 'false light'; (4) appropriating the claimant's name or likeness for private advantage.[131] The English tort of wrongful disclosure of private information covers 'unreasonable publication of private facts', and, as we explained above, the new English tort of wrongfully obtaining access to private information *may* cover some forms of 'unreasonable intrusion into private situations'. So – here we will briefly consider some of the difficulties which might be involved in creating *limited* torts to cover: (1) intrusion that does not involve obtaining access to private information; (2) placing the claimant in a 'false light'; and (3) appropriating the claimant's name or likeness. So far as there are *distinct* problems with developing each of these limited torts, these will tend to confirm Lord Hoffmann's opinion that a *general* tort of invasion of privacy should not be created because of the need to fashion conditions of liability and appropriate defences reflecting the differences between the areas where the value of privacy may be invoked.[132]

A. Intrusion

A tort covering this form of invasion would encompass behaviour such as *Fan* disturbing *Striker*'s meal with his family in a restaurant in order to seek an autograph, or perhaps simply staring at him, or snapping a picture of him with a camera-phone.[133] While many people would castigate *Fan*'s behaviour in these scenarios, perhaps calling it 'impolite' or 'distasteful', the question whether a tort should be created to cover it is more difficult.

We saw in the previous chapter that Parliament has enacted that a 'course of conduct', and not a one-off event, can amount to *harassment* under the Protection from Harassment Act 1997. This *might* be taken to suggest that Parliament believes that single instances of rude and irritating behaviour are too trivial to warrant the attention of the civil law. It appears that there is a special problem, however, where the cumulative effect of rude and irritating behaviour by a number of unconnected people is intolerable: for example, where *Snapper* is one of a number of freelance photographers who wait outside the restaurant where *Striker* was dining in order to shout questions at him and take pictures as he heads home. One can easily imagine how *Striker* and his family could be affected if they regularly had to confront such photographers, even if different individuals were involved on each occasion. We think that there is a strong case for making it a tort to be part of a group of individuals collectively acting in such a way as to *unreasonably intrude* on an individual's *solitude*. We suggest, however, that such a tort would have to be created by *legislation* since great care would have to be taken to define each of the key elements: when an individual would be (1) *part of a group*, (2) *collectively acting*, so as to (3) *unreasonably* intrude (4) on an individual's *solitude*.

B. False light

A tort covering this form of invasion would extend over behaviour such as publishing the false information that the claimant was romantically involved with a celebrity or a false version of a dramatic event involving the claimant. Clearly, if *Tabloid* published the

---

[131] See, for instance, Prosser 1960; Rest 2d, Torts § 652A.

[132] *Wainwright* v *Home Office* [2004] 2 AC 406, at [31]–[33].

[133] We noted above that *staring* or *taking photographs* might amount to the new tort of *wrongfully obtaining private information* – but only if *obtaining* is defined broadly, and the requirement for *secrecy* is abandoned. See above, § 21.7.

information that *Starlet*, a single woman, was dating *Prince Harry*, a single man, this would usually not be defamatory of *Starlet* even if it was wholly false.[134] It would be likely, however, to subject *Starlet* to a significant degree of unwanted public attention and it is easy to see why people might want to be protected from such attention. But the issue whether a tortious duty should be created to confer such protection raises two subsidiary questions.

First, whether the degree of annoyance likely to be suffered by someone subjected to such attention is sufficiently significant to warrant such a step, given that there cannot be a duty to avoid all potentially annoying forms of conduct.[135]

Secondly, whether the existence of such a duty might unduly restrict the activities of those who want to retell recent events in a dramatically engaging manner, such as the authors of docudramas and unauthorised biographies. It would certainly be a burden on modern historians and unauthorised biographers if they could be liable for non-defamatory factual errors, and we think that the complexity of the current law of libel – a product of both complex case law and detailed statutes – provides a good reason why courts should be cautious about presuming that they have the capacity to develop a new privacy tort in this area.

C. Appropriation of personality

A tort covering this form of invasion would extend over behaviour such as using a photograph of a person in an advertisement without his consent. For instance, if an airline published an advertisement for its flights using the picture of a person recently involved in a criminal case with the slogan 'for a quick getaway fly with our airline'[136] then the person depicted might be able to claim. Similarly, this tort might cover a case where a photograph of a teenager taken in a public place without obtaining her consent was used to illustrate a magazine article.[137] From a privacy perspective the utility of the tort is that it gives a person control over *how* her image and identity is used, and prevents that image and identity being treated as a mere tool by others. In practice, however, such a tort might primarily benefit those celebrities who do not want their images and identities to be used in advertising.[138]

One difficulty with creating a tort to cover this form of invasion of privacy would be defining the scope of a claimant's protected interest. Where a photograph of the claimant is used the matter is straightforward, but more difficult cases might involve use of a distinctive catchphrase, mannerism or vocal characteristic.[139] It might be possible to get round this problem by defining the tort so that it covered only *intentional* appropriation,

---

[134] It might be defamatory in unusual circumstances: for instance, if *Starlet* was a nun.

[135] Such a duty would be unsatisfactory because it would impinge on so many aspects of ordinary social life. It would be extraordinarily ironic if many everyday encounters became subject to legal regulation in the interests of protecting *privacy*!

[136] EasyJet issued similar advertisements during 2003.

[137] *Aubry* v *Editions Vice-Versa Inc* [1998] 1 SCR 591.

[138] The extension of the tort of passing off in *Irvine* v *Talksport Ltd* [2002] 1 WLR 2355 (discussed above, § 18.3) will protect the interest of a celebrity who has acquired a valuable reputation or goodwill from misrepresentations which enable a defendant to make use of or take advantage of that reputation (at [38], per Laddie J). The tort of passing off will not, however, protect an unknown teenager like the claimant in the *Aubry* case, above, and may not protect a claimant who has attained *notoriety*.

[139] Cases from the United States have involved the use of a television presenter's catchphrase to market a portable toilet (*Carson* v *Here's Johnny Portable Toilets Inc*, 698 F 2d 831 (1983)), the use of a singer who sounded like Bette Midler to advertise cars (*Midler* v *Ford Motor Co*, 849 F 2d 460 (1988)), and the use of a robot dressed like a gameshow hostess to advertise videorecorders (*White* v *Samsung Electronics America Inc*, 971 F 2d 1395 (1992)).

but this would not avoid all difficulties.[140] A further difficulty would be defining the situations where use of a person's image without consent is legitimate. For instance, photographs are commonly used without the consent of those depicted to illustrate legitimate news stories, in protest and in satire.[141] In Germany a person's image is protected and in an important decision the Bundesgerichtshof had to determine *when* it was permissible for Greenpeace to use the name and picture of the president of a chemical company on a campaign poster.[142] No doubt English courts could solve similar disputes, but it is important to note that extending tort law to cover this form of invasion of privacy would be likely to involve a move away from the traditional preference for clear legal duties in commercial settings.[143]

In *Douglas* v *Hello! Ltd (No 3)* (2008)[144] a majority of the House of Lords held that a private event, such as a wedding in a hotel, could be organised so that the information that would be disclosed by a *photographic* image of the event became a commercial secret, which could be protected by the wrong of breach of confidence. This may provide a person with some degree of control over exploitation of images of *what they looked like during such an event*. But the duty not to publish such confidential information is, naturally, far narrower than a *general* duty not to appropriate another's image would be.

Further reading

Because the two torts we have discussed in this chapter have developed quite quickly, and are still developing, many of the articles which have focused on the law have already been overtaken by new cases.

If we were asked to select two articles from the last decade that usefully analyse the issues confronting the developing law then we would opt for two by **Nicole Moreham: 'The protection of privacy in English common law: a doctrinal and theoretical analysis'** (2005) 121 *Law Quarterly Review* 628 and **'Privacy in public places'** (2006) 65 *Cambridge Law Journal* 606. Dr Moreham is also one of the editors of an excellent practitioners' work, which is invaluable for anyone seeking to explore the *details* of the law: **Warby, Moreham and Christie (eds),** *Tugendhat and Christie: The Law of Privacy and the Media*, 2nd edn (Oxford University Press, 2010).

Looking beyond tort law, for those interested in exploring the problems faced by anyone brave enough to attempt to *define* 'privacy' we would recommend **Daniel J. Solove's** *Understanding Privacy* (Harvard University Press, 2008). And for those seeking insights into the question whether new technology, such as the Internet, and new practices, such as social networking, spell the end for privacy, we would recommend **Saul Levmore and Martha Nussbaum (eds),** *The Offensive Internet* (Harvard University Press, 2010).

---

[140] For instance, if the defendant argued that he intended to invoke a *generic* athlete of the 1970s and the claimant argued that his individual image was appropriated. (In 2003 David Bedford, the athlete who held the world record for the 10,000 metres from 1973 until 1977, became involved in a dispute with a directory enquiries company which he claimed had appropriated his image.)

[141] The short phrase 'for private advantage' used in the summary of the tort clearly does not go very far towards answering the difficult issues raised, since newspapers and satirists generally seek to make a profit.

[142] BGH, 12 October 1993, NJW 1994, 124 (Federal Court of Justice, Germany).

[143] In *Von Hannover* v *Germany* (2005) 40 EHRR 1, the European Court of Human Rights held (at [72]) that states have undertaken a 'positive obligation under the Convention to protect private life *and the right to control the use of one's image*' (emphasis added). See also [57]. One way in which the United Kingdom could fulfil this obligation would be for the *courts* to create a new tort making appropriation of personality actionable.

[144] [2008] 1 AC 1 (heard alongside *OBG Ltd* v *Allan*).

Visit **www.mylawchamber.co.uk/mcbride** to access tools to help you develop and test your knowledge of Tort law, including interactive multiple choice questions, practice exam questions with guidance, weblinks, legal newsfeed, additional case summaries, legal updates and tips on answering problem and essay questions.

Use **Case Navigator** to read in full some of the key cases referenced in this chapter with commentary and questions:

- Wainwright *v* Home Office

22 Breach of statutory duty

22.1 The basics *626*

22.2 Resolving hard cases *630*

22.3 Health and safety at work *634*

22.4 Highways *635*

22.5 Defective premises *636*

22.6 Equality Act 2010 *637*

Overview

In this chapter, we look at some situations where a claimant can sue a defendant in tort based merely on the fact that the defendant has breached a statutory duty that was imposed on him for the claimant's benefit. Section 22.1 sets out the core principles underpinning this area of law. Section 22.2 deals with the difficult issue of how we determine whether or not Parliament intended that the breach of a statutory duty owed to another would be civilly actionable in a case where it has not made its intentions clear. Sections 22.3 to 22.6 deal with some concrete instances of situations where the breach of a statutory duty owed to another will give rise to a civil remedy.

22.1 THE BASICS

We have already seen a number of different situations where a defendant who has breached a statutory duty can be sued for damages by a claimant. So, for example, a defendant who has – contrary to s 1 of the Protection from Harassment Act 1997 – unreasonably subjected a claimant to a course of conduct that he knows, or ought to know, amounts to harassment, can be sued for damages by that claimant under s 3 of the 1997 Act. The same point applies to breaches of statutory duties imposed on defendants by the Occupiers' Liability Acts 1957 and 1984, the Copyright, Designs and Patents Act 1988, and the Human Rights Act 1998.

All of these are examples of situations where a claimant can sue a defendant for *breach of statutory duty* – in other words, for breaching a duty that arises under an Act of Parliament, not under the common law. But not every breach of statutory duty ('SD' for short) is civilly actionable – that is, capable of entitling someone to sue the person committing the breach for the sort of remedies (damages or an injunction) dealt with in this book. In fact, most SDs are not enforceable by private persons. Most SDs are *only* enforceable by the *State*, either by bringing a criminal prosecution against a defendant for breaching an SD, or by obtaining an order from the courts (known as a *public law remedy*) requiring the defendant to stop acting unlawfully, or to undo the effect of his earlier unlawful conduct.

This chapter is concerned with situations where a claimant can bring a civil action to enforce an SD that a defendant is subject to. We can distinguish three different situations where a claimant might be interested in bringing such an action:

A. Breach of duty owed to no one in particular

The first situation is where a defendant has breached an SD that was imposed on him for the benefit of the community as a whole. The general rule here is that the defendant's breach will *not* be civilly actionable. There are two exceptions to this rule.[1]

The first is where the defendant's breach amounts to a *public nuisance*. In that case, anyone who has suffered *special damage* as a result of the defendant's breach of duty will be entitled to sue the defendant for compensation for that damage. (We will talk about public nuisance in the chapter immediately following this one.) The second is where the defendant is a public official and he has committed the tort of *misfeasance in public office* in acting as he did. (We will talk about the tort of misfeasance in public office in chapter 25, below.)

An example of the general rule set out here is provided by *Lonrho Ltd v Shell Petroleum (No 2)* (1982). In that case, Lonrho owned an oil pipeline that ran into Southern Rhodesia. (Southern Rhodesia was at the time (1965) part of the British Empire; on independence, it was renamed Zimbabwe.) Oil companies would pay the claimants to use the oil pipeline to transport oil into Rhodesia. Rhodesia had voted in favour of becoming an independent state, but the UK government was not willing to grant independence unless the black majority in Rhodesia was fairly represented in the government of an independent Rhodesia. The white-dominated Rhodesian government refused to agree to this demand and unilaterally declared Rhodesia independent of the UK in November 1965. In response, the UK government made it illegal to supply oil to Rhodesia with the result that Lonrho pipeline fell into disuse.

Shell secretly continued to supply oil to Rhodesia, in breach of the sanctions applied by the UK government to Rhodesia. Had they not, it was likely that the Rhodesian government would have collapsed sooner than it did (in 1979); that the sanctions against Rhodesia would have been lifted earlier than they were (also in 1979); and that Lonrho's pipeline would not have been out of use for as long as it was. Lonrho sued Shell for compensation for the loss of business that they had suffered as a result of Shell's sanctions breaking. Its claim was dismissed. The SD breached by Shell in this case was imposed for the benefit of the UK as a whole, which had an interest in bringing down the Rhodesian government through the use of sanctions. It was therefore owed to no one in particular.

The SD that was breached in *Lonrho* was clearly imposed for the benefit of the community as a whole, and not for any particular individual's benefit. However, not all cases are so clear-cut. For example, in *X v Bedfordshire County Council* (1995), the claimants were five children who suffered years of abuse at home. Despite being alerted to this, the relevant local authority failed to initiate proceedings to take the claimants into care, thereby breaching various SDs which required it to intervene to protect 'at risk' children. The claimants sued the local authority for compensation in respect of the losses they had suffered as a result of the local authority's breaches of statutory duty. The House of Lords dismissed the claim on the basis that the SDs breached in this case had not been imposed for the benefit of any particular individuals, such as children at risk of being abused, but

---

[1] The High Court of Australia suggested a further exception in *Beaudesert Shire Council v Smith* (1966) 120 CLR 145, holding (at 160) that if A's breach of statutory duty was intentional, and B suffered loss as an inevitable consequence of A's breach, then B would be able to sue A for compensation for that loss. However, the House of Lords ruled in *Lonrho v Shell Petroleum (No 2)* [1982] AC 173, at 188 that this was *not* the law in England. (Nor is it now the law in Australia: *Northern Territory v Mengel* (1995) 185 CLR 307.)

were 'all concerned to establish an administrative system designed to promote the social welfare of the community'.[2]

Again, in *Cutler* v *Wandsworth Stadium* (1949), the claimant was a bookmaker who sued a dog racing track for breaching its SDs under s 11 of the Betting and Lotteries Act 1934 'not [to] . . . exclude any person from the track [because] he proposes to carry on bookmaking on the track' and to 'take such steps as are necessary to secure that . . . there is available for bookmakers space on the track where they can conveniently carry on bookmaking in connexion with dog races run on the track on that day'. The House of Lords dismissed the claimant's claim, holding that the SDs arising under s 11 of the 1934 Act were not imposed for the benefit of bookmakers like the claimant, but for the benefit of members of the general public who might want to lay a bet at the races, and whose interests might be prejudiced if the owners of racing tracks had a monopoly over betting at their tracks.

B. Breach of a duty owed to a third party

The second situation is where a defendant has breached an SD that was imposed on him for the benefit of someone other than the claimant. The general rule here is that the claimant will *not* be entitled to bring an action for breach of statutory duty against the defendant. (However, the defendant might have committed some *other* tort in relation to the claimant in acting as he did. This possibility is explored in the chapter on the 'Economic Torts', two chapters on from this one.)

An example of the general rule is provided by *Wingrove* v *Prestige & Co Ltd* (1954). In that case, the claimant was a clerk of works employed by Middlesex County Council to supervise the defendants as they built a school for the council. The claimant was blinded in both eyes as a result of an accident on the construction site. The accident occurred because the defendants committed a breach of their statutory duty to ensure that 'suitable and safe scaffolds shall be provided for all work that cannot be safely done on or from the ground or from part of the building . . .'[3] The claimant sued the defendants for compensation for his injury but his claim was dismissed. The statutory duty that the defendants breached had been imposed for the benefit of the defendants' employees, not the claimant.

Another example is provided by *Bretton* v *Hancock* (2006). That case was concerned with the situation where *Owner* allows *Poor* to drive her car without insurance, in breach of the SD she owes other drivers on the road to ensure that people who drive her car carry insurance. While driving *Owner*'s car, *Poor* drives the car so badly that she causes an accident in which *Unlucky* is injured. The accident was also caused in part by a third party *Driver*'s negligence. So *Unlucky* could sue *Driver* and *Poor* in negligence for her injuries. Suppose she sues *Driver* and recovers full compensation for her injuries from *Driver*. And suppose *Driver* wants to make a claim in contribution against *Poor*, arguing, 'You were also liable for what happened to *Unlucky*; you have to contribute your fair share of what I had to pay *Unlucky*' but *Poor* is not worth suing because *Poor* has no money. Can *Driver* bring a claim for breach of statutory duty against *Owner*, arguing 'Had you ensured that *Poor* was insured in driving your car, *Poor* would be able to contribute his fair share of my liability to *Unlucky*'? The answer is 'no' because *Owner*'s SD to ensure that *Poor* was insured in driving her car was imposed on her for the benefit of *Unlucky* – to help ensure that he would be able to recover adequate compensation for his injuries – and not for the benefit of *Driver*.

---

[2] [1995] 2 AC 633, 747 (per Lord Browne-Wilkinson).
[3] Building (Safety, Health and Welfare) Regulations 1948, reg 5.

C. Breach of a duty owed to the claimant

The third situation where a claimant might be interested in bringing a claim for breach of statutory duty against a defendant is where the SD breached by the defendant was imposed on him for the benefit of the claimant, or the benefit of a limited class of people that included the claimant. In this sort of case, the rule is that the defendant's breach of duty *will* be civilly actionable by the claimant, so long as: (1) the defendant's breach has resulted in the claimant suffering the kind of loss that the SD breached by the defendant was imposed on him in order to avoid; and (2) Parliament intended that a breach of the SD that the defendant breached should be civilly actionable.

(1) *Wrong kind of loss.* We are already quite familiar with the idea that you cannot sue in tort for a loss suffered as a result of a breach of duty if the loss is the wrong kind of loss – not the sort of loss that the duty breached was imposed in order to avoid.[4] And we have already mentioned[5] *Gorris v Scott* (1874), the leading case that establishes that that rule applies to actions for breach of statutory duty. That was the case where the defendant shipowner failed – in breach of his statutory duty to do so – to keep the claimant's sheep in pens while he was transporting them, with the result that the sheep were washed overboard when a big wave crashed onto the deck of the defendant's ship. It was held the claimant could not bring a claim for breach of statutory duty against the defendant for the loss of his sheep as the SD breached by the defendant in that case was imposed on him in order to stop disease spreading among the sheep, not to protect them from being washed overboard.

(2) *Parliamentary intention.* If a defendant has breached an SD owed to the claimant, and the claimant has suffered the right kind of loss as a result, the claimant will still not be entitled to bring a claim for breach of statutory duty against the defendant unless Parliament intended that breach of the defendant's SD should be civilly actionable. As Lord Browne-Wilkinson observed in *X v Bedfordshire County Council* (1995):

> The basic proposition is that in the ordinary case a breach of statutory duty does not, by itself, give rise to any private law cause of action. However a private law cause of action will arise if it can be shown, as a matter of construction of the statute, that the statutory duty was imposed for the protection of a limited class of the public *and that Parliament intended to confer on members of that class a private right of action for breach of that duty.*[6]

Whether or not Parliament could be said to have intended that breach of a particular SD should be civilly actionable depends, the courts say, on the proper construction of the statute that created that SD. However, it can often be very difficult to determine what Parliament's intentions were in creating a particular SD, as to whether breach of that SD should be civilly actionable. Sometimes Parliament makes it clear that breach of a particular SD should not be civilly actionable.[7] Sometimes – as is the case with the Occupiers' Liability Acts, or the Human Rights Act, or the Protection from Harassment Act – Parliament makes it clear that breach of a particular SD should be civilly actionable. But more often than not

---

[4] See above, § 10.3.

[5] See above, § 10.1(2).

[6] [1995] 2 AC 633, 731–2 (emphasis added).

[7] For example, s 9 of the Post Office Act 1969 provides that 'It shall be the duty of the Post Office . . . to provide throughout [the British Islands] . . . such services for the conveyance of letters . . . as satisfy all reasonable demands for them' but section 9(4) of the Act makes it clear that a breach of this duty will *not* be civilly actionable: 'Nothing in this section shall be construed as imposing upon the Post Office . . . any form of . . . liability enforceable by proceedings before any court.'

Parliament does not make it clear one way or the other whether it intended that the breach of an SD which exists for the benefit of a limited class of people should be civilly actionable if one of those people suffers the right kind of loss as a result of the breach of that SD. In such cases – what we can call *hard cases* – Lord Denning MR despairingly observed that 'you might as well toss a coin to decide'[8] what Parliament's intentions were. However, we should not be so quick to despair. There are in fact two different approaches available to us to determine in a hard case whether or not Parliament intended breach of a particular SD should be civilly actionable. Those two approaches are the subject of the next section.

22.2 RESOLVING HARD CASES

The first approach to determining in a hard case whether or not Parliament intended that breach of a particular SD should be civilly actionable is exemplified by the recent Supreme Court decision in *Morrison Sports Ltd* v *Scottish Power Plc* (2010). In that case, the claimants owned properties that had been damaged by a fire which had originated from an electricity meter cupboard. The claimants brought an action for breach of statutory duty against the defendant electricity supplier, arguing that the fire was the result of the defendant's breach of its statutory duty under reg 17 of the Electricity Supply Regulations 1988 to ensure that its works were 'so constructed, installed, protected . . . used and maintained as to prevent danger . . . so far as is reasonably practicable.' Through a close analysis of the history of the 1988 Regulations, and the scheme of statutory duties set up by the Regulations, the Supreme Court concluded that Parliament did not intend that a breach of reg 17 should be civilly actionable:

> Looked at as a whole . . . the scheme of the legislation, with its carefully-worked out provisions for various forms of enforcement on behalf of the public, points against individuals having a private right of action for damages for contravention of regulations made under it.[9]

While the courts always adopt this kind of *analytical approach* nowadays to the question of whether – in a hard case – Parliament intended that breach of a particular SD should be civilly actionable, this approach is of no use to students who will often by asked to determine whether a claimant can bring a claim for breach of statutory duty when the SD that has been breached has been *made up*, and very limited information about that fictional SD is supplied to the student. In determining whether breach of that kind of SD was intended to be civilly actionable, a different approach is needed – one we will call the *presumption approach*.[10]

Under the *presumption approach*, we start off by presuming that if a defendant has breached an SD that was imposed on the defendant for the benefit of the claimant and that claimant has suffered the right kind of loss as a result of that breach (the sort of loss that the breached SD was imposed in order to avoid), then Parliament intended that the claimant should be able to bring a claim for breach of statutory duty against the defendant. We then look to see whether there is any reason to think that Parliament did *not* in fact intend that breach of the SD that was breached by the defendant would be civilly actionable. If we can find sufficient indicators that Parliament did *not* intend that breach of that SD would be civilly actionable, then that is what we will conclude, and find that the claimant

---

[8] *Ex parte Island Records* [1978] 1 Ch 122, 135A.
[9] [2010] 1 WLR 1934, at [37].
[10] Following Stanton 2003, 25–6.

will not be able to bring an action for breach of statutory duty against the defendant. If we cannot make a convincing case for thinking that Parliament did not intend that breach of the defendant's SD would be civilly actionable, we will conclude that Parliament intended that breach of that SD should be civilly actionable and find that the claimant can bring a claim for breach of statutory duty against the defendant.

In looking for indications that Parliament did *not* intend that breach of the SD breached by the defendant would be civilly actionable, we look at a wide number of factors.

(1) *Alternative means of enforcement.* As Lord Rodger observed in the *Morrison* case:

> if a statute provides some means, other than a private law action for damages, of enforcing any duty which it imposes, that will normally indicate that the statutory right was intended to be enforceable by those means and not by private right of action.[11]

In the *Morrison* case itself, the extensive powers given to the relevant Secretary of State to enforce proper observance of the regulations in question in *Morrison* counted heavily against the Supreme Court finding that breach of those regulations was intended to be civilly actionable. In *Scally* v *Southern Health and Social Services Board* (1992), the House of Lords held that an employer's breach of his statutory duty to give his employees a written statement detailing the particulars of their contracts of employment was not intended by Parliament to be civilly actionable. This was because Parliament had specified precisely what should happen when that statutory duty was breached: an affected employee would have the right to go to a tribunal to get the terms of his employment detailed there.

The existence of a criminal penalty for breach of a given SD may count as an indication that Parliament intended that breach of that SD should be sanctioned through the criminal law, and not through a civil action. However, the existence of such a penalty will not be a *conclusive* indication that Parliament did not intend that breach of the SD in question should be civilly actionable, as well as the sort of thing that could give rise to a criminal prosecution. For example, in *Groves* v *Wimborne* (1898), the claimant's employer breached the statutory duty he owed the claimant under s 5 of the Factory and Workshop Act 1878 to ensure that all dangerous machinery used by the claimant was securely fenced. As a result of this breach, the claimant was injured by some unfenced cogwheels. Section 82 provided that an employer breaching his duty under s 5 could be fined. No provision was made in the Act for anyone to bring a civil claim for breach of the duty created by s 5. Despite this, the Court of Appeal still found that when Parliament created the statutory duty contained in s 5 of the 1878 Act, it intended that a breach of that duty should be civilly actionable. Vaughan Williams LJ observed that

> where . . . a remedy is provided in cases of nonperformance of the statutory duty, that is a matter to be taken into consideration for the purpose of determining whether [Parliament intended that breach of that duty should be civilly actionable], or whether [Parliament] intended that there should be no other remedy than the statutory remedy; *but it is by no means conclusive or the only matter to be taken into consideration for that purpose.*[12]

(2) *Floodgates.* Among the other matters 'to be taken into consideration' is whether finding that breach of a given SD is civilly actionable would create an oppressive burden of litigation for those who are subject to that SD.

---

[11] [2010] 1 WLR 1934, at [29].
[12] [1898] 2 QB 402, 416 (emphasis added). See also *Phillips* v *Britannia Hygienic Laundry Co* [1923] 2 KB 832, 841 (per Atkin LJ).

For example, in *Atkinson v The Newcastle and Gateshead Waterworks Company* (1877), the defendants supplied Newcastle and surrounding towns with water. Under the Waterworks Clauses Act 1847, they had a statutory duty to install fire hydrants and supply water to those hydrants at a certain pressure. They breached this duty with the result that firefighters could not obtain any water from one of the defendants' fire hydrants to put out a fire in the claimants' house. As a result, the claimants' house burned down. The claimants brought a claim for breach of statutory duty against the defendants. Their claim was rejected. The Court of Appeal thought that when Parliament created the duty breached by the defendants it could not have intended that a breach of that duty should be civilly actionable:

> it certainly appears a startling thing to say that a company undertaking to supply a town like Newcastle with water, would not only be willing to be put under [a statutory] duty to supply gratuitously for the purpose of extinguishing fire an unlimited quantity of water at a certain pressure ... but would further be willing in their contract with [P]arliament to subject themselves to the liability to actions by any number of householders who might happen to have their houses burnt down in consequence [of the company's non-performance of this duty]; and it is, *a priori*, equally improbable that [P]arliament would think it a necessary or reasonable bargain to make ... [T]he company would virtually become gratuitous insurers of the safety from fire, so far as water is capable of producing that safety, of all the houses within the district over which their powers were to extend.[13]

(3) *The public interest.* It is also material to ask whether it would be contrary to the public interest for breach of a given SD to be civilly actionable. If so, we can safely assume that Parliament did not intend that breach of that SD should be civilly actionable.

This was one of the considerations that led the House of Lords to conclude in *X v Bedfordshire County Council* (1995) that when Parliament imposed duties on local authorities to safeguard the welfare of children in their jurisdiction, Parliament did not intend that the breach of those duties should be civilly actionable. As Lord Browne-Wilkinson observed:

> the Acts in question are all concerned to establish an administrative system designed to promote the social welfare of the community. The welfare sector involved is one of peculiar sensitivity, involving very difficult decisions how to strike the balance between protecting the child from immediate feared harm and disrupting the relationship between the child and its parents. Decisions often have to be taken on the basis of inadequate and disputed facts. In my judgment in such a context it would require exceptionally clear language to show a parliamentary intention that those responsible for carrying out these difficult functions should be liable in damages if, on subsequent investigation with the benefit of hindsight, it was shown that they had reached an erroneous conclusion and therefore failed to discharge their statutory duties.[14]

(4) *Useful purpose.* We could also ask whether finding that a breach of a given SD is civilly actionable would serve some useful purpose. If the answer is 'no' then that may indicate that when Parliament created that SD, it did *not* intend that a breach of that duty would be civilly actionable.

For example, in *McCall v Abelesz* (1976) the claimant let a room in a house owned by the defendants. Through no fault of the claimant the authorities cut off the supply of gas and electricity to his room and the defendants did nothing to get the supply reconnected in the hope that if the gas and electricity supply to the claimant's room remained cut off,

---

[13] (1877) 2 Ex D 441, 445–6.
[14] [1995] 2 AC 633, 747.

the claimant would be persuaded to take up alternative accommodation that they were offering him. The defendants owed the claimant a statutory duty not to do this under statutory provisions forbidding landlords from harassing their tenants into giving up their tenancies. The claimant brought a claim for breach of statutory duty against the defendants. The claim was dismissed by the Court of Appeal. One of the reasons the Court of Appeal gave for finding that Parliament did not intend that the SD breached by the defendants would be civilly actionable was that making breach of this duty civilly actionable would serve little useful purpose. A tenant who was being harassed by his landlord would usually have a range of remedies available to him, and so there would be little point in adding one more remedy on top of those.

Again, in *Cullen* v *Chief Constable of the Royal Ulster Constabulary* (2003), the claimant was arrested under suspicion of being involved in an act of terrorism. During his time in police custody, the police denied him access to a solicitor and in doing so committed a breach of statutory duty. The claimant suffered no loss as a result of being denied access to a solicitor but still sued the police for nominal damages. A bare majority of the House of Lords held that the claim should be dismissed. The majority thought that Parliament had not intended that the SD breached by the police in this case would be civilly actionable even if the victim of the breach suffered no loss as a result of the breach. The best explanation of this decision is that no useful purpose would be served if denial of access to a solicitor were actionable *per se*. Of course, if unlawfully denying someone access to a solicitor were actionable *per se*, then someone who was denied access to a solicitor could bring a claim in tort against the police straightaway, without having to wait for the denial of access to cause him some kind of loss. He would thereby be provided with a speedy means of getting a court to determine whether or not he was entitled to a solicitor. However, someone who is denied access to a solicitor while in custody *already* has a speedy means of getting a court to determine whether or not he is entitled to see a solicitor – he can make an application for judicial review of the decision to deny him access.[15]

(5) *State of mind*. One factor which the courts have taken into account in the past in determining – in a hard case – whether Parliament intended that breach of a particular SD would be civilly actionable is whether the existence of that SD was dependent on the person who was subject to that duty having a certain state of mind. If it was, the courts have taken that as indicating that Parliament did *not* intend that breach of that SD would be civilly actionable.

For example, s 2(2) of the Child Care Act 1980 provided that:

> Where it appears to a local authority with respect to a child in their area . . . that his parents are . . . prevented . . . from providing for his proper accommodation, maintenance and upbringing . . . [and] that the intervention of the local authority . . . is necessary in the interests of the welfare of the child, it shall be the duty of the local authority to receive the child into care.

---

[15] [2003] 1 WLR 1763, at [34]–[40] (per Lord Hutton). Lords Bingham and Steyn dissented, on the ground (at [20]) that someone who is denied access to a solicitor will hardly be in a position to make an application for judicial review to get a court to determine whether the denial of access is lawful or not. However, it is hard to see how being allowed to sue for nominal damages would assist such a detainee – the lack of access to a solicitor would make it just as difficult for him to bring a claim in tort against the police. The only possible advantage of allowing claims for nominal damages to be made in cases like *Cullen* is that if such claims could be made, then a detainee who was denied access to a solicitor while in custody would be able to bring a claim in tort against the police months or years after he was detained for the *sole* purpose of having it established in a public forum whether or not the police acted lawfully in denying him access to a solicitor. But it is hard to see what *useful* purpose would be served in allowing him to do this.

One of the reasons the House of Lords gave in *X v Bedfordshire County Council* (1995) for thinking that Parliament did not intend that breach of this statutory duty would be civilly actionable was that if it were, the following paradoxical result would obtain. An *Incompetent* local authority that thought a child in its area needed to be taken into care but then failed to follow through and take the child into care would be subject to an action for breach of statutory duty. In contrast, a *Callous* local authority that perversely refused to recognise that a child in its area needed to be taken into care could not be sued for breach of statutory duty because it would not have the state of mind required for that duty to kick in. So *Incompetent* local authorities would be treated more severely under the law than *Callous* local authorities, if breach of the statutory duty in s 2(2) of the Child Care Act 1980 were civilly actionable.

Again, s 65 of the Housing Act 1985 provides that if a housing authority is:

> satisfied that [an applicant for accommodation] has a priority need and [is] not satisfied that he became homeless intentionally, [it] shall . . . secure that accommodation becomes available for his accommodation.

In *O'Rourke v Camden London Borough Council* (1998), Lord Hoffmann thought that when Parliament enacted this section, it could not have intended that a breach of this duty would be actionable in tort. If it *had* had such an intention then the following 'anomalous' result would obtain: 'a housing authority which accepts it has a duty to house the applicant but does so inadequately will be liable in damages, but an authority which perversely refuses to accept it has any such duty will not.'[16] As Lord Hoffmann observed, 'This seems to me wrong.'[17]

By attending to factors such as the five set out above, most hard cases where Parliament has not expressly made it clear whether or not it intended that breach of a given SD would be civilly actionable can be resolved using the *presumption approach*.

The following sections will not be concerned with hard cases. In the following sections we will look at some statutory duties breach of which, Parliament has made it clear, *will* be civilly actionable.

22.3 HEALTH AND SAFETY AT WORK

An employer cannot be sued for breach of statutory duty if he breaches the general duty that he will owe all of his employees under s 2 of the Health and Safety at Work Act 1974 'to ensure, so far as is reasonably practicable, the health, safety and welfare at work of all his employees'. This is because s 47(1)(a) of the 1974 Act makes it clear that breach of *that* duty will not be civilly actionable.

However, s 15 of the 1974 Act gave the government power to introduce statutory regulations governing health and safety in the workplace and s 47(2) of the 1974 Act provides that a breach of a duty arising under these regulations will be civilly actionable unless the regulations provide otherwise. Section 15 has been used to introduce a huge number of regulations governing health and safety in the workplace, such as the Workplace (Health, Safety and Welfare) Regulations 1992, the Personal Protective Equipment at Work Regulations 1992, the Construction (Health, Safety and Welfare) Regulations 1996, the Fire

---

[16] [1998] AC 188, 196.
[17] ibid.

Precautions (Workplace) Regulations 1997, the Provision and Use of Work Equipment Regulations 1998[18] and the Control of Substances Hazardous to Health Regulations 2002.[19]

Particularly significant are the Management of Health and Safety at Work Regulations 1999, which require an employer, among other things, to make a 'suitable and sufficient assessment of . . . the risks to the health and safety of his employees to which they are exposed while they are at work' and to take 'preventive and protective measures' to protect the health and safety of his employees on the basis of that risk assessment.[20] It used to be that a breach of duty under the 1999 Regulations would not be civilly actionable[21] but this has now been reversed by the Management of Health and Safety at Work and Fire Precautions (Workplace) (Amendment) Regulations 2003.[22] As virtually any accident at work can be said to be attributable to an employer's failure to implement a 'suitable and sufficient' risk assessment, it is likely that the 1999 Regulations will provide a fertile source of litigation.

22.4 HIGHWAYS

Under s 41(1) of the Highways Act 1980, the highway authority for a particular highway will owe the users of that highway 'a [statutory] duty to maintain the highway'.[23] Section 41(1A) provides that 'In particular, a highway authority are under a duty to ensure, so far as is reasonably practicable, that safe passage along a highway is not endangered by snow or ice.'[24]

A breach of these duties will give rise to an action for breach of statutory duty. However, s 58(1) of the 1980 Act provides that in

> an action for damages against a highway authority in respect of damage resulting from their failure to maintain a highway . . . it is a defence . . . to prove that the authority had taken such care as in all the circumstances was reasonably required to secure that the part of the highway to which the action relates was not dangerous for traffic.

So, in effect, a user of a highway who is injured or whose property has been harmed[25] because the relevant highway authority failed to ensure that the highway was properly

---

[18] Remarkably, the House of Lords had to interpret these particular regulations on no less than three different occasions, in all cases finding that the cause of the harm counted as 'work equipment': *Robb v Salamis* [2006] UKHL 56 (ladder on bunk bed provided to oil rig worker); *Spencer-Franks v Kellogg, Brown and Root Ltd* [2008] UKHL 46 (closer on door: five different judgments, 100 paragraphs long!); *Smith v Northamptonshire County Council* [2009] UKHL 27 (wooden ramp at day centre).

[19] Most of these regulations have been introduced in response to EU Directives.

[20] Regs 3–4.

[21] This was by virtue of Reg 22(1), which provided that 'Breach of a duty imposed by these Regulations shall not confer a right of action in any civil proceedings.'

[22] The 2003 Regulations do this in a somewhat backhanded way, amending Reg 22 of the 1999 Regulations so that it says: 'Breach of a duty imposed on an employer by these Regulations shall not confer a right of action in any civil proceedings insofar as that duty applies for the protection of persons not in his employment.' Thus, but only by implication, a breach of a duty arising under the 1999 Act *will* be actionable if an *employee* was affected by the breach. The somewhat grudging wording of the new Reg 22 is no doubt attributable to the fact that the government was forced into changing the old Reg 22 on the ground that the old Reg 22 failed properly to implement EU health and safety directives.

[23] It has been held that this duty does not go so far as to require the highway authority to erect traffic signs along the highway to reduce the risk of accidents: *Lavis v Kent County Council* (1992) 90 LGR 416; *Gorringe v Calderdale MBC* [2004] UKHL 15.

[24] This provision was inserted by s 111 of the Railways and Transport Safety Act 2003 and has the effect of reversing the decision of the House of Lords in *Goodes v East Sussex County Council* [2000] 1 WLR 1356, which held that a highway authority will *not* be required under s 41 to keep the highways under its jurisdiction free from ice.

[25] It appears no action can be brought under the Highways Act 1980 for pure economic loss resulting from a highway authority's breach of its duty to maintain the highway: *Wentworth v Wiltshire CC* [1993] QB 654.

maintained will *not* be able to sue the highway authority for damages *if* the highway authority can prove that it took reasonable steps to see that the highway in question would be reasonably safe to travel on. (In cases of harm caused by a highway authority's failure to clear the highway of snow or ice, it seems unlikely that the highway authority will need to take advantage of s 58(1) as its duty in relation to snow or ice is already, under s 41(1A) limited to doing what is *reasonably practicable* to clear the highway of snow or ice.)

22.5 DEFECTIVE PREMISES

Section 1(1) of the Defective Premises Act 1972 provides that:

> A person taking on work for or in connection with the provision of a dwelling (whether the dwelling is provided for by the erection or by the conversion or enlargement of a building) owes a duty –
> (a) if the dwelling is provided to the order of any person, to that person; and
> (b) without prejudice to paragraph (a) above, to every person who acquires an interest (whether legal or equitable) in the dwelling;
> to see that the work which he takes on is done in a workmanlike or, as the case may be, professional manner, with proper materials and so that as regards that work the dwelling will be fit for habitation when completed.[26]

It is quite clear that a breach of this duty will be civilly actionable: both ss 1(5) and 2(1) of the 1972 Act contemplate that someone who breaches this duty may be sued by a victim of the breach who has suffered loss as a result. Three points may be made about this statutory duty.

(1) *Approved scheme.* Section 2(1) of the 1972 Act provides that if someone breaches the duty set out in s 1(1) in doing work on a dwelling, no action may be brought against him for breaching the duty set out in s 1(1) if the dwelling in question is covered by an 'approved scheme' which protects people who acquire interests in houses which prove to suffer from structural defects. For a long time, most houses in the UK were covered by an approved scheme operated by the National House Building Council with the result that during that time most people who discovered they lived in houses which suffered from structural defects because of the way they were built were barred from suing for breach of the statutory duty owed to them under s 1(1) of the 1972 Act. However, the National House Building Council no longer submits its scheme for approval and so the existence of this scheme no longer stands in the way of an action being brought in respect of a breach of the duty set out in s 1(1) of the 1972 Act.

(2) *Who is subject to the duty?* Because the National House Building Council's scheme worked for a long time to prevent actions being brought for breach of the duty set out in s 1(1) of the 1972 Act, there is very little caselaw on this section. So it remains uncertain *who* is subject to the duty set out in s 1(1): the duty could apply not only to builders and engineers but also to architects and surveyors. Section 1(4) provides that

---

[26] Why did we not mention this duty when setting out the situations in which it has been established one person will owe another a duty of care? (See above, chapters 5–7.) The reason is that the duty set out in s 1(1) of the 1972 Act is *not* a duty of care – it is much stricter than that. It requires someone who takes on work in connection with the provision of a dwelling to *ensure* that the work is done in a workmanlike manner, with proper materials and done in such a way that the house will be fit for habitation.

A person who –

(a) in the course of a business which consists of or includes providing or arranging for the provision of dwellings or installations in dwellings; or

(b) in the exercise of a power of making such provision or arrangements conferred by or by virtue of any enactment;

arranges for another to take on work for or in connection with the provision of a dwelling shall be treated for the purposes of this section as included among the persons who have taken on the work.

(3) *Work done to order.* Section 1(2) of the 1972 Act provides that if A takes on work in connection with the provision of a dwelling on B's behalf and does so on the understanding that he is to do that work in accordance with B's instructions, A will be treated as having discharged the duty set out in s 1(1) of the 1972 Act if he does the work in accordance with B's instructions.

22.6 EQUALITY ACT 2010

We have already come across the horrifically complicated Equality Act 2010, in chapter 20 (on 'Harassment'). We saw there that the 2010 Act imposes a huge number of statutory duties on service-providers, people exercising public functions, people disposing of premises, employers, education providers, and associations not to 'harass' other people in various different ways. Breach of all of these duties will be civilly actionable in the county court, unless the defendant is an employer – in which case a remedy may be sought from an employment tribunal.

The main target of the Equality Act 2010 is not, however, harassment, but 'discrimination'. 'Discrimination' takes a variety of forms under the Act. The direct form is defined in s 13 of the Act as treating someone less favourably than you would others because they have a 'protected characteristic' – where s 4 of the Act picks out the following characteristics as being 'protected characteristics': 'age; disability; gender reassignment; marriage and civil partnership; pregnancy and maternity; race; religion or belief; sex; sexual orientation.' The dual form is defined in s 14 as treating someone less favourably than you would others because they have two or more 'protected characteristics'. The indirect form is defined in s 19 as applying to a class of people – including someone with a 'protected characteristic' – a 'provision, criterion or practice' under which the person with a 'protected characteristic' will be disadvantaged as compared with the other members of the class, when applying that 'provision, criterion or practice' to the class is not 'a proportionate means of achieving a legitimate aim'.

Parts 3 to 7 of the Act impose statutory duties on service-providers, people exercising public functions, people disposing of premises, employers, education providers, and associations not to discriminate against other people in various ways, and on various grounds. A breach of any of these duties will be civilly actionable either in the county court or (if the defendant is an employer) in an employment tribunal.[27]

Beyond that, it is not possible for us to go in a book of this kind. The reader who is interested in exploring this subject further should consult a specialist guide to the Equality Act 2010.

---

[27] Sections 114 and 120.

Further reading

In *R* v *Saskatchewan Wheat Pool* [1983] 1 SCR 205, the Supreme Court of Canada ruled that it would no longer recognise a free-standing right to sue a defendant for damages based on the fact that the defendant had breached a statutory duty owed to the claimant. A claim for such damages would have to be brought under the law of negligence (with the breach of duty going to indicate fault on the part of the defendant) or nothing. Academics periodically discuss whether the UK courts should abolish the action for breach of statutory duty. For us, the proposal (as stated) is a non-starter: if we recognise the sovereignty of Parliament, we have to also recognise that Parliament has the power to make certain breaches of statutory duty civilly actionable. Whether the courts should adopt a hardline position that a breach of statutory duty will not be civilly actionable if Parliament has not expressly indicated that it will be is another matter. Certainty would indicate that the courts should. On the other hand, justice may demand that an inadvertent failure by Parliament to say that it wants a breach of a given SD to be civilly actionable should not count against someone's being able to bring a claim for breach of that SD if it is plain that that is what Parliament actually wanted to happen. Anyone who is interested in exploring this topic further should definitely read **Neil Foster's 'The merits of the civil action for breach of statutory duty' (2011) 33 *Sydney Law Review* 67** as well as **James L.R. Davis' 'Farewell to the action for breach of statutory duty?' in Mullany and Linden (eds), *Torts Tomorrow: A Tribute to John Fleming* (LBC Information Services, 1998).**

23 Public nuisance

23.1 The basics *639*

23.2 Unreasonable interference *641*

23.3 Responsibility *647*

23.4 Special damage *650*

Overview

In this chapter we look at a very odd and ill-defined area of the law of tort – the law on public nuisance. As we explain in section 23.1, a claimant who has suffered special damage as a result of the existence of a public nuisance can sue for damages a defendant who was responsible for the existence of that public nuisance. In section 23.2, we explain what sorts of interferences fall within the scope of public nuisance; in section 23.3, when a defendant can be held responsible for public nuisance; and in section 23.4, when a claimant can say that she has suffered special damage as a result of the existence of a public nuisance.

23.1 THE BASICS

A defendant will commit a public nuisance if:

(1) he creates, authorises, adopts or continues a state of affairs which
(2) unreasonably interferes with *either* (a) a public right *or* (b) the comfort, convenience or safety of the public,
(3) he knew, or ought to have known (because the means of knowledge were available to him), that would be the consequence of what he did or omitted to do.

Public nuisance is a strange sort of tort, if it is a tort at all.[1] Why? For a start it is a crime as well as a tort. But this is not particularly odd, even though it may surprise those who misguidedly equate tort law with the tort of negligence. There are actually many well-established torts that are crimes as well as torts: assault and battery, for example. What makes public nuisance odd is what *sort* of wrong it is. The duty that someone breaches when they commit a public nuisance is a duty imposed for the benefit of the public as a whole, not for the benefit of any particular individual. And tort law normally deals – as we have seen just in the last chapter – with breaches of duties owed to particular individuals.

So how did public nuisance end up on the contents page of tort books? The answer is 'By accident – and not just one accident, but two.' As John Spencer's excellent article 'Public nuisance – a critical examination' explains, the first accident was the responsibility of medieval writers on the law who associated public nuisance (a crime) with private nuisance

---

[1] For discussion, see Merrill 2011 – though it should be noted that he is writing from a distinctly American perspective, where government bodies have far more powers to bring civil actions on behalf of the public than is the case in the UK. (His concern is to determine whether public nuisance claims should be brought by government bodies, rather than private individuals.)

(a well-established tort) simply because they shared half a name and shared some very rough similarities in terms of the problems they dealt with:

> it became usual for legal writers who were explaining private nuisance to add a discussion of nuisances to public rights of way either immediately before or afterwards. When the concept of private nuisance later grew to include stinking neighbours out with pigs as well as flooding them and blocking up their access, the writers naturally added to their discussion of obstructing the highway a sentence or two on depasturing pigs in city streets – a practice all too common in days when citizens used the streets as dustbins as well as highways – and which like blocking the highway was a criminal matter for the local courts.[2]

The second accident was the fault of the judges. As Spencer explains: 'It was once a settled rule that no civil action lay for damage resulting from a [public] nuisance, [public] nuisances being exclusively a matter for criminal proceedings.'[3] Given the association that medieval legal writers had drawn between public and private nuisances, this must have given rise to the question – Why aren't public nuisances civilly actionable, if private nuisances are? In a classic example of the dangers of reaching the right conclusion but for the wrong reasons, the judges did *not* say that public nuisances were not civilly actionable because committing a public nuisance involved a wrong to the public, and not any particular claimant. Instead the reason why public nuisances were not civilly actionable

> as given in 1535 by Baldwin CJ in a case where the [claimant] tried unsuccessfully to sue the defendant for damages for blocking the public highway was that 'if one person shall have an action for this, by the same reason every person shall have an action, and so he shall be punished a hundred times on the same case' . . .[4]

But this *floodgates argument* for the non-actionability of public nuisances inevitably led the judges (including Fitzherbert J, in the very same case as the one from which Baldwin CJ's *dictum* was taken)[5] to accept that if a claimant had suffered *special damage* – over and above that suffered by everyone else – as a result of a public nuisance, then that claimant *would* be entitled to sue the defendant who was responsible for that public nuisance. Allowing *that* claimant to sue would not open the floodgates to hundreds of other actions against the defendant for the same thing.

And that is how something that had nothing to do with tort law ended up in the tort books: because public nuisance shares half a name with a well-established tort, private nuisance, and the judges came up with the wrong reason to explain why public nuisances were not civilly actionable in the same way as private nuisances are. But we are now stuck with the rule that if a defendant commits a public nuisance – as defined at the start of the section then – a claimant can bring a civil claim for damages against that defendant if: (4) the claimant suffered special damage as a result of that state of affairs.

The next three sections are devoted to explaining the key elements in the definition: (a) what sorts of things will be held to unreasonably interfere with *either* a public right *or* the comfort, convenience or safety of the public; (b) when a defendant will be held responsible for a state of affairs as a result of having created, authorised, adopted or continued it; and (c) what will count as special damage.

---

[2] Spencer 1989, 58.
[3] Spencer 1989, 73.
[4] Spencer 1989, 73.
[5] For criticism of Fitzherbert J's *dictum*, see Newark 1949, 483.

23.2 UNREASONABLE INTERFERENCE

It is difficult to define what a public nuisance is in any helpful way.[6] Most books rely on Archbold's definition, according to which A will commit the crime of public nuisance if he:

> commits an act not warranted by law, or omits to discharge a legal duty, where the effect of the act or omission is to endanger the life, health, property, [morals,] or comfort of the public or to obstruct the public in the exercise of rights common to all Her Majesty's subjects.[7]

But this definition is very vague. What, for instance, is 'an act not warranted by law'?[8] The Second US Restatement of Torts notes that English judicial decisions have held that public nuisance covers:

> interference with the public health, as in the keeping of diseased animals . . . ; with the public safety, as in the case of storage of explosives in the midst of a city . . . ; with the public morals, as in houses of prostitution . . . ; with the public peace, as by loud and disturbing noises; with the public comfort, as in the case of widely disseminated bad odors, dust, and smoke; with the public convenience, as by obstruction of a public highway or navigable stream; and with a wide variety of miscellaneous public rights of a similar kind.[9]

This catalogue usefully illustrates the width of public nuisance in practice. But it is also misleading so far as it suggests that *any* interference with these public interests will be sufficient. This is incorrect. If we take the example of storage of explosives and inflammable substances, it is not the law in England that someone will commit public nuisance whenever he stores the slightest amount of these.[10] Similarly, a defendant will not commit a public nuisance whenever he obstructs the highway to a minor extent.[11] What is crucial is whether the substances are stored *to an unreasonable extent or in an unreasonable way*, and whether the highway is obstructed *to an unreasonable extent*.[12] Thus we think that someone who commits a public nuisance breaches one or both of the following two overlapping duties:

---

[6] Spencer 1989 scathingly criticises the current scope of the concept of a 'public nuisance'.

[7] Archbold's definition was approved by the House of Lords in *R v Rimmington, R v Goldstein* [2006] 1 AC 459, subject to removal of the reference to morals (per Lord Bingham at [36], per Lord Rodger at [45]), which is why we have put that word in square brackets. Archbold's definition follows *Stephen's Digest of the Criminal Law*, 9th edn (1900), at 184: 'A common nuisance is an act not warranted by law or an omission to discharge a legal duty, which act or omission obstructs or causes inconvenience or damage to the public in the exercise of rights common to all His Majesty's subjects.'

[8] In *R v Rimmington, R v Goldstein* [2006] 1 AC 459, the House of Lords held that the definition of public nuisance is not so vague that it violates human rights standards because it is (at [36]): 'clear, precise, adequately defined and based on a discernible rational principle. A legal adviser asked to give his opinion in advance would ascertain whether the act or omission contemplated was likely to inflict significant injury on a substantial section of the public exercising their ordinary rights as such: if so, an obvious risk of causing a public nuisance would be apparent; if not, not.'

[9] Restatement of Torts 2d, §821B, comment b.

[10] *R v Lister* (1856–7) 7 Dears & B 209, 169 ER 979; *R v Chilworth Gunpowder Co* (1888) 4 TLR 557.

[11] *Trevett v Lee* [1955] 1 All ER 406, CA (temporarily placing a hosepipe across a country lane).

[12] Support for this proposition can be found in the Court of Appeal decision of *Harper v G N Haden & Sons Ltd* [1933] Ch 298 concerning whether builders' scaffolding which obstructed a pavement amounted to a public nuisance. Lord Hanworth MR said (at 302): 'A temporary obstruction to the use of the highway or to the enjoyment of adjoining premises does not give rise to a legal remedy where such obstruction is reasonable in quantum and in duration.' Romer LJ drew an express parallel with the standard of unreasonableness in private nuisance cases and stated (at 317): 'The law relating to the user of the highway is in truth the law of give and take.' However, in the recent case of *Westminster City Council v Ocean Leisure Ltd* [2004] EWCA Civ 970, the Court of Appeal treated Lord Hanworth's dictum as too wide (at [24]). The Court preferred (at [42]) the view that a limited restriction on the ability of the public to use the highway will be lawful if the restriction is a consequence of a reasonable incident of use of the highway, for instance parking, or of reasonable access to or maintenance of premises alongside the highway.

(PND1) a duty not to create, authorise, adopt or continue a state of affairs which *interferes unreasonably with a public right*; and

(PND2) a duty not to create, authorise, adopt or continue a state of affairs which *interferes unreasonably with the comfort, convenience or safety of the public.*

A. Unreasonable interference with public rights

Claims based on a breach of duty PND1 raise the question of what counts as a public *right*. Some of the uncertainties as to the scope of public nuisance flow from the fact that it is easy to use the word *right* in a loose sense. It is important not to assume that there is a *right* to all benefits which are widely enjoyed. The rights which are most often relied on in public nuisance cases are the right to free passage along public highways and the right to free navigation along a public river.

As an example of the law in action we will focus on unreasonable interferences with the right to free passage along public highways. Free passage along the public highway will be unreasonably interfered with if the highway is unreasonably *obstructed* or users of the highway are unreasonably *endangered*. So, what will count as an actionable *obstruction*? And what will count as an actionable *endangerment*?

(1) *Obstruction*. Whether an obstruction to the highway will amount to an unreasonable obstruction depends on the degree of interference created by the obstruction and the reasonableness of causing that degree of interference. Where the obstruction is not such as is likely to inconvenience the public, such as a lamp-post on a pavement, the court will usually hold that there is no unreasonable obstruction.[13] Further, even when an obstruction does cause inconvenience, the person creating the obstruction may be able to demonstrate that there was no *unreasonable* obstruction because it was reasonable to use the highway in the way that he did:

> No member of the public has an exclusive right to use the highway. He has merely a right to use it subject to the reasonable use of others, and if that reasonable user causes him to be obstructed he has no legal cause of complaint.[14]

Thus it is not a public nuisance to block a highway with a cart in order to unload it.[15] But it is a public nuisance to block a highway so regularly as effectively to prevent it from being used by others.[16] Similarly, it is a public nuisance to block a highway for some reason other than reasonable use of the highway for passage, incidents of passage, access to premises alongside the highway, or building work on premises alongside the highway.[17] In such cases the interferences cannot be defended by appealing to some advantage that might flow to

---

[13] *W H Chaplin & Co Ltd v Mayor of Westminster* [1901] 2 Ch 329.

[14] *Harper v G N Haden & Sons Ltd* [1933] Ch 298, 317 per Romer LJ. See also, *Herring v Metropolitan Board of Works* (1865) 19 CB NS 510, 144 ER 886.

[15] *R v Jones* (1812) 3 Camp 230, 231; 170 ER 1364, 1365: 'A cart or wagon may be unloaded at a gateway; but this must be done with promptness' (per Lord Ellenborough).

[16] *R v Cross* (1812) 3 Camp 224, 227, 170 ER 1362, 1363: 'No one can make a stable yard of the king's highway' (per Lord Ellenborough, finding against the proprietors of the Greenwich stagecoach which made two 45-minute stops each day near Charing Cross). But it seems that in rare circumstances even this may be reasonable: *Dwyer v Mansfield* [1946] 1 KB 437, where the obstruction was caused by queues at a greengrocer's shop during wartime rationing.

[17] *Westminster City Council v Ocean Leisure Ltd* [2004] EWCA Civ 970, where the state of affairs (that would have been a public nuisance had it not been authorised by statute) involved obstruction of the highway in order to build a new footbridge across the River Thames.

the public interest from such an obstruction continuing.[18] An unreasonable obstruction does not always have to be physical. For example, in *Wandsworth LBC v Railtrack PLC* (2001) the obstruction took the unusual form of users being discouraged from using a particular footpath by the risk of falling pigeon excrement. Gibbs J held that this state of affairs amounted to a public nuisance even without consideration of the possible health risks.

No right to persist with an obstruction of the highway can be obtained by long use,[19] but if an obstruction pre-dates dedication of the road as a highway then the dedication may be treated as subject to the reservation of the obstruction being continued.[20]

(2) *Endangerment.* As we have said, a state of affairs which unreasonably endangers users of the highway will amount to an unreasonable interference with free passage. It might be thought that where a claimant alleges that he was unreasonably endangered *and then injured* by a state of affairs which the defendant created, authorised, continued or adopted, the claimant ought really to allege that the defendant committed the tort of negligence.[21] After all, this is the tort which is – in large part – built around the existence of duties to avoid creating unreasonable risks of others suffering physical injury.[22] But there is no rule that prevents a claimant from bringing a claim in public nuisance, rather than negligence, if she has been injured as a result of a defendant creating, authorising, continuing or adopting a state of affairs that poses an unreasonable danger to users of the highway. This is probably because many states of affairs that are dangerous involve a degree of *obstruction*, and there is no doubt that unreasonable obstruction of the highway can give rise to a claim for public nuisance.

B. Interference with the public's comfort and convenience

Claims based on a breach of duty PND2 raise the difficult question of how we draw the line between situations where we say 'this has interfered with the comfort, convenience or safety of *some individuals*' and those where we say 'this has interfered with the comfort, convenience or safety of *the public*'. We think that the line depends on two factors: (1) how many people were affected, or potentially affected, and (2) whether the effect was 'common' to them. We will discuss each of these factors in turn, and then also discuss: (3) when an interference with comfort, convenience or safety will be *unreasonable*; and (4) whether a breach of duty PND2 requires more than a single, isolated incident.

(1) *How many people were affected?* In *Attorney-General v PYA Quarries* (1957), Denning LJ refused to stipulate that some minimum number of people had to be affected, and instead said that for an interference to amount to a public nuisance it would have to be

---

[18] In *R v Train* (1862) 2 B & S 640, 121 ER 1129, the King's Bench ruled that a tramway in Lambeth was a public nuisance since it withdrew part of the highway from ordinary use. As Crompton J pointed out, the effect of such a ruling was merely to insist that those who wanted to promote such projects had to obtain a private Act of Parliament. Some 'technical' obstructions may, however, be held to be reasonable because they 'enable the public to exercise their right with greater facility and more convenience', such as a barrier preventing unauthorised vehicles from using a towpath: *Attorney-General v Wilcox* [1938] 3 All ER 367, 372 (liability found on the facts).

[19] *R v Cross* (1812) 3 Camp 224, 227, 170 ER 1362, 1363: 'It is immaterial how long the practice may have prevailed, for no length of time will legitimate a nuisance' (per Lord Ellenborough).

[20] *Fisher v Prowse* (1862) 2 B & S 770, 121 ER 1258. This explains the legality of maintaining, for instance, stone steps leading down from an old house onto a pavement, and the cellar-flaps of an ancient public house.

[21] See *Hunter v Canary Wharf* [1997] AC 655, 692. The question whether public nuisance *should* be restricted to exclude claims for personal injuries is discussed in detail below, § 23.4(D).

[22] For an account of the principle that foreseeability of physical injury gives rise to a duty of care, which underlies the existence of a large number of duties of care in negligence, see above, § 6.2.

so widespread in its range or so indiscriminate in its effect that it would not be reasonable to expect one person to take proceedings on his own responsibility to put a stop to it, but that it should be taken on the responsibility of the community at large.[23]

This statement has been regularly cited and has made its way into almost all the tort textbooks. But in our opinion, it must be treated with caution.

Our main quarrel with Denning LJ's statement is that it seems to assume that every public nuisance is also a private nuisance to a large number of claimants.[24] This overlooks the fact that the public interest (protected by public nuisance) is not simply a conglomeration of private interests *in land* (protected by private nuisance). Many cases of public nuisance do not involve interferences with private interests *in land* at all. For instance, in *R v Vantandillo* (1815) the defendant created a public nuisance by carrying a child with smallpox through the streets and it is unlikely that this was an interference with the interests in land of a substantial number of citizens.[25] Similarly, in *R v Madden* (1975) the Court of Appeal stated that the crime of public nuisance could be committed by making a hoax bomb threat if a considerable number of persons was affected, but there was no suggestion that there had to be any possibility of those affected being able to sue for private nuisance. And in the important recent case of *Corby Group Litigation Claimants v Corby BC* (2009) the claimants established that the defendant was responsible for a state of affairs that unreasonably endangered the *health* of the public, not one that unreasonably interfered with private interests *in land*.[26]

Thus our view is that Denning LJ should have made no reference to the reasonableness or otherwise of expecting *individuals* to sue. We think that the appropriate test should be whether the interference was so widespread in its range or so indiscriminate in its effect that it is appropriate to treat it as a wrong to the community at large. This modified test preserves an important element in Denning LJ's statement: the interference can amount to a wrong to the *community* because it is either (1) 'widespread in its range' or (2) 'indiscriminate in its effect'.

For the avoidance of doubt we should make clear that although it is *not* the case that *every* public nuisance is made up of multiple instances of private nuisance, *some* public nuisances will involve widespread effects that can *also* give rise to claims in private nuisance. If the interference in question has caused any claimant to suffer *both* special damage and an unreasonable interference with land in which she has an interest, then that claimant can make a claim in *both* public nuisance and private nuisance against anyone who created, authorised, adopted or continued the interference in question.[27] Claims in public nuisance and private nuisance are not mutually exclusive.[28]

---

[23] [1957] 2 QB 169, 191.

[24] This assumption can best be seen by going through the following steps. (1) Denning LJ's test for a public nuisance depends on whether it *would be reasonable to expect* an individual to sue. (2) The question whether it is *reasonable to expect* an individual to sue assumes that the individual *could sue*. (3) The most obvious thing individuals could be suing for is private nuisance.

[25] See also *R v Henson* (1852) Dears 24, 169 ER 621 (taking a horse with an infectious disease into a public place).

[26] The reference here is to the first instance trial: [2009] EWHC 1944 (TCC). Before this trial was held the Court of Appeal ruled on whether the public nuisance claim should be 'struck out': *Corby Group Litigation Claimants v Corby BC* [2009] QB 335.

[27] For example, in the case of *Jan de Nul (UK) Ltd v AXA Royale Belge SA* [2000] 2 Lloyd's Rep 700 (upheld on appeal, [2002] 1 Lloyd's Rep 583) Jan de Nul (UK) Ltd conducted dredging operations in Southampton Water in such a way as to cause silt to be deposited elsewhere in the estuary. Some of the users who were inconvenienced by this *possessed* parts of the river bed and could have sued in private nuisance, while others could only have sued for public nuisance by interference with the public right of navigation or the public right to take fish.

[28] See *Colour Quest Ltd v Total Downstream UK PLC* [2009] EWHC 540 (Comm), at [432]–[434]. The Court of Appeal dealt with an appeal against part of David Steel J's decision in *Shell UK Ltd v Total UK Ltd* [2011] 1 QB 86, but his conclusion on this point was not re-examined.

We still have to face the question of *how many* people, in practice, must be inconvenienced or discomforted or subjected to an indiscriminate risk before a defendant will be held to have committed a public nuisance by breaching duty PND2.[29] Our view is that the most useful discussion of how many people must be affected before the effects will be sufficiently widespread is found in Romer LJ's judgment in *Attorney-General* v *PYA Quarries* (1957). He suggests that a judge should ask whether 'the neighbourhood' is affected by the defendant's activity and should then consider whether 'the local community within that sphere comprises a sufficient number of persons to constitute a class of the public'.[30] These issues are described by Romer LJ as 'questions of fact', which seems to mean that they are matters for the judgment of trial judges rather than for appellate rules. On the particular facts of the *PYA Quarries* case the Court of Appeal held that there were no grounds for interfering with the trial judge's conclusions that flying rocks which disturbed 30 petitioners and vibrations which prompted fewer complaints were both sufficiently widespread. It is common to cite *R* v *Lloyd* (1802) as a case on the other side of the line. In this case it was held that the defendant did not create a public nuisance when he created a noise which disturbed only three houses in Clifford's Inn.

(2) *Was the effect 'common'?* Recall, we are explaining how the law decides when to say 'this has interfered with the comfort, convenience or safety of *the public*' rather than 'this has interfered with the comfort, convenience or safety of *some individuals*'. While this depends in part on how many people were affected, or potentially affected – the issue we explored under the previous sub-heading – it also depends on whether the effect on them was 'common'. When we say that the effect must have been 'common', we do not mean 'common' as opposed to rare, but that it must have been 'common' in the sense of 'shared'. The nature of this requirement is illustrated by *R* v *Rimmington* (2006).[31] In this case the House of Lords held that a defendant had not committed the crime of public nuisance by sending 538 letters and packages containing racially offensive material to a large number of people. The defendant had offended a large number of people; but the effect on them was not 'common'.[32] The outcome might have been different if the defendant had set up a loudspeaker system through which he broadcast racially offensive material so that it could be heard by 538 people in a particular area. In such a case all the people living in a particular 'community' would have been subjected to the 'common' annoyance of disturbance by the defendant's obnoxious broadcasts. So far most English cases have involved injuries that were 'common' because they affected a sufficient number of people in a particular geographical location; the English appellate courts have not decided whether public nuisance can also protect communities that are not defined by geographical propinquity.[33]

An effect does not cease to be 'common' just because the interference simultaneously affects a significant number of individual interests. Thus the explosion at the Buncefield Oil Storage Depot in 2005 disrupted over 600 nearby businesses, led to 2000 people being

---

[29] Where the defendant breaks duty PND1 – that is, 'interferes unreasonably with a public right' – there is no need for any minimum number of people to be affected. As Denning LJ said in *Attorney-General* v *PYA Quarries* [1957] 2 QB 169, 191, 'Take the blocking up of a public highway or the non-repair of it. It may be a footpath very little used except by one or two householders. Nevertheless, the obstruction affects everyone indiscriminately who may wish to walk along it.'

[30] [1957] 2 QB 169, 184–5.

[31] *R* v *Rimmington*, *R* v *Goldstein* [2006] 1 AC 459.

[32] Similarly, the House of Lords held that making obscene telephone calls to a large number of different people will not amount to a public nuisance.

[33] Suppose, for instance, that a defendant was responsible for a state of affairs that interfered with the 'comfort, convenience or health' of the users of a particular online service, perhaps by interrupting all those who were playing a popular online game by streaming violent pornography to their computers.

evacuated from their homes, and damaged houses throughout the St Albans district. In the litigation that followed David Steel J ruled that the fact that many of the claimants had suffered sufficient interferences with their private interests in land to enable them to sue for *private* nuisance did not mean that there was not also a 'common injury' sufficient to give rise to a claim for public nuisance: 'while a private owner's right to the enjoyment of his own land is not a right enjoyed by him in common with other members of the public, nonetheless any illegitimate interference, being the very same interference contemporaneously suffered by other members of the public, constitutes a common injury satisfying the public nature of a public nuisance'.[34]

(3) *Unreasonable interference.* Clearly, not every interference with comfort, convenience or safety will amount to a wrong, even if it is widespread; for example, the fact that residents near major football stadia will regularly be inconvenienced by crowded streets, and disturbed by chanting fans, does not mean that they are victims of public nuisance. In such cases the pivotal question is whether the interference is *unreasonable*.

Many of the factors that courts will take into account when considering whether an interference is unreasonable will parallel those taken into account in private nuisance cases;[35] for example: (a) an insubstantial interference will not be unreasonable; (b) an interference resulting from a wholly ordinary use of land will not be unreasonable; (c) when considering whether an interference is unreasonable a court will ignore any amplification of its effects that can be attributed to the hypersensitivity of those affected; (d) what is unreasonable will be considered in the context of what is ordinarily to be expected in a locality of a similar character; and (e) the significance of an interference will vary in accordance with how regularly it occurs, the time when it occurs, and its duration and intensity. Thus in *Shoreham-by-Sea UDC v Dolphin Canadian Proteins Ltd* (1973),[36] in considering whether the smell emanating from the defendant's factory amounted to a public nuisance, Donaldson J took into account that it was situated in 'an industrial area' – 'the local inhabitants are not entitled to expect to sit in a sweet-smelling orchard' – and that mechanical failure or human error would almost inevitably lead to the emission of offensive smells two or three times a year, but concluded that the particular smell's frequency and unattractive and strong character meant that it was a public nuisance. But while *many* of the factors will have a parallel in the tort of private nuisance we think that it is important for a court always to bear in mind that in private nuisance cases the essential question is what a landowner in a particular locality ought to be expected to tolerate, while in public nuisance the essential question is whether the state of affairs is such that it should be condemned as a *wrong to the community*.[37]

(4) *Isolated incidents.* It has sometimes been asked whether an isolated incident can amount to a public nuisance. In *Stone v Bolton* (1949), Oliver J stated that 'an isolated act of hitting a cricket ball on to a road, cannot, of course, amount to a nuisance . . . nuisance must be a state of affairs'.[38] Oliver J's opinion was supported by Professor Newark, though he seems

---

[34] *Colour Quest Ltd v Total Downstream UK PLC* [2009] EWHC 540 (Comm), at [430]. The Court of Appeal dealt with an appeal against part of David Steel J's decision in *Shell UK Ltd v Total UK Ltd* [2011] 1 QB 86, but this point was not re-examined.

[35] See above, §§ 15.4–15.5.

[36] *Shoreham-by-Sea UDC v Dolphin Canadian Proteins Ltd* (1973) 71 Local Government Reports 261.

[37] This may mean that planning permission should be treated as more relevant in cases of *public* nuisance than in cases of *private* nuisance. But this point has not been explored in the cases or in recent academic commentary: for example, Parpworth 2008, Bishop and Jenkins 2011.

[38] [1949] 1 All ER 237, 238e. This point was not discussed when the case reached the House of Lords: [1951] AC 850.

to have been chiefly motivated by the fear that if this opinion was rejected then a skidding bus might constitute a public nuisance.[39] If Oliver J's opinion represents the law,[40] then it is necessary to determine: (1) how long a single incident must last in order to amount to a 'state of affairs'; and (2) whether, and, if so when, a series of single incidents can amount to a 'state of affairs'. In our opinion there is no good reason of principle for getting enmeshed in such arcane questions. Rather courts should concentrate on the central question whether there was an unreasonable interference or not.[41]

23.3 RESPONSIBILITY

Where a claimant has suffered special damage (a term still to be explained) as a result of the existence of a public nuisance, he will only be entitled to sue a defendant for damages if the defendant *created, authorised, adopted or continued* the public nuisance. We can split these ways of establishing that a defendant was responsible for a public nuisance into two.

A. Creating or authorising

A person who *creates* a state of affairs that amounts to a public nuisance can be held responsible for it. And a person who *authorises* someone else to create a state of affairs that amounts to a public nuisance can *also* be held responsible for it. But in both situations the defendant will only be responsible if he knew, or ought to have known (because the means of knowledge were available to him[42]), that such an interference would be the consequence of what he did or omitted to do.

The importance of knowledge in this context was established by the House of Lords in the criminal case of *R* v *Goldstein* (2006). The defendant had enclosed a small amount of salt in a letter which he posted. This was intended as a harmless joke but some of the salt leaked from the envelope in a postal sorting office and because of fears that it might be anthrax the building was evacuated and the police called in. The House of Lords held that a defendant is only responsible for a public nuisance which 'he knew, or ought to have known (because the means of knowledge were available to him), would be the consequence

---

[39] Newark 1949, 486, 488. There are more convenient ways of avoiding inconsistency with the tort of negligence in road accident cases. Thus it could be argued that (1) it is not an unreasonable use of the highway to drive a reasonably safe bus on it, (2) such buses sometimes skid without anyone having been careless, and (3) consequently, the non-careless skidding of a bus is not an unreasonable interference with the safety of other road users.

[40] It is doubtful whether the case law supports Oliver J. Thus public nuisance can cover situations where a mass of snow suddenly falls off a roof onto a claimant (*Slater* v *Worthington's Cash Stores (1930) Ltd* [1941] 1 KB 488, decided by Oliver J!), where a building next to the highway suddenly collapses (see, for instance, *Wringe* v *Cohen* [1940] 1 KB 229 and *Mint* v *Good* [1951] 1 KB 517) and where an isolated incident, such as the discharge of oil, creates a longer term interference (see, for example, *Southport Corporation* v *Esso Petroleum Co Ltd* [1954] 2 QB 182, 197 per Denning LJ). It may be that the first two situations can be explained on the basis that the mass of snow and buildings were public nuisances even before they collapsed because of the *danger* they posed to users of the highway.

[41] In *Colour Quest Ltd* v *Total Downstream UK PLC* [2009] EWHC 540 (Comm), David Steel J ruled (at [408]–[421]) that there is no rule preventing a claim in *private* nuisance being based on a 'single isolated escape', and the defendants did not attempt to argue that such a rule existed in *public* nuisance. The Court of Appeal dealt with an appeal against part of David Steel J's decision in *Shell UK Ltd* v *Total UK Ltd* [2011] 1 QB 86, but this point was not re-examined.

[42] In *Sedleigh-Denfield* v *O'Callaghan* [1940] AC 880, 904, Lord Wright treated the phrase 'means of knowledge' as equivalent to what an occupier should have realised 'with ordinary care in the management of his property'. If we can generalise from this that 'means of knowledge' refers to 'the capacity to know through the exercise of reasonable care', then this guidance is likely to be useful.

of what he did or omitted to do'.[43] Applying this test, the House of Lords held that Goldstein should not have been convicted because it had not been proved that he ought to have known that the salt would escape.

The House of Lords adopted this test from the Court of Appeal in *R v Shorrock* (1994), which had itself adopted it from Lord Wright in *Sedleigh-Denfield* v *O'Callaghan* (1940). The relevant passage in Lord Wright's speech states:

> Though the rule has not been laid down by this House, it has I think been rightly established in the Court of Appeal that an occupier is not prima facie responsible for a nuisance created without his knowledge and consent. If he is to be liable a further condition is necessary, namely, that he had knowledge or means of knowledge, that he knew or should have known of the nuisance in time to correct it and obviate its mischievous effects . . . The responsibility which attaches to the occupier because he has possession and control of the property cannot logically be limited to the mere creation of the nuisance. It should extend to his conduct if, with knowledge, he leaves the nuisance on his land. The same is true if the nuisance was such that with ordinary care in the management of his property he should have realised the risk of its existence. This principle was affirmed in *Barker* v *Herbert*[44] . . . Though the nuisance [in *Barker* v *Herbert*] was a public nuisance, and though a public nuisance in many respects differs or may differ from a private nuisance, yet there is in my opinion no difference, in the respect here material, which is that if the defendant did not create the nuisance he must, if he is to be held responsible, have continued it, which I think means simply neglected to remedy it when he became or should have become aware of it.[45]

In this passage Lord Wright was only purporting to discuss what had to be proved as to the defendant's state of mind in order to establish liability in cases where the defendant was an occupier of land who had *not* created or authorised the nuisance. *Sedleigh-Denfield* involved a flood arising from work done on the defendant's land by a trespasser and earlier in his speech Lord Wright had bluntly stated that: 'If the work had been done by or on behalf of the [defendant], the conditions requisite to constitute a cause of action for damages for a private nuisance, would be beyond question complete.'[46] Similarly, *R v Shorrock* (1994) involved potential liability of an occupier for a public nuisance caused by the acts of others on his land. In this case the event that amounted to a public nuisance was an 'acid house party' attended by between 3,000 and 5,000 people, and the defendant was the farmer whose field had been the venue. The farmer had been convicted despite testifying that he had gone to Harrogate for the weekend to celebrate his anniversary after allowing an acquaintance to use the field for what the acquaintance had described as a 'disco' to raise money for charity. The farmer appealed against his conviction on the grounds that the judge ought to have directed the jury that actual knowledge had to be proved, but the Court of Appeal held that the trial judge's direction in accordance with Lord Wright's speech had been correct.

This suggests that if knowledge is now required in a case where a defendant *created or authorised* the state of affairs that amounted to a public nuisance then the House of Lords *changed the law* in *Goldstein's* case: a rule that was developed for one group of cases – those where the defendant was an occupier of land who had *not* created or authorised the state of affairs concerned – was extended to another group of cases – those where the defendant *had* created or authorised the state of affairs.

---

[43] [2006] 1 AC 459, at [39] (per Lord Bingham) and [56] (per Lord Rodger).
[44] [1911] 2 KB 633.
[45] [1940] AC 880, 904–5.
[46] [1940] AC 880, 902.

Some subsequent cases *seem* to have overlooked that the House of Lords changed the law in this way. For example, in the litigation arising from the explosion at the Buncefield Oil Storage Depot nobody seems to have argued that the claimants could only succeed in their public nuisance claim if they could show that the defendant knew (or ought to have known) that an explosion 'would be the consequence' of what they did (overfilling a storage tank with petrol).[47] But perhaps the explanation for this is that where a public nuisance involves *endangering* the public the claimant only has to show that the defendant knew (or ought to have known) that the public would be *endangered*: it is not also necessary for the defendant to show that the defendant knew exactly how the danger would end up bringing about injury. Similarly, in a case of public nuisance by obstruction of the highway perhaps it would be enough to show that the defendant knew (or ought to have known) that he had created an obstruction, and it would not be necessary to show that he knew exactly who would be obstructed.

A controversial line of cases suggests that a defendant may be liable, even if he has not *personally* created or authorised a public nuisance, if he has engaged a contractor to perform some task which involves an obstruction of the highway or endangers users of the highway, and the *contractor* has created an *unreasonable* obstruction or *unreasonably* endangered other users of the highway. The cases indicate that in these circumstances the defendant will be responsible for the public nuisance created by the contractor unless the contractor's behaviour was collateral to what he was instructed to do.[48] This rule has been relied on principally against bodies with special statutory powers allowing them to arrange for the digging up of the highway. In *Rowe* v *Herman* (1997), the Court of Appeal suggested that the rule would not make a householder liable if builders she engaged failed to put lights on a skip which they placed in the road.[49] Thus it seems possible that this rule applies only to those with special statutory powers.

B. Adopting or continuing

An owner or occupier of land can be held responsible for an interference caused by a state of affairs which she did not create or authorise. This will be the case if the state of affairs in question arose on land *owned*[50] or *occupied*[51] by her and she *continued* or *adopted* the state of affairs in question.[52] She will be held to have continued or adopted the state of affairs in question if: (1) she knew, or ought to have known (because the means of knowledge were available to her), that such a state of affairs would be the consequence of what she did or omitted to do; and (2) a reasonable owner or occupier in her position would have taken steps to prevent the state of affairs from arising or to deal with it once it had arisen.

Owners and occupiers are often held to have *continued* or *adopted* a state of affairs directly caused by the workings of nature. For instance, if a tree on A's land falls into the highway, A may be held liable for the interference with the highway this causes if he

---

[47] *Colour Quest Ltd* v *Total Downstream UK PLC* [2009] EWHC 540 (Comm).

[48] *Hardaker* v *Idle DC* [1896] 1 QB 335; *Penny* v *Wimbledon Urban District Council* [1899] 2 QB 72; *Holliday* v *National Telephone Co* [1899] 2 QB 392.

[49] [1997] 1 WLR 1390, 1394.

[50] In *Mint* v *Good* [1951] 1 KB 517 the Court of Appeal held that the rule set out in the text applied to owners who were not in possession as well as to occupiers.

[51] For instance, a tenant at will can be held liable under this rule: *R* v *Watts* (1703) 1 Salk 357, 91 ER 311.

[52] The Court of Appeal has held that a Highway Authority does not count as an owner or occupier of a highway for the purpose of these rules: *Ali* v *City of Bradford MDC* [2010] EWCA Civ 1282. Thus a Highway Authority will not be liable for public nuisance if it fails to use its powers to clear debris from a highway.

carelessly failed to inspect that tree to determine whether or not it was likely to fall into the road or otherwise obstruct the highway.[53] Similarly, in *Wandsworth LBC* v *Railtrack PLC* (2002), the defendant, which owned a railway bridge over Balham High Road, was held liable for failing to take reasonable steps to prevent pigeons roosting under the bridge and inconveniencing passing pedestrians.

Owners and occupiers can also be held to have continued or adopted a state of affairs directly caused by trespassers.[54] Thus in *Attorney-General* v *Tod Heatley* (1897) the owner of a building site in Westminster was held to have continued a public nuisance by failing to take sufficient steps to remove from the site dead dogs, cats, fish and offal which had been dumped by unknown trespassers.[55]

The rules concerning when owners and occupiers will be held to have adopted or continued a state of affairs directly caused by a *building* falling into a state of disrepair are relatively stringent. Thus courts tend to take the robust view that 'there must be some fault on the part of someone or other for that to happen'.[56] Further, if a defendant is aware of the disrepair, or ought to be, her duty to take reasonable steps to deal with the problem will be non-delegable; as a result, if contractors appointed by the defendant carelessly fail to deal with the problem, she will still be held liable.[57] She will avoid liability, however, if she can establish that the danger was purely the result of 'latent defects'. Historically, the non-delegable duty owed by an owner or occupier which allows claims by those injured by a thing falling from the owner's or occupier's land onto the highway, was probably related to the rule in *Rylands* v *Fletcher*.[58] Now, however, only an extraordinary or unusual use of land falls within the ambit of the rule in *Rylands* v *Fletcher*, while public nuisance covers a far broader range of uses of land. The public nuisance duty is also distinct in that where the complaint is of an unreasonable interference with the highway users of the highway will be able to make claims, while claims under the rule in *Rylands* v *Fletcher* must be made by persons with interests in neighbouring land.[59]

23.4 SPECIAL DAMAGE

If A has created a public nuisance and B has suffered some harm as a result, B will only be entitled to sue A for damages in respect of that harm if that harm counts as 'special

---

[53] *Noble* v *Harrison* [1926] 2 KB 332; *Caminer* v *Northern & London Investment Trust Ltd* [1951] AC 88; *British Road Services* v *Slater* [1964] 1 WLR 498.

[54] *Barker* v *Herbert* [1911] 2 KB 633.

[55] A decision which was approved by the House of Lords in *Sedleigh-Denfield* v *O'Callaghan* [1940] AC 880, and held still to represent the law by the Court of Appeal in *Wandsworth LBC* v *Railtrack PLC* [2002] QB 756, [26].

[56] *Mint* v *Good* [1951] 1 KB 517, 526–7, per Denning LJ. Though in *Wringe* v *Cohen* [1940] 1 KB 229, 233, the Court of Appeal suggested that where premises were undermined by 'a secret and unobservable operation of nature, such as subsidence under or near the foundations' the owner or occupier might not be liable.

[57] *Tarry* v *Ashton* (1876) 1 QBD 314.

[58] See chapter 16 for a discussion of this rule. It will be noted that Blackburn J played a pivotal role in both *Rylands* v *Fletcher* and *Tarry* v *Ashton*, and that both cases involved independent contractors carrying out operations on the defendants' land.

[59] In *Wringe* v *Cohen* [1940] 1 KB 229 the Court of Appeal held that the non-delegable duty only attached to 'premises on a highway' but that both passers-by and owners of adjoining property could take advantage of the duty. It seems to us, however, that it would be implausible for an adjoining owner to claim that he had been a victim of unreasonable interference with the public right to use the highway. Consequently, we think that if the owner of adjoining property has a claim at all it certainly is not a claim for *public* nuisance. Instead it may be a claim for continuing a *private* nuisance (see above, § 15.9(C)). In *Mint* v *Good* [1951] 1 KB 517, 527, Denning LJ stated that the decision in *Wringe* v *Cohen* was 'clearly correct in regard to the responsibility of an occupier to *passers-by*' (emphasis added).

damage'. For these purposes 'special damage' means damage which is different in nature or extent to that suffered by the other members of the public affected by the nuisance. Thus if A creates a public nuisance by unreasonably obstructing a highway, if all that B suffers as a result is the inconvenience of having to go round by another route or being delayed then B probably will not have suffered 'special damage'. But if B trips on the obstruction and is injured, or damages her personal property, then she will have suffered 'special damage'. The difficulty comes with deciding how to deal with cases that fall between these extremes. Four situations which have caused difficulty will be discussed.

A. Special costs from obstruction

In some cases courts have decided that a particular person suffered 'special damage' because the obstruction suffered by all was, in practice, far more inconvenient for that person. The best example of this is provided by *Rose* v *Miles* (1815)[60] where the defendant was alleged to have moored a barge across a public navigable creek and the claimant had to incur the expense of unloading goods from his barges and conveying them by land. The court seems to have thought that the claimant's damage was 'special' to him because he had already loaded his goods before the time of the obstruction and consequently he was unable to avoid the extra expenses. Dampier J said, 'If this be not a particular damage, I scarcely know what is'.[61]

A similar approach was taken in *Jan de Nul (UK) Ltd* v *AXA Royale Belge SA* (2000), where Moore-Bick J considered the liability of a dredging company responsible for siltation interfering with freedom of navigation in an estuary. He held that in such circumstances,

> any significant interference with an individual's commercial operations or the enjoyment of private rights resulting from the obstruction to navigation would in my judgment represent damage over and above that suffered by the public at large and would be sufficient to support an action.[62]

B. Interference with customers

Where an obstruction is particularly harmful to B because it interferes with his ability to receive customers it seems that B will be able to establish 'special damage'. In *Iveson* v *Moore* (1699), the claimant alleged that he had lost customers and the profits of his colliery because of the obstruction of the highway near his colliery. The Court of King's Bench split 2:2 on whether this was sufficiently 'special damage'. But it seems that the case was later argued before all the judges of the Common Pleas and Exchequer, and their opinions unanimously supported the claimant's claim.[63] Similarly, in *Wilkes* v *Hungerford Market Co* (1835) a bookseller successfully claimed that the loss he suffered through his customers being inconvenienced by an obstructed highway was sufficiently distinct to constitute 'special damage'. The correctness of *Wilkes* was doubted by Lord Chelmsford LC in the case

---

[60] See also *Walsh* v *Ervin* [1952] VLR 361.

[61] (1815) 4 M & S 101, 104; 105 ER 773, 774. 'Particular damage' is a phrase that some judges and authors use instead of 'special damage'.

[62] [2000] 2 Lloyd's Rep 700, [44]. This point was not challenged on appeal: [2002] 1 Lloyd's Rep 583.

[63] It is worth noting that in this case the defendant was a rival colliery owner and it was alleged that he obstructed the road with the aim of harming the claimant. In such a situation a modern claimant might prefer to rely on the tort of intentional infliction of harm by unlawful means (discussed in chapter 24) rather than alleging public nuisance. Such a claimant would have to establish that the means used were 'unlawful' (see below, § 24.4) and that the defendant was 'aiming' to cause harm to him. It would not be necessary, however, to demonstrate 'special damage'.

of *Ricket* v *Metropolitan Railway* (1867). But the case was treated as correct by the Court of Appeal in *Blundy, Clark & Co Ltd* v *London North Eastern Railway* (1931). In that case Greer LJ stated that:

> Where a [claimant] has property near a highway which he uses for the purposes of his business, and the highway . . . is unlawfully obstructed, and he is thereby put to greater expense in the conduct of his business, or suffers loss by the diminution of his business, he is entitled to recover damages as a person who has suffered special or peculiar damage beyond that which has been suffered by other members of the public wanting to use the highway.[64]

C. Costs of removing the public nuisance

In *Winterbottom* v *Lord Derby* (1867) the Court of Exchequer held that the claimant could not rely on the expense he had incurred in removing an obstruction as 'special damage' since otherwise any person could give to himself the opportunity to sue. But in *Tate & Lyle Industries Ltd* v *GLC* (1983),[65] the House of Lords held that the claimant *could* claim for the expense it had incurred in dredging the River Thames in order to remove the obstruction to free navigation for which the defendant was responsible. The majority of the House of Lords seems to have held that the 'special damage' was not the cost of dredging itself, but the special loss that the claimant suffered because ships of particular dimensions were unable to progress up the channel. This is important, because it clarifies that the claimant had suffered 'special damage' *before* the dredging was undertaken, and thus does not conflict with the decision in *Winterbottom*.

Lord Diplock disagreed with the majority and argued that 'special damage' arising from the claimant's choice about how it used public rights could not be the basis for a claim for public nuisance.[66] We think, however, that Lord Diplock's dissent was out of line with the cases we have just been discussing under (1) and (2), above. It is clear that the fact that a claimant has *chosen* to make use of a particular highway or river for delivering goods or receiving customers does not prevent an action against someone responsible for an unreasonable obstruction. Further, there is no obvious reason for distinguishing between choosing to use a highway for making deliveries and choosing to use a river for receiving supplies.

The position is different where the body which incurs costs to remove the public nuisance is fulfilling a statutory function by doing so. In *Jan de Nul (UK) Ltd* v *AXA Royale Belge SA* (2002) the Court of Appeal held that where a dredging company had caused quantities of silt to be deposited in such a way as to interfere with the public right of

---

[64] [1931] 2 KB 334, 369. See also *Lyons, Sons & Co* v *Gulliver* [1914] 1 Ch 631; *Walsh* v *Ervin* [1952] VLR 361; and *Colour Quest Ltd* v *Total Downstream UK Plc* [2009] EWHC 540 (Comm), at [459]: 'I conclude that there is long standing and consistent authority in support of the proposition that a claimant can recover damages in public nuisance where access to or from his premises is obstructed so as to occasion a loss of trade attributable to obstruction of his customers' use of the highway and liberty of access' (per Steel J). Stevens 2007 objects to *Wilkes* (at 186–8) because he believes that the bookseller's claim was not based on interference with *his own* right to use the highway but interference with the rights of his *customers*. See also Neyers and Diacur 2012. This assumes, however, that a person's right to use the highway does not include a right to use it as a way of *being reached* by customers, guests, etc. Similarly, courts have allowed the occupiers of piers and those with businesses at the water's edge to bring cases based on interference with public rights of navigation when the difficulty was in *being reached* by others: *Jan de Nul (UK) Ltd* v *AXA Royale Belge SA* [2000] 2 Lloyd's Rep 700 (upheld on appeal, [2002] 1 Lloyd's Rep 583).

[65] Neyers 2010 argues *that Tate & Lyle Industries Ltd* v *GLC* (1983) is a 'landmark case' in the law of torts. This assessment, however, is based on the rejection by the House of Lords of Tate & Lyle's claims in negligence and private nuisance rather than its acceptance of the claim for public nuisance.

[66] [1983] 2 AC 507, 547.

navigation in a river, a harbour authority could sue that company in public nuisance for the cost of dredging the river bed, if either it was its duty to dredge the river bed or it had a statutory power to do so.[67]

D. Personal injuries

There is no real dispute over whether personal injuries can be sufficiently 'special' to an individual claimant. Instead, the debate is over whether personal injuries should be actionable at all in public nuisance cases. The Court of Appeal addressed this question in *In re Corby Group Litigation* (2009).

In that case, the claimants were children who claimed that they were born suffering from various deformities because the defendant council's programme of reclaiming and detoxifying land that formerly belonged to the British Steel Corporation had released, and exposed their mothers to, toxic materials while the claimants were in their mothers' wombs. One of the grounds on which the claimants sued the defendant was public nuisance. The defendant applied to have this particular aspect of the claimants' claim struck out arguing that compensation for personal injuries could not be sued for under the law on public nuisance, by analogy with the position established by the House of Lords in private nuisance cases in *Hunter v Canary Wharf Ltd* (1997)[68] and *Transco plc v Stockport Metropolitan Borough Council* (2004).[69]

The Court of Appeal held that there was nothing in those two decisions that would entitle them to depart from the long line of precedents[70] where damages were awarded for personal injuries in public nuisance cases. The Court of Appeal went on to doubt the argument of the counsel for the defendant – borrowed from F.H. Newark's article 'The boundaries of nuisance' – that public nuisance was, like private nuisance, concerned to protect claimants' interests in exercising 'rights over land in the amplest manner'.[71] Dyson LJ argued that:

> The essence of the right that is protected by the crime and tort of public nuisance is the right not to be adversely affected by an unlawful act or omission whose effect is to endanger the life, safety, health etc of the public.[72]

Given this, he found it hard to understand why damages for personal injury should not be recoverable in a public nuisance case.[73]

---

[67] [2002] 1 Lloyd's Rep 583, at [60]. For a similar case involving a highway authority see *Louth District Council v West* (1896) 65 LJ (QB) 535.

[68] Discussed above, § 15.12. In *Hunter v Canary Wharf* [1997] AC 655, at 692, Lord Goff drew attention 'to the fact that although, in the past, damages for personal injury have been recovered at least in actions of public nuisance, there is now developing a school of thought that the appropriate remedy for such claims as these should lie in our now fully developed law of negligence, and that personal injury claims should be altogether excluded from the domain of nuisance'.

[69] Discussed above, § 16.3(B).

[70] See, for example, *Castle v St Augustine's Links* (1922) 38 TLR 615, and, more recently, *Mistry v Thakor* [2005] EWCA Civ 953.

[71] See Newark 1949, 489.

[72] [2009] QB 335, at [29].

[73] [2009] QB 335, at [30]. At a subsequent trial, *Corby Group Litigation Claimants v Corby BC* [2009] EWHC 1944 (TCC), the claimants demonstrated that the defendant was responsible for a public nuisance, and that the toxic materials that were emitted had the ability to cause the type of limb defects that all except two of the claimants complained of. In April 2010 the defendant dropped plans to appeal, and reached a settlement with the claimants: Ben Quinn, 'Poisoned children win compensation fight against Corby borough council' (published on guardian.co.uk, 16 April 2010).

Further reading

The most important article about public nuisance is clearly **J.R. Spencer, 'Public Nuisance – A Critical Examination' (1989) 48** *Cambridge Law Journal* **55**. Readers will want to assess for themselves whether the House of Lords in *R v Rimmington; R v Goldstein* (2006) sufficiently addressed the concerns raised in it.

Visit **www.mylawchamber.co.uk/mcbride** to access tools to help you develop and test your knowledge of Tort law, including interactive multiple choice questions, practice exam

questions with guidance, weblinks, legal newsfeed, additional case summaries, legal updates and tips on answering problem and essay questions.

Use **Case Navigator** to read in full some of the key cases referenced in this chapter with commentary and questions:

- Hunter *v* Canary Wharf Ltd
- Transco plc *v* Stockport Metropolitan Borough Council

24 The economic torts

24.1 The basics *655*

24.2 Inducing a breach of contract *660*

24.3 Analogous torts *672*

24.4 Intentionally causing loss by unlawful means *672*

24.5 Two-party cases *681*

24.6 Lawful means conspiracy *683*

24.7 Unlawful means conspiracy *688*

24.8 Deceit *692*

24.9 Malicious falsehood *696*

24.10 Recoverable harm *698*

Overview

In this chapter, we look at one of the most interesting, but also least-taught, areas of the law of tort: the economic torts. We deal with six economic torts in this chapter: section 24.2 is about the tort of inducing a breach of contract (roughly, persuading someone to break their contract with someone else) and section 24.3 is about other torts that involve inducing someone to do something wrong. Section 24.4 is about the major tort of intentionally causing another to suffer loss by using unlawful means. In recent years, this tort has been defined as only applying where A intentionally causes B loss by unlawfully interfering with C's freedom to deal with B. In section 24.5 we see what scope there is for saying that the same tort applies in a case where A directly causes B loss, and not by interfering with a third party's relationship with B. Sections 24.6 and 24.7 are concerned with torts that are committed when someone is intentionally caused harm pursuant to an agreement that the defendant has entered into with one or more people. Sections 24.8 and 24.9 are about cases where a claimant is caused loss as a result of lies told by the defendant: either lies told to the claimant (section 24.8) or lies told about the claimant to third parties (section 24.9). Section 24.10 concludes by discussing whether the only sort of harm you can sue for under these torts is economic harm, or whether other – more intangible – harms such as pure distress can be sued for under these torts.

24.1 THE BASICS

In this chapter, we deal with a number of different torts that are conventionally grouped under the name 'the economic torts'. There are six of them.

The first is the tort of *inducing a breach of contract*, which is primarily committed where A persuades C to breach a contract that C has with B. In such a case, A will normally be found to have committed the tort of inducing a breach of contract in relation to B, and will be held liable to compensate B for any losses that she has suffered as a result of C's breach.

The second tort is the tort of *intentional infliction of harm by unlawful means*. As currently defined, this tort is committed where A intentionally harms B by committing (or threatening to commit) a civil wrong – a breach of contract, a tort, or an equitable wrong – in relation to C.

The third and fourth torts we will be discussing in this chapter are both *conspiracy* torts. The tort of *lawful means conspiracy* is committed where A and C combine together to inflict loss on B for no legitimate reason. The tort of *unlawful means conspiracy* is committed where A and C combine together to inflict loss on B using unlawful means to do so.

The final two torts that we will be discussing in this section both involve deceiving someone else. The first such tort is the tort of *deceit*, which is committed where A deliberately lies to B with the object of inducing B to do *x*, B is induced by A's lie to do *x*, and B suffers loss as a result. The second deception tort is the tort of *malicious falsehood*. This tort is committed where A deliberately tells a lie to C about B and B suffers loss as a result.

There is a seventh economic tort – the tort of *passing off*. The principal way in which A will commit this tort is if people are induced to buy A's goods because he is selling them in a way that makes it look like they are made by B. We have already discussed this tort in chapter 18 ('Torts to Intangible Property') and will not talk about it again here.

These torts are known as 'the economic torts' because: (1) they are normally committed by one person causing another to suffer some form of pure economic loss; (2) someone who has suffered a form of pure economic loss will find it easiest to recover compensation for that loss if he can show that he has been the victim of one of these torts; and (3) the existence of these torts consequently helps to protect claimants from suffering pure economic loss at other people's hands.[1] However, giving these torts the name 'the economic torts' is regrettable, for three reasons.

First, the name suggests that these torts can *only* be committed by causing another person to suffer some form of pure economic loss. Consequently, the question of whether these torts might operate to protect a claimant from (say) being caused pure distress by someone else tends not even to be raised when these torts are discussed. (We will, however, discuss this question below in section 24.10.)

Secondly, giving all these torts a common name tends leads many to think that these torts must have something *more* in common than the fact that they all usually involve one person causing another to suffer some kind of pure economic loss. And so in books and articles we find wistful references to the fact that the economic torts have so far 'lacked their Atkin'[2] – some genius who will finally discern the principle that underlies all the economic torts and unify them as a single tort.

These tendencies to mono-mania must be resisted. There is absolutely no good reason to think that the torts gathered together in this section have anything in common except for the accidental fact of the kind of loss that tends to be suffered by someone who is a victim of these torts. All attempts to find a unifying rule or principle that underlies all of these torts have so far failed. For example, it has been suggested[3] that all of the economic torts give effect to a rule that A will commit a tort in relation to B if he intentionally causes B to suffer some kind of loss using unlawful means. So – according to this view – all of the economic torts are examples of, or species of, the tort of *intentional infliction of harm by unlawful means.* But this view is unsustainable. It does not have to be shown that A had an intention to harm B in order for it to be established that A committed the tort of inducing a breach of contract in persuading C to breach his contract with B. Nor does it have to be shown that A acted unlawfully in persuading C to breach his contract with B. The same is true of the deception torts. To establish that A committed one of those torts in

---

[1] It is important to remember that a claimant's economic loss counts as being *pure* economic loss when it is *not* a consequence of the claimant's person or property being harmed.
[2] See Wedderburn 1983, at 229.
[3] See Weir 1997.

relation to B, it does not have to be shown that A acted as he did because he was trying to harm B.[4]

Thirdly, giving these torts the name 'the *economic* torts' tends to ghettoise them as being primarily about money and business, and about regulating what businesses can do to each other by way of competition.[5] As a result, 'the economic torts' are widely viewed as only being of importance to lawyers specialising in competition law and commercial law. They are certainly not thought of as being centrally important to the law of tort, and tend not to be even mentioned to first-year law students. This is highly regrettable. The torts dealt with in this chapter raise fundamental issues about the limits of individual freedom under the law. *Allen* v *Flood* (1898) – a case we discussed in the opening chapter of this book[6] – is one of the key cases on the economic torts and has been hailed by Tony Weir as 'arguably the most important case' in his *A Casebook on Tort*:

> The case is important because it is about freedom. It holds that, whatever morality might say, in law one is free to beggar one's neighbour provided one neither does anything unlawful oneself nor gets anyone else to do anything unlawful.[7]

In *Allen* v *Flood*, it might be recalled, the claimants were employed on a day-to-day basis to do woodwork on a ship. The defendants objected to the claimants' being employed to work on the ship as the claimants had done ironwork on another ship that the defendants regarded as the exclusive province of ironworkers whom they represented. The defendants threatened the claimants' employers that if the claimants were asked to come back to work the next day, the employers' ironworkers would not turn up for work (as they were entitled to do, as they were also employed on a day-to-day basis). The claimants' employers told the claimants their services would no longer be required.

A nine judge House of Lords ruled, by six to three, that the claimants could *not* sue the defendants for putting them out of work.[8] The defendants had not induced the claimants' employers to breach any contract that the employers had with the claimants, and while the defendants had intentionally harmed the claimants, they had not used unlawful means to do so. There was, Lord Herschell held, a 'chasm' between using lawful means to harm someone else and unlawful means:[9]

> In my opinion a man cannot be called upon to justify either act or word merely because it interferes with another's trade or calling; any more than he is bound to justify or excuse his act or word under any other circumstances, *unless it be shewn to be in its nature wrongful*, and thus to require justification.[10]

The debate still goes on as to whether the House of Lords made the right choice in *Allen* v *Flood* by deciding that intentionally harming someone else will *not* amount to a tort unless independently unlawful means are used to inflict the harm. Some American states have

---

[4] See, in relation to the tort of deceit, *Polhill* v *Walter* (1832) 3 B & Ad 114, 110 ER 43. The fact that the tort of deceit can be committed without any intention to harm the victim of the deceit means that Weir 1964 (at 226), Cane 1996 (at 152, n 9) and Sales and Stilitz 1999 (at 432) are *wrong* to suggest that deceit can be seen as an instance of the tort of using unlawful means to harm another.

[5] See Carty 2010, 2–4. Deakin and Randall 2009 go so far as to argue (at 533) that the torts *should* only protect certain economic interests: 'unless a direct interference with trade, business or employment is made out, a vital element of the wrong is missing, even if loss or damage is also present'.

[6] See above, § 1.2.

[7] Weir 2004, 604.

[8] For an account of the litigation see Heuston 1986.

[9] The point is actually slightly better put by Lord Reid in *Rookes* v *Barnard* [1964] AC 1129, at 1168–9: 'I agree with Lord Herschell [in *Allen* v *Flood* [1898] AC 1, at 121] that there is a chasm between doing what you have a legal right to do and doing what you have no legal right to do.'

[10] [1898] AC 1, 139 (emphasis added).

made a different choice. For example, in *Tuttle* v *Buck* (1909), the defendant and the claimant both lived and worked in the village of Howard Lake, Minnesota. The defendant was a banker and the claimant was a barber. The claimant complained that the defendant had developed a grudge against him and had opened up a rival barbershop in the village, with the intention of undercutting the claimant's prices, and driving the claimant out of business. The Supreme Court of Minnesota held that:

> To divert to one's self the customers of a business rival by the offer of goods at lower prices is in general a legitimate mode of serving one's own interest, and justifiable as fair competition. But when a man starts an opposition place of business, not for the sake of profit to himself, but regardless of loss to himself, and for the sole purpose of driving his competitor out of business, and with the intention of himself retiring upon the accomplishment of his malevolent purpose, he is guilty of a wanton wrong and an actionable tort.[11]

The legal philosopher John Finnis has argued that this is correct: 'A sound tort law identifies as tortious every act *intended* precisely to cause harm to another person . . .'[12] And as we will see, English law has gone some way towards adopting Finnis' position in relation to *conspiracies* to harm someone else: an agreement between *Chum* and *Mate* to harm *Target*, if carried out successfully, will amount to a tortious conspiracy if there was *no good reason* for the conspirators to have sought to harm *Target*. Such lack of good reason is most easily made out if the conspirators were acting as they did out of malice towards *Target*.

For what it is worth, we think that the House of Lords was right in *Allen* v *Flood not* to adopt the position that it is a tort intentionally to harm someone else for no good reason. This is for four reasons.

(1) *The difficulty of ascertaining someone's motives.* It can be very difficult to determine *why* someone acted as they did. But such an inquiry would have to be made in applying a rule under which it was a tort intentionally to harm someone else for no good reason.[13] For example, when *Allen* v *Flood* was being argued, one of the judges asked: If a cook, wishing no longer to work alongside her master's butler because she did not get on with him, said to her master 'I will leave you at the end of my current engagement unless you dismiss the butler at the end of his' and the master, in consequence, dismissed the butler at the end of his engagement, will the cook have committed a tort?[14] The result of the decision in *Allen* v *Flood* was that the answer is 'no' – the cook used no unlawful means to induce the master not to re-employ the butler. And no doubt, on the example as given, it would not be a tort for the cook to do what she did even under a rule which said that it is a tort to harm someone intentionally for no good reason, as the cook *did* have a good reason for not wanting to work with the butler anymore. But in the real world, it might be very difficult to determine *why* the cook made the threat that she did. Was it that she only wanted to work alongside people she liked and the butler did not fit the bill (which would give her a good reason for acting as she did) or was is that she wanted to take revenge on the butler for refusing her advances (which would not give her a good reason for acting as she did)?

[11] (1909) 107 Minn Rep 145 (per Elliott J). The judges deciding the case disagreed on whether the facts as stated by the claimant came within this principle. The only judgment (by Elliott J) was actually a dissenting judgment, arguing that the facts – as pleaded – 'do not . . . tend to show a malicious and wanton wrong to the [claimant].' But the other judges disagreed.

[12] Finnis 2002, 46 (emphasis in original). See also Dietrich 2000.

[13] See Restatement 2d, Torts, § 870, Comment i.

[14] [1898] AC 1, 36 (per Cave J), 179 (per Lord James). Lord Herschell (at 138–9) and Lord Shand (165–6) had a different recollection of what was said in argument: they thought it had been asked what the position would be if a butler threatened not to renew his contract with his master unless the cook were let go.

It would be very difficult to tell. As we are not blessed with the ability to peer inside other people's souls, we would do well to steer clear of legal rules that require us to do this.

(2) *Legitimacy of reasons*. Even if we could determine in a given case why a defendant intentionally harmed a claimant, it might be a controversial question whether the defendant had a *good* reason for harming the claimant.[15] For example, suppose A drove B out of business because B had beaten up A's son – would A have had a good reason for acting in the way he did? What if A acted as he did because B had seduced A's wife, or offered A's daughter drugs? These are very difficult questions and it is not clear the courts are the right institutions to answer them.[16] Under the ruling in *Allen* v *Flood* these questions never arise. If A intentionally ruins B using unlawful means to do so he will commit a tort – the question of whether or not A had a good reason for acting as he did never arises because you can never be said to have a good reason for breaking the law.[17]

(3) *Certainty*. The third reason why the English courts have not adopted the *Tuttle* v *Buck* position emerges out of the first two: if the law said that A will commit a tort in relation to B if he intentionally harms B for no good reason, the law would become intolerably uncertain. Take the example of the cook and butler that we have already discussed. Were the law to take the *Tuttle* v *Buck* position, the cook would not be able to tell with any degree of certainty whether or not her procuring the butler's dismissal would amount to a tort or not. Maybe it would, maybe it wouldn't – it would all depend on how the courts, acting after the event, construed her motives and how much sympathy they had for the reasons why she acted as she did. This is unsatisfactory: as Tony Weir asks, 'Is it not important that people should be able to be told in advance what they may or may not do . . . ?'[18]

(4) *Freedom*. In Wainwright v Home Office (2004), the House of Lords considered whether they should recognise that A would commit a tort in relation to B if he intentionally caused B distress when he had no good reason for doing so. Lord Hoffmann, delivering the leading judgment, thought that they should not take such a step:

> In institutions and workplaces all over the country, people constantly do and say things with the intention of causing distress and humiliation to others. This shows lack of consideration and appalling manners but I am not sure that the right way to deal with it is always by litigation . . . it might not be in the public interest to allow the law to be set in motion for one boorish incident.[19]

The fear underlying Lord Hoffmann's judgment here is that were English law to take the step of recognising that it is a tort intentionally to cause someone else distress when one has no lawful justification or excuse for so doing, then our freedom to do and say what we like would be radically curtailed.[20] It seems likely that freedom would be similarly curtailed

[15] See Weir 1997, 74–5.

[16] Had *Allen* v *Flood* [1898] AC 1 gone the other way, it would have been – at that time – up to a jury to determine these issues, and the House of Lords' distrust of juries' abilities to determine correctly whether or not someone had had a *good* reason for intentionally harming someone else undoubtedly influenced the House of Lords' decision.

[17] Though Parliament has taken the view that a trade union official who uses unlawful means to inflict harm on an employer in the course of a trade dispute should not be held liable for so acting: see the Trade Union and Labour Relations (Consolidation) Act 1992, s 219 (summarised below, § 26.5).

[18] Weir 1997, 68.

[19] [2004] 2 AC 406, at [46].

[20] In the United States, where a tort of intentionally causing another emotional distress without lawful justification or excuse is recognised, this concern is addressed by requiring that the defendant's conduct has been so 'extreme and outrageous' that it goes beyond 'all possible bounds of decency . . . and [is] utterly intolerable in a civilised community': see Rest 2d, Torts, § 46, Comment *d*.

if it was a tort intentionally and for no good reason to cause another person to incur any additional cost or loss of profit. Under the ruling in *Allen* v *Flood*[21] no such concern arises. If A intentionally causes B to suffer some kind of harm, A will only commit a tort in relation to B if the means he uses to inflict that loss are already means that are unlawful. So *Allen* v *Flood* does not have the effect of curtailing our liberties in any way at all.

Whether these argument are correct or not, we hope it is now clear to the reader just how important the torts dealt with in this chapter are, and how fundamentally important the issues governing the contours of these torts can be. We will now turn to look at each of these torts in turn.

24.2 INDUCING A BREACH OF CONTRACT

A will have committed the tort of inducing a breach of contract in relation to B *if*:

(1) B had a contract with a third party, C; *and*
(2) A induced C to breach that contract;[22] *and*
(3) A was in a certain state of mind – defined below – when A induced C to breach that contract; *and*
(4) A had no justification for acting as he did.

So – in *Lumley* v *Gye* (1853), Johanna Wagner, a well-known soprano, made a contract with Lumley to sing at Her Majesty's Theatre, and not to sing anywhere else. Gye, a rival opera impresario, was alleged to have persuaded Wagner to sing for him at the Royal Italian Opera – and therefore to break her contract with Lumley. The Court of Queen's Bench held that if Gye *had* persuaded Wagner to break her contract with Lumley then Gye would have committed a tort in relation to Lumley.[23]

The tort in *Lumley* v *Gye* is usually described as either 'the tort of procuring a breach of contract' or 'the tort of inducing a breach of contract'. At one time it was thought that the tort might extend beyond situations where A induced C to breach her contract with B – for instance, to situations where A made it *impossible* for C to perform her contract with B. In such situations, C's failure to perform might not actually amount to a breach of contract: C's non-performance as a result of forces beyond her control might have been expressly excused under the contract or A's intervention might have had the effect of frustrating the contract. The apparent extension of the tort to cover situations where there was no breach led to suggestions that it should be renamed 'the tort of interference with contract'.[24]

But in *OBG Ltd* v *Allan* (2008)[25] the House of Lords held that it was an error to think that the tort in *Lumley* v *Gye* extends to situations where A has made it impossible for C to perform her contract with B. It is clear after *OBG* that A will *not* commit a tort in relation to B by making it impossible for C to perform her contract with B *unless* he uses *unlawful means* to make it impossible *and* he intends to cause harm to B. And then the tort A will

---

[21] Strangely, *Allen* v *Flood* was not cited at all in *Wainwright* v *Home Office* even though, had the House of Lords declared that it is a tort intentionally to cause another distress without lawful justification or excuse, they would have created a large exception to the principles laid down in *Allen* v *Flood*.

[22] *Important note.* The term 'induce' as used in this chapter does not bear its normal meaning of 'cause' or 'bring about': see below, § 24.2(B).

[23] In fact, at the later trial of the facts, a jury found that Gye had not committed the tort because he had honestly believed that Wagner was at liberty to terminate her agreement with Lumley: for further details, see Waddams 2001.

[24] For instance, Fleming 1998, 756–7.

[25] The case is reported at [2008] 1 AC 1, and is referred to hereafter as '*OBG*'.

commit in relation to B will be 'the tort of intentionally causing loss by the use of unlawful means' – the tort discussed in the next section[26] – *not* 'the tort of inducing a breach of contract'.

We will now look at the elements required to commit the tort of inducing a breach of contract.

A. Breach

The House of Lords' decision in *OBG* made it clear that C's committing an *actionable breach of contract* is a necessary element of the tort discussed here.[27] The tort was explained as involving a form of *secondary liability* and, for A's liability to be secondary, C must also be liable: 'No *secondary liability* without primary liability.'[28]

So A will not have committed the tort discussed here if he persuaded C to terminate her contract with B in a *lawful* manner, as there will be no primary liability in this situation.[29] This is consistent with the famous case of *Allen* v *Flood* (1898), which we have just discussed, and which established that A will not commit a tort in relation to B if he persuades C by lawful means *not to make* a contract with B.

The decision in *OBG* also seems to indicate that it is *not* a tort to persuade someone to rescind a contract that is voidable.[30] In *Proform Sports Management Ltd* v *Proactive Sports Management Ltd* (2006), Judge Hodge QC had to consider the separate question whether it is a tort to persuade someone to *breach* a contract which *could have been* lawfully avoided by the party who was induced to breach it.[31] The judge decided that there was no good reason for imposing a duty not to induce a breach of any contract which *could be* lawfully avoided by the party who was induced to breach it.

B. Inducing

What sort of thing does A have to do before he will be found to have *induced* C to breach a contract with B? A number of different forms of conduct can be distinguished.

---

[26] See below, § 24.3.

[27] Ong 2008 points out (at 731) that the courts have not clarified 'how severe the breach of contract must be before tortious liability is imposed.' We think that this is because there is no severity threshold. But Deakin and Randall 2009 (at 538) would not allow the tort to cover breaches where there was an exemption clause (or significant limitation clause) in the contract.

[28] *OBG*, at [44] (per Lord Hoffmann). See also [5] (per Lord Hoffmann), [172] (per Lord Nicholls), [320] (per Lord Brown).

[29] The position was less clear before *OBG*. In *Torquay Hotel Co Ltd* v *Cousins* [1969] 2 Ch 106, Winn LJ stated *obiter* (at 147): 'For my part I think that it can at least be said, with confidence, that where a contract between [B and C] exists which gives [C] an optional extension of time or an optional mode for his performance of it, or of part of it, but, from the normal course of dealing between them, [B] does not anticipate such postponement, or has come to expect a particular mode of performance, [inducing C] to exercise such an option should, in principle, be held actionable if it produces material damage to [B].' This view was contrary, however, to that expressed by Morris LJ in *DC Thomson & Co Ltd* v *Deakin* [1952] Ch 646, 702. The High Court of Australia accepted in *Sanders* v *Snell* (1998) 196 CLR 329, at [23], that Morris LJ had correctly stated the law on this point.

[30] There is clear authority that someone will not commit the tort discussed here if he induces someone not to perform a contract which is void: *Joe Lee Ltd* v *Lord Dalmeny* [1927] 1 Ch 300. On whether it is a tort to induce someone to rescind a voidable contract, Slade J found the authorities conflicted in *Greig* v *Insole* [1978] 1 WLR 302, at 333, but decided to assume that it was not.

[31] The party could have avoided the contract because he was a minor when he entered it and it did not fall into any of the exceptional classes of contract which are binding on minors. The contract concerned was one in which the footballer Wayne Rooney appointed the claimant company as his exclusive representative in contract negotiations and transfers for two years for a management fee calculated as a percentage of his earnings.

(1) *Persuading*. There is no doubt that if A has *persuaded* C to break a contract with B then A will be held to have induced C to breach that contract. Some commentators have argued that the tort should extend no further than this: 'liability should attach under *Lumley* v *Gye* only when the defendant has persuaded the [claimant's] contractor deliberately to break his contract.'[32] Persuasion in this context could involve either an enticing offer or an unattractive threat – either 'carrot or stick'.[33] However, there are some cases when A has been held to have induced C to breach her contract with B even though it would be difficult to describe the part he played in bringing about that breach as *persuasion*.

(2) *Advice*. Suppose that *Singer* has contracted to sing at a theatre in London and that *Singer's Aunt* has advised her not to go to London because a wealthy relative is dying and this relative is likely to give bequests only to family members who pray at his bedside. If *Singer* takes this advice and breaks her contract, should *Aunt* be held to have induced the breach?

Those who argue that *Aunt* should not be held to have induced *Singer* to breach her contract assert that there is an important distinction between *creating* a reason to break a contract and *pointing out* that a reason exists.[34] But Winn LJ showed no sympathy for such a distinction when it was pressed in *Torquay Hotel* v *Cousins* (1969), and suggested that a father who told his daughter that her fiancé had been convicted of indecent exposure would have induced her to break her engagement even if the information was true.[35] Certainly there would be a risk, if the courts drew a distinction between persuasion and advice, that the line between making a soprano a generous offer to *persuade* her to break her contract and merely *advising* her that such an offer was likely to be available if she broke her contract would be difficult to draw in practice.

(3) *Harbouring*. Can A be said to have induced a breach of a contract between B and C if C's breach of that contract happened *before* A became involved? Suppose, for example, that *Soprano* contracted to perform exclusively for *Impresario*. Suppose that *Soprano* then walked out on *Impresario* in breach of contract and was later engaged by *Rival*. Can *Rival* be said to have induced *Soprano* to breach her contract with *Impresario*? It seems that the English courts have taken the view that *Rival can* be held liable if *Soprano's* breach of her contract with *Impresario* was still 'retrievable'.[36] This is often referred to as liability for 'harbouring' – the idea being that in the case just described, *Rival*, by providing *Soprano* with a 'harbour', made it less likely that *Soprano* would return and perform for *Impresario*.[37]

(4) *Facilitating*. In *British Motor Trade Association* v *Salvadori* (1949), C sold a car to A, in breach of a contractual undertaking that C had made with B that he would not sell the car to anyone within a year of purchasing it. A argued that C had been willing to sell the car

---

[32] Weir 1997, 35. See also Carty 2010, 37: 'Persuasion . . . is the necessary link'.

[33] Weir 1997, 34. Likewise, in *OBG*, [20], Lord Hoffmann treats persuasion to breach a contract by a threat of assault as falling within the tort of inducing a breach of contract *as well as* potentially falling within the tort of three-party intimidation.

[34] Carty 2010, 37, citing Hart and Honoré 1985, 54.

[35] [1969] 2 Ch 106, 147. Of course, in such a case the father might be able to rely on the defence of justification. In *Camden Nominees Ltd* v *Slack (or Forcey)* [1940] Ch 352, Simonds J was equally clear that 'advice which is intended to have persuasive effects is not distinguishable from inducement', but also held that a person who provided advice could rely on the defence of justification if the law recognised a moral duty to give the advice.

[36] *Blake* v *Lanyon* (1795) 6 TR 221, 101 ER 521; *De Francesco* v *Barnum* (1890) 63 LT 514.

[37] If it was clear that *Soprano* would never have returned to perform for *Impressario* then *Impressario* might be unable to sue *Rival* because *Rival's* 'harbouring' would not have caused *Impressario* any actionable loss: *Jones Brothers (Hunstanton) Ltd* v *Stevens* [1955] 1 QB 275.

and break his contract with B without any influence from him, and that consequently he could not be said to have induced the breach. Roxburgh J held, however, that C could not break the contract *not to sell* without *someone* being willing to buy, and that 'any active step taken by a defendant ... by which he facilitates a breach' was sufficient to fall within the scope of the tort.[38] Some commentators, however, have expressed strong doubts about this statement because the courts have refused to adopt a general principle that anyone who assists another to commit a tort will be held liable.[39] It must be noted, however, that the cases which have rejected this principle have not involved defendants who both *knew* that they were bringing about a wrong and *intended* to do so.

(5) *Inconsistent dealing.* The situations we mean to describe as involving 'inconsistent dealing' are those where A does something that puts C in breach of a contract with B, usually after A has made a deal with C that removes C's power to control whether he performs the contract and instead allocates that power to A. Two examples may help.

First, suppose that *Owner* contracts with *Neighbour* that no building will be erected during *Neighbour's* lifetime on a particular plot of land ('Whiteacre') belonging to *Owner*. *Owner* then sells Whiteacre to *Rich*. Secondly, suppose *Owner* owns a boat (the '*Prima Donna*') which she hires to *Neighbour* for two years. During this period, *Owner* sells the *Prima Donna* to *Rich*. Clearly in each example *Owner* has relinquished her power to control whether the contract is performed – having sold Whiteacre and the *Prima Donna* to *Rich* it is *Rich* who now can decide whether to build on Whiteacre or to take the *Prima Donna* back from *Neighbour*. But does he have power to do these things? Or would it be a tort for *Rich*, assuming that he knows about the contracts that *Owner* has made, to build on Whiteacre[40] or to take the *Prima Donna* back?

We think that it would be better not to treat 'inconsistent dealing' as falling within the scope of the tort. If it were within the scope then there would be a risk of the tort being inconsistent with the special set of rules about when a covenant relating to land can be enforced against a subsequent owner of the land.[41] There might also be inconsistency with the rules that establish that where a contract between A and B creates an *equitable interest* in an item of property then this will bind a subsequent purchaser of the property unless he was a bona fide purchaser for value without notice.[42] Thus we think a good case can be made for drawing a line between (1) A doing something that *facilitates* a breach of contract by C,[43] and (2) A acquiring property which enables him to control whether a contract made by C is performed.[44]

---

[38] [1949] Ch 556, 565.

[39] See below, § 36.3.

[40] The Whiteacre scenario is similar to the situation in *Sefton (Earl)* v *Tophams* [1965] Ch 1140, where Stamp J found that the defendant would have committed the tort of inducing a breach of contract if he built. The Court of Appeal continued an injunction against the defendant, requiring him not to build, without finding that the defendant would commit the tort of inducing a breach of contract if he did build, and the House of Lords did not consider this point: *Sefton (Earl)* v *Tophams* [1967] 1 AC 50.

[41] For these rules see, Smith 2011, chapter 24.

[42] *Swiss Bank Corp* v *Lloyds Bank Ltd* [1982] AC 584, 598, 613. When such an equitable interest will arise is a controversial question. Compare *Lord Strathcona SS Co* v *Dominion Coal Co* [1926] AC 108 with *Port Line Ltd* v *Ben Line Steamers Ltd* [1958] QB 146.

[43] *British Motor Trade Association* v *Salvadori* [1949] Ch 556, discussed in the previous section.

[44] If this view is correct it follows that *Rich* should not be held liable for *inducing a breach of contract* in either of our two examples. Carty 2010, 55 argues that 'inconsistent transactions should not be seen as tortious per se'. Indeed she would also exclude 'facilitating', and perhaps 'harbouring' from the scope of the tort. See also Smith 1977.

(6) *Preventing performance*. Suppose A *prevented* C from performing a contract with B and B suffered some kind of financial loss as a result, and A did this knowing of the contract and intending that C should be unable perform it. In *OBG* the House of Lords decided that A will *not* commit a tort in relation to B by making it impossible for C to perform her contract with B *unless* he uses *unlawful means* to make performance impossible *and* intends to cause harm to B.[45] And then the tort A will commit in relation to B will be 'the tort of intentionally causing loss by the use of unlawful means' – the subject of the next section – not 'the tort of inducing a breach of contract'.

Since A will not be held to have *induced* C to breach a contract if A takes steps which prevent C from performing, it follows that A will also not be held to have *induced* C to breach a contract if A *omits to take steps which would have enabled C to perform*. Thus if *Speculator* contractually agrees to sell a painting to *Investor*, and *Owner*, who currently owns the painting, refuses to sell it to *Speculator*, then *Owner* will not have committed a tort in relation to *Investor even if Owner*'s only reason for refusing to sell was because he wanted to cause *Speculator* to be in breach of his contract with *Investor*. Indeed, even if *Owner* had already contractually agreed to sell the painting to *Speculator before Speculator* made his contract with *Investor*, a failure by *Owner* to perform this contract will not be held to have *induced Speculator* to breach his contract to sell it to *Investor*. In this latter case, however, *Owner*'s breach of contract will amount to the use of 'unlawful means', so *Owner* may have committed the tort of 'intentionally causing loss by the use of unlawful means' in relation to *Investor*, depending on whom (if anyone) he intended to harm through his non-performance.

The two main arguments[46] in favour of fixing the limit on what counts as 'inducing' between persuading and preventing are that it is easier to draw this line than the principal alternative[47] and that there is a moral difference between seducing C into committing a wrong and merely rendering C unable to perform.[48] But the clarity of the persuasion/prevention distinction should not be exaggerated: there are some forms of behaviour which must be assessed, particularly *harbouring* and *facilitating*, that cannot be easily described as *either* persuasion *or* prevention.[49] Similarly, the significance of the moral difference should not be overplayed: B may find it difficult to share the philosopher's view that if A persuades C to break her contract with B by *threatening* to have her tied up[50] he

---

[45] This point was expressed most clearly by Lord Nicholls: *OBG*, at [178]–[180]. Lord Hoffmann did not make the same point *explicitly*. But such a point is consistent with Lord Hoffmann's insistence that there can be no liability for inducing breach of contract unless there has been a breach of contract, because preventing performance will not always result in a breach. In *Meretz Investments NV v ACP Ltd* [2008] Ch 244 the Court of Appeal confirmed that preventing performance could not amount to inducing a breach of contract and that Lord Hoffmann had not intended to disagree with Lord Nicholls on this point.

[46] A wider range of arguments for and against such a distinction are reviewed in Bagshaw 2000.

[47] The principal alternative is to draw a line between *direct* and *indirect* interferences with contract. But this distinction is not easy to draw and was expressly condemned as 'unsatisfactory' by Lord Hoffmann in *OBG*, at [38].

[48] Simester and Chan 2004 argue (at 152) that *persuading* C to break a contract is essentially different from *preventing* C from performing because only the former 'attacks the very status of [the contractual] undertaking as a reason-generating promise'. But while this argument identifies a way in which *persuasion* is different from *prevention* it does not explain why the law of torts ought to *use* the distinction. Similarly, Stevens 2007 (at 280) offers an explanation more likely to appeal to an outside observer than to the victim: 'Where the promisor has no choice [because he has been prevented from performing], the damage to the convention of promising, and consequently our ability to place trust in one another, is not undermined to the same degree [as it is when the defendant induces a voluntary breach by the promisor].'

[49] Neyers 2009 argues (at 174–5) that in order to make the tort of inducing breach of contract consistent with a corrective justice account of the law it would be better if the law held that A had induced a breach of contract by C only where A has 'intentionally appropriated' B's right to C's performance of the contract.

[50] Recall that for Weir and Lord Hoffmann *persuasion* can involve 'carrot or stick': see above, n. 33.

commits a different wrong from D who keeps C away by *actually* tying her up. But while B may think that he suffers the same harm – non-fulfilment of his contractual expectation – *OBG* treats A and D as having committed different torts in relation to B.

C. Fault elements

Suppose A induced C to breach a contract that she had made with B. A will not have committed the tort of inducing a breach of contract in so acting unless he had the *requisite state of mind* when he brought about the breach.

So what sort of state of mind does it have to be shown A was in before we will find that A committed the tort of inducing a breach of contract in inducing C to breach her contract with B? The short answer is that when A induces C to breach the contract A must: (1) *know* that he is inducing a breach of contract *and* (2) *intend* to induce a breach of contract. But both of these elements require further discussion.

(1) *Knowledge that a breach is being induced.* In *OBG*, Lord Hoffmann explained the knowledge element in the following way:

> To be liable for inducing a breach of contract, you must know that you are inducing a breach of contract. It is not enough that you know that you are procuring an act which, as a matter of law or construction of the contract, is a breach. You must actually realise that it will have this effect.[51]

This means that if A mistakenly but genuinely believes that what he is procuring will *not* amount to a breach of contract then he will not be liable, even if that belief is unreasonable.[52] In one of the cases heard by the House of Lords alongside *OBG* – the case of *Mainstream Properties Ltd* v *Young* – two employees of the claimant had told the defendant that they were at liberty to purchase a particular plot of land for development. That was wrong; it was a breach of their contracts with their employer, the claimant, for them to divert the purchase to their joint venture with the defendant. But because the defendant believed what he had been told – that the two employees were at liberty to do what they did – he was not liable for inducing a breach.[53] Of course, the two employees were liable; they broke their contracts. Any mistake they made as to their contractual obligations, even if honest and reasonable, could not help them.

While a defendant who mistakenly believes that he is *not* bringing about a breach will not commit the tort, a defendant who makes a conscious decision not to find out how things stand will be liable. In *Emerald Construction* v *Lowthian* (1966), the defendants, the officers of a building trade union, sought to persuade the main contractor building the Fiddlers Ferry power station to terminate a labour-only subcontract.[54] The defendants knew of the subcontract but were not aware of its terms. The main contractor terminated

---

[51] *OBG*, at [39].

[52] *British Industrial Plastics* v *Ferguson* [1940] 1 All ER 479, HL.

[53] In *Meretz Investments NV* v *ACP Ltd* [2008] Ch 244, the Court of Appeal dealt with a case where the defendant had received legal advice about the action which brought about a breach of contract; he had *not* been advised that the action would not induce a breach, but had been advised that he was *legally* entitled to act in this way. The Court concluded, at [124], that a defendant's honest belief that he was *legally* entitled to act in a particular way was sufficient to preclude his state of mind being held to have been an intention to induce a breach of contract. This seems doubtful, particularly since it might have the effect of protecting from liability a range of defendants who *mistakenly* believe themselves to enjoy a defence of justification.

[54] The defendants objected to workers being employed on labour-only subcontracts because the subcontractor (in this case, a company with only two shareholders, a joiner and his wife) tended to have no assets, and as a result any workers employed by the subcontractor would have no effective recourse if the subcontractor went bust.

the subcontract and committed a breach of contract in so doing; the subcontract did not permit the main contractor to terminate it in the way that it did. The defendants were held liable for inducing a breach of contract even though they had not known *for certain* that the main contractor would commit a breach of the subcontract if it terminated it. Lord Denning MR remarked:

> Even if they did not know the actual terms of the contract, but had the means of knowledge – which they deliberately disregarded – that would be enough. Like the man who turns a blind eye. So here, if the officers deliberately sought to get this contract terminated, heedless of its terms, regardless of whether it was terminated by breach or not, they would do wrong. For it is unlawful for a third person to procure a breach of contract knowingly, or recklessly, indifferent whether it is a breach or not.[55]

This passage was quoted with approval by Lord Hoffmann in *OBG*.[56] He made clear that the crucial line was to be drawn between an honest belief – even if it stems from gross negligence – that a breach would not be induced, and a conscious decision not to confirm a suspicion that a breach would be induced.

(2) *Intention to induce a breach*. A will only have committed the tort of inducing a breach of contract in relation to B *if* when A induced C to breach her contract with B he *intended to induce a breach of contract*. So we must ask what state of mind will count as 'intention' in this context. The simple answer to this is that A will be held to have intended to induce a breach of contract *if* A *aimed* to induce C to commit a breach of contract, either as an end in itself or (much more commonly) as a means of achieving some other end. But A will not be held to have intended to induce a breach of contract if such a breach was merely an unaimed-for *side effect* of A's actions, albeit one which A knew was very likely to occur as a consequence of his actions. There are three points of detail that we must clarify.

First, where a defendant sets out to achieve his end by means of inducing a breach of contract then he will be held to have intended to induce a breach of contract *even if* he would have preferred it to have been possible to achieve his end in some other way. Thus if *Antville Football Club* persuaded *Cobweb* to break his contract with *Bugtown Football Club*, by persuading *Cobweb* to refuse to play for *Bugtown* until they agree to transfer him to *Antville*, then it will not assist *Antville* for them to claim that they would have much preferred the transfer to have been arranged without such steps being taken by *Cobweb*.

Secondly, a difficult issue concerns the position of a defendant who is determined to achieve a particular end but is unsure what means will be necessary to achieve it. For instance in *Emerald Construction* v *Lowthian* (1966), as we have seen, the defendants' end was to terminate a labour-only subcontract but they were not sure if the main contractor would have to breach the subcontract in order to achieve this. Lord Denning MR's comments, quoted above, suggest that he thought that defendants could commit the tort if they suspected that it might be necessary for a contract to be breached in order to achieve their end but went ahead without investigating whether this was the case because they did not care. Given that Lord Hoffmann cited these comments with approval in *OBG*,[57] it seems likely that a defendant will be held to have intended to induce a breach of contract by C if

---

[55] [1966] 1 WLR 691, 700–1.

[56] *OBG*, at [40]–[41].

[57] *OBG*, at [40]–[41]. At this point in his speech Lord Hoffmann is discussing 'knowledge' rather than 'intention', but there would be little point in holding that turning a blind eye to whether a contract would have to be broken is sufficient to constitute 'knowledge' if such reckless indifference could not also constitute 'intention'. Moreover, in a later passage in his speech (at [69]–[71]), Lord Hoffmann seems to assume that it would be actionable for A to encourage C to terminate a contract with B with reckless indifference as to whether C will have to breach this contract.

he intends to induce C to *take whatever means are necessary* to achieve a particular end, and he knows that it may be necessary for C to breach a contract with B, but he does not care. This is not, of course, to say that a defendant will be held to have intended to induce a breach of contract by C whenever he was recklessly indifferent as to whether a consequence of his conduct would be to persuade C to breach a contract with B. There is an important difference between being recklessly indifferent between different means of achieving your object and being recklessly indifferent as to the likely consequences of achieving your object.

Thirdly, in deciding what a defendant intends it is necessary to distinguish carefully between what is *part of* the defendant's end or means and what is a consequence of achieving that end or using those means. An outcome will count as *part of* the defendant's end if it is 'simply the other side of the same coin' *and* the defendant knows that this is the case.[58] An example of such a situation may be provided by the facts of *Lumley* v *Gye*: if Gye had known that Wagner had made a valid contract with Lumley not to sing elsewhere than at Her Majesty's Theatre then he must also have known that she could not sing for him at the Royal Italian Opera without breaching this contract. Thus he could *not* say that he intended to induce her to sing at the Royal Italian Opera but did not intend to induce her to break her contract with Lumley to sing nowhere except at Her Majesty's Theatre.

(3) *Summary.* So – to sum up: before we can find that A committed the tort of inducing a breach of contract in inducing C to breach her contract with B, it will have to be established that when A acted as he did:

(a) he *knew* that he was inducing a breach of contract; *and*
(b) he *intended* to induce a breach of contract.

But (a) will also be satisfied if A *suspected* that he might have been inducing a breach of contract but he did not bother to find out. And (b) will be satisfied if A intended to achieve an end by whatever means were necessary, and A did not care that the necessary means might involve a breach of contract by C.

(4) *Intention to harm.* We have just explained the fault requirements that have to be satisfied before it will be found that A committed a tort in relation to B by inducing C to breach a contract that C has with B. It may be worth emphasising that it does *not* have to be shown that A *intended to harm* B when he acted as he did. This was confirmed by the House of Lords in *South Wales Miners' Federation* v *Glamorgan Coal Co Ltd* (1905),[59] where the defendant miners' union had induced miners to break their contracts of employment in order to raise the price of coal (at the time the wages of miners were pegged to the price of coal) and argued that this would *benefit* the claimant colliery owners rather than harming them. The House of Lords held that the defendants' expectation that the claimants might benefit from their actions was irrelevant because to establish the tort it was sufficient to demonstrate an intention to induce the claimants' employees to breach their contracts.

D. Absence of justification

Suppose A has induced C to breach her contract with B. Suppose further that A acted with the requisite mental element when he induced C to breach that contract. If A had a *justification* for inducing C to breach her contract with B, the courts will *not* find that A committed the

---

[58] *OBG*, at [134] (per Lord Hoffmann), [167] (per Lord Nicholls).
[59] [1905] AC 239. This case was cited with approval as authority for this point by Lord Hoffmann in *OBG*, at [8].

tort of inducing a breach of contract in acting as he did. It is important to note that the pivotal question is not whether *C's breach* was justified but whether *A's inducing C to breach* her contract was justified.

English law has recognised the validity of both legal and moral justifications for inducing a breach. A can claim to have had a *legal* justification if he had a legal right which was inconsistent with B's contractual rights and was superior or equal in status to those contractual rights. A simple example of this situation would be if Johanna Wagner had foolishly made two contracts with rival impresarios promising to sing exclusively for each. In such circumstances either impresario would be justified in seeking to persuade Johanna Wagner to break her contract with the other.

A more complex example was provided by *Edwin Hill* v *First National* (1989). In this case the defendant was a finance company which had loaned money to a property developer to enable him to purchase Wellington House for development. Unfortunately the project stalled and the developer became unable to repay. This meant that the defendant had the power to force the sale of Wellington House. Instead of exercising this power of sale, the defendant agreed to finance the project itself, but, as a condition of doing so, insisted that the property developer should break his contract with the architects who he had previously engaged. The architects then sued the defendant for inducing the developer to breach this contract. The defendant claimed that it had been justified in doing so.

The complexity in the case comes from the fact that although the defendant had a (superior) legal right in the form of its power to force the sale of Wellington House, it had not actually exercised *this* power. It had instead used the bargaining position that this power provided in order to put together a different deal (which included the breach of contract). Despite this complexity the Court of Appeal thought that the defendant could rely on the defence of justification. Two explanations were provided. First, the court identified the legal right which the defendant had which might justify it in interfering with the architects' contractual right against the developer as the right to receive payment of what was due. Given this, one could say that the defendant acted reasonably[60] to protect its right to be repaid the money it had lent the developer. Secondly, the court pointed out that the end result was no worse for the architects than if the power to force the sale had been exercised and that in such circumstances it made no sense for the law to prohibit a different deal which was better for both defendant and developer.

To establish a defence of *moral* justification the defendant must show that he was impelled to act by a sense of moral duty. It is not sufficient merely to claim that there were good reasons for inducing a breach or that the person breaking the contract might gain some valuable benefit from doing so: 'The fact that their motives were good in the interests of those they moved to action does not form any answer to those who have suffered from the unlawful act.'[61] In practice the defence of moral justification has been successfully deployed very infrequently. A rare example is provided by *Brimelow* v *Casson* (1924), where the defendant induced theatre proprietors to break their contracts with a stage show producer in order to pressurise him into paying higher wages to the chorus girls he engaged. The supposed moral necessity was provided by the belief that the wages were so low that his employees were being forced into lives of immorality and prostitution.

---

[60] The reasonableness of changing architects was not considered in detail. But it should have been, because it is important to establish some inconsistency between the architect's right to the continuation of his contract and the defendant's right to be repaid.

[61] *South Wales Miners' Federation* v *Glamorgan Coal Co Ltd* [1905] AC 239, 252 (per Lord James). See also *Greig* v *Insole* [1978] 1 WLR 302, 341.

E. Is it a tort?

We have now described the various elements required to establish the tort of inducing a breach of contract. However, two issues in relation to this tort still need discussing. First of all, is inducing a breach of contract a tort at all, or is it some other form of liability masquerading as a tort?

In *OBG*, the House of Lords held that liability for inducing a breach of contract is not an *independent* tort but is actually a form of *accessory* liability – the defendant is held liable because he participated in the contract-breaker's wrong.[62] This point has been used as a foundation for arguing that liability for inducing a breach of contract should be studied alongside liability for participating in torts committed by others, and should be reformulated to make it conform to a *general* model of *accessory* liability for torts.[63] The *general* model, however, treats a defendant who is an *accessory* to another's tort as if he *also* committed the same tort, and is *jointly* liable for it. Of course, if liability for inducing a breach of contract is a form of *accessory* liability it may remain convenient to *talk about it* as if it were a tort because it sounds so odd to say that a person who was never a party to a contract is *jointly* liable for breaching it. But there are at least three reasons for doubting whether a defendant who has induced a breach of contract will, even after the *OBG* case, *be treated* as if he is jointly liable for having breached a contract.[64]

(1) *Different remedies.* Suppose that A has induced C to breach her contract with B. If A's liability to B in this situation is genuinely *secondary* in nature – and does not arise out of the fact that A committed a tort in relation to B in acting as he did – then it follows that the remedies available against A should be similar to those available against C. But the available evidence suggests that *different remedies* will be available against A and C.[65]

(2) *Different defences.* If a defendant's liability for inducing a breach of contract is genuinely *secondary* it seems odd that the defendant can rely on a defence of *justification* to escape being held liable even when the contract-breaker has undoubtedly committed the wrong of breach of contract. In such a case, after all, the defendant may have knowingly and intentionally *persuaded* the contract-breaker to commit the wrong.

(3) *Vicarious liability for inducing breach.* Suppose that A induces C to breach her contract with B – and that A, in so acting, was acting in the course of his employment by E. If A's liability for inducing C to breach her contract with B were genuinely secondary in nature then B could not sue *E* for damages in respect of the losses suffered by him as a result of C's breach.[66] But it seems likely that if *Lackey* was employed by *Impresario* and in the course

---

[62] *OBG*, at [5] (per Lord Hoffmann), [172] (per Lord Nicholls), [320] (per Lord Brown). Similar views were expressed by academics before the *OBG* case: see Sales 1990, 503–4. The law on when someone will be held secondarily liable as an accessory to a tort committed by someone else is dealt with in chapter 32, below.

[63] Carty 1999, 506–10; Carty 2010, 319–20.

[64] Deakin and Randall 2009, Neyers 2009 and Lee 2009 also conclude that the tort is not an instance of secondary liability, though their reasons diverge from ours.

[65] The cases where damages have been assessed do not seem to have proceeded by considering how much would be awarded in an action for breach of contract. See eg *Goldsoll* v *Goldman* [1914] 2 Ch 603, 615–16. Indeed, in *Lumley* v *Gye* (1853) 2 E & B 216, 230, one of the reasons that Crompton J gave for the existence of the tort was that the measure of damages might be different from that in an action for breach of contract. Moreover, as Stevens 2007 has pointed out (at 277), courts readily grant injunctions against defendants ordering them not to *induce* employees to breach their contracts of employment while they would not usually grant injunctions against the employees ordering them not to breach the same contracts.

[66] There is no precedent for an employer being held vicariously liable for an employee's breach of contract – whether that breach of contract was personally committed by the employee or whether the employee has been held to have committed that breach of contract because he was an accessory to it.

of his employment *Lackey* persuaded *Soprano* to breach her contract with *Rival* the courts *would* want to hold *Impresario* vicariously liable for *Lackey's* wrong.

Is there an alternative way of explaining the existence of the tort? Robert Stevens has written:

> The better view is that all contractual rights carry with them a right good against everyone else that they do not induce the infringement of the contractual right. The secondary right is accessory to the primary right and its infringement is a free-standing tort.[67]

This explanation insists that a defendant who induces someone to breach a contract is *not* jointly liable for committing the same wrong as the contract-breaker. It is not, however, an explanation that can draw any support from the *OBG* case.

F. Should the tort exist?

The second issue that we still need to discuss is whether defendants should be held liable *at all* for inducing other people to breach their contracts. Some legal commentators[68] have criticised the existence of the tort of inducing a breach of contract. The foundation for their criticisms is that if A has committed the tort by inducing C to breach her contract with B, B will be able to make a claim for breach of contract against C. Why, they ask, should B be given a claim against A as well?

Part of the answer may be that occasionally a claim against A will be more attractive than a claim against C. For instance, in *South Wales Miners' Federation* v *Glamorgan Coal Co Ltd* (1905), the defendant organisation had persuaded miners in South Wales to break their contracts with the coal companies which employed them and stop working for a one-day protest. Regardless of what we may think about such protests, we can easily imagine why the coal companies did not want to sue the people who had broken their contracts, the miners. It would not have been good for labour relations to have made legal claims against the miners as soon as they returned to work. There might also have been doubts about whether the miners would have had the money to pay for any losses suffered through stopping production for a day. Furthermore, from the point of view of the coal companies we can see why the defendant organisation might appear to have been 'the real authors of the mischief'.[69] The miners would not have stopped work for the protest without the encouragement of the defendant organisation. To use a biblical metaphor, the defendant organisation played a role similar to that of the serpent in the Garden of Eden.

But showing why victims of a breach of contract would like a tort of inducing a breach of contract to exist is not enough to satisfy all of its critics. One common criticism is that the tort fails to advance economic efficiency because it tends to discourage the *efficient breach* of contracts. A second common criticism is that the tort reduces the capacity of workers to organise effective industrial action and consequently facilitates oppression by powerful employers. Can these criticisms be answered?

---

[67] Stevens 2007, 281. Bagshaw 2000 identifies (at 132–7) some reasons for recognising such 'a right good against everyone else'. Lee 2009 argues (at 524) that the claimant's right is a right to 'exclusive access (vis-à-vis third parties) to the peremptory status of the promisor's promise'.

[68] See, for example, Howarth 2005b; and Fridman 2009, at 234: 'what was done in 1853 was something that was contrary to precedent and a step in the wrong direction, and . . . capable of producing undesirable consequences.'

[69] [1905] AC 239, 246 (per Lord Macnaghten).

(1) *Efficient breach.* The notion of 'efficient breach' is based on the idea that it may be better for the wealth of society as a whole if particular contracts are broken.[70] Suppose, for example, that *Seller* owns the only widget in the world and he has contracted to sell it to *Buyer*, who will use it to generate 40 units of wealth each year. *Seller* discovers that *Rival* could use the widget to generate 50 units of wealth each year and is therefore willing to pay *Seller* more for the widget than *Buyer* is. In such a case, *it might be thought* that it would be better for *Seller* to break his contract with *Buyer*, pay her compensation for the loss of profits resulting from her not getting the widget, and sell the widget to *Rival* instead.[71] But the existence of the tort of inducing a breach of contract means that it would be wrongful for *Rival* (or anyone else) to *persuade Seller* to break his contract with *Buyer* in order to ensure that the widget goes to the person who can make the most productive use of it.

So far it looks as if the critics of the tort have a good case. But we have ignored two things. First, the tort does not stop *Rival* negotiating with *Buyer* and *Seller*[72] to try to persuade them to cancel their contract so that the widget can be sold to him – and if *Rival* can make more money than *Buyer* using the widget then *Rival* should be capable of making very attractive offers to both *Buyer* and *Seller* to induce them to cancel their contract. Secondly, in our discussion we have assumed that everyone knows how much *Rival* and *Buyer* can make with the widget. In real life such information is often not available. In particular, it is unlikely that *Seller*, if approached by *Rival*, will be in any position to know who is likely to make best use of the widget. Consequently, it might again be better to encourage *Rival* to negotiate with both *Buyer* and *Seller*. A further benefit of encouraging such negotiations rather than allowing *Rival* to persuade *Seller* to break his contract with *Buyer* is that it will avoid the courts having to spend valuable time and effort calculating how much by way of damages *Seller* should pay *Buyer* in the aftermath of his breaching his contract to sell the widget to her.[73]

(2) *Industrial oppression.* One answer to the second criticism of the tort of inducing a breach of contract that was advanced above might be that the tort of inducing a breach of contract has a role to play only where there is a contract between two parties. Now – an employee must have voluntarily (to the extent that the law of contract demands) agreed to the terms of his contract of employment. Given this, there is only limited scope for the employee to argue that it is oppressive to impose a duty on others not to *persuade* him to break his contract. But this argument only really works at a formal level. In practice, we know that in many circumstances employees (and others) have little control over the terms of the contracts that they enter. The South Wales miners had little opportunity when

---

[70] For a presentation of the doctrine of 'efficient breach' see Posner 2003, 119–21. But note that Posner has argued that the existence of the tort can be justified in most of the circumstances in which it is used: Landes and Posner 1987, 224.

[71] See, for example, Perlman 1982, at 128, 'In cases of [inducing breach of contract by] otherwise lawful acts, tort liability works at cross-purposes with contract policies. Contract remedies seem to promote efficiency, whereas the addition of inducer liability inhibits efficient outcomes.'

[72] If *Rival* wants the identical widget which *Seller* has contracted to supply to *Buyer* he may be able to negotiate solely with *Buyer* – but in other cases, where, for instance, *Seller* has contracted to supply the output of his widget factory to *Buyer*, and *Rival* instead wants *Seller*'s factory to make slightly different widgets for him, all three parties will have to be involved in the negotiations.

[73] See Macneil 1982, at 957–60, for discussion of how it can only be determined whether a breach will be 'efficient' in the light of 'transaction costs' – that is, broadly speaking, the relative costs of negotiations and of sorting out breaches.

applying for jobs to influence the terms of any employment offered. Parliament has recognised that in practice employees are empowered by the possibility of collective industrial action and has provided a statutory immunity for economic torts committed in the furtherance of trade disputes.[74] There is no doubt, however, that the law in this area does still restrict liberty. The core issue is whether this restriction on liberty is justified by the protection that this area of the law provides for contractual rights. Our view is that for many people and companies their contractual rights are one of their most valuable assets, and that consequently it makes sense for the law to offer them some protection.[75]

24.3 ANALOGOUS TORTS

If inducing breach of contract is a form of *accessory* liability which is *talked about* as a tort because it *sounds* odd to say that a person who was never a party to a contract is *jointly* liable for breaching it,[76] then we should ask whether there are similar torts covering the inducing of other similar wrongs.

English cases have recognised liability for inducing the violation of obligations which are somewhat similar to contractual obligations. For example, the Court of Appeal held in a case involving an employment relationship that was governed by statute rather than contract, that A could commit a tort in relation to B by inducing C to breach a statutory obligation to work provided that such a breach by C could give rise to a civil action by B.[77] It may also be a tort for A to persuade C to break a duty to grant a particular private law remedy to B.[78]

By contrast, in *Metall und Rohstoff AG v Donaldson Lufkin & Jenrette Inc* (1990), the Court of Appeal refused[79] to recognise that it was a tort to induce someone to commit a breach of trust, principally to avoid any conflict with the well-developed equitable wrong of dishonestly assisting another to commit a breach of trust.[80] And in *Credit Lyonnais* v *Export Credit Guarantee Department* (2000), the House of Lords refused to find that it is a tort to assist someone else to commit a tort on the ground that there was no authority in favour of the existence of such a tort, and creating such a tort would be inconsistent with clear authority which stated that someone who assists someone else to commit a tort will not be held liable as an accessory to that tort.[81]

---

[74] This immunity is now conditional on certain procedures being followed in the organisation of the industrial action: see below, § 26.5.

[75] See further, Bagshaw 2000, at 132–7.

[76] Normally, where A has procured B to commit a tort against C the law holds that A and B are *jointly* liable for committing the tort against C. See below, chapter 36.

[77] *Associated British Ports* v *Transport and General Workers' Union* [1989] 1 WLR 939, 952, 959–60, 964–5. Liability for inducing a breach of a statutory duty is not confined to statutory duties similar to employment obligations: *Meade* v *Haringey LBC* [1979] 1 WLR 637.

[78] This was assumed by the Court of Appeal in *Law Debenture Corp* v *Ural Caspian Ltd* [1995] Ch 152, although it went on to hold that there was no right to an equitable remedy until it had been granted. The matter is somewhat complicated, however, by the fact that the reasoning of the court invokes both (1) a *broader* version of the tort of inducing breach of contract than is authoritative after the *OBG* case, and (2) the case of *Acrow (Automation) Ltd* v *Rex Chainbelt Inc.* [1971] 1 WLR 1676, which was founded on a *broader* version of the tort of intentionally causing loss by the use of unlawful means than is authoritative after the *OBG* case.

[79] [1990] 1 QB 391, at 481.

[80] See *Royal Brunei Airlines* v *Tan* [1995] 2 AC 378.

[81] [2000] 1 AC 486, at 500. See below, chapter 36, for an account of when someone will be held liable as an accessory to a tort committed by someone else.

24.4 INTENTIONALLY CAUSING LOSS BY UNLAWFUL MEANS

A will have committed the tort of *intentionally causing loss by unlawful means*[82] in relation to B if:

(1) A caused B to suffer some kind of loss;
(2) by interfering with the freedom of a third party, C, to deal with B; and
(3) the means by which A interfered with C's freedom to deal with B were unlawful; and
(4) A acted in the way he did with the intention of harming B.[83]

This tort developed as a *generalisation* of two more narrowly defined torts.

The first of these torts will be committed by A in relation to B if A makes use of unlawful threats in order to intimidate a third party, C, into not dealing with B, or ceasing to deal with B.[84] This tort is usually referred to as *three-party intimidation*.[85]

The second of these torts will be committed by A in relation to B if A makes use of unlawful means in order to interfere with a third party, C's, performance of a contract with B. For instance, in *Merkur Island Shipping Corp* v *Laughton* (1983), the claimants owned a ship, the *Hoegh Apapa*, which docked at Liverpool. The defendant union officials made it impossible for the claimants to perform their charter-contract with C to 'prosecute . . . voyages with the utmost despatch', and under the terms of the charter-contract C was not obliged to pay hire for the days when the ship was trapped in Liverpool. The defendant union officials achieved this by persuading the employees of a tug company to break their contracts of employment with the tug company by refusing to assist the tug company in fulfilling its obligation to tow the ship from its berth; in other words the means used by the defendants to injure the claimants was to commit the tort of inducing breach of contract *in relation to the tug company*.

The claimants sued the defendants, arguing that the defendants had committed a tort in relation to the *claimants* in indirectly interfering with the claimants' ability to perform their charter-contract and that the defendants were therefore liable to compensate the claimants for the loss of hire suffered by them as a result of the defendants' interference. The House of Lords agreed, referring to the tort committed by the defendants as 'the common law tort of actionable interference with contractual rights'.[86] But the House of Lords also acknowledged that the case could fit within the general tort of 'interfering with the trade or business of another person by doing unlawful acts'.[87] Persuading the tug company's employees to break their contracts of employment was identified as the necessary 'unlawful means'. At one time this tort, 'actionable interference with contractual rights', was treated as an *extension* of the tort of inducing breach of contract. But in *OBG*, the House of Lords firmly stated that this had been an error.

---

[82] In *OBG*, this tort is referred to by Lord Hoffmann, Baroness Hale and Lord Brown as 'the tort of causing loss by unlawful means', but by Lord Nicholls as 'interference with a trade or business by unlawful means or, more shortly, the tort of unlawful interference'. We discuss below, § 24.10, whether the tort should cover only economic losses associated with 'trade or business' interests.

[83] Fridman 1993 suggests (at 113) that for this tort to be committed, 'It is only necessary to show that the defendant's acts caused the loss of which the [claimant] complains, and that the defendant knew, or presumably could have appreciated, that such would be the effect or consequence of his acts.' This is wrong: if it were right, then *Lonrho* v *Shell Petroleum (No 2)* [1982] AC 173 (summarised above, § 22.1(A)) would have been decided differently.

[84] *Garret* v *Taylor* (1620) Cro Jac 567, 79 ER 485; *Tarleton* v *M'Gawley* (1790) Peake NPC 270, 170 ER 153.

[85] The qualifying term *three-party* is necessary because a tort of *two-party* intimidation *may* also exist. See below, (§ 24.5).

[86] [1983] 2 AC 570, 609.

[87] ibid.

Between them, the two narrowly defined torts of *three-party intimidation* and *actionable interference with contractual rights* provided a good basis for recognising a more general tort. This is because the tort of *actionable interference with contractual rights* focused on a particular way in which a claimant might suffer loss (interference with his contractual rights) – but could be committed by the use of any type of *unlawful means*. In contrast, the tort of *three-party intimidation* put no limit on the way in which a claimant might suffer loss – but focused on a particular type of *unlawful means* (unlawful threats). Thus the two narrowly defined torts suggested that it ought to be a tort to use *unlawful means* (including, but not limited to, unlawful threats) to cause loss (including, but not limited to, interference with contractual rights), though some features of this general tort of *using unlawful means to cause loss to another*, such as what might count as 'unlawful means', what the defendant's state of mind would have to be, and what loss it would protect against, remained to be settled. We will discuss each of these features below.

A. Unlawful means

In defining what amounts to 'unlawful means' for the purpose of the tort of *using unlawful means to cause loss to another*, the law draws on definitions of what is unlawful found in other areas of the law.

(1) *Tort*. It is clear that if A has caused B to suffer some kind of loss by committing a *tort* in relation to C which interferes with C's freedom to deal with B, A will be found to have caused B to suffer that loss through unlawful means.

In *OBG*, Lord Hoffmann stated that A's behaviour would also amount to 'unlawful means' if the only reason that it did not amount to a *tort* in relation to C was that C did not suffer any kind of actionable loss.[88] An example of this extension of the meaning of 'unlawful means' may be provided by *Lonrho v Fayed* (1990) where it was alleged that the defendant had caused loss to the claimant by using the unlawful means of making a deceitful statement to the Secretary of State for Trade and Industry, but it was not alleged that the Secretary of State had suffered any actionable loss as a result of this statement. It seems that Lord Hoffmann thought that this extension was also wide enough to cover cases where A *threatened to commit a tort* in relation to C but did not have to go through with the threat because C 'gave in' and caused loss to B in the way which A sought.[89]

(2) *Breach of contract*. The question whether a *breach of contract* will amount to 'unlawful means' for the purposes of the tort discussed here might seem to be more difficult. If A has breached a contract with C in order to harm B, one can clearly castigate what A has done as unlawful vis-à-vis C, but is there any reason to treat A's action as unlawful vis-à-vis B? The law of contract would not, after all, usually give B any right to insist on the contract being performed.[90] Nonetheless, it was decided in *Rookes v Barnard* (1964) that a threat to

---

[88] *OBG*, at [49]–[50].

[89] *OBG*, at [49], 'In the case of intimidation, for example, the threat will usually give rise to no cause of action by the third party because he will have suffered no loss. If he submits to the threat, then, as the defendant intended, the claimant will have suffered loss instead. It is nevertheless unlawful means. But the threat must be to do something which *would* have been actionable if the third party had suffered loss.' There is a risk that this definition of which threats will count as 'unlawful means' will prove to be too narrow. For instance, if A threatens C that he will kill C's friend unless C acts in a way which will cause loss to B, and C submits, then the threat which A will have used will *not* have been a threat of behaviour which would have been actionable by C if he suffered loss.

[90] For an exception, see the Contracts (Rights of Third Parties) Act 1999.

break a contract was an unlawful threat for the purposes of the tort of three-party intimidation, which tort – as we have seen – forms part of the *general* tort. A major strand in the reasoning which supported this conclusion was that there was 'no difference in principle between a threat to break a contract and a threat to commit a tort'.[91] In *OBG* Lord Hoffmann also stated that 'In principle, the cases establish that intentionally causing someone loss by interfering with the liberty of action of a third party in breach of contract with him is unlawful.'[92] In other words, a *breach of contract* will count as 'unlawful means' for the purposes of the tort discussed here, and so will a *threat to breach a contract*.

(3) *Crime*. Will the commission of a *criminal offence* count as 'unlawful means' for the purposes of the tort discussed here? This question does not cause any problems when the behaviour that constitutes the criminal offence could also be actionable as a tort, because we have already seen that all torts count as unlawful means.[93] The question is difficult, however, when we think about minor crimes such as regulatory offences.[94] Here the main controversy flows from the fact that the definition of 'unlawful means' helps to determine what, for instance, traders can do to each other by way of competition, while Parliament may have defined certain things as minor crimes for reasons completely different from any considerations of what should be legitimate behaviour between competitors.

For example, many competitors try to persuade each other's customers to switch allegiances by sending out small free gifts with advertising slogans. If *Upstart* decided to try and take customers from *Rival* by sending *Rival's* customers free calculators, would we want to say that *Upstart* committed the tort of using unlawful means to harm another in relation to *Rival* if its campaign was successful – and caused loss to *Rival* – but it later turned out that the batteries in these calculators contained a chemical which can cause severe pollution, so that it was a statutory offence to supply them? The dilemma here is that 'unlawful means' is meant to be a clearly defined concept and consequently there is an attraction to the answer that *all* criminal offences should count as 'unlawful means'. On the other hand, however, if the role of the tort is to define what methods it is wrongful for A to use against C in an attempt to cause loss to B, it makes nonsense of the tort to make it cover methods which nobody thinks are improper. Does anyone think if *Upstart* sends *Rival's* customers defective calculators (instead of some other advertising gift) he is behaving wrongfully vis-à-vis *Rival*?

The question whether *criminal offences* should count as 'unlawful means' divided the House of Lords in the *OBG* case. Lord Hoffmann thought that they should not. He stated:

> In my opinion, and subject to one qualification, acts against a third party count as unlawful means only if they are actionable by that third party. The qualification is that they will also be unlawful means if the only reason why they are not actionable is because the third party has suffered no loss.[95]

---

[91] [1964] AC 1129, 1168 (per Lord Reid).

[92] OBG, at [48].

[93] Neyers 2009 suggests (at 188–97) that the tort would be easier to justify from a corrective justice perspective if *only* serious criminal offences, and not civil wrongs, were treated as 'unlawful means'.

[94] An overlapping question is whether the breach of a statutory duty will count as 'unlawful means' for the purposes of the tort discussed here if the breach of the duty in question is *not* civilly actionable.

[95] OBG, at [49]. Lord Hoffmann explained that the qualification included cases where A had done everything necessary to commit a tort in relation to C but C had suffered no loss *and also* cases where A had threatened to use unlawful means on C but never had to go through with the threat because C surrendered to it and acted in a way which harmed B.

By contrast, Lord Nicholls preferred the view that 'In this context the expression "unlawful means" embraces all acts that a defendant is not permitted to do, whether by the civil law or the criminal law'.[96] In discussion, he seemed to qualify this view by suggesting that committing a criminal offence might *only* count as unlawful means if: (a) the defendant's crime was committed 'against' the claimant, *or* (b) the defendant intentionally caused loss to the claimant by committing (or threatening to commit) a crime against a third party in order to cause a loss to the claimant 'through the *instrumentality* of'[97] that third party.[98]

A majority in the House of Lords expressly adopted Lord Hoffmann's view.[99] There seem to be three reasons why the majority in *OBG* rejected Lord Nicholls' views.

First, we have already considered the example of *Upstart* trying to take customers from *Rival* by sending her customers free calculators, where this scheme involved a criminal offence because the calculators contained a chemical which can cause severe pollution. Lord Hoffmann thought that this sort of example demonstrated that it would be *arbitrary* to allow the question of whether *Upstart* had committed a tort in relation to *Rival* to turn on the question whether a criminal offence had been committed. In this example the aspect of *Upstart*'s scheme which is criminal has no effect on the likelihood of the free gifts influencing *Rival*'s customers to cease trading with her.

Lord Nicholls might respond to this argument by claiming that in this example, *Upstart*'s offence would not count as 'unlawful means' because *Upstart*'s offence could only count as 'unlawful means' (in his view) if it amounted to a crime *against Rival*'s customers and that offence enabled *Upstart* to cause loss to *Rival* 'through the instrumentality of' the third party. And he might argue that neither of these conditions are made out in this case. But this leads on to the second reason why the majority in *OBG* might have rejected Lord Nicholls' position. If Lord Nicholls' position were to be adopted, we would have to define what the terms used to qualify his position on what amounts to 'unlawful means' actually mean. And this can be very difficult. Suppose, for example, that the night before *Salesman* is due to pitch for a multi-million pound contract for the company he works for, *Rival* plies *Salesman* with copious quantities of illegal drugs, so that *Salesman* will be in no condition to pitch for business the next day, and *Rival* can pick up the contract instead. Would we say in this situation that *Rival* has committed a crime *against Salesman*? It is very hard to say – *Rival*'s crime here is regarded by some people as 'victimless', by others as an offence 'against society', and by a third group of people as an example of the law trying to protect people like *Salesman* from themselves.

A third reason for rejecting Lord Nicholls' position was that many crimes are created by statute and it would be undesirable to treat the fact that a given form of conduct contravenes a statutory provision as a reason for bringing it within the ambit of a tort in

---

[96] *OBG*, at [162].

[97] *OBG*, at [159] (emphasis in original).

[98] *OBG*, at [159]–[162]. The relevant passages are not easy to follow. The House of Lords seems to have been concerned to define the tort of causing loss by the use of unlawful means so that it would *not* cover a delivery company gaining an advantage over its rivals by offering a faster service premised on its agents ignoring speed limits and traffic lights. With reference to a similar example Lord Nicholls states, at [160], that the reason why this would not be a tort is because 'The couriers' criminal conduct is not an offence committed against the rival company in any realistic sense of that expression'. The case is an unusual one because it involves a *promise* to third parties – potential customers – to commit crimes to their advantage, rather than the more familiar variation of a *threat* to commit crimes to their disadvantage. If we consider the more familiar variation – *threats* to commit crimes – it is not clear why the tort ought to cover only threats to commit crimes 'against' third parties. For instance, what if a defendant intentionally intimidated third parties into not trading with the claimant by *threatening* to commit blasphemy or to be cruel to animals?

[99] *OBG*, at [266]–[270] (Lord Walker), [302] and [306] (Baroness Hale), [320] (Lord Brown).

the absence of evidence that Parliament intended the provision to be used in this way. The proposition that A will commit a tort in relation to B if A intentionally causes loss to B by committing a crime against him seems capable of converting a large number of minor regulatory offences into torts, and it must be doubtful whether it would be appropriate for the judiciary to do this.

(4) *Two-party cases.* In *OBG*, Lord Walker predicted that neither Lord Hoffmann's nor Lord Nicholls' judgments would be regarded as 'the last word on this difficult and important area of the law.'[100] His prediction came true within less than a year when, in the conspiracy case of *Revenue & Customs Commissioners* v *Total Network* (2008), members of the House of Lords suggested *obiter* that Lord Nicholls' approach to the question of what amounted to unlawful means for the purpose of the tort discussed here might be adopted in a *two-party case* where a defendant intentionally caused loss to a claimant but did so directly, and not through interfering with a third party's freedom to deal with the claimant.[101] In making this suggestion, their Lordships focused on a passage in Lord Hoffmann's speech in *OBG* where he said:

> I would only add one footnote to this discussion of unlawful means. In defining the tort of causing loss by unlawful means as a tort which requires interference with the actions of a third party in relation to the [claimant], I do not intend to say anything about the question of whether a claimant who has been compelled by unlawful intimidation to act to his own detriment, can sue for his loss.[102]

Though the first sentence in this paragraph refers to 'unlawful means', it is clear that Lord Hoffmann did not mean to suggest that in *two-party cases* a different test of unlawful means should be adopted. He was merely pointing that the *next* requirement for the tort of intentionally inflicting loss using unlawful means (which we will discuss now) might not apply in all cases. It remains to be seen whether the suggestions in the *Total Network* case that 'unlawful means' might have a different meaning in *two party cases* (which we will discuss in the next section) than it does in *three party cases* (where the majority's view in *OBG* is authoritative) will be taken up by the courts.

B. Interference with a third party's freedom

A claimant's economic interests will often depend on third parties being willing and able to deal with him. For example, if B runs a business then he will clearly lose money if his customers take their business elsewhere or his employees resign or his suppliers refuse to sell him what he requires or if it becomes impossible for any of these groups to deal with him. But in such cases the customers, employees and suppliers *are likely* to be able to act in this way *without* committing any civil wrong to B. (The most obvious exception to this would be where by acting in this way the customers, employees or suppliers would be breaching a *contract* with B.)

In circumstances where B's economic interests depend on third parties remaining willing and able to deal with him, he will be potentially vulnerable to A taking steps to *interfere* with that willingness or ability. For instance, he will be potentially vulnerable to A

[100] *OBG*, at [269].
[101] [2008] 1 AC 1174, at [43] (per Lord Hope), [99] (per Lord Walker), [124] (per Lord Mance], [223] (per Lord Neuberger).
[102] *OBG*, at [61].

scaring off his potential customers by threats of violence or preventing his suppliers from making deliveries by damaging their vehicles. A, of course, is likely to owe a duty *to the potential customers* not to act violently towards them and a duty *to the suppliers* not to damage their vehicles. But the tort of *using unlawful means to cause loss to another* is based on a further duty, owed *to B*, not to use such unlawful means with the intention of causing loss to him.

So, for example, if *Driver* runs down *Striker*, a well-known footballer, with the intention of causing economic loss to *Club*, which employs *Striker*, then *Club* will be able to make a claim against *Driver* on the basis that *Driver*, in acting as she did, committed the tort of using unlawful means to cause loss to another in relation to *Club*. Such a claim will be supplementary to *Striker*'s claim for the wrong done *to him* when *Driver* ran him down. Moreover, such a claim is permitted even though *Club* could *not* claim for its losses if all that happened was that *Driver* negligently ran down *Footballer*. It is a crucial feature of the tort that *Driver* must have acted as she did with the *intention* of causing loss to *Club*.

In *OBG*, Lord Hoffmann distinguished between situations where A uses unlawful means to *interfere with the freedom* of a third party to deal with B and situations where A uses unlawful means to *reduce the value* to B of his freedom to deal with a third party.[103] For instance, in the case of *RCA Corp* v *Pollard* (1983), the claimant had the exclusive right to exploit records made by Elvis Presley and the defendant sold 'bootleg' recordings that had been made at concerts without the consent of Elvis. Lord Hoffmann stated that, assuming that this behaviour amounted to 'unlawful means',[104] and *even if* the defendant had used such means with the intention of causing loss to the claimant,[105] he would still *not* have committed the tort of using unlawful means to cause loss in relation to the claimant. This is because the defendant's conduct did not interfere with the ability of Elvis's estate to perform its contract with the claimant.[106]

What forms of conduct will be regarded as 'interfering with the freedom' of a third party? The examples discussed by Lord Hoffmann in the *OBG* case suggest that the list includes:

(1) Making it *impossible* for a third party to behave in a particular way towards B, including preventing a third party from performing a contract with B.
(2) *Threatening* a third party to persuade him to behave in a particular way towards B.
(3) *Misleading* a third party to lead him to behave in a particular way towards B.

In situations (2) and (3) the threat or misleading statement can be used *either* to cause a third party to refrain from dealing with B *or* to take some *positive steps* which will cause loss to B.

---

[103] *OBG*, at [51], 'Unlawful means therefore consists of acts intended to cause loss to the claimant by interfering with the freedom of a third party in a way which is unlawful as against that third party and which is intended to cause loss to the claimant. It does not in my opinion include acts which may be unlawful against a third party but which do not affect his freedom to deal with the claimant.'

[104] The behaviour was clearly criminal and might have also amounted to the tort of breach of statutory duty in relation to Elvis Presley: see *Lonrho Ltd* v *Shell Petroleum Co Ltd (No 2)* [1982] AC 173, at 187 (per Lord Diplock).

[105] Carty 2010 argues (at 97–98) that the requirement of 'interference with a third party's freedom' would have been unnecessary if the House of Lords in *OBG* had insisted that the tort required 'targeted harm'. But this would mean that a bootlegger that had the primary goal of damaging a record company's profits would be liable to the record company.

[106] *OBG*, at [53].

There is a question whether the list should also include the following forms of conduct:

(4) Making it *less attractive* for a third party to behave in some way towards B which would be advantageous to B, with the result that the third party does not act in that way.
(5) Making it *more attractive* for a third party to behave in some way towards B which would be disadvantageous to B, with the result that the third party acts in that way.

Arguably, using unlawful means to *steer* a third party's behaviour should be covered because it is sufficiently similar to using a misleading statement or a threat of unlawful conduct to do so. For instance, if A used unlawful means to make it far more expensive for C to perform a contract with B, with the intention of causing C to terminate the contract lawfully and cause loss to B, it is hard to see why this would interfere with C's freedom *less than* misleading C as to the additional profits that he could make if he terminated the contract. Thus it is arguable that (4) and (5) should also be treated as situations which may involve *interference* with the freedom of a third party.

One curious consequence of the requirement for A's use of unlawful means to interfere with the freedom of a third party to deal with B is that in certain circumstances A may be liable to B for *threatening to do x* to C, even though he would *not* have been liable if he had *actually done x* to C.

For instance, suppose *Publisher* has the contractual right to publish a book that *Author* is about to complete. If *Jealous* seriously defames *Author* by calling him a 'Nazi sympathiser', with the result that the contractual right to publish *Author's* book is rendered valueless (as no one is likely to buy the book until *Author* clears his name), *Publisher* will be unable to sue *Jealous* even if *Jealous's* intention when he defamed *Author* was to cause loss to *Publisher*. This is because *Jealous's* defamatory words will not have interfered with *Author's* liberty to deal with *Publisher*. By contrast, if *Jealous* threatens *Author* that he will seriously defame him unless *Author* terminates his relationship with *Publisher*, then if *Author* gives in to this threat *Publisher* will be able to sue *Jealous* if *Jealous's* intention when he threatened *Author* was to cause loss to *Publisher*.

C. Intention to cause loss

B will only be able to base a claim on A's use of unlawful means to interfere with a third party's freedom to deal with him if A acted in the way he did with the intention of causing loss to B. So we must ask what state of mind will count as 'intention' in this context.

The simple answer to this is that A will have intended to cause loss to B if he aimed to cause B loss, either as an end in itself or as a means of achieving some other end. But A will not be held to have intended to cause loss to B if such loss was merely a unaimed-for side effect of A's actions, albeit one that he knew was very likely to occur. There are four points of detail that we must clarify.

(1) *Undesired harms.* If causing loss to B was either A's end or the means by which he was seeking to achieve that end then A *will* be held to have intended to cause loss to B *even if* he would have preferred not to have been put in a position where he had to adopt such an end or would have preferred not to have had to resort to such means to achieve his end.[107] For instance, the defendants in the case of *Rookes* v *Barnard* (1964) used unlawful means – a threat to commit a breach of contract – to persuade BOAC to dismiss the claimant,

---

[107] *OBG*, at [165] (per Lord Nicholls).

Rookes. The defendants might have preferred Rookes to have resigned his post voluntarily so that they did not have to persuade his employer to dismiss him – indeed, they might have preferred to avoid the dispute that led to them targeting Rookes – but such preferences would not negate the fact that when they threatened BOAC they intended to cause loss to Rookes.

(2) *The other side of the coin.* A defendant will be held to have aimed to cause a claimant loss if the claimant's suffering a loss was 'simply the other side of the same coin' as the defendant's achieving his aim, and the defendant knew that this was the case.[108] For instance, if *Chancer* takes a horse which *Owner* was about to deliver to *Stirrup*, and *Chancer* knows that *Owner* was about to do this, then *Chancer* cannot simultaneously maintain that he intended to obtain the horse for himself but also that he did not intend to prevent *Stirrup* from obtaining it. The courts will find that it was part of *Chancer*'s aim to prevent *Stirrup* from obtaining the horse, as *Stirrup*'s being prevented from obtaining the horse was – as *Chancer* knew – the inevitable flipside of his achieving his aim of taking the horse for himself.

In *Douglas* v *Hello! (No 3)* (2008), one of the appeals heard by the House of Lords alongside *OBG*, the defendants and claimants were respectively the publishers of two rival celebrity magazines, *Hello!* and *OK!* The claim resulted from the defendants' publishing unofficial photographs of the wedding of Michael Douglas and Catherine Zeta-Jones in *Hello!* shortly before the claimants were due to publish official photographs in *OK!* The trial judge found that the defendants had not intended to cause loss to the claimants on the basis of evidence from the controlling shareholder of *Hello!*'s Spanish holding company that his intention was only to avoid a loss of sales for *Hello!* and not to reduce sales of *OK!* But Lord Hoffmann identified this as a situation where the loss to *OK!* was necessarily intended because it was simply the flipside of the preserved sales of *Hello!*, presumably because a substantial proportion of the preserved sales would be to purchasers who would otherwise have bought *OK!* instead.[109]

Lord Hoffmann distinguished this situation from one where a customer suffered loss as a result of action directed against its supplier.[110] If, for instance, *Saboteur* used unlawful

---

[108] *OBG*, at [134] (per Lord Hoffmann), [167] (per Lord Nicholls). Carty (2010), 82–84, criticises this aspect of the decision.

[109] *OBG*, at [134]. Suppose that a substantial number of readers usually buy only one magazine or the other, and that the defendants knew that. The defendants might say that they *could* achieve their aim – maintain sales of their own magazine – *without* reducing sales of the claimant's magazine, provided that more readers than usual bought *both* magazines. But it is hard to believe that the defendants really intended to preserve their sales only by persuading *more* readers to buy two magazines; surely they intended to persuade some readers not to switch to their rival's publication.

[110] *OBG*, at [64]. The case Lord Hoffmann cited, *Barretts & Baird (Wholesale) Ltd* v *Institution of Professional Civil Servants* [1987] IRLR 3, involved a strike in support of a pay claim by Fatstock Officers (FOs) employed by the Meat and Livestock Commission (MLC), which caused loss to private abattoirs because they could not get their meat certified for export. But the basic factual pattern is the same as that found in the more common scenario of action directed against a supplier which will almost inevitably harm the supplier's customers. Henry J described the defendants' state of mind in *Barretts & Baird* as follows, at [70]: 'Clearly, damage to the various [claimants] was an unavoidable by-product of that withdrawal of labour and was a readily foreseeable consequence and, perhaps, in the case of some FOs, a not undesired consequence on the basis that the greater the disruption caused the greater the pressure for a satisfactory settlement with the MLC and the sooner the return to normal working. But there is no evidence to suggest that the FOs would not have struck if their industrial action had not injured these plaintiffs. On the evidence the desire to strike was the cause of the injury to the plaintiffs rather than the desire to injure the [claimants] being the cause of the strike.' Lord Hoffmann said, in *OBG*, at [64]: 'I think Henry J was right . . . when he decided a strike by civil servants in the Ministry of Agriculture in support of a pay claim was not intended to cause damage to an abattoir which was unable to obtain the certificates necessary for exporting meat and claiming subsidies. The damage to the abattoir was neither the purpose of the strike nor the means of achieving that purpose, which was to put pressure on the government.'

means to prevent trains from running with the intention of causing loss to a train operating *Company*, although *Saboteur* would probably know that some passengers would suffer loss as a result of his activities he would *not* be held to have intended to cause passengers to suffer such losses because he could achieve his aim – causing loss to *Company* – even if all *Company*'s passengers unexpectedly found cheaper and more convenient ways of travelling when their trains were cancelled. In such a case any loss suffered by passengers would *not* be the inevitable flipside of the defendant's achieving his aims. The situation would, of course, be different if one of the defendant's objectives was to inflict loss on the passengers *in order to* prompt them to put pressure on the train operating company.

(3) *No need for an intent to cause the type of loss suffered by the claimant.* In *OBG*, Lord Hoffmann repeatedly stated that what is required is an intention to cause loss to the claimant rather than an intention to cause the particular type of loss which the claimant ends up suffering. This might be significant if, for instance, *Rival* made threats of violence against *Trader*'s potential customers with the intention of persuading them not to trade with *Trader*, but *Trader* avoided this type of loss either by paying for additional security for his potential customers or by reducing his prices so that his customers became convinced that the risk of violence was worth taking. It would be odd if in either of these circumstances *Rival* could avoid liability by objecting that the type of loss which *Trader* had suffered was not the type that he had intended to cause.

(4) *Breach of contract cases.* The state of mind that the tort of intentionally causing loss by the use of unlawful means requires – an intention to cause loss to B – is different from the state of mind required in order to establish the tort of inducing a breach of contract. We saw above that to show that a defendant has committed the tort of inducing a breach of contract it is necessary to show that he intended *to induce a breach of contract*, and a defendant will not avoid liability by demonstrating that he honestly expected the breach to cause no loss.[111] The distinction is potentially significant because where a defendant causes loss to a claimant by persuading a third party to break a contract with the claimant he may commit a tort if he intended *to induce a breach of contract*, while if a defendant causes loss to a claimant by preventing a third party from performing a contract with the claimant, he will only commit a tort if he *intended to cause loss* to the claimant.

24.5 TWO-PARTY CASES

We have seen that in the *OBG* case the House of Lords defined the tort of intentionally causing loss by unlawful means so that A could only commit it in relation to B if he interfered with C's freedom to deal with B. In other words, the tort was defined so as to cover only situations involving *three* parties.

It might be thought that there is no need for a similar tort in situations involving only *two* parties because the tort requires unlawful means, and, as we have seen, a defendant will only *usually* be held to have used unlawful means if he has committed a 'civil wrong'. Thus in situations involving only two parties the claimant can usually simply sue for this 'civil

---

[111] See above, § 24.2(C)(2).

wrong'.[112] But we have also seen that a defendant will be held to have used unlawful means if he has *threatened* to commit a 'civil wrong', but has not had to do so because the person threatened *submits*. This means that there is one situation involving *two* parties where the claimant cannot simply sue for a 'civil wrong': where A threatens B that he will commit a civil wrong in relation to B unless B acts in some way that will cause him loss, and A makes his threat with the intention of causing B to suffer loss. Would A commit a tort in relation to B in this situation if B submitted to the threat and acted in such a way as to cause himself some loss?

There is good evidence that such a tort of *two-party intimidation* exists. The Court of Appeal recognised the existence of the tort in *Godwin* v *Uzoigwe* (1993) and awarded £20,000 to a teenager who had been coerced into working without pay for two and a half years by the defendant's violence and mistreatment. It was also recognised by Lord Devlin in *Rookes* v *Barnard* (1964), who stated that 'an action will doubtless lie at the suit of a trader who has been compelled to discontinue his business by means of threats of personal violence made against him by the defendant with that intention'.[113] And although in the *OBG* case Lord Hoffmann defined the tort of intentionally causing loss by unlawful means so that cases of two-party intimidation would *not* fall within it, he expressly stated that he was not discussing 'the question of whether a claimant who has been compelled by unlawful intimidation to act to his own detriment, can sue for his loss'.[114]

One reason why Lord Hoffmann did not simply *confirm* the existence of the tort may have been the uncertainty which surrounds some elements of it. Three factors help to explain this uncertainty.

First, threats are often made in two-party situations where there is a genuine dispute. For example, if A threatens to breach a contract with B unless B pays him a sum of money which is now due it may be the case that A *honestly believes* that all he is threatening is to exercise his right to refuse to perform until he receives a sum that he is owed. If B pays the sum in this situation then the law may have an interest in treating the payment as the settlement of a dispute rather than a tort.

Secondly, and relatedly, where B makes a contract with A after a threat, or pays money to A after a threat, the doctrines of duress and economic duress determine whether A can enforce that contract, or will have to repay the money. Clearly it would be unsatisfactory if these doctrines said that the contract was enforceable, or the money could be retained, but tort law insisted that B should be compensated by A for the loss caused by the threat.

Thirdly, in a two-party situation B has a better opportunity to protect himself, by refusing to submit, than in a three-party situation where C's response to the threat is out

---

[112] It has sometimes been suggested that a claimant might be able to obtain a greater measure of damages by framing his claim as one for a two-party version of the tort of intentionally causing loss by unlawful means rather than simply relying on the 'civil wrong'. For instance, if B could show that A intentionally caused loss to him by breaching a contract with him then perhaps he would be entitled to a greater measure of damages than would usually be awarded for a breach of contract. The measure of damages might be different because, for example, exemplary damages are not available for a breach of contract but are available for an intentional tort. It must be doubtful, however, whether the courts would be willing to establish a two-party version of the tort in order to allow a claimant to circumvent the rule that exemplary damages are not available for breach of contract. In an attempt to avoid such a consequence, Carty 2010 argues (at 118–119) that an actual breach of contract should only constitute 'unlawful means' in a case involving *three* parties. Similarly, Sales and Stilitz 1999 argue (at 424) that in a case only involving *two* parties, a threat to break a contract should constitute 'unlawful means' but an actual breach of contract should not.

[113] [1964] AC 1129, 1205. Lord Devlin was quoting, with approval, from the contemporary edition of *Salmond on The Law of Torts*.

[114] *OBG*, at [61].

of B's hands. Thus a tort of two-party intimidation should *perhaps* be defined so as to require a claimant not to submit too readily to an insignificant threat. Cumulatively, these factors suggest that a two-party tort might not rely on elements precisely parallel to those found in the three-party tort. But because such matters have not been discussed by the courts they remain uncertain.

24.6 LAWFUL MEANS CONSPIRACY

In the mid-1880s one group of shippers entered into an association in order to try to squeeze rival shippers out of the China tea shipping market. The association offered discounts on freight charges to shipping agents who only ever used ships owned by association members, and association members agreed between themselves that if a non-association ship tried to find a cargo of tea, they would immediately send association ships to the same port to offer to carry the cargo at a cheaper freight rate, even if they had to carry it at a loss. The defendants in the action were members of this association.

The claimants owned ships which had previously taken part in the China tea trade, and indeed had been part of the association in previous years, but had been excluded in 1885 because the claimants only sent their ships to China for the three-week tea season when shipping was most profitable while the other association members operated shipping links between China and Europe all year round. Despite being excluded, the claimants sent their ships to China to load tea during the 1885 season. The association responded by sending ships to undercut their rates, and the claimants were forced to make their rates so low that they made a loss in order to get any cargo at all.

The claimants then sued the defendants, but the House of Lords held in *Mogul Steamship Co Ltd* v *McGregor, Gow & Co* (1892) that the defendants had not committed a tort in relation to the claimants. Lord Watson explained that although the defendants had agreed to band together and pursue the course of action which caused loss to the claimants

> If neither the end contemplated by the agreement [between members of the association], nor the means used for its attainment were contrary to law, the loss suffered by the [claimants] was *damnum sine injuria*.[115]

This sentence reflects the fact that there are *two* forms of tort involving a conspiracy. One form depends on the *end* contemplated by the agreement being unlawful; the other form depends on the *means* used to attain the end being contrary to law. The claimants lost in the *Mogul* case because they could not establish that the defendants had committed either form of conspiracy tort.

Although the claimants *alleged* that the defendants had made use of unlawful means in conspiring against them, they failed to substantiate this: they failed to prove that unlawful threats had been made, and although the contract which held the association together might have been unenforceable the *making of* such an agreement was not, at that time, unlawful. With regard to the 'end contemplated', Lord Watson dismissed the suggestion that this had been unlawful:

> There is nothing in the evidence to suggest that the parties to the agreement had any other object in view than that of defending their carrying trade during the tea season against the encroachments of the [claimants] and other competitors, and of attracting to themselves custom which might otherwise have been carried off by these competitors. That is an object which is strenuously

---

[115] [1892] AC 25, 42. '*Damnun sine injuria*' means 'damage which it is not a legal wrong to inflict'.

pursued by merchants great and small in every branch of commerce; and it is, in the eye of the law, perfectly legitimate.[116]

The argument that the object of the conspiracy in *Mogul* was lawful because the defendants in *Mogul* were seeking to promote their business interests proved to have momentous consequences. In later cases, it was held that where the *predominant purpose* of a conspiracy was *not* to promote the conspirators' business interests, but was simply to hurt the claimant, then the conspiracy would have an unlawful object and would be actionable.

So *Mogul* contemplated that there could exist two forms of actionable conspiracy: the first where people banded together with the object of harming the claimant and they used unlawful means to do so; the second where people banded together with the object of harming the claimant and used lawful means to do so, but the conspirators had no good reasons for wanting to harm the claimant. The first sort of conspiracy became known as *unlawful means conspiracy*. The second as *lawful means conspiracy*.[117] We will discuss the second type of conspiracy first, because – as we will see – its existence has had some effect on the shape of the tort of unlawful means conspiracy.

A. Definition

A defendant will commit the tort of *lawful* means conspiracy in relation to a claimant where:

(1) someone intentionally harmed the claimant; and
(2) in so doing, they were acting in pursuance of a plan that had been agreed upon by the defendant and one or more other people; and
(3) the parties to that agreement had no good reason for wishing to harm the claimant.

Below we will discuss the three central elements of this tort in turn, and then consider some criticisms that have been raised against it.

B. Intention to harm

We discussed when a defendant would be found to have intended to cause loss to a claimant in detail when we were describing the tort of intentionally causing loss by unlawful means. Consequently, here we will simply state that A will have intended to cause harm to B if he aimed to cause B harm, either as an end in itself or as a means of achieving some other end. But A will not be held to have intended to cause harm to B if such harm was merely an unaimed-for side effect of A's actions, albeit one that he knew was very likely to occur. Anyone who wants a more detailed account should refer back to section 24.4(C).

C. Agreement

There can be no conspiracy unless there was an agreement to harm the claimant which was subsequently carried out. So if *Boss* takes against *Enemy* and orders his employees to spend their days ringing up *Enemy*'s customers and attempting to persuade them to stop doing business with *Enemy*, *Boss* cannot be said to have committed the tort of lawful means

---

[116] ibid.
[117] Lord Walker referred to this tort as 'unlawful object' conspiracy in *Revenue & Commissioners v Total Network SL* [2008] 1 AC 1174, at [66] and [73].

conspiracy as he has not reached an *agreement* with his employees that they will try to harm *Enemy*.[118]

D. Absence of good reason

This is the most important element in the tort of lawful means conspiracy: the conspirators must have no good or legitimate reason for seeking to harm the claimant. The *Mogul* case (1892) made it clear that protecting your own business interests was an acceptable reason for intentionally harming someone else.[119] Subsequent cases have taken their cue from that to say that a defendant will only have committed the tort of unlawful means conspiracy if he acted maliciously in seeking to hurt the claimant, or with the predominant purpose of harming the claimant.[120]

The first case to find someone liable for lawful means conspiracy on this ground was *Quinn v Leathem* (1901). In that case, Leathem was a wholesale butcher. The Belfast Journeymen Butchers and Assistants' Association was upset that Leathem did not exclusively employ men who belonged to that union. In fact, none of Leathem's employees belonged to that union and neither did Leathem. Leathem attended a meeting of the union and offered to make his employees members of the union. The union insisted that he dismiss his employees and employ existing members of the union instead. Leathem refused to do this. The defendants, officials of the union, resolved to punish Leathem for taking this stand and did so by threatening Leathem's customers that union members employed by those customers would walk out on their jobs if they continued to deal with Leathem. As a result, Leathem lost a lot of custom. On these facts, the House of Lords held that the defendants had committed a tort. They had organised together and intentionally caused Leathem to suffer loss and had no good reason for doing so – they did not act as they did

---

[118] See *Crofter Hand Woven Harris Tweed Co v Veitch* [1942] AC 435, 468 (per Lord Wright). On the other hand, see Viscount Simon LC, at 441: 'It was argued that the [defendant] Mackenzie should not be regarded as acting in combination with the [defendant] Veitch, so as to establish the element of agreement between them in the tort of conspiracy, because Veitch held the responsible position of Scottish area secretary to the union, whereas Mackenzie was only branch secretary for Stornoway. This, I think, is an unsound contention. The respective position of the two men in the hierarchy of trade union officials has nothing to do with it. *Even if Mackenzie could be regarded as only obeying orders from his superior, the combination would still exist if he appreciated what he was about*' (emphasis added).

[119] See also *Sorrell v Smith* [1925] AC 700 (union of retail newsagents attempts to limit the competition in their area by agreeing not to deal with any wholesaler who supplies newspapers to an 'unauthorised' newsagent; no lawful means conspiracy committed when the members of the union switched their trade away from the claimant wholesaler, who had supplied an 'unauthorised' newsagent).

[120] *Crofter Hand Woven Harris Tweed Co v Veitch* [1942] AC 435, 445 (per Viscount Simon LC); *Lonrho plc v Fayed* [1992] 1 AC 448, 465 (per Lord Bridge of Harwich). In previous editions, we criticised the emphasis placed by the cases on it having to be established that the defendant had the 'predominant purpose' of harming the claimant, and urged that the courts instead focus on whether the defendant had a good reason for acting as he did. Some partial vindication for this view was provided by the case of *Customs & Excise Commissioners v Total Network SL* [2008] 1 AC 1174, where the claimant was defrauded out of almost £2m by the defendant and other conspirators. The claimant brought an action for unlawful means conspiracy against the defendant (which we discuss below). An invitation to plead lawful means conspiracy was turned down, presumably on the ground that the claimant thought that it could never establish that the defendant's predominant purpose was to harm the claimant as the predominant purpose of the fraud was, of course, to enrich the defendant. Had the courts emphasised that the key issue in lawful means conspiracy was whether the defendant had a *good reason* for seeking to harm the claimant, then the claimant would not have hesitated to plead lawful means conspiracy as there was obviously no good reason for inflicting loss on the public revenue. As it was, some of the judges who decided *Total Network* were reduced to saying that they thought it was strongly arguable that a predominant purpose to harm the claimant was made out here (ibid, at [34] in the Court of Appeal, and at [228], per Lord Neuberger) – an obvious abuse of language that could not do anyone any good.

to advance the interests of their union or the members of the union, but simply out of a vindictive desire to see Leathem punished for acting as he did.

Since then, the courts have been careful to make it clear that trade unionists will not commit the tort of lawful means conspiracy so long as in intentionally harming an individual they have been honestly seeking to promote the best interests of their union.[121] If – as was suggested in *Revenue & Commissioners v Total Network* (2008)[122] – the tort of lawful means conspiracy had its origin in

> the deep suspicion which the governing class had, in Georgian and Victorian England, of collective action in the political and economic spheres, as potential threats to the constitution and the framework of society[123]

the law seems to have outgrown that by the 1930s. But even after then, the tort of lawful means conspiracy was a weapon that could be used against trade unionists who used their power to punish individuals who had sought to challenge them,[124] or who used their power in a disproportionate way to obtain recourse from individuals who had wronged them,[125] or who simply hired out the trade union's services as an 'enforcer' to the highest bidder in return for a donation to union funds.[126]

If, on a moral scale, intentionally harming someone for vindictive or malicious reasons is at one end, and intentionally harming someone out of self-interest is somewhere in the middle, intentionally harming someone for altruistic reasons would be at the other end of the scale. Given the courts' willingness to find 'just cause or excuse for the action taken'[127] when a defendant uses lawful means to harm someone out of self-interest, it comes as no surprise that the courts will find that an agreement to harm someone using lawful means that has been entered into for altruistic reasons does not amount to a lawful means conspiracy.

So in *Scala Ballroom (Wolverhampton) Ltd v Ratcliffe* (1958), the claimants were proprietors of a ballroom. They operated a 'colour bar', excluding people who were not white from the dance floor. At the same time, they allowed non-white musicians to play in the orchestra. The defendants were officials of the Musicians' Union. They attempted to bring the 'colour bar' to an end by warning the claimants that members of the Musicians' Union would not be allowed to play at the claimants' ballroom while the 'colour bar' was in place. The Court of Appeal held that the defendants had committed no tort in so acting.

---

[121] *Crofter Hand Woven Harris Tweed Co Ltd v Veitch* [1942] AC 435 (no lawful means conspiracy committed when union dockers refused to handle bales of 'Harris tweed' that had been produced so cheaply, it threatened to put out of business various spinning mills that produced more expensive 'Harris tweed' using union labour).

[122] Reported at [2008] 1 AC 1174, and referred to hereafter simply as '*Total Network*'.

[123] *Total Network*, at [78] (per Lord Walker).

[124] As in *Quinn v Leathem* or *Huntley v Thornton* [1957] 1 WLR 321 (tort of lawful means conspiracy committed against a shipworker who had broken a strike for one day only and subsequently found he could not obtain work anywhere due to lawful threats that the union had made to prospective employers).

[125] *Giblan v National Amalgamated Labourers' Union of Great Britain and Ireland* [1903] 2 KB 600 (tort of lawful means conspiracy committed in ensuring that former official of union who was alleged to owe the union money could not get permanent work anywhere; the union should have sued him for the money rather than trying to starve him into giving them the money he owed).

[126] *Crofter Hand Woven Harris Tweed Co Ltd v Veitch* [1942] AC 435, 446 (per Viscount Simon LC): 'If . . . the mill-owners in the present case had promised a large subscription to the trade union funds as an inducement to bribe the [defendants] to take action to smash the [claimant's] trade, I cannot think that the [defendants] could excuse themselves for combining to inflict this damage merely by saying that their . . . purpose was to benefit the funds of the union thereby.' Also Viscount Maugham, to the same effect, at 451.

[127] *Sorrell v Smith* [1925] AC 700, 712 (per Viscount Cave LC). See also *Crofter Hand Woven Harris Tweed Co v Veitch* [1942] AC 435, 451–2 (per Viscount Maugham).

What is the position if the defendant and his co-conspirators had different reasons for seeking to harm the claimant? The law seems to say that if the defendant had a good reason for seeking to harm the claimant, he will still have committed the tort of lawful means conspiracy if he knew his co-conspirators did not have a good reason.[128] If the defendant had a bad reason for seeking to harm the claimant, he will have committed the tort of lawful means conspiracy if at least one of his co-conspirators – all of whom had good reasons for harming the claimant – knew this.

E. Criticisms

Two criticisms are commonly made of the tort of lawful means conspiracy.

The first is that the existence of this tort cannot stand beside the decision of the House of Lords in *Allen v Flood* (1898). As Lord Diplock observed in *Lonrho Ltd v Shell Petroleum (No 2)*, 'Why should an act which causes economic loss to A but is not actionable at his suit if done by B alone become actionable because B did it pursuant to an agreement between B and C?'[129]

The second is that the existence of this tort plunges the courts into all the difficulties regarding ascertaining people's motives for acting that the decision of the House of Lords in *Allen v Flood* helped the courts avoid in cases where a single defendant, acting alone, intentionally causes harm to a claimant. For example, in *Quinn v Leathem* (1901), it must have been very difficult to determine why the defendants victimised the claimant. On the one hand, it was argued that they acted as they did because they were outraged at the way the claimant had stood up to them and they wanted to teach him a lesson. On the other hand, it could just as well have been argued that the defendants had sought to harm the claimant in order to promote the interests of their trade union, by making it clear to everyone that anyone who failed to go along with their demands would incur severe sanctions.

Both of these criticisms seem to us to be convincing, but there is no realistic possibility of the tort of lawful means conspiracy disappearing from our law.[130] In the *Total Network* case, the House of Lords expressed itself very content with the existence of lawful means conspiracy as a tort, with Lord Scott arguing that it was an example of a situation where 'the conduct of the authors of the harm had been sufficiently reprehensible to require the conclusion that they ought to be held responsible for the harm'[131] and Lord Walker arguing that the law is acting in a 'principled' way in holding people liable where their 'object is simply to do harm, and not to exercise [their] own just rights.'[132] And, as we will now see, in *Total Network* the existence of the lawful means conspiracy tort was allowed to have a big effect on the definition of when someone would commit the tort of unlawful means conspiracy.

---

[128] *Crofter Hand Woven Harris Tweed Co Ltd v Veitch* [1942] AC 435, 495 (per Lord Porter). See also *Huntley v Thornton* [1957] 1 WLR 321 (two union officials committed no tort in helping other union officials prevent the claimant getting work as they had no idea the other union officials were doing this out of petty vindictiveness).

[129] [1982] AC 173, 188.

[130] In *Lonrho Ltd v Shell Petroleum (No 2)* [1982] AC 173, 188–9, Lord Diplock stated that the tort 'must I think be accepted by this House as too well-established to be discarded however anomalous it may seem today' but 'unhesitatingly' chose to confine it to the 'narrow limits that are all that common sense and the application of the legal logic of the decided cases require'.

[131] *Total Network*, at [56].

[132] *Total Network*, at [77], quoting Bowen LJ in *Mogul Steamship Co Ltd v McGregor, Gow & Co* (1888) 23 QBD 598, at 616.

24.7 UNLAWFUL MEANS CONSPIRACY

A defendant will commit the tort of *unlawful* means conspiracy in relation to a claimant where:

(1) someone intentionally harmed the claimant using unlawful means to do so; *and*
(2) in so doing, they were acting in pursuance of a plan that had been agreed upon by the defendant and one or more other people.

The main differences between this tort and the lawful means conspiracy tort are that for this tort: (a) it has to be shown that the claimant was harmed using unlawful means, and (b) it does not have to be shown that the conspirators had no good reason for harming the claimant.

The only real issue in relation to unlawful means conspiracy has been what counts as 'unlawful means'. In *Powell* v *Boladz* (1998), Stuart-Smith LJ had held that for the tort of unlawful means conspiracy to be committed, the person who harmed the claimant must have done so by committing an actionable wrong in relation to the claimant.[133] But in the *Total Network* case, the House of Lords said that this was wrong.

Total Network concerned what is known as a 'carousel fraud'. It is a fraud on the taxpayer, and it works like this. Under the rules governing the charging of VAT (value added tax) in the UK, a business pays VAT on its purchases ('input tax') and charges VAT on its sales ('output tax'). So suppose a business buys a widget and pays a certain amount of input tax on that widget and then sells the exact same widget and charges a certain amount of output tax on that widget. If the output tax exceeds the input tax (if the business charges more VAT on the sale of the widget than it had to pay on purchasing the widget), then the business has to account for the difference. If the input tax exceeds the output tax, then the taxman has to refund the difference to the business.

No VAT is payable to the British tax authorities on imports into the UK from somewhere else in the European Union, or exports out of the UK to somewhere else in the European Union. This is what enables a carousel fraud to work. Fraudsters find a company somewhere outside the UK but inside the European Union, selling (say) mobile phones. They then set up two or more companies based in the UK to buy and sell mobile phones. Let's call the company outside the UK 'E', and the two companies inside the UK, B1 and B2. B1 buys 4,000 mobile phones from E for £1.5m. No VAT is chargeable on that transaction. B1 then sells the phones to B2. This time VAT is chargeable, as B1 and B2 are both inside the UK. B1 sells the phones to B2 for £1.76m, of which £260,000 is VAT.

B1 – having paid no VAT on the phones when he bought them, and having charged £260,000 VAT on selling the phones – should pay the taxman £260,000. But B1 doesn't do this. B1 'disappears' – but not before B1 gives B2 a receipt showing that B2 paid £260,000 in VAT when it bought the phones. B2 then sells the phones back to E, thereby exporting them out of the UK to somewhere else in the EU. No VAT is chargeable on that transaction. So B2 can then go to the taxman and say, 'Look – I paid £260,000 in VAT when I bought these phones, and I could not charge any VAT when I sold them on, so you owe me £260,000.' The taxman – being completely unaware that he has not actually received the VAT that B2 paid when buying the phones from B1 – pays £260,000 to B2. At that point, the fraud is complete. The fraudsters who set up B1 and B2 have obtained £260,000 from

---

[133] [1998] Lloyd's Rep Med 116, 126. The same conclusion was reached by Laddie J at first instance in *Michaels* v *Taylor Woodrow Developments Ltd* [2001] Ch 493.

the UK taxpayer, merely as a result of shuffling money and phones (none of which may have actually existed, and if they did, they will never have actually changed hands) between these three companies. (Hence the phrase '*carousel* fraud'.)

Total Network concerned 13 such 'carousel frauds' involving mobile phones, and which earned the fraudsters behind the frauds approximately £2m. The defendant in *Total Network* was one of the parties to the fraud – a Spanish company from whom the mobile phones had been bought. The claimant was the Customs & Excise Commissioners, who had lost almost £2m as a result of the fraud. Lawful means conspiracy should have been pleaded, but was not – for reasons we explore in a note above.[134] Instead, the claimant based its case on unlawful means conspiracy.

The relevant unlawful means by which the claimant had been harmed was a common law crime – that of cheating the revenue. The question was whether that crime amounted to sufficient 'unlawful means' for the purpose of the tort of unlawful means conspiracy. Two arguments were made for why it did not.

A. Unlawful means conspiracy as accessory liability

The first argument was that unlawful means conspiracy gives effect to a form of accessory liability, where A is held liable for a wrong committed by B to C because A agreed with B that B should commit that wrong to C. If this view of unlawful means conspiracy were correct, then if B had not in fact done any wrong to C, but had instead caused loss to C by committing some crime, then there would be no basis for making A liable for that loss as an accessory – B would have done no wrong to C to which A could be an accessory. The House of Lords firmly rejected this view – the *secondary liability view* – of unlawful means conspiracy as 'unsustainable'.[135]

The main problem[136] with the *secondary liability view* is that in a case of *conspiracy to commit a tort against C*, where B intentionally causes loss to C by committing a simple tort in relation to C, such as battery or deceit, the *secondary liability view* renders the tort of unlawful means conspiracy completely redundant. If you want to make A liable for C's loss you can simply do so on the basis that A is an accessory to B's tort.[137] Unlawful means conspiracy does not need to come into it.

B. The argument from *OBG v Allan* (2008)

The second argument was much more powerful. It was that the House of Lords had already agreed only a few months before in *OBG* (2008) that for the purposes of the tort of intentionally causing loss using unlawful means, 'unlawful means' meant an actionable wrong (or one that would have been actionable had the victim suffered some loss as a result). It was argued that for the sake of consistency, the same test for 'unlawful means' should apply in unlawful means conspiracy cases.

The House of Lords had two reasons for rejecting this argument, and the differences between these reasons are important – so it is worth spelling both of them out carefully.

---

[134] See above, fn 120.
[135] *Total Network*, at [103] (per Lord Walker). Also [123] (per Lord Mance) and [225] (per Lord Neuberger).
[136] We also set out a second problem below, § 36.2(D).
[137] Accessory liability is discussed below, chapter 36.

(1) *OBG only applies to three-party cases.* The first reason was that they thought Lord Hoffmann's views in *OBG* as to what amounted to 'unlawful means' for the purpose of the tort of intentionally causing loss using unlawful means might not have been intended to apply in *two-party cases*; that is cases where a defendant intentionally caused a claimant harm directly rather than by interfering with a third party's freedom to deal with the claimant. *Total Network* was in this sense a *two-party case*, since the conspirators directly caused the claimant loss, without the intervention or manipulation of any intermediary. Given this, the House of Lords in *Total Network* thought that saying that the crime of cheating the revenue amounted to sufficient 'unlawful means' in this case might not be directly inconsistent with Lord Hoffmann's views as to what should amount to 'unlawful means' for the purpose of the tort of intentionally causing loss by unlawful means.[138]

(2) *Lawful means conspiracy.* The second reason was provided by the existence of the tort of lawful means conspiracy. Lord Neuberger expressed it very well:

> a claim based on conspiracy to injure can be established even when no unlawful means, let alone any other actionable tort, is involved . . . In my judgment, given the existence of that tort, it would be anomalous if an unlawful means conspiracy could not found a cause of action where, as here, the means 'merely' involved a crime, where the loss to the claimant was the obvious and inevitable, indeed in many ways the intended, result of the sole purpose of the conspiracy, and where the crime involved, cheating the revenue, has as its purpose the protection of the victim of the conspiracy.[139]

Lord Hope and Lord Scott expressed similar views: if a claimant can sue in lawful means conspiracy where no one has actually done anything wrong to cause the claimant that loss, it would seem strange if a claimant were barred from suing in unlawful means conspiracy just because the means used to cause the claimant that loss were merely criminal and did not amount to an actionable wrong to the claimant.[140]

The significance of the distinction between these reasons arises in a *three-party* conspiracy case where harm has been caused to a claimant via the intervention or manipulation of a third party. For example, suppose that *Trader* is desperate to stop a *Rival* firm getting a multi-million pound contract for which *Rival's* star *Salesman* will be pitching next week. So *Trader* agrees with *Dick* that *Dick* will supply *Salesman* with a generous quantity of illegal drugs the night before his pitch, in the hope that this will make his pitch incoherent and prevent *Rival* getting the contract. The plan works and *Rival* does not get the contract. Can *Rival* – when it discovers what happened – sue *Trader* for unlawful means conspiracy?

According to the first reason for distinguishing Lord Hoffmann's views on 'unlawful means' in *OBG*, the answer would seem to be 'no'. This is a *three-party* case, where *Trader* has caused *Rival* harm by interfering with *Salesman*, and so Lord Hoffmann's views in *OBG* on what amounts to 'unlawful means' would seem to apply here to determine whether the

---

[138] See *Total Network*, at [43] (per Lord Hope), [99] (per Lord Walker), [124] (per Lord Mance), [223] (per Lord Neuberger).

[139] *Total Network*, at [221].

[140] *Total Network*, at [44] (per Lord Hope: 'If . . . it is in the fact of the conspiracy that the unlawfulness resides, why should that principle not apply here? As a subspecies of the tort of unlawful means conspiracy, the case is virtually indistinguishable from the tort of conspiracy to injure') and at [56] (per Lord Scott: 'the proposition that a combination of two or more people to carry out a scheme that is criminal in its nature and is intended to cause economic harm to some person does not, when carried out with that result, constitute a tort actionable by that person is, in my opinion, unacceptable. Such a proposition is . . . inconsistent with the jurisprudence of tortious conspiracy . . . ').

right kind of unlawful means have been used here to harm *Rival*. And they have not – no actionable wrong has been done to *Salesman* here.[141] But the second reason for distinguishing Lord Hoffmann's views on 'unlawful means' in *OBG* would tend to indicate that his views are *never* relevant to the issue of whether someone has committed the tort of unlawful means conspiracy. On this view, the courts are free to develop their own rules as to what amounts to 'unlawful means' for the purpose of the law on unlawful means conspiracy, free from any requirement that those unlawful means should in *any* cases amount to an actionable wrong.

We think that the courts are very likely to go down the second road and will interpret *Total Network* as ruling that the tort of intentionally causing loss using unlawful means and the tort of unlawful means conspiracy should from now on develop along their own lines. So we think it unlikely that any court will in future apply Lord Hoffmann's views in *OBG* on 'unlawful means' to a *three-party* unlawful means conspiracy case. Instead, an independent set of rules on what amounts to 'unlawful means' for the purpose of unlawful means conspiracy, which will apply in *all* unlawful means conspiracy cases, will be developed.

The House of Lords made a start on developing such a set of rules in *Total Network* itself. Two main ideas emerge from the judgments in *Total Network* as to when unlawful conduct will amount to 'unlawful means' for the purpose of the tort of unlawful means conspiracy.

First, what made the conduct unlawful must have played a part, or been *instrumental*, in causing the claimant loss. This requirement was most prominent in Lord Walker's judgment: 'in the phrase "unlawful means" each word has an important part to play. It is not enough that there is an element of unlawfulness somewhere in the story.'[142] So, for example, suppose that in *Lonrho Ltd v Shell Petroleum (No 2)* (1982),[143] Shell and other oil companies had agreed, 'This is our chance to do down our enemy Lonrho. The longer we can keep the Rhodesian government propped up by supplying it with oil in breach of the sanctions imposed on Rhodesia, the more likely it is that Lonrho will go bust because its business interests in Rhodesia will remain frozen.' On Lord Walker's view, that would *not* amount to an unlawful means conspiracy.[144] What makes Shell and the other companies' sanctions-breaking unlawful (it is contrary to the interests of the UK, which wants to bring the Rhodesian government down) is not what would be helping it and the other companies do down Lonrho.

Secondly, the rules that were breached by the unlawful conduct must have existed for the *benefit* of the claimant. This requirement was emphasised most strongly by Lord Mance, who pointed out that the crime of cheating the revenue existed for the benefit of the claimant in *Total Network*.[145] In contrast:

> The pizza delivery business which obtains more custom, to the detriment of its competitors, because it instructs its drivers to ignore speed limits and jump red lights . . . should not be liable, even if the claim be put as a claim in conspiracy involving its drivers and directors.[146]

---

[141] Though note that Stuart-Smith LJ in *Powell v Boladz* [1998] Lloyd's Rep Med 116 would have said that even committing an actionable wrong to *Salesman* would not be enough for a claim in unlawful means conspiracy to be made out here: it would have to be established that *Dick* committed an actionable wrong in relation to *Rival*. However, *Rival* would probably be able to overcome that hurdle in the case where *Dick* committed an actionable wrong to *Salesman*, by arguing that *Dick* simultaneously committed the wrong of intentionally causing loss by unlawful means to *Rival*.

[142] *Total Network*, at [96].

[143] Discussed above, § 22.1(A).

[144] *Total Network*, at [95].

[145] *Total Network*, at [120].

[146] *Total Network*, at [119].

The rules breached by the pizza firm's drivers here exist for the benefit of other motorists and pedestrians, not for the benefit of the pizza firm's rivals. Some support for Lord Mance's views may also be obtained from Lord Walker's otherwise mysterious remark that

> I would accept that the sort of considerations relevant to determining whether a breach of statutory duty is actionable in a civil suit . . . may well overlap . . . with the issue of unlawful means in the tort of conspiracy.[147]

He may well have been referring there to the requirement that a claimant who wants to bring a claim for breach of statutory duty must show, at the very least, that that statutory duty was imposed on the defendant for the benefit of the claimant, or a limited class of people that included the claimant.[148]

24.8 DECEIT

A will have committed the tort of deceit (or fraud) in relation to B if:

(1) he made a representation of fact to B which was untrue; *and*
(2) when he made that representation to B he did not honestly believe that it was true;[149] *and*
(3) he intended, in making that representation to B, to induce B to act in a particular way; *and*
(4) B was induced to act in that way by A's representation; *and*
(5) B suffered loss as a result.[150]

It is worth saying more about three elements of this tort.

A. Representation of fact

(1) *Conduct.* Someone can obviously make a representation of fact by words or writing, but they can also do so by conduct. If A has conducted himself in such a way that B *reasonably* inferred from A's conduct that *x* was true, then it is fair to say that A represented to B that *x* was true.[151]

---

[147] *Total Network*, at [96].
[148] See above, § 22.1(C).
[149] We explain this further below, § 24.8.B.
[150] There is no further requirement that A's representation must have been made in a commercial context: see *P v B* [2001] 1 FLR 1041 and *Magill v Magill* (2006) 226 CLR 551 (both cases allowing a claimant to bring an action for deceit against his ex-partner, claiming that she lied to him in telling him that he was the father of her child).
[151] This requirement was not satisfied in *Ward v Hobbs* (1878) 4 App Cas 13. In that case, Hobbs sold pigs to Ward at the Newbury market. Ward later discovered that the pigs were suffering from typhoid fever; all but one of the pigs died and some other pigs of Ward's also died, having been infected by the pigs bought from Hobbs. Ward sued Hobbs claiming, *inter alia*, that Hobbs had committed the tort of deceit. The claim failed: Hobbs had made no representation that his pigs were free from illness and of good quality. Ward argued that Hobbs's act of driving the pigs to market when he had a statutory duty not to do so if they were suffering from a contagious disease meant that he represented to Ward that his pigs were free from disease. However, even if Ward inferred from Hobbs's driving his pigs to market that the pigs were free from disease, this was not a reasonable inference to draw; it was not *reasonable* to think that Hobbs would observe his statutory duty and not drive his pigs to market if they were suffering from a contagious disease. As Lord Selborne remarked (at 29): '[t]o say that every man is always to be taken to represent, in his dealings with other men, that he is not, to his knowledge, violating any statute, is a refinement which . . . would not I think appear reasonable to any man.'

(2) *Representation of opinion.* A representation of opinion always carries with it a representation of fact that can ground an action for deceit. This is because if A says to B, 'I think that *x* is true' he makes a representation that it is a fact that he thinks *x* is true. So if A says to B 'I think that *x* is true' when he does not actually think *x* is true then A makes an untrue representation of fact to B – he represents to B that he thinks *x* is true when this is not true. Some judges have gone further and said that if A says to B 'I think that *x* is true' when A is in a much better position than B to know whether or not *x* is true, then A's representation 'I think that *x* is true' will amount to a representation of fact that there is *good reason* to believe that *x* is true.[152] Some judges have gone even further than this and said that in such a case, A's representation 'I think that *x* is true' will amount to a representation of fact that *x is* true.[153]

(3) *Representation of intention.* Similarly, a representation of intention always carries with it a representation of fact that can ground an action for deceit. This is because if A says to B, 'I intend to do *x*', he makes a representation that it is a fact that he currently has an intention to do *x*. So if A says to B 'I intend to do *x*' when he has no such intention, A makes an untrue representation of fact – he represents to B that it is currently his intention to do *x* when this is not true.

For example, in *Edgington* v *Fitzmaurice* (1885), the directors of a company issued a prospectus inviting subscriptions for debentures issued by the company. The prospectus stated that the object of the issue was to raise money to allow the company to complete alterations in the buildings of the company, to purchase horses and vans and to develop the company's trade. In fact the directors intended to use the money raised to pay off some of the company's debts. It was held that the directors had made an untrue representation of fact in the prospectus – they had represented that it was their intention to invest the money raised by the issue of debentures when it was actually their intention to use the money to pay off some of the company's debts. Bowen LJ put the point memorably: '[t]here must be a misstatement of an existing fact [for an action in deceit to be maintained]: but the state of a man's mind is as much a fact as the state of his digestion.'[154]

Similarly, in *East* v *Maurer* (1991), the defendant ran two hairdressing salons in neighbouring areas. The defendant decided to sell one of the salons and devote all his efforts to working in the other salon. The claimants were interested in purchasing the salon the defendant wanted to sell and, in order to encourage them to buy the salon, the defendant assured them that he did not intend to work regularly in the other salon. In so assuring the claimants, the defendant made an untrue representation of fact: he represented that he had no intention of working regularly in his other salon when, in fact, he had every intention of doing so.

(4) *Ambiguous representations.* What if a representation is ambiguous? In *Smith* v *Chadwick* (1884), a company's prospectus claimed that the 'present value of the turnover or output of the entire works is over £1m per annum'. This was ambiguous: it could have meant that the company's entire works *had actually* produced £1m worth of produce in one year (which was not true) or it could have meant the company's entire works were *capable* of producing £1m worth of produce in one year (which was true). The claimant

---

[152] *Brown* v *Raphael* [1958] 1 Ch 636.
[153] *Bisset* v *Wilkinson* [1927] AC 177.
[154] (1885) 29 Ch D 459, 483.

was induced by this statement to buy shares in the company. He then sued the directors of the company in deceit, seeking to recover the money he had paid for the shares.

To succeed in his claim the claimant would have had to show: (i) that he understood the statement in the company's prospectus to mean that the company's entire works had actually produced £1m worth of produce in one year;[155] (ii) that the directors had intended to encourage people like the claimant to think this; (iii) the directors did not honestly believe that the company's entire works had actually produced £1m worth of produce in one year;[156] and (iv) the directors intended, by encouraging people to believe that the company's entire works had actually produced £1m worth of produce in one year, to induce people to buy shares in the company. As things turned out, the claimant's claim failed: he could not prove that (i) was true.

B. Lack of honest belief

In *Derry* v *Peek* (1889), Lord Herschell observed that, 'in order to establish an action of deceit, there must be proof of fraud, and nothing short of that will suffice ... fraud is proved when it is shewn that a false representation has been made (1) knowingly, or (2) without belief in its truth, or (3) recklessly, careless whether it be true or false.'[157] But if (1) is true, (2) is true. And if (3) is true, (2) is true. So we can reduce Lord Herschell's statement down to: 'fraud is proved when it is shewn that a false representation has been made ... without belief in its truth' without losing anything.

What if a defendant believed that a fact was true at the time that he made a representation but subsequently discovered that it was not true? So, suppose that A made a representation of fact to B intending to induce B to do x, and B was induced to do x by that representation. And suppose further that at the time A made that representation, he honestly believed that it was true but before B did x, A discovered that his representation was untrue. What is the position?

The law, as it stands now, seems to say that if A did not warn B in time that his representation was untrue, then A committed the tort of deceit.[158] So, it will be recalled, in *East* v *Maurer* (1994) the defendant assured the claimants – who were interested in buying one of his hairdressing salons – that he did not intend to work regularly at his other salon. This assurance induced the claimants to buy the defendant's salon, just as the defendant intended. The defendant was held to have committed the tort of deceit – at the time he gave the assurance he had every intention of working regularly at his other salon. The result would have been the same if the defendant had been telling the truth when he assured the claimants that he did not intend to work regularly at his other salon, but before the sale went through, he – without telling the claimants – changed his mind and decided that he would after all work regularly at his other salon.

---

[155] The claimant's claim could not have succeeded if he had understood the statement in the company's prospectus to mean that the company's entire works were capable of producing £1m worth of produce in one year because, in that case, the claimant would not have been deceived when he bought shares in the company – just like the claimant in *Ship* v *Crosskill*.

[156] *Akerhielm* v *De Mare* [1959] AC 789, 805.

[157] *Derry* v *Peek* (1889) 14 App Cas 337, at 374.

[158] *Brownlie* v *Campbell* (1880) 5 App Cas 925; *Briess* v *Woolley* [1954] AC 333.

C. Inducement

The courts will hold that A's representation of fact to B induced B to do x if A's representation *played some part* in B's decision to do x.[159]

In *Smith* v *Chadwick* (1884), the claimants claimed that they were induced to buy shares in a company because its prospectus falsely represented that G was a director of the company. This claim was dismissed. The claimants could not have been induced to buy shares in the company by the representation in the prospectus that G was a director of the company because, by their own admission, the claimants had never heard of G before the prospectus was issued. The representation in the prospectus that G was a director of the company could not therefore have played any part in the claimants' decision to take up shares in the company.

In *JEB Fasteners Ltd* v *Marks Bloom & Co* (1983) (*not* a deceit case) the claimants started negotiations to take over a company which had recently started trading in the same products as the claimants. In the course of negotiations, the defendants drew up and showed to claimants the company's accounts, which accounts gave a false picture of the financial health of the company. The claimants decided to take over the company. When the takeover proved unsuccessful the claimants sued the defendants, claiming that they had been induced to take over the company by the misrepresentations as to the company's profitability contained in the company's accounts. The claimants' claim was dismissed. The judge was satisfied that the company's accounts had played *no* part in the claimants' decision to take over the company. Two considerations played a large part in this finding. First, the claimants' main object in taking over the company was to secure the services of the company's two directors. Secondly, the claimants knew before they took over the company that its accounts were unreliable.

Sometimes it is very difficult to know whether a given person was induced to act in a certain way by a representation that was made to him or her. So, for example, suppose *Driver* bought a car from *Trader*. Suppose further that, while *Driver* was inspecting the car before making up her mind whether or not to buy it, *Trader* told *Driver* that the car had just passed its MOT. Did that representation induce *Driver* to buy the car? In other words, did that representation play any part in *Driver's* decision as to whether or not to buy the car? It is very hard to say. To assist them in resolving difficult questions like this, the courts have adopted a principle that if:

(1) A made a representation to B with the object of inducing B to do x; *and*
(2) it would have been reasonable for B to have taken that representation into account in deciding whether or not to do x; *and*
(3) B did x after A made that representation to her; *then*
(4) it is presumed that A's representation induced B to do x.[160]

---

[159] It does *not* have to be shown that B would not have done x *but for* A's representation: *Downs* v *Chappell* [1997] 1 WLR 426 (action for deceit available when claimants bought bookstore having been shown a set of accounts for the bookstore which made the bookstore out to be a lot more profitable than it was: the fact that the state of the accounts played some part in the claimant's decision to buy the bookstore was enough to ground an action for deceit – it was irrelevant that the claimants might well have bought the bookstore anyway had they never seen the accounts).

[160] *Smith* v *Chadwick* (1884) 9 App Cas 187, 196 per Lord Blackburn: 'if it is proved that the defendants with a view to induce the claimant to enter into a contract made a statement to the claimant of such a nature as would be likely to induce a person to enter into a contract, and it is proved that the claimant did enter into the contract, it is a fair inference of fact that he was induced to do so by the statement.'

This principle allows us to presume in the situation just discussed that *Driver was* induced to buy the car from *Trader* by *Trader*'s representation. *Trader* made that representation in order to induce *Driver* to buy the car; it would have been reasonable for *Driver* to have taken *Trader*'s representation into account in deciding whether or not to buy the car; and *Driver* did buy the car.

D. A difficult scenario

An interesting problem arises where a fact that was untrue when the representation was made later becomes true. Suppose that A made a representation of fact to B intending to induce B to do *x* and B was induced to do *x* by that representation. Suppose further that A's representation of fact was – to A's knowledge – untrue at the time he made it, but, by the time B came to do *x*, A's representation of fact was no longer untrue. What is the position?

This question came up in *Ship* v *Crosskill* (1870). In that case, a company issued a prospectus which said, *inter alia*, that more than half the capital of the company had been subscribed. At the time the prospectus was issued, this was not true. However, by the time the claimant applied for, and was sold, shares in the company, this was true. It was held that the claimant could *not* bring an action in deceit to recover the money he had paid for shares in the company. At the time he bought the shares in the company, he was not deceived.

24.9 MALICIOUS FALSEHOOD

As a general rule, A will commit the tort of malicious (or injurious) falsehood in relation to B if he maliciously makes a false statement to C that refers to B or B's property and B suffers loss as a result.

The term 'maliciously' needs some explanation. A will have acted maliciously in making a false statement to C if: (1) he knew the statement was untrue when he made it; *or* (2) he did not care whether or not the statement was true when he made it; *or* (3) he made that statement for some dishonest or improper reason.[161]

A couple of examples of this tort being committed will help to illustrate its role. In *Ratcliffe* v *Evans* (1892), the *County Herald*, a Welsh newspaper, incorrectly said that the claimant had ceased to trade as an engineer and boilermaker and that the claimant's firm had ceased to trade. As a result the claimant experienced a loss of business. He was held entitled to sue the *County Herald* on the ground that it had committed the tort of malicious falsehood. The *County Herald* had not acted in good faith in publishing its story about the claimant and the claimant had suffered loss as a result of its publication.

In *Khodaparast* v *Shad* (2000), the claimant was an Iranian woman who worked in an Iranian community school. She had an affair with the defendant and when she brought it to an end, the defendant sought to take some revenge by circulating photocopies of pages from pornographic magazines which appeared to contain photographs of the claimant advertising telephone sex services. In fact the claimant had nothing to do with telephone sex services; the defendant's photocopies were made by photocopying pages from pornographic magazines on which he had artfully superimposed revealing pictures of the claimant that he had taken during their affair. As a result of the defendant's circulating these photocopies, the claimant was dismissed from her job. The claimant successfully sued

---

[161] *Dunlop* v *Maison Talbot* (1904) 20 TLR 579.

the defendant for committing the tort of malicious falsehood – the defendant had, through his photocopies, maliciously misled people into thinking that the claimant was involved in telephone sex services and the claimant had suffered loss as a result.[162]

Four further points can be made about the tort of malicious falsehood:

(1) *The difference between malicious falsehood and defamation.* There are three differences.

First, malicious falsehood extends to cases where a defendant causes a claimant loss by making non-defamatory statements about the claimant to third parties. For example, the statement in *Ratcliffe* v *Evans* (above) was not defamatory of the claimant – right-thinking people would not think less well of the claimant on hearing that he had closed down his business – but that did not prevent a finding that the defendant had committed the tort of malicious falsehood in making that statement.

Secondly, to bring an action for malicious falsehood, you have to prove that the statement you are complaining of was untrue; to bring an action for defamation, all you need do is prove that the statement you are complaining of was defamatory – it is for the defendant to prove that it was true.

Thirdly, to bring an action for malicious falsehood, you have to prove that the defendant acted maliciously in making the statement which you are complaining about; in an action for defamation, you will not normally need to show that the defendant acted maliciously to succeed in your claim.

If a defendant maliciously published a false and defamatory statement about you to someone else and you suffered loss as a result, you will be able to sue either for malicious falsehood or defamation, depending on which way of presenting your action is more advantageous.[163]

(2) *Presumption of loss.* The normal rule in a malicious falsehood case is that the claimant has to prove that the defendant's statement caused her to suffer some kind of loss. However, s 3(1) of the Defamation Act 1952 qualifies this rule. It provides that in an action for malicious falsehood:

it shall not be necessary to allege or prove special damage –

(a) if the words upon which the action is founded are calculated to cause pecuniary damage to the claimant and are published in writing or other permanent form; or

(b) if the said words are calculated to cause pecuniary damage to the claimant in respect of any office, profession, calling, trade or business held or carried on by him at the time of the publication.

(3) *An exception to the rule.* A claim for malicious falsehood will not be available in a case where *Trader* has lured customers away from *Rival* by alleging that his goods are of better quality than *Rival*'s: the courts will not want to get into the business of adjudicating whether or not *Trader*'s boasts were justified or not.[164] However, if *Trader* alleges to *Rival*'s customers that *Rival*'s goods suffer from specific defects, an action for malicious falsehood

---

[162] The House of Lords refused leave to appeal: [2001] 1 WLR 126.

[163] *Joyce* v *Sengupta* [1993] 1 WLR 337.

[164] See the remarks of Lord Herschell LC in *White* v *Mellin* [1895] AC 154, 164–5: 'My Lords, I cannot help saying that I entertain very grave doubts whether any action could be maintained for an alleged disparagement of another's goods, merely on the allegation that the goods sold by the party who is alleged to have disparaged his competitor's goods are better either generally or in this or that particular respect than his competitors' are . . . I think it is impossible not to see that . . . a very wide door indeed would be opened to litigation, and that the Courts might be constantly employed in trying the relative merits of rival productions, if an action of this kind were allowed.'

may be available to *Rival* as the courts will have no problem determining in this case whether or not *Trader*'s allegations were correct.[165]

(4) *Ambiguous representations.* In *Ajinomoto Sweeteners SAS* v *Asda Stores Ltd* (2011), the defendant supermarket had marketed its own brand of health foods. The packaging of these health foods said 'No hidden nasties' and 'No artificial colours and flavours and no aspartame.' (Aspartame is an artificial sweetener often used as a substitute for sugar in low calorie foods.) The claimant manufacturers of aspartame sued the defendant in malicious falsehood, claiming that the combination of these statements on the defendant's packaging amounted to a false representation that aspartame might be harmful. The defendant argued that in making these statements on its packaging, it was merely saying that its health foods were suitable for customers who objected to foods that contained aspartame.

The Court of Appeal rejected the contention that it should – as happens in defamation cases[166] – find that the statements on the packaging had one single meaning, and attempt to determine what that meaning was. Instead, they held that the claimants would be able to sue the defendant for malicious falsehood if: (a) the defendant had known that its packaging was capable of bearing the meaning that the claimants complained of; (b) the defendant had acted maliciously in marketing its health foods in packaging that was capable of bearing that meaning; (c) some of the defendant's customers had understood the defendant's packaging to suggest that aspartame might be harmful; and (d) the claimants had suffered loss as a result of (c).

24.10 RECOVERABLE HARM

So far, we have presented the economic torts in the way that most lawyers think of them – as a way for claimants to recover compensation for pure economic loss that they have suffered.[167] (Where that loss usually takes the form of a loss of profits or business, or loss of one's job, or frustration of one's abilities to find a job.) However, in this final section we would like to question the assumption that the economic torts are purely *economic* in nature and ask whether the torts examined in this chapter could be used as the foundation of a claim for some other form of loss. It is useful to begin, however, by considering the recent argument of Deakin and Randall[168] that the economic torts should be confined to protecting only economic interests associated with 'trade, business or employment'.

A. Trade, business and employment

In their challenging recent article[169] Deakin and Randall argue that the economic torts should only protect economic interests associated with 'trade, business and employment'[170] Their reasoning is that the primary role of the economic torts is to 'maintain the integrity of the competitive process' and consequently courts should focus on designing torts to achieve this goal, without the distraction of protecting interests that are not associated with it.

---

[165] *De Beers Abrasive Products Ltd* v *International General Electric Co of New York* [1975] 1 WLR 972.

[166] See above, § 19.3(10).

[167] Injunctions are often also sought as a remedy where commission of an economic tort is imminent, continuing, or regularly repeated. See below, chapter 33 for discussion of injunctions.

[168] Deakin and Randall 2009.

[169] ibid.

[170] ibid, 533. Sometimes they say 'trade, business and livelihood' instead.

We think that there are three reasons why 'the economic torts' should not be re-fashioned and confined in the way that Deakin and Randall suggest.

Firstly, Deakin and Randall do not provide much evidence to suggest that any problems that the courts have had in deciding the scope of the economic torts have been caused by a failure to focus on cases involving competition. Difficult questions, such as how to define the requisite mental states and what should count as 'unlawful means', are not easy to answer even in cases that obviously involve business competition.

Secondly, if Deakin and Randall's proposal was adopted then the courts would have to decide the scope of the limiting concept: 'trade, business and employment'. This would not be straightforward. For example, they think that a central question in the *Total Network* case should have been whether the claimant, the collector of tax, came 'within the range of claimants with relevant economic interests at stake in the competitive process'.[171] What should the answer have been?

Thirdly, as we argue in the next two sections, we think that there are good reasons for recognising that 'the economic torts' can protect a wider range of interests than those that are *purely economic*.

B. Personal injury and property damage

We think that a claimant could sue for personal injury or property damage that was caused as a result of several of these torts being committed if a suitable case arose.

Suppose, for example, that *Doctor* had made a contract with *Patient*, promising to visit him in a remote location and provide some form of treatment necessary to prevent his health from deteriorating, and *Weevil* intentionally persuaded *Doctor* to breach this contract with the result that *Patient*'s health deteriorated. In such a case we do not think that there is a strong argument for preventing *Patient* from suing *Weevil* for the tort of inducing a breach of contract and recovering damages for the deterioration of his health. Why would tort law distinguish between contracts that confer purely economic benefits and contracts which are designed to protect property or health?[172]

Variations on the same example can be used to test whether the other economic torts also ought to be available to be used where a claimant has suffered personal injury or property damage. Suppose, for instance, that *Doctor* has not made a contract with *Patient* but nonetheless invariably visits him each Monday to provide the necessary treatment. If *Weevil* prevented *Doctor* from visiting by, for example, threatening to commit a tort against her if she visits, then why – assuming that *Weevil* can be shown to have the requisite mental element – should *Patient* not be able to sue *Weevil* for the tort of causing loss by the use of unlawful means (intimidation)?

No doubt the main reason why it is rarely asked whether claimants can sue for physical injury or property damage on the basis of the economic torts is that it is assumed that in such cases *Weevil* could be straightforwardly held liable in negligence for what he has did. But we are not sure that this is straightforward. Suppose, for example, *Weevil* commits the tort of trespass to land by parking his car on *Doctor*'s land, and as a result blocks *Doctor* from getting her own car onto the public highway. Suppose further that *Doctor* asks *Weevil* to move his car, and explains that she needs to set off to visit *Patient* in order to provide

---

[171] Deakin and Randall 2009, 534.
[172] Deakin and Randall might argue for such a limit: see Deakin and Randall, 2009, 537–8. We discussed their views in the previous section.

him with crucial treatment. In such circumstances it is not straightforward to establish that *Weevil* will owe a duty to *Patient* to move his car, because *not moving* the car might be classified as an omission. But surely it ought to amount to a tort (causing loss by the use of unlawful means), if *Weevil* refuses to remove his car, and thus continues to commit the tort of trespass, with the intention of thereby causing harm to *Patient*.

We must acknowledge, however, that there is currently clear authority concerning the tort of *malicious falsehood* which confines it to protecting claimants against economic harm.[173]

C. Pure distress

Even if the economic torts will rarely be required in cases involving personal injury or property damage, we must discuss whether a claimant could bring a claim for *pure distress* off the back of any of the torts discussed in this chapter. This issue is important because, as we have seen, *pure distress* – that is, mental suffering not serious enough to qualify as a psychiatric illness and which does not result from the sufferer's experiencing some other loss, such as physical injury or damage to property or economic loss – is hardly ever actionable in negligence. We will consider each tort in turn.

(1) *Inducing a breach of contract.* In a case where a claimant can sue a contract-breaker for damages for pure distress, there does not seem to be any reason why the claimant should not also be able to sue anyone who culpably induced the breach for such damages. So in a case where *Soprano* contractually agrees to sing for *Aesthete* and his guests at a dinner party *Aesthete* is holding, and then breaks her contract because she has received a better offer (made in the knowledge of the *Soprano–Aesthete* contract) from *Impresario*, *Aesthete* will be able to sue *Soprano* for the loss of the pleasure that having her sing for him and his guests would have given him (as that was the main object of the contract) and there seems no reason why *Aesthete* should not be also allowed to sue *Impresario* for that loss of pleasure.

(2) *Intentionally causing loss by unlawful means.* In *OBG*, Lord Hoffmann said that the 'essence' of this tort 'appears to be (a) a wrongful interference with the actions of a third party in which the claimant *has an economic interest* and (b) an intention thereby to cause loss to the claimant.'[174] He later said that this tort was 'designed *only* to enforce basic standards of civilised behaviour in *economic competition*, between traders or between employers and labour.'[175] These *dicta* strongly suggest that the tort of intentionally causing loss by unlawful means will only ground an action for economic loss.

Moreover, Lord Hoffmann's requirement that this tort will only be committed in *three-party cases* if the defendant has committed a wrong to a third party which has interfered with the third party's 'freedom to deal with the claimant'[176] ensures in a lot of cases that the *three-party* version of this tort can only be committed where the defendant's conduct has caused the claimant to suffer some kind of economic loss. Consider, for example, the **Tiger Kidnapping Problem**:[177]

---

[173] Carty 2010, 216–18.
[174] *OBG*, at [47] (emphasis added).
[175] *OBG*, at [56] (emphasis added).
[176] *OBG*, at [51].
[177] The crime described in the problem is known generally as '*tiger* kidnapping' because of the amount of stalking and planning that is required beforehand to pull the crime off.

Gangster rings up *Bank Manager* at work and tells him that he has kidnapped *Manager*'s wife and children. He allows *Manager* to speak to his wife and children on the 'phone to confirm that this is correct. He instructs *Manager* to take £100,000 out of the bank's vault and deposit it at a location that will be given to *Manager* at a later stage. If he follows the instructions precisely, *Manager* will be reunited with his family. *Manager* does so, but it is many hours before his wife and children are picked up by the police walking down the side of a motorway, and he is informed they are safe. Until then, and since receiving *Gangster*'s 'phone call, *Manager* has been undergoing horrendous mental suffering, wondering what has happened to his family. That suffering was, however, completely normal and did not amount to a recognised psychiatric illness.

Although *Gangster* has committed a wrong (false imprisonment) in relation to *Manager*'s family here, and he committed that wrong with the object of causing *Manager* mental distress (as a means of persuading *Manager* to obey *Gangster*'s instructions), it seems that *Gangster* will *not* have committed the tort of intentionally causing *Manager* loss using unlawful means here as *Gangster*'s wrong to *Manager*'s family did not interfere with the family's freedom to 'deal' with *Manager*.

However, there are some *three-party cases* where the claimant will only have suffered pure distress and which will fit Lord Hoffmann's definition of when the tort of intentionally causing loss using unlawful means will be committed in a three party case. In their excellent article, 'Intentional infliction of harm by unlawful means', Daniel Stilitz and Philip Sales suggest the example of a case where a defendant who was in a dispute with a train company wrongfully interferes with the running of the company's trains. They observe that if the passengers sought to sue the defendant on the basis that he had committed in relation to *them* the tort of intentionally causing loss using unlawful means (because he aimed to disrupt the passengers' journeys as a way of putting pressure on the train company to yield in its dispute with him), 'It would be invidious . . . if the business passengers could recover, but those on a day trip could not.'[178] A passenger who was planning to spend the day at the seaside with his family but whose journey was ruined by the defendant's actions could bring himself within Lord Hoffmann's definition of the *three-party* version of the intentional harm tort, as the defendant's actions have interfered with the train company's freedom to provide its services to the passenger. We see no reason why such a passenger should not be able to sue for having his day ruined.

So far as possible *two-party* forms of the tort of intentionally causing loss using unlawful means are concerned – that is, cases where a defendant directly causes harm to a claimant without going through a third party – the picture is mixed. On the one hand, in *Godwin* v *Uzoigwe* (1993), the Court of Appeal gave damages for distress to a claimant who had been bullied into working for the defendants for two and a half years. On the other hand, in *Mbasogo* v *Logo Ltd* (2007) – where the head of state of Equatorial Guinea tried to sue for damages for pure distress resulting from the defendants' (allegedly) financing an abortive coup attempt against him – the Court of Appeal refused to extend the tort of intentionally causing another loss using unlawful means to this kind of harm because they thought that doing so might have the side effect of granting victims of harassment a common law right to sue for such harassment, thereby undermining the rules for when such a claim could be brought under the Protection from Harassment Act 1997. But the Court did accept – in line

---

[178] Sales and Stilitz 1999, 431.

with the decision in *Godwin v Uzoigwe* – that intimidation was a 'paradigm' example of a tort where compensation could be awarded for injury to feelings.[179]

(3) *Unlawful means conspiracy*. In *three-party* cases, we see no reason why damages for pure distress should not be available. For example, suppose that *Angry* and his *Friend* agree that *Friend* will blow up the *Hotel* where *Angry*'s *Ex* is due to get married, so as to ruin her big day. *Friend* does so, and *Ex* is very distressed at having her wedding ruined. We cannot see why *Ex* should not be able to sue *Friend* and *Angry* in unlawful means conspiracy for damages for her distress.

In *two-party* cases (that is, cases where there is a conspiracy to commit a tort directly against the claimant) the Court of Appeal's decision in *Mbasogo v Logo Ltd* (2007) – which was pleaded as an unlawful means conspiracy case – stands in the way of damages for pure distress being easily available. If *Husband* agrees with *Chancer* that *Chancer* should kill *Husband*'s *Wife*, and the police get wind of the plot and tell *Wife* with the result that she has to go into hiding while the police try to track down *Husband* and *Chancer*, it seems unlikely at the moment that *Wife* could sue either of them for damages for the distressing experience she has been through as a result of their agreement.

(4) *Lawful means conspiracy*. It seems very unlikely that damages for pure distress could be sued for under this head. Allowing such damages to be sued for would run into two objections. The first is the *anomaly objection* – if a defendant acting alone could not be sued for damages for pure distress for successfully causing a claimant to suffer pure distress, it would seem wrong that he could be sued if he did what he did pursuant to an agreement that he had reached with someone else. The second is what we can call the *Wainwright objection* – so-called because Lord Hoffmann set out this objection to damages being made available for pure distress in *Wainwright v Home Office* (2004):

> In institutions and workplaces all over the country, people constantly do and say things with the intention of causing distress and humiliation to others. This shows lack of consideration and appalling manners but I am not sure that the right way to deal with it is always by litigation.[180]

Allowing damages for pure distress to be sued for in lawful means conspiracy would open the doors to claims being made for 'lack of consideration and appalling manners' so long as it could be shown that more than one person was in on a plan to treat the claimant that way.

(5) *Deceit*. Allowing claims for pure distress in deceit might also fall foul of the *Wainwright* objection, as it would open the doors to litigation against pranksters who induced a claimant to humiliate themselves by telling them a lie. (For example, telling a new employee, 'The last Friday of every month is "Batman Day" in this office – everyone comes in dressed as a character from Batman' and the employee duly turns up to the office on the last Friday of the month dressed as the Penguin . . .) Given this, we think the better view is that damages for deceit cannot be given for pure distress.[181]

(6) *Malicious falsehood*. It was assumed by Eady J in *Quinton v Peirce* (2009) – a case concerning an election leaflet criticising the claimant, who was standing for election – that

---

[179] [2007] QB 846, at [97].
[180] [2004] 2 AC 406, at [46].
[181] Carty 2010 argues (at 194) that damages for distress *can* be sued for in deceit, citing *Shelley v Paddock* [1980] QB 348. In that case, the claimant was deceived into paying the defendant £9,420 to purchase a house in Spain which the defendant had no power to transfer into her name. The trial judge awarded the claimant £500 for the distress she had suffered as a result of losing her money. However, the distress in that case was not *pure*, as it was consequent on the economic loss the claimant had suffered as a result of the defendant's deceit.

damages could only be awarded in malicious falsehood if the defendant's falsehood resulted in the claimant suffering 'actual financial loss'.[182] So losing one's seat as a council member, or being very distressed at false allegations that were made against you in the election would not count as compensable losses so far as the law on malicious falsehood is concerned – but losing your right to claim expenses as a council member would![183]

In *Ajinomoto Sweeteners SAS v Asda Ltd* (2011), the Court of Appeal said that it did not 'find at all helpful' the suggestion that malicious falsehood was a purely economic tort, though its alternative analysis that malicious falsehood is concerned with 'the reputation of property, typically in the form of the goodwill of a business'[184] is – we think – not at all consistent with the caselaw on malicious falsehood. Nonetheless, the Court of Appeal's remarks might indicate some slight weakening towards the possibility of claims being made in malicious falsehood for non-pecuniary loss, and when one contemplates the facts of *Khodaparast v Shad* (2000), it would be natural to think that the claimant in that case should have been awarded some kind of remedy even if she had been merely upset by her ex-boyfriend leading everyone to believe that she was a telephone sex worker, and had not lost her job.[185] However, allowing a claim to be made for pure distress in a case like *Khodaparast* again runs into the *Wainwright* objection – that it is not uncommon for people to make up distressing lies about other people's sex lives or past histories, particularly in the workplace, and it is not clear that litigation is the best way of dealing with that problem.

Further reading

Anyone interested in exploring this area of law further should consult **Hazel Carty's An Analysis of the Economic Torts, 2nd edn (OUP, 2010)**. While rendered slightly out of date by recent developments, **Tony Weir**'s discussions of the economic torts in his *An Introduction to Tort Law*, **2nd edn (Clarendon, 2006), chapter 13**, and the 'Introduction' to Part VIII ('Deception and other wrongful conduct' of his *A Casebook on Tort*, **10th edn (Sweet & Maxwell, 2004)** are impeccably clear and extremely stimulating. Also somewhat out of date is **Philip Sales and Daniel Stilitz's 'Intentional infliction of harm by unlawful means' (1999) 115** *Law Quarterly Review* **411**. The law seems to have ended up saying the complete opposite of what Sales and Stilitz wanted it to say, in that the law now has a very restrictive test for what amounts to unlawful means for the purposes of the tort of intentionally causing another loss using unlawful means to do so, and a much wider test for what amounts to unlawful means for the purposes of the tort of unlawful means conspiracy. Sales and Stilitz favoured a very wide test for the intentional harm tort, and a very narrow test for unlawful means conspiracy. However, their article is still worth reading, if only to see what the road not taken by English law in this area might have looked like. Getting more up to date, we have already referred to **Deakin and Randall's 'Rethinking the economic torts' (2009) 72** *Modern Law Review* **519**. **David Howarth's 'Against *Lumley* v Gye' (2005) 68** *Modern Law Review* **195** and **Jason Neyers' 'The economic torts as corrective justice' (2009) 17** *Torts Law Journal* **164** are also worth reading, not least because they promulgate views very different from those found in our chapter.

---

[182] [2009] EWHC 912 (QB), at [86]. Similarly, in *Joyce v Sengupta* [1993] 1 WLR 337, 347–9, Sir Donald Nicholls V-C said *obiter* that 'injury to feelings alone will not found a cause of action in malicious falsehood.'

[183] [2009] EWHC 912 (QB), at [85].

[184] [2011] QB 497, at [28].

[185] In *Khodaparast v Shad* (2000) the Court of Appeal upheld the trial judge's decision to award the claimant *aggravated damages* to reflect the 'injury to her feelings', at [42] and [44]. We discuss below, § 29.3, whether it is appropriate to award aggravated damages to compensate for distress.

Visit **www.mylawchamber.co.uk/mcbride** to access tools to help you develop and test your knowledge of Tort law, including interactive multiple choice questions, practice exam questions with guidance, weblinks, legal newsfeed, additional case summaries, legal updates and tips on answering problem and essay questions.

Use **Case Navigator** to read in full some of the key cases referenced in this chapter with commentary and questions:

- Wainwright *v* Home Office

25 Abuse of power torts

25.1 The basics *705*

25.2 Malicious prosecution *706*

25.3 Analogous torts *707*

25.4 Misfeasance in public office *709*

Overview

In this chapter we look at how the law of tort controls and sanctions the abuse of *public power* (as opposed to private power, which was very much the concern of the previous chapter). This chapter is concerned with two torts – malicious prosecution (dealt with in section 25.2) and misfeasance in public office (dealt with in section 25.4). We also briefly mention some torts that are analogous to the torts of malicious prosecution in section 25.3.

25.1 THE BASICS

Cases like *Allen* v *Flood* (1898)[1] show how unwilling the English common law courts[2] have been to sanction the abuse of *private* power (in the case of *Allen* v *Flood*, the power to withhold one's labour from someone with whom you are not in a contractual relationship). However, when it came to *public* powers or *quasi-public* powers, the courts were much more willing to intervene. It may be that the law on conspiracy can be seen in this way – as an attempt by the courts to ensure that the quasi-public power to associate with other people and to pursue common goals was not abused. In this chapter we look at two torts which are concerned to stop public powers being abused. The first tort focuses on a specific power – the power to bring criminal prosecutions. The abuse of that power will amount to the tort of *malicious prosecution*. The second tort focuses on public officials generally, and makes it a tort – the tort of *misfeasance in public office* – for a public official to abuse his powers when he knows that a particular claimant is likely to suffer loss as a result.

---

[1] And also the earlier case of *Bradford* v *Pickles* [1895] AC 587, where the defendant landowner was held to have had a perfect right to take as much as he liked of water flowing under his land in an undefined channel, even though he was only appropriating that water in order to annoy the claimants into whose reservoirs the water would have otherwise flown. *Bradford* v *Pickles* is not, however, as good an example of the courts' unwillingness to impose liability for 'abuse of rights' as *Allen* v *Flood*. This is because there is an alternative analysis of why the claimants were not entitled to sue in *Bradford* v *Pickles*. According to this analysis, the claimants could not sue because you cannot complain that your use of land has been interfered with as a result of something being prevented from coming onto your land unless you had a right to receive that thing – and the claimants in *Bradford* v *Pickles* had no right to receive any of the water that was flowing under the defendant's land. So it could be argued that the claimants could not sue in *Bradford* v *Pickles* not because the defendant had a perfect right to take as much as he liked of the water flowing under his land, but because the claimants had no right to receive that water. See further § 15.5(D), above.

[2] As we have already seen (see above, § 1.9), the Courts of Equity were much more interventionist, restraining people from relying on their strict legal rights when it would be 'unconscionable' to do so. But they never asserted a power to make someone pay damages for abusing their legal rights.

25.2 MALICIOUS PROSECUTION

A will have committed the tort of malicious prosecution in relation to B if:

(1) A prosecuted B for committing a criminal offence; *and*
(2) the prosecution ended in B's favour;[3] *and*
(3) A had no reasonable and probable cause to prosecute B for that offence; *and*
(4) A acted maliciously in prosecuting B for committing that offence.[4]

Four points should be made about this tort:

(1) *Prosecution.* In order to show that A has committed the tort of malicious prosecution in relation to B, it is first necessary to show that A prosecuted B for committing a criminal offence. This requirement will obviously be satisfied if A is a private citizen and brings a private prosecution against B for committing an offence. Similarly, if A works for the Crown Prosecution Service and in that capacity prosecutes B for committing an offence.

Outside these simple cases, the House of Lords has made it clear that A will be held to have prosecuted B for committing a criminal offence if he was *directly responsible* for B's being prosecuted for committing that offence.[5] So, for example, if *Informer* supplied information to the police which indicated that *Suspect* had committed some offence and *Suspect* was subsequently prosecuted for that offence, *Informer* will only be held to have 'prosecuted' *Suspect* if: (i) *Informer* supplied his information to the police with the intention of persuading the police to prosecute *Suspect*; *and* (ii) the facts of *Suspect*'s case were such that it was impossible for the police to exercise any independent judgment as to whether or not *Suspect* should be prosecuted.[6]

However, even if (i) and (ii) are satisfied, and *Informer* maliciously supplied false information about *Suspect* to the police, he may still be protected from being sued for malicious prosecution by the decision of the Court of Appeal in *Westcott* v *Westcott* (2009), which held that statements made to the police for the purpose of encouraging them to investigate a crime were protected by absolute immunity, which means they cannot be made the basis of a tort claim under any circumstances.

(2) *Termination of prosecution in claimant's favour.* The courts will refuse to say that A committed the tort of malicious prosecution in prosecuting B for committing a particular criminal offence if B was found guilty of committing that offence and her conviction has not yet been reversed. This is to stop B from reopening the question of whether or not her conviction was valid by bringing an action for malicious prosecution against A.[7]

---

[3] That is, B was not found guilty of committing that offence or B was found guilty of committing that offence but her conviction was subsequently reversed.

[4] For a general discussion of the tort, see Fridman 1963.

[5] *Martin* v *Watson* [1996] 1 AC 74.

[6] *Mahon* v *Rahn (No 2)* [2000] 1 WLR 2150, at [269]. Also *Martin* v *Watson* [1996] 1 AC 74 (W's allegation that M had indecently exposed himself to her capable of giving rise to action for malicious prosecution). In *H* v *AB* [2009] EWCA Civ 1092 – a case where the subject of an overturned conviction for rape sued the woman who claimed he had raped her for malicious prosecution – Sedley LJ held that: (i) the defendant could not be sued for malicious prosecution because the police had approached her, not the other way round; and (ii) even if the defendant had approached the police, claiming that she had been raped, she could only be sued for malicious prosecution if she had done something 'improper . . . designed to cause . . . [the] authorities to take a course [they] would not otherwise have taken' (at [46]–[47]).

[7] *Basébé* v *Matthews* (1867) LR 2 CP 684, 687 (per Byles J): 'there is [no] doubt that the criminal proceeding must be determined in favour of the accused before he can maintain an action for malicious prosecution. If this were not so, almost every case would have to be tried over again upon its merits . . . It makes no difference that the party convicted has no power of appealing.'

(3) *Reasonable and probable cause*. A *Prosecutor* will only have had reasonable and probable cause to prosecute *Defendant* for an offence if, when he brought the prosecution: (i) *Prosecutor* thought that *Defendant* had probably committed that offence;[8] *and* (ii) it was reasonable for *Prosecutor* to think this, given the evidence available to him at the time he prosecuted *Defendant*.[9] If (i) or (ii) are missing, there will be no reasonable and probable cause for the prosecution.[10]

(4) *Malice*. It seems that *Prosecutor* will act maliciously in prosecuting *Defendant* for committing a criminal offence if his predominant purpose in prosecuting B for committing that offence is *not* to ensure that justice is done to B with respect to that offence.[11]

It was suggested in *Glinski* v *McIver* (1962) that the police prosecuted the claimant for conspiracy to defraud not

> in order to bring him to justice for that offence, but to punish the claimant for having a week before given evidence, which the police believed then to have been perjured, for the defence in the case of *Reg* v *Comer*.[12]

On another reading of the facts in *Glinski* v *McIver*, the police prosecuted the claimant in order to induce him to admit that he had perjured himself in the *Comer* case the week before. Even on this reading, the police acted maliciously in prosecuting the claimant: their object in prosecuting the claimant was not to ensure that justice was done to the claimant – if the claimant had admitted his perjury, they would have dropped the prosecution.

25.3 ANALOGOUS TORTS

It seems well established that:

(1) *Arrest warrant*. A will commit a tort if he maliciously and without reasonable and probable cause procures the issue of a warrant for B's arrest.[13]

(2) *Search warrant*. A will commit a tort if he maliciously and without reasonable and probable cause procures the issue of a search warrant authorising the police to search B's premises.[14]

---

[8] See Lindley J in *Shrosbery* v *Osmaston* (1877) 37 LT 792, 794: 'if a man believes that another is not guilty of a criminal charge, and prosecuted unsuccessfully, I confess I have the greatest difficulty in seeing that such a man can be held to have reasonable and probable cause for prosecuting.' But it does not have to be shown that *Prosecutor positively believed* that *Defendant* was guilty: *Tempest* v *Snowden* [1952] 1 KB 130, 139 (per Denning LJ), *Glinski* v *McIver* [1962] AC 726, 758 (per Lord Denning). All that has to be shown is that he thought *Defendant* was *probably* guilty.

[9] *Glinski* v *McIver* [1962] AC 726, 766 (per Lord Devlin): 'there must [have been] cause (that is, sufficient grounds . . .) for thinking that [*Defendant*] was probably guilty of the offence imputed.'

[10] It may be more difficult than one might think to show that either (i) or (ii) are missing. Most of the leading cases on 'reasonable and probable cause' are cases where 'reasonable and probable cause' was established: *Hicks* v *Faulkner* (1878) 8 QBD 167 (not unreasonable to rely on own memory of events in support of view that claimant had committed an offence); *Dawson* v *Vansandau* (1863) 11 WR 516 (not unreasonable to rely on testimony of purported accomplice to form view that claimant had probably committed offence); *Abbott* v *Refuge Assurance Co Ltd* [1962] 1 QB 432 (not unreasonable to rely on not obviously defective advice from counsel that prosecution of claimant would probably succeed).

[11] See Alderson B's observation in *Stevens* v *Midland Counties Railway* (1854) 10 Ex 352, 356; 156 ER 480, 482: 'Any motive other than that of simply instituting a prosecution for the simple purpose of bringing a person to justice, is a malicious motive on the part of the person who acts in that way.'

[12] [1962] AC 726, 766 (per Lord Devlin).

[13] *Roy* v *Prior* [1971] AC 470.

[14] *Reynolds* v *Commissioner of Police of the Metropolis* [1984] 3 All ER 649.

(3) *Liquidation proceedings*. A will commit a tort if he maliciously and without reasonable and probable cause starts liquidation proceedings against a trading company or bankruptcy proceedings against an individual.[15]

(4) *Disciplinary proceedings*. There is *no* tort of maliciously and without reasonable and probable cause instituting disciplinary proceedings against someone else. So if A maliciously and without reasonable cause institutes disciplinary proceedings against B and does not in doing so commit one of the torts mentioned in this book, he will not commit a tort.[16]

(5) *Civil proceedings*. There is *no* tort of maliciously and without reasonable and probable cause bringing a civil action against someone else. So if A maliciously and without reasonable cause brings a civil action against B and does not in doing so commit one of the torts mentioned in this book, he will not commit a tort.[17]

Does this make sense? Why will the law protect B from having arrest warrants issued against her for no good reason or from her being subject to unwarranted bankruptcy proceedings while it does not take any special steps to ensure that B is not subjected to groundless disciplinary proceedings or to ensure that B is not the victim of unjustified civil suits? The traditional explanation for the distinctions drawn by the law in this area is that the law in this area is designed to prevent people suffering three kinds of harm: harm to their reputation, harm to their person (including the loss of liberty), and harm resulting from having to spend money defending oneself from proceedings being taken against one.[18] So where B is liable to suffer one of these kinds of harm as a result of proceedings being taken against her, A will owe B a duty to ensure that he does not maliciously start such proceedings when he has no reasonable and probable cause to do so.

This traditional explanation does not quite explain why the law does *not* protect people against the malicious initiation of disciplinary or civil proceedings without reasonable or probable cause. After all, someone who is subjected to such proceedings will be put to a lot of expense defending them, which is one of the heads of damage that this area of law is designed to protect people against suffering. So far as civil proceedings are concerned, Bowen LJ in *Quartz Hill Consolidated Gold Mining Co* v *Eyre* (1863) that:

> The bringing of [a civil] action does not as a natural or necessary consequence involve any injury to a man's property, for this reason, that the only costs which the law recognises, and for which it will compensate him, are the costs properly involved in the action itself. For those the successful defendant will have been already compensated, so far as the law chooses to compensate him.[19]

However, this is not true. The costs awarded to a successful defendant to a civil action will always be less than the true costs incurred by the defendant in defending that action.[20]

In *Gregory* v *Portsmouth City Council* (2000), the House of Lords expressed some unease at the state of the law in this area but refused to disturb it. It thought the jump from imposing common law duties on people not to start *criminal* proceedings maliciously and without

---

[15] *Quartz Hill Consolidated Gold Mining Co* v *Eyre* (1863) 11 QBD 674.

[16] *Gregory* v *Portsmouth City Council* [2000] AC 419, 432.

[17] *Metall und Rohstoff AG* v *Donaldson Lufkin & Jenrette Inc.* [1990] 1 QB 391, 471–2; *Gregory* v *Portsmouth City Council* [2000] AC 419, 432–3.

[18] The threefold division of the harms concerned to be prevented by the law in this area goes back to a *dictum* of Holt CJ's in *Savill* v *Roberts* (1698) 12 Mod Rep 208, 88 ER 1267.

[19] (1863) 11 QBD 674, 690.

[20] This will certainly be true if the civil justice reforms contained in the government's Legal Aid, Sentencing and Punishment of Offenders Bill go through unamended as they will require a successful claimant to pay out of his damages any 'success fee' that his law firm charges him. So a claimant who is represented by a law firm on a no win, no fee basis will never recover in full the amount of the costs incurred in winning his case.

reasonable and probable cause to imposing common law duties on people not to start *private disciplinary* proceedings maliciously and without reasonable and probable cause was too large a jump for the law to take.[21] It thought that there was a stronger case for changing the law so as to protect people from being subjected to malicious and groundless civil actions but expressed the hope that other areas of the law such as the law on defamation, conspiracy and malicious falsehood would suffice to protect the interests of people who were subject to malicious civil actions without reasonable and probable cause.[22]

(6) *Judicial review.* An attempt to revive the tort of 'abuse of process' was made in the case of *Land Securities plc* v *Fladgate Fielder* (2010). In that case, the claimants were developers who had been granted planning permission to develop one site on terms that would allow them to proceed with plans to develop another site opposite the defendants' offices. The defendants applied for judicial review of the decision to grant the claimants planning permission to develop the first site. The claimants sued the defendants for 'abuse of process', claiming that their sole reason for applying for judicial review was to delay the claimants' developments, and thereby put pressure on the claimants to abandon their plans to develop the site opposite the defendants' offices. The Court of Appeal noted that there were, at best, two cases[23] in the history of English law where a claim for 'abuse of process' had been allowed – the first was 170 years ago; the second 140 years ago.[24] The Court of Appeal was prepared to admit that there existed a tort of 'abuse of process' but held that

> even if the tort can be committed outside circumstances of compulsion by arrest, imprisonment or other forms of duress, there is no reasonably arguable basis for extending the tort beyond the other particular heads of damage . . .[25]

which the torts analogous to malicious prosecution exist to protect people against (that is, harm to reputation, harm to the person (including loss of liberty), and harm resulting from the expense of defending oneself from proceedings that have been initiated against one). Accordingly, the Court of Appeal refused to find that the tort of abuse of process could be committed by making an application for judicial review, even if the intended effect of that application was to cause the claimant to suffer business losses.

25.4 MISFEASANCE IN PUBLIC OFFICE

Public officials have a special capacity to cause harm by abusing their official powers or neglecting their official duties.

> The rationale of the tort [of misfeasance in public office] is that in a legal system based on the rule of law executive or administrative power 'may be exercised only for the public good' and not for ulterior and improper purposes.[26]

---

[21] [2000] AC 419, 431–2.

[22] [2000] AC 419, 432–3.

[23] *Grainger* v *Hill* (1838) 4 Bing NC 212, 132 ER 769 (defendant sued claimant for debt, and had officers threaten to take claimant to prison unless he gave up register of ship of which he was the master (and which he could have sailed away in, with the register): held, abuse of process to use legal proceedings to obtain property to which the defendant was not entitled); *Gilding* v *Eyre* (1861) 10 CB NS 592, 142 ER 584 (claimant had judgment entered against him for debt; overpaid the money he owed because of threat of being arrested for failure to pay full amount of debt).

[24] [2010] Ch 467, at [41].

[25] [2010] Ch 467, at [68].

[26] *Three Rivers DC* v *Governor and Company of the Bank of England (No 3)* [2003] 2 AC 1 (henceforth, *Three Rivers (No 3)*), 190 (per Lord Steyn, quoting Nourse LJ in *Jones* v *Swansea CC* [1990] 1 WLR 54, 85).

In many situations a public official who abuses his or her powers will commit one of the other torts discussed in this book. For instance, if a public official physically detains someone when he has no lawful authority to do so, he will commit the tort of false imprisonment. Similarly, a public official will commit the tort of conversion if she seizes someone else's property when she has no lawful authority to do so. But in some situations an abuse of power by a public official will not fall within the ambit of any other tort. This will be the case, for example, if a public official refuses to grant a licence to someone when such a licence would normally have been granted,[27] or orders someone not to carry out a profitable activity when such an order should not have been given, or neglects his or her official duties.[28] The tort of misfeasance in public office is normally the only tort that *could* have been committed in these situations.

A, a public official, will commit the tort of misfeasance in public office in relation to B if:

(1) in bad faith he misuses his powers or neglects his duties with the specific intention of injuring B *and* B suffers material damage; *or*
(2) in bad faith he acts in a way that he knows is beyond his powers or is inconsistent with his duties and he knows that his acting in that way is likely either to injure B or to injure a class of people of which B is a member *and* B suffers material damage.

In the case of *Three Rivers DC v Bank of England (No 3)* (2003)[29] the members of the House of Lords expressed different views as to whether (1) and (2), above, amount to two different forms of the tort or not. Lord Steyn suggested that it was 'conducive to clarity to recognise' that (1) and (2) are alternative forms of the tort with a 'unifying element of conduct amounting to an abuse of power accompanied by subjective bad faith'.[30] By contrast, Lord Millett argued that 'the two limbs are merely different ways in which the necessary element of intention is established'.[31] On this question we prefer the view of Lord Steyn because we doubt whether anything properly called intention can be inferred from the proof of (2). We would describe the relationship between the two forms in this way – form (2) is an *extension* of the scope of the tort beyond form (1).

Several elements of the definition are worth further discussion.

(1) *Public official.* This is defined broadly. Best CJ was of the opinion that 'every one who is appointed to discharge a public duty, and receives a compensation in whatever shape,

---

[27] Many of the cases on misfeasance in public office involve abuses of licensing powers. For example, *Roncarelli* v *Duplessis* [1959] SCR 121 involved an abuse of the power to grant liquor licences to restaurants, *David* v *Abdul Cader* [1963] 1 WLR 834 involved an abuse of the power to license cinemas, and *Three Rivers (No 3)* involved allegations of abuse of the power to license banks. Another group of cases involve alleged abuses of planning powers: see, for example, *Dunlop* v *Woollahra MC* [1982] AC 158 and *Barnard* v *Restormel BC* [1998] 3 PLR 27. Recently, many claims have alleged abuse of powers relating to immigration and asylum.

[28] Some of the claims in *Three Rivers (No 3)* involved allegations that the defendant had deliberately decided not to perform the duties imposed on it by the statutes which made it the regulator of deposit-taking institutions. In *Odhavji Estate* v *Woodhouse* [2003] 3 SCR 263, the Supreme Court of Canada expressly rejected the argument that the tort only covered the abuse of powers. The Court held (at [30]) that the tort should cover both abuse of powers and neglect of duty because they were 'equally inconsistent with the obligation of a public officer not to intentionally injure a member of the public through deliberate and unlawful conduct in the exercise of public functions'.

[29] The House of Lords dealt with the issues raised by this case in two separate sets of speeches that are reported sequentially at [2003] 2 AC 1. Only the second set of speeches used numbered paragraphs. Thus our references to the first set of speeches use page numbers and our references to the second set use paragraph numbers.

[30] [2003] 2 AC 1, 191–2.

[31] [2003] 2 AC 1, 235.

whether from the Crown or otherwise, is constituted a public officer'.[32] Most cases involve officers who are members of the executive, but the Court of Appeal of New Zealand has held that the tort can also be committed by a judge.[33] Public bodies, such as local councils, can be liable, as well as individual public officials.[34] If A is a public official, he can commit the tort of misfeasance in public office by abusing *any* of the powers attached to his post: 'It is not the nature of the power which matters. Whatever its nature or origin, the power may be exercised only for the public good. It is the office on which everything depends.'[35] Thus an official who works for a particular public body can commit the tort by abusing the powers which come from the public body being a landlord,[36] or which come from the fact that the body has the capacity to make contracts, and not just by abusing the special statutory and prerogative powers that the public body may have.[37] Indeed, it seems that a public official can also commit the tort by using his or her position to lay claim to powers that he or she does not legally have. In the Australian case of *Northern Territory* v *Mengel* (1995), the defendant public officials committed the tort of misfeasance in public office by asserting a power to stop the Mengels transporting their cattle to market when, in fact, they did not have such a power.

(2) *Acts and omissions.* Obviously, a public official may commit the tort of misfeasance in public office if he performs a *positive act* that is unlawful, such as issuing an unlawful order. If B wants to claim that A committed the tort of misfeasance in public office by performing some kind of positive act, it will be important for B to identify the act in question since a pivotal issue will be A's state of mind in performing the act in question.[38]

A difficult question is whether the tort also covers situations where a public official *fails to act*, knowing that this is likely to lead to B suffering some kind of harm. Different members of the House of Lords gave different answers to this question in *Three Rivers (No 3)*, where some of the claims were based on *failure* to revoke a licence.[39] Lord Hobhouse stated that

> If there is a legal duty to act and the decision not to act amounts to an unlawful breach of that legal duty, the omission can amount to misfeasance for the purpose of the tort . . . What is not covered is a mere failure, oversight or accident.[40]

This answer suggests that two separate conditions must be fulfilled before an omission can amount to misfeasance: there must be (i) a breach of a *legal duty* to act, and (ii) a *decision* not to act. Lord Hutton also seemed to support (ii) and said that where the claim was based

---

[32] *Henly* v *Mayor of Lyme* (1828) 5 Bing 91, 107, 130 ER 995, 1001. In *Stockwell* v *Society of Lloyd's* [2008] 1 WLR 2255 the Court of Appeal concluded that Lloyd's was *not* a public officer for the purposes of the tort.

[33] *Rawlinson* v *Rice* [1998] 1 NZLR 454.

[34] Further, a public body may be held vicariously liable if one of its employees commits the tort of misfeasance in public office: *Racz* v *Home Office* [1994] 2 AC 45. For the rules governing when an employer will be vicariously liable in respect of a tort committed by one of his employees, see below, chapter 37.

[35] *Jones* v *Swansea CC* [1990] 1 WLR 54, 85 (per Nourse LJ).

[36] As was the case in *Jones* v *Swansea CC* where the claimant alleged that the council had maliciously refused to allow a change of use of premises that she leased from the council.

[37] Aronson 2011 argues that it would be better if the tort focused on abuse of *public power* rather than the defendant's office. Thus he would extend liability to abuse of *public power* by government contractors.

[38] *Calveley* v *Chief Constable of the Merseyside Police* [1989] AC 1228, 1240.

[39] *Three Rivers (No 3)*, involved claims that the Bank of England, as regulator of deposit-taking institutions, was liable to compensate depositors who lost money on the collapse of the Bank of Credit and Commerce International (BCCI). The claims alleged that the Bank of England had acted unlawfully in licensing BCCI and in not intervening sooner to control its activities.

[40] *Three Rivers (No 3)*, at 230. See also 237 (per Lord Millett).

on an omission it 'must be a deliberate one involving an actual decision'.[41] By contrast, Lord Hope stated 'I would reject the argument that proof of conscious decisions to act or not to act is required. In my view the tort extends to a deliberate or wilful failure to take those decisions.'[42]

There can be little doubt that condition (1) must be satisfied when a claim is based on an omission because the tort of misfeasance requires *unlawful* behaviour and an omission will not be unlawful unless there was a duty to act. It is important to remember, however, that public law insists that where an official has a *power* to act: (a) that official will be under a legal *duty* to exercise the power if, in the circumstances, it would be utterly unreasonable[43] not to do so, and (b) that official will be under a legal duty *to consider* whether to use that power or not. Lord Hope's reason for rejecting condition (2) was that he thought it would benefit a defendant who repeatedly procrastinated and refused to make a decision. But it is arguable that such a defendant could be described as having *decided* to breach legal duty (b).[44]

(3) *State of mind.* The state of mind which it must be proved a public official had at the time of his unlawful act or omission is different for the two forms of the tort. To prove that A has committed form (i) of the tort in relation to B, B must prove that A 'specifically intended' to injure B (or a class of persons of which B was a member) when he misused his powers or neglected his duty. It is probably also necessary to show that A knew that it was not lawful to injure B – otherwise the tort might cover cases where a public official honestly believed that punishing someone else was legally authorised.[45]

Suppose now that B wants to establish that A, in acting beyond his powers or inconsistently with his duties, committed form (ii) of the tort of misfeasance in public office. What will B have to prove was A's state of mind when he acted in this way? In addressing this question, it is important to distinguish between what must be shown to have been A's state of mind *towards the unlawfulness of his act* and what must be shown to have been A's state of mind *towards B*.

As to the first, in the *Three Rivers (No 3)* case Lord Steyn said that 'only reckless indifference in a subjective sense will be sufficient'.[46] So, at the very least, B will have to 'prove that [A] acted with a state of mind of reckless indifference to the illegality of his act'.[47] This means that B must show that A knew that the act was unlawful, or suspected that the act was unlawful but did not bother to check further because he or she did not care whether it was or not.

As to A's state of mind *towards B*, Lord Steyn said that at the very least B must prove that A acted 'in the knowledge that his act would probably injure [B] or a person of a class of

---

[41] *Three Rivers (No 3)*, at 228.
[42] *Three Rivers (No 3)*, at [69].
[43] Those who have studied administrative law will be familiar with this concept being called 'Wednesbury unreasonableness', after the case of *Associated Provincial Picture Houses Ltd* v *Wednesbury Corp* [1948] 1 KB 223.
[44] The House of Lords in *Three Rivers (No 3)* split 3:2 over whether the claims should be permitted to proceed to trial. The dissentients, Lord Hobhouse (at [172]–[173]) and Lord Millett (at [191]) regarded the claims based on omissions to revoke the licence as flawed by a failure to establish a legal duty to revoke. Lord Hope was willing to allow the case to proceed on the basis of the general allegation that 'the Bank deliberately ran away from its responsibility as the relevant supervisory authority' (at [68]).
[45] The formulation of the tort in *Three Rivers (No 3)* does not mention this element, but both forms of the tort require 'bad faith' and in our opinion it is obvious that 'bad faith' requires not just an intention to injure but also knowledge that such injury is not lawful.
[46] *Three Rivers (No 3)*, at 193.
[47] ibid.

which [B] was a member'.[48] But again, proof of actual knowledge is not necessary and it would be sufficient for B to prove that A suspected that injury to B would probably be caused but did not bother to check further because he or she did not care.

In *Akenzua v Secretary of State for the Home Department* (2003), the Court of Appeal considered whether Lord Steyn's statement that A must know that 'his act would probably injure [B] or a person of a class of which [B] was a member' meant that the tort could not catch a defendant who unlawfully acted in a way which imperilled people indiscriminately. The Court held that it did not matter whether the defendant could contemplate harm to a particular *group of persons* provided that the *way in which the harm was caused* was the same sort of way as the defendant had in contemplation at the time of his unlawful act or omission. Thus if A unlawfully released C knowing him to be an arsonist, A might be liable to B if she was injured by a fire started by C, but not if she was injured by C's negligent driving.

(4) *Bad faith*. The speeches in *Three Rivers (No 3)* have not settled the role 'bad faith' plays in the tort of misfeasance in public office. Lord Hope suggested that 'bad faith' was *demonstrated* by proof of the relevant state of mind.[49] Thus, for him at least, 'bad faith' was not an *additional* ingredient. By contrast, Lord Hutton treated 'bad faith' as requiring an evaluation of the defendant's *motive*.[50] If a bad motive is an additional ingredient then a public official who knowingly acted unlawfully, and knew of the risk of probable harm to the claimant, could nonetheless avoid liability if he acted for the purest of motives, for instance, because he believed that the unlawful behaviour was in the public interest. This has been criticised on the ground that 'there should be no encouragement given to [public officials] to dream up arguments as to why it was a good idea to deliberately choose not to comply [with legislation]'.[51] But Lord Hutton's view seems to give more weight to the function of the tort as being to control *abuse* of the official's position. The official's pure motive clearly cannot make his unlawful behaviour lawful, but we think that it may be sufficient to prevent it from falling within this tort.

(5) *Lord Steyn's error?* In *Three Rivers (No 3)* Lord Steyn stated that

> in both forms of the tort the [state of mind] required *must be directed at the harm complained of,* or at least to harm of the type suffered by the plaintiffs.[52]

If Lord Steyn's view is correct then what follows from it? Consider the **Unpredictable Criminal Problem**:

> *Turnkey*, a corrupt prison officer, unlawfully releases *Thug* from prison before the end of his sentence, knowing that *Thug* has vowed to take revenge on *Citizen*, whose testimony led to *Thug* being imprisoned. *Turnkey* believes that it is very likely that *Thug* will physically attack *Citizen* but he does not care. *Thug* goes to *Citizen*'s house with the intention of attacking her, but after he has let himself into the house he finds that she owns a large amount of valuable jewellery and decides it would be better to steal this and make a new life for himself. *Thug* steals *Citizen*'s jewellery.

---

[48] *Three Rivers (No 3)*, at 196.
[49] *Three Rivers (No 3)*, at [44].
[50] *Three Rivers (No 3)*, at [121]–[125].
[51] Stanton 2003, 134.
[52] *Three Rivers (No 3)*, at 195–6 (emphasis added).

The difficulty raised by this problem stems from the fact that *Turnkey*, the public official, expected *Thug* to cause one *type* of harm to *Citizen* – physical injuries – but *Thug* has actually caused a different *type* of harm – loss of personal property. If we apply Lord Steyn's rule, *Turnkey* will not be held liable to compensate *Citizen* for the harm suffered by her as a result of *Turnkey*'s act of misfeasance; his state of mind was *not* directed at 'the harm complained of, or at least to harm of the type suffered by' *Citizen*. This result is contrary to the usual rules as to the extent of a defendant's liability where a defendant has committed an *intentional* tort.[53] Moreover, Lord Steyn did not expressly consider what the correct legal outcome should be in such a case. Consequently there are grounds for arguing that Lord Steyn made an error.

In our opinion, he should have said that in order to have committed the tort of misfeasance in public office in relation to *Citizen*, *Turnkey* must, when misusing his powers, have intended *Citizen* to suffer harm, or known that *Citizen* would probably suffer harm, or suspected that *Citizen* would probably suffer harm and not cared, but that if *Turnkey* has committed the tort, the separate and further question of what damages are recoverable should be governed by the usual rules governing the extent of an intentional tortfeasor's liability.[54]

(6) *Material damage.* In *Watkins v Secretary of State for the Home Department* (2006), the House of Lords considered whether three prison officers had committed the tort of misfeasance in public office in relation to Watkins, a serving prisoner, when they unlawfully and in bad faith opened his correspondence. The case was difficult because Watkins had suffered no 'material damage', that is, no economic loss or physical or mental injury,[55] as a result of these unlawful acts. Indeed the trial judge had found that he appeared 'to thrive on these conflicts'. The House of Lords concluded that the three prison officers had not committed the tort of misfeasance in public office in relation to Watkins *because* he had not suffered 'material damage'. One factor that seems to have particularly influenced the judges who decided the case is that they did not want the tort to be available as a vehicle for claimants whose sole object was to punish public officials through obtaining awards of punitive damages.[56]

---

[53] An intentional tort is one which can only be committed deliberately. On the rules governing the extent of an intentional tortfeasor's liability, see above, § 10.2(D).

[54] In *Watkins v Secretary of State for the Home Department* [2006] 2 AC 395, at [72], Lord Rodger referred to these rules in connection with the tort of misfeasance in public office. He did not draw attention, however, to their inconsistency with Lord Steyn's statement in *Three Rivers (No 3)*.

[55] In the subsequent case of *Karagozlu v Metropolitan Police Comr* [2007] 2 All ER 1055 the Court of Appeal held that a claim for misfeasance in public office could also be based on a 'loss of liberty', including the loss of residual liberty that a prisoner would suffer if he was unlawfully moved from an open prison to a closed prison. See also *Iqbal v Prison Officers Association*, [2010] QB 732, at [41]–[42].

[56] For further discussion of the case, see below, § 27.3(A).

Further reading

On the tort of misfeasance in public office we particularly recommend **Mark Aronson, 'Misfeasance in public office: a very peculiar tort'** (2011) 35 *Melbourne University Law Review*, which discusses a substantial number of significant questions about the future of the tort, and draws on a great wealth of knowledge about both public and private law in a range of Commonwealth jurisdictions.

Some see the torts dealt with in this chapter as examples of defendants being held liable for an 'abuse of rights': see, for example, **Jason Neyers, 'Explaining the inexplicable? Four manifestations of abuse of rights in English law'** in Nolan and Robertson (eds), *Rights and Private Law* **(Hart Publishing, 2011), chapter 11**. The difficulty with this view is that it is hard to see that there is a *right* to bring an unjustified prosecution, or a *right* in a public body to act unlawfully. For this reason we prefer to characterise these torts as being directed at abuses of *power*, rather than abuses of *right*.

Visit **www.mylawchamber.co.uk/mcbride** to access tools to help you develop and test your knowledge of Tort law, including interactive multiple choice questions, practice exam questions with guidance, weblinks, legal newsfeed, additional case summaries, legal updates and tips on answering problem and essay questions.

premium
my**law**chamber
unrivalled support for legal education

26 Defences

26.1   The basics 716

26.2   Lack of capacity 718

26.3   Act of state 720

26.4   Sovereign and diplomatic
       immunity 720

26.5   Trade union immunity 721

26.6   Witness immunity 721

26.7   Abuse of process 723

26.8   Death 725

26.9   *Volenti non fit injuria* 725

26.10 Exclusion of liability 728

26.11 Illegality (1): the common law 730

26.12 Illegality (2): statute 737

26.13 More good than harm 738

26.14 Limitation 739

26.15 Contributory negligence 743

26.16 The impact of Article 6 of the
       ECHR 743

Overview

In this chapter we gather together a large number of defences that might be raised to defeat a claim in tort. The most important for students' purposes are *volenti* (section 26.9), exclusion of liability (section 26.10) and illegality (sections 26.11 and 26.12). Contributory negligence is mentioned in section 26.15, but dealt with in detail in chapter 28 (section 28.5). The other defences dealt with in this chapter are not without interest. In particular the defences dealt with in sections 26.3–26.7 and 26.14 reflect a perception that there are some things more important than tort law, and some priorities more pressing than upholding the rights tort law gives us.

26.1 THE BASICS

In this chapter we look at some general pleas that a defendant in a tort case might be able to make to defeat the claim that is being made against him. Some of these pleas involve the defendant in denying that he is liable to the claimant because he did nothing wrong to him. A defence such as *volenti non fit injuria* ('no wrong is done to the willing') is of this type. Unsurprisingly, we are already very familiar with this defence as it is an important feature of all of the torts set out in this book that the claimant did not consent to be treated in the way he was. Other defences take the form of the defendant arguing he is not liable to the claimant because, even if he did something wrong to the claimant, the claimant still cannot sue him for reasons of public policy, or the proper administration of justice.

James Goudkamp draws a similar distinction between what he calls 'absent element' defences – which are 'denials by the defendant of an element of the tort in which the plaintiff sues'[1] – and 'public policy defences' which 'exempt the defendant from liability even though he committed a tort.' 'Public policy defences', Goudkamp argues:

> are insensitive to the rational defensibility of the defendant's conduct. In other words, when advancing a public policy defence, the defendant does not attempt to explain why he committed

---

[1] Goudkamp 2011b, text at n 2.

a tort. He does not endeavour to show that what he did was supported by the balance of reasons. Public policy defences exist in recognition of the fact that the goals of tort law must on occasion play second fiddle to other social concerns. Liability must sometimes be withheld from a tortfeasor in order to promote some aim external to tort law.[2]

We will not seek rigorously to classify all the defences set out below as either being 'absent element defences' (arguing 'I did no wrong') or 'public policy defences' (arguing 'Even if I did do something wrong, considerations of the public interest require that I not be held liable for what I did'). (To save words, from now on we will call an 'absent element defence', an 'AED'; and a 'public policy defence', a 'PED'.) It seems to us that there are some defences that could be classified either way. For example, when a trade union calls its members out on strike, thereby inducing them to breach their contracts of employment, the trade union cannot be sued for inducing a breach of contract, provided it has followed the proper procedures before calling the strike. It is hard to tell, in such a case, whether the trade union's *immunity* from being sued in this case should be classified as an AED ('We did no wrong in calling our members out on strike') or as a PPD ('We did wrong, but we cannot be sued for it because public policy dictates that the interests of trades unions in being allowed to call strikes over their grievances should prevail over the interest employers have in keeping their employees working').

Difficult though the distinction might be to apply in concrete cases, the distinction is important for the purpose of evaluating whether or not a particular defence should be recognised or not. AEDs need no justification – if the defendant did not do anything wrong to the claimant, he should not be held liable to the claimant, and that is that. But PPDs are in need of very strong justification if they are to be recognised. This is because 'the rule of public policy that has first claim on the loyalty of the law [is] that wrongs should be remedied.'[3] We have already come across this *dictum* before, as a factor that the courts consider in determining whether or not one person owed another a duty of care.[4] We attacked the relevance of this factor to the inquiry as to whether the defendant owed a duty of care to the claimant – because it presupposes precisely what is at issue in that inquiry: whether the defendant did anything wrong to the claimant. But this *dictum* comes into its own in this chapter, so far as PPDs are concerned. If the defendant *has* done something wrong to the claimant, that is something – as we will see later on, when we consider the basis of claims for compensatory damages – that calls out to be repaired or rectified.[5] The existence of a PPD leaves the hole created by the defendant's tort unfilled. And that is something that requires substantial justification.

So in going through the defences set out below, it is worth asking yourself – is this defence an AED or PPD? And if it is a PPD, ask yourself whether the reasons for the defence justify overriding the normal right that the victim of a tort would have to seek some kind of remedy from the person who committed that tort.

---

[2] Goudkamp 2011b, text near nn 14 and 15. Goudkamp identifies (text at n 12) a third type of defence – a justificatory defence that relieves 'the defendant of liability on the basis that he acted reasonably in committing a tort.' However, the suggestion that the law recognises such a defence is far more problematic than the suggestion that some defences can be classified as being 'absent element defences' and others as 'public policy defences'.

[3] See *X v Bedfordshire CC* [1995] 2 AC 633, at 663 (per Sir Thomas Bingham MR); *Gorringe v Calderdale MBC* [2004] 1 WLR 1057, at [2] (per Lord Steyn); *A v Essex CC* [2004] 1 WLR 1881, at [43]; *D v East Berkshire Community NHS Trust* [2005] 2 AC 373, at [24]–[25] (per Lord Bingham).

[4] See above, § 5.3(K).

[5] See below, § 28.7.

26.2 LACK OF CAPACITY

We start with a defence that very rarely applies. It is very rare for a person to be able to plead that they lacked the capacity to commit a tort. Three types of person who might want to make such a plea can be distinguished.

A. Children[6]

Under the criminal law, children under the age of 10 are incapable of committing crimes.[7] The same is not true of tort law. A child who has fulfilled all the requirements for a tort to have been committed will have committed that tort, whatever their age. This position is of very long standing. For example, in *Jennings v Rundall* (1799), Lord Kenyon CJ remarked, '. . . if an infant commit an assault, or utter slander, God forbid that he should not be answerable for it in a Court of Justice.'[8]

The seeming harshness of tort law in subjecting children to the same legal requirements as adults is substantially mitigated by the fact that in so far as foreseeability of harm is a prerequisite either to finding a defendant has committed a tort or to holding the defendant liable for the consequences of a tort that he or she has committed, the courts will take into account the defendant's age in judging what sort of harm was reasonably foreseeable.[9] So, for example, we have already seen that in *Mullin v Richards* (1998)[10] – where Mullin and Richards, both 15-year-old schoolgirls, were playfully fencing with plastic rulers when one of the rulers shattered and Mullin was blinded in her right eye – Richards was held not to have committed the tort of negligence in play fighting with Mullin as a typical 15 year old could not have been expected to foresee that Mullin would be injured as a result of their play. In so ruling, the Court of Appeal followed the approach of the High Court of Australia in *McHale v Watson* (1966), where a 12 year old was being sued in negligence for throwing a spike at a wooden post. Unfortunately, the spike cannoned off the post and hit the claimant in the eye. The High Court found that the defendant was not liable in negligence for the claimant's injury as it would not have been reasonably foreseeable to a typical 12 year old that throwing the spike would result in injury to the claimant:

> It is, I think, a matter for judicial notice that the ordinary boy of twelve suffers from a feeling that a piece of wood and a sharp instrument have a special affinity. To expect a boy of that age to consider before throwing the spike whether the timber was hard or soft, to weight the chances of being able to make the spike stick in the post, and to foresee that it might glance off and hit the girl, would be, I think, to expect a degree of sense and circumspection which nature ordinarily withholds till life has become less rosy.[11]

---

[6] See Bagshaw 2001.

[7] Children and Young Persons Act 1933, s 50.

[8] (1799) 8 TR 335, 337; 101 ER 1419, 1421–2.

[9] The courts will also not allow a claim in tort to be made against a child where doing so would subvert the rules protecting children from being bound by contracts. So a claim in tort cannot be made against a child who has purportedly hired a horse and ridden it for longer than the contract of hire permitted as the contract of hire was not binding on the child (*Jennings v Rundall* (1799) 8 TR 335, 101 ER 1419), but a claim in tort can be made against a child who has purportedly hired a horse and injured it by making it do something that the child could foresee was dangerous (*Burnard v Haggis* (1863) 14 CB (NS) 45, 143 ER 360).

[10] Discussed above, § 6.2.

[11] (1966) 115 CLR 199, at 216.

B. Persons suffering from mental illness

Tort law does not make any special exceptions for people suffering from mental illness.[12] If such a person has fulfilled all the requirements for committing a tort, then he will be held to have committed that tort. So, for example, in *Morriss* v *Marsden* (1952), the defendant suffered from schizophrenia and attacked the claimant, the manager of a hotel at which the defendant was staying. The court found that the defendant knew what he was doing at the time he attacked the claimant, but his mental condition meant that he did not know what he was doing was wrong. Under the criminal law, the defendant would have been found not guilty 'by reason of insanity' of committing an offence against the person in attacking the claimant.[13] However, the defendant *was* found to have committed the tort of battery in attacking the claimant as he had the requisite intention to commit that tort – an intent to apply force to the claimant's person – and was held liable to pay the claimant almost £6,000 in damages.[14]

It does not seem – in terms of determining what was reasonably foreseeable to the defendant in a tort case – that the courts will make the same concession to defendants who are mentally ill as they do to children. That is, they will *not* judge what was reasonably foreseeable by adopting the point of view of a reasonable person with the defendant's mental incapacities.[15] However, the objectivity of the standard of care that defendants are expected to live up to in performing a task such as driving will be relaxed where a defendant's mental incapacity meant that he was incapable of driving to the same standard as a ordinary, reasonable driver *and* the onset of that incapacity was sudden and could not have been foreseen by the defendant.[16]

C. The Crown

It used to be believed that 'The King can do no wrong', with the result that it used to be the case that it was simply not possible to bring a claim in tort against the 'Crown' – a term which includes the monarch, government departments, and heads of government departments acting in an official capacity. (Of course, an employee of the Crown could always be held personally liable if he or she had committed a tort in relation to the claimant.) The Crown Proceedings Act 1947 abrogated this rule to some extent. Section 2 of the Act provides that the Crown can be sued in tort, in the same way that an ordinary person can be: (1) in respect of torts committed by its servants or agents; (2) in respect of a breach of a duty of care it owes one of its employees as that employee's employer; (3) in respect of a breach of a duty attaching to 'the ownership, occupation, use or control of property'; or (4) in respect of the breach of a statutory duty which is binding on people 'other than the Crown and its officers' and breach of which is normally actionable in tort. Otherwise the old rule of Crown immunity from being sued in tort remains.

---

[12] See Goudkamp 2012 for arguments that insanity should be a defence to being sued in tort.

[13] This is under the *M'Naghten* rules on when a criminal defendant will be found not guilty by reason of insanity, under which rules a defendant will be able to take advantage of a defence of insanity if he was suffering from 'a disease of the mind' which meant either that he did not know what he was doing, or if he did know what he was doing, that he did not know it was wrong (legally *and* morally).

[14] A huge sum of money at that time: worth approximately £135,000 in today's money.

[15] See Moran 2003, 18–26.

[16] *Mansfield* v *Weetabix* [1998] 1 WLR 1263.

26.3 ACT OF STATE

This is another defence that will rarely be available. It classically applies in a case where the Crown, or someone whose acts have been authorised or ratified by the Crown, has deliberately injured a claimant who is not British and where the injury occurred outside British territory.[17] In such a case, any attempt by the claimant to argue that he has been the victim of a tort can be defeated by the plea of 'act of state'.[18] It is doubtful whether 'act of state' could be successfully pleaded to defeat the claim of a British citizen who is injured abroad,[19] and impossible that the plea could be successfully made where anyone – whether British or not – is injured on British soil.[20] In such cases, an attempt might be made to defeat the claim by relying on s 11 of the Crown Proceedings Act 1947, which provides that the Crown cannot be sued in tort for exercising its powers under the royal prerogative or under statute. However, it has been held that the Crown enjoys no powers under the royal prerogative to seize or destroy a British subject's property without compensating the property owner for the loss of his property.[21] So where the Crown has used its prerogative powers to seize or destroy the property of a British subject, it will still have to compensate the property owner for the loss of his property even if the property owner cannot sue the Crown in *tort* for what it has done.

26.4 SOVEREIGN AND DIPLOMATIC IMMUNITY

On 17 April 1984, WPC Yvonne Fletcher was killed by a shot fired from the Libyan Embassy in London, while she helped to control a demonstration outside the Embassy. Could (1) the Libyan government and/or (2) the person who fired the gun have been held liable for Yvonne Fletcher's death?

The answer to (1) is contained in the State Immunity Act 1978. Section 1(1) sets up the basic rule that 'A State is immune from the jurisdiction of the courts of the United Kingdom . . .'. However, the Act immediately goes on to create a number of exceptions to that basic rule, which operate where: (a) a State has submitted to the jurisdiction of the UK courts; (b) proceedings are brought against a State in respect of death or personal injury, or damage to or loss of tangible property, caused by an act or omission in the UK;

---

[17] See, for example, *Buron v Denman* (1848) 2 Exch 167, 154 ER 450, where Rear Admiral Joseph Denman burned down some depots at the mouth of the Gallinas river in Africa (on the current border between Sierra Leone and Liberia) where almost 850 slaves were being held. The Spanish slave dealer who owned the depots sued for damages. Denman's actions having been ratified by the Crown, it was held that the claim must be dismissed on the ground of 'act of state'.

[18] It is questionable, though, whether UK law would even apply nowadays to such a case (that is, the case where a foreigner has suffered some kind of harm outside the UK): see the Private International Law (Miscellaneous Provisions) Act 1995, Part III. (Though see *Bici v Ministry of Defence* [2004] EWHC 786 (QB), where it was agreed that two Albanian Kosovars who had been shot at by UK soldiers working for the UN in Kosovo could have their claims for damages against the UK government tried under UK law.) It is different with the Human Rights Act 1998, which can apply to protect foreigners living outside the UK: *R (Al-Skeini) v Secretary of State for Defence* [2008] 1 AC 153 and *R (Smith) v Oxfordshire Assistant Deputy Coroner* [2011] 1 AC 1. In those cases, the Supreme Court ruled that the Human Rights Act 1998 applied in UK military bases on foreign soil. The European Court of Human Rights has recently gone much further by ruling in *Al-Skeini v United Kingdom* (July 7 2011) that the European Convention on Human Rights applies not just in UK military bases abroad, but more generally in territories or areas which are controlled by the UK, or over which the UK has assumed some governmental powers.

[19] *Nissan v Attorney-General* [1970] AC 179, 213 (per Lord Reid).

[20] *Johnstone v Pedlar* [1921] 2 AC 262.

[21] *Attorney-General v De Keyser's Royal Hotel* [1920] AC 508; *Burmah Oil Co Ltd v Lord Advocate* [1965] AC 75; *Nissan v Attorney-General* [1970] AC 179, 227–8 (per Lord Pearce).

(c) proceedings are brought against a State in respect of an 'obligation of the State arising out of its interest in, or its possession or use of' immoveable property in the UK; (d) proceedings are brought against a State in respect of various infringements of intellectual property rights in the UK. Yvonne Fletcher's murder would have fallen under exception (c) and, indeed, in July 1999 the Libyan government accepted responsibility for her murder and paid compensation to her family.

The answer to (2) is contained in the Diplomatic Privileges Act 1964, which gives the force of law to the 1961 Vienna Convention on Diplomatic Relations. Article 31 of the Vienna Convention provides that a 'diplomatic agent' will enjoy immunity from the criminal law of the 'receiving State' as well as immunity from the receiving State's 'civil and administrative jurisdiction' (except in actions relating to land located in the receiving State, wills, and professional or commercial activity undertaken by the diplomatic agent outside his or her normal functions). The immunity is an immunity from being sued, not from being liable – with the result that the immunity does not protect anyone (such as an insurer or an employer) who is liable for the diplomatic agent's liabilities. And a diplomatic agent is always vulnerable to having his immunity from suit being waived under Article 33 by the State for which he or she works. So if Yvonne Fletcher was shot by a 'diplomatic agent' – that is, the head of the Libyan Embassy, or a member of the staff at the Embassy enjoying diplomatic status – then he could not have been sued for her death unless the Libyan government waived his immunity from suit.

26.5 TRADE UNION IMMUNITY

If A, a trade union member, has committed a tort in relation to B, B will be barred from bringing a claim in tort against A under s 219 of the Trade Union and Labour Relations (Consolidation) Act 1992 Act *if*: (1) A committed his tort in the 'contemplation or furtherance of a trade dispute';[22] *and* (2) the tort committed by A was one of the following torts: inducing a breach of contract, interfering with the performance of a contract, interfering with B's business using the unlawful means of threatening a breach of contract, lawful means conspiracy; *and* (3) none of the qualifications to s 219 of the 1992 Act apply in A's case.[23]

26.6 WITNESS IMMUNITY

The basic rule is that the testimony a witness gives in court cannot give rise to a claim in tort against that witness. The reason for giving witnesses such an immunity from being sued in tort is the importance the law attaches to witnesses in judicial proceedings being able to say what they want in court free from the fear that they might be sued for what they

---

[22] Section 244 of the 1992 Act defines a 'trade dispute' as involving a 'dispute between workers and their employer which relates wholly or mainly' to such things as – the workers' terms and conditions of employment, the employer's actions in firing or refusing to engage one or more workers; matters of discipline; a worker's membership or non-membership of a trade union; facilities for officials of trade unions.

[23] *Very broadly speaking*, s 219 will not work to protect A from being sued by B if: (1) A's tort was committed by him in the course of picketing which was not rendered lawful by s 220 of the 1992 Act (s 219(3)); (2) A's tort was committed because B proposed to employ a non-union member or refused to discriminate against a non-union member (s 222); (3) A's tort was committed because B dismissed an employee for unofficial trade union action (s 223); (4) B was not party to the trade dispute in the furtherance of which A's tort was committed (s 224, though A will still be protected if his tort was committed in the course of lawfully picketing B's premises); (5) A's tort was committed in order to pressure B into recognising a trade union (s 225).

say.[24] Witness immunity will normally protect witnesses from being sued for defamation, but it will also protect them from being sued for conspiracy (where the claimant's claim will be that the testimony was given with the object of harming the claimant, in furtherance of a conspiracy to injure the claimant),[25] or even negligence (where the claimant's claim will be that the witness acted carelessly, and breached a duty of care owed to the claimant, in giving the testimony she did). Witness immunity will also protect an actual or potential witness from being sued for pre-trial statements made to lawyers who are building a case.[26] The reason for this is that the protection given to witnesses for what they say in court would be easily eroded if claimants could simply refocus their claims on what the witness said before trial.

An important limit on the scope of witness immunity was created by the decision of the Supreme Court in *Jones* v *Kaney* (2011), which dealt with whether witness immunity protected an *expert witness* who was hired by the claimant to give his views about a case the claimant was involved in. The Supreme Court ruled by five Justices to two that witness immunity does not apply to expert witness. In *Jones* v *Kaney* itself, the claimant was negligently run over by a drunk driver. The claimant sued for compensation claiming that she had, among other things, suffered post-traumatic stress disorder (PTSD) as a result of being run over. There was some dispute over whether the claimant was actually suffering from PTSD, and the claimant hired the defendant to give her view as a consultant clinical psychologist. The defendant initially agreed that the claimant was suffering from PTSD but after a judge ordered the defendant and an expert witness on the other side to come up with a joint opinion, the defendant signed a report prepared by the other expert witness which said that the claimant was *not* suffering from PTSD and was deliberately exaggerating some of his symptoms. Faced with this joint report, the claimant's claim for damages was settled for a lot less than it might have been. The claimant sued the defendant in negligence, alleging that as he had hired her to work for him as an expert witness, she had owed him a duty to do that work with a reasonable degree of care and skill and had breached that duty in simply going along with the opinion of the expert witness on the other side. The Supreme Court ruled that there was no reason why expert witnesses should be protected by witness immunity. Holding that expert witnesses could be sued by their clients in negligence would not, they thought, have an adverse effect either on the quality of the testimony given by expert witnesses,[27] or the willingness of expert witnesses to give evidence in court.

While the Supreme Court's decision in *Jones* v *Kaney* has limited the scope of witness immunity – at least in so far as claims against *expert* witnesses by their *clients* are concerned – there are other authorities that have *extended* witness immunity to protect defendants from being sued for statements that have been made in the course of an *investigation* into actual or alleged criminal offences. For example, in *X* v *Bedfordshire County Council* (1995),

---

[24] Witnesses who knowingly give false testimony in court are, of course, liable to be prosecuted for perjury. However, the prospect of a prosecution for perjury is not likely to have any 'chilling' effect on what (honest) witnesses say in court. Witnesses will know that prosecutions for perjury are very rare and are only brought in blatant cases of dishonesty, so there is little or no likelihood of a witness who gives his testimony in good faith being prosecuted for perjury.

[25] *Marrinan* v *Vibart* [1963] 1 QB 528.

[26] *Watson* v *M'Ewan* [1905] AC 480 (no claim for defamation would be allowed in respect of statements about the claimant made to the barrister who was acting for the claimant's wife, and gathering evidence for the wife's impending divorce proceedings).

[27] Indeed, Lord Brown thought that being exposed to the risk of being sued in negligence might improve the quality of such testimony, as expert witnesses would become more cautious about making bold claims on behalf of their client that would later prove impossible to sustain: [2011] UKSC 13, at [67].

Lord Browne-Wilkinson held that a psychiatrist who was employed by the police to determine who had sexually abused a child could not be sued in negligence for mistakenly reporting that the child had been sexually abused by the child's mother's lover; her report was protected by witness immunity.[28] In *Taylor v Director of the Serious Fraud Office* (1999), the defendant was a lawyer in the Serious Fraud Office. She suspected that the claimant, a lawyer practising in the Isle of Man, was engaged in a major fraud with one F. She wrote to the Attorney-General of the Isle of Man, requesting his assistance in her investigation. When F was eventually charged and prosecuted, the Serious Fraud Office's files on him were disclosed to F. These files included a copy of the defendant's letter which F showed to the claimant. The claimant sued the defendant for libel. The claim was dismissed; it was held that the statements made in the letter were protected by witness immunity. In *Westcott v Westcott* (2009), the Court of Appeal held that witness immunity covered the case where the defendant made a complaint to the police about the claimant, thus triggering an investigation into the claimant; though this may have gone too far and is hard to reconcile with other authorities which hold out the possibility that such a complainant might, in the right circumstances, be sued for false imprisonment or malicious prosecution.[29]

The House of Lords has placed one limit on this extension of the law on witness immunity to cover statements made in the course of an investigation, holding in *Darker v Chief Constable of the West Midlands Police* (2001) that the law on witness immunity does not protect an investigator from being sued on the basis that he committed a tort *by encouraging other people to fabricate evidence or by concealing evidence.*

26.7 ABUSE OF PROCESS

If A has committed a tort in relation to B, B will sometimes be barred from suing A for compensatory damages on the ground that B will only be able to establish that she is entitled to sue A for such damages by bringing into question – in other words, by making a *collateral attack* on – the correctness of an earlier decision of the courts. In such a case, B may be barred from suing A for compensatory damages on the ground that bringing such an action would involve an *abuse of process*. It is hard to tell *when* B will be barred from suing A on this basis but the following test may be suggested: B will be barred from suing A on the ground of abuse of process if it would not be legitimate to allow B to challenge the correctness of the earlier judicial decision by bringing a claim in tort against A.

For instance, in *Hunter v Chief Constable of the West Midlands Police* (1982), the claimants were the Birmingham Six. They had been convicted of causing two bomb explosions which killed 21 people and injured 161 others. They were convicted largely on the basis of written and oral confessions that they made while in police custody. At their trial, they had claimed that these confessions had been beaten out of them. The trial judge held a hearing on the matter and concluded that the claimants had not been beaten by the police and held that their confessions were admissible in evidence. After the claimants were convicted, they sued the police for assault. Their claims were struck out on the ground that they involved an abuse of process. The claimants' claims sought to challenge the correctness of the trial judge's decision that the claimants had not been beaten and, in the absence of any fresh evidence that was unavailable to the trial judge at the time he made his decision, it would not be legitimate to allow the claimants to attack the correctness of that earlier decision by bringing a claim in tort against the police.

---

[28] [1995] 2 AC 633, 755.
[29] See above, §§ 2.2, 25.2.

Similarly, in *Smith* v *Linskills (a firm)* (1996), the claimant was convicted of aggravated burglary at the Crown Court and sent to prison. On his release, the claimant sued the defendants, the solicitors who had acted for him during his trial, claiming that they had breached the duty they owed him to represent him with a professional degree of care and skill. The claimant's claim was dismissed on the ground that it amounted to an abuse of process. The claimant's claim involved an attack on the correctness of his conviction – he could only show that the defendants' negligence had caused him to suffer some kind of loss by showing that 'if his criminal defence had been handled with proper care he would not, and should not, have been convicted'.[30] In the absence of any fresh evidence that was unavailable to the Crown Court when the claimant was convicted, it would not be legitimate to allow the claimant to cast doubt on the correctness of his conviction by bringing a claim in tort against the defendants.

In contrast, in *Walpole* v *Partridge & Wilson (a firm)* (1994), the claimant was convicted of obstructing a veterinary officer in the execution of his duty in that he tried to prevent the officer taking blood samples from the pigs at his farm. The claimant instructed the defendants, his solicitors, to appeal against the decision. He thought that as the officer had no reason to suspect that his pigs were diseased, he had not committed any offence in attempting to prevent the officer taking blood samples from them. The defendants failed to lodge an appeal in time and the claimant sued them in negligence. The Court of Appeal refused to strike out the claimant's claim on the ground that it amounted to an abuse of process. While the premise of the claimant's claim was that his conviction would have been overturned on appeal and therefore that he should not have been convicted in the first place, the claimant's claim that he should not have been convicted in the first place was based on a point of law which was not considered by the court which convicted the claimant. Given this, it was not illegitimate to allow the claimant to bring a claim in tort against the defendants even though the bringing of such a claim would inevitably challenge the correctness of his conviction.

All these cases concerned claimants who claimed to have been convicted of some *criminal* offence due to the negligence of their lawyers.[31] What is the position if, say, A, a barrister, represented B in a *civil case* and B lost her case? Could B sue A in negligence for damages, alleging that A failed to conduct her case with a professional degree of care and skill and that had A conducted her case properly she would have won the case? The question was considered in *Arthur J S Hall* v *Simons* (2002), which established that a barrister who represented a client in court would owe that client a duty to represent that client with a reasonable degree of care and skill. Lord Hoffmann thought that in the situation just described, any claim by B would *not* normally be struck out as involving an abuse of process.[32]

---

[30] [1996] 1 WLR 763, 768–9.

[31] An attempt by a still convicted criminal to sue an expert witness who had been hired to give testimony on his behalf at his trial would also founder on the shoals of abuse of process: *Jones* v *Kaney* [2011] UKSC 13, at [60] (per Lord Phillips).

[32] [2002] 1 AC 615, 706–7. He did suggest one exception. Suppose *Barrister* represented *Client* in a defamation case where *Angry* was suing *Client* for defaming her. Suppose further that C admitted that her statements about A were defamatory but claimed that they were true. Suppose finally that B did not do a very good job of arguing C's case with the result that the court found that C's statements were not true and found for A, awarding substantial damages against C. In such a case, Lord Hoffmann suggested, if C then sought to sue B in negligence, her claim might be struck out on the ground that it amounted to an abuse of process. In order to make out her claim against B, C would have to show that but for B's negligence, the courts would have accepted that her statements about A were true. So C's claim would amount to an attack on the correctness of the court's decision that her statements about A were not true. Lord Hoffmann thought it might be improper to allow C to attack this decision. This must be right: it would surely be wrong to allow C to bring an action against B which, if successful, would have the effect of blackening A's name without giving A any opportunity to defend herself.

26.8 DEATH

It used to be the rule at common law that if A committed a tort in relation to B and A subsequently died, B would be barred from suing A (or, more accurately, A's estate) for compensatory damages. Similarly, it used to be the rule at common law that if A committed a tort in relation to B and B subsequently died, B (or, more accurately, B's estate) would be barred from suing A for compensatory damages in respect of the losses suffered by B as a result of A's tort before she died. These rules were, for the most part, abolished by s 1(1) of the Law Reform (Miscellaneous Provisions) Act 1934. However, the 1934 Act left the old common law rules intact in one respect. Section 1(1) of the 1934 Act provides that 'this subsection shall not apply to causes of action for defamation'. So suppose that *Journo* libelled *Celeb* and shortly after this happened *Celeb* died. In such a case, *Celeb*'s estate will be barred from suing *Journo* for damages. Alternatively, suppose that *Journo* died before *Celeb* could sue her for damages. *Journo*'s death will mean that *Celeb* cannot sue *Journo*'s estate for damages; though *Celeb*'s independent action against *Journo*'s newspaper for publishing her story about him will still survive.

26.9 *VOLENTI NON FIT INJURIA*

A. The rule

The rule that *volenti non fit injuria* ('no wrong is done to the willing') applies in two situations.

(1) A claimant cannot complain that a defendant committed a tort in relation to her by acting in a particular way if the claimant fully consented to the defendant's acting in that way.

(2) If a defendant has committed a tort in relation to a claimant and the claimant has suffered some kind of loss as a result, the claimant will normally be barred from suing the defendant for compensation for that loss on the ground that *volenti non fit injuria* if she willingly took the risk that *she would suffer that kind of loss in the way that she suffered it*.

We are already very familiar with the law on *volenti* as it applies in the first situation.[33] That the defence of *volenti* applies in the second situation is more controversial,[34] and so its application in this kind of case will be discussed in detail here.

A good example of the defence of *volenti* being applied in the second kind of situation is provided by the case of *Morris* v *Murray* (1991). In that case, Morris and Murray went drinking together. At the end of the evening Murray suggested that they go for a ride in his light aircraft. Both men were quite drunk at this stage but Morris agreed to Murray's suggestion. Once both men were inside the plane, Murray – in his drunken state – just managed to get the plane airborne but it crashed soon after. Morris was badly injured and Murray was killed. Morris sued Murray's estate for damages in respect of his injuries, claiming that Murray had been negligent in the way he had piloted the plane.

---

[33] See above, §§ 2.4, 6.2.

[34] For example, Jaffey 1985 does not think that *volenti* applies at all in the second situation, arguing that the defence will only be available if the claimant expressly agreed that the defendant's conduct would not be actionable before he did what he did. However, this view is too narrow; it is certainly not consistent with the authorities mentioned below.

The Court of Appeal dismissed Morris's claim.[35] In climbing into the plane he had willingly taken a risk that Murray would fail to pilot the plane properly and that he would be injured as a result. It would have been different, it might be suggested, if – once Morris and Murray were airborne – Murray had suddenly been overcome by suicidal feelings and had deliberately targeted the plane at the ground. While Morris willingly took the risk when he climbed into the plane that he would be injured as a result of the plane being badly piloted, he did not willingly take the risk that he would be injured as a result of Murray's deliberately crashing the plane into the ground. Given this, in our alternative scenario, Morris would not have been barred from suing Murray's estate for damages on the ground that *volenti non fit injuria*.

That this is correct is confirmed by the decision of the Court of Appeal in *Slater* v *Clay Cross Co Ltd* (1956). In that case, the defendants operated a railway which passed through a tunnel. For many years, local residents walked through the tunnel to get to a village. One day the claimant happened to be walking through the tunnel when she was hit by one of the defendants' trains and was injured. The claimant sued the defendants, claiming that the defendants' driver had been negligent in the way he had driven the train; he had not kept a proper look-out and so on. The defendants argued that the claimant's claim should be dismissed on the ground that when the claimant walked through the tunnel she had voluntarily taken a risk that she would be hit by an oncoming train. However, the Court of Appeal dismissed this argument, holding that when the claimant walked through the tunnel she did not willingly take a risk that a train driver would *negligently* run into her.

It should be emphasised that for the *volenti* defence to be raised in the sort of situation we are discussing here, it must be shown that the claimant – who is seeking compensation for some loss that she has suffered – *willingly* took the risk that she would suffer that loss in the way that she did. So in *Haynes* v *Harwood* (1935) the defendant negligently left some horses unattended in the street.[36] A boy threw a stone at the horses and as a result they bolted. The claimant, a nearby police constable, threw himself in the way of the horses and seized their reins and brought them under control – but in doing so he suffered various personal injuries. The claimant successfully sued the defendant in negligence for compensation for his injuries. The Court of Appeal held that the defence of *volenti non fit injuria* was not available here. While the defendant had taken the risk when he tried to stop the horses bolting that he would be injured, he did not *willingly* take that risk – he had only acted as he did because it was an emergency.

B. Exceptions to the rule

A couple of exceptions and one non-exception to the rule that *volenti non fit injuria* are worth mentioning.

(1) *Paternalistic duties.* If A owes B a duty to stop B harming herself, then if A breaches that duty with the result that B harms herself, A will not be able to defeat B's claim for damages on the ground that *volenti non fit injuria*. While B – when she harmed herself – willingly took the risk that she would suffer that harm in the way she did, if the *volenti* defence were available to A here A's duty would become meaningless. A would be completely free to

---

[35] The House of Lords refused leave to appeal: [1991] 1 WLR 1362.
[36] 'Negligently' because it was reasonably foreseeable that the horses might bolt and injure passers-by if they were left unattended in the street.

breach it, safe in the knowledge that if B took advantage of his breach to harm herself, he would be able to raise a *volenti* defence to any subsequent claim she might bring against him for compensation for the harm she had suffered.[37]

(2) *Traffic accidents.* Section 149(3) of the Road Traffic Act 1988 provides that, 'The fact that a [passenger] has willingly accepted as his the risk of negligence on the part of the [driver] shall not be treated as negativing any . . . liability of the [driver].'[38] This meant that a defence of *volenti* was unavailable in *Pitts* v *Hunt* (1991), where the claimant and defendant stole a motorbike and took it for a joyride. The defendant drove the motorbike and the claimant sat behind him. The defendant – with the encouragement of the claimant – drove the bike faster and faster, and finally crashed the bike. While the claimant was *volenti* as to the risk of being injured in the way he was, his claim for damages in respect of the injuries he suffered in the crash could not be dismissed on that ground because of the statutory provision preventing the defence of *volenti* applying in that case.[39] The provision is an unprincipled one, designed to ensure that the costs of looking after the victims of motor accidents stay with insurance companies and are not shifted onto the State through the National Health Service and disability allowances.

(3) *The 'fireman's rule'.* This is the non-exception. Some American states have adopted what is known as the *fireman's rule* under which someone whose job involves running the risk of suffering a particular kind of loss cannot seek to recover compensatory damages if he actually suffers that kind of loss in doing his job.[40]

So if *Fool* negligently starts a fire in his house and *Fireman* is injured in the course of fighting the fire, then – under the *fireman's rule* – *Fireman* will be barred from suing *Fool* for damages. Again, the *fireman's rule* would operate to bar a police officer who developed a psychiatric illness as a result of what he saw or heard in dealing with a particularly traumatic incident from suing the person responsible for causing that incident for damages.

The reason for the rule is clear enough: if you have been paid to run a particular risk, you should not complain if that risk materialises and you suffer loss as a result. However, in *Ogwo* v *Taylor* (1988) the House of Lords refused to adopt the *fireman's rule* in English law and allowed a fireman to sue a householder for damages in respect of injuries suffered by him in fighting a fire negligently started by the householder.[41] The House of Lords had another opportunity to adopt the 'fireman's rule' in *Frost* v *Chief Constable of West Yorkshire Police* (1999) where – it will be recalled – the claimant policemen sought to recover damages in respect of the psychiatric illnesses they claimed to have developed as a result of the work they did helping out in the aftermath of the Hillsborough tragedy. However, their Lordships again showed no sign that they were in any way inclined to adopt the *fireman's rule*.

---

[37] *Reeves* v *Commissioner of Police of the Metropolis* [2000] 1 AC 360, 375–6 (per Lord Jauncey of Tullichettle).

[38] So the result in *Morris* v *Murray* would have been different if Murray had invited Morris to come for a drive in his car and had driven the car so badly that it crashed with the result that Morris was injured. In such a case, s 149(3) of the Road Traffic Act 1988 would have applied to prevent Morris's claim being barred on the ground that *volenti non fit injuria.*

[39] The claimant's claim was, however, dismissed on the ground of illegality: see below, § 26.11.

[40] California: *Walters* v *Sloan*, 571 P 2d 609 (1977); Michigan: *Kreski* v *Modern Wholesale Electric Supply Co*, 415 NW 2d 178 (1987) (though see also *Miller* v *Inglis*, 567 NW 2d 253 (1997) and *Gibbons* v *Caraway*, 565 NW 2d 663 (1997), holding that the 'fireman's rule' does not apply in cases where defendant wilfully and wantonly created a risk that the claimant would be injured).

[41] [1988] AC 431, 449, approving *Salmon* v *Seafarer Restaurants Ltd* [1983] 1 WLR 1264.

26.10 EXCLUSION OF LIABILITY

Three cases where a defendant (D) might be able to rely on a contractual term to defeat a claim in tort that has been made against him by a claimant (C) need to be distinguished.

A. Term in contract between D and C

If there is a term in a contract between D and C that, properly interpreted, excludes or limits C's right to sue D for the tort that he has committed, then D will normally be able to take advantage of that term to defeat C's claim against him (if the term is an exclusion clause) or limit his liability to C (if it is a limitation clause).

We say 'normally' because there are statutory limits on when a defendant will be able to take advantage of a contract term to defend a claim in tort that is being made against him:

(1) *Section 2(1) of the Unfair Contract Terms Act 1977* ('UCTA') provides that a term that purports to exclude or limit a business's liability in negligence for death or personal injury will always be invalid.

(2) *Section 2(2) of UCTA* provides that a term that purports to exclude or limit a business's liability in negligence for any other kind of loss (such as property damage or economic loss) will be invalid if it is unreasonable.

(3) *Section 3 of the Misrepresentation Act 1967* provides that a term that purports to exclude or limit someone's (not necessarily just a business's) liability for misrepresentation will be invalid if it is unreasonable.

(4) *The Unfair Terms in Consumer Contracts Regulations 1999* provides that a term in a contract between a business and a consumer that purports to exclude or limit the business's liability to the consumer will be invalid if the term was not individually negotiated *and* 'contrary to the requirement of good faith', the existence of the term caused a 'significant imbalance' in the parties' rights and obligations under the contract to the detriment of the consumer.

(5) *Section 149 of the Road Traffic Act 1988* provides that a term in a contract between a driver and a passenger that purports to exclude or limit the driver's liability for injuring the passenger will be invalid.

Readers wishing to find out more about how these provisions will apply in practice should consult a specialist textbook on contract law.

B. Term in a contract between C and a third party

In this sort of case, D wants to take advantage of a term in a contract between C and a third party which purports to exclude or limit C's right to sue D for the tort that he has committed. So, for example, if C has employed *Shipper* to deliver some goods for him to C's new home, *Shipper* might have inserted into his contract with C a provision saying that C would not be entitled to sue any of *Shipper*'s employees for negligently damaging those goods. So if D, one of *Shipper*'s employees, does negligently damage those goods, and is subsequently sued by C, D will want to take advantage of the term in the contract between C and *Shipper* to defeat C's claim against him.

Traditionally, the doctrine of *privity of contract* – which said that someone could not take advantage of, or be burdened by, a contract to which he was not party – would stand in D's way here. As D was not a party to the contract between C and *Shipper*, he could not take advantage of the term in that contract that had been inserted for his benefit. Attempts were made to get round this by, for example, finding that there existed a contract between C and D which included this term,[42] or by saying that C could not sue D because the existence of the term in the C – *Shipper* contract meant that C had willingly taken the risk of his goods being negligently damaged by D.[43] However, such arguments were always quite artificial and the need to make them has been substantially reduced by the Contracts (Rights of Third Parties) Act 1999, which has created a major exception to the doctrine of privity.

Under the 1999 Act, D will be able to take advantage of a term in a contract to which he is not a party if: (1) D is expressly identified in the contract as being someone who should be able to take advantage of that term; or (2) the term purports to be for D's benefit and the parties to the contract have *not* indicated that D should *not* be able to take advantage of that term. While the 1999 Act is primarily concerned with allowing third parties to a contract to *sue* when that contract has been breached, s 1(6) of the Act makes it clear that the Act also applies to cases where a third party to a contract *who is being sued* wants to take advantage of a term in that contract to defend the claim that is being made against him.

So, in the concrete example we are considering, the 1999 Act will probably apply here to allow D to take advantage of the term in the contract between C and *Shipper* to exclude or limit his liability to C. However, D may still be barred from relying on that term to exclude or limit his liability to C by one of the statutory provisions set out above.[44]

C. Term in a contract between D and a third party

In this sort of case, a third party has agreed in a contract with D that if something goes wrong, D will not be liable or his liability will be limited to a certain amount. Something has gone wrong and C, as a result, is entitled in principle to sue D in tort for what has happened. D wants to take advantage of the term in his contract with the third party to say either that C cannot sue him, or that his liability to C is limited to a certain amount.

Understandably, D will find it very hard to do this. The courts are highly resistant to the notion that provisions in a contract which might have been made without C's knowledge or agreement could limit C's rights to sue D in tort. However, there are occasions where C will be bound by a term in a contract to which she was not a party (provided, of course, that the term is not rendered invalid by the statutory provisions set out above).

For example, if *Keeper* held C's goods as a bailee for C, and C authorised *Keeper* to hand those goods over to D for safekeeping on terms which limited D's liability in the event that the goods were lost or damaged, then C will be bound by any such terms in the contract between *Keeper* and D.[45] Again, where C is essentially suing D in tort for failing to perform properly a contract with a third party – as is the case with a claim for pure economic loss under *White* v *Jones* (1999)[46] or *Junior Books Ltd* v *Veitchi* (1983)[47] – then C will be bound by any terms in the contract between D and that third party which specified what the scope

---

[42] *New Zealand Shipping Co Ltd* v *A M Satterthwaite & Co Ltd, The Eurymedon* [1975] AC 154.
[43] *Scruttons Ltd* v *Midland Silicones Ltd* [1962] AC 446, 488–9 (per Lord Denning, dissenting); *Norwich City Council* v *Harvey* [1989] 1 WLR 828.
[44] Contracts (Rights of Third Parties) Act 1999, s 3(6).
[45] *Morris* v *C W Martin* [1966] 1 QB 716, 729 (per Lord Denning MR); *The Pioneer Container* [1994] 2 AC 324.
[46] See above, § 6.13.
[47] See above, § 6.11.

of D's liability would be if he breached that contract.[48] C cannot pick and choose: she cannot sue D for failing to perform a responsibility that he assumed in a contract and ignore the terms on which he was prepared to assume that responsibility.[49]

26.11 ILLEGALITY (1): THE COMMON LAW[50]

In medieval times, someone who was declared to be an 'outlaw' had all his civil rights suspended. The result was that anyone could do anything they liked to an outlaw, without any legal sanction at all. The outlaw was outside the law's protection. Outlawry as an institution has long fallen into disuse, but it remains the case that people who have committed criminal offences will sometimes enjoy less protection from the law of tort than the rest of us do. Roughly speaking, the defence of *illegality* (otherwise known as the defence of '*ex turpi causa non oritur actio*', or '*ex turpi causa*' for short)[51] will apply to prevent C suing D in tort where:

(1) D committed a tort in relation to C and C, in consequence, committed a criminal offence and suffered loss as a result; in such a case, the defence of illegality will usually operate to bar C from suing D for compensation for that loss;

(2) C committed a serious criminal offence and D, in consequence, committed a tort in relation to C; in such a case, if there was a sufficiently close relationship between C's crime and D's tort, the defence of illegality will usually operate to bar C from suing D for committing that tort.

The defence of illegality now exists both at common law and under statute. This section is devoted to the defence as it exists under the common law. The following section will look at the particular form of the defence of illegality that was created by s 329 of the Criminal Justice Act 2003.

A. Lord Hoffmann's restatement

In *Gray* v *Thames Trains Ltd* (2009), Lord Hoffmann followed counsel for the defendants in that case by distinguishing between a 'wider' and a 'narrower' form of the common law defence of illegality.[52]

The narrower form of the defence says that 'you cannot recover for damage which is the consequence of a sentence imposed on you for a criminal act.' This form of the defence is based on the need for consistency across the legal system: if the criminal law has imposed a particular punishment on an offender, the civil law would subvert what the criminal law is trying to do if it allowed the offender to sue for damages to compensate him for the harm caused to him by that punishment.[53]

---

[48] *White* v *Jones* [1995] 2 AC 207, 268 (per Lord Goff); *Junior Books Ltd* v *Veitchi Co Ltd* [1983] 1 AC 520, 546 (per Lord Roskill).

[49] Though in a *Junior Books* type situation it might be different if D got the job of working as a subcontractor on a job that *Contractor* was doing for C by assuring C that he would do an excellent job and would take full responsibility if his work turned out to be imperfect, and then secretly inserted a provision in his contract with *Contractor* specifying that he could not be sued, or only sued for a limited amount, if his work was not up to scratch.

[50] See, generally, Glofcheski 1999.

[51] 'From a shameful cause, no action will arise.'

[52] [2009] 1 AC 1339, at [29] and [32].

[53] [2009] 1 AC 1339, at [37].

The wider form of the defence says that 'you cannot recover for damage which is the consequence of your own criminal act'. Lord Hoffmann thought that this version of the defence was

> justified on the ground that it is offensive to public notions of the fair distribution of resources that a claimant should be compensated (usually out of public funds) for the consequences of his own criminal conduct.[54]

This seems weak. This form of the defence of illegality is more likely to be based on the ground that it is offensive for someone who has previously flouted the law to then turn round and demand that *his* legal rights be respected.

Lord Hoffmann's narrower and wider versions of the defence of illegality provide a useful starting point for discussing the common law form of the defence; not least because the narrower version of the defence is a lot less controversial than the wider form.

B. The narrower form of the defence

It seems well-established now that the victim of a tort who has gone on, as a result of that tort being committed, to commit a criminal offence will not be allowed to sue for damages to compensate him for the fact that he has been punished for committing that offence.

For example, in *Clunis* v *Camden and Islington Health Authority* (1998) the claimant was found guilty of manslaughter on grounds of diminished responsibility and was detained under the Mental Health Act 1983. An attempt by the claimant to sue the defendant health authority for damages to compensate him for his loss of liberty – arguing that he would never have killed anyone had the health authority taken better care of this mental health – was dismissed on the ground of illegality.[55]

Although the claimant in *Clunis* was not technically being punished in being detained after having been found guilty of manslaughter – he was detained so that his mental problems could be treated – the House of Lords confirmed in *Gray* v *Thames Trains Ltd* (2009) that the Court of Appeal had been right to apply the narrower form of the defence of illegality in that case: the courts would get into real difficulties in applying the narrower form of the defence of illegality if they sought to distinguish between sentences imposed for curative purposes and sentences imposed for punitive purposes.[56]

The House of Lords also thought that *Gray* was a case where the narrower form of the defence of illegality applied. In that case, the claimant was injured in a train accident as a result of the defendants' negligence. His injuries meant he was permanently laid off work, and also had the effect of changing his personality for the worse with the result that he ended up stabbing someone to death and was found guilty of manslaughter on grounds of diminished responsibility and detained under the Mental Health Act 1983, just like the claimant in *Clunis*. However, *Gray* was a different case from *Clunis*. In *Clunis*, the claimant wanted to be compensated for the loss of liberty that he had suffered as a result of being

---

[54] [2009] 1 AC 1339, at [51].
[55] *Meah* v *McCreamer* [1985] 1 All ER 367 was distinguished. In that case, the claimant was involved in a car crash that was caused by the defendant's negligence. The injuries sustained by the claimant in the car crash had the effect of changing the claimant's personality for the worse, with the result that he sexually assaulted two women. The claimant was imprisoned and recovered damages from the defendant for the losses suffered by him as a result of his being imprisoned. However, unaccountably, the judge in *Meah* v *McCreamer* was not invited to dismiss the claimant's claim on the ground of illegality, and so the decision in *Meah* v *McCreamer* was no authority at all on the issue of whether the defence of illegality would be available in cases like *Meah* or *Clunis*.
[56] [2009] 1 AC 1339, at [41].

found guilty of manslaughter. So, in effect, he was arguing that his criminal act meant he should be paid *more* compensation than he would have been entitled to sue for had he stayed out of trouble. In *Gray*, the defendants claimed that the damages payable to the claimant for the loss of earnings he had experienced as a result of the defendants' negligence should not include anything for the money he would have earned in the years that he was now going to be spend detained in hospital. So, in effect, in *Gray*, the defendants were arguing that the claimant's criminal act meant he should be paid *less* compensation than he would have been entitled to sue for had he stayed out of trouble.

Despite these differences, the House of Lords accepted the defendants' argument in *Gray*. The decision is not an easy one to explain but can be rationalised on the basis that:

(1) not allowing the claimant to sue for the earnings he would have made in the years he was going to be detained in hospital ensured that he was not better off than other people who had been detained for manslaughter and could not earn anything during their period of detention;[57] *or*

(2) on a proper understanding of the law on causation, the defendants' negligence did not cause the claimant to lose any earnings for the period for which he was going to be detained in hospital, and this is so even though the claimant would not have been detained had the defendants not been negligent in the first place.[58]

C. The wider form of the defence

In *Gray*, Lord Hoffmann seemed to endorse the principle that 'you cannot recover for damage which is the consequence of your own criminal act' without any qualification, other than that damage should truly be *caused* by the claimant's criminal act.[59] However, as he noted, other judges have been much more cautious, and have only been willing to say that the wider form of the defence of illegality will apply where 'The facts which give rise to the claim [are] inextricably linked with . . . criminal conduct [which is] sufficiently serious to merit the application of the [defence].'[60]

In order to make sense of this area of the law, it might be worth distinguishing two different situations where the wider form of the defence of illegality might apply. In the first – the *Crime Before Tort* situation – A commits a crime, and as a result B commits a tort in relation to A for which A now wants to sue B. In the second – the *Tort Before Crime* situation – B commits a tort in relation to A, and as a result A commits a crime, and suffers some loss (not involving being punished for his crime) for which A now wants to sue B.

(1) *Tort Before Crime.* In this kind of situation, there are strong reasons why the courts should not allow the claimant to sue the defendant for damages. If you tell someone who is thinking about committing a crime that they might be able to sue for compensation for any adverse consequences (other than being punished for that crime) that committing that crime has for them, the inevitable consequence will be to encourage them to commit that crime. So it would seem to be contrary to public policy for the courts to allow damages for the adverse consequences of committing a criminal act to be claimed in a *Tort Before Crime* situation.

---

[57] See above, § 10.8.
[58] See above, § 9.11.
[59] [2009] 1 AC 1339, at [54].
[60] *Vellino* v *Chief Constable of Manchester Police* [2002] 1 WLR 218, at [70] (per Sir Murray Stuart-Smith).

So, for example, in *Vellino v Chief Constable of Manchester Police* (2002), the claimant was a career criminal who was seriously injured when, in an attempt to escape police custody, he jumped out of the kitchen window of his flat. His claim for damages was dismissed on the ground that the police had not owed him a duty to stop him trying to escape. However, Sir Murray Stuart-Smith went on to hold that even if the police had owed him such a duty and breached it, the claimant would still have been barred from suing the police for damages in respect of his injuries on the ground of illegality. This seems right. One of the incentives that people have not to attempt to escape from police custody – that they could get injured in the course of the escape – would be substantially weakened, and their incentives to attempt an escape correspondingly strengthened, if the courts held out any prospect that they might be able to sue the police for compensation if they are injured in the course of escaping.

There is one possible *Tort Before Crime* situation where damages should be payable to a criminal who has suffered loss (other than being punished for his crime) as a result of committing that crime. This is the situation where the defendant has negligently or intentionally deceived the claimant into committing a crime.[61] In this kind of case the demand of public policy that potential criminals should not be assured that they will be indemnified against any adverse consequences (other than being punished) that their crime might have for them is considerably weakened, as the claimant was never aware he might be breaking the law.[62]

An example of this kind of situation is provided by *Griffin v UHY Hacker Young & Partners* (2010) where the claimant committed a criminal offence by getting involved with a company that was trading under a similar name to a company that the claimant had previously managed and that had gone insolvent. As a result of being convicted, the claimant had to give up his investment in another company and suffered various losses of earnings. He sued his accountants for negligently failing to warn him that he might be

---

[61] No similar exception to the narrower version of the illegality defence exists. If A deceives B into committing a crime and B is punished for it, B cannot sue A for compensation for the fact that he has been punished. Part of the reason for this is identified by Lord Hoffmann in *Gray v Thames Trains Ltd* [2009] 1 AC 1339, at [41]: 'It must be assumed that the sentence . . . was what the criminal court regarded as appropriate to reflect the personal responsibility of the accused for the crime he had committed.' This does not explain the result in *Safeway Stores Ltd v Twigger* [2011] 2 All ER 841, where a company that had been fined for anti-competitive behaviour because of the conduct of its employees was prevented by the defence of illegality from suing its employees for compensation for the fact that it had been fined. As the company had no personal responsibility for what happened, Lord Hoffmann's *dictum* does not apply. *Safeway* can be explained on the basis that the company's fine had to be borne by the company, and not shifted onto anyone else via a tort claim, in order to encourage the company to take positive steps to ensure that its employees did not step out of line in future.

[62] We assume that the deception concealed from the claimant that his conduct was criminal, not that he was deceived into doing something that he knew to be criminal. For an example of the latter type of case, see *Nayyar v Denton Wilde Sapte* [2009] EWHC 3218 (QB), where the claimant travel agents were encouraged by the defendant to pay a bribe in an attempt to secure the exclusive rights to sell tickets for a particular airline. The bribe did not work and the claimants sued the defendant in negligence for the money they had spent on the bribe and associated costs. The claim was dismissed on grounds of *ex turpi causa*. If paying the bribe was a criminal offence this was right: holding out to the claimants that they might be able to get back the cost of their bribe if it did not work could only encourage them to pay the bribe. However, the judge indicated that his decision would have been the same even if the payment of the bribe was not criminal, on the basis that *ex turpi causa* 'can extend to immoral as well as illegal acts' (at [92]). Whether *ex turpi causa* should apply to *Tort Before Immorality* cases is a very difficult question. For example, suppose that *Fool* advises *Lustful* that if he pays *Beauty* £1,000, she will sleep with him. If *Beauty* accepts the money but refuses to sleep with *Lustful*, could he sue *Fool* on the basis that *Fool* negligently gave him bad advice? It might be that the claim should be turned down on the ground of *ex turpi causa* because allowing it might have the effect of encouraging people to act immorally by offering people money to sleep with him, safe in the knowledge that if the payment does not come off, they might be able to sue someone for encouraging them to waste their money. For a different view, see Goudkamp 2011a.

committing an offence. It was held that the defendant accountants could not rely on a defence of illegality to defeat the claim against them.

(2) *Crime Before Tort*. This kind of situation is much more difficult to resolve. The reason is that giving full-blown effect to Lord Hoffmann's wider form of the illegality defence in a *Crime Before Tort* situation threatens to revive the institution of outlawry. Saying 'you cannot recover for damage which is a consequence of your own criminal act' in a *Crime Before Tort* situation would seem to suggest that if A breaks into a shed on B's land, and B (observing this) releases his dogs to hunt down A, with the result that the dogs savage A, then B's conduct will incur no sanction under the law of tort.[63]

Lord Hoffmann attempted to get round this problem in *Gray* by suggesting that there is a distinction between 'causing something and merely providing the occasion for someone else to cause something'[64] and it might be possible to draw on this distinction to argue that A's breaking into B's shed did not actually cause him to be savaged by B's dogs. But the safer route to ensuring that the defence of illegality does not operate unacceptably in this area would seem to lie in adopting the approach of the Court of Appeal in *Cross* v *Kirkby* (2000) and *Vellino* v *Chief Constable of Manchester Police* (2002), under which the defence of illegality will only be available in a *Crime Before Tort* situation if the claimant's crime was *sufficiently serious*[65] and there was a *sufficiently close connection* between the defendant's tort and the claimant's crime.

The twin cases of *Revill* v *Newbery* (1996) and *Cross* v *Kirkby* (2000) illustrate this test at work. In *Revill* v *Newbery*, Revill attempted to break into a shed on an allotment owned by Newbery. Newbery – having had his shed broken into many times before – was ready and waiting for him. Intending to scare Revill away, he put a gun to a hole in the door of the shed and fired it. Revill was standing just outside the door; the shot blew a hole in his arm and wounded his chest. Newbery was held liable to pay £4,000 in damages to Revill. It was held that no defence of illegality could be pleaded in this case, as Newbery's actions had been 'out of all proportion' to the threat posed to him by Revill.

It was different in *Cross* v *Kirkby*. In that case, Cross – a hunt saboteur – attacked Kirkby – a farmer who was allowing the local hunt to ride across his lands – with a baseball bat. Kirkby seized the baseball bat and hit Cross with it on the head. When Cross sued Kirkby, the Court of Appeal dismissed Cross's claim on the ground that Kirkby had acted reasonably in self-defence in striking Cross. The Court of Appeal went on to hold that even if Kirkby *had* acted unreasonably in striking Cross, they would have still allowed Kirkby to rely on the defence of illegality to defeat Cross's claim for damages. There would still have been a sufficiently close connection between Cross's criminal conduct in threatening Kirkby and Kirkby's striking him.

One *Crime Before Tort* situation where a defence of illegality will always be available is where the defendant's tort was committed in furtherance of a criminal joint venture between the defendant and the claimant. For example, in *National Coal Board* v *England* (1954), Lord Asquith considered what the position would be if 'A and B, agree to open a safe by means of explosives, and A so negligently handles the explosive charge as to injure B'.[66] His Lordship thought that, in this case, A would be able to raise a defence of illegality

---

[63] Though there is always the criminal law as a long-stop.
[64] [2009] 1 AC 1339, at [54].
[65] Defined by Sir Murray Stuart-Smith in *Vellino* v *Chief Constable of Greater Manchester* [2002] 1 WLR 218 as being one which is punishable with imprisonment (at [70]).
[66] [1954] AC 403, at 429.

to any claim B might make against A for damages. In this case there would be a very close connection between A's tort and the illegal venture that A and B were engaged on at the time A committed his tort, as that tort was committed in the course of furthering the illegal venture.[67] Lord Asquith thought it would be different if 'A and B are proceeding to . . . premises which they intend burglariously to enter, and before they enter them, B picks A's pocket and steals his watch.'[68] In this sort of case there would be less of a connection between A's tort and the illegal venture that A and B were engaged on. As a result, Lord Asquith thought that in this second case, A would *not* be entitled to rely on a defence of illegality to defeat B's claim against him for damages.

D. Loss of criminal earnings or property

Lord Hoffmann's restatement of the scope of the common law defence of illegality was confined to cases where a claimant was attempting to sue for compensation for a loss that he had suffered as a result of committing a criminal offence. But what about cases where a claimant is suing a defendant on the basis that the defendant's tort deprived him of an advantage that he had obtained, or was going to obtain, through committing a criminal act?

The general rule is that the claimant will not be entitled to sue the defendant for the loss of such an advantage. For example, in *Hewison* v *Meridian Shipping Services Pte Ltd* (2002), the claimant worked for the defendant shipping company as a crane operator. The claimant suffered from epilepsy and should therefore not have been put in charge of a crane. However, the claimant concealed his epilepsy from the defendants, thereby committing a criminal offence under s 16 of the Theft Act 1968.[69] Due to the defendants' negligence, the claimant was injured on the job. The injuries suffered by the claimant caused him to have three epileptic fits. As a result, the defendants became aware of the claimant's condition and were forced to dismiss him. The Court of Appeal held that the claimant could sue for damages for his injuries – there was no connection between the claimant's criminality and the defendant's negligence – but he could not sue for the money he would have earned in the future working for the defendants, had he not been negligently injured by them. Such earnings would have represented the proceeds of a criminal act, with the result that the loss of those earnings could not be sued for.[70]

There is one important exception to this general rule. The exception arises where the defendant is in possession of property that has been obtained from the claimant, and to which the claimant has a better title than the defendant. In such a case, the claimant will be entitled to sue the defendant for the value of the property even if that property was

---

[67] The decision of the Court of Appeal in *Pitts* v *Hunt* [1991] 1 QB 24 bears out Lord Asquith's point. The claimant and defendant in that case went joyriding on a motorbike – the defendant drove the bike and the claimant travelled in the pillion car attached to the motorbike. The claimant urged the defendant to drive faster and faster and when the defendant complied, he crashed the bike and the claimant was injured. The claimant's claim for damages in respect of his injuries was thrown out on the ground of illegality – there was a very close connection between the defendant's negligent driving and the joint illegal venture which the claimant and the defendant were engaged on at the time the defendant negligently crashed the bike.

[68] [1954] AC 403, at 429.

[69] The (now abolished) offence of obtaining a pecuniary advantage by deception.

[70] It is hard to see why Ward LJ, who dissented, thought the claimant's claim for this loss of (future) earnings might have merit. After all if *Householder* beat up *Burglar* so badly that *Burglar* had to give up his 'career' as a burglar, he could hardly be allowed to sue for the money he would have made in the future had he been allowed to continue burgling people's houses. Perhaps the real reason for Ward LJ's dissent was that he did not think that the claimant's offence in lying about his health was actually that serious.

stolen from a third party, or represents the proceeds of crime. In *Webb* v *Chief Constable of Merseyside Police* (2000), the Court of Appeal held that this exception applied even in the case where the police were in possession of money that had been seized on suspicion that it represented the proceeds of drug trafficking. Once the statutory powers under which that money had been seized ceased to apply, the money had to be returned to its original owners, even if it *did* represent the proceeds of drug trafficking. The constitutional importance of not allowing property to be expropriated by the State unless authorised by statute overrode any other consideration militating against finding for the claimants in this case.

E. The position of companies

We saw in chapter 8 – on 'Breach of Duty' – how, because a company is an artificial legal person, we need to adopt 'attribution rules' that tell us whose conduct we should look at for the purposes of determining what the company has done and has not done. Those rules are as relevant here as they are in cases where a company is alleged to have breached a duty of care owed to a claimant. The reason why they are relevant here is that if a defendant wants to raise a defence of illegality to a company's claim for damages against him, the defendant will have to show that the company has behaved illegally. And in order to determine whether or not the company has behaved illegally, we need to know whose actions represent the company's actions.

For example, in *Stone & Rolls Ltd* v *Moore Stephens* (2009), the claimant company (S&R) was a one-man company. It was owned and controlled by one man: Zvonko Stojevic (ZS). ZS was a fraudster, who used S&R and an Austrian company to defraud a Czech bank (KB) of over $100m. The fraud worked like this. S&R would pretend to be selling goods – which, in fact, never existed – to the Austrian company. KB would issue a letter of credit to S&R, guaranteeing that S&R would be paid for the goods if they presented certain documents to S&R's bank, proving that the goods had been shipped to the Austrian company. When the letter of credit was presented to S&R's bank, the bank would pay the sum on the letter of credit, and that bank would then be entitled to be reimbursed by KB. KB, in turn, would expect to be paid back by the Austrian company. In fact, KB was never paid back all of the monies it paid out, and owed other banks, under the letter of credit that it issued.

KB successfully sued ZS and S&R for damages. S&R – which was by then in the hands of administrators – sued its auditors in negligence for failing to detect that it was being used as a vehicle for fraud. The House of Lords turned down the claim, by a majority of 3:2. Because ZS represented the company's controlling mind and will, what ZS did as S&R's managing director, S&R did. So S&R was as much guilty of criminal fraud as ZS was. S&R was therefore in the position of suing its auditors for failing to expose its own criminal wrongdoing. As such, it was barred from suing its auditors by the defence of illegality. However, the majority thought that it was crucial that S&R's sole shareholder (ZS) was behind S&R's criminal conduct. Had S&R had shareholders who were innocent of any wrongdoing, S&R would still have been guilty of criminal wrongdoing under the rules of attribution for companies, but at least some of the majority thought it possible that S&R would not have been barred by the defence of illegality from suing its auditors for failing to expose its wrongdoing.[71] The reason, presumably, is that a company's auditors are not

---

[71] [2009] 1 AC 1391, at [86] (per Lord Phillips), [173] (per Lord Walker, though less sure at [192]), [203] (per Lord Brown).

supposed just to protect the company's interests, but also the interests of the shareholders behind the company.

26.12 ILLEGALITY (2): STATUTE

Politicians have been unable to resist the temptation to meddle in this area. When the then Criminal Justice Bill was introduced to Parliament in 2002, Tony Blair – the then Prime Minister – boasted that it was a 'victim's justice bill'. Section 329 of what became the Criminal Justice Act 2003 was designed to provide 'justice' for victims of crime who had gone 'over the top' in injuring a criminal who was threatening them, or who had broken into their house. Section 329 would ensure – it was thought – that the injured criminal would not be able to sue for compensation for his injuries. It has had a very different effect.

A. The section

Section 329 of the 2003 Act provides that if:

(1) B is suing A for damages on the basis that A committed the tort of *assault, battery or false imprisonment* in relation to B by doing *x*; *and*
(2) B's actions round about the time A did *x* resulted in B's being convicted of an imprisonable offence; *and*
(3) A did *x* because he honestly believed at the time: (i) that B was about to commit an offence or had committed an offence or had just committed an offence; *and* (ii) that it was necessary to do *x* in order to protect himself or another person, or to protect or to recover property, or to prevent the commission or continuance of an offence, or to apprehend B or secure B's conviction of having committed an offence; *and*
(4) A's doing *x* was not grossly disproportionate to whatever B did, *then*
(5) A will be able to raise a defence to B's claim against him.

B. The effect

So far as anyone knows, this provision has *never* been relied upon by an ordinary person who has used unreasonable force against a criminal who has been threatening her, or who has broken into her house, and who is now being sued by the criminal for damages. In a stunning illustration of the law of unintended consequences, s 329 has only ever been used by the *police* to avoid being sued for using unreasonable force on members of the public.

The courts drew attention to this scandal in the case of *Adorian v Commissioner of Police of the Metropolis* (2009). In that case, Adorian was arrested by the police for disorderly behaviour and was subsequently convicted of obstructing the police in the execution of their duty. In the course of being arrested, Adorian suffered multiple hip fractures of a type normally only associated with being hit by a car, or falling from a significant height. Adorian sought to sue the police for assault and battery, claiming that they had used unreasonable force in arresting him. The police argued that Adorian's claim should be struck out, on the ground that s 329 of the 2003 Act applied to his case. The Court of Appeal refused to strike out the claim, holding that there was evidence in this case that 'grossly disproportionate' force had been used on Adorian.[72] The Court of Appeal also expressed grave concern that the police were attempting to use s 329 in order to shield themselves from claims in tort being made against them by the general public. As Sedley LJ observed:

> **6** One cannot fail to notice that this section has nothing on the face of it to do with policing. In what one can call the Tony Martin situation – a sudden encounter with a crime – it gives the individual a defence of honest, even if unreasonable, belief in the need for his or her act; and it forfeits the defence only if the act was grossly disproportionate. There is nothing on the face of the section or in its shoulder note which manifests an intention to afford the police a novel protection from claims by offenders for objectively unreasonable or unnecessarily violent arrests.
>
> **7** The section nevertheless inexorably covers police officers as well as civilians. Indeed, so far as counsel have been able to tell us, since it was brought into force in January 2004 it is only police defendants who have invoked it. The consequences should not go unnoticed. In place of the principle painstakingly established in the course of two centuries and more, and fundamental to the civil rights enjoyed by the people of this country – that an arrest must be objectively justified and that no more force may be used in effecting it than is reasonably necessary – the section gives immunity from civil suits, not confined to those involving personal injury, to constables who make arrests on entirely unreasonable grounds, so long as they are not acting in bad faith, and accords them impunity for using all but grossly disproportionate force in so doing. Conscious of article 9 of the Bill of Rights 1689[73] we say only that there is no indication that Parliament was aware, much less intended, that what it was enacting would have this effect.

For good measure, the Court of Appeal also went out of its way to question whether it was true that 'section 139 would nullify not only a claim for trespass to the person but also any other claim – [such as a] claim in negligence – based on the same facts.'[74] This *dictum* might be taken as encouraging litigants against the police to evade the effect of s 329 by framing their claims as ones in negligence or under the Human Rights Act 1998.

26.13 MORE GOOD THAN HARM

In *The Tojo Maru* (1972), Lord Reid considered what would be the position in the following situation:

> Suppose a house is on fire. It contains a valuable collection of, say, china. There is little or no hope of saving the collection but a passer-by, with or without the consent of the owner, goes in and brings most of the collection to safety. But owing to some gross negligence on his part some of the china is smashed.[75]

In principle, one would have thought that *Passer-By* could be sued for the loss of the smashed china: when he went into the house, he owed the owner of the china a duty to take care not to smash it, he breached that duty, and the china was destroyed as a result of that

---

[72] When the case went to trial, His Honour Judge O'Brien rejected all claims that the police had used unreasonable force in arresting Adorian: [2010] EWHC 3861 (QB).

[73] 'That the freedom of speech and debates and proceedings in Parliament ought not to be impeached or questioned in any court or place outside of Parliament.'

[74] [2009] 1 WLR 1859, at [43].

[75] [1972] AC 242, 268.

breach. However, subject to a couple of qualifications that we will set out below, Lord Reid thought that the *Owner* of the china would not be able to sue for the loss of the china in this case: he said it would be 'most unjust'[76] if *Passer-By* were held liable for the destruction of the china.

In this sort of situation we can say that *Passer-By* is entitled to take advantage of a 'I did more good than harm' defence[77] to being sued for the loss of the china.[78] What are the limits on this defence? Lord Reid said that *Passer-By* should not be allowed the defence if he deterred other people from rescuing the china by rushing in to rescue it himself or if there was no immediate emergency requiring the china to be saved.[79] It is also doubtful whether *Passer-By* could take advantage of the defence if he – having seized the china in an attempt to rescue it – deliberately smashed one cup to see what noise it would make when it broke. We also think that the defence can only apply in cases where the defendant went above and beyond the call of duty to help the claimant. If the defendant was duty bound to help the claimant and did more good than harm for the claimant in performing that duty – say, for example, the defendant was a doctor who saved the claimant's life by operating on him, but left a swab inside the claimant's body when closing him up, the removal of which necessitated a further operation – the defendant will be liable for the harm he did the claimant, irrespective of how much good he might have simultaneously done for the claimant.

26.14 LIMITATION

In the interests of justice, the law places time limits on when a tort claim can be brought against a defendant. If those limits are exceeded, the defendant will normally be able to raise a defence of *limitation* to the claim being made against him. When we say 'In the interests of justice' we refer both to: (1) the fact that it may become very hard to do justice in a case that is heard long after the facts of that case occurred, when relevant documents may have been lost and memories may be impaired; and (2) the fact that it would be unjust to potential defendants to tort claims to allow them to go through their lives, year after year, with the prospect that they might be sued in tort constantly hanging over them: at some point, people are entitled to face, and plan for, the future free of the burden of what they might have done in the past.

The law on when a claimant will be barred on grounds of limitation from suing a defendant in tort is very complicated and a detailed account is beyond the scope of this book. However, a brief summary of the law in this area can be given. The *general rule* is that if A has committed a tort in relation to B, B will be barred from suing A for committing

---

[76] ibid.

[77] *Passer-By* could say to *Owner*: 'Had I done nothing, you would have ended up with nothing. As a result of my doing something, you have ended up with something. So I have done more good than harm, overall.'

[78] Notice that *Passer-By* could not argue that his liability should be very small because the destroyed china was 'doomed' anyway (see above, § 9.6, and below, § 28.3(C)). It was not: had *Passer-By* not been negligent, the china would have been saved. Notice also that *Passer-By* could not argue either that his liability to compensate for the loss of the china should be reduced to take account of the benefits obtained by *Owner* as a result of his negligence (see below, § 28.4). *Owner* obtained no benefit from *Passer-By*'s carelessly smashing the china – *Owner* only obtained a benefit from *Passer-By*'s rushing in and rescuing the china (in the course of which he smashed some of it).

[79] [1972] AC 242, 268.

that tort if she does not sue A within *six years* of the date she was first entitled to obtain a remedy in respect of A's tort.[80]

However, this general rule is subject to various qualifications.

A. Ignorance

What if B was first entitled to obtain a remedy in respect of A's tort in June 2005 – but she only found out that she was entitled to obtain such a remedy in January 2009? As a general rule, if it was A's *fault* that B did not know she was entitled to sue A for committing his tort until January 2009, then the limitation period will be extended and B will have six years from January 2009 to bring an action against A, not six years from June 2005.[81]

If it wasn't A's fault that B was left in ignorance for so long that she was entitled to sue A, then B will normally be stuck – the limitation period for suing A having elapsed in June 2011, she will be barred from suing A. However, it is different if the tort committed by A was *negligence* and A's negligence caused B to suffer various actionable losses which B only found out about in January 2009. In such a case, B will have three years to sue A from the date that she could first have *reasonably been expected* to find out about those losses. So if B could only have been reasonably expected to find out about the actionable losses which A's tort caused her to suffer in August 2008, she will have until August 2011 to sue A.[82]

B. Physical injury

If A has committed a tort in relation to B and B has suffered some kind of physical injury as a result, a special limitation regime will often apply to B's action against A under s 11 of the Limitation Act 1980. Section 11 will apply in cases where a claim is made for physical injury resulting from 'negligence, nuisance or breach of duty'.[83] If s 11 applies to B's claim against A, then B will normally have three years from the date she was injured as a result of A's tort to sue A for damages in respect of that injury.

---

[80] Limitation Act 1980, s 2. Assume that A committed his tort in January 2009. If that tort was actionable *per se* (that is, the tort committed by A was actionable even if it did not cause B to suffer any actionable loss), then B will normally have until January 2015 to sue A for committing that tort. The reason for this is that because A's tort was actionable *per se* B was entitled to obtain a remedy in respect of that tort as soon as it was committed. If, on the other hand, A's tort was not actionable *per se* (that is, the tort committed by A was only actionable if it caused B to suffer an actionable loss), then B will *normally* have six years from the date she first suffered an actionable loss as a result of A's tort to sue A for committing that tort. So if A's tort was not actionable *per se* and B first suffered an actionable loss as a result of A's tort in June 2010, B will *normally* have until June 2016 to sue A for committing that tort. The reason for this is that because A's tort was not actionable *per se*, the first time B was entitled to obtain a remedy in respect of A's tort was in June 2010. In *Hedley Byrne* cases – where the claimant is entitled to sue the defendant in negligence for pure economic loss – it can be very difficult to say when exactly the claimant first suffered a pure economic loss for which she could sue. See, for example, *Shore* v *Sedgwick Financial Services Ltd* [2008] EWCA Civ 863 (time to bring a claim started running as soon as claimant invested in inferior pension scheme on defendant's advice, not when the value of his investment depreciated) and *Law Society* v *Sephton & Co* [2006] 2 AC 543 (solicitor misappropriated client money and Law Society had to pay out to clients from Solicitor's Compensation Fund; sued defendant accountants for misrepresenting state of solicitor's accounts and lulling Law Society into false sense of security about solicitor's honesty; time to bring claim started running from moment Law Society had to pay out to defrauded clients, not moment when it failed to strike off solicitor or moment when solicitor misappropriated client money).

[81] Limitation Act 1980, ss 32(1)(b), 32(2). It appears this qualification to the general rule does not apply to actions under the Defective Premises Act 1972: *Warner* v *Basildon Development Corp* (1991) 7 Const LJ 146.

[82] Limitation Act 1980, s 14A. This rule is not meant to prejudice the limitation period for suing A that B would enjoy under the general rule that you have six years to sue from the first time you were entitled to sue the defendant.

[83] Section 11(1).

There are two exceptions to this rule. First, if it took B some time for her to realise that she had suffered a 'significant injury'[84] and to identify A as being the person whose act or omission was responsible for her suffering that injury, then she will have three years from the date she found that A was responsible for her suffering a significant injury to sue him for that injury.[85] Secondly, if the applicable limitation period for suing A in respect of B's injury has elapsed, the courts may nevertheless allow B to sue A for compensation for her injury under s 33 of the Limitation Act 1980 if it would be 'equitable' to do so.[86]

C. Sexual abuse

The House of Lords has had to decide on two different occasions whether the victim of sexual abuse comes within the special limitation regime created by s 11 of the Limitation Act 1980 – that is, the limitation regime that applies where the victim of 'negligence, nuisance or breach of duty' suffers physical injury as a result. The question is of vital importance because victims of sexual abuse tend only to bring claims many years after they were abused, and as a result their claims will normally fail on the ground of limitation unless they come within the special limitation regime described above. If they do, then claims for sexual abuse that have been brought years after the acts of abuse might not be defeated on grounds of limitation if it would be 'equitable' to allow the claims to continue under s 33 of the Limitation Act 1980 despite the lapse of time between the acts of abuse and the bringing of the claim.

In the first case dealing with this issue – *Stubbings v Webb* (1993) – the House of Lords decided that the phrase 'negligence, nuisance or breach of duty' did not cover the case where one person sexually abused another. In particular, the House of Lords did not think that the phrase 'breach of duty' covered a case involving a trespass to the person. Lord Griffiths remarked:

> I should not myself have construed breach of duty as including a deliberate assault. The phrase lying in juxtaposition with negligence and nuisance carries with it the implication of a breach of duty of care not to cause personal injury, rather than an obligation not to infringe any legal right of another person. If I invite a lady to my house one would naturally think of a duty to take care that the house is safe but would one really be thinking of a duty not to rape her?[87]

The issue came back to the House of Lords in *A v Hoare* (2008). The House of Lords refused to follow *Stubbings v Webb* and held that a trespass to the person *did* involve a breach of duty, as that phrase is used in s 11 of the Limitation Act 1980.[88] As Lord Hoffmann observed, 'there could be no moral or other ground for denying to a victim of intentional injury the more favourable limitation treatment [under s 11 of the 1980 Act] for victims of injuries caused by negligence.'[89]

---

[84] Section 14. On when the victim of sexual abuse can first be said to have realised that they have suffered a 'significant injury' see *A v Hoare* [2008] 1 AC 844, at [34]–[35] (per Lord Hoffmann), [66]–[68] (per Lord Carswell); and *B v Nugent Care Society* [2010] 1 WLR 516, at [108]–[114].

[85] Section 11(5).

[86] Section 33.

[87] [1993] AC 498, at 508.

[88] Approving the views of Lord Greene MR in *Billings v Riden* [1945] KB 11, at 19 that 'trespass to the person . . . is certainly a breach of duty'; and Adam J in the Australian case *Kruber v Grzesiak* [1963] VR 621, at 623 that 'do not all torts arise from breach of duty – the tort of trespass to the person arising from the breach of a general duty not to inflict direct and immediate injury to the person of another either intentionally or negligently in the absence of lawful excuse?'

[89] [2008] 1 AC 844, at [14].

Right though that undoubtedly is, the decision in the *Hoare* case placed a possibly unwelcome burden on the courts to decide in sexual abuse cases where the cases were brought years after the acts of abuse whether it would be 'equitable' to allow those cases to continue under s 33 of the Limitation Act 1980. In the *Hoare* case, Lord Brown went out of his way to warn that

> By no means everyone who brings a late claim for damages for sexual abuse, however genuine his complaint may in fact be, can reasonably expect the court to exercise the section 33 discretion in his favour. On the contrary, a fair trial (which must surely include a fair opportunity for the defendant to investigate the allegations ...) is in many cases likely to be found quite simply impossible after a long delay.[90]

However, it would require remarkable steeliness on the part of a trial judge not to be swayed by the opprobrium he would undoubtedly receive if he concluded that it would not be 'equitable' to allow a claim for sexual abuse to be brought years after the acts of sexual abuse occurred. In the *Hoare* case itself – where the defendant attempted to rape the claimant in 1988, was sentenced to life imprisonment, was released in 2005, having won £7m on the National Lottery on day release in 2004, and was sued by the claimant when she heard the news about his lottery win – Coulson J held that it would be 'equitable' to exercise his discretion under s 33 to allow the claimant to sue the defendant for trespass to the person, some 17 years after the trespass occurred, because the defendant had not been worth suing up until 2004.[91]

In the subsequent case of *B v Nugent Care Society* (2010), the Court of Appeal considered when the courts should exercise their discretion under s 33 to allow a 'late' claim for damages for sexual abuse to be brought. The Court made it clear that relevant factors to be considered included:

(1) The quality of the evidence that was now likely to be available to determine whether the claimant has a good claim against the defendant. The narrower the basis of the claimant's claim the more likely it is that the lapse of time in bringing the claim will not prevent the courts from properly disposing of his case.[92]

(2) The reasons for the claimant's delay in bringing the case. Particularly relevant will be the issue of 'whether the claimant, taking into account his psychological state in consequence of the injury, could reasonably have been expected to institute proceedings.'[93]

(3) The strength of the claimant's case, as it appears at the preliminary hearing to determine whether the discretion under s 33 should be exercised:

> if the claimant's case is beset by inconsistencies and the claimant shows himself in evidence to be unreliable, the court may conclude that the delay is likely to prejudice the defendant in [that he will be] put to the trouble and expense of successfully defending proceedings and then not [be]

---

[90] [2008] 1 AC 844, at [86].

[91] *A v Hoare* [2008] EWHC 1573 (QB).

[92] [2010] 1 WLR 516, at [14]–[15]. For an example of where the complexity of the claimants' claims led the Court of Appeal to refuse to find that it would be equitable to allow them to continue under s 33 after such a long lapse of time, see *AB v Ministry of Defence* [2010] EWCA Civ 1317 where the claimants sued the Ministry of Defence in negligence in 2004 for cancers that they claimed had developed as a result of the claimants' being exposed to radiation from nuclear tests carried out between 1952 and 1958. The difficulties in establishing causation, and the effect that the lapse in time in bringing the claims would have had on the MoD's ability to counter the claimants' allegations of negligence, led the Court of Appeal to refuse to exercise its discretion under s 33 to allow the claims to continue. The Supreme Court has now given leave to appeal.

[93] [2010] 1 WLR 516, at [16]; also [43]–[44].

able to recover costs . . . In those circumstances . . . it may well be that it would not be equitable to allow the claimant to proceed. On the other hand, if the evidence of the claimant is compelling and cogent that the abuse occurred, and it is said that it was the abuse that inhibited him from commencing proceedings, that is surely a compelling point in favour of the claimant.[94]

(4) The size of the claimant's claim. The smaller the claimant's claim is, the less compelling his case will be for arguing that it would be 'equitable' to allow the claim to be brought despite the lapse of time in bringing the claim.[95]

D. Defamation, malicious falsehood and deceit

If A has committed one of these torts in relation to B, a special limitation period will apply. In cases of defamation and malicious falsehood, B will normally have only a year to sue A from the moment she was first entitled to obtain a remedy in respect of A's tort.[96] In the case of deceit, B will have six years from the time A's deceit first came to light to sue A.[97]

26.15 CONTRIBUTORY NEGLIGENCE

This defence is often discussed in tort textbooks in this kind of chapter. However, there is an important distinction between this defence and all the other defences we have considered so far. The defences we have looked at so far operate to bar a claimant from suing a defendant. Contributory negligence does not: it merely operates to reduce the amount of compensatory damages a claimant can sue a defendant for in respect of some loss the claimant has suffered if the claimant is judged also to have been at fault for the fact that that loss has been suffered. Accordingly, we will postpone any discussion of contributory negligence until the chapter on 'Compensatory Damages' below.[98]

26.16 THE IMPACT OF ARTICLE 6 OF THE ECHR

Thus stands the law at the moment on when a defendant will be able to raise a defence to a claim in tort that has been made against him. However, for the sake of completeness we should note one further point. Claimants who have been faced with having their claims in tort dismissed because the defendant can raise a defence to their claim have sometimes sought in the past to argue that dismissing their claim would violate their rights under Article 6(1) of the European Convention on Human Rights, which provides, so far as is relevant, that:

> In the determination of his civil rights and obligations . . . everyone is entitled to a fair and public hearing within a reasonable time by an independent and impartial tribunal established by law.

The claimant's argument would be that throwing out his case just because the defendant is able to raise a defence to that claim means that his case is not being given a 'fair and public hearing'. It may be that such arguments will not be made in future. Law is as much subject to fads and fashions as any other human institution, and our sense is that arguments that

---

[94] [2010] 1 WLR 516, at [22].
[95] [2010] 1 WLR 516, at [63].
[96] Section 4A. However, the limitation period may be extended under s 14A. If the applicable limitation period for B's suing A has expired, the courts may still allow B to sue A if it would be 'equitable' to do so: s 32A.
[97] Section 32(1)(a).
[98] See § 28.5.

throwing out a claim because you have *no claim* violates your rights under Article 6(1) are going out of fashion at the moment. However, just in case we are wrong on this, we will briefly try to sum up how and when Article 6(1) could have an impact on a defendant's ability to rely on a defence to defeat a claim that is being made against him in tort.

So – let's assume that C is suing D for damages in tort and D wants to defeat C's claim by relying on a *Killer* defence. C wants to argue that throwing out her claim because of *Killer* will violate her rights under Article 6(1). To make out this argument, she will have to do two things:

(1) Show that allowing D to rely on *Killer* to defeat her claim *could* violate her Article 6(1) rights. If she can do this, we can say that her case is *covered* by Article 6(1).

(2) Show that allowing D to rely on *Killer* to defeat her claim will serve no legitimate purpose *or* will serve some legitimate purpose but do so in a disproportionate way.

If C can do (1) *and* (2) then she will be able to argue that her Article 6(1) rights *will* be violated if D is allowed to rely on *Killer* to defeat her claim. The real difficulty for C will be in doing (1) – showing that her case is covered by Article 6(1). The law on when a claimant can argue that throwing out her claim *could* violate her Article 6(1) rights is very confused. However the following points can be made.

(1) A claimant cannot argue that her Article 6(1) rights have been violated just because she is not allowed to sue a defendant.[99]

(2) The law on the scope of Article 6(1) draws a distinction between cases where a claimant has been prevented from suing a defendant because the domestic law governing her case put a *procedural* bar in the way of the claimant suing the defendant and cases where a claimant has been prevented from suing a defendant because the domestic law governing her case put a *substantive* bar in the way of her suing the defendant.

(3) A claimant who has been prevented from suing a defendant will be able to argue that her case is covered by Article 6(1) if she was prevented from suing the defendant because the law put a *procedural* bar in the way of her suing the defendant.[100]

So, for example, a prisoner who was prevented from suing his prison governor for libel because, under UK law, he was not allowed access to a solicitor was able to establish that Article 6(1) covered his case.[101] Similarly, when the claimant in *Stubbings v Webb* (1993) was prevented from suing the defendant for sexually abusing her as a child on grounds of limitation, it was held that her case was covered by Article 6(1).[102] The law on limitation of actions created a procedural bar to her claim.[103]

(4) By contrast, Article 6(1) will not cover the case where a claimant has been prevented from suing a defendant because the law put a *substantive* bar in the way of her suing the defendant. If the claimant's claim against the defendant failed because she had *no right* to sue the defendant under the law applicable to her claim, then we would *normally* say that

---

[99] *Z v United Kingdom* [2001] 2 FLR 612, at [88].

[100] *James v United Kingdom* (1986) 8 EHRR 123, at [81].

[101] *Golder v United Kingdom* (1975) 1 EHRR 524, discussed above, p 90. The prisoner's Art 6(1) rights were found to have been violated.

[102] *Stubbings v United Kingdom* [1997] 1 FLR 105. The European Court of Human Rights went on to find that the claimant's Art 6(1) rights had not actually been violated: the laws on limitation which prevented the claimant suing the defendant pursued a legitimate goal, and in a proportionate way.

[103] See *Matthews v Ministry of Defence* [2003] 1 AC 1163, at [128] (per Lord Walker): 'Bars arising from statutes of limitation are . . . generally regarded as procedural.

there existed a *substantive* bar which prevented her from suing the defendant. However, it is clear from the decided cases that a claimant whose claim against a defendant has failed because she had no right to sue him will *sometimes* be able to argue that the bar on her suing the defendant that existed in her case was actually *procedural* in nature and *not* substantive.

(5) The European Court of Human Rights (ECtHR for short) has held in a number of cases that a claimant who has been prevented from suing a defendant because she had no right to sue him will be able to argue that a *procedural* bar stood in the way of her suing the defendant if the reason why she had no right to sue him was that the domestic law governing her claim conferred an *immunity* on the defendant from being sued by the claimant.[104] These cases take their inspiration from the following *dictum* of the ECtHR in *Fayed* v *United Kingdom* (1994):

> it would not be consistent with the . . . basic principle underlying Article [6(1)] . . . – namely that civil claims must be capable of being submitted to a judge for adjudication – if, for example, a State could, without restraint or control by the Convention enforcement bodies, remove from the jurisdiction of the civil courts a whole range of civil claims or confer immunities from civil liability on large groups or categories of persons . . .[105]

The ECtHR has never explained when exactly a defendant can be said to enjoy an *immunity* from being sued by a claimant. Some cases seem to suggest that a defendant will enjoy an immunity from being sued by a claimant if:

(a) the claimant wants to bring an action against the defendant which is well recognised under the domestic law governing her case; *and*

(b) the domestic law governing the claimant's case provides that the claimant has no right to bring such an action against the defendant, but it does so for reasons that have nothing to do with the merits of the claimant's case.[106]

If (a) and (b) are made out then, according to these cases, the claimant will be able to argue that the domestic law governing her case has put a *procedural* bar in the way of her suing the defendant and that therefore her case is covered by Article 6(1).[107]

(6) The House of Lords has, however, taken a much narrower view as to when a claimant who has no right to sue a defendant can argue that the bar which the law places on her suing the defendant is procedural in nature, rather than substantive.

In *Matthews* v *Ministry of Defence* (2003), the claimant was an electrical mechanic who suffered various asbestos related injuries as a result of working in the Royal Navy between

---

[104] *Tinnelly & Sons Ltd* v *United Kingdom* (1998) 27 EHRR 249, at [71]–[72]; *Al-Adsani* v *United Kingdom* (2001) 34 EHRR 273, at [46]–[48]; *Fogarty* v *United Kingdom* (2001) 34 EHRR 302, at [25]–[26]; *McElhinney* v *Ireland* (2001) 34 EHRR 322, at [23]–[25].

[105] (1994) 18 EHRR 393, at [65].

[106] See above, n 104.

[107] It could be argued that our account of the scope of Art 6(1) is inconsistent with the decision of the ECtHR in *Powell and Rayner* v *United Kingdom* (1990) 12 EHRR 355. In that case the claimants were prevented from suing the defendants in private nuisance because of s 76(1) of the Civil Aviation Act 1982, which provides that no claims in private nuisance can be brought in respect of 'the flight of an aircraft over any property at a height above the ground which is . . . reasonable.' It was held that the bar on the claimants' suing the defendants here was a substantive one and that Art 6(1) did not therefore cover the claimants' case. However, two points can be made in response to this. First, it is not clear that the bar which existed in *Powell and Rayner* had nothing to do with the merits of the claimants' case: if the flight of aircraft over the claimants' property was 'reasonable' that would weaken the strength of the claimants' claim that they were entitled to sue the defendants in private nuisance. Secondly, the decision in *Powell and Rayner* antedated the decision in *Fayed*, and it may well be that if a case like *Powell and Rayner* came up again today, the decision would be very different.

1955 and 1968. He sued the Ministry of Defence for compensation. Under the law that was applicable to his claim, he would have had no right to sue the Ministry of Defence for compensation *if*: (i) his injuries were suffered as a result of the condition of any ship used by the armed services; *and* (ii) the relevant Secretary of State issued a certificate to that effect.[108] Such a certificate was issued in the claimant's case and as a result his claim for damages was thrown out.[109]

The claimant argued that his rights under Article 6(1) were violated when his claim was thrown out. The House of Lords disagreed: they held the bar which prevented the claimant suing the Ministry of Defence in this case was substantive, not procedural, in nature and that therefore the claimant's case was not covered by Article 6(1). The House of Lords was prepared to admit that a *no right* case might in certain circumstances be covered by Article 6(1). At the same time, it is clear that their Lordships took a very narrow view of what those circumstances might be. Lord Hoffmann suggested that a *no right* case would be covered by Article 6(1) if the reason why the claimant had no right to sue a defendant was that the government had been given an 'arbitrary power' to declare that the claimant had no right to sue the defendant and thereby stop her case in its tracks.[110] Lord Millett took the view that a *no right* case would be covered by Article 6(1) if the reason why the claimant had no right to sue the defendant was that the government had passed a statute stripping people like her of the right to sue people like the defendant for reasons which were unrelated to the reason why people like her had a right to sue people like the defendant in the first place.[111] In so ruling, the House of Lords took the view that the object of Article 6(1) is to prevent the government arbitrarily interfering with people's enjoyment of the rights that they are afforded under the law – either through using procedural tricks designed to prevent them getting a full hearing of their case or by using its legislative power to strip people of rights to sue that they would otherwise enjoy. Seen in this way, it was obvious that the claimant's case in *Matthews* was not covered by Article 6(1). Section 10 of the Crown Proceedings Act 1947 was not intended to deprive people of any rights that they previously enjoyed under statute or the common law. Instead it preserved, in part, the old rule that people had *no rights* to sue the Crown, while at the same time ensuring – through the certification procedure – that those prejudiced by the preservation of that rule would obtain an alternative means of compensation for the harm they had suffered through the award of a pension.[112]

(7) In *Roche* v *United Kingdom* (2006), the ECtHR had the opportunity to address the question of whether the bar to bringing a civil claim considered in the *Matthews* case was substantive or procedural in nature. Of the 17 judges who decided the case, nine agreed with the House of Lords in *Matthews* that the bar was substantive in nature and therefore the claimant in *Roche* could not complain that applying it to prevent him suing the Ministry of Defence for damages violated his Article 6(1) rights. The remaining eight judges took the position set out in point (5), above, and held that the bar was procedural in nature, with the result that applying that bar to stop the claimant suing the Ministry of

---

[108] Crown Proceedings Act 1947, s 10. This provision was later repealed by the Crown Proceedings Act 1987, and therefore does not figure in our account of the scope of Crown immunity set out above, at § 26.2(C). As the claimant's injuries in *Matthews* were suffered by him as a result of his working in the Royal Navy between 1955 and 1968, his claim for compensation for those injuries was governed by s 10.

[109] Though the issuing of the certificate meant that the claimant became entitled to a pension which would help compensate him for the injuries he had suffered.

[110] [2003] 1 AC 1163, at [35].

[111] [2003] 1 AC 1163, at [79].

[112] [2003] 1 AC 1163, at [73] (per Lord Hope).

Defence might have violated his Article 6(1) rights. The decision in *Roche* makes it difficult to know what position the ECtHR will take in the future as to when a *no right* case will be covered by Article 6(1).

(8) The difference between the position taken by the minority in *Roche* as to when a *no right* case will be covered by Article 6(1) and the position taken by the House of Lords in *Matthews* v *Ministry of Defence* may be better appreciated through the use of a concrete example. We have already seen that if *Journo* libels *Celeb* and subsequently dies, *Celeb* will not be allowed to sue *Journo*'s estate for damages.[113] Whether or not *Celeb* will be able to argue that this violates his rights under Article 6(1) will depend on whether the bar on *Celeb*'s suing *Journo*'s estate here is procedural or substantive in nature.

It is not hard to imagine that the minority in *Roche* would rule that the bar here is *procedural* in nature: *Celeb* wants to sue *Journo*'s estate for damages in defamation – a cause of action which is well acknowledged in UK law – but he is prevented from doing so by s 1(1) of the Law Reform (Miscellaneous Provisions) Act 1934 and for reasons which have nothing to do with the merits of her claim. So the minority in *Roche* might well rule that Article 6(1) covers *Celeb*'s claim here.[114] Equally, it seems to follow from the decision in *Matthews* that the Supreme Court would rule that there exists a *substantive* bar in the way of *Celeb*'s suing *Journo*'s estate here. Section 1(1) of the 1934 Act does not deprive people like *Celeb* of any rights that people like him previously enjoyed. Instead it preserves, in part, the old rule that the victim of a tort would have *no rights* to sue the person who committed that tort if he died after he committed that tort. So the Supreme Court – if asked – might well rule that Article 6(1) does *not* cover *Celeb*'s case here, with the result that *Celeb* will *never* be able to claim that the courts will violate his Article 6(1) rights if they throw out his claim, no matter how silly or disproportionate the rule embodied in s 1(1) of the 1934 Act is.

Now that we have a firmer grasp of what sort of cases are covered by Article 6(1), we can return to our original case – where D is seeking to rely on *Killer* to defeat C's claim against him in tort. When will C be able to argue that her claim against D is covered by Article 6(1)? It is clear that if *Killer* is a limitation defence then C's case will be covered by Article 6(1). C will have no problem establishing that the bar on her suing D created by *Killer* is procedural in nature. It is much more uncertain what the position is in relation to the other defences that D might raise to defeat C's claim. Normally one would think that these defences create a substantive bar to C's suing D: if D is able to take advantage of any of these defences, C will have *no right* to sue D. But, as we have seen, even some *no right* cases will be treated by the courts as cases where the law has placed a *procedural* bar in the way of a claimant suing a defendant. Can any of the defences considered here be treated as creating a procedural bar in the way of C's suing D?

If we follow the approach of the minority in *Roche* to the question of when a *no right* case will involve a procedural bar, then the following defences might well be regarded as creating a procedural bar to C's suing D if they are relied upon by D to defeat C's claim: Crown immunity, witness immunity, trade union immunity and abuse of process. All of these defences will operate to prevent C from bringing a tort claim for damages against D

[113] See above, § 26.8.
[114] Of course, if Article 6(1) does cover *Celeb*'s case here, dismissing *Celeb*'s claim will not necessarily violate his Article 6(1) rights: it depends on whether dismissing his claim will serve a legitimate purpose and in a proportionate way. It is hard to think that it will. Given this, the issue of whether Article 6(1) covers *Celeb*'s claim becomes vitally important – it seems that if Art 6(1) covers *Celeb*'s claim, then *Celeb* will have a good chance of arguing that dismissing his claim against *Journo*'s estate *will* violate his Art 6(1) rights.

– a claim which is well acknowledged under UK law – and for reasons that have nothing to do with the merits of C's claim. The defences of *volenti*, exclusion of liability and illegality will also prevent C bringing a tort claim for damages against D but the defences in those cases will be centrally concerned with the merits of C's claim.

If, on the other hand, we follow the House of Lords' approach to this question, then trade union immunity is probably the only defence (other than the obvious one of limitation) that could be said to raise a procedural bar to C's suing D. It could be argued that Parliament, in creating this immunity, stripped people of rights they previously enjoyed under the common law. If this is right then, under the House of Lords' approach to the scope of Article 6(1), cases where a defendant is able to take advantage of the defence of trade union immunity may well be covered by Article 6(1). An employer who is prevented from suing a trade union for damages under s 219 of the Trade Union and Labour Relations (Consolidation) Act 1992 might therefore be able to argue that his Article 6(1) rights have been violated – though whether they have or not will depend on whether s 219 serves a legitimate purpose in a proportionate way.[115] By contrast, it is hard to argue that the existence of defences such as witness immunity, Crown immunity, *volenti*, exclusion of liability and illegality strip people of rights that they previously enjoyed before those defences were created. The defences came with the rights: they did not post-date them.

So it is very uncertain what effect Article 6(1) of the European Convention on Human Rights has on the availability of the defences dealt with in this chapter. If the House of Lords' view as to the scope of Article 6(1) is correct, then the effect is very small – Article 6(1) will not prevent a tortfeasor relying on most of the defences set out in this chapter. If the ECtHR follows the view of the minority in *Roche* – and the ECtHR case law that preceded the decision in *Roche* – then the impact of Article 6(1) should be more far-reaching.

Further reading

A lot of writing on defences focuses on the illegality defence. The House of Lords' decision in *Gray* v *Thames Trains Ltd* provoked a flurry of comment: see **Paul Davies, 'The illegality defence and public policy'** (2009) 125 *Law Quarterly Review* 556 and **Po Jen Yap, 'Rethinking the illegality defence in tort law'** (2010) 18 *Tort Law Review* 52. A good overview of the entirety of the law on illegality is provided by **Rick Glofcheski's 'Plaintiff's illegality as a bar to the recovery of personal injury damages'** (1999) 19 *Legal Studies* 6.

On *volenti*, see **A.J.E. Jaffey, 'Volenti non fit injuria'** (1985) 44 *Cambridge Law Journal* 87 and **Mark Lunney, 'Personal responsibility and the "new" volenti'** (2005) 13 *Tort Law Review* 76.

Visit **www.mylawchamber.co.uk/mcbride** to access tools to help you develop and test your knowledge of Tort law, including interactive multiple choice questions, practice exam questions with guidance, weblinks, legal newsfeed, additional case summaries, legal updates and tips on answering problem and essay questions.

premium mylawchamber
unrivalled support for legal education

---

[115] It is likely, though, that s 219 would survive this process of scrutiny, given that it is so severely qualified.

27 Nominal damages

27.1 The basics *749*

27.2 Reasons *750*

27.3 Theories *751*

Overview

This chapter is the first of seven chapters dealing with the remedies that are available to the victim of a tort. We start with one of the most minor: the right of the victim of a tort who has not been harmed as a result of that tort being committed to sue for nominal damages so long as the tort is actionable *per se* (actionable without proof of loss). Section 27.1 explains what nominal damages are, and which torts are actionable *per se*. Section 27.2 sets out the reasons why a claimant might sue for nominal damages. Section 27.3 deals with the issue of why some torts are actionable *per se* while others are not.

27.1 THE BASICS

If the victim of a tort has suffered no loss as a result of that tort being committed, he or she might still be entitled to sue the person who committed that tort for *nominal damages* – usually £5.[1] Whether she will be entitled to sue for such damages will depend on whether the tort that she is the victim of is *actionable per se* – that is, actionable without her having to prove that she has suffered any loss as a result of that tort.

The following torts are actionable *per se*: torts involving a trespass to someone's person;[2] trespass to land; private nuisances involving an interference with someone's right to light or other rights attached to his land.[3] The classic example of a tort that is *not* actionable *per se* is negligence. So if *Driver*'s bad driving results in his *almost* running over *Pedestrian*, *Pedestrian* will *not* be entitled to sue *Driver* for nominal damages. Private nuisances not involving an interference with someone's right to light or other rights attached to his land do not seem to be actionable *per se*.[4] It is unclear whether the tort of trespass to goods is actionable *per se*. Ancient authority indicates that it is not,[5] but the Court of Appeal assumed – though without the benefit of any argument on the matter – that trespass to

---

[1] See, for example, *Brandeis Goldschmidt & Co v Western Transport* [1981] QB 864, 874; *Watkins v Secretary of State for the Home Department* [2004] EWCA Civ 966, at [61]. Until the 1980s, the conventional sum awarded in making an award of nominal damages was £2: see, for example, *Child v Stenning* (1879) 11 Ch D 82; *Sykes v Midland Bank Executor & Trustee Co* [1971] 1 QB 113. The press release accompanying the Supreme Court decision in *Lumba v Secretary of State for the Home Department* [2011] UKSC 12 – in which the claimants were awarded nominal damages – said that the claimants in that case were only awarded £1 in nominal damages; but the judgments in the case make no mention of the sum that should be awarded in nominal damages.
[2] That is, assault, battery and false imprisonment.
[3] See *Nicholls v Ely Beet Sugar Factory Ltd* (No 2) [1936] 1 Ch 343, 348–9.
[4] Though see *Dobson v Thames Water Utilities Ltd* [2009] EWCA Civ 28, where it was suggested (at [34]) that a claimant might be entitled to sue in private nuisance, but obtain no more than nominal damages where the nuisance had not caused them an *actual* loss of amenity.
[5] *Slater v Swann* (1730) 2 Stra 872, 93 ER 906.

goods could be actionable *per se* in *White* v *Withers* (2009).[6] The House of Lords has made it clear that the tort of misfeasance in public office is not actionable *per se*.[7] It seems that it will be very rare for the breach of a statutory duty owed to another to be actionable *per se*.[8]

Libel is often said to be a tort that is actionable *per se*. This is because if A publishes to C a statement referring to B that is defamatory of B, B will still be entitled to sue A for damages even if she cannot show that she suffered any loss as a result of A's publication. However, the better analysis of what is going on in a libel case such as B's is that B does not have to *prove* that she has suffered any loss as a result of A's libel. Instead, it will be *presumed* that she did suffer some loss as a result of A's libel and it will be up to a jury or a judge to put a figure on how much of a loss she suffered.[9] If the loss suffered by B seems to the jury or judge to be very small because, for example, C did not believe A's statement or because B was of such bad character that she had no reputation to lose, then B will not be awarded very much by way of damages[10] – but the damages paid to her will still be *compensatory in nature, not nominal*.[11]

27.2 REASONS

Why would a claimant want to sue a defendant for nominal damages? Four reasons might be given.

(1) *Unlocking further remedies*. Suing a defendant for nominal damages may open the door to obtaining further, more substantial, remedies such as aggravated damages (awarded when the defendant's conduct in committing the tort was particularly outrageous), or exemplary damages (damages designed to punish a defendant for his conduct in committing a tort). These types of damages are awarded on top of a basic award of compensatory or nominal damages. So in a case where the victim of a tort has suffered no loss as a result of a tort being committed, she will only be able to access these special awards of damages by bringing a claim for nominal damages.

(2) *Setting the record straight*. If A has committed a tort that is actionable *per se* in relation to B but B has suffered no actionable loss as a result, B might want to sue A for nominal damages in order to have it publicly established that A committed a tort in acting as he did. This may be especially important where A defamed B: she will want it to be publicly established that whatever A said about her was untrue.[12]

---

[6] [2009] EWCA Civ 1122, at [62] (per Ward LJ), and [71] (per Sedley LJ).

[7] *Watkins* v *Secretary of State for the Home Department* [2006] 2 AC 395.

[8] In *Cullen* v *Chief Constable of the Royal Ulster Constabulary* [2003] 1 WLR 1763 (discussed above, § 22.2), Lord Hutton held that the breach of a statutory duty owed by A to B might be actionable *per se* if the statutory duty was contained in a written constitution, but if the duty in question was imposed by an ordinary statute, A's breach of that duty would only be actionable if it caused B to suffer 'loss or injury of a kind for which the law awards damages' (ibid, at [47], quoting *Pickering* v *Liverpool Daily Post* [1991] 2 AC 370, at 420 (per Lord Bridge)).

[9] To the same effect, see Mitchell 2005, 53.

[10] In *Newstead* v *London Express Newspaper* [1940] 1 KB 377, the claimant was awarded one farthing. In *Reynolds* v *Times Newspapers Ltd* [2001] 2 AC 127, the claimant was awarded one penny.

[11] If the damages payable to B are extremely small because she had no reputation to lose when A libelled her, they will be known as *contemptuous* or *derisory* damages.

[12] Of course, a finding of liability in a defamation case does not indicate that what the defendant said about the claimant was untrue; it merely indicates that the defendant could not prove that what he said about the claimant was true (see above, § 19.1(5)).

(3) *Assertion of right*. If A has committed a tort that is actionable *per se* in relation to B by doing *x* but B has suffered no actionable loss as a result, B might still want to sue A for nominal damages because if she does not sue him for doing *x*, he might acquire a licence to do *x* in the future.

Suppose, for example, that *Trespasser* regularly walks across *Owner's* land without her permission but she does not suffer any loss as a result of his walking across her land. Because *Trespasser* is committing the tort of trespass to land, *Owner* will be entitled to sue *Trespasser* for nominal damages here. Now: *Owner* will have an incentive to sue A for such damages, because if she does not *Trespasser* might – if he continues to walk across her land – acquire a *right by prescription* to walk across *Owner's* land.

Similarly, in *Bower* v *Hill* (1835), the defendant blocked a drain which lay between the claimant's land and a nearby river. In so doing he committed a tort: the claimant had a right of way over the drain. The claimant did not suffer any loss as a result of the defendant's blocking the drain as it was already choked with mud. However, the claimant still sued the defendant for nominal damages (as he was entitled to do as the tort committed by the defendant in blocking the drain was actionable *per se*) because, as Tindal CJ noted, if '[the claimant] acquiesced in [the blockage of the drain] for twenty years, [that] would become evidence of a renunciation and abandonment of the [claimant's] right of way'[13] and everyone would, after that time, be free to block the drain.

(4) *Punishment*. If A commits a tort that is actionable *per se* in relation to B but B has suffered no actionable loss as a result, B might want to sue A for nominal damages as a way of punishing A for committing that tort. The punishment would not, of course, consist in having to pay B £5 in nominal damages; the punishment would consist in having to repay the legal costs incurred by B in bringing her case against A – which would, obviously, come to a lot more than £5. However, nowadays such a plan might well backfire on B: if the courts thought that B's sole motivation in suing A for nominal damages was to inflict a bill for her legal costs on him, then they might well refuse to award B costs and she would have to bear those costs herself.[14] As Sedley LJ remarked in *White* v *Withers* (2009): 'The claim for a shilling in damages in order to prove a point and obtain an award of costs is history.'[15]

27.3 THEORIES

Why are some torts actionable *per se* and other torts only actionable if the victim can show that she has suffered some loss as a result of that tort being committed? Some people think that the reasons for this are *deep*; other people think that the reasons are relatively *shallow*.

(1) *Shallow theories*. A theory as to why some torts are actionable *per se* and others are not is *shallow* if it explains the distinction on purely pragmatic grounds. So such a theory might say that the tort of trespass to land is actionable *per se* because that enables landowners to stop harmless trespassers acquiring a licence to go over their land; while negligence is not actionable *per se* because there does not seem to be much point in allowing *Pedestrian* to

---

[13] (1835) 1 Bing NC 549, 555; 131 ER 1229, 1231.
[14] See Devlin J's remarks in *Anglo-Cyprian Agencies* v *Paphos Industries* [1951] 1 All ER 873, at 874 doubting whether a claimant who has obtained nominal damages from a defendant should always be entitled to recover the costs incurred by him in suing the defendant for such damages.
[15] [2009] EWCA Civ 1122, at [72].

sue *Driver* for *almost* running her over. Such a theory might go on to say that libel is actionable *per se* (if it is) because that enables the subject of defamatory but harmless allegations that have been published in permanent form to get a judgment that she can point to should anyone in the future see those allegations and be tempted to think less well of her. But you will not normally be entitled to sue for slanderous but harmless words, because the fact that those words are not in a permanent form means that it is unlikely that people will revisit those words in future and need to be told that those words were the subject of a successful claim for defamation.

Some support for the idea that the reasons why some torts are actionable *per se* and others not are relatively shallow is provided by the decision of the House of Lords in *Watkins* v *Secretary of State for the Home Department* (2006), where their Lordships gave relatively shallow reasons why misfeasance in public office should not be actionable *per se*. They did not see any real need for the tort to be made actionable *per se*: abuses of public power that did not cause any harm could be sanctioned through disciplinary proceedings, and corrected through applications for judicial review.[16] They were also concerned that making the tort actionable *per se* would unlock the door to exemplary damages being awarded in cases where a claimant had not suffered any loss as a result of an abuse of public power: they doubted whether exemplary damages should be awarded in such a case.[17]

(2) *Deep theories*. A theory as to why some torts are actionable *per se* and others not is *deep* if it explains the distinction as resting on fundamental ideas about the nature of a tort or the basis of tort liability.

For example, Robert Stevens concedes that the reasons why torts such as slander (in most of its forms) and misfeasance in public office are not actionable *per se* are shallow in nature.[18] But he thinks the reason why negligence is not actionable *per se* is *deep*. The reason why *Pedestrian* cannot sue *Driver* for nominal damages in the case where *Driver* almost runs over *Pedestrian* is that *Driver* has done nothing wrong – committed no tort – to *Pedestrian*. The only duty of care *Driver* owed *Pedestrian* was a CPR-focused duty to take care not to injure *Pedestrian* by driving carelessly.[19] As *Driver*'s bad driving did not result in injury to *Pedestrian*, *Pedestrian* cannot say that *Driver* has done anything wrong to her in this case.

John Goldberg and Benjamin Zipursky disagree with this, and agree with us,[20] that *Driver* owed *Pedestrian* a C-focused 'duty of non-injuriousness' to take care not to drive dangerously. But they argue[21] that negligence is not actionable *per se* because – they argue – *Driver*'s breach of this duty will not amount to a tort. A breach of duty only amounts to a tort, they argue, if it so serious as to entitle the victim of that breach to some form of civil redress for what has been done to her. This will not be the case where *Driver* almost runs over *Pedestrian*. *Driver*'s bad driving will only amount to a tort to *Pedestrian* if it causes *Pedestrian* to suffer some kind of *injury*.[22]

---

[16] [2006] 2 AC 395, at [26] (per Lord Bingham), [65] (per Lord Rodger), [81] (per Lord Carswell).
[17] [2006] 2 AC 395, at [32] (per Lord Hope), [64] (per Lord Rodger), [81] (per Lord Carswell).
[18] Stevens 2007, 88.
[19] On CPR-focused duties of care, see above, § 5.5.
[20] Ibid.
[21] See Goldberg and Zipursky 2002.
[22] Goldberg and Zipursky 2010a, 954: 'there is never a tort without an *injury*.'

We have already explained the problems with Stevens' deep theory as to why negligence is not actionable *per se*.[23] Goldberg and Zipursky's deep theory rests on even deeper foundations – their *civil recourse theory* of tort liability, which we will look at and criticise in the next chapter.[24]

Visit **www.mylawchamber.co.uk/mcbride** to access tools to help you develop and test your knowledge of Tort law, including interactive multiple choice questions, practice exam questions with guidance, weblinks, legal newsfeed, additional case summaries, legal updates and tips on answering problem and essay questions.

premium
my**law**chamber
unrivalled support for legal education

---

28 Compensatory damages

28.1 The basics *754*

28.2 Techniques *755*

28.3 Assessment *758*

28.4 Reduction (1): receipt of benefit *765*

28.5 Reduction (2): contributory
negligence *773*

28.6 Third party losses *779*

28.7 Theories *781*

Overview

In this chapter, we look at the principal remedy available to the victim of a tort: compensatory damages. Most of this chapter is quite technical, dealing with the details of how the courts assess how much a claimant should be paid in compensatory damages, and how the compensation should be delivered to the claimant. But the final section is very theoretical: it deals with the issue of why the victim of a tort should be entitled to sue for compensatory damages *at all*.

28.1 THE BASICS

This chapter is concerned with the victim of a tort's right to sue for compensatory damages in respect of the actionable losses that that tort has caused her to suffer, and may cause her to suffer in the future. The rights of a third parties to a tort to sue for compensation for losses they have suffered as a result of that tort being committed will be dealt with in chapters 34 and 35.

Much of the work that should be done in this chapter has already been done. We have looked at when the victim of a tort can argue that that tort has *caused* her loss in chapter 9, and set out the rules on when a loss suffered by the victim of a tort as a result of that tort being committed will be *actionable* in chapter 10. With those fundamental matters of principle already settled, much of this chapter is quite technical in nature.

In the next section we look at the different ways in which the victim of a tort might be compensated for the past, present and future actionable losses that that tort has caused, or might cause, her to suffer. Traditionally, the victim of a tort has been awarded a *lump sum* to cover all these losses. As this sum is intended to cover future losses as well as past and present losses, it is invariably speculative in nature. In order to avoid this speculation, new methods for awarding compensatory damages have been developed in recent years, such as making *periodical payments* of damages.

Having looked at these different techniques for awarding compensatory damages, we will go on to take a much more detailed look in section 28.3 at how, in a case where a claimant is to be compensated through the award of a lump sum, the courts go about assessing how much the claimant should, in principle, be awarded. We say 'in principle' because any damages award (however made) to a claimant is liable to be reduced because, for example: (1) the claimant was *partly to blame* for the losses she has suffered, or is liable to suffer, as a result of the defendant's tort; or (2) the claimant has received some kind of *benefit* from the defendant's tort which should go to offset the damages she would normally be entitled to sue the defendant for. In sections 28.4 and 28.5, we look at when compensatory damages normally payable to a claimant will be reduced because of either (1) or (2).

So far, we have been assuming when the victim of a tort sues for compensatory damages, she will be simply suing for damages in respect of the losses that *she* has suffered as a result of that tort being committed. However, there are occasions when she will be entitled to sue for damages in respect of the losses suffered by *third parties* to the tort (which damages will then be held *on trust* for those third parties) in section 28.6.

In section 28.7, we look at the various theories that have been presented to explain why the victim of a tort is entitled to sue for compensatory damages. Most such theories are either *economic* or *rights-based* in nature. An *economic* theory says that the victim of a tort is allowed to sue for compensatory damages because it makes economic sense to allow her to sue for such damages. *Rights-based* theories take a variety of forms. One theory says that the victim of a tort is allowed to sue for compensatory damages as a 'second best' way of giving her what she had a legal right to in the first place, and was deprived of when that tort was committed. Another theory – 'civil recourse theory' – says that the victim of a tort is allowed to sue for compensatory damages because she has a moral right to seek redress for that wrong, and allowing her to sue for compensatory damages provides her a civilised way of achieving that redress.

28.2 TECHNIQUES

Where A has committed a tort in relation to B, the courts will normally aim – in awarding compensatory damages to B – to give B a *lump sum* sufficient to compensate her for the actionable losses that A's tort *has caused* her to suffer and the losses that A's tort *may* cause B to suffer in the future.

So suppose that *Driver* negligently runs over *Injured* and one of *Injured*'s legs has to be amputated as a result. *Injured* currently works in an office and her terms of employment are unaffected by the fact that she has lost one leg, though she did of course have to take some time off work to have her injuries treated. In this situation *Driver*'s tort *has caused Injured* to suffer three kinds of losses. First, physical injury – *Injured* was injured in the accident caused by *Driver*'s negligence and one of her legs had to be amputated. Secondly, distress – *Injured* will have experienced a great deal of pain and suffering as a result of being injured in the accident, as well as distress at the fact that she will now have to live with having only one leg. Thirdly, economic loss – as a result of the fact that she had to take time off work to have her injuries treated, *Injured* will have suffered some kind of diminution in income. However, in this situation, *Driver*'s tort *may cause Injured* to suffer a further kind of loss *in the future.* If *Injured* loses her current job in the future, the fact that she has only one leg may make it difficult for her to find alternative employment. So *Injured* may suffer economic loss in the future as a result of *Driver*'s tort.

So the lump sum payable to *Injured* in this situation will be designed to compensate her for: (1) the fact that *Driver*'s tort has *caused* her to suffer physical injury, distress and economic loss; *and* (2) the fact that *Driver*'s tort *may* cause her to suffer economic loss in the future because her capacity to find alternative employment if she loses her current job has been diminished.[1] Inevitably, in awarding damages designed to compensate *Injured* for (2), she will not be awarded damages equal to the *full* amount of money she would lose if

---

[1] Damages that are designed to compensate the victim of a tort for the fact that she may suffer economic losss in future because the tort has reduced her capacity to find alternative employment are known as damages for 'loss of earning capacity' or '*Smith* v *Manchester* damages' after one of the cases in which such damages were awarded: *Smith* v *Manchester* (1974) 17 KIR 1. In the situation we are considering, such damages will only be awarded to *Injured* if there is in fact a *real or substantial* risk that she will lose her job in the future and that her disability will make it difficult for her to find alternative employment: *Moeliker* v *Reyrolle* [1977] 1 All ER 9.

she lost her job and found it difficult, because of her disability, to find alternative employment. Because there is a chance that she will not lose her job, the damages payable to *Injured* will be *discounted* to take account of that chance. However, this creates a problem.

The problem arises out of the fact that once *Injured* is awarded a lump sum in damages that is designed to compensate her for (1) and (2), *that is it.* If the lump sum proves inadequate to cover the losses that *Injured* has suffered as a result of *Driver*'s tort, she will not be able to go back to court to obtain a larger amount. Similarly, if it proves that *Driver* has overpaid and the lump sum award turns out in fact to be larger than was necessary to compensate *Injured* for the losses that she has suffered as a result of *Driver*'s tort, then *Driver* will not be able to go back to court to claw back the overpayment.

Now – because the lump sum payable to *Injured* in this case will be designed in part to compensate her for (2), that lump sum will *inevitably* either undercompensate or overcompensate *Injured* for the losses she has suffered as a result of *Driver*'s tort.[2] Either *Injured* will at some stage in the future lose her job and find it difficult to find alternative employment because she has only one leg – in which case the lump sum award will undercompensate her because that part of the award which was designed to compensate her for the fact that this might happen was discounted to take account of the possibility that *Injured* might *not* lose her job. Or *Injured* will never lose her current job and will sail on to retirement, with her earning capacity undisturbed by the fact that she has only one leg – in which case *Injured* will be overcompensated, because the lump sum paid to her included an element designed to compensate her for the possibility that she might suffer a loss that, as things turned out, she never did.

Given this problem, the law has started to move towards different systems of awarding damages:

(1) *Provisional damages.* Under an award of provisional damages, the victim of a tort is awarded a sum designed to compensate her for the losses that she *has* suffered as a result of that tort being committed; and then, if it turns out that that tort has caused her to suffer some futher losses, she is able to go back to court and sue for further damages, designed to compensate her for those losses. Section 32A of the Senior Courts Act 1981[3] allows[4] the courts in a personal injury case to make a provisional award of damages which would be later topped up with further awards of damages if:

> there is proved or admitted to be a chance that at some definite or indefinite time in the future the injured person will, as a result of the act or omission which gave rise to the cause of action, develop some serious disease or suffer some serious deterioration in his physical or mental condition.

---

[2] See Lord Scarman's remarks in *Lim v Camden Area Health Authority* [1980] AC 174, at 182–3: '[There are] insuperable problems implicit in a system of compensation for personal injuries which (unless the parties agree otherwise) can yield only a lump sum assessed by the court at the time of judgment. Sooner or later . . . if the parties do not settle, a court (once liability is admitted or proved) has to make an award of damages. The award, which covers past, present, and future injury and loss, must, under our law, be of a lump sum assessed at the conclusion of the legal process. The award is final; it is not susceptible to review as the future unfolds, substituting fact for estimate. Knowledge of the future being denied to mankind, so much of the award as is to be attributed to future loss and suffering – in many cases the major part of the award – will almost surely be wrong. There is really only one certainty: the future will prove the award to be either too high or too low.' See also Lord Steyn in *Wells v Wells* [1999] 1 AC 345, at 384.

[3] As amended by s 6 of the Administration of Justice Act 1982.

[4] Under rule 25.7 of the Civil Procedure Rules 1998, the courts are only allowed to exercise this power in cases where the defendant is insured or is a public authority – the idea being that in such cases, there is no real injustice to the defendant in having the possibility of a further award of damages being made against him sometime in the future hanging over his head.

(2) *Periodical payments.*[5] An award of periodical payments is designed to deal with the following kind of situation: A has tortiously injured B and she is disabled and unable to work as a result. She needs to be compensated for the future loss of income that she will suffer as a result of A's tort, but no one can be certain how much longer B will live. Under the lump sum system, the courts simply have to make a guess as to how much longer B is likely to live and award her a lump sum that – when properly invested – will yield her an annual income over her remaining (estimated) lifespan equivalent to the money she would have earned each year but for A's tort. But if B dies earlier than expected, the lump sum awarded her to compensate her for her future loss of income will prove to have been too much; and if she dies later than expected, the lump sum awarded her will prove to have been too little. An award of periodical payments solves this problem: A is simply required to pay B a regular sum to cover her loss of income for as long as she lives. Section 2(1) of the Damages Act 1996[6] now provides that 'A court awarding damages for future pecuniary loss in respect of personal injury . . . may order that the damages are wholly or partly to take the form of periodical payments.' Under s 2(3): 'A court may not make an order for periodical payments unless satisfied that the continuity of payment under the order is reasonably secure.'

(3) *Flexible periodical payments.* Suppose that in the above case B's injuries were such that she was unable to continue working as a high-flying legal executive, but she is still able, despite her injuries, to take a lower paid, but far less stressful, job teaching A-Level Law in a school. Suppose further that there is a chance that B's injuries might get worse in the future and she might be unable to carry on teaching. In such a case regular periodical payments designed to compensate B for the difference in her current income teaching A-Level Law and the income she would have been earning but for A's tort might end up seriously under-compensating or over-compensating her. They will under-compensate her if her condition gets worse and she has to give up teaching: she will not be compensated for the loss of the income from teaching that A's tort has caused her to suffer. They will over-compensate her if she suddenly gets a lot better and she can go back to work as a high-flying legal executive: A will continue having to pay B a regular sum to cover a loss of income that she is no longer experiencing. To cover this possibility, the Damages (Variation of Periodical Payments) Order 2005[7] provides that:

> If there is proved to be a chance that at some definite or indefinite time in the future the claimant will –
>
> (a) as a result of the act or omission which gave rise to the cause of action, develop some serious disease or suffer some serious deterioration, or
> (b) enjoy some significant improvement in his physical or mental condition, where that condition had been adversely affected as a result of that act or omission,
>
> the court may, on the application of a party, with the agreement of all the parties, or of its own initiative, provide in an order for periodical payments that it may be varied.

So in the case we are imagining, when the initial order for periodical payments is made against A, provision can be made for the payments to go up or down in the future depending on what happens in the future.

---

[5] See Lewis 2007.
[6] As amended by the Courts Act 2003, s 100.
[7] SI 2005/841.

Despite the advantages involved in making awards of damages in these new and more flexible ways, it should be noted that there are some disadvantages involved in making awards of damages in these ways.

First, all the parties to litigation will have an interest in not letting litigation 'drag on'. The victim of a tort's ability to get on with her life will be impeded if she is left in constant uncertainty as to how much compensation she will get in respect of the losses suffered by her as a result of that tort being committed. At the same time, the tortfeasor (or his insurer) will have an interest in knowing as soon as possible what his total liability to the victim of his tort is going to be for the purpose of financial planning.

Secondly, the victim of a tort may well have other reasons for preferring to receive a lump sum award designed to compensate her for *all* the losses that she has suffered as a result of that tort being committed and the losses that she may suffer in the future as a result of that tort being committed, rather than receiving small periodic payments designed to compensate her for the losses that, it turns out, she has suffered as a result of that tort being committed. She will be able to do more things with a lump sum: for instance, armed with a lump sum award of damages, she could purchase a business which would be out of her financial reach if she received her damages in small periodic payments over a number of years.[8]

28.3 ASSESSMENT

In this section, we will look at some typical cases where the victim of a tort might sue the person who committed that tort for compensatory damages and see how the courts assess how large the lump sum that is payable to the victim of the tort should be.

A. Physical injury

Let us consider first a standard case where *Driver* negligently caused a crash in which *Pedestrian* ('P') was injured. P's injuries were such that she has become permanently disabled and, as a result, she has had to take a job which pays less than the job she was working in before the crash. P had to take six months off work so as to have her injuries treated with the result that she did not receive any wages for those six months. P opted to have her injuries privately treated and as a result she incurred substantial medical bills. So *Driver's* negligence will have caused P to suffer a mixture of *non-pecuniary* and *pecuniary* losses.

(1) *Non-pecuniary losses*. P's *non-pecuniary* losses include: (a) the *physical injury* that P sustained in the car crash; (b) the consequential *pain and suffering* P experienced as a result of being injured; (c) the *inconvenience* that P's disability causes her to suffer in trying to get around and cope with life generally; (d) the *loss of amenity* (or enjoyment of life) that P's disability will cause her to suffer.

---

[8] At the same time, the victim of a tort who has suffered large losses as a result of that tort being committed might not want to shoulder the burden of managing the large lump sum that she will be awarded to compensate her for her losses. If this is the case *and* liability is undisputed *and* the person who committed the tort in question is insured, the victim of the tort will have the option of entering into what is called a 'structured settlement' with the tortfeasor's insurer. Under this arrangement, a proportion of the damages that would be paid to the victim of the tort in a lump sum if she went to court are paid over to the victim of the tort upfront and the rest is invested by the tortfeasor's insurer in annuities that will produce a regular, tax-free, yearly income for the victim of the tort.

Inevitably, the process of determining how much P should be paid to compensate her for the fact that she has suffered losses (a)–(d) is arbitrary in the sense that there is no demonstrably correct answer as to how much P should be awarded so as to compensate her for the fact that she has suffered these losses. We could easily award P £10,000 or we could award her £20,000; neither figure seems more appropriate. In assessing the figure payable, the courts will merely seek to be *consistent*. So if someone in a previous case who suffered a similar injury to P was awarded £15,000 in respect of that injury and consequential non-pecuniary loss, then the courts will almost certainly award the same amount to P. Moreover, if someone in a previous case who suffered a much more serious injury than P was awarded £20,000 in respect of that injury and consequential non-pecuniary loss, the courts will not give P more than that. In this way, a body of caselaw has been built up on how much will be customarily awarded to compensate people who suffer certain 'standard' injuries and consequential non-pecuniary losses, details of which can be found in advanced works on damages. At the prompting of the Law Commission, the Court of Appeal has sought to update this caselaw, finding that in the past personal injury victims have been undercompensated by the courts for the non-pecuniary losses suffered by them as a result of their injuries. From now on, if the victim of a tort who has suffered a personal injury as a result of a tort being committed would have been entitled – under the old caselaw – to sue for more than £10,000 in respect of that injury and consequential non-pecuniary losses, her award should be increased by up to one-third, depending on what she would have obtained under the old caselaw.[9]

Whatever sum is payable to P to compensate her for the fact that she has suffered losses (a)–(d), it will normally be discounted somewhat to take account of the possibility that had P not become disabled as a result of *Driver*'s negligence, she might have become disabled at some stage in the future. So if P was 'doomed' to become disabled even if *Driver* had not been negligent, then the damages payable to P to compensate her for the fact that she has suffered losses (a)–(d) will be substantially reduced.[10]

(2) *Pecuniary losses*. P's *pecuniary* losses include: (e) the income she lost as a result of having to take six months off work to have her injuries treated; (f) the money P spent on having her injuries privately treated; (g) the loss of income she has suffered and will suffer as a result of having to take a job that pays less than the one she had before she was injured.

In considering how much P should be paid so as to compensate her for the pecuniary losses that she has suffered or may suffer in the future as a result of *Driver*'s negligence, we should draw a distinction between the pecuniary losses that P *has* suffered as a result of *Driver*'s negligence and the pecuniary losses that P will probably suffer in the future as a result of *Driver*'s negligence.

It is quite easy to determine how much P should be paid to compensate her for the loss of wages suffered by her when she had to take time off work to have her injuries treated. She should be paid a sum equivalent to the *net* loss suffered by her: that is, a sum equal to how much P would have taken home after tax had she not had to take time off work. Again, it is not difficult to determine how much P should be paid to compensate her for the fact that she incurred medical bills as a result of having her injuries treated. She should be paid a sum equivalent to the amount she was charged for medical treatment.[11]

---

[9] *Heil* v *Rankin* [2001] QB 272.
[10] *Jobling* v *Associated Dairies Ltd* [1982] AC 794.
[11] Though the sum payable will be reduced if the medical bills covered the cost of food and laundry: see below, §
28.4(A).

Assessing the amount payable to P in respect of the future loss of income that she will probably suffer as a result of *Driver's* negligence is much more problematic. Let us suppose that before she was injured, P was earning £20,000 a year net of tax. P's disability means that she is now in a job where she earns £12,000 a year net of tax. Let us further assume that P was 40 when she was injured.

It is *not* possible to say that had P not been injured she would probably have earned £8,000 a year more than she is currently earning up until retirement age (65) and that she should therefore be awarded (£8,000 × (65–40) =) £200,000 to compensate her for the future loss of income that she will probably suffer as a result of A's negligence. This is for three reasons.

First, P might not live until 65. If P's medical health is such that an actuary would predict that P will not survive beyond 60, then the damages payable to P in respect of the loss of income that she will probably suffer in the future as a result of P's negligence should be assessed on the basis that P will die at 60.

Secondly, P might not have continued to earn £20,000 a year net of tax but for P's negligence for the rest of her expected working lifespan. P might have been sacked, or been made redundant and found it difficult to find alternative employment. The damages payable to P to compensate her for the loss of income that she will probably suffer in the future as a result of A's negligence should be adjusted to take account of these possibilities.

Thirdly, suppose that we estimate that P will probably work for 20 more years and that, but for *Driver's* negligence, P would have earned £8,000 a year more over those years than she actually will. The damages paid to P *now* in respect of the loss of income that she will probably suffer in the future as a result of *Driver's* negligence should not equal the total amount of extra income P would probably have earned over her expected working lifespan, that is, (£8,000 × 20 =) £160,000. If they did, then P could invest the damages and earn a yearly income with them – made up of interest plus yearly withdrawals of portions of the capital sum invested – which would exceed the yearly income loss suffered by her as a result of *Driver's* negligence. So awarding P damages equal to the total amount of extra income P would have obtained over her expected lifespan had *Driver* not negligently injured her would overcompensate P: it would make P better off than she would have been had *Driver* not been negligent. To avoid this possibility, the damages payable to P should amount to a capital sum which, when properly invested, will yield P an annual income – made up of interest plus a proportion of the capital sum – equivalent to £8,000 a year for 20 years; at the end of which 20 years the capital sum will be used up. This capital sum will be considerably smaller than £160,000.

So one way of assessing how much P should be paid to compensate her for the loss of income that she will probably suffer in the future as a result of *Driver's* negligence would be to proceed as follows. First, ask: What is the difference between what P is earning now net of tax and what she would have been earning now net of tax had *Driver* not been negligent? (Say this is £8,000.) Then ask: How much of a working life has P probably got left to her? (Say this is 20 years.) Next, multiply £8,000 by 20 to get a rough idea of how much the total loss of income will be that P will suffer over the rest of her working life as a result of *Driver's* negligence: this gives us £160,000. Next, discount that sum to take account of the possibility that had *Driver* not been negligent, P would have been sacked or made redundant and might not have earned as much as £8,000 more over the rest of her working life than she will now earn over the rest of her working life. So if we discount £160,000 by 25%, this gives us a figure of £120,000, equivalent to a loss of income of £6,000 a year over the rest of P's expected working life.

Then we assess what sort of capital sum, properly invested, would produce a yearly income stream – made up of interest plus a proportion of the capital sum – of £6,000 a year over 20 years. Obviously this depends a lot on how we might expect P to invest the capital sum awarded. If we can expect P to invest the money only in very safe investments which produce a low rate of interest, then more of a capital sum must be awarded to P to produce the necessary income stream. If, on the other hand, we can expect P to invest her money in more risky investments which produce a higher rate of interest, then less of a capital sum must be awarded to P to produce the necessary income stream. In *Wells* v *Wells* (1999), the House of Lords ruled that in assessing the damages payable in respect of future loss of income it must be assumed that the payee will invest the damages in very safe, low-interest investments such as government index-linked bonds. The capital sum we finally come up with (say £112,000) is the sum P should be paid to compensate her for the loss of income that she will probably suffer in the future as a result of *Driver*'s negligence.

Instead, the courts adopt a slightly different method of assessing how much P should be paid by way of damages to compensate her for the loss of income that she will probably suffer in the future as a result of *Driver*'s negligence. This method is known as the *multiplier method*. What the courts do is assess the difference between what P now earns net of tax and what she would have been earning now net of tax had *Driver* not been negligent. This figure (here, £8,000) is known as the *multiplicand*. They then multiply the multiplicand by a figure (known as the *multiplier*) which takes into account: (a) the number of years that P can be expected to suffer that yearly loss of income; (b) the possibility that P would not actually have earned as much in the future as she was earning at the time *Driver* injured her; and (c) the fact that P is being awarded damages *now* in respect of future income loss and can therefore be expected to earn interest with those damages which will help to cover that future income loss.

The end result is exactly the same as is yielded by the approach suggested in the above paragraph (the courts might be expected to apply a multiplier of about 14 in the above case,[12] resulting in a damages award of £112,000). The multiplier approach simply represents a slightly different way of going about assessing the damages payable to P in respect of the loss of income that she will probably suffer in the future as a result of *Driver*'s negligence.

B. Loss of life expectancy

Suppose A has negligently injured B. Suppose further that B was 35 when she was injured and before she was injured she could have been expected to live to 70. However, B's injury now means that she can only be expected to live to 45.

B will, of course, be entitled to sue A for damages in respect of: her injury and any consequential non-pecuniary losses suffered by her as a result of that injury; any medical expenses incurred by her as a result of being injured; and any loss of income that she has suffered or is likely to suffer as a result of A's injuring her between the date of her injury and the date of her death (now anticipated to occur at 45).

It is, however, well established that B will *also* be entitled to sue A for damages in respect of the money she could have earned during the years that are now 'lost' to her as a result of

---

[12] Of course, if B had been younger when she was injured, a higher multiplier would be used to assess the damages payable to her. In practice, the courts will rarely apply a multiplier greater than 17 or 18 in assessing how much should be paid to compensate someone for a future loss of income.

A's negligence[13] provided that such an award would not be too speculative.[14] This is a bit puzzling: what earthly good would awarding B such damages do her? However, the point of awarding B such damages is *not* actually to compensate B but to ensure that any dependants of B – who would have been supported by B in the years that are now 'lost' to her – do not lose out as a result of B's expectation of life being reduced.[15] B can sue for damages in respect of the money she would have earned in the years that are now lost to her and thereby create a fund that will help to support her dependants after she dies.[16]

How do we assess how much B should be entitled to recover in respect of this loss of income? The courts again use a 'multiplier' approach. They first assess how much B could have been expected to earn per year net of tax in the years that are now 'lost' to her: say this is £50,000. They then deduct from that the yearly amount B would have spent on supporting herself in the years that are now 'lost' to her: call this £35,000.[17] Thus, £15,000 (the difference between £50,000 and £35,000) is the multiplicand used by the courts to determine how much B should be paid in damages. The courts then arrive at a multiplier, which takes into account the following factors: (i) the fact that B could have been expected to earn money for 20 of the 25 years that are now 'lost' to her as a result of A's negligence; (ii) the fact that had B not been injured she might not have earned £50,000 per year in the years that are now 'lost' to her: she might have been made redundant and found it difficult to find alternative employment; (iii) the fact that any damages awarded to B can be invested and produce an income stream which will help replace the yearly net amount that B would

---

[13] *Pickett v British Rail Engineering Ltd* [1980] AC 126, overruling *Oliver v Ashman* [1962] 2 QB 210. Section 1(1)(a) of the Administration of Justice Act 1982 prevents victims of torts who have suffered a 'loss of expectation of life' suing for damages to compensate them for that fact (so no action for loss of amenity can be brought in respect of the pleasures that a victim of a tort would have enjoyed in the years that are now 'lost' to her as a result of that tort being committed). However, s 1(2) of the same Act provides that s 1(1)(a) does not apply to actions for 'damages in respect of loss of income'.

[14] It was for this reason that the Court of Appeal ruled in *Croke (a minor) v Wiseman* [1982] 1 WLR 171 that damages for the years that have been 'lost' could *never* be awarded to a young child whose life expectancy has been reduced by the defendant's tort. The Court of Appeal expressed some unhappiness with this decision in *Iqbal v Whipps Cross University Hospital NHS Trust* [2007] EWCA Civ 1190 (life expectancy of infant reduced to 41 due to negligence of defendants when he was being born) but held that as *Croke* was not 'manifestly wrong', they were bound by it.

[15] However, B will be entitled to sue A for damages in respect of the money she would have earned in the years that are now lost to her even if she has no dependants who would have been supported by her in those years.

[16] See Lord Diplock's explanation of the decision in *Pickett v British Rail Engineering Ltd* in *Gammell v Wilson* [1982] AC 27, at 64–5; also Lord Phillips MR in *Gregg v Scott* [2005] 2 AC 176, at [177]–[181]. An alert student might raise the following objection to this explanation. 'Surely after B dies, B's dependants will be entitled in any case to bring a claim for loss of support against A under the Fatal Accidents Act 1976? So why would the law go to such lengths to allow B to protect her dependants while she is still alive?' However, if B sues A for damages before she dies, B's dependants will lose any rights they might otherwise have had to sue A under the 1976 Act – and B will almost certainly want and need to sue A before she dies in order to get some compensation for the losses that she is *currently* suffering as a result of A's negligence. However, on this point, see: (1) Lord Phillips MR in *Gregg v Scott* [2005] 2 AC 176, arguing at [182] that 'It would be much better if [B] had no right to recover for such loss of earnings [that would have been made in the 'lost years'] and the dependants' right to claim under [s] 1(1) of the Fatal Accidents Act 1976 subsisted despite the claimants' recovery of damages for his injury. I am not persuaded that this result could not be achieved by a purposive construction of that section.' (2) Section 3 of the Damages Act 1996, which provides that 'The award of provisional damages [to the victim of a tort] shall not operate as a bar to an action in respect of that person's death under the Fatal Accidents Act 1976', though the award may be taken into account in judging how much a claimant bringing a claim under the 1976 Act has in fact lost by way of a loss of support.

[17] This is consistent with the reason why B is allowed to sue A for damages in respect of the money she would have earned in the years that are now 'lost' to her. As the object of awarding her such damages is really to compensate B's dependants, if any, for the loss of support that they will suffer on B's premature death, there is no reason to allow B to claim damages in respect of any income that she would have earned in the years that are now 'lost' to her that she would merely have spent on supporting herself.

have earned and not spent on herself in the years that are now 'lost' to her. They then multiply the multiplier and multiplicand together to arrive at the figure B should be awarded in damages to compensate her for the money she would have made in the years that are now 'lost' to her.

C. Property damage

Let us now consider what the position is if *Driver* negligently damages property belonging to *Owner*. Assuming that the damage to property is actionable, how do we go about determining how much *Owner* should be paid so as to compensate him for the fact that his property has been damaged?

The courts' answer is: *As a general rule*, *Owner* should be paid damages equal to the amount of money it would have cost *Owner* to repair the property in question had he repaired that property at the time it was first reasonable for him to do so.

So, for example, in *Dodd Properties (Kent) Ltd* v *Canterbury City Council* (1980), the defendants built a multi-storey car park beside a building owned by the claimants. The building work took place in 1968. Due to the defendants' negligence in carrying out pile-driving operations for the foundations, serious structural damage was done to the claimants' building. The earliest time the claimants could have repaired the building was in 1970 when it would have cost £11,375 to repair the building. However, the claimants could not easily raise the funds to do the repairs at that date and were in any case uncertain as to whether or not they would be able to claim back the cost of the repairs from the defendants. Given this, they decided to hold off doing any repairs until they had sued the defendants. The claimants' case was heard in 1978, by which time the cost of doing the repairs had risen to £30,327. The Court of Appeal held that the claimants had acted reasonably in delaying repairing their building until they had sued the defendants and therefore held that the claimants should be awarded damages in respect of the damage done to their property equal to the cost of repairing the building in 1978. The Court of Appeal therefore awarded the claimants £30,327 in damages.[18]

The general rule set out above is subject to three exceptions.

(1) If, when *Owner*'s property was damaged, it would have been *cheaper to replace* it rather than repair it then the compensation for the damage done to *Owner*'s property will *usually* be assessed by reference to the cost of replacing it rather than repairing it. The cost of repair measure of compensation will still be used if the property in question was so special to *Owner* that it would have been unreasonable to expect him to have replaced it rather than repaired it.

So in *O'Grady* v *Westminster Scaffolding Ltd* (1962), the defendant negligently damaged the claimant's 1938 MG motor car. The claimant could have bought a replacement car for about £185 but his MG was his 'pride and joy' and so he decided to keep it and spent about £250 repairing it. It was held that the claimant was entitled to damages for the damage done to his car assessed according to the cost of repair measure: given his special attachment to his car, it would have been unreasonable to expect him to have scrapped it and bought a replacement car.

---

[18] See also the Privy Council decision in *Alcoa Minerals of Jamaica Inc* v *Broderick* [2002] 1 AC 371, which endorsed the decision in *Dodd Properties*.

It was different in *Darbishire* v *Warran* (1963). In that case, the claimant's car was badly damaged in a collision caused by the defendant's negligence. The claimant had owned the car for about four years and it had always proved reliable. Rather than look for a replacement – which would have cost about £80 – the claimant chose, more out of inertia than anything, to have the car repaired instead. The repairs cost him about £192. The court held that the claimant was entitled to damages for the damage done to his car assessed according to the cost of replacement measure: it would not have been unreasonable to expect the claimant to have bought a new car rather than have his old, damaged, one repaired. So the claimant was awarded £80 as compensation for the damage done to his car, with the result that he was left out of pocket by £112.

(2) If the property that was damaged by *Driver*'s negligence was *valueless* to *Owner* – for example, *Owner* was going to scrap it – then *Owner* will not be entitled to recover the cost of repairing that property from *Driver*.

(3) If the property that was damaged by *Driver*'s negligence was *in need of repair anyway* and performing that repair work would at the same time repair the damage done by *Driver*'s negligence, *Owner* will not be entitled to recover anything for the cost of repairing the damage done to his property by *Driver*'s negligence.

So in *Performance Cars Ltd* v *Abraham* (1962), the defendant negligently drove his car into the claimant's Rolls-Royce. The front wing of the claimant's Rolls-Royce was damaged as a result. It was agreed that in order to repair the damage the whole of the lower part of the Rolls-Royce would need to be resprayed. However, at the time of the collision, the rear wing of the Rolls-Royce was already damaged and *that* damage could only be repaired by respraying the whole of the lower part of the Rolls-Royce. The Court of Appeal held that the claimant was not entitled to sue the defendant for anything by way of damages: at the time of the accident, the Rolls-Royce was already in need of a respray and carrying out that respray would, as well as repairing the damage to the rear wing of the Rolls-Royce, at the same time repair the damage done by the defendant to the front wing of the Rolls-Royce.

Now let's consider the situation where *Driver* has negligently damaged a car belonging to *Owner*, and *Owner* is entitled to sue *Driver* for the reasonable costs of repairing that car. While the car is being repaired, *Owner* will be deprived of the use of that car, and will be entitled to sue for damages in respect of that. However, the basis on which such damages should be assessed has occasioned some controversy. If *Owner* has hired a replacement car, and has acted reasonably in hiring the car at the rate he did, then *Owner* can sue for the costs of hiring that replacement car.[19] But other cases are not so simple.

The first variation we can call *No Hire*. In this variation, *Owner* never hired a replacement car: he simply used another car that he had in his garage to get around, or borrowed a replacement from his neighbour. The second variation we can call *Unreasonable Hire*. In this variation, *Owner* hired a replacement car but it was unreasonable for him to do so. For example, while his car was being repaired, *Owner* was going on holiday anyway, so had no need for a replacement car – but he hired one anyway, which he left outside his house while

---

[19] *Lagden* v *O'Connor* [2004] 1 AC 1067 (discussed above, § 9.12). *Bee* v *Jenson* [2007] 4 All ER 791 seems to suggest (at [15] and [22]) that *Owner* can recover the cost of hiring the replacement car even if someone else covered the cost for him. It is not clear that the suggestion is limited to the situation considered in *Bee*, where an insurer covers the cost of hiring the replacement car; and if it is not so limited (and a friend paid for the replacement car) whether any damages payable for the cost of hire would be held on trust for the person who actually incurred that cost.

he was away. In both the *No Hire* and *Unreasonable Hire* case, *Owner* will *not* be entitled to sue for the costs of hiring a replacement car.[20] But can he get anything for the fact that he has been deprived of the use of his car while it is being repaired?

The Court of Appeal has ruled in *Beechwood Birmingham Ltd* v *Hoyer Group UK Ltd* (2011) that in a *No Hire* or *Unreasonable Hire* case, we need to distinguish between cases where *Owner* is a private person and where *Owner* is a company. Damages for the loss of the use of a car that belongs to a *company* while it is being repaired will – in a *No Hire* or *Unreasonable Hire* situation – equal the interest payable on the capital value of the car for the period that it is being repaired.[21] In contrast, where the owner of the damaged car that is being repaired is a private person, damages for the loss of the use of the damaged car while it is being repaired will simply aim to compensate *Owner* for any inconvenience he may suffer as a result of being deprived of the use of that car.[22] So in the situation where *Owner* is on holiday anyway while his car is being repaired, no such damages will be payable.

28.4 REDUCTION (1): RECEIPT OF BENEFIT

In this section, we look at when the compensatory damages payable to the victim of a tort will be reduced because the victim obtained some benefit from that tort being committed. The *general rule* is that the damages payable to the victim of a tort will be reduced to take account of a benefit that she has obtained as a result of that tort being committed, unless there is some good reason why they should not be. We will now look at a range of benefits that the victim of a tort might obtain from that tort being committed and see which will work to reduce the damages payable to the victim, and which will not.

A. Savings on food and other necessities

Suppose that *Careless* negligently injured *Unlucky*, with the result that *Unlucky* had to stay for a few weeks in a private hospital, having his injuries treated. Suppose further that while he was in the hospital, the hospital provided him with meals. *Careless* will of course be liable to compensate *Unlucky* for the medical bills he has incurred in being treated.

However, in this situation *Careless*'s negligence will have resulted in *Unlucky* receiving a benefit: while he was in hospital, he did not have to buy his own food. *Careless*'s liability will be reduced to take account of this saving that *Unlucky* has made.[23] So suppose that *Unlucky*'s medical bills came to £10,000; but in the time *Unlucky* was in hospital, he would have spent £500 on buying food for himself. On these figures, *Careless* will only be liable to pay *Unlucky* £9,500 in compensatory damages – *Careless*'s *prima facie* liability to pay *Unlucky* £10,000 in damages will be reduced to take account of the fact that *Unlucky* saved £500 that he would otherwise have spent on buying food for himself while he was in hospital.[24]

---

[20] In *Unreasonable Hire*, this will be either because *Owner*'s unreasonable hiring of a replacement car broke the chain of causation between *Driver*'s negligence and the expenses incurred by *Owner* in hiring the replacement car, or because *Owner* unreasonably failed to mitigate the loss suffered by him as a result of *Driver*'s negligence in unreasonably incurring the expense of hiring a replacement car.

[21] [2011] QB 357, at [52].

[22] [2011] QB 357, at [48]–[49].

[23] *Shearman* v *Folland* [1950] 2 KB 43.

[24] Of course, *Unlucky*'s medical bills will almost certainly include a charge for the food *Unlucky* received while he was in hospital but that is immaterial. At the same time as *Unlucky* was paying the hospital for the food that the hospital served him, he was saving money which he would have spent had *Careless* not injured him on buying food for himself.

The same point will apply if, had *Unlucky* not been in hospital, he would have spent money on necessities that were provided by the hospital, such as washing *Unlucky*'s clothes. The damages payable to *Unlucky* will be reduced to take account of this saving.

B. Compensation payments from other defendants liable in tort

Suppose that *Driver* negligently ran over *Pedestrian*'s leg, but a failure to treat the leg properly in hospital by *Doctor* resulted in *Pedestrian* ('P') losing the leg. Suppose that £100,000 would be sufficient to compensate P for the loss of his leg. Each of *Doctor* and *Driver* will be liable to pay this sum to P. If *Doctor*'s settles P's claim against him for a certain sum of money, this will reduce the amount of money P is entitled to sue *Driver* for: the compensation payment from *Doctor* will count as a benefit that P has received as a result of *Driver*'s tort.

The difficult question is by how much *Driver*'s liability to P will be reduced. Obviously, if *Doctor*'s compensation payment to P came to £100,000, then *Driver* will not be liable to pay P anything. P will be fully compensated for the losses that she suffered as a result of *Driver*'s tort and will therefore not be entitled to sue *Driver* for anything.[25] But what if *Doctor*'s compensation payment came to only £80,000? The normal rule is that P will be entitled to sue *Driver* for £20,000 – the balance of the uncompensated loss that she suffered as a result of *Driver*'s tort. However, there are two situations in which *Doctor*'s compensation payment to P of £80,000 will have the effect of extinguishing *entirely* *Driver*'s liability to P.

(1) It used to be the case that if A and C were *jointly liable* to compensate B for the losses suffered by her, then any compensation payment by C to B would have the effect of discharging A's liability to B. However, the position nowadays is a bit more complicated.

If C's compensation payment was made because B won a *judgment* against C, then C's payment will not have the effect of extinguishing B's rights to sue A for compensation: A will therefore be liable to make up any shortfall in the compensation paid by C to B.[26] If, on the other hand, C's compensation payment was made to B under a settlement that he reached with B, then the old rule will apply – and A's liability to B will be extinguished – *unless* B's settlement with C preserved her rights to sue A for damages in respect of the losses suffered by her:[27] in which case, A will again be liable to make up any shortfall in the compensation C has paid B.

As it happens the law on joint liability will not apply in *Driver*'s case. This is because joint liability will only arise where one defendant is vicariously liable, or liable as an accessory, for another's tort.[28] Neither apply here: *Driver* and *Doctor*'s torts were committed independently of each other. So in this situation *Driver* and *Doctor* will be *jointly and severally* liable to compensate P for the loss of her leg.[29]

---

[25] However, *Doctor* will be entitled to make a claim in contribution against *Driver*, forcing *Driver* to shoulder a 'just and equitable' share of the burden of compensating P for the losses she has suffered: see above, § 5.3(F) (2).

[26] Civil Liability (Contribution) Act 1978, s 3: 'Judgment recovered against any person liable in respect of any . . . damage shall not be a bar to an action . . . against any other person who is . . . jointly liable with him in respect of the same . . . damage.'

[27] *Gardiner* v *Moore* [1969] 1 QB 55.

[28] See chapters 36–37, below.

[29] See by *The Koursk* [1924] P 140. In that case, two ships – the *Clan Chisholm* and the *Koursk* – collided with each other. The collision occurred as a result of the negligence of both the owners of the *Clan Chisholm* and the negligence of the defendants, the owners of the *Koursk*. As a result of the collision, the *Clan Chisholm* collided with the claimants' vessel, the *Itria*, which sank. In this case the owners of the *Clan Chisholm* and the defendants, the owners of the *Koursk*, were each liable in tort to compensate the claimants for the loss of the *Itria*: each of

(2) Even though *Doctor* and *Driver* were *jointly and severally* liable to compensate P for the loss of her leg, a compensation payment of £80,000 by *Doctor* to P will still have had the effect of extinguishing *Driver*'s liability to P if P treated *Doctor*'s payment of £80,000 to her as *fully compensating* her for the loss of that leg. This odd rule owes its existence to the decision of the House of Lords in *Jameson v Central Electricity Generating Board* (2000). The rule exists for the protection of *Doctor* who, having settled P's claim against him, might find – if P subsequently dies because of medical complications arising out the loss of his leg – that *Driver* has been found liable to pay a substantial sum to P's dependants for the loss of support that they have suffered as a result of P's death, and that *Driver* now wants *Doctor* to contribute to his liability. In the interests of allowing *Doctor* to wash his hands of any further liabilities that he might incur as a result of what has happened to P, the House of Lords ruled in *Jameson* that if *Doctor*'s compensation payment to P is treated by P as fully compensating P for the loss of her leg, P will then lose her right to sue *Driver* for compensation for the loss of her leg. This means that if P subsequently dies of complications arising out of the loss of his leg, P's dependants will not be able to sue *Driver* for loss of support under the Fatal Accidents Act 1976 (and *Doctor* will not have to fear *Driver* subsequently making a contribution claim against him). This is because P's dependants will not be able to show – as they are required to under the 1976 Act – that had P lived longer, she would have been entitled to sue *Driver* for damages.[30]

C. Redundancy payments

Suppose that *Careless* negligently injured *Employee* and as a result *Employee* was unable to continue in her job and was made redundant. Any redundancy payment received by *Employee* on leaving her job will operate to reduce the damages payable by *Careless* to *Employee*.[31]

D. Social security payments

Suppose that A negligently injured B and B was incapacitated as a result. Suppose that as a result of her being incapacitated, B received quite a lot of money in social security payments. The Social Security (Recovery of Benefits) Act 1997 establishes that the social security payments that B received as a result of her being incapacitated in the first *five* years after A injured her will be taken into account in determining the damages payable to B; however, any subsequent social security payments will be disregarded. At first sight, the Act seems to work in A's favour. However, the Act also provides that if A makes a compensation payment to B, he will be liable to compensate the State for *all* the social security payments that B received as a result of her being incapacitated in the first five years after A injured her. This can cause injustice if A is not wholly to blame for the fact that B was injured.

---

them committed the tort of negligence in relation to the claimants and the *Itria* would not have been sunk had not each of them been negligent. However, as their negligent acts were unconnected, the owners of the *Clan Chisholm* and the defendants were not *jointly* liable to compensate the owners of the *Itria* for the loss of the *Itria*; they were jointly and severally liable. So when the owners of the *Clan Chisholm* made a compensation payment to the owners of the *Itria*, that did not have the effect of extinguishing the liability of the defendants to the owners of the *Itria*. The defendants were still liable to compensate the owners of the *Itria* for the balance of the uncompensated loss that they had suffered as a result of the sinking of the *Itria*.

[30] See below, § 34.4.

[31] *Colledge v Bass Mitchells & Butlers Ltd* [1988] 1 All ER 536.

E. Gifts

The damages payable to the victim of a tort will *not* be reduced to take account of the value of any gifts that she received from sympathetic friends and relatives who wanted to help or comfort her in the aftermath of the tort. Suppose, for example, that *Driver* negligently ran over *Builder* and as a result *Builder* was laid up for a while. *Friend* gave *Builder* £500 'to tide you over until you are back on your feet and able to work again'. The damages payable to *Builder* will not be reduced to take account of the £500 that *Builder* has received from *Friend*, even though *Builder* would not have received that money but for *Driver*'s tort. There are two reasons for this. First, if the damages were reduced, then *Friend*'s gift would end up working to benefit *Driver*, not *Builder*. As the gift was made for *Builder*'s benefit, and not *Driver*, this would be unfair. Secondly, if the damages were reduced, *Friend* might be discouraged from helping *Builder* out, on the basis that in the long run, his helping *Builder* would only benefit *Driver*.

F. Insurance payments

In *Bradburn* v *Great Western Railway Co* (1874), the defendant railway company's negligence caused the claimant to be injured while he was travelling on the defendants' line. The claimant sued the defendants for compensatory damages. Compensation for the actionable losses suffered by the claimant as a result of his injuries was assessed at £217. However, the claimant had received, on account of his injuries, £31 from his insurance company, the Accidental Insurance Company. The question was whether the claimant was entitled to recover £217 or (£217 − £31 =) £186 in compensatory damages from the defendants. It was held that even though the £31 received by the claimant was a benefit which he received as a result of the defendants' negligence – had the defendants not been negligent he would never have received that £31 – the claimant was still entitled to recover £217 from the defendants in compensatory damages.[32]

Why didn't the court hold that the claimant could only sue the defendants for £186? The reason is that had they done this all the premiums paid by the claimant on his insurance policy with the Accidental Insurance Company would have gone to waste. He would have obtained no benefit from them. Instead, the defendants would have been the ones who benefited from the insurance premiums paid by the claimant. As the claimant paid those premiums for his benefit and not for the benefit of anyone else, this would have been unfair. As Asquith LJ remarked in *Shearman* v *Folland* (1950):

---

[32] The claimant – having obtained those damages – would have been entitled to keep the damages for himself. What is the position if A negligently destroys B's property, B obtains the value of the property from his property insurer, and then sues A for damages equal to the value of the property? B will be entitled to recover the full value of the property from A – for the reasons set out below, the damages payable to B will not be reduced to take account of the insurance payment that B has already obtained in respect of the destruction of his property – but B's insurance company will then have a charge over those damages for the value of the insurance money it paid out to B: *Lord Napier and Ettrick* v *Hunter* [1993] AC 713. The reason why B's insurance company will have a charge over the damages is to prevent double recovery. (For the same reason, if A tortiously causes B to suffer some kind of pure economic loss that B was insured against, B will be entitled to claim on her insurance policy but will then hold any damages obtained against A subject to a charge for the insurance company.) The reason why contracts of insurance against physical injury – such as the contract of insurance in *Bradburn* – are 'different' is that the concern to prevent double recovery will not apply in the cases where a claimant suffers physical injury as a result of someone's committing a tort in relation to her. The courts acknowledge that it is impossible to determine what would amount to an 'adequate' level of compensation for the physical injury suffered by the claimant – so people should be left free to insure their persons so as to 'boost' the amount of money they will be able to recover if someone physically injures them.

If the wrongdoer were entitled to set-off what the wrongdoer was entitled to recoup or had recouped under his policy, he would, in effect, be depriving the claimant of all benefit from the premiums paid by the latter and appropriating that benefit to himself.[33]

Three points may be made about this:

(1) There could have been no objection if the Court in *Bradburn* had held that the claimant would only be entitled to recover £186 in compensatory damages from the defendants *if* the defendants repaid all the premiums paid by the claimant on his insurance policy with the Accidental Insurance Company.[34] However, it probably did not occur to the court to decide the *Bradburn* case in this way.

(2) What would have been the position if the *defendants* had paid the insurance premiums on the claimant's insurance policy with the Accidental Insurance Company? Say, for example, that the claimant had been an employee of the defendants and they had taken out the insurance policy for his benefit to protect him against the risk of being killed or injured while he worked for them. Recent authority indicates that if this had been the case, then the claimant would have been limited to suing the defendants for £186.[35] This is quite right: in the case just described, no injustice would have been done to anyone if the defendants had been allowed to take advantage of the premiums paid on the claimant's insurance policy – after all, they paid those premiums in the first place.

(3) What would have been the position if a *Third Party* had paid the premiums on the claimant's insurance policy with the Accidental Insurance Company for him? If this had been the case, should the court have held that the claimant could only sue the defendants for £186? Subsequent authorities seem to say that the answer to this question is 'yes'.[36] However, it is more complex than that. We can imagine two variations on the situation we are now imagining obtained in *Bradburn*, where *Third Party* paid the insurance premiums on the claimant's policy with the Accidental Insurance Company.

In the first case, *Third Party* intended, when he paid the premiums, that the claimant and no one else should get the benefit of those premiums. If this had been the case, it would have been unfair – unfair on *Third Party* – for the court to allow the defendants to take advantage of the payment of those premiums and hold that the claimant was only entitled to recover £186 in compensatory damages from the defendants. The right decision would have been to hold that the claimant could sue the defendants for £217.

In the second case, *Third Party* paid the premiums because he was contractually obliged to do so under an arrangement with the claimant – say John was the claimant's employer – and, in paying the premiums, had no intention one way or the other as to who should benefit from the payment of those premiums. If this had been the case, it would *not* have been unfair for the court to allow the defendants to take advantage of the payment of those premiums and hold that the claimant could sue the defendants for £186. Given this, that is what the court should have held.

---

[33] [1950] 2 KB 43, 46.
[34] *Bristol & West Building Society* v *May, May & Merrimans (No 2)* [1998] 1 WLR 336, 356.
[35] *Gaca* v *Pirelli General plc* [2004] 1 WLR 2683.
[36] *Hussain* v *New Taplow Paper Mills* [1988] 1 AC 514, 527; *Hodgson* v *Trapp* [1989] 1 AC 807, 819; *Bristol & West Building Society* v *May, May & Merrimans (No 2)* [1998] 1 WLR 336, 358–9.

G. Pension payments[37]

In *Parry* v *Cleaver* (1970), the claimant was prevented from carrying on working as a police constable as a result of injuries he sustained in a traffic accident caused by the defendant's negligence. At the time of the accident the claimant was 35 years old and had worked as a police constable for 12 years. Throughout his time in the force the claimant had made a weekly contribution to the police pension fund. On being invalided out of the force, the claimant obtained an invalidity pension of £204 a year. It was found that had the claimant not been injured, he would have continued working as a police constable until the age of 48 and would then have retired on a pension of £515 a year and found work in the civilian sector. As it was, the claimant's injury meant he had to find work in the civilian sector at the age of 35 and he did not receive a retirement pension at all.

So the defendant's negligence caused the claimant to suffer two losses: (1) the loss of the extra money the claimant would have earned net of tax between the ages of 35 and 48 had he continued working for the police and not been forced to work in the civilian sector (say this loss was worth £5,000); (2) the loss of the extra pension money the claimant would have received from the age of 48 until the end of his life had he not been invalided out of the police force (this was worth £311 a year: the difference between the retirement pension that the claimant would have received had he stayed on in the police force until he was 48 and the invalidity pension that the claimant actually did receive as a result of being invalided out of the police force).

However, the defendant's negligence also meant that the claimant would receive a benefit between the ages of 35 and 48: an invalidity pension payment of £204 a year. Had the defendant not been negligent, the claimant would not have received that payment. The House of Lords held that this benefit should not be taken into account in determining the damages payable to the claimant, on the ground that if it were then the claimant would lose the benefit of his 12 years' worth of contributions to the police pension fund that he made before he was injured.[38]

Parry v *Cleaver* was followed in *Smoker* v *London Fire Authority* (1991). In that case, the claimant was employed as a firefighter by the defendants. Under the terms of his employment, he was a member of a pension scheme to which he contributed approximately 11% of his wages. The defendants contributed twice as much as the claimant towards his pension. In 1985 the claimant was disabled as a result of the defendants' negligence and his disability meant he had to retire from the force in December 1985. Had the defendants not been negligent, the claimant would have continued to work as a firefighter until December 1987, when he was due to retire.

The defendants' negligence therefore resulted in the claimant suffering a loss of income: the money the claimant would have earned in the two years between December 1985 and December 1987 had he been allowed to continue to work for the defendants. This loss was worth about £13,500. At the same time the defendants' negligence resulted in the claimant obtaining a benefit during those two years. The claimant received about £10,000 in invalidity pension payments in the two years between December 1985 and December 1987.

---

[37] See Lewis 1999, 81–6.

[38] This is not quite true. The claimant was allowed to sue the defendant for the extra pension money he would have received after the age of 48 had he not been invalided out of the police force and that extra pension money would have been payable in part because of the 12 years' worth of contributions that the claimant made to the police pension fund. So the claimant would still have obtained something for those 12 years' worth of contributions even if the damages payable to him had been reduced to take account of the invalidity pension payments he was going to receive between the ages of 35 and 48 as a result of the defendant's negligence.

These payments were made out of the claimant's pension scheme in consideration of the contributions that he and the defendants made to that pension scheme.

The House of Lords held, following *Parry* v *Cleaver*, that the invalidity pension payments made to the claimant between December 1985 and December 1987 were not to be taken into account in calculating the damages payable to the claimant. So the claimant was entitled to recover £13,500 in compensatory damages from the defendants in respect of the loss of income suffered by him between December 1985 and December 1987: no deduction would be made to take account of the fact that the claimant had in fact received a benefit of about £10,000 in invalidity pension payments as a result of the defendants' negligence during those two years. This decision can be criticised. The pension payments that the claimant received between December 1985 and December 1987 could be split into two. One-third of those payments (approximately £3,300) were attributable to the contributions that the claimant made to his pension scheme. Two-thirds (approximately £6,700) were attributable to the contributions that the defendants made to the claimant's pension scheme.

Now it might be conceded that the £3,300 that the claimant received in pension payments between December 1985 and December 1987 and that were attributable to the claimant's contributions to his pension scheme should not have been taken into account in determining the damages payable to the claimant, on the ground that if they were that would be unfair on the claimant. However, it would not have been unfair – either on the claimant or on the defendants – to deduct the remaining pension payments, that were attributable to the *defendants'* contributions to the claimant's pension scheme, from the damages payable to the claimant.

The House of Lords recognised the strength of this point in the case of *Hussain* v *New Taplow Paper Mills Ltd* (1988). In that case the claimant was injured in an accident due to the negligence of the defendants, his employers, and was unable, due to his injuries, to continue working for the defendants. For 15 months after the accident, the defendants continued to pay the claimant his full pay – even though he was not doing any work for them – under their 'permanent health insurance scheme'. This scheme was paid for by the defendants: the defendants' employees, including the claimant, made no contribution to this scheme. The claimant sued the defendants in negligence for damages to compensate him for the loss of income that he had suffered as a result of the defendants' negligence.

The House of Lords held that the health insurance payments that the claimant had received for 15 months after he had stopped work should be taken into account in determining the damages payable to the claimant. The House of Lords held that deducting these payments from the damages payable to the claimant would not be unfair on the claimant. The claimant could not claim that making such a deduction would result in him receiving no benefit from the contributions he had made to the defendants' health insurance scheme: the claimant made no such contributions.

H. Windfall payments

In *Needler Financial Services Ltd* v *Taber* (2002), the defendants negligently advised the claimant to switch pension schemes. The claimant did so and lost out as a result: the pension scheme that he switched into (with the Norwich Union) was not as profitable as his original pension scheme. He sued the defendants for damages. The defendants admitted liability but claimed that the damages payable to the claimant should be reduced because the claimant received a windfall payment of about £7,800 when the Norwich Union demutualised. Sir Andrew Morritt V-C held that this benefit – which the claimant had received as a result of the defendants' negligent advice – should *not* be taken into account in determining the damages payable to the claimant. It is hard to understand why it should not have been. However, one possible explanation is that the claimant might have already spent the windfall payment that he received from the Norwich Union. If he had, then taking that windfall payment into account in determining the damages payable to the claimant would have made him, through no fault of his own, worse off overall – which would have been unfair to the claimant.

I. Gains made through the exercise of skill and judgment

In *Hussey* v *Eels* (1990), the defendants fraudulently induced the claimants to buy their house. The house was, to the defendants' knowledge, affected by subsidence but the defendants told the claimants that to their knowledge the property had not been subject to subsidence. The claimants purchased the defendants' house for approximately £53,000. The true value of the house was about £36,000 as repairing it would have cost in excess of £17,000. So the defendants' fraud caused the claimants to lose £17,000. However the claimants, having discovered the problem with subsidence, then began to turn things around. They decided not to have the house repaired. Instead, they demolished it and sought planning permission to build two bungalows on the vacant plot. This was granted and the claimants then sold the land to a developer with the planning permission for £78,500.

So – having initially lost £17,000, the claimants' ingenuity meant that they made a gain of £42,500 on selling the land on which their house was originally built: they obtained £78,500 in return for an asset which was originally worth £36,000 in their hands. The claimants then sued the defendants for the original £17,000 that they had lost in buying the defendants' house. The defendants claimed that the £42,500 profit that the claimants made on selling the land on which the house was built should be taken into account in assessing the damages payable to the claimants. So in effect they argued that they should not be held liable to the claimants at all. The Court of Appeal rejected the defendants' claim. This was quite right: had the claimants' profit been taken into account, all the work and planning they did in improving the value of their land would have redounded to the benefit of the defendants. So the defendants were correctly held liable to pay the claimants £17,000 in damages.

J. Psychic benefits

In *Wise* v *Kaye* (1962), Sellers LJ remarked that:

> The complete loss of sight may bring, and I think often does, a serenity and calm of life which might lead to a happiness hitherto unknown, but I cannot think that a defendant is entitled to pray that in aid in order to reduce the damages he has to pay to the sufferer. [Similarly if] [i]nfirmity which cripples and incapacitates a man . . . [brings] him a sympathy and attention which reveals in him an inward comfort which he has never previously known [making him] happier than he has ever been.[39]

[39] [1962] 1 QB 638, 651.

28.5 REDUCTION (2): CONTRIBUTORY NEGLIGENCE

Section 1(1) of the Law Reform (Contributory Negligence) Act 1945 provides that where:

> any person suffers damage as the result partly of his own fault and partly of the fault of any other person or persons ... the damages recoverable in respect thereof shall be reduced to such extent as the court thinks just and equitable having regard to the claimant's share in the responsibility of the damage.

Section 4 of the 1945 Act provides that:

> 'fault' means negligence, breach of statutory duty or other act or omission which gives rise to liability in tort or would, apart from this Act, give rise to a defence of contributory negligence.

A number of different points need to be made about the scope of the defence of contributory negligence.[40]

A. Defendant's conduct

The 1945 Act says that the defence of contributory negligence can be pleaded where the damage suffered by the claimant was 'the result ... partly of the fault of [some] other person' where 'fault' is defined as meaning 'negligence, breach of statutory duty' or some other form of conduct which, before 1945, would have given rise to a defence of contributory negligence. So contributory negligence will *not* be available as a defence to *all* torts. There will be some torts where the fact that the claimant was partly to blame for the fact that she suffered the loss she did will not go to reduce the damages payable to the claimant. If the tort committed by A was conversion or amounted to an intentional trespass to B's goods, then the defence will not apply;[41] nor will it if the tort committed by A was deceit[42] or involved dishonesty of any kind[43] (as will be the case if the tort committed by A was conspiracy or inducing a breach of contract). In *Standard Chartered Bank v Pakistan National Shipping Corporation (Nos 2 and 4)* (2003), Lord Rodger of Earlsferry stated that 'contributory negligence [has] never been a defence open to a defendant who ... intended to harm the [claimant]'.[44] Although a defendant may assault or batter a claimant without necessarily having an intention to harm the claimant,[45] the Court of Appeal ruled in *Co-operative Group* v *Pritchard* (2011) that 'the 1945 Act cannot, in principle, be used to reduce damages in cases where claims are based on assault and battery ...'.[46]

B. Claimant's conduct

If A has committed a tort in relation to B to which the defence of contributory negligence applies, then the compensatory damages payable to B will be reduced if it was 'partly [her] own fault' that she suffered the losses she did as a result of A's tort. The House of Lords made it clear in *Reeves v Commissioner of Police of the Metropolis* (2000) that 'fault' does not

---

[40] On which, see generally Gravells 1977.

[41] Section 11 of the Torts (Interference with Goods) Act 1977 provides that 'Contributory negligence is no defence in proceedings founded on conversion, or on intentional trespass to goods.'

[42] *Alliance & Leicester Building Society* v *Edgestop Ltd* [1993] 1 WLR 1462; *Standard Chartered Bank* v *Pakistan National Shipping Corporation (Nos 2 and 4)* [2003] 1 AC 959.

[43] *Corporacion Nacional de Cobre* v *Sogemin* [1997] 1 WLR 1396.

[44] [2003] 1 AC 959, at [45].

[45] See above, § 2.3.

[46] [2011] EWCA Civ 329, at [62] (per Aikens LJ), disapproving Lord Denning MR's suggestion to the contrary in *Murphy v Culhane* [1977] QB 94, at 98–9.

just cover an inadvertent act by the victim of a tort that contributed to her own loss – it also covers a deliberate act (here, self-harm) that contributed to the losses that the victim of a tort suffered as a result of that tort being committed.[47] However it should be noted that where A has committed a tort in relation to B and that tort has resulted in B suffering some kind of loss because B did something deliberate *after* A committed his tort, B may be barred *completely* from suing for that loss, either on the basis that B's deliberate act broke the chain of causation between A's tort and B's loss,[48] or on the basis that B's deliberate act meant she failed to mitigate the loss suffered by her as a result of A's tort.[49]

In judging whether the losses suffered by the victim of a tort were 'partly [her] own fault', one first asks whether the victim of a tort did anything to contribute to the fact that she suffered those losses, and if she did, one then asks whether a reasonable person of her age[50] and in her physical condition[51] would have acted in the way she did. Subject to one doubt, if a reasonable person of the victim's age and in the victim's physical condition would not have acted as she did, then we would find that the losses suffered by the victim were 'partly [her] own fault'.

The one doubt arises in the case where the victim of a tort suffered from a mental illness that led her to do something that contributed to the losses that she suffered as a result of that tort. For example, consider the **Horrible Seat-Belt Problem**:

> *Teen* suffered from a mental illness that meant that she could not bear the feeling of a seat-belt against her body. One day, she was travelling in the back of a car that *Driver* negligently crashed into. *Teen* was badly injured in the crash. Had she been wearing a seat belt, she either would not have been injured at all, or her injuries would have been substantially mitigated.

Should the damages payable to *Teen* by *Driver* be reduced for contributory negligence? There is no doubt that a reasonable person of *Teen*'s age and in her physical condition would have been wearing a seat-belt at the time of the crash. But does that mean we should say that *Teen*'s injuries were 'partly [her] own fault'? There is authority that says 'yes' to this question, and holds that the damages payable should be reduced for contributory negligence.[52] However, the recent case of *Corr* v *IBC Vehicles Ltd* (2008)[53] (which we discuss in detail below) indicates that we should adopt a more nuanced approach. If *Teen*'s mental illness meant that she literally had *no choice* whether or not to wear the seat-belt, then the Law Lords in *Corr* were agreed that the damages payable to *Teen* should not be reduced for contributory negligence. On the other hand, if *Teen*'s mental illness meant that she *could* have worn a seat-belt, but it would have been *very difficult* for her to do so, then three of the Law Lords in *Corr* were agreed that the damages payable to *Teen* should be reduced for contributory negligence to recognise 'the element of choice'[54] that *Teen* enjoyed in this case. (Though the damages payable to *Teen* will not be reduced by anywhere near as much as they would have been in the case where *Teen* did not have any good reason not to wear a seat-belt.)

[47] [2000] 1 AC 360, at 370 (per Lord Hoffmann), 377 (per Lord Jauncey), 383 (per Lord Hope), 385 (per Lord Hobhouse).
[48] See above, § 9.12.
[49] See above, § 10.6.
[50] *Yachuk* v *Oliver Blais Co Ltd* [1949] AC 386, *Gough* v *Thorne* [1966] 1 WLR 1387.
[51] *Daly* v *Liverpool Corporation* [1939] 2 All ER 142.
[52] *Baxter* v *Woolcombers Ltd* (1963) 107 SJ 553.
[53] Reported at [2008] 1 AC 884, and referred to as '*Corr*' below.
[54] *Corr*, at [52] (per Lord Mance).

C. Assessment of reduction

(1) *Two party cases*. If A has committed a tort in relation to B but can raise a defence of contributory negligence to reduce the damages payable to B in respect of the losses suffered by B as a result of A's tort, the courts determine by how much the damages payable to B should be reduced by assessing the *comparative blameworthiness* of A and B for the losses suffered by B. So if they were equally to blame for the fact that B suffered those losses, the damages payable will be reduced by 50%;[55] if A was four times as much to blame as B for the losses suffered by B, the damages will be reduced by 20%.[56]

(2) *Three party cases*. The position is a bit more complicated in a case which involves two tortfeasors. Suppose that *Careless* and *Heedless* each committed a tort in relation to *Silly* and *Silly* suffered various losses as result but *Silly* was partly to blame for the fact that he suffered those losses. We determine by how much the damages payable to *Silly* should be reduced by lumping *Careless* and *Heedless* together and asking: as compared to *Silly*, how much to blame were *Careless* and *Heedless together* for the losses suffered by *Silly*?

So in *Fitzgerald* v *Lane* (1989), *Pedestrian* ('P') walked across a road when the lights were against him. He was struck by a motor car being negligently driven by *Driver One*. While he was lying in the road he was struck by a motor car which was negligently driven by *Driver Two*. It was held that *One* and *Two both* caused P to suffer the injuries he suffered as a result of the second collision[57] and so P was entitled to sue either *One* or *Two* or both for compensation for the fact that he received those injuries. However, P was partly to blame for the fact that he suffered those injuries: he would not have been injured had he not acted unreasonably by walking across the road when the lights were against him. Given this, the damages payable to P were liable to be reduced for contributory negligence. It was found that P was twice as much to blame as *each* of *One* and *Two* for the injuries that he suffered in the second collision – that is, P was 50% to blame for what happened, *One* was 25% to blame, and *Two* was 25% to blame. It followed that P was just as much to blame for the injuries that he suffered as *One* and *Two* were *together*. The damages payable to the claimant were therefore reduced by 50%.

D. Self-harm

The question of whether the defence of contributory negligence should be applied in a case where the victim of a tort has deliberately harmed herself (in the worst case, killed herself) and the person who committed that tort is being sued for the loss resulting from that act of self-harm has troubled the courts.

Let us first of all consider the case where the victim of a tort was mentally ill when he or she harmed herself. In *Corr* v *IBC Vehicles* (2008), an employee injured in a workplace accident caused by his employer's negligence developed post-traumatic stress disorder with the result that he eventually killed himself. The Law Lords were deeply divided over whether the damages payable to the employee's dependants in respect of his death should be reduced on the ground of contributory negligence. Lords Bingham and Walker thought

---

[55] The deduction made in *Reeves* v *Commissioner of Police of the Metropolis* [2000] 1 AC 360 (prisoner took advantage of defendants' negligence to commit suicide).

[56] The deduction made in *Froom* v *Butcher* [1976] QB 286 (claimant's failure to wear seat belt contributed to the injuries she suffered in car accident caused by defendant's negligence).

[57] For an explanation of this point, see above, § 9.1.

that the fact that the employee killed himself in a depressed state meant that he was not *at all* to blame for his death and thought that the damages payable to the employee's dependants should *not* be reduced *at all* for contributory negligence.[58] The other Law Lords – Scott, Mance, and Neuberger – disagreed. They took the view that *if* the employee was not an automaton at the time he killed himself,[59] then his death was, in part, something for which he was responsible, and the damages payable to the employee's dependants in respect of that death should be reduced for contributory negligence. Lord Scott would have been in favour of the damages being reduced by 20% in *Corr*.[60] Lords Mance and Neuberger thought that as the questions of (i) whether the employee was in an autonomous state at the time he killed himself, and if so, (ii) what his degree of responsibility for his own death was, had not been addressed at first instance, it would be inappropriate for them to make a finding on those questions. So they decided that the damages in *Corr* should not be reduced for contributory negligence;[61] but because of a lack of evidence rather than a matter of principle.

Given the willingness of three of the five Law Lords in *Corr* to allow a defence of contributory negligence to be pleaded against someone who was *mentally ill* but still enjoyed some degree of autonomy when they harmed themselves, it is clear that the decision of the House of Lords in *Reeves v Commissioner of Police of the Metropolis* (2000) – which dealt with the case where someone of *sound mind* harmed themselves – remains good law. In *Reeves*, someone who had been charged with credit card fraud and was remanded in police custody and was known to be a suicide risk took advantage of the police's carelessness to kill himself in his cell. The prisoner – 'surprising thought it might seem'[62] – was found to have been of sound mind when he killed himself. The House of Lords held that the damages payable to the prisoner's dependants in respect of his death should be reduced by 50% for contributory negligence, as the prisoner was as much responsible for his death as the police were.

E. Contributory negligence and *Hedley Byrne*

Two problems need to be addressed under this heading. First, will a defendant who has breached a duty of care owed to another under one of the principles in *Hedley Byrne* be entitled to rely on the defence of contributory negligence to reduce the damages payable to that other? Secondly, if he is, how does the defence of contributory negligence interact with the limit placed by the *SAAMCO* principle on what damages can be sued for in a *Hedley Byrne* case?

On the first question, suppose that A advised B that a car that she was thinking of buying was in good condition and that he indicated to her that she could safely rely on his advice. Suppose further that she did rely on A's advice and bought the car. However, the car later proved to be so defective that it was not worth repairing and had to be given away to some scrap metal merchants. If B sues A in negligence, can A attempt to raise a defence of contributory negligence to B's claim on the basis that she was partly to blame for the fact that she lost the money she spent on the car because it was very foolish of her to rely on his

---

[58] *Corr*, at [22] (per Lord Bingham), [44] (per Lord Walker).
[59] *Corr*, at [31] (per Lord Scott), [51] (per Lord Mance), [65] (per Lord Neuberger).
[60] *Corr*, at [32].
[61] *Corr*, at [47] (per Lord Mance), [70] (per Lord Neuberger).
[62] *Corr*, at [64] (per Lord Neuberger).

advice? It is unlikely that A would be allowed to make such an argument.[63] Having earlier indicated to B that she could safely rely on his advice, it is likely that A would be prevented (estopped) from subsequently arguing that B was foolish to rely on his advice for the purpose of raising a defence of contributory negligence to her claim for damages.

However, if the *extent* of the losses suffered by B as a result of acting on A's advice was partly B's fault, then there is no reason why A should not be allowed to raise a defence of contributory negligence to reduce the damages payable to B. This was what happened in *Platform Home Loans* v *Oyston Shipways Ltd* (2000), a case which also dealt with the interaction between the *SAAMCO* principle and the defence of contributory negligence. Simplifying the facts of the case slightly, the claimant lent £1m to a Mr Hussain secured by a mortgage of Hussain's home. The home was negligently valued by the defendant as being worth £1.5m: it was in fact worth only £1m. Four years later, Hussain defaulted on repaying the loan and the claimant sought to recoup the money he had lent by selling Hussain's house, which was worth only £400,000 at that stage. So the claimant lost £600,000 as a result of the defendant's negligence.[64] But two points complicated the case.

The first was that under the *SAAMCO* principle, the defendant should only have been entitled to sue the claimant for £500,000 – that was the loss which the defendant had suffered that was attributable to the fact that it had loaned money to Hussain on inadequate security.[65] The second point was that the claimant was – as compared with the defendant – 20% to blame for the fact that he lost the money he did on the loan to Hussain. The reasons for this were: (1) he had failed to check whether or not Hussain was a credit risk; and (2) he had loaned Hussain more than was reasonable given the defendant's valuation of Hussain's house. So the defendant was entitled to raise a defence of contributory negligence to reduce the damages that he had to pay the claimant.

The problem faced by the courts in the *Platform Home Loans* case was – how did these two points relate to each other? Do you say that the defendant was *prima facie* liable to pay the claimant £600,000, deduct 20% for contributory negligence, turning the defendant's liability into one to pay the claimant £480,000, and then allow the claimant to claim for the whole of that on the basis that doing so would not violate the *SAAMCO* principle (under which the most the claimant could have sued the defendant for was £500,000)? Or do you say that the *SAAMCO* principle means that the defendant was *prima facie* liable to pay the claimant £500,000 and then knock 20% off *that* figure, turning the defendant's liability into one to pay the claimant £400,000? The Court of Appeal preferred the latter approach; but the House of Lords ruled that the former approach was correct. In so doing, the House of Lords reinterpreted the *SAAMCO* principle as one which does not determine *which* of the losses suffered by a claimant in a *Hedley Byrne* case can be sued for by that claimant, but as one which places a 'cap' on the potential liability of a defendant to a claimant in a *Hedley*

---

[63] See *Gran Gelato Ltd* v *Richcliff (Group) Ltd* [1992] Ch 560, 574 (per Sir Donald Nicholls V-C), doubting whether the damages payable to a claimant in a *Hedley Byrne* case could be reduced for contributory negligence where it was alleged that the claimant was contributorily negligent because she should not have done the very thing that she was advised to do by the defendant.

[64] It was established that if the defendant had taken care in his valuation, he would have accurately valued the house as being worth only £1m; as a result, the claimants would have offered to lend Mr Hussain only £700,000 and he would have declined the loan.

[65] Had the claimant lent the £1m to Hussain on adequate security – that is, in return for a mortgage of a house worth £1.5m – when Hussain defaulted, the security would have been worth £900,000 and the claimant would have lost £100,000 on the loan. So £100,000 of the £600,000 loss suffered by the claimant would have been suffered by the claimant anyway, even if he had lent Hussain money on adequate security. Therefore, £500,000 of the money lost by the claimant was lost by the claimant because he lent money to Hussain on inadequate security.

Byrne case. It is, however, doubtful whether that interpretation of the *SAAMCO* principle is reconcilable with the reasons for its adoption by Lord Hoffmann in the *SAAMCO* case.

F. Contributory negligence and *White* v *Jones*

Suppose that A asked C to prepare a will for him under which B would inherit £9,000. C prepared the will but only had one person witness A's signing the will, thus making the will invalid. A – who had some knowledge of the law relating to wills – thought that more than one witness was required but did not raise any objections because he thought C 'knew best'. Shortly afterwards, A died and his will was declared to be invalid with the result that B did not receive her legacy. B will, of course, be able to sue C for damages under the principle in *White* v *Jones* (1995),[66] but will C be able to raise a defence of contributory negligence to her claim on the basis that *A* was partly to blame for the fact that B did not receive her legacy? The question was raised in *Gorham* v *British Telecommunications plc* (2000). Of the three members of the Court of Appeal who decided that case, Pill and Schiemann LJJ preferred to leave the matter to be decided another day,[67] though Pill LJ thought the argument that a defence of contributory negligence should be available in this kind of case had its 'attractions'.[68] Sir Murray Stuart-Smith thought that the defence *would* be available in this kind of case.[69]

G. One final limit

Suppose that A has committed a tort in relation to B and B has suffered various losses as a result, for which she was partly to blame – she would not have suffered those losses had she not acted unreasonably in some way. It seems to be the case that if the reason why B suffered those losses has nothing to do with the reason why it was unreasonable for B to act in the way she did, A will not be able to raise a defence of contributory negligence to B's claim to be compensated for those losses.

So, for example, in *Jones* v *Livox Quarries Ltd* (1952), Denning LJ considered whether the defence would be available in the following case. A negligently fires a gun and the bullet fired from the gun happens to hit and injure B while she was dangerously perched on the back of a moving lorry. Now – it was clearly unreasonable for B to stand on the back of the lorry and had she not done this she would not have been hit by the bullet: it was because she was on the lorry that she was in the wrong place at the wrong time. Does this mean that A can raise a defence of contributory negligence to any claim B makes against him for damages? Denning LJ thought not.[70] But the only explanation as to why the defence would not be available here is that the reason why it was unreasonable for B to perch on the back of the lorry had nothing to do with the reason why B was hit by the bullet.

In *Westwood* v *The Post Office* (1974), the claimant worked for the Post Office at a telephone exchange. His place of work was a three-storey building with a flat roof. Workers at the exchange, including the claimant, would frequently take short breaks on the roof although they were not authorised to do so and not permitted to gain access to the roof. While on his way back from one such break on the roof, the claimant fell through a

---

[66] Discussed above, § 6.13.
[67] [2000] 1 WLR 2129, 2144 (per Pill LJ), 2145 (per Schiemann LJ).
[68] [2000] 1 WLR 2129, 2144.
[69] [2000] 1 WLR 2129, 2149.
[70] [1952] 2 QB 608, 616.

defective trapdoor and was injured. The claimant sued the Post Office for damages in respect of his injuries, claiming that he had been injured because the Post Office had breached the duty it owed him under s 16 of the Offices, Shops and Railway Premises Act 1963 to ensure that the floors in the claimant's workplace were of sound construction. The Post Office admitted liability but sought to raise a defence of contributory negligence to the claimant's claim. The Post Office argued that the claimant was partly to blame for his injuries because he would not have been injured had he not acted unreasonably in trespassing on the flat roof of the telephone exchange. The House of Lords held that no defence of contributory negligence could be raised here: the reason why the claimant was injured (he trod on a trapdoor which was not soundly constructed) had nothing to do with the reason why it was unreasonable for the claimant to trespass on the flat roof of the telephone exchange (he had no business being up there).

In *St George* v *Home Office* (2009), the claimant – who was addicted to alcohol and drugs – was sentenced to four months in prison. On arrival at the prison, he informed the staff that he was prone to epileptic seizures when in withdrawal from alcohol and drugs. Despite this, he was allocated the top bunk in his cell. While lying on the top bunk, the claimant had a withdrawal-induced epileptic seizure, fell off the bunk, and hit his head on the floor. The head injury caused the claimant to have continual seizures for over an hour, and he suffered severe brain damage as a result. He successfully sued the prison authorities in negligence for allocating him a top bunk when they knew he was prone to epileptic seizures when withdrawing from alcohol and drugs. An attempt to plead that the damages payable to the claimant should be reduced for contributory negligence, on the ground that the claimant was to blame for the fact that he was addicted to alcohol and drugs in the first place, was dismissed. The reason why the claimant suffered brain damage in this case (withdrawing from alchol and drugs resulted in his suffering an epileptic seizure) had nothing to do with the reason why it was unreasonable for the claimant to get addicted to alcohol and drugs (addictions are enslaving).

28.6 THIRD PARTY LOSSES

So far, we have been looking at cases where the victim of a tort wants to sue for compensation for losses that *she* has suffered as a result of that tort being committed. Occasionally, however, the law will allow the victim of a tort to sue for compensatory damages in respect of losses that have been suffered by a *third party* as a result of that tort being committed. We have already seen an example of this.

If A has committed a tort in relation to B and B has been so badly injured as a result that her expectation of life has been reduced, she will be allowed to sue A for damages in respect of the money she would have earned and not spent on herself in the years that are now 'lost' to her.[71] The point of allowing B to sue for such damages is essentially to ensure that any dependants that B has, who would have been supported by her in the years that are now 'lost' to her, do not lose out as a result of A's tort. By allowing B to sue A for damages in respect of the money she would have earned in the years that are now 'lost' to her, the law enables B to set up a fund which will look after her dependants after she has died.

---

[71] See above, § 28.3(B). Though no such damages will be awarded if B is so young that any estimate as to how much she earned in the years that are now 'lost' to her would be purely speculative: *Gammell* v *Wilson* [1982] AC 27, 78 (per Lord Scarman, suggesting there might be an exception in the case where a child was already earning money at the time her expectation of life was cut short as a result of someone's negligently injuring her; which would be the case if the child was a movie star).

Another example is provided by what we can call the *principle in Donnelly v Joyce*.[72] (Though '*Hunt v Severs* damages'[73] is also a popular way of referring to the damages awarded under this principle.) This principle applies in the following kind of situation. Suppose that A tortiously injured B and B, as a result, was incapacitated and needed to be looked after. Suppose further that C – a friend or relative[74] of B's – looked after B without charging her anything for the work done by him in looking after her.[75] The principle in *Donnelly v Joyce* says that in this situation, B will be entitled to sue A for damages equal to the value of the work that C did in looking after B.[76] That such damages are designed to compensate C for the effort he put in looking after B is shown by two things.

First, the damages payable will depend on what sort of sacrifices were incurred by C in looking after B; the greater the sacrifices, the greater the damages payable.[77]

Secondly, if B does sue A for damages equal to the value of the work done by C in looking after her, she will hold those damages on trust for C.[78] This feature of the law had an unexpected effect in *Hunt v Severs* (1994), where the defendant in that case negligently injured his girlfriend in a car accident and then spent a lot of time looking after her while she was incapacitated. The girlfriend then sued the defendant for damages, which would – in effect – be paid by the defendant's liability insurer. The House of Lords held that the girlfriend could *not* sue the defendant for damages in respect of the work that he had done in looking after her because if such damages were awarded to her, they would have to be

---

[72] After the decision in *Donnelly v Joyce* [1974] QB 454.

[73] After the decision in *Hunt v Severs* [1994] 2 AC 350.

[74] It is uncertain whether the principle in *Donnelly v Joyce* will apply in the situation where a complete stranger looks after the victim of a tort without charging her anything for doing so. In Scotland, only care provided by a relative is covered by their version of the principle in *Donnelly v Joyce*: Administration of Justice Act 1982, s 8. It seems implicit in *Islington LBC v University College London Hospital NHS Trust* [2005] EWCA Civ 596 (noted, Stanton 2007a) that the position is the same in England (though care provided by friends is also covered). In that case, the claimant local authority sought to sue the defendant hospital in negligence for the money it had spent providing residential care to Mrs J, a woman who had had a stroke as a result of the defendant's negligence. The claim was dismissed – the defendant had not owed the claimant a duty of care. It seemed to be assumed that suing in negligence was the only way for the claimant to recover the money it had spent caring for Mrs J; that is, Mrs J could not have sued herself for the costs of her care by the claimant. But, on the other hand, Clarke LJ wondered (at [45]) whether if Mrs J had been looked after by a friend, the friend could have compelled Mrs J to have made a claim for the cost of her care by the friend, and if so, whether Islington LBC could have done so as well.

[75] If C had *charged* B for looking after her, then A would of course be liable to compensate B for the money she spent on getting C to look after her – so long, of course, as the money she paid C for looking after her was reasonable.

[76] So – in *Donnelly v Joyce* [1974] QB 454 itself, the claimant was a child who was negligently injured by the defendant and as a result needed to spend six months at home having his injuries treated. The claimant's mother took time off work to look after the claimant. The claimant was allowed to sue the defendant for damages equal to the value of the work done by the claimant's mother in looking after him.

[77] *Housecroft v Burnett* [1986] 1 All ER 332, 343. However, the damages payable will not be allowed to exceed the going market rate for the kind of services that C provided B: ibid. So, for example, suppose *Careless* negligently injured *Wife* and *Wife's* injuries were so serious that she needed to be looked after 24 hours a day for six months. *Husband* – who earned £400 a hour working as a lawyer – decided to quit his legal practice to look after *Wife* full time for the six months she was laid up, thereby forgoing roughly £400,000. *Wife* would not be able to sue *Careless* for that £400,000; instead she will be limited to suing *Careless* for the market value of the services provided by her husband in looking after. The reason why *Wife* will not be able to sue *Careless* for £400,000 under the principle in *Donnelly v Joyce* is that by having her husband look after her, she and *Husband* will have failed to mitigate the loss suffered by them as a result of *Careless's* tort: it would have been much cheaper to hire a nurse to look after *Wife* and have *Husband* carry on working.

[78] It is a difficult question whether B will also hold her *right to sue* A for those damages on trust for C; if she does, then C will be allowed to *compel* B to sue A for those damages. Degeling 2003 takes the view that, as the law stands, C will not be able to compel B to sue. However, she goes on to argue that C *should* be subrogated to B's rights to sue A for damages in respect of the cost of caring for her – which would allow C to sue A for such damages in B's name.

paid straight back to the defendant. So the principle against *circuity of actions* worked against a finding of liability in this case. (Of course, in reality, the girlfriend and the defendant would have benefited a great deal from an arrangement where the defendant had to pay damages to his girlfriend in respect of the care she had received and then the girlfriend had to pay those damages straight back to the defendant. As the damages would have come from the defendant's liability insurer in the first place, allowing the girlfriend to sue for the care she had received would have been a way of enriching the defendant at his insurer's expense.) The logic of the decision is impeccable, but it has been criticised on the ground that its effect is to encourage a husband who has negligently injured his wife to contract out her care to a complete stranger rather than looking after her himself. The Law Commission has accordingly recommended that the result in *Hunt* v *Severs* be reversed.[79]

There are other situations where the victim of a tort will be entitled to sue for damages in respect of losses suffered by third parties to that tort – though it must be emphasised that these situations are exceptional in nature; the normal rule is that the victim of a tort is confined to suing for compensatory damages in respect of the losses that *she* has suffered as a result of that tort being committed. So –

(1) If A tortiously injures a housewife with the result that she can no longer do any housework, she will be entitled to sue A for damages in respect of the work done by any members of her family in filling in for her.[80]

(2) If B regularly looked after C, a family member, but is now no longer able to do so because she was tortiously injured by A, with the result that another family member has to look after C, B will be entitled to sue A for damages equal to the value of the work she used to do in looking after C.[81]

(3) If A negligently damages B's car and C – a friend of B's – lends B a replacement car while his car is being repaired, then B *may* be entitled to sue A for damages equal to the rent that he would normally have had to pay to rent that kind of replacement car.[82]

28.7 THEORIES

Having looked at the law governing the victim of a tort's right to sue the person who committed that tort for compensatory damages, we will now address an issue which lies at the heart of tort law: *why* does the law give the victim of a tort a right to sue for compensatory damages? In order to sharpen the discussion, we will consider a hypothetical situation adapted from Jeremy Waldron's excellent essay 'Moments of carelessness and massive loss':

---

[79] Law Comm No 262, *Damages for Personal Injury* (1999), paras 3.67–3.76.

[80] *Daly* v *General Steam Navigation Co Ltd* [1981] 1 WLR 120. But if A negligently injures a businessman and as a result the businessman can no longer run his business and has his wife fill in for him, he will not be able to sue A for damages in respect of the work done by his wife running the business for him: *Hardwick* v *Hudson* [1999] 1 WLR 1770.

[81] *Lowe* v *Guise* [2002] QB 1369. Rix LJ suggested in that case (at [38]) that the damages, once paid over, 'may' be held on trust for the family member who took B's place in looking after C. What if C responded to B's being incapacitated by paying someone else to look after him, C? Presumably in that case the damages payable to B might then be held on trust for C.

[82] The point was left open in *Giles* v *Thompson* [1994] 1 AC 142, at 166–167. However, it is implicit in the House of Lords' decision in *Dimond* v *Lovell* [2002] 1 AC 384 that such a claim will be available to B, and may even be available where C was not a friend but a complete stranger. No such claim could be made on the facts of *Dimond* v *Lovell*, however – where the replacement car was provided by a finance company under a hire agreement that was void under the Consumer Credit Act 1974 – because to allow such a claim would have subverted the 1974 Act.

As *Fate* drove his car through a shopping district, he took his eyes off the road, turning his head for a moment to look at the bargains advertised in a shop window. Distracted by a bargain advertised in a shoe shop, he failed to notice that the traffic ahead of him had slowed down. His car ploughed into a motorcycle ridden by *Hurt*. *Hurt* was gravely injured: his back was broken so badly that he would spend the rest of his life in a wheelchair. When the police arrived, *Fate* readily admitted he had been driving carelessly. *Hurt* successfully sued *Fate* for £5 million to cover his medical costs, to compensate him for the extreme pain in which he would live for the rest of his life, and to make up the earnings he could have expected from the career he was pursuing at the time.[83]

The question we want to address here is – *why* is *Hurt* entitled to sue *Fate* for compensation for the losses that he has suffered as a result of what *Fate* has done?

A. Economic theories

In the 1970s, the most popular explanations as to why someone like *Hurt* is entitled to sue for compensatory damages were economic in nature. The idea was that *Hurt* is allowed to sue *Fate* for compensatory damages, because giving him such a right produced economically beneficial results.

According to one such theory,[84] the person who could have avoided the accident in which *Hurt* was injured was *Fate*: by keeping a proper look-out, *Fate* could have easily avoided hitting *Hurt*. By telling *Fate* that if he does not keep a proper look-out, he will be held liable to pay compensatory damages to *Hurt*, the law gives *Fate* an incentive to keep a proper look-out, and ensures that *Fate* will keep a proper look-out and avoid hitting *Hurt* *unless* it makes economic sense for him not to pay proper attention to what is happening in front of him. This will be the case if he can make more money by focusing on something other than the traffic ahead of him (for example, a business deal that has to be concluded right there and now on *Fate*'s mobile phone) than he would have to pay out if his failure to keep a proper look-out resulted in someone like *Hurt* being injured.

The problem with all such economic theories of tort law – and the reason why they have fallen into disrepute nowadays – is that they assume that tort law is made up of *liability rules*: rules which are intended to give people an incentive to act in economically sensible ways by telling them 'If you do *x*, then you will have to pay price *P*'. But – in the language of adherents to such explanations of tort law – tort law is made up of *property rules*.[85] That is, tort law is made up of rules which tell people 'Don't do *x*' or 'Do *x*', and what we need to explain is why violation of one of *those* rules gives rise to a right on the part of the person for whose benefit that rule exists to sue for compensatory damages.[86] We cannot explain this right by recharacterising the rules of tort law as liability rules – by imagining that, in the case we are considering, the law actually permitted *Fate* to drive badly so long as he could make driving badly pay by making more money from driving badly than he would have to pay out to those injured by his bad driving. The law does not *ever* permit *Fate* to drive badly, and an explanation of the basis of *Fate*'s liability to pay compensatory damages to *Hurt* that forgets that fact is missing something important.

---

[83] Waldron 1995, 387 (paraphrased).
[84] Calabresi 1970.
[85] See Calabresi and Melamed 1972.
[86] See, generally, Nance 1997.

B. Next best theories

The same accusation cannot be made of the next explanation as to why *Hurt* is allowed to sue *Fate* for compensatory damages. According to this explanation, allowing *Hurt* to sue *Fate* for such damages is the next best way of upholding the right that *Fate* violated by carelessly crashing into *Hurt*. This is because paying compensatory damages to *Hurt* puts him – so far as money can do such a thing – in the position he would have been in had *Fate* been more careful. Ernest Weinrib, John Gardner, Robert Stevens, and Arthur Ripstein have all advanced such *next best theories* of the foundation of a victim of a tort's right to sue the person who committed that tort for compensatory damages:

> When [a] defendant . . . breaches a duty correlative to the [claimant's] right, the [claimant] is entitled to reparation. The remedy reflects the fact that even after the commission of the tort the defendant remains subject to the duty with respect to the [claimant's] right. The defendant's breach of . . . duty . . . does not, of course, bring the duty to an end . . . With the materialization of wrongful injury, the only way the defendant can discharge his or her obligation respecting the [claimant]'s right is to undo the effects of the breach of duty . . . Thus tort law places the defendant under the obligation to restore the [claimant], so far as possible, to the position the [claimant] would have been in had the wrong not been committed.[87]

> When I fail to perform a duty that I owe to someone, there is something that I still owe that person afterwards. Strictly speaking, I still owe him performance of the duty, which continues to bind me. But if it is too late to perform – the dirty deed is done – I now owe him the next best thing. I owe it to him to put him back, so far as it can now be done, into the position he would have been in if I had done my duty in the first place.[88]

> Where [a] wrong has been committed, the secondary obligation to pay money imposed upon the wrongdoer can be seen as the law's attempt to reach the 'next best' position to the wrong not having been committed by him in the first place. Where the defendant is required to make good the claimant's . . . loss . . . this is the law's attempting to reach this nearest approximation of the wrong not having occurred.[89]

> Damages are not awarded to compensate for the awful things that people do to each other, but rather to make it as if [people] had the means that they would have had if others had not wrongfully deprived them of them.[90]

The difficulty with all such *next best theories* is that they conceal a problem that needs to be addressed. It is *tempting* to think that because it is justified for the law to impose on *Fate* a duty to take care not to crash into *Hurt* (or, to put it another way, give *Hurt* a right that *Fate* take care not to crash into him), the law is *also* justified – now that that primary duty/right has been violated – in requiring *Fate* to repair his violation by putting *Hurt* back in the position he would have been in had that duty/right not been violated. But, like most temptations, this is one that needs to be resisted. The reason for this is that repairing *Fate*'s breach of duty/violation of right is *a lot* more burdensome than observing the primary duty/right that was violated in this case. Requiring *Fate* to pay *Hurt* £5 million pounds is unimaginably more burdensome than requiring *Fate* to keep a proper look-out while he is driving his car. So it would be wrong to think that *just because* the primary duty that *Fate* owed *Hurt* (or the right *Hurt* had against *Fate*) is justified, then requiring *Fate* to repair his

---

[87] Weinrib 1995, 135.
[88] Gardner 2011, text at n 20.
[89] Stevens 2007, 59.
[90] Ripstein 2007a, 1968.

violation of that duty/right is *also* justified. What we need is an argument that it would *not be unfair* on *Fate* to require him to repair that violation – and the above theorists do not supply us with such an argument.[91] But someone *has* made such an argument, and we will look at whether that argument works right now.

C. Outcome responsibility

Tony Honoré's theory of 'outcome responsibility' – first presented in his *Law Quarterly Review* article 'Responsibility and luck: the moral basis of strict liability'[92] – purports to offer an explanation as to why it might *not be unfair* to impose a liability on *Fate* to compensate *Hurt* for the losses that he has suffered here.[93]

Honoré argues that we live in a society that generally allocates 'credit and esteem and . . . discredit and resentment'[94] according to the outcomes of our actions. When our actions go well, we make money and enjoy a good reputation. When our actions go badly, we lose money and incur other people's resentment. This is so even though it is often just a matter of luck whether our actions go well or badly. But the fact that our society operates a system of outcome responsibility will not be unfair so long as its operation is 'impartial, reciprocal and over a period beneficial':

> It must apply impartially to all those who possess a minimum capacity for reasoned choice and action. It must be reciprocal in that each person is entitled to apply it to others and they to him. It must work so as to entitle each person to potential benefits which are likely on the whole to outweigh the detriments to which it subjects him. This makes it unfair to apply the system to the incapable, for whom there is no likely surplus of benefit over detriment. But for the capable the three conditions are normally satisfied. All those who possess a minimum capacity stand to profit from the system of outcome-allocation most of the time . . .[95]

Seen as part of a general social system in which credit and discredit are allocated to us according to the outcomes of our actions, and under which we all end up winning more credit than we lose, it is not unfair on *Fate* to impose on him a duty to compensate *Hurt* that has the effect of allocating the responsibility for what has happened to *Hurt* to *Fate*. Indeed, *Fate* should welcome being subjected to such a system of outcome responsibility. It is only by ascribing outcomes – good and bad – to *Fate* that *Fate* acquires the characteristics of a person: someone who has 'a history, an identity, and a character.'[96]

---

[91] Of course, *Fate* will have been carrying liability insurance which means that requiring her to pay *Hurt* £5 million will not impose an undue burden on her. However, it is not clear that this gets the 'second-best' theorists off the hook. Liability insurers only undertake to cover the insured's legal liabilities. The legal liabilities therefore come first, and have to be justified without reference to the fact that they might end up being insured against. So if we are to explain why it would not be unfair to make *Fate* pay *Hurt* £5 million, as part of a project of justifying imposing such a liability on *Fate*, we must do so on the basis that that liability will be borne by *Fate* and ignore the possibility that it might end up being insured against.

[92] Honoré 1988.

[93] Honoré is careful not to say that he is offering a reason why *Fate* *should* be held liable to *Hurt* here: his theory 'does not entail that whenever a harmful outcome is properly allocated to someone this justifies imposing on him a strict liability to compensate for that outcome' (Honoré 1988, 541): it merely explains why it might be *not unfair* to hold *Fate* liable to *Hurt* here for *other reasons*. (For Honoré, these other reasons normally reduce to saying that *Fate* was at fault for what happened to *Hurt*, or that what *Fate* did carried with it a special risk of *Hurt* suffering harm: see Honoré 1988, 542.)

[94] Honoré 1988, 540.

[95] Honoré 1988, 540–1.

[96] Honoré 1988, 543.

The fairness of holding *Fate* liable for what has happened to *Hurt* here crucially depends – according to Honoré's theory – on whether *Fate* is likely to be a long-term winner under a system of outcome responsibility, where credit and demerit attaches to *Fate* according to the outcome of his actions. Honoré assumes that *Fate* is likely to be a long-term winner, but it is not clear that this is so. As Stephen Perry observes,

> the claim that the system of [outcome responsibility] is beneficial to all [people who 'possess a minimum capacity for reasoned choice and action] seems to be, empirically, false. We all know people, or know of people, who apparently possess whatever minimum capacity is required to get by in the world and be properly regarded as a person, who nonetheless seem to be (and to be destined from the outset to be) life's perennial losers.[97]

Fate could very easily turn out to be one of those long-term 'losers' once he is saddled with a £5m debt. We can test Honoré's assumption that people of minimum capacity will turn out to be long-term winners under a system of outcome responsibility another way. Suppose we applied Honoré's system of outcome responsibility to *Hurt*'s choice to go out riding on a motorbike the day *Fate* would be distracted while driving behind *Hurt*, and allocated the responsibility for the outcome of *Hurt*'s choice to *Hurt*, so that he was not entitled to sue anyone for being permanently disabled as a result of *Fate*'s running into him.[98] Having done this, do we think that *Hurt* is still likely to be a long-term winner from living under a system of outcome responsibility? It seems very doubtful that *Hurt* will be a long-term winner: it is much more plausible to think that he will end up being a long-term loser.

So Honoré's optimism is unjustified. Some perfectly capable but unlucky people can end up being long-term losers under a system of outcome responsibility; and we have no reason to think that *Fate* would not be one of those people were he held accountable for the outcome of his choice to go out driving on the day when traffic would slow down while he was distracted by an advertisement in a nearby shop window. The truth is that outcome responsibility only *seems* fair because it is surrounded by a battery of institutions (the family, the State, insurance, employment law) that help to catch people who lose out under outcome responsibility. Outcome responsibility *on its own* is unfair, and cannot explain *on its own* why it is not unfair to hold *Fate* liable to pay *Hurt* £5 million in the situation we are considering.

If this is right, Tony Honoré's theory of outcome responsibility does not work to explain why it would not be unfair to make *Fate* pay *Hurt* £5m, so as to force him to do the 'next best' thing to what he should have done in the first place. It follows that theorists who advance 'next best' theories as to why we make people pay compensatory damages still have to explain why it would not be unfair to make someone do the 'next best' thing to what they should have done in the first place, even when doing the 'next best' thing is hugely more burdensome than doing what they should have done in the first place. And it is not clear that such an explanation can be offered.

---

[97] Perry 2001, 67.

[98] Honoré would not personally be in favour of doing this as there seems to be no positive reason for making *Hurt* responsible for the outcome of his choice. But that does not matter. If Honoré's assumption that everyone of minimum capacity benefits under a system of outcome responsibility, then the assumption should hold in this situation or any other situation where outcome responsibility applies.

D. Civil recourse theory

Finally, we come to the theory of tort liability that John Goldberg and Benjamin Zipursky have been developing over last 15 years or so: the civil recourse theory of tort law.[99] This theory makes a number of connected claims, which we can set out as follows:

(1) There are some moral wrongs that morally entitle the victim of one of those wrongs to seek some form of redress against the perpetrator of that wrong. We can call such a wrong, 'a redress-entitling wrong'.[100]

(2) However, the State – in order to preserve a monopoly of force within society – prevents the victim of a redress-entitling wrong from taking direct action against the perpetrator of that wrong to obtain redress for the fact that that wrong has been committed.

(3) As a result, victims of redress-entitling wrongs have a right against the State that it provide them with a peaceful means of seeking redress against the person or persons who have committed those wrongs against them.

(4) Tort law exists to provide victims of redress-entitling wrongs with such a peaceful means of seeking redress. The function of tort law is to determine when someone has been the victim of a redress-entitling wrong and to provide a means of redress where something that is recognised as a redress-entitling wrong by the law of tort has been committed.

So in the situation we are considering, *Hurt* is entitled to sue *Fate* for £5 million because the law recognises that *Fate* has committed a redress-entitling wrong in this situation and allowing *Hurt* to sue *Fate* for compensatory damages is the law's way of providing *Hurt* with a civilised, peaceful and orderly way of obtaining redress for *Fate*'s wrong.

It seems to us that there are three problems with the civil recourse theory of tort law. First of all, it is not clear that the side of our characters that wants to obtain redress for wrongs that other people do to us is a particularly attractive one, or one that the State should pander to by providing each of us with a civil means of obtaining redress from those that the State thinks have committed a redress-entitling wrong in relation to us.[101] However, it may be that forgiving those who trespass against us is beyond most of us, and that the State would be faced with a serious social problem if it did not do something to help us obtain some redress against those who have seriously wronged us. So this first objection does not provide a clinching argument against the truth of the civil recourse theory of tort law.

The second objection is more serious. The objection is that the State's catalogue of wrongs that it recognises as torts does not correspond with any plausible list of what we might regard as being redress-entitling wrongs. The lack of match-up is on both sides: there are torts that are so trivial it is hard to believe the State seriously thinks they are redress-entitling wrongs, and there are redress-entitling wrongs (if there are any redress-entitling wrongs) that the State does not recognise as torts. For example, if *Hiker* innocently wanders onto *Owner*'s land, no one would seriously think that *Owner* was entitled at a

---

[99] Citing all the articles in which this theory has been developed would not assist the reader very much, such is Goldberg and Zipursky's prodigious productivity. Key articles (in chronological order) are: Zipursky 1998a, Goldberg and Zipursky 2002, Zipursky 2003, Goldberg and Zipursky 2010a.

[100] Note that the phrase 'redress-entitling wrong' is a phrase we have coined to make it easier to set out and understand Goldberg and Zipursky's civil recourse theory of tort law: it is not a phrase that occurs in Goldberg and Zipursky's work.

[101] See Finnis 2002, 656.

moral level to seek some redress for what *Hiker* has done: but *Hiker*'s conduct will still amount to the tort of trespass to land. On the other side of the line, if *Social Services*, on virtually no evidence, seize *Child* from his *Parents* and give the child up to be adopted, with the result that *Parents* are then legally disabled from ever regaining custody of *Child*, most people would regard *Social Services*' conduct as a classic example of a redress-entitling wrong, and would not be at all surprised if *Parents* wanted to maim the people responsible for what *Social Services* did. But *Social Services*' conduct will not amount to a tort to the *Parents*.[102]

The third objection is that it is not clear why the means of redress that the State provides to the victim of (what the State perceives to be) a redress-entitling wrong should take the form of holding the person who committed that wrong liable to pay *compensation* to the victim of his wrong. Holding the person who committed that wrong liable to pay a fixed sum to the victim of his wrong – assessed according to the nature of the wrong and how it was committed – would provide an altenative way of allowing the victim of wrong a way of making the person who committed that wrong pay for what he did, and this alternative means of civil recourse might work in a much fairer way in a case like *Fate*'s where a momentary lack of attention has resulted in a huge loss.

E. Conclusion

Our conclusion from reviewing these various theories is a pessimistic one: there is no completely satisfactory way of explaining why *Fate* is held liable to pay compensatory damages to *Hurt* in the case we are considering. Our guess is that the explanation that comes closest to being 'correct' is a *next best theory*, but allowing the victim of a tort to claim *full* compensation for the losses he has suffered as a result of a tort being committed cannot be justified in today's society (where the losses that might be suffered by the victim of a tort are potentially massive), and is only tolerated because of the existence of liability insurance.

Further reading

Many of the articles referred to in the further reading to chapter 1 are also relevant to this chapter.

In discussing the various theories as to why a tortfeasor is held liable to pay compensatory damages to the victim of his tort, we have not used the phrases *corrective justice* or *distributive justice*. This would puzzle many tort theorists who think that a tortfeasor is required as a matter of 'corrective justice' to compensate the victim of his tort. But when one asks what corrective justice requires, the normal answer is – that wrongful losses be rectified, or that wrongdoers are made to repair their wrongs. (The notion of 'corrective justice' comes from Aristotle's *Nicomachean Ethics* – actually, a set of notes on some lectures on ethics delivered by Aristotle round about 350BC, and prepared by or dedicated to his son Nicomachus. This fact has given rise to countless and utterly pointless articles discussing what Aristotle really meant by 'corrective justice' and whether theorist X's account of corrective justice is compatible with what Aristotle had to say about it.)

But if this is right, then appeals to 'corrective justice' do not tell us anything about why tortfeasors are held liable to pay compensatory damages to the victims of their torts: 'Why

→

---

[102] See above, § 1.3.

does the law require a wrongdoer to undo the harmful consequences that his wrong has had on the victim of his wrong?' 'Because corrective justice demands it' 'And what does corrective justice demand?' 'That wrongdoers undo the harmful consequences that their wrongs have had on the victims of their wrongs' 'Oh . . .' Still, for those wishing to explore the notion of corrective justice further, **John Gardner's 'What is tort law for? Part 1: the place of corrective justice' (2010, available on SSRN)** is as good a place as any to start. **Scott Hershowitz's 'Harry Potter and the trouble with tort theory' (2011) 63** *Stanford Law Review* **67 (also available on SSRN)** wonderfully explores the limitations of corrective justice and economic accounts of the basis of tort law.

Principles of distributive justice – which tell us how things that need to be distributed should be distributed – are relevant to tort law in two ways: (1) they are relevant to the issue of who is given what rights under tort law; (2) insofar as principles of distributive justice are relevant to how much wealth people should have (something some people would dispute as they do not think wealth is something that is up for distribution) they may limit how much one person can sue another for in tort, where allowing a claim in tort would have unacceptable effects on the distribution of wealth. (1) is not really relevant to this chapter, and – as we have just observed – it is debatable whether distributive justice has anything to do with (2). **Tsachi Keren-Paz** explores the relevance of distributive justice to tort law in his monograph *Torts, Egalitarianism and Distributive Justice* **(Ashgate Publishing, 2007)**; the book was reviewed by **William Lucy in (2009) 72** *Modern Law Review* **1048** and by **Ariel Porat in (2009) 29** *Legal Studies* **509**.

The judges have eagerly seized on the language of corrective and distributive justice to make sense of what they are doing in deciding tort cases: see, for example, **Lord Steyn's 'Perspectives of corrective and distributive justice in tort law' in (2002) 37** *Irish Jurist* **1**. (The slight awkwardness of the title may bespeak an unconscious unconfidence in the concepts of corrective and distributive justice.) It is also worth reading the reflections of another Law Lord (and now Supreme Court Justice), **Lord Scott, on 'Damages' in [2007]** *Lloyd's Maritime and Commercial Law Quarterly* **465**.

Tony Weir's 'All or nothing' (2003–4) 78 *Tulane Law Review* **512** is a typically brilliant survey of the trend across the whole of the common law, including tort law, away from either awarding a claimant *everything* he is suing for or *nothing*, towards awarding a claimant *some* of what he is suing for.

29 Aggravated damages

29.1 The basics *789*

29.2 Requirements *789*

29.3 Theories *792*

Overview

In this chapter we look at aggravated damages, which are awardable where a tortfeasor has 'added insult to injury' in the way he committed his tort, or treated the victim of his tort after the tort was committed. The basic requirements that have to be satisfied before an award of aggravated damages will be made are dealt with in section 29.2. Section 29.3 lays out the various theories as to what awards of aggravated damages are meant to achieve.

29.1 THE BASICS

Where a tortfeasor is liable to pay the victim of his tort compensatory damages, or nominal damages (in the case where the tort is actionable *per se* and the victim has suffered no loss as a result of that tort being committed), *aggravated* damages may also be awarded to the victim of the tort if the tortfeasor has behaved in an *arrogant and high-handed* way, either in committing that tort, or in the way he treated the victim of the tort after it was committed.

29.2 REQUIREMENTS

A. Arrogant and high-handed conduct

The principal requirement that has to be satisfied before a claimant can sue a defendant in tort for aggravated damages is that the claimant has to show that the defendant treated her in an arrogant and high-handed way, either (1) in the way he acted in committing a tort in relation to the claimant; or (2) in the way he treated the claimant after he had committed the tort. When will a claimant be able to show that either (1) or (2) are true?

(1) *Conduct in committing the tort.* A defendant who *knowingly* committed a tort can be said to have acted in an arrogant and high-handed way in committing that tort. For example, in *Thompson* v *Hill* (1870), the claimant's business as a tailor was disrupted when the defendant built some extra floors on his house, thus blocking off the light to the premises in which the claimant conducted his business. The defendant knew that his building the extra floors on his house would amount to a nuisance because it would prevent the claimant's premises receiving light that he had a right to receive. Aggravated damages were awarded against the defendant and the award was upheld on appeal. Again, in *McMillan* v *Singh* (1984), the claimant was a tenant of the defendant's, paying £16 a week rent. The defendant realised that if the claimant left, he could rent out the claimant's room for £26 a week. As a result the defendant threw the claimant out along with his belongings.

The defendant knew that he had no right to do this and therefore knew that in throwing the claimant and his belongings out of his room, he was committing a tort. Aggravated damages were awarded against the defendant.

The authorities also indicate that someone who has *unknowingly* committed a tort can still be said to have acted in an arrogant and high-handed way in committing that tort if he *humiliated or insulted* the victim of that tort in committing the tort in question. So, for example, in *Thompson v Commissioner of Police of the Metropolis* (1998), the Court of Appeal held that police officers who commit the tort of false imprisonment by arresting someone when they are not entitled to do so can be sued for aggravated damages if, in making the arrest, they humiliated the person being arrested or otherwise behaved in a 'high-handed, insulting, malicious or oppressive manner [in conducting] the arrest',[1] and this is so even if the police officers thought they were entitled to make the arrest in question and therefore did not knowingly commit the tort of false imprisonment in making the arrest.

(2) *Conduct after the tort was committed.* In *Sutcliffe v Pressdram Ltd* (1991), the Court of Appeal held that if A has wrongfully defamed B, A will act in an arrogant and high-handed manner in dealing with B's claims to be compensated for the actionable losses suffered by her as a result of A's defaming her if: (i) he fails to make any or sufficient apology for and withdrawal of his defamatory statement; (ii) he repeats the statement; (iii) he tries to deter B from proceeding with her claim against A; (iv) he tries to defeat B's claims by persisting, 'by way of a prolonged or hostile cross-examination of [B] or in turgid speeches to the jury, in a plea of justification which is bound to fail';[2] (v) he tries to give wider publicity to his defamatory statement in the preliminaries to the trial of B's action against A or in the trial itself; (vi) he engages in a general persecution of B.[3]

In *Ley v Hamilton* (1935), the claimant libelled the defendant by publishing to some business partners of the defendant a letter which alleged that the defendant had embezzled money. This was completely untrue. When the claimant sued the defendant for libel, the defendant unsurprisingly did not seek to rely in his pleadings on a defence of justification but instead claimed that his statement to the claimant's business partners was protected by qualified privilege. However, when the case came to trial and the defendant was cross-examined, he persisted in claiming that the claimant *had* embezzled money. The claimant won his case and was awarded aggravated damages as well as damages to compensate him for the actionable losses suffered by him as a result of the defendant's libel. The award of aggravated damages was upheld by the House of Lords.

In *Alexander v Home Office* (1988), the Court of Appeal held that if A commits a tort by unlawfully discriminating against B on grounds of her race, A will act in an arrogant and high-handed way in dealing with B's claims to be compensated for the actionable losses suffered by her as a result of A's discrimination if: (1) he makes untrue and injurious allegations about B in an attempt to establish that his acts of discrimination against B were not racially motivated; *or* (2) he conspicuously fails to acknowledge that his acts of discrimination against B were unjustified.[4] Similarly, if A commits the tort of false imprisonment by arresting B when he had no right to do so, he will act in an arrogant and high-handed way in dealing with B's claims to be compensated for the losses suffered by

---

[1] [1998] QB 498, 516.
[2] [1991] 1 QB 153, 184.
[3] ibid.
[4] [1988] 1 WLR 968, 979.

her as a result of A's falsely imprisoning her if he attempts, through making untrue allegations about B, to justify his arrest of B.[5]

B. Negligence

It seems to be that aggravated damages will not be awardable against a defendant who is being sued for *negligence*.[6] There seems to be no good reason why this should be so. After all, someone can breach a duty of care owed to another in an arrogant and high-handed manner. (For example, suppose an employer deliberately refused to install necessary safety equipment in his factory on the ground that his employees' safety didn't matter to him.) In *Kralj v McGrath* (1986), Woolf J said that

> it would be wholly inappropriate to introduce into claims . . . for . . . negligence, the concept of aggravated damage. [Making such damages available in negligence cases would] be wholly inconsistent with the general approach to damages in this area, which is to compensate the [claimant] for the loss that she has actually suffered, so far as it is possible to do so, by the award of monetary compensation and not to treat those damages as being a matter which reflects the degree of negligence . . . of the defendant.[7]

But this just begs the question as to whether damages in negligence should be purely compensatory in nature.

In *AB v South West Water Services Ltd* (1993), Sir Thomas Bingham MR said: 'I know of no precedent for awarding damages for indignation aroused by a defendant's conduct [where the defendant has merely acted negligently or committed some other non-intentional tort].'[8] But the fact that there is no precedent for awarding aggravated damages in a negligence case is a poor justification for refusing to award such damages when they are merited.

However, it may be that the courts are moving towards the position that in appropriate cases, aggravated damages may be awarded in negligence cases. In *Ashley v Chief Constable of Sussex Police* (2008),[9] the police were sued in negligence and assault and battery for shooting a man dead in the course of a drugs raid on his house. It was argued that the police had been negligent in organising the raid on the man's house, and had committed

---

[5] *Thompson v Commissioner of Police of the Metropolis* [1998] QB 498, 518.

[6] Aggravated damages have been awarded for: (i) assault or battery in *W v Meah* [1986] 1 All ER 935; (ii) false imprisonment in *Thompson v Commissioner of Police of the Metropolis* [1998] QB 498; (iii) defamation in *Ley v Hamilton* (1935) 153 LT 384, and *Sutcliffe v Pressdram Ltd* [1991] 1 QB 153; (iv) trespass to land in *Drane v Evangelou* [1978] 1 WLR 455 and *McMillan v Singh* (1984) 17 HLR 120; (v) private nuisance in *Thompson v Hill* (1870) LR 5 CP 564; (vi) intentionally inflicting harm on another using unlawful means in *Messenger Newspapers Group Ltd v National Graphical Association* [1984] IRLR 397; (vii) deceit in *Archer v Brown* [1985] QB 401; (viii) malicious falsehood in *Khodaparast v Shad* [2000] 1 WLR 618 (ix) malicious prosecution in *Thompson v Commissioner of Police of the Metropolis* [1998] QB 498; (x) discriminating against another on grounds of race in *Prison Service v Johnson* [1997] ICR 275; and (xi) discriminating against another on grounds of sex in *Ministry of Defence v Meredith* [1995] IRLR 539.

[7] [1986] 1 All ER 54, 61e–g.

[8] [1993] QB 507, 532. It is necessary to insert the passage in square brackets because otherwise Sir Thomas Bingham's remarks may be read as indicating that aggravated damages may never be awarded to the victim of a tort. See Smith J's remarks in *Prison Service v Johnson* [1997] ICR 275, at 286–7: '[It has been suggested] that Sir Thomas Bingham MR was [in *AB v South West Water Services Ltd*] making a statement of general application that there is not or should not be any such thing as an award of aggravated damages . . . [However it must be] realised that those remarks were made in the context of a claim for damages . . . based upon the torts of negligence, non-intentional nuisance and non-intentional breach of statutory duty . . . [Sir Thomas Bingham MR's] dicta were not [therefore] of general application and were not intended to change the law relating to aggravated damages . . .'.

[9] Discussed in detail above, § 2.7.

an unlawful trespass to his person when they shot him. The defendant chief constable was willing to settle the claim in negligence, and pay the dead man's estate aggravated damages as part of that settlement. In regard to that concession, Lord Scott observed that aggravated damages 'would not *normally* be available in a negligence claim.'[10] Lord Neuberger went further:

> I cannot see why [aggravated] damages should not ... be recoverable in some categories of negligence claims ... It appears to me that it would be reminiscent of the bad old days of forms of action if the court held that the Ashleys' claim could result in aggravated damages if framed in battery, but not if framed in negligence.[11]

29.3 THEORIES

Issues of whether aggravated damages can be sued for in negligence aside, the law is clear as to when aggravated damages will be available. What is less clear is *why* the law allows the victim of a tort who has been treated in an arrogant and high-handed way by the person who committed that tort to sue him for aggravated damages. Three theories may be considered.

A. Compensation for distress

There are many *dicta* in the cases which take the view that aggravated damages are really compensatory in nature, and they are designed to compensate the victim of a tort for any *distress* that she has been caused as a result of the way that tort was committed, or as a result of the way she was treated in the aftermath of that tort.[12] However, there are two problems with this view.

First, there is no requirement that the claimant in a tort case show that the defendant's conduct *upset* or *distressed* her before she can be awarded aggravated damages. If the claimant was merely *indignant* or *outraged* at the defendant's conduct, aggravated damages may still be payable to the claimant. Outrage is not the same as distress. Secondly, in some cases where the claimant *was* distressed at the arrogant and high-handed way in which she was treated by the defendant, the court dealing with her claim made her an award of damages for her distress and gave her a *separate* award of aggravated damages.[13] If aggravated damages were meant to compensate for distress, the court would be guilty of double counting here.

B. Civil recourse theory[14]

There is no doubt that we feel entitled to hit back at those who treat us as though we are worthless, and it might be argued that suing for aggravated damages provides us with a civilised, peaceful and orderly way of achieving this goal. On this view, aggravated damages

---

[10] [2008] 1 AC 962, at [23] (emphasis added).
[11] [2008] 1 AC 962, at [102].
[12] *Rookes* v *Barnard* [1964] AC 1129, 1221 (per Lord Devlin); *McCarey* v *Associated Newspapers Ltd (No 2)* [1965] 2 QB 86, 104–105 (per Pearson LJ); *Broome* v *Cassell & Co Ltd* [1972] AC 1027, 1124 (per Lord Diplock); *Archer* v *Brown* [1985] QB 401, 424–5 (per Peter Pain J); *Thompson* v *Commissioner of Police of the Metropolis* [1998] QB 498, 512. See also Scott 2007.
[13] See *Duffy* v *Eastern Social Health and Services Board* [1992] IRLR 251 (£15,000 damages awarded for distress, as well as £5,000 in aggravated damages). Also *Deane* v *Ealing LBC* [1993] ICR 329, 335.
[14] Discussed in detail above, § 28.7(D).

exist to assuage the outrage we feel at the way a tortfeasor has treated us, by allowing us a peaceful way of hurting the tortfeasor for treating us with contempt. As Windeyer J observed in the Australian case of *Uren* v *John Fairfax & Sons Pty Ltd* (1965): 'the satisfaction that the [claimant] gets [from an award of aggravated damages] is that the defendant has been made to pay for what he did.'[15] The difficulty with this view is that it tends to obliterate the distinction between aggravated damages and exemplary damages, that we will look at in the next chapter. However, it could be argued in response that there is in fact no real distinction between the two forms of damages,[16] and we should stop acting as though there is one.

C. Dignity

Theorists who are unhappy with the first two explanations have tended to argue that aggravated damages are awarded to compensate the victim of a tort for the injury to his *dignity* that has been occasioned by the way in which that tort was committed.[17] As John Murphy argues:

> wherever an individual is subjected to conduct that constitutes or implies some form of disregard for the innate values associated with personhood – be it their deliberate humiliation or objectification (in the sense of treatment as though a mere thing or object) – that person can be said to have suffered an affront to his or her dignity. It is the explicit or implicit treatment of another in a manner which undermines or demeans their human status or moral worth that comprises an affront to dignity. It is treating them as though they were somehow worth less than oneself, or simply worthless.[18]

This theory chimes in well with the requirement that it be shown that the defendant treated the claimant in an 'arrogant and high-handed manner' before aggravated damages will be awarded against him. However, there are two aspects of the current law on aggravated damages that may stand in the way of our accepting this theory as correct.

First, companies have no dignity – so, if this theory were correct, we would not expect companies to be able to sue for aggravated damages. The courts have proved themselves divided on the issue of whether companies can sue for aggravated damages. In *Messenger Newspapers Group Ltd* v *National Graphical Association* (1984), Caulfield J said that: 'aggravated damages can be awarded against inanimate legal entities like limited companies, and I cannot see any reason why the same legal entities cannot be awarded aggravated . . . damages'.[19] On the other hand, in *Columbia Picture Industries Inc* v *Robinson* (1987), the defendants wrongfully and arrogantly seized a number of video tapes which were on sale in a video shop run by one Robinson and a company controlled by him. Scott J held that Robinson and the company were entitled to sue the defendants for damages. Robinson was allowed to sue the defendants for compensatory damages and aggravated damages. The company was only allowed to sue the defendants for compensatory damages. The reason

[15] (1965–66) 117 CLR 118, 151.

[16] Murphy 2010a does point out (at 355) that there may be a distinction where the victim of a tort dies: in such a case exemplary damages cannot be sued for by the victim's estate (see below, § 30.3(4)), but the House of Lords saw no problem in *Ashley* with allowing the dead man's estate to sue for aggravated damages in that case.

[17] Beever 2003a; Murphy 2010a. Birks 1996a argues that aggravated damages are not compensatory but instead mark the fact that a tortfeasor has, in the way he treated the victim of his tort, committed the distinct tort of using unlawful means to treat someone with less than an 'equality of respect'.

[18] Murphy 2010a, 360.

[19] [1984] IRLR 397, at [77].

why the company was only allowed to sue the defendants for compensatory damages but not aggravated damages was that 'contumely and affront affect individuals, not inanimate corporations'.[20]

The second objection is more serious. John Murphy's explanation of the concept of dignity suggests that someone's dignity can be injured without their being aware of it. If, *in fact*, A has treated B as 'worthless' then A has injured B's dignity, whether B is aware of it or not. (Suppose, for example, that A turned B's application for a job down because she was a woman, but he convinced her that he had turned it down because she lacked the necessary qualifications.) But it is not clear that aggravated damages can be awarded simply on the basis that the victim of a tort has suffered an *objective* insult to her dignity.

For example, in *Ministry of Defence v Meredith* (1995), the defendants unlawfully sacked the claimant when she became pregnant. The claimant sued the defendants for compensatory *and* aggravated damages. As part of her case, she sought to obtain discovery of documents that would indicate whether or not the defendants had *known* they were acting unlawfully in sacking her because she was pregnant. The Employment Appeal Tribunal held that the claimant was not entitled to discovery of those documents as they had no relevance to her claim. They obviously had no relevance to her claim for compensatory damages; and they had no relevance to her claim for aggravated damages as – they held – she would *only* have been entitled to claim such damages from the defendants if she *already knew* that the defendants had acted in an arrogant and high-handed manner in sacking her.

Again, in *Ashley v Chief Constable of Sussex Police* (2008) the deceased knew nothing about the circumstances leading up to his shooting before he was shot dead by the police. So he could not have known whether the drugs raid on his house had been organised or conducted by the police in an 'arrogant and high-manner'. Lord Carswell thought this fact made it difficult to see how the police could be sued for aggravated damages.[21]

If – as these cases suggest – something more than an objective injury to the claimant's dignity is required before aggravated damages can be awarded, this tends to undermine the strength of dignity-based explanations of such awards. If an on-going *awareness* that you have been treated with contempt by the defendant is required, then we seem to tip back towards the idea that aggravated damages are awarded to assuage the victim of a tort's outrage at having been treated with contempt, and satisfy their desire to see the tortfeasor pay for treating them that way. If this is right then two things follow. First, companies should *still* not be allowed to sue for aggravated damages. (Companies don't feel outrage and certainly shouldn't be allowed to pursue desires to hurt someone else who has wronged them.) Secondly, the whole of this chapter should be swallowed up by the next chapter, on exemplary damages.

---

[20] [1987] 1 Ch 38, 88.

[21] [2008] 1 AC 962, at [80]. Lord Neuberger was willing to award aggravated damages on the basis that it was reasonably foreseeable that 'a negligently mishandled armed police raid could result in just the sort of mental distress and shock that aggravated damages are intended to reflect'. But if no such mental distress or shock was experienced because the deceased in *Ashley* was shot dead before he could gather his thoughts, it is hard to see how aggravated damages could be awarded in this case.

Further reading

John Murphy's piece on aggravated damages – **'The nature and domain of aggravated damages'** (2010) 69 *Cambridge Law Journal* 353 – is well worth reading in full and currently represents the state of the art in thinking about the nature and function of aggravated damages. Students should never pass up the chance to read anything by **Peter Birks**, and they should definitely not miss the chance to read **'Harassment and hubris: the right to an equality of respect'** (1997) 32 *Irish Jurist* 1, even though we would disagree with his claim that there exists a distinct tort of committing some other tort in an arrogant or high-handed manner, and that aggravated damages are awarded in response to that distinct tort.

Visit **www.mylawchamber.co.uk/mcbride** to access tools to help you develop and test your knowledge of Tort law, including interactive multiple choice questions, practice exam

questions with guidance, weblinks, legal newsfeed, additional case summaries, legal updates and tips on answering problem and essay questions.

30 Exemplary damages

30.1 The basics *796*

30.2 Requirements *797*

30.3 Further points *801*

30.4 Reform *802*

Overview

This chapter is concerned with exemplary damages – damages that are designed to punish a tortfeasor for the way he has behaved in committing a tort. After introducing the concept of exemplary damages in section 30.1, we set out in section 30.2 the many requirements that have to be satisfied before an award of exemplary damages may be made against a tortfeasor. Section 30.3 is quite technical, making four points about the assessment and award of exemplary damages. In section 30.4 we examine the different options for reforming this area of law, including abolishing it altogether.

30.1 THE BASICS

This chapters deals with one of the most controversial areas of tort law, as it seems to intrude on the proper function of the criminal law – that of punishing people who have knowingly or recklessly violated other people's rights. The power that the courts currently enjoy in civil cases to award exemplary damages against a tortfeasor whose conduct was so outrageous as to be worthy of punishment has long been regarded with suspicion, as undermining the protections that the criminal law affords to those whom the State wishes to punish.

In *Rookes* v *Barnard* (1964), the House of Lords made a major effort to place major limits on this power, ruling that exemplary damages could only be awarded in tort where: (1) the defendant was a public body and acted in an 'arbitrary, oppressive or unconstitutional manner' in committing a tort; or (2) the defendant committed a tort because he figured he would make more money from committing that tort than he would have to pay out in compensatory damages to the victim of that tort. But within those limits, the power to award exemplary damages in tort cases remained.

Since 1964, academic and judicial opinion has been deeply divided on the future of exemplary damages. Nobody seems that happy with *Rookes* v *Barnard*. Some argue that the *Rookes* v *Barnard* limits on when exemplary damages should be abolished, pointing out that no other common law jurisdiction has followed the House of Lords' example in *Rookes* v *Barnard* and sought to limit its powers to award exemplary damages in civil cases. Others regret that the House of Lords in *Rookes* v *Barnard* 'was willing to wound and yet afraid to strike'[1] down the institution of exemplary damages altogether. We will make our position clear in the final section of this chapter. But first we will set out the current law on when a claimant can sue a defendant in tort for exemplary damages.

---

[1] Alexander Pope, *An Epistle to Dr Arbuthnot* (1734).

30.2 REQUIREMENTS

A. Desert

The most fundamental requirement is that the defendant must *deserve* to be punished for what he has done. But when will this be the case? In *A v Bottrill* (2003) – a Privy Council case – the minority (Lords Hutton and Mustill) argued that exemplary damages should only be awarded against a tortfeasor who was *aware* that his conduct amounted to a tort. But the majority took a more expansive approach, holding that exemplary damages could be awarded against a tortfeasor who was unaware that he was doing anything wrong at the time he acted if his conduct was so *outrageous* as to be worthy of condemnation.

So in *Bottrill*, the claimant had four cervical smear tests over four years. In each case, the smear test was examined by the defendant pathologist and in each case he gave the claimant a clean bill of health. However, the defendant failed in each case to inspect the claimant's smear test properly. Had he done so, he would have spotted that the claimant was in danger of developing cervical cancer and the claimant would have received treatment that would have prevented the cancer developing. However, because the claimant's smear tests were not properly examined, the claimant's condition went untreated and she developed cervical cancer. The Privy Council held, by a 3:2 majority, that exemplary damages could be awarded against the defendant.[2] While the defendant may have *thought* that he was adopting an adequate procedure for inspecting the claimant's smear tests, he had acted so outrageously in adopting a procedure for inspecting smear tests that had a 50% error rate[3] that his conduct was worthy of punishment.

It is now clear that the English courts are following the approach laid down by the majority of the Privy Council in *Bottrill* and asking themselves whether the defendant's conduct was so outrageous as to be worthy of punishment. For example, in *Muuse v Secretary of State for the Home Department* (2010),[4] the claimant was detained by the Home Office after serving four months in custody for a criminal damage offence. The Home Office was not entitled to do this: the claimant was a Dutch national who could not be deported from the UK, or detained in the UK once his prison sentence had been served. Unfortunately, no one who handled the claimant's case could be bothered to ascertain his true nationality – despite the claimant's repeated protestations that he was Dutch and the fact that he had actually handed over to officials a Dutch ID card in his name – and handled his case on the basis that he was a Somali national. Even if he had been, the claimant's case was still handled improperly: he was detained without any of the correct procedures for notifying him of the grounds of detention having been followed. Eventually the claimant was released, after having been detained for about four months.

The judge at first instance found the Home Office liable for false imprisonment, and awarded the claimant £27,500 in exemplary damages. The Court of Appeal upheld the award, expressly disapproving the suggestion that 'malice, fraud, insolence [or] cruelty' has to be shown before exemplary damages may be awarded against a defendant.[5] It is enough

---

[2] As the case occurred in New Zealand, she was not allowed to sue the defendant for compensation for the fact that she developed cervical cancer: that was covered under the New Zealand Accident Compensation Scheme (summarised below, § 38.3(A)). However, s 396 of the Accident Insurance Act 1998 preserved the powers of the courts in New Zealand to award exemplary damages against defendants in personal injury cases.

[3] That is, the procedure failed to recognise the signs of cancer in every other smear test inspected that objectively did show signs of cancer.

[4] Noted, Stanton 2010, Varuhas 2011.

[5] [2010] EWCA Civ 453, at [71].

to show that the defendant's conduct was so 'outrageous' as to be worthy of punishment.[6] So in *Muuse*, while no one involved in handling the claimant's case may have been *aware* they were unlawfully detaining the claimant, their 'manifest incompetence', their repeated and unexplained failures to follow proper procedures, and the Home Office's systemic failure to put any checks in place on officials acting incompetently meant that the claimant's detention was so 'outrageous' as to be worthy of punishment.[7]

B. *Rookes* v *Barnard* (1964)

Even if a tortfeasor's conduct in committing that tort was so outrageous as to be worthy of punishment, exemplary damages can only be awarded against him if his case falls into one of the situations in which the House of Lords held in *Rookes* v *Barnard* (1964) that exemplary damages can be awarded. The House of Lords held[8] in *Rookes* v *Barnard* that if A has committed a tort, exemplary damages can only be awarded against him if:

(1) A was a 'servant of the government' at the time he committed his tort and he acted in an 'oppressive, arbitrary or unconstitutional' manner in committing that tort;[9]
(2) A committed his tort because he figured that he would make more money committing that tort than he would have to pay out in damages to the victim of that tort; or
(3) statute law authorises an award of exemplary damages to be made against someone who has committed the kind of tort that A committed.

If A's case does not fall into one of these categories, then exemplary damages *cannot* be awarded against him. We will now look at each of these categories in turn.

(1) *Torts committed by public officials*. It is clear from the judgments in *Broome* v *Cassell & Co Ltd* (1972) that the phrase 'servant of the government' should be construed broadly: it covers anyone 'purporting to exercise powers of government, central or local, conferred on them by statute or at common law'.[10] So the police would be counted for these purposes as being servants of the government; as would officials of a local authority. In *AB* v *South West Water Services Ltd* (1993), the Court of Appeal held that a nationalised corporation which supplied water to the inhabitants of Camelford was not a 'servant of the government' for the purpose of determining whether or not it could be sued for exemplary damages; it did not exercise any governmental powers but was merely a commercial operation.[11]

(2) *Gain-seeking torts*. Lord Devlin made it clear in his judgment in *Rookes* v *Barnard* that this category does not just cover cases where someone deliberately commits a tort because he thinks that he will make more money by committing that tort than he will have to pay the victim of the tort in compensatory damages:

---

[6] [2010] EWCA Civ 453, at [70], quoting Lord Hutton in *Kuddus* v *Chief Constable of Leicestershire* [2002] AC 122, at [89].

[7] [2010] EWCA Civ 453, at [73]–[74].

[8] Or rather Lord Devlin: he was the only Law Lord in *Rookes* v *Barnard* to address the issue of when exemplary damages could be awarded against a defendant in a tort case. The other Law Lords were content to indicate that they agreed with this aspect of Lord Devlin's judgment.

[9] [1964] AC 1129, 1226.

[10] [1972] AC 1027, 1130 (per Lord Diplock). See also 1077–8 (per Lord Hailsham LC) and 1087–8 (per Lord Reid).

[11] [1993] QB 507, 525 (per Stuart-Smith LJ), 532 (per Sir Thomas Bingham MR).

It extends to cases in which [someone deliberately commits a tort in order] to gain ... some object – perhaps some property which he covets – which either he could not obtain at all or not obtain except at a price greater than he wants to put down.[12]

For example, in *Drane v Evangelou* (1978), the defendant let some premises to the claimant. He then unlawfully evicted the claimant from the premises so that they could be occupied by his in-laws. It was held that the case fell within *Rookes v Barnard*'s second category of situations where exemplary damages could be awarded: the defendant deliberately committed the tort of trespass because he thought he would gain more by committing that tort – possession of the premises occupied by the claimant – than he would have to pay the claimant in damages.

For a case to fall under this category, it does not have to be shown that the defendant did a precise calculation as to how much he stood to gain and lose from commiting his tort.[13] It is enough to show the tort was committed with a view to a gain: from that it can be inferred that the tortfeasor calculated he could make more than he would lose from committing the tort.[14]

(3) *Statutory authorisation*. There are very few examples of statutes which authorise the victim of a tort to sue the person who committed that tort for exemplary damages. Perhaps the only example is provided by s 13(2) of the Reserve and Auxiliary Forces (Protection of Civil Interests) Act 1951, which provides that exemplary damages may be awarded against someone who converts goods that are covered by the Act.

C. Compensatory and aggravated damages not enough to punish

If a defendant's conduct in committing a tort was so outrageous as to be worthy of punishment, *and* the circumstances in which he committed that tort fall within one of the three *Rookes v Barnard* categories of situation where exemplary damages may be awarded, exemplary damages will still not be awarded against the defendant if requiring him to pay compensatory and aggravated damages to the victim of his tort will punish him adequately for what he has done.[15]

D. No double punishment involved

Until recently, it had been thought that exemplary damages could not be awarded against a defendant who had been criminally punished for his conduct.[16] The reason for this is pretty obvious: the law should not punish people twice for the same offence. If a defendant's conduct has already been the subject of criminal punishment, it is inappropriate for the civil law to come in and add to his punishment.

This seemed obvious until the decision of the Court of Appeal in *Borders v Commissioner of Police of the Metropolis* (2005), and the decision of Treacy J in *AT v Dulghieru* (2009). In the *Borders* case, £100,000 was awarded in exemplary damages against a book thief who had

---

[12] [1964] AC 1129, 1227.

[13] *Broome v Cassell & Co Ltd* [1972] AC 1027, 1078–9 (per Lord Hailsham LC), 1094 (per Lord Morris).

[14] *John v Mirror Group Newspapers Ltd* [1997] QB 586, 619A.

[15] *Rookes v Barnard* [1964] AC 1129, at 1228: jury is only allowed to award exemplary damages against a defendant in a tort case if 'the sum which they have in mind to award as compensation (which may, of course, be a sum aggravated by the way in which the defendant has behaved ...) is inadequate to punish him for his outrageous conduct ...'.

[16] See, for example, *Archer v Brown* [1985] QB 401 (no award of exemplary damages against a defendant who had committed the tort of deceit because he had already been sent to prison for his fraud).

already been sentenced to 30 months in prison for his activities. In the *AT* case, the two defendants had been involved in a sex trafficking network which had resulted in the four claimants in *AT* being forced to have sex with clients over one or two months. £60,000 in exemplary damages was awarded against the defendants, even though they had already been sentenced to long terms in prison for their activities.

These cases are an illustration of the saying that 'ideas have consequences'. And really bad ideas have really bad consequences. The really bad idea[17] here – endorsed by Sedley LJ in the *Borders* case,[18] and adopted by Treacy J in the *AT* case[19] – is that exemplary damages that are awarded under the second *Rookes v Barnard* head are not really designed to punish the defendant for his behaviour, but are really a form of gain-based damages, designed to strip the defendant of the profits he has made from committing a tort. (Gain-based damages are discussed in the next chapter.) So if this is true, then there can be no objection to awarding exemplary damages against a defendant under the second head in *Rookes v Barnard* even though the defendant has already been criminally punished for his behaviour, as the award of exemplary damages under that head is not intended to punish, but to strip the defendant of the gains he has made from his behaviour.

Why is it such a bad idea to say that exemplary damages awarded under the second head in *Rookes v Barnard* are really a form of gain-based damages? There are two reasons. First, and most importantly, it's just *not true*. There is no reason to think that a defendant *actually* has to have made a gain from his tort for exemplary damages to be awarded against him under the second head in *Rookes v Barnard*. All that has to be shown is that he *aimed* to make a gain. And even if he did make a gain from his tort, there is no reason to think that the exemplary damages that will be awarded against him under the second head in *Rookes v Barnard* will precisely match the gain that he has made.[20] As we will see, exemplary damages that are awarded against a defendant are designed to make the defendant 'smart'. How much is required to do that will depend on the defendant's overall resources, not the size of the gain that he made from committing his tort.

Secondly, legal fictions are always and everywhere a bad idea in the long run. Awarding gain-based damages under the heading of exemplary damages can only result in the law becoming confused and unprincipled. For example, until *AT v Dulghieru*, there had been no authority in English law that allowed gain-based damages to be sued for in a case involving a trespass to the person, and at the time *AT v Dulghieru* was decided, two significant Court of Appeal cases had set their face against any extensions being made in awards of gain-based damages.[21] So allowing an award of what was meant to be, effectively, gain-based damages in the *AT* case raised important issues of precedent and principle, that were never addressed at all by Treacy J in *AT* because the damages were being awarded as 'exemplary damages' rather than 'gain-based damages'. If Treacy J had thought it desirable to award gain-based damages in the *AT* case, he should have proceeded by declining to award exemplary damages (on the basis that the defendants had already been punished for their conduct) and then made an award of gain-based damages, having first explained how such an award was justified in principle and consistent with the authorities that were binding on him.

---

[17] First propounded by restitution scholars casting around for authorities that would support the idea that there was such a thing as gain-based damages under the common law. See, for example, Edelman 2006, at 149.

[18] [2005] EWCA Civ 197, at [25]–[27].

[19] [2009] EWHC 225, at [68].

[20] For example, £60,000 represented about half of what the defendants might have been expected to make from forcing the claimants in the *AT* case to have sex with clients. See, further, Keren-Paz 2010a.

[21] *Devenish Nutrition Ltd v Sanofi-Aventis SA* [2009] Ch 390; *Forsyth-Grant v Allen* [2008] EWCA Civ 505.

30.3 FURTHER POINTS

Here are four more important points about the law on exemplary damages:

(1) *Quantum of damages.* In a case where it would be appropriate to award exemplary damages against a defendant, the damages payable will be just enough to bring the entire amount of damages that the defendant has to pay to the claimant up to a level sufficient to punish him for his conduct.[22]

For example, in *Duffy* v *Eastern Health and Social Services Board* (1992), the defendants unlawfully discriminated against the claimant on grounds of her religion. The claimant was entitled to sue the defendants for £15,000 in compensatory damages and for £5,000 in aggravated damages. The court held that the claimant was entitled to sue the defendant for exemplary damages and found that the defendants would only be sufficiently punished for behaving in the way they did if they were made to pay the claimant £25,000 in damages. So they held that the claimant was entitled to sue the defendant for £5,000 in exemplary damages.

This general rule is subject to two qualifications. First, in *Holden* v *Chief Constable of Lancashire* (1987), the Court of Appeal held that the exemplary damages payable to the victim of a tort might be reduced if he or she provoked the person who committed that tort into committing that tort.[23]

Secondly, in a case where a defendant's conduct has resulted in his committing torts in relation to multiple claimants, the Court of Appeal held in *Riches* v *News Group Newspapers* (1986) that the size of the exemplary damages payable by the defendant should be assessed by: (a) assessing how much of a sum the defendant would have to pay to punish him for his conduct; (b) subtracting from that the total sum of compensatory and aggravated damages that the defendant must pay to *all* the claimants; (c) and awarding the difference between (a) and (b) as exemplary damages against the defendant, shared out in equal shares between the claimants.[24]

(2) *Standard of proof.* In a criminal case, a defendant can only be found guilty and punished if it is proved *beyond a reasonable doubt* that he committed the offence with which he is charged. But, as we have seen already in the context of the law on causation,[25] that in civil cases, a defendant can be held liable if it is proved *on the balance of probabilities* that the defendant committed a tort and caused the claimant actionable harm. It is one of the main criticisms of the law on exemplary damages that a defendant can end being punished for committing a particular tort when it has merely been established that it is was more likely than not that he committed that tort.[26] It seems right that the courts should

---

[22] What level of damages will be sufficient to punish A for committing his tort will, of course, depend on his means and how badly he behaved in committing his tort: *Rookes* v *Barnard* [1964] AC 1129, 1228.

[23] [1987] 1 QB 380, 388 (per Purchas LJ).

[24] It seems that the exemplary damages will be split equally between the claimants even if one claimant was more affected by the defendant's conduct than the others. So the exemplary damages payable in *AT* v *Dulghieru* [2009] EWHC 225 were split equally among the four claimants in that case, even though two of the claimants had each been forced to work as prostitutes for two months, and the other two for a month each.

[25] See above, § 9.4.

[26] As happened to O.J. Simpson. He was charged with murdering his ex-wife, Nicole Brown Simpson and her friend, Ron Goldman, and acquitted on the ground that the jury thought it could not be proved beyond a reasonable doubt that he had committed the murders. Ron Goldman's estate then sued O.J. Simpson in tort. It was found that it was more probable than not that O.J. Simpson had murdered Ron Goldman and Ron Goldman's estate was held to be entitled to sue O.J. Simson for $33.5m, most of which was exemplary damages. (O.J. Simpson's desire to avoid paying these damages led him to place a large amount of sports memorabilia in his house in the hands of 'friends'. In attempting to get these pieces of memorabilia back, he committed offences of kidnapping, armed robbery, and burglary that resulted in his being sentenced to 15 years in prison.)

only award exemplary damages against a defendant who has *clearly* done what he is alleged to have done. (Having said that, there is no English case – so far as we know – where exemplary damages have been awarded against a defendant where there was any doubt about what the defendant had done.)

(3) *Vicarious liability*. If *Employee* has committed a tort in the course of his employment, the *Victim* of that tort will be entitled to sue the employee's *Employer* for whatever *Victim* could sue *Employee* for by way of compensatory and aggravated damages.[27] But if exemplary damages may be awarded against *Employee*, could they also be awarded against *Employer*? One would have thought that, in principle, the answer should be 'no' – why should *Employer* be punished for what his *Employee* has done?[28] But a number of cases seem to assume that if *Employee* is liable to pay *Victim* exemplary damages, then so should *Employer*.[29]

(4) *Death*. Section 1(2)(a)(i) of the Law Reform (Miscellaneous Provisions) Act 1934 provides that if the victim of a tort dies before she has had a chance to sue the person who committed that tort for damages, any right she might have had to sue the tortfeasor for exemplary damages will die with her.

30.4 REFORM

A. Functions

In order to assess whether the law on exemplary damages is in need of reform, we need to determine whether it serves any useful purpose. It could be argued that awards of exemplary damages serve not one, but two useful functions.

(1) *Vindicating the rule of law*. The House of Lords in *Rookes v Barnard* (1964) clearly thought that awards of exemplary damages served a useful purpose in giving people an incentive to obey the law.[30] This was why they limited such awards to cases where a public official had acted outrageously in committing a tort, and cases where someone had committed a tort figuring he could make more money by committing that tort than he would have to pay out in damages. In each of these cases, the standard incentives that the tortfeasor has to obey the law are significantly weakened. In the second case, the prospect of having to pay compensatory and aggravated damages to the victim of his tort will not put the tortfeasor

---

[27] See below, § 37.1.

[28] See *Kuddus v Chief Constable of Leicestershire* [2002] 2 AC 122, at [137].

[29] See *Lancashire County Council v Municipal Mutual Insurance Ltd* [1997] QB 897 (not improper for local authority to insure against exemplary damages because such awards could be made against it under the law on vicarious liability, and if such an award were made, it would not be to blame for the conduct that was being punished); *Thompson v Commissioner of Police of the Metropolis* [1998] QB 498 (not only can exemplary damages be awarded against an employer under the law on vicarious liability, they could actually exceed the exemplary damages that the employee would be liable to pay because the employer would have more means than the employee); *Muuse v Secretary of State for the Home Department* [2010] EWCA Civ 453 (exemplary damages awarded against Home Office because of 'manifest incompetence' of its employees). See also *New South Wales v Ibbett* [2006] HCA 57, where the High Court of Australia upheld an award of exemplary damages against the State of New South Wales on the ground that it was vicariously liable for two police officers' torts (trespass to land and assault), holding (at [51]) that the award was necessary to bring home to the State that police officers employed by the State had to be trained not to engage in the sort of conduct that the police officers in *Ibbett* had engaged in.

[30] See *Rookes v Barnard* [1964] AC 1129, 1226 ('an award of exemplary damages can serve a useful purpose in vindicating the strength of the law'); also *Kuddus v Chief Constable of Leicestershire* [2002] 2 AC 122, at [63] (per Lord Hutton): 'the power to award exemplary damages ... serves to uphold and vindicate the rule of law because it makes clear that the courts will not tolerate such conduct.'

from committing his tort. In the first case, the public official might think it unlikely that his outrageous behaviour will receive any sanction from his superiors or the police. The tendency of the State to look after its own was remarked on by the Court of Appeal in the *Muuse* case:

> There has been no Parliamentary or other enquiry into Mr Muuse's case. No Minister or senior official has been held accountable. We were not told of any internal or other enquiry conducted by the Permanent Secretary or Head of the Immigration Directorate (or as it now is the UK Border Agency). The only way in which the misconduct of the Home Office has been exposed to public view and his rights vindicated is by the action in the High Court.[31]

The Court of Appeal went on to observe that:

> Given the absence of Parliamentary accountability for the arbitrary and unlawful detention of Mr Muuse, the lack of an enquiry and the paucity of the measures taken by the Home Office to prevent a recurrence, it is difficult to see how such arbitrary conduct can be deterred in the future and the Home Office made to improve the way in which the power to imprison is exercised other than by the court making an award of exemplary damages . . . [The] award of [such] damages . . . has a real role in restraining the arbitrary use of executive power and buttressing civil liberties, given the way the United Kingdom's Parliamentary democracy in fact operates.[32]

(2) *Civil recourse theory.* We saw in the previous chapter that it is normal for people to feel entitled to strike back at those who treat them with contempt. It could be argued that allowing a claimant to sue a defendant in tort for exemplary damages when conditions (1) ('desert'), (3) ('compensatory and aggravated damages not enough to punish') and (4) ('no double punishment involved') in section 30.2, above, are satisfied gives the claimant a civilised, peaceful and orderly way of satisfying his natural desire to see the defendant pay for treating her in such an outrageous fashion.[33] While we might be initially skeptical as to whether awards of exemplary damages play a role in allowing a claimant to ensure the defendant gets what he deserves for treating her with contempt, it should be noted that this view of exemplary damages explains s 1(2)(a)(i) of the Law Reform (Miscellaneous Provisions) Act 1934, which prevents exemplary damages being awarded to the estate of the victim of a tort who died after that tort was committed. If the victim of a tort is no longer around, there is no longer anyone whose desire to strike back at the person who committed that tort needs to be assuaged.

B. Options for reform

Now that we have identified the functions played by awards of exemplary damages, we can canvass the two main options for reform of this area of the law.

(1) *Abolition.* This is not a possibility we should seriously entertain. Abolishing awards of exemplary damages would clearly weaken the force of the rule of law among those defendants at whom *Rookes* v *Barnard* currently directs such awards. Purists like Allan Beever object to the damage done to the 'integrity' of tort law by allowing claimants to make claims for exemplary damages on the basis that allowing such claims to be made is

---

[31] [2010] EWCA Civ 453, at [75].
[32] [2010] EWCA Civ 453, at [77].
[33] See Zipursky 2005 (at 151–61), defending awards of exemplary damages on the ground that, on occasion, the victim of a tort has a 'right to be punitive' towards the person who committed that tort, because of the manner in which it was committed. See Stevens 2007, at 85–7, and Sebok 2007 for similar arguments.

in the public interest.[34] Why should only the *victim* of a tort be allowed to sue for such damages? Why should it only be *damages* that can be sued for? However, impurity is not always a bad thing. Pearls come from a bit of grit that finds its way into an oyster shell. It seems that we would be throwing away a valuable pearl if in the interests of purity, we abolished the ability of civil courts to award exemplary damages.

(2) *Reversing Rookes* v *Barnard.* Should we follow the example of other common law jurisdictions and get rid of the *Rookes* v *Barnard* limits on when exemplary damages may be awarded in a tort case?

Rule of law considerations do not strongly indicate that there is a problem with *Rookes* v *Barnard*. Where a private actor is thinking about committing a tort, but not for gain, the existing incentives that he has to obey the law (the prospect of having to pay damages to the victim of his tort, and possible criminal prosecution for what he has done, as well as extra-legal sanctions such a losing his job) will usually prove sufficient to keep him straight; and where they do not, it is not clear that the prospect of an award of exemplary damages will make any difference.

From the point of view of an adherent to civil recourse theory, *Rookes* v *Barnard* looks more problematic – it stands in the way of a claimant suing for exemplary damages to make a defendant pay for treating her in an outrageous fashion, when the defendant was a private person and his tort was not committed for gain. However, even from this perspective, something can be said for *Rookes* v *Barnard*. It might be argued that there is something especially outrageous about committing a tort for financial gain or in your capacity as a public servant. Public servants are supposed to work for us, not against us. And treating someone's interests as less important than making a financial gain for yourself is especially insulting. So it might be argued that in the situations currently covered by *Rookes* v *Barnard*, a claimant's desire to strike back at the defendant for what he has done will be especially strong; and there is not much of a case for extending the availability of exemplary damages to cases where the desire to see the defendant pay for what he has done will be less strong.

Further reading

The case for and against abolishing awards of exemplary damages is considered in **Birks (ed),** *Wrongs and Remedies in Private Law* **(OUP, 1996)** (see the chapters by **McBride** ('Punitive damages') and **Burrows** ('Reforming exemplary damages')) and **Rickett (ed),** *Justifying Private Law Remedies* **(Hart Publishing, 2008)** (see the chapters by **Edelman** ('In defence of exemplary damages') and **Beever** ('Justice and punishment in tort: a comparative theoretical analysis')).

Visit **www.mylawchamber.co.uk/mcbride** to access tools to help you develop and test your knowledge of Tort law, including interactive multiple choice questions, practice exam questions with guidance, weblinks, legal newsfeed, additional case summaries, legal updates and tips on answering problem and essay questions.

premium
mylawchamber
unrivalled support for legal education

---

[34] Beever 2003a.

31 Gain-based damages

31.1 The basics *805*

31.2 Disgorgement damages *810*

31.3 Licence fee damages *814*

31.4 Theories *816*

Overview

This chapter deals with a very difficult and controversial question – when will the victim of a tort be entitled to sue a tortfeasor because he has made some sort of gain from committing his tort? Section 31.1 explains why precisely this area of law is so difficult to understand and make sense of. Sections 31.2 to 31.3 set out the different types of damages that might be awarded against a tortfeasor who has made a gain from committing his tort. Section 31.4 discusses why such damages are awarded at all.

31.1 THE BASICS

In this chapter we are concerned with situations when the victim of a tort can recover damages from the person who committed that tort assessed not according to the *loss* the victim has suffered as a result of that tort being committed, but according to the *gain* made by the tortfeasor as a result of committing that tort. The law on when the victim of a tort is entitled to sue the person who committed that tort for *gain-based damages* is extremely difficult to set out correctly and discuss intelligently, for four reasons.

A. Interpretation

First of all, it is a matter of dispute as to what cases provide genuine examples of a victim of a tort being allowed to sue for gain-based damages, and what cases only *seem* to provide examples of gain-based damages being awarded and can be more accurately explained on some other basis.

We saw an example of this in the previous chapter with awards of damages under the second head in *Rookes* v *Barnard* (1964). Some say damages awarded under this head are intended to strip a tortfeasor of the gain he has made by committing a tort. But this does not seem plausible: no gain has to be proved before such damages can be awarded, and the damages awarded under this head are not calculated by seeing what gain has been made by the tortfeasor. The better explanation is that such damages are designed to *punish* a tortfeasor for his outrageous conduct in committing a tort with the *aim* of making a gain for himself.

Again, some say that damages that are awarded in lieu of an injunction are gain-based, and argue on that basis that gain-based damages are available when someone commits the tort of private nuisance, as damages in lieu of an injunction are often awarded in such cases.[1] The reason why damages awarded in lieu of an injunction *seem* to be gain-based is

---

[1] See above/below, §§ 15.12(A)(2), 33.4(C).

this. Consider a situation where A is, in principle, entitled to an injunction to stop B polluting A's land with so much smoke from B's factory, but – because the loss A is suffering from the pollution is relatively small and the inconvenience to B of an injunction is relatively large – the courts award A damages in lieu of an injunction instead. The courts assess how much to award A in damages by seeing how much A and B would *hypothetically* agree A should be paid for giving up his right[2] to an injunction, were each party to negotiate in good faith and not hold out grimly for the best possible deal for themselves. Were such a *hypothetical bargain* to be entered into, A would insist on B paying him enough money to cover any losses he might suffer as a result of B's pollution *but he would also* want B to add something on top of that to give A a share of any gain B might make from being allowed to carry on polluting A's land. It is only fair that if A is giving up his right to an injunction, that he should get a proportion of the profits that B will make as a result of not being subject to that injunction. It is because damages in lieu of an injunction contain this gain-based element that some people argue that they are gain-based *in nature*.

The better view, we would submit, is that damages in lieu of an injunction are not gain-based at all. They are *compensatory*: they exist to compensate A for the fact that he has been forced to sell his right to an injunction by giving him a fair price for giving up that right.[3] The fact that that fair price has a gain-based element to it, does not make damages in lieu of an injunction gain-based in nature. So there is no inconsistency between the cases in which damages in lieu of an injunction that included a gain-based element were routinely awarded in private nuisance cases,[4] and cases in which it was denied that gain-based damages could be awarded to the victim of a private nuisance.[5] The two sets of authorities are dealing with completely different things.

B. Measures

The second source of difficulty in discussing this area of law is that not all gain-based damages are the same. Consider the following two situations:

> *Thief* steals *Owner*'s horse and sells it to *Third Party* for £10,000. *Owner* can sue *Thief* for the £10,000 made from selling his horse.[6]
>
> *Chancer* goes for a ride on *Owner*'s horse without *Owner*'s permission, and brings the horse back to *Owner* in good condition. *Owner* can sue *Chancer* for a reasonable sum for the use he has made of the horse.[7]

We would submit that the damages awarded in *each* of these cases are gain-based in nature. But there are significant differences between the two sets of awards of damages. The damages awarded against *Thief* are designed to make *Thief* hand over to *Owner* the value

---

[2] Technically, no one has a right to an injunction (injunctions are awarded as a matter of discretion by the courts) but for the purposes of the hypothetical bargain, it is assumed that A does have such a right, which gives him a bargaining chip and something to sell in his negotiations with B.

[3] *Carr-Saunders* v *Dick McNeil Associates Ltd* [1986] 1 WLR 922, 931; *Jaggard* v *Sawyer* [1995] 1 WLR 269, 291; *Stoke-on-Trent County Council* v *Wass* [1988] 1 WLR 1406, 1420.

[4] *Carr-Saunders* v *Dick McNeil Associates Ltd* [1986] 1 WLR 922, *Tamares Ltd* v *Fairpoint Properties Ltd (No 2)* [2007] EWHC 212 (QB).

[5] *Stoke-on-Trent City Council* v *W & J Wass Ltd* [1988] 1 WLR 1406, *Forsyth-Grant* v *Allen* [2008] EWCA Civ 505.

[6] See below, § 31.2.

[7] See below, § 31.3.

of a money gain he has made by converting *Owner*'s property. The damages awarded against *Chancer* do not have this effect. *Chancer* has not made any kind of money gain from riding on *Owner*'s horse. In fact, he may not have made any tangible gain at all: the experience of riding on *Owner*'s horse may have proved to have been an utterly miserable one for *Chancer*. But *Chancer* seems to be made to pay a reasonable sum here for the *privilege* he has enjoyed of going for a ride on *Owner*'s horse. It is the fact that *Chancer* is being made to pay for enjoying this privilege that entitles us to say that the damages paid by *Chancer* here are gain-based: but they are not gain-based in the same way that the damages payable by *Thief* are.

The damages payable by *Thief* are usually known as *disgorgement damages*.[8] Another name – borrowed from the law of Equity – for the remedy that *Owner* can obtain here is *account of profits*. But we will stick with 'disgorgement damages'. In the next section, we discuss when the victim of a tort will be entitled to sue the person who committed that tort for disgorgement damages.

There is no consensus over what we should call the damages payable by *Chancer*. They have been called, alternatively, 'user damages', 'reasonable fee damages', 'negotiating damages',[9] 'restitutionary damages',[10] and '*Wrotham Park* damages'.[11] In the last edition of this book, we followed Peter Jaffey in proposing that this second measure of gain-based damages be called 'licence fee damages'.[12] We see no reason for departing from that usage in this edition. It seems to us that phrase 'licence fee damages' expresses very accurately what these damages are designed to do: to make a tortfeasor pay a reasonable sum for the licence he has been allowed to enjoy in committing his tort. In section 31.3, we will discuss when the victim of a tort will be allowed to sue the tortfeasor for licence fee damages.

C. The impact of *Attorney-General* v *Blake* (2001)

Blake was a landmark case in which the House of Lords held that gain-based damages might be awarded against a defendant who had committed a breach of contract. Lord Nicholls, giving the leading judgment, could see no reason why the victims of proprietary torts could sue for gain-based damages while the victim of a breach of contract could not:

> it is not easy to see why, as between the parties to a contract, a violation of a party's contractual rights should attract a lesser degree of remedy than a violation of his property rights.[13]

It seems that the decision in *Blake*, in using the law on when gain-based damages are available in tort as basis for developing the law on remedies for breach of contract, *may* have a disruptive, feedback effect on the area of law discussed in this chapter. This is in two ways.

---

[8] Smith L 1992, Edelman 2002b.

[9] *Lunn Poly Ltd* v *Liverpool and Lancashire Properties Ltd* [2006] EWCA Civ 430, at [22] (per Neuberger LJ).

[10] See Edelman 2002b. (The idea is that *Chancer* is not allowed to deny that he has had obtained a benefit from riding on *Owner*'s horse, as he voluntarily took *Owner*'s horse for a ride, and must now 'return' that benefit to *Owner* by paying *Owner* a reasonable sum for it: Edelman 2009, 227)

[11] After the case of *Wrotham Park Estate Company Ltd* v *Parkside Homes Ltd* [1974] 1 WLR 798. This was a case involving damages awarded in lieu of an injunction for breach of a restrictive covenant not to develop land without the neighbouring claimant's consent. Even though damages in lieu of an injunction are not gain-based in nature, some academics still like to call the damages that *Chancer* is liable to pay owner '*Wrotham Park* damages' because they are assessed in the same way as damages in lieu of an injunction are assessed: that is, by asking how much money *Chancer* and *Owner* would have hypothetically agreed that *Chancer* should have to pay for the privilege of riding *Owner*'s horse, had each party negotiated in good faith with the other.

[12] See Jaffey 2007, 100.

[13] [2001] AC 268, 283.

(1) *Adequate remedy.* In order to prevent the new remedy of 'account of profits' for breach of contract getting out of control, Lord Nicholls held that this remedy should *not* be made available when the normal remedies for breach,

> damages, specific performance and injunction . . . will provide an adequate response to a breach of contract. It will only be in exceptional cases, where those remedies are inadequate, that any question of accounting for profits will arise.[14]

It has *never*, traditionally, been the rule that gain-based damages would only be available in tort if suing the tortfeasor for compensatory damages would provide the victim of the tort with an 'inadequate' remedy. The law has long contemplated that gain-based damages might be sued for in tort where the victim of the tort could also sue the tortfeasor for substantial compensatory damages. In such a case, the law has always been that the victim of the tort had to *elect* whether to sue for compensatory damages or to sue for gain-based damages.[15]

However, in the case of *Devenish Nutrition* v *Sanofi-Aventis* (2009) (where the defendants operated an illegal price-fixing cartel), Arden and Tuckey LJJ seemed to take the view that gain-based damages would not be available in tort where alternative remedies would provide an 'adequate remedy' for that tort:

> it is a condition of a restitutionary award that exceptional circumstances of the kind described in *Blake*'s case . . . should be shown. That condition is not satisfied in this case, principally because on the assumed facts damages would be an adequate remedy.[16]

> an account of profits is available only where it is necessary to do justice in the case . . . it is not an appropriate remedy in principle where damages are an adequate remedy.[17]

This, we would submit, is incorrect so far as the availability of gain-based damages in tort is concerned. As Longmore LJ observed in *Devenish Nutrition*, 'The concept of damages being an inadequate remedy . . . is a treacherous one if it is used as a supposedly principled reason for the disgorgement of profits'. He then went on to observe that '*apart from* cases of the misuse of the claimant's own property, an account of profits . . . is only to be made in "exceptional" cases'[18] – the implied suggestion being that in a case involving the misuse of the claimant's own property, there is no need to prove that that case is 'exceptional' before an award of gain-based damages can be made.

(2) *Scope of torts for which gain-based damages are available.* By breaking awards of gain-based damages out of the enclave of proprietary torts, and allowing them to be awarded in breach of contract cases, the House of Lords' decision in *Blake* raised the question of whether, now that gain-based damages are available in breach of contract cases, they should also be made available for other non-proprietary torts. If you can have gain-based damages in a breach of contract case, why not in a case involving a trespass to the person, or defamation? Some support was expressed in *Devenish Nutrition* for the idea that *Blake*

---

[14] [2001] AC 268, 285.
[15] *United Australia Ltd* v *Barclays Bank Ltd* [1941] AC 1 (election only has to take place once the claimant knows how much she could recover under either head); *Tang Man Sit* v *Capacious Investments Ltd* [1996] AC 514 (an election to sue for compensatory damages can be reversed even after the damages have been paid if it was made in ignorance of the fact that gain-based damages would have been a better remedy).
[16] [2009] Ch 390, at [4] (per Arden LJ).
[17] [2009] Ch 390, at [104] (per Arden LJ).
[18] [2009] Ch 390, at [148] (emphasis added).

implies that gain-based damages should be available across the board for *all* torts, where normal damages would be an 'inadequate remedy':

> The overall holding in *Blake*'s case is that the law on remedies . . . should be coherent and that the same remedies should be available in the same circumstances, even if the cause of action is different.[19]

Despite this, Arden and Tuckey LJJ took the view that gain-based damages could not be awarded for the defendant's committing the tort of breach of statutory duty in *Devenish Nutrition* because they were bound by Court of Appeal authority that gain-based damages could only be awarded in tort where a proprietary tort had been committed. But their judgments plant the idea that if it were not for some pesky previous decisions of the Court of Appeal, *Blake* would have already ushered in a brave new world where gain-based damages would be available across the board in *all* tort law cases where normal damages are an 'inadequate remedy'.

D. Explanations

The final point that makes this area of law difficult to come to grips with is that some arguments that academics make as to *why* victims of torts are allowed to sue for gain-based damages, look good but are actually bad. Because of this, it is very easy to fall into accepting these bad arguments – with the result that one fails ever to understand why victims of torts are *actually* allowed to sue for gain-based damages.

For example, why is *Owner* allowed to sue *Thief* for £10,000 in the case where *Thief* sells his horse for £10,000? A lot of academics would say that this is because 'no man should be allowed to profit from his wrong.'[20] But this is an example of what philosophers call a 'concealed tautology'. What is being argued here is that:

(1) *Thief* should be required to hand over £10,000 to *Owner* because someone like *Thief* – a wrongdoer – should not be allowed to profit from his wrong.

If we change the language of (1) a little bit – without altering its sense in any way at all – the tautology involved in (1) is revealed, or is stated in its 'open' form:

(2) *Thief* should made be made to give up the profit he has made from wronging *Owner* because *Thief* should not be allowed to keep the profit he has made from wronging *Owner*.

If (2) is not 'open' enough for the concealed tautology in (1) to be revealed, (2) can be restated even more baldly as:

(3) *Thief* should be made to give up the profit he has made from wronging *Owner* because *Thief* should be made to give up the profit he has made from wronging *Owner*.

(1), (2) and (3) say exactly the same thing, but whereas (1) seems like it might amount to a good argument as to why *Thief* is held liable to pay disgorgement damages to *Owner*, (2) and (3) show that (1) is actually saying the same thing twice – a wrongdoer should be made to give up the profits from his wrong because a wrongdoer should be made to give up the profits from his wrong.

---

[19] [2009] Ch 390, at [4] (per Arden LJ).
[20] See, for example, Burrows 2011, at 623: 'Restitution for a wrong directly reflects the idea that "no person shall profit from his or her wrong".'

Alternatively, it could be argued that *Thief* is held liable to pay *Owner* disgorgement damages because holding him liable to pay such damages to *Owner* will *deter* him from selling *Owner*'s horse.[21] This seems like a good argument – *Thief* would surely be putting off selling *Owner*'s horse if he knew that he would not be allowed to keep any money he made from selling the horse. But it is not, because *Thief* does not know that it is *certain* he will be held to account for selling the horse. Given this, *Thief* might think it worth his while to sell the horse and *take the chance* of being held liable to give up the proceeds of the sale. In economic terms, if *Thief* knew that he could make £10,000 by selling the horse, and there was a 60% chance that he will get away with selling the horse, he would value the opportunity to sell the horse as being worth up to how much he would be willing to pay for a 60% chance of keeping £10,000. Let's say this is £200 – that anyone, including *Thief*, would be willing to stake £200 for a 60% chance of winning £10,000. So in this situation *Thief* would *not* be deterred from selling *Owner*'s horse just by the prospect of being made to give up the proceeds of the sale if he were caught. He would still have an incentive to sell the horse in that situation as selling the horse would give him free of charge an opportunity to make a gain that he would be willing to pay up to £200 for. The only effective way of deterring *Thief* from selling *Owner*'s horse is to threaten him with an award of *exemplary* damages that would come to *at least £200 more* than *Thief* would make from selling *Owner*'s horse. Only if *Thief* was confronted with the prospect of being made to pay *Owner* £200 or more on top of what he made from selling *Owner*'s horse would he think twice about selling the horse.

There are better arguments than these that can be advanced for making gain-based damages available to the victims of torts, and we will discuss these in section 31.4.

31.2 DISGORGEMENT DAMAGES

Disgorgement damages are available for the following torts:

(1) *Conversion.* In *Kuwait Airways Corpn* v *Iraqi Airways Co (Nos 4 & 5)* (2002), Lord Nicholls remarked that 'all those who convert [someone else's goods] should be accountable for the *benefits* they receive';[22] and indeed it has long been established that disgorgement damages may be claimed against someone who commits the tort of conversion.

So, for example, in *Oughton* v *Seppings* (1830) the defendant, a sheriff's officer, received a warrant authorising him to seize the property of one Winslove and sell it in order to pay off a debt which Winslove owed. The defendant met Winslove driving a pony cart. The defendant seized the pony cart and the pony and sold both items of property. In selling the pony, the defendant committed the tort of conversion as the pony belonged to the claimant, Winslove's landlord, and not Winslove, at the time it was sold. The claimant was held entitled to sue the defendant for the value of the money he obtained in return for the claimant's pony.[23]

---

[21] See Edelman 2002b.

[22] [2002] 2 AC 883, at [79] (emphasis added).

[23] Of course, the defendant no longer had that money – he would have handed it over to Winslove's creditors. However, it is generally accepted that there is no defence of what is called 'change of position' to a claim for disgorgement damages against a wrongdoer: see *Lipkin Gorman* v *Karpnale* [1991] 2 AC 548, 580 (per Lord Goff). This is rough on a defendant who has *innocently* converted someone else's property, and Lord Nicholls suggested in the *Kuwait Airways* case that a defence of change of position should be available to such a defendant: [2002] 2 AC 883, at [79].

In *Oughton*, the defendant converted the claimant's property by selling it. May disgorgement damages be awarded against a defendant who converts another's property by *using* it? There is no English authority where disgorgement damages have been awarded against someone who has converted another's property by using it.[24] However, there is an American case where such damages were awarded. In *Olwell* v *Nye & Nissen* (1946), the defendant converted a machine belonging to the claimant by using it in his factory. It was held that the claimant was entitled to sue the defendant for the profits the defendant had made by using that machine.

(2) *Passing off*. Disgorgement damages may be awarded against someone who has *deliberately* committed the tort of passing off.[25] So in *My Kinda Town* v *Soll* (1982), the defendants deliberately dressed up their restaurant in such a way that people would be deceived into thinking that the defendants' restaurant was a branch of a chain of restaurants run by the claimants. Slade J held that the claimants were entitled to sue the defendants for the money they had made by passing off their restaurant as being one of the claimants' restaurants. But the claimants were only entitled to sue the defendants for the money they had made by deceiving people into believing that their restaurant was run by the claimants: the claimants were not entitled to sue the defendants for the money they had made from customers who had not entered the defendants' restaurant in the belief that it was run by the claimants. Quantifying how much money the claimants could sue the defendants for therefore proved a very difficult exercise: the court had to estimate how many of the defendants' customers had walked into the restaurant in the belief that it was run by the claimants and what the profits were on the meals sold to those customers.

(3) *Infringement of intellectual property rights*. Disgorgement damages (under the name 'account of profits') may be awarded against someone who infringes another's copyright[26] or someone who infringes another's design right.[27] In the case where a defendant has infringed another's patent, disgorgement damages may be awarded if the defendant knew or ought to have known of the existence of the patent at the time he infringed it.[28]

(4) *Invasion of privacy*. The equivalent of disgorgement damages are routinely awarded against defendants who commit equitable wrongs such as a breach of trust, a breach of fiduciary duty, or a breach of confidence.[29] The fact that the new tort of wrongful disclosure of private information has its origins in the equitable wrong of breach of confidence makes it likely that disgorgement damages will be routinely awarded against defendants who commit this tort. Indeed, in *Douglas* v *Hello! Ltd (No 3)* (2006), the Court of Appeal accepted that if the defendants in that case had made a profit from publishing unauthorised photographs

---

[24] See McInnes 2003, at 712: '[The] precedents consistently indicate that while the defendant is required to give up his entire gain if he wrongfully *sells* the claimant's property, he merely is required to pay a hiring fee [i.e. licence fee damages] for improper *usage*' (at 712).

[25] *Edelsten* v *Edelsten* (1863) 1 De G J & S 185, 46 ER 72.

[26] Copyright, Designs and Patents Act 1988, s 96(2). It is not thought that s 97(1) of the 1988 Act affects this point. That subsection provides that: 'Where in action for infringement of copyright it is shown that at the time of the infringement the defendant did not know, and had no reason to believe, that copyright subsists in the work to which the action relates, the claimant is not entitled to damages against him, but without prejudice to any other remedy.' It is thought that the reference to *damages* in this section is a reference to *compensatory* damages.

[27] Section 229(2). Again, it is not thought that s 233(1) of the 1988 Act – which provides that the owner of a design right which has been infringed will not be entitled to sue the person who infringed the design right for damages if he did not know of, and had no reason to know of, the existence of the design right infringed by him – affects this point.

[28] Patents Act 1977, s 62(1).

[29] See, for example, *Attorney-General* v *Guardian Newspapers Ltd* (No 2) [1990] 1 AC 109.

of the claimants' wedding celebrations, then the claimants would have been entitled to sue the defendants for a sum equal to that profit.[30] However, it was found that the defendants had paid so much for the photographs, they did not in the end make a profit from the extra sales of their magazine that resulted from their publishing the photographs.[31]

It is currently *uncertain* whether disgorgement damages will be available for the following proprietary torts:

(5) *Private nuisance.* In *Stoke-on-Trent County Council* v *Wass* (1988), the Court of Appeal refused to award disgorgement damages against a trader who had committed the tort of private nuisance by running a market in an area where the claimants had the exclusive right to run a market. As the private nuisance in this case took the anomalous form of an interference with the claimant's monopoly right to hold a market in a particular area, the case is not a particularly strong one on whether disgorgement damages can ever be sued for in private nuisance.

The issue was raised again in *Forsyth-Grant* v *Allen* (2008), a 'proper' private nuisance case in which the defendant interfered with a hotel owner's right to light by building two houses on the defendant's land. The hotel owner wanted to sue the defendant for the profit he had made (which was assessed at almost £7,000) from building in an area that interfered with the hotel owner's right to light. Patten J (with whom Mummery LJ agreed) thought that if gain-based damages were available in a private nuisance case, they could only be awarded in 'exceptional circumstances', and the damages that would be awarded in such a case would be licence fee damages, rather than disgorgement damages.[32] As the claimant in this case was suing for disgorgement damages rather than licence fee damages, his claim was dismissed. Toulson LJ also thought that 'in an appropriate case' damages in a private nuisance could be assessed on a licence fee basis.[33] He did not think this was an appropriate case, as the hotel owner had been given ample opportunity by the defendant to reach an agreement as to how the defendant should develop his land, and had refused to have any dealings with the defendant. As for disgorgement damages, Toulson LJ thought that making them available in nuisance cases would give rise to a 'legion of questions' concerning to assess the profit made by a defendant as a result of polluting a *particular* claimant's land. Given this, he thought that the courts should be cautious about awarding disgorgement damages in private nuisance cases, but did not rule out such awards.[34]

Toulson LJ's judgment aside, the decision in *Forsyth-Grant* seems to indicate that disgorgement damages will *not* be available in a private nuisance case, until the Supreme Court rules otherwise.

(6) *Trespass to land.* The American case of *Edwards* v *Lee's Administrators* (1936) provides an example of disgorgement damages being made available in a trespass to land case. That case concerned a long cave that contained some very interesting rock formations. The entrance to the cave was on the defendants' land and they would charge people to enter the cave and look around. Unfortunately, a third of the cave stretched under the claimants' land. So the defendants committed the tort of trespass to land whenever they allowed

---

[30] [2006] QB 125, at [249].
[31] [2006] QB 125, at [245].
[32] [2008] EWCA Civ 505, at [31]–[32].
[33] [2008] EWCA Civ 505, at [38].
[34] [2008] EWCA Civ 505, at [46]–[47].

customers to view that part of the cave that was under the claimants' land. The claimants were held entitled to sue the defendants for damages equal to the money the defendants had made by allowing people to look at that part of the cave that was under the claimants' land.

It has however been doubted whether the same approach would be adopted here.[35] James Edelman has argued that *Livingstone v Rawyards Coal Company* (1880) is authority for the proposition that if A *deliberately and in bad faith* trespasses on B's land and makes a gain as a result, he will be liable to pay disgorgement damages to B.[36] However, the only statement in the case that can be taken as supporting that idea is the following:

> There is no doubt that if a man furtively and in bad faith robs his neighbour of property . . . the person [will be held liable for] the value of the whole of the property which he has so furtively taken, and . . . no allowance [will be made] in respect of what he has so done as would have been justly made to him if the parties had been working by agreement, or if, as in the present case, they had been the one working and the other permitting the working through a mistake.[37]

But that statement is considering the case where A has stolen B's property (a case of conversion), rather than the case where A trespasses on B's land and makes a profit for himself as a result without actually stealing anything from B.

The Court of Appeal's decision in *Devenish Nutrition v Sofia-Aventis* (2009) makes it fairly clear that – until the Supreme Court rules otherwise – disgorgement damages will *not* be available for the following *non-proprietary* torts:[38] (7) breach of statutory duty; (8) deceit; (9) trespass to the person; and (10) defamation. A claim for disgorgement damages for breach of statutory duty was explicitly ruled out in *Devenish Nutrition*. A claim for such damages in the case of deceit was ruled out by the Court of Appeal in *Halifax Building Society v Thomas* (1996), where the defendant obtained a mortgage by lying about his indebtedness to the claimant building society and was held entitled – once the building society affirmed the mortgage by foreclosing it and forcing a sale of the house that the defendant bought with the mortgage – to keep any profits from the increase in the value of the house after the defendant had bought it.[39] No attempt to disapprove *Thomas* was made in *Devenish Nutrition*. By holding itself unable to award disgorgement damages in any cases other than proprietary torts, the Court of Appeal has effectively ruled out for itself the possibility of making such awards in trespass to the person or defamation cases. (However, in such cases, an award of exemplary damages may well be available.)

---

[35] See McInnes 2003, at 712: '[It] is quite likely that an English claimant, in the same circumstances, would be limited to reasonable rental value [i.e. licence fee damages]'; to the same effect, Cooke 1994, 428–9; also *Severn Trent Water Ltd v Barnes* [2004] EWCA Civ 570 (disallowing anything but an award of licence fee damages against a defendant who had trespassed on the claimant's land by laying a water mains under the land); and *Stadium Capital Holdings (No 2) Ltd v St Marylebone Property Co Ltd* [2010] EWCA Civ 952 (trespass by fixing advertisement hoarding to claimant's wall; held, first instance judge should *not* have awarded damages equal to entire amount of profit made from hoarding).

[36] Edelman 2006, at 147.

[37] (1880) 5 App Cas 25, at 34 (per Lord Hatherley).

[38] It is true, as Burrows 2011 notes at 659, that in *Devenish Nutrition* Longmore LJ took the view that there was no authority binding on the Court of Appeal that held that disgorgement damages could only be awarded in cases of a 'tortious claim[s] for breach of a proprietary right' (at [145]) and went on to say (at [148]) that 'an account of profits outside the established categories is only to be made [and therefore by implication *can* be made] in "exceptional" cases' but Longmore LJ was in the minority on this point.

[39] See also *Renault UK Ltd v Fleetpro Technical Services Ltd* [2007] EWHC 2541 (QB), where the judge refused to award disgorgement damages against a defendant who, by deceit, persuaded the claimant to manufacture and sell to him some cars that he then sold on at a profit.

31.3 LICENCE FEE DAMAGES

Licence fee damages are available for the following torts:

(1) *Conversion*. It is well established that licence fee damages may be awarded against someone who has committed the tort of conversion.[40]

So, for example, if A has converted B's property by using it, B will be entitled to sue A for damages designed to make A pay B a reasonable sum for the use he has made of B's property.[41] What if A did not *use* B's property but converted it by doing something to prevent B getting hold of it? It does not matter: B will still be entitled to sue A for damages designed to make A pay B a reasonable sum for the *dominion* he has enjoyed over B's property.[42]

(2) *Trespass to land*. It is also well established that licence fee damages may be awarded against someone who has committed the tort of trespass to land.

So – if *Tenant* stays in *Landlord*'s house beyond the term of the lease, *Landlord* will be entitled to sue *Tenant* for a reasonable sum – known as *mesne*[43] *profits* – for the use *Tenant* made of *Landlord*'s house by staying in it beyond the term of his tenancy.[44]

More generally, if A commits the tort of trespass to land by using B's land without his consent for some purpose, B will be entitled to sue A for damages designed to make A pay B a reasonable sum for the use he has made of B's land.[45] The sum payable normally equals the going market rate for the use B has made of A's land, though that measure was displaced in favour of a lower sum in the unusual case of *Ministry of Defence v Ashman* (1993).[46] Where there is no going market rate, the sum payable is assessed by imagining how much A and B would have agreed B should have to pay for using A's land, assuming that they had each been bargaining in good faith and trying to reach a reasonable agreement.[47]

What if A commits the tort of trespass to land not by using B's land but by preventing B gaining access to his land? A will still have to pay B a reasonable sum for the dominion

---

[40] See *Kuwait Airways Corpn v Iraqi Airways Co (Nos 4 and 5)* [2002] 2 AC 883, at [87] (per Lord Nicholls).

[41] See, for example, *Strand Electric Engineering Co. Ltd v Brisford Entertainments* [1952] 2 QB 246 (defendants converted claimants' switchboards by using them in various theatre productions staged at the defendants' theatre; they were held liable to pay the claimants a reasonable sum for the use they had made of the switchboards).

[42] So if A takes one of B's chairs away for a year but does not use it, B will be entitled to sue A for damages designed to make A pay B a reasonable sum for the dominion he has enjoyed over the chair for a year – and this is so even if B did not miss the chair at all in the year A had it: *Mediana (Owners of Steamship) v Comet (Owners of Lightship)* [1900] AC 113, 117 (per Earl of Halsbury LC).

[43] Pronounced 'mean'.

[44] *Swordheath Properties v Tabet* [1979] 1 WLR 285; *Ministry of Defence v Ashman* [1993] 2 EGLR 102; *Ministry of Defence v Thompson* [1993] 2 EGLR 107.

[45] See *Whitwham v Westminster Brymbo Coal & Coke Company* [1896] 2 Ch 538 (defendants who committed the tort of trespass to land by tipping refuse from their colliery onto the claimants' land held liable to pay the claimants a reasonable sum for the use they had made of the claimants' land); and *Penarth Dock Engineering Co v Pounds* [1963] 1 Lloyd's Rep 359 (defendant committed the tort of trespass to land by keeping his boat tied up in the claimants' docks; he was held liable to pay the claimants a reasonable sum for the use he had made of their land).

[46] In that case the defendant was a military wife whose husband left her, and she was forced to stay on in military quarters as the local council could not re-house her and her children. Hoffmann J refused to hold the defendant liable to pay the going market rate for living in quarters like the ones she was trespassing on, and instead only held her liable to pay the rent she would have had to pay had she been in council accommodation.

[47] See *Bocardo SA v Star Energy UK Onshore Ltd* [2011] 1 AC 380 (trespass to claimant's land by allowing pipelines to intrude under the claimant's land, while extracting oil from under the land; held, had the claimant and defendants bargained in good faith as to how much the defendants should pay the claimant to be allowed to drill under his land, the defendants would not have ended up paying very much as they could at any point have obtained a licence from the Crown entitling them to insert pipelines under the claimant's land).

he has enjoyed over B's land while B was kept out. So in *Inverugie Investments Ltd* v *Hackett* (1995), the claimant leased 30 apartments in a hotel in the Bahamas but was then kept out of them for 15 years by the defendants, who owned the hotel. During those 15 years, the defendants let the apartments out to guests but at any one time only about 40% of the apartments were let out. So the defendants used only about 40% of the claimant's apartments during the 15 years they kept him out of them. However, during those 15 years they enjoyed dominion over all the claimant's apartments, 365 days a year. Accordingly, it was held that the claimant was entitled to sue the defendant for damages designed to make the defendants pay the claimant the going rate for renting apartments like the claimant's 365 days a year for 15 years.

(3) *Private nuisance.* The Court of Appeal decision in *Forsyth-Grant* v *Allen* (2008) seems to indicate that in an 'exceptional' case (Patten J, with Mummery LJ agreeing) or an 'appropriate' case (Toulson LJ), licence fee damages may be awarded against a defendant who commits the tort of private nuisance. In such a case, the damages would be 'calculated by reference to the price, which the defendant might reasonably be required to pay for a relaxation of the claimant's rights so as to avoid an injunction.'[48]

(4) *Inducing a breach of contract.* It seems that licence fee damages *may* be awarded against someone who commits the tort of inducing a breach of contract. So, for example, in *Lightly* v *Clouston* (1808) the defendant persuaded the claimant's apprentice to work as a mariner on his ship instead of working on board the claimant's ship. Mansfield CJ held that the claimant was entitled to compel the defendant to pay him a reasonable sum for the work that his apprentice did for the defendant.[49] However, these cases may be based on an old-fashioned idea that someone's servants were his property.

(5) *Non-proprietary torts.* Depending on how one reads the Court of Appeal's decision in *Devenish Nutrition* v *Sofia Aventis* (2009), the Court of Appeal *may* have ruled out licence fee damages being awarded in *any* case involving a non-proprietary tort. It depends on whether one thinks that the Court of Appeal, in ruling out awards of disgorgement damages for non-proprietary torts, was also ruling out the award of licence fee damages for such torts. One *dictum* that makes one wonder is this:

> It is now clear that the principle underlying user damages [what we have been calling 'licence fee damages'] does not depend on there being some misuse of a property right of the claimant. It was awarded in the . . . case [of *Experience Hendrix* v *PPX Enterprises* (2003)] on the basis of a breach of a contractual obligation. This is an important point. It is paradigmatic of a cultural change in the law in favour of the classification of remedies on a coherent basis rather than on the basis of some formulaic division between different wrongs. As Lord Nicholls observed in *Blake*'s case . . . 'it is not clear why it should be any more permissible to expropriate personal rights than it is permissible to expropriate property rights.'[50]

We can test whether licence fee damages should be awarded in cases where a non-proprietary tort has been committed by asking whether we should allow such a claim to be made in the case where *Thug* beats up *Teen*. We would suggest there is a serious problem in the way of allowing licence fee damages to be awarded in such a case. We cannot assess what a 'reasonable sum' might be for the privilege of being allowed to beat someone else up. And

---

[48] [2008] EWCA Civ 505, at [32] (per Patten J).
[49] See also *Foster* v *Stewart* (1814) 3 M & S 191, 105 ER 582.
[50] [2009] Ch 390, at [68] (per Arden LJ).

it would be contrary to public policy for the courts to engage in the exercise of imagining *Thug* and *Teen* bargaining to determine how much *Thug* should pay *Teen* for the privilege of beating him up. Any such bargain would be unenforceable in real life as contrary to public policy – so giving effect to such a 'hypothetical bargain' would also be contrary to public policy. The same point applies even more strongly to the sort of case presented by *AT* v *Dulghieru* (2009), where the claimants were forced by the defendants to have sex with clients. The courts would bring themselves into disrepute if they attempted to determine what a 'reasonable sum' might be for hiring out your body for sex. Similar considerations would, we think, rule out awards of licence fee damages for almost all non-proprietary torts.

31.4 THEORIES

We have done our best to set out above the current law on when gain-based damages will be available in tort. However, it has to be conceded that the law is in an unholy mess at the moment. The principal cause of the confusion is the current lack of any convincing theory as to *why* gain-based damages should ever be awarded against a tortfeasor. We have already considered, and dismissed, two bad arguments that academics commonly make in favour of such awards being made – that 'no man should profit from his wrong' and that making such awards helps to deter tortfeasors from committing torts. But can a convincing account of why gain-based damages are claimable in tort be offered? We think two such accounts can be offered. The first offers *one* explanation as to why *both* disgorgement damages *and* licence fee damages can be sued for in tort. We can call this the *monist* account. The second account gives one explanation as to why disgorgement damages can be sued for in tort, and a quite different explanation as to why licence fee damages can be sued for in tort. We can call this the *plural* account.

A. The monist account

According to the *monist* account, this area of law is not based on the principle that 'no man should profit from his wrong' but that 'the victim of a wrong should not be deprived of the benefits he would have obtained had that wrong not been committed.' Seen in this way, disgorgement damages and licence fee damages have more in common with compensatory damages than might first be supposed: they all aim to put the victim of a tort in the position he would have been in had that tort been committed. It is just that the tort that has been committed is characterised differently in the case where compensatory damages are being sued for than it is when disgorgement damages and licence fee damages are being sued for. In a case where a tortfeasor is being sued for compensatory damages, he is being sued on the basis that he committed a tort by doing something that caused the victim of the tort loss. In a case where he is being sued for disgorgement damages or licence fee damages, he is being sued on the basis that he committed a tort by failing to do something that would have benefited the victim of his tort.

To illustrate this point, suppose that *Chancer* goes for a ride on *Owner*'s horse without *Owner*'s permission. The ride goes disastrously: the horse is lamed and is unable to run in the race that *Owner* had entered him for the following weekend. In this kind of case, there are two ways of characterising the wrong that *Chancer* committed:

(1) *Chancer* went for a ride on *Owner*'s horse.
(2) *Chancer* went for a ride on *Owner*'s horse without first having obtained *Owner*'s permission.

If *Owner* sues *Chancer* on the basis that *Chancer* committed wrong (1), then he will be suing to be put in the position he would have been in had *Chancer* not gone for a ride on the horse. Had *Chancer* not gone for a ride on *Owner*'s horse, the horse would not have been lamed, and *Owner* would have a chance of winning the race the following weekend. *Owner* will therefore be entitled to sue *Chancer* for compensatory damages, including damages designed to compensate for the loss of the chance of winning next weekend's race.

But if *Owner* elects to sue *Chancer* on the basis that *Chancer* committed wrong (2), then he will be suing to be put in the position he would have been in had *Chancer* obtained *Owner*'s permission to ride on *Owner*'s horse. Had *Chancer* obtained that permission, he would have been made to pay *Owner* a reasonable sum for the privilege of riding on *Owner*'s horse, and *Owner* will be entitled to sue *Chancer* for licence fee damages equal to the value of that reasonable sum.[51]

Again, suppose *Thief* sells a horse belonging to *Owner* for £10,000 when *Owner* had planned to give the horse away the following day to a school for autistic children. In this kind of case, there are two ways of characterising the wrong that *Thief* committed:

(1) *Thief* sold *Owner*'s horse.
(2) *Thief* sold *Owner*'s horse for his own gain, and not on behalf of *Owner*.

If *Owner* sues *Thief* on the basis that *Thief* committed wrong (1), he will be suing to be put in the position he would have been in had his horse not been sold. This is problematic given that had the horse not been sold, *Owner* would have given it away anyway.

But if *Owner* elects to sue *Thief* on the basis that *Thief* committed wrong (2), he will be suing to be put in the position he would have been in had *Thief* sold *Owner*'s horse on *Owner*'s behalf and not for his own gain. Had *Thief* done this, *Owner* would now be in receipt of the £10,000 made from the sale of the horse, and so *Owner* is entitled to sue for that sum.[52]

Now consider the case where *Thug* beats up *Teen*, either for pleasure, or because he has been paid £10,000 to do so by *Enemy*. We could try to characterise the wrong committed by *Thug* in one of three ways:

(1) *Thug* beat up *Teen*.
(2) *Thug* beat up *Teen* without first obtaining *Teen*'s permission to do so.
(3) *Thug* beat up *Teen* for his own selfish gain, and not on behalf of *Enemy*.

No court would allow *Teen* to frame a case against *Thug* on the basis of (3), as (3) is too bizarre to be pleaded. And it does not seem that suing *Thug* on the basis of (2) would do *Teen* any good. No court would allow *Teen* to argue that he would only have given *Thug* permission to beat him up if *Thug* had paid him a reasonable sum for doing so – such a

---

[51] This argument finds strong echoes in the argument that the licence fee damages payable by *Chancer* are ultimately compensatory, in that they compensate *Owner* for the loss of the opportunity to make *Chancer* pay to ride his horse that *Chancer* deprived Owner of by riding the horse without *Owner*'s permission: see Sharpe and Waddams 1982; Scott 2006; Giglio 2007; *WWF v WWF* [2006] EWHC 184 (QB), at [137] (per Peter Smith J); and *Devenish Nutrition v Sanofi-Aventis* [2009] Ch 390, at [40]–[41] (per Arden LJ). These arguments are criticised in Burrows 2011, 635–638, on the ground that *Chancer* will still have to pay licence fee damages to *Owner* even if he can show that *Owner* would never have allowed *Chancer* to ride his horse for any money. But the argument made above is not vulnerable to this objection as *Owner* is being allowed to *elect* to sue *Chancer* on the basis that he *would* have given his permission, had a reasonable fee been paid.

[52] This argument finds weak echoes in Arthur Ripstein's argument, in Ripstein 2007a (at 1993) that a claimant's 'property is to be used only for her purposes. If it is used for a purpose she has not authorised, the law must make it as if the wrong had never happened. It cannot undo the fact of [the] defendant's use of the property, but the law can treat it as it were [the claimant's] own use by requiring [the] defendant to disgorge his gains.'

bargain would have been unlawful and unenforceable. So the only basis on which *Teen* can sue *Thug* is on the basis of wrong (1) – in which case *Teen* would simply be suing to be put in the position that he would have been in had *Thug* not beaten him up; a claim which only allows *Teen* to sue *Thug* for compensation for his injuries.

B. The plural account

According to the *plural* account, awards of *disgorgement* damages are based on the idea that property is *multiplicative*. You are not just entitled to the thing that is your property, but also the fruits of that thing – what can be obtained in return for that thing. So property has an *exchange* value as well as a *use* value: property is not only good for what you can use it for, but also for what you can get in return for it. Disgorgement damages recognise that fact by allowing the *Owner* of a thing to claim that whatever money has been obtained in returned for that thing belongs to him.[53]

According to this explanation, it is obvious why disgorgement damages are available in a case like *Oughton* v *Seppings* (1830) (sale of claimant's pony) but are not available in a case like *Stoke-on-Trent County Council* v *Wass* (1988) (violation of claimant's monopoly right to hold a market in a given area) or a case like *AT* v *Dulghieru* (2009) (claimants forced to work as prostitutes). In *Oughton* v *Seppings* (1830), the money obtained from the sale of the claimant's pony belonged to her, because it had been obtained in return for her property. She was therefore entitled to sue for that money. In the *Wass* case, the defendants' conduct in running a market violated a property right of the claimant's, but none of the money earned by the defendants in running that market was obtained *in return for the claimant's property*. So there was no basis on which the claimant could argue that that money belonged to it. In the *Dulghieru* case, the claimants' bodies may have – in some sense – belonged to them, but the law does not recognise bodies as having an exchange value. So whatever money the defendants earned in that case from prostituting the claimants was not earned in return for property that was tradeable under the law. So the claimants could not say that that money belonged to them.

Turning to *licence fee* damages, according to this account, licence fee damages exist to protect the integrity of rules that have been laid down by the law that specify how one might lawfully achieve one's goals.[54] So – if you want to take a ride on *Owner's* horse, there is a way of doing that lawfully. You go to see *Owner*, ask him for permission, and negotiate and pay a fee if one is required. It is important that the law work effectively to 'channel' someone like *Chancer* into following this procedure for achieving his goal of riding on *Owner's* horse; otherwise there is no point in the law's specifying how to achieve this goal in the first place. The award of licence fee damages can be seen as being part of this attempt to channel people like *Chancer* into respecting the law's rules on how to achieve their goals. By awarding licence fee damages against someone like *Chancer* the law is making it clear that there is no point in someone like *Chancer's* trying to achieve his goals outside the law. He will be no better off if he simply gets hold of *Owner's* horse and rides off on him – he will still have to pay a reasonable sum for the ride.

---

[53] See Weinrib 2000, 12. Arguably, the decision of the House of Lords in *Foskett* v *McKeown* [2001] 1 AC 102, in rejecting the view that an owner's right to what has been obtained for his property arises out of 'unjust enrichment' but is instead property-based, can be read as supporting this analysis of the basis of disgorgement damages.

[54] This explanation finds strong echoes in Jackman 1989's argument (at 304) that gain-based damages are awarded when it is necessary to do so to protect 'facilitative institutions' such as 'contracts, trusts and private property'.

Contrast *Chancer*'s case with the *Dulghieru* case, where the defendants made the claimants work as prostitutes. Here, there is no proper procedure laid down by the law for getting someone to work for you as a prostitute. This is something that simply should not be done – not something that can be done, but in a different way from the way the defendants chose to do it. So there were no rules that needed their integrity protecting in *Dulghieru*. Given this, there was no basis for awarding licence fee damages in that case.

Further reading

Discussion of what is known as 'restitution for wrongs' got off to a bad start in the UK through adoption of two assumptions: (1) that in all restitution for wrongs cases, the wrongdoer is stripped of a gain he has made from his wrong; and (2) that all restitution for wrongs cases can be explained as giving effect to the principle that 'no wrongdoer should profit from his wrong'. The academic literature on this area of law has yet to recover fully from these two historic errors, and should as a result be approached with care and skepticism.

James Edelman's monograph *Gain-Based Damages* (**Hart Publishing, 2002**) was a major achievement, in that it brought into question whether (1) and (2) were true, but only at the expense of endorsing another major misconception: (3) that awards of disgorgement damages are designed to deter people from wronging others.

Craig Rotherham is emerging as a major thinker on this area of law: see his **'The conceptual structure of restitution for wrongs' (2007) 66** *Cambridge Law Journal* 172; **'*Wrotham Park* damages and accounts of profits: compensation or restitution?' [2008]** *Lloyd's Maritime and Commercial Law Quarterly* 25; **'The normative foundations of restitution for wrongs: justifying gain-based relief for nuisance'** in Robertson and Tang (eds), *The Goals of Private Law* (Hart Publishing, 2009); **'Gain-based relief in tort after *Att-Gen* v *Blake*' (2010) 126** *Law Quarterly Review* 102.

Sarah Worthington's **'Reconsidering disgorgement for wrongs' (1999) 62** *Modern Law Review* **219** is also worth reading.

Visit **www.mylawchamber.co.uk/mcbride** to access tools to help you develop and test your knowledge of Tort law, including interactive multiple choice questions, practice exam questions with guidance, weblinks, legal newsfeed, additional case summaries, legal updates and tips on answering problem and essay questions.

32 Vindicatory damages

32.1 The basics *820*

32.2 Examples? *822*

32.3 The *Lumba* decision *827*

32.4 The future *829*

Overview

In this chapter, we look at a new type of damages that the courts have only recently started awarding. After introducing the notion of 'vindicatory damages' in section 32.1, in section 32.2 we look at some examples of awards of damages that might be analysed as 'vindicatory' in nature. In section 32.3 we take a detailed look at the important decision of the Supreme Court in *Lumba* v *Secretary of State for the Home Department* (2011), which is likely to have a big impact on future awards of vindicatory damages. Section 32.4 concludes by looking at what should happen in the future with regard to such awards of damages.

32.1 THE BASICS

Vindicatory damages are designed to vindicate a claimant's rights by making a defendant pay the claimant a significant sum for the mere fact that he has violated the claimant's rights. Previous editions of this textbook did not mention the concept of 'vindicatory damages'. The law of tort seemed not to recognise such a head of damages. A claimant could not (it seemed) go to court and simply say, 'D violated my rights; make him pay me substantial damages.'[1] However, in recent years, an increasing number of judges[2] and academics[3] have argued that: (1) at least in some tort cases, a claimant should be able to claim vindicatory damages; and (2) a number of established damages awards should be re-analysed as being vindicatory in nature. In other words, they argue that we *should* allow claimants to sue for vindicatory damages (at least in some tort cases), and that we *already do* allow claims for vindicatory damages to be made in some tort cases (though we may currently and inaccurately call such damages something else (such as 'compensatory' or 'gain-based') when they are claimed).

A major impetus behind this development has been the widespread adoption of human rights legislation. In a case where A's human rights have been violated but A has suffered no or very little loss as a result (for example, where A's telephone has been unlawfully tapped by the police, or where A has been unlawfully denied access to a solicitor while in custody), allowing A to sue the government for a small sum in compensatory damages would seem to make a mockery of his rights. Hence the suggestion that in this sort of case,

---

[1] Of course, in the case where a tort is actionable *per se*, a claimant could go to court and say, 'D violated my rights; make him pay me nominal damages'. But vindicatory damages are distinct from nominal damages in that vindicatory damages are substantial.

[2] See Scott 2007.

[3] Notably, Stevens 2007, 59–91.

A should be allowed to sue for vindicatory damages – a significant sum to mark the significance of the violation of his rights that has occurred in this case.[4]

So, for example, in *Attorney-General of Trinidad and Tobago* v *Ramanoop* (2006), the claimant was assaulted by a police officer both while he was being arrested and then again at the police station to which he was taken. The claimant sued for damages, arguing that the assault violated his 'right to life, liberty, [and] security of person' under s 4(a) of the Constitution of Trinidad and Tobago, and that he was entitled to 'redress' under s 14 of the Constitution. The first instance judge held that all he could award the claimant under s 14 was compensatory damages. The Judicial Committee of the Privy Council (which was, and still is, the supreme appellate court over issues of law in Trinidad and Tobago) held that this was wrong. Lord Nicholls observed that:

> An award of compensation will go some distance towards vindicating the infringed constitutional right. How far it does will depend on the circumstances, but in principle it may well not suffice. The fact that the right violated was a constitutional right adds an extra dimension to the wrong. An additional award, not necessarily of substantial size, may be needed to reflect the sense of public outrage, emphasise the importance of the constitutional right, and the gravity of the breach, and deter further breaches.[5]

It is this 'additional award' that has come to be known as 'vindicatory damages',[6] and *Ramanoop* is now routinely cited by judges and academics in favour of the proposition that a tort claimant may be able to sue for vindicatory damages if the tort for which she is suing involved a violation of some 'constitutional right' of hers.

However, it is still not clear whether vindicatory damages have a place in the law of tort. The issue of whether the victim of a tort can sue for vindicatory damages was addressed by the Supreme Court in the recent case of *Lumba* v *Secretary of State for the Home Department* (2011),[7] and the Supreme Court Justices could not reach agreement on this issue.

Of the nine Justices who decided *Lumba*, Lords Dyson and Collins came out strongly against the notion that vindicatory damages could be sued for in a tort case.[8] Lord Phillips went out of his way to express his agreement with Lords Dyson and Collins on this point.[9] Lord Brown (with whom Lord Rodger agreed) dissented on the issue of whether a tort had been committed in *Lumba*, with the result that the issue of whether vindicatory damages should be awarded did not arise for him.[10] But Lord Brown went on to say that he was in 'respectful agreement with Lord Dyson's judgment' on everything save the issue of whether

---

[4] See, in addition to the case cited below, *Vancouver* v *Ward* [2010] 2 SCR 28, at [25]–[29], and *Taunoa* v *Attorney General* [2007] NZSC 70, at [109], [255], [372], as well as the cases on awards of damages under the Human Rights Act 1998 cited above, § 3.2.

[5] [2006] 1 AC 328, at [19]. See also *James* v *Attorney General of Trinidad and Tobago* [2010] UKSC 23, at [35]: 'A risk of the devaluation of [constitutional] rights would obviously arise if the state could expect that the most significant sanction for their being flouted was a declaration that they had been breached' and *Inniss* v *Attorney-General of Saint Christopher & Nevis* [2008] UKPC 42, at [27]: '. . . vindication involves an assertion that the rights is a valuable one, as to whose enforcement the complainant herself has an interest. Any award of damages for its contravention is bound, to some extent at least, to act as a deterrent against further breaches. The fact that it may be expected to do so is something to which it is proper to have regard.'

[6] Lord Nicholls did not himself give a name to this 'additional award' but did say that 'the expressions "punitive damages" or "exemplary damages" are better avoided as descriptions of this type of additional award' on the ground that 'punishment . . . is not [the] object [of this award]' (ibid). In cases involving violations of human rights legislation, such damages are alternatively known as 'constitutional damages' or, sometimes, 'public law damages'.

[7] Reported at [2011] UKSC 12, and referred to below as '*Lumba*'.

[8] *Lumba*, at [101] (per Lord Dyson) and [237] (per Lord Collins).

[9] *Lumba*, at [335].

[10] *Lumba*, at [361].

a tort had been committed in *Lumba*[11] – which might be taken as indicating that he shared Lord Dyson's hostility to vindicatory damages.[12] The other four Justices (Lord Hope, Lord Walker, Lady Hale, and Lord Kerr) were willing to allow awards of vindicatory damages to be made in certain circumstances to tort claimants – but there was no agreement among them as to what those circumstances would be.

Depending, then, on how you read Lord Brown's judgment in *Lumba* there were either: (1) five Justices who were against awards of vindicatory damages being made in tort, and four in favour in certain circumstances; or (2) three Justices who were against such awards being made, and four who were in favour in certain circumstances, and two who expressed no clear opinion on the issue. So *Lumba* cannot be said to have finally decided – either positively or negatively – whether vindicatory damages are available in tort, and if so, when.

32.2 EXAMPLES?

It could be argued that even under the law as it as the moment, damages that are essentially vindicatory in nature can be sued for in a wide range of situations. We set these situations out below.

A. Other awards of damages

As we have seen, some theorists analyse other types of damages that we have already discussed as being truly vindicatory in nature.[13]

For example, *nominal* damages look vindicatory in nature: if they do not exist to mark the fact that the claimant's rights have been violated, and to mark the courts' disapproval of that fact, it is hard to see why they exist. Some theorists – as we have seen – re-analyse *compensatory* damages as serving a vindicatory purpose: that of giving the claimant in money form what he was entitled to in the first place from the defendant.[14]

Robert Stevens argues that *exemplary* damages are vindicatory in nature,[15] quoting in support Lord Nicholls in *A v Bottrill* (2003): '[Exemplary damages] serve as an emphatic vindication of the [claimant's] rights.'[16] John Goldberg takes a similar view of exemplary damages. In *Huckle v Money* (1763), the claimant printer was falsely imprisoned under a general warrant for six hours (and treated to beef steaks and beer while imprisoned!) by royal agents, because the claimant had been involved in producing a newspaper that was critical of the government. A jury awarded the claimant £300 in damages (about £22,500 in today's money). Only about £20 of that award (about £1,500 in today's money) could be justified as genuinely compensatory. The Court of King's Bench refused to set aside the award:

---

[11] *Lumba*, at [362].

[12] Such a position would be consistent with Lord Brown's observation in *Van Colle v Chief Constable of the Hertfordshire Police* [2009] 1 AC 225, at [138] that claims under the Human Rights Act 1998 or under the European Convention on Human Rights 'have very different objectives from civil actions. Where civil actions are designed essentially to compensate claimants for their losses, Convention claims are intended rather to uphold minimum human rights standards and to vindicate those rights.'

[13] Cf. Witzleb and Carroll 2009, at 42: 'vindication of the [claimant's] legal right is the effect and purpose of *all* private law remedies' (emphasis added).

[14] See above, § 28.7(B).

[15] Stevens 2007, 85–88.

[16] [2003] 1 AC 449, at [29].

the small injury done to the plaintiff, or the inconsiderableness of his station and rank in life did not appear to the jury in that striking light in which the great point of law touching the liberty of the subject appeared to them at the trial; they saw a magistrate over all the King's subjects, exercising arbitrary power, violating Magna Charta, and attempting to destroy the liberty of the kingdom, by insisting upon the legality of this general warrant before them; they heard the King's Counsel, and saw the solicitor of the Treasury endeavouring to support and maintain the legality of the warrant in a tyrannical and severe manner. These are the ideas which struck the jury on the trial; and I think they have done right in giving exemplary damages.[17]

John Goldberg argues that the exemplary damages in this case were awarded in order to satisfy or vindicate the claimant's rights: 'the jury acted appropriately "in giving exemplary damages" because a relatively large award accurately reflected the enormity of the wrong that the victim had suffered at the hands of his government captors.'[18]

B. *Ashby* v *White* (1794)

In *Ashby* v *White*, the electors of Aylesbury were called upon to elect two people to represent them in Parliament. Ashby was entitled to vote in the election and duly turned up to vote. Unfortunately, the four constables – including White – who were charged with conducting the election refused to allow Ashby to vote, and refused to count his vote. Ashby sued, claiming that he had a right to vote and that the constables had committed a tort in acting as they did. His claim was turned down in the Court of King's Bench by four votes to one. However, the House of Lords reversed this decision (by 50 votes to 16), preferring the opinion of the judge who dissented in the Court of King's Bench: Holt CJ. It is plain from Holt's judgment that he thought Ashby had to be given a remedy in this case in order to vindicate his right to vote:

> it is a great privilege to vote for a Parliament-man; and sure every one that has that great privilege has a right in it; and if so, of necessary consequence he has an action to vindicate and maintain that right . . . it is a vain thing to imagine that there should be a right without a remedy . . .[19]

What is interesting is how much Ashby sued for in damages, and was presumably awarded when his case was reinstated in the House of Lords. He sued for £200, which is the equivalent of about £11,000 in today's money. Such a sum could not possibly be equivalent to any loss he suffered as a result of being denied the right to vote. The damages Ashby would have recovered on winning his case therefore look vindicatory in nature: they were awarded in order to ensure that Ashby's right to vote was not made meaningless. As Holt CJ remarked, 'the encouraging of remedies for injuries is the most effectual way to make these officers honest and observant of the constitutions of their cities and boroughs'.[20]

C. Property torts

In *Mediana (Owners of Steamship)* v *Comet (Owners of Lightship)* (1900), Lord Halsbury LC observed that: 'the unlawful keeping back of what belongs to another person is of itself

---

[17] (1763) 2 Wils KB 205, 206–7; 95 ER 768, 769.
[18] Goldberg 2006, 460–1.
[19] (1794) 6 Mod 45, 53; 87 ER 810, 815.
[20] (1794) 6 Mod 45, 55; 87 ER 810, 817.

a ground for real damages, not nominal damages at all.'[21] In support of this proposition, he gave as an example:

> Supposing a person took away a chair out of my room and kept it for twelve months, could anybody say you had a right to diminish the damages by shewing that I did not usually sit in that chair, or that there were plenty of other chairs in the room?[22]

In such a case, he thought substantial damages would be payable (calculated by reference to how much it would cost to rent a chair for a year) even if no actual loss had been suffered by the claimant as a result of being deprived of the chair. It is possible to argue that such damages are gain-based – the defendant is being held liable to pay a reasonable sum for the privilege of keeping the chair for a year – but it must be admitted that analysing these damages as vindicatory in nature is equally attractive.

People's property rights would become much weaker if people were only held liable to pay compensatory damages on violating them. In cases where the violation caused no loss at all, the right would melt away and become ineffectual. In order to stop this happening, it could be argued that the law adopts the position that vindicatory damages are the *normal* remedy when someone's property rights are violated, and compensatory damages are awarded *on top* of vindicatory damages when a violation of someone's property rights caused the property owner special loss. This is the position adopted by Robert Stevens, citing two strong cases in favour of this position.[23]

The first is *The Sanix Ace* (1987), where the owner of goods that were being shipped to someone who had contracted to buy the goods in whatever condition they were delivered (so the risk of the goods being damaged mid-shipment was on the buyer) was held entitled to sue for damages in respect of the damage negligently done to the goods mid-shipment; and this was so, even though the buyer (having a right to be paid full value for those goods) was not made any worse off as a result of the goods being damaged. The second is the already mentioned *Mediana* (1900), where a ship belonging to the claimants was negligently damaged by the defendants. The ship was used to provide light to vessels wanting to use the claimants' port at night. The claimants had a replacement lightship in storage which they used while the damaged lightship was being repaired. It was held that they were entitled to sue for a reasonable sum for the loss of the use of the lightship while it was being repaired, even though the claimants had not really made been any worse off as a result of being deprived of the lightship's services for the period in which it was being repaired.

Stevens' position has come under attack from Andrew Burrows,[24] who thinks that when a property tort has been committed, the normal remedy should be compensation, and that the awards in cases like *The Sanix Ace* (1987) and *The Mediana* (1900) can be re-analysed as truly compensatory in nature.[25] For example, it could be argued that in *The Sanix Ace* the owner's normal right to sue for compensation for the damage to his goods should not be suspended just because he had a contractual right to be paid the full value of those goods, when contracts are often broken and are expensive to enforce when they are broken. And it could be argued that in *The Mediana* the owner of the damaged lightship was really being compensated for

[21] [1900] AC 113, 118.
[22] [1900] AC 113, 117.
[23] Stevens 2007, 73–74. Though Stevens would use the word 'substitutive' rather than 'vindicatory' in this context, and strongly disapprove of the pragmatic explanation advanced in the text for the availability of vindicatory/ substitutive damages in this context, arguing that the claimants are entitled to vindicatory/substitutive damages as of right (see above, § 28.7(B)).
[24] Drawing on the arguments of Edelman 2009, 213–6.
[25] Burrows 2011, 638–640.

the fact that while the damaged lightship was being repaired he would have to hire a *third* lightship to serve as cover for the replacement lightship that had been brought out of storage and was being used to fill in for the damaged lightship.[26] Alternatively, it could be argued that the owner's cleverness in having a substitute lightship in storage to cover for the damaged lightship should not work for the benefit of the defendant who negligently damaged that lightship, and who would – had the owner been less resourceful – have been liable for the cost of hiring a replacement lightship while the damaged one was being repaired.[27]

D. Trespass to the person

In *Ashley* v *Chief Constable of Sussex Police* (2008), Ashley was shot dead during a police raid on his house. In the course of his judgment, Lord Scott suggested that vindicatory damages might be awardable to Ashley's estate.[28] The suggestion is an attractive one because it fills whatever otherwise might be regarded as a loophole in the law. The loophole is illustrated by the **Murdered Tramp Problem:**

> *Tramp* lives on the streets and has no job and no prospects. One night, *Killer* walks up behind *Tramp* and shoots him through the head. *Tramp* dies instantly.

In this sort of case, if *Killer* cannot be sued for vindicatory damages, it does not seem that he will be liable to pay damages to *anyone* in this case. *Tramp* has no dependants who could sue for damages under the Fatal Accidents Act 1976. And *Tramp*'s estate cannot sue for damages under the Law Reform (Miscellaneous Provisions) Act 1934, as *Killer*'s tort in shooting *Tramp* caused *Tramp* no loss before he died. It might be thought that is unsatisfactory: that if we leave *Killer* to be dealt with by the criminal law, and leave his case untouched by tort law, we will be giving the poor and homeless less protection under the law than we would give the rich and privileged.

E. Defamation

We have already seen that damages in defamation cases have a vindicatory function: part of the reason for giving a claimant substantial damages at the end of a defamation case is to send out a signal to the public at large that what was said about the claimant was untrue.[29] However, it is not clear that such damages are vindicatory in the sense that that term is being used here. Damages in defamation cases are intended, in part, to vindicate the claimant's *reputation*, not to vindicate his *right that the defendant not unjustly defame him.*[30]

F. Invasion of privacy

In *Mosley* v *News Group Newspapers* (2008), Eady J held that the damages payable for a wrongful invasion of privacy could include a vindicatory component 'to ensure that an

---

[26] Edelman 2009, 216.

[27] Either of these alternative explanations of *The Mediana* are weakened by the fact that damages payable in that case were for the cost of *maintaining* a replacement lightship, not for the cost of *hiring* a replacement lightship.

[28] [2008] 1 AC 962, at [22]. None of the other Law Lords who decided *Ashley* expressed agreement with Lord Scott on this issue.

[29] See above, § 19.13.

[30] The distinction is marked by Eady J in his judgment in *Mosley* v *News Group Newspapers* [2008] EWHC 1777 (QB), at [216].

infringed right is met with "an adequate remedy".'[31] So in a case where a wrongful invasion of privacy had caused little or no loss, substantial damages could still be awarded to a claimant 'to [mark] the fact that an unlawful intrustion has taken place.'[32]

G. *Rees* v *Darlington Memorial Hospital NHS Trust* (2004)

The most obvious example of vindicatory damages being awarded in the law of negligence is the House of Lords' decision in *Rees* v *Darlington Memorial Hospital NHS Trust* (2004) that a claimant who gives birth to an unwanted baby due to a defendant's negligence will be entitled to sue the defendant for a fixed sum of £15,000. Although such a sum is supposed to compensate the claimant for the 'loss of autonomy' she will suffer as a result of having to bring up an unwanted child, Lord Hope convincingly criticised this view of the award in *Rees* on the basis that it makes no sense to compensate for such a loss through a *fixed* award.[33] However, Lord Bingham argued that the fixed sum of £15,000 was not intended to be compensatory at all:

> The conventional award would not be, and would not be intended to be, compensatory. It would not be the product of calculation. But it would not be a nominal, let alone a derisory, award. It would afford some measure of recognition of the wrong done.[34]

Lord Bingham's emphasis on 'the wrong done' suggests that the fixed sum award made in *Rees* is vindicatory in nature – intended both to mark the fact that the claimant in a wrongful birth or wrongful pregnancy case has suffered a wrong and to ensure that the defendant incurs some sanction for violating the claimant's rights to be treated properly by the defendant.[35]

H. *Chester* v *Afshar* (2005)

Another example of vindicatory damages being awarded in the law of negligence is provided by the case of *Chester* v *Afshar* (2005). In that case, it will be recalled, the claimant was partially paralysed when an operation carried out by the defendant resulted in her suffering nerve damage in her back.[36] The defendant had wrongfully failed to warn the claimant of the very small (1–2%) risk that the operation would result in her suffering such harm. Lord Hoffmann, in the minority, took the view that the claimant's claim for compensation for her paralysis should be dismissed, but that there was a case for awarding her a 'modest solatium'.[37] Such an award looks vindicatory in nature – it is intended to give the claimant something for the fact that her right to be treated properly by the defendant (which right encompasses a right to be told about the risks associated with her operation)

---

[31] ibid.
[32] [2008] EWHC 1777 (QB), at [231].
[33] [2004] 1 AC 309, at [71]–[73].
[34] [2004] 1 AC 309, at [8].
[35] Nolan 2007b objects (at 79) to this analysis on the ground that negligence is not actionable in the absence of proof of damage: so 'while torts such as battery can vindicate rights in the absence of harm, negligence cannot'. Meh. If duties of care are conduct-focused (as we have argued, above § 5.5) and a duty of care has been breached without causing the claimant harm, there may still be reasons why the courts should make an award to mark the fact that the claimant's rights (the flipside of the duties owed to her) have been breached. If those reasons exist, why should the courts be prevented from responding to them simply because there is a mantra that 'damage is the gist of negligence'?
[36] The case is discussed in detail above, at § 9.10.
[37] [2005] 1 AC 134, at [34].

has been violated. The majority – it could be argued – took a different route to vindicating the claimant's right to be treated properly. Even though the defendant's failure to treat the claimant properly did not *cause* her to become paralysed,[38] the majority still allowed the claimant to sue the defendant for compensation for her paralysis in order to ensure that her right to be treated properly did not become meaningless. As Lord Hope observed, in terms reminiscent of Holt CJ's judgment in *Ashby* v *White*, over 200 years earlier:

> The function of the law is to enable rights to be vindicated and to provide remedies when duties have been breached. Unless this is done the duty is a hollow one, stripped of all practical force and devoid of all content. It will have lost its ability to protect the patient and thus to fulfil the only purpose which brought it into existence. On policy grounds therefore I would hold that the test of causation is satisfied in this case.[39]

32.3 THE *LUMBA* DECISION

The case of *Lumba* v *Secretary of State for the Home Department* (2011) provided the Supreme Court with an ideal opportunity to clarify the position of vindicatory damages in the law of tort. A majority of the Supreme Court held that the claimants had been falsely imprisoned by the government in being detained pursuant to a secret and blanket policy that was inconsistent with the government's official position as to when people like the claimants would be detained. At the same time, the Supreme Court took the view that the claimants had not suffered any loss as a result of being falsely imprisoned as they could have been legitimately detained even under the government's announced policy. So the Supreme Court had a choice between awarding the claimants merely nominal damages for being falsely imprisoned, or awarding them something more substantial by way of vindicatory damages to mark the fact that their rights not to be falsely imprisoned had been violated by the government.

The result of the *Lumba* case was a signal lack of clarity as to when vindicatory damages will be available in tort. Of the six Supreme Court Justices who thought the claimants had been falsely imprisoned, three (Lords Walker and Hope and Lady Hale) thought the claimants should be awarded vindicatory damages, and three (Lords Dyson, Collins and Kerr) thought that the claimants should be awarded nominal damages. Because the remaining three Supreme Court Justices who decided *Lumba* (Lords Phillips, Brown and Rodger) were in favour of giving the claimants nothing at all on the ground that they had not been falsely imprisoned, the claimants ended up merely getting nominal damages. On the issue of when vindicatory damages should be available in tort:

(1) Lord *Dyson* thought that vindicatory damages should *never* be available: he could see 'no justification for letting such an unruly horse loose on our law.' 'Undesirable uncertainty would result' from opening the door to such awards being made, both in terms of for what torts vindicatory damages would be available, and as against which defendants. He thought that the purpose of vindicating claimants' rights was adequately served through remedies such as compensatory damages, declarations that a wrong had been committed, and awards of exemplary damages.[40]

---

[38] Because there was a merely coincidental connection between the defendant's wrong and the claimant's paralysis: see above, § 9.10.
[39] [2005] 1 AC 134, at [87].
[40] *Lumba*, at [101].

(2) Lord *Collins* agreed, arguing that there was no authority that justified 'a conclusion that there is a separate head of vindicatory damages in English law' and there was no case for recognising one here.[41] The award of a fixed sum of £15,000 in wrongful birth and wrongful pregnancy cases 'served a vindicatory purpose' but did not amount to 'vindicatory damages'.[42]

(3) Lord *Phillips* (dissenting on the issue of whether the government had falsely imprisoned the claimants) said that had he 'agreed with Lord Dyson on liability, I would have shared his approach to damages. I also endorse Lord Collins' conclusions in relation to vindicatory damages.'[43]

(4) Lord *Brown* (also dissenting on the issue of whether the tort of false imprisonment had been committed in *Lumba*) did not say anything about vindicatory damages in his judgment, but did say that 'insofar as this judgment indicates the area of my disagreement with Lord Dyson's judgment, I wish to say that I am in respectful agreement with it and feel unable to add anything of value on the various other issues arising for decision.'[44]

(5) Lord *Rodger* agreed with Lord Brown.

(6) Lord *Kerr* did not rule out the possibility that vindicatory damages could be available in tort, but thought that 'such an award could only be justified where the declaration that a claimant's right has been infringed provides insufficiently emphatic recognition of the seriousness of the defendant's default.' He thought that was not the case here: 'The defendant's failures have been thoroughly acknowledged and exposed.'[45]

(6) Lord *Walker* seemed to take the view that vindicatory damages should be available in cases where a claimant's 'constitutional rights' have been violated or where there has been 'an assault on individual's person or reputation'. He was in favour of awarding £1,000 in vindicatory damages to each of the claimants in *Lumba*.[46]

(7) Lord *Hope* seemed to think that vindicatory damages should be available in tort where a claimant had suffered a serious violation of her 'fundamental rights'. He thought *Lumba* (unlike *Rees* v *Darlington Memorial Hospital NHS Trust* (2004))[47] was such a case:

> the conduct of the officials in this case amounted . . . to a serious abuse of power and it was deplorable. It is not enough merely to declare that this was so. Something more is required, and I think this is best done by making an award of damages that is not merely nominal.[48]

Lord Hope was content to agree with Lord Walker's suggested damages of £1,000 for each claimant 'although I, for my part, would have arrived at a substantially lower figure.'[49]

(8) Lady *Hale* seemed to think that vindicatory damages should be available where 'important rights' of the claimant had been violated. As examples of such 'important rights' she instanced 'the rights to bodily integrity and personal autonomy, the right to limit one's

---

[41] *Lumba*, at [237].
[42] *Lumba*, at [236].
[43] *Lumba*, at [335].
[44] *Lumba*, at [362].
[45] *Lumba*, at [256].
[46] *Lumba*, at [195].
[47] Lord Hope reaffirmed his opposition to the conventional award in Rees in *Lumba*, at [180].
[48] *Lumba*, at [176].
[49] *Lumba*, at [180].

family and to live one's life in the way planned' (which rights justified a vindicatory award in *Rees*)[50] and 'the right to be free from arbitrary imprisonment by the state.'[51] Accordingly, she thought that *Lumba* was an appropriate case for an award of vindicatory damages:

> perhaps £500 rather than the £1,000 suggested by Lord Walker, designed to recognise that the claimant's fundamental constitutional rights have been breached by the state and to encourage all concerned to avoid anything like it happening again.[52]

None of the judgments in *Lumba* on whether and when vindicatory damages will be available in tort are at all impressive. Lords Hope and Walker and Lady Hale's vacillation on the issue of how much the claimants in *Lumba* should have been awarded only strengthens Lord Dyson's argument that undesirable uncertainty might be injected into the law by the widespread availability of vindicatory damages; as does their failure to agree on what sort of rights the violation of which should give rise to a right to sue for vindicatory damages. On the other hand, Lords Dyson, Collins and Phillips failed to address the argument that vindicatory damages are *already* being awarded by the courts, and their existence cannot simply be wished away. In particular, Lord Collins' assertion that the conventional award of £15,000 in a wrongful birth or a wrongful pregnancy case serves a 'vindicatory purpose' but does not amount to a form of vindicatory damages is mystifying.

32.4 THE FUTURE

The *Lumba* decision amounted to a missed opportunity to clarify the role of vindicatory damages in the law of tort. In this section, we will set out how we think this area of law should develop in the future. A useful starting point is provided by Lord Dyson's judgment in the *Lumba* case. In criticising the suggestion that vindicatory damages should be awarded in *Lumba*, he remarked:

> If they were awarded here, then they could in principle be awarded in any case involving a battery or false imprisonment by an arm of the state. Indeed, why limit it to such torts? And why limit it to torts committed by the state?[53]

These are good questions that we want to address here. *In principle*, we see no reason why vindicatory damages should not be made available whenever someone has committed a tort and the standard remedies for that tort do not provide an adequate sanction for that tort being committed. We think that vindicatory damages have a useful role to play in ensuring that *no one* feels that they can ride roughshod over *any* of the rights that the law of tort recognises us as having against other people.

However, *in practice*, we recognise that making vindicatory damages so widely available is liable to overburden the courts' limited resources with a multiplicity of tort claims. Given this, we would suggest that the availability of vindicatory damages be limited to cases where the standard remedies for a particular tort will almost always tend to be quite weak and limited. This will be the case where tort law provides us with rights that are designed to protect intangible interests of ours – in particular, our interest in being able to *choose* for ourselves what happens to us and what happens to our property. It is no accident, we think,

---

[50] *Lumba*, at [216].
[51] *Lumba*, at [217].
[52] ibid.
[53] *Lumba*, at [101].

that vindicatory damages have in the past tended to be awarded where a defendant has violated a right of the claimant's that was designed to allow the claimant to make a choice – for example, who to vote for in an election, or whether to have a particular medical procedure, or whether to have a baby, or whether to reveal some intimate detail about one's private life to someone else, or whether to allow someone else to use one's property. Where what we can call a *choice right* is violated by someone else, the standard remedies for committing a tort are liable to be particularly weak because it will be hard for a claimant to prove that being deprived of a particular choice has actually made her financially worse off in any way. In such cases, vindicatory damages have a vital role to play in ensuring that people are not allowed to override the law's decision that a particular choice should be made by the claimant and not by anyone else.

So we think vindicatory damages should be available for torts involving the appropriation of someone else's property; invasion of privacy; battery (where the battery involves unwanted medical treatment or physical attention); false imprisonment (where the imprisonment involves preventing someone going where they have the power and desire to go); and negligence (where the negligence results in someone not being able to make an informed choice about their medical treatment, or having an unwanted baby). In contrast, we do not think that a particularly strong case can be made for extending the availability of vindicatory damages to cases of wrongfully damaging someone else's property or person or reputation. In such cases, the standard remedies for committing a tort will normally prove sturdy enough to provide sufficient sanction for the defendant's wrongdoing.

Turning to the second question posed by Lord Dyson – whether vindicatory damages should be limited to cases of torts committed by the State – again, *in principle*, we see no reason why vindicatory damages should not be made available against *anyone* who has committed a tort where the standard remedies for that tort are not likely to provide an adequate sanction for that kind of wrongdoing. However, *in practice*, it has to be admitted that the concern underlying awards of vindicatory damages – that the law provide an adequate sanction for violating someone else's rights – is magnified in cases where a defendant is wealthy or powerful enough not to have to worry very much about the consequences of violating someone else's rights. In such cases, it is especially important that vindicatory damages be made available so that even the richest and most powerful defendant will be given pause for thought before trampling on someone else's rights. So in practice, we think that vindicatory damages should be made available in cases where the State or a company or an employee of the State or a company has committed one of the torts set out in the previous paragraph. In cases where a private individual, not working for the State or a company, has committed one of those torts, we think the case for making vindicatory damages available against such a defendant is not especially strong.

Further reading

Anyone wishing to explore this new area of law still further must read two things. **Robert Stevens'** chapter on 'Remedies' (chapter 4) in his *Torts and Rights* (OUP, 2007), and **Normann Witzleb and Robyn Carroll's** article 'The role of vindication in tort damages' (2009) 17 *Tort Law Review* 16.

Visit **www.mylawchamber.co.uk/mcbride** to access tools to help you develop and test your knowledge of Tort law, including interactive multiple choice questions, practice exam questions with guidance, weblinks, legal newsfeed, additional case summaries, legal updates and tips on answering problem and essay questions.

premium
my**law**chamber
*unrivalled support **for** legal education*

Use **Case Navigator** to read in full some of the key cases referenced in this chapter with commentary and questions:

• Chester *v* Afshar

POWERED BY ⬤ LexisNexis

33 Injunctions

33.1 The basics *832*

33.2 Classification of injunctions *834*

33.3 When will an interim injunction be granted? *834*

33.4 When will a final injunction be granted? *837*

33.5 Reform *841*

Overview

In this chapter we focus on the judicial remedy of injunctions; that is, court orders that prohibit people from doing specified things or require them to do specified things. We explain that there are different types of injunction that can be sought; in particular, that they can be sought as a final remedy or as an interim measure to preserve the status quo until a later trial. The tests for whether an interim injunction will be granted, given that these are orders that will restrict the liberty of people who have not as yet been proved to be tortfeasors, tend to involve a careful balancing of competing interests. In section 33.3 we describe the basic 'balance of convenience' test for awarding an interim injunction, and then set out the situations where other tests will be used instead. In section 33.4 we move on to presenting the law that governs whether a final injunction will be granted against someone who has been proved to be a tortfeasor, focusing in particular on when a court may decide that it would be appropriate to refuse a final injunction and award a special measure of damages for anticipated future harm instead. In the final section we investigate whether there is a good case for granting injunctions more readily in order to prevent torts being committed that may lead to personal injury or death, and whether it is legitimate to criticise English law for being too ready to grant injunctions in cases involving torts to property.

33.1 THE BASICS

An injunction is 'a court order prohibiting a person from doing something or requiring a person to do something'.[1] In some circumstances a claimant will seek an injunction to prevent a defendant from committing a tort in relation to him or her.[2] In particular, a claimant may find this remedy attractive if the defendant is continuously doing something that amounts to a tort, or regularly does something that amounts to a tort, or seems to be on the verge of doing something that will amount to a tort.

For example, if *Hornblower* regularly encourages his hounds to run across *Reynard*'s land in order to chase foxes, and *Hornblower* has continued to do this despite knowing that

---

[1] Civil Procedure Rules, glossary. The general authority of the High Court to grant injunctions is found in Senior Courts Act 1981, s 37(1).

[2] Injunctions are also available in many circumstances outside tort law. For example, s 34 of the Policing and Crime Act 2009 empowers a court to award a 'gang injunction' to help prevent gang-related violence. Clearly many of the things that a 'gang injunction' can prohibit a person from doing, such as wearing particular gang-related articles of clothing in particular places, would not amount to *torts* if the person concerned was to do them. This chapter is focused on injunctions *in tort law*.

Reynard objects to it, then *Reynard* may want to seek an injunction which will order *Hornblower* not to commit the tort of trespass to land by encouraging his hounds to act in this way in the future. If such an injunction is issued against *Hornblower* then he is very likely to obey it; a defendant who ignores a court order will commit a contempt of court and render himself liable to be criminally punished. Moreover, if *Reynard* expects *Hornblower* to continue sending his hounds across his land then it will obviously be to his advantage to obtain such an order rather than having to keep returning to court to seek damages for *Hornblower*'s latest trespass.

Continuing, or regularly repeated, torts are only one example of a situation where a claimant may have good reasons for seeking an injunction. Another common situation is where the claimant is likely to suffer some form of harm that can never be fully redressed by an award of damages if a tort is committed, or continues to be committed. For example, if *Diva* learns that *Redtop* is about to commit the tort of wrongful disclosure of private information in relation to her, by publishing a salacious account of her unusual sexual behaviour with a former lover, then she is likely to want a remedy that will prevent this tort from being committed: obtaining damages *after* the account has been published will never re-establish *Diva's* privacy, and she may already have more money than she knows how to spend.

While claimants may often regard injunctions as an attractive remedy the examples concerning *Reynard* and *Diva* also suggest why courts have to be cautious about granting this remedy: injunctions restrict the liberty of those they are granted against in a far more direct way than awards of damages, and may sometimes impose a disproportionate burden on those who are subject to them. An example of a severe restriction on liberty can be based on the hunting case: suppose that *Hornblower* claims that the open nature of the countryside in the region where he hunts makes it very difficult for him to know where the boundaries between the properties of different landowners are, and consequently if he is ordered not to send his hounds across *Reynard*'s land, on pain of punishment for contempt of court, he will probably also have to stop hunting on land near *Reynard*'s land, even though the owners of the nearby plots of land are very happy for him to hunt there. In such circumstances *Hornblower* may ask if it is really appropriate to grant a remedy that will restrict his liberty to such a great extent simply in order to avoid a minor annoyance to *Reynard*. Similarly, suppose that *Redtop* can plausibly argue that if it is ordered not to publish the story about *Diva* then it will have to recall and pulp a large number of newspapers that it has already printed and distributed to wholesalers, and this will cause it financial loss out of all proportion to the amount of damages that *Diva* might expect to be awarded if the story is published. These concerns – about the effects injunctions have on liberty and the risk they create of putting a disproportionate burden on defendants – help to explain why courts do not automatically grant injunctions whenever a tort has been committed. Instead, injunctions are regarded as a 'discretionary' remedy.

Saying that injunctions are a discretionary remedy does not, of course, mean that a court has a *free* choice as to whether to grant an injunction or not; it simply means that courts will not *automatically* grant an injunction. Instead they will usually make a judgment about whether an injunction is appropriate in the particular circumstances, taking into account the suitability of *other* possible remedies. Moreover, certain rules – some of which we will discuss in more detail in sections 33.3 and 33.4 – guide the courts when making these judgments. For example, an injunction will not be granted unless the court can clearly specify what it is that the defendant must cease doing (or must do), and an injunction will not be granted if a claimant waits too long before seeking it.

33.2 CLASSIFICATION OF INJUNCTIONS

(1) *Interim and final injunctions.* Injunctions granted as a remedy at the conclusion of a trial are referred to as *final* or *perpetual* injunctions. English civil procedure also allows a party to seek an injunction to protect his or her position before trial. Such injunctions are referred to as *interim* (formerly *interlocutory*) injunctions.[3] *Interim* injunctions are particularly important where there is a risk that a claimant will suffer *irreparable* damage if the defendant is not prevented from doing something which is arguably a tort. But *interim* injunctions also give rise to special concern because they restrict a defendant's liberty *before* it has been established whether what he is doing, or proposes to do, is, or will be, a tort. In chapter 21 we discuss in detail some special issues relating to interim injunctions which arise most commonly in cases of invasion of privacy. In particular, it is in that chapter that we discuss the effects that interim injunctions may have on third parties, when the parties to a claim for an injunction will be anonymised, and when, if ever, it will be appropriate to grant a super-injunction, which forbids disclosure of the fact that an interim injunction has been obtained.[4]

(2) *Mandatory and prohibitory injunctions.* If an injunction instructs someone to take positive action, for example, to repair a wall, then the injunction is called a *mandatory* injunction. On the other hand, if an injunction instructs someone to cease behaving in a particular way the injunction is called a *prohibitory* injunction. The distinction is one of substance rather than form. A good rule of thumb is that if fulfilling an injunction requires the expenditure of money then the injunction is, in substance, *mandatory*. English courts are more cautious about granting *mandatory* injunctions than *prohibitory* injunctions.[5]

(3) *Quia timet injunctions.* Most injunctions will instruct someone either not to *continue* committing a tort or to undo the consequences which followed the commission of a tort (for example, to destroy all copies of a document that they received as a result of a tort). It is also possible, however, for someone to obtain an injunction if she can establish that she is *about* to be the victim of a tort to be committed by A. Such an injunction, known as a *quia timet* injunction, will order A not to commit the tort. For example, in *Litchfield-Speer v Queen Anne's Gate Syndicate (No 2) Ltd* (1919), Lawrence J held that the claimants were entitled to an injunction to restrain the defendants from erecting a new building, which, had it been built, would have amounted to a private nuisance because its presence would have unreasonably interfered with the claimants' right to light.

33.3 WHEN WILL AN INTERIM INJUNCTION BE GRANTED?

We have already noted that interim injunctions are particularly important where A proposes to do something, or continue doing something – *x* – which will cause damage to B *before* there is any opportunity to hold a trial to determine whether A's doing *x* will be, or is, a tort to B, and where the damage which will be caused to B as a result of A doing *x* is of a type that could not be properly reversed by a payment of damages. In such a case, B may be able to obtain an *interim* injunction against A, requiring him not to do *x* until some future time. But since A may dispute that doing *x* will be, or is, a tort to B, and may even

---

[3] We will not discuss certain specialised interim injunctions, such as 'asset freezing injunctions', which help to ensure that money can be obtained from a defendant if he is eventually held liable to pay damages.

[4] See above, § 21.8.

[5] The reasons for this are explained below, § 33.4.

insist that preventing him from doing *x* will in turn cause *him* irreparable damage, it is necessary to determine what test a court will use when deciding whether such an injunction should be granted.

A. The 'balance of convenience' test[6]

The general rule is that B will be required to do three things before an interim injunction will be granted:

(1) B must establish that there is a serious question to be tried as to whether if A does *x* he will commit a tort to B.[7]
(2) B will have to undertake that if an interim injunction is granted against A and it is later found that *x* would not have involved A committing a tort to B, she will compensate A for any losses suffered by him as a result of that injunction's being granted.[8]
(3) B will have to convince the court that the 'balance of convenience' favours granting an interim injunction.

The 'balance of convenience' is determined by balancing B's need to be protected against any harm (for which she could not be adequately compensated in damages) that she might suffer if A were allowed to do *x* against A's need to be protected against any harm (for which he could not be adequately compensated in damages under the claimant's undertaking) that he might suffer as a result of being prevented from doing *x*.

Thus if *Draughtsman* wanted to cut down an old tree he believes to be on his land so as to allow more light to reach his office window, and *Eco* claimed that the old tree was on her land so cutting it down would be a tort to her, then the court would balance the extent to which *Eco* would be adequately compensated if the tree was cut down and it turned out to be her tree, against the extent to which *Draughtsman* could be adequately compensated by damages if he was prevented from cutting down the tree until trial and it turned out that cutting the tree down would not involve a tort to *Eco*. In such circumstances a pivotal issue would be what harm, if any, *Draughtsman* might suffer if he had to delay cutting down the tree, and whether it could be adequately compensated by damages.

B. Exceptions

There are four situations which commonly arise in tort cases where the courts will *not* use the 'balance of convenience' test:

(1) *Time is of the essence.* In some situations ordering A not to do something until trial will effectively preclude him from ever doing it, since he may only want to do it at a particular

---

[6] This test was set out by Lord Diplock in *American Cyanamid* v *Ethicon Ltd* [1975] AC 396, and is commonly referred to as 'the *American Cyanamid* test'. For its detailed application, and some of the criticisms that have been made of it, the reader is advised to consult a specialist book on civil procedure.
[7] This is not a high hurdle. In *American Cyanamid* v *Ethicon Ltd* [1975] AC 396, Lord Diplock explained (at 407) that there was a 'serious question to be tried' if the court was satisfied that the claim was not 'frivolous or vexatious'. He also stated that, 'It is no part of the court's function at this stage of the litigation to try to resolve conflicts of evidence on affidavit as to facts on which the claims of either party may ultimately depend nor to decide difficult questions of law which call for detailed argument and mature considerations. These are matters to be dealt with at the trial.' Zuckerman 2006 (at 9.45) suggests that many judges are reluctant to use such a *low* hurdle when they feel able to reach a preliminary view on the merits and that there is a 'widespread but unstated practice' of using a *higher* hurdle: 'as every lawyer should know, a clear probability of success on the merits is bound to figure in judges' calculations when they come to decide whether to grant interim relief.'
[8] Civil Procedure Rules, Practice Direction 25, 5.1(1).

time. Consequently, in some tort cases the question whether an interim injunction will be granted effectively determines the whole dispute. An example might be where *Airline* seeks an order that *Union* should not organise some industrial action. By the time that a full trial can be arranged to determine whether *Union* was on the verge of committing a tort the dispute which generated the threat of industrial action may have been resolved, and neither party may have much desire to establish whether *Union's* proposed action would have been lawful. In such an exceptional case a judge who is asked to grant an interim injunction should not consider merely whether there is a serious question to be tried, but whether *Airline* will be likely to obtain a *final* injunction if the case is fully tried.[9]

(2) *Defamation cases*. '[T]he importance of leaving free speech unfettered is a strong reason in cases of libel for dealing most cautiously and warily with the granting of interim injunctions.'[10] This caution is reflected in the rule[11] that interim injunctions will not generally be granted in cases where B claims that a proposed publication by A will libel or slander her[12] but A intends to argue at trial that his statement is not defamatory,[13] or intends to put forward a defence of justification,[14] fair comment on a matter of public interest,[15] or privilege.[16] If, however, it is clear that the defence is doomed to fail, an interim injunction may still be granted.[17]

(3) *Freedom of expression cases*. Section 12(3) of the Human Rights Act 1998 provides that:

> No . . . relief [affecting the exercise of the Convention right to freedom of expression] is to be granted so as to restrain publication before trial unless the court is satisfied that the applicant is likely to establish that publication should not be allowed.

This provision has not altered the common law rule discussed in the previous paragraph, which applies in cases of libel and slander.[18] But the statutory provision means that the 'balance of convenience' test will *also* not apply in other situations where an interim injunction is sought to prevent the commission of a wrong involving publication, such as the wrongful disclosure of private information.[19]

In *Cream Holdings Ltd* v *Banerjee* (2005), the House of Lords noted the difficulty of defining 'likely' in this provision because the test must be applied in such a wide range of situations. In some cases (for instance, those involving allegedly confidential information about the dealings of a company) the claimant might be seeking to protect a financial interest and the defendant relying on the public interest, but in others (for instance, those

---

[9] *NWL Ltd* v *Woods* [1979] 1 WLR 1294, 1306–7.

[10] *Bonnard* v *Perryman* [1891] 2 Ch 269, 284 (per Lord Coleridge).

[11] Commonly referred to as 'the rule in *Bonnard* v *Perryman*'.

[12] Similar rules probably apply to the tort of malicious falsehood, and courts will be careful not to allow the rules to be evaded by claims that the publication may amount to some other tort, such as lawful means conspiracy (discussed in chapter 24, above): see *Gulf Oil (Great Britain) Ltd* v *Page* [1987] Ch 327, 333–4; *Femis-Bank* v *Lazar* [1991] Ch 391.

[13] *Coulson* v *Coulson* [1887] 3 TLR 846.

[14] *Bonnard* v *Perryman* [1891] 2 Ch 269.

[15] *Fraser* v *Evans* [1969] 1 QB 349, 360.

[16] *Quartz Hill Consolidated Mining Co* v *Beal* (1882) 20 Ch D 501; *Harakas* v *Baltic Mercantile and Shipping Exchange Ltd* [1982] 1 WLR 958.

[17] *Holley* v *Smyth* [1998] QB 726, holding that a claimant is allowed to adduce evidence to show that a defence of justification is bound to fail; *Herbage* v *Pressdram* [1984] 1 WLR 1160, 1164, discussing a situation where there was overwhelming evidence of malice which would negate a defence of qualified privilege.

[18] *Greene* v *Associated Newspapers Ltd* [2005] QB 972.

[19] Discussed in Chapter 21, above. In *A* v *B* [2003] QB 195, at [11], the Court of Appeal set out guidelines for judges asked to decide whether an interim injunction should be granted to prevent commission of this tort.

involving protecting the new identity of a released criminal) the claimant might be seeking to protect his right to life. Lord Nicholls solved this difficulty by holding that Parliament intended the word 'likely' to be able to change meaning:

> The intention of Parliament must be taken to be that 'likely' should have an extended meaning which sets as a normal perquisite to the grant of an injunction before trial a likelihood of success at the trial higher than the commonplace *American Cyanamid* standard of 'real prospect' but permits the court to dispense with the higher standard where particular circumstances make this necessary.[20]

Later in his speech he identified the degree of likelihood that an applicant would have to establish in a normal case (that is, not one involving particularly severe potential consequences, and not one involving a very brief injunction pending the judge being able to read the papers or an appeal being considered) as being that the claim would 'more likely than not' succeed at trial.[21]

The approach under s 12(3) is distinct from that under the ordinary 'balance of convenience' test not only because it asks whether the claimant is 'likely to establish that publication should not be allowed' instead of whether there is 'a serious question to be tried', but also because under s 12(3) the court must reach a provisional view on disputes of fact and questions of law in order to reach a view on the merits of the claim. In considering the merits the court must consider not merely the likelihood of the claimant establishing the defendant's *liability* but also the likelihood of the claimant convincing the court that a *final* injunction is appropriate.

(4) *Trade disputes*. The fourth exception is where A claims that his proposed course of action will be performed in contemplation or furtherance of a trade dispute. In such a case, before granting an interim injunction a court must consider the likelihood that A will be able to establish the defence of trade union immunity[22] at trial.[23]

33.4 WHEN WILL A FINAL INJUNCTION BE GRANTED?

A. The general rule

The general rule is that courts will grant a *final* injunction against someone who has committed a tort to prevent the continuation or repetition of such a tort where there is a sufficient basis for believing that without an injunction there will be a continuation or repetition of such a tort.

In practice this means that injunctions are far more common where certain types of tort are alleged. Torts that are usually committed by isolated impacts, such as negligence, are unlikely to give rise to claims for injunctions,[24] while torts which are often committed by

---

[20] [2005] 1 AC 253, at [20].
[21] [2005] 1 AC 253, at [22].
[22] The immunity is found in Trade Union and Labour Relations (Consolidation) Act 1992, ss 219–220. These provisions are discussed above, at § 26.5.
[23] Trade Union and Labour Relations (Consolidation) Act 1992, s 221(2).
[24] Cf Lord Denning MR's remark in *Miller* v *Jackson* [1977] QB 966, 980: 'there is no case, so far as I know, where [an injunction] has been granted to stop a man being negligent.' This is disputed, however, in McBride 2004, pointing to the American cases of *Shimp* v *New Jersey Bell Telephone Co.*, 368 A 2d 408 (1976) and *Smith* v *Western Electric Co.*, 643 SW 2d 10 (1982), where in each case an injunction was granted against an employer, compelling him to comply with the duty of care he owed his employees to take reasonable steps to see that they would be reasonably safe in working for him.

interference over a longer period with someone's interests, such as private nuisance, commonly give rise to such claims. It is worth noting, however, that because injunctions are intended to deal with future continuation or repetition of the wrongful behaviour, a claimant seeking an injunction will often *also* claim damages for past injury – and where a court finds that A has committed and is committing a tort by engaging in a continuous course of conduct, it will often award *both* an injunction against A to prevent the tort being committed in the future *and* damages for any past injury caused by A's tort.

The remedy of injunction was initially developed in the Courts of Equity and consequently it conforms to general equitable principles about remedies. The central general principle is that remedies developed by the Courts of Equity (known as 'equitable remedies') are 'discretionary'. What this means is that even where a claimant has established the conditions sufficient to be awarded a remedy a court will not necessarily grant it – it can still refuse. In practice, the courts' choices as to whether or not to grant someone an equitable remedy are usually directed by well-developed rules. Thus an injunction will not be awarded where justice can be done by ordering the defendant to pay damages to the claimant,[25] where granting the injunction would be oppressive,[26] where the claimant seeking the injunction does not have 'clean hands',[27] where the claimant seeking the injunction is unwilling to 'do equity',[28] where the claimant initially allowed the defendant to do what she is now seeking an injunction against,[29] or where there has been unacceptable delay on the part of the claimant in seeking an injunction against the defendant. But even beyond these rules there exists a degree of residual flexibility.

Courts are generally more cautious about granting mandatory injunctions than prohibitory injunctions for two principal reasons. First, if a mandatory injunction is awarded against a defendant, the court must specify what the defendant must do to comply with it. Where it is impossible to state clearly what it is that the defendant is being required to do a mandatory injunction will be refused.[30] Secondly, there is a concern that if a mandatory injunction is awarded against A for B's benefit, A may be compelled to spend more money complying with that injunction than B will gain from that injunction being complied with. This might be regarded as wasteful. Consequently, it is necessary to pay particular attention to whether damages will be an *adequate* remedy for any future harm, and how much it will cost a defendant to obey a mandatory injunction.[31] However, if the cost to A of complying with the injunction that B is seeking far outweighs whatever benefits B will reap from that injunction being awarded against A, an injunction may still be awarded against A if A has acted with wanton disregard of B's interests.

---

[25] Damages are generally not thought to be adequate where the harm caused is to non-pecuniary interests, such as health or amenity, or where the damages would be hard to quanitfy. Consequently, this basis for refusing an injunction is rarely relied on in tort cases.

[26] This concept is discussed in detail below.

[27] This basis for refusing an injunction allows a court to take account of any misconduct by a claimant seeking an injunction. Of course, the courts will not refuse to grant an injunction because of a trivial act of misconduct by the claimant.

[28] This basis for refusing an injunction allows a court to consider whether the claimant is willing to perform any duties that she owes the defendant.

[29] An injunction might be refused on this basis if, for instance, B stood by and watched A expend money on a project before objecting to it and seeking an injunction. In *Jaggard* v *Sawyer* [1995] 1 WLR 269 the claimant warned the defendant that the defendant's proposed action was wrongful but did not seek an interim injunction. The Court of Appeal treated this failure to seek an interim injunction as relevant to the decision whether to grant a final injunction: 283 (Sir Thomas Bingham MR), 289 (Millett LJ).

[30] *Redland Bricks Ltd* v *Morris* [1970] AC 632.

[31] ibid.

B. Final injunctions affecting freedom of expression

Where a court is considering whether to grant any relief which, if granted, might affect the exercise of the Convention right to freedom of expression then:

> The court must have particular regard to the importance of the Convention right to freedom of expression and, where the proceedings relate to material which the respondent claims, or which appears to the court, to be journalistic, literary or artistic material (or to conduct connected with such material), to –
>
> (a) the extent to which –
>> (i) the material has, or is about to, become available to the public; or
>> (ii) it is, or would be, in the public interest for the material to be published;
>
> (b) any relevant privacy code.[32]

Clearly an injunction forbidding someone from publishing something may affect freedom of expression to a greater extent than an award of damages after it has been published. Thus before granting an injunction which will interfere with freedom of expression a court will want to be convinced that the proposed interference is supported by 'relevant and sufficient grounds', will respond to a 'pressing social need' and will not interfere to any extent greater than necessary to meet the legitimate aim pursued. The Court of Appeal has held that s 12(4) does not require a court to attribute *extra* weight to the listed factors: it 'does no more than underline the need to have regard to contexts in which [the European Court of Human Rights'] jurisprudence has given particular weight to freedom of expression, while at the same time drawing attention to considerations which may none the less justify restricting that right'.[33] Equally, s 12(4) is not intended to give one Convention right (Article 10, freedom of expression) pre-eminence in a case where another Convention right (eg Article 8, privacy) is also involved.[34]

C. Damages in lieu of final injunctions

If B applies to a court for a final injunction which would require A not to continue committing a particular tort in relation to B in the *future*, the choice for the court which is considering B's application is not a straightforward one between granting an injunction and leaving B, for the time being,[35] without any remedy. The court may refuse to award B an injunction but at the same time award B damages *in lieu of* (instead of) an injunction.[36]

The result of refusing to grant an injunction in a case where it has been established that A will almost certainly continue to commit a tort in relation to B in the future will be to leave the defendant *in effect* free to commit that tort. We say '*in effect* free', rather than simply 'free', because refusing an injunction does not mean that it is not a *wrong* for the defendant to go ahead and commit the tort in relation to B: doing so will remain *wrongful*,

---

[32] Human Rights Act 1998, s 12(4).

[33] *Ashdown v Telegraph Group Ltd* [2002] Ch 149, [27].

[34] The court should not give either right precedence over the other, should focus intensely 'on the comparative importance of the specific rights being claimed in the individual case', should take account of 'the justifications for interfering with or restricting each right' and should apply the proportionality test to each right: *In re S (A Child) (Identification: Restrictions on Publication)* [2005] 1 AC 593, at [17].

[35] If no remedy is granted and A *does* continue to commit the tort in the future then B will be able to come back to court to seek *damages* at that stage.

[36] The Chancery Amendment Act 1858, better known as Lord Cairns's Act, allowed the Court of Chancery to award damages in lieu of an injunction. This statute has been repealed, but s 50 of the Senior Courts Act 1981 preserves the court's jurisdiction to award damages in lieu of an injunction.

and as a result it may be appropriate to make A pay damages – *in lieu of injunction* – in advance. Such damages are, in effect, a reasonable sum for the privilege of being allowed to continue committing that tort.

In order to calculate how much a claimant should be awarded by way of damages in lieu of injunction a court will not simply estimate how much damage the claimant will suffer if the tort continues to be committed. Instead, it will assess how much should be paid by way of damages in lieu by asking: How much would a reasonable person in the claimant's shoes charge the defendant for the privilege of being allowed to continue committing the tort complained of?[37]

Because an injunction will usually protect a claimant's interests more completely than receiving some money in advance, and because calculating damages in lieu necessarily requires courts to attempt to predict what the effects of tortious behaviour stretching into the future might be, the courts have traditionally been cautious about using their power to award damages in lieu of injunctions. In the leading case of *Shelfer* v *City of London Electric Lighting Co* (1895), A.L. Smith LJ stated,

> In my opinion it may be stated as a good working rule that – (1) If the injury to the claimant's legal rights is small, (2) And is one which is capable of being estimated in money, (3) And is one which can be adequately compensated by a small money payment, (4) And the case is one in which it would be oppressive to the defendant to grant an injunction: – then damages in substitution for an injunction may be given.[38]

And in *Jaggard* v *Sawyer* (1995), the Court of Appeal treated A.L. Smith LJ's list of four factors as having 'stood the test of time'.[39]

The question whether a court should also take into account the *public interest* in a defendant being left free to continue committing a tort in the future has proved controversial. In *Shelfer*, Lindley LJ expressed the strong view that the fact that a wrongdoer was 'in some sense a public benefactor' had never 'been considered a sufficient reason for refusing to protect by injunction an individual whose rights are being persistently infringed'.[40] In chapter 15 we explain in detail the different views expressed by judges as to the relevance of the public interest when a court is deciding whether to grant an injunction against a defendant who is conducting an activity which is of some social benefit but also involves commission of the tort of private nuisance because of the disturbance that it causes to neighbouring landowners.[41] Here we will simply note that the current orthodox position was confirmed by Sir Andrew Morritt in *Watson* v *Croft Promosport Ltd* (2009):[42] 'in a marginal case where the damage to the claimant is minimal' it is legitimate, consistently with *Shelfer*, to take into account the effect on the public interest of awarding an injunction; but the public interest cannot negate the key requirements under *Shelfer* that an injunction should only be refused 'in exceptional circumstances' *and* when it would be 'oppressive' to grant one.[43]

---

[37] *Jaggard* v *Sawyer* [1995] 1 WLR 269.

[38] [1895] 1 Ch 287, 322–3.

[39] [1995] 1 WLR 269, 287 (per Millett LJ). We discuss these factors in more detail in the section on remedies in private nuisance: see, above, § 15.12.

[40] [1895] 1 Ch 287, 315–6.

[41] Above, § 15.12.

[42] In the *Watson* case the defendant was committing private nuisance because of the noise which resulted from a rural motor-racing circuit being used for events where members of the public could drive fast cars. At first instance Simon J held that there was a public interest in this being allowed to continue because the circuit created employment locally and allowed those who gained pleasure from driving cars at high speed to do so legally and in relative safety. (The claimants in the *Watson* case did not seek to prevent the circuit from pursuing its 'core activity' of holding car and motorcycle racing fixtures.)

[43] [2009] EWCA Civ 15, at [51].

33.5 REFORM

In this section we will consider two ways in which it has been argued that the law relating to injunctions ought to be reformed.

A. Should *quia timet* injunctions be granted more readily?

John Murphy argues that a court should have power to grant an injunction against A where he wantonly or recklessly acts in such a way as to create an unjustifiable risk to B's physical well-being.[44] This would probably require a change in the law because currently a court would probably say that A had not yet committed a tort in relation to B (because the most obviously applicable tort, negligence, is not complete until damage has been caused to B) and an injunction will only be granted *before* a tort is committed if a tort that will cause serious damage is imminent.[45] If the law were to be changed in the way that Murphy suggests then it might allow an injunction to be granted in the **Regular Menace Problem**:

> *Newman* lives next to *Gordon*. Nearly every morning *Newman* plays with his young children on a communal paved area situated in front of his house and Gordon's house. And nearly every morning *Newman* sees *Gordon* drive out of his garage and across the paved area with a mobile phone awkwardly held between his ear and his shoulder. On several occasions *Gordon* has narrowly avoided running over *Newman* and his children, apparently because he has been so distracted by his telephone conversations that he has failed to notice them. *Newman* protests to *Gordon* about this dangerous and unlawful behaviour but *Gordon* tells him to 'piss off and ring Special Branch'. *Newman* forms the view that *Gordon* poses an unjustifiable risk to his safety and that of his children.

But should the law be changed to enable *Newman* to obtain an injunction against *Gordon* in this case? Murphy argues that the law should be changed because it is important to protect people like *Newman* and his children from physical harm[46] and equally important to prevent people like *Gordon* from wantonly or recklessly ignoring the duties of care that tort law imposes on them. We agree that these are important factors. But we also think that there are two countervailing reasons that must also be considered.

First, if injunctions could be granted to people facing a significant risk of being injured by a tort, rather than just to those who are at *imminent* risk, then many more people would become eligible to seek injunctions. Tort claims are expensive to process, and it cannot be taken for granted that the cost of dealing with any additional applications for injunctions will be counter-balanced by a reduction in the number of injuries as a result of more injunctions being granted against those who create 'unjustifiable risks'.

Secondly, if such injunctions were granted then the effect would be to create something like a 'two-tier' criminal law: most drivers who were subsequently caught recklessly using mobile phones while driving in the vicinity of *Newman* and his children would be subject to the ordinary criminal law, but if *Gordon* was caught doing this then – if an injunction

---

[44] Murphy 2007b.

[45] Murphy accepts that this is the law, quoting Chitty J's statement (in *Attorney-General* v *Manchester Corporation* [1893] 2 Ch 87, at 92) that: 'The principle which I think may be properly and safely extracted from the *quia timet* authorities is, that the [claimant] must shew a strong case of probability that the apprehended mischief will, in fact, arise.'

[46] Oddly, Murphy 2007b suggests that one of the reasons that the law does not currently grant injunctions in situations such as the Regular Menace Problem is because courts are more ready to grant injunctions to protect property. We do not think that this is the case: we think that *Newman* would find it no easier to obtain an injunction against the unjustifiable risk that *Gordon* might be posing to his garden fence.

had been granted against him – he would be subject to more serious punishment for committing a contempt of court. Why, *Gordon* might ask, should a private citizen who has not been injured be able to increase the penalties that another citizen will face if he continues to behave in a dangerous way? To put the same point a different way, there are concerns about making it too easy for private litigants to increase the penalties that some others will be subject to if they behave wrongfully *but cause no harm by doing so*.

B. Should final injunctions be granted less often in cases involving property torts?

One question which has excited legal economists is whether the readiness with which courts grant final injunctions in cases involving property torts, in particular trespass to land and private nuisance, prevents land from being used in the most productive way.

Professor Coase argued in a famous article[47] that if 'bargaining costs' were ignored, then the initial decision in a private nuisance case would have no effect on how land was actually used. Whatever the decision, the parties would end up using their land in the most profitable way: if the party engaged in the more profitable use won the case then all would be fine, and if the party engaged in the less profitable use won the case then the losing – more profitable – side would bargain with the winner so as to reverse the result.[48] All the decision would determine is how the profits garnered from using the land in that way would be shared between them.[49] In the real world, however, there are 'bargaining costs', and these make it important whether a court which finds that A has committed a tort in relation to B chooses to grant an injunction or merely awards damages in lieu: for example, if the court grants an injunction to B against A even though A's use of land is much more profitable than B's then there is a risk that A will be unable to go ahead and use his land in the more profitable way because the 'bargaining costs' will prevent him from reaching an appropriate agreement with B.

An example might help to illustrate this point: suppose that *Hotelier* obtains an injunction against *Promoter* preventing him from holding a very noisy rock festival on his land because if the festival goes ahead it will disturb *Hotelier's* guests to such an extent that he will lose all business for a week. If *Promoter* stands to make ten times as much profit from the festival than *Hotelier* can make from her business in a week then clearly *Promoter* ought to be able to reach an agreement with *Hotelier* which will allow the festival to go ahead and leave them both better off than they would be if the injunction was complied with and the festival cancelled. But if 'bargaining costs' are high, say because *Hotelier's* accounts are in such a mess that she does not really have a clue as to how much profit she will lose if she closes her hotel for a week, then there is a risk that the parties will not reach

---

[47] Coase 1960.

[48] You can work through to these propositions by considering a simplified case where *Sweet-tooth* wants to use his land for a noisy factory, which will make a profit of £100,000 per year, and *Consultant* wants to use his neighbouring land for practising medicine (which will be impossible if *Sweet-tooth's* noisy factory remains in operation). If *Consultant's* medical practice will be more profitable – suppose it will make a profit of £200,000 per year – then if he obtains an injunction against *Sweet-tooth* then his profitable practice will go ahead, and if he loses the case his practice will still be able to go ahead because his superior profitability means he will be able to bargain for *Sweet-tooth's* silence by offering him more than the profit he can make from the factory. Similarly, if Consultant's medical practice will be less profitable – suppose it will make a profit of only £50,000 per year – then if *Consultant* fails to obtain an injunction then the more profitable factory will continue to operate, and if he obtains an injunction *Sweet-tooth* will nonetheless be able to continue operating the more profitable factory by buying a right to make the noise: his superior profitability will mean he can offer *Consultant* more for such a right than *Consultant* can make from his practice.

[49] Of course, the fairness of the distribution of the profits is a perfectly legitimate concern for English law. It is worth remembering throughout this section that economic efficiency is not all-important.

an agreement. Of course, if the court did not grant an injunction to *Hotelier*, but awarded her damages *in lieu*, then the court would have to try and calculate these, which would be difficult given the state of the accounts.

Legal economists[50] commonly argue that if 'bargaining costs' between *Promoter* and *Hotelier* are *low* then an injunction should be granted against *Promoter*. This way, the parties can reach whatever agreement is appropriate and the courts will not have to spend time trying to calculate how much a reasonable hotel owner would charge a festival promoter for the right to make so much noise.[51] If, however, 'bargaining costs' are high, it may be better to refuse to grant *Hotelier* an injunction and instead award her damages in lieu of an injunction. As long as these damages are calculated correctly, *Promoter* will end up holding the festival on his land if he will make more money from it than *Hotelier* would make if she were able to keep the hotel open, and will cancel the festival if he cannot make enough profit to cover the damages.

If this is correct then it means that – from the perspective of ensuring that land is used in the most productive way – English courts should only grant final injunctions *readily* if they think that 'bargaining costs' are low. Unfortunately, what evidence there is suggests that 'bargaining costs' between parties in the aftermath of private nuisance cases *are* high. A careful study of 20 American nuisance cases found that there was no serious bargaining after judgment in any of them.[52] This was in part because the litigation seemed to have resulted in animosity between the parties; also, winning claimants often seemed unwilling to treat their rights – for example, to freedom from noise, or freedom from smell – as things which could be commodified and sold.

This last point is, of course, important. If most claimants who obtain final injunctions as a remedy for a property tort think that the rights which are being protected are *priceless*, then this tends to challenge the very premise of any inquiry into whether the courts' readiness to grant such injunctions may prevent land from being used in the most productive way: how can anything be more productive than protecting what is priceless?

Further reading

In his thought-provoking article, **'Rethinking Injunctions in Tort Law' (2007) 27** *Oxford Journal of Legal Studies* **509, John Murphy** laments that there is so little academic writing about injunctions in tort law. Fortunately his article helps to fill the gap. Anyone inclined to research the law on the topic in depth would probably be well-advised to start with the relevant chapter in **Clerk & Lindsell on Torts (20th edn, 2010)**. But for a very different perspective on the role of injunctions, that has stimulated many academic articles in the United States, we would recommend **Guido Calabresi and A. Douglas Melamed, 'Property Rules, Liability Rules, and Inalienability: One View of the Cathedral' (1972) 85** *Harvard Law Review* **1089**.

Visit **www.mylawchamber.co.uk/mcbride** to access tools to help you develop and test your knowledge of Tort law, including interactive multiple choice questions, practice exam questions with guidance, weblinks, legal newsfeed, additional case summaries, legal updates and tips on answering problem and essay questions.

premium
mylawchamber
unrivalled support for legal education

---

[50] See, for instance, Ogus and Richardson 1977; Tromans 1982.
[51] As we explained above, § 33.4, this is how courts calculate damages *in lieu of* injunction.
[52] Farnsworth 1999.

34 Wrongful death claims

34.1 The basics *844*

34.2 Dependant *845*

34.3 The parasitical nature of wrongful death claims *845*

34.4 Loss of support *846*

34.5 Bereavement *851*

34.6 Funeral expenses *852*

34.7 Limitation *852*

34.8 Non-wrongful death *852*

Overview

This chapter looks at a major exception to the general rule that only the victim of a tort will be entitled to sue for damages in respect of that tort. Where the victim of a tort died as a result of that tort being committed, his or her dependants may be entitled to bring a claim for *wrongful death* against the person who committed that tort. Section 34.1 sets out the basic conditions that have to be satisfied for such a claim to be brought. Section 34.2 explains who a 'dependant' is. Sections 34.3 to 34.5 run through the different types of wrongful death claim that a dependant might be able to make. Section 34.6 deals with situations where a dependant will be able to bring a claim for wrongful death against a defendant even though the deceased's death was not necessarily the result of anything wrong being done to him.

34.1 THE BASICS

We saw, all the way back in chapter 1, how tort law remedies are usually only made available to the *victim* of a tort.[1] Third parties who suffer losses as a result of a tort that has been committed in relation to someone else are usually left to bear those losses themselves.[2] The most important exception to this rule – by far – is created by the Fatal Accidents Act 1976.

That Act enables a *Dependant* of the *Victim* of a tort who has died as a result of that tort being committed to sue the person who committed that tort for: (a) any *loss of support* that *Dependant* has suffered as a result of *Victim*'s death; (b) *bereavement damages*, in the case where *Dependant* and *Victim* were married or where *Victim* was *Dependant*'s child and still a minor; and (c) *Victim*'s *funeral expenses*, in the case where *Dependant* paid for those expenses.

The general conditions that have to be satisfied before a *wrongful death* claim can be brought against a defendant under the 1976 Act are:

(1) the defendant – or someone for whose actions the defendant is liable[3] – must have committed a tort *in relation to the deceased*;

---

[1] See above, § 1.5.

[2] For further examples, see Stanton 2007a.

[3] See chapters 36 and 37 below, for an account of when someone can be held liable for a tort committed by someone else.

(2) that tort must have *caused* the deceased's death, and the death must have been a *non-remote* consequence of that tort;[4]

(3) had the deceased not died, she would have been entitled to sue the defendant for damages.

If (1), (2) and (3) are made out, then a dependant of the deceased's *may* be entitled to bring a *wrongful death* claim under the 1976 Act for loss of support, bereavement damages or funeral expenses.

All of this needs much more explanation, which we aim to provide in this chapter.

34.2 DEPENDANT

Section 1(3) of the 1976 Act provides that if someone commits a tort that causes another to die, the deceased's dependants will be:

(1) the wife or husband or former wife or husband of the deceased;

(2) the civil partner or former civil partner of the deceased;

(3) any person who was living with the deceased at the time of the deceased's death as the deceased's husband or wife and had been living with the deceased in such a capacity for at least two years before the deceased's death;

(4) any parent or other ascendant of the deceased;

(5) any person who was treated by the deceased as being his or her parent;

(6) any child or other descendant of the deceased;

(7) anyone who was treated by the deceased as if he or she were his child, as a result of his being married or in a civil partnership with someone else;

(8) anyone who was, or was the issue of, the deceased's brother, sister, uncle or aunt.

34.3 THE PARASITICAL NATURE OF WRONGFUL DEATH CLAIMS

A dependant's ability to bring a claim under the 1976 Act is conditional on it being shown that had the deceased not been killed as a result of the defendant's tort, she would have been entitled to sue the defendant for damages. This limit on the right to sue a defendant for wrongful death covers – somewhat uneasily – two entirely different situations, which need to be considered separately.

(1) *Instantaneous death.* Suppose that A's tort caused B to die instantaneously. In order to see whether a dependant of B's can to sue A under the 1976 Act, we have to ask: had B survived the shooting and *merely been injured by it*, would she have been entitled to sue A for damages? If the answer is 'no' – because, for example, A could have raised a defence of illegality to any claim for personal injury that B might have brought against him – then no claim for wrongful death can be brought against A under the 1976 Act.[5]

---

[4] Section 1(1) of the 1976 Act merely says that 'If death is *caused* by any wrongful act . . . the person who would have been liable had death not ensued shall be liable to an action for damages . . .' (emphasis added). However, it has been accepted by both the Law Commission (Law Com No 263, *Claims for Wrongful Death* (1999), para 2.4) and the courts (*Corr* v *IBC Vehicles Ltd* [2008] 1 AC 884) that a wrongful death claim cannot be brought under the 1976 Act if the deceased's death was a remote consequence of the defendant's tort.

[5] See *Murphy* v *Culhane* [1977] QB 94. In that case, Culhane struck Murphy on the head with a plank of wood and killed him. M's widow brought a claim for wrongful death against C. It was alleged that C had struck M only after M, along with some other men, had attempted to attack C. The Court of Appeal held that if that allegation were made out then the widow's claim would fail. On the facts as they were alleged to be, had M survived C's attack and merely been injured by it, he would *not* have been allowed to sue C for damages: had he attempted to do so, C would have been able to raise a defence of illegality to defeat M's claim.

(2) *Tort causing injury which results in death some time after.* Suppose that A's tort caused B to suffer some kind of injury and B died some time after that because she suffered that injury. In order to see whether a dependant of B's is entitled to sue A under the 1976 Act, we have to ask: had B not died when she did *but had lived a little longer*, would she have been entitled to sue A for damages in respect of her injury? If the answer is 'no' – because, for example, before B died she had already obtained a compensation payment from A in respect of that injury,[6] or a compensation payment from a third party that had the effect of extinguishing her right to sue A for damages in respect of that injury[7] – then no claim for wrongful death can be brought against A under the 1976 Act.[8]

The parasitical nature of claims under the 1976 Act is also reflected by the fact that s 5 of the 1976 Act provides if – had the deceased sued the defendant for damages – the damages payable to the deceased would have been reduced for contributory negligence, then any damages awarded under the 1976 Act 'shall be reduced to a proportionate extent.'

34.4 LOSS OF SUPPORT

As we have seen, there are basically three kinds of claims that can be brought under the 1976 Act by a dependant who has suffered loss as a result of the victim of a tort's death. The most important is the claim for *loss of support*.

A. Requirements

In order to bring a claim for loss of support under the 1976 Act, a dependant of the deceased has to show that:

(1) there was a reasonable prospect that had the deceased not died, the dependant would have obtained some kind of financial benefit from the deceased in the future; *and*

(2) the dependant would have obtained that benefit by virtue of the fact that he was a dependant of the deceased's.

The following cases demonstrate these rules in action. For example, in *Franklin v The South Eastern Railway Company* (1858), the claimant's son was killed as a result of the defendants' negligence. At the time his son was killed, the claimant was getting old and infirm but was not receiving any assistance from his son, who was earning 3s 6d a week at the time he was killed. It was held that had the son not been killed there was a reasonable prospect that as the claimant grew older and weaker, the son would have paid the claimant some money so as to assist him financially. As a result the claimant was held entitled to bring an action for loss of support against the defendants.

In *Barnett v Cohen* (1921), the claimant's four-year-old son was killed as a result of the defendant's negligence. The claimant brought an action for loss of support against the defendant, claiming that had his son not been killed and had instead grown up to earn a

---

[6] Section 3 of the Damages Act 1996 provides that if A's payment to B took the form of provisional damages, then that payment will not bar anyone from bringing a claim against A under the Fatal Accidents Act 1976.

[7] See above, § 28.4, for discussion of when this will be the case.

[8] See, for example, *Read v The Great Eastern Railway Company* (1868) LR 3 QB 555. In that case, the claimant's husband was injured as a result of the defendant railway company's negligence. The claimant's husband died of his wounds but not before he accepted a sum of money from the defendants in full and final settlement of all his claims against the defendants. Once the claimant's husband died the claimant brought a claim for loss of support against the defendants. Her claim was dismissed: at the time of her husband's death, he was not entitled any more to sue the defendants for damages.

living, his son would have paid him some money to assist him financially. The claim was dismissed: the claimant had not established that there was a reasonable prospect he would have received such assistance from his son had his son not been killed and grown up instead. This was for two reasons. First, the age of the claimant's son when he was killed made it impossible to predict what would have happened had he not been killed as a result of the defendant's negligence. Secondly, the claimant was a very wealthy man (earning £1,000 a year at the time of his son's death) and it was therefore hardly likely that the claimant's son would have had any reason to give the claimant anything by way of financial assistance if he had been allowed to grow up.

In *Davies* v *Taylor* (1972), the claimant's husband was killed in a road accident that was caused by the defendant's negligence. At the time the claimant's husband died, the claimant and her husband were separated and the claimant's husband was in the process of divorcing the claimant for adultery. The claimant brought an action for loss of support against the defendant, claiming that had her husband not been killed, there was a reasonable prospect her husband would have spent money on her. The claimant's claim was dismissed: had the claimant's husband not been killed, the claimant's husband would only have spent money on the claimant if they had been reconciled and the claimant had not established that there was a reasonable prospect that she and her husband would have been reconciled had he not been killed as a result of the defendant's negligence.

In *Berry* v *Humm* (1915), the defendant negligently knocked down and killed the claimant's wife. At the time of her death, the claimant's wife stayed at home and did all the domestic chores while her husband worked in the docks. Had the claimant's wife not been killed there was every prospect that the claimant's wife would have continued to do work around the claimant's house for free, thereby conferring a financial benefit on the claimant. As a result, the claimant was held entitled to bring a claim for loss of support against the defendant.

In *Burgess* v *Florence Nightingale Hospital for Gentlewomen* (1955), the claimant and his wife were professional dance partners. The claimant's wife was killed as a result of the defendant's negligence. There was a reasonable prospect that had the wife not been killed the claimant and his wife would have continued to dance together and would have earned a certain amount of prize money. It was held that the claimant – in bringing a claim against the defendant for loss of support – could *not* sue for the prize money he would have earned in the future had his wife not been killed. The reason was that the prize money that the claimant would have earned if his wife had not been killed would not have been obtained by him by virtue of the fact that he was one of his wife's dependants. That money would have been obtained by him because he was his wife's *dancing partner*, not because he was *married* to her.[9] The claimant *was*, however, entitled, in bringing a claim for loss of support against the defendant, to sue the defendant for damages in respect of the money his wife would have given him as a contribution towards their household expenses had she not been killed. *That* money *would* have been obtained by him as a result of the fact that he was married to his wife and therefore one of his wife's dependants.

In *Malyon* v *Plummer* (1964), the claimant and her husband ran a business selling and distributing portable electrical machinery to builders and farm machinery suppliers in East Anglia. The business was run through a company which paid the claimant a salary of about

---

[9] See also *Cox* v *Hockenhull* [2000] 1 WLR 750. The claimant's wife was killed in a car accident that the defendant negligently caused. The claimant's wife was disabled and at the time of the accident the claimant was her full-time carer and as such received an invalidity care allowance. Held: the claimant could not sue the defendant for the loss of the invalidity care allowance that he experienced after his wife's death as that allowance had not been received by the claimant because he was his wife's husband but because he was his wife's carer.

£600 a year. The claimant did not do much work for the company in return for her salary; the claimant's husband did most of the work drumming up business and collecting and processing orders. In fact, the value of the work done by the claimant for the company came to only about £200 a year: the remaining £400 a year paid to the claimant essentially amounted to a gift to the claimant. When the claimant's husband was killed in a car crash caused by the defendant's negligence, the business collapsed. The company through which the business was run went into insolvency and the claimant lost her £600 a year salary.

Of course, had the claimant's husband not been killed there was every prospect that the family business would have flourished and the claimant would have continued to draw a salary of £600 a year from their company, but £200 of that £600 a year salary would have been obtained by the claimant by virtue of the work done by her for the company she and her husband owned; only £400 of that £600 a year salary would have been paid to her by virtue of, or in recognition of, the fact that the claimant was married to her husband and therefore one of her husband's dependants. The claimant could therefore only bring a claim for loss of support against the defendant in respect of two-thirds of the £600 a year salary she would have continued to draw had her husband not been killed.

B. Limits

Two limits on a dependant's ability to bring a claim for loss of support under the 1976 Act should be noted.

(1) *Illegality*. No claim for loss of support can be made in respect of any proceeds of crime that the dependant would have received from the deceased had the deceased not been killed.

For example, in *Burns* v *Edman* (1970), the claimant's husband was killed in a motor accident caused by the defendant's negligence. The claimant's husband had never had a job and what money he gave her (£20 a week) invariably represented the proceeds of crime. The claimant brought an action for loss of support against the defendant but her claim was dismissed. While there was more than a reasonable prospect that the claimant would have received a weekly allowance of £20 a week from her husband had he not been killed, there was no prospect that that weekly allowance would have represented anything but the proceeds of crime.

(2) *No loss of benefit*. No claim for loss of support can be brought if the deceased's death did not actually prevent the dependant receiving a financial benefit that she would have received had the deceased not died.

In *Auty* v *National Coal Board* (1985), the claimant's husband was killed due to the defendants' negligence. Her husband was 55 when he died. When he died the claimant received a widow's pension under the Mineworkers' Pension Scheme. Had the claimant's husband not been killed, there was a reasonable prospect that he would have died before retiring at 65 and the claimant would have received a widow's pension. The claimant brought an action for loss of support against the defendants and included in her claim a claim for the fact that had her husband not been killed as a result of the defendant's negligence there was a reasonable prospect he would have been killed before retiring and she would have received a widow's pension. This element of her claim was thrown out: her husband's death had not actually prevented her from receiving a widow's pension as when he died as a result of the defendants' negligence, she received a widow's pension.

This case can be contrasted with *Welsh Ambulance Services NHS Trust* v *Williams* (2008), where the claimants' husband and father was killed when an ambulance belonging to the defendants negligently crashed into his car. The deceased was a businessman who operated a very substantial family business from which the claimants benefited a great deal financially. After his death, the deceased's son and one of his daughters took over the running of the business and managed to keep it going as a successful enterprise from which they and their mother and their sister obtained a substantial income. Counsel for the defendants argued that this meant that no claim for loss of support could be made against the defendants: as things had turned out, the claimants were just as well off after the deceased's death as they had been before. This argument was rejected at first instance. The Court of Appeal upheld the decision of the first instance judge, holding that

> He was correct when he said that nothing that a dependant (or for that matter anyone else) could do after the death could either increase or decrease the dependency. The dependency is fixed at the moment of death; it is what the dependants would probably have received as benefit from the deceased, had the deceased not died. What decisions people make afterwards is irrelevant.[10]

The value of the benefit that the claimants were receiving from the deceased at the time of his death was valued at the cost of replacing his services in running the family business, and this is what the claimants were awarded.

What we might call the *Williams principle* that the value of someone's dependency is fixed at the moment of death and cannot be affected by what happens afterwards might also be said to underlie the decision of the Court of Appeal in *Hay* v *Hughes* (1975). In that case, the parents of two boys were killed in a motor accident caused by the defendant's negligence. The boys were then taken in by their grandmother and looked after by her. The boys were held entitled to sue for the loss of care that they would have received (free of charge) from their parents until they were grown-up. The fact that they were now getting the same sort of care, free of charge, from their grandmother was held not to affect their right to sue the defendant. An alternative explanation of the decision in this case was that allowing the boys to sue for the loss of care from their parents was the Court of Appeal's roundabout way of making up for the fact that the law, strangely, does not allow children to bring claims for bereavement damages when one or both of their parents die.

The *Williams principle* also seems to underlie s 3(3) of the 1976 Act which provides that:

> In an action under this Act where there fall to be assessed damages payable to a widow in respect of the death of her husband there shall not be taken into account the re-marriage of the widow . . .

So a widow who re-marries within six months of her husband's death and gets everything from her new husband that she was accustomed to getting from her deceased husband will still be entitled to sue in full for the loss of financial benefits that she stood to receive from her first husband had he not died.

C. Assessment

The rules on assessing how much can be sued for by way of loss of support where A and B were married and childless,[11] and both A and B were earning money, and A died as a result of the defendant's tort, are quite complex.

[10] [2008] EWCA Civ 81, at [50].

[11] For simplicity, we assume that A and B are childless, but even if they do have children, the rules for assessing loss of support remain much the same. It is assumed that before A died, a third of A and B's income went on A, and the rest on B and the children and any joint expenditures from which all the family benefited. And now that A has died, all of B's money will go on her and the children. So the net loss of support suffered by B and the children as a result of A's death will be calculated by taking two thirds of A and B's projected joint income in the future and deducting from that B's projected income in the future.

It is assumed that had A not died, he would have spent a third of his earnings exclusively on himself, a third exclusively on B, and a third on joint expenditures from which both A and B profited. And B would have done the same: spent a third of her earnings exclusively on herself, a third on A, and a third on joint expenditures from which both A and B profited. So had A not died, B would have profited from two-thirds of A's earnings and two-thirds of her earnings.

Now that A has died, B will no longer receive anything from A's earnings, but *all* of her own earnings will now be spent on herself instead of a third being spent exclusively on A. So the *net* loss of support that B will suffer each year as a result of A's death is calculated by –

(1) adding together the yearly income that A and B could each have been expected to earn in the future;
(2) multiplying (1) by two-thirds to put a value on the financial support B could have expected to receive each year in the future had A not died; and
(3) deducting from (2) the income that B can be expected to earn in the future to give the difference between the financial support that B could have expected to receive each year in the future had A not died and the financial support that B will now receive each year in future given that A has died.

B's award for loss of support will aim to give her a lump sum which, if appropriately invested, will give her the value of (3) each year for the rest of her life.[12]

In assessing the damages payable to a dependant for loss of support, s 4 of the 1976 Act provides that *no* reduction will be made in respect of any benefits that the dependant has received as a result of the deceased's death. So, for example, if – in the case we have just been considering – on A's death, the mortgage on A and B's house was paid off with the result that B no longer has to make any mortgage payments, that will *not* go to reduce the amount of damages payable to B for loss of support.[13]

There seem to be two situations where the courts will still reduce the damages payable to a claimant under the 1976 Act because they have received a benefit from the deceased's death.

(1) *Receipt of benefit from defendant.* In *Hayden* v *Hayden* (1992), the claimant's mother was killed as a result of the negligence of the defendant, the claimant's father, in driving the car in which they were travelling. The defendant gave up his job to look after the claimant full-time. The claimant sued the defendant (in reality, his liability insurer) for the loss of her mother's services in caring after her. It was held that the damages payable to the claimant should be reduced to take account of the value of the care that he was now receiving from the defendant and that he would not have received had his mother not died.

However, the decision of the Court of Appeal in *Arnup* v *White* (2008) has made it very difficult to say – as we did in previous editions – that benefits received from the defendant as a result of the deceased's death will go to reduce the damages for loss of support that are payable to a claimant under the 1976 Act. In that case, the claimant's husband was killed at

---

[12] See § 28.3, above, for discussion as to how such a lump sum is calculated.

[13] See *Pidduck* v *Eastern Scottish Omnibuses Ltd* [1990] 1 WLR 993 (payment of widow's allowance to claimant on death of her husband not to be taken into account in assessing damages payable to widow under 1976 Act); *McIntyre* v *Harland & Wolff plc* [2006] 1 WLR 2577 (payments made by employer's provident fund to claimant's husband before he died, and which then formed part of his estate that claimant inherited, should be disregarded in assessing damages payable to claimant under 1976 Act).

work as a result of his employer's negligence. Shortly after his death, the claimant received cheques for £129,600 and £100,000, the first from a death in service benefits scheme set up by the defendant, and the second from a trust fund set up by the defendant. The Court of Appeal strictly applied s 4 and held that these benefits were not to be taken into account in assessing the damages payable for loss of support to the claimant. A payment by the defendant to the claimant after the deceased's death would only go to reduce the damages payable to the claimant under the 1976 Act if the payment was made subject to the stipulation that he 'wishes to have it taken into account when damages are assessed ... Then it will not be a benefit, caught by section 4, it will be a conditional payment on account.'[14]

Where the decision in *Arnup* leaves the decision in *Hayden* v *Hayden* is very hard to say. *Hayden* was cited in argument in *Arnup*, but was not mentioned by the Court of Appeal.

(2) *Adoption*. In *Watson* v *Willmott* (1991), the claimant's mother was killed in a car accident caused by the defendant's negligence. The claimant's father, depressed at the death of his wife, committed suicide and the claimant was adopted. The claimant sued for the loss of care that he would have received from his parents (free of charge) until he was grown-up. The damages payable to the claimant were reduced to take account of the value of the care he had received and would receive from his adoptive parents. The court felt it was authorised to depart from the rule set out in s 4 of the 1976 Act by virtue of para 3 of Sch 1 of the Children Act 1975 under which 'An adopted child shall be treated in law ... where the adopters are a married couple, as if he had been born as a child of the marriage'. As such, the decision in *Watson* v *Willmott* is to be confined strictly to the case where a child's parents have been killed as a result of a tort committed in relation to them and the child has been subsequently adopted.

34.5 BEREAVEMENT

The second kind of action that can be brought under the 1976 Act is a claim for bereavement damages. Section 1A of the Fatal Accidents Act 1976 provides that such damages can be sued for by:

(a) ... the wife or husband or civil partner of the deceased; and
(b) where the deceased was a minor who was never married or a civil partner –
   (i) ... his parents, if he was legitimate; and
   (ii) ... his mother, if he was illegitimate.

The damages payable for bereavement are fixed at £11,800. They cannot vary according to how upset the claimant was at the deceased's death. This leads Tony Weir to argue that the damages payable for bereavement are

not designed as compensation for grief but [are] simply ... a replacement in money for a life lost. The lump sum is standard because people are equal, not because they are equally regrettable.[15]

Weir's view is supported by the fact that £11,800 is the maximum a defendant can be held liable to pay by way of bereavement damages. So if more than one claimant is entitled to

---

[14] [2008] EWCA Civ 447, at [26].
[15] Weir 2006, 215.

claim such damages – which will be the case where a legitimate child with two parents still alive is killed as a result of the defendant's tort – the lump sum has to be shared out between them. Double the grief does not result in double the damages for bereavement.

34.6 FUNERAL EXPENSES

Section 3(5) of the 1976 Act provides that:

> If the dependants [of the victim of a tort who was killed as a result of that tort being committed] have incurred funeral expenses in respect of the deceased, damages may be awarded in respect of those expenses.

Such a claim will of course be available only if the conditions that have to be satisfied before a claim can be brought under the 1976 Act are satisfied.

34.7 LIMITATION

Section 12(2) of the Limitation Act 1980 provides that, in the case where the victim of a tort has died as a result of that tort having been committed, a claimant will not be able to bring an action under the 1976 Act more than three years after the *later* of the following two dates: (1) the date the victim of the tort died; (2) the date the claimant first learned, or could have reasonably been expected to learn, that the victim of the tort had died. Section 33 of the Limitation Act 1980 creates an exception to this rule: it provides that a claimant who attempts to bring a claim under the 1976 Act outside the limitation period set out in s 12(2) may be allowed to do so if it would be 'equitable' to do so.

34.8 NON-WRONGFUL DEATH

The 1976 Act is meant only to apply in cases where the victim of a *tort* has died as a result of that tort being committed. The requirement that a *wrong* must have been committed before a claim can be brought under the 1976 Act can sometimes create problems.

For example, if A's cat caused B some kind of physical harm due to the cat's having an uncommon characteristic, known to A, that meant the cat was likely to cause that sort of harm, A will be held strictly liable to compensate B for that harm under s 2(2) of the Animals Act 1971.[16] A's liability in this case is not based on his having done anything *wrong* to B. Section 2(2) merely sets up a liability rule: if B is harmed, then A is liable. But if B dies as a result of his injuries, we might well want his dependants to be able to bring a claim for wrongful death against A. In order to allow them to do this – to bring a claim for wrongful death even though no wrong has necessarily been committed – s 10 of the Animals Act 1971 provides that 'For the purposes of the Fatal Accidents Acts . . . any damage for which a person is liable under sections 2 to 4 of this Act shall be treated as due to his fault.'

The same trick is pulled in relation to the Consumer Protection Act 1987, which again sets up a liability rule: if you are injured as a result of a product being dangerously defective, then the producer will be liable for your injury.[17] In order to allow the dependants of someone who has been killed by a dangerously defective product to bring a claim for loss

---

[16] See above, § 13.1.
[17] See above, § 21.1.

of support under the Fatal Accidents Act 1976 – again, to bring a wrongful death claim where no wrong has necessarily been committed – s 6(1) of the Act sets up a fiction that 'Any damage for which a person is liable under [the Act] shall be deemed to have been caused . . . for the purposes of the Fatal Accidents Act 1976, by that person's wrongful act, neglect or default.'

35 Other third party claims

35.1 The basics *854*

35.2 Congenital disabilities *854*

35.3 Recovery of state losses *857*

35.4 The principle of transferred loss *858*

Overview

This chapter completes the discussion begun in the previous chapter of when the law will allow a third party to a tort to sue for compensation for losses suffered by them as a result of that tort being committed. Sections 35.2 and 35.3 set out the two main further exceptions (in addition to the exceptions created by the Fatal Accidents Act 1976, discussed in the previous chapter), and section 35.4 discusses an abortive attempt to introduce a further such exception into English law.

35.1 THE BASICS

Having dealt with the Fatal Accidents Act 1976 in the previous chapter, this chapter is about the remaining few exceptions to the general rule that only the victim of a tort can obtain a remedy in respect of that tort. What exceptions there are are attributable either:

(1) to the fact that a child that has been injured in the womb will sometimes be unable to argue that he or she was the victim of a tort and would as a result be left without a remedy for his disabilities were the general rule applied to his case; or

(2) the State using its law-making powers to protect itself from being left without a remedy when it has spent money looking after the victim of a tort; or

(3) a perception that there is something unsatisfactory about applying the general rule to a situation where the victim of a tort has suffered no loss, but a third party has.

35.2 CONGENITAL DISABILITIES

The Congenital Disabilities (Civil Liability) Act 1976 ('CDCLA' for short) allows a child that has been born disabled to sue a defendant for damages in respect of its disabilities if those disabilities were caused by a tort that the defendant committed in relation to one or both of the child's parents.

It is arguable that the 1976 Act is unnecessary, at least in the following type of case:

Pregnant is involved in a car *Accident* that was a foreseeable result of *Defendant*'s carelessness. The foetus inside *Pregnant*'s womb is injured in the accident, but *Pregnant* does not miscarry and carries the foetus to term, when she gives birth to a disabled baby *Boy*.

This is because the Court of Appeal decided in *Burton v Islington Health Authority* (1992) that in this kind of case *Boy* would be able to sue *Defendant* in negligence for his disabilities, arguing that the defendant owed him – while he was in *Pregnant*'s womb, in the form of a foetus – a duty to take care not to cause *Accident* as it was reasonably foreseeable that if *Driver* caused *Accident*, *Boy* would be born disabled. In *Burton*, it was argued that no such duty of care could have been owed by *Defendant* to *Boy* while he was in *Pregnant's* womb because at that point he was just a foetus and enjoyed no legal personality. So arguing that such a duty of care was owed by *Defendant* would be like arguing that *Defendant* owed a duty to *Pregnant's car* not to cause *Accident* on the basis that it was reasonably foreseeable that if he did so, the car would be damaged. The Court of Appeal disagreed:

> while there are cases . . . which establish the general proposition that a foetus enjoys, while still a foetus, no independent legal personality . . . [there] are other contexts . . . in which the English courts have adopted as part of English law the maxim of the civil law that an unborn child shall be deemed to be born whenever its interests require it . . .[1]

So the Court of Appeal thought that there was no problem in finding that, in the case we are considering, *Defendant* owed *Boy* a duty to take care not to cause *Accident*, even though at the relevant time *Boy* was merely a foetus. *Boy* could argue that: 'When I was in my mother's womb, you owed me a duty to take care not to cause *Accident* because it was reasonably foreseeable that if you did, I would be born disabled as a result. You breached that duty and I have suffered the right kind of loss as a result – I have been born disabled, as opposed to being killed in the womb. So pay up.'

The existence of the CDCLA makes it unnecessary for such an argument to be made anymore.[2] Moreover, the CDCLA applies in cases where the law of negligence cannot go – for example, to cases where a defendant was not at fault for a child's disabilities, or cases where a child's disabilities were due to something that the defendant did before the child was even conceived. The CDCLA does all this by creating an exception to the general rule that you can only sue for compensation for losses suffered as a result of a tort being committed if you were a victim of that tort. It basically provides that a child that has been born disabled will be entitled to sue a defendant for damages in respect of his or her disabilities if:

(1) the child's disabilities are the result of the defendant committing a tort in relation to either of its parents which had the effect of impairing their ability to have a normal, healthy child,[3] *or*
(2) the child's disabilities are the result of the defendant committing a tort in relation to the child's mother during her pregnancy or while the child was being born,[4] *or*
(3) the child's disabilities are the result of the defendant committing a tort in relation to the child's parents when artificially inseminating the child's mother.[5]

A number of different points need to be made about the CDCLA.

(1) *Wrongful life.* A child can only sue under the CDCLA if its *disabilities* are attributable to a tort that the defendant has committed in relation to one of its parents. So no action can be brought by the child under the CDCLA in the case where *Doctor* scans a pregnant *Mother* to see if her child is disabled, *Doctor* negligently fails to spot that the child is disabled and fails to give *Mother* the opportunity of having the child aborted, and *Mother* ends up giving birth to a disabled child. While *Doctor* will be liable to pay damages to *Mother* in this case,[6] he will not be liable to pay the child damages under the CDCLA. The child's being *born* is attributable to the *Doctor's* negligence here, not the child's being *disabled*.

---

[1] [1992] 3 All ER 833, 838 (per Dillon LJ).
[2] In *Burton*, the claimants were all children who were not entitled to sue under the CDCLA as the events giving rise to their disabilities had all occurred before the Act came into force.
[3] Section 1(2)(a).
[4] Section 1(2)(b).
[5] Section 1A.
[6] See above, § 10.5.

Any claim that the child might make here is known as a claim for 'wrongful life'. The child's claim is basically: 'Had you not been negligent, I would not have been born and so I would not be suffering these disabilities.' The courts have made it clear that they will not countenance claims for 'wrongful life' being made under the CDCLA.[7] Not only does the wording of the Act not cover this kind of case,[8] the courts think that it would be wrong in principle to allow claims for 'wrongful life' to be brought.[9] The courts will not accept that a child that has escaped being aborted and has been born alive can claim that he or she has suffered a loss as a result. In their view, the gift of life is so immense that it outweighs any number of disabilities that might come with that gift – so the courts simply will not allow a claimant to say, 'It would have been better for me had I never existed.'

(2) *Assumption of risk.* Under ss 1(4) and 1A(3) of the CDCLA, no claim can be brought by a *Child* that has been born disabled if the defendant's tort occurred *before the child was conceived* and at least one of the child's parents were aware at that time that the defendant's tort might have the effect of causing *Child* to be born disabled. The idea is that if the child's parents or one of the child's parents consciously took a risk of having a disabled child as a result of what the defendant did, that is their responsibility, not the defendant's.

There is an exception under s 1(4) where the defendant is the *father.* So suppose *Husband* gave *Wife* some weedkiller in an attempt to kill her, but the dose was too small to affect her, or even be noticeable. If he was aware that even that small dose might cause any child she subsequently conceived to be disabled, and he did not tell her about that, then if *Wife* subsequently conceives a *Child* with *Husband* and *Child* is born disabled, then *Child* can sue *Husband* for damages for his disabilities under the CDCLA.

(3) *Action against the mother.* Section 1(1) of the CDCLA makes it clear that claims cannot be brought under the CDCLA against the mother of a disabled child. (The wording of the various provisions of the Act probably make it impossible for the mother to fall under any of them in any case.) There is one exception to this, though. This is created by s 2 of the CDCLA, which provides that:

> A woman driving a motor vehicle when she knows (or ought reasonably to know) herself to be pregnant is to be regarded as being under the same duty to take care for the safety of her unborn child as the law imposes on her with respect to the safety of other people; and if in consequence of her breach of that duty her child is born with disabilities which would not otherwise be present, those disabilities are to be regarded as damages resulting from her wrongful act and actionable at the suit of the child.

As we have already explained,[10] the reason for this provision lies in its opening words. 'A woman driving a motor vehicle' will be carrying liability insurance, and so any damages

---

[7] *McKay* v *Essex Area Health Authority* [1982] 1 QB 1166, 1178 (per Stephenson LJ), 1186–7 (per Ackner LJ), 1192 (per Griffiths LJ).

[8] While s 1(1) does simply refer to a child being 'born disabled' as a result of the defendant's actions – a phrase that would cover a wrongful life case – s 1(1) makes it clear that the defendant's actions have to fall within s 1(2), which says that the defendant's actions must have: '(a) affected either parent of the child in his or her ability to have a normal, healthy child; or (b) affected the mother during her pregnancy . . . so that the child is born with disabilities which would not otherwise have been present.' The case of the *Doctor* who negligently fails to spot that *Mother* is pregnant with a disabled child does not fall within (a) or (b). *Child* may be born with disabilities as a result of *Doctor's* negligence, but it can hardly be said that those disabilities 'would not otherwise have been present' had *Doctor* not been negligent. The disabilities would not have existed had *Doctor* not been negligent – but only because the child bearing those disabilities would not have existed either. For a different view of the scope of the CDCLA, see Ellis and McGivern 2007.

[9] In addition to *McKay* v *Essex Area Health Authority* [1982] 1 QB 1166, see the High Court of Australia's decision in *Harriton* v *Stephens* (2006) 80 AJLR 791 (criticised, Teff 2007).

[10] See above, § 1.14(B)(3).

award to her child for the disabilities he or she is born with as a result of her bad driving will not come from her, but her liability insurer.

(4) *Defective product*. Because a defendant's liability under the Consumer Protection Act 1987 for damage caused by a dangerously defective product is not contingent on its being shown that the defendant did anything *wrongful* in producing or supplying that product,[11] special provision had to be made in s 6(3) of the 1987 Act to allow a child who had been born disabled as a result of a product being dangerously defective to bring a claim for his disabilities under the CDCLA. Section 6(3) basically provides that if a child is born disabled as a result of a product being dangerously defective under the 1987 Act, the child will be able to sue a defendant for compensation for his disabilities under the CDCLA if the defendant would have been held liable to the child's parents under the 1987 Act had the product harmed one of them.

The framers of the 1987 Act would have been especially aware of the need to make provision for the effects of dangerously defective products on unborn children as one of the most notorious cases of dangerously defective products causing harm in the second half of the 20th century was provided by the drug thalidomide, that was licensed in the UK in 1958 as a cure for morning sickness in pregnant women. Soon after it was licensed, women who had taken thalidomide while pregnant gave birth to disabled children. The connection between thalidomide and the disabilities was quickly established, and the drug was withdrawn in 1961, but not before 2,000 babies were born with thalidomide-linked disabilities, of which about 1,500 subsequently died.

Were a comparable tragedy to occur again today as a result of a drug affecting babies in the womb, the children that were born with disabilities might be able to sue the producers of the drug under the CDCLA, on the basis that the producers would have been liable to their mothers under the Consumer Protection Act 1987 had the drug harmed them. However, the producers might be able to escape liability by invoking the 'development risks defence',[12] under which they could not be held liable to anyone for the harm done by their drug if the state of scientific and technical knowledge at the time the drug was marketed was not such as to enable the drug's defective nature to be discovered. (A provision that would have arguably protected the manufacturers of thalidomide.)

35.3 RECOVERY OF STATE LOSSES

In two situations, the State is allowed to sue someone who has committed a tort for compensation in respect of the losses that it has suffered as a result of that tort being committed.

(1) *The Social Security (Recovery of Benefits) Act 1997*. Roughly speaking, this Act provides that someone who has made a compensation payment to the victim of a tort will be held liable to the State for the value of *all* the social security payments that have been made to the victim of that tort as a result of her being a victim of that tort.[13]

(2) *The Health and Social Care (Community Health and Standards) Act 2003*. Section 150 of this Act covers the situation where B, the victim of a tort, has suffered some kind of injury ('physical or psychological')[14] as a result of that tort being committed. If B has

---

[11] See above, § 12.8.
[12] Discussed further above, § 12.6(5).
[13] Space does not allow us to say more than this. For a *very* detailed treatment of the Act, see Lewis 1999, 113–222.
[14] Section 150(5) provides that ' "Injury" does not include any disease.'

received treatment on the National Health Service (NHS) for that injury, or has been provided with an ambulance service on the NHS as a result of suffering that injury, then anyone who makes a compensation payment to B in respect of that injury will be liable to pay charges to the NHS for the treatment, or ambulance services, received by B. If B was partly to blame for her injury so that the compensation payable to her is liable to be reduced for contributory negligence, the charges payable in respect of the NHS services received by B will be reduced by a corresponding amount.[15]

35.4 THE PRINCIPLE OF TRANSFERRED LOSS

Section 3 of the Latent Damage Act 1986 covers the situation where A committed a tort in relation to B and B's property was damaged as a result, but before the damage was discovered B transferred the property to C. In such a case, s 3 provides that if B would have been entitled to sue A for damages in respect of the damage done to his property had he discovered it in time, C will be entitled to sue A for damages in respect of the damage done to that item of property.

Section 3 could be seen as giving effect to what has become known as the 'principle of transferred loss'. An attempt to introduce this principle as a wide-ranging principle of liability was made by Robert Goff LJ in *The Aliakmon* (1986). In that case, Leigh & Sillavan had agreed to buy some steel coils from Kinso-Mataichi. The coils were to be shipped to L&S by Aliakmon Shipping. L&S weren't able to pay for the coils when they were shipped, but promised to pay for them when the coils were delivered. K-M agreed to send the coils to L&S, but on the understanding that the coils remained their property until L&S paid for them, on delivery. K-M also insisted that L&S should be what is called 'on risk' as to the coils being damaged mid-voyage. What that meant was that if the coils were damaged during the voyage, L&S still had to pay full price for them when they were delivered. Unfortunately, the coils were damaged mid-voyage as a result of AS's negligence, and L&S ended up paying far more for the coils than they were actually worth.

L&S wanted to sue AS for compensation but faced the problem that when the coils were damaged, they were not L&S's property. So the duty to take care not to damage the coils that AS breached in this case was owed to K-M, not L&S. In order to overcome this problem, when the case of *The Aliakmon* was heard by the Court of Appeal, Robert Goff LJ suggested that English law should recognise a 'principle of transferred loss' according to which if

> A owes a duty of care in tort not to cause physical damage to B's property, and commits a breach of that duty in circumstances in which the loss of or physical damage to the property will ordinarily fall on B but (as is reasonably foreseeable by A) such loss or damage, by reason of a contractual relationship between B and C, falls upon C, then C will be entitled, subject to the terms of any contract restricting A's liability to B, to bring an action in tort against A in respect of such loss or damage to the extent that it falls on him, C.[16]

When *The Aliakmon* fell to be decided by the House of Lords they roundly rejected the idea that English law should give effect to this principle of transferred loss. Lord Brandon of Oakbrook remarked:

> With the greatest possible respect to Robert Goff LJ, the principle of transferred loss . . . is not only not supported by authority, but is on the contrary inconsistent with it.[17]

[15] Section 153(3).
[16] [1985] QB 350, 399. For discussion of this principle and how it works, see Cane 1996, 327–9.
[17] [1986] AC 785, 820.

In *White* v *Jones* (1995) (*not* a case which was covered by the principle of transferred loss)[18] Lord Goff (as he had by then become) did not renew the attempt he made in *The Aliakmon* to introduce the principle of transferred loss into English law, beyond observing that recognition of such a principle might serve to fill some lacunae in English law.[19] Subsequently, in the case of *Alfred McAlpine Construction Ltd* v *Panatown Ltd* (2001), Lord Goff seemed to disown the principle of transferred loss entirely, remarking that the principle 'is not an easy one for a common lawyer to grasp' and observing that he did not feel 'sufficiently secure' in his understanding of how it would apply to employ it in deciding the case at hand.[20]

With Lord Goff now long retired from the bench, it must be doubted whether anyone else will attempt to introduce the principle of transferred loss into English law and thereby create another exception to the general rule that if A has committed a tort in relation to B and a third party, C, has suffered loss as a result, C will *not* be entitled to sue A for damages in respect of that loss.

Further reading

While *White* v *Jones* (1995) was not a case covered by the principle of transferred loss, some of the appeal of that principle lies in an idea that may also have motivated the decision in *White* v *Jones* – the idea that the law is not working in the way it should if 'the only person who may have a valid claim has suffered no loss, and the only person who has suffered a loss has no claim' (*White* v *Jones* [1995] 2 AC 207, 262 (per Lord Goff)). The question of whether this is actually a problem is wonderfully explored in **Nicholas Davidson QC, 'The law of black holes?' (2006) 22 *Professional Negligence* 54.**

Visit **www.mylawchamber.co.uk/mcbride** to access tools to help you develop and test your knowledge of Tort law, including interactive multiple choice questions, practice exam questions with guidance, weblinks, legal newsfeed, additional case summaries, legal updates and tips on answering problem and essay questions.

premium
mylawchamber
unrivalled support for legal education

---

[18] In *White* v *Jones* [1995] 2 AC 207, it will be recalled, a father instructed his solicitor to make a will under which his daughters would receive £9,000 each. The solicitor was unacceptably tardy in drawing up the will and it was not signed and witnessed by the time the father died. As a result the father's daughters did not receive their bequests. In this case, the father did *not* suffer any loss as a result of his solicitor's negligence which was then passed on to his daughters.
[19] [1995] 2 AC 207, 264–6.
[20] [2001] 1 AC 518, 557.

36 Accessory liability

36.1 The basics *860*

36.2 Requirements *860*

36.3 Limits *862*

Overview

In this chapter, we look at the situations in which someone can be held to have committed a tort because of his participation in that tort being committed by someone else. The basic idea behind this area of law is set out in section 36.1. Section 36.2 sets out the situations where someone will be held to have committed a tort on the ground that they were an accessory to someone else's committing that tort. Section 36.3 discusses why *assisting* someone to commit a tort will not make you an accessory to that tort.

36.1 THE BASICS

So far, we have assumed that there is only *one* way of committing a particular tort: you commit the tort of negligence by breaching a duty of care owed to another; the tort of battery by unlawfully and directly applying force to another's person; the tort of defamation by making a defamatory and untrue statement about another person to a third party; and so on.

In fact, there are *two* ways of committing a tort: committing a tort yourself, or by being an accessory to a tort committed by someone else. So you will commit the tort of battery if you hit B unlawfully; but you'll also commit the tort of battery if you successfully encourage A to hit B unlawfully. In the second situation, you will be held to have committed the tort of battery because you were an accessory to the battery carried out by A. So if A hits B with your encouragement, B will be able to sue you, or A, or both you and A, for damages; and you and A will be *jointly* liable to pay the damages that are due to B.[1]

There are basically four ways in which you can become an accessory to somebody else's tort: (1) by *procuring* the tort; (2) by *authorising* the tort; (3) by *ratifying* the tort; (4) as a result of the tort having been committed in furtherance of a *common design* that you and the tortfeasor agreed to carry out. The next section will explore these different ways of becoming an accessory to a tort committed by someone else.

36.2 REQUIREMENTS

(1) *Procuring.* In *John Hudson & Co Ltd* v *Oaten* (1980), Oliver LJ said, 'A man who procures the commission by another person of a tortious act becomes liable because he then becomes principal in the commission of the act. It is his tort.'[2]

---

[1] The significance of two or more people being *jointly* liable to pay damages to a claimant was explored above: see § 28.4(B).

[2] 19 June 1980 (unreported), quoted by House of Lords in *Credit Lyonnais NV* v *ECGD* [2000] 1 AC 486, 497–8.

In *CBS Songs* v *Amstrad* (1988), Lord Templeman made it clear that 'A defendant may procure [someone to commit a tort] by inducement, incitement or persuasion.'[3] He then went on to observe that 'Generally speaking, inducement, incitement or persuasion to [commit a tort] must be by a defendant to an individual tortfeasor and must identifiably procure a particular [tort] in order to make the defendant liable as a joint [tortfeasor].'[4] Two points need to be made about this way of becoming an accessory to a tort.

First, if A has committed a tort by doing *x*, C can only be held to have procured A to commit that tort if his words of inducement, incitement or persuasion *played some part* in A's decision to do *x*. It would be going too far to demand that it be shown that A would *not* have done *x* but for C's words; but it must be shown that A took C's words into account in deciding to do *x*.

Secondly, if something C said to A led A to commit a tort by doing *x*, C can only be held to have procured A to commit that tort if C *intended to encourage* A to do *x* when he spoke to A. So, for example, suppose *Friend* told *Husband* that his wife was having an affair. As a result, *Husband* beat his wife up, thereby committing the tort of battery. *Friend* can only be said to have procured *Husband* to commit the tort of battery if, when he told *Husband* of his wife's affair, he intended to encourage *Husband* to beat his wife up.

(2) *Authorisation*. If A commits a tort by doing *x*, and C has granted A permission to do *x* then C will be held to be an accessory to A's tort.[5]

It does not have to be shown that A would not have committed his tort but for C's giving him permission. For example, if *Landlord* has agreed that *Tenant* can use the house for *Tenant*'s band to rehearse in, it is no defence – when *Landlord* is sued by his neighbours for private nuisance – for *Landlord* to argue that had he not given his permission, *Tenant* would still have used the house for band rehearsals.

However, if A has committed a tort by doing *x*, C can only be held to have been an accessory to A's tort under this head if C had the authority, or purported to have the authority, to permit A to do *x*.[6] So if *Teen* produces an illegal copy of a CD or a DVD on her computer, the manufacturer of that computer cannot be said to have 'authorised' *Teen* to commit this breach of copyright because the manufacturer does not have, and does not pretend to have, the authority to permit *Teen* to produce illegal CDs and DVDs on her computer.[7]

(3) *Ratification*. If A commits a tort by doing *x*, and C subsequently treats A as though A did *x* on C's behalf, then C will be held to be an accessory to A's tort.

For example, in *Hilbery* v *Hatton* (1864), a ship called *John Brooks* was stranded off the coast of Africa. A man called Ward – who owned cargo on board the ship – unlawfully took charge of the ship and sold it to the defendants' agent, a man called Thompson, who was principally employed by the defendants to buy palm oil for them. Thompson subsequently wrote to the defendants announcing that he had purchased *John Brooks* for them; presumably, he thought the defendants could use the ship in their business. The defendants wrote back, approving the purchase. It was held that Thompson had committed the tort of conversion in buying, and taking possession, of the ship, and that the defendants also committed the tort of conversion when they approved the purchase of the ship on their behalf.

---

[3] [1988] AC 1013, at 1058.

[4] ibid.

[5] For further discussion of this point in relation to the tort of private nuisance, see above, § 15–8(2).

[6] See *CBS Inc* v *Ames Records & Tapes Ltd* [1982] Ch 91, at 106 (per Whitford J): 'authorisation can only come from somebody having or purporting to have authority . . . an act is not authorised by somebody who . . . does not purport to have any authority which he can grant to justify the doing of the act.'

[7] *CBS Songs* v *Amstrad plc* [1988] AC 1013, 1053–5.

(4) *Common design*. In *The Koursk* (1924), the Court of Appeal endorsed the proposition that 'Persons are said to be joint tortfeasors when their respective shares in the commission of the tort are done in furtherance of a common design.'[8] So if A commits a tort by doing *x*, and in doing *x*, he was carrying out a plan of action agreed on between him and C, then C will be an accessory to A's tort.

Some have argued that liability for committing the tort of unlawful means conspiracy[9] has its origins in this rule of accessory liability.[10] However – as the House of Lords observed in *Revenue & Customs Commissioners* v *Total Network SL* (2008) – this is incorrect.[11] Suppose that *Rogue* and *Villain* agree to imprison a famous opera *Singer* so as to disrupt a performance of *Le Nozze di Figaro* which *Impresario* is putting on. *Rogue* subsequently kidnaps *Singer* and the opera performance has to be cancelled.

It is well established that in this situation *Impresario* can bring a claim for unlawful means conspiracy against both *Rogue* and *Villain*. It is not clear how *Impresario*'s claim can be rationalised as being based on a form of accessory liability. Clearly, *Rogue* committed the tort of false imprisonment in kidnapping *Singer*, and *Villain* will be liable to *Singer* for false imprisonment as an accessory to *Rogue*'s tort. But that does not explain the basis of *Impresario*'s claims against *Rogue* and *Villain* as it was *Singer* who was the victim of *Rogue*'s act of false imprisonment, not *Impresario*.

It is possible to argue that in kidnapping *Singer*, *Rogue* committed the tort of intentional infliction of harm by unlawful means[12] in relation to *Impresario*, and that *Villain* is an accessory to *that* tort. Given this, one could argue that the real reason why the courts allow *Impresario* to sue *Rogue* and *Villain* for unlawful means conspiracy is that *Rogue* committed the tort of intentional infliction of harm by unlawful means in relation to *Impresario*, and *Villain* is an accessory to that tort. However, this seems implausible – the tort of unlawful means conspiracy existed long before the tort of intentional infliction of harm by unlawful means was explicitly recognised by the courts.

36.3 LIMITS

The decision of the House of Lords in *CBS Songs* v *Amstrad plc* (1988) makes it clear that merely assisting someone to commit a tort will *not* make you an accessory to that tort.[13] So in the *Amstrad* case, CBS Songs argued that Amstrad were liable for all the breaches of copyright that were committed by people who used stereos manufactured by Amstrad to produce copies of cassette tapes bought in the shops. The House of Lords held that this would only be the case if Amstrad had procured or authorised people to make these copies, or that these copies were produced as part of a common design between Amstrad and their customers. The mere fact that Amstrad was helping its customers commit breaches of copyright by manufacturing their stereos was not enough to make it liable as an accessory for those breaches of copyright.

The fact that there is no accessory liability for assisting someone to commit a tort creates a puzzle in the law. The puzzle is that it *is* an equitable wrong dishonestly to assist someone

---

[8] [1924] P 140, 151, 156, 159. (*The Koursk* is discussed further above, § 28.9, fn 29.)
[9] Discussed above, § 24.7.
[10] For arguments that the tort of unlawful means conspiracy is rooted in this rule of accessory liability, see Sales 1990, and Stevens 2007, 249.
[11] [2008] 1 AC 1174, at [103] (per Lord Walker) and [225] (per Lord Neuberger).
[12] Discussed above, § 24.4.
[13] See also *Credit Lyonnais NV* v *Export Credit Guarantee Department* [2000] 1 AC 486, discussed below, § 37.8.

else to commit a breach of trust.[14] Moreover, someone who aids or abets someone to commit a crime will be held to have committed that crime.[15] So why is the common law so reluctant to impose liability in tort on someone who assists someone else to commit a tort?[16] The answer may lie in the fact that there are a huge number of perfectly legitimate actions that may end up assisting someone to commit a tort. Some random examples are: selling someone a knife or a bottle of bleach, creating a computer on which DVDs or CDs can be created, giving someone lessons in self-defence, and telling someone where a particular person lives or what their phone number is.

In a recent article, Paul Davies argues that we can impose liability for assisting someone else to commit a tort without unacceptable side effects if we only make people liable for assisting a tort if they *knew* that their actions would have the effect of assisting that *particular* tort to be committed.[17] Under this formula, A would be held liable if he saw B beating up C, and A threw a knife to B, which B then used to stab C.[18] But a computer *Manufacturer* would not be held liable for assisting *Pirate* to copy DVDs or CDs using one of the manufacturer's computers, merely because it knew that 30% – or even 90% – of its computers would be used for such an illegal purpose.[19] When *Manufacturer* shipped out the computer that *Pirate* used to produce his illegal DVDs or CDs, *Manufacturer* did not know that its shipping out *that computer* would have the effect of assisting *Pirate* to commit a breach of copyright. Even in a case where a defendant like Twitter knows that it is assisting *Gossip* to unlawfully violate *Celebrity*'s privacy by maintaining the Twitter account on which *Gossip* is revealing *Celebrity*'s secrets, Davies argues that Twitter should be able to take advantage of a defence of *justification*. This should be made available where someone has created a product or technology in good faith, and 'the product or technology at issue is capable of substantial lawful uses.'[20]

There are two problems with Davies' position. The first is that while he insists that *actual* knowledge that you are assisting someone else to commit a tort should be required before assistance liability is imposed,[21] the courts have in the past found themselves incapable of sticking to such a position. Once liability based on actual knowledge is allowed, the courts invariably expand liability to cases of 'Nelsonian knowledge' (turning a blind eye to the effects of one's actions),[22] and once they have made that move away from requiring actual knowledge, they are unable to find any natural stopping place in determining what sort of knowledge will make a defendant liable and what will not. The law on liability for knowingly assisting someone to commit a tort would soon turn into the same sort of legal quagmire that, for example, the law on when someone will be held liable for knowingly receiving assets disposed of in breach of trust has become.

---

[14] Authorities on the modern form of this wrong are: *Royal Brunei Airlines* v *Tan* [1995] 2 AC 378, *Twinsectra Ltd* v *Yardley* [2002] 2 AC 164, and *Barlow Clowes International* v *Eurotrust International* [2006] 1 WLR 1476.

[15] Accessories and Abettors Act 1861, s 8.

[16] This reluctance carries over into the law of negligence, where the courts take a very cautious approach to finding that a defendant owed a claimant a duty of care not to do something that enabled a third party to commit a tort in relation to the claimant: see above, § 6.3.

[17] Davies 2011, 378. Dietrich 2011 takes a very similar position (at 247).

[18] Davies 2011, 368.

[19] Davies 2011, 376–8.

[20] Davies 2011, 380.

[21] Davies 2011, 376.

[22] Called 'Nelsonian knowledge' because at the Battle of Copenhagen in 1801, Vice-Admiral Nelson disregarded a signal to retreat from his commanding officer by looking with his blind eye through a telescope at the flags signalling that he should retreat and remarking 'I really do not see the signal!'

Secondly, Davies argues that any unacceptable side effects caused by adopting an expanded definition of what amounts to culpable knowledge that your actions will assist someone else to commit a tort can be avoided through making a defence of justification available to defendants. However, as Davies himself points out, 'Justification is a flexible defence which is difficult precisely to define' and 'The scope of this defence will probably only become clear through decided cases'.[23] Given this, the prospect of possibly being able to take advantage of a defence of justification is likely to provide little reassurance to companies like Twitter or Craigslist, that would want to know in advance whether they could be held liable for assisting someone to commit an invasion of privacy, or to commit a rape, when the services they provide are abused.

It seems that if the law were to open the door to defendants being held liable simply on the basis that they assisted someone to commit a tort, the law would soon become unacceptably uncertain and inhibit many perfectly legitimate activities.[24] Not holding A liable in a case where he throws a knife to B, which is then used to stab C, is a price we have to pay in the interests of legal certainty and the public welfare.

Further reading

Anyone wishing to explore this area of law further should read **Carty, 'Joint tortfeasance and assistance liability'** (1999) 19 *Legal Studies* 489; Dietrich, 'Accessorial liability in the law of torts' (2011) 31 *Legal Studies* 231; and Davies, 'Accessory liability for assisting torts' (2011) 70 *Cambridge Law Journal* 353.

Visit **www.mylawchamber.co.uk/mcbride** to access tools to help you develop and test your knowledge of Tort law, including interactive multiple choice questions, practice exam questions with guidance, weblinks, legal newsfeed, additional case summaries, legal updates and tips on answering problem and essay questions.

premium
mylawchamber
unrivalled support for legal education

---

[23] Davies 2011, 379.
[24] A criticism that can already be levelled at the criminal law, which *does* make people criminally liable for culpably assisting someone else to commit a crime.

37 Vicarious liability

37.1 The basics *865*

37.2 Situations of vicarious liability *867*

37.3 Who is an employee? *869*

37.4 'Borrowed' employees *873*

37.5 The Salmond test *874*

37.6 The *Lister* test *878*

37.7 Theories of vicarious liability *886*

37.8 Two final points *890*

Overview

This chapter is concerned with one of the most practically important features of tort law – vicarious liability. The law on vicarious liability allows a defendant to be held liable for a tort committed by someone else. Section 37.1 sets out some basic features of the law on vicarious liability, and distinguishes it from other forms of liability that may arise when a third party has committed a tort. Section 37.2 sets out the basic situations where someone will be held vicariously liable in respect of a tort committed by someone else – the most important of which is the situation where an employee commits a tort in the course of his employment. Sections 37.3 to 37.6 focus on this situation, with sections 37.3 and 37.4 explaining when someone will be held to be someone else's *employee*, and sections 37.5 and 37.6 explaining when an employee will be held to have committed a tort *in the course of his employment*. Section 37.7 considers various different theories as to why tort law has a doctrine of vicarious liability. Section 37.8 rounds off the discussion by making two final, technical points about the application of the law on vicarious liability.

37.1 THE BASICS

Vicarious liability is not accessory liability. In a situation where A has committed a tort in relation to B and C is vicariously liable in respect of that tort, C will *not* be held to have committed that tort.[1] But the courts will treat C *as though* he had committed that tort along with A. So if B can sue A for compensatory damages, she will also be able to sue C for such damages.[2]

Three points need to be emphasised about this form of liability:

A. Joint liability

In the situation where C is vicariously liable in respect of a tort that A has committed in relation to B, A and C will be *jointly* liable to pay damages to B. So if B releases A from liability, all her rights to sue C for damages will usually also be extinguished.[3]

---

[1] Though some would dispute this. See § 37.7(6), below, for further discussion of this point.

[2] Birks 1995 observes at 41 that: 'A "vicarious" liability is a liability which one person takes over from another, and as such [is] not his but that other's, just as a "vicar" was originally a person in holy orders who occupied a place which was not his but the rector's whose substitute he was.' This is not quite right: A's liability to pay damages to B is not shifted on to C, but is shared with C.

[3] See above, § 28.4(B).

B. Vicarious liability and personal liability

It is very easy to get into the habit of thinking that whenever A does something that results in C being held liable in tort to pay damages to B, that is an example of vicarious liability. But if we are to think clearly about the law on vicarious liability, we have to resist this temptation. Consider the **Fur Coat Problem** (though it is not really a problem at all):

> *Rich* entrusts her fur coat to *Store*'s care, and *Store* gives the coat to *Shifty* to look after. *Shifty* then steals the coat.

It is well-established that in this situation, *Rich* will be entitled to sue *Store* for damages for the loss of her coat.[4] At first sight, this looks like an example of vicarious liability.[5] *Shifty* has done something wrong by stealing the coat, and *Store* ends up being held liable to compensate *Rich* for the loss caused by *Shifty*'s wrong, as though *Store* had stolen the coat itself.

But appearances mislead. The real reason that *Store* is liable to *Rich* here is that it owed *Rich* a non-delegable duty[6] to take reasonable steps to safeguard *Rich*'s coat and *Shifty*'s actions put *Store* in breach of this duty: *Store* gave *Shifty* the job of looking after the coat and *Shifty* failed to look after the coat properly.[7] So *Store* is not held liable to pay *Rich* damages here under the law on vicarious liability. It is *personally liable* under the law of bailment (or negligence, or conversion, as one prefers) to compensate *Rich* for the loss that she has suffered as a result of *Store*'s breach of the duty of care it owed *Rich* to take reasonable steps to safeguard her coat.

There are some who argue that even though the law may say that *Store* has committed a tort here, and that is what *Store* is being held liable for, what is *really* going on is that *Store* is being held vicariously liable in respect of *Shifty*'s tort. So, for example, Gleeson CJ, of the High Court of Australia, urged in *Leichhardt Municipal Council* v *Montgomery* (2007) that the law should 'frankly acknowledge' that in cases where someone is held liable for breaching a non-delegable duty of care owed to another, 'what is involved is not the breach by the defendant of a special kind of duty, but an imposition upon a defendant of a special kind of vicarious [liability].'[8]

With all due respect to Gleeson CJ, and those who think like him,[9] the law on when someone will be held liable for breaching a non-delegable duty of care *cannot* be subsumed within the law on vicarious liability.[10] Consider the **Slippery Canteen Floor Problem**:

> Part of the floor of the canteen at *Boss*'s factory is slippery because someone spilled a drink on it. *Boss* tells one of his employees, *Lackey*, to clean up the spillage. *Lackey* fails to do so for no good reason. Subsequently, another one of *Boss*'s employees, *Unlucky*, slips on the spilled drink and breaks his leg.

It is well-established that in this situation, *Unlucky* will be entitled to sue *Boss in negligence* for damages for his broken leg. *Lackey*'s failure to clean up the spillage put *Boss* in breach

---

[4] *Morris* v *CW Martin & Sons Ltd* [1966] 1 QB 716.
[5] It was assumed that this is an example of vicarious liability in *Lister* v *Hesley Hall Ltd* [2002] 1 AC 215, at [19] (per Lord Steyn), [46] (per Lord Clyde), [57] (per Lord Hobhouse), [75]–[76] (per Lord Millett). See also *Dubai Aluminium Co Ltd* v *Salaam* [2003] 2 AC 366, at [129] (per Lord Millett).
[6] Any reader currently unacquainted with the concept of a non-delegable duty of care should read § 8.6(B), above, before proceeding further.
[7] See Weir 2006, 111–12. Also *New South Wales* v *Lepore* (2003) 212 CLR 511, at [127] (per Gaudron J) and at [147], [161] (per McHugh J).
[8] [2007] HCA 6, at [24].
[9] See, for example, Williams 1956b; Fleming 1998, 434.
[10] Stevens 2007, 118.

of the non-delegable duty he owed *Unlucky* to take reasonable steps to see that the canteen would be safe for her to use. We *cannot* re-explain *Boss*'s liability in this case as being a form of vicarious liability because *Lackey* did not do anything wrong *to Unlucky* in failing to clean up the spillage. *Lackey* did not owe *Unlucky* a duty to clean up the spillage. So if *Boss* is held liable here, it can only be because *Boss* did something wrong to *Unlucky*, not because *Lackey* did something wrong to *Unlucky*.

C. Vicarious liability and accessory liability

Consider the following two situations:

(1) *Boss* successfully encourages *Tough* to beat *Victim* up.
(2) *Tough*, *Boss*'s employee, beats *Victim* up with the result that *Boss* is held vicariously liable for *Tough*'s battery.

In situation (1), *Boss* will be held to have committed the tort of battery in relation to *Victim*. In situation (2), *Boss* will *not* be held to have committed the tort of battery, but will otherwise be treated by the courts *as though* he had beaten *Victim* up and will consequently be held liable to pay damages to *Victim*. But what practical difference does it make whether *Boss* is held to have committed the tort of battery, or is treated *as though* he has committed the tort of battery? There are two potential effects:

First, in situation (1), *Boss* is a wrongdoer and a court may award exemplary damages – damages designed to punish *Boss* for his conduct – against him. In situation (2), it would be much more controversial to award exemplary damages against *Boss*. After all, if *Boss* is not *actually* a wrongdoer – but is merely treated for one reason or another as though he were one – how can it be legitimate to punish him for what he has done in this situation?

Secondly, because *Boss* is an actual wrongdoer in situation (1), there is a possibility that someone else – say, *Chief* – might be vicariously liable in respect of *Boss*'s wrong to *Victim*. So it might end up that *Victim* could sue *three* people for damages in situation (1): *Tough* (for battery), *Boss* (for battery), and *Chief* (on the basis that he is vicariously liable for *Boss*'s battery). In situation (2), because *Boss* is not an *actual* wrongdoer, no one else can be held vicariously liable for what *Boss* has done in this situation. So *Victim* will be confined to suing *Tough* and *Boss* for damages here.[11]

37.2 SITUATIONS OF VICARIOUS LIABILITY

There are many different[12] situations in which one person will be vicariously liable in respect of a tort committed by another:

---

[11] See *Credit Lyonnais Bank Nederland NV* v *Export Credit Guarantee Department* [2000] 1 AC 486 (discussed below, § 37.8).

[12] It should be noted that the Supreme Court of Canada takes the view that these situations are not so different and that there is a general rule underlying all these instances of vicarious liability, namely that A may be held vicariously liable for a tort committed by B if the relationship between A and B at the time B committed his tort was 'sufficiently close as to make a claim for vicarious liability appropriate': see *KLB* v *British Columbia* [2003] 2 SCR 403, at [18] (per McLachlin CJ). In order to judge whether this requirement is satisfied, we must determine whether B was ' "acting on his own account" or acting on behalf of [A]' at the relevant time (at [21]) – and this in turn will depend, in part, on how much 'control' A exerted over B at the relevant time (at [22]). Accordingly, it was held in the *KLB* case (Arbour J dissenting) that the government could not be held vicariously liable for various assaults that a foster parent committed on a child placed in his care by the government: foster families do not operate under 'close government control' and, as a result, while they do 'indeed [act] in the service of a public goal, their actions are too far removed from the government in the sense necessary to justify vicarious liability' (at [23], [25]).

(1) *Employment*. If A is B's *employer*, A will be vicariously liable in respect of a tort committed by B if that tort is committed by B 'in the course of his employment'.[13] On the other hand, if A gets B to do some work for him as an *independent contractor*, A will *never* be vicariously liable in respect of a tort committed by B, even if B commits that tort in the course of doing the work that A has hired him to do.[14]

(2) *Police*. If A is the chief police officer in charge of an area in which B, a police officer, is working, A will be vicariously liable in respect of a tort committed by B in performing his functions as a police officer.[15]

(3) *Agency*.[16] If A appoints B to act as his agent,[17] and B commits a tort while acting within the actual or ostensible scope of her authority as A's agent, A will be vicariously liable in respect of B's tort.[18]

(4) *Car owners*. Suppose that A requested B to perform some task for him which required B to drive A's car. Suppose further that in performing that task B negligently crashed A's car and in so doing injured C. It has been held – perhaps by analogy to the above rule dealing with vicarious liability for the acts of one's agents – that in this situation, A will be vicariously liable in respect of B's negligence.[19]

(5) *Partnership*. Under s 10 of the Partnership Act 1890, the partners in a firm will be vicariously liable in respect of a tort committed by one of the partners in that firm so long as the partner in question was acting 'in the ordinary course of the business of the firm'.[20]

(6) *Joint venture*. If A and B embark on a joint venture, and B commits a tort in the course of furthering that venture, then A will be vicariously liable in respect of B's tort.

---

[13] It used to be the case that if an employee of the Crown committed a tort in the course of his employment, the Crown would not be held vicariously liable in respect of that tort. That rule has now been abolished by s 2(1)(a) of the Crown Proceedings Act 1947.

[14] Of course, if A was subject to a non-delegable duty and he gave B – an independent contractor – the job of discharging that duty, then B might put A in breach of that duty and A might incur some sort of liability as a result. However, as has already been made clear, that liability will be personal in nature, not vicarious.

[15] Police Act 1996, s 88.

[16] See Watson and Noonan 2009.

[17] An 'agent' is someone who acts as someone else's representative for legal purposes.

[18] *Lloyd v Grace, Smith & Co* [1912] AC 716 (for an alternative explanation of the decision in this case, see above, § 8.6(B)); *Uxbridge Permanent Benefit Building Society v Pickard* [1939] 2 KB 248; *Armagas Ltd v Mundogas Ltd, The Ocean Frost* [1986] AC 717.

[19] See *Ormrod v Crosville Motor Services Ltd* [1953] 1 WLR 1120 (criticised, Brooke-Smith 1954). The defendant asked O to drive his car down to Monte Carlo so that the defendant could drive it in a motor rally there. In doing so, O negligently crashed the car into a bus. It was held that the defendant was vicariously liable in respect of O's negligence. *Ormrod* did *not* apply in *Klein v Caluori* [1971] 1 WLR 619, where F borrowed the defendant's car without his consent; when the defendant discovered this, he told F to bring the car back. As F was driving the car back, he negligently crashed into the claimant's car. Held, the defendant was not vicariously liable in respect of F's negligence because F was not performing a task for the defendant in bringing the car back – the job of bringing the car back was always F's to perform, not the defendant's. Neither did it apply in *Morgans v Launchbury* [1973] AC 127, where the defendant's husband went to the pub in the defendant's car. Realising he was too drunk to drive himself home, he had C drive him home in the defendant's car. On the way home, C drove the car so negligently that the claimants were injured. It was held that the defendant was not vicariously liable in respect of C's negligence as the defendant did not ask C to drive her husband home. See also *Nelson v Raphael* [1979] RTR 437.

[20] It is worth noting that vicarious liability used to arise in the context of a very different kind of partnership: a husband used to be held vicariously liable in respect of any torts committed by his wife, but that rule was abolished by s 3 of the Law Reform (Married Women and Joint Tortfeasors) Act 1935.

In *Brooke* v *Bool* (1928), the defendant let to the claimant a shop on the ground floor of a house next door to the defendant's home. The claimant agreed that each day the defendant could enter the shop after the claimant had left it to check that it was securely locked up. One night a lodger in the defendant's home told the defendant that he thought he could smell gas coming from the claimant's shop. The defendant and the lodger both went to investigate. They inspected a gas pipe which passed down a wall in the claimant's shop, the defendant inspecting the lower half of the pipe and the lodger the upper half. The lodger used a naked light to inspect his half of the gas pipe. Unfortunately, the upper half of the gas pipe was leaking gas and when the gas came into contact with the lodger's light there was an explosion which damaged the claimant's goods. The lodger had been negligent in using a naked light to inspect the gas pipe and the defendant was held to be vicariously liable in respect of the lodger's negligence: he and the lodger had been engaged in a joint venture (checking for a gas leak) and the lodger had been attempting to further that venture when he acted as he did.[21]

Of these six situations in which one person will be held vicariously liable in respect of a tort committed by someone else, the most important by far is the first. The rule that an employer will be held vicariously liable for a tort committed by one of her employees if that tort was committed in the course of the employee's employment raises two key issues: (1) When can someone be said to be someone else's *employee*? and (2) When can a tort committed by an employee be said to have been committed *in the course of his employment*? Most of the rest of this chapter will be devoted to answering these questions.

37.3 WHO IS AN EMPLOYEE?

Suppose that A committed a tort while working for C. When can we say that A was working for C as an employee of C's?[22] The basic answer is – we look at the nature of the contract between A and B that governed A and B's relationship. If it was a contract *of service* then A was working for C as an *employee*. If it was a contract *for services* then A was working for C as an *independent contractor*.

This does not get us very far. (Though it does emphasise that you can only be said to be working for someone else as their employee if you are contractually bound to work for them. So a wife who types up some documents for her husband as a favour to him is not acting as an employee in typing the documents.)[23] We need to know how to determine whether A's contract with C is a contract of service or a contract for services.

For a long time, the courts thought the distinction between a contract of service and a contract of services lay in the amount of *control* the contract gave C over *how* A did his work. If C was allowed under the contract to dictate how A did his work, then it was a contract of service. If, on the other hand, the contract merely specified what work A was supposed to do, and it was left up to A to decide how to do it, then it was a contract for

---

[21] Stevens 2007, at 248–9, seems to treat this case as an example of accessory liability, but as there was no agreement between the defendant and the lodger that the lodger should use a naked light to inspect the pipe (and no encouragement from the defendant that the lodger should do so), we would prefer to see it as an example of vicarious liability. Even Carty 1999 (at 500) concedes that if *Brooke* v *Bool* is an example of accessory liability, it is 'probably at the outer limits' of such liability.

[22] See, generally, Kidner 1995.

[23] See *Carmichael* v *National Power plc* [1999] 1 WLR 2042 (tour guides who worked for defendant on casual basis, turning up for work as and when they were required to do so, could not claim to be employees of the defendant as they were under no obligation to turn up for work when they were asked to do so).

services.[24] However, the courts have now rejected the 'control test' as an unsatisfactory means of determining whether a contract to do work for someone else is a contract of service or a contract for services. In cases where an employee has very specialised skills, an employer cannot hope to control how the employee does her work: but the employee remains an employee for all that.[25] The modern approach to this issue[26] is more impressionistic. We look at a range of different factors and form an impression as to whether we are dealing with a contract of service or a contract for services. Relevant factors will include:

(1) *Scope of duty.* A key difference between employees and independent contractors is that employees are employed to work for a particular period of time, whereas independent contractors are normally hired to perform a particular job – how long they take over it is up to them.[27]

The fact that an independent contractor can be hired to work for a particular period of time (for example, a nanny being hired to babysit for a certain number of hours in the evening) means this factor cannot provide a foolproof method of determining whether a contract is a contract of service or a contract for services. However, if C hires A to perform a particular job, and leaves A completely free to determine how he will do that job and how long he will spend on it, it is almost inevitable that A will be classified as an independent contractor, rather than an employee.

(2) *Payment.* Following on from the last point, employees are paid according to the time they have worked for their employer. In most cases, they are paid *wages* (an amount per week worked) or a *salary* (an amount per month worked).[28] Independent contractors, by

---

[24] See *Performing Right Society Ltd* v *Mitchell & Booker (Palais de Danse) Ltd* [1924] 1 KB 762 (finding that a dance hall band was employed by the owner of the dance hall because the contract under which they worked gave the owner 'the right of continuous, dominant and detailed control on every point, including the nature of the music to be played [by the band]' (at 771)). See also *Yewens* v *Noakes* (1880) 6 QBD 530, 532–3: 'A servant is a person who is subject to the command of his master as to the manner in which he shall do his work' (per Bramwell LJ) and *Honeywill and Stein Ltd* v *Larkin Brothers Ltd* [1934] 1 KB 191, 196: 'The determination whether [someone] is a servant ... on the one hand or an independent contractor on the other depends on whether or not the employer not only determines what is to be done, but retains control of the actual performance, in which case the doer is a servant ...; but if the employer, while prescribing the work to be done, leaves the manner of doing it to the control of the doer, the latter is an independent contractor' (per Slesser LJ).

[25] See *Gold* v *Essex County Council* [1942] 2 KB 293, 305 (per Mackinnon LJ, giving the example of the master of a ship).

[26] 'Modern' is a relative term here. The approach set out here dates back to Lord Thankerton's judgment in *Short* v *J W Henderson Ltd* (1946) 62 TLR 427, setting out (at 429) 'four indicia' that we should look at in determining whether a given contract is a contract of service or a contract for services. See also Cooke J's judgment in *Market Investigations Ltd* v *Minister of Social Security* [1969] 2 QB 173, 184-5 (endorsed by the Privy Council in *Lee Ting Sang* v *Chung Chi-Keung* [1990] 2 AC 374, at 382), setting out a range of factors to be considered in determining whether someone who has contracted to work for another is 'in business on his own account' (if yes, he is an independent contractor; if no, he is an employee).

[27] See *WHPT Housing Association Ltd* v *Secretary of State for Social Services* [1981] ICR 737, 748 (per Webster J): 'the difference between a contract of service and one for services must reside, essentially, in the terms of the principal obligation agreed to be undertaken by the employee – a word which I use without begging the question. In a contract of service ... the principal obligation undertaken by the employee is to provide himself to serve: whereas in a contract for services the principal obligation is not to provide himself to serve the employer but his services for the use of the employer.'

[28] One of Lord Thankerton's 'four indicia' of whether A is working for C under a contract of employment was whether the contract provided for A to be paid a wage (see above, n 26).

contrast, are normally paid a *fee* for doing a particular job. Again, payment by way of a fee would almost inevitably indicate that the person receiving the fee should be classified as an independent contractor rather than an employee. But a contract providing for payment for time worked will not always be a contract of service.[29]

(3) *Personal nature of duty.* Contracts of employment are like prison sentences: the work to be done under the contract has to be done by the employee, and cannot be done by anyone else. In contrast, an independent contractor will usually be free to subcontract the work to be done under the contract to somebody else. The important thing, where someone hires an independent contractor to work for him, is that the job be done; not who will do it. However, there are exceptions: if C hires A to paint his portrait, A will be an independent contractor, but will also be required under the contract to paint the portrait himself and will not be allowed to delegate the job to anyone else.

(4) *Identity of the person for whom the work is being done.* Employees are not usually employers. So if A is working for C, and C earns his money by working as employee for D, it will not usually be the case that A is an employee of C's. It is far more likely to be the case that A is an independent contractor, hired by C to help out with some job that C is too busy – because of his employment commitments – to do himself. However, there are (as usual) exceptions. Some employees (usually bankers or lawyers!) are paid so much they can afford to pay for a nanny to live with their family to help out with looking after children and doing various domestic chores. Such a live-in nanny would count as being an employee, rather than an independent contractor – she will be paid to work for a particular period of time; her contractual obligations are personal to her and cannot be discharged by anyone else; her major source of income will be from the family that she looks after (see (6), below); and the family for which she works will have a great deal of control over how she does her job (see (7), below).

(5) *Identity of the person doing the work.* The fact that employees are rarely employers (see (4), above) gives us an additional ground for distinguishing between a contract of service and a contract for services. If A contracts to do work for C, and A employs people to help him do that work, then A will normally be working for C as an independent contractor, and not as an employee.[30] And if A is a company, then A will definitely be an independent contractor. Companies can only be employers, or independent contractors, or both: they can never be employees. Only human beings can be employees.

(6) *Source of income.* Employees normally rely on their employer as their sole, or primary, source of income. In contrast, independent contractors normally earn money by working for a range of different people.

---

[29] See, for example, *Argent v Minister of Social Security* [1968] 1 WLR 1749, where a school drama teacher (an actor who was normally out of work) was paid on an hourly basis, but was still found to be an independent contractor by virtue of the fact that whenever he found a paying job as an actor he would take a 'leave of absence' from his school duties in order to perform. This was not a vicarious liability case and the decision might have gone the other way had the teacher sexually abused a student and the issue was whether the school was vicariously liable for his actions. We could well expect the courts' decisions as to who is an employee and who is not to depend on the context in which that question arises.

[30] Cooke J suggested in *Market Investigations v Minister of Social Security* [1969] 2 QB 173, at 185 that someone who 'hires his own helpers' would tend to be regarded as an independent contractor.

The courts have sought to articulate this relatively simple point in a variety of different ways. For example, in *Stephenson Jordan & Harrison Ltd* v *MacDonald & Evans* (1951), Denning LJ suggested that 'under a contract of service, a man is employed as part of the business and his work is done as an integral part of the business: whereas under a contract for services his work, although done for the business, is not integrated into it but is only accessory to it.'[31] Cooke J's suggestion in *Market Investigations* v *Minister of Social Security* (1969) that an independent contractor was 'in business on his own account' and that an employee was not[32] may be taken as making much the same point.

(7) *Control.* While the courts have rejected the idea that you can determine whether A's contract to work for C is a contract of service or a contract for services by looking solely at how much control C is allowed to exercise under the contract over how A does his work, the degree of control that C has over A under the contract is still a relevant factor to be looked at in determining whether A is an employee of C's or an independent contractor.[33] Employees *are* normally subject to more control than independent contractors are.

(8) *Equipment.* A final factor that the courts will look at in determining whether A's contract to work for C is a contract of service or a contract for services is whether C supplies A with the equipment that he needs to do his work.[34] Employees tend to turn up to work and have the equipment they need to do their job supplied to them by their employer. By contrast, independent contractors tend to supply their own equipment. Again, this factor is not determinative – it is possible to think of cases that go the other way (for example, a chef who is an employee but turns up to work with his own knives and other cooking equipment; and a motivational speaker who visits firms as an independent contractor to speak to their employees, but expects the firms to provide all the presentational equipment he requires to do his job).

The table below sums up this section. Where A contracts to do work for C, we take into account a variety of different factors in determining whether A is an employee (working for C under a contract of service) or an independent contract (working for C under a contract for services):

---

[31] (1951) 69 RPC 10, 22. See also *Bank voor Handel en Scheepvart NV* v *Slatford* [1953] 1 QB 248, where Denning LJ suggested (at 295) that 'the test of being a servant does not rest nowadays on submission to orders. It depends on whether the person is part and parcel of the organisation.' This test was criticised for being unduly vague by MacKenna J in *Ready Mixed Concrete (South East) Ltd* v *Minister of Pensions and National Insurance* [1968] 2 QB 497, at 524.

[32] See above, fn 26.

[33] See, for example, *Montgomery* v *Johnson Underwood Ltd* [2001] EWCA Civ 318 (held, a temp is not employed by the employment agency which places her with various employers on a temporary basis because the employment agency had no control over how she did her work) – though note again that this was not a vicarious liability case, but an unfair dismissal case (where again the issue of whether someone is an employee (and thus qualifies for various employment rights) is very important). The inconvenience of burdening temp agencies with unfair dismissal legislation may well have played an important part in the courts' decision not to find that the worker here was an employee.

[34] This factor was mentioned by Cooke J as a relevant factor in *Market Investigations* v *Minister of Social Security* [1969] 2 QB 173, 185.

Factors to be considered	The question to be asked:	The answer:	
		YES	NO
Scope of duty	Is A required to work for a particular time for C?		
Payment	Will A be paid according to how long he has worked for C?		
Nature of duty	Is A under a duty to carry out the work himself?		
Nature of C	Is C an employee himself?		
Nature of A	Is A an employer himself?		
Source of income	Is C A's primary source of income?		
Control	Does the contract give C control over how A does his work?		
Equipment	Does C provide A with the equipment he needs for his work?		

The more ticks that appear in the shaded boxes, the more likely it is that A is an employee of C's, rather than an independent contractor.

37.4 'BORROWED' EMPLOYEES

In a 'borrowed' employee situation, the problem is not so much determining whether someone who has committed a tort was an employee – there is no question about that – but *whose* employee he was at the time he committed his tort.

The basic situation we are concerned with is this: A is an employee of B's, and then A is sent by B to work for C. While A was working for C, he committed a tort. We need to determine who A's employer was at the time he was working for C so as to know who is vicariously liable in respect of A's tort. So the question is: When A committed his tort, whose employee was he? Was he B's employee, or was he C's, or was he, perhaps, employed by *both* B *and* C at the time he committed his tort?

Two Court of Appeal decisions have provided some guidance as to how we determine who will be said to have been A's employer at the time he committed his tort.[35] The following propositions can be extracted from the cases:

(1) *Initial presumption.* For the purposes of the law on vicarious liability, the initial presumption will be that when A was working for C, he was *still* employed *solely* by B. This presumption will be difficult to displace.[36]

(2) *Shifting the presumption.* However, this initial presumption will be displaced if A was so much under C's control while he was working for C that we can say that C had the power and responsibility to stop A committing the tort that he committed.[37]

(3) *Settling the question.* If the initial presumption that A was B's employee at the time he committed his tort can be displaced, then we find out who was A's employer at the time he committed his tort by asking – Who had the power and responsibility to stop A committing

---

[35] See *Viasystems (Tyneside) Ltd* v *Thermal Transfer (Northern) Limited* [2006] QB 510 ('*Viasystems*'); *Hawley* v *Luminar Leisure Ltd* [2006] EWCA Civ 18 ('*Hawley*').

[36] *Viasystems*, at [16] (per May LJ); *Hawley*, at [28].

[37] *Hawley*, at [28].

that tort? If the answer is: 'C, and no one else' then we should say that A was C's employee, and not B's, at the time A committed his tort. If, on the other hand, the answer is: 'B and C *both* had the power and responsibility to stop A committing his tort' then we should say that A was employed by *both B and C* at the time he committed his tort.

So – in *Mersey Docks & Harbour Board* v *Coggins & Griffith (Liverpool) Ltd* (1947), A was a crane operator, B was a harbour authority that owned the crane operated by A, and C was a firm of stevedores that had hired the crane to help unload a ship. A was negligent in operating the crane, and as a result the claimant was injured. The House of Lords held that in this case the initial presumption that A was B's employee when he was working for C was not displaced. When A went to work for C, C obtained no kind of control over how A did his work. All they could do was direct him what to do. They had no power over *how* A operated the crane.

In contrast, in *Hawley* v *Luminar Leisure Ltd* (2006), A was a nightclub 'bouncer', B was a firm that supplied bouncers to nightclubs, and C was a firm that operated a nightclub. A was sent by B to work at C's nightclub. One evening, a fracas broke out outside C's nightclub, and in the course of dealing with the fracas, A punched the claimant in the face. The Court of Appeal found that C exercised a great deal of control over how A discharged his duties as a bouncer at C's nightclub. So the initial presumption that A was B's employee at the time he hit the claimant was displaced. The Court of Appeal went on to find that C exercised so much control over how A did his job as a bouncer at C's nightclub compared with B that the sole power and responsibility of stopping A beating up customers outside C's nightclub rested with C. Given this, the Court of Appeal found that when A hit the claimant, he was employed solely by C. It followed that only C could be held vicariously liable for the tort A committed in hitting the claimant.

Finally, in *Viasystems (Tyneside) Ltd* v *Thermal Transfer (Northern) Limited* (2006), A was an apprentice metalworker, learning his trade under the supervision of a 'fitter'. B was a firm that supplied metalworkers to help out on building sites. C was a firm that had been engaged to install some airducts in the claimants' factory. B supplied C with a fully trained 'fitter' to work on the installation job, and sent A along with the 'fitter' to help out. While A was fetching some equipment, he carelessly set off the factory sprinkler system, which caused a flood. The Court of Appeal found that C exercised enough control over how A did his work to displace the initial presumption that A was B's employee when he negligently damaged the claimants' factory. The Court of Appeal went on to find that the power and responsibility of stopping A being negligent was shared between C and B. (In the case of B, the fully trained 'fitter' supplied by B to C had the task of supervising A's work.) So the Court of Appeal found that at the time A was negligent, he was employed by *both B and C*, with the result that both B and C could be held vicariously liable for A's negligence.

37.5 THE SALMOND TEST

We can now turn to the second of the two issues raised by the rule that an employer will be held vicariously liable in respect of a tort committed by one of his employees if that tort was committed *in the course of the employee's employment*: when we can we say that a tort was committed in the course of an employee's employment?

Before the decision of the House of Lords in *Lister* v *Hesley Hall Ltd* (2002), one would use the *Salmond test* to determine whether an employee's tort was committed in the course of his employment. Under this test – set out by the great tort lawyer Sir John Salmond in the first edition of his *Law of Torts* – an employee's tort will have been committed in the course of his employment if it was:

> either (a) a wrongful act authorised by [the employee's employer], or (b) a wrongful and unauthorised mode of doing some act authorised by [the employee's employer][38]

To put the test another way, under the Salmond test, an employee's tort will have been committed in the course of his employment if *the employee did something he was employed to do by committing that tort.*

For example, in *Poland* v *John Parr & Sons* (1927), a carter who was employed by the defendants to accompany a cart carrying sugar bags as it travelled through Liverpool hit a claimant schoolboy who he mistakenly thought was trying to steal a bag from the cart. The boy fell under the impact of the blow and one of the wheels of the cart rolled over the boy's foot, breaking it. It was held that the defendants were vicariously liable in respect of the carter's battery. The carter had been acting in the course of his employment in hitting the claimant because he was doing something he was employed to do – prevent people stealing sugar from the cart – by hitting the claimant. True, the defendants may have been horrified at the *way* in which the claimant went about his job of preventing people stealing sugar; they may even have expressly forbidden him from using force to prevent people stealing sugar from the cart. But that is immaterial under the Salmond test. The only issue is whether the employee was doing something he was employed to do by committing the tort: whether he was allowed or forbidden to act in the way he did makes no difference.

Similarly, and much more recently, in *Bernard* v *Attorney-General of Jamaica* (2004) – a Privy Council case – a policeman wanted to use a public payphone to call for assistance but the claimant – who was using the payphone at the time – refused to hang up. The policeman took out his gun (the case occurred in Jamaica) and shot the claimant through the head. (Amazingly, the claimant survived the shooting.) The policeman's employers were found to be vicariously liable for the policeman's battery. The policeman had been doing something he was employed to do – freeing up the payphone so that he could call for assistance – by committing his tort. Getting hold of the phone by shooting the person currently using it was completely uncalled for and unauthorised, but that is – again – immaterial under the Salmond test.[39]

In contrast, in *Heasmans* v *Clarity Cleaning Co* (1987), the claimants engaged the defendant cleaning company to clean its offices. One of the cleaners employed by the defendants to clean the claimants' offices made a number of long-distance telephone calls on the claimants' telephones while cleaning their offices, thereby committing the tort of conversion. The claimants sued the defendants, claiming that they were vicariously liable in respect of their cleaner's acts of conversion. The claim was dismissed on the ground that, under the Salmond test, the cleaner did not act in the course of his employment when

---

[38] Salmond 1907, 83. It should be pointed out that an employer will be held liable as an accessory for an employee's tort if the tort was committed with the employer's authority (see above, § 36.2(2)), and so there is no need in this kind of case (situation (a) in the Salmond test) to say that the employer will be held vicariously liable in respect of his employee's tort.

[39] See also *Limpus* v *London General Omnibus Company* (1862) 1 H&C 526; 158 ER 995 (bus company vicariously liable for bus driver's breaking of speed limit while driving buses on route); *Rose* v *Plenty* [1976] 1 WLR 141 (defendant employers vicariously liable in respect of milkman's negligent driving in driving milk float on his round); *Brown* v *Robinson* [2004] UKPC 56 (in an attempt to maintain order in a crowd of people waiting to get into a football stadium, a security guard got into an altercation with the claimant which resulted in his shooting the claimant; held that defendant employers of security guard were vicariously liable for the shooting as the security guard acted as he did to maintain some discipline in the crowd).

he made his international telephone calls. The cleaner was not doing anything he was employed to do by making the international telephone calls.[40]

For the most part, the Salmond test for determining whether or not an employer would be vicariously liable in respect of a tort committed by one of his employees was straightforward to apply. However, in certain marginal cases there were difficulties – arising out of the fact that it is not always clear how widely or narrowly we should characterise what an employee was employed to do. For example, in *London County Council* v *Cattermoles (Garages) Ltd* (1953), the defendants employed one Preston to work in their garage. One of Preston's duties was to move cars that had been left at the garage when they were in the way of other cars using the garage. He was told to move any cars by hand as he did not have a driving licence. Preston was instructed to move a van which was obstructing access to the defendants' petrol pumps. Preston got into the van and drove it into the road. However, he did not keep a proper lookout in driving the van into the road and it collided with the claimant's vehicle. The claimant sued the defendants claiming that they were vicariously liable in respect of Preston's negligence.

The case turned on the question: What was Preston employed to do? If he was employed to move cars in the defendants' garage *by hand* then Preston did *not* do anything he was employed to do by *driving* the van into the road without keeping a proper lookout. If he was simply employed to *move* cars in the defendants' garage, then Preston *did* do something he was employed to do by driving the van into the road without keeping a proper lookout. The Court of Appeal took a wide view of what Preston was employed to do in this case and found that Preston was employed to move cars in the defendants' garage. So the court concluded that Preston *was* acting in the course of his employment when he drove the van into the road without keeping a proper lookout.

Other cases are more difficult. For example, suppose A was an employee of B's and one day he drove to work at 100 mph, with the result that he negligently crashed into someone's car. Could we say – for the purposes of applying the Salmond test to determine whether B are vicariously liable in respect of A's negligence – that A was doing something he was employed to do when he *drove to work* at 100 mph? The House of Lords addressed this issue in the case of *Smith* v *Stages* (1989). Lord Lowry sought to deal with it by setting out some guidelines which are worth setting out in full:

> 1. An employee travelling from his ordinary residence to his regular place of work, whatever the means of transport and even if it is provided by the employer is not on duty and is not acting in the course of his employment, but, if he is obliged by his contract of service to use the employer's transport, he will normally, in the absence of an express condition to the contrary, be regarded as acting in the course of his employment while doing so.

---

[40] See also *Warren* v *Henleys Ltd* [1948] 2 All ER 935 (a petrol pump attendant struck a customer in the course of an altercation about whether or not the customer had paid for petrol taken from the petrol pump; held, that the employers of the attendant were not vicariously liable in respect of the battery committed by the attendant as the attendant did not do anything he was employed to do by striking the passenger); *Keppel Bus Co* v *Sa'ad bin Ahmed* [1974] 1 WLR 1082 (bus conductor swore at passenger and then hit him when the passenger protested; held, bus company not vicariously liable in respect of conductor's battery as he did not do anything he was employed to do in hitting the passenger); *Deatons Pty Ltd* v *Flew* (1949) 79 CLR 370 (defendant hotel owners not vicariously liable in respect of tort committed by employee tending bar in hotel when she reacted to lewd suggestion by a patron of the bar by throwing beer, and subsequently an empty glass, in his face); *Storey* v *Ashton* (1869) LR 4 QB 476 (two employees of defendant's went by horse and cart to deliver some wine to a customer of the defendant's; on the way back, one employee persuaded the other to make a diversion and pick up a cask of wine from the first employee's brother-in-law; held, defendant not vicariously liable in respect of negligent way in which second employee drove horse and cart on the way to the home of the first employee's brother-in-law as second employee not employed to drive horse and cart to that destination).

2. Travelling in the employer's time between workplaces (one of which may be the regular workplace) or in the course of a peripatetic profession, whether accompanied by goods or tools or simply in order to reach a succession of workplaces . . . will be in the course of the employment.

3. Receipt of wages (though not receipt of a travelling allowance) will indicate that the employee is travelling in the employer's time and for his benefit and is acting in the course of his employment, and in such a case the fact that the employee may have discretion as to the mode and time of travelling will not take the journey out of the course of his employment.

4. An employee travelling in the employer's time from his ordinary workplace to a workplace other than his regular workplace or in the course of a peripatetic profession or to the scene of an emergency (such as a fire, an accident or mechanical breakdown of plant) will be acting in the course of his employment.

5. A deviation from or interruption of a journey undertaken in the course of employment (unless the deviation or interruption is merely incidental to the journey) will for the time being (which may include an overnight interruption) take the employee out of the course of his employment.

6. Return journeys are to be treated as on the same footing as outward journeys.[41]

It should also be noted that the application of the Salmond test in particular cases to determine whether an employer was vicariously liable in respect of a tort committed by one of his employees was sometimes affected by the following legal rule: In any proceedings between a claimant and an employer of an employee who has committed a tort, the employer will be *estopped* (or prevented) from denying that the employee in question was employed to do *x* if the employer led the claimant to believe that the employee was employed to do *x* and the claimant relied on that belief.

For example, in *Conway* v *George Wimpey & Co Ltd* (1951), the defendant building company took on some construction work at an airport and to help out their employees they had some of their employees drive lorries around the perimeter of the airport – the idea being that if any of the defendants' employees wanted a lift to another area of the airport, they could hitch a lift on one of these lorries. The claimant – who was not one of the defendants' employees – hitched a ride on one of these lorries and was injured as a result of the fact that the driver was negligent in driving the lorry. The Court of Appeal applied the Salmond test and held that the defendants were *not* vicariously liable in respect of their driver's negligence because he was not employed to give rides to people like the claimant: he was only employed to give rides to the defendants' employees of the defendant company who were working at the airport.

But it would have been different if the defendants had led the claimant to believe that their drivers were employed to give rides to *anyone* working in the airport and the claimant had relied on that belief by hitching a ride on one of the defendants' lorries. In such a case – when the claimant sued the defendants on the basis that they were vicariously liable in respect of their driver's negligence – the defendants would have been estopped (or prevented) from denying that their driver was employed to give rides to people like the claimant. The defendants would therefore have been unable to deny that their driver was acting in the course of his employment when he drove the claimant to his chosen destination in a negligent fashion. As it happened, the defendant company had done nothing to induce the claimant to believe that its lorry driver was employed to pick up people like him and give them lifts to where they wanted to go and so the defendant company was not estopped from denying that its lorry driver was employed to pick up people like the claimant.

---

[41] [1989] 1 AC 928, 955–6.

This principle of estoppel is often said[42] to underlie the decision of the House of Lords in *Lloyd* v *Grace, Smith & Co* (1912).[43] In that case, the claimant owned two cottages. She was dissatisfied with the income she received from her assets and consulted the defendant firm of solicitors for advice. Her case was handled by one Sandles, the managing clerk of the firm. He tricked her into transferring the two cottages to him. The House of Lords held that the defendants were liable to compensate the claimant for the losses suffered by her as a result of Sandles's deceit. It is possible to argue that the source of the defendants' liability in this case was that they were vicariously liable in respect of Sandles's deceit – and the reason why they were vicariously liable in respect of Sandles's deceit was that they were estopped from denying that Sandles did something he was employed to do when he persuaded the claimant to sign over her cottages to him. After all, the defendants did lead the claimant to believe that Sandles was acting with their authority in *whatever* he did in relation to the claimant's affairs and the claimant relied on that belief by allowing Sandles to handle her affairs.

37.6 THE *LISTER* TEST

We are now in a position to understand the radical change in the law that was brought about by the decision of the House of Lords in *Lister* v *Hesley Hall Ltd* (2002). In that case, the defendants ran a boarding house for children who attended a nearby school. The defendants employed a married couple, Mr and Mrs Grain, to run the boarding house and maintain discipline. Unfortunately, Mr Grain used his position to sexually abuse a number of the children staying at the boarding house. The claimant sued the defendants for compensation, claiming that the defendants were vicariously liable in respect of the torts committed by Grain when he sexually abused them.

Had the Salmond test been applied to determine whether or not Grain was acting in the course of his employment when he sexually abused the claimants, the claimants' claims for compensation would certainly have been dismissed. There was no way it could be said that Grain did something he was employed to do by sexually abusing the claimants. Indeed, in an earlier case the Court of Appeal had applied the Salmond test to determine whether a local education authority was vicariously liable in respect of the torts committed by a deputy headmaster in sexually assaulting a student when they were on a school trip together, and had concluded that the deputy head had not been acting in the course of his employment when he sexually assaulted the student.[44]

However, the Salmond test was *not* applied in the *Lister* case to determine whether or not Grain was acting in the course of his employment when he sexually abused the claimants. The House of Lords swept that test away. In its place, the House of Lords adopted a quite different test for determining whether or not an employee was acting in the course of his employment when he committed a tort. This test was first adopted by the Supreme Court of Canada in the cases of *Bazley* v *Curry* and *Jacobi* v *Griffiths* (both 1999).[45] Under this test, an employee will be held to have acted in the course of his employment when he committed a tort if that tort was:

---

[42] See *Dubai Aluminium Co Ltd* v *Salaam* [2003] 2 AC 366, at [28] (per Lord Nicholls); *New South Wales* v *Lepore* (2003) 212 CLR 511, at [108]–[111] (per Gaudron J) and [232] (per Gummow and Hayne JJ).

[43] For an alternative explanation of the case, see above, § 8.6(B).

[44] *Trotman* v *North Yorkshire County Council* [1999] LGR 584.

[45] Noted, Cane 2000a.

so closely connected with his employment that it would be fair and just to hold the [employee's employer] vicariously liable [in respect of that tort].[46]

The House of Lords held that under *this* test – what we might call the 'sufficiently close connection' test, Grain *had* acted in the course of his employment when he sexually abused the claimants.[47] Their main reason for so finding was that the defendants had owed the claimants a duty to look after them; that they tried to discharge that duty by having Grain look after the claimants; and Grain conspicuously failed to look after the claimants when he sexually abused them.[48]

Three criticisms may be made of the House of Lords' decision in *Lister*:

(1) *Constitutionality*. It may be wondered whether the House of Lords acted entirely constitutionally in sweeping aside a test for determining whether an employee acted in the course of his employment when he committed a tort that had stood the test of time for almost a century. It was surely a job for Parliament, acting in conjunction with the Law Commission, to bring about such a radical change in the law on vicarious liability.[49]

Perhaps recognising this, their Lordships in *Lister* attempted to argue that there was nothing *new* about the 'sufficiently close connection' test that they adopted in *Lister*.[50] They argued that there were plenty of cases where this test had *already* been used to determine whether an employee acted in the course of his employment in committing a tort. Unfortunately, it could be argued that two of the cases mentioned – *Morris* v *C W Martin & Sons Ltd* (1966) and *Photo Production* v *Securicor* (1980) – are not vicarious liability cases at all but cases where the defendant was put in breach of a non-delegable duty of care by the acts of one of his employees.[51] A similar analysis could be made of the third case mentioned by their Lordships – *Lloyd* v *Grace, Smith & Co* (1912).[52] But even if that case *is* regarded as a vicarious liability case, the decision in that case is compatible with the Salmond test for determining whether an employee acted in the course of his employment in committing a tort and cannot be read as supporting the 'sufficiently close connection' test adopted by their Lordships in *Lister*.[53]

(2) *Necessity*. Had the House of Lords wanted to rule in favour of the claimants in *Lister*, they had no need to alter the law on vicarious liability to do so. They could have easily

---

[46] *Lister* v *Hesley Hall Ltd* [2002] 1 AC 215 (henceforth '*Lister*'), at [28] (per Lord Steyn). See also [70] (per Lord Millett: 'What is critical is . . . the closeness of the connection between the employee's duties and his wrongdoing'). An alternative formulation of the same test was offered by Lord Nicholls in *Dubai Aluminium Co. Ltd* v *Salaam* [2003] 2 AC 366, at [23]: 'the wrongful conduct must be so closely connected with acts the . . . employee was authorised to do that, for the purpose of the liability of the . . . employer to third parties, the wrongful conduct *may fairly and properly be regarded* as done by the [employee] while acting in the ordinary course of the . . . employee's employment' (emphasis in original).

[47] They also found that under this test the deputy headmaster in the *Trotman* case (see above, fn 44) *had* been acting in the course of his employment when he sexually assaulted the student in that case and, accordingly, the House of Lords overruled the Court of Appeal's decision in that case that the local education authority was not vicariously liable in respect of the torts committed by the deputy head in sexually assaulting the student.

[48] *Lister*, at [25]–[28] (per Lord Steyn), [50] (per Lord Clyde), [59]–[61] (per Lord Hobhouse), [82]–[83] (per Lord Millett).

[49] It was argued by counsel for the defendants that 'Any radical expansion or development of liabiliy in this area of law should be left to Parliament' (*Lister*, at 218) but that argument was ignored by their Lordships.

[50] *Lister*, at [15] (per Lord Steyn), [69] (per Lord Millett). Cf. *New South Wales* v *Lepore* (2003) 212 CLR 511, at [319]: '[The House of Lords] did not depart from precedent in establishing the "close connection" analysis. They merely developed and elaborated the traditional approach' (per Kirby P).

[51] For such an explanation, see above, § 8.6(B).

[52] ibid.

[53] See above, § 8.6(B).

found that the defendants in *Lister* were *personally* liable to compensate the claimants for the harm they suffered as a result of being sexually abused by Grain. Their Lordships could have reached this conclusion using the device of a non-delegable duty of care. They could have ruled that: (1) the defendants owed the claimants a non-delegable duty of care to look after them; (2) the defendants gave Grain the job of looking after the claimants; and (3) Grain put the defendants in breach of the non-delegable duty of care that they owed the claimants when, by sexually abusing the claimants, he failed to look after the claimants properly. It is hard to understand why the House of Lords did not decide *Lister* in this way – particularly as these were the *very* reasons why the House of Lords found that there *was* a 'sufficiently close connection' between the torts committed by Grain in the *Lister* case and what he was employed to do so as to make the defendants *vicariously* liable in respect of those torts.[54]

(3) *Certainty*. The third criticism that may be made of the House of Lords' decision in *Lister* is that the 'sufficiently close connection' test is so vague and open-ended that it is now very hard to tell when exactly an employee will be held to have committed a tort in the course of his employment.[55] As Lord Nicholls observed in *Dubai Aluminium Co Ltd* v *Salaam*:

> the 'close connection' test ... affords no guidance on the type or degree of connection which will normally be regarded as sufficiently close to prompt the legal conclusion that the risk of the wrongful act occurring, and any loss resulting from the wrongful act, should fall on the firm or employer rather than the third party who was wronged ... [Under the 'sufficiently close connection' test, the] crucial feature or features, either producing or negativing vicarious liability, [will] vary widely from one case or type of case to the next. Essentially the court makes an evaluative judgment in each case, having regard to all the circumstances ...[56]

It is not clear that the judges who decided *Lister* would regard the lack of certainty inherent in the 'sufficiently close connection' test as a problem; they might even regard it as a virtue. It is obvious that in the *Lister* case, their Lordships wanted to come up with a test for when an employee would be held to have acted in the course of his employment in committing a tort that would allow them to do 'practical justice'[57] in individual cases.[58] But, as Lord Millett observed in *Lister*, it is doubtful whether anyone can come up with a test that is sufficiently flexible as to allow the courts to do 'practical justice' in individual cases but at

---

[54] See Glofcheski 2004, 27; also *New South Wales* v *Lepore* (2003) 212 CLR 511, at [208]: 'The analyses of Lord Hobhouse and Lord Millett [in *Lister*] have strong echoes of non-delegable duties' (per Gummow and Hayne JJ).

[55] Cf. Callinan J's criticisms of the 'sufficiently close connection' test for determining whether an employee committed a tort in the course of his employment in *New South Wales* v *Lepore*: '[If such a test were to be adopted in Australia] [d]istinguishing between [cases where there was a "sufficiently close connection" between an employee's tort and what he was employed to do and cases where there was not] would be very difficult. Cases would, as a practical matter, be decided according to whether the judge ... thought it "fair and just" to hold the employer liable. Perceptions of fairness vary greatly. The law in consequence would be thrown into a state of uncertainty. I would not therefore be prepared to adopt their Lordships' or any like test' (ibid., at [345]). Only one of the seven judges who decided *New South Wales* v *Lepore* in the High Court of Australia expressed any enthusiasm for the 'sufficiently close connection' test (Kirby P). Callinan, Gaudron, Gummow, Hayne JJ and (less clearly) Gleeson CJ all held that Australian courts should continue to use the Salmond test to determine whether an employee committed a tort in the course of his employment. McHugh J declined to express an opinion on the issue.

[56] [2003] 2 AC 366, at [25]–[26].

[57] *Lister*, at [16] per Lord Steyn.

[58] For a fine critique of judicial attempts to do 'practical justice' in individual cases, see Beever 2003b.

the same time sufficiently precise so as 'to enable the outcome of a particular case to be predicted'.[59] Any test which did work in a predictable fashion would be 'rigid and possibly inappropriate . . . as a test of liability' in particular cases.[60]

However, in their desire to do 'practical justice' in individual cases, the Law Lords who decided *Lister* forgot or disregarded the primary responsibility that they owe the public at large, which is to ensure that the law is stated in clear and certain terms, so that we can all know where we stand when we get involved in disputes with other people. For this reason, it is to be hoped that the Supreme Court will abandon the 'sufficiently close connection' test for determining whether an employee committed a tort in the course of his employment in favour of another test which will work in a more predictable fashion.[61]

Until that day comes, in any case where an employee has committed a tort, the courts will have to determine whether the employee committed that tort in the course of his employment by asking – Was there a sufficiently close connection between the employee's tort and what he was employed to do so as to make it 'fair and just' that the employer should be held vicariously liable in respect of the employee's tort? When are the courts likely to find that this test is satisfied?

Obviously, in a case where the Salmond test is satisfied, it seems almost inevitable that the courts will find that there was a 'sufficiently close connection' between the employee's tort and what he was employed to do.[62] The real problem arises in cases where an employee commits a tort in circumstances where we *cannot* say she was doing what she was employed to do by committing that tort. The decision in *Lister* makes it clear that in such a case, the courts might still find that there was a 'sufficiently close connection' between the employee's tort and what he was employed to do. But when will they?

Two key ideas emerge from the *Lister* decision as to when a 'sufficiently close connection' will still exist between an employee's tort and what the employee was employed to do even though the employee was not doing what he was employed to do in committing that tort.

[59] *Lister*, at [66].

[60] ibid.

[61] Such a test would have to identify exactly *when* it is 'fair and just' to hold an employer vicariously liable in respect of a tort committed by one of his employees in terms which make it possible to predict with a fair degree of success in any given case whether an employer will be held vicariously liable in respect of a tort committed by one of his employees. The Supreme Court of Canada attempted to come up with such a test in *Bazley v Curry* [1999] 2 SCR 534, holding that 'the policy purposes underlying the imposition of vicarious liability on employers are served *only* where the wrong *is so connected with the employment that it can be said that the employer has introduced the risk of the wrong* (and is thereby and usefully charged with its management and minimization)' (at [37], per McLachlin J, emphasis added). However, members of the High Court of Australia expressed themselves doubtful in *New South Wales v Lepore* (2003) 212 CLR 511 whether that test was expressed in sufficiently clear terms as to make its application predictable: see [126] (per Gaudron J) and [212] (per Gummow and Hayne JJ). If it is not possible to identify in clear and certain terms *when* it would be 'fair and just' to hold an employer vicariously liable in respect of a tort committed by one of his employees (and Lord Millett seemed to think in *Lister* that it was not: see above, fn 59) 'second-best' test would have to be formulated which worked in a predictable fashion *and* served to make employers vicariously liable for their employees' torts in *most* situations where it it would be 'fair and just' to make them so liable. It may be that the only such 'second-best' test on offer is the Salmond test.

[62] It can hardly be supposed that for nearly 100 years before *Lister* was decided, the courts acted unfairly or unjustly by holding employers vicariously liable for their employees' torts when the Salmond test was satisfied. But see Lord Millett's observation in *Dubai Aluminium Co Ltd v Salaam* [2003] 2 AC 366 that 'the Salmond test is only that – a test. It is not a conclusive definition of the circumstances in which vicarious liability arises. *Even if it is satisfied, the facts, taken as a whole, may nevertheless show that the employee was not acting in the course of his employment*' (at [128], emphasis added).

A. Delegation[63]

Various *dicta* in *Lister* seems to suggest that if *Employer* was under a duty to do *x*, and he instructed *Employee* to discharge that duty, then if *Employee* failed to follow instructions and in so doing committed a tort, there will exist a 'sufficiently close connection' between *Employee*'s tort and what he was employed to do. For example, Lord Hobhouse suggested that:

> Whether or not some act comes within the scope of the servant's employment depends upon an identification of what duty [of the employer's][64] the servant was employed by his employer to perform ... If the act of the servant which gives rise to the servant's liability to the [claimant] amounted to a failure by the servant to perform that duty, the act comes within 'the scope of his employment' and the employer is vicariously liable.[65]

In order to show a 'sufficiently close connection' under this head, it is crucial to show that *Employee* was entrusted by *Employer* with the job of discharging one of *Employer*'s duties. So it was vital that the employee in the *Lister* case was employed to discharge the duty that the defendants were under to look after the children staying at their boarding house. Had the claimants in *Lister* been abused by a handyman who was employed by the defendants merely to do odd jobs around the boarding house, then it is unlikely that the House of Lords would have found a 'sufficiently close connection' between the torts committed by the handyman in abusing the claimants and what he was employed to do.[66] It could not have been said that the defendants employed the handyman to discharge the duty they were under to look after the children staying at their boarding house.

B. Special risk[67]

In the *Lister* case, Lord Steyn made clear that the decisions of the Supreme Court of Canada in *Bazley* v *Curry* and *Jacobi* v *Griffiths* (both 1999) should form the 'starting point' of any inquiry into whether there was a 'sufficiently close connection' between what an employee was employed to do and a tort committed by the employee.[68] Those decisions indicate that if an employee is employed to do a particular job and there is a *special risk*[69] associated with that job that he will commit a particular kind of tort, then if the employee in question commits that tort, there will be a 'sufficiently close connection' between the employee's tort and what he was employed to do.

This requirement was held to be satisfied in *Bazley* v *Curry* (1999), where the defendants unknowingly employed a paedophile to work in a home for disturbed children and the paedophile used his position to sexually abuse some of the children in the home. It was held that there was a special risk that people who work in children's homes will sexually

---

[63] See Giliker 2009, at 42–53.

[64] It is quite clear from Lord Hobhouse's judgment (in particular [54]–[55]) that the word 'duty' here refers to a duty that the *employer* is subject to, not a duty that the employee is subject to. In the situation he is discussing, the employee is given the job of performing the employer's duty.

[65] *Lister*, at [59]. See also [50] (per Lord Clyde), and [82] (per Lord Millett). The House of Lords did not feel it necessary to explain *why* it is 'fair and just' to hold an employer vicariously liable in respect of a tort committed by one of his employees in this situation: Lord Steyn thought that it was a clear case where vicarious liability should be imposed (at [28]).

[66] See *Jacobi* v *Griffiths* [1999] 2 SCR 570, at [45] (per Binnie J); also *EDG* v *Hammer* [2003] 2 SCR 459, at [36] (per Arbour J).

[67] See, generally, Brodie 2010.

[68] [2002] 1 AC 215, at [27].

[69] The decisions actually talk in terms of an 'increased or materially enhanced ... risk' (*Bazley* v *Curry* [1999] 2 SCR 534, at [39] (per McLachlin J)) but it is simpler to use the term 'special risk'.

assault the children there. This is because, McLachlin J explained, people who work in children's homes occupy a position of 'power and intimacy' in relation to the children at the homes – as a result, if they have paedophiliac tendencies, they will feel emboldened to sexually abuse the children in their care and the children in their care will be more likely to submit to being assaulted without complaint.[70]

In contrast, the special risk requirement was held not to be satisfied in *Jacobi v Griffiths* (1999). In that case, the defendants set up a club for children. They employed a Harry Griffiths to act as programme director at the club. His job was to organise recreational activities at the club and the occasional outing. Griffiths used his position to befriend a couple of the children who used the club and he ended up inviting them to his home, where he sexually assaulted them. The Supreme Court of Canada held, by four to three, that there was *not* a 'sufficiently close connection' between what Griffiths was employed to do and the torts that he committed in sexually assaulting the children.

The fact that Griffiths had been employed to work at the club had of course given him the opportunity to sexually assault the children, but that was not enough to establish the requisite connection between his torts and what he was employed to do.[71] There was no special risk that someone employed in Griffiths' capacity would sexually abuse children who used the club: there was no special reason to think that someone employed to work as a programme director at a children's club would develop a relationship of 'power and intimacy' with the children at the club that might embolden him to assault the children at the club and lead them to submit to the assaults without complaint.[72]

The fact that the Supreme Court of Canada divided four to three in *Jacobi* over whether the special risk requirement was satisfied in that case indicates that it will often be very difficult to tell whether or not there was a special risk associated with what an employee was employed to do that he would commit a particular kind of tort. The difficulty lies in distinguishing between cases where an employee's employment creates a *special risk* that an employee will commit a particular kind of tort and cases where an employee's employment merely gives him a *good opportunity* to commit a particular kind of tort. All of the judges in *Lister*, *Bazley v Curry* and *Jacobi* were agreed that a 'sufficiently close connection' between an employee's tort and what he was employed to do would *not* be established in a case where an employee's employment merely gave him a good opportunity to commit that tort.[73] But it is not clear that it is possible to draw a clear line between *special risk* cases and *good opportunity* cases.

In some cases, the requirement of a 'special risk' has been clearly satisfied. In *Weir v Chief Constable of Merseyside Police* (2003), the defendant chief constable in that case was held vicariously liable in respect of an assault committed by an off-duty police officer on the claimant in a police van which the officer had borrowed in order to help a friend move some belongings. (The police officer suspected that the claimant had attempted to pilfer some of the friend's belongings while they were awaiting removal.) The Court of Appeal's main

---

[70] [1999] 2 SCR 534, at [44]. See also *New South Wales v Lepore* (2003) 212 CLR 511, at [216] (per Gummow and Hayne JJ).

[71] If the same case occurred in the United Kingdom, could a court find the defendants vicariously liable for the programme director's acts of sexual abuse using the 'delegation' idea set out above? It depends on whether it could be said that the programme director in *Jacobi v Griffiths* was employed by the defendants in that case to discharge the duty the defendants owed the children at the club to take reasonable steps to see that they were reasonably safe in using the club.

[72] [1999] 2 SCR 570, at [79]–[86] (per Binnie J).

[73] *Lister*, at [45] (per Lord Clyde), [59] (per Lord Hobhouse), [65] (per Lord Millett); *Bazley v Curry* [1999] 2 SCR 534, at [40] (per McLachlin J); *Jacobi v Griffiths* [1999] 2 SCR 570, at [81] (per Binnie J).

reason for finding the defendant vicariously liable in respect of the officer's assault was that, before he took the claimant into the police van and assaulted him, 'he . . . confirmed to, and the [claimant] understood, that he was a police officer' (at [12], per Rt Hon Sir Denis Henry).[74] It may be that there is a special risk that police officers will commit assaults on ordinary citizens whenever they act in their capacity as police officers: they may feel that they are more likely to 'get away' with assaulting people when they act in their official capacity.

In *Mattis* v *Pollock* (2003), the claimant was stabbed by a nightclub bouncer employed by the defendants; the bouncer had earlier had an altercation with the claimant and was seeking to take revenge on him for this. The Court of Appeal held that the defendants *were* vicariously liable in respect of the bouncer's attack on the claimant. The court held that a sufficiently close connection was established between the bouncer's attack and what he was employed to do because: (1) using violence on other people was part of his job; *and* (2) the earlier altercation between the bouncer and the claimant had arisen out of the bouncer's doing what he was employed to do and the bouncer's stabbing the claimant was directly linked to the earlier altercation. It could be argued that the nature of a bouncer's employment does create a special risk that: (1) he will get into altercations with customers of the type that happened in *Mattis* and (2) that those altercations will result in the kind of violence that happened in *Mattis*.[75]

Gravil v *Carroll* (2008) was a case that arose out of a rugby match between Halifax RFC and Redruth RFC in 2005. Andrew Gravil was playing for Halifax when he was punched by Richard Carroll, a Redruth player, in a melee that developed following a scrum. Gravil sued Redruth RFC for damages, claiming that they were vicariously liable in respect of Carroll's battery. The Court of Appeal held that there was a sufficiently close connection between Carroll's employment and his punch:

> . . . the throwing of punches is not uncommon in situations like this, when the scrum is breaking up after the whistle has done. Indeed, they can fairly be regarded as an ordinary (though undesirable) incident of a rugby match.[76]

Given this, it could be argued that a rugby player's employment as a rugby player does create a special risk that he will engage in violent acts of the type that Carroll was guilty of.

However, the difficulty of distinguishing between 'special risk' cases and 'good opportunity' cases has meant that the courts have found it difficult not to fall into finding a sufficiently close connection between an employee's tort and his employment *simply* on the basis that the employee's employment gave him or her a good opportunity to commit that tort. The Privy Council tried to hold the line in *Attorney-General for the British Virgin Islands* v *Hartwell* (2004), holding that it was 'clear cut' that a police officer's employers were not vicariously liable for the actions of the police officer in firing four shots into a bar

---

[74] [2003] EWCA Civ 111, at [12] (per Rt Hon Sir Denis Henry).

[75] The pre-*Lister* Court of Appeal decision in *Fennelly* v *Connex South Eastern Ltd* [2001] IRLR 390 is more marginal. An initial altercation between a passenger and a ticket inspector over the passenger's failure to produce his ticket escalated and the ticket inspector ended up putting the passenger into a headlock. The Court of Appeal held that the inspector's employers were vicariously liable in respect of the tort committed by the inspector in laying his hands on the passenger. It may be that the nature of a ticket inspector's employment creates a special risk of his getting into arguments with customers, but there is nothing in a ticket inspector's training that creates a special risk that those arguments will spill over into violence of the type perpetrated in *Lister*. Of course, if the ticket inspector thought that putting the passenger into a headlock was the best way of getting the passenger to pay the right fare, then the decision that he was acting in the course of employment could be straightforwardly supported by reference to the Salmond test. However, it seems in this case that the ticket inspector was out for blood, rather than pursuing his employer's interests.

[76] [2008] EWCA Civ 689, at [23].

where his ex-girlfriend was sitting with her new lover;[77] this despite the fact that the police officer used a gun issued to him by his employers and must have received training from them in how to use it. However, two recent decisions of the Court of Appeal seem to collapse the (already tenuous) distinction between cases where an employee's employment gives him a 'good opportunity' to commit a particular tort and cases where an employee's employment creates a 'special risk' that he will commit a particular tort.[78]

The first case is *Maga v Trustees of the Birmingham Archdiocese of the Roman Catholic Church* (2010). In that case, the claimant was sexually abused by a Roman Catholic priest, Fr Clonan, between the ages of 12 and 13. They met when the claimant was admiring the priest's car. The priest invited the claimant to a few discos organised by his church, and had the claimant do some odd jobs for him. Most of the priest's acts of abuse were carried out in the priest's residence attached to his local church. In finding that there was sufficiently close connection between the priest's employment by the church and his acts of sexual abuse, all three members of the Court of Appeal placed great emphasis on the *opportunities* that the priest's job gave him to carry out those acts of sexual abuse – in particular, the fact that because part of his job involved counselling young people, he was allowed to spend time alone with the claimant without being challenged by anyone.[79]

The second case is *Brink's Global Services Inc v Igrox Ltd* (2010). In that case, Igrox was hired to fumigate some pallets of silver bars that were going to be shipped to India. Two of Igrox's employees were given the job of fumigating the pallets. For some reason, they never fumigated the pallets, but one of the employees took the chance to come back later in the day, gain access to the container containing the pallets, and steal 15 silver bars. The owners of the bars sued Igrox, arguing that they were vicariously liable for the theft. Counsel for Igrox argued forcefully that this was simply a case where the employee's employment merely gave him an opportunity to steal the silver bars and that this could not give rise to a finding of vicarious liability – any more than it did in *Heasmans v Clarity Cleaning Co* (1987), a case we have already discussed, where an office cleaner made long distance telephone calls on the telephones in the offices he was supposed to be cleaning.[80] Despite this, the Court of Appeal found that there was a sufficiently close connection between the employee's employment and the employee's theft. Just as in *Maga*, emphasis was placed on the fact that the nature of the employee's employment meant that he could spend time around the pallets of silver bars without being challenged.[81] For good measure, the Court

---

[77] [2004] 1 WLR 1273, at [16]–[17].

[78] Though see Hoyano 2010, arguing that one of these cases (*Maga*) involved a straightforward application of the 'special risk' idea.

[79] [2010] 1 WLR 1441, at [50] ('[T]he fact that Father Clonan was spending time alone with the claimant for illegal sexual purposes is [irrelevant]: the *opportunity* to spend time alone with the claimant, especially in the presbytery, arose from Father Clonan's role as a priest employed by the Archdiocese' per Lord Neuberger MR), [84] ('the progressive stages of intimacy were . . . only *possible* because Father Clonan had the priestly status and authority which meant no one would question his being alone with the claimant. It is this that provides the close connection between the abuse and what Father Clonan was authorised to do' per Longmore LJ), [94]–[95] ('I do not think that, if a priest or pastor of an non-evangelical church had the ostensible authority to befriend and develop intimacy with a young person by reason of his pastoral duties and if he then abused the *opportunities* given by that ostensible authority, the position of that church would be any different from the position of the Roman Catholic Church in this case' per Smith LJ); emphasis added in every case.

[80] [2010] EWCA Civ 1207, at [14], [28].

[81] [2010] EWCA Civ 1207, at [36]: '[The defendants] clothed [the employee] with the outward appearance of being their employee . . . so that no one would be suspicious if he were seen alone near the container. The closed circuit TV system showed that he was indeed around the container at the relevant time and it was only because he had the outward appearance of an Igrox employee that such a position could be allowable and understandable' (per Longmore LJ).

of Appeal also went out of its way to express the view that post-*Lister*, *Heasmans* would probably be decided differently nowadays.[82]

The decisions of the Court of Appeal in *Maga* and *Brink's* illustrate how difficult it is to tell with any certainty when the courts will, and when they will not, find that the *Lister* test for determining whether an employee's tort was committed in the course of his employment is satisfied. The courts deny that the *Lister* test will be satisfied merely by showing that the employee's tort was in some way connected with, or enabled by, his employment. However, it seems that in *any* case where such a connection, or enablement, is established, there is a *chance* that a court will find that the *Lister* 'sufficiently close connection' test is satisfied – and whether the court will so find simply depends on who happens to be hearing the case.[83]

37.7 THEORIES OF VICARIOUS LIABILITY

We could be more certain about how the *Lister* test for vicarious liability will apply in practice if we knew exactly *why* it is 'fair and just' to hold an employer vicariously liable for torts committed by his employee in the course of his employment. After all, under the *Lister* test, the courts are only supposed to find that an employee's tort was committed in the course of his employment when the degree of connection between the tort and the employment is such as to make it 'fair and just' to hold the employer vicariously liable for that tort.[84] Unfortunately, no one has ever managed to explain what exactly is 'fair and just' about holding an employer vicariously liable for torts committed by his employees.[85]

(1) *Deep pockets.* It is argued, first of all, that in a case where *Employee* commits a tort in the course of employment, it is 'fair and just' to hold *Employer* vicariously liable for that tort because doing so will allow the victim of *Employee*'s tort to recover damages from someone worth suing.[86] This theory does not work, either at a normative or descriptive level. At a normative level, there is nothing 'fair or just' about giving effect to a principle of 'can pay, will pay'. At a descriptive level, if the law on vicarious liability were designed to give the victim of a tort a cash-rich defendant to sue, it is hard to see why the victim of a

---

[82] [2010] EWCA Civ 1207, at [31] ('In light of more recent decisions I think it is doubtful whether the case would now be decided in the same way . . . The theft of office equipment which a cleaner is employed to clean is now likely to be regarded as a wrong committed in the course of his employment and it is doubtful whether other forms of misuse of the same equipment are to be viewed in a different light' per Moore-Bick LJ) and [37] ('An office cleaner illegitimately using telephones to make long-distance calls is a more borderline case . . . [but] if the same facts arose today, the result would probably be different' per Longmore LJ).

[83] It is interesting to note that in four of the Court of Appeal cases discussed above – *Weir*, *Mattis*, *Gravil* and *Maga* – the first instance judge refused to find vicarious liability, and was in each case overturned by the Court of Appeal. Are first instance judges getting *Lister* wrong, or are they simply less pro-claimant and more sympathetic to the concerns of employers than the Court of Appeal?

[84] *Lister*, at [28] (per Lord Steyn).

[85] Cf. *Hollis v Vabu Pty Ltd* (2001) 207 CLR 21, at [35] (per Gleeson CJ, Gaudron, Gummow, Kirby and Hayne JJ): 'a fully satisfactory rationale for the imposition of vicarious liability . . . has been slow to appear'; also *New South Wales v Lepore* (2003) 212 CLR 511, at [106] (per Gaudron J, remarking on the 'absence of a satisfactory and comprehensive jurisprudential basis for the imposition of liability on a person for the harmful acts or omissions of others'), and [299] (per Kirby P: 'The history of the imposition of vicarious liability demonstrates that the foundation of such liability has been uncertain and variable').

[86] Cf. *Limpus v London General Omnibus Company* (1862) 1 H&C 526, 529; 158 ER 995, 998: 'It is well-known that there is virtually no remedy against the driver of an omnibus, and therefore it is necessary that, for injury resulting from an act done by him in the course of his master's service, the master should be responsible; for there ought to be a remedy against some person capable of paying damages to those injured by improper driving' (per Willes J). Also Baty 1916, 152; Atiyah 1967, 22; Feldthusen 1998, 224–5.

tort is only allowed to sue the tortfeasor's employer when the tort was committed *in the course of the employee's employment.*[87]

(2) Loss spreading. It is argued, secondly, that it is 'fair and just' to hold *Employer* vicariously liable for a tort committed by *Employee* in the course of his employment because doing so will shift the loss caused by that tort onto the shoulders of someone who can then spread the loss throughout the community – either by recovering the loss from *Employer's* liability insurer, which will then spread the loss to all its customers through higher premiums; or by spreading the loss among *Employer's* customers in the form of higher prices.[88]

A variant on this loss-spreading argument is made by Tony Weir, who argues that vicarious liability seems to be designed to allow losses to be shifted from human beings (in the shape of the victims of torts) to companies (in the shape of employers), which are in a better position to absorb and spread those losses:

> [S]uppose that one were challenged to produce formal rules with the substantial effect that companies must pay for people but not *vice versa*. One could hardly do better than lay down that liability should attach to employers but not to customers, that one should be liable for one's permanent staff but not for any other bodies whom or which one might pay to do things or get things done – in brief, that there should be liability for employees but not for independent contractors.[89]

This explanation again suffers from problems at both a normative and descriptive level. There seems nothing 'fair and just' about shifting a loss onto someone else simply because he or she can absorb and spread it more easily than the person currently suffering that loss. And if a desire to spread losses did underlie the law on vicarious liability, it is hard to see why the loss suffered by the victim of a tort will *only* be shifted and spread if the tort was committed in the course of an employee's employment.

(3) Relative blame. In *Hern* v *Nichols* (1700), Holt CJ explained that *Employer* will be vicariously liable in respect of a tort committed by *Employee* in the course of his employment because 'seeing somebody must be a loser [as a result of a tort committed by an employee] it is more reason that he that employs and puts a trust and confidence in [the employee] should be a loser than a stranger'.[90] But if this is right it is hard to see why someone who engages someone else to work for him as an independent contractor should not be vicariously liable in respect of any torts committed by that contractor in doing the work he is engaged to do.

(4) Deterrence. It is also said that holding *Employer* vicariously liable in respect of a tort committed by *Employee* in the course of his employment will encourage *Employer* to take

---

[87] Fleming 1998 argues (at 410) that the law does not hold employers liable for torts committed by their employees outside the course of their employment because it does not want to 'foist an undue burden on business enterprise'. But there is more than a whiff of *ex post facto* rationalisation about this explanation.

[88] See *Bazley* v *Curry* [1999] 2 SCR 534, at [31]: 'the employer is often in the best position to spread the losses [caused by an employee's tort] through mechanisms like insurance and higher prices, thus minimizing the dislocative effect of the tort within society' (per McLachlin J); also *Various Claimants* v *The Catholic Child Welfare Society* [2010] EWCA Civ 1106, at [35]: 'There is not much doubt about the principal rationale for this non-fault liability, which is loss distribution, [the employer] being more able to bear the loss than [the employee], often (though not always) because he can and will in practice insure against it. Where there is such insurance, the cost is often passed on to the buyers or users of the service or goods provided by [the employer]' (per Hughes LJ).

[89] Weir 2004, 269.

[90] (1700) 1 Salk 289, 91 ER 256. See also *Bazley* v *Curry* [1999] 2 SCR 534, at [50] and [54] (per McLachlin J).

steps to see that his employees do not act wrongfully while they work for him.[91] For example, in *Gravil v Carroll* (2008), the Court of Appeal justified imposing vicarious liability on the defendant rugby club for a punch thrown by their player in a melee following a scrum on deterrence based grounds:

> There is an obvious temptation for clubs to turn a blind eye to foul play. They naturally want their side to win and, no doubt, to play hard to do so. The line between playing hard and playing dirty may be seen as a fine one. The temptation for players to cross the line in the scrum may be considerable unless active steps are taken by clubs to deter them from doing so . . . It is . . . striking that here the club did not take any disciplinary action against [their player]. Perhaps it would have done if it had appreciated that there was a risk of liability in such cases in the future.[92]

The difficulty with all such explanations of vicarious liability is that it makes no difference *at all* to an employer's liability whether or not he has taken all reasonable steps, or has done everything he can, to prevent his employees committing torts while working for him. Suppose that in *Gravil v Carroll* (2008) the defendant rugby club had regularly disciplined any of their players who stepped out of line on the field of play. That would have made no difference to their vicarious liability for any future infractions.

(5) *Enterprise risk.* Another explanation as to why the law will sometimes hold *Employer* vicariously liable in respect of a tort committed by an *Employee* in the course of his employment goes as follows. Elementary fairness dictates that if you seek to make money from engaging in some activity and other people suffer loss as a result of your engaging in that activity, you should compensate them for that loss – if you want to obtain the gains resulting from engaging in that activity, then you should bear the losses as well.

This principle of fairness applies here.[93] An employer sets up in business for himself, and employs people to work for him and make money for him. If the sort of work an employee is employed to do carries with it a special risk that the employee will commit a particular kind of tort, when that risk materialises, it is only fair that the employer should bear the loss resulting from that risk materialising.[94]

This explanation of the law on vicarious liability makes sense of the current state of the law, post-*Lister*, as to when an employer will be held vicariously liable for a tort committed by one of his employees. However, it suffers from a major flaw. The law on

---

[91] See *Bazley v Curry* [1999] 2 SCR 534, at [32]–[33]: 'Fixing the employer with responsibility for the employee's wrongful act, even where the employer is not negligent, may have a deterrent effect. Employers are often in a position to reduce accidents and intentional wrongs by efficient organization and supervision . . . Beyond the narrow band of employer conduct that attracts direct liability in negligence lies a vast area where imaginative and efficient administration and supervision can reduce the risk [of wrongdoing by the employer's employees]. Holding the employer vicariously liable for the wrongs of its employee may encourage the employer to take such steps and, hence, reduce the risk of future harm' (per McLachlin J). Also *New South Wales v Lepore* (2003) 212 CLR 511, at [305] (per Kirby P); Pollock 1882, 130.

[92] [2008] ICR 1222, at [26]–[27].

[93] It may also underlie the Consumer Protection Act 1987, in so far as it makes a manufacturer who manufactures goods for profit liable for the harm caused by any of his goods being defective. See Stapleton 1994a, 185–217; Waddams 1998, 124–5. The 1987 Act is discussed in detail above, in chapter 12. The rule in *Rylands v Fletcher* (discussed above, chapter 16), might also be said to rest on this principle of fairness: Cane 1999, 202.

[94] Cf. *Dubai Aluminium v Salaam* [2003] 2 AC 366, at [21]: 'The . . . legal policy [underlying the law on vicarious liability] is based on the recognition that carrying on a business enterprise necessarily involves risks to others. It involves the risk that others will be harmed by wrongful acts committed by the [employees] through whom the business is carried on. When those risks ripen into loss, it is just that the business should be responsible for compensating the person who has been wronged' (per Lord Nicholls). See also *Lister v Hesley Hall Ltd* [2002] 1 AC 215, at [65] (per Lord Millett); *Bazley v Curry* [1999] 2 SCR 534, at [22], [30] (per McLachlin J); *New South Wales v Lepore* (2003) 212 CLR 511, at [303] (per Kirby P); *Majrowski v Guy's and St Thomas's NHS Trust* [2007] 1 AC 224, at [9] (per Lord Nicholls); Pollock 1882, 122.

vicarious liability applies to *all* employers, and not just employers who are in business for themselves and out to make a profit for themselves. In recent years, lawyers have argued in court that it is unfair to make their clients vicariously liable for the torts of their employees because their clients are non-profit making bodies. However, the courts have always set their face against such arguments, and held that churches, charities, clubs and government bodies are just as much subject to the rules on vicarious liability as businesses are.[95]

(6) *Master's tort.* We began this chapter by saying that vicarious liability is not accessory liability – that is, an employer whose employee has committed a tort in the course of his employment is not held to have committed a tort *himself* but is instead treated *as though* he had committed the employee's tort along with the employee. There is, however, a very old theory of vicarious liability – known as the 'master's tort' theory – which says that this is not true. In the case where *Employee* commits a tort in the course of his employment (so the theory goes) *Employer* is held liable because *he* has committed a tort. *Employer* is held to have done what *Employee* did, and is held liable accordingly. So suppose *Employee* punched *Victim* in the course of his employment. Because the punch occurred in the course of *Employee's* employment, the punch is attributed to *Employer*. So *Employer* is held to have punched *Victim* and as a result is held liable in battery to pay damages to *Victim*.

The master's tort theory of vicarious liability has long been unfashionable.[96] However, it has recently been revived by academics who are hostile to policy-based explanations of tort law in general, and the sort of policy-based explanations of vicarious liability that have been canvassed above and found wanting. Chief among these academics is Robert Stevens, whose book *Torts and Rights* (2007) contains a powerful defence of the 'master's tort' theory of vicarious liability:

> A close analogy is with the rules of games. In the 1966 World Cup Final, the person whose physical actions caused the last goal to be scored was Geoff Hurst. However, the rules of the game also attribute his physical actions to his team, England. Both Geoff Hurst and England scored the goal. Beyond the selection of 11 players, it is not possible for either side to choose for itself who can score its goals, or perhaps more pertinently commit a foul. If a player kicks the ball into his own team's net, this will be considered to be an own goal. It does not matter that he was acting contrary to the express instructions of his team manager; nor does it matter if he did so deliberately in a fit of anger. If the words or actions of another person are attributed to the defendant, and those actions infringe the claimant's rights, the defendant will be liable. The law, like the game of football, has rules for determining this.[97]

However, there are a number of problems with the 'master's tort' theory.

First, the fact that we *can* attribute the acts of an employee to an employer does not establish that we *should*. Robert Stevens attempts to counter this argument by saying that:

> the liability of corporate bodies for misfeasance demonstrates that rules for the attribution of words and actions are *indispensable* . . . Corporations are legal constructs and do not exist in the

---

[95] *Bazley* v *Curry* [1999] 2 SCR 534, at [47]–[56]; *Gravil* v *Carroll* [2008] ICR 1222, at [9]; *Various Claimants* v *The Catholic Child Welfare Society* [2010] EWCA Civ 1106, at [38].

[96] Until recently, the last defence of the 'master's tort' theory of vicarious liability could be found in Williams 1956a. Recent decisions have had no hesitation in (implicitly) rejecting this theory of vicarious liability: see *Dubai Aluminium Co Ltd* v *Salaam* [2003] 2 AC 366, at [155] (per Lord Millett): '[In a vicarious liability case] [t]he employer is not a wrongdoer; he is not liable in respect of his own conduct. He is answerable for his employee's wrongdoing, and his liability is coextensive with that of his employee. He is personally innocent, but he is liable because his employee is guilty.' To the same effect, see also *Majrowski* v *Guy's and St Thomas's NHS Trust* [2007] 1 AC 224, at [7] and [15] (per Lord Nicholls), and [68] (per Baroness Hale).

[97] Stevens 2007, 261.

physical world. When we refer to the conduct of a corporation, this is a form of shorthand for the acts of a corporation's human agents, usually its employees.[98]

But not all employers are corporations – so why should a living, breathing employer be fixed with any of the actions of his employees?

Secondly, we *already have* a set of rules for attributing actions to corporations. We discussed them above, in the chapter on 'Breach of duty'.[99] According to those rules, a corporation is normally only held to have done what those who represent its 'directing mind and will' have done. Given this, why would the law on vicarious liability supply us with a *second* set of rules for attributing actions to corporations, according to which a corporation is supposed to have done whatever *any* of its employees, however lowly and subordinate, have done so long as those employees were acting in the course of their employment?

Thirdly, the 'master's tort' theory of vicarious liability tells us *nothing* about *what* rules we should adopt for attributing an employee's actions to his employer. Given this, the 'master's tort' theory of vicarious liability gives us no basis for criticising or praising the decision to find vicarious liability in cases like *Lister* or *Maga* and the decision not to find vicarious liability in a case like *Jacobi v Griffiths*. All the 'master's tort' theory tells us that when vicarious liability is found, it is because the employee's actions were attributed to his employer; and when vicarious liability was not found, the employee's actions were not attributed to his employer. It tells us nothing about when we *should* attribute an employee's actions to his employer and when not.

Fourthly, the 'master's tort' theory of vicarious liability is inconsistent with a fairly basic fact about vicarious liability. An employer whose employee has punched someone else in the course of employment is *not* held liable for 'battery'. He is instead held liable on the basis that he is vicariously liable in respect of the *employee*'s battery.

The truth is that vicarious liability is a bit of a mystery: something without which hardly any tort cases would be brought to court, but the existence of which has no rational justification. It is an area of law that is desperately in need of reform and rationalisation.[100]

37.8 TWO FINAL POINTS

A couple of final points about the law on vicarious liability remain to be made:

A. Contribution and indemnity

Suppose that A has committed a tort and B is vicariously liable in respect of that tort. Suppose further that B is held liable to pay compensatory damages to the victim of A's tort. In such a case B will be entitled to bring a claim in contribution against A under the Civil Liability (Contribution) Act 1978 because they were both liable to make the compensation payment that B made. This will allow B to recover from A a 'just and equitable' *proportion* of the compensation payment that he made.

However, if the reason why B was vicariously liable in respect of A's tort was that A was her employee and he committed his tort in the course of his employment by B, then B will be entitled to bring a claim for breach of contract against A: he will have invariably

---

[98] Stevens 2007, 262 (emphasis in original).

[99] See above, § 8.6.

[100] Amazingly, the Law Commission – that cannot stop fiddling with certain areas of law, such as the criminal law – seems never to have thought it worth its while to have a look at the law on vicarious liability.

breached his contract of employment in committing his tort. If B does bring a claim for breach of contract against A, she will be allowed to sue A for damages equal to the *entire* amount of money that she had to pay out to the victim of A's tort: the entire amount will count as a loss that B has suffered as a result of A's breach of contract.

So – in *Lister* v *Romford Ice and Cold Storage Co Ltd* (1957), Lister, who was employed by the claimants as a lorry driver, drove his lorry into a slaughterhouse yard to pick up some waste. Lister's father accompanied him and got out of the lorry before Lister had parked it. In parking the lorry, Lister negligently knocked down and injured his father. Lister's father sued the claimants, claiming that they were vicariously liable in respect of his son's negligence, and recovered £1,600 from the claimants in compensatory damages. The claimants then sued Lister, claiming that he had breached his contract of employment when he negligently knocked down his father and that they were therefore entitled to sue him for damages equal to the £1,600 that they had to pay out to Lister's father as a result of Lister's negligence. The House of Lords allowed the claim, agreeing that Lister had breached his contract of employment in negligently knocking down his father: they found that there was an implied term in Lister's contract of employment with the claimants that he would perform his duties under his contract of employment with reasonable skill and care and that when Lister negligently knocked down his father he breached that implied term.

B. Vicarious liability for the acts of accessories

We have already noted that if A has committed a tort in relation to B, and C is an accessory to A's tort with the result that the courts will hold that A's tort was committed by both A *and* C, then it may be possible for *someone else* to be vicariously liable in respect of the tort that the courts will hold C has committed.[101] The decision of the House of Lords in *Credit Lyonnais* v *Export Credit Guarantee Department* (2000) emphasises that if, in this situation, C's employer is to be held vicariously liable for C's tort, then *all* of the actions that made C an accessory to A's tort have to have been committed in the course of C's employment.

In the *Credit Lyonnais* case, the claimants were defrauded of a substantial amount of money by one Mr Chong. The fraud worked like this. Chong forged some bills of exchange – promises to pay for goods received – and offered them for sale to the claimants. Obviously the claimants wanted some assurance that they would be paid under the bills of exchange before they bought them. This is where Chong's accomplice, a man called Mr Pillai, came in. Pillai was employed by the defendants, a government agency called the Export Credit Guarantees Department. Pillai – who knew very well that Chong's bills of exchange were forged – arranged for the defendants to guarantee that they would pay the claimants 90% of the value of the bills of exchange if they were not paid. Encouraged by this guarantee, the claimants paid Chong £10m for the bills of exchange. Chong then disappeared. The bills of exchange were worthless. So was the defendants' guarantee: it was conditional on the claimants' having taken reasonable steps to assure themselves that the bills of exchange were genuine, and the claimants had not done this. The claimants sued the defendants for damages, claiming that Pillai had committed a tort in acting as he did, and that the defendants were vicariously liable for that tort.

But what tort had Pillai committed? Pillai had not committed the tort of deceit through his own actions because the claimants had not been deceived by the defendants' guarantee.

---

[101] See above, § 37.1.

Chong *had* committed the tort of deceit in relation to the claimants. Was Pillai an accessory to Chong's deceit, so that it could be said that Chong's deceit was committed by both Chong *and* Pillai? The answer was 'yes' – Chong deceived the claimants as part of a common design agreed on between Pillai and Chong.[102] Unfortunately, when Pillai and Chong agreed on their scheme for defrauding the claimants, Pillai was not acting in the course of his employment by the defendants. The only thing Pillai did in the course of his employment was have the defendants issue their guarantees to the claimants. Pillai's doing this *did* help Chong defraud the claimants but, unfortunately for the claimants, merely helping someone commit a tort does not make you an accessory to that tort.[103] So Pillai had not done anything in the course of his employment that made him an accessory to Chong's tort. As a result, Pillai had not committed any tort in the course of his employment for which the defendants could be held vicariously liable.[104]

Further reading

The undoubted master of this area of law is **Paula Giliker**: see her **'Rough justice in an unjust world'** (2002) 65 *Modern Law Review* 269, **'Making the right connection: vicarious liability and institutional responsibility'** (2009) 17 *Torts Law Journal* 35, and **'Lister revisited: vicarious liability, distributive justice, and the course of employment'** (2010) 126 *Law Quarterly Review* 521. She has also written a monograph on *Vicarious Liability in Tort: A Comparative Perspective* (CUP, 2010).

Po Jen Yap's article **'Enlisting close connections: a matter of course for vicarious liability'** (2008) 28 *Legal Studies* 197 is also worth reading for an excellent summary of the law post-*Lister*.

The old 'master's tort' theory of vicarious liability is discussed in **Glanville Williams'** **'Vicarious liability: tort of the master or tort of the servant?'** (1956) 72 *Law Quarterly Review* 522 and wonderfully revived in **Robert Stevens'** *Torts and Rights* (OUP, 2007), chapter 11.

Visit **www.mylawchamber.co.uk/mcbride** to access tools to help you develop and test your knowledge of Tort law, including interactive multiple choice questions, practice exam questions with guidance, weblinks, legal newsfeed, additional case summaries, legal updates and tips on answering problem and essay questions.

premium **mylaw**chamber
unrivalled support for legal education

Use **Case Navigator** to read in full some of the key cases referenced in this chapter with commentary and questions:

- Lister *v* Hesley Hall Ltd

POWERED BY LexisNexis

---

[102] For this ground of accessory liability, see above, § 36.2.
[103] See above, § 36.3.
[104] An argument that there is a tort of 'assisting someone to commit a tort' which Pillai committed in the course of his employment by the defendants was rejected by the House of Lords: see above, § 24.3.

38 Loss compensation schemes

38.1 The basics *893*

38.2 Features of loss compensation schemes *893*

38.3 Four loss compensation schemes *895*

38.4 Evaluation of loss compensation schemes *899*

Overview

In this chapter, we leave the rules and principles of tort law behind and look at some loss compensation schemes which might (in our view, wrongly) be argued to perform tort law's functions better than it can. Section 38.2 provides an overview of the different features that a loss compensation scheme might have. Section 38.3 looks in detail at four actual loss compensation schemes. Section 38.4 is intended to help the reader form some views about whether such schemes should be implemented, either alongside tort law, or as a substitute for it.

38.1 THE BASICS

Although we are not inclined to think of tort law purely as a scheme for getting compensation to those who deserve it, there are many people who do. Such people ask whether tort law might be better replaced with an *alternative* loss compensation scheme. This chapter is intended to help with such discussions, by setting out a variety of different possible loss compensation schemes and discussing their merits and demerits.

38.2 FEATURES OF LOSS COMPENSATION SCHEMES

The dominant model for a loss compensation scheme involves the State compelling contributions to a fund, with the fund then paying compensation to a defined range of claimants. A variety of schemes can be based on this simple model, but there are five principal variables.

(1) *Conditions for entitlement.* There are a range of options as to the conditions for entitlement to claim against the fund. A common feature of all schemes is that the claimant's ability to prove that a particular defendant was at fault is *not* a condition for entitlement. Thus such schemes are often referred to as *no-fault compensation schemes.* But beyond this common feature there are many possibilities. An ambitious *general* scheme might attempt to assist all victims of serious adverse events, including illness, a less ambitious *general* scheme might attempt to assist all victims of *accidents,* and a sector-limited scheme might attempt to assist only victims of a particular type of accident or adverse event, eg road accidents or adverse events during medical treatment. Schemes might be further refined by making particular categories of people ineligible, eg victims of self-inflicted injury or drivers who were drunk when injured.

(2) *Contributors and their contributions.* There is a range of options as to who is compelled to contribute to the fund and in what proportions. For instance, a State could seek to compel

contributions by risk creators in proportion to the risks that they create, or it could seek to compel contributions from potential claimants in proportion to the potential benefits that they might claim, or it could add the cost to the burden of general taxation, or it could adopt some combination of these approaches.

(3) *Levels of compensation*. There is scope for defining the level of compensation to be paid by the fund. Some schemes involve the payment of compensation at a level equivalent to what would be awarded in a successful tort claim, while others award more limited payments (eg only 80% of lost earnings). Some more complicated schemes, particularly those which involve contributions from potential claimants, allow contributors to select their own possible level of compensation when their contributions are calculated.[1]

(4) *Relationship to tort claims*. A fourth variable is the relationship between the scheme and tort claims. In some jurisdictions where a loss compensation scheme has been set up it operates parallel to tort law[2] while in others tort law has been abolished for incidents falling within the scope of the scheme. A more complicated option involves the scheme as the exclusive way of dealing with minor injuries, but the scheme being supplemented by the possibility of tort claims for more serious injuries.[3]

(5) *Who administers the fund*. The fifth and final variable is the question of who administers the fund. Although such funds are usually created by statute[4] they can be operated either by a public body or by private organisations such as insurance companies. More complicated possibilities are also sometimes used. For instance, where contributions are paid by potential injurers (for instance, employers) to a scheme which will cover possible injuries to a fixed class (for instance, their employees) it is possible that a public body will operate the scheme for small employers and large employers can choose to opt out, and take full responsibility themselves for providing benefits equivalent to those under the scheme.[5]

Clearly when it comes to designing or evaluating a scheme these five variables cannot be considered in isolation. For instance, the wider the scope of entitlement to claim, and in particular the further that the entitled group extends beyond the range of those who might be able to claim in tort, the greater the pressure to cap the level of payments and the greater the pressure to raise some proportion of the contributions from the potential beneficiaries. As a second example, it is where the entitled group is limited to the victims of a particular type of accident that it may be most practical to compel contributions from risk creators, to quantify awards in line with tort, and to abolish tort claims.

---

[1] A greater contribution is demanded in exchange for the promise of a higher level of compensation.

[2] Where a loss compensation scheme operates parallel to tort law it will be necessary to define the relationship between the two types of claims. One possibility would be to reduce the tort claim by any amount recovered under the scheme. But an alternative would not reduce the tort claim but would instead allow the operators of the scheme to recoup any tort damages paid to compensate for loss that the scheme had already compensated. The Criminal Injuries Compensation Scheme, which pays compensation to those suffering personal injuries as a result of being a victim of crime, or seeking to prevent a crime or apprehend a criminal, is an example of a scheme which is supplementary to tort law. Such victims are entitled to sue the perpetrators in tort if such a course is likely to be worthwhile.

[3] For an example of a scheme like this see the discussion below of road traffic accident schemes in use in some American states.

[4] Of course operators of activities may also set up contractual insurance pools as a supplement to tort rights. Many climbing gyms, for instance, require users to purchase insurance which will cover all accidents and mishaps.

[5] A variation on this model is used in New Zealand.

The interrelationship of the five factors set out above may become clearer by considering some specific schemes.

38.3 FOUR LOSS COMPENSATION SCHEMES

A. The New Zealand Accident Compensation Scheme

This came into operation on 1 April 1974, and has been regularly amended since then. The 1974 scheme covered all personal injuries suffered in accidents and tort law claims were abolished for injuries falling within it.[6] Contributions were raised from three groups: employers paid a levy on wages (and the self-employed made similar payments) to cover the costs of injuries to earners (other than in road accidents); owners of motor vehicles paid a levy to cover the costs of injuries in road accidents; and the government funded the costs of injuries to non-earners, such as students, the unemployed, the retired and visitors from abroad. The level of compensation was reasonably close to tort law. The scheme covered a victim's medical expenses, 80% of their loss of earnings after the first week, and also provided a lump sum for pain, suffering and loss of amenity.

One criticism of the 1974 scheme was that it was unfair to make employers pay contributions to cover the cost of all accidental injuries suffered by their employees, including those not associated with work. A second criticism was that it was unfair not to distinguish between employers with good and bad safety records when setting contribution levels. A third criticism was that it was unfair to treat the victims of accidents more generously than victims of illness and those born disabled.

The scheme has been amended to respond to the first and second criticisms. Thus employees now pay a special contribution towards the cost of non-work injuries which is collected from them by the Inland Revenue and the levy on employers takes into account how many claims have been made by their employees in the previous three years.[7] The third criticism has proved more difficult to meet, however, and the only significant move in that direction has been the extension of the scheme to cover injuries caused by medical 'treatment injuries'.[8]

Some other significant changes to the scheme have also been tried but then reversed. Thus at one stage lump sum payments were abolished and replaced by 'independence allowances'. This, however, has now been reversed, and other attempts are being made to encourage rehabilitation. A second experiment was 'privatisation' of the scheme by allowing private insurance companies to compete to provide scheme-style cover to employers. This, however, has also been reversed and the scheme is once again administered by the Accident Compensation Corporation,[9] a Crown entity.

---

[6] Claims for exemplary damages can still be brought.

[7] The regulations introducing 'experience rating' came into force on 1 April 2011. For large employers they operate by comparing the employers' claims record with other employers in the same industry, or similar industries: employers with better-than-average records receive a discount on their levy for the next year, and employers with worse-than-average records pay an additional percentage.

[8] 'Treatment injuries' are adverse medical events causally linked to treatment (including non-treatment and diagnosis) by a registered health professional, as opposed to adverse events which are a necessary part or ordinary consequence of treatment. Thus injury caused by an allergic reaction to a medicine will be covered, but an ordinary side effect will not be. For assessment see Oliphant 2007.

[9] Details of the history and operation of the New Zealand scheme can be found at http://www.acc.co.nz/.

B. Road traffic accident schemes in use in some American states[10]

It is often argued that there are strong reasons for introducing a limited scheme covering personal injuries suffered in road accidents because: (i) drivers are already used to paying for insurance which covers the cost of some[11] such personal injuries; (ii) the class of people who create the risk of road accidents and might be expected to pay for them (that is, drivers) are also by-and-large those who might make most claims from a compensation scheme;[12] but (iii) it is costly and slow to sort out road accidents through the tort system, and (iv) there are significant classes of victims who excite sympathy but are left uncompensated by tort (for example, children who unpredictably run into the road). Given these factors any scheme which will cost drivers no more than current insurance premiums while offering a better protection for victims could gain popular support.

The model scheme which is most common in the United States involves contributions from road users and is administered by private insurance companies. Under the scheme all victims of road accidents are entitled to compensation even if they cannot prove that another driver was at fault, but in exchange for this wider-than-tort scope of entitlement the level of compensation is reduced to below the tort level for victims of *minor* accidents. Usually tort claims are abolished for minor accidents. Private insurance companies sell membership of these schemes and pay out benefits, and treat them alongside other insurance policies.[13] Thus drivers pay to their insurers amounts covering the risk that they will be injured in a road accident (and the risk that they will injure a person who is not a driver and will consequently not have a policy of his own), while claims are made by injured drivers against their insurers, and by injured non-drivers against the insurers of the driver who injured them.

Three arguments are commonly raised against such schemes. The first objection is that it seems unfair that where a victim was undoubtedly injured by the negligence of another the scheme leaves her with less compensation than tort law would have provided. This first objection is often augmented by the fact that when it is a driver who was undoubtedly injured by the negligence of another then the scheme adds insult to injury by making the innocent victim claim on her own policy (perhaps forfeiting a no-claims bonus).

The first objection is partially met by preserving the possibility of a tort claim if the injury suffered goes above a certain level of seriousness. This means that no victim suffering a *serious* injury will be left significantly worse off by the scheme. Unfortunately, however, the use of seriousness hurdles, especially if seriousness is measured by the cost of medical treatment, creates an incentive for fraud, in the form of exaggerated medical bills.[14]

---

[10] We concentrate on American schemes because they are well established and have been carefully studied. Similar schemes are also in place, however, in several Canadian provinces, Australian states, and European countries, eg France.

[11] Not all. Currently it is not compulsory in England and Wales for a driver to insure against injury to *himself* or *herself*, though it is compulsory to insure against the possibility of *negligently* injuring a *third party*. Nonetheless, many drivers purchase insurance against injury to themselves.

[12] To spell this out the risk of road accidents is created by drivers and people injured in road accidents are generally also drivers (even though they may be travelling as passengers or be pedestrians at the time when they are injured).

[13] Indeed, often insurers sell to drivers a 'package' which includes (1) scheme membership, which is often called 'personal injury protection' (PIP); (2) liability insurance, covering the risk of being held liable in tort for causing personal injuries not covered by the scheme; and (3) insurance covering property damage, which is usually outside the scheme.

[14] After Massachusetts raised its tort threshold from $500 to $2,000 in 1988, the median number of treatment visits rose from 13 to 30 per auto injury claim: Marter and Weisberg 1992, 488.

The second objection is that drivers who drive badly, and know that this is the case, will still be able to claim compensation for their own injuries if they cause an accident and will not have to pay damages to other motorists, except those suffering serious injuries. Given this, the incentive to drive carefully may be reduced, and accident rates may rise. Studies trying to determine whether the introduction of no-fault schemes has led to an increase in accident rates have yielded mixed results, and are discussed in the final section of this chapter.

The third objection is that experience has shown that what motorists must pay in no-fault states is not always less than what they would have to pay in states that kept ordinary tort law. Thus the authors of a major study in 2010 reported that:

> between the 1980s and 2006, both average liability premiums and premium growth were higher in no-fault states than other states, particularly tort states. These differences persist after adjusting for property-damage costs to account for variation in general inflation and accident prevalence across states. We also found that states that repealed no-fault laws saw substantial drops in liability premiums. Taken together, these facts indicate that no-fault has been a more expensive auto-insurance system.[15]

The reasons why no-fault schemes have proved more expensive than their designers expected are not wholly clear. The authors of the same study conclude that no-fault schemes do not lead to more accidents, nor make injured people more willing to claim, but instead lead to claimants seeking a greater amount on average being for medical expenses.[16]

Currently, 12 American states have no-fault road accident schemes.[17] All of these allow tort claims to be brought if the victim's injury exceeds a particular threshold of severity, with seven expressing that threshold in terms of the medical bills ($2,000 in Massachusetts, $4,000 in Minnesota) and five using a phrase such as 'serious injury' (New York) or 'significant and permanent loss of an important bodily function' (Florida). Usually such a threshold is sufficient to keep most claims out of tort law.[18] When the claim is below the threshold then the schemes differ as to the level of compensation provided. In New York, for instance, the scheme covers up to $50,000 in total by way of hospital and medical expenses and 80% of lost wages up to a maximum of $2,000 per month for a period not exceeding three years. In Florida, by contrast, the scheme covers only 80% of hospital and medical expenses up to a maximum of $10,000. Moreover, it is only if any of the $10,000 is left that a claim can be made for loss of earnings, and then only for 60%. Michigan is the only state which has extended its no-fault scheme beyond personal injuries: it also covers up to $1 million of damage to the property of others, with the exception of moving or improperly-parked cars.

C. Vaccine damage schemes

Many vaccines that are routinely administered have a small risk of very serious adverse consequences. The Vaccine Damage Payments Act 1979 set up a scheme under which

---

[15] Anderson, Heaton and Carroll 2010, at 76.

[16] ibid, 131–2.

[17] As of July 2011. In nine of these states the no-fault scheme is mandatory, while in three a driver can choose whether to participate in the no-fault scheme (in which case her insurance premium will be lower) or to keep full tort rights. At the peak of the popularity of no-fault road schemes during the late 1970s, 16 states had some form of no-fault scheme.

[18] Estimated to be kept out of tort law in 1997, 58% of claims in Kentucky, 70% in Colorado, 78% in New York and 66% in Florida: Insurance Research Council 1999.

people who have been left severely disabled[19] by vaccination are awarded a lump sum, currently £120,000. This is clearly far less than such a child might expect to be awarded if the disability was caused by a tort, but an award does not preclude a tort claim. The scheme is funded by the state from general revenue and administered by the Department for Work and Pensions. The justification for such a scheme was explained by the Pearson Commission: 'There is a special case for paying compensation for vaccine damage where vaccination is recommended by a public authority and is undertaken to protect the community.'[20]

The United Kingdom scheme is far less generous than the scheme operating in the United States. In the United States, the National Childhood Vaccine Injury Act of 1986 established a Federal *no-fault* scheme to compensate those injured by certain listed childhood vaccines, whether administered in the private or public sector. Awards under the scheme are substantial, covering medical and rehabilitative expenses, and in certain cases, pain and suffering and future lost earnings.[21] Eligibility and appropriate compensation are decided by the US Federal Court of Claims[22] but legal fees are covered provided that there was a reasonable basis for the claim and it was made in good faith, and many hearings are simplified by the statutory presumption that the victim is eligible if he suffered an 'adverse event' appearing in the 'Vaccine Injury Table'.[23] The scheme is funded by an excise tax of 75 cents on each dose of covered vaccine. One of the reasons why a generous scheme exists is that before its creation tort claims led to vaccine prices soaring and several manufacturers halted production. A vaccine shortage resulted and public health officials became concerned about the return of epidemic disease. The statute requires victims to file claims for compensation under the *no-fault* scheme before commencing tort litigation, and if a claimant accepts an award under the scheme he is precluded from pursuing a tort claim.

D. Professor Atiyah's first-party insurance scheme

Patrick Atiyah has suggested that 'the personal injury tort system should be abolished, but *not* replaced by a universal state compensation system. Instead, we should be willing to leave its replacement largely to the operation of the free market.'[24] He predicted that many people would choose to go into the market to buy insurance covering themselves against income lost as a result of non-trivial accidents (regardless of who, if anyone, was at fault) but usually would not buy coverage for pain and suffering or medical costs. Moreover, such people would consider carefully how far they needed protection for loss of income.[25] Perhaps the government would have to intervene to compel people to buy at least a minimum level of coverage against common types of serious accidents, such as road accidents, but in other spheres of life, for instance the workplace, institutions such as unions might arrange convenient mass cover.

---

[19] This requires at least 60% disability: Vaccine Damage Payments Act 1979, s 1(4), as amended by the Regulatory Reform (Vaccine Damage Payments Act 1979) Order 2002 (SI 2002/1592). The sum of £120,000 was set by the Vaccine Damage Payments Act 1979 Statutory Sum Order 2007 (SI 2007/1931).

[20] Pearson 1978, para 1398.

[21] The average award is currently (January 2008) just over US $1 million (with a maximum of $250,000 in cases of death).

[22] At first instance by 'special masters' appointed by the Court.

[23] This lists particular 'adverse events' and 'time windows' for each vaccine covered by the scheme.

[24] Atiyah 1996, 35. See also Atiyah 1997, ch 8.

[25] For example, professional footballers might conclude that if they were injured in an accident they could 'get by' in future on less than £90,000 per week.

It is worth representing Atiyah's proposals in terms of the five factors which we have used when describing loss compensation schemes. Under Atiyah's proposals the contributions are paid by potential victims in proportion to the degree of risk that they face, and such potential victims choose for themselves what events they want to be covered against and what level of compensation they want should such events occur; these choices will be made at the time of buying a policy from a private insurance company and tort law will be abolished for personal injuries.

Many students' first reaction to Atiyah's proposals is that it is unfair to make potential victims pay for their own protection, and indeed many could not afford to do so. But it may be the case that the costs of liability policies (that is, of potential tort claims) are already passed on to potential victims in the form of higher prices for products and services, and that the cost of choosing a low level of general coverage under one of Atiyah's insurance policies will be *cheaper* than the total of all these passed-on costs.[26] Moreover, it is generally assumed that Atiyah's scheme would be cheaper to administer and claimants would get their payments more quickly.

This should not suggest, however, that we think that Atiyah's proposals should be accepted without further debate. At the very least we think that there are major practical issues to be thought through concerning the position of those who could not reasonably be expected to buy policies, such as children and the insane, and those who foolishly failed to buy any cover, or bought less cover than they later turned out to need. We also think that there are broader issues to be considered when evaluating loss compensation schemes which are intended to replace tort law, and these are considered in the next section.

38.4 EVALUATION OF LOSS COMPENSATION SCHEMES

In evaluating a particular scheme we recommend considering it from five perspectives.

First, the *fairness of the funding arrangements* should be considered. It is commonly argued that there are justifications for internalising the costs associated with particular risks to those that create the risks, and this could support a particular approach to funding. But other approaches might also be justified, for instance, by a person who believes that it is fair to redistribute resources from profit-making enterprises to potential victims of the industrial society.

Secondly, the *cost of administering the scheme* should be considered. This should include consideration of the costs of collecting contributions and of deciding whether claimants are entitled to claim. Clearly with a sector-limited scheme, such as one covering only the

---

[26] In particular, it may be cheaper for a low earner to buy an *Atiyah*-policy which offers him better coverage than to buy an ordinary *liability*-policy. For instance, imagine that the chance for all drivers of being involved in a serious collision with another car is 1 in 1,000 per year; and that the chance of that accident being caused by your own negligence is 40%, by the other driver's negligence 40%, and by nobody's negligence 20%. Imagine further, that in such accidents both drivers have to take one year off work. Now let us consider the position of A, who earns £10,000 per year, which is less than the £30,000 per year earned by the average driver. The cost of an *Atiyah*-policy for A will reflect his risk of being a victim, which is £10 ($1/1,000 \times £10,000$). The cost of a *liability*-policy for A will reflect his risk of negligently injuring another, which is £12 ($40\% \times 1/1,000 \times £30,000$). Of course, the average driver's *Atiyah*-policy will be more expensive (£30) than a *liability*-policy (£12), but that is because an *Atiyah*-policy will compensate him for his loss of earnings in 100% of accidents, while a liability-policy will only help him in 40% of accidents. Moreover, the example has been kept artificially simple by considering only loss of earnings. Currently a *liability*-policy also has to cover possible claims for pain and suffering and private medical care. If we added to the example the extra fact that all such accidents involve £20,000 of pain and suffering and £25,000 of medical bills then the average driver's earnings-only-*Atiyah*-policy would be the same price (£30) as his current *liability* policy (40% 3 1/1,000 3 £75,000).

victims of road accidents, there may be costs involved in determining which claims properly fall within the scheme and which do not.

Thirdly, the *fairness of the definition of those qualified to claim* should be considered. Here an important issue may be whether there is any sufficient reason for distinguishing between those qualified to claim and other people suffering similar injuries or disabilities who are not entitled to assistance from the fund.

Fourthly, the *effect of the scheme on accident rates* should be considered. Many defenders of tort law argue that it plays a role in reducing the number of accidents to an efficient minimum, or (to put the same point a different way) in deterring inefficient risk-creating behaviour.[27] Consequently, if a scheme is promoted with the intention that tort law is abolished it will be necessary for the scheme's supporters to explain whether they believe that the scheme will continue to provide such incentives (as might be the case if contributions to the scheme are truly proportionate to risk created), whether such incentives will be sufficiently provided by some other area of law (eg criminal law), or whether they believe that the beneficial effect of tort law on accident rates was always exaggerated and will not be much missed.

Fifthly, it must be considered whether *tort law performs any irreplaceable tasks* which a loss compensation scheme would not perform.

(1) *Fairness of the funding arrangements*. Some of the questions concerning the fairness of funding arrangements, such as whether it is fair to redistribute the cost of accidental injuries from the rich to the poor, require deeper analysis of competing models of justice than is appropriate in a tort book. That said, many of the proposals for schemes which have failed to attract support have been unpopular because their funding arrangements did not actually achieve what the proponents of the scheme thought that they would achieve. For instance, at one time advocates of road-accident schemes proposed that contributions should be funded by a levy on petrol, a so-called 'pay-at-the-pump' scheme.[28] These advocates thought that it would be fair for those who drove further to pay more since they would be likely to be involved in more accidents. In fact this was a false premise, since accident rates are more closely related to traffic density than to mileage,[29] and if the scheme had ever been put into practice it would have led to those driving long distances in rural areas subsidising the accident costs of those making short journeys in busy cities!

(2) *Cost of administration*. It has sometimes been suggested that the main problem with ambitious state-run schemes, such as the New Zealand scheme, is that they create massive bureaucracies which cost too much to operate. But, in fact, the bureaucracies that are created are many times less costly than the networks of professionals and officials who are required to operate the tort system. The real problem with ambitious state-run schemes is that the *total* cost of achieving their goals is high. Let us imagine (for the sake of argument) that the tort system compensates only 20% of accident victims, that the total

---

[27] This is not to say, of course, that tort liability exists *in order to* deter wrongful behaviour. Our intention here is merely to consider what effect a switch to a loss compensation scheme might have on incentives to behave reasonably.

[28] The Pearson Commission recommended a 'pay-at-the-pump' scheme (Pearson 1978, paras 1054, 1057) though this was intended as a supplement to tort law rather than an alternative.

[29] Though there are more fatalities per mile driven on rural roads, perhaps because of the speed of collisions and the distance to hospitals.

compensation bill is £n per year, and that the administration costs are a further 40% on top of the total compensation bill. Given these figures we can say that the tort system costs £1.4n per year. So what might an accident compensation scheme cost by comparison? Let us assume that such a scheme will compensate 90% of accident victims, will pay them each only 75% of what they would have received had they successfully sued in tort and will cost only 10% on top of the total compensation bill to administer. Such a compensation scheme requires £3.7n per year.[30] So it requires more than two-and-a-half times as much as the tort system in total despite the fact that it is paying less per claimant and is more efficient.

Some people find it baffling that a more efficient system which pays less per claimant ends up being more expensive. But the key to avoiding bafflement is to realise that the current tort system leaves such a high proportion of accident victims uncompensated.[31] Currently members of this large group obtain medical care through the NHS, but beyond that are left to struggle through life as best as they can with assistance from savings, family, friends, charities and the social security safety net. One major cost of an ambitious loss compensation scheme is that many in this group will now qualify for the far better benefit of an award at 75% of tort levels and such awards add up. Of course, a good case can be made for conferring such a benefit on this group. But the proposition, 'we should pay more tax to ensure better provision for those injured in accidents which they cannot demonstrate were caused by anyone else's fault' is not uncontroversial.

(3) *Fairness of qualification.* Those who have advocated loss compensation schemes have often relied on the argument that because claimants can only obtain remedies in tort law if they prove that the defendant's breach of a duty caused them compensatable damage, and because the breach and causation elements of such claims are often difficult to prove in practice, many claimants who were *in fact* victims of torts are *in practice* unable to obtain remedies. Thus some of the beneficiaries of loss compensation schemes are persons who *ought to have been* compensated in tort law.

It is usually impossible, however, to define those entitled to claim so as to include *only* persons who *ought to have been* compensated in tort law; any attempt to do so is likely to make it costly to determine whether any particular individual is entitled or not. Consequently, it is common to define the class of those entitled to claim in terms of the type of accident which *caused* their injuries, such as 'victims of road accidents' or 'victims of vaccine'. It is not easy to explain why accident victims generally, or victims of specific types of accidents, should be treated better than those who succumb to illness or who are born with disabilities. But, as the discussion under the previous sub-heading suggests, one of the major problems with compensation schemes has been their total cost. Consequently, any proposal to extend qualification far beyond accident victims would probably cost more than most governments would be willing to raise by way of taxation.[32]

---

[30] This figure is derived in the following way: If compensating 20% of victims at tort law levels costs £n, then compensating 90% of victims at 75% of tort law levels will cost £3.38n (n × 4.5 × 0.75). Add to that administration costs of 10% (£0.338n) and the total is £3.7n (£3.38n + £0.338n).

[31] Harris 1984 found (at 51) that tort damages were recovered by 19% of work accident victims, 29% of road accident victims, and 2% of victims of other accidents. Because accidents in the home make up such a high proportion of all accidents the overall figure was that 12% of accident victims obtain tort compensation.

[32] In 1989 the New Zealand government (Labour) announced that the compensation scheme would be extended to cover those incapacitated by sickness or disease, but the Labour Party lost the election in 1990 to the National Party and no such change was made when the scheme was reformed in 1992.

(4) *Effect on accident rates.* Some studies have suggested that no-fault road accident schemes lead to higher accident rates.[33] For instance, Cummins, Weiss and Phillips modelled the effect of road accident schemes in the United States and concluded that no-fault is associated with higher fatality rates than tort: two models yielded estimates of 12.8–13.8% and 7.2–7.5% higher than tort.[34] A subsequent empirical study by Cohen and Deheija estimated that no-fault led to a 10% increase in fatalities.[35] These effects seem severe, but are actually more moderate than McEwin's estimate of 16% higher fatalities in Australia and New Zealand.[36] By contrast Loughran concluded that his comparison of fatal accident, car damage and negligence rates in tort and no-fault states cast 'serious doubts on contentions that no-fault auto insurance as implemented in the United States has led to greater driver negligence and higher accident rates'.[37] Loughran pointed out that most people avoid driving negligently because they do not want to risk being injured, that if they thought that others were driving less safely they might alter their own behaviour so as to drive more safely, and that because most road accidents involve damage to cars and most no-fault schemes do not cover property damage tort law still provides some incentives. Likewise, a study by Heaton and Helland which used data relating to non-fatal accidents found 'little evidence that no-fault coverage is associated with more numerous accidents . . . Overall, our results suggest that the behavioral adjustments of drivers induced by no-fault, if any, are modest and affect accident severity more than accident incidence.'[38]

(5) *Effect on tort law's functions.* Does tort law perform any tasks that a loss compensation scheme cannot perform? It will be recalled that tort law is made up of two parts, each of which performs a different function. The duty-imposing part of tort law helps to determine what duties we owe each other; while the remedial part of tort law determines what remedies will be available when one of these duties is breached. Obviously no loss-compensation scheme could perform the first function – that of helping to determine what duties we owe each other. So if tort law were abolished outright in favour of a loss-compensation scheme, the task of determining what duties we owe each other would be shouldered by the criminal law and contract law. Whether this would be a good thing or a bad thing is too complex a question to be addressed in this book.

What of the remedial part of tort law? *As this part of tort law currently stands*, the remedial part of tort law performs a number of different tasks:

(a) Requiring wrongdoers to repair their wrongs by putting the victim of a tort in (roughly) the position he or she would have been in had that wrong not been committed.
(b) In a case where a tort has been committed in a particularly outrageous manner, satisfying the victim of a tort's perception that the person who committed that tort must be made to pay for the fact that he has ridden roughshod over the victim's rights.

---

[33] There is less evidence available as to the effect that schemes might have on accident rates in sectors other than road accidents. Rubin and Shepherd 2007, have suggested that several reforms aimed at *reducing* tort damages in the United States have led to a *reduction* in death rates. Their explanation for this effect is that many tort claims are directed at defendants who are in the business of reducing risks, for instance medical professionals and the producers of pharmaceuticals and safety devices, and reforms which reduce the exposure of such defendants to heavy liability bills may lead to their services and products becoming both cheaper and more widely available.
[34] Cummins, Weiss and Phillips 2001, 455.
[35] Cohen and Deheija 2004, 360, 382.
[36] McEwin 1989.
[37] Loughran 2001.
[38] Heaton and Helland 2008, 20.

(c) Giving the victim of a tort that is being committed on an ongoing basis the ability to bring that wrongdoing to an end by allowing him or her to obtain an injunction, requiring the person who is committing that tort to stop what he or she is doing.

The existence of a loss-compensation scheme would mean that the law no longer needed to give effect to perform function (a) in respect of losses covered by that loss-compensation scheme. The existence of the loss-compensation scheme would mean that there was nothing for a tortfeasor to repair, in so far as his tort had caused the victim of that tort to suffer a loss that is covered by a loss-compensation scheme. But a loss-compensation scheme cannot perform the other tasks that the remedial part of tort law currently performs. Given this, we would suggest that any proposal to abolish tort law *altogether* in favour of a loss-compensation scheme would be seriously defective. Before such a proposal could be countenanced, some other mechanism would need to be found to perform tasks (b) and (c), above.

Further reading

Patrick Atiyah's work has been tremendously influential in this area. **P.S. Atiyah, *The Damages Lottery* (Hart Publishing, 1997)** manages to be powerful, provocative, and easy to read. Peter Cane is now the author of ***Atiyah's Accidents, Compensation and the Law* (7th edn, Cambridge University Press, 2006)**, which continues to pose an important challenge to orthodox visions of tort law. **Don Dewees, David Duff and Michael Trebilcock, *Exploring the Domain of Accident Law – Taking the Facts Seriously* (Oxford University Press, 1996)** collects and analyses a vast amount of data about tort law and alternative schemes; it is an essential source for anyone who wants to consider what the benefits and pitfalls of replacing tort law with an alternative scheme might be. With respect to the automobile schemes that operate in some parts of the USA we particularly recommend **Gary Schwartz, 'Auto no-fault and first party insurance: advantages and problems' (2000) 73 *Southern California Law Review* 611.**

Visit **www.mylawchamber.co.uk/mcbride** to access tools to help you develop and test your knowledge of Tort law, including interactive multiple choice questions, practice exam questions with guidance, weblinks, legal newsfeed, additional case summaries, legal updates and tips on answering problem and essay questions.

premium
mylawchamber
unrivalled support for legal education

Bibliography

Abel, R. 1994. 'A critique of torts' *Tort Law Review* 2:99.

Abraham, K.S. 2003. '*Rylands* v *Fletcher*: tort law's conscience' in Rabin and Sugarman 2003, 207–28.

Allen, C.K. 1931. *Legal Duties and Other Essays in Jurisprudence*. Clarendon Press.

Allen, J. 2009. 'Variable standards of care in negligence' *Tort Law Review* 17:5.

Ames, J.B. 1908. 'Law and morals' *Harvard Law Review* 22:97.

Andenas, M. and Fairgrieve, D. 2000. eds. *Judicial Review in International Perspective: II*. Kluwer Law International.

Anderson, J.M., Heaton, P. and Caroll, S.J. 2010. *The US Experience With No-Fault Automobile Insurance: A Retrospective*. RAND Institure for Civil Justice.

Arden, M. 2010. 'Human rights and civil wrongs: tort law under the spotlight' *Public Law* [2010]:140.

Armour, J. 1999. 'Corporate personality and asssumption of responsibility' *Lloyd's Maritime and Commercial Law Quarterly* [1999]:246.

Aronson, M. 2011. 'Misfeasance in public office: a very peculiar tort' *Melbourne University Law Review* 35.

Atiyah, P.S. 1967. *Vicarious Liability in the Law of Torts*. Butterworths.

——. 1996. 'Personal injuries in the twenty-first century: thinking the unthinkable' in Birks 1996b, 1–46.

——. 1997. *The Damages Lottery*. Hart Publishing.

Bagshaw, R. 1998. 'Can the economic torts be unified?' *Oxford Journal of Legal Studies* 18:729.

——. 1999. 'The duties of care of emergency service providers' *Lloyd's Maritime and Commercial Law Quarterly* [1999]:71.

——. 2000. 'Inducing breach of contract' in Horder 2000, 131–50.

——. 2001. 'Children through tort' in Fionda 2001, 127–50.

——. 2004a. 'Private nuisance and the defence of the realm' *Law Quarterly Review* 120:37.

——. 2004b. 'Rylands confined' *Law Quarterly Review* 120:388.

——. 2004c. 'Children as actionable damage' *King's College Law Journal* 15:117.

——. 2009a. 'Negligently making business activities illegal: *Jain* v *Trent Strategic Health Authority*' *Torts Law Journal* 17:295.

——. 2009b. 'Tort law, concepts and what really matters' in Robertson and Tang 2009, 239–260.

——. 2011a. 'Causing the behaviour of others and other causal mixtures' in Goldberg 2011.

——. 2011b. 'The edges of tort law's rights' in Nolan and Robertson 2011, 405–32.

Bailey, S.H. 2010. 'Causation in negligence: what is a material contribution?' *Legal Studies* 30:167.

Bailey, S.H. and Bowman, M.J. 2000. 'Public authority negligence revisited' *Cambridge Law Journal* 59:85.

Bailey, S.H. and Nolan, D. 2010. 'The *Page* v *Smith* saga' *Cambridge Law Journal* 69:495.

Baker, T. 2005. 'Liability insurance as tort regulation: six ways that liability insurance shapes tort law in action' *Connecticut Insurance Law Journal* 12:1.

Barendt, E. 1993. 'Libel and freedom of speech in English law' *Public Law* [1993]:449.

——. 1999. 'What is the point of libel law?' *Current Legal Problems* [1999]:110.

Barker, K. 1993. 'Unreliable assumptions in the law of negligence' *Law Quarterly Review* 109:461.

——. 'Economic loss and the duty of care: a study in the exercise of legal justification' in Rickett 2008, 175–203.

Bartle, R. 2004. 'Virtual worldliness: what the imaginary asks of the real' *New York School Law Review* 49:19.

Baty, T. 1916. *Vicarious Liability*. Clarendon Press.

Beever, A. 2003a. 'The structure of aggravated and exemplary damages' *Oxford Journal of Legal Studies* 23:87.

——. 2003b. 'Particularism and prejudice in the law of tort' *Tort Law Review* 11:146.

——. 2004. 'A rights-based approach to the recovery of economic loss in negligence' *Oxford University Commonwealth Law Journal* 4:25.

——. 2007. *Rediscovering the Law of Negligence.* Hart Publishing.

——. 2008. 'Justice and punishment in tort: a comparative theoretical analysis' in Rickett 2008, 249–298.

——. 2009. 'Transferred malice in tort law?' *Legal Studies* 29:400.

Beitz, C. 2009. *The Idea of Human Rights.* Oxford University Press.

Benson, P. 1995. 'The basis for excluding liability for economic loss in tort law' in Owen 1995, 427–58.

Berkowitz, R. 2010. *The Gift of Science: Leibniz and the Modern Legal Tradition.* Fordham University Press.

Bingham, Lord. 2010. 'The uses of tort' *Journal of European Tort Law* 1:3.

Birks, P.B.H. 1983. 'Obligations: one tier or two?' in Stein and Lewis 1983, 18–38.

——. 1989. *Introduction to the Law of Restitution,* revised edn. Clarendon Press.

——. 1994. ed. *The Frontiers of Liability: Volume 2.* Oxford University Press.

——. 1995. 'The concept of a civil wrong' in Owen 1995, 31–51.

——. 1996a. *Harassment and Hubris: The Right to an Equality of Respect.* University College, Dublin.

——. 1996b. ed. *Wrongs and Remedies in the 21st Century.* Clarendon Press, Oxford.

——. 1997a. 'Definition and division: a meditation on Institutes 3.13' in Birks 1997b, 1–35.

——. 1997b. ed. *The Classification of Obligations.* Clarendon Press.

——. 1997c. ed. *Privacy and Loyalty.* Clarendon Press.

——. 2000a. 'Personal property: proprietary rights and remedies' *King's College Law Journal* 11:1.

——. 2000b. 'Rights, wrongs and remedies' *Oxford Journal of Legal Studies* 20:1.

Bishop, P. and Jenkins, V. 2011. 'Planning and nuisance: revisiting the balance of public and private interests in land-use development' *Journal of Environmental Law* [2011]:285.

Bitensky, S. 1998. 'Spare the rod, embrace our humanity: towards a new legal regime prohibiting corporal punishment of children' *University of Michigan Journal of Law Reform* 31:353.

Bjorge, E. 2011. 'Torture and "ticking bomb" scenarios' *Law Quarterly Review* 127:196.

Bloustein, E. 1964. 'Privacy as an aspect of human dignity: an answer to Dean Prosser' *New York University Law Review* 39:962.

Bohlen, C. 1926. 'Incomplete privilege to inflict intentional invasions of property and personality' *Harvard Law Review* 39:307.

Bowman, M.J. and Bailey, S.H. 1984. 'Negligence in the realm of public law – a positive obligation to rescue?' *Public Law* [1984]:277.

Bright, S. 2000. 'The third party's conscience in land law' *Conveyancer and Property Lawyer* 64:398.

——. 2001. 'Liability for the bad behaviour of others' *Oxford Journal of Legal Studies* 21:311.

Brodie, D. 2010. *Enterprise Liability and the Common Law.* Cambridge University Press.

Brooke-Smith, B.J. 1954. 'Liability for the negligence of another' *Law Quarterly Review* 70:253.

Buckland, W. 1935. 'The duty to take care' *Law Quarterly Review* 51:637.

Burrows, A. 1996. 'Reforming exemplary damages' in Birks 1996b, 153–74.

——. 2004. *Remedies in Contract and Tort,* 3rd edn. Oxford University Press.

——. 2011. *The Law of Restitution,* 3rd edn. Oxford University Press.

Burrows, A. and Peel, E. 2003. eds. *Commercial Remedies: Current Issues and Problems.* Oxford University Press.

Burrows, A. and Rodger, Lord 2006. eds. *Mapping the Law: Essays in Memory of Peter Birks.* Oxford University Press.

Butler, D. 2002. 'An assessment of competing policy considerations in cases of psychiatric injury resulting from negligence' *Torts Law Journal* 10:13.

Butler, R. 2003. 'SAAMCO in practice' in Burrows and Peel 2003, 71–90.

Butler, S. 2006. ed. *Discovering the Law.* Law Matters Publishing.

Calabresi, G. 1970. *The Cost of Accidents*. Yale University Press.

Calabresi, G. and Melamed, D. 1972. 'Property rules, liability rules and inalienability: one view of the cathedral' *Harvard Law Review* 85:1089.

Calnan, A. 2005. 'In defense of the liberal justice theory of torts: a reply to Professors Goldberg and Zipursky' *New York University Journal of Law & Liberty* 1:1023.

Cane, P. 1982. 'Justice and justifications for tort liability' *Oxford Journal of Legal Studies* 2:30.

———. 1996. *Tort Law and Economic Interests*, 2nd edn. Clarendon Press, Oxford.

———. 1998. 'Retribution, proportionality and moral luck in tort law' in Cane and Stapleton 1998, 141–74.

———. 1999. 'Fault and strict liability for harm in tort law' in Swadling and Jones 1999, 171–206.

———. 2000a. 'Vicarious liability for sexual abuse' *Law Quarterly Review* 116:21.

———. 2000b. 'Consequences in judicial reasoning' in Horder 2000, 41–59.

———. 2001a. 'The temporal element in law' *Law Quarterly Review* 117:5.

———. 2001b. 'Distributive justice and tort law' *New Zealand Law Review* 4:401.

———. 2002. *Responsibility in Law and Morality*. Hart Publishing.

———. 2004. 'The doctor, the stork and the court: a modern morality tale' *Law Quarterly Review* 120:23.

———. 2006. *Atiyah's Accidents, Compensation and the Law*, 7th edn. Cambridge University Press.

Cane, P. and Gardner, J. 2001. eds. *Relating to Responsibility*. Hart Publishing.

Cane, P. and Stapleton, J. 1998. eds. *The Law of Obligations: Essays in Honour of John Fleming*. Oxford University Press.

Cane, P. and Tushnet, M. 2003. eds. *The Oxford Handbook of Legal Studies*. Oxford University Press.

Carty, H. 1999. 'Joint tortfeasance and assistance liability' *Legal Studies* 19:489.

———. 2010. *An Analysis of the Economic Torts*. 2nd edn. Oxford University Press.

Case, P. 2010. 'Now you see it, now you don't: black letter reflections on the legacies of *White* v *Chief Constable of South Yorkshire Police*' *Tort Law Review* 18:33.

Chambers, R., Mitchell, C. and Penner, J. 2009. *Philosophical Foundations of the Law of Unjust Enrichment*. Oxford University Press.

Clarkson, C.M.V., Keating, H.M. and Cunningham, S.R. 2010. *Clarkson and Keating's Criminal Law: Text and Materials*. 7th edn. Sweet & Maxwell.

Coad, J. 2007. '*Reynolds* and public interest – what about truth and human rights?' *Entertainment Law Review* 18:75.

———. 2011. '*Reynolds, Flood* and the King's new clothes' *Entertainment Law Review* 22:1.

Coase, R. 1960. 'The problem of social cost' *Journal of Law and Economics* 3:1.

Cohen, A. and Dehejia, R. 2004. 'The effect of automobile insurance and accident liability laws on traffic fatalities' *The Journal of Law and Economics* 47:357.

Coleman, J. 1993. *Risks and Wrongs*. Cambridge University Press.

———. 2001. *The Practice of Principle*. Clarendon Press, Oxford.

Coleman, J. and Shapiro, S. 2002. eds. *The Oxford Handbook of Jurisprudence and Philosophy of Law*. Oxford University Press.

Compton, B. and Hand, J. 2009. 'The Animals Act 1971 – where are we now?' *Journal of Personal Injury Law* [2009]:1.

Conaghan, J. and Mansell, W. 1999. *The Wrongs of Tort*, 2nd edn. Pluto Press.

Cooke, E. 1994. 'Trespass, mesne profits and restitution' *Law Quarterly Review* 110:420.

Cooke, Lord. 1991. 'An impossible distinction' *Law Quarterly Review* 107:46.

———. 1998. 'The right of Spring' in Cane and Stapleton 1998, 37–57.

Cornford, T. 2008. *Towards a Public Law of Tort*. Ashgate Publishing.

Craig, P. 2002. 'Contracting out, the Human Rights Act and the scope of judicial review' *Law Quarterly Review* 118:551.

Cross, G. 1995. 'Does only the careless polluter pay? A fresh examination of the nature of private nuisance' *Law Quarterly Review* 111:445.

Cummins, J.D., Weiss, D. and Phillips, M. 2001. 'The incentive effects of no-fault automobile insurance' *Journal of Law and Economics* 44:427.

Dagan, H. 1997. *Unjust Enrichment: A Study of Private Law and Public Values*. Cambridge University Press.

Dalphond, P. 2002. 'Duty of care and the supply of alcohol' *Supreme Court Law Review (2d)* 17:97.

Davidson, N. 2006. 'The law of black holes?' *Professional Negligence* 22:54.

Davies, P.S. 2009. 'The illegality defence and public policy' *Law Quarterly Review* 125:556.

——. 2011. 'Accessory liability for assisting torts' *Cambridge Law Journal* 70:353.

Davis, J.L.R. 1998. 'Farewell to the action for breach of statutory duty?' in Mullany and Linden 1998, 69–83.

——. 2000. 'Liability for careless acts or omissions causing purely economic loss: *Perre v Apand Pty Ltd*' *Torts Law Journal* 8:123.

Deakin, S. and Randall, J. 2009. 'Rethinking the economic torts' *Modern Law Review* 72:519.

Degeling, S. 2003. *Restitutionary Rights to Share in Damages: Carers' Claims*. Cambridge University Press.

Degeling, S., Edelman, J. and Goudkamp, J. 2011. *Torts in Commercial Law*. Thomson Reuters.

Depoorter, B. 2011. 'Fair trespass' *Columbia Law Review* 111:1090.

Descheemaeker, E. 2011. ' "Veritas non est defamatio"? Truth as a defence in the law of defamation' *Legal Studies* 31:1.

Dewees, D., Duff, D. and Trebilcock, M. 1996. *Exploring the Domain of Accident Law – Taking the Facts Seriously*. Oxford University Press.

Dietrich, J. 2000. 'Lawful coercive threats and the infliction of harm' *Torts Law Journal* 8:187.

——. 2011. 'Accessorial liability in the law of torts' *Legal Studies* 31:231.

Donnelly, C. 2007. *Delegation of Governmental Power to Private Parties: A Comparative Perspective*. Oxford University Press.

Douglas, S. 2009. 'The nature of conversion' *Cambridge Law Journal* 68:198.

——. 2011. 'Re-examing trespass', unpublished manuscript on file with the authors.

D'Souza, D. 2002. *Letters to a Young Conservative*. Basic Books.

Duff, D. and Trebilcock, M. 1996. *Exploring the Domain of Accident Law – Taking the Facts Seriously*. Oxford University Press.

Duff, R.A. and Marshall, S.E. 2006. 'How offensive can you get?' in Von Hirsch and Simester 2006, 57–90.

Dugdale, T. 2000. 'The impact of SAAMCO' *Professional Negligence* 16:203.

Duncan Wallace, I. 2000. '*Donoghue v Stevenson* and "complex structures": *Anns* revisited?' *Law Quarterly Review* 116:530.

Dworkin, R. 1977. *Taking Rights Seriously*. Duckworth.

——. 1986. *Law's Empire*. Fontana Publishing.

Dziobon, S. and Tettenborn, A. 1997. 'When the truth hurts: the incompetent transmission of distressing news' *Professional Negligence* 13:70.

Economides, K. 2000. et al. eds. *Fundamental Values*. Hart Publishing.

Edelman, J. 2002a. 'Equitable torts' *Torts Law Journal* 10:64.

——. 2002b. *Gain-Based Damages*. Hart Publishing.

——. 2006. 'Gain-based damages and compensation' in Burrows and Rodger 2006, 141–60.

——. 2008. 'In defence of exemplary damages' in Rickett 2008, 225–48.

——. 2009. 'The meaning of loss and enrichment' in Chambers, Mitchell and Penner 2009, 211–41.

Eekelaar, J. 2003. 'Corporal punishment, parent's religion and children's rights' *Law Quarterly Review* 119:370.

Ellis, E. and McGivern, B. 2007. 'The wrongfulness or rightfulness of actions for wrongful life' *Tort Law Review* 15:135.

Elvin, J. 2003a. 'Liability for negligent refereeing of a rugby match' *Law Quarterly Review* 119:560.

——. 2003b. 'The duty of schools to prevent bullying' *Tort Law Review* 11:168.

Epstein, R.A. 1973. 'A theory of strict liability' *Journal of Legal Studies* 2:151.

——. 2010. 'Towards a general theory of tort law: strict liability in context' *Journal of Tort Law* 3:Article 6.

Evans, H. 2001. 'The scope of the duty revisited' *Professional Negligence* 17:147.

Fairgrieve, D. 2001. 'The Human Rights Act 1998, damages and tort law' *Public Law* [2001]:695.

——. 2005. ed. *Product Liability in Comparative Perspective*. Cambridge University Press.

Fairgrieve, D. and Howells, G. 2007. 'Rethinking product liability: a missing element in the European Commission's third review of the

Product Liability Directive' *Modern Law Review* 70:962.

Fairgrieve, D., Adenas, M. and Bell, J. 2002. eds. *Tort Liability of Public Authorities in Comparative Perspective*. BIICL.

Farnsworth, W. 1999. 'Do parties to nuisance cases bargain after judgment? A glimpse inside the cathedral' *University of Chicago Law Review* 66:373.

Feldman, D. 1997. 'Privacy-related rights and their social value' in Birks 1997c, 15–50.

Feldthusen, B. 1991. 'Economic loss in the Supreme Court of Canada: yesterday and tomorrow' *Canadian Business Law Journal* 17:356.

——. 1997. 'Failure to confer discretionary public benefits: the case for complete negligence immunity' *Tort Law Review* 5:17.

——. 1998. 'Vicarious liability for sexual torts' in Mullany and Linden 1998, 221–43.

Ferran, E. 2011. 'Corporate attribution and the directing mind and will' *Law Quarterly Review* 127:239.

Finnis, J. 1980. *Natural Law and Natural Rights*. Clarendon Press.

——. 1995. 'Intention in tort law' in Owen 1995, 229–48.

——. 2002. 'Natural law: the classical tradition' in Coleman and Shapiro 2002, 1–60.

——. 2011. *Natural Law and Natural Rights*, 2nd edition. Clarendon Press.

Fionda, J. 2001. ed. *Legal Concepts of Childhood*. Hart Publishing.

Fischer, D. 1992. 'Causation in fact in omission cases' *Utah Law Review* 41:1335.

Fleming, J. 1997. 'Preventive damages' in Mullany 1997, 56–71.

——. 1998. *The Law of Torts*, 9th edn. LBC Information Services.

Fletcher, G. 1972. 'Fairness and utility in tort theory' *Harvard Law Review* 85:537.

Foot, P. 1967. 'The problem of abortion and the doctrine of double effect' *Oxford Review* 7.

Fordham, M. 2010. 'Saving us from ourselves – The duty of care in negligence to prevent self-inflicted harm' *Torts Law Journal* 18:22.

Foster, N. 2011. 'The merits of the civil action for breach of statutory duty' *Sydney Law Review* 33:67.

Fridman, G.H.L. 1963. 'Compensation of the innocent' *Modern Law Review* 26:481.

——. 1993. 'Interference with trade or business – part 2' *Tort Law Review* 1:99.

——. 2009. '*Lumley* v *Gye* and the (over?) protection of contracts' in Neyers, Bronaugh and Pitel 2009, 225–35.

Fried, C. 1968. 'Privacy' *Yale Law Journal* 77:475.

Fuller, L. 1964. *The Morality of Law*. Yale University Press.

Gardner, J. 2002. 'Obligations and outcomes in the law of tort' in Cane and Gardner 2001, 111–43.

——. 2010. 'What is tort law for? Part 1: the place of corrective justice', available on SSRN.

——. 2011. 'Punishment and compensation: a comment', available on SSRN.

Gearty, C. 1989. 'The place of private nuisance in a modern law of torts' *Cambridge Law Journal* 48:214.

Giglio, F. 2007. 'Restitution for wrongs: a structural analysis' *Canadian Journal of Law and Jurisprudence* 20:5.

Giliker, P. 2002. 'Rough justice in an unjust world' *Modern Law Review* 65:269.

——. 2009. 'Making the right connection: vicarious liability and institutional responsibility' *Torts Law Journal* 17:35.

——. 2010a. *Vicarious Liability in Tort: A Comparative Perspective*. Cambridge University Press.

——. 2010b. 'Lister revisited: vicarious liability, distributive justice, and the course of employment' *Law Quarterly Review* 126:521.

Glofcheski, R. 1999. 'Plaintiff's illegality as a bar to recovery of personal injury damages' *Legal Studies* 19:6.

——. 2004. 'A frolic in the law of tort: expanding the scope of employers' vicarious liability' *Tort Law Review* 12:18.

Goff, R. 1983. 'The search for principle' *Proceedings of the British Academy* 69:169.

——. 1986. *Judge, Jurist and Legislature*. Child & Co Oxford Lecture.

Goldberg, J. 2000. 'Duty and the structure of negligence' *Kansas Journal of Law and Public Policy* [2000]:149.

——. 2002. 'Unloved: tort law in the modern legal academy' *Vanderbilt Law Review* 55:1501.

——. 2003a. 'Tort' in Cane and Tushnet 2003, 21–47.

——. 2003b. 'Twentieth-century tort theory' *Georgetown Law Journal* 91:513.

——. 2003c. 'Rethinking injury and proximate cause' *San Diego Law Review* 40:1315.

——. 2006. 'Two conceptions of tort damages: fair vs full compensation' *DePaul Law Review* 435.

——. 2008. 'Ten half-truths about tort law' *Valparaiso University Law Review* 42:1221.

Goldberg, J. and Zipursky, B. 1998. 'The moral of *MacPherson*' *University of Pennsylvania Law Review* 146:1733.

——. 2001. 'The Restatement (Third) and the place of duty in negligence law' *Vanderbilt Law Review* 54: 657.

——. 2002. 'Unrealized torts' *Virginia Law Review* 88:1625.

——. 2006. 'Seeing tort law from the internal point of view: Holmes and Hart on legal duties' *Fordham Law Review* 75:1563.

——. 2007. 'Tort law and moral luck' *Cornell Law Review* 92:1123.

——. 2009. 'Intervening wrongdoing in tort: The Restatement (Third)'s unfortunate embrace of negligent enabling' *Wake Forest Law Review* 44:1211.

——. 2010a. 'Torts as wrongs' *Texas Law Review* 88:917.

——. 2010b. 'The easy case for products liability law' *Harvard Law Review* 123:1919.

Goldberg, R. 2011. ed. *Perspectives on Causation*. Hart Publishing.

Goodhart, A.L. 1938. 'The foundations of tortious liability' *Modern Law Review* 2:1.

Goodin, R.E. 1989. 'Theories of compensation' *Oxford Journal of Legal Studies* 9:56.

Gordley, J. 1995. 'Tort law in the Aristotelian tradition' in Owen 1995, 131–58.

——. 1998. 'Responsibility in crime, tort and contract for the unforeseeable consequences of an intentional wrong: a once and future rule?' in Cane and Stapleton 1998, 175–208.

Goudkamp, J. 2011a. '*Ex turpi causa* and immoral behaviour in the tort context' *Law Quarterly Review* 127:354.

——. 2011b. 'A taxonomy of tort law defences' in Degelman, Edelman and Goudkamp 2011.

——. 2012. 'Insanity as a tort defence' *Oxford Journal of Legal Studies* 32.

Goymour, A. 2011. 'Conversion of contractual rights' *Lloyd's Maritime and Commercial Law Quarterly* [2011]:67.

Gravells, N. 1977. 'Three heads of contributory negligence' *Law Quarterly Review* 93:581.

Gray, K. 1991. 'Property in thin air' *Cambridge Law Journal* 50:255.

Gray, N. and Edelman, J. 1998. 'Developing the law of omissions: a common law duty to rescue?' *Torts Law Journal* 6:240.

Greasley, K. 2010. 'A negligent blow to children at risk: *MAK and RK v United Kingdom*' *Modern Law Review* 73:1026.

Green, S. 2010. 'Understanding the wrongful interference actions' *Conveyancer and Property Law* 74:15.

Gronow, M. 1995. 'Conspiracy: the tort that failed?' *Torts Law Journal* 3:255.

Guest, A.G. 1961. ed. *Oxford Essays in Jurisprudence 1st Series*. Clarendon Press.

Guy, S., Richardson, K. and Hocking, B. 2010. 'The liability of publicans: rejection of the Canadian approach' *Tort Law Review* 18:117.

Haberfield, L. 1998. '*Lowns v Woods* and the duty to rescue' *Tort Law Review* 6:56.

Handford, P. 2007. 'Psychiatric injury in breach of a relationship' *Legal Studies* 27:26.

Handley, E. and Davis, G. 2001. 'Defamation and satire: *Hanson v Australian Broadcasting Corporation*' *Torts Law Journal* 9:1.

Harmon, S. and Laurie, G. 2010. '*Yearworth v North Bristol NHS Trust*: property, principles, precedents and paradigms' *Cambridge Law Journal* 69:476.

Harris, D. 1984. et al. *Compensation and Support for Illness and Injury*. Oxford University Press.

Harris, J. 1961. 'The concept of possession in English law' in Guest 1961, 69–106.

——. 1986. 'Who owns my body?' *Oxford Journal of Legal Studies* 16:55.

Hart, H.L.A. 1994. *The Concept of Law*. 2nd edn. Clarendon Press.

Hart, H.L.A. and Honoré, A.M. 1985. *Causation in the Law*, 2nd edn. Oxford University Press.

Hartstone, J. 2008. 'Confusion, contradiction and chaos within the House of Lords post *Caparo v Dickman*' *Tort Law Review* 16:8.

Heaton, P. and Helland, E. 2008. *No-Fault Insurance and Automobile Accidents: RAND Working Paper WR-551-ICJ*. RAND Institute for Civil Justice.

Hepple, B. 1997. 'Negligence: the search for coherence' *Current Legal Problems* [1997]:69.

Herring, J. and Palser, E. 2007. 'The duty of care in gross negligence manslaughter' *Criminal Law Review* [2007]:24.

Hershowitz, S. 2011. 'Harry Potter and the trouble with tort theory' *Stanford Law Review* 63:67.

Heuston, R.F.V. 1970. 'Who was the third Law Lord in *Rylands* v *Fletcher*?' *Law Quarterly Review* 86:160.

———. 1986. 'Judicial prosopography' *Law Quarterly Review* 102:90.

Hill, T. 1991. 'A lost chance for compensation in the tort of negligence by the House of Lords' *Modern Law Review* 54:511.

Hoffmann, D. 2011. ed. *The Impact of the UK Human Rights Act on Private Law*. Cambridge University Press.

Hoffmann, Lord. 2005. 'Causation' *Law Quarterly Review* 121:592.

Holmes, O.W. 1873. 'The theory of torts' *American Law Review* 7:652.

Honoré, A.M. 1988. 'Responsibility and luck: the moral basis of strict liability' *Law Quarterly Review* 104:530.

Hope, Lord. 2003. 'James McGhee – a second Mrs Donoghue?' *Cambridge Law Journal* 62:587.

Horder, J. 2000. ed. *Oxford Essays in Jurisprudence 4th Series*. Clarendon Press.

Howarth, D. 1997. 'Is there a future for the intentional torts?' in Birks 1997b, 233–81.

———. 2004. 'Public authority non-liability: spinning out of control?' *Cambridge Law Journal* 63:546.

———. 2005a. 'Poisoned wells: "proximity" and "assumption of responsibility" in negligence' *Cambridge Law Journal* 64:23.

———. 2005b. 'Against *Lumley* v *Gye*' *Modern Law Review* 68:195.

———. 2006. 'Many duties of care – or a duty of care? Notes from the underground' *Oxford Journal of Legal Studies* 26:449.

———. 2011. 'The cost of libel actions: a skeptical note' *Cambridge Law Journal* 70:397.

Howells, G. 2005. 'Defect in English law – lessons for the harmonisation of European product liability' in Fairgrieve 2005, 138–152.

Howells, G. and Mildred, M. 2002. 'Infected blood: defect and discoverability' *Modern Law Review* 65:95.

Hoyano, L. 1995. 'The dutiful tortfeasor in the House of Lords' *Tort Law Review* 3:63.

———. 1999. 'Policing flawed police investigations: unravelling the blanket' *Modern Law Review* 62:912.

———. 2002. 'Misconceptions about wrongful conception' *Modern Law Review* 65:883.

———. 2010. 'Ecclesiastical responsibility for clerical wrongdoing' *Tort Law Review* 18:154.

Hunt, M. 1998. 'The "horizontal" effect of the Human Rights Act' *Public Law* [1998]:422.

Hyman, D. 2005. 'Rescue without law: an empirical perspective on the duty to rescue' *Texas Law Review* 84:653.

Ibbetson, D. 1999. *A Historical Introduction to the Law of Obligations*. Oxford University Press.

———. 2003. 'How the Romans did for us: ancient roots of the tort of negligence' *University of New South Wales Law Journal* 26:475.

Insurance Research Council. 1999. *Injuries in Auto Accidents: An Analysis of Auto Insurance Claims*. Insurance Research Council.

Jackman, I. 1989. 'Restitution for wrongs' *Cambridge Law Journal* 48:302.

Jaffey, A.J.E. 1985. 'Volenti non fit injuria' *Cambridge Law Journal* 44:87.

Jaffey, P. 2007. *Private Law and Property Claims*. Hart Publishing.

Jolowicz, J.A. 2008. 'Civil litigation: what's it for?' *Cambridge Law Journal* 67:508.

Keating, G. 1997. 'The idea of fairness in the law of enterprise liability' *Michigan Law Review* 95:1266.

Kelley, P.J. 1990. 'Who decides? Community safety conventions at the heart of tort liability' *Cleveland State Law Review* 38:315.

Kelly, R. 1967. 'The inner nature of the tort action' *Irish Jurist (New Series)* 2:279.

Keren-Paz, T. 2007. *Torts, Egalitarianism and Distributive Justice*. Ashgate Publishing.

———. 2010a. '*AT* v *Dulghieru* – compensation for victims of trafficking, but where is the restitution?' *Torts Law Journal* 18:87.

———. 2010b. 'Poetic justice: why sex slaves should be allowed to sue ignorant clients in conversion' *Law and Philosophy* 29:307.

Kessler, D.P. and McClellan, M. 1996. 'Do doctors practise defensive medicine?' *Quarterly Journal of Economics* 111:353.

Kidner, R. 1991. 'The variable standard of care, contributory negligence and volenti' *Legal Studies* 11:1.

———. 1995. 'Vicarious liability: for whom should the "employer" be held liable?' *Legal Studies* 15:47.

Kimel, D. 2003. *From Promise to Contract: Towards a Liberal Theory of Contract*. Hart Publishing.

Klar, L. 1998. 'Downsizing torts' in Mullany and Linden 1998, 305–20.

Koenig, T.H. and Rustad, M.L. 2001. *In Defense of Tort Law*. New York University Press.

Koziol, H. and Steininger, B. 2005. eds. *European Tort Law 2004: Tort and Insurance Yearbook*. Springer.

Laddie, H. 2008. 'The insatiable appetite for intellectual property rights' *Current Legal Problems* 61:401.

Landes, W.M. and Posner, R.A. 1987. *The Economic Structure of Tort Law*. Harvard University Press.

Lastowka, F.G. and Hunter, D. 2004. 'The law of the virtual worlds' *California Law Review* 92:1.

Lee, J. 2009. 'The fertile imagination of the common law: *Yearworth* v *North Bristol NHS Trust*' *Torts Law Journal* 17:130.

Lee, M. 2003. 'What is private nuisance?' *Law Quarterly Review* 119:298.

——. 2011. 'Safety, regulation and tort: fault in context' *Modern Law Review* 74:555.

Lee, P.W. 2009. 'Inducing breach of contract, conversion and contract as property' *Oxford Journal of Legal Studies* 29:511.

Levmore, S. and Nussbaum, M. 2010. *The Offensive Internet*. Harvard University Press.

Lewis, R. 1999. *Deducting Benefits from Damages for Personal Injury*. Oxford University Press.

——. 2007. 'Tort law in practice: appearance and reality in reforming periodical payments of damages' in Neyers, Chamberlain and Pitel 2007, 487–508.

Lewis, R., Morris, A. and Oliphant, K. 2006. 'Tort personal injury claims statistics: is there a compensation culture in the United Kingdom?' *Torts Law Journal* 14:158.

Loughran, D. 2001. *The Effect of No-Fault Automobile Insurance on Driver Behaviour and Automobile Accidents in the United States*. Rand Corporation.

Loveland, I. 2000a. 'Political libels – whose right is it anyway?' *Current Legal Problems* 53:333.

——. 2000b. *Political Libels*. Hart Publishing.

Low, K. 2010. 'Equitable title and economic loss' *Law Quarterly Review* 126:506.

Lucy, W. 2009. Review of Keren-Paz, *Torts, Egalitarianism and Distributive Justice*. *Modern La Review* 72:1048.

Lunney, M. 2005. 'Personal responsibility and the "new" *volenti*' *Tort Law Review* 13:76.

MacDonald, A. 1936–1938. '*Hollywood Silver Fox Farm* v *Emmett*' *Alberta Law Quarterly* 2:99.

Machin, E.A. 1954. 'Negligence and interest' *Modern Law Review* 17:405.

Macneil, I. 1982. 'Efficient breach of contract: circles in the sky' *Virginia Law Review* 68:947.

Madden, M.S. 2005. *Exploring Tort Law*. Cambridge University Press.

Mahoney, F. 1997. 'Defamation law – time to rethink' in Mullany 1997, 261–73.

Marter, S. and Weisberg, H. 1992. 'Medical expenses and the Massachusetts automobile Tort Reform Law: a first review of 1989 bodily injury liability claims' *Journal of Insurance Regulation* 10:462.

Mason, J.K. 2002. 'Wrongful pregnancy, wrongful birth and wrongful terminology' *Edinburgh Law Review* 6:46.

Matthews, P. 1983. 'Whose body? People as property' *Current Legal Problems* [1983]:193.

Matula, M.L. 1996. 'Manufacturers' post sale duties in the 1990s' *Tort and Insurance Law Journal* 32:87.

McBain, G. 2008. 'Modernising and codifying the law of bailment' *Journal of Business Law* [2008]:1.

McBride, N.J. 1996. 'Punitive damages' in Birks 1996b, 175–202.

——. 2000. 'On the conceptual and philosophical foundations of tort law' in Horder 2000, 219–36.

——. 2004. 'Duties of care: do they really exist?' *Oxford Journal of Legal Studies* 24:417.

——. 2006a. 'Tort law' in Butler 2006, 26–35.

——. 2006b. 'Negligence liability for omissions – some fundamental distinctions' *Cambridge Student Law Review* 2:10.

——. 2011. 'Rights and the basis of tort law' in Nolan and Robertson 2011.

McBride, N.J. and Hughes, A. 1995. '*Hedley Byrne* in the House of Lords: an interpretation' *Legal Studies* 15:376.

McEwin, I.R. 1989. 'No-fault and road accidents: some Australasian evidence' *International Review of Law and Economics* 9:13.

McInnes, M. 2003. 'Interceptive subtraction, unjust enrichment and wrongs – a reply to Professor Birks' *Cambridge Law Journal* 62:697.

Merkin, R. 2010. 'Tort and insurance: some insurance law perspectives' *Professional Negligence* 26:194.

Merrett, L. 2009. 'Costs as damages' *Law Quarterly Review* 125:468.

Merrill, T.W. 2011. 'Is public nuisance a tort?' *Journal of Tort Law* 4(2):4.

Mildred, M. 2005. 'The development risks defence' in Fairgrieve 2005, 167–91.

Miles, J. 2000. 'Standing under the Human Rights Act 1998: theories of rights enforcement and the nature of public law adjudication' *Cambridge Law Journal* 59:133.

Mitchell, H.C. 2005. *The Intellectual Commons*. Lexington Books.

Mitchell, C. and Mitchell, P. 2010. eds. *Landmark Cases in the Law of Tort*. Hart Publishing.

Mitchell, P. 1999. 'Malice in qualified privilege' *Public Law* [1999]:328.

——. 2005. *The Making of the Modern Law of Defamation*. Hart Publishing.

Moore, M. 2009. *Causation and Responsibility*. Oxford University Press.

Moran, M. 1997. 'Rethinking *Winnipeg Condominium*: restitution, economic loss, and anticipatory repairs' *University of Toronto Law Journal* 47:115.

——. 2003. *Rethinking the Reasonable Person*. Oxford University Press.

——. 2010. 'The reasonable person: a conceptual biography in comparative perspective' *Lewis & Clark Law Review* 14:1233.

Moreham, N. 2005. 'The protection of privacy in English common law: a doctrinal and theoretical analysis' *Law Quarterly Review* 121:628.

——. 2006. 'Privacy in public places' *Cambridge Law Journal* 65:606.

Morgan, J. 2003. 'Lost causes in the House of Lords: *Fairchild* v *Glenhaven Funeral Services*' *Modern Law Review* 66:277.

——. 2004. 'Tort, insurance and incoherence' *Modern Law Review* 67:384.

——. 2006. 'The rise and fall of the general duty of care' *Professional Negligence* 22:206.

Morris, A. 2007. 'Spiralling or stabilising? The compensation culture and our propensity to claim damages for personal injury' *Modern Law Review* 70:349.

——. 2011. ' "Common sense common safety": the compensation culture perspective' *Professional Negligence* 27:82.

Moyn, S. 2010. *The Last Utopia: Human Rights in History*. Harvard University Press.

Mulheron, R. 2010. 'Trumping *Bolam*: a critical legal analysis of *Bolitho*'s "gloss" ' *Cambridge Law Review* 69:609.

Mullany, N. 1997. ed. *Torts in the Nineties*. LBC Information Services.

——. 1998. 'Liability for careless communication of traumatic information' *Law Quarterly Review* 114:380.

Mullany, N. and Handford, P. 1993. *Tort Liability for Pyschiatric Damage*. LBC Information Services.

Mullany, N. and Linden, A.M. 1998. eds. *Torts Tomorrow: A Tribute to John Fleming*. LBC Information Services.

Mullender, R. 2000. 'Negligence, the personal equation of defendants and distributive justice' *Tort Law Review* 8:211.

——. 2005. 'The reasonable person, the pursuit of justice, and negligence law' *Modern Law Review* 68:681.

——. 2008. 'Negligence law and the concept of community' *Tort Law Review* 16:85.

——. 2011. 'Blame culture and political debate: finding our way through the fog' *Professional Negligence* 27:64.

Murphy, J. 1996. 'Expectation losses, negligent omissions and the tortious duty of care' *Cambridge Law Journal* 55:43.

——. 2004. 'The merits of *Rylands v Fletcher*' *Oxford Journal of Legal Studies* 24:643.

——. 2007a. 'Juridical foundations of common law non-delegable duties' in Neyers, Chamberlain and Pitel 2007, 369–91.

——. 2007b. 'Rethinking injunctions in tort law' *Oxford Journal of Legal Studies* 27:509.

——. 2010a. 'The nature and domain of aggravated damages' *Cambridge Law Journal* 69:353.

——. 2010b. *The Law of Nuisance*. Oxford University Press.

Nance, D. 1997. 'Guidance rules and enforcement rules: a better view of the cathedral' *Virginia Law Review* 83:837.

Nelson, J.W. 2010. 'The virtual property problem: what property rights in virtual resources might look like, how they might work, and why they are a bad idea' *McGeorge Law Review* 41:281.

Newark, F.H. 1949. 'The boundaries of nuisance' *Law Quarterly Review* 65:480.

Neyers, J. 2002. 'Distilling duty: the Supreme Court of Canada amends *Anns' Law Quarterly Review* 118:221.

——. 2005. 'A theory of vicarious liability' *Alberta Law Review* 43:287.

——. 2009. 'The economic torts as corrective justice' *Torts Law Journal* 17:162.

——. 2010. '*Tate & Lyle Food Distribution Co Ltd* v *Greater London Council (1983)*' in Mitchell and Mitchell 2010, 227–50.

——. 2011. 'Explaining the inexplicable? Four manifestations of abuse of rights in English law' in Nolan and Robertson 2011, 309–330.

Neyers, J., Bronaugh, R. and Pitel, S. 2009. *Exploring Issues in Contract Law*. Hart Publishing.

Neyers, J., Chamberlain, E. and Pitel, S. 2007. eds. *Emerging Issues in Tort Law*. Hart Publishing.

Neyers, J. and Diacur, J. 2012. 'What is a nuisance? *Antrim Truck Centre Ltd* v *Ontario (Minister of Transportation)*', forthcoming.

Nolan, D. 2001. 'Risks and wrongs – remoteness of damage in the House of Lords' *Tort Law Review* 9:101.

——. 2004. 'Psychiatric injury at the crossroads' *Journal of Personal Injury Law* 1:1.

——. 2005. 'The distinctiveness of *Rylands* v *Fletcher*' *Law Quarterly Review* 121:421.

——. 2007b. 'New forms of damage in negligence' *Modern Law Review* 70:59.

——. 2009. 'Causation and the goals of tort law' in Robertson and Tang 2009, 165–90.

——. 2011a. 'The liability of public authorities for failure to confer benefits' *Law Quarterly Review* 127:260.

——. 2011b. ' "A tort against land": private nuisance as a property tort' in Nolan and Robertson 2011, 457–88.

Nolan, D. and Robertson, A. 2011. *Rights and Private Law*. Hart Publishing.

Nwabueze, R. 2007. 'Interference with dead bodies and body parts: a separate cause of action in tort?' *Tort Law Review* 15:63.

Ogus, A. and Richardson, G. 1977. 'Economics and the environment – a study of private nuisance' *Cambridge Law Journal* 36:284.

Oliphant, K. 2005. '*Rylands* v *Fletcher* and the emergence of enterprise liability in the common law' in Koziol and Steininger 2005, 81–120.

——. 2007. 'Beyond misadventure: compensation for medical injuries in New Zealand' *Medical Law Review* 15:357.

——. 2011. et al. *On A Slippery Slope: A Response to the Jackson Report*.

Oliver, D. 2000. 'The frontiers of the State: public authorities and public functions under the Human Rights Act' *Public Law* [2000]:476.

——. 2004. 'Functions of a Public Nature under the Human Rights Act' *Public Law* [2004]:329.

Ong, B. 2008. 'Two tripartite economic torts' *Journal of Business Law* [2008]:723.

Orr, G. 1995. 'Is an innkeeper her brother's keeper? The liability of alcohol servers' *Torts Law Journal* 3:239.

O'Sullivan, J. 1997a. 'Negligent professional advice and market movements' *Cambridge Law Journal* 56:19.

——. 1997b. 'Nuisance in the House of Lords – normal service resumed' *Cambridge Law Journal* 56:483.

——. 1999. 'Liability for fear of the onset of future medical conditions' *Professional Negligence* 15:96.

Owen, D. 1995. ed. *Philosophical Foundations of Tort Law*. Clarendon Press.

Palmer, S. 2008. 'Public functions and private services: A gap in human rights protection' *International Journal of Constitutional Law* 6:585.

Parfit, D. 2011. *On What Matters, Volume One*. Oxford University Press.

Parpworth, N. 2008. 'Public nuisance in the environmental context' *Journal of Planning and Environmental Law* [2008]:1526.

Pearson, Lord. 1978. *Royal Commission on Civil Liability and Compensation for Personal Injury*. HMSO.

Pedain, A. 2005. 'Requiem for a fairytale' *Cambridge Law Journal* 64:11.

Peel, E. 2003a. 'SAAMCO revisited' in Burrows and Peel 2003, 55–70.

——. 2003b. ' "Loss of a chance" revisited: *Gregg* v *Scott*' *Modern Law Review* 66:623.

Perlman, H. 1982. 'Interference with contract and other economic expectancies: a clash of tort and contract doctrine' *University of Chicago Law Review* 49:61.

Perry, S. 1992. 'Protected interests and undertakings in the law of negligence' *University of Toronto Law Journal* 42:247.

——. 2001. 'Honoré on responsibility for outcomes' in Cane and Gardner 2001, 61–80.

Polinsky, A.M. and Shavell, S. 2010. 'The uneasy case for products liability' *Harvard Law Review* 123:1437.

Pollock, F. 1882. *Essays in Jurisprudence and Ethics*. Macmillan, London.

Porat, A. 2009. Review of Keren-Paz, *Torts, Egalitarianism and Distributive Justice*. *Legal Studies* 29:509.

Porat, A. and Stein, A. 2003. 'Indeterminate causation and apportionment of damages: an essay on *Holtby, Allen* and *Fairchild*' *Oxford Journal of Legal Studies* 23:667.

Posner, R.A. 2003. *Economic Analysis of Law*. 6th edn. Aspen.

Postema, G. 2001. ed. *Philosophy and the Law of Torts*. Cambridge University Press.

Priaulx, N. 2007. *The Harm Paradox: Tort Law and the Unwanted Child in an Era of Choice*. Routledge.

Prosser, W. 1960. 'Privacy' *California Law Review* 48:383.

Rabin, R. 1999. 'Enabling torts' *DePaul Law Review* 49:435.

Rabin, R. and Sugarman, S. 2003. eds. *Torts Stories*. West Law School.

Rawls, J. 1971. *A Theory of Justice*. Harvard University Press.

Reece, H. 1996. 'Losses of chance in the law' *Modern Law Review* 59:188.

Reed, A. 1996. 'The professional liability of agents in tort' *Tort Law Review* 4:62.

Reid, G. 2005. '*Gregg v Scott* and lost chances' *Professional Negligence* 21:78.

Rickett, C. 2008. ed. *Justifying Private Law Remedies*. Hart Publishing.

Ripstein, A. 1998. 'Some recent obituaries of tort law' *University of Toronto Law Journal* 48:561.

——. 2002. 'Philosophy of tort law' in Coleman and Shapiro 2002, 656–86.

——. 2006a. 'Private order and public justice: Kant and Rawls' *Virginia Law Review* 92:1391.

——. 2006b. 'Beyond the harm principle' *Philosophy and Public Affairs* 34:215.

——. 2007a. 'As if it had never happened' *William and Mary Law Review* 48:1957.

——. 2007b. 'Tort law in a liberal state' *Tort Law Journal* 1:Article 3.

——. 2009. *Force and Freedom: Kant's Legal and Political Philosophy*. Harvard University Press.

Ripstein, A. and Zipursky, B. 2001. 'Corrective justice in an age of mass torts' in Postema 2001, 214–49.

Robertson, A. 2011. 'Rights, pluralism and the duty of care' in Nolan and Robertson 2011.

Robertson, A. and Tang, H.W. 2009. *The Goals of Private Law*. Hart Publishing.

Rotherham, C. 2007. 'The conceptual structure of restitution for wrongs' *Cambridge Law Journal* 66:172.

——. 2008. '*Wrotham Park* damages and accounts of profits: compensation or restitution?' *Lloyd's Maritime and Commercial Law Quarterly* [2008]:25.

——. 2009. 'The normative foundations of restitution for wrongs: justifying gain-based relief for nuisance' in Robertson and Tang 2009, 389–418.

——. 2010. 'Gain-based relief in tort after *Att-Gen v Blake*' *Law Quarterly Review* 126:102.

Rubin, P.H. and Shepherd, J.M. 2007. 'Tort reform and accidental deaths' *The Journal of Law and Economics* 50:221.

Rudden, B. 1991–1992. 'Torticles' *Tulane Civil Law Forum* 6/7:105.

Sales, P. 1990. 'The tort of conspiracy and civil secondary liability' *Cambridge Law Journal* 49:491.

Sales, P. and Stilitz, D. 1999. 'Intentional infliction of harm by unlawful means' *Law Quarterly Review* 115:411.

Salmond, J. 1907. *Law of Torts*. Sweet & Maxwell.

Schwartz, G. 1991. 'The myth of the Ford Pinto case' *Rutgers Law Review* 43:1013.

——. 2000. 'Auto no-fault and first party insurance: advantages and problems' *Southern California Law Review* 73:611.

Scott, Lord. 2007. 'Damages' [2007] *Lloyd's Maritime and Commercial Law Quarterly* 465.

Sebok, A. 2007. 'Punitive damages: from myth to theory' *Iowa Law Review* 92:957.

Seneviratne, M. 2001. 'The rise and fall of advocates' immunity' *Legal Studies* 21:644.

Sharpe, R.J. and Waddams, S.M. 1982. 'Damages for lost opportunity to bargain' *Oxford Journal of Legal Studies* 2:290.

Shears, P. 2007. 'The EU Product Liability Directive – twenty years on' *Journal of Business Law* [2007]:884.

Sherwin, E. 2003. 'Compensation and revenge' *San Diego Law Review* 40:1387.

Shmueli, B. 2010. 'Love and the law, children against mothers and fathers: or, what's love got to do with it' *Duke Journal of Gender Law & Policy* 17:131.

Simester, A. and Chan, W. 2004. 'Inducing breach of contract: one tort or two?' *Cambridge Law Journal* 63:132.

Simpson, A.W.B. 1984. 'Bursting reservoirs: the historical context of *Rylands* v *Fletcher*' *Journal of Legal Studies* 13:209.

——. 1995. *Leading Cases in the Common Law.* Oxford University Press.

Smith, J.C. and Burns, P. 1983a. '*Donoghue* v *Stevenson* – the not so golden anniversary' *Modern Law Review* 46:147.

——. 1983b. 'The good neighbour on trial: good neighbours make bad law' *University of British Columbia Law Review* 17:93.

Smith, R. 1977. 'The economic torts: their impact on real property' *Conveyancer and Property Lawyer* 41:318.

——. 2011. *Property Law.* 7th edn. Pearson Education.

Solomon, R. and Payne, J. 1996. 'Alcohol liability in Canada and Australia: sell, serve and be sued' *Tort Law Review* 4:188.

Solove, D. 2008. *Understanding Privacy.* Harvard University Press.

Spencer, J. 1989. 'Public nuisance – a critical examination' *Cambridge Law Journal* 48:55.

——. 2010. 'Compensation for wrongful imprisonment' *Criminal Law Review* [2010]:803.

Sprankling, J.G. 2008. 'Owning the center of the Earth' *UCLA Law Review* 55:979.

Stallybrass, W.T.S. 1929. 'Dangerous things and non-natural user of land' *Cambridge Law Journal* 3:376.

Stanton, K. 1997. 'Incremental approaches to the duty of care' in Mullany 1997, 34–55.

——. 2003. et al. *Statutory Torts.* Sweet & Maxwell.

——. 2007a. 'Pure economic loss: back to basics in the 21st century' *Tort Law Review* 15:5.

——. 2007b. 'Decision-making in the tort of negligence in the House of Lords' *Tort Law Review* 15:93.

——. 2009. 'Burying the dead: developing a modern approach to vicarious liability' *Tort Law Review* 17:9.

——. 2010. 'Tort and wrongful detention' *Tort Law Review* 18:69.

Stapleton, J. 1991. 'Duty of care and economic loss: a wider agenda' *Law Quarterly Review* 107:249.

——. 1994a. *Product Liability.* Butterworths.

——. 1994b. 'In restraint of tort' in Birks 1994, 83–102.

——. 1995. 'Duty of care: peripheral parties and alternative opportunities for deterrence' *Law Quarterly Review* 111:301.

——. 1997. 'The normal expectancies measure in tort damages' *Law Quarterly Review* 113:257.

——. 1998. 'Duty of care factors: a selection from the judicial menus' in Cane and Stapleton 1998, 59–95.

——. 2001. 'Unpacking causation' in Cane and Gardner 2001, 145–85.

——. 2002a. 'Comparative economic loss: lessons from case-law-focused "middle theory"' *University of California, Los Angeles Law Review* 50:531.

——. 2002b. 'Lords a-leaping evidentiary gaps' *Torts Law Journal* 10:276.

——. 2003a. 'Cause-in-fact and the scope of liability for consequences' *Law Quarterly Review* 119:388.

——. 2003b. 'The golden thread at the heart of tort law: protection of the vulnerable' *Australian Bar Review* 24:135.

——. 2005. 'Bugs in Anglo-American product liability' in Fairgrieve 2005, 295–333.

——. 2006a. 'Evaluating Goldberg and Zipursky's civil recourse theory' *Fordham Law Review* 75:1529.

——. 2006b. 'Occam's razor reveals an orthodox basis for *Chester* v *Afshar*' *Law Quarterly Review* 122:426.

——. 2008. 'Choosing what we mean by "causation" in the law' *Missouri Law Review* 73:433.

Stauch, M. 2001. 'Risk and remoteness of damage in negligence' *Modern Law Review* 64:191.

Steel, S. and Ibbetson, D. 2011. 'More grief on uncertain causation in tort' *Cambridge Law Journal* 70:451.

Steele, J. 2008. 'Damages in tort and under the Human Rights Act: remedial or functional separation?' *Cambridge Law Journal* 67:606.

Stein, P.G. and Lewis, A.D.E. 1983. eds. *Studies in Justinian's Institutes*. Sweet & Maxwell.

Stevens, R. 2005. 'An opportunity to reflect' *Law Quarterly Review* 121:189.

——. 2007. *Torts and Rights*. Oxford University Press.

——. 2009. 'The conflict of rights' in Robertson and Tang 2009, 139–164.

——. 2011. 'Rights and other things' in Nolan and Robertson 2011, 115–150.

Stevens, R. (2). 1964. '*Hedley Byrne* v *Heller* – judicial creativity and doctrinal possibility' *Modern La Review* 27:121.

Steyn, Lord. 2002. 'Perspectives of corrective and distributive justice in tort law' *Irish Jurist* 37:1.

Stigglebout, M. 2009. 'The scope and rationale of the principle that the defendant "take his victim as he finds him"' *Tort Law Review* 17:140.

Stone, J. 1946. *The Province and Function of Law*. Associated General Publications.

Sugarman, S. 2002. 'A new approach to tort doctrine: taking the best from the civil law and common law of Canada' *Supreme Court Law Review (2d)* 17:375.

Swadling, W. and Jones, G. 1999. eds. *The Search for Principle: Essays in Honour of Lord Goff of Chieveley*. Oxford University Press.

Taggart, M. 2002. *Private Property and Abuse of Rights in Victorian England*. Oxford University Press.

Tan, K.F. 1981. 'A misconceived issue in the tort of false imprisonment' *Modern Law Review* 44:166.

Teff, H. 1996. 'The requirement of "sudden shock" in liability for negligently inflicted psychiatric damage' *Tort Law Review* 4:44.

——. 1998. 'Liability for negligently inflicted psychiatric harm: justifications and boundaries' *Cambridge Law Journal* 57:91.

——. 2007. 'Condoning wrongful suffering' *Tort Law Review* 15:7.

Tettenborn, A. 1993. 'Damages in conversion – the exception or the anomaly?' *Cambridge Law Journal* 52:128.

——. 1994. 'Reversionary damage to chattels' *Cambridge Law Journal* 53:326.

——. 1996. 'Trust property and conversion: an equitable confusion' *Cambridge Law Journal* 55:36.

——. 2000a. 'Professional negligence: free riders and others' in Economides 2000, 295–311.

——. 2000b. 'Components and product liability: damage to "other property"' *Lloyd's Maritime and Commercial Law Quarterly* [2000]:338.

Todd, S. 2007. 'Policy issues in defective property cases' in Neyers, Chamberlain and Pitel 2007, 199–232.

Tomlinson, E.A. 2000. 'The French experience with duty to rescue: a dubious case for criminal enforcement' *New York Law Journal of International and Comparative Law* 20:451.

Treiger-Bar-Am, L.K. 2000. 'Defamation law in a changing society: the case of *Youssoupoff* v *Metro-Goldwyn-Mayer*' *Legal Studies* 20:291.

Trindade, F. 1982. 'Intentional torts: some thoughts on assault and battery' *Oxford Journal of Legal Studies* 2:211.

Tromans, S. 1982. 'Private nuisance – prevention or payment' *Cambridge Law Journal* 41:87.

Tunc, A. 1972. 'Tort law and the moral value' *Cambridge Law Journal* 30:247.

Turner, P. 2010. 'Consequential economic loss and the trust beneficiary' *Cambridge Law Journal* 69:444.

Varuhas, J.N.E. 2009. 'A tort-based approach to damages under the Human Rights Act 1998' *Modern Law Review* 72:750.

——. 2010. 'False imprisonment of prisoners: lawful authority, omissions and damages' *Cambridge Law Journal* 69:438.

——. 2011. 'Exemplary damages: "public law" functions, *mens rea* and quantum' *Cambridge Law Journal* 70:284.

Veitch, E. and Miers, D. 1975. 'Assault on the law of tort' *Modern Law Review* 38:139.

Von Hirsch, A. and Simester, A. 2006. *Incivilities*. Hart Publishing.

Waddams, S. 1998. 'New directions in products liability' in Mullany and Linden 1998, 119–29.

——. 2001. 'Johanna Wagner and the rival opera houses' *Law Quarterly Review* 117:431.

——. 2003. *Dimensions of Private Law: Categories and Concepts in Anglo-American Legal Reasoning.* Cambridge University Press.

Waldron, J. 1995. 'Moments of carelessness and massive loss' in Owen 1995, 387–408.

Warby, M., Moreham, N. and Christie, I. 2010. *Tugendhat and Christie: The Law of Privacy and the Media.* 2nd edn. Oxford University Press.

Watson, S. and Noonan, C. 2009. 'The widening gyre of vicarious liability' *Torts Law Journal* 17:144.

Wedderburn, Lord. 1983. 'Rocking the torts' *Modern Law Review* 46:224.

Weinrib, E. 1980. 'The case for a duty to rescue' *Yale Law Journal* 90:247.

——. 1995. *The Idea of Private Law.* Harvard University Press.

——. 2000. 'Restitutionary damages as corrective justice' *Theoretical Inquiries in Law* 1:1.

——. 2005. 'The disintegration of duty' in Madden 2005, 143–86.

Weir, J.A. 1964. 'Chaos or cosmos? *Rookes, Stratford* and the economic torts' *Cambridge Law Journal* 23:225.

——. 1995. 'A damnosa hereditas' *Law Quarterly Review* 111:357.

——. 1997. *Economic Torts.* Clarendon Press.

——. 1998a. 'The staggering march of negligence' in Cane and Stapleton 1998, 97–138.

——. 1998b. 'Suicide in custody' *Cambridge Law Journal* 57:241.

——. 2001. 'The maddening effect of consecutive torts' *Cambridge Law Journal* 60:237.

——. 2003–4. 'All or nothing' *Tulane Law Review* 78:512.

——. 2004. *A Casebook on Tort.* 10th edn. Sweet & Maxwell.

——. 2006. *An Introduction to Tort Law.* 2nd edn. Clarendon Law Series, Oxford.

Weston, C.A.R. 1999. 'Suing in tort for loss of computer data' *Cambridge Law Journal* 58:67.

Whittaker, S. 1989. 'European product liability and intellectual products' *Law Quarterly Review* 105:125.

——. 1997. 'The application of the "broad principle of *Hedley Byrne*" as between parties to a contract' *Legal Studies* 17:169.

Williams, G. 1939–1941. 'The foundation of tortious liability' *Cambridge Law Journal* [1939-41]:111.

——. 1956a. 'Vicarious liability: tort of the master or servant?' *Law Quarterly Review* 72:122.

——. 1956b. 'Liability for independent contractors' *Cambridge Law Journal* 15:180.

Williams, K. 2000. 'Defaming politicians: the not so common law' *Modern Law Review* 63:748.

——. 2001. 'Medical Samaritans: is there a duty to treat?' *Oxford Journal of Legal Studies* 21:393.

——. 2005. 'State of fear: Britain's compensation culture reviewed' *Legal Studies* 25:499.

Winfield, P. 1926. 'The history of negligence in the law of torts' *Law Quarterly Review* 42:184.

——. 1927. 'The foundation of liability in tort' *Columbia Law Review* 27:1.

——. 1931. *The Province of the Law of Tort.* Cambridge University Press.

——. 1934. 'Duty in tortious negligence' *Columbia Law Review* 34:41.

Witting, C. 2000a. 'Negligent inspectors and flying machines' *Cambridge Law Journal* 59:544.

——. 2000b. 'Liability to third parties for negligent misstatements' *Oxford Journal of Legal Studies* 20:615.

——. 2001. 'Distinguishing between property damage and pure economic loss in negligence: a personality thesis' *Legal Studies* 21:481.

Witzleb, N. and Carroll, R. 2009. 'The role of vindication in torts damages' *Tort Law Review* 17:16.

Wolfe, J. 1995. 'Casinos and the compulsive gambler: is there a duty to monitor the gambler's wagers?' *Mississippi Law Journal* 64:687.

Woolf, Lord. 2000. 'The Human Rights Act 1998 and remedies' in Andenas and Fairgrieve 2000, 429–36.

Worthington, S. 1999. 'Reconsidering disgorgement for wrongs' *Modern Law Review* 62:218.

——. 2009. 'Art, law and creativity' *Current Legal Problems* 62:168.

Wright, C. 1944. 'Introduction to the law of torts' *Cambridge Law Journal* 8:238.

———. 1961. 'The English law of torts – a criticism' *University of Toronto Law Journal* 11:84.

Wright, J. 2012. *Tort Law and Human Rights*. 2nd edn. Hart Publishing.

Wright, R. 1985. 'Causation in tort law' *California Law Review* 73:1735.

———. 1988. 'Causation, responsibility, risk, probability, naked statistics and proof: pruning the bramble bush by clarifying the concepts' *Iowa Law Review* 73:1001.

———. 1995. 'The standards of care in negligence law' in Owen 1995, 249–275.

———. 2001. 'Once more into the bramble bush: duty, causal contribution, and the extent of legal responsibility' *Vanderbilt Law Review* 53:1071.

———. 2003. 'Hand, Posner and the myth of the "Hand Formula"' *Theoretical Inquiries in Law* 4:145.

———. 2011a. 'The NESS account of natural causation: a response to criticisms' in Goldberg 2011.

———. 2011b. 'Private nuisance law: a window on substantive justice' in Nolan and Robertson 2011, 489–522.

Yap, P.J. 2008. 'Enlisting close connections: a matter of course for vicarious liability?' *Legal Studies* 28:197.

———. 2009. 'Pure economic loss and defects in the law of negligence' *Tort Law Review* 17:80.

———. 2010. 'Rethinking the illegality defence in tort law' *Tort Law Review* 18:52.

Zipursky, B. 1998a. 'Rights, wrongs and recourse in the law of torts' *Vanderbilt Law Review* 51:1.

———. 1998b. 'Legal malpractice and the structure of negligence law' *Fordham Law Review* 67:649.

———. 2002. 'Philosophy of private law' in Coleman and Shapiro 2002, 623–55.

———. 2003. 'Civil recourse, not corrective justice' *Georgetown Law Journal* 91:695.

———. 2005. 'A theory of punitive damages' *Texas Law Review* 84:105.

———. 2007. 'Sleight of Hand' *William and Mary Law Review* 48:1999.

Zuckerman, A. 2006. *Zuckerman on Civil Procedure – Principles of Practice*. 2nd edn. Sweet & Maxwell.

Zweigert, K. and Kötz, H. 1998. *An Introduction to Comparative Law*. 3rd rev'd edn. (trans Weir, J.A.). Oxford University Press.

Index of problems

Blinded Gardener 421, 422, 464

Careless-Careful Driver 306
Changing Mind 62
Chemical Vats 462–3
Concerned Sister 616, 617
Cracked Vase 166

Dead Man Walking 51
Deceptive Appearances 610, 617
Defective Car 245, 247, 256
Desperate Academic 546
Disabled-Blind Footballer 309, 310
Drunken Student 612
Dog Whistle 421
Double Poison 300, 303, 319, 321
Doube Poison Reversed 319, 321
Dramatic Detective 550, 552

Electrocuted Couple 374
Exploding Car 413

Falling Sign 209, 210
Forgetful Investor 100, 125, 329
Fur Coat 866

Gullible Lovers 10, 11
Gullible Student 62, 63

Healed Victim 305, 306
Hollywood Dog 336
Horrible Seat-Belt 774

Injured Prostitute 356

Julius Caesar 318

Learner Driver 277
Lightning 314
Lost Ring 166
Lottery Ticket 293

Misdiagnosed Patient 345
Murder on the Orient Express 318
Murdered Tramp 825

Regular Menace 841
Restaurant-Dungeon 49

Second Misdiagnosed Patient 346
Slippery Canteen Floor 866
Slippery Floor 369
Suicidal Prisoner 260

Three References 300–1, 302, 303
Tiger Kidnapping 700–1
Trolley 212
Two Burglars 9–10
Two Fires 300, 301, 302, 303, 304, 305, 317, 320
Two Flats 461, 462
Two Hunters 284, 290, 291
Two Negligent Doctors 304, 305

Unconscious Man 220, 221
Unfortunate Rock Star 93, 316
Unpredictable Criminal 713
Unreliable Paparazzi 614
Useless T-Shirts 166

Water Bottle 272, 303, 320

Index

Abuse of process
  defence, 66, 502, 524, 541–2, 543, 723–4, 747
  tort, 709
Accessory liability
  assisting, 672, 862–4
  authorising, 861
  common design, 862
  definition, 860
  joint liability, 860
  procuring, 860–1
  ratifying, 861
  vicarious liability and, 867
Accord and satisfaction: *see* Settlements
Act of God
  Animals Act 1971, 404
  nuclear installations, 484
  private nuisance, 448
  Rylands v *Fletcher*, 467, 478
Act of State, 720
Actionable *per se*
  definition, 14, 749
  significance of some torts being, 740, 749, 751–3
  what torts are, 65, 94, 414, 749–50
  what torts are not, 462, 633, 749–50
Aggravated damages
  civil recourse and, 792–3
  companies, 793–4
  defamation, 790
  dignity and, 793–4
  discrimination, 790–1
  distress and, 792–3
  ECHR and, 83
  false imprisonment, 790, 791
  negligence, 97, 791–2
  privacy, 617
  private nuisance, 789, 791
  requirements, 789–91
  theories, 792–4
  torts for which awarded, 791
  trespass to land, 789–90, 791
Animals
  see also Animals Act 1971

cattle trespass, 407, 483
  conversion, 498
  duty to control, 231
  trespass to land, 407–8
Animals Act 1971
  Act of God, 404
  act of stranger, 404
  antecedents, 398
  contributory negligence, 404
  dangerous species, 398–9
  fatal accidents, 852
  fault of claimant, 404
  keeper, 399
  knowledge, 400, 401, 402
  liability rules, 398–9
  property damage, 398
  section 2(2), 399–403
  straying livestock, 399, 404
  trespassers, 404
  volenti non fit injuria, 404
Arrest
  right to, 56, 58, 64, 65
Arrest warrant
  procuring issue of, when a tort, 707
Assault
  actionable *per se*, 65, 749
  aggravated damages, 65, 791
  conduct required, 39–40
  definition, 36
  fault required, 43–44
  silence, 39
Assisting
  breach of contract, 662–3
  breach of trust, 672, 863
  crime, 863
  tort, 672, 862–4
Assumption of responsibility
  critics, 18, 174, 184
  definition, 173–4, 175, 181
  duty of care, basis of, 174, 175, 217, 252
  economic loss and, 187–8
  examples of, 175–80, 181–2, 182–7
  omissions, 217–222
  reality of, 174–5

Bailment
  at will, 492
  conversion, 237, 497
  definition, 503
  duty of bailee, 503
  exclusion clause, 729
  negligence and, 237
  non-delegable duty, 262
  presumption of breach, 269
  sub-, 503–4, 729
Barrister
  duty of care, 182, 724
  no immunity, 116
Battery
  actionable *per se*, 65, 749
  aggravated damages, 65, 791
  conduct required, 38–9
  consent, 45–9
  contributory negligence, 773
  corporal punishment, 55
  definition, 36
  fault required, 42–3
  hostility, 43
  intention to harm, 43
  limitation, 741–3
  mistakes, 62–4
  necessity, 50–8
  vindicatory damages, 65–7
  voluntary assumption of risk, 48–9
Breach of duty of care
  burden of proof, 267–9
  companies, 265–7
  degree and foreseeability of risk,
    252–6
  delegable and non-delegable, 260–5
  emergencies, 250–1
  games, 251
  intention to harm, 93–4
  objectivity, 248–52
  professional standards, 257–8
  public interest, 255–6
  public law, relevance of, 258–60
  res ipsa loquitur, 268
  warnings, 370–1
Breach of statutory duty
  child protection, 632, 633–4
  defective premises, 636–7
  discrimination, 637
  health and safety, 634–5
  highways, 635–6
  inducing, 672
  third parties, 628

  when tort, 7, 21–22
  wrong kind of loss, 329, 341–2, 629
Builders
  duties of, 131, 183–4, 636–7

Case, action on, 36
Causation
  break in chain, 311–7
  but for test, 272–3, 275–9, 300–3
  evidential difficulties, 281–96
  Fairchild exception, 285–91
  material contribution, 279–80
  material increase in risk test, 273, 305–9
  NESS test, 317–20
  overdetermination, 300–5
  public policy, 325–7
  views on, 317–25
Chance, loss of
  economic loss, form of, 294
  establishing, 292–4
  physical injury causing, 294, 341
  property damage causing, 294
  pure, 294–9
Child care services, 240–1, 632, 633–4
Children
  see also Congenital disabilities
  capacity, 718
  consent, 47–8
  contributory negligence, 774
  corporal punishment, 55
  cost of bringing up, 346–50
  duties owed by, 134, 718
  duties owed to, 238–41, 632, 633–4, 854–5
  duty to control, 232–3
  immaturity, relevance of, 47–8, 134
  medical treatment, 47–8
Civil proceedings
  instituting, not a tort, 708–9
Civil recourse theory
  aggravated damages and, 792–3
  compensatory damages and, 786–7
  exemplary damages and, 803
  property and, 510–1
Civil wrong
  definition, 8–9
  public wrong and, 8–9
Companies
  act of company, 265–7, 736–7
  aggravated damages, 793–4
  defamation, 543–4, 575
  illegality, 736–7
  privacy, 603–4

Compensatory damages
  actionability, 328–55
  assessment, 758–64
  contributory negligence, 773–9
  defences, 716–43
  distress, 158–61, 162, 340, 460–2, 581–2, 700–3, 755, 792
  failure to mitigate, 314, 350–2
  Human Rights Act 1998, 81–5
  judgment, 766
  loss of amenity, 758–9, 762
  loss of chance, 292–9, 341
  lump sum awards, 755–6
  non-tortious claim for, 14, 15, 397
  periodical payments, 757–8
  property damage, 763–5
  provisional damages, 756
  receipt of benefit, 765–73
  SAAMCO principle, 342–6, 776–8
  theories, 781–7
  third parties, suing for, 779–81
  third parties, liability to pay to, 844–59
Confidence, breach of
  equitable wrong, 20–1
  gain-based damages, 811
  law on privacy and, 591–2
Congenital disabilities
  general rule, 855
  limits on right to sue, 855–6
  product liability and, 857
  wrongful birth, 855–6
Consent
  see also Volenti non fit injuria
  battery, 45
  belief in, 62
  capacity to give, 47–8
  children, 47–8
  defamation, 546–7
  informed, 46
  negligence, 132
  parental, 48
  Rylands v *Fletcher*, 478–9
  validity, 45–6
  withdrawal, 46–7
Conspiracy
  contributory negligence, 773
  lawful means, 683–8
  relationship with other torts, 689–92
  terminology, 683–4
  unlawful means, 688–92
Consumer Protection Act 1987
  antecedents, 381–3

basic rule, 382
contributory negligence, 394
damage, 388–90
defect, 384–7
defences, 390–3, 394
development risks defence, 391–2
exclusion of liability, 394
fatal accidents, 852–3
negligence and, 381–2, 389
producer, 387–8
product, 383–4
supplier, liability of, 388
theories, 394–7
tort law and, 396–7
Contemptuous damages, 371, 750
Contract,
  conversion of?, 516–9
  exclusion of liability, 359, 374–5, 394, 728–30
  inducing breach of, 660–72
  interfering with, 664–5
  tort and, 17–8
Contribution,
  assessment of amount payable, 113, 353
  vicarious liability, 890
Contributory negligence
  Animals Act 1971, 404
  assessment of reduction, 773, 775
  battery, 773
  concept of, 773–4
  conspiracy, 773
  Consumer Protection Act 1987, 394
  conversion, 773
  deceit, 773
  effect of, 773
  Fatal Accidents Act 1976, 846
  Hedley Byrne, 776–8
  inducing a breach of contract, 773
  SAAMCO principle, 777–8
  trespass to goods, 773
  White v *Jones*, 778
Conversion
  animals, 498
  bailee's liability, 237, 497
  cheques, 517, 518
  consent, 497
  contract, 516–9
  contributory negligence, 773
  damages, 504–7
  definition, 494
  delivery to third party, 496–7
  destruction of goods, 497

distress damage feasant, 498
finding, 494
gain-based damages, 506, 810–1, 814
modes, 494–7
money, 500
police, 499, 735–6
recaption, 498–9
restoration of goods, 499–500
retention of goods, 495–6
taking possession, 494–5
things that may be converted, 487–9, 516–9
title to sue, 491–3
use of property, 497
Corporal punishment, 55
Corporations: *see* Companies
Corrective justice, 664, 675, 787–8
Course of employment
assault, 875, 876
Lister test, 878–86
estoppel, 877–8
Salmond test, 874–8
scope of employment, 876–7
sexual abuse, 878–9, 882–3, 885
Crime
see also Breach of statutory duty
defence of acting to prevent, 55
liability for failing to prevent, 102–3, 112–3,
223–4, 232–4, 241–2, 376–7
public nuisance, 639
tort and, 23–4
Criminal Injuries Compensation Scheme, 894
Crown immunity, 719

Damage to property
assessment of damages, 763–5
complex products, 167–70, 388–9
Consumer Protection Act 1987, 388–90
definition, 165–6, 420–1
insurance and, 27–8
Damages: *see* Aggravated damages;
Compensatory damages; Contemptuous
damages; Exemplary damages; Gain-
based damages; Nominal damages;
Provisional damages; Vindicatory
damages
Dangerous premises
damage to other property, 169–70
physical injury, 131
negligence and, 131, 340–1, 377–9
occupiers' liability and, 358–76
restitution and, 131, 203, 341
private nuisance and, 439, 442–6

public nuisance and, 641, 643
Rylands v *Fletcher* and, 480
statute and, 636–7
Death
see also Wrongful death
losses consequent on, 761–2, 779
defence, 725, 747, 802, 803
defamation, 543, 725, 747
Deceit
aggravated damages, 791
ambiguous representations, 693–4
change in circumstances, 696
contributory negligence, 773
definition, 692
distress, 702
fault requirement, 694
gain-based damages, 813
inducement, 695–6
intention, statement of, 693
intention to harm, 657
limitation, 743
third party to, 10–11
vicarious liability, 878
Defamation
absolute privilege, 555–7
abusive words, 531
actionable *per se*, whether, 750
aggravated damages, 791
American law, 524, 576
assessment of damages, 570–2
bad character, relevance of, 549, 571
companies, 543–4
consent, 546–7
death, 543, 725, 747
definition, 530
exemplary damages, 571–2
ECHR and, 91, 523, 530, 545–6, 572, 575
fair comment, 549–5, 575–6
freedom of speech, 522–6, 529, 530, 545–6,
572, 575
honest comment, 549–5, 575–6
innocent dissemination, 568–70
innuendo, 534–5
juries, 531, 571–2
jurisdiction, 524, 525–6
justification, 547–9
libel, 544–6, 750
limitation, 743
offensive words, 531
offer to make amends, 529, 570
partial justification, 548–9
political speech, 543–4, 576–7

Defamation (*continued*)
  presumption of loss, 544, 545–6, 750
  privilege, 555–68
  publication, 538–43
  public interest, 523, 549, 552–3, 563, 564, 566, 568, 576–7
  qualified privilege, 557–68
  reference to claimant, 535–8
  reform of law, 529, 530, 531, 543, 547, 548, 553, 554, 563, 567, 572–8
  ridicule, 531
  satire, 531
  slander, 544–6
  title to sue, 543–6
Defective products
  auto-destruction, 167–70, 388–9
  Consumer Protection Act 1987, 388–90
  negligence, 1–2, 130, 167–70
Defence of person, 50–2, 63–4, 737
Defence of property, 446–7, 498
Defences
  abuse of process, 66, 502, 524, 541–2, 543, 723–4, 747
  act of state, 720
  capacity, 718–9
  children, 718
  Consumer Protection Act 1987, 390–3
  Crown immunity, 719
  defamation, 546–70
  ECHR, effect of on, 743–8
  exclusion of liability, 728–9
  Human Rights Act, 80–1, 85
  illegality, 354–6, 730–8
  insanity, 719
  limitation, 739–43
  private nuisance, 446–8
  trade unions, 721
  types of, 716–7
  volenti non fit injuria, 18, 132, 235–6, 478–9, 716, 725–7, 748
  witness immunity, 721–3
Delegable and non-delegable duties of care
  see also Vicarious liability
  bailment, 262
  concept, 260–1
  danger, 263
  employers, 261–2
  Hedley Byrne, 263–4
  hospitals, 263
  occupiers, 261, 365–6
  significance of distinction, 261
  vicarious liability and, 866–7

Deterrence
  exemplary damages and, 802–3
  gain-based damages and, 810
  vindicatory damages and, 821
Disciplinary proceedings
  instituting, not a tort, 708
Disgorgement damages, see Gain-based damages
Discrimination
  aggravated damages, 790–1
  tort, when, 637
Distress, 42, 83, 158–61, 162, 340, 460–2, 581–2, 700–3, 755, 792
Distributive justice, 787–8
Doctors
  battery and, 43, 46, 47–8, 52–5
  duties of, 181, 182–3, 257, 281
  more good than harm defence, 352, 739
  standard of care, 182–3, 257
Dogs
  dangerous, 399
  guard, 404
  liability for straying, 408
  protection of livestock against, 399, 404
Duress, 406, 682, 709
Duties
  owed to another, 3, 9
  public, 9
  rights and, 3
  skepticism about, 119–21
Duty of care
  see also Breach of duty of care; Negligence
  adoption agencies, 131–2
  alcohol, 112, 138, 139–40, 223–4, 225
  ambulance services, 220–1, 228
  architects, 182
  accountants, 177, 182
  assumption of responsibility, 18, 173–87, 217–222, 252
  auditors, 344–5
  bailees, 116, 182, 274
  barristers, 116, 182, 274
  betting agency, 276
  builders, 131, 183–4
  Caparo test, 104, 107–8
  carriers, 237–8, 360
  certification bodies, 111, 132, 170–1
  child care services, 240–1
  children, 134, 238–41
  consent, 132, 235–6, 365
  control principle, 231–4
  creation of danger, 222–8
  credit agency, 199

dangerous chattels, 129, 130, 137
dangerous persons or animals, 138–40, 231–4
death or injury, 130, 136–7
dentists, 181
dependency, 197–9
distress or humiliation, foreseeable, 158
doctors, 181, 182–3
Donoghue v *Stevenson*, 1–2, 7, 104, 105–6, 129–30
drivers, 130, 237–8, 360
duty to rescue, 109, 207–42
ECHR, 89, 241–2
educational authorities, 232, 239, 263
employers, 235–7
enabling tort, 138–40
engineers, 182, 210
exclusion of duty, 175–6, 373–4
factors, 108–19
fair, just and reasonable, 6, 104, 107, 108, 112, 117, 125, 138, 208, 217, 240
fire brigade, 208, 219
footballers, 251
foreseeability, 108, 127–9, 134–6, 139, 141–2, 155, 718
freedom, loss of foreseeable, 95, 200
freedom, relevance of, 214
health inspectors, 114–5, 176, 192–3
hydrographers, 109
Hedley Byrne, 172–87
highway authorities, 130, 209, 223
incremental approach, 104, 106–7, 117–8
injunction, 98, 837
interference, 228–31
judges, 114
landlords, 234–5
military, 114, 133–4
manufacturers, 7, 129–30
morality, 122, 212–3, 214
neighbour principle, 104, 105–6, 130
neighbours, 96, 377–9
occupiers, 234, 358–80
omissions, 109, 207–42
parents, 115, 238–9
paternalistic, 137–8, 229
pension advisers, 202
physical danger, 129–40
police, 102–3, 241–2
primary and secondary victims, 141, 148–9
principle, 101–4
prison authorities, 224, 229
property harm, 162–72

property rights and, 163–5, 191–2, 204
proximity, 104, 107–8, 109, 125, 149, 188, 198
psychiatric illness, 125–7, 137–58
psychiatrists, 233, 722–3
psychologists, educational, 190–1, 198
public policy, 13, 31, 101–4, 114–7, 118–9, 133–4, 216, 241, 242
pure economic loss, 125, 172–205
referees (games), 182
referees (jobs), 95, 116, 189–90, 198
regulatory authorities, 114–5, 176, 179, 192–4, 200, 208
rescuers, 131, 145–6
rights and, 4, 204
rule of law and, 108
self-harm, duty not to, 150–1
self-harm, duty to protect against, 137–8, 229
sellers, 130
social services, 8, 103, 115, 221, 240–1
solicitors, 177, 181, 191, 200–1
statutory authority, effect on, 113–4
stress at work, 154–6
suicide, 229
surveyors, 188–9, 197–8
teachers, 239
tests, 104–8
types of, 99–100
vets, 181
White v *Jones*, 191, 200–1
Duty to act: *see* Omissions
Duty to mitigate: *see* Mitigation of loss

Easement
    interference with, 411, 436–7, 445
    nature of, 162–3, 437
Economic loss
    duty of care and, 125, 172–205
    Hedley Byrne, 172–88
    intentional infliction, 5, 11, 657–60, 672–92
    loss of a chance, 294
    physical injury causing, 335, 759–61
    property damage causing, 336, 764–5
    pure, 101
    restitution, 131, 203, 341
    White v *Jones*, 191, 200–1
Economic torts, 6, 657
    see also Conspiracy; Deceit; Inducing a breach of contract; Intentional infliction of loss using unlawful means; Intimidation; Malicious falsehood; Passing off

Eggshell skull rule, 335
Employers
    definition, 869–73
    discrimination, 637
    duties of care, 235–7
    statutory duties, 634–5
    vicarious liability, 867–91
Enterprise risk liability, 26–7, 395, 468, 484,
    888–9
Equity, 16, 19–20
Equitable proprietary rights, 19
    conversion and, 493
    negligence and, 163–5
Equitable wrong
    breach of confidence, 20–1, 591–2
    intellectual property, 509
    invasion of privacy, 20–1, 591–2
    remedies, 21, 811
    torts and, 20–1
Estoppel
    consent, 62
    misrepresentation, 777
    vicarious liability, 877–8
    visitor, 361–2
European Convention on Human Rights
    conversion and, 519
    defences and, 743–8
    direct effect on law, 74–85
    duty of care and, 87–8, 89, 241–2
    exemplary damages and, 572
    defamation and, 91, 523, 530, 545–6, 572, 575
    false imprisonment and, 37, 88
    families, protection of, 8, 115
    indirect effect on law, 85–91
    privacy and, 91, 589, 592–3, 605, 611
    private nuisance and, 453–4
    rights under, 70
Exclusion clauses
    bailment, 729
    Consumer Protection Act 1987, 394
    effect on third parties to contract, 728–30
    Hedley Byrne, 175–6
    occupiers' liability, 359, 371–5
    validity, 176, 359–60, 371–5, 728
Exemplary damages
    assessment, 801
    availability, 797–800
    criminal punishment and, 799–800
    death, effect on right to sue for, 802
    gain-based damages and, 800
    reform, 802–4
    Rookes v Barnard, 798–9

    standard of proof, 801–2
    vicarious liability, 802
Ex turpi causa non oritur actio, 354
    see also Illegality

False imprisonment
    actionable per se, 65, 749
    aggravated damages, 65, 790, 791
    arrest, 40, 55, 56, 58, 64
    assumption of risk, 49–50
    conduct required, 40–2
    creditors, 49
    definition, 36
    fault required, 44–5
    imprisonment, 40
    intention, 44
    miscarriage of justice, 57
    mistakes, 64–5
    necessity, 55, 56–8
    prison authorities, 64–5
    public law, relevance of, 58–61
    responsibility, 40–1
    vindicatory damages, 65, 67, 827–9
Fatal Accidents Act 1976: see Wrongful death
Fault
    negligence and, 248, 269
    no-fault defence, 635
Fire
    common law rule, 480, 481, 482
    negligence, 377–8
    occupiers' liability, 377–8
    Rylands v Fletcher, 478, 482
    strict liability, 480, 482–3
Fireman's rule, 727
Foreseeability
    age, 134, 718
    defamation, 337, 539–40
    dependency, 198–200
    determining, 127–9
    mental age, 135
    negligence, 108, 127–9, 134–6, 331–4
    privacy, 613–4
    private nuisance, 443, 462–3
    psychiatric illness, 126–7, 141–2, 155, 336–7
    remoteness of damage, 331–9
    rule of law and, 108
    Rylands v Fletcher, 476–7
    third parties, actions of, 139
Fraud: see Deceit
Freedom of speech
    defamation, 522–6, 529, 530, 545–6, 572, 575
    protection of privacy, 605–13

Gain-based damages
  availability, 808–9, 810–6
  basis, 809–10, 816–9
  change of position, 810
  compensatory damages and, 414, 806, 817
  conversion, 506, 810–1, 814
  deceit, 813
  disgorgement damages, 807, 810–3
  election, 808
  inducing breach of contract, 815
  intellectual property, 811
  invasion of privacy, 618, 811–2
  licence fee damages, 506, 807, 814–6
  private nuisance, 812, 815
  rationale, 809–10, 816–9
  trespass to land, 812–3, 814–5
  trespass to person, 813, 815–6
  types of, 806–7
Goods
  see also Bailment; Conversion; Trespass to
    goods
  immediate right to possess, 491–3
  possession, 490–1
  specific restitution of, 506
  wrongful interference with, 493–4

Harassment
  course of conduct needed?, 582, 585
  distress and, 581–2, 701
  Equality Act, 579–80, 585–8
  Protection from Harassment Act, 579, 580–5
  remoteness, 339
Hedley Byrne
  see also Negligent misstatement
  assumption of responsibility, 174–87
  basic principle, 172–80
  extended principle, 180–7
  limitation period, 740
  limits of, 175–6, 177–8, 178–80, 183–4,
    188–96
  non-delegable duties, 263–5
  SAAMCO principle and, 342–6
Highway authorities
  duty not to endanger others, 130, 210
  duty to prevent harm, 209, 223, 368, 635–6
  no-fault defence, 635
  snow, 635, 636
Human Rights Act 1998
  damages, 81–5
  direct effect, 72, 74–85
  indirect effect, 72–4, 85–91
  judges, 85

liability for failure to act, 71, 72
  Parliament, 85
  public authority, 71
  remedies, 81–85
  rights protected by, 70
  statutory authority, 80–1
Hunt v *Severs* damages, 780–1
Husband and wife: *see* Marriage

Illegality
  companies, 736–7
  ex turpi causa, 354
  immoral conduct, 356, 733
  police, 737–8
  rationale of defence, 355, 730–1, 732
  requirements (common law), 354–6, 730–7
  requirements (statute), 737–8
  serious offence, need for, 734
  unlawful gains, 735–6, 848
Immorality
  see also Morality
  defence, 356, 603, 607, 608, 733
  ground of liability, 7, 658
  private nuisance, 438–9
Immunity
  Crown, 719, 747
  diplomatic, 721
  human rights and, 745–7
  military, 134
  negligence and, 89
  police and, 89, 738
  sovereign, 720–1
  trade union, 672, 721, 747, 837
  witness, 40, 706, 721–3, 747, 748
Independent contractor, 261, 262, 365, 478,
    481, 482, 868, 869, 870, 871, 872, 873
Inducing
  see also Inducing a breach of contract
  breach of statutory duty, 672
  breach of trust, 672
  someone to commit a tort, 860–1
  violation of right to private law remedy,
    672
Inducing a breach of contract
  breach, need for, 661
  conduct required, 661–5
  contributory negligence, 773
  criticisms, 670–2
  definition, 660–1
  fault required, 665–7
  gain-based damages, 815
  justification, 667–8

Injunction
  damages in lieu, 839–40
  final, 837–9
  interim, 834–7
  mandatory, 834
  negligence, 98, 837
  prohibitory, 834
  public interest, 456–8, 836–7, 839, 840
  quia timet, 834
  reform, 841–3
  types of, 834
Insurance
  subrogation, 27–8, 390
  first party, 27–8, 898–9
  liability (third party), 28–9, 31
Intellectual property
  basis, 508–11
  gain-based damages, 811
  types, 512–3
Intention
  finding, 43, 679–81
  need for, 42–3, 44, 408–9, 679–81, 685–7
  negligence and, 93–4
  to harm, 43, 679–81
  to commit tort, 337–8
  remoteness and, 337–8
Intentional infliction of loss using unlawful
      means
  aggravated damages, 97
  conspiracy and, 689–92
  definition, 673
  distress, 700–2
  'genus' tort, 674, 675
  history, 673–4
  intention to harm, 679–81
  interference with contract and, 664–5
  intimidation and, 673, 674, 675
  loss, type required, 698–9, 700–2
  two party form of tort, 677, 681–3
  unlawful means (definition), 674–7
  unlawful means (requirement), 657–60
Intimidation,
  by threatening breach of contract, 674–5
  instance of 'genus' tort, 675
  two-party form, 673, 682
Invasion of privacy
  see also Freedom of speech, Wrongful
      disclosure of private information,
      Wrongfully obtaining access to private
      information
  appropriating name or likeness, 623–4
  breach of confidence and, 591–2
  disclosure of private information, 591–613
  false light, 622–3
  intrusion, 622
  no general tort of, 589
  obtaining access to private information, 614–7
Ius tertii, 412, 450

Joint liability, 669, 670, 672, 766, 767, 860, 865
Joint and several liability, 766, 767
Judgment (legal)
  effect of, 766–7
  lump sum rule, 755–6
  periodical payments, 757–8
  provisional damages, 756
Judicial review
  application for, whether tort, 709
  false imprisonment, establishing, 58–61
  grounds for, 58–9
Justice
  corrective, 664, 675, 787–8
  distributive, 787–8
  practical, 165, 201, 880–1

Kantian Right, 16

Land
  easements over, 162–3, 411, 436–7, 445
  possession of, 411–3
  restrictive covenants and, 436, 807
  rights over, loss of, 163
Landlords
  duty of care, owed by, 234–5
  liability for acts of tenants, 112, 223, 225, 226,
      441–2, 448
Lawful means conspiracy: *see* Conspiracy
Libel: *see* Defamation
Licence fee damages: *see* Gain-based damages
Limitation
  battery, 740
  deceit, 743
  defamation, 743
  Consumer Protection Act 1987, 392–3
  fatal accidents, 852
  Hedley Byrne, 740
  malicious falsehood, 743
  negligence, 740
  physical injury, 740–1
  sexual abuse, 741–3
  six year rule, 739–40
  torts actionable *per se*, 740
Liquidation proceedings
  starting, when a tort, 708

Loss
   presumption of, 544, 545–6, 750
   types of, 125, 758–9
Loss compensation schemes
   Criminal Injuries Compensation Scheme, 894
   first party insurance, 898–9
   New Zealand Accident Compensation
     Scheme, 895
   replacement for tort law, 899–903
   types of, 893–5
   vaccine damage, 897–8
Loss of chance *see* Chance, loss of

Malice
   conspiracy, 685
   defamation, 549, 555, 557, 576–7
   private nuisance, 432–4
   malicious falsehood, 696
   malicious prosecution, 707
   transferred, 43
Malicious falsehood, 696–8, 743
Malicious prosecution, 706–7
   see also Arrest warrant; Civil proceedings;
     Disciplinary proceedings; Judicial review;
     Liquidation proceedings; Search warrant
Marriage
   see also Parents
   interference with, not a tort, 7
   statements between spouses, 538–9
   vicarious liability, 868
Mesne profits, 814
Minors *see* Children
Misfeasance in public office
   definition, 710
   not actionable *per se*, 714, 750
   omissions, 711–2
   public official, 710–1
   state of mind, 712–3
   two forms, 710
Mistakes
   arrest, 64, 65
   belief in consent, 62
   duration of prison term, 64–5
   maps (product liability), 384
   maps (trespass), 26
   use of force, 63–4, 737–8
Mitigation of loss
   abortion and, 351–2
   causation, relation to, 314
   'duty' to mitigate, 351
   failure to seek medical treatment, 314
   White v *Jones* and, 352

Morality, 16, 122, 197, 200, 212–3, 214, 439,
   510–1, 657, 664, 668, 686, 786–7, 793
   see also Immorality
More good than harm defence
   Consumer Protection Act 1987, 392
   doctors, 392, 739
   negligence, 739

Necessity
   battery, 50–8
   imprisonment, 55, 56–8
   private nuisance, 446–7
   trespass to land, 410–1
Negligence
   see also Breach of duty of care, Duty of care
   aggravated damages, 97, 791–2
   basis of liability, 119–21
   carelessness and, 92–3
   damage, gist of, 121, 826
   definition, 5–6, 92
   duty and, 92–3, 99–123
   fault and, 92–3
   injunction, 98, 837
   intention and, 93–4
   not actionable *per se*, 121, 749
   requirements, 92
Negligent misstatement
   auditors, 344–5
   books, 178–9
   dependency and, 197–9
   directors, 179–80
   experts, 178, 184
   health inspectors, 176
   Hedley Byrne, 172–4, 175, 176
   off-the-cuff statements, 177
   official registers, 179
   professionals, 178, 184
   physical danger and, 187, 210
   referees, 95, 116, 189–90, 198
   social occasions, 177–8
   solicitors, 177
   surveyors, 188–9, 197–8
Nervous shock: *see* Psychiatric illness
New Zealand loss compensation scheme, 895
Nominal damages
   availability of, 14, 749–50
   contemptuous damages and, 371, 750
   defamation, 750
   misfeasance in public office, 714, 750
   negligence, 121, 749
   reasons for seeking, 750–1
   vindicatory damages and, 65

Non-delegable duties of care: *see* Delegable and
    non-delegable duties of care
Nuclear installations, 294, 484, 742
Nuisance: *see* Private nuisance, Public nuisance

Occupiers
    definition, 360–1
    duties of care, 360, 367, 369–70, 376–80
    exclusion of duty, 359, 371–4
    fire, 378, 481–2
    lawful entrants, 361, 363, 367–8, 376–7
    negligence, 234, 376–80
    neighbours, 377–9, 442–6
    passers-by, 379–80, 649–50
    premises, 360, 363–4
    private nuisance, 442–6
    public nuisance, 649–50
    trespassers, 362–3, 366–7, 377
    visitors, 361, 362–3, 376–7
    warnings by, 370–1
Omissions
    definition, 209–11
    Human Rights Act 1998, 71, 72
    morality, 212–3, 214
    negligence, 207–39
    private nuisance, 442–6

Parents
    duty owed to children, 238–9
    duty owed to unborn child, 28–9, 856–7
    parental consent, effect of, 48
    rights where family interfered with, 8, 115
Partners
    vicarious liability, 868
Passing off
    appropriation of goodwill, 513–5
    damage to goodwill, 515–6
    gain-based damages, 516, 811
Paternalism, 52–4, 137–8, 229
Periodical payments, 754, 757–8
Personal injury: *see* Physical injury
Physical injury
    assessment of damages for, 758–61
    concept of, 136–7, 295
    Consumer Protection Act 1987, 388
    exclusion of liability for, 22, 359, 375, 728
    insurance against, 27
    losses consequent upon, 140, 335–6, 758–9
    negligence, 129–40
    private nuisance, 421–2, 464
    psychiatric illness and, 126–7, 140–1,
        336–7

public nuisance, 653
Rylands v *Fletcher*, 471–2
Police
    authority to seize goods, 499, 735–6
    lawful arrest, 55, 56, 58, 64
    failure to rescue, liability for, 89, 102–3,
        228–9, 241–2
    vicarious liability, 868
Possession: *see* Goods, Land
Practical justice, 165, 201, 880–1
Privacy: *see* Freedom of speech, Invasion of
        privacy, Wrongful disclosure of private
        information, Wrongfully obtaining access
        to private information
Private nuisance
    actionable *per se*, whether, 462, 749
    Act of God, 448
    adopting or continuing, 442–6
    affront, 438–9
    aggravated damages, 789, 791
    amenity value of land, 417, 418, 419–20, 421,
        424–5, 430–2, 451–2, 454, 460–1, 462, 464
    authorising, 441–2
    creating, 440–1
    damage to land, 417–8, 420–1
    definition, 415
    emanation, 417, 419–34, 436
    encroachment, 417, 434–5
    ECHR, 453–4
    forms of, 416–9, 464
    franchise to run ferry, 464
    gain-based damages, 812, 815
    hypersensitivity, 423, 429–30, 433
    ius tertii, 450
    landlord's liability, 441–2, 448
    landlord's right to sue for, 420
    locality rule, 424–5, 430–2
    malice, 432–4
    necessity, 446–7
    negligence and, 96, 378, 426–8, 445
    obstruction, 435–7
    occupier's liability, 442–6
    occupier's right to sue for, 449–50
    physical injury, 421–2, 464
    planning permission, 430–2
    property damage, 421, 463–4
    public nuisance and, 639–40
    reasonable user, 426–9
    recoverable harm, 459–64
    rival market, organising, 464, 812
    rule in *Rylands* v *Fletcher* and, 469–70
    third parties, liability for acts of, 441–6

title to sue, 448–54
tort to land, 451
trespass to land and, 406, 407
unreasonable interference, establishing,
    429–34, 435, 438
Product liability
    see also Consumer Protection Act 1987
    congenital disabilities, 857
    negligence, 1–2, 130, 167–70
    theories, 394–7
Property
    body parts, 488–9
    definition, 488
    equitable, 19, 163–5, 493
    immediate right to possess, 491–3
    intangible, 508–21
    interests in,
    possession, 411–13, 490–1
    rights over, 489–50, 508
    tangible, 488–9
    virtual, 519–20
Property damage: see Damage to property
Provisional damages, 756, 762, 846
Proximity, 104, 107–8, 109, 125, 149, 188, 189
Psychiatric illness
    bad news causing, 152–3
    close and loving relationship, 141, 142–5,
        148, 149
    Consumer Protection Act 1987, 388
    death or injury (third party's) causing,
        141–51
    exposure to danger causing, 126–7, 140–1,
        156–8
    feelings of responsibility causing, 146–7
    foreseeability, 126–7, 141–2, 155, 336–7
    humiliating treatment causing, 153–4
    injury (claimant's) causing, 140
    physical injury and, 126–7, 140–1, 336–7
    primary and secondary victims, 141, 148–9
    proximity, requirement of, 125, 142, 144–5,
        146–7
    rescue causing, 145–6
    self-harm causing, 150
    stress causing, 154–6
Public interest
    see also Public policy
    breach of duty of care, 255–6
    breach of statutory duty, 632
    defamation, 523, 549, 552–3, 563, 564, 566,
        568, 576–7
    distress, claim for, 659
    injunctions, 456–8, 836–7, 839, 840

privacy, invasion of, 606–11
private nuisance, 427–9
tort law, contrary to? 29–32
trespass torts, 36–8, 55–8
Public law
    breach of duty of care and, 258–60
    false imprisonment and, 58–61
    grounds of judicial review, 58–9
Public nuisance
    crime, 639, 641
    danger to public, 643, 649–50
    definition, 639
    highway, 642–3
    physical injury, 653
    private nuisance and, 639–40
    public wrong, 17, 639–40
    isolated incidents, 646–7
    knowledge, 647–50
    responsibility for, 647–50
    special damage, 640, 650–3
    tort, 16–17
    types of, 641–2
Public policy
    see also Public interest
    actionability, 330, 353–6
    causation, 323, 325–7
    defamation, 523, 555, 562–8
    defences, 716–7
    duty of care, 13, 31, 101–4, 114–7, 118–9,
        133–4, 170–1, 192–3, 195, 216, 241, 242
    exemplary damages, 804
    relevance of, 101–4, 325–7
    remedying wrongs, 13, 118–9, 717
Public/private distinction
    abuse of power, 705
    defamation, 524–5, 543–4, 575–6, 576–7
    exemplary damages, 798, 804
    Human Rights Act 1998, 74–9
    negligence, 208, 215
    privacy, 607–10

Reasonable foreseeability: see Foreseeability
Reasonable user, 426–9
Remoteness,
    breach of statutory duty, 339, 583–4
    eggshell skull rule, 335
    foreseeability test, 331–4
    intentional torts, 337–8
    Page v Smith, 126, 336–7
    Rylands v Fletcher, 476–7
    wrong kind of loss and, 339–40
Res ipsa loquitur, 268

Rescue
  break in chain of causation, 311
  duty to, 207–9
  more good than harm, 738–9
  physical injury caused by, 131, 311
  psychiatric illness caused by, 145–6
Restitution
  see also Gain-based damages
  dangerous premises and, 131, 203, 341
  necessity and, 411
Restitutionary damages: see Gain-based damages
Rights
  concept of, 2–5
  duties and, 2–3
  exclusivity, 508
  human, 69–72
  property, 489–90, 508
  tort as violation of, 1–2, 4
  types of, 2–4
  use, 508
Rule of law, 60, 108, 709, 802–3, 804
Rylands v Fletcher, The rule in
  Act of God, 478
  act of stranger, 478
  ascription of liability, 471
  basis of rule, 468–71
  consent, 478–9
  definition, 467–8
  escape, need for, 476
  exceptional danger, 472
  fault of claimant, 478
  fire, 481–3
  litigation in Rylands v Fletcher, 466–7
  non-natural use, 472–5
  physical injury, 472
  private nuisance and, 471–2
  remoteness of damage under, 476–7
  statement of, 467–8
  title to sue, 471–2
  tort law and, 468, 470

SAAMCO principle, 342–6, 777–8
Search warrant
  procuring issue of, when a tort, 707
Self-defence, 50–2, 737
Self-harm
  duty not to, 150–1
  duty to prevent, 137–8, 229
Sexual abuse
  duty to prevent, 115, 240, 241
  limitation period, 741–3
  vicarious liability, 878–9, 882–3, 885

Settlements
  effect of, 766
  structured, 758, 846
Slander: see Defamation
Social security, 767, 857, 901
Specific restitution of property, 506
Statutory authority, effect of
  Consumer Protection Act 1987, 390
  false imprisonment, 58
  Human Rights Act 1998, 80–1
  negligence, 113–14
  private nuisance, 447
Statutory discretion, 113–4
Strict liability
  see also Animals Act 1971, Consumer
    Protection Act 1987, Fire, Nuclear
    installations, Rylands v Fletcher, The rule
    in, Water
  definition, 25, 478
  enterprise risk, 26–7, 395, 468, 484, 888–9
  potential unfairness, 26, 486–7
  tort liability, 25–6, 42, 396–7, 408, 486–7
Subrogation, 27–8, 390

Teachers
  corporal punishment, 55
  duties of, 239
Thin skull rule: see Eggshell skull rule
Third parties to tort
  see also Accessory liability, Congenital
    disabilities, Hunt v Severs damages, Social
    security, Subrogation, Wrongful death
    claims
  general rule (no recovery), 10–13, 844
  latent damage to property, 858
  NHS costs, 28, 857–8
  principle of transferred loss, 858–9
Tort
  see also Tort law, Torts
  civil wrong, 8–10
  contract and, 17–19
  crime and, 23–4
  duty and, 2–3, 9
  equitable wrong and, 20–1
  intentional, 329, 337–8, 714
  range of conduct amounting to, 5–8
  rights and, 1–2, 4–6
Tort law
  functions of, 1–2
  loss-compensation and, 13–16
  residual wrongs model, 16–17
  scope of, 5–8, 396–7, 468, 470

Torts
    actionable *per se*, 14, 749
    how many, 5
    names of, 5–7, 35
Torture, 51–2, 70, 71, 84, 87, 241
Trade unions
    defamation of, 543
    immunity, 672, 721, 747, 837
Trespass, 35–6
Trespass to goods
    actionable *per se*, whether, 502, 749–50
    contributory negligence, 773
    definition, 500
    direct interference, 501
    private documents, 501–2
    title to sue, 502–3
    wheel clamping, 501
Trespass to land
    abuse of power to enter land, 362–3
    actionable *per se*, 749
    aggravated damages, 789–90, 791
    airspace, 412
    conduct required, 406–8
    consent, 409
    definition, 405
    fault required, 408–9
    gain-based damages, 812–3, 814–5
    ius tertii, 412
    necessity, 410–1
    private nuisance and, 406, 407
    remoteness of damage, 413–4
    title to sue, 411–3
    trespass *ab initio*, 409
    trespass by relation, 411
Trespass to the person: *see* Assault, Battery, False
    imprisonment

Unlawful means
    see also Intentional infliction of loss using
        unlawful means
    breach of contract, 674–5
    conspiracy, 688–92
    crime, 675–7
    need to establish, 657–60
    threats, 675, 682–3
    tort, 674

Vicarious liability
    see also Delegable and non-delegable duties
        of care
    accessory liability and, 867, 891–2
    agency, 868

    assault, 875, 876, 883–5
    borrowed employee, 873–4
    breach of non-delegable duty and, 262,
        866–7, 879–80
    contribution, 890
    conversion, 875–6, 885–6
    course of employment, 874–96
    employee, 869–73
    employer's indemnity, 890–1
    estoppel, 877–8
    exemplary damages, 802
    husband and wife, 868
    independent contractor, 869, 870, 871, 872,
        873
    joint liability, 865
    Lister test, 878–86
    partners, 868
    police, 868
    rationale, 886–90
    reform, 890
    Salmond test, 874–8
    sexual abuse, 878–9, 882–3, 885
    situations of, 867–9
Vindicatory damages
    availability, 65–7, 821–2
    defamation, 571, 825
    deprivation of vote, 823
    examples, 822–7
    future, 829–30
    human rights, 820–1
    nature, 65–6, 820
    negligence, 826–7
    trespass, 65–7, 822–3, 823–5, 827–9
Volenti non fit injuria
    see also Consent
    Animals Act 1971, 404
    Consumer Protection Act 1987, 392
    duty of care and, 132, 235–6, 365
    employers' liability, 235–6
    exceptions to rule, 726–7
    fireman's rule, 727
    games, 48–9
    imprisonment, 47, 49
    knowledge, 365
    occupiers' liability, 365
    paternalism, 726–7
    rationale, 18
    risk, acceptance of, 48–9, 725–6
    Rylands v *Fletcher*, 478–9
    road accidents, 727
    sado-masochism, 45
    trespass to goods, 49–50, 501

Voluntary assumption of risk: *see* Consent, *Volenti non fit injuria*

Warnings
  occupiers' liability, 370–1
  product liability, 386, 392
Water
  rights to, 433–4, 435, 437
  strict liability for escape of, 476, 483
White v *Jones*
  contributory negligence, 778
  conveyance of land, 201
  dependency, 200–1
  duty to mitigate, 352
  intermeddling, 201
  lacuna in law, filling, 201
  pensions, 202
  practical justice, 201
  vasectomy, 202
  wills, 191
Wife and husband: *see* Marriage
Wilkinson v *Downton*
  negligence and, 131, 153, 161–2
  recoverable harm, 161, 162
  redundant, 161
  requirements, 161
Witness immunity, 721–2
  expert witnesses, 722
  informants, 40, 706, 723
  investigators, 723
Wrong kind of loss
  breach of statutory duty, 329, 342, 629
  definition, 329
  distress, 158, 340
  negligence, 127, 329–30, 339–42, 366

  remoteness and, 339–40
  SAAMCO test and, 342
Wrongful death claims
  Animals Act 1971, 852
  bereavement, 851–2
  conditions for, 844–6
  contributory negligence, 846
  Consumer Protection Act 1987, 852–3
  dependants, 845
  funeral expenses, 852
  limitation, 852
  loss of support, 846–51
  receipt of benefit, 850–1
Wrongfully obtaining access to private information
  see also Invasion of privacy
  intention, 615
  intrusion and, 615–6, 622
  justification, 616–7
  now a tort, 614–5
  private documents, 616
Wrongful disclosure of private information
  see also Invasion of privacy
  companies, 603–4
  freedom of speech and, 605–13
  gain-based damages, 618, 811–2
  is it a tort, 20–1, 589, 591–2
  knowledge, 613–4
  photographs, 600–2
  private information, 594–605
  public interest, 606–11
  sexual relationships, 599
  structure, 593–4
Wrongful interference with goods, 493–4
  see also Conversion, Trespass to goods